SERVICE RECORD

NAME _____

BRANCH OF SERVICE _____ **PLACE OF ENTRANCE** _____

DATE _____

RANK _____

FIRST ASSIGNMENT _____

RECORD OF PROMOTION
_____
_____
_____

RECORD OF CITATIONS AND AWARDS
_____
_____

PHOTOGRAPH HERE

RECORD OF TRAINING AND DOMESTIC SERVICE
_____ _____
_____ _____

RECORD OF FOREIGN SERVICE AND COMBAT
_____ _____
_____ _____
_____ _____
_____ _____
_____ _____
_____ _____

RELEASED FROM SERVICE _____ **DATE** _____ **RANK** _____

SERVICE RECORD

NAME
BRANCH OF SERVICE   PLACE OF ENTRANCE
                         DATE
                         RANK
                         FIRST ASSIGNMENT

PHOTOGRAPH HERE

RECORD OF PROMOTION

RECORD OF CITATIONS AND AWARDS

RECORD OF TRAINING AND DOMESTIC SERVICE

RECORD OF FOREIGN SERVICE AND COMBAT

RELEASED FROM SERVICE   DATE   RANK

SERVICE RECORD

NAME _____

BRANCH OF SERVICE _____ PLACE OF ENTRANCE _____

DATE _____

RANK _____

FIRST ASSIGNMENT _____

PHOTOGRAPH HERE

RECORD OF PROMOTION
_____
_____
_____

RECORD OF CITATIONS AND AWARDS
_____
_____

RECORD OF TRAINING AND DOMESTIC SERVICE
_____ _____
_____ _____
_____ _____

RECORD OF FOREIGN SERVICE AND COMBAT
_____ _____
_____ _____
_____ _____
_____ _____
_____ _____

RELEASED FROM SERVICE _____ DATE _____ RANK _____

WORLD WAR II's MOST FAMOUS PICTURE
Iwo Jima, 1945

THE COMPLETE HISTORY
OF
WORLD WAR II

BY

FRANCIS TREVELYAN MILLER, Litt.D., LL.D.

WITH A BOARD OF HISTORICAL AND
MILITARY AUTHORITIES

WAR PHOTOGRAPHS

OFFICIAL RECORDS

MAPS

Progress Research Corporation

3210 N. DAYTON ST. CHICAGO 13, ILL.

also publishers of
AMERICAN LIFE MAGAZINE
1949

COPYRIGHT, 1948
ANN WOODWARD MILLER

Copyright, 1945, by A. W. M.

Copyright in Great Britain and in the
British Dominions and the Possessions

Copyright in the Republic of the Philippines

MADE IN THE UNITED STATES OF AMERICA

BOARD OF HISTORICAL AND MILITARY ANALYSTS

DR. CURT L. HEYMANN: Authority on invasions of Holland, Belgium, Norway, Greece, and the Balkans; also on the diplomatic conferences. Scholar and lifetime observer from a family of distinguished Dutch diplomatists, he has lived in the capitals of Europe and been intimately associated with the great statesmen of his time. Noted as a foreign journalist and essayist he came to America. Engaged on editorial staff of *New York Times* until officially delegated by the Government for special service in occupied countries during the last year of World War II.

BENEDICT FITZPATRICK: British authority, formerly on foreign editorial staff of *London Daily Mail*. Contributor to leading encyclopedias and standard histories. Author of some thirty works, including monumental *Ireland and the Foundations of Europe,* and *Ireland and the Making of Britain*. Contributing editor London and continental journals, special writer *London Illustrated News*. Educated at Ushaw College, University of London; Bonn University, Germany; LL.D. Holy Cross, United States. Conducted researches into foundations of European civilization.

KARL BURGER: Authority on Central Europe in intimate contact with Government officials and State documents. Engaged with Division of Psychological Warfare with Allies in World War II. Formerly editor-in-chief *Oesterreichische Illustrierte Zeitung* (Vienna, Austria). Editor with *Wegweiser-Verlag* (German Book of the Month Club, Berlin-Vienna). Correspondent leading German and Austrian dailies: *Berliner Lokal-Anzeiger, Berliner Tag, Leipziger Illustrierte Muenchner Jugend, Simplicissimus, Neus Wiener Tageblatt, Der Wiener Tag, Tageblatt-Wochenausgabe,* Editor Paramount newsreel for seven European countries; shortwave pickups for United Press.

CHARLES LAM MARKMANN: Authority on campaigns in France, North Africa, Italy, and invasions of Germany. On cable desk *New York Times* during World War II, editing, collating, rewriting foreign dispatches from war fronts. Translator of official documents from French, Italian, German; also French volume on Belgian Underground; University of Pennsylvania (A.B.); New York University (LL.B.). Experience and knowledge on foreign events qualified him as analyst of all military campaigns, for this history commanded by General Eisenhower.

VICTOR H. LAWN: Authority on campaigns in Far East; Japanese invasions, war in China, India, Philippines and islands of the Pacific. University of Michigan (A.B.). Formerly director of information, ERB; Executive Secretary Committee for National Morale; research and surveys on economic phases of war; confidential work in coöperation with Government agencies to counter subversive activities. On cable desk *New York Times* in World War II. Public relations counselor for large industrial organizations. Special investigator for ten years on *New York World, Philadelphia Evening Ledger, Detroit News,* and leading American newspapers.

CRERAR HARRIS: Authority on Russian affairs and military campaigns covering German invasions of Russia for this history, and all subsequent drives of Russian Armies to regain lost territory and their counter invasions of Poland, Rumania, and the liberation of all conquered countries, with final Russian conquest of Germany. Educated at University of Rochester. Served on staff of *Rochester Democrat and Chronicle* and *San Francisco Examiner*. Edited and contributed to *News Letter* and *Wasp* (California) ten years. Conducted syndicated column from New York. On cable desk *New York Times*.

WERNER LOEB: Authority on German activities in World War II, organization of Nazi political party and youth movements in Germany. Lived in Dusseldorf, Rhineland, in Hague, Holland, and Switzerland. Educated in America at Bucknell University and New York University for degree of B.S. On editorial staffs of *New York Post, New York News,* and Standard News subsidiary to Allied Press. Researcher on editorial staff for first biography of General Eisenhower. Conducted exhaustive researches into causes of World War II.

ANN WOODWARD MILLER
Director of Research

HENRY FEINSTEIN
Research in London

WILL H. JOHNSTON
Chronologist

With board of 200 historical and military authorities from 30 nations.

HISTORIAN'S FOREWORD

This is the first History of World War II to present a complete panorama of the greatest struggle in human history, with authentic text, official photographs, maps, records, and documents in a single volume.

Its service is to give homes, schools, and libraries a standard work in which the reader may obtain a comprehensive understanding of the epoch-making events through which we have passed. Here we witness the organization of the greatest armies, navies, and air forces the world has ever known—the gigantic battles on land, sea, and in the air—the might of industrial power and production.

We have lived through the most stupendous struggle in the 7,000 years of recorded history. The destiny of 70 nations and 2,000,000,000 people has been at stake. The homelands of more than three quarters of the population of the earth have felt the iron heel of war. More than 100,000,000, one out of every twenty human beings on the globe, have been engaged in the fighting forces of belligerent nations.

The records of World War II, as set forth in this volume, challenge the imagination. The official lists of numbers killed and wounded are a tragic commentary on civilization: more than 20,000,000 casualties; 30,000,000 more men, women, and children driven from their homes; 10,000,000 more massacred; hundreds of thousands of homes left in ruins.

The cost of this "War for Survival," with its destruction, devastation, and economic losses, is estimated at the sum of $1,000,000,000,000. The great wealth of the world, with its resources, industrial power, and man power, has been concentrated on destruction. Nations have accumulated an indebtedness which far exceeds all the money in the world. The responsibility for meeting this obligation is placed upon future generations to carry the burden.

This is the price we have paid for human freedom. The amount of money consumed in this war is sufficient to build a home for every family in the world, or to give an education to every child on earth. It is far greater than all the moneys ever expended for schools, churches, and hospitals since the beginning of the human race.

We have, therefore, endeavored to make this History of World War II a human history, treating men and events as they directly affect our own lives. The causes which created this human tragedy are herein analyzed, with sketches of the leading personalities and backgrounds of the nations involved.

Military events are clearly visualized from the outbreak of the war to its final battles. Our purpose has been to present these with such clarity that you may follow your own "boys" through to the final victory and re-live the experiences through which they passed.

This service has been accomplished through the organization of a staff of experts, specialists, and analysts under the direction of a historian-general. (The list of staff authorities and writers is given on pages iii and iv, and in the section, "Authorities and Official Sources" on pages 939-941. Divisional chiefs were "on duty" at desks over which more than 60,000 words from the battlefronts passed every day.

Official communiqués from all parts of the world were analyzed each day, with reports and proclamations issued by all the Governments. As each event was officially confirmed, it was transcribed into historical narrative for this book and coördinated by the historian-general.

Throughout the war, conferences were held with official sources, military authorities, and communications with diplomats and statesmen, supplemented by the information organizations representing thirty nations.

While it was the first great "War in the Air," coördinated with land and sea forces, it may also be called the "War of the Scientists," in which invention, discovery, mechanical genius, and mass production take a foremost part. Through this new age of radio, with the elimination of time and space the whole world was in instant communication. Through cinematography and radio photography, the scenes of action were brought immediately into our homes. The war passed before our eyes on motion picture screens and was preserved on films to pass before the eyes of generations to come.

Another war on this gigantic scale, with further development of instruments for destruction by scientific genius, would place the human race in danger of self-annihilation. Therefore, a clear understanding of World War II is essential for our own self-preservation. The time has come, if we are to survive as peoples and nations, when some coöperative plan must be agreed upon whereby wars can be stopped at their point of inception—some plan whereby we can all live together in peace and security.

This History of World War II is dedicated to that great forward step in human progress. It stands also as a memorial to those who fought and died for this achievement. The colossal magnitude of this war may be visualized when we state that the armies and navies engaged in World War II would form a marching line of men in combat reaching four times around the earth in continuous procession.

May it never happen again.

Francis Trevelyan Miller

CONTENTS

1. Victory of the United Nations—Causes and Results of World War II . . . 3
2. Last Days of World's Greatest War—New Age of the Atomic Bomb . . . 14
3. Historic Scenes at Surrender of Japan—118 Days After Germany . . . 27
4. Triumph of Democracy—MacArthur in Tokyo—Eisenhower in Germany . . . 39
5. The Phenomenon of Hitler . . . 51
6. Nazi Plot to Conquer the World . . . 64
7. Raising a Generation for Human Slaughter . . . 74
8. Rise and Fall of Benito Mussolini . . . 84
9. Austria First to Fall to Nazi Conspirators . . . 93
10. Fascism and Nazism in Violent Action . . . 103
11. Czechoslovakia Falls Into Grip of Despots . . . 109
12. Invasion of Poland—Hitler Ignites the Fuse of World's Greatest War . . . 120
13. Denmark Falls Into Captivity . . . 127
14. Norway Under Iron Heel of Invaders . . . 137
15. Belgium in Path of Blitzkreig . . . 153
16. German Invasion of the Netherlands . . . 167
17. Why the British Entered World War II . . . 178
18. France Meets the Crisis in Defense of Liberty . . . 192
19. German Juggernaut Hurls Its Power at France . . . 199
20. The Battle of France—"Vive La Republique" . . . 214
21. The Battle of Britain—Fortitude of a Great People . . . 224
22. Occupation of France by Nazis—A Story of Infamy . . . 234
23. De Gaulle Rallies Free French Under Tricolor . . . 248
24. Blitz in the Balkans—"Cockpit of Europe" . . . 261
25. Rumania—The Battleground for Oil . . . 267
26. Battle of Yugoslavia—"Cradle of the Slavs" . . . 272
27. Modern Iliad of the Heroic Greeks . . . 282
28. Behind Veil of Japanese Treachery . . . 292
29. How America Was Drawn Into Vortex of World War II . . . 308

Contents

30. "Day of Infamy"—Stabbed in the Back at Pearl Harbor . . 324
31. War in the Pacific—Its Magnitude and Problems . . . 336
32. MacArthur Leads Fight to Save Philippines—The Fall of Manila 347
33. Russo-Finnish Conflict—Its Causes and Results . . . 353
34. Rising Power of Russia in World Arena 359
35. Germany Pits Her Might Against Russia 364
36. Battle for Moscow—Russian Cities Aflame 369
37. Battle of Stalingrad—Gate to the East 375
38. The Red Army Strikes Back—141 Crucial Days . . . 380
39. Russia's Fate on the Rivers of Destiny 387
40. Red Army's Mighty Surge Drives Germans from Soil of Russia 392
41. Rape and Rapine in Wake of Nazi Armies 398
42. Invaders Stopped at Gates to Egypt—1,750 Mile Retreat Across Desert 410
43. Commando Raid on Dieppe—Test Tube for Invasion of Europe 415
44. Courageous China's Long Defense of Her Homeland . 429
45. India, Goal of the Axis—Burma, Malaya, and Fall of Singapore 437
46. Japs Sweep Through the Islands of the Pacific . . . 442
47. Last Stand at Bataan—Corregidor Surrender and March of Death 452
48. Australia—Land Where the Tide Was Turned Back . 465
49. MacArthur Starts Back—Fighting Through Jungles of New Guinea 471
50. United States Becomes "Arsenal of Democracy"—A Nation in Action 478
51. Rebirth of American Sea Power Into World's Greatest Navy 487
52. "Shangri-La"—First Raid on Tokyo—Crisis on Continent of Asia 497
53. Battle of Coral Sea 503
54. Battle of Midway—And the Aleutians 510
55. Battles of Guadalcanal and the Solomons—Land, Sea, and Air 517
56. Naval Battles at the "Dead End" in the Southwest Pacific 525

Contents

57. AMERICANS LAND IN NORTH AFRICA—FIRST GREAT ALLIED OFFENSIVE 533
58. EISENHOWER STRATEGY AT GATES OF TUNISIA 543
59. GREAT BATTLES IN LIBERATION OF AFRICA 551
60. CASABLANCA—ROAD TO VICTORY AND "UNCONDITIONAL SURRENDER" 556
61. BATTLE OF KASSERINE PASS ON THE ROAD TO TUNIS . . . 565
62. ROMMEL ROUTED ON MARETH LINE 574
63. BATTLES LEADING TO HILL 609 AND TRIUMPH 587
64. FALL OF TUNIS AND BIZERTE—FIRST GREAT ALLIED VICTORY 598
65. PANORAMA OF 15,000 MILES IN EAST—AND BATTLE OF BISMARCK SEA 607
66. JAPANESE SUN BEGINS TO SET OVER INDIA—BURMA—CHINA 618
67. TARAWA—CONQUEST OF THE ATOLLS—STEPPING-STONES IN THE PACIFIC 625
68. "I SHALL RETURN"—MACARTHUR ON ROAD BACK TO KEEP HIS PLEDGE 634
69. FINAL STAGE IN GREAT SWING FROM PIVOT AT NEW GUINEA 643
70. SMASHING JAP DEFENSES—BATTLES OF SAIPAN AND PHILIPPINE SEA 649
71. BOMBING 5,000,000 SQUARE MILES IN PACIFIC—GUAM REDEEMED 654
72. AMERICAN NAVY WITH THE AIR FORCES BLAST ROADS FOR MACARTHUR'S ARMY 657
73. "PEOPLE OF THE PHILIPPINES, I HAVE RETURNED!" MACARTHUR AT LEYTE 661
74. INVASION OF SICILY—DOORSTEP TO CONTINENT OF EUROPE . 667
75. ABDICATION OF MUSSOLINI—AND THE FALL OF SICILY . . 677
76. BATTLE OF SALERNO 686
77. FALL OF NAPLES—FIERCE FIGHTING ALONG THE VOLTURNO . 691
78. ITALY SURRENDERS—FIRST AXIS POWER TO COLLAPSE . . 698
79. CRUCIAL BATTLES AT CASSINO AND ANZIO 703
80. LIBERATION OF ROME—ALLIES RESTORE FREEDOM TO THE ETERNAL CITY 711
81. BATTLES FROM ROME TO FLORENCE—PISA—AND THE GOTHIC LINE 715
82. D-DAY—ALLIED FORCES LAND IN FRANCE—START OF WESTERN FRONT 726
83. BATTLES OF NORMANDY 739

Contents

84. Conquest of Caen by Canadians—Americans Capture St. Lô 746
85. Liberation of France—Victory March Into Paris . 754
86. Belgium and Netherlands Liberated—Allies Invade German Soil 765
87. Americans Cross German Border—Allies on the Rhine 772
88. Sack of Warsaw—German Massacre of the Polish Patriots 779
89. Last Battles in Italy—Execution of Mussolini—Germans Surrender 783
90. Battle of the Bulge—Germany's Last Attempt to Come Back 788
91. Last Battles in Germany—Great Cities Fall in Ruins 798
92. Russians Push on Toward Berlin—From the Vistula to the Oder 806
93. Fall of Budapest and Vienna as Red Army Sweeps On 820
94. Fall of Berlin—The Proud German Capital Lies in Ruins 829
95. Unconditional Surrender! Decisive Defeat of Germany 842
96. Last Scenes in Tragedy of War—Collapse of German Might 852
97. Truth About Torture Chambers in Axis Prison Camps 862
98. War in the Pacific—Decisive Battle for Leyte Gulf . 872
99. "Home Again!" MacArthur at Luzon—Enters Manila in Triumph 889
100. Fall of Iwo Jima—Battering Down the Inner Defenses of Japan 900
101. Japanese Empire Crumbles in the Pacific and on Continent of Asia 910
102. Okinawa—Last Great Battle in the Pacific—At Doorway to Japan 921

Authorities and Official Sources 939
Chronology 943

Supreme Headquarters
ALLIED EXPEDITIONARY FORCE
Office of the Supreme Commander

It gives me great pleasure to contribute in the name of the Allied Expeditionary Forces under my command to your invaluable and essential compilation of the History of World War II.

The keynote of success of these forces was Allied unity of thought, purpose and deed in all ranks and echelons, without which the utter military defeat of Germany could not have been achieved. I must pay equal tribute to every soldier of the United Nations who fought with me, Great Britain, Canada, and her other Dominions, France, Belgium, Holland, Luxembourg, Poland, Czechoslovakia, Norway and Denmark, as well as to our Comrades in Arms, the gallant men and women of the Soviet Armies.

To this fine fighting team the American soldier brought the best American traditions both as representatives of our nation and as fighting men. Moulded by long months of varied and arduous training in the United States, he has been tried and tested in all aspects of combat under the most rigorous conditions of weather and terrain against a vicious and fanatical enemy. He repeatedly demonstrated a high degree of individual initiative, resourcefulness, energy and physical and moral stamina until now he has emerged victorious.

The success of our Armies would have been utterly impossible without the magnificent support of the American people in supplying an almost insatiable demand for the sinews of war. For they made our country the "Arsenal of Democracy" and made good our boast as the best fed, best clothed, best equipped, and best medically cared-for Army in history. Equally impossible would this feat of arms have been without complete coöperation on land, on the sea, and in the air. Through the combined and coördinated efforts of all arms and services the final goal was achieved. Commanders, staffs, and men are worthy of the highest praise which can be paid them. And to those who died that this great victory might be won, we can repay them only by ensuring that the peace will be as surely won as the military victory for which they gave their lives.

The keynote of a successful peace is teamwork and unity of purpose among the free nations of the world; that same teamwork which brought us through the dark days of Nazi triumphs to the final defeat of Germany.

Dwight D. Eisenhower

Contributed by GENERAL DWIGHT D. EISENHOWER to this History of World War II—Supreme Commander of Allied Expeditionary Forces writes this tribute to his comrades for permanent record in this historical repository.

GENERAL HEADQUARTERS
SOUTHWEST PACIFIC AREA
OFFICE OF THE COMMANDER-IN-CHIEF

Words alone are inadequate to describe the noble heights to which our fighting men have risen in the campaigns culminating in Philippine liberation. Of a peace-loving race and stranger to the sword, in our Country's cause they have perfected mastery of the sword. Through a valor unsurpassed in military annals and with an unconquerable spirit which is the very cornerstone to our country's greatness, they have forced the enemy relentlessly back to his own Empire fortress or destroyed him where he elected to stand. Neither the worst of Nature's barriers, deadly disease and pestilence, nor the defensive dispositions of a fanatical enemy could halt them in this resolute forward advance.

These men from every state in the American Union—indeed from every city in every state—are a cross section of our people. In theirs, the future of our country—in peace or war—rests in strong and reliable hands. On their record, written unforgettably throughout the Far East, all Americans may find justifiable pride—on it Our Flag has been enshrined in new glory, new dignity, and new honor.

Very sincerely,

Douglas MacArthur

MESSAGE SENT BY GENERAL MacARTHUR FROM THE PHILIPPINES TO THIS MEMORIAL HISTORY OF WORLD WAR II

WHAT WE FOUGHT FOR IN WORLD WAR II

Official Statements By
FRANKLIN DELANO ROOSEVELT
President of the United States during World War II—
Commander in Chief of the Army and Navy

President Roosevelt, upon request of the historians for this volume, sent from the White House a personal letter in which he stated: "I have had some extracts made from my addresses and messages from which I think you may gather suitable material." These selections from his writings, presented to us under title, "Some Pertinent Statements by the President on What We Are Fighting For," are herewith given historical record. They constitute what may be called by historians the "Ten Commandments of World War II."

I. We are not a warlike people. We have never sought glory as a nation of warriors. We are not interested in aggression. We are not interested—as the dictators are—in looting. We do not covet one square inch of the territory of any other nation. Our vast effort, and the unity of purpose which inspires that effort are due solely to our recognition of the fact that our fundamental rights are threatened by Hitler's violent attempt to rule the world. These rights were established by our forefathers on the field of battle. They have been defended—at great cost but with great success—on the field of battle, here on our own soil, and in foreign lands, and on all the seas all over the world. There has never been a moment in our history when Americans were not ready to stand up as free men and fight for their rights.

II. Together with other free peoples, we are now fighting to maintain our right to live among our world neighbors in freedom and in common decency, without fear of assault.

III. We are fighting today for security, for progress and for peace, not only for ourselves, but for all men, not only for one generation but for all generations. We are fighting to cleanse the world of ancient evils, ancient ills. We are fighting as our fathers have fought, to uphold the doctrine that all men are equal in the sight of God.

IV. On the desert sands of Africa, along the thousands of miles of battle lines in Russia, in New Zealand and Australia and the islands of the Pacific, in war-torn China and all over the seven seas, free men are fighting desperately—and dying—to preserve the liberties and the decencies of modern civilization.

V. The essence of our struggle is that men shall be free. There can be no real freedom for the common man without enlightened social policies. In last analysis they are the stakes for which democracies are today fighting.

VI. We are figting to free the people of this earth from the most powerful, the most ruthless, the most savage enemy the world has ever seen. We are dedicating all that we have and all that we are to the combat. We will not stop this side of victory.

VII. It is useless to win battles if the cause for which we fought these battles is lost. It is useless to win a war unless it stays won. We, therefore, fight for the restoration and perpetuation of faith and hope throughout the world. The objective of today is clear and realistic. It is to destroy completely the military power of Germany, Italy, and Japan to such good purpose that their threat against us and all the other United Nations cannot be revived a generation hence.

VIII. The overwhelming majority of all the people in the world want peace. Most of them are fighting for the attainment of peace—not just a truce, not just an armistice—but peace that is as strongly enforced and as durable as mortal can make it.... American boys are fighting today in snow-covered mountains, in malarial jungles, etc., and the thing for which they struggle is best symbolized by the message that came out of Bethlehem.

IX. Today this nation, which George Washington helped so greatly to create, is fighting all over this earth in order to maintain for ourselves and for our children the freedom which George Washington helped so greatly to achieve.

X. In this war of survival we must keep before our minds not only the evil things we fight against but the good things we are fighting for. We fight to retain a great past—and we fight to gain a greater future. The issue of this war is the basic issue between those who believe in mankind and those who do not—the ancient issue between those who put their faith in the people and those who put their faith in dictators and tyrants.

The foregoing statements selected at the White House for this History of World War II are from the following official documents: (I) Radio Address from Hyde Park Library, September 1, 1941—(II) Radio Address December 9, 1941—(III) Message to Congress January 6, 1942—(IV) Statement July 4, 1942—(V) Address to ILO November 6, 1941—(VI) Presidential Release May 9, 1943—(VII) Radio Address October 12, 1942—(VIII) Radio Address December 24, 1943—(IX) Radio Address February 22, 1943—(X) Message to Congress January 7, 1943.

HEADQUARTERS, ARMY AIR FORCES
WASHINGTON

First of all, may I tell you how much I appreciate your asking me to participate in your historical record. I must warn you, however, that any record of the accomplishments of the Army Air Forces in the past three years is in my mind a more fit subject for a thousand-page volume than a letter, however heartfelt. Therefore, I believe it will be more fruitful if I confine myself to a few of the highlights of our history in the past few years....

Remember, if you will, what the Japanese did to our Air Force in the first weeks of this war. We had 526 airplanes deployed to meet possible attacks on Hawaii and the Philippines. Within a few hours that number was reduced to 176. In the Philippines were our last two worn-out P-40's and a couple of Japanese ships with 500-pound bombs hitched to the wings—and then they, too, were lost.

Exactly two and a half years after those P-40's went down, twenty thousand American airmen flew over the English Channel on their zero hour D-Day mission....

One of the basic elements of aërial offensive is, of course, strategic bombardment—one of the great developments of modern warfare. Complex as its separate aspects appear, its basic principles are simple. At the Casablanca conference the Combined Chiefs of Staff were able to state the aims of our bombing offensive in a single sentence. Our objective was "the progressive destruction and dislocation of the German military and economic system and the undermining of the morale of the German people to a point where their capacity for armed resistance is fatally weakened."

We knew that, to accomplish this, the United States had to produce enough airplanes, build enough bases, train enough men to make up the largest and best Air Force in the world. And we could not wait to begin operations until all the aircraft were built and all the crews ready.

The 17th of August, 1942, was D-Day for the AAF's offensive against Germany. On that day, our first heavy bombers took off from English bases to bomb a target at Rouen. Less than two years later, on the 6th of June, 1944, the Luftwaffe was unable to offer serious opposition to the landing of our Ground Forces in Normandy....

Our heavy bomber missions brought cumulative disruption into the entire German war economy. When we stopped production in the ball-bearing factories in Schweinfurt and Berlin, we created shortages that effected the making of tanks, artillery, engines—in fact of any of the special weapons of modern war. We diverted millions of able-bodied Germans to the jobs of aircraft defense, plant dispersal and camouflage, shelter building wreckage, disposal, and warning services.

We did not, of course, neglect our tactical air arm. Tactical Air Forces are composed of lighter aircraft—the medium bombers and fighters—although heavy bombers are sometimes used for tactical purposes. By tactical purposes I mean the attainment of more or less immediate objectives.

In our implement of tactical air power we have arrived at what appears to be an extremely sound set of basic principles. We have found these principles as simple as they are effective.

First, we neutralize the enemy's air power by hitting his airdromes or taking out his planes in aërial combat.

Second, we isolate a battle area of our own choice by cutting enemy supply and communication lines, such as bridges and railroads. We call this process interdiction.

Third, and last, our tactical Air Forces coöperate in the closest possible way with our advancing or defending ground troops.

These were our guiding principles in the drive against North Africa and up the Italian peninsula, in France, in Germany, as well as in New Guinea, and along the last of the long road to Japan. In this war, control of the air has come to be an absolute prerequisite of success on land or sea....

But the Army Air Forces must never rest on their laurels—not even after the defeat of Japan.

An Air Force can never stand still; it must either go forward or be left hopelessly behind. The aircraft types of a year ago are today either obsolete, obsolescent, or about to become so. And the same will hold true for our present types in the very near future. The battle of the laboratories knows no armistice.

At the same time an Air Force is not a question of laboratories alone. We do not dare ever again to cut our best in training facilities down below the needs of the largest and best Air Force the world has known. We must never again relinquish the leadership first seized by Wilbur and Orville Wright. To retain that leadership will not be an easy matter. It must be done. I am confident the American people will see to it that we shall.

Sincerely,

HHArnold

Commanding General,
Army Air Forces.

UNITED STATES FLEET
HEADQUARTERS OF THE COMMANDER IN CHIEF
NAVY DEPARTMENT
WASHINGTON 25, D. C.

We have every reason to be proud of what our military and naval forces have achieved in Europe. However, we cannot—and must not—entertain any belief that, because organized resistance has ceased on the part of the German enemy, the war is "about over."

We congratulate the United States Army—and the armed forces of our Allies—for effecting the actual entry into Germany and destroying her ability to make war. We congratulate the air forces for their victory over the Luftwaffe, and for their support of those engaged in fighting on the ground.

Though there were few naval surface actions in the Atlantic in the traditional sense, the Navy's contribution to the European victory was substantial. The winning of the Battle of the Atlantic against the U-boats was a requisite to the winning of the Battle of Europe. The Allied navies landed our ground forces on the soil of Normandy and, despite the enemy's U-boat campaigns, maintained the flow of supplies. The Navy further assisted Allied ground forces in the climactic crossing of the Rhine barrier. This operation, as all others, required the closest coöperation between the United States Army and Navy.

While we now congratulate those who have achieved victory in Europe we must not forget those thousands who gave their lives fighting to make this victory possible. They died that we might have the privilege of continuing to enjoy American liberty as we have known it. Our sympathy and our humble appreciation go out to their bereaved families and friends.

During the past year the war in the Pacific has progressed at an accelerated tempo. In that area we are still securing positions from which to launch heavier and more concentrated offensives against the Japanese homeland. At the same time, the closer we get to the heart of Japan, the stronger we find her resistance—as we experienced on Saipan, and on Iwo Jima, and, more recently, on Okinawa. The farther we advance the longer our vital supply lines become, further complicating our already complex logistic system.

The problem of convoying the millions of troops now in Europe halfway around the world to the Far East is one of the most immense which any naval force ever faced. To supply them once they get there will be almost equally difficult. These problems must be—and are being—solved even as we continue to press home the campaigns now under way in the far Pacific. Coördination of effort among the fighting forces and the efforts of workers on the home front have made possible our success so far and will continue to be essential to ultimate victory.

We sincerely wish that this could have been a day of victory on all fronts, but we know that the tough kernel of Japanese resistance remains to be crushed. Hence, we must pursue the war in the Pacific with increased determination, and with the maximum of equipment and trained personnel. Therefore make this not a day of celebration primarily, but rather a day of rededication to the task that yet remains ahead of us—total and rapid defeat of the Japanese enemy.

E J King

E. J. KING,
Fleet Admiral, U. S. Navy.

V-E DAY (MAY 8, 1945) RADIO STATEMENT BY FLEET ADMIRAL
E. J. KING, U. S. NAVY

HEADQUARTERS U. S. MARINE CORPS
WASHINGTON

It is a pleasure to accept the kind invitation of the Historical Foundations of World War II to outline the achievements of the men of the Marine Corps during this war.

The Marine Corps is an integral part of the United States Navy. As the land-arm of the Navy, the Corps is prepared by study, practice, and tradition to carry out the land-fighting phases of amphibious operations. The men of our Fleet Marine Force are especially trained for ship-to-shore assault and the subsequent hard fighting usually necessary to wrest the objective from hostile defending forces.

Since the war against Japan has been predominately amphibious in nature—has, in fact, been by far the greatest amphibious conflict of all time, the Marine Corps has been committed almost entirely to the War in the Pacific.

The men of the Corps have fought throughout the war with unsurpassable heroism and skill, in keeping with the traditions of their Corps and their national heritage. Their record of indomitable fighting service in defense of their country began in the very first hours of the war, when the Japanese struck at Pearl Harbor, Wake Island, the Philippines, and Guam.

Aboard ships and ashore, Marines bore their share of the fighting and the maintenance of order throughout the enemy's sudden air attack on Pearl Harbor on December 7, 1941. Casualties in our ranks, as among all other service personnel there, were heavy.

In the Philippines a Marine force, drawn mostly from the Fourth Marine Regiment, fought alongside Army troops throughout the heroic delaying struggle against overwhelming enemy ground and air power on Bataan Peninsula and Corregidor.

The first all-Marine action of World War II was the epic stand at Wake Island where a garrison of only four hundred Marines and a Marine air fighter squadron held off for fourteen days a major Japanese task force attempting to make a landing. Actually, the fighter squadron never had more than four planes in operation (others were damaged on the ground by enemy air action), but the dauntless pilots of those four planes at one time forced the task force to retreat and sank a large cruiser. The enemy, after suffering sharp losses in ships and men, finally effected a landing and overran the island on December 23.

Our naval base at Guam also was attacked on December 7 and captured by the Japanese after its garrison of slightly more than one hundred Marines and a small naval complement put up a gallant but futile fight.

At Guadalcanal, on August 7, 1942, our First Marine Division Reenforced drove ashore in the first American ground offensive of the war, beginning a long but steady march by Allied forces 3,000 miles across the Pacific to the Japanese homeland.

From Guadalcanal on, our men never were turned back. Every landing operation ended in the complete seizure of the objective. In almost every instance, the Japanese garrisons fought to stem the advance with desperate fanaticism. To defeat them—to break through and crush them in their huge blockhouses, their pill boxes, and their mazes of heavily fortified positions—called for the highest in courage and skill. And the highest never was lacking....

The Marine Corps also has taken a vital part in the aërial offensive in the Pacific, Marine pilots, flying both land and carrier-based planes, have served in many capacities throughout the Pacific battle area. From Midway to the Philippines, from Wake Island to a carrier off Tokyo, they have supported ground operations, destroyed enemy shipping, immobilized by-passed enemy strongholds, attacked enemy airdromes, scouted enemy activities, defended American-held bases, and carried troops, cargo, and mail to front-line fields.

Marine airmen have distinguished themselves unfailingly in every operation to which they have been assigned.

Throughout our history, Marines have served aboard the capital warships of the Navy. In this war, our fighting ships' complements have proudly maintained the high traditions established and upheld by the seagoing Marines of the past.

Please extend to the Board of Historians my sincerest thanks for the kind regards expressed in your letter, and also my best wishes in respect to the preparation of your History of World War II.

Sincerely yours,

General A. A. Vandegrift
Commandant of the United States
Marine Corps

**UNITED STATES PACIFIC FLEET
AND PACIFIC OCEAN AREAS
HEADQUARTERS OF THE COMMANDER IN CHIEF**

This is a day for which the world's people who understand freedom and justice have long prayed. The forces of tyranny and aggression in Europe are crushed. The way is open there for the resumption of the onward march of progress and civilization.

The victory of the allied forces is the work of many hands and many minds. It is a victory for our armed forces but also a victory for the industries that armed them. It is a victory won by united effort at home and in the zones of combat.

This is particularly a day of glory for General Dwight D. Eisenhower, supreme Allied commander, and for the leaders of our gallant Army. Generals Marshall, Arnold, McNair, Stilwell, Somervell, Bradley, Patch, Hodges, Simpson, Patton, Spaatz, and others have earned the admiration and gratitude of this and future generations.

Today we also honor our staunch Allies: The British Commonwealth of Nations, which never faltered, never flinched in spite of setbacks and the dark outlook when she stood alone; Russia, which was nearly overrun by Hitler's legions in 1942 but staged a magnificent rally unmatched in military history to eject the attackers from her soil; and our other allies who, with more limited military resources, nevertheless extended to us unlimited coöperation.

Above all, today we honor the valiant men of the United Nations who gave their lives in defense of their homes, and all things enlightened people hold dear. The record of their victories, and the memory of their valor will never die.

C. W. NIMITZ,
Fleet Admiral, U. S. Navy.

Excerpt of tribute radioed to victorious Allied Forces on V-E Day by Fleet Admiral C. W. Nimitz, U. S. Navy, Commander in Chief U.S. Pacific Fleet and Pacific Ocean Areas—Contributed by Admiral Nimitz for historical record.

WAR DEPARTMENT
WASHINGTON

We have deep and just cause to be thankful to a beneficent Providence on this day—thankful for the strength and endurance of our Allies, thankful that we have been able to raise up a mighty Army in time to meet the dangers that confronted us, thankful for the skill of our commanders and the courage and initiative of our soldiers that have brought to successful conclusion one of the great military feats of history. We should be deeply grateful also, that science, industry and labor have wrought the wonders of production that have allowed our fighting forces to confound the enemy with speed and fire power at sea, on land, in the air.

We have won a mighty victory in less time and with less loss than we had any right to expect. And as we pay solemn tribute to those who have died to save our civilization we thank the God who has blessed our cause to this present victory and pray for His continued help until the task is done.

The German nation united science and industry to the cause of degenerate barbarism. They turned their full manpower, long trained to war, to the conquest of the world that they might banish from it all the higher aspirations of mankind.

Their vile ambitions are shattered. Their leader is no more. The savage ambition he taught them is defeated. But the void in their character and the infection of their depravity still abides with them.

They must be watched lest they again poison civilization.

On the other side of the world the Japanese have likewise taken savage conquest and brutal rule as a national aspiration and justified it, like the Germans, by a self-adjudged superiority. Hirohito follows the downward paths of Mussolini and Hitler. His fading power for evil must and shall be utterly destroyed.

We are fighting one vast war for a decent world. We shall continue that war wherever it has to be fought with all our righteous might until the last sign of power in our enemies has disappeared from sight.

Henry L. Stimson

Secretary of War

HISTORICAL RECORD OF SECRETARY OF WAR HENRY L. STIMSON'S STATEMENT TO THE NATION OVER THE RADIO ON V-E DAY—AUTOGRAPHED BY HIM FOR PRESERVATION IN THIS MEMORIAL HISTORY OF WORLD WAR II

THE SECRETARY OF THE NAVY
WASHINGTON

This war has demonstrated these four primary truths about the sea and air power of our Navy:

First: That possession of such power, giving us control of the great reaches of sea in both oceans, means that our enemies cannot bring attacks to our home shores.

Second: That the corollary of the above statement is that the places where we fight any nation with which we go to war will be of our choosing and not theirs.

Third: That possession of sea power mutiplies the effectiveness of land forces, and may give us what Mahan said British sea power gave Wellington, the multiple use of the limited forces at his disposal—they were available to fight Napoleon in Spain and they could be shifted by water to fight in the Low Countries.

Fourth: That however powerful our land and air armies may be, it is command of the sea that enables their power to be applied, whether it is on the coast of North Africa, the beaches of Normandy, the jungles of Luzon, or in the skies over Tokyo.

These fundamentals make possible our victory in this war. We should never forget them or neglect the Navy which embodies them.

Sincerely yours,

James Forrestal

James Forrestal
Secretary of the Navy

STATEMENT CONTRIBUTED BY SECRETARY FORRESTAL FOR RECORD IN THIS HISTORY OF WORLD WAR II

The peoples of the British Commonwealth are proud to have had a part in the victory over Germany. We knew the dark days of 1940. In five and a half years we had more than a million casualties. We were mobilised for total war and all that it involved. In Britain we suffered the ruthless bombing of our cities and a wartime way of life made hard by strict rationing, the blackout, and unremitting work. We accepted every burden cheerfully because we knew that it was necessary and regarded it as our contribution to the common effort and sacrifice of the free peoples of the world.

In the same spirit we are now marching with our Allies to final victory over Japan and an enduring peace. For this we need above all the unity that has been forged in war. One of the sharpest weapons in the armory of the enemy was a propaganda which aimed at creating disunity and mutual mistrust among the peoples about to be attacked. That weapon was effective until at last it broke on the shield of Allied unity. For with the gallantry of those who fought, the skill of those who planned and the ungrudged service of those who worked, we must rate as a major factor in our victory over Germany the coöperation and comradeship of the peoples of our great alliance.

Halifax

(The Rt. Honorable, the Viscount Halifax, K. G., Ambassador to the United States from Great Britain)

WRITTEN BY LORD HALIFAX FOR MEMORIAL RECORD IN THIS HISTORY OF WORLD WAR II

HISTORY OF WORLD WAR II

VICTORY OF THE UNITED NATIONS
CAUSES AND RESULTS OF WORLD WAR II

WE who lived through World War II witnessed the mightiest struggle the world has ever known—the war waged by the dictators against the democracies, in which tyranny and despotism threatened to destroy civilization.

After six years and one day the gigantic conflict came to its dramatic climax with the unconditional surrender of Japan on September 2, 1945, the last of the sinister forces of the Axis "master races" which had started out on the debauched adventure of world conquest.

Germany, starting the war on the European front on September 1, 1939, had fallen in ruins, the victim of her own mad ambitions, on May 7, 1945, with her great cities in flames and wreckage—cities of the dead. The unconditional surrender in Berlin had come 118 days before the surrender of Japan in Tokyo. Italy, the third of the great Axis partners had fallen by the wayside and surrendered on September 8, 1943, nearly two years before the final triumph of the Allied democracies.

Japan, following Germany into the war on the side of the Axis when she infamously attacked the United States at Pearl Harbor on December 7, 1941, had been left to fight it out alone on the Asiatic and Pacific fronts. The triumvirate met the most disastrous defeat in history.

V-E Day (May 7, 1945) and V-J Day (September 2, 1945) were celebrated throughout the free nations of the world. Millions knelt in the churches in thanksgiving. Millions of soldiers began their preparations for the grand homecoming—the war was over.

The Germans, who had invaded and subjugated fifteen nations to their iron rule, were now held fast by the great powers of liberation. They had lost every conquered country and themselves been conquered, to be placed under strict guardianship until their military spirit was broken, their lust for conquest was completely eradicated, and they proved themselves worthy to reënter the family of nations.

Herr Hitler was variously reported a suicide, to have been murdered by his own comrades, to have become violently insane, and to have fled into hiding. Himmler, Goebbels, and most of the Nazi leaders had committed suicide. Goering and a host of others had been taken prisoner to be placed on trial for their "war crimes."

Generals, field marshals, admirals had shot themselves or been captured. Mussolini had met ignominious death at the hands of Italian patriots and his body hanged in a public square while throngs jeered and spat upon it, kicking and trampling on the lifeless El Duce as he fell to the gutter. Never before in history had such grim retribution come to tyrants and despots.

Tragedies were taking place in Japan where Tojo and many of the warlords were attempting suicide, committing hara-kiri, or being placed on trial for their crimes. No war in history had ever ended with such a wave of self-destruction and confessions of guilt. Never before had the war-makers been stamped as criminals, placed under arrest, found guilty by juries of their fellowmen and executed.

The cost of World War II in human lives on all fronts, civilian and military, is estimated as high as fifty million men, women, and children. The military losses in killed, wounded, and missing total over twenty million and may eventually be found to reach thirty million. The homeless exceed twenty-five million.

The direct cost in money, as stated in the Historian's Foreword, passed a trillion dollars. The economic cost in destruction and loss of potential life earnings adds another trillion dollars to this colossal expenditure. This sum directed into the constructive channels of peace is sufficient to give every family on earth a substantial home, and a college education to every boy and girl in the world. It is more money than has been expended for schools, churches, and hospitals since the birth of Christ.

The Axis Powers, plotting to overthrow democracy and establish world dictatorship under Germany, Italy, and Japan, were able to gather but five satellites around them. Fifty nations joined the United Nations in preservation of human freedom; five remained neutral.

Historians are in agreement that World War II was the "unfinished phase" of the First World War—the inevitable result of the failure to crush the military power of the exponents of world conquest, which, between the two wars, developed into a "super-race" mania.

Documentary evidence proves irrefutably that the Axis plague threatened to set up a reign of terror throughout the earth, overthrow every form of human freedom, destroy Church and State, and revert to medieval despotism. To accomplish this their leaders had raised and trained a generation for human slaughter.

Mankind was to lose everything it had gained through seventy centuries of human progress. Every race, nationality, and creed was to be subjected to a paganistic system of slavery. The rights of "life, liberty and the pursuit of happiness" were to be abolished. The world was to be ruled by a "master race" which declared that morality, mercy, humanity, were weaknesses not to be tolerated by the "new order."

The direct roots of this gigantic conspiracy lie deeply planted in the age-old war system with its centuries of conquest. During the last three thousand years there has been a war in some part of the world twelve out of every thirteen years.

The League of Nations, magnificent in its conception, the first organized effort to protect nations against future wars, was deprived of power to enforce its edicts. A deliberative body, it advised, suggested, and applied economic sanctions, without being given the means to apply them, if necessary, by united action. It functioned successfully in more than a thousand disputes, but found itself without "police power" in the last crucial test.

The Treaty of Versailles has been criticized as both too severe and too lenient—events have proved that it was too lenient. It failed to recognize the psychology of Europe which for three hundred years has been a "breeding ground" for war. In its compromises, with its diplomatic exchanges, it placed too great faith in the pledges of the war-mongers.

It failed to lock the doors of opportunity through which the Hitlers and Mussolinis and Tojos of the world were later to step. It failed to comprehend the greed and avarice of men imbued with the ambition for world conquest. Provisions, which constricted them for a time, were not vigorously enforced. It placed too great stress on economic reconstruction and restoration of trade, without taking into consideration the elements in human nature which plot and conspire against the world's peace.

With this encouragement, sinister forces in Germany, Italy, and Japan, believing that the United States would not engage in disturbances outside our own borders, began to defy the League of Nations.

On September 18, 1931, Japan sent up the first "trial balloon" to test the reactions of the United States and the rest of the world. This was the famous "Mukden Incident" when Japan felt her way into Manchuria. The South Manchurian Railway track five miles north of Shenyang was blown up. The Japanese declared that Chinese soldiers were responsible—and on this pretext Japan took possession. When the world's reactions proved to be nothing more than words—diplomatic notes, statements, resolutions of protest—Japan, Germany, and Italy were convinced the road to world conquest was clear.

Four months later Japanese Marines landed at Chapei in Shanghai, setting off the flames that were to sweep China. Then Italy dared to invade Ethiopia—and in quick succession followed the Saar "plebiscite" —the Franco Revolution in Spain—Hitler's defiance of the Versailles Treaty, Locarno Pact, and League of Nations by reoccupation of the Rhineland—annexation of Austria by Germany—seizure of Albania by Mussolini—and the other steps leading through the Sudetenland and Munich to the invasion of Poland on September 1, 1939. The "day of infamy" at Pearl Harbor, December 7, 1941, was a logical climax to the alleged bombing of a railroad in Mukden ten years before.

Students of World War II, and especially servicemen and their families, will find the issues for which they fought consistently stated and re-stated in President Roosevelt's messages to Congress and his frequent reports to the nation. He never equivocated; he never deviated from the cardinal principles of justice and humanity. These moral and spiritual appeals stand as memorial documents in striking contrast to the paganistic and sadistic proclamations of Germany and Japan. It is the voice of civilization *versus* barbarism. In his address to Congress on January 6, 1941, he set forth the cause of the democracies in these immortal words:

"In the future days, which we seek to make secure, we look forward for a world founded upon the four essential human freedoms:

"The first is freedom of speech and expression—everywhere in the world.

"The second is freedom of every person to worship God in his own way—everywhere in the world.

"The third is freedom from want—which, translated into world terms, means economic understandings which will secure to every nation a healthy, peaceful life for its inhabitants—everywhere in the world.

"The fourth is freedom from fear—which, translated into world terms, means a world-wide reduction of armaments to such a point and in such a thorough fashion that no nation will be in a position to commit an act of aggression against any neighbor—anywhere in the world."

This clarion call resounded through the world. It became the modern "Sermon on the Mount" to the distressed peoples and nations of the earth, the soul expression of the hopes and ambitions of the human race which proclaimed Roosevelt as the "hope of humanity."

His fundamental principles were the motivating forces behind every edict and action of the Allies throughout the war. They were the spiritual power behind every war conference leading to the establishment of the United Nations of the World organized in San Francisco to provide ways and measures to save the human race from the causes which create wars.

The first of these history-making conferences was held "somewhere in the Atlantic" early in August, 1941. President Roosevelt and Prime Minister Churchill were the architects of the future when they issued a joint declaration of the peace aims of the United States and Great Britain—the Atlantic Charter. This was a mutual expression of the principles involved rather than an official document for preservation in Government archives. Their purpose was to establish a moral understanding between the democracies of the Anglo-Saxon world in contravention to the unmoral and medieval promulgations of the totalitarian nations who were engaged in loot and plunder.

The Atlantic Charter was the first direct reply to German attacks on shipping and the submarine warfare being conducted against the freedom of transportation of American products. This "War in the Atlantic" began more than two years before the United States was drawn into the conflict and was a brazen warning of Hitler's plans while he was organizing the Axis assaults on the civilized world. The Charter, announced from Washington on August 14, 1941, stated:

"The President of the United States of America and the Prime Minister, Mr. Churchill, representing His Majesty's Government in the United Kingdom, being met together, deem it right to make known certain common principles in the national policies of their respective countries on which they base their hopes for a better future for the world.

"First, their countries seek no aggrandizement, territorial or other;

"Second, they desire to see no territorial changes that do not accord with the freely expressed wishes of the peoples concerned;

"Third, they respect the right of all peoples to choose the form of government under which they will live, and they wish to see sovereign rights and self-government restored to those who have been forcibly deprived of them;

"Fourth, they will endeavour, with due respect for their existing obligations, to further the enjoyment by all states, great or small, victor or vanquished, of access on equal terms to the trade and to the raw materials of the world which are needed for their economic prosperity;

"Fifth, they desire to bring about the fullest collaboration between all nations in the economic field with the object of securing, for all, improved labor standards, economic adjustment, and social security;

"Sixth, after the final destruction of the Nazi tyranny, they hope to see established a peace which will afford to all nations the means of dwelling in safety within their own boundaries, and which will afford assurance that all the men in all the lands may live out their lives in freedom from fear and want;

"Seventh, such a peace should enable all men to traverse the high seas and oceans without hindrance;

"Eighth, they believe that all the nations of the world, for realistic as well as spiritual reasons, must come to the abandonment of the use of force. Since no future peace can be maintained if land, sea, or air armaments continue to be employed by nations which threaten, or may threaten, aggression outside of their frontiers, they believe, pending the establishment of a wider and permanent system of general security, that the disarmament of such nations is essential. They will likewise aid and encourage all other practicable measures which will lighten for peace-loving peoples the crushing burden of armaments."

FRANKLIN D. ROOSEVELT
WINSTON S. CHURCHILL

These high concepts of social justice and unity of purpose commanded the immediate attention of the world. They gave to the nations not only a new Declaration of Independence, but the first great Declaration of Interdependence, a structural plan for collective security.

Less than five months later this inspired conception began to take form. On January 2, 1942—twenty-six days after the consummation of the Axis plot which stabbed the United States into the war at Pearl Harbor—all the twenty-six countries then at war with one or more of the Axis partners entered into concerted action by signing at Washington a pledge bearing the title: Declaration of the United Nations.

This document, the first practical result of the Four Freedoms and the Atlantic Charter, formulated the plan which was eventually to win the war and later to organize the brotherhood of nations to protect the world from future wars.

One year later, on January 24, 1943, the ten-day Casablanca Conference in North Africa—where General Eisenhower was commanding the forces against the Axis—set in operation the first United Nations offensive which was to lead to "unconditional surrender" of the Axis Powers. While decisive blows were being struck on the battlefronts the architects of the future drew the blueprints for the winning of the war, the re-creation of Europe, the rehabilitation of Asia, and world reconstruction.

The guideposts were set up at the First Quebec Conference in Canada where the whole field of world operations was surveyed on August 11-24, 1943.

In the Moscow Conference in Russia from October 19-30, 1943, the Foreign Secretaries of the United States and Great Britain established the relationship with the Soviet Union "essential to their own national interests and in the interest of all peace-loving nations to continue close collaboration in the solution of world problems."

Then came the Cairo Conference in Egypt, on November 22-26, 1943, where President Roosevelt and Prime Minister Churchill met with Generalissimo Chiang Kai-shek to agree upon the future military operations against Japan. They resolved to bring "unrelenting pressure against their brutal enemies," to "strip Japan of all the islands in the Pacific which she had seized or occupies," to "expel the Japanese from all the territories which she has taken by violence and greed" and to restore the Republic of China.

The first meeting of President Roosevelt and Prime Minister Churchill with Premier Stalin of the Soviet Union took place at the Teheran Conference in Iran (ancient Persia), November 26-December 2, 1943. Here these three great leaders "shaped and confirmed our common policy," with "determination that our nations shall work together in the war and in the peace that will follow." The statesmen of the three nations signed a pact of coöperation which includes these pledges:

"The common understanding which we have here reached guarantees that victory will be ours.... We recognize fully the supreme responsibility resting upon us and all the United Nations to make a peace which will command good will from the overwhelming masses of the peoples of the world and banish the scourge and terror of war for many generations.... We shall seek the coöperation and active participation of all nations, large and small, whose peoples in heart and in mind are dedicated, as are our own peoples, to the elimination of tyranny and slavery, oppression, and intolerance.... We look with confidence to the day when all the peoples of the world may live free lives untouched by tyranny and according to their varying desires and their own consciences."

This same spirit and purpose was affirmed at the Second Quebec Conference in Canada, on September 11-16, 1944, when President Roosevelt and Prime Minister Churchill reached decisions to crush tyranny by speeding the defeat of Germany and Japan. Plans were made "for as far ahead as any men could see with things changing as rapidly in the world as they are today." The conference was conducted in a blaze of friendship.

In the blood and travail of the battlefields the outlines of a rainbow of hope could be discerned spanning the earth. A New Age was in the making. Out of the thunder and flame of war, the day of resurrection was dawning.

On October 9, 1944—seven months before the end of the war—four great nations, the United States, Great Britain, Russia, and China, gathered in Washington, and after seven weeks' discussions announced the momentous decision of the Dumbarton Oaks Conference to recommend "the creation of an international security organization to be known as the United Nations."

The purpose of this world body was to stop future wars instantly at their point of inception with the authority for forcing peace and making future aggressions impossible. It was proposed to set up a General Assembly of all peace-loving nations which would make recommendations for maintaining world peace and security, a Security Council, and an Economic and Social Council of eighteen nations to seek "solutions of international economic, social, and other humanitarian problems and promote respect for human rights and fundamental freedoms."

The last of the great conferences between President Roosevelt, Prime Minister Churchill, and Premier Stalin was held on Russian soil at Yalta, on February 4-11, 1945, while the war was drawing rapidly to its close. Here the death strokes against the tottering Axis were planned, with the specified duties of each nation in Europe after the fall of the Axis until the various countries could establish self-government on democratic principles which would guarantee their own security and the preservation of peace.

The life work of President Roosevelt was nearing its consummation—the "greatest idea in history" for which he labored throughout the war. To establish some plan whereby the age-old system of war could be abolished from the earth, he ordained that a United Nations Conference be called in San Francisco beginning April 25, 1945. The goal of this Conference would be to perfect international organization and formulate a charter which would guarantee the collective security of the nations of the world.

Avoiding the weaknesses of the League of Nations following World War I, he warned that the United Nations Charter at the end of World War II must be invested with power to enforce its edicts, to take such immediate force as necessary against future aggressors *before* rather than after they had made war. The denial of this power to the old League of Nations was the cause of its failure.

The inscrutable processes of history, the destiny of mankind, were in spiritual evolution in the midst of revolution. Out of the carnage could be seen evolving the shape of things to come.

President Roosevelt, his faith strong in God and man, envisioned the future for which he was giving his life. The burdens of humanity had weighed heavily on his shoulders. Seeking a few days of rest he left Washington to relax in the countryside he loved at Warm Springs, Georgia.

At 5:49 on the afternoon of Thursday, April 12, 1945, the world was startled by words which began to flash over the radios: *"President Roosevelt is dead."*

While renewing his strength in the peaceful hills preparatory to the arduous duties of the San Francisco Conference, he had slipped quietly into eternity and immortality. The end came during the afternoon, as he sat in his chair talking with his friends, with the sudden stroke of a cerebral hemorrhage.

On the desk in his room lay the manuscript he had written the night before—the words he had intended to broadcast to the nation as a Jefferson Day address, Friday, the day following his death. As we read the message we find these stirring sentences: "Today, this nation, which Jefferson helped so greatly to build, is playing a tremendous part in the battle for the rights of man all over the world....

"We are part of the vast Allied force—a force composed of flesh and blood and steel and spirit—which is today destroying the makers of war, the breeders of hate, in Europe and in Asia....

"We seek peace—enduring peace. More than an end to war, we want an end to the beginnings of all wars—yes, an end to this brutal, inhuman, and thoroughly impractical method of settling the differences between governments by the mass killings of peoples....

"The mere conquest of our enemies is not enough. We must go on to do all in our power to conquer the doubts and fears, the ignorance and the greed, which made this horror possible....

"Today as we move against the terrible scourge of war—as we go forward toward the greatest contribution that any generation of human beings can make in this world—the contribution of lasting peace—I ask you to keep up your faith....

"To you, and to all Americans who dedicate themselves with us to the making of an abiding peace, I say: *The only limit to our realization of tomorrow will be our doubts of today. Let us move forward with strong and active faith.*"

The great leader of humanity was gone, but the inspiration of his words and deeds lives on. Never has a man received higher tributes than those which came like a mighty flood from all parts of the world. Memorials over the radio and in the press placed him among the great men of all time. He was proclaimed "a citizen of the world"; "a valiant soldier who had died in battle"; "a brother of mankind"; "a man with great love for the people"; "the savior of humanity." His position in history was immediately established.

The body of the Commander in Chief was carried through the streets of Washington to the White House on a black army caisson, drawn by six white horses with a seventh for a guide, along the route of his former inaugural processions. Hundreds of thousands lined the way. Many wept. Soldiers and sailors and women in the uniforms of the armed forces "marched in slow, measured cadence ahead of the flag-draped catafalque as service bands played the dirge of a Commander in Chief fallen in war."

Franklin Delano Roosevelt lies in the flower garden—back home in the village of Hyde Park, New York, on the banks of the Hudson River. He, like Lincoln, "belongs to the ages." Lincoln gave his life for the emancipation of three million slaves; Roosevelt gave his life for the emancipation of two billion human beings from the age-old scourge of war.

When Vice President Harry S. Truman took the oath of office as President of the United States, he pledged himself to carry on the mission of his fallen friend, and issued orders that the United Nations Conference on International Organization in San Francisco be held as Roosevelt had planned—it must "go forward."

It was at this assembly that the representatives of fifty nations, after eight weeks of continuous discussions, signed on June 25, 1945, the Charter of the United Nations to preserve world peace through collective security. This charter was later confirmed by the United States Senate and the Governments of the signatory world powers.

Its structure and functions in stopping future military aggressions, and in building solid foundations for economic security of all law-abiding nations, avoided the pitfalls of the League of Nations. It established a strong international organization with power to take action by force, if need be, to stop future wars before they can flame into conflagrations. This was the first pracical result of World War II —the dream of the ages come true.

Twenty-two days after organization of the United Nations in San Francisco, President Truman sat with Prime Minister Churchill and Premier Stalin in Berlin, the fallen capital of the conquered enemy of human freedom. This was the first meeting of the three great nations since the surrender of Germany. Symbolically it was held in Potsdam, the figurative birthplace of Prussian militarism, where from July 17 to August 2, 1945, was written the Potsdam Declaration which doomed the war-making nations.

Here, in the almost fabulous Cecilienhof Palace of the late Kaiser's days of splendor, the democracies issued their proclamation which pronounced retributive penalties against tyranny, despotism, and aggression. American, British, and Russian flags draped the huge oak-paneled chamber, symbols of the birth of a new epoch.

Around the table, reminiscent of the elegance and luxury of a profligate age, sat the leaders of the United Nations with their official staffs, President Truman presiding. Telephones and radio connected them with every point in the world, providing instantaneous communication with every nation and people of the earth. Here they delivered a final ultimatum to the Japanese Government to surrender or be crushed. Here they pronounced the fate of Germany, and set the plans for the future of Europe and the world.

At 10:30 A.M., on August 2, 1945, the Potsdam Conference came to its formal close. In Washington, London, and Moscow, the epoch-making document that recorded the results of the deliberations was broadcast. The first section of the 7,000-word document dealt with world peace. A council of foreign ministers of the "Big Three" with China and France was empowered to "continue the necessary preparatory work for the peace settlements," with the belligerent countries of the fallen Axis. The remainder of the decisions was devoted largely to Germany, with provisional agreements on territorial re-adjustments and reparations terms.

The section dealing with Germany took proper note of the fact that the German people were equally guilty with their leaders. It made it plain that the Allies intended neither to destroy nor to enslave the German people, but rather to rehabilitate them and make them fit to exist in modern civilization. The basic aims were the disarmament and demilitarization of Germany and her industries, the abolition of all her military, quasi-military, and political forces that existed up to the time of her surrender.

War criminals were to be arrested and tried, including political and military figures. All highly placed Nazis and sympathizers were to be interned, and no Nazi was to be left in a responsible position, public or private. Education was to be controlled to eliminate Nazism. The judicial system was included in similar plans. Decentralization was emphasized in the political future of Germany and for the time being the establishment of a central German Government was forbidden, while democracy was to guide local self-government. The basic freedoms of speech, religion, and the press were to be permitted within the limits of military security, and free trade unions were allowed.

It was declared that the United Nations would accept applications from all "peace-loving states who accept the obligations contained in the present Charter, and, in the judgment of the organization, were able and willing to carry out these obligations."

Human consciousness and conscience, as a result of World War II, have been awakened to a realization that only through some plan of world coöperation, endowed with power to stop war at its point of inception, can future catastrophies be averted.

The end of this first chapter of World War II seems a fitting place to include a message that has been sent to the historian by General Dwight D. Eisenhower from his Headquarters in Europe:

"The United Nations have been engaged in a great war for freedom. The military conflict has been won and there now remains the necessity of developing the victory into a secure, peaceful, and prosperous future.

"During the war the sons and daughters of free nations have demonstrated a capacity for sacrifice of self and for uniting in a common cause that can now be turned into the more fruitful task that lies ahead. My faith and my belief in the democratic peoples of the world leave no doubt in my mind as to ultimate success."

LAST DAYS OF WORLD'S GREATEST WAR —NEW AGE OF THE ATOMIC BOMB

HOW civilization on the brink of the abyss of war was saved by the indomitable will and superhuman courage of men, with the power of science, inventive genius, and industry behind them, is the greatest story in the annals of mankind. The fourth decade of the twentieth century surpasses in its astounding revelations any other period in history, and it marked the end of a war far more devastating than the human mind was hitherto able to conceive.

In these pages we shall survey the world's first great war in the air through the developments of the aëronautical sciences, the first great mechanized war on land and sea, the first war with implements of modern industry, the first war conducted by vast organization and engineering directed by the science of radio. It was a war in which time and space were eliminated to such an extent that they were mastered by men—a war that proved to be the beginning of an era of marvels in which radar and atomic energy made their first appearance on the human stage.

Mighty forces were released whose utility in times of peace, having first served as powers of destruction, can revolutionize life on this earth and help solve many of the economic, social, and political problems of the future. These, with awakened spiritual conceptions, under the guidance of the United Nations, give men and nations the opportunity to create a new civilization rising out of the ashes of World War II. If, through greed and avarice, man fails to take advantage of these opportunities, he will sign his own death warrant and perish through the power of his own inventive genius.

As historians, it is our duty to portray the bloodshed which led to this new epoch, the battles in which millions of men fought and died, or survived to come home to take leadership in the creation of this new world. We advise our readers to study the time-table of events which appears in the Chronology at the end of this book, as it is impossible within the scope of our narrative to present more than the highlights.

The greatest moment in any war is the moment it ends. Therefore we are presenting the last days of World War II before discussing the start of the war and the long train of events which followed in rapid succession until it reached its climax.

Inasmuch as the fall of the Axis in Europe on May 7, 1945, is

Last Days of War

described in the closing chapters, we take you to the Pacific to witness the final scenes of the world conflict—the last battles in the Far East where the war ended.

After the celebrations of V-E day (Victory in Europe) and the triumph of the Allies, the world's attention was directed toward Japan. It was estimated that it would require one more year and possibly 4,000,000 men to bring the cataclysmic struggle to its conclusion. How this schedule was reduced to a few weeks is here related. Japan was fighting desperately alone as the last of the Axis in these final weeks. In one of the most brilliant campaigns of the war the tide in Burma, which had been turned at Imphal, Kohima, and Myitkyina, surged over that country of towering mountains and abysmal jungles until the Japanese were driven from Mandalay, Akyab, Rangoon, and all the rest of the stolen territory except a corridor along the Sittang River which provided a tenuous escape route into Thailand.

The enemy fought with everything he possessed, but later engaged in a series of wide withdrawals behind the screen of desperate suicide rear-guards. The entire Japanese Army in Burma, with the exception of scattered elements, was wiped out.

In China, the Japanese had achieved for a brief moment their long objective of gaining full possession of the Canton-Hankow Railway and other main lines, cutting Free China off from its coastal provinces. The campaign captured eleven bases of the United States Fourteenth Air Force, depriving the Americans of every forward field other than a few isolated, hidden emergency fields, and pushing them back hundreds of miles to Kunming. Generalissimo Chiang's troops, in a sudden resurgence, were bolstered by the Sixth Army that had driven into Burma through the Salween Valley. The United States Tenth Air Force, shifted to China from Burma, unleashed powerful attacks in the late spring of 1945 that reopened long stretches of the railways and culminated in the liberation of hundreds of miles of the country's coastline within two hours' flight from Okinawa. In China, as in Burma, the Japanese began a series of retreats, clinging desperately to certain areas to prevent a rout.

At sea the Fifth and Third Fleets, subsequently revealed to have been one and the same thing under different names to confuse the enemy, closed in on the main islands of Japan. Under Admiral Halsey it was the Third Fleet, under Admiral Spruance it was the Fifth with only a few changes in composition. Week after week it sailed deep into enemy waters, launching as many as 1,400 planes from its carrier decks against Tokyo, Kobe, Kure, the Inland Sea, and a host of other targets. The main objective of the fleet's bombers was to keep the enemy air force pinned to the ground and destroy as much in the way of installations and war potential as possible.

During June and July they caught the remnants of the Japanese

Fleet hiding in the Inland Sea and at the Yokosuka naval base below Tokyo and virtually wiped out what was left of the world's third largest navy. Battleships and other surface units pumped thousands of tons of shells into coastal cities virtually without opposition from shore batteries or from the air.

When Admiral Halsey again took over the naval forces, on May 28, Japan was free of Third Fleet attacks only at rare intervals. Despite raging typhoons 105 American warships and twenty-eight British combat vessels under Admiral Fraser, attached to the Third Fleet, drew the net tighter. By the middle of August this armada, headed by nine battleships including the new *Missouri, Iowa, Wisconsin,* and the British *King George V,* twenty carriers, and twenty-five cruisers, shot down 290 enemy planes in combat, destroyed 1,301 on the ground, and damaged 1,374 more. Forty-eight enemy warships from battleships down were sunk, 100 more were battered and 1,500 merchantmen were sunk or damaged. In the last thirty-seven days of operations the only Third Fleet damage was to one light surface unit.

By the second week in August Japan's naval war loss totaled twelve battleships, nineteen carriers, thirty-six cruisers, 126 destroyers, and 125 submarines. Only a dozen destroyers and nine coast defense vessels were left in good enough condition to be able to take to sea duty within ten days. Submarines, under Vice Admiral Charles A. Lockwood, Jr., had played a big part in this destruction. Since Pearl Harbor they had definitely sunk 167 warships and 1,089 transports, tankers, and merchantmen, with hundreds more probably sunk or damaged. Japan's pre-war merchant fleet of 7,000,000 tons had been cut to less than 1,500,000.

In the air the United States dealt the most crippling blows against the enemy, with the giant B-29's leading the way. Capture of Iwo and Okinawa made it possible to provide the Superfortresses with escort craft. Okinawa was quickly being converted into a base large enough to keep the B-29's on Japan's doorstep.

When the war in Europe ended, Lieutenant General Doolittle was sent to Okinawa with his Eighth Air Force to spearhead the final pre-invasion assault and continue the job he had begun from "Shangri-la." General Carl A. Spaatz, who had directed the strategic bombing of Germany, was placed in command of the new Strategic Air Forces built around the B-29's and also sent to the Pacific. General Arnold told the Japanese that the country would be hit with bombs at the rate of 2,000,000 tons a year.

The B-29's had increased so vastly in number and power that the original flight of eleven planes carrying scarcely 100 tons of bombs grew to a mission of 820 Superfortresses which, on August 6, dropped 6,600 tons of demolition and fire-bombs on a series of targets. From

November 24, 1944, to August 14-15, 1945, the Superfortresses had flown some 325 missions involving 32,612 individual sorties, totaling a distance of more than 100,000,000 miles during which 169,421 tons of bombs were dropped on 581 important factories, six major arsenals, 102 airfields, and other targets in sixty-four industrial areas with a combined population of nearly 25,000,000. In addition, mines had been laid in forty-five stretches of enemy home waters, completely ringing Japan and isolating her from the rest of the world. In all these operations 437 B-29's and 297 crew members were lost; over 600 of the men were rescued from the sea.

The rapidly approaching end of the aërial war was evident when the B-29's came in low to drop the new gelatin fire-bombs which defied all man-made fire breaks. Tokyo was the target. Conflagrations raged up to the high embankments surrounding Emperor Hirohito's palace. The incendiary attack was so successful that from then on most of the aërial assaults were of this type.

General Kenney's fliers, from the time he took over at the gates of Australia in the middle of 1942 until his Far East Air Forces began to operate from Okinawa, had destroyed 11,900 enemy planes and probably destroyed 4,676 more. They also had sunk 1,700,000 tons of shipping and damaged 3,000,000 more. The Fifth Air Force which had been the core of the climb up the Pacific was subsequently joined by the Thirteenth, which had been based in the Solomons, and in June by the Seventh, which, in fightng westward from Pearl Harbor to Okinawa, had covered 16,000,000 square miles of the Pacific.

Three devastating blows in four days struck Japan during the first week of August. These blows, with the atomic bombs to follow, quickly drove Japan out of the war and brought World War II to its sudden and completely victorious close. On August 6 "the force from which the sun draws its powers" was "loosed against those who brought the war to the Far East."

The words are those of President Truman who, in a dramatic statement issued aboard the cruiser *Augusta,* on which he was returning home from the Potsdam Conference, announced that the world's first atomic bomb had been dropped from an American B-29 upon the Japanese city and army base of Hiroshima on the Inland Sea.

The 350,000 residents of that city had rushed to air raid shelters shortly before nine o'clock on that Monday morning when two B-29's appeared overhead. The big planes circled Hiroshima two or three times and then moved away. The "all-clear" sounded. The Japanese did not know that those two planes were checking the weather, visibility, wind, etc., for a third B-29, which came over as the people began to go about their usual business.

At 9:15 a parachute dropped from the bomb bay. At its end was a bomb-casing containing a small explosive charge. When the parachute was about 1,500 feet from the ground, it seemed as if the world had suddenly come to an end. A tremendous flash, like a ball of fire, illuminated everything for scores of miles; it was visible from the air 170 miles away. Then a funnel of smoke, dust, fire, and color mounted like a waterspout up, up, up ever higher until the pillar of boiling dust had reached the stratosphere. In two minutes the head was 40,000 feet above the ground and was still rising. It took hours for the air to clear sufficiently to see what had happened.

In a split second 60 per cent of Hiroshima had been wiped off the map. The new weapon was the atomic bomb, which harnessed the basic power of the universe. It obliterated buildings, trees, and everything else within a wide range. One tenth of Hiroshima's population was killed instantly, as many more died of their injuries, and more than 30,000 just disappeared.

Colonel Paul W. Tibbets, Jr., of Miami, Florida, piloted the *Enola Gay,* which dropped the bomb. With him was Captain William S. Parsons, U.S.N., of Chicago, who had designed the bomb. Captain Parsons made it possible to drop the tiny device containing the atom-splitting miracle by adding a casing to give it weight, a timing apparatus to make it begin functioning at the proper height, and the essential military apparatus for the release of the destructive energy—an explosive force equivalent to 20,000 tons of TNT which would have required 2,000 Superfortresses to carry.

The man who released the first atomic bomb was Major Thomas W. Ferebee, of Mocksville, N. C. The co-pilot was Captain Robert A. Lewis, Ridgefield Park, New Jersey, the navigator Captain Theodore J. Van Kirk, North Cumberland, Pennsylvania. The other members of that epoch-making crew were: Staff Sergeant Wyatt E. Duzenbury, Lansing, Michigan, flight engineer; Pfc. Richard N. Nelson, Los Angeles, California, radio operator; Sergeant Joe A. Steiborik, Taylor, Texas, radar operator; Staff Sergeant George R. Ceron, Lynbrook, Long Island, tail gunner, and Lieutenant M. U. Jeppson, electronics officer.

President Truman characterized the development of the atomic bomb as "the battle of the laboratories," a battle just barely won over Germany by the heroic efforts of Allied fighting men which retarded enemy progress on the one hand while hastening military defeat on the other. It was also won by the superhuman efforts of scientists.

The first real progress came when President Roosevelt and Prime Minister Churchill agreed to pool the knowledge of Great Britain and the United States on the development of this scientific marvel. Experimental work was begun in 1940 in the United States.

What transpired after that and until August 6, 1945 was the world's best kept secret, despite the fact that at one time 125,000 persons were engaged in extracting the uranium element and producing the other essentials for the attainment of what scientists call "atomic fission" that releases the almost limitless energy.

Three hidden cities with a total population of 100,000 sprang into being to produce the atomic bomb. One was at Oak Ridge, Tennessee. It rose from an area of oaks, pines, and small farms to become the state's fifth largest city. It was operated under the name "Manhattan Engineer District," and was also known as the Clinton Engineer Works. A second town was isolated in the New Mexico mesa near Santa Fe, where experimental work was carried on and near which the first bomb constructed was exploded to observe the results. Richland Village, or the Hanford Engineers Works, was constructed near Pasco, Washington. Hundreds of the nation's leading scientific and industrial concerns contributed vital parts to the entire project.

It was the scientists of the United States, Great Britain, and Canada, who made the bomb possible. President Roosevelt, in 1941, created a special group in the Office of Scientific Research and Development to supervise the delicate task, with Dr. Vannevar Bush in direct charge. Vice President Wallace, Secretary of War Stimson, General Marshall, and President James B. Conant of Harvard constituted, with Dr. Bush, a General Policy Group. Major General Leslie R. Groves, of Albany, New York, was placed in executive charge of the program. Dr. J. Robert Oppenheimer, of the University of California, was director of the New Mexico laboratory where the first atomic bomb was exploded on July 16, only three weeks before it went into actual use at Hiroshima. Colonel Franklin T. Matthias headed the Washington project, and Colonel Kenneth D. Nichols the Tennessee work. Brigadier General Thomas F. Farrell was first assistant to General Groves. Dr. Richard C. Tolman of the California Institute of Technology was the scientific adviser, and Dr. Conant served as counselor.

The undertaking was a joint Anglo-American project and Great Britain was fully represented in all stages. Field Marshal Sir John Dill, Colonel J. J. Llewellin, Sir Ronald I. Campbell, the Earl of Halifax, Field Marshal Sir Henry Maitland Wilson represented the United Kingdom, and C. D. Howe represented Canada on the combined policy committee. Sir James Chadwick and Dean C. J. Mackenzie were scientific advisers. Hundreds of physicists participated in the work, including Dr. A. H. Compton, Prof. Harold Urey, Dr. Niels Bohr, Prof. Ernest Lawrence, Dr. Enrico Fermi, and Dr. Lise Meitner, the latter a refugee from Nazi Germany.

President Truman's announcement of the atomic bomb produced an effect upon Japan's rulers equal to the shock suffered by the people of Hiroshima.

"The Japanese began the war from the air at Pearl Harbor," he said. "They have been repaid many fold. And the end is not yet. We are now prepared to obliterate more rapidly and completely every productive enterprise the Japanese have above ground in any city. We shall destroy their docks, their factories, and their communications. Let there be no mistake; we shall completely destroy Japan's power to make war.

"It was to spare the Japanese people from utter destruction that the ultimatum of July 26 was issued at Potsdam. Their leaders promptly rejected that ultimatum. If they do not now accept our terms they may expect a rain of ruin from the air, the like of which has never been seen on this earth. Behind this air attack will follow sea and land forces in such numbers and power as they have not yet seen and with the fighting skill of which they are already aware."

As if to implement his words the second atomic bomb fell on Nagasaki, Japan, three days later. It was an improved version of the first. While it did not destroy as great an area as the 4.1 square miles of Hiroshima, the devastation was more complete and final. The buildings of Nagasaki were devastated. In the center of the area where, according to witnesses, a vacuum was created, there was no sign of any buildings whatsoever. Everything had vanished. Of Nagasaki's 50,000 buildings 18,000 were destroyed and few of the others escaped damage. Nearly 30,000 persons were killed. Among them were eight Allied prisoners of war who had been among those interned in a prison camp located in the heart of the great Mitsubishi arms plant, contrary to all international rules.

Great Britain and the United States had reluctantly unleashed the atomic bomb against Japan. The decision was reached only when it became evident that the war would be shortened and tens of thousands of American lives would be saved. Behind these new bombs was to come a giant invasion of Kyushu and Honshu in the late months of 1945 and early months of 1946. Japan, it was discovered, had an army of 7,000,000 men, nearly double the highest estimates, of which 3,000,000 were on the home islands. More were being withdrawn from the continent.

The enemy also had from 6,000 to 9,000 planes he was hoarding to use against the invasion, explaining the lack of opposition encountered by the Allied bombers and warships. These planes the Japanese intended to hurl in suicide attacks against the troopships and covering vessels. They planned to inflict so much damage that the American troops would be insufficient in number and equipment to cope with the islands' defenders. That there was some justification to this hope was evidenced by the fact that more than 250 American ships had been hit by the Kamikaze squads during the Okinawa campaign.

More than thirty American ships were sunk, with casualties of 10,000 killed, missing, and wounded.

It was Japanese lives against Allied lives that cast the die in favor of using the atomic bomb against Japan. The British and Americans were so fearful of future developments that they decided to entrust its secret to a special commission that would study ways in which the illimitable energy might be converted to constructive purposes for the good of mankind.

Then came another shock to Japan. Between the Hiroshima and Nagasaki blows Russia entered the Pacific war, fulfilling her promise at Yalta to join the United Nations against Japan after the defeat of Germany.

President Truman, at Potsdam, had won one of his greatest victories in persuading Premier Stalin to enter the conflict at once.

On August 8, 1945, Foreign Commissar Molotov handed Japanese Ambassador Sato in Moscow a note stating that Russia was joining the other Allied Powers in the war against Japan and that from August 9, 1945 "the Soviet Government will consider itself to be at war with Japan."

Promptly on the morning of August 9 the Red Army swept into Manchuria against Japan's vaunted Kwantung Army.

Included also in the Russian note was the first intimation to the world that the Japanese had broached the subject of peace. Rumors had been numerous but remained unconfirmed or denied. In view of Tokyo's subsequent attempts to attribute Japan's defeat to the atomic bomb, Moscow's disclosure proved that the enemy had realized he was defeated long before Hiroshima. Premier Stalin rejected Japan's first proposal on the ground that it was too general to submit. Then Tokyo wanted to send a delegation to Europe during the Potsdam Conference, but before this could be settled the ultimatum of July 26 was issued and it was too late.

The Red Army started to move at 12:10 A.M. on August 9—nine minutes after the declaration of war had become effective. One attack was launched on Manchuria's northeast border, the other on the west, where Outer Mongolia and Manchuria join. Korea was invaded the next day. In rapid strides of eighty, ninety, and more than one hundred miles a day the Russians, under supreme command of Marshal Alexander M. Vasilevsky, former Chief of Staff of the Red Army, closed in on Harbin in their typical "pincers" style that had beaten Germany's best troops.

Rashin, Japanese naval base in Korea and the nearby port of Yuki were quickly captured by the Soviet Pacific Fleet of Admiral Ivan Yumasheff. General Oto Yamada's Kwantung Army was no more able to stop the Russians than the Germans had been.

Things started to break with incredible rapidity and bewildering contradiction. On Friday, August 10, the Tokyo radio broadcast that Japan was ready to surrender if the Emperor's "prerogatives" were not prejudiced. The next day the United States, on behalf of the Allies, replied that the Emperor and his Government would be subject to the direction of the Allied Supreme Commander. The following day there was a false radio flash that the Japanese had agreed. Following more days of contradictory reports, blended with abysmal silence from Tokyo, word finally reached the White House early in the evening of Tuesday, August 14, that the terms had been accepted. The incredible delays stirred fears of Japanese treachery. While the pace of fighting was slowed, combat conditions were maintained everywhere.

The Japanese Domei news agency broadcast of August 10 that startled the world read: "Demarche First: Japanese Government today addressed following communications to Swiss and Swedish Governments, respectively, for transmission to the United States, Great Britain, China, and Soviet Union:

"In obedience to the gracious command of His Majesty the Emperor, who, ever anxious to enhance the cause of world peace, desires earnestly to bring about an early termination of hostilities with a view to saving mankind from the calamities to be imposed upon them by further continuation of the war, the Japanese Government asked several weeks ago the Soviet Government, with which neutral relations then prevailed, to render good office in restoring peace vis-a-vis the enemy powers. Unfortunately these efforts in the interest of peace having failed, the Japanese Government, in conformity with the august wish of His Majesty to restore the general peace and desiring to put an end to the untold sufferings entailed by war as quickly as possible, have decided upon the following:

"The Japanese Government are ready to accept the terms enumerated in the joint declaration which was issued at Potsdam on July 26, 1945, by the heads of the Governments of the United States, Great Britain, and China, and later subscribed to by the Soviet Government, with the understanding that the said declaration does not comprise any demand which prejudices the prerogatives of His Majesty as a sovereign ruler. The Japanese Government hopes sincerely that"—and here the Tokyo radio went off the air for several hours. A later broadcast completed the sentence as follows—"this understanding is warranted and desire keenly that an explicit indication to that effect will be speedily forthcoming."

The wording of the note carried an additional significance in that it presented the Emperor as a peace-loving man and, by implication, denied responsibility for having plunged China and the other nations into war.

President Truman immediately conferred with the heads of the other nations. On behalf of the Big Four, Secretary of State James F. Byrnes (who had succeeded Edward R. Stettinius, Jr., when the latter took over the State Department at the time Secretary Hull was forced to relinquish that post because of ill health) dispatched the following answer through the Swiss Legation, on the morning of August 11:

"With regard to the Japanese Government's message accepting the terms of the Potsdam Proclamation but containing the statement, 'with the understanding that the said declaration does not comprise any demand which prejudices the prerogatives of His Majesty as a sovereign ruler,' our position is as follows:

"From the moment of surrender the authority of the Emperor and the Japanese Government to rule the State shall be subject to the Supreme Commander of the Allied Powers, who will take such steps as he deems proper to effectuate the surrender terms.

"The Emperor will be required to authorize and insure the signature by the Government of Japan and the Japanese Imperial General Headquarters of the surrender terms necessary to carry out the provisions of the Potsdam Declaration, and shall issue his commands to all the Japanese military, naval, and air authorities, and to all of the forces under their control wherever located to cease active operations and to surrender their arms, and to issue such other orders as the Supreme Commander may require to give effect to the surrender terms.

"Immediately upon the surrender the Japanese Government shall transport prisoners of war and civilian internees to places of safety, as directed, where they can quickly be placed aboard Allied transports.

"The ultimate form of government of Japan shall, in accordance with the Potsdam Declaration, be established—by the freely expressed will of the Japanese people.

"The armed forces of the Allied Powers will remain in Japan until the purposes set forth in the Potsdam Declaration are achieved."

This answer withdrew not in the least from the previously stated Allied position. It suited the victors' purpose to have the Emperor remain temporarily in power because of the implicit obedience he commanded from the people. It said nothing about his prerogatives except that he must accept the orders of the Allied Supreme Commander—that he was to do as he was told. From the Japanese standpoint it gave the enemy an opening to "save face," so vital to the Orientals. It also furnished the basis for the propaganda that Japan had not been invaded—therefore that her soil was held inviolate.

The Potsdam Declaration was couched in simple, forthright words.

It said, among other things: "The following are our terms; we will not deviate from them; there are no alternatives; we shall brook no delay.

"There must be eliminated for all time the authority and influence of those who have deceived and misled the people of Japan into embarking on world conquest, for we insist that a new order of peace, security, and justice will be impossible until irresponsible militarism is driven from the world.

"Until such a new order is established and until there is convincing proof that Japan's war-making power is destroyed, points in Japanese territory to be designated by the Allies shall be occupied to secure the achievement of the basic objectives we are here setting forth.

"The terms of the Cairo Declaration shall be carried out and Japanese sovereignty shall be limited to the islands of Honshu, Hokkaido, Kyushu, Shikoku, and such minor islands as we determine.

"We do not intend that the Japanese shall be enslaved as a race or destroyed as a nation, but stern justice shall be meted out to all war criminals, including those who have visited cruelties upon our prisoners. The Japanese Government shall remove all obstacles to the revival and strengthening of democratic tendencies among the Japanese people. Freedom of speech and religion and of thought, as well as respect for the fundamental human rights, shall be established.

"Japan shall be permitted to maintain such industries as will sustain her economy and permit the payment of just reparation in kind, but not those industries which will enable her to rearm for war. To this end access to, as distinguished from control of, raw materials shall be permitted. Eventual Japanese participation in world trade relations shall be permitted.

"The occupying forces of the Allies shall be withdrawn from Japan as these objectives have been accomplished and there has been established in accordance with the freely expressed will of the Japanese people a peacefully inclined and responsible Government.

"We call upon the Government of Japan to proclaim now the unconditional surrender of all Japanese armed forces, and to provide proper and adequate assurances of their good faith in such action. The alternative for Japan is prompt and utter destruction."

Days followed which were so aptly described as "the war of nerves" before final Japanese acceptance came. President Truman immediately announced the appointment of General Douglas MacArthur as Supreme Commander for the Allies. Fighting continued on all fronts during the interval. It was not until the B-29's went out on their final attack, and heavy assaults were launched elsewhere that this reply was received from Tokyo:

"1. His Majesty the Emperor has issued an imperial rescript regarding Japan's acceptance of the provisions of the Potsdam Declaration.

"2. His Majesty the Emperor is prepared to authorize and insure the signature by his Government and the Imperial General Headquarters of the necessary terms for carrying out the provisions of the Potsdam Declaration. His Majesty is also prepared to issue his commands to all the military, naval, and air authorities of Japan, and all the forces under their control, wherever located, to cease active operations, to surrender arms, and to issue such other orders as may be required by the Supreme Commander of the Allied Forces for the execution of the above mentioned terms."

Secretary Byrnes immediately replied, instructing the Emperor to "direct prompt cessation of hostilities" and to send fully empowered emissaries to deal with General MacArthur for the formal surrender as he directed.

General MacArthur immediately went into action. He ordered the Japanese emissaries to start for Manila on the 17th. The code word for communication between the Allies and Japan was "Bataan." In Japan the Suzuki Government resigned. Then followed another series of delays before the enemy envoys finally took off as ordered for Ie Island, where they were transferred to an American plane for the final flight to Manila.

The Japanese emissaries upon their arrival in Manila were coldly and formally received although some brought flowers and gifts. General MacArthur refused to see them personally. They gave his officers full detailed answers on military dispositions and other vital questions preliminary to surrender. After the sixteen-man enemy delegation had started back to Tokyo, General MacArthur announced on August 20 that, subject to weather, he would move to Japan to accept the formal surrender within ten days.

During the next few days MacArthur announced that the United States Sixth and Eighth Armies, with Marines and naval detachments, would occupy the main islands of Japan on a definite schedule, and that the Tenth Army would occupy southern Korea. The Russians were to occupy northern Korea and Manchuria and regain possession of southern Sakhalin and the Kurile Islands. China would accept the surrender for all China, except Outer Mongolia and Hongkong, which latter the British would occupy, and also move into part of French Indo-China. The British would accept at Singapore the surrender of all Southeast Asia. Australian and New Zealand forces would take over the islands in the Southwest Pacific.

The formal signing of the general surrender was scheduled to take place on the U.S.S. *Missouri,* Admiral Halsey's flagship, in Tokyo

Bay, on August 31. The Pacific Fleet sailed into Sagami Gulf cautiously, after the mines had been cleared, and then proceeded into Tokyo Bay.

Caution dominated every move at this stage. No chances were being taken. This consideration, plus the appearance of typhoons, delayed the signing of the surrender until September 2.

Meanwhile, fighting was going on in various degrees on many fronts. Fanatical suicide groups continued their resistance in Burma. The Russian Marshal Vasilevsky curtly ordered the Kwantung Army in Manchuria and Korea to quit or be annihilated. General Yamada and his Chief of Staff Lieutenant General Hata decided on the latter course. On August 23 Premier Stalin proclaimed complete victory in the Pacific and the internment of Henry Pu Yi, Japan's puppet "Emperor" of Manchuria.

Thus far no Japanese spokesman had used the word "defeat" or "surrender." The Tokyo propaganda version for historical purposes as well as home consumption was that the atomic bomb threatened to wipe out the Japanese race. The Emperor could not sit idly by and watch his people annihilated. The home radio and newspapers printed only those things that supported this thesis.

Subtly, but unmistakably, there was being bred in the people a conviction that the war had been called off only temporarily by the Emperor until such time as Japan felt itself strong enough to resume the conflict. Fear and suspicion were inculcated in the populace.

Even before the formal surrender of Japan, the Americans began the occupation of the enemy's home islands. The first landing was made at 9:00 A.M., local time, on Tuesday, August 28, when 150 technicians from the Fifth Air Force and other units arrived at the Atsugi Airfield to prepare it for the main landings by General MacArthur and his airborne occupation troops. The task of this first group was to ascertain that all the installations of the field would be ready to receive the main body, that communications and supply facilities were operating, and that the Japanese were keeping their pledges.

The first American flag raised in victory over the soil of Japan was unfurled on August 29, at Atsugi, just below Tokyo.

It was originally intended that the real occupying force should fly to Atsugi two days after the first landings there, but a series of storms prevented the planes from taking off for several days. Meanwhile, ten ships of the Third Fleet entered Tokyo Bay to make similar preparations for the landing of 10,000 sailors and Marines at the Yokosuka naval base. Though the narrow Uraga channel was lined with coastal guns of heavy caliber, these were silent. American carrier planes roared overhead, prepared for any eventuality.

The world waited in tense expectation—waited for the end of the world's greatest war.

HISTORIC SCENES AT SURRENDER OF JAPAN—118 DAYS AFTER GERMANY

DRAMATISTS have never conceived a plot of more intense suspense and more gripping situations than unfolded on the Asiatic stage in the last hours of the war: The rescue of the long-lost General Jonathan Wainwright from a Manchurian prison; his reunion with General MacArthur; the revelations of Japanese atrocities; and the final minutes on the ship in Tokyo Bay on September 2, 1945.

The first thought of the Allied leaders as Japan collapsed was for the safety of more than 150,000 prisoners of war and internees. They were scattered in numerous camps from Manchuria and the home islands through the Continent of Asia to Thailand and in the hundreds of Japanese-held Pacific islands. The task was a formidable one, but it was the first job the victorious nations undertook. Army-navy task forces were created to land with advanced units and scour all areas for prisoner-of-war camps.

The Americans did not wait for occupation details to be concluded. Rescue teams were organized in China and dropped by parachute in nine places from Manchuria to French Indo-China, where, at the risk of their lives, they brought food, medical aid, and hope to about 20,000 prisoners and 15,000 civilian internees in more than thirty camps.

On August 19 word was flashed from Chungking that General Wainwright, hero of Bataan and Corregidor, had been freed from the camp near Mukden with many of his comrades, including Major General George M. Parker Jr., and Lieutenant Colonel James P. S. Devereux, commander of the Marines in their heroic stand at Wake Island.

At first slowly, but then at an ever-increasing tempo, the prison camps began to yield their human wreckage. Of the more than 200,000 Allied men and women incarcerated by the enemy at least 50,000 had died in camps or been torpedoed on prison ships. Japan's home islands held nearly 40,000 of the survivors; 2,500 more were in Korea and Manchuria, among whom were the highest captured officers; camps in China held 15,000 more, those in Indo-China, Thailand, and Malaya numbered 50,000. There were 60,000 in the Netherlands East Indies, and thousands more on scattered islands of the Pacific.

When General Wainwright emerged after 1,201 days as a prisoner he was a ghastly sight. Always so thin that he had earned the sobriquet "Skinny," he presented the appearance of a yellow parchment spread over a cadaver. He was so weak when he greeted his liberators that his entire weight rested on a cane. At his side, ready to catch him should he fall, were General Parker, and Lieutenant General Sir Arthur E. Percival, British commander at Singapore who had surrendered to Yamashita. General Wainwright was deaf from the effects of the gunfire at Corregidor and the subsequent neglect and hardships suffered in the numerous prison camps in which he had been held.

The sufferings of the hero, who celebrated his sixty-second birthday four days after his liberation, were to be forgotten in a round of honors such as he had never dreamed. The vanquished had become the victors. It was not until August 28 that he reached Chungking and made his first statement. It was typical of the man that he should express his deep gratitude for the "forbearance and generosity greater than any in the experience of any other defeated commander" with which the American people had accepted his surrender at Corregidor.

General MacArthur, in the first of a series of generous gestures embodying the feelings of the entire Allied world, invited General Wainwright and General Percival to go with him to Tokyo and witness the formal surrender of the Japanese. Beyond that, the Allied Supreme Commander arranged for General Wainwright to accept the final surrender of Japanese in the Philippines from the once proud "Tiger of Malaya," General Yamashita.

As American troops and ships closed in on Tokyo in preparation for the capitulation ceremonies more and more accounts of enemy savagery were brought out by released prisoners.

The *Houston* and *Perth* survivors managed to exist in Thailand camps despite lack of medical attention, despite starvation diets and physical brutalities. Two of the men escaped and, aided by Thai guerrillas, struggled through the jungles into a secret camp set up by the Office of Strategic Services "Cloak and Dagger Outfit" at the end of July. They revealed that 300 of their comrades were at the end of their physical and spiritual resistance and begged for prompt rescue. They also solved the mystery of the fate of their ships by saying the cruisers, trying to flee from the scene of the Java Sea disaster had dashed for Sunda Strait between Sumatra and Java. Just as escape seemed near they ran into a Japanese convoy at night, escorted by eight cruisers and a dozen destroyers, which opened up with all guns and launched more than 100 torpedoes. Eight found their mark in the two Allied ships which went down with a loss of more than 1,100 lives.

Fifteen hundred men were jammed into the hold of a prison ship and limited to one canteen cup of water for three men every two days. Thirst drove them crazy. When the vessel, known as *Beecher's Boat,* reached Japan after a twenty-two day horror trip 1,000 of the Americans had died.

Guards treated them like caged animals. On Truk men were brutally beaten; and so it went wherever they were held.

More than 20,000 Allied prisoners were "murdered" by starvation, disease, and fantastic cruelties in Burma, and 3,500 others perished on a "death march" of 140 miles through Thailand. In China, where the Japanese for years had indulged their delicate skill in torture, the victims were numbered in hundreds of thousands.

The variety of tortures devised by the Japanese was infinite, but the climax was reached in sheer cannibalism. The Australian Government officially declared that, not satisfied with raping nuns, flogging missionaries, and stabbing others to death, human flesh had been found in Japanese mess kits and over camp fires.

Those days and nights of hell were now over. American officers dressed in work clothes stepped on Japanese soil and were greeted on Atsugi airfield by Japanese generals resplendent in full-dress uniforms, Samurai swords, and medaled blouses. The Americans landed on August 28, the vanguard of the occupation forces. Two days later General MacArthur arrived in his plane, so appropriately named "Bataan," with General Eichelberger and Lieutenant General Richard K. Sutherland, the Supreme Commander's Chief of Staff who had handled negotiations with the enemy envoys in Manila.

"Well, we got here, didn't we," General MacArthur beamed, when he stepped from the "Bataan" onto the soil of Japan.

"From Melbourne to Tokyo was a long road," he told the cheering soldiers. "It has been a long, hard road, but this looks like the payoff."

The Supreme Commander went directly to his headquarters in the New Grand Hotel at Yokohama without deigning to see the Japanese liaison officers. American planes by the score and soldiers by the hundreds guarded the route from Atsugi to the headquarters General MacArthur was to occupy until he entered Tokyo. He busied himself with details of the occupation and the surrender ceremonies. The ventilator head on the galley deck of the *Missouri* was selected as the "table" on which the formal surrender would be signed. The United States flag, that Commodore Perry had flown on his historic mission to Japan ninety-two years before, was flown to the battleship to be raised at the time of the surrender.

The final week was ushered in when Admiral Halsey took his Third Fleet including the British warships into Sagami Bay on Monday, August 27. Japanese envoys boarded the *Missouri* and were given instructions for clearing necessary channels and for the occupation of the big naval base at Yokosuka, thirty miles south of Tokyo.

On Tuesday: 150 American air force technicians landed on Atsugi, between Tokyo and Yokosuka, raised the American flag and prepared for the stream of transport planes that was to bring in the first large body of occupying forces. The Third Fleet entered Tokyo Bay.

On Wednesday: General MacArthur reached Okinawa on the way from Manila to Japan. Admiral Nimitz arrived from Guam and raised his flag on the battleship *South Dakota*.

On Thursday: General MacArthur landed at Atsugi accompanied by thousands of troops including the 11th Airborne Division, victors of Luzon, and the 27th Division. Simultaneously, 10,000 Marines and bluejackets took over Yokosuka and neighboring fortress islands. The two forces spread out and reached to the outskirts of Tokyo.

Friday: It was a great day! General Wainwright arrived at Yokohama and was greeted by General MacArthur. The two men uttered their one thought: "I'm glad to see you," and clasped each other by the hand and shoulder. The Supreme Commander could not disguise his pain and concern at "Skinny's" appearance. It was the first time the two had met since March, 1942.

"The last surrender I attended the shoe was on the other foot," General Wainwright remarked. "It's good to be back a free man and an American soldier wearing a gun again."

On Saturday: the Marines occupied the naval base at Tatayama, across the bay from Yokosuka, and the entire area south of Tokyo was firmly held by United States troops. Under the orders issued by General MacArthur the Japanese had removed all troops to a safe distance and had disarmed everyone except the police. Marines also occupied the Kurihama naval base at which Commodore Perry had landed in 1853.

Sunday: September 2, 1945, dawned gray and sullen. Fujiyama's white crest reflected no rays of the rising sun. No sun rose over Tokyo this day and the Japanese saw in this a celestial manifestation that their "divine ancestors" were weeping. This was the day of formal surrender —the first in Japan's long history. Before the day was over—at the very moment that the twenty-minute ceremony ended—the sun broke through and beamed its radiance upon a world at peace.

About 8:30 that memorable morning General MacArthur and Admiral Halsey came aboard the *Missouri* and entered Admiral Halsey's quarters. Coveys of naval craft, great and small, maintained a tight patrol around the surrender ship. Overhead the best fliers in the army and navy carried on a similar vigil. The flags of the United States, Britain, the Union of Soviet Socialist Republics, China, and France fluttered from the veranda deck while on the mainmast hung Admiral Perry's flag with its thirty-one stars. More than 100 high-ranking military and naval officers of the United Nations looked down upon the space in front of the captain's cabin where the ceremony was to take place. Every vantage point from lowest deck to bridge was lined with spectators in uniform, eager to watch the proceedings. A green-baize table stood midway between Number 2 turret and the rail; a chair was on either side.

Ten minutes to nine—the Allied leaders went on deck. Personnel speed boats were loading the Japanese mission which was obeying the command of their Emperor's proclamation: "Accepting the terms set forth in the declaration issued by the heads of the Governments of the United States, Great Britain, and China on July 26, 1945, at Potsdam and subsequently adhered to by the Union of Soviet Socialist Republics, I have commanded the Japanese Imperial Government and the Japanese Imperial General Headquarters to sign on my behalf the instrument of surrender presented by the Supreme Commander for the Allied Powers and to issue general orders to the military and naval forces in accordance with the direction of the Supreme Commander of the Allied Powers.

"I command all my people forthwith to cease hostilities, to lay down their arms and faithfully to carry out all the provisions of the instrument of surrender and the general orders issued by the Japanese Imperial General Headquarters hereunder."

The voice was that of Hirohito, but the words were those of MacArthur, who had drawn the proclamation.

At 8:55 A.M. Sunday, September 2, Tokyo Time and 7:55 P.M. Saturday, September 1, Eastern War Time, Foreign Minister Mamoru Shigemitsu climbed stiffly up the ladder on the side of the *Missouri*. He limped as the result of an artifical leg which replaced the one that was blown away by a bomb thrown by a Korean at a celebration of the Emperor's birthday in Shanghai many years before.

Shigemitsu was followed by General Yoshijiro Umezu, chief of the Imperial General Staff, who was to sign for the military. Not a word was spoken or sign of greeting exchanged as the Japanese walked to their places. Every one in the delegation of eleven was sullen and grim.

General MacArthur, who was to act as master of ceremonies, was flanked on one side by Generals Wainwright and Percival, on the other by Admirals Nimitz and Halsey. The representatives of the other Powers, some in resplendent uniforms, stood behind. At nine o'clock General MacArthur stepped forward and spoke into a microphone:

"We are gathered here, representative of the major warring Powers, to conclude a solemn agreement whereby peace may be restored. The issues, involving divergent ideals and ideologies, have been determined on the battlefields of the world and hence are not for our discussion or debate. Nor is it for us here to meet, representing as we do a majority of the peoples of the earth, in a spirit of distrust, malice, or hatred. But rather it is for us, both victors and vanquished, to rise to that higher dignity which alone befits the sacred purposes we are about to serve, committing all of our peoples unreservedly to faithful compliance with the undertakings they are here formally to assume....

"The terms and conditions upon which the surrender of the Japanese imperial forces is here to be given and accepted are contained in the instrument of surrender now before you.

"As Supreme Commander for the Allied Powers, I announce it my firm purpose, in the tradition of the countries I represent, to proceed in the discharge of my responsibilities with justice and tolerance, while taking all necessary dispositions to insure that the terms of surrender are fully, promptly, and faithfully complied with.

"I now invite the representatives of the Emperor of Japan and the Japanese Government and the Japanese Imperial General Headquarters to sign the instrument of surrender at the places indicated."

Foreign Minister Shigemitsu doffed his top hat and approached the chair on the opposite side of the table from which General MacArthur was standing. He signed first the American copy, a sheet about twelve by eighteen inches, then the duplicate copy for Japan.

General Umezu, following him, sat down resolutely and scrawled his name with terrific haste.

"The Supreme Commander for the Allied Powers will now sign on behalf of all the nations at war with Japan," exclaimed General MacArthur. "Will General Wainwright and General Percival step forward and accompany me while I sign?"

The two Allied commanders, finally in their hour of triumph, advanced. General MacArthur signed the document with five pens. The first went as far as "Doug" and he stopped, handed the pen to General Wainwright, wrote "las" with the second which he handed to General Percival. The third pen wrote "MacArthur" and was presented to the United States Government archives; the fourth went to the Military Academy at West Point. The fifth, a small red one he pulled from his pocket, belonged to Mrs. MacArthur.

MacArthur arose and proceeded: *"The representative of the United States of America will now sign."*

Admiral Nimitz stepped up, flanked by Admirals Halsey and Sherman, signed swiftly and stepped back.

"The Representative of the Republic of China will now sign." It was General Hsu Yung-chang, chief of military operations for the Chinese National Council.

"The representative of the United Kingdom will now sign." Admiral Sir Bruce Fraser affixed his signature.

"The representative of the Union of Soviet Socialist Republics will now sign." Lieutenant General Kuzma Niokolaevich Derevyanko signed.

"The representative of Australia will now sign." General Sir Thomas

Blamey, Commander in Chief of Australian Military Forces, quickly signed both documents.

"The representative of Canada will now sign." And Colonel Lawrence Moore-Cosgrave, military attaché in Australia, placed his signature on the two copies.

"The representative of France will now sign." General Jacques Pierre Leclerc acted for his country.

"The representative of the Netherlands will now sign." It was Admiral Conrad E. L. Helfrich.

"The representative of New Zealand will now sign." Air Vice Marshal Leonard M. Isitt affixed the final signature.

General MacArthur spoke reverently: *"Let us pray that peace be now restored to the world, and that God will preserve it always.* These proceedings are closed."

The first signature was affixed to the documents at 9:03 and General MacArthur signed at 9:07. At 9:20 the Japanese picked up their copy, bowed stiffly and started to depart. Simultaneously more than 250 American planes led by fifty B-29's and followed by scores of carrier fighters roared over the *Missouri* in a mighty display of air power, and at the same moment the sun came from behind the clouds and blessed the sight of peace on earth. World War II was over.

Distinguished spectators of the army and navy had witnessed the ceremonies. One of the happiest was Vice Admiral John S. McCain. His last sea assignment in thirty-nine years in the navy was to witness the surrender. The next day "Uncle John" was to return to Washington for a desk job. But he never reached the capital. Three days later, shortly after he had arrived at his home port in San Diego, he died of a heart attack.

This is the surrender instrument that was signed in twenty minutes.

"(1) We, acting by command of and in behalf of the Emperor of Japan, the Japanese Government, and the Japanese Imperial General Headquarters, hereby accept provisions in the declaration issued by the heads of the Governments of the United States, China, and Great Britain July 26, 1945, at Potsdam, and subsequently adhered to by the Union of Soviet Socialist Republics, which four Powers are hereafter referred to as the Allied Powers.

"(2) We hereby proclaim the unconditional surrender to the Allied Powers of the Japanese Imperial General Headquarters and of all Japanese armed forces and all armed forces under Japanese control wherever situated.

"(3) We hereby command all Japanese forces, wherever situated, and the Japanese people to cease hostilities forthwith, to preserve and save from damage all ships, aircraft and military and civil property and to comply with all requirements which may be imposed by the

Supreme Commander for the Allied Powers or by agencies of the Japanese Government at his direction.

"(4) We hereby command the Japanese Imperial General Headquarters to issue at once orders to the commanders of all Japanese forces and all forces under Japanese control, wherever situated, to surrender unconditionally themselves and all forces under their control.

"(5) We hereby command all civil, military, and naval officials to obey and enforce all proclamations, orders, and directives, deemed by the Supreme Commander for the Allied Powers to be proper to effectuate this surrender and issued by him or under his authority, and we direct all such officials to remain at their posts and to continue to perform their noncombat duties unless specifically relieved by him or under his authority.

"(6) We hereby undertake for the Emperor, the Japanese Government and their successors to carry out the provisions of the Potsdam Declaration in good faith, and to issue whatever orders and take whatever action may be required by the Supreme Commander for the Allied Powers or by any other designated representative of the Allied Powers for the purpose of giving effect to that declaration.

"(7) We hereby command the Japanese Imperial Government and the Japanese Imperial General Headquarters at once to liberate all Allied prisoners of war and civilian internees now under Japanese control and to provide for their protection, care, maintenance, and immediate transportation to places as directed.

"(8) The authority of the Emperor and the Japanese Government to rule the state shall be subject to the Supreme Commander for the Allied Powers, who will take such steps as he deems proper to effectuate these terms of surrender."

The Japanese delegation also took ashore "Order No. 1 issued by the Japanese Imperial General Headquarters under the orders of the Supreme Allied Commander." It bore detailed directions for the surrender of local commanders over the entire vast Pacific War area, for the disarmament and demobilization of Japan, for the release of Allied prisoners of war and civilian internees, and promised to follow the orders of General MacArthur.

Immediately after the Japanese had left the *Missouri,* General MacArthur broadcast a moving message to the American people:

"My fellow countrymen:

"Today the guns are silent. A great tragedy has ended. A great victory has been won. The skies no longer rain death—the seas bear only commerce—men everywhere walk upright in the sunlight. The entire world lives quietly at peace.

"The holy mission has been completed and in reporting this to you, the people, I speak for the thousands of silent lips, forever stilled among the jungles and the beaches and in the deep waters of the Pacific which marked the way. I speak for the unnamed brave millions homeward bound to take up the challenge of that future which they did so much to salvage from the brink of disaster....

"A new era is upon us. Even the lesson of victory itself brings with it profound concern, both for our future security and the survival of civilization....

"The problem basically is theological and involves a spiritual recrudescence and improvement of human character that will synchronize with our almost matchless advance in science, art, literature, and all material and cultural developments of the past 2,000 years.

"It must be of the spirit if we are to save the flesh....

"The energy of the Japanese race, if properly directed, will enable expansion vertically rather than horizontally. If the talents of the race are turned into constructive channels, the country can lift itself from its present deplorable state into a position of dignity.

"To the Pacific basin has come the vista of a new emancipated world.

"Today, freedom is on the offensive, democracy is on the march.

"Today, in Asia as well as in Europe, unshackled peoples are tasting the full sweetness of liberty, the relief from fear....

"And so, my fellow countrymen, today I report to you that your sons and daughters have served you well and faithfully with the calm, deliberate, determined fighting spirit of the American soldier and sailor, based upon a tradition of historical trait, as against the fanticism of an enemy supported only by mythological fiction. Their spiritual strength and power has brought us through to victory.

"They are homeward bound—take care of them."

Surrenders by local enemy commanders followed quickly, some falling like ripe plums, others dragging on for weeks. The garrison on Marcus Island had given up on August 31; Truk, Pagan, Rota, and others in the Marianas yielded September 2; the Bonins and the Philippines the next day; and the American flag was run up on Wake Island on the 4th, the same day that Penang surrendered. Singapore was reoccupied on the 5th. September 7 saw the capitulation of the Ryukyus and the 9th brought surrender of 1,000,000 Japanese in China and the enemy in southern Korea. Malaya yielded on the 12th; Burma the 13th; and in between all these dates New Guinea, New Britain, and other enemy territory surrendered. It was a total surrender of the Japanese, as the throne of feudalism tottered.

The final act was played in Washington where, on September 10, General Wainwright, elevated to a full General, received the Congressional Medal of Honor and two days later deposited the original surrender documents in the National Archives Building.

Pearl Harbor was avenged by the soldiers, sailors, and Marines of the United States who had suffered over a quarter of a million casualties between December 7, 1941 and September 2, 1945, to restore the honor and the security of their country—and more than a million casualties throughout the entire battlefronts of the war.

Back home in the nation's capital on that great day of the war's ending, seated in the White House, President Truman, surrounded by members of his cabinet, had awaited the signing of the unconditional surrender terms in Japan, which he termed "the victory of liberty over tyranny." When the official word came that the war was ended the President spoke to the world over the radio:

"My fellow Americans:

"The thoughts and hopes of all America—indeed of all the civilized world—are centered tonight on the battleship *Missouri*. There on that small piece of American soil anchored in Tokyo harbor the Japanese have just officially laid down their arms.

"They have signed terms of unconditional surrender.

"Four years ago the thought and fears of the whole civilized world were centered on another piece of American soil—Pearl Harbor. The mighty threat to civilization which began there is now laid at rest.

"It was a long road to Tokyo—and a bloody one.

"We shall not forget Pearl Harbor.

"The Japanese militarists will not forget the U.S.S. *Missouri*.

"The evil done by the Japanese war lords can never be repaired or forgotten. But their power to destroy and kill has been taken from them. Their armies and what is left of their navy is now impotent.

"To all of us there comes first a sense of gratitude to Almighty God who sustained us and our Allies in the dark days of grave danger, who made us to grow from weakness into the strongest fighting force in history, and who now has seen us overcome the forces of tyranny that sought to destroy His civilization.

"God grant that in our pride of the hour, we may not forget the hard tasks that are still before us; that we may approach these with the same courage, zeal, and patience with which we faced the trials and problems of the past four years.

"Our first thoughts, of course—thoughts of gratefulness and deep obligation—go out to those of our loved ones who have been killed or maimed in this terrible war.

"On land and sea and in the air, American men and women have given their lives so that this day of ultimate victory might come and assure the survival of a civilized world.

"No victory can make good their loss.

"We think of those whom death in this war has hurt, taking from them husbands, sons, brothers and sisters whom they loved. No victory can bring back the faces they long to see.

"Only the knowledge that the victory, which these sacrifices have made possible, will be wisely used, can give them any comfort. It is our responsibility—ours, the living—to see to it that this victory shall be a monument worthy of the dead who died to win it.

"We think of all the millions of men and women in our armed forces and merchant marine all over the world who after years of sacrifice and hardship and peril, have been spared by Providence from harm. We think of all the men and women and children who during these years have carried on at home, in lonesomeness, anxiety, and fear.

"Our thoughts go out to the millions of American workers and businessmen, to our farmers and miners—to all those who have built up this country's fighting strength, and who have shipped to our Allies the means to resist and overcome the enemy.

"Our thoughts go out to our civil servants and to the thousands of Americans, who, at personal sacrifice, have come to serve in our Government during these trying years; to the members of the Selective Service Boards and Ration Boards; to the Civilian Defense and Red Cross workers; to the men and women in the USO and in the entertainment world—to all those who have helped in this coöperative struggle to preserve liberty and decency in the world.

"We think of our departed gallant leader, Franklin D. Roosevelt, defender of democracy, architect of world peace and coöperation.

"And our thoughts go out to our gallant allies in this war: To those who resisted the invaders; to those who were not strong enough to hold out, but who nevertheless kept the fires of resistance alive within the souls of their people; to those who stood up against great odds and held the line, until the United Nations together were able to supply the arms and the men with which to overcome the forces of evil.

"This is a victory of more than arms alone. This is a victory of liberty over tyranny.

"From our war plants rolled the tanks and planes which blasted their way to the heart of our enemy; from our shipyards sprang the ships which bridged all the oceans of the world for our weapons and supplies; from our farms came the food and fiber for our armies and navies and for all our allies in all the corners of the earth; from our mines and factories came the raw materials and the finished products which gave us the equipment to overcome our enemies.

"But back of it all were the will and spirit and determination of a free people—who know what freedom is, and who know that it is worth whatever price they had to pay to preserve it.

"It was the spirit of liberty which gave us our armed strength and which made our men invincible in battle. We now know that that spirit of liberty, the freedom of the individual, and the personal dignity of man are the strongest and toughest and most enduring forces in all the world.

"And so on V-J Day, we take renewed faith and pride in our own way of life. We have had our day of rejoicing over this victory. We have had our day of prayer and devotion.

"Now let us set aside V-J Day as one of renewed consecration to the principles which have made us the strongest nation on earth and which, in this war, we have striven so mightily to preserve.

"Those principles provide the faith, the hope, and the opportunity which helped men to improve themselves and their lot. Liberty does not make all men perfect nor all society secure.

"But it has provided more solid progress and happiness and decency for more people than any other philosophy of government in history. And this day has shown again that it provides the greatest strength and the greatest power which man has ever reached.

"We know that under it we can meet the hard problems of peace which have come upon us. A free people with free allies, who can develop an atomic bomb, can use the same skill and energy and determination to overcome all the difficulties ahead.

"Victory always has its burdens and its responsibilities as well as its rejoicing. But we face the future and all its dangers with great confidence and great hope. America can build for itself a future of employment and security. Together with the United Nations, it can build a world of peace founded on justice and fair dealing and tolerance.

"As President of the United States, I proclaim Sunday, September 2, 1945, to be V-J Day—the day of formal surrender by Japan.

"It is not yet the day for the formal proclamation of the end of the war or of the cessation of hostilities. But it is a day which we Americans shall always remember as a day of retribution—as we remember that other day, the day of infamy.

"From this day we move forward. We move toward a new era of security at home. With the other United Nations we move toward a new and better world of peace and international good will and coöperation.

"God's help has brought us to this day of victory. With His help we will attain that peace and prosperity for ourselves and all the world in the years ahead."

4

TRIUMPH OF DEMOCRACY—MacARTHUR IN TOKYO—EISENHOWER IN GERMANY

THE last scene in this greatest drama in the world's history was MacArthur's entrance into Tokyo on Sunday, September 9, 1945. Here he established his rule over the Japanese Empire until such time as it should prove itself willing and able to live among the democratic nations as a law-abiding people.

The great Commander took possession of the ancient Japanese capital with simple dignity, in keeping with the democratic spirit and American character. There was no pretentiousness of grandeur or triumph. It was a peaceful occupation of a mission endowed with nobility of purpose. As he established himself under the Stars and Stripes of freedom at the American Embassy, near the palace of Emperor Hirohito, he assumed full authority over the Emperor and the Empire. He felt the tremendous responsibility which rested on his shoulders and prayed for God's guidance.

Far away in Germany, his friend, General Eisenhower, was carrying the burden of a similar responsibility with the same resoluteness of purpose, aiding the Allied leaders in reëstablishing peace for the rebuilding of Europe on the principles of human freedom and amity between nations.

Before we consider the problems which confronted them let us spend a few minutes with General MacArthur at Tokyo as the outlines of American policy began to take shape. His desire was to assure tranquillity with as little disturbance as possible to the Japanese people, who were confused by the presence of a victorious "foreign power" in their homeland for the first time in 2,500 years; not to placate them, but to give them a practical demonstration of the meaning and methods of democracy at work. Thus the occupation was to be gradual. The extension of the firm hand of justice, if received in a coöperative spirit, would lead them back to the friendship of democratic nations and give them a place of restored integrity in the civilized world— the world of the Twentieth Century, not the isolation and insecurity of the medieval ages in which they had so long lived only to meet disaster.

It was the intention of MacArthur to move quietly, and give the national temper an opportunity to adjust itself and manifest its intentions. But he was prepared for every emergency and moved with determination and decision.

In many quarters there was considerable fear that the enemy had deliberately stalled his acceptance of the Allies' surrender terms in order to gain time for last-minute preparations for either Underground resistance early in the occupation or the concealment of leaders, men, and materials for an eventual uprising; or even for the formation of the nucleus for a new war, against the day when the occupation should end.

It was apparent that the Allies were proceeding as warily on the political front as in the actual physical occupation. Coöperation with the Imperial House and the new cabinet of Prince Higashi-Kuni was obviously to be the guiding principle. This administrative policy was purely one of expediency, it was admitted to the critics who protested on moral and ideological grounds. These critics had made one point that was hard to deny; it was best summed up by the Netherlands' Ambassador to the United States, Alexander Loudon, who found the Japanese situation an almost exact analogy to the German situation in 1918: the enemy had surrendered when his own soil had not yet been entered by his opponents and when his own troops still held virtually all that they had seized in the whole war of aggression.

In Japan herself, politicians, editors, and ordinary citizens were indeed saying exactly what Germans had said twenty-seven years before: "We were not defeated, we were tricked. We have not lost the war." That this attitude would persist and be assiduously fostered was undeniable; to combat it was one of the hardest jobs before the Allies.

Events proved that the Allies' occupation of Japan was to be little like the occupation of Germany after the Second World War. The press was allowed to continue functioning, even though under the Allies' censorship; the Government that signed the surrender was to remain in power subject to the military control of the Allies. The elimination of Japanese fanatics, whether prominent or unknown, would be a difficult, continuous task.

We have seen that the American flag was raised for the first time on Japanese soil as a sign of victory on August 29, 1945. The little party of technicians that had flown into Atsugi raised Old Glory on that historic landmark without ceremony as MacArthur arrived on Okinawa en route to Japan.

From that conquered island the General flew the next day to Atsugi in his own C-54 transport plane, which he had christened "Bataan," to lead a veritable sky parade of airborne occupation troops.

The Allies' Supreme Commander was accompanied by Lieutenant General Robert Eichelberger, the commander of the American Eighth Army, and Lieutenant General Richard K. Sutherland, MacArthur's chief of staff. Behind them, as both American and Japanese photographers filmed the historic landing, streamed hundreds of transports, just as other hundreds had preceded, members of the 11th Airborne Division pouring from the planes to take up their work.

The planes that brought them there had been taken off every Air Transport Command route throughout the world for this task and massed for days on Okinawa's fields, almost wing to wing. Now they were swooping down out of the sun onto Japan and pouring out upon her shattered soil the hardened veterans of Luzon and Leyte. Among the troops were eighty-six Red Cross men and women, the vanguard of that force which had stood beside our soldiers through all their hardships to bring them as much comfort as the exigencies of war would allow.

When the formalities of the surrender had been concluded aboard the *Missouri,* the occupation went ahead at greatly accelerated pace. Within the first four days, 25,000 troops, including 3,000 Marines, had been landed by sea and air, principally at Atsugi and Yokosuka. By September 3 they had occupied more than seven hundred square miles up to the "line of evacuation" on the southern limits of Tokyo. When they would actually enter the capital was the major topic of interest not only among the troops but also in many a far-off city in America and Europe. That time was to be set by MacArthur.

One of the problems which confronted him was the lack of vital transport. In the air- and seaborne landings it had been possible to bring in only a limited number of motor vehicles. The Japanese, who were bound to supply the Allies' needs as far as they could, had considerable difficulty in rounding up serviceable vehicles in their bomb-wrecked country. Many of those they did furnish were to break down en route.

There was the problem of health, for example: tuberculosis and dysentery had made great strides in the enemy's country before the surrender. The Medical Corps had to take every possible measure to prevent the infection of our men. Sanitation was poor. To meet this as well as other, graver civil problems, MacArthur planned to set up a Four Power board, similar to the Allied Control Council in Berlin. This board would consist of representatives of the United States, Britain, Russia, and China. The American representative was to be Admiral Nimitz.

It was announced on September 5 that Major General William C. Chase's First Dismounted Cavalry Division would occupy Tokyo three days later. These men, the first to reënter Manila in the re-invasion of the Philippines, were already stationed between the capital and the great port city of Yokohama. The 27th Infantry was to join the occupation later.

General Eichelberger summoned Field Marshal Sugiyama, former chief of the Japanese General Staff and military adviser to the Emperor, to his headquarters and laid down to him the Americans' orders for their entry into Tokyo.

All roads and cities were to be marked in English. More important, the enemy was to prepare complete lists of all prisoners, including the names and burial places of those who had died, and to turn over prison camps to the ranking officer in each, making full provision for food, shelter, and health.

Similar arrangements applied to southern Honshu, under the command of Lieutenant General Walter Krueger of the Sixth Army; and Korea, where Lieutenant General John R. Hodge of the 24th Corps would take charge. MacArthur also ordered the Japanese to provide ships and skilled labor as he should direct, meanwhile demobilizing their forces as speedily and efficiently as possible. Office buildings, hospitals, and any other facilities for which need might arise were to be furnished as the Americans called for them. The Tokyo radio, which, like all others, was eventually to be handed over, was ordered to cease all foreign-language broadcasts.

Reluctantly, it seemed, Tokyo admitted that the American troops already landed were conducting themselves properly. In a veiled attempt to discredit the Americans, however, it falsely alleged a few cases of brutality, rape, and looting. It urged the population to behave circumspectly, lock its doors, and in general keep out of the way. In Yokohama, the City Council urged all women to flee to the country at once to avoid a "fate worse than death." There was a complete cessation of street-car service, since all the operators were women. Generally, however, public transport, both urban and interurban, was kept functioning.

The enemy's Domei news agency was being retained and, many Americans alleged, was being allowed to "scoop" them on important developments. The army could not permit reporters for the Allies in Tokyo because it might result in "spearheading the occupation." Some had gone in before the troops' entry but they had sent out little information of value and certainly none of military or political importance.

The vanguard of the First Cavalry rumbled through Tokyo in trucks on September 5 to prepare the city for MacArthur. Their job was to find suitable quarters for offices, for residences and similar purposes, and to see that the enemy was carrying out Eichelberger's orders to disarm all troops, including the M.P.'s, leaving only the civilian police armed. In Tokyo and Yokohama the Japs were already piling up their side arms neatly and lining up heavy equipment in designated places. But so far no war criminals had been turned over; the Allies had not yet published their lists of the men they would accuse. Some members of Japan's disbanded Gestapo, the Kimpei-Tai, were being impressed into the civilian police force and might eventually be used to trap the war criminals.

One of these, however, fell right into the Allies' hands. This was a woman, Iva Togori, a native of California who had gone to Japan before the war and become one of the four women known as "Tokyo Rose" who regaled American troops nightly with broadcasts of popular music and clumsy, amateurish propaganda.

The time for the official entry into the capital, with all that it would symbolize, approached. American forces began to feed famished Japanese civilians in the Yokosuka area. This was a practical matter of preventing disorders that might otherwise plague the occupation forces. General MacArthur declared that he would need between 300,000 and 400,000 men for the occupation of Japan proper and all the territory that the enemy had seized; though the Japs had kept ten times that number overseas alone. The Japanese had been occupying hostile territory; the Americans would be restoring liberated lands.

Similar arrangements were being made for the occupation of other areas that the Japanese had held for years. In Korea, the citizens, who expected that the end of the war would mean their liberation from Japanese rule, had a rude surprise when they learned that, until an American military government could be organized, the Japanese officials who had controlled their country since its invasion would temporarily continue in power under American supervision. The Koreans protested vigorously as they could not understand the reasoning of expediency behind the move.

As the formal occupation of Tokyo was taking place a Japanese offer was made to line the twenty-mile route from Yokohama to Tokyo with armed police. General MacArthur declined all pomp and ceremony and drove into the shattered capital accompanied only by a single squadron of the 7th Cavalry Regiment of the First Division, to establish the Allies' authority over Japan. With MacArthur rode Generals Eichelberger and Sutherland, Brigadier General Bonner D. Fellers, his military secretary, and an aide, Colonel Roger Egeberg.

The General's party drove directly to the compound of the American Embassy and alighted from its cars. Though the American flag had previously been unofficially raised over the Nippon Times building, MacArthur ignored the incident. He stood alone before Eichelberger and in a calm, virile tone issued the historic order:

"General Eichelberger, have our country's flag unfurled, and in Tokyo's sun let it wave in its full glory as a symbol of hope for the oppressed and as a harbinger of victory for the right."

Eichelberger saluted briskly, repeating the order. A band of honor played The Star-Spangled Banner. All present saluted as the flag was slowly raised to a height from which it could be seen from almost anywhere in those portions of Tokyo which remained intact. A First Division chaplain gave the benediction and the ceremony was over.

The flag that had flown above the national capital in Washington on December 7, 1941, above Casablanca, above Berlin, and above the *Missouri* on the day when Japan surrendered now waved majestically above the enemy's capital, a symbol of the United Nations' victory.

The greatest task in the United States' military history had now officially begun: the administration of conquered Japan. Further occupation operations were scheduled, to embrace eventually the entire Japanese Empire.

MacArthur had already announced that courts-martial would try the men whom the Allies regarded as guilty of war crimes. No sooner had the occupation begun than certain Japanese groups began preparing their own list of criminals for presentation to the Allies. Premier Hideki Tojo, who headed the Government responsible for the Pearl Harbor attack, led the list; but it included, as well, former Premier Prince Fumimaro Konoye, now Vice Premier, and Foreign Minister Shigemitsu, who had signed the surrender aboard the *Missouri*. He, it was charged, had long been instrumental behind the scenes in preventing a peaceful solution of the war in China.

What the Allies would do with this list was a subject for speculation; it was known only that they were already taking extensive steps to round up every war criminal from the top to the bottom. This procedure had been begun with the liberation of the first Japanese prison camps, when former captives and internees were asked to record the names and crimes of all those Japs who had practiced barbarities on them.

Even before the formal surrender in Tokyo Bay, the new Japanese Government had announced that it would permit the formation of six political parties and would hold elections as soon as possible. While little faith was placed in the integrity of these parties, since they were really nuclei of the old Japanese Fascist groups, the step was at least a nominal recognition of the Allies' demand for democratic rule. MacArthur's statement of policy on September 10 made it plain that Japan would be aided in every genuine effort to achieve democracy, rehabilitate herself, and reënter the society of civilized nations.

MacArthur ordered the immediate dissolution of the enemy's High Command, to be completed within three days. Henceforth the Allies would deal only with the Government. He then established a firm censorship over press and radio, revealing that his interim policies had been psychological tests of Japanese character. During the initial days of the occupation, every Japanese had been free to speak his mind as critically as he chose: thus all who were determined to incite their fellows to opposition had fallen into the trap and "tipped their hands." There was no need to search for these dissidents: they had betrayed themselves. At the same time, MacArthur made it plain that his power transcended that of all Japanese authorities, civil or military.

MacArthur made it equally plain that the Potsdam declaration issued by Truman and Churchill and endorsed by Chiang would govern his policies in dealing with Japan. Under its terms, the ultimate form of the country's government would be determined by the freely expressed will of its people. Meanwhile, the authority of the Emperor and the Government would be subject to the Allies' Supreme Commander.

The first instance of this came on September 11, when MacArthur ordered the arrest of forty prominent Japanese, including the entire Cabinet, headed by Premier Hideki Tojo, that had been in power at the time of the Pearl Harbor treachery; also Lieutenant General Masaharu Homma, the evil genius of the infamous "death march" in the Philippines after the fall of Corregidor and Bataan; Jose P. Laurel, the Filipino traitor who had served as puppet Premier for the Japanese, and Heinrich Stahmer, the German Ambassador to Tokyo.

Armed forces were dispatched to take all these men into custody as war criminals. One of the first to be taken was Tojo himself—the "Razor," as he had long been known among military men because of his quick brain and also because of his utter disregard for human life. Only the day before, Tojo had told an American reporter that, while victory might give the Americans the right to declare him a war criminal, history would vindicate him and his country.

When the troops knocked at the door of his suburban home, it was locked. Tojo refused to have it opened. While the Americans waited outside the house, they heard a shot. They smashed the door and rushed into the house. The former Premier stood before them with blood welling from his chest and his automatic revolver pointed at them. The Americans' guns were drawn too, and Tojo subsided into a chair, coughing and choking, confident that he had cheated the justice of the Americans.

The American officers rushed him immediately to a hospital where doctors worked over him in an effort to keep him alive until he could be brought to trial for all his outrages. The bullet that he fired into his chest had been aimed at his heart and passed through his back near the left shoulder blade. The best medical men available to the Americans in Japan gave him an even chance to live until his doom could be imposed on him in a manner befitting his life.

MacArthur announced that he would issue instructions to the Emperor and the Government, giving them every opportunity to carry them out without further compulsion. He warned that the Allies' troops were held in constant readiness to enforce the Commander's orders if the Japanese proved lax or treacherous. Japan's economy, he said, would be controlled only in so far as it was necessary to the achievement of the United Nations' objectives.

The keystone of his proclamation was his pledge that the occupying forces would treat the civilian population, the ordinary man and woman of Japan, only in such a way as to "develop respect for and confidence in the United Nations and encourage coöperation." The Japanese people, he promised, "would be completely free from all unwarranted interference with their individual liberty and property rights."

Democracy had been brought to Japan. From now on, it was up to the Japanese to accept or reject it, to determine their own fate by their choice.

On the other side of the world General Eisenhower and his allies, the British, Russians, and French, were laying the foundations for the "Europe of the future." Following the unconditional surrender of Germany on May 7, 1945, the Potsdam Conference had drafted the plans for its restoration on democratic principles.

Even before the Berlin Conference, the Allies had made it plain that their purpose in occupying Germany was to rid it of Nazism and militarism and to prevent it from again periling the peace of Europe and the world. To that end, one of their first acts was to place the country under control of the four occupying Powers. This meant the dissolution of SHAEF, that marvelous composite organization that Eisenhower had blended into an integral whole for the conquest of Europe. When SHAEF was disbanded, General Eisenhower's title of Supreme Commander, Allied Expeditionary Force, was changed to that of Commanding General of the United States Forces in the European Theatre, known thereafter as USFET.

Not only Germany as a whole but Berlin itself was divided into four zones of occupation. In each case the occupying Powers were the United States, Britain, France (whose share in both was the smallest), and Russia (whose share was the largest). The commanders of the four Allies' armies in occupation of Germany became the Allied Control Council, which was invested with full legislative and executive powers.

This council—composed of General Eisenhower for the United States, Field Marshal Montgomery for Britain, General Joseph-Pierre Koenig for France, and Marshal Zhukov for Russia—had absolute power to lay down the broad general policies of occupation, to which the military governments of the various occupation zones had to adhere in administering their respective territories, and to provide for necessary inter-zone passage of men and materials. To preclude national rivalries it was arranged that the chairmanship of the Council should rotate monthly among the four commanders.

The same procedure was followed with the Kommandatur, the Four Power governing body for Berlin composed of the military commanders of the various occupation areas of the capital. The Russians controlled the eastern part of Berlin, while the Americans, British, and French shared the western and southern areas.

Germany herself was divided similarly. The entire eastern half of the country, except for what had been temporarily ceded to Poland in the Berlin Conference, was in Russian hands. In the west, the British occupied the northern half and the Americans the southern half, except for a strip in the southern Rhineland Province and some territory farther south that was in French hands. In each case, subject to the directives laid down by the Control Council, the occupying Power ruled its area autonomously.

The major purpose of this division was to prevent the centralization —political and economic—that had always enabled the German Empire to wage war. Everything that contributed to the war potential in any way was subject to confiscation or destruction by the Allies; they were determined to prevent its restoration.

In the course of the invasion of Germany many of the leading war criminals had been arrested. When the conquest had been completed, the occupying authorities pressed a relentless search in all zones.

Here arose the first great problem of the occupation for the western Powers. The Russians used the simple method of ousting every Nazi official. Every non-Nazi who could not show a genuinely anti-Nazi record was replaced with men of coöperative tendencies.

In the western Powers' zones there was a temporary experiment. The military-government authorities tested the plan of retaining efficient and experienced officials, regardless of their Nazi records; the civilian groups advocated weeding out every Nazi and replacing all with our own men, if necessary, until democratic Germans could be trained to take over the task of running their own country.

In the early stages of the occupation the first school was dominant. Every officeholder and aspirant had to file an exhaustive questionnaire concerning his activities since the First World War. Many of these were filled with perjury and known Nazis continued in office. In Bavaria it was discovered that Nazism was being perpetuated virtually under the aegis of the American military government. In Berlin a similar situation arose when the Nazi system of street, block, and house "leaders" was retained. Here the Nazi incumbents were immediately ousted, but the men with whom the Allies replaced them, despite the known anti-Nazi records of many, proved quite as tyrannical in a petty way as the little Fuehrers who had preceded them.

Assigned to their posts in order to assure equitable distributions of food, clothing, fuel, and other necessities, and the maintenance of order, they lost no time in employing the same brutality, bribery, and extortion that their predecessors had used, in order to protect their friends, procure favors for themselves, and generally increase their power at the expense of those for whose benefit, supposedly, they had been appointed. The Germans were not yet ready for democracy.

The Russian zones permitted both trade unions and political parties to reappear. All groups, whatever their labels, were firmly dominated by the Red Army and its military-government units. Those who were friendly to the Russian ideology were the strongest of all in power if not in numbers. The western Allies were much more reluctant to permit the resurgence of any German political or economic organizations, for they had neither the machinery nor the desire to take political control, and they feared the results of independent action.

The Allies made it plain, however, that de-Nazification and demilitarization would be a definite reality. To this end they stated explicitly that the category of war criminals would embrace not only military and political leaders on the highest levels but also all minor party functionaries and members of Nazi affiliates who had taken any part, active or passive, in any war crimes or any persecutions. They let it be known unequivocally that they would root out the last vestige of Nazism.

They put their intentions into vigorous practice when the first formal indictments were presented, preparatory to the war-crimes trials to be held in Nuremberg, the party's shrine city.

The list included not only Goering, von Ribbentrop, Keitel, Jodl, Rosenberg, Frank, Seyss-Inquart, Doenitz, Raeder, Streicher, and others who had served as government officials, military commanders, commissioners of occupied territory, and persecutors of Jews, but also such men as Robert Ley, head of the Labor Front; Fritz Sauckel, Commissioner for Imported Labor; Wilhelm Frick, Minister of the Interior; Walther Funk, Minister of Economics and President of the Reichsbank, and Gustave Krupp von Bohlen und Halbach, head of the famous Essen arms plant bearing his family's name.

Three men who had never joined the Nazi Party were also indicted: Baron Konstantin von Neurath, former Foreign Minister who became the first "Protector" of Bohemia-Moravia after the absorption and dismemberment of Czechoslovakia; Franz von Papen, spy and intriguer par excellence of the First World War, servant of the Weimar Republic and later of the Nazi Reich; and Hjalmar Horace Greeley Schacht, former President of the Reichsbank and financial wizard.

Omitted from this first list was Martin Niemoeller, the Lutheran pastor who declared, on his liberation from a German concentration camp by the Americans, that Germany had a just cause in the war and that he regretted his Government's refusal of his offer to command a U-boat in this war as he had done in the preceding one. His only "anti-Nazi" act had been to object to the state's encroachment on what he regarded as the exclusive rights of the church.

All the liberated countries lost no time in bringing their traitors to justice. Among them were Marshal Pétain of France and Major Quisling of Norway, the man whose name had already become a synonym for traitor in every language of the world.

Pétain's trial was a drama that held all the world's interest. Political and military leaders of every French faction since 1934 paraded across the witness stand to denounce or to exonerate the Marshal, and above all to try to clear themselves.

The height of brazen hypocrisy was reached when Pierre Laval, himself facing death for treason, threw the onus for all his own actions on Pétain and wound up by declaring: "I was never a Facist! I love the Republic!" Reynaud, Daladier, Gamelin, Weygand, and dozens of others testified to what the accused Pétain had said and done in the collapse of France. In all the mass of accusation, recrimination, and self-defense one fact stood out: Pétain in 1940 was Pétain in 1916, the defeatist who refused to believe that the enemy could be beaten, the man who had to be relieved of his command at Verdun on the direct order of Marshal Joffre because he wanted to surrender France then. He stood as the firm disciple of authoritarianism and the foe of democracy. His collaboration with the Germans was proved in the trial.

The jury of twenty-four members was unanimous in pronouncing Marshal Pétain guilty. Conviction meant death under the law but, in view of his age—Pétain was then eighty-nine—a majority recommended executive clemency. General de Gaulle, as President of the Provisional Government of the French Republic, granted this request, permitting the old but still vigorous traitor to end his life in prison.

Quisling's trial in Norway was shorter and more clear-cut. He could find few witnesses to defend him. His counsel had to be appointed by the court; not a lawyer in Norway was willing to defend him. On the stand, he denied that he had helped the Germans and attempted to justify his embezzlements of state and royal property.

Flushed with anger at direct evidence of his complicity in the German invasion of 1940, he professed never to have known until he heard it mentioned in the courtroom that the sixteen hundred Norwegian Jews whose deportation to Germany he had ordered would be doomed to extermination. He did not know, he said, that the Germans killed Jews. Quisling was convicted and doomed to execution.

In mid-August the American military government of Germany called a three-day conference of its key men. Among the scheduled speakers was special Ambassador Robert D. Murphy, who had been made political adviser to Eisenhower. His speech was read for him. It was largely advice to coöperate. Lieutenant General Lucius Clay, who was Eisenhower's deputy, restated the Allies' policy and aims for the occupation of Germany in a way that made it plain that those Americans who, three months after the surrender, were proclaiming that Nazism had already been extirpated and the duration and strength of the occupation could be materially reduced were grievously deluded.

Nazism and Germanism, Clay insisted, were almost indistinguishable. Every German, high and low, had told the Allies that he had never been a Nazi, even when the Party records were there to refute him. As soon as they realized that they had been conquered, they had dropped their guns for the new weapons of guile ("Nordic guile," Hitler used to call it approvingly).

Other officers, working in the field with military-government units, reiterated the vital fact that already the Germans were scheming for the restoration of their State, their armies, and their conquests.

Clay declared that the Allies had no desire to reduce Germany to starvation and serfdom but that, on the other hand, they were not consciously going to assist her to regain her power of aggression. The restoration of Germany's economy beyond the bare level needed to maintain her population, he asserted, was not among the Allies' objectives. Only when—and if—Germany had proved a genuine willingness to adopt and practice democratic principles would she be readmitted to the society of civilized nations.

A month later the Four Power Allied Control Council manifested its complete endorsement of these views by calling on all neutral nations to surrender immediately to the Allies any Germans within their jurisdictions who were members of the Government or agents of any of its instrumentalities at the time of the surrender of Germany, as well as their families and "other obnoxious Germans" who might be demanded by the United Nations at any time. The Control Council added that it was taking this step in view of the continuing peril of a renewal of the German war effort at any future date.

The Second World War was unquestionably a triumph of democracy. It was the democratic nations that were the victims of the initial aggressions of German and Japanese nationalism and imperialism. The victory was essentially that of democratic peoples. The world's two leading practitioners of genuine democracy—the British Commonwealth and the United States—stood out for more than a year utterly alone against the greatest military might that the world had yet seen.

Only because the spiritual power of a free people made possible the organization of their latent power, were the enemies of democracy crushed and the world rescued from impending barbarism.

THE PHENOMENON OF HITLER

GREAT events are but the sum total of the personalities behind them. They generally start in the mind of one individual or a small group which motivates them. How Adolf Hitler rose out of obscurity, set the world aflame, and met his tragic end, is a study in human psychology. The "case history" of this phenomenon gives a clear insight into the simmering elements which exploded into World War II.

Psychiatrists diagnose Hitler as a "psychopathic escapist type with a complex effecting megalomania." Historians find him a man who escaped from his case history, before the psychiatrists got him, into world history. Projected on a world-wide canvas, we find in him the elements of frustration with an undercurrent of persecution mania, and an all-consuming "will to power" that knows only the alternatives: *Domination or annihilation.*

The historical analysis of Adolf Hitler is based on the testimony of members of his own family and his most intimate associates. This enigmatic personality, who declared he would conquer the earth or "pull the world down with me in ruins," is the key to the events herein recorded. This key unlocks the door to a full revelation of the sinister influences behind this war.

Was Hitler a genius or a madman? The evidence proves that he was but the puppet of stronger forces behind him. As the stooge for powerful interests in the background, he seized the opportunity to fulfil his own consuming ambitions. He originated nothing, pilfered the ideas of others, betrayed his associates, and gained power. Defying God and man, he gained his place in history as the "greatest criminal of all times." He was neither a Napoleon nor a Hannibal, a "military genius" nor a statesman: he was an ignorant "rabble-rouser."

While fighting small, defenseless nations, he met with success; through plot and conspiracy he undermined larger nations. When forced to face the world powers in actions or in decisive battles, he was a confused, deluded, and frightened desperado, turning against his own armies and dragging his own people down to disaster.

This is the man, who, through his machinations with Japan, finally brought America into World War II and pulled the democracies of the world down on his own head. Adolf Hitler was born on April 20, 1889, at Braunau, a little border town in Upper Austria looking across the river Inn into Bavaria. Independent biographers, such as Rudolf

Olden and Konrad Heiden, make it evident that Hitler's autobiography in *Mein Kampf* was concocted by obscuring, twisting, eliminating, and patching facts of his early life, with the obvious intent to create a Messianic legend about himself. It, nevertheless, contains valuable hints for his case history.

His father was Alois Schicklgruber, the illegitimate child of a peasant girl, who bore his mother's name until he was forty. Alois started out as a shoemaker's apprentice. Conscripted into the army, he rose to the rank of sergeant. That was much above a mere cobbler, so he stayed with the army for fifteen years. After his discharge, he received a so-called "certificate appointment" that made him a minor customs official with the Imperial Civil Service. He had "worked up" to what seemed to him high above the scorned classes of common people, the peasants, and the poor little workingmen. That trait had its influence on his son, Adolf.

Alois Schicklgruber married three times. His first wife, fourteen years older than he, divorced him. While his first marriage was still valid another girl, Franziska Matzelsberger, bore him a son, Alois. Schicklgruber married her after his divorced wife died. Two months after their marriage she bore him a daughter, Angela. One year later his second wife died. Ten months thereafter he married Klara Poelzl, who was his junior by twenty-three years. He was forty-seven, then, and had in the meantime changed his name (to obtain a legacy) to Hitler. From his third marriage sprang five children, of whom three died in infancy; the two surviving were Adolf and Paula.

Adolf Hitler's half brother, Alois, ran away from home, complaining about cruel treatment by his father. He worked as a waiter in England, married an Irish girl, treated her cruelly, and begot a son, William Patrick Hitler. After Adolf came to power Alois returned to Germany, leaving wife and son behind, and became a prosperous innkeeper. Adolf's half sister, Angela, also followed him to Germany from Austria, to care for his households in Munich and Berchtesgaden. She was the mother of unhappy Grete Gele Raubal, the girl who was said to have committed suicide after becoming enamored of her Uncle Adolf.

His sister, Paula, considered a queer person, lived a troublesome life in Vienna and became an ardent Nazi. William Patrick Hitler broke away from the Hitler clan and came with his mother to the United States to fight against the world scourge of Nazism. This young man, imbued with the spirit of freedom inherited from his liberty-loving Irish mother, joined the United States Navy.

The historians of this volume held confidential talks with Hitler's nephew, some of which can be related here. He placed before us official documents which threw light on the background of Adolf Hitler. He told us about the years when he lived with his uncle at Berchtesgaden, the conduct and habits of the Fuehrer. How in his mountain retreat, the most strongly fortified in the world, Hitler planned and plotted world conquest. The nephew related to us the "secrets" of the mysterious Rudolf Hess and Ernst "Putzie" Hanfstaengl, who fled to England, the latter being held prisoner in Canada and later coming to the United States. Letters were submitted to document the facts.

These are books in themselves which undoubtedly will be revealed in future years. It is sufficient to state here that young Patrick Hitler fled from Berchtesgaden when he became convinced that his uncle was suffering from delusions of grandeur and a Messianic complex which endangered his own nephew's life as well as Germany and the whole world. Having "disposed of" a thousand of his intimates, Adolf Hitler's own family was not safe from attack. He would break into his nephew's room in the midnight hours to rant about how he would "conquer the world."

As a child, he was as difficult as Alois, his father. Father Alois was a tyrannical egotist with a mania for cruelty. Young Adolf liked to rage in rabid oratories, audience or no audience. His father called him daffy and lazy. He wanted his son to become an important personage like himself. But eleven-year-old Adolf revolted against going to school and exposing himself to the heavy task of book learning. He hated his teachers and schoolmates.

Faced by the odious realities of life as they were fearfully represented to him by a father with a big stick and an inclination for alcohol, Adolf wanted only to escape. He was thirteen at the time of his father's death, and nineteen when his mother died. Of the six years between those two events little is known about the boy's doings, except that he prevailed upon his mother to take him out of the hated secondary school, and that she encouraged him in his hobby of making drawings until his ego became inflated to the point of believing himself a genius. He lived on his mother's pension until her death.

With his mother and her income gone, the escapist days were over. He had to face life. A misfit, uneducated, arrogant, undeveloped in mind, stubborn and quarrelsome, without any moral concepts, such was young Adolf Hitler when he entered Vienna at the beginning of 1909. Here his ego was deflated for the first time. He could not even pass his entrance examinations to the Academy of Arts; his drawings were considered crude imitations—counterfeits. When a jury at the Academy in Munich refused a painting he submitted for exhibition, he stormed back to inquire who composed the jury. He learned that among them was a Jew, who ranked as one of the outstanding masters of German art. At once he blamed the jury's decision to exclude his work upon this Jew, declaring, "They shall pay for this."

Precipitated from vainglory, Hitler woke to find himself an obscure outcast. In his despair, he stooped so "low" in his own estimation as to take up work as an unskilled laborer. To carry mortar on scaffolding was far beneath his dignity. He had not yet conceived the idea that "Providence had chosen him" to be "the leader of the master race." He propped up his conceit by hating his fellow workers; he would not mix with the "scum."

"I was studying my surroundings," he later asserted. "But I was not one of those poor, low-grade creatures around me." His account of those days is dripping with self-pity. It sheds a good deal of light upon the Fuehrer whom official Germany was later to put up as the sublime symbol of the German worker.

The workers requested him to join their union. Hitler refused. Unable to grasp how far more intelligent the workers were than he, he tried to argue with them. Only a nineteen-year-old, he thought he knew everything there was to be known. He hated education and educated people as he did the workers, and made a nuisance of himself with his heated arguing and quarreling. Here is his own confession: "A few of the opposition leaders forced me to either leave the building at once or be thrown from the scaffolding. Since I was alone and resistance seemed futile I preferred to follow the former advice." To him the workers were already "opposition leaders." He swore he would "get even with them." A man without a job, he was "filled with disgust" for workers.

He jeered at cultural organizations, open to everyone free of charge, the evening schools, public libraries, and lecture courses at the People's Educational Society and the People's Academy. "I did not have to learn much to add to what I created for myself," he boasted. He went panhandling in the streets, took shelter in flophouses, and snatched bowls of soup from the hands of mercy at the back doors of nunneries and monasteries. And sneered to himself: "They will have to pay for this!"

Such were the "five years of misery and grief" he spent in Vienna, mostly in the Asylum for the Poor and Homeless, a derelict among derelicts, alluding to his occupation only with occasional remarks such as, "I had been a decorator's man." He was copying postcards which a flophouse companion tried to sell. He grew a beard on his hollow cheeks and let his hair grow long to support his posing as a misunderstood genius in the world of arts.

Between twenty and twenty-two, still a provincial vagrant, mentally stunted, he was completely lost in gay Vienna, then the metropolis of the Hapsburg Empire and a colorful spectacle of many nations and cultures. That spectacle was beyond the grasp of the young Hitler, who was becoming concerned about the "pollution of the German nation." He began to rant about the "seduction of hundreds of thousands of blond girls by repulsive, dark-haired, bow-legged Jews." Eventually he linked this with another obsession that "Jews and Marxists are identical." Not because Social-Democratic masons had chased him (a querulous crank) from a construction scaffolding, but because Jew-baiting provided him with the prejudices upon which he based his intolerance. An arrogant ignoramus, he took whatever things were beyond his grasp for enemies, and covered up his fear with violent hatred.

The smattering of "big words," which he was later to use in exhibitionist speeches before awe-struck masses, he acquired from anti-Semitic newspapers and pamphlets (stacks of which he collected) and from the demogogic speeches he listened to avidly. The neurotic Hitler needed plenty of scapegoats for his own many shortcomings. Here was one ready-made, and already implanted into the group psychology of the masses. Thus he adopted persecution as the basic symbol of wisdom and power.

A "wretched crackpot," a nobody with a mad urge to be a somebody of excessive superiority, driven to overcompensate his festering inferiority complex, he availed himself of any means within his grasp. His "anti-Semitism," and fictional "Aryanism" he pilfered from Gobineau and Houston Stewart Chamberlain. His Nazi philosophy he stole from Alfred Rosenberg. Hitler did not create anything original. His sole resource was his capacity for vitriolic hate. He hated cosmopolitan Vienna, the polyglot Austro-Hungarian Dual Monarchy, the Hapsburgs, the aristocracy, the bourgeoisie, the proletariat, the reactionists, the Socialists, the intellectuals and the churches, because he was an outsider. This was how Hitler, under the chaotic post-war conditions in Germany, finally got his first chance to show his skill in stirring up the stew of all-round bad feelings, grievances, and factional hatreds. He succeeded in sneaking into the most promising power groups, and used that compound of devil's brew for his own rise to power. Under stabilized economic conditions, and in a comparatively sane atmosphere, "politicians" of Hitler's ilk explode harmlessly like firecrackers.

One talent Hitler unquestionably possessed: rabble-rousing. He practiced it freely in those Vienna days in flophouses, only to be told by his fellow tramps to "shut up" when he grew too noisy. His hate-filled speeches found not even an echo among the dregs of society.

The year before World War I, Hitler made up his mind. He moved to Germany, to Munich. There he took up where he had left off in Vienna: reading rabid newspaper editorials and arguing violently whenever he found a chance to provoke discussions, around beer tables now, because this was Munich. His favorite topic was his contempt for that "mummy state" Austria; "unworthy little neighbor of the Great German Empire." Erupting into these speeches relieved his boiling emotions. The Munich people of those days were a tolerant lot (if no Prussian were near them). They were accustomed to Bohemians, eccentrics, quacks, and queer prophets. Over their beer they listened with great composure.

A door of glorious escape opened for Hitler with the outbreak of World War I. He relates: "To me those hours came like a salvation from the bitter vexations of my youth. Even today I am not ashamed to say I was overcome with impetuous enthusiasm. Falling on my knees, I thanked Heaven from an overflowing heart for having been granted the happiness to live at this time." War was now the goal of his life; brutal conflict against democracies, against freedom, liberty, peace.

He emerged from World War I unknown, a nervous wreck. The rest is legend, including his having been wounded, poisoned and blinded by mustard gas, and having earned the Iron Cross of the First Class.

Diligent and meticulous searches by independent biographers have established the following facts: Hitler joined the Bavarian Army as a volunteer (no proof could be found as to whether he joined in 1914 or 1916); he served as an orderly with the regimental staff of the Sixteenth Bavarian Reserve Infantry Regiment during the entire campaign, never saw trench-warfare, and stayed a sub-corporal. In the middle of October, 1918, he arrived at a hospital at Pasewalk, near Berlin, where he remained during the time of the armistice and the revolution. At this hospital no medical report could be found. Neither could there be unearthed any official record to the effect that Hitler had been awarded the Iron Cross. It was an ardent National Socialist, and former comrade of Hitler on the regimental staff, who first supplied the information that Adolf Hitler had frequently suffered from pathological depressions.

"I have decided to become a politician," Hitler declared after the revolution which gave birth to the German Republic. The political Hitler was born, fed, clothed, sheltered, and reared by the German Army. And what he later propagated as his new "Weltanschauung" was neither new, nor his, nor Weltanschauung. It was the exclusive viewpoint of the three powerful groups of the German ruling class: the Army, the Junkers, and the heavy industry. These found a unified expression in the Pan-German Union, a central organization created by an ingenious anti-Semitic intriguer, Justizrat Heinrich Class. In fact, the atmosphere in Germany was saturated with such elements as generated the complex of Hitler's pathological personality. Thus, instead of landing in an asylum, he landed on top of a Germany fermenting with power-crazy monomaniacs.

To understand this situation one has to bear in mind that the German Republic was established by the people against the nationalist ruling strata of German "upper-class" society. These chauvinists, who never conceded defeat, needed no Hitler to tell them that they were superior in every respect—"supermen" of a "master race" destined to rule the world. Hitler came in quite handy for them as a "drummer," a nationalist circus barker, a vulgarizer of their ambitions. It was they who were to unchain Hitler so that he could drug the masses with wild harangues and propaganda, with uniforms, flags, parades—and terror.

The Junkers remained the real behind-the-scenes rulers of Germany, notwithstanding the Weimar Constitution with Social Democrats in leading State positions; they engineered as early as 1919 the German war production, the international maze of cartel interests as a power resort of their own. They staged the *Kapp-Putsch* in Berlin in 1920; and they took over Bavaria to make what they called an *ordhungszelle* (nucleus of order), after the first Prime Minister of the Bavarian Republic, Socialist Kurt Eisner, was murdered. This was, in fact, their plotting center against the German Republic. The German Imperialists survived all debacles unscathed.

Hitler had no part in all this. Leaving the Pasewalk Hospital in a confused state of mind, hungry, penniless, and homeless, he returned to the reserve regiment in Munich toward the end of November in 1918. Finding Socialists of all shades in power, he tried to palm himself off as a Social Democrat. Failing in this attempt, he retreated to a military camp in Traunstein, again steeped in depression, and returned to barracks in Munich when the camp was closed. Until April, 1920, he wore his field uniform and loafed about, living on the pay and food he received from the army.

His first chance came when, after the bloody overthrow of the Bavarian "Raete-Republic" by the corps of General von Epp, reaction set in, with the army assuming power. Hitler became "informer" for the army. Soldier comrades, with whom he had lived in the barracks, were pointed out by him as "Reds" and dragged before execution squads. Thus he made himself a spy for Reichswehr officers. Among them was Captain Roehm, who later was to become SA Leader, and was "liquidated" by his "dearest friend, Adolf," in the bloody purge of the Nazi Party in 1934.

It was during this work that he met Gottfried Feder, a civil engineer with a foggy idea of a new Socialism to end all Socialisms. Feder had much in common with Hitler—neither of them had read *Das Kapital* by Karl Marx and both were out to destroy Marxism. The very abstruseness of Feder's theory hit Hitler with the impact of a revelation. He immediately appropriated Feder's phrases, and also his little mustache brush by cutting off the long ends of his own. Later he appointed Feder as Secretary of the Labor Department of the Reich.

While a spy, Hitler discovered the "German Workers' Party." He was sent out by his officers to "investigate" a small political group by that name. He tracked them down at a small meeting hall, where were assembled about two dozen little people listening to Gottfried Feder exhort on his favorite theme, the "bondage of interest." When a man got up to argue against Feder, Hitler forgot that he was supposed to be only a spy; he jumped to his feet and attacked the speaker with a broadside of bombast. He reaped applause. The chairman of the party, Anton Drexler, shook hands with him. A week later, the German Workers' Party notified Corporal Hitler that he had been accepted as a member—number 7.

Without transition, he soared from a state of deepest depression to highest exaltation. He designed party emblems, banners, uniforms. From Mussolini he appropriated the party shirt and the Fascist salute. Thus Hitler's National Socialist German Workers' Party was born; fostered by the army, running wild on propaganda orgies, and pampered by heavy industry and foreign money.

Among its outstanding early supporters were: Captain Roehm, General Staff Officer of the Reichswehr; Rudolf Hess, an unemployed former air force lieutenant, who became Hitler's secretary and his closest associate; General Erich Ludendorf, first Quartermaster General during World War I (already involved in the Berlin *Kapp-Putsch*) and who later broke with Hitler; Hermann Goering, former air force captain, drug addict, and adventurer with a dubious past; Ernst Poehner, Police President of Munich, who, at a court trial called the Republic which paid him, and to which he had sworn allegiance, "the foulest kind of popular deception"; Wilhelm Frick, Poehner's adjutant, whom Hitler later appointed Minister of the Interior; Alfred Rosenberg, professional anti-Christian and anti-Semite, and expounder of German paganism, who was made Nazi Party "philosopher"; Gottfried Feder, originator of the Hitler mustache; and Lieutenant Colonel Kriebel.

Hitler had reached the initial stage of his career as a politician. It was also the initial stage of his power megalomania.

The party grew through its circus propaganda methods and its guerrilla-civil-war technique, or, as Hitler put it with cynical candor, through "exploiting the weakness and the beastliness of the masses." Three years later, on November 8, 1923, Hitler thought himself already strong enough to reach out for dictatorship.

The Munich *Buergerbrau* (Beer Hall) *Putsch* failed because his reactionary co-conspirators (General von Lossow, Commander of the Reichswehr in Munich, Gustav von Kahr, Bavarian Prime Minister, and von Seisser, Chief Constable of the Bavarian Police), whom he tried to double-cross, double-crossed him in the end. Instead of jointly "marching on Berlin" to overthrow the hated parliamentary government of the Reich, as originally planned, a shooting fray started. Fourteen Nazis fell. Hitler fled for his life to hide at the country place of his friend, Hanfstaengl. Goering escaped to the Tyrol.

In February-March, 1924, Hitler, General Ludendorf, Hess, and seven others were brought to trial for high treason. The trial before the

Munich People's Court turned out to be a farce. Accused and witnesses reproached each other with having broken their "word of honor." A howling Nazi mob in the background cheered. Ludendorf, who had marched with Hitler at the head of 2,000 Nazi revolutionists, was acquitted. Hitler and the other eight were sentenced to five years' imprisonment—and released after six months. In the Fortress Prison at Landsberg, where they settled down as distinguished guests, they received visitors and held conferences. And Hitler conceived there that incoherent document destined to become the Nazi Bible—*Mein Kampf*.

He had learned his lesson. A *Putsch* would not do the trick. From now on the wolf was to wear the sheep's clothing of "legality." He would play his part in the parliamentary game and take advantage of the rights and privileges of democracy, without obeying its rules of fair play, while sowing dissension and stirring up group hatred from within. There was no risk for him in that game. At his disposal were frauds, lies, perjury, violence, rape, and murder. Such means would tip the scales in his favor. In a deal between a gentleman and a scoundrel it will always be the gentleman who will lose; this was no original discovery of Hitler's. It is the well-known formula of the outlaw. The only thing new was his open and determined application of this nefarious formula to national politics. After he had Germany in his grip, he applied the same tactics to international politics.

It took Hitler four years to readjust the party after the *Putsch* failure. The Briand-Stresemann rapprochement period was 1924-1928, with peace plans in the air, and economic recovery. It was a clear air, hard to breathe for Nazis. In the May, 1928, elections they won only 12 out of 465 seats in the Reichstag. On the other hand, Hitler found new "accessories" in the brothers Gregor and Dr. Otto Strasser, and Dr. Joseph Goebbels, the club-footed "Mephisto" who proved to be Hitler's equal in craftiness, mendacity, and villainy. Goering returned from exile. Roehm also returned to take over command of the SS (Storm Troopers). Julius Streicher, anti-Semitic editor of the pornographic scandal sheet, *Der Sturmer,* rose to party honors. Heinrich Himmler became leader of the SS and proved his mettle as chief murderer and executioner after he had been appointed Chief of the Gestapo.

And the Nazis suddenly began to roll in money that was never accounted for. The party leaders took to a luxurious standard of living. Hundreds of Nazi papers mushroomed all over the country. Avalanches of propaganda were pouring forth. Party palaces were built. The army of SA mercenaries grew to 400,000 men. The party organization became a state within a state, with an annual budget that rose, in 1931, to ninety million marks.

Where did the money come from? The first representatives of the heavy industries to support Hitler's Workers' Party lavishly were the industrial magnates, Emil Kirdorf and Fritz Thyssen (coal and steel barons from the Rhineland). Why? The heavy industries required rearmament to flourish again. And Stresemann had refused to rearm—he was working for peace. Why not bet on Hitler who was, incidentally, splitting the Pacifist Socialist workers' front? Gerling Insurance Company stepped in as a heavy financial supporter. And in the middle of 1929, Geheimrat Alfred Huggenberg became Hitler's patron. He was the multimillionaire "lord over press and film," Chairman of the German Nationalist Party, and as respectable and cunning a Pan-German Imperialist as his friend, Justizrat Class. Common hatred against Stresemann, who was about to pacify and stabilize the German Republic and to save fever-ridden Europe, made haughty Huggenberg stoop to little Hitler. The fight of the reactionaries against the "Young Plan" made this unholy alliance click. For this they would have united with the devil.

All they wanted was to make use of Hitler to attain their own ends. They thought him a despicable, unscrupulous rogue, but a valuable tool. With their money they increased his power and his political prestige and made the influence of the Nazi Party grow with breath-taking speed. Warmongers for profit, they were willing to gamble with the lives of the German people, and drag their nation into infamy and disaster, while they piled up their fortunes in foreign banks.

Rearmament! Rearmament! Hitler called it "Liberation of an enslaved Germany turned into a Young Colony." After Stresemann died at the end of 1929, the political wire-puller, Reichswehr-General Kurt von Schleicher, made Heinrich Bruening Chancellor. The rearmament started at the expense of a starving population. It made the entire economic and political structure of the Republic crumble; unemployment rose to over six million; foreign credits were withdrawn; the people were bled white. But the heavy industries got their money back. And Hitler reaped his profit in growing power.

His propaganda lines to the despairing people were now: "You see? The Republic is ruining you. I told you so!" And to the ruling powers: "I shall save you from Bolshevism. Leave it to me!"

In the September elections of 1930, the Nazis got 107 seats in the Reichstag (instead of 12). And in the elections of July 1932 the Nazis won 230 seats (*i.e.,* 13,700,000 votes; 37 per cent of the total number cast). That was the most Hitler ever bagged. New Nazi enthusiasts rushed to climb on Hitler's bandwagon. Among these were Prince August Wilhelm, one of the Kaiser's sons; the Duke of Coburg; General Frank Ritter von Epp, the conqueror of Munich; General Karl Leitzmann; Count von Helldorf, a rowdy nobleman; and Dr. Hjalmar Schacht, President of the Reichsbank.

A period of intrigues, plots, political trickeries, and financial scandals followed. General Schleicher, who had made Bruening the Chancellor, threw him over for Franz von Papen as Bruening's successor. Von Papen turned off the flow of money to Hitler at its source in an attempt to entrench himself. Schleicher threw von Papen out and took over the reins himself, whereupon von Papen turned on the money flow to Hitler again. He introduced Hitler, who was already on the verge of bankruptcy and despair, to the Cologne banker, Baron Schroeder. The Baron had not only the confidence of the steel and coal magnates, but also first-class connections with London's financial center. To spite Schleicher, von Papen saved Hitler at the last moment and introduced him later to Reichspräsident von Hindenburg.

Bruening had to go because he antagonized Hitler. Von Papen had to go because he set up a dictatorship of his own, and thereby antagonized the Reichswehr. Schleicher fell because he antagonized the Junkers when he revealed their grand larceny by appropriating taxpayers' money under the guise of "Eastern Farmers' Help." Hitler, who never antagonized the money interests, was the benefactor as the proponent of "victory of the strong and the annihilation of the weak."

The road for Hitler was clear. He ingratiated himself with the Junkers by one of his famous promises. And they put pressure on President von Hindenburg, himself a Junker, to appoint Hitler as Chancellor of Germany. Hindenburg but three weeks before had assured Gregor Strasser: "I give you my word of honor as a Prussian General that I will never make this sub-corporal Chancellor of the German Reich!" The old Field Marshal suffered from a poor memory. Hitler was "in."

The ruling powers had him tied to a cabinet of trustworthy, dependable men—a "foolproof" cabinet. They made Hitler give his word of honor that he would make no changes without Hindenburg's consent. They made von Papen Vice Chancellor as an additional safeguard. Roehm, Goebbels, and Rosenberg were not let "in." But Goering became Commissioner for the Prussian Ministry of the Interior, under von Papen. They forgot that this morphine addict, Goering, President of the Reichstag since July, 1932, was the man who had roared at a meeting: "It is not my province to do justice, but to destroy and exterminate!" Hitler, to whom legality was only a sheepsclothing disguise, would, once in power, feel perfectly safe to interpret legality in the shifty terms peculiar to his own distorted psychology.

Four weeks after Hitler became Chancellor, the "Reichstag Fire" startled the German people. It happened on February 27, 1933, exactly the way it had been planned four weeks in advance by Hitler and his accomplices, a "flaming signal for a Bolshevist Revolution." It was Hitler's "legal" way of putting his terror machine into action with violence, sadism, and murder raging unchecked for days. The victims were Social Democrats, Freemasons, Communists, liberal writers, journalists, and Jews.

Germany became a military camp bristling with arms. The SA formations alone had grown to three million gunmen. The Reichwehr had accepted the swastika as its official emblem, yet it was jealously guarding its dominant position. After all, it, with the financiers, had made Hitler. Hitler himself said to his cohorts a few months after his appointment: "If the army had not stood on our side in the days of the revolution, we should not be standing here today."

He could not do without his hoodlum troops. So he staged the "St. Bartholomew Night" of June 30, 1934. This time he invented (in place of the conventional "Bolshevist Revolution") an "SA Mutiny" to "legalize" the killing of more than a thousand of his own leading SA men. This was an opportunity to get rid of the two who had done more than any others to help him climb to power: SA Chief Ernst Roehm and Dr. Gregor Strasser. Both were murdered.

Again murders raged throughout Germany for three days, personally supervised by Hitler from Munich and by Goering from Berlin. During this massacre many persons were killed: General von Schleicher and his wife; Schleicher's collaborator, General von Bredow; Gustav von Kahr, once Hitler's co-conspirator who had turned state's witness against him after the Munich *Putsch;* Catholic politicians, among them Ministerial-Director Klausner, and other leaders of the "Catholic Action" and von Papen's closest friends. Von Papen and Bruening escaped by a hair's breadth. Hitler was in his stride. He had himself appointed not only executioner but the "Supreme Court of Justice of the German people" (his own words).

The SA dropped from three million to a quarter of a million. Its rôle now was that of extras for mass meetings, enacting "the spontaneous outbursts of the German people"; *i.e.,* burning of churches and synagogues, and plundering. The German Army repaid its debt of gratitude. When von Hindenburg died, it immediately took the oath of allegiance to Hitler. All Hitler and his accomplices had to do after that was to produce a forged Hindenburg testament to make Adolf Hitler the successor of the great German idol.

Hitler became dictator supreme of the German Reich. He instituted the Third Reich—the totalitarian National Socialist State. He declared: "One cannot train an army to a proper state of efficiency if preparation for battle is not its *raison d'être*. There is no such thing as an army to preserve peace, but only for the victorious conduct of war."

And there lies the story of Hitler's rise to power, the forces behind him which created World War II. Hitler, who had a Napoleonic complex without any of the great General's genius, based his life creed on Napoleon's dictum: "If you want to get on in this world make many promises, but do not keep them." To this Hitler added his own axiom: "Any lie if big enough and told often enough will be believed."

Let us look further into the character of this man, through transcripts from the mass of evidence in his own proclamations, subsidized press, conferences with his own associates at Berchtesgaden, including the testimony of Dr. Hermann Rauschning in the valuable historical records which he gave the world:

"My purpose," declared Hitler, "is the subjugation of all races and peoples and to set up our master race to rule the world.... Empires are made by sword ... by theft and robbery ... by brute force.... We shall proceed step by step with iron determination ... we shall be master of the earth."

"I have no conscience," he boasted to his inner cabinet. "I shall shrink from nothing ... we have no scruples.... There is no such thing as truth.... We are at the end of the Age of Reason ... the Ten Commandments have lost their validity ... the Sermon on the Mount is for idiots. ... Promises, agreements, treaties are sheer stupidity ... they are made to be broken.... Anyone whose conscience is so tender is a fool."

These self-confessions give us a life-size portrait of the man who railed against the Americans: "It is a simple matter for me to produce unrest and revolt in the United States ... these gentry will have their hands full with their own affairs ... they are permanently on the brink of revolution.... We shall break down the enemy psychologically before the armies begin to function.... The enemy must be demoralized into moral passivity.... We shall not shrink from plotting revolutions.... We shall have friends who will help us in all enemy countries ... they will come of their own accord.... Ambition and delusion, party squabbles and self-seeking arrogance will drive them into mental confusion ... indecision ... panic ... these are our first weapons."

"Democracy," he sneered, "is the disgusting death-rattle of a corrupt and worn-out system ... the falsity of liberty and equality ... the masses are doomed to decay and self-destruction ... they are fools, donkeys and sterile old men.... Our aim is to appeal to their baser instincts.... The masses shall be eternally disfranchised ... we need not hesitate to call them the modern slave class.... I shall not be deceived by Captains of Industry ... they are stupid fools who cannot see beyond the wares they peddle.... Damn your economic science ... bring me money. I don't care how you get it."

It is sufficient from these attested records to leave Hitler for the time being as he rants: "I am freeing man from the restraints of intelligence ... from the dirty and degraded self-mortifications called conscience and morality.... The world can be ruled only by fear.... We are above clinging to the old bourgeois notions of honor and reputation. ... We have no time for fine sentiments.... It will be unbelievably bloody and grim.... Yes, we are barbarians ... we may fail, but if we do, we shall drag the world down with us ... a world in flames."

NAZI PLOT TO CONQUER THE WORLD

THE plot which instigated the greatest holocaust in history was conceived and nourished in Germany, with collusion in Japan. This is proved by overwhelming evidence. It is further established by the fact that the democracies were caught unprepared. They had failed to heed the advice: "Eternal vigilance is the price of liberty."

Let us survey briefly what was happening in Germany while other nations were content in their illusions of peace and security. Self-government was placed in the hands of the Germans by the new Republic following the First World War. They elected as their first president, not a Prussian Junker, not one of the old ruling class, but a humble saddler and son of a tailor—Frederick Ebert (1919-25). He was as truly representative of the people as Lincoln. A man with nobility of soul and love for humanity, he began under the most difficult circumstances to lay the foundations for a great free nation.

During those years, the old military clique with their armament makers and groups which profited by war, were insidiously working to regain control of Germany. Behind them were international money-lenders and investors seeking to share in the profits. Taking advantage of the struggles of the new Republic, its economic problems in reconstruction on a basis of peace, the unparalleled inflation, unemployment and hunger, they were again waiting *Der Tag*.

Their first opportunity came when Ebert, father of the Republic, died in 1925. Shrewdly seeking a successor who was in sympathy with the old system, they found their man—Field Marshal Paul von Beneckendorf und von Hindenburg. He had been built up as a national symbol and idol. He could be used in his venerable years for their sinister purposes. They would figuratively walk over his aged body as if it were a bridge leading back to militaristic control.

Von Hindenburg, a great man in his years of vigor, was their victim. He was elected president in 1925 and reëlected in 1932. When the world-wide depression gripped Germany, as it did the rest of the world, the people were led to believe it was the plot of foreign powers to heap suffering and indignity upon them as a result of their defeat in World War I. They were told that they "were not defeated and must rise again to protect their homeland."

The stage was being set for World War II. We have seen in the preceding chapter how von Hindenburg, feeble and in fear of death,

From *The War in Maps* by permission of Oxford University Press, New York.

How the map of Western Europe looked in September, 1939.

was induced to set up Adolf Hitler, the Junkers' "dummy" as Chancellor of Germany—endorsed by the electorate with an overwhelming vote. The German people had fallen into the trap; now they must pay the penalty. Hitler proceeded to rouse them to fever heat. As their Fuehrer he would "right all their wrongs, remove unemployment, rehabilitate them as a prosperous nation, and restore them to their former position as a world power."

The ruination of Germany by the Nazis is one of the blackest pages in history. Partially owing to their distress, then under fear of death, the German people were led and coerced by their military masters, until they fell instinctively back into the goose-step.

The Hitlerian method, in collusion with militarists, backed by industrialists with both domestic and foreign capital, is simple to decipher: to rouse the people by stirring up their hatreds, to make everything but Nazism their enemy. This was his first "secret weapon" which he turned against his own people.

The Nazi régime began with a reign of terror. They desecrated, tortured, killed, and enslaved without conscience and without mercy, prompted by the lowest motives of greed and bloodthirst. They held nothing holy, and respected neither human life nor divine teachings. They overthrew and made a farce of all the social institutions of civilization, the Church, the schools, and the courts.

It is a deplorable fact that the democracies watched this grow and allowed it to continue for six years without interfering, a mistake for which they paid in blood and sacrifice. At first it was only Germany which saw its religions persecuted and its people murdered, but other nations soon followed. It was the same Heinrich Himmler, who had persecuted and tortured in Germany, who later undertook to wipe out the entire Polish nation. It was the same Himmler who had charge of prisoners of war. Free speech, free press, and religion became heresies whose advocates were branded and treated as criminals. Arrest, seizure of property without payment, trial in secret, and conviction without evidence became the ordinary functions of the police and courts.

Goebbels was the minister of propaganda; Goering the minister of war; von Schirach the minister of youth; Heinrich Himmler became the head of all German police, the Gestapo, and the Schutzstaffel (SS), also organizer and chief of the concentration camps, executioner, inciter of pogroms and mass murder.

It was Himmler who organized the butchery of thousands of party men in the purge of June, 1934. He called the Jews "the true creators of all suffering" and promised to wipe them out. As soon as Hitler came to power he began to fight the Catholics, under the pretense of fighting "political Catholicism." The Catholic Zentrum Party was dissolved on January 5, 1933. Ludwig Mueller took the place of the anti-Nazi Bishop Bodelschwingh as head of the Protestant Church, and decreed the suppression of self-government in the churches, instituted German racial theories as a teaching of the church and disciplinary punishment against anti-Nazi clergy.

The Social Democratic Party of Germany was dissolved in 1933, and many of its members and most of its leaders placed in "protective custody" in concentration camps. A law was passed making the NSDAP the only party which was allowed to function in the Reich. Leaders of all other parties were jailed in concentration camps.

Hitler declared war on all political opposition. The procedure was arrest, secret and unexplained, by the Gestapo or the SS, and trial in secret, without defense. Mobs were incited to riot by constant needling through the press and other propaganda sources.

Concentration camps were the invention of Goering, "improved upon" by Himmler. Their ostensible function was the housing of political prisoners in "protective custody." Their factual function was to drive inmates mad through torture, and allow them to make hopeless attempts to escape ending in certain death. The British Government issued a White Paper describing conditions in the camps.

The Nazis took great care to hide the true conditions in their concentration camps. When a prisoner was released, he was inspected carefully for signs of mistreatment. If any were too obvious he was never released. Others were required to sign a document which stated that they had never been mistreated, acquired no infectious diseases, and received all their personal belongings. They were threatened with reprisals if they told the truth, and were then released without any assistance for their return home. Officially none of the atrocities occurred. When prisoners were driven to death, their families learned that they were "shot trying to escape," "committed suicide," "died of illness," or they were just never heard from again.

There were four large concentration camps in Germany: Dachau, near Munich; at Sachsenhausen, near Oranienburg; at Lichtenburg, near Torgau; and at Sachsenburg, near Chemnitz, as well as several smaller camps. A conservative estimate places the number who died in these camps at over 150,000 before the outbreak of war.

Mass persecutions, prevalent against those considered hostile to the Nazis, were carried out by official party groups under direct orders of the government. Nazi papers had for weeks been playing up the shooting of Herr von Rath, an unimportant attaché, by a half-crazed Jewish youth, Herschel Grynzpan, whose parents had been victims of the Nazis. As von Rath lay hovering between life and death, propaganda sources promised reprisals against all German Jewry should he die. This was intended to stir the population to a fever heat of anti-Semitism.

Von Rath did die in November, 1938, and the following order sent by Himmler, was received over the police telegraph in Cologne. (1) At 4:00 A.M. the synagogues and chapels were to be set afire. (2) At 6:00 A.M. looting and destruction of shops was to begin. (3) At 8:00 A.M. the same was to happen in the suburbs. (4) All action was to cease at 1:00 P.M. The order was carried out by the SS, SA and a fringe of hoodlums and looters, but was described the next day as an uprising of "an angry and excited folk."

In Munich, in 1935, a Catholic charity collection drive resulted in a riot in which 4,000 volunteers were set upon by Nazi Storm Troopers in civilian clothes. A half hour after the charity workers appeared on the street the Storm Troopers, obviously by a prearranged plan, began hawking the morning editions of the *Voelischer Beobach,* the Nazi daily, which featured a headline concerning a report from Berlin that a Catholic nun had been sentenced to five years in prison on a charge of exchange smuggling. The Troopers shouted: "Don't give to the traitors!" Protesting Catholics were immediately set upon by organized Nazi Brown Shirts and Black Shirts. The day ended in city-wide anti-Catholic riots with thousands fleeing to churches for protection.

Protestants had a large following in Germany. It was Hitler's intention to make the Protestant Church semi-official, a fact shown by his appointment of Mueller as *Reichsbishopf*. Instead of open persecutions, police raids were employed. All mail to clergy was opened for "Red" propaganda, secret raids by police on Protestant homes were constant, and the arrest of clergy commonplace.

German courts and trials during the period became hatchers of and preludes to further atrocities. Sterilization became a common practice sanctioned by law and imposed as a punishment. A law went into effect providing for the sterilization of 400,000 Germans suffering from "hereditary" diseases. Over 1,700 hereditary health courts were set up. Physicians were required by the law to report all persons subject to sterilization under the law, and they assiduously picked cases that were anti-Nazi. After trial before the court, the victims either had to arrange for their sterilization or were sterilized by force. A new crime, *Rassemschande* (Race Shame), which was committed by sexual intercourse between Aryans and Jews, was punishable by sterilization, and also by prison and possible death sentence.

Laws were used to persecute religious groups. The Nuremberg Laws of September, 1935, created two types of citizens: Those with rights and those without rights. The latter group consisted of Jews, who had previously been excluded by law from all trades, professions, and business enterprises. The destitution and poverty following these laws were then augmented by refusing, through the Nuremberg Laws, right to trial, police protection, and other civic freedoms. Nazi greed put into effect in 1938 a law imposing extra taxes upon the Jewish citizen "with no rights." Trapped in a land that would not allow them to leave until they had been bled white, they could earn nothing. When savings gave out, only death remained. Suicides ran high.

The government, in 1938, decreed that Jews had to register all property, and gave Goering the right to seize any and all Jewish property whenever he pleased. Through this process of law they had no rights, no property, no money, no passports, were unable to work, were subject to persecution at the whim of any Nazi, and were rapidly being forced into extinction. As soon as war broke out, the deportation to Poland began. Those who survived the trip were killed by the thousands by what the Nazis had decided on as the cheapest and most efficient method, the injection of air bubbles into the blood stream.

Courts and laws were used against the Catholics. Hundreds of priests, lay brothers, nuns, and lay members of the Church were unjustly persecuted by the Nazis on trumped-up charges, and subsequently sentenced to prisons and concentration camps. The two most infamous charges against the Catholic Church were the currency trials of 1935 and the morality trials of 1937. In the former, hundreds of German priests, nuns, and other church members were accused of smuggling money out of Germany. Actually, these priests and others had collected charities for use in Germany, and some of the money had found its way out of the country for use in charities elsewhere, but none of the money was ever used to the personal gain of anyone accused.

Vatican protests were disregarded. Through German laws and courts the persecution of Catholics was inexorably perpetrated.

Even more shocking were the morality trials. These were preceded by a violent propaganda campaign, and a speech by Goebbels in which he threatened to close the monasteries and expel the monks and Jesuits. He accused the Catholics of the foulest of sex perversions, then said they had incited the trials by attacking Hitler from their pulpits.

Sworn records reveal that in order to build a case the Nazis bribed children with candy, and then threatened them with concentration-camp sentences. Witnesses were beaten, and threatened with guns. Lay brothers and children were asked the vilest questions and forced to testify under duress. Over three hundred priests were charged with sexual crimes, and hundreds were imprisoned.

Hundreds of former members of the Socialist party were sentenced together to prison terms for having belonged to the party prior to 1933. Thus German courts and laws became instruments of fanatics in an attempt to kill and torture all opposition.

"Honor the worker, and you honor the people!" shouted Hitler, and labor's millions cheered. A scant twenty-four hours later all union offices in Germany were seized by his armed SA and SS men under his orders. All important labor leaders were arrested.

"Gentlemen, the second phase of the National Socialist revolution began today!" he announced triumphantly. "We have watched the actions of trade union leaders much too long." Three days later, Dr. Robert Ley became the director of German labor as head of the *Arbeitsfront,* the national strait-jacket built by the Nazis to replace the ousted unions. One year later, the betrayal of German labor was completed when a law ended labor's right to strike, bargain collectively, or establish or maintain unions. It empowered the employer, as the leader of his shop, to fix all wages. The worker was officially relegated to the position of a slave to the state, when a decree in 1935 announced: "The whole labor market will be consolidated under state domination."

The class to which everyone belonged proved to be a slave class, as soon as Hitler's ideas were put into practice: slaves to the state. And the state was Adolf Hitler. He first began to gain control of labor in the twenties when he established Nazi cells in Germany's unions, following his plan of using organizations and facilities already in existence: the school system, the banks, the government and Nazifying them. Slowly the great middle class capitulated, while organized labor squabbled ineffectually and feared to act.

The Nazis promised the industrialists free reign in return for support. They gave this support and the industrialists also were betrayed.

The contemptuous Doctor Ley was a strange labor leader indeed, one who believed only in the iron fist and the cocked pistol as a compulsion. A confirmed drunkard, he had risen in the party because he was a notorious street fighter and bully. He had joined forces with Hitler in 1925 when he saw in the sub-corporal a fellow plotter.

Appointed the Reichsinspector of the political organizations of the NSDAP in 1931, the *Reichsorganisationsleiter* following Strasser's resignation a year later, he brought together the units of the party and made ready for the organized *Putsch* that was to land the Nazis in jail as a prelude to power. After his appointment as *Reichsarbeitleiter* he realized to his regret that he could not throw into concentration camps all the five million workers who had voted against Hitler. He decided instead to wipe out the organizations, and made all workers join the *Arbeitsfront.* Anyone who did not join this organization was "investigated" by the Gestapo, and ended his days in a concentration camp or starved to death. The law of 1933 ruled that the industries could only hire *Arbeitsfront* members; unemployment relief could be granted only to members.

The *Arbeitsfront* grew to a membership of twenty millions in 1939. Its members were continually under observation. This rank and file was at the bottom of a tremendous hierarchy of leaders and sub-leaders. A law had decreed: "Until the reorganization of the social constitution, *Truehaender der Arbeit* (trustees of labor) will take the place of the workers' trade unions, as well as of the employers and their organizations."

Thus labor and capital were lumped together and subordinated to despotic state rule, a rule which deliberately used labor and capital for the instigation of war. Only war could absorb the millions of unemployed in Germany, Hitler and his economists reasoned, and set about creating work by beginning the manufacture of war implements.

Hitler knew that within the working classes lay the seed of revolt against his tyranny. Therefore they would have to be under "control." For this reason, Ley established his "Strength through Joy" movement. These groups forced the worker to "have a good time." Rallies, picnics, social affairs occupied him, and always the bayonet of the Gestapo was pointed at his back. He could not speak, lest he be thrown into a concentration camp or forced to starve by expulsion from the *Arbeitsfront*.

As low wages helped the Nazis in their muddled economy, there were few scruples exercised. The result was that by 1937 the average German worker made 510 marks in a year and was able to save about four of them. Inflation was prevented by keeping the worker at the borderline of support, while the large industrialists, many of whom, like Goering, held high government positions, waxed prosperous.

This exploitation was not limited to labor. The businessman was trapped in a maze of bureaus and officials which finally culminated, as in all other branches, in the hands of one sub-dictator who was a Nazi and had the avaricious Nazi characteristics. The small employer became the tool of the state, and through him labor exploitation was enforced. Even if he wished to treat his workers fairly, he could not. The Labor Front decided all labor policies for him. He was no better off than the worker, for he, too, was a slave to the state economy.

When Hitler took power his most urgent task was to reduce unemployment. There were approximately 5,800,000 unemployed workers in Germany in 1933. Hitler proceeded to absorb these by placing the country on a war footing. He thought only in terms of total war as a normal condition. He proceeded to use up the national wealth of Germany at an appalling rate. Germany spent in the first four years of Hitler government (when there was no war) twelve billion, five hundred million dollars on war armaments.

As the armament industry grew, labor became scarcer. As a result Hitler decided to create a slave class. All youths under twenty-five had been previously dismissed *en masse* from industry, and were now utilized as a source of cheap labor after the law of June, 1935: "All young Germans of both sexes are obliged to serve their nation in the labor service. The function of this service is to inculcate in German youth a communal spirit, a spirit of the community of the nation and a true concept of the dignity of work."

Thus the young workers-to-be were seized by the Nazi Party as soon as they emerged from the Hitler Youth organizations. In the forced labor service they were even more Nazified than previously. Inoculated with the poison virus of serfdom they became human robots, manipulated by a dictator who held over them the goading lash.

Step by step labor was delivered into the Nazis' hands. The record is its own indictment: On May 2, 1933, when it was decreed that all unions would come under the party supervision and officers would be replaced by trusted Nazis, union officials and editors were taken into custody. Labor's funds, amounting to the equivalent of sixty millions of dollars, were seized. On January 16, 1934, when the new German Labor Code was formulated, it ended the right to strike, to collective bargaining, unofficial and unsupervised meetings, and free unions. On December 31, a law decreed that youths under twenty-five could not be employed without the consent of the *Arbeitsfront* and, as a result, youth was forced into labor organizations which inculcated militaristic nationalism and Nazism, and whose function it was to still forever the drive for free work on the part of German labor.

Ley again demonstrated his unique qualifications as a leader of labor in 1935 by steadfastly erasing more of labors' erstwhile rights. On February 26 a law was passed ordaining *Arbeitsbuecher* (Labor Books) which were passports issued to workers. The effect was to limit completely the workers' freedom of movement and to eradicate his choice of work. He had to stay where he was put.

On March 26 of that year, Ley and Doctor Schacht, the Minister of Economics, met and drafted an agreement whereby the Reich Chamber of Economics joined the *Arbeitsfront*. The chamber was a federation of all German employers and corresponded to the *Arbeitsfront* in organization, inasmuch as the final power of decision lay in the hands of Nazi officials. This management group felt itself in opposition to labor, as it was their task to maintain their business as economically as possible. This group was now given the incongruous name of "Leaders of Labor." It became the economic department of the *Arbeitsfront* and thus the employer was granted two voices in governing labor: In its shop labor was governed by an employer, and in its organization it was governed in the economic sense by a group of employers. As a result, such matters as pay, length of working hours, and working conditions rested entirely with the employer.

Thus is exposed the fraudulent claim of "full employment" under the Nazi system. There were 5,800,000 unemployed in Germany in 1933 and the official figure in 1935 was 4,000,000. But this did not include "blind unemployment." Jews were not counted among the

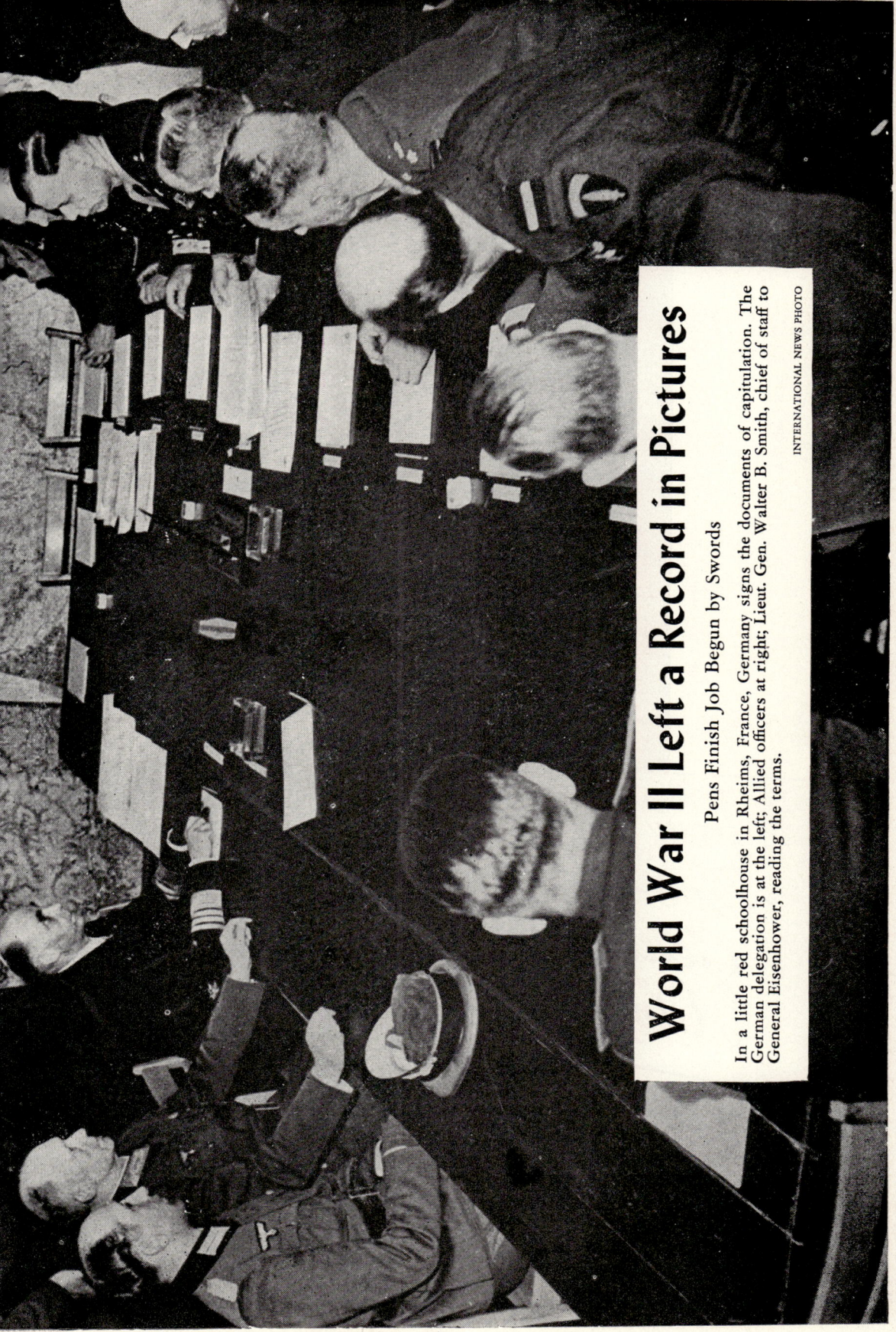

World War II Left a Record in Pictures

Pens Finish Job Begun by Swords

In a little red schoolhouse in Rheims, France, Germany signs the documents of capitulation. The German delegation is at the left; Allied officers at right; Lieut. Gen. Walter B. Smith, chief of staff to General Eisenhower, reading the terms.

INTERNATIONAL NEWS PHOTO

TO THE AMERICAN PEOPLE:

Your sons, husbands and brothers who are standing today upon the battlefronts are fighting for more than victory in war. They are fighting for a new world of freedom and peace.

We, upon whom has been placed the responsibility of leading the American forces, appeal to you with all possible earnestness to invest in War Bonds to the fullest extent of your capacity.

Give us not only the needed implements of war, but the assurance and backing of a united people so necessary to hasten the victory and speed the return of your fighting men.

from our...
Five-Star Generals and Admirals

COURTESY, AMPRO CORPORATION

SIGNAL CORPS PHOTO
General of the Army, George C. Marshall

OFFICIAL PHOTO, U.S. A.A.F.
General Henry H. Arnold

SIGNAL CORPS PHOTO
General Douglas MacArthur

OFFICIAL U. S. NAVY PHOTOGRAPH
Fleet Admiral Chester William Nimitz, U. S. Navy

SIGNAL CORPS PHOTO
General Dwight D. Eisenhower

OFFICIAL U. S. NAVY PHOTOGRAPH
Fleet Admiral William D. Leahy, U. S. Navy

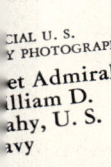

OFFICIAL U. S. NAVY PHOTOGRAPH
Fleet Admiral Ernest J. King U. S. Navy

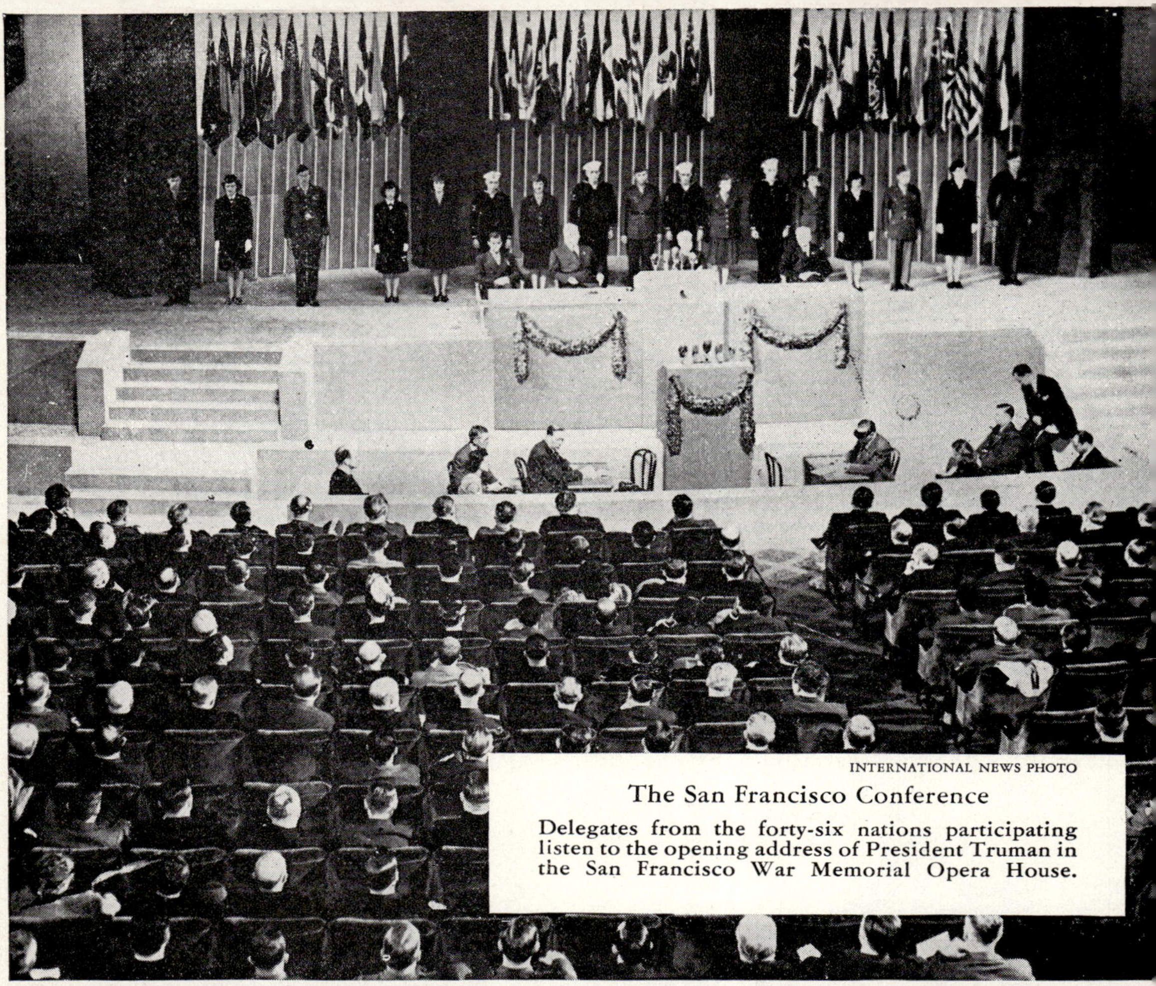

INTERNATIONAL NEWS PHOTO

The San Francisco Conference

Delegates from the forty-six nations participating listen to the opening address of President Truman in the San Francisco War Memorial Opera House.

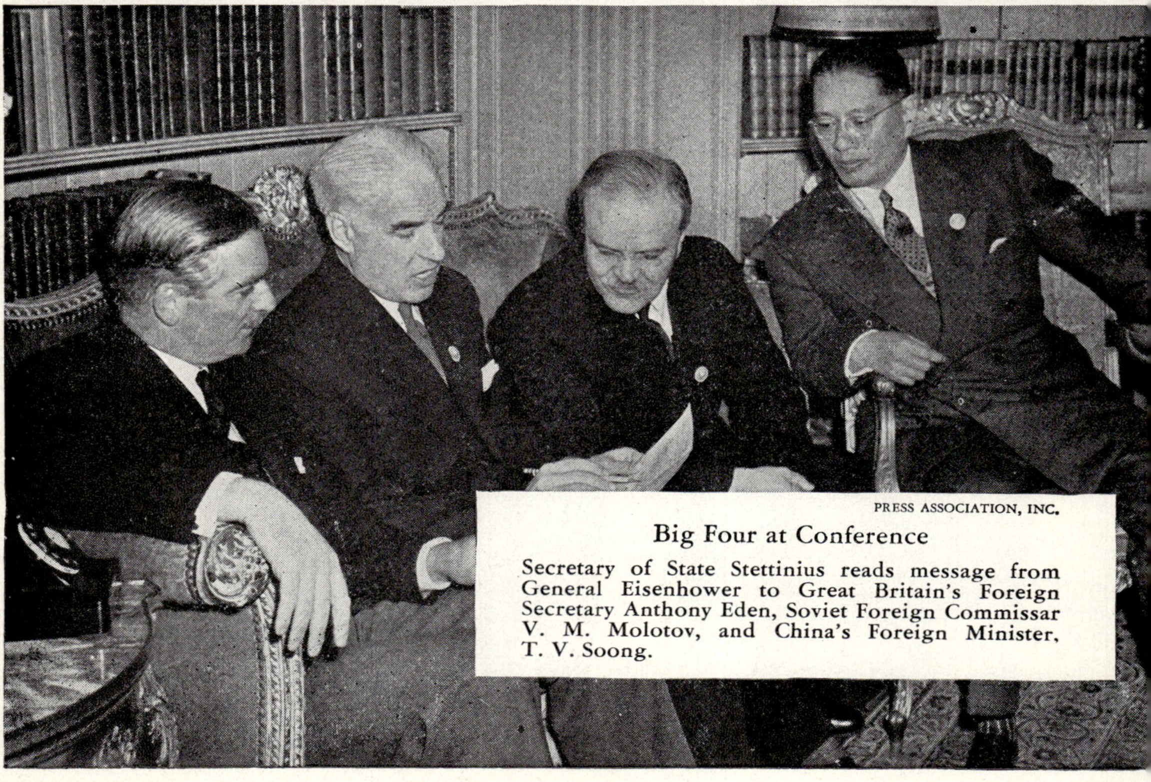

PRESS ASSOCIATION, INC.

Big Four at Conference

Secretary of State Stettinius reads message from General Eisenhower to Great Britain's Foreign Secretary Anthony Eden, Soviet Foreign Commissar V. M. Molotov, and China's Foreign Minister, T. V. Soong.

The Men Who Planned the Victory
Churchill, Roosevelt, Stalin at Yalta

INTERNATIONAL NEWS PHOTO

One of the War's Most Famous Pictures
Fifth Division Marines of the 28th Regiment hoist to the top of an improvised flagpole the flag they carried to the summit of Mount Suribachi on Iwo Jima.

ACME NEWSPICTURES, INC.

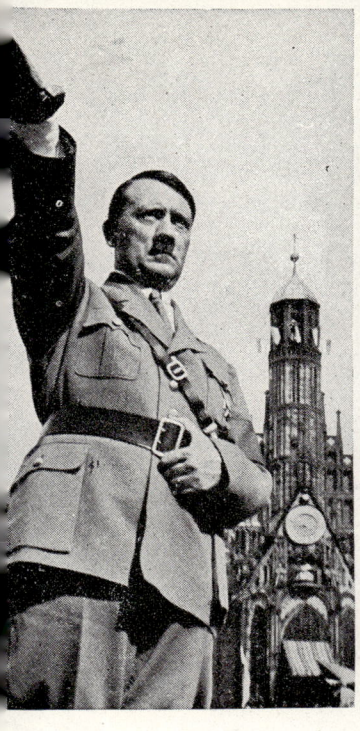

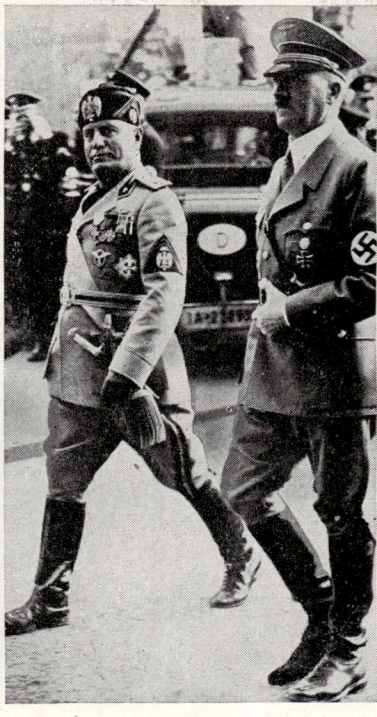

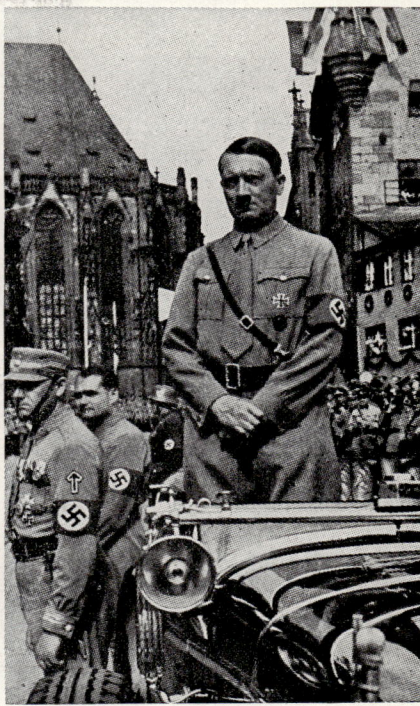

Adolf Hitler and his friend, Benito Mussolini, when they were both at the peak of their glory. (The first and third photographs were found in an apartment in Germany by a United States Army captain.)

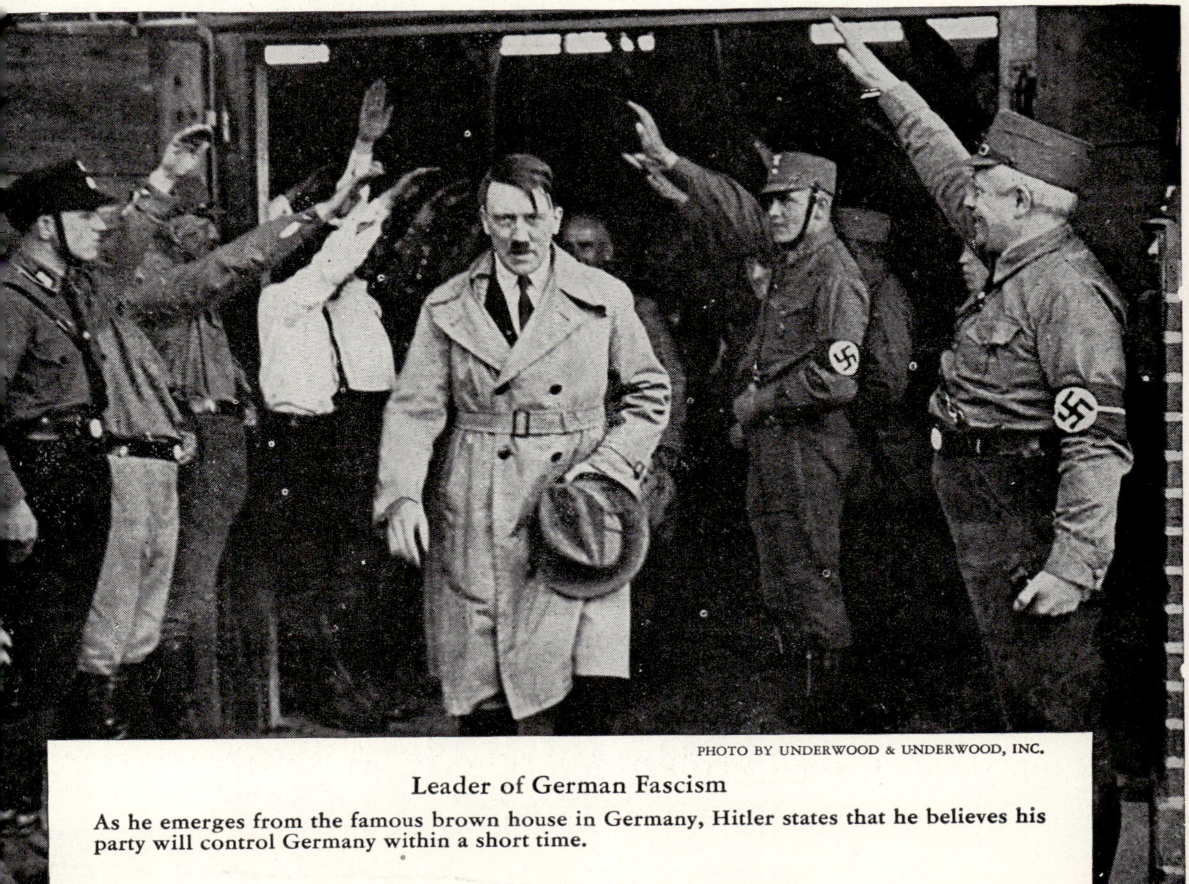

PHOTO BY UNDERWOOD & UNDERWOOD, INC.

Leader of German Fascism

As he emerges from the famous brown house in Germany, Hitler states that he believes his party will control Germany within a short time.

Triumphal Entry Into Vienna

Reichsfuehrer Adolf Hitler riding into Vienna between masses of cheering Austrians. The next day Austria was annexed as a German province.

The Munich Pact

In September, 1938, Prime Minister Chamberlain of England, Premier Daladier of France, Chancellor Hitler of Germany, Premier Mussolini of Italy, and his son-in-law, Count Ciano, meet to decide whether Europe would be plunged into another war.

PHOTO, ACME NEWSPICTURES, INC.

War Trophy for Nazis
Hitler, hands on hips, inspects a Polish gun somewhere in Poland.

INTERNATIONAL NEWS PHOTO

Visiting Scene of Victory
Adolf Hitler, pictured with aides at Danzig, shortly after his arrival at Westerplatte.

Nazi Occupation of Oslo

A street scene in Oslo where Nazis question pedestrians. This picture was smuggled over the Swedish border.

Nazi Traffic Control

A Nazi soldier directing traffic in Copenhagen, capital of Denmark, soon after this tiny country was invaded by the Reich.

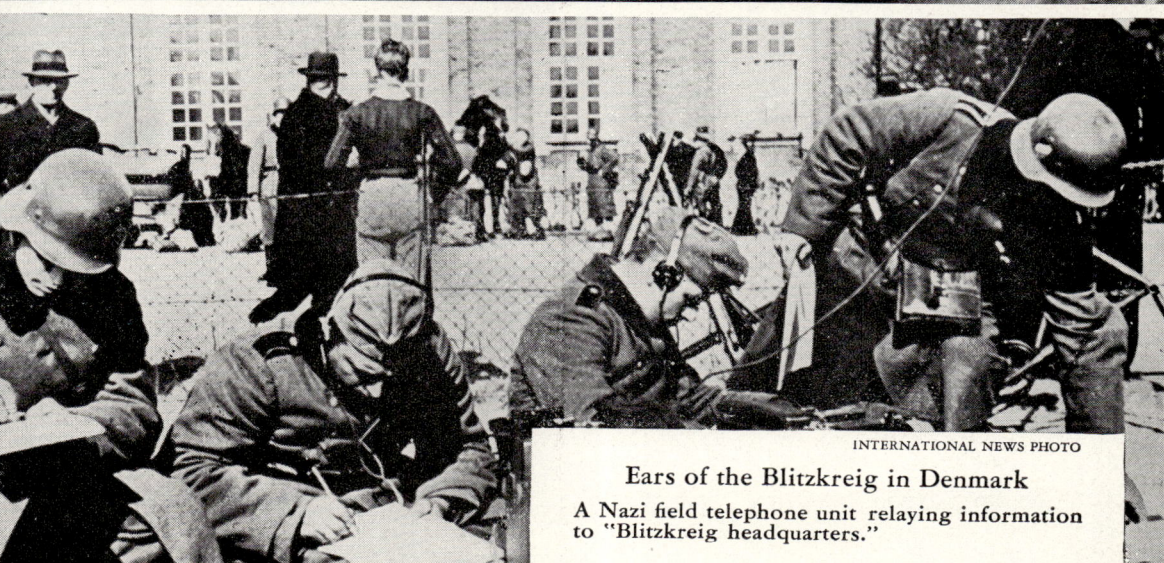

Ears of the Blitzkreig in Denmark

A Nazi field telephone unit relaying information to "Blitzkreig headquarters."

Nazi Invaders

German troops in dress rehearsal disembark at Hamburg, Germany, preparatory to the Nazi thrust at Norway.

INTERNATIONAL NEWS PHOTO

Vaagso—Maaloy Commando Raid

The British fleet carries the war into Norwegian waters.

BRITISH OFFICIAL PHOTOGRAPH

Marching Through Oslo
Led by a German band, the first German troops enter the Norwegian capital.

Battleship Covers Landing

Somewhere in Norway a German battleship covers landing of German troops.

Expedition to the Lofoten Islands

German troops were landed to blow up the oil tanks, and then returned to their ships, after completing work of destruction.

BRITISH OFFICIAL PHOTOGRAPH

Canadian Naval Cadets

Canada trains her captains courageous, many of whom were attached to the British fleet.

The White Cliffs of Dover

Famous in song and motion picture, these chalk cliffs of England still stand untroubled and untouched.

BRITISH OFFICIAL PHOTOGRAPH

Minesweeping Off English Coast

The crew of a British minesweeper at work seeking and rendering harmless enemy mines.

INTERNATIONAL NEWS PHOTO

BRITISH OFFICIAL PHOTOGRAPH

"Action Stations" on Gibraltar

An everyday scene on "the Rock," where a Bofors S-S site is at action 1,330 feet above sea level.

Home Defense

Antiaircraft battery in operation in England and British troops in France on guard at night.

BRITISH OFFICIAL PHOTOGRAPHS

"The Thin Red Line"

British troops on the shores of Dunkirk, waiting for their ships to pick them up, after their escape in Flanders.

PRESS ASSOCIATION, INC.

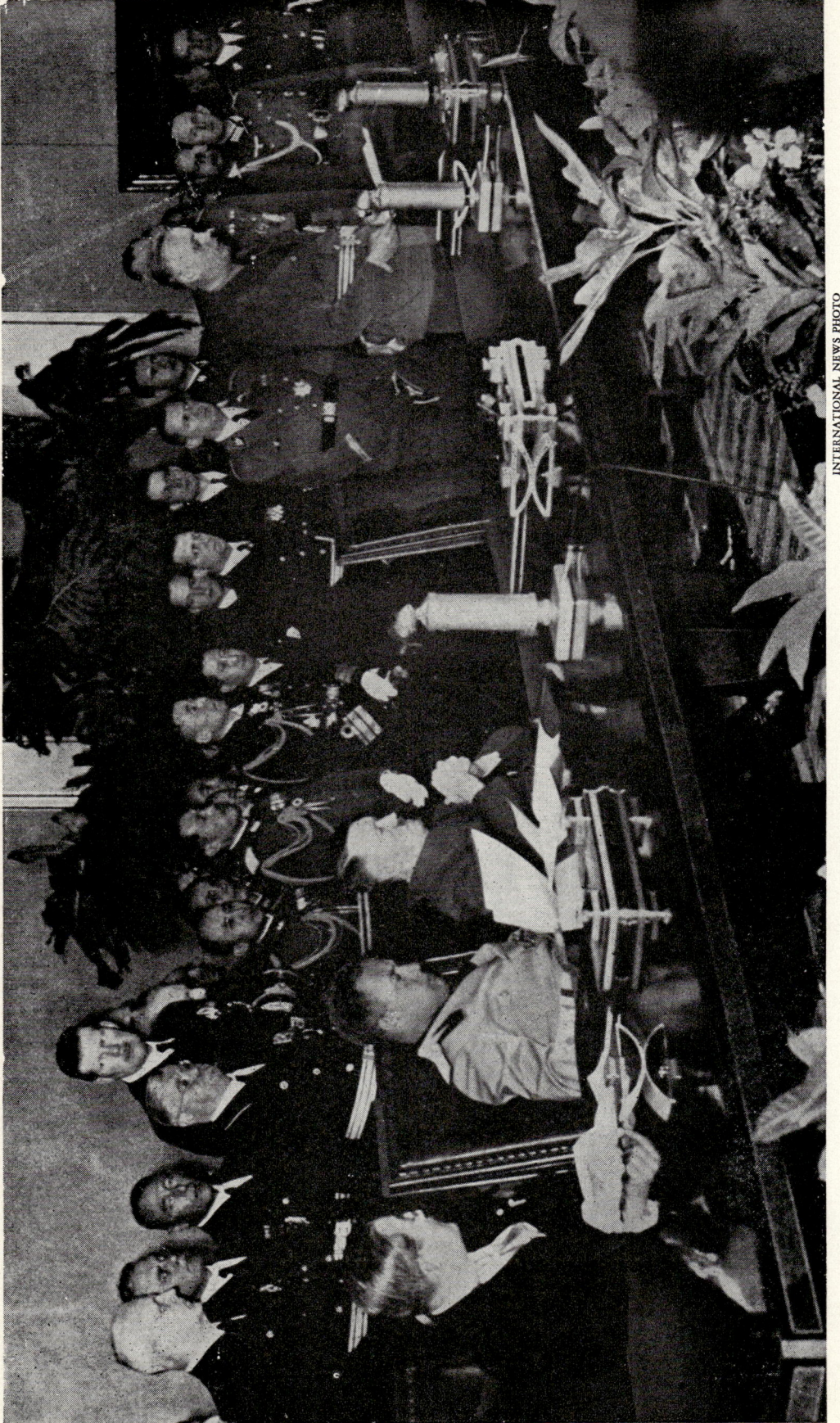

As Japan Signed Up with the Axis

The ten-year pact, signed in 1940, whereby Japan, Italy, and Germany pledge to go to the aid of any one of the others if he is attacked.

unemployed; women who had been forced to stop working were not counted; no one under twenty-five was counted; and the state-subsidized labor-creation programs were not included. Actually the drop in unemployment was negligible or non-existent. Much of middle-class unemployment was erased by the creation of a tremendous bureaucratic class. The *Arbeitsfront* alone absorbed 55,000 Nazi officials. The SS and SA were also brought to full strength and numbered at least a million members, while the Gestapo had 25,000 agents, besides a great clerical staff.

Furthermore, labor's standard of living had gone down precipitously. Wages had dropped to 22 marks per week and prices had risen. There was grumbling among the workers, but this was cruelly quelled by the usual methods. German wage earners were being "prepared for war." At the Nuremberg Congress the Four Years Plan for raw-material self-sufficiency was announced. Its declared purpose was to establish independence from foreign supplies of textiles, oils, and rubber as well as other scarce products. The eight-hour day was extended to ten hours by a decree in 1939. This included women, and children under sixteen. Many cases of regular sixteen-hour working days for skilled and unskilled male labor were recorded.

Remembering the revolt that ended Germany's part in World War I, Hitler carefully deprived labor of all its rights, to prevent another revolt. He reduced them to the slave level in order to make their dependence on the state complete. He theorized that those who were dependent on a state for their food would not revolt against it, even though their sons were slaughtered and they slowly starved to death.

Labor at the beginning of the war already knew what was in store. They remembered the thousands who had starved at the end of the last war, and the belt was already tight at the beginning of World War II. The Nazis resorted finally to importing paid labor and later slave labor from conquered territories.

Labor was secure during the period of the Republic. It had six and a half million in unions. The eight-hour day was prevalent, social security assisted the worker when he was unemployed, and Labor courts protected the legal rights of the worker. The lower middle class, consisting of small salaried employees was unorganized. As a result they were willing to follow anyone who would promise them more security. Hitler did this, being careful not to say that he would revoke all promises whenever he so desired.

This is what Nazism meant in Germany. The indictment would require many legal volumes. Germans whose hearts revolted against these Nazi practices were unable to lift their voices in protest. Bewildered and helpless, they must remain silent. Against the might of government and military power, the price of protest was death.

RAISING A GENERATION FOR HUMAN SLAUGHTER

NAZI guilt is completely revealed in the official documents of their own party. These records show clearly the methods by which Hitler and his cohorts planned to sacrifice an entire generation for their own diabolical schemes. These documents reveal to us the real causes for which our young men and women were fighting in their epoch-making crusade for human freedom.

Hitler systematically raised a generation of boys for "gun fodder" to gratify his own ambition to conquer the world. He broke down all standards of morality, taught them to hate, robbed them of religious training, defiled the names of God and Jesus Christ. For the young women of Germany he destroyed the sanctity of marriage and home, and exhorted them to become "brood mares" in common prostitution in order to give more sons for world conquest.

The methods used for this corruption and degradation of a formerly great people are startling. The avowed aim of education in Germany under the Nazi régime was the creation of a race of warriors. Hitler, while in prison at Landsberg following the failure of his Munich *Putsch,* set down the aim of education for boys in *Mein Kampf* which was to become the Bible of the new generation.

All education in schools and homes was based on preparation for slaughter. He said blandly, "It is to change the young man into a soldier.... Of secondary importance is the training of mental abilities." Later he gave a clear clue to the Nazi aims of education: "His (the boy's) entire education and devotion has to have the aim of giving him the conviction of being absolutely superior to others. Through this he has to win the belief in the invincibility of the entire nationality, the 'super-race.'"

Hitler devoted but a few lines to the education of girls: "Here, too, the main stress should be put on physical training, and only after this on the promotion of spiritual, and, last of all, intellectual values." The *goal* of female education invariably was to make them breeders for the war machine. He turned each subject into an instrument for the development of national egotism: "It is the task of a folkish state to see to it that at last a world history is written in which the race question is raised to a predominant position."

It remained only for the Nazis to install their own teachers and curricula. The *Nationalsozialistischer Deutscher Lehrersbund* (NSLB

National Socialist German Teachers' Union) had been formed in 1927 as a branch of the party and was strong enough in 1933 to organize all the teachers in Germany. With its *Reichswalter* and *Gauleiter,* Fritz Waechtler, the NSLB decreed that all public school teachers had to belong to a NSDAP fighting organization, come to school in uniform whenever possible, know military sports, and be proficient in them. All non-Aryan teachers were removed and all teachers left were commanded to serve and teach for the NSDAP or be purged.

Hitler assumed complete control over Germany's schools on April 30, 1934, when Dr. Bernard Rust was appointed Reich Minister of Science, Education, and Culture for the people. Official new textbooks and curricula were imposed on the school system. Rust had been a party member since 1922. Promoted to *Gauleiter* of Hanover and Brunswick, and later promoted to head all German schools, he made the schools political-party incubators. "All educational agencies have one common goal: The formation of the National Socialist man."

German schools were used as a political instrument in the creation of a generation of brute force. They indulged in the Hitlerian methods of inculcation, propagandizing, teaching of untruths and half truths, and the prostitution of psychology to the nefarious ends of the NSDAP. Knowledge admittedly was looked down upon and discouraged. When taught, it was merely to make the pupil a more rabid Nazi. History was used only to distort all facts. The pupil who already had swallowed the race theories was made to believe that all cultures and civilizations started and ended with the Nordic German race. Their superiority was therefore present in all Germans.

Biology textbooks were interpreted with super-race theory. Mendelian laws were used as a basis.

Subtly but surely, the institution of the family was undermined: The high calling of motherhood was debased to brood mares for soldiers. Through the most insidious methods of education a philosophy of ruthlessness, blind obedience, hate, and falsehood was inculcated. The systematic assumption of control over Germany's educational system included the universities and colleges. Balder von Schirach arranged for Hitler to speak at Munich University. The speech resulted in bringing most of the listeners into the NSDAP. Party units were subsequently organized on many German campuses, and the *Studentenbund* (Students' Union) was formed with von Schirach as leader. NSDAP established central offices, with branches in every German university and college. Its function was to spy on all students and professors to see that they adhered strictly to the party line.

An analysis of the catalog of the University of Berlin in 1941 revealed that all phases of knowledge had been twisted in much the same way as the public-school curriculum. Courses in religion were devoted to proving the evil influences of the Bible and Christianity with its Hebraic foundations. National leader worship was declared to be the highest form of religion. History of religion was given a degenerate church background to pervert its old form and to replace it with National Socialism as the only religion.

Law and economics courses enhanced the virtues of the new German system and condemned or ridiculed all others. Medical courses emphasized the race biology and geopolitical teachings of the Nazis. Surgery classes concentrated only on war problems, following the usual Nazi point of view, which saw the normal state of the world as a continued state of partial or total war.

The more important part of this paganistic system of education lay in the *Jugend* (Hitler Youth). Every German boy belonged to one of the branches of this all-inclusive organization from the time he was five until he was eighteen, and every girl until she was twenty-one. The Hitler Youth was already a strong organization in 1933. Even as far back as 1921 Kurt Gruber had begun an unofficial organization of Nazis in *Vogtland*. At the same time, in Munich, Adolf Lenks formed the *Jungsturm Adolf Hitler* (Young Storm Troopers of Adolf Hitler). Rudolf Gugel started similar groups in Nuremberg and Franken territory.

At the *Reichsparteitag* (National Party Day) in Weimar in 1926, the Hitler Youth was officially ordained as part of the party by Hitler, and named *Hitler Jugend* by Julius Streicher. During this period Kurt Gruber was its *Reichsfuehrer* (National Leader). In 1929, two thousand members of *Hitler Jugend* marched before Hitler in Nuremberg. In 1932, one hundred thousand marched before him, and by the end of 1933 the numbers had swelled to over three million.

The organization of Germany's youth under the NSDAP was largely the work of Baldur von Schirach, the molder of German youth under the Third Reich. In 1924, at the age of seventeen, he heard Hitler speak at Munich, where the corporal had gone five years before and had allied himself with Drexel's *Deutsche Arbeiter Partei* (German Workers' Party). Fanatically attached to Hitler, he worked for him in the German universities throughout the '20's and early '30's. Von Schirach became the first *Reichsjugendfuehrer* (State Youth Leader) in 1931 and, upon assumption of power by Hitler, was named *Jugendfuehrer des Deutschen Reiches* (Youth Leader of the German Nation). Many independent youth groups began to ally themselves with the HJ. For example, in December, 1933, the German Evangelical Youth entered the HJ after a "conference" between von Schirach and the Reichsbishop of the church. Other groups, such as the *Wandervoegel* and *Sportjugend* (Wanderbirds—Sport Youth) quickly joined.

As in the schools system, the various Hitler Youth groups were divided through the convenient machinisms of age and sex. A boy, at the age of six, had already learned the basic *Fuehrer Prinzip* (leader principles) in the *Kindertagestaedte* (day nurseries) where he was left by his working parents. At the age of six he was ready to enter the *Pimpfs*. The purpose of this organization was to lay the foundation for the *Hitler Jugend*. The boy was given a *Leistugbuch* (achievement record) which he kept throughout his membership in Hitler Youth Groups. His record in *Weltanschauliche Shulung* (world-point-of-view training) was kept, as well as *Ausland Kenntnisse* (knowledge of foreign affairs) which were taught him, distorted, by the German point of view.

He was told that the Versailles Treaty had been a masterpiece of treachery; that the name of the President of the United States was Rosenfeldt, and that he was a Jew; that the democracies were decadent and "unnatural"; that in nature only do the strong survive, whereas in democracy the weak are also given a chance. He learned that only might makes right; that the strong must kill the weak; and that Germany would act on this principle in conquering the world. He learned above all the *Fuehrer Prinzip*. If, upon his *Pimpfenprobe* (*Pimpf* examination) the boy showed a definite devotion to the party, he was promoted to the *Jungvolk* (Young Folk).

Home and religion were expected to count as nothing. Devotion to the party was the culmination of all ideals, the giver and taker of all love and emotion, the provider of life itself, and the institution to which life was a debt to be repaid in blood. The slogan of the *Pimpf* group of six- to ten-year-olds was *"Zaehne zusammen! Aushalten!"* (Teeth clenched! Endure!) The basic principles taught the *Pimpf* were: (1) Hitler was the saviour and above all. (2) Foreigners were to be hated and revenge taken against them. (3) The strong rightfully kill the weak. This is nature. The survival of the fittest is the basic principle of life. (4) A pure race is the only good race, and the German race to which the *Pimpf* belong is that race.

Cases on record reveal that children who thought themselves weak were still devoted to Hitler and ready to die for him in the *Hitlerkammer* (Hitlerchamber). Thus the will to live was actually degenerated into a desire to die for the Fuehrer's glory.

The next group was the *Jungvolk* (Young People), for boys between the ages of ten and fourteen. Here the same principles were taught as in the *Pimpf* group, but life became more rigid and Spartan. The leaders knew psychology and used it to direct all the aims of a boy of this age toward the making of a Nazi. The third group for boys was the *Hitler Jugend* (Hitler Youth) into which they graduated at the age of fourteen. This was the secondary army. At this stage the boys were already well equipped, both physically and mentally, to fight for and die for Hitler. It remained merely to round out the curriculum. Thus the boys were taught *Deutschkunde* as a final inculcation to embue them with Nazism. Again the great lesson was pounded into them that the nation is a blood unit, a fighting unit, a working unit, and that each party member is a cog in that unit existing only for the state.

All girls up to the age of fourteen were members of the *Jungmaedel* (Young Girls). In this organization they were to acquire the rudiments of Nazi education. The entire system was integrated to accomplish Hitler's aim, and thus the main trend of studies was toward the development of the subject of sex, eugenics, and domestic science, which were studied from early childhood.

From the ages of fourteen to twenty, girls were members of the *Bund Deutscher Maedel's* (Union of German Girls), BDM. Here they were encouraged to mix with boys from labor camps and to begin to have illegitimate children. Legitimacy was of no consequence. German girls were prostituted into the mothers of Nazis. About 550,000 were initiated into the BDM yearly and trained under the careful supervision of leaders developed at special leader training schools.

Hitler Youth leaders used every sinister method in accomplishing their purpose of making Nazis. They knew the tastes of children at each stage of their development and catered to them, always slyly injecting their poisonous philosophy. Books were written by HJ leaders on the effectiveness of uniforms. Hitler himself mentions the uniform in *Mein Kampf* as a valuable method of emotional satisfaction, and this lure was held out to the Hitler Youth. The love for adventure was capitalized upon in the formation of the HJ Marines, fliers, and motorized division, which had at their disposal real motorcycles, airplanes, and other military equipment.

The need for something to worship was cunningly devised by the state religion. How far this was blasphemously carried is proved by a prayer for the youth written by Baldur von Schirach: "Adolf Hitler, we believe in Thee. Without Thee we would be alone. Through Thee we are a people. Thou hast given us the greatest experience of our youth, comradeship. Thou hast laid upon us the task, the responsibility, the duty. Thou hast given us Thy name (*Hitler Jugend*), the most beloved name that Germany has ever possessed. We speak it with reverence, we bear it with faith and loyalty. Thou canst depend upon us, Adolf Hitler, Leader and Standard-Bearer. The youth is Thy name, Thy name is the youth. Thou and the young millions can never be sundered."

The official handbook of the HJ reveals a strange mixture of truth and falsehood. It launches into a discussion of races, to which the first four chapters are devoted. The Christian teaching "Before God all men are equal" is derided as false. Christianity, Freemasonry, Marxism, and Judaism are lumped together and condemned.

The German youngster was told it was advisable to sterilize or kill those with diseases, or those hopelessly degraded by mixing: "In mixing, only the worst features are inherited by the hybrids." In explaining man's adjustment to his environment, they are warned that only in having children and more children could the German race survive.

A discussion of German territory inculcated the conquest microbe: "By German territory we mean every region of Europe which is inhabited by Germans and which has received its cultural imprint from the German people." The groundwork was further laid for the idea that the world is German in a three-chapter discussion of the German political area, the German population area, and the German culture area, which means every place on earth where there "happens" to be a German. All activities of the German youth were integrated to produce in the child a lust for conquest, fighting, and dying; a blind obedience to his leaders, a conviction that he and his were ordained to take their place as the greatest race on the earth.

So Hitler built his Nazi Frankenstein. He overthrew all human values; the home was turned to the Nazi's own uses; religion was displaced by the state religion; love was interpreted only as a medium for an ascending birth rate; morality and marriage were discounted by sanctioned illegitimacy; and God was displaced by Herr Hitler.

Upon his graduation from the HJ a boy was ready to subscribe to the following rules: The leader is always right ... never violate discipline. ... The program is your dogma, it demands your complete surrender to the cause.... Whatever serves the interest of the movement, and through it Germany and the German people, is *right*.

Hitler's legions, coldly and scientifically, were deprived of moral and spiritual values and were reared for ruthless conquest. They were never given an opportunity to know human brotherhood. They knew only hate. Their characters were twisted, their instincts inflamed. A race indeed was created, a race of barbarous automatons who goosestepped forth to conquer the world. They were prostituted *en masse*.

Like every other democratic principle, the freedom of the press was eradicated in Germany soon after Hitler succeeded to power. The Nazis stole the press from its former owners and turned it into a great lie factory, from which they derived tremendous profits for individuals and the party.

Dr. Joseph Goebbels, as Propaganda Minister, on June 30, 1933, became the Reich Minister of National Enlightenment and Propaganda. He assumed unlimited power over the press, radio, motion pictures, periodicals, books, advertising, and all other "molders of the public mind."

The new propaganda machine was tested on June 24, 1933. Scare headlines fabricated this falsehood: "Red Plague Over Berlin—Foreign planes of an unknown type escaped unrecognized—Defenseless Germany—Tomorrow it might be gas or incendiary bombs."

This startling "news," including the assertion that foreign planes had dropped propaganda leaflets over Berlin denouncing the new government, was published in large type on the front page of all German newspapers. This was the beginning of a campaign for the establishment of a German air force, as indicated by this paragraph: "Is it not the most natural thing to assume that Air Police shall be in a position to interfere at once and prevent foreign attackers.... Every bird is allowed to defend itself if its nest is attacked. Only Germany has to look on, with her wings clipped and her claws blunted, while her nest is being defiled and may soon be destroyed." Goebbels' first demonstration with the German press frightened the people into a belief they were to be attacked.

Goebbels, a small, deformed Aryan with an insatiable sex appetite, had started out as a left-wing sympathizer. Born a Roman Catholic and married to the stepdaughter of a respectable Jewish family, he became anti-Catholic, anti-Semitic, rightist, and Hitler's mouthpiece for his own political advancement. Opportunism and treachery marked his rise. He began as the leftist Strasser's secretary in 1922, and betrayed him four years later when he joined the Hitler faction. Hitler appointed him *Gauleiter* of Berlin in 1926.

Unscrupulous, misshapen, and perverted, he made an ideal Nazi chieftain. He enjoyed nothing better than to browbeat strong men, probably in compensation for his own weakness, and as a result, he was hated by all subordinates. He was described by his fellow Nazi, Max Amann, as the "Mephisto of the party, an unsympathetic fellow, one marked by the Almighty with a club foot, of whom one must beware." This was the man in whose hands the "national enlightenment of the German people" was placed. It was he who eradicated freedom of thought in Germany.

The first law decreed by the Nazis suspended the Constitution and all civil rights, including the freedom of the press. The Reich Kultur Chamber was established a few months later. This was a corporation headed by Goebbels, which included all the heads of public information concerns. The press was divided, like industry, into two groups: the employers, who were the "leaders," and the employees, who were the "followers." Both groups were headed by Nazi officials who controlled their two organizations. Working journalists were forced to join the Reich Press Association, a group of similar design and objectivity. All executive positions in these organizations were appointive, the power of appointment lying with Goebbels. No journalist could work if he did not belong to the association; no publisher could publish without belonging to an official publishers' group. All non-Aryan journalists were immediately barred from membership in the groups.

The concentration camp waited for violators of the law. This regulation could naturally be applied to anything and anyone whom the Nazis wished to single out. Each day the Propaganda Ministry issued its orders. News was suppressed, untruths were ordered to be printed, and the manner of presentation prescribed. Any journalist who revealed what went on at "press conferences" was subject to severe punishment. There are cases on record of sentences of life imprisonment and beheading for the revelation of the procedures.

The seizure of the press was not accomplished without blood. On the day the Nazis took power hundreds of newspapers were smashed, and editors were forced to flee or be killed. One of the newspapers hated most by the Nazis was the *Gerade Weg* of Munich. It was invaded and smashed to bits. Its editor, Dr. Fritz Gerlich, was taken into "protective custody" and later beheaded. Others, such as Theodore Wolff, editor of the *Berliner Tageblatt,* and the Ullstein family, owners of one of the greatest press syndicates, were forced to flee for their lives in 1933. Anyone who had written against the Nazis prior to their accession to power was in danger of the concentration camp and death. Herr Schaefer, editor of the *Koelnische Zeitung,* was taken into "protective custody" because he had given an account of the methods of canvassing employed by the Nazi *Westdeutsche Boebachter* in competition with his newspaper.

Whenever antagonism was to be created against any group, the press pounded away for months beforehand to prepare the way for the persecution or injustice sure to follow. The persecution of the Roman Catholics is a good example. Prior to the morality trials in 1937, the press hammered at the Roman Catholic Church with a torrent of abuse unparalleled in journalistic history. Cartoons depicting priests in disgusting positions were printed daily, and headlines screamed the terms: "Black-robed hypocrites." Columns were filled with foul descriptive matter and alleged "testimony" from students in the parochial schools. By lies, repetition, and a monopoly of the press, the public was prepared gradually for the events which would have caused a great shock and uproar without the propagandistic softening.

Foreign news was always carefully scrutinized and rewritten to the Nazi point of view. When President Roosevelt made his plea for peace at the time of the Czechoslovakian crisis, the publication of the message was delayed for forty-eight hours in order to let Hitler make a similar plea. The news was presented to the German people in reverse order, and the impression was conveyed that the President had followed and supported Hitler's action.

American womanhood was a continual object of Nazi press attack. The impression conveyed to the German people was that American women were parasites and prostitutes, and that they spent their time loafing at bars and in night clubs while their children grew into degenerates and criminals.

The Nazis then instituted "law for the preservation of the independence of the German press," which prohibited organizations formed for religious, professional, or political purposes, coöperative societies, joint stock companies, limited liability companies, and public bodies of any kind from owning newspapers. Furthermore, the Aryan origin of every stockholder, as well as anyone connected with the newspaper had to be proved to the year 1800. Any newspaper could henceforth be closed by the Reichs Press Chamber if that body decided that the market serviced by such newspapers could not support two or more papers. This opened the way for the seizure and closing of Roman Catholic presses, all opposition party presses, and all newspapers which detracted from the circulation of official party organs.

In charge of the "financial aspects" of the press was Max Amann, one of Hitler's closest friends. He was the Chairman of the German Press Chamber, to which he succeeded after a lifelong career of petty thievery and shady dealing. He was the lord of the publishing world in the Reich. He was Czar over the Official *Franz Eher Verlag,* the publisher of the official party organ, the *Voelkischer Beobachter,* and of *Mein Kampf;* he was the head of the *Berliner Kampfverlag,* and overlord of every other sizable publishing company. As soon as Hitler seized power, Amann seized or began to gain control of the large, independent publishers, including Ullstein, Sherl, and others. SA men and party members began compulsory subscription campaigns, which included door-to-door canvassing by armed thugs who intimidated everyone into subscribing. Those who were reluctant to subscribe were threatened with the loss of jobs.

Nearly all the important party leaders had private newspapers which they used as mouthpieces. Goebbel's *Angriff* which he founded in the pre-Nazi days, grew to tremendous size after Hitler's accession to power, and became so successful financially that Amann transferred it to the party *Franz Eher Verlag* in 1935. These newspapers served as individual sources of income for the Nazi chieftains, and their success was insured by enforced circulation methods. All Germans had to buy the journals issued by their superiors. Dr. Robert Ley, leader of the *Arbeitsfront* derived great personal benefit from his *Der Deutsche,* the former organ of the Christian trade unions. It was seized by Ley after the law forbidding the publication of newspapers by public bodies.

The function of the press as a weapon of international aggression was first used in 1933 when the initial attempt was made to incorporate

Austria with Germany. The press began to attack the Austrian Government violently until the first Nazi *Putsch* in July, 1934, failed in Austria. Truth was completely thrown aside. The main assertion was that the National Socialists in Austria were being persecuted by the Communist Government which was ostensibly in control. Thus by pretending to be attacked itself, instead of being the attacker, the Nazi Government prepared the way for every act of aggression. The same method was used in 1938 in the Sudetenland; in Czechoslovakia in 1939, and finally in Poland, France, Belgium, Holland, Norway, the Balkans, Greece, and all countries marked for conquest.

Flagrant examples of fraudulent attack on foreign powers are numerous. Throughout the war, the German people were flagrantly misinformed by the German press regarding losses and military defeats. As the situation grew worse for the Germans, the "verbal newspaper" rumors became more and more prevalent. These began to offset the fantastic lies issued by the DNB, the German news agency. Journalism in the Third Reich became a farce of propaganda and falsehood.

German mothers, with fear and anguish, saw what was happening to their sons and daughters. Many were filled with pride; many grieved at the spectacle. The house was divided against itself. In some homes youth was arrayed against old age; sons against fathers; daughters against mothers. In other homes the family unitedly followed Hitler.

These were the processes of disintegration through which the German people passed. These are the processes which Hitler and his cohorts reached out to inflict on the rest of the world. The German people were forced to live in almost complete darkness about events taking place, for all news which reached them was brazen distortion. Those who dared to question were warned of "sudden death" to them or to their loved ones. It is known that millions of German people prayed for deliverance behind drawn curtains in their homes. Aged fathers and mothers saw their sons and grandsons either engulfed by the emotional waves of Nazism or driven into it by force. The new generation of the "New Order" knew nothing else.

Many great scientists, scholars, physicians, lawyers, and intellectuals were driven from their country. Many famous "Aryans" who were loyal to the republic refused to live under the Nazi reign and managed to escape to Switzerland, England, and America. Thus these nations were enriched by the brains and character of the old Germany which had given the world science, art, and culture.

Germany was swiftly plunging headlong into destruction; it was starting on a road which would eventually lead to its devastation. It was pulling down the pillars of the temple of civilization which would annihilate a large portion of its own manhood, leave its cities in ruins, and its homeland in seething flames of a just retribution.

8

RISE AND FALL OF BENITO MUSSOLINI

WHEN two dictators meet to divide the world between them in a Bacchanalian feast, there is bound to be trouble ahead. Behind the "love feast" is a clash of inordinate ambitions. The dictators stick together only because they do not wish to "hang together." Behind the thin disguise each detests the other.

The personality of Adolf Hitler has already been discussed; let us now look upon his friend Benito Mussolini, the imitation Cæsar behind whose twentieth-century chariot the Italian people were to be lashed and dragged into World War II.

Italy, once the seat of the mighty Roman Empire, had for generations been a nation of liberty-loving people. Garibaldi was their emancipator. Proud of their traditions, its more than 45,000,000 people lived under sunny skies at peace with the world, except when driven into wars by intriguing men in power.

The record of Mussolini, in whom the Italian people placed their trust, is one of treachery and tragedy. It is related here with reverence and affection for Italy. The historical facts may astound the Italians, for while held in bondage they knew little of the true background of the pompous dictator whom they vociferously cheered as he stood on the balcony overlooking the excited throngs, his chin and chest thrust out in emulation of a modern Cæsar.

The historical record of Mussolini is made from documents, eye-witnesses, and intimates of Mussolini, some of whom stood by his side in his inner councils both before he was dictator and while he held office. Americans know him only through his orations which came to them over the radio. His powerful voice and vigorous excitations made him for a time assume the proportions of a modern Cæsar. The time has now come, in justice to the Italian people, to remove his Roman toga and let the world see the actual man who had been hiding beneath it.

Life stories of great men of a faraway past represent an amalgam of facts and legend. Students of modern history have grown up within the same span of time with Benito Mussolini, and have thus been in a position to witness the fabrication of the Mussolini legend woven before their very eyes. The legend presented Mussolini as "the greatest man of our sphere and time," quoting the late Ambassador to Italy, Hon. Richard Washburn Child. Students of contemporary history, alert enough to salvage the facts behind Mussolini's life story, wonder how the world could have been so grossly misled by pomp and bombast, by the wizardry of modern, high-pressure press agentry.

Here are the facts: Born in Predappio, Italy, on July 28, 1883, the son of a blacksmith and a schoolteacher, the boy Benito was a little rogue with an early predilection for violence. He not only bullied and beat children weaker than himself, but was expelled from two schools, once for stabbing an older boy with a penknife, and the second time for using an undisclosed weapon in a fracas with three boys. His father whipped him; his mother pampered him. He grew up like a vicious little animal.

His father, Alessandro Mussolini, was a rebel with an ideal for which he lived, fought, and suffered jail terms—Socialism. Progressing from blacksmith to tavern-keeper, he became mayor of his district and formed one of the first labor unions. Young Benito took to Socialism as an outlet for his irresistible urge to violent action, A terrorist by temperament, he became a histrionic, double-crossing radical, true to his excessive ego exclusively. Hitching himself to political programs only as long as they served him, he pushed himself up to power. The charlatan radical claimed, by turns, to be attached to Karl Marx, Babeuf, Blanqui, Sorel, Schopenhauer, Stirner, Nietzsche, but Machiavelli was the only patron saint governing his mind. He studied the life of Machiavelli, and in one instance underlined in the text: "All armed prophets have conquered and the unarmed have been destroyed."

Before he arrived at his height of Napoleonic and Cæsarean poses, he traveled many devious ways, being in and out of jail, without leaving a record of any human deed pointing at greatness. When he taught in the elementary schools, he frightened the children away from classes, was charged with blasphemy, and had to leave a town after a lodging-house brawl for the affection of the landlady.

He fled to Switzerland at twenty years of age to escape military conscription. His life there was hard, for he muddled through as a mason's apprentice, a butcher boy, and a porter, sometimes sleeping under bridges and driven by hunger to go begging, sometimes helped along by revolutionaries. He joined and passed through Socialist, anarchist, pacifist, antireligionist and other groups. He became a soap-box orator, strike organizer and propagator of atheism. The first article that he ever had published was entitled *"Dieu N'Exist Pas"* (God Does Not Exist).

His Swiss police record bears entries for vagabondage, for the theft of a gold watch, for using a forged passport. After having been expelled from one canton after another for violation of "State rights," he was finally expelled from Switzerland altogether. Thus it came about that at the end of 1904, Benito Mussolini appeared in Trento, Austria, with the halo of a "Socialist martyr."

Trento, in the South Tyrol, was the center of activities of the Italian Irredenta, so Mussolini joined the Irredentists. When the King of Italy granted an amnesty to political refugees and deserters in 1905, Benito slipped quietly back to Italy, where the army seized him. His military duty completed, he went to jail for a strike-terror act in Oneglia in 1908. Then back to Austria and Irredenta, where he got into conflict with Austrian authorities and returned again to Italy, leaving a common-law wife and a child behind in Trento. In 1910, his radical weekly, *Lotta di Classe* (Class Struggle), advocated syndicalism, direct action, and a blood-bath of the proletariat. Another arrest followed, after which he acquired a second common-law wife who bore him two children. Finally, in 1911, he achieved something that, for the first time, made him a nationally known figure—he was sentenced to seven months' imprisonment for a popular cause.

The cause was opposition to Italy's war on Tripoli. The war was going badly and, therefore, unpopular. Not only were the Socialists opposed to it but also the broad public. Mussolini, riding the wave of mounting pacifism, made himself its most rabid spokesman, started strike riots, and committed acts of violence and sabotage.

"This Libyan adventure means only useless and stupid bloodshed!" declared the glorifier of blood-letting, who, when he had become duce and war lord, exclaimed on his visit to Tripoli in 1926: "Rome carried the beacon lamp of strength to the shores of the African sea. No one can stop our inexorable will!" In 1911, he went proudly to jail for resisting that "beacon lamp of strength."

Stepping out of prison as an exalted Socialist, he began to show that he knew the ropes of demagoguery. He went to the Socialist Party congress at Reggio Emilia in July, 1912, and accused the intellectual Socialist leaders, Bissolati, Bonomi, and Cabrini, of being slackers. They were not revolutionary enough, not radical, not antimonarchist, not antimilitarist enough he declared, and he demanded their expulsion from the party.

His emotional oratory turned the congress into a madhouse. Bissolati, democrat and humanist, and others were forced out of the party. Mussolini, the apostle of violence, rose to leadership. Six months later the party entrusted the promising radical with the editorship of its paper, *Avanti*. He became head of the Socialist Party and one of the influencing factors of Italian politics.

The Triple Alliance contracted Italy to fight for Germany and Austro-Hungary. Mussolini headlined his editorial on July 27: "Our Neutrality Must Be Absolute!" The editorial struck a popular tune. Mussolini mocked the "sentimental farce staged by these two old gossips, France and Belgium." On September 21, at the Socialist Party convention at Bologna, he outdid himself (and Lenin, across the border, in Switzerland) by threatening open revolt and dictatorship of the working class in case of war.

Four days later, on September 25, something incredible happened. The same Benito Mussolini called for intervention on the side of "poor, ravished France and atrociously martyred Belgium." He was ready to march straight to the front, and he urged all Italy to follow him.

What had happened in the intervening four days? The Italian workers were dumbfounded. Their first outcry was: *"Chi paga?"* (Who's paid for this?) Their next: *"Traditore!"* (Traitor!) Mussolini, with offended innocence and wounded pride, resigned from *Avanti* with the vow: "I will never write another word."

Eight days later he produced his own paper in Milan, *Il Popolo d'Italia,* crying out in the leading editorial that one rebellious and terrifying word: "WAR!"

The blunt fact, as later documented by notables, among them the great French liberal, Maître Torrés, was this: The French Government had bought Benito Mussolini with a considerable sum of money and subsidized *Il Popolo d'Italia* generously until 1919. "If the Kaiser had offered him a double sum he would have defended neutrality," wrote an Italian who knew Mussolini well. It did not deter "the greatest man" from writing in his autobiography: "To me money is detestable," nor his admirers from asserting he started his paper "with empty hands." Neither did French money keep Il Duce from drilling his Fascist cohorts later to roar in unison: *"Abbasso la Francia!"* Nor from giving France in her hour of greatest stress his patented "stab in the back."

The first time in his life that Mussolini refrained from acting rashly was when Italy entered the war in May, 1915. He confined his braggadocio to his editorials and waited until his class was called. His war-hero career was about as brilliant as that of Corporal Hitler, only shorter. Corporal Mussolini was thirty-eight days in the trenches, without having taken part in action. He managed to get splendid publicity, though, in his own paper. Published photographs show him posing heroically on top of parapets, leaving melées around him to the imagination. When he was accidentally injured during grenade practice in a training school, he quit the war for good to take his "place as a fighter in my newspaper office," as he records.

The Italians who won their only "victories" after the armistice, when they rushed across the undefended Austrian border to capture whole armies of homeward-bound Austrian soldiers, were craving for an achievement to be proud of. They also were raging against Woodrow Wilson who had denied them Fiume which was on Yugoslavian territory.

"Fiume o Morte!" (Fiume or Death!) became their new war cry.

Although the government complied with the decisions of the Allies, Gabriele d'Annunzio and Mussolini rebelled. D'Annunzio gathered the *Arditi* around him, young ex-soldiers, officers, unemployed, and adventurous loafers. They equipped the men with black shirts, black fezzes, stilettos, and all other paraphernalia later adopted by Mussolini for his own armed legions.

Mussolini built up his own troops of armed Fascist gangs. Money and troops, both supposed to be shipped to Fiume, somehow loyally stuck to Mussolini. He ignored the desperate pleas of d'Annunzio for immediate financial support and for arms, troops, and food, because Fiume was literally starving.

Mussolini was busy running for parliament and had to finance his own election campaign. True, he received almost no votes, but he had now a private militia on his hands. And, in addition, he noticed that Prime Minister Giolitti was determined to liquidate that Fiume adventure which threatened to become an incident with international implications. Giolitti suspected that Mussolini was ready for a deal. The Government was willing to sponsor Fascism, to take care of the financing and armament of the Fascisti, provided that Mussolini forsook Fiume and made use of the Fascists against the "Bolshevists."

Benito Mussolini, whose French subsidies had stopped in 1919, took his "thirty pieces of silver" in silence, and kept quiet when government troops surrounded Fiume and began bombarding it on Christmas Eve, 1920. "Fiume or Death?" It was Fiume *and* Death for four days and four nights. Whereupon d'Annunzio, tumbled from his cloud castles, walked out by the stage door, followed by thousands of his disillusioned, hungry extras.

This was the fateful year of 1920, when Mussolini showed himself in his best turncoat style. Who was the leader of the "Bolshevists" that the government was determined to crush? It was none other than Mussolini himself. It was he who backed the railroad strikers and incited them to seize the railroads. It was he who, not satisfied with agrarian reform, called for land seizure. He supported the strikes of the metal workers, the bakery workers, the waiters, the teachers. He exhorted the workers to seize factories and exclaimed, with that theatrical gesture so typical of him: "Your rights are sacred and I am with you!"

Before making his deal with Giolitti, he had approached both the Federation of Metal Workers, trying to sell them his idea of social revolution and civil war, and the top organization of the big industrialists, offering them his protection against any revolutionary uprising. Thus, he adopted the modern racketeer principle by offering the service of his hired thugs to the highest bidder.

The organized workers preferred legality. The metal-works owners, afraid of his grim countenance, paid; so did the large land proprietors.

The Milan bankers, the Turin industrialists, the steamship companies also paid. Thus the Fascist movement grew.

Mussolini again had sold out. He was the new boss of the money bags. In July, 1921, Mussolini was so well satisfied with the way affairs were going that he proposed a truce between the Fascists and their opponents, the Socialists, Catholics, and Democrats, for the realization of the return of "normalcy." The Fascists were not at all satisfied with stopping their gory guerrilla warfare against democracy. Large factions of them revolted against Mussolini. He resigned! The big industrialists and landowners simply took over the management.

Blazing a trail that was later eagerly followed by "coal and steel" in Germany, they began to hire thousands of unemployed army officers, setting up new branches and headquarters all over the country, buying arms and military supplies, and training their growing, illegal army.

Mussolini realized before long that it was high time for him to do another about-face. He rushed to the Fascist congress in Rome, in November, 1921. An old hand in taking in others by outdoing them in mouthy radicalism, he pledged the use of violence in the "holy crusade against the enemies." These "enemies" were the Socialists, the Catholic workers, the peasants' party or Popolari, led by the courageous social-minded priest, Don Sturzo; the democratic liberals; and the Freemasons. Mussolini was now the new master of the Fascisti will. "Down with Parliament!" the cry arose. For, in spite of all the money behind them, and intimidation and assassination, the Fascists had won only thirty-two seats out of 502 in the last general election.

The most momentous turn was now to come. With Mussolini, the most unscrupulous agitator and inciter to violent action, out of the labor movement, Bolshevism had died in Italy. The small faction of Communists had been driven out by the Socialist Party congress in Leghorn in January, 1921. That was unfortunate for the Fascists and their wire-pullers in the background because they had pledged themselves to "save Italy from Bolshevism." This was their only justification for brute violence and civil war. How else could they crush organized labor and all other institutions of democracy, get the state in their grip and seize upon absolute power, than by waging civil war? There was one thing left for them to do and that was to create the legend that they had "saved the country from Bolshevism." This astute deliberation became article one of the Fascist credo and wherever poisonous totalitarianism reared its ugly head.

Thus, it came one year later on that "victorious march on Rome" in which the great Mussolini acted the part of the "little man who wasn't there." It was not a Fascist exploit, either. It was a common army general *Putsch,* backed by the plotting Duke of Aosta who wanted to sit on the throne occupied by his cousin, Victor Emmanuel III.

The ambitious Duke had many followers in the army, including General Vaccari, chief of staff. The generals De Bono, who was to become one of the most vicious Fascist leaders, Fara, Magiotto, Tibby, and Zamboni, ready to junk the oath of loyalty to the King, took over the Black Shirt legions and put many soldiers into black shirts. Mussolini, after his fireworks oratory at the Fascist congress at Naples on October 24, 1922, hurried back to his newspaper office in Milan to await the outcome. The generals with whom he had conspired made about 8,000 Fascists "march." It was a ragged crowd that roamed the countryside toward Rome, seizing public buildings, railroad stations, and communication centers.

Prime Minister Facta and the King were actually running around in circles. Martial law was declared on the 28th of October and withdrawn on the 29th. The imperialists and the stooges of the industrialists of the north whispered gleefully in the ear of the King that the Duke of Aosta was besieging Rome with 80,000 men and that the army had refused to fight them.

The King, panicky that his crown might slip, gave in, and while Mussolini showed himself as an intrepid revolutionary by frantically barricading his newspaper building in entirely calm and peaceful Milan, the frightened King sent him a telegram begging him to come to Rome and form a government.

This was the signal for the Fascists to rejoice, cease marching, and hop railroad trains, trucks, and mules headed for Rome. In their exhilaration, they forgot that there was supposed to be a revolution.

When Mussolini arrived a few days later, he bowed gallantly and kissed the King's hand. Big parades were staged, and Il Duce posed before the cameras, his chin thrust out boldly. The pictures went around the world with the caption: "Il Duce leading his Fascist legions in their victorious march on Rome." This was the first trickle of that deluge of globe-enveloping frauds and lies of official Fascism.

Prime Minister Benito Mussolini entered on an entirely new rôle: he started out playing the lamb. He formed a parliamentary coalition government. "Patience," he whispered aside toward the Fascist benches. Immediately he clamped down press censorship, but in Parliament he fluted: "Patience! We'll remedy that. Liberty is not only a right, it is a duty." After the free press had been wiped out for years, he still exhorted a congress of journalists in 1927: "You are in error if you suppose I have suppressed liberty of the press."

"Mussolini always is right!" This was the dictum he established. When the opposition in Parliament pointed out the fact that he had no program at all, not even a new one, to offer, since he had discarded that 1919 election program of the *Fascio di Combattimento,* he shed his sheepsclothing. From this moment he roared like a lion launched on a bloody terror campaign of personal vendetta. He snapped back into the character rôle that was genuinely his.

While acting before the world on the dimly lighted European stage the part of the head of government of the Kingdom of Italy, statesman and diplomat, he increased the strength of his Black Shirt legions to about half a million, thus outnumbering the regular army. He organized a powerful secret murder organization, the existence of which he continually denied, although he could not deny the pile of corpses of its victims, until 1926, when he "legalized" it as the OVRA, *Organizzazione Vigilanza Repressione Antifascismo*. He boasted that he had destroyed the other three underworld organizations known as Mafia, Camorra, and Black Hand. He closed up their private business and "nationalized" it by putting their members, so efficient in racketeering, blackmail, and murder, in the service with the OVRA.

Having accomplished this, he went ahead with "launching the laws for the defense of the régime." He abolished the free press; crushed the organizations and institutions of the Socialists, Catholics, and Freemasons; dissolved all other non-Fascist groups; abolished universal suffrage and Parliament.

Mussolini at last had a program. He suppressed free speech; abolished the liberty of teaching and liberty of the magistracy. He "Fascistized" law courts; abolished the inviolability of private homes and private correspondence; abrogated the right of non-Fascists to choose or exercise a business or a profession. He suppressed municipal liberty; cut down wages and pushed up taxes.

He militarized the entire population from the cradle to the grave— all this "to make of Fascism the sacred religion of every Italian."

At one particular time, in 1924, there was a fateful moment when a word from the King, or a single courageous act on the part of the leaders of the opposition parties, could have cut short that perennial nightmare of Mussolini's political tyranny. That was shortly after the assassination of the distinguished speaker of the five opposition parties, Socialist Deputy Giacomo Matteotti. This created an uproar in Italy and reverberations in Europe as no other Fascist murder before or since has done, although the anti-Fascists listed at that time 4,000 dead.

Cardinal Maffi of Pisa telegraphed to Mussolini: "As a priest I weep. As an Italian I am ashamed." The King, again frightened, waved a threatening finger, more he dared not do because with the other nine fingers he had to clasp his crown. The press cried out, demanding punishment of the murderers and challenging the throttling grip of political hooliganism. The people rose in panic, tearing the million pictures of Mussolini from the walls all over Italy and smearing them with the words "assassin" and *"morte a Mussolini,"* while the swaggering Fascists, crestfallen, shed their black shirts and hid.

Mussolini, before the Chamber, put on an act of utter contrition, claiming to be "heartbroken over this horrible crime" (which he had ordered). With tears in his eyes, he recited dramatically false oaths, resigned from one of his many offices, promised justice, return to legality, and disbandment of the "militia." He disowned his accomplices.

The storm blew over because that one word of deliverance was not spoken, that one courageous action that could have brought about salvation was not taken. One of the most sinister figures among Mussolini's right-hand men, Roberto Farinacci, secretary-general of the Fascist Party, known as "the Sadist," redeemed Mussolini's promises with terror, massacre, fire, and wholesale destruction all over the country. Within a few months the opposition was paralyzed. It took Mussolini almost two years to recover sufficiently to stage that farcical "trial" of the actual killers of Matteotti: Amerigo Dumini, Albino Volpi, Amleto Poveromo, Augusto Malacria, and Giuseppe Viola, all of them members of Mussolini's "Secret Service," and jail-hardened criminals. The first three were found guilty, sentenced and amnestied shortly after. The glorious murder régime was now firmly established.

Fascist heroes came and went in those days. General Italo Balbo, who commanded mass transatlantic flights to America, became governor of Libya and lost his life in a mysterious airplane accident. General de Vecchi, who led the Massacre of Turin, became governor of Somaliland, later ambassador to the Vatican, and then member of the Cabinet. General de Bono, coörganizer of the assassination of Matteotti and the attack on minister Giovanni Amandola, became Colonial Minister. Farinacci, the Sadist, became bank manipulator and later leader of the Nazi-controlled Fascist Party in Northern Italy.

Dino Grandi, who was accused of pocketing graft money amounting to 300 million lire, and who hired a physician to poison his accuser, Baroncini, with disease germs, became Mussolini's representative at the League of Nations. Another representative of Mussolini in the League of Nations, Belloni, contrived to have a thirty-million-dollar loan to the city of Milan, which was floated in America, "vanish" to the last cent. Belloni went to the penal islands. Filippelli was caught in a municipal swindle. Augusto Turati, once Mussolini's most powerful assistant, disappeared in an insane asylum.

Cæsar Mussolini stayed on. He grew. It was the roaring Mussolini who led the Italian people through the blood bath of World War II. And these same peace-loving people were to be delivered from their bondage by American and British troops who came not as conquerors but with the hand of good-fellowship and brotherhood.

The hand of deliverence was to reach out to the Italian people—the hand of democracy. Again they could raise their heads and cry with the rest of the world: *"Viva Italia!"*

9

AUSTRIA FIRST TO FALL TO NAZI CONSPIRATORS

FIRST testing ground for the gigantic Nazi conspiracy was Austria. While Hitler was building his war machine, his secret agents were sent out to create ferment in all parts of the world. With Sudetenland as a trial balloon for future aggression, Austria was the underground political kettle of plot, counterplot and assassinations.

Spies and Fifth Columnists were dispatched from Berlin to every nation around the globe. Bribery and corruption were used to undermine France and all the nations of the European continent. Great Britain was planted with informers and "wolves in sheep's clothing." Africa and Asia became hunting grounds for fellow travelers. But it is in Austria that we first find the pot boiling over.

After World War I, the Dual Monarchy of Austria-Hungary, one of the six great Powers of Europe, had disintegrated almost overnight. The might of the long reign of the Hapsburg dynasty collapsed. The nation which for five hundred years had helped to shape the destiny of Western civilization chose the wrong side in the First World War and paid the price for doing so.

The House of Hapsburg gambled on power politics as a consort of Germany, and lost. With the liquidation of the Dual Monarchy—that arena which had been a continuous Hapsburg brawl—its dismemberment was believed to be completed. Of all the heirs to the ancient domain, the German-Austrians, Czechs, Slovaks, Poles, Ruthenians, Slovenes, Croats, Serbs, Rumanians, Italians, it was the German-Austrians who were to keep alive the enmities.

With the founding of the Austrian Republic, as a result of World War I, the stage for the tragedy was set. What was once an empire of 261,000 square miles, with a population of 51,000,000, had for the German-speaking Austrians become a state of 32,000 square miles with a population of 6,500,000. Of these almost 2,000,000 lived in the city of Vienna. About 3,800,000 German-Austrians living in Czechoslovakia and in the South Tyrol were left outside the boundaries of the new Austrian state, a fact which Hitler later exploited with shrewdness.

Austria, shrunk to a small, landlocked country, had but one solution —democracy! The leaders of the Social Democratic Party: Dr. Victor Adler, Dr. Karl Renner, Jakob Reumann, Karl Seitz, Dr. Otto Bauer, Dr. Julius Deutsch, immediately took up the fallen reins of government. It was due to the inner logic of political facts of pre-war Austria that this party should at the outset become the dominating factor in the new republican state, which was to be founded according to democratic ideals. Having represented the modern labor movement in the old Empire, it had been in opposition to the dominating groups on which the system of the Hapsburg régime rested. It was the only political party that was never involved in the scuffle of nationalities, nor could it be blamed for the catastrophe that had befallen the country under the previous régime.

The Social Democratic Party embraced republicanism as suiting perfectly its democratic principles. It did not have to revise or retract its policies. It did not have painfully to re-orientate itself and yield to temporary confusion. The two other political factions were the ultra-conservative Christian Socialist Party which traditionally tied up with the dominating forces of the Hapsburg Monarchy, and the Pan-German Party which was always a fluctuating political factor likely to compromise with any other faction that suited its Pan-German policies.

The problems of the new republic were many. Soldiers came flooding back from the fronts in unemployed masses. There were bloody border clashes with Hungarians. A threatening revolt broke out in the Provinces of Tyrol and Salzburg where the inhabitants were attempting to force the issue of incorporation with Germany.

Austria's plight attracted the attention of the world. Public loans from the four principal Allied Powers, and credits from neutral countries, helped tide the struggling republic over the inflationary period for the first three years after World War I. Yet the conditions grew from bad to worse. The coalition government into which the Social Democrats had entered with the Christian Socialists and the Pan-Germans broke up. The Social Democrats, in a wrangle over a universal conscription bill, went again into opposition. The second *Putsch* attempt of Karl Hapsburg across the border in Hungary fizzled out like a carnival spree.

Elections gave the Social Democrats the majority of votes. They had the backing of the million members of the trade unions and of the liberal and progressive elements of the population. They launched an ambitious reform program, introduced far-reaching social legislation, reorganized school life and adult education. Their rebuilding scheme for the Municipality of Vienna was a model of its kind that evoked international admiration.

A momentous turn in the history of Austria came in 1922. It brought to the fore Dr. Ignatz Seipel, who promised Austria a solid economic foundation. Under Chancellor Seipel, Austria's financial reconstruction period was started. League of Nations' loans were secured; connections with international finance were revived; the currency was stabilized; and industry and commerce began to recover. In a purely economic sense the prospects warranted optimism but politically the situation was dangerous.

A most bitter antagonist of the Social Democrats, Seipel filled his Christian Socialist Party anew with a militant spirit. He brought the police force and a reorganized army, with an aristocratic officer caste bent on boosting the old monarchic army traditions, under his party's influence. These became, unofficially, the rallying point of reactionary groups stirred up by political adventurers and fostered by those who could not get over their resentment against the Republic that deprived them of those royal prerogatives they had enjoyed under the Hapsburg régime.

Armed gangs began to mushroom in the provinces of Seipel's Austria. They grew to semimilitary organizations, partly made up of war-veteran groups, partly of mercenaries hired from among the unemployed youths by self-made chieftains with burning ambitions. There were such monarchists as Major Emil Fey, a narrow-minded *condottiere* type; Austro-Fascist Doctor Steidle; pro-Nazi Dr. Walter Pfriemer; and the Vienna night-life playboy, Prince Ernst Ruediger von Starhemberg, who was involved in Hitler's first Munich *Putsch*. He raised afterwards his own private troop in Upper Austria to become a professional reactionary opportunist ready to step into any fray if it served both his ambition and the destruction of democracy. A Prussian *Putsch* expert, Major Waldemar Pabst, was imported; he traveled between Germany and Italy and started to unify those formations.

Thus, the *Heimwehr* was born. Money and arms from antirepublican sources in Germany and from Fascist Italy followed across both borders into Austria.

The countermove of the Social Democrats, having the choice of defense or surrender, was the building up of a semimilitary organization of their own: The Republican Defense Corps. Frequent parades of the uniformed formations of both *Heimwehr* and Republican Defense Corps increased the restlessness of the population. Minor clashes in the provinces followed. Rifles began to shoot. Except for frequently discovering and confiscating arms hidden by Social Democrats, while the armament of the *Heimwehr* went unmolested, the Government made no move. This game kept on for years.

The first explosion occurred on July 15, 1927. The occasion was a court decision which the workers considered a miscarriage of justice. *Heimwehr* men, firing from ambush on parading Social Democrats in a Burgenland village, had killed one man and a child; they were brought to trial and acquitted. Hundreds of thousands of Vienna workers dropped their tools and streamed from workshops and factories to the streets of the Inner City, there to demonstrate their indignation by parading past the Parliament and the Palace of Justice.

Mounted police charged the milling crowd with sabers. When the first gunshots rang out, the unarmed paraders turned into an infuriated mob. The Palace of Justice was set on fire, and the police went on a shooting spree. Result: eighty-five civilians and four policemen killed. The Social Democratic Party proclaimed a general strike which was broken within three days, with the help of the *Heimwehr*.

Four years later, Doctor Pfriemer led the Styrian *Heimwehr* to open revolt against the State, seized public buildings, and established martial law. He issued proclamations to the army and police, requesting their oath of loyalty to him as dictator of Austria. Social Democrats resisting the *Putsch* action were killed; Doctor Pfriemer was allowed to escape across the border after the Government had restored order. Prince Starhemberg was arrested and later released. But the *Heimwehr* was kept in training to be at hand for a better-planned revolution.

A bank crash and a new wave of financial and economic crises shook Austria, while the double conspiracy against the Republic went on. Engelbert Dollfuss became Chancellor in 1932, securing the Lausanne Loans, and indebting himself personally to Mussolini who was encouraging the Fascist element in Austria while at the same time carrying on underground relations with leading German Nazis. Doctor Goebbels addressed the Nazi gathering in Vienna. Nazi Storm Troopers, brought from Germany, staged the first anti-Semitic riots to occur on Austrian soil.

A behind-the-scenes tug-of-war between Austro-Fascists and Nazis threatened a serious rift within the *Heimwehr*.

Dollfuss, a product of stubborn, shortsighted provincialism, was gradually slipping into an internal two-front war. His aim was the destruction of parliamentarianism, which was the most troublesome obstacle on his way towards "unifying" Austria as Mussolini had already unified Italy—as Hitler was about to unify Germany. Dollfuss invariably rejected compromises proffered by the Social Democrats, who represented the largest and most united party. Totalitarianism was his goal.

Nazi bombs exploded suddenly all over Austria after Hitler came to power in Germany in 1933. The brown flood of terrorism began to rise. As the security of the State was now threatened by both *Heimwehr* and Nazis, Dollfuss appointed the most cold-blooded *Heimwehr condottiere*, Major Fey, as Minister of Security. Fey's first move was to prohibit parades of the Republican Defense Corps and step up the activity of the *Heimwehr*, making its parading an official function. Stumbling upon an anti-Dollfuss plot, in which Prince Starhemberg's *Heimwehr* section was caught conspiring with the German Government, he went on smoking out the Nazis within the *Heimwehr*. Then the armament scandal broke. It added the final incentive to Dollfuss' determination to throw democracy overboard and come out in the open as the dictator of the Fascist-State Austria.

It was the Social Democrats who aired the facts of the illegal arms traffic between Italy, Austria, and Hungary, in defiance of the Treaty of St. Germain. Its principal figures were Prince Starhemberg and Fritz Mandl, Austrian munitions magnate connected with the international armament ring. Implicated were Mussolini, Dollfuss, General Goemboes, the Hungarian Minister of War, and General von Seeckt, Commander in Chief of the German Reichswehr. It was revealed that forty truckloads containing rifles and machine guns were shipped from Italy to Mandl's factory in Austria, described as "scrap metal."

International agitation flared up. Czechoslovakia, in constant fear of Hungary's rearmament, brought the incident before the League. The Dollfuss Government, in a painful position, pleaded complete innocence: "It was transit goods. How can anyone know what transit goods had contained?" Czechoslovakia's insistence prevailed upon France and Britain to demand that the arms be returned to Italy. Dollfuss promised to comply. Soon afterwards the head of Austria's railroadmen's trade union revealed that the General Manager of the State Railroad had offered him a large bribe to divert the arms to Hungary. When he refused to comply with this request, the arms were "stolen" by the *Heimwehr*.

With the help of legalistic trickeries based on an old Imperial wartime emergency measure, and the support of massed police and *Heimwehr* forces, Dollfuss closed the Parliament and issued about three hundred illegal and unconstitutional decrees diminishing the social rights of the wage earners, increasing the rents of property owners, subsidizing his peasant followers at the expense of low-income city dwellers, restricting the rights of trial by jury, abolishing freedom of the press and of assembly.

The Republican Defense Corps and other organizations of the Social Democratic Party were dissolved, and went underground. And as the excesses of Nazi terrorism with bombings, dynamitings, and killings had reached a new climax, the Nazi Party was dissolved, and went underground. The death penalty, abolished by the Republic, was restored. "Lightning Courts" with traveling executioners were established. But only the Social Democrats accused of resisting *Heimwehr* actions were hanged.

Hitler had been in power in Germany but one year when Major Fey, at a great *Heimwehr* parade in Austria, promised "the big clean-up." On February 12, 1934, the storm broke. Overnight, leaders of the Social Democratic Party were arrested and imprisoned. The answer was a general strike. Dollfuss proclaimed martial law. *Heimwehr* forces besieged party buildings, press plants, and workers' dwelling-houses all over the country. The Republican Defense Corps frantically unearthed its hidden arms. Futile as resistance seemed against the combined forces of *Heimwehr,* police, gendarmery and army, the workers defended themselves with their backs against the wall. It was their last stand for democracy, political freedom, and the Austrian Republic. It took massed artillery, shelling their great apartment houses in Vienna for three days, to fell them.

The Dollfuss Government boasted that it had "successfully nipped a Bolshevist uprising in the bud." The Nazis stepped up their regular terror campaign, infiltrating at the same time into government circles and executive officialdom, with the German Embassy as their ghost center. On July 15, they sprang their surprise, a concerted attack on government buildings in the provinces, and on the Chancellery and the official radio station in Vienna. To the consternation of Europe, Dollfuss was assassinated by a band of Nazi gunmen who broke into the Chancellery, shot the Chancellor and let him bleed to death. Mussolini, Premier of Fascist Italy, massed Italian troops on the Austrian border and threatened action if the German Nazis attempted to take advantage of the situation. (This was before Italy began the invasion of Ethiopia and before the Rome-Berlin Axis came into being.)

War was in the air of Europe, but the critical moment passed without any action by Germany. Indeed, Hitler officially denounced the "Austrian rebels," and withdrew his minister in Vienna, Doctor Rieth, who, said Hitler, "has involved the German Reich without any justification in an internal Austrian affair." A more subtle intriguer was sent in his place: Franz von Papen, well remembered for his conspirator rôle in the United States in World War I, and sometimes referred to as the man who made a career of "waging war in a top hat."

Kurt von Schuschnigg became Chancellor, and for a few years there was comparative calm. He dismissed Fey and Starhemberg, and dissolved the *Heimwehr,* part of it fusing with a Fatherland Front Militia. All seemed well; but Schuschnigg did not know that, about the same hour, he himself, together with Austria, was being dropped by his guarantor, Mussolini.

The Rome-Berlin Axis was already taking shape when Schuschnigg on his next visit to Rome learned with a shock that Mussolini would not make any further promises for Austro-Italian coöperation, until an Austro-German settlement of differences was completed. At this point von Papen stepped in. In collaboration with Mussolini, he forced upon Schuschnigg, on July 11, 1936, the signing of the Austro-German Agreement as a "pacific gesture" on both sides. It brought the Trojan Horse of Nazism inside Schuschnigg's fortified position. For, against Hitler's worthless promise of recognizing the sovereignty of Austria and his worthless pledge not to interfere in Austrian international affairs, it made Schuschnigg agree that he would admit to his Cabinet two thinly camouflaged Nazis: Dr. Guido Schmidt, Foreign Secretary, and Glaise von Horstenau. The first, conniving with von Papen, betrayed Schuschnigg into his final disastrous step, the visit to Hitler in Berchtesgaden in February, 1938; and the latter was the bearer of Hitler's ultimatum, coupled with the invasion threat on March 11.

The spirit of the Austro-Nazis rose anew to a feverish pitch. Noisy demonstrations became again an everyday affair. Fights between the Fatherland Front Militia and the Nazis in the provinces assumed alarming proportions. The "gentleman's agreement," of two years before, bore its fruits. One by one, the Nazi stooges appointed by Schuschnigg under that Pact to "pacify the internal situation in Austria" were caught red-handed at plottings organized in Germany.

Schuschnigg, cold-shouldered by Mussolini, hurriedly made a trip to Hitler, into which he was lured by the assurance of a new friendship pact with Germany. Here he found himself face-to-face with His Excellency Adolf Hitler. Surrounded by the General Staff of the German Army, Hitler peremptorily demanded from Schuschnigg an agreement that amounted to "unconditional surrender."

Under the almost paralyzing pressure of personal insult, vilification, and blackmail, Schuschnigg kept his composure. He stalled for terms. For making three minor concessions, he demanded that Hitler guarantee, publicly in his forthcoming Reichstag speech, both Austria's independence and the severance of connections between the illegal Austrian Nazi conspirators and the Third Reich. Hitler gave his "word of honor." He granted Schuschnigg three days for the surrender of Ministries of Foreign Affairs, War, Security, Justice and Education to his Nazi appointees. The German Army would remain ready for invasion on the frontiers.

Why Schuschnigg on his return tried to keep his Berchtesgaden visit a secret in Austria, and even fed the foreign press with optimistic reports, is a mystery. Von Papen was making his propaganda-drummers work. The news spread, and struck the Austrian people like a bolt from the blue.

Guido Schmidt was made Foreign Minister. Dr. Seyss-Inquart, another camouflaged Nazi, was appointed Minister for Security. They took the oath of loyalty to Schuschnigg, as did General Glaise von Horstenau. But eighteen hours after his appointment Seyss-Inquart, in whose hands police and gendarmery were laid, traveled to Berlin for further instructions. The imprisoned Nazi bomb-throwers and murderers were granted amnesty.

Undercover Nazis within the police force, protected by Seyss-Inquart, began to fraternize with Nazi Storm Troopers who emerged in full uniform from their hiding places. Again it was the Social Democrats who were beaten and arrested. Thousands of Nazis sped throughout the provinces from city to city. Mass demonstrations were held to make it appear as if they were numberless, spreading over all the country in an overwhelming majority which it would be a hopeless task to suppress.

Hitler's Reichstag speech, with not a word in it about Austria's independence, shocked Schuschnigg. It contained a stirring encouragement for a Nazi rebellion. Schuschnigg, in a rage, rose to defy Hitler and his Third Reich. His frantic attempts to reach Mussolini by telephone were of no avail; Mussolini was said to be skiing in the Alps. He started negotiations with the surviving successors of the leaders of the former Social Democratic movement working in the underground trade and workers' unions. He launched on his last-minute attempts to right the wrongs committed by Fascist foes of democracy which had opened the backdoors to Nazi inroads. He made his last great speeches in Vienna and in Innsbruch—the desperate efforts of a forlorn man to rally the Austrian people against the common foe: the Nazi Moloch. He proclaimed a plebiscite to be held within three days, calling on the whole people to answer the question of Austria's independence simply with "Yes" or "No."

It was too late.... Seyss-Inquart and General Glaise von Horstenau dropped their disguise and appeared openly in their rôles as Hitler's messenger boys. Hitler would not allow a plebiscite; he demanded that it be cancelled—or the German Army would march in.

The plebiscite was canceled to avoid an invasion. Hitler followed up with another ultimatum, demanding Schuschnigg's resignation and the establishment of a full Nazi Cabinet headed by Seyss-Inquart. Schuschnigg wanted to avoid bloodshed. He broke down and resigned. His farewell speech over the air ended in his prayerful words: "God protect Austria!" They were still ringing in the ears of the Austrian people when motorized columns of the German Army, with Goering's massed air fleet thundering overhead, crossed the Austrian border.

On the night of March 11, 1938, the rape of Austria was in full swing. Among the very first to flee Austria in time to save their lives were Guido Zernatto, Secretary-General of the Fatherland Front; Stockinger, a former peasant leader, who as a friend of Dollfuss had amassed a fortune; Fritz Mandl, Austrian munitions king, who had supplied both the *Heimwehr* and the Nazis with Mussolini's arms (and later had transferred his millions safely to the Argentine); the two Hapsburgs, Adelheid and Felix Franz; and Dollfuss' widow.

The Vienna populace was taken completely by surprise. There were still groups of Fatherland Front members and columns of workers parading in the streets, carrying propaganda banners for the plebiscite, when squads of police traitors suddenly attacked them, screaming *"Heil Hitler!"* They beat the confused paraders down with a hail of truncheon blows.

Before Schuschnigg's speech ended, 6,000 Nazi Storm Troopers and 800 SS men marched from their places of concealment toward the Chancellery where a mob of 100,000 had gathered. Five minutes after the speech they stormed the broadcasting station and seized all public buildings. Secret Nazis among the guards opened the gates from the inside for the plunderers. Schuschnigg, who had flatly refused to leave Austria, was placed under "protective arrest" by Seyss-Inquart.

In the streets of Vienna a veritable witches' sabbath broke loose. Motor trucks filled with heavily armed Storm Troopers, flaunting big swastika flags, raced up and down. Brown-Shirt boys with cartridge belts and rifles embraced the police traitors who turned up with swastika armlets. Hysterically shrieking women were trampled down by torch-bearing crowds. Scenes of frenzy dragged on all night.

Window-smashing marauders were only the vanguard of the triumphant Nazi mob. Gangsters attacked anyone who dared to show himself on the street without a swastika badge on his lapel. Wholesale plundering of the Jews in their homes by ruthless, armed Nazi gangs set in.

And then, as inevitably as night follows day, law and order as known to the civilized world gave place to a shameless orgy under Fascist rule. Nazi experts from the Third Reich, conspicuous for organizing German efficiency, stepped in. Making use of the black lists of anti-Nazis, on which the Austro-Nazis had methodically worked for years, they systematized the rule of terror. The ring of the doorbell produced a nervous shock in any person, no matter how clean his conscience. It could be the Gestapo waiting outside the door and, once taken away by them, there was a slim chance of ever returning to the living. Thousands were arrested without a pretense of a charge.

Austria was swallowed up by a Germany turned Nazi monster. Hitler had made his first step across the boundary of pre-war Germany—on the road to world conquest.

The first German invasion troops, already on the march to the frontier in the noon hour of March 11, crossed the Austrian frontier exactly at 9:03 P.M., about one hour after President Miklas, a mere figurehead of the Austrian State, had accepted Schuschnigg's "resignation as Chancellor." Miklas removed him "together with all other Ministers and Secretaries of State" (according to the last state document to which Schuschnigg put his signature). Thus, there was no "National Socialist Government in Vienna" when the German Army crossed the frontiers. It was not before 11:00 P.M. that President Miklas, as a prisoner of Seyss-Inquart, who at this hour was neither a minister nor had he any public function at all, was forced to appoint as Chancellor the man who had placed him under arrest, while at the same time taking his fresh oath of "loyalty to the State."

And as for the German Army being "summoned by the new National Socialist Government in Vienna itself": On March 12, the German official news agency published, concurrently with Hitler's proclamation, a statement to the effect that "Chancellor" Seyss-Inquart had cabled to the German Government to send troops to maintain order against the armed Socialists and Communists. And Seyss-Inquart himself told the correspondent of a Paris news agency that "Socialists and Communists in Vienna had risen to bloody attacks in which Nazis were massacred." There we have the whole Fascist-Nazi pattern. Against these arrogant falsehoods stands Doctor Schuschnigg's last declaration in his farewell speech over the air—that Hitler's stories of workers' disorders "were lies from A to Z." And the master of prevarication, Reichskanzler Hitler, who did not mind if his many lies crowded up to offset each other, declared in his Reichstag speech of March 18: "Not a single shot had fallen or a single victim been made." The German puppet Reichstag applauded this statement... not a single voice mentioned the victims who died in prisons, concentration camps, and ghettos.

A villain behind the scenes was Doctor Seyss-Inquart, whose treachery was rewarded by Hitler's making him *Statthalter* (Governor) of Austria. He became a member of the German Reichstag. Despised among his compatriots who had been handed over to the German Nazis, he ruled later as German Governor over occupied Holland.

And Schuschnigg went to a German concentration camp, where he was held incommunicado for the next seven years. He was literally raised from the dead when the American Armies of liberation defeated, imprisoned, and drove to suicide the persecutors of Schuschnigg.

Thus we have witnessed the disintegration of a republic—how Austria fell to the Nazis. It reveals to us the sinister forces at work which were to strike out for world conquest to destroy democracy. And in another two years America was to be drawn into the vortex.

FASCISM AND NAZISM IN VIOLENT ACTION

STEPPING-STONES over which Hitler and Mussolini started on the road to world conquest led us directly into World War II and the epoch-making events to follow. The occupation of Austria by the Nazis was for the purpose of "feeling the way," to "try it out" on their first victims.

When Mussolini invaded Ethiopia, it was but another natural sequence of his "feelers." Franco in Spain had set up a "test case." On the other side of the globe, the Japanese made their first test in Manchuria. It was a logical consequence that these three war machines, Germany, Italy, and Japan, would, at the "psychological moment," synchronize their actions in all-out war against the democratic nations of the world.

Mussolini's aim was, in the beginning, a comparatively modest one: aggrandizement of Italy, with a vision of restoring the ancient, all-powerful Roman Imperium. Hitler's megalomania was nothing less than world conquest. To attain their ends, both men resorted to the totalitarian method as a means first to dehumanize the people ruled by them and then mold them into a robot-like war machine.

Mussolini had an eleven-year start when Hitler climbed to power. The conqueror schemes of the two did not match at all. They were rivals—suspicious of each other. Mussolini considered Hitler a poor rival in the struggle for power in Europe, an "upstart" trying to imitate him. To check Hitler's ambitions, Mussolini attempted to take over Austria by making it a Fascist protectorate of his; that also would protect his back against Hitler.

As Hitler's power grew, Mussolini meanwhile was busily raiding Ethiopia. Il Duce gave the whole situation a second thought. He became not only afraid of his rival, but he saw Hitler's value as an equally ruthless and treacherous accomplice.

With the destruction of Austria, Hitler gained the "missing link" with his brother-in-thievery, later to be known as Berlin-Rome axis. He succeeded at the same time in encircling the last bastion of democracy in Central Europe: Czechoslovakia.

With the destruction of democracy in Spain, and after foisting a Fascist régime upon the Spanish people, both Mussolini and Hitler succeeded in closing up the Mediterranean and, at the same time, in threatening France from the rear. Balkan dominance was Mussolini's own pet ambition; without Balkan dominance there could be no Roman Imperium. So Mussolini surprised Hitler by rushing across the Adriatic and snatching Albania away for his own pocket. He was not very successful in this raid. Hitler, finally, had to help him out; he did so because it was a thrust at Yugoslavia.

What makes a close scrutiny of Austria so important is the fact that events spanning roughly the period between the two world wars present a textbook of the pattern by which Fascism and Nazism work out their successful campaigns. They show that the first step of totalitarian invasion is to obscure the political atmosphere of the country to be conquered by denouncing the democratic element of that country as "Bolshevist." Their next step is to secure the assistance of reactionary elements with grievances against the democratic way of life, toward breaking down the resistance of the democratic element.

The first chance to stop short Hitler's career was lost on March 8, 1936. The day before, Germany's Reichs-Chancellor had torn up the Locarno Treaty and set the *Reichswehr* marching to occupy the demilitarized zone of the Rhineland. He was still relying mainly on treachery and bluff. He knew as well as the nervous *Reichswehr* generals that the German Army was at that time neither prepared nor equipped to fight the regular French Army. The German Army marched with sealed orders, allowing them to beat a hasty retreat should the French actually oppose them. That would have meant Hitler's end, and a new turn for world history.

The invasion of Austria was another lost chance. All the world listened to the loud-speakers shouting the official communiqués on Hitler's new triumph. They did not know that the invasion of Austria was a military debacle. True, about 50,000 highly armed and mechanized forces started the invasion at nightfall on March 11, 1938. Although any opposition by the Austrian Army was called off by Doctor Schuschnigg in his last radio address "to avoid bloodshed," the German war machine, under command of Hitler's favorite "Nazi general," von Reichenau, Commander of Army Group IV, bogged down near Linz in Upper Austria. The advance guard became disorganized. Tanks creaked and ditched. The motorized heavy artillery developed defects and blocked the roads. Inadequate gasoline provisions added to the confusion. The 10th Infantry Division had to waste four days in making detours around blocked highways.

Hitler, waiting in Linz to start his march of triumph into Vienna, raged with fury. He had to summon the non-Nazi General von Bock from Dresden to take charge. Then he turned his wrath against his generals, von Reichenau and von Brauchitsch, Guderian, and von Keitel. They were backed up by General Beck, Chief of the General Staff, and they reminded the Fuehrer that he had refused to listen to the repeated warnings of General von Fritsch that Germany was not ready yet to face a major war: neither at the time of the Rhineland occupation, nor during the intervention in Spain, nor when the invasion of Austria was mapped out.

The army was now stuck on the road between Linz and Vienna, helpless, a perfect target for bombings from the air. Twice the German Minister in Prague, Eisenlohr, asked the Czechoslovakian Government for assurances that Czechoslovakia would not mobilize. He promised in Hitler's name, that the German troops would not trespass on Czechoslovakian territory, and would, in fact, keep a distance of ten miles away from the borders. In those frantic forty-eight hours the flower of the German Army could have been bombed out of existence on the Linz-Vienna road, but, again, there was no one to call Hitler's bluff.

On March 13, the annexation of Austria was announced. President Miklas was ordered by Seyss-Inquart, who had just made an oath of loyalty to him, to resign. This made Seyss-Inquart Chancellor and President at the same time. A "Federal and Constitutional Law" was made public, proclaiming Austria to be part of the German Reich. It fixed April 10 as the date on which a plebiscite would be held "to ratify" the annexation.

On the evening of March 14, after careful preparations by the Gestapo, Hitler made his belated triumphal entry into the capital of Austria. On that very day, the suicide rate in Vienna rose to three figures, the daily average for many weeks.

This stands in striking contrast to the "enthusiastic welcome given Hitler by the people of liberated Austria," a welcome flashed over the air by Goebbels' propaganda machine. The only enthusiasm was the hysterics of the Nazi masses brought together from the provinces and from Germany for this occasion. One should not forget that the huge military occupation forces employed in taking over Austria are a rather odd accompaniment to an "enthusiastic welcome." There were in all 9,000 SA men in Vienna on March 11, 1938, and in the whole of Austria some 90,000 members of all Nazi organizations. Many had turned Nazi out of sheer opposition to oppressive Fascist rule. The Nazis' own estimate confessed that not more than a sixth of Austria's whole population was within their ranks. Moreover, four weeks after it had been taken over by Seyss-Inquart, the police and the gendarmery contained only 5 per cent Nazis; the army even less.

This explains Hitler's determination to resort to a gamble of force rather than let Schuschnigg carry through his plebiscite. He knew quite well he would not have to be afraid of the results of a "plebiscite" staged by himself under the Nazi gangster rule.

All day long and most of the night the radio blared out its propaganda in restaurants, cafés, and all other public places. The wholesale dismissal from public office began—all were surreptitiously ousted who either were "political suspect," meaning, loyal to their oath to the Austrian State before Hitler took over, or could not prove their "pure Aryan" descent for eight generations.

Motor trucks laden with official plunder streamed back to the Third Reich. The 400,000,000 shillings worth of gold of the Austrian National Bank was stolen for the coffers of the impoverished Reichsbank in Berlin. Private plundering by uniformed Nazi gangs was carried out unchecked for many weeks. Jews, a sixth of the population of Vienna, had become pariahs overnight. They were excluded from citizenship and deprived of all their civil rights, including the right to retain property large or small, to enter restaurants, coffee houses, bathing beaches, baths, or public parks. They stayed behind drawn curtains in their homes. All motor cars were immediately stolen from them, with the plunderers demanding contributions "for gasoline and upkeep."

It became quite a common sight in the streets of Vienna to see trucks lined up in front of stores, and armed Storm Troopers loading them with stolen goods. Police stood by to keep the curious from interfering with the hard work of "Aryanizing." Whenever the hushed grumbling of the Viennese about this unashamed plundering grew too loud, the police issued communiqués warning the population. Stern measures were taken whenever they were caught. The police had to take orders from the SS squads. The Jews were rounded up for menial tasks like washing the motor cars of the Nazis, or cleaning the bowls of the toilets in the SS barracks with their naked hands, or scrubbing the pavements on the streets with lye that was poured over their hands.

Dr. Arthur von Seyss-Inquart, with a diplomatic smile on his clean-shaven face, publicly declared: "In following our unchangeable course, we neither wish nor enjoy individual hardships which it may involve. But neither do we seek to avoid their infliction." One could read in the *Voelkischer Beobachter* (April 27, 1938): "Jews, abandon all hope! Our net is so fine that there is not a hole through which you can slip!"

Constant threat of an omnipresent Gestapo and the horror of concentration camps was hanging above everybody's head like the sword of Damocles. Freemasons, and all Austrians who were not among the illegal Nazis before the downfall of Austria, were likewise exposed to "liquidation." Two printed slips, which were received by women whose husbands had been arrested a week before without any charge, tell their own story: One slip reads: "The relatives of ——— are informed herewith that he died today at Dachau Concentration camp. (Signed) GESTAPO HEADQUARTERS." The other slip, attached to a small parcel, reads: "To pay, 150 marks, for the cremation of your husband—ashes enclosed from Dachau."

Postal and telephone services in Vienna, whose Austrian chiefs had been dismissed, were taken over by a highly trained army of spies and censors sent from Berlin. The German system of terror by informers was established amongst the general population. It had its eyes and ears on the streets, in all public places, offices, stores, schools, organizations, work shops, and even invaded dwelling-houses and homes.

Whoever could muster enough courage, and find ways and means, fled. Physicians of world-wide fame, psychoanalysts, scientists, architects, educators, musicians, writers, opera singers, lawyers departed. Within four weeks Vienna ceased to be even a shadow of what it was once: a center of international culture in the heart of Europe. It became the Eastern outpost of Nazi savagery. And Austria became a German Gau (province)— the *Gau Ostmark*.

Hitler's Austrian plebiscite farce came on April 10, 1938. The Nazis decided who was permitted to vote. Three days before the voting day such persons as were found "eligible" received postcards with instructions. Persons who did not receive such cards were not eligible.

Nazi officials stood near the voting booths, supervising the act of voting. Among the Viennese the joke went the rounds that the only danger was that in adding together the votes the total would come out at 102 per cent "Yes" votes. Goebbels was seemingly smart enough to circumvent this danger. He announced the same night that the Austrian people had voted 99 per cent "Yes."

Taking the voting result at its face value, without regard to the blackmail and fraud involved, the question arises: Who were the "Austrians" that wished upon their homeland complete obliteration and "jungle laws" of usurpers deriving their authority from systematic terror, torture, assassination, and wholesale killing? The Nazis themselves totaled only 16 per cent in Austria. Surely, the tradition-bound Catholic masses of the peasants and middle-class people were not for a Nazified Austria. And neither were the other victimized groups, the intellectuals, and the workers. The adherents of the former Social Democratic Party, though decimated by Fascist and Nazi persecutions alike, could still be estimated as embracing about 40 per cent of Austria's population. This analysis should give an inkling of the brazenness which called this voting farce of a 99 per cent Yes-result a plebiscite.

The Germans took over in Austria with their habitual ruthless efficiency. Joseph Buerckel, the hard-faced, square-jawed German Nazi, who had Nazified the Saar district and the Rhineland, was made *gauleiter* of the *Ostmark* to expedite the Nazification. General von Bock became Commander in Chief of the armed forces in Austria. The Austrian industries, immediately geared to the German war machine, were sucked up by the "Hermann Goering Werke."

In the workers' ranks there was, at first, only silent hatred and passive sabotage; their leaders disappeared in concentration camps.

SS Leader Heydrich, who became known as "Butcher Heydrich," was put in charge of the Gestapo in Austria. Austria was divided into seven separate parts, each with its own German-ruled administration. Anyone who tried to get in contact with someone living across the boundaries of his province aroused the suspicions of the Gestapo. When Hitler launched on his greatest adventure, the all-out war, on September 1, 1939, Austria's manpower was drained away. All Austrians between the ages of seventeen and fifty were forced into the German Army, or set to work in factories and on the land in faraway conquered countries.

Immediately following the death of Heydrich, who was killed by Czech patriots, a new wave of terror swept over Austria, worse than any previous one. In each Austrian province, Gestapo committees for the registration of asocial elements were set up, with sub-committees in every region and district. They were given full and unrestricted power to send to concentration and forced-labor camps anyone "not meeting the requirements of national unity." Any person "dissatisfied with the existing situation," or inclined to believe rumors spread by "enemy propaganda," was marked for "elimination." All administrative organs had to obey the decisions of these Gestapo committees. The victims were threatened with sterilization. Mass arrests, with not even pretense of a trial, were carried out throughout all Austrian provinces. In Vienna, Baldur von Schirach, the leader of the Hitler Youth organization, became ruler supreme.

The official Nazi paper, *Jugendfuehrer* (Youth Leader) announced the dissolution in Vienna of fourteen branches of the Hitler Youth organization on the grounds that "they have become imbued with rebellious spirit." Active Catholic youth were deported on the pretense that they "proved themselves to be unfit to live in Austria."

Hundreds of Austrians, formed into separate Austrian battalions, began fighting in the ranks of the Yugoslavian Volunteer and Guerrilla Army. Whole trainloads of rifles and ammunition were sent to the guerrillas by Austrian railroadmen of the large rail junction of Villach, Carinthia.

The German masters, finally, decided to drop the many fake nonpolitical reasons given by the special courts for the execution of their opponents. Death sentences were passed on large groups of Austrian patriots. Another group was sentenced to hard labor for life. And this in Graz, the city which was once looked upon as a center of Nazi activity and given the name "City of the German national uprising" after Austria's annexation. Organized opposition was finally admitted. Daily lists of "Austrian saboteurs" were published in the papers, followed by the line "beheaded with the ax." The chopping block became the "court of law." Such is the story of Austria under Nazi rule.

CZECHOSLOVAKIA FALLS INTO GRIP OF DESPOTS

CZECHOSLOVAKIA'S struggle for survival as a free nation is a Slovakian chronicle, a *hrdiniska utalost* with all the realism of a Capek drama. The martyrdom of Lidice magnified many thousandfold the fourteenth-century sacrifice of Jan Hus.

The Czechs were the first people, after Austria, to fall into the grip of the Nazi despots; this was in March, 1939, five months before the outbreak of World War II. This was the direct result of the betrayal at Munich, which delivered them into the hands of the Germans. After centuries of struggles for freedom, Czechoslovakia attained its goal after World War I. With Woodrow Wilson and the United States as godfather, she gained her independence on October 28, 1918, after the break-up of Austria-Hungary. Her constitution was adopted on February 29, 1920, with the great Dr. Thomas Garrigue Masaryk as "Father of the Republic."

Masaryk, the "George Washington of Czechoslovakia," who had spent many years in America and married an American woman, was a philosopher, scholar, and statesman of the highest rank. After laying the foundations of a great nation, he retired in 1935. He died in 1937. Masaryk was succeeded as President by Eduard Benes, a statesman who had gained world-wide eminence. Benes, one of the foremost exponents of world peace, was in power when the Nazis gambled for his country at Munich and won. Because he was subjected to the most outrageous conspiracy ever directed against a peaceful nation, he resigned as President and went into exile, where he later set up a Government-in-exile in London and became the vigorous supporter of the United Nations. Jan Masaryk, son of the first President, and Ambassador to London, who had also married an American, was one of the leading patriots in the restoration of Czechoslovakia.

Czechoslovakia, located in the heart of Europe and one of the richest territories on the Continent, because of her natural resources and great industries, was on Hitler's agenda. Her allegiance to democracy aroused the despot's hatred. He vowed to destroy the nation. More than 60,000 liberty-loving Czechs were executed by the Nazi terrorists. More than 250,000 were sent to concentration camps. Nearly 2,000,000 were taken into slavery.

"The master of Bohemia is the master of Europe." These words, spoken by Bismarck at the end of the last century, supplied the formula for the more modern Nazi aggression and subjection of central Europe. It is one of the shameful chapters of modern history that the appeasement policy followed by the western European democracies handed over the strategic territory of Czechoslovakia to the land-hungry Hitler without the firing of a shot.

It was in September and October, 1938, that the final and greatest blunder of appeasement was committed with the conclusion of the Munich Agreement. This agreement, concluded by France, Great Britain, Germany, and Italy, forced Czechoslovakia to give to Germany the frontier area, designated as the Sudetenland, on the Wilsonian principle of national self-determination. Paradoxically, Hitler the aggressor turned the doctrine of Wilson to his own use at this time, claiming that the area he demanded was actually dominantly German in population.

"The Sudetens are the last territorial demand I shall make in Europe. I have no further interest in the Czech state, and I can guarantee it if necessary. We want no Czechs at all." Thus spoke Hitler on September 26, 1938. Apparently western Europe believed him, for it was at this time that articles like the following by Sir Thomas Cunninghame were current in the British press: "Yet there are, to this day, many idealistically minded people who, in their indignation at such events as the absorption of Czechoslovakia and Austria by Germany, call upon us to exert our force to prevent further consolidation in central Europe and even to take the Government of Great Britain to task for not having defended the independence of the fallen states, regardless of the fact that their existence was not only no concern of ours but was the cause of deep-seated unrest in central Europe for which, as long as they remained there, there could be no cure."

Only one man saw the danger and spoke. On October 5 Winston Churchill made the following statement in the House of Commons: "All is over. Silent, mournful, and broken, Czechoslovakia recedes into the darkness."

The Sudetenland was handed over to the Germans in four stages between October 1 and 7, 1938. The fixing of further stages was left to an international commission in Berlin. By October 10, the final frontiers were to be fixed. Poland and Hungary were also to receive certain concessions.

Through the Munich Agreement and other settlements, the Republic of Czechoslovakia lost 4,992,400 inhabitants and 19,000 square miles of territory—nearly a quarter of its area and a third of its population. More than a million Czechs found themselves outside the frontiers of the Czechoslovak Republic; one Czech in every eight was put at the mercy of the Nazis; one Slovak in every five or six was handed back to the Magyars, ill-famed from the time of the Hapsburg Empire for ruthless oppressions of non-Magyar minorities. Sub-Carpathian Russia lost 220,000 inhabitants out of a total population of 725,000.

Nevertheless, the Czech people did not despair. On October 4, a new government was formed under General Syrovy. President Benes resigned the following day upon German demand and left the country. During the next two months the Czech nation underwent a tremendous revolution before, on November 30, a new president, Dr. Emil Hacha, was elected. On October 3, the minority party of Slovak autonomists, incited by the Nazis who intended to use them as their Fifth Column, presented to the Czechoslovakian Government a demand for Slovakian autonomy and recalled their member from the Czechoslovak Government.

After some negotiation, agreements were reached with the Slovaks and the Sub-Carpathian Russians which embodied the minority demands in two autonomy laws. The laws were passed by the National Assembly on November 19. The first effort of Germany to split the Czech nation had succeeded. The Czechoslovak Republic ended and became a hyphenated federation, akin to the federation of states prior to the adoption of the United States Constitution, and was known as the Czech-Slovak Republic, often referred to as the Second Republic.

Now the Hitlerian totalitarianism was high-pressured into Slovakia by German influence. On November 8 the Prime Minister of Slovakia, Joseph Tiso, declared himself in favor of a totalitarian state in that country and advocated the abolition of all parties with the exception of the Hlinka Party. At first the totalitarian idea made little headway in the Czech half of the state. The Fifth Column made itself felt in the Government after Hacha's election, with the appointment of Rudolf Beran as Prime Minister. Following his appointment he persuaded Parliament to pass an enabling act and was vested with full powers. He thereupon adjourned the Parliament *sine die*.

The Fifth Column had already manifested itself under the Syrovy Government. In his capacity as the newly appointed Foreign Minister, Dr. Frantisek Chvalkovsky visited Hitler on October 14. In the course of his lengthy diplomatic appointments as Czechoslovakian envoy to Berlin and Rome he had been won over to totalitarianism. As soon as he returned from Berlin, the German ideas that he brought back began to make themselves felt. On October 20, the Government dissolved the Communist Party. The next day the Foreign Minister informed the Soviet Minister in Prague that his Government was no longer interested in any pact with the Russian Government. On November 14 the Government began to arrest Communist Party officials and to confiscate their property. The post-Munich Government could not risk entering into a conflict with Germany, for the Nazi system of using the slightest grievance for marching into any country they desired would make

Czechoslovakia vulnerable to the Nazis. Thus in a final effort to remain an independent country, German demands were granted in silence. Failure of this aim was inevitable.

In the first appendix to the Munich Agreements the British and French Governments had repeated their offers to guarantee the Czech frontiers. Germany and Italy had done likewise, promising no unprovoked attack and guaranteeing the new frontiers as soon as the Munich territorial adjustments had been cleared up. On November 22, the Czech Government approached the Great Powers with the request that they keep their promise and guarantee the new Czech frontiers.

Dr. Chvalkovsky discussed the matter of the guarantee with von Ribbentrop, German Foreign Minister, during his visit to Berlin in January, 1939. The Nazi brazenly declared he could not grant the guarantee to a state that had "not solved the Jewish problem in accordance to the German Nuremberg laws," the most nefarious anti-Semitic legislation ever perpetrated by a sovereign state. As a result of these laws, most of the German Jews were starving or thrown into concentration camps. "Germany refuses to live on equal terms with any nation in which Jews exercise any political or economic influence," von Ribbentrop explained to the receptive Chvalkovsky. He issued the ultimatum that Czechoslovakia must grant her Germans far-reaching minority rights. He demanded that she reduce her army even beyond the point it had already done by an agreement of November, 1938. Von Ribbentrop peremptorily demanded that Czechoslovakia again declare her complete neutrality. As if its termination were not enough, the Nazis began to blackmail the Czechs into denouncing their earlier pact with the Comintern, forcing them to join the Axis anti-Comintern Pact. The mailed fist was in action. Berlin badgered Czechoslovakia to repudiate her treaty with France and to withdraw from the League of Nations, in which she had been an active democratic member.

Germany then began to impose her will in the economic sphere. She demanded a part of the gold reserve and insisted that no new industries be set up, industries that would compete with those of the "Sudetengau," as the territories taken from Czechoslovakia were known.

The Munich surrender of September 29 and the Vienna award of November 7, now had hacked from Czechoslovakia 41,266 square miles of territory, 4,700 towns and villages, 5,344,000 inhabitants (one-third of her population). Of the people annexed by Germany, Hungary, and Poland, 1,189,000 were Czechs and Slovaks, who lost their press, their schools, their political rights, their cultural life, and most of them their occupations. There was no gain to anyone but Germany, for the Nazis later swallowed Poland and Hungary also.

This robbery under the guise of legality took much more loot into the German bag. The Republic was stripped of her own defense line,

70 per cent of her steel industry, 80 per cent of her textile mills, and most of her glass, porcelain, paper, and lumber industries so important to her export trade. Czechoslovakia lost 40 per cent of her national revenue; all her main railway lines were severed by new frontiers; the electric power plants of her three largest cities and the water supply of many others were placed outside the country. The new frontiers came within five miles of two of her great steel cities, Pilsen and Ostrava. These boundaries were not justified on any ethnological grounds. No new fortifications or even customhouses were permitted on the new frontiers, for Berlin intended to occupy the whole country within a few months.

German greed knew no bounds. All these humiliations and concessions could not bring Berlin to give the guarantee promised. On February 8, the French and British Governments, through their ambassadors at Berlin and Rome respectively, sounded out the German Government about the guarantees. There was no reply from the Wilhelmstrasse until March 2. In a statement repudiating all pledges, the Nazis declared their opposition against any kind of guarantee of Czechoslovakia by the western Powers. The note from Berlin warned that the responsibility for the development of this part of Europe fell "within the German sphere of influence."

As the Nazis slowly dropped their masks of innocence, it became clear that they would be satisfied with nothing less than possession of Czechoslovakia herself.

German intrigue fomented the Slovak autonomous movement by sending emissaries and observers to Czechoslovakia. They encouraged the Ukranian autonomists through the staff of the Consulate General that had been set up at Chust, the new capital of Sub-Carpathian Russia. The autonomy of Slovakia within a federated Czechoslovakia did not satisfy the extremists in the Slovak Autonomous Party, especially Bela Tuka, who had been released from internment, to which he had been condemned for high treason by the courts of the Republic. These extremists regarded the Second Republic only as a step toward complete independence. The agitation directed by German agents with ample funds demanded immediate expulsion of all Czechs from Slovakia and the transfer of all official positions to Slovakia. Slovakia was made a dictatorship under Tiso, modeled after Hitler Germany.

On Christmas, 1938, President Hacha and a number of Czech ministers visited Slovakia. The Slovaks needed a loan from the Czechs to balance their budget, but all efforts at agreement failed. Over the head of the Minister of Foreign Affairs in Prague, the Slovak extremists friendly with the Nazis were already negotiating in Berlin on economic coöperation between Slovakia and the Reich. They demanded the division of the army into Czech and Slovak sections.

The conspiracy was fully revealed. On March 8, 1939, the Prague Government decided on an extreme step. It broke off negotiations with the Slovak representatives about autonomy and refused to meet the deficit in the Slovak budget until the Slovak Government clearly declared its loyalty to the state. The Czech Government was fully aware of the risk it ran in taking the measure. It realized that the Reich might use its intervention in Slovak affairs as an excuse for intervention of its own to "protect" the Slovaks.

On orders from Bratislava and on German instigation, delegates of the Slovak Government in Prague refused to proclaim the loyalty of the Slovak Government to the Czechoslovakian Republic. Instead, they demanded that the Czechs make a loan to Slovakia and allow her to have her own diplomatic representatives in certain states. The Prague Government refused to do so and dismissed the Slovak Prime Minister, Tiso, and others. In addition to dismissing Tiso, the Prague Government ordered the arrest of certain extremist politicians, the disarming of the Hlinka Guard, and the occupation of the garrison towns by Czech troops.

Martial law was proclaimed at Bratislava. Slovakia was occupied by such troops as the Germans had not demobilized, and order was restored on March 10. But all was far from well. Durcansky, one of the most extreme separatists, managed to escape. The Nazis allowed him to use the Vienna broadcasting station for Slovak broadcasts, thus publicly revealing their direct participation in what was going on in Slovakia. As a representative of the regular Slovak Government, Durcansky, fully backed by the Germans, appealed for armed resistance to the Czech troops. The Reich leaders who directed these actions waited for the right moment to step in. The signal was soon given. The German press began to denounce the Czech occupation of Slovakia, a sure sign of military action to follow. Events moved rapidly to a crisis. On March 13, a telegram from Hitler reached Bratislava, asking ex-Prime Minister Tiso to visit him in Berlin. Tiso discussed the matter with his friends, and left for Berlin with Durcansky. There he was cynically told by Hitler that it lay with the Slovak people to decide their own fate. They were informed that only an independent Slovakia would enjoy the protection of the Third Reich. The Slovak Parliament was summoned at short notice for a session on March 14. Intimidated by Hitler's threats, they voted for an independent Slovakia.

Czechoslovakia was thus reduced to a Nazi vassal. Then followed the fateful scene in the Berlin Chancellery on the night of March 14, 1939. On the table lay two documents, ready to be signed by President Hacha, who had been summoned by Hitler. In order that history may not wholly discredit President Hacha for placing his signature on these documents, we record the following report from M. Coulondre,

French Ambassador in Berlin, to M. Georges Bonnet, French Minister of Foreign Affairs, as presented on March 17, 1939:

"Immediately on arrival, M. Hacha and his minister, who were received with military honors, were taken to the Chancellery, where Hitler, Goering, von Ribbentrop, and Keppler were waiting for them. The document to be signed lay on the table, as well as a memorandum relating to the future statute for the administration of Bohemia and Moravia. The Fuehrer stated very briefly that the time was not one for negotiation, but that the Czech ministers had been summoned to be informed of Germany's decisions, that these decisions were irrevocable, that Prague would be occupied the following day at nine o'clock, Bohemia and Moravia incorporated within the Reich and constituted a protectorate, and whoever tried to resist would be trodden under foot. With that the Fuehrer wrote his signature and went out.

"A tragic scene then took place between the Czech ministers and the three Germans. For hours Dr. Hacha and M. Chvalkovsky protested against the outrage done to them, declared that they could not sign the document presented to them, pointed out that were they to do so they would be forever cursed by their people. Dr. Hacha, with all the energy at his command, fought against the Statute of Protectorate which it was intended to impose on the Czechs, observing that no white people were reduced to such a condition.

"The German Ministers were pitiless. They literally hunted Dr. Hacha and M. Chvalkovsky round the table on which the documents were lying, thrusting them continually before them, pushing pens in their hands, incessantly repeating that if they continued in their refusal, half of Prague would lie in ruins from aërial bombardment within two hours, and this would be only the beginning. Hundreds of bombers were only awaiting the order to take off, and they would receive that order at six in the morning if the signatures were not forthcoming by then.

"President Hacha was in such a state of exhaustion that he more than once needed medical attention from the doctors, who, by the way, had been there ready for service since the beginning of the interview. The Czech ministers, having stated they could not take such a decision without the consent of their Government, received the answer that a direct telephonic line existed to the Cabinet of Ministers then in session at Prague and that they could get in touch immediately.

"It is a fact that such a line had been laid down in Czech territory by members of the German minority, without the knowledge of the authorities.

"At 4:30 in the morning, Dr. Hacha, in a state of total collapse, and kept going only by means of injections, resigned himself with death in his soul to give his signature. As he left the Chancellery, M. Chvalkovsky declared: 'Our people will curse us, and yet we have saved their existence. We have preserved them from a horrible massacre.'"

German infamy, with intimidations of murder and reigns of terror, had won its first battle in Czechoslovakia. The Czech President and envoys would never have reached their homeland alive if they had not signed the German document, figuratively with a revolver at their heads.

Thus ended Czech independence. Bohemia and Moravia became a protectorate of the German Reich. The Czech nation fell under the domination of Hitler.

The Nazis set up a vassal state, the strange political mongrel known as the protectorate, in itself an invention of the Nazi mind and with no historic precedent. It gave the Protector, Freiherr Konstatin von Neurath, the power to veto any act of the puppet Czech administration. Not even the courts remained free. The press was gagged and forced repeatedly to publish articles of German origin under the signatures of Czechs who had not even seen them. Hundreds of students and teachers were murdered; schools were closed in an effort to deprive the nation of intelligent leaders. Many leaders and administrators were arrested merely for being veterans of the First World War. Seventy thousand people were tortured and killed in concentration camps by the most bestial methods because they refused to divulge military secrets.

Protector Von Neurath's office was a great graft-ridden machine supported by Czech taxes. No political parties were allowed, no public or private meetings could be held, no newspaper comments could be made, save those dictated by the German office of propaganda.

The gold reserve was the first thing to be attacked and carried to Germany, along with all reserves of foreign currency in the National Bank. Then followed the seizure of all military equipment, food reserves, the best locomotives and cars, and coal, oil, and construction supplies for the railways. For weeks long trains and fleets of trucks were busy carrying the plunder to the Reich. At the end of this looting, all shops were empty of all commodities, even to the last cigarette and bar of soap. This was henceforth to be rationed to the previously prosperous nation now basking in the munificent "protection" of the German Third Reich. No houses save those of Germans were heated during the winter. Epidemics of various kinds were also part of the "protection." Jewish property, businesses, and other sources of income were submitted to a unique process of Aryanization, a Nazi method through which any German could buy non-Aryan materials at a fraction of their value and enjoy the protection of the Gestapo and other law-enforcing agencies in the process.

Graft reached such proportions that even the German governors were appalled and sent their petty officials back home, only to have them replaced by a new loot-hungry gang of international gangsters.

The Czechs had no legal protection, for Germans had to be tried in German courts, where they were granted all favor due a true Aryan subject of the German Reich. By means of Aryanization, which was extended beyond Jews to Rotarians, Masons, and Benes sympathizers, the Escompt Bank in Prague and the Bank of Commerce and Industry were given to the Dresdener Bank. The Union Bank of Bohemia went to the Deutsche Bank. Thus the Germans took over the groundwork of the Czech economic system, which was vested in these two banks. Dresdener Bank also acquired the two great munitions plants, the Skoda works and the Brno Zbrojovka.

The Republic owned several thousand acres of forests, large estates, experimental farms, immense fisheries in fresh-water lakes, sugar refineries, distilleries, and other agricultural industries. All such state property, both in the Sudeten area and throughout the protectorate, was taken by the Germans at one stroke. It was handed to the Organization for German Colonization. The Czech officials of the Land Reform Office and Bureau of Forests and Lands were arrested and all records were seized to prevent the public being informed about these confiscations.

Hitler had stated in *Mein Kampf* that he intended to move the Slavic races bodily out of central Europe to regions in the east. In the first two years the German occupation authorities specified five large areas of Bohemia and Moravia from which all Czechs were forced to move by certain dates to make way for German colonists. By September 1, 1941, these areas were emptied of their Czech population, and Germans were settled there. The Czechs were forbidden to take with them anything except clothing. Their farm tools and stock, their businesses, even their kitchen utensils, had to be left for the German settlers.

The position of labor under Nazi domination was, if anything, worse than that of the farmers. Labor organizations were disbanded, their funds confiscated, and their leaders jailed. At least 400,000 workers were taken to German factories chiefly in the Rhineland, often in mass removals in order to give their places at home to Germans. Stocks of raw materials were seized from Czech factories that competed with those of the Reich, such as textiles. Even the machinery, if it was modern, was carted off to Germany. Any factories that the Nazis wished to undermine were refused quotas of raw materials and fuels. No care was taken of workers left unemployed by such steps except to offer them work in the bombed areas of the Reich. In many instances Czech factory owners, whose shops were closed, were offered quotas and permission to reopen if they would employ only German workers.

Every influx of German workers or colonists brought an immediate demand for German schools, German courts, German postal, police, and administrative officials. Women and children were evacuated to Czech cities by the tens of thousands to escape British bombings. Teachers and their families were brought from the German Reich, all to be paid from Czech taxes, since evacuees pay no taxes.

The Czechs, like all the victims of the Nazi aggression, did not submit docilely. Resistance invariably followed the use of force and the abolition of freedom. When the Protector, Von Neurath, arrived in Prague, all school children were ordered to turn out and watch a parade in his honor. Few came. Those who did turned their backs as the Protector's car passed. A secret underground press was formed. The secret radio transmitter *Na zdar* began operation. When orders were issued forbidding Jews to eat in Aryan restaurants, the Czechs ate with the Jews in Jewish restaurants. When Jews were banned from trains, the trains were boycotted. Workmen rose early in the morning to walk to work rather than ride.

A German army of at least a quarter of a million was tied up in Bohemia and Moravia. October 28, the anniversary of the founding of the republic, found the people wearing the national tricolor and taking a holiday. Many Czechs were arrested and tortured. The next day demonstrations even larger were staged. The Protector appealed to the populace to abandon the tricolor and wear a button with the initials N.S., *Narodni Sourucenstvi,* National Solidarity. The buttons appeared on the lapels of the people upside down, as S.N., *Smrt Nemcum,* Death to Germans!

Deputy Protector Frank threatened to shoot 7,000 hostages unless leading Czechs publicly declared their loyalty to the new order. The Czechs refused. The Boy Scouts were disbanded, and then the Sokol, a national youth movement. Demonstrations followed, and barefisted Czechs fought Germans armed to the teeth.

Neurath screamed: "I shall not hesitate to set up a military dictatorship if necessary. The spirit of the Czechs must be broken." But he did not succeed. Sabotage in the factories reached a peak, and damaged war supplies flowed from the hands of Czech slaves. Planes exploded in midair, locomotives fell to pieces, shells blew the cannons apart. Arrests and deportation of factory workers began. In the spring of 1941, sixty workers of the munitions factory at Strakonice were arrested and later shot.

Conditions became so bad for the Nazis that in 1941 Heinrich Himmler advised Hitler to remove von Neurath and replace him with Reinhard Heydrich, General of Police. During the next 105 days German courts passed 394 death sentences against Czechs for noncriminal reasons and handed over 1,134 prisoners to the butchers of the Gestapo. On the morning of May 27, two Czechs killed Heydrich. The same day the Nazis announced that "anyone harboring the culprits or ... helping them will be shot with all his family." A reign of terror began and many families were wiped out in mass murders. Between May 28 and July 3, 1,228 Czechs were executed. The names of many families thus out were on file and documentary proof of these atrocities exists.

This blood bath was not enough for the Germans. In June the village of Lidice was completely destroyed. The Germans killed every man, woman, and child in that town, and leveled it to the ground. Newborn babies and old people alike were mowed down by machine guns. Ten days later the village of Lezaky suffered the same fate. This was German revenge for the assassination of the butcher Heydrich. The exact number of those who died resisting the Nazis is not known. Despite the ever-growing number, the people fought on to victory.

Meanwhile the Czechs fought gallantly in the armed forces of the United Nations. During the first year of occupation Czechs and Slovaks, from cabinet ministers to private soldiers and students, escaped over the heavily guarded borders to fight abroad for liberty. At the risk of their lives, some 30,000 crossed to Poland and organized Czech units in the Polish Army when the nation was attacked by Germany. After the defeat of Poland about 10,000 Czechs fought in France. Hundreds of them had suffered imprisonment in Hungary, traveled through the Balkans, the Near East, and Africa to join their free comrades. A thousand Czech aviators reached England. Many Czech infantrymen fought at Dunkirk. Czech aviators had their own squadrons in the R.A.F. Czech brigades fought in Russia, and on all fronts.

Dr. Benes formed a Free Czech Government in London which was recognized by all the United Nations. Through this agency the Czech people saw their way through to a victorious peace and a continuance of the principles of freedom that sustained them not only during their twenty years of freedom but also during the black days of their Nazi subjugation.

The spirit of the Czechs was never broken. The martyrdom of Lidice became a flaming sword. In tribute to the dead, they marched on with the Allied armies, strong in the ranks of the Russians and formidable in the ranks of the Americans, the British, and the French. Their soldiers were with Eisenhower in the liberation of Europe and with MacArthur in the liberation of the islands of the Pacific. The character and intrepidity of the Czechs rose to majestic heights. In the final days of the war and the restoration of peace, they had their part in the plans to abolish from the face of the earth the age-old system of war.

INVASION OF POLAND—HITLER IGNITES FUSE OF WORLD'S GREATEST WAR

ON September 1, 1939, the Germans invaded Poland and touched off the match which exploded a world conflagration. Repudiating his pledges and defying all other nations, Adolf Hitler started World War II for the deliberate purpose of subjugating Europe and establishing eventual world rule of his "master race."

At 4:50 in the dawn of this September day, without declaration of war, the 35,000,000 people of Poland were aroused by swarms of German warplanes dropping bombs on their homeland. Within the next few hours more than thirty cities were in flames. War was being waged on women and children. Homes, hospitals, churches, and schools were indiscriminately bombed along with military objectives. Museums, libraries, and shrines were wantonly destroyed. Roads crowded with fleeing refugees were machine-gunned.

We have the official documents before us as we record these facts: The first German bombs fell on the station of the Polish Naval Air Force at Puck, killing an officer—the first casualty of the war. From there the bombers spread over the country in a reign of destruction.

The proclamation of President Ignace Moscicki of the Republic of Poland, issued in Warsaw immediately upon the attack, declared: "Citizens: During the course of last night our age-old enemy commenced offensive operations against the Polish State. I affirm this before God and History. At this historic moment I appeal to all citizens of the country in the profound conviction that the entire nation will rally around its Commander in Chief and armed forces to defend its liberty, independence, and honor, and to give the aggressor a worthy answer, as has happened already more than once in the history of Polish-German relations. The entire nation, blessed by God in its struggle for a just and sacred cause, and united with its army, will march in serried ranks to the struggle and the final victory."

This undeclared war by the Germans was in direct violation of the Ten-Year Non-Aggression Pact between Germany and Poland. Hitler struck nearly five years before its expiration date, 1944, thus carrying on the old German custom of tearing up treaties as "scraps of paper."

Hitler's perfidy shocked the moral conscience of the world. Americans felt a close kinship with Poland; there were many ties of common interests. The 3,000,000 Polish-American citizens in the United States were loyal adherents of democratic principles. At the end of the First

World War President Woodrow Wilson had fathered the cause of Polish independence, with Premier Ignace Jan Paderewski—great Polish statesman and world-famous pianist—sitting by his side at the Versailles Conference. With Josef Pilsudski as chief of state, Poland in 1921 adopted a constitution combining features of the Constitution of the United States of America and the Constitution of the Republic of France. Poland, therefore, was to some extent a godchild of the United States, as was Czechoslovakia.

When the Germans attacked Poland in 1939, thus starting World War II, Paderewski was urged by his people to become their President. Declining health would not permit him to assume this tremendous responsibility, but he later went to Paris and became Premier of the Polish Republic-in-exile. A year later, when France was attacked, he came to America. He died in New York in June, 1941—six months before the United States was precipitated into the world conflict.

Invasion of Poland had been preceded by campaigns of falsehoods against the Polish people. There were faked names, figures, and incidents of "ill treatment of German minorities" in Poland—the same method of falsification used in Danzig, in Polish Pomerania, and in the Sudeten campaign against Czechoslovakia.

Again government documents reveal Germany's machinations: Strategy of a war for world domination made it imperative for her first to conquer Poland in order to secure a supply of many raw materials essential for modern armament. Russia was the richest prize, since it had oil, iron, manganese, and other minerals in abundance, and was one of the world's most productive agricultural countries. Russia also offered unbounded opportunities for future industrial development and was an inexhaustible reservoir of manpower. Between Germany and Russia, however, lay Poland. Poland had rejected Germany's repeated suggestions that she should join in an attack upon Russia, the reward for which was to be part of the Russian territory conquered.

Polish "Facts and Figures" expose Germany's double-dealing. Unable to draw Poland into the Machiavellian conspiracy, Hitler entered into a secret agreement with Moscow—the Ribbentrop-Molotov pact of August 23, 1939, seven days before his invasion of Poland. This was another Hitlerian non-aggression pact which the Fuehrer had no intention of keeping, for Russia was his ultimate destination. The pact stated explicitly: "The two contracting parties bind themselves to refrain from any act of force, and aggressive action, and any attack on one another, both singly and also jointly with other powers."

How this worked out was to be quickly unfolded by events. Hitler's own chicanery was one of the decisive factors in his eventual defeat. Moscow, which undoubtedly knew his intentions, quite evidently was sparring for time to build up Soviet defenses. Russia also had a nonaggression pact with Poland which did not expire until December 31, 1945. An alliance between Poland and France had kept them natural allies through the years.

Two days after Hitler and von Ribbentrop had apparently tricked Russia into inactivity, Great Britain and Poland entered into a Mutual Assistance Agreement, signed by Lord Halifax and Count Edward Raczynski. It read in part: "Should one of the contracting parties become engaged in hostilities with a European power in consequence of aggression by the latter against that contracting party, the other contracting party will at once give the contracting party engaged in hostilities all the support and assistance in its power."

Hitler, blind and deaf to its import, failed to read the handwriting on the wall. Von Ribbentrop, the crafty wine salesman turned diplomat, still sold the Fuehrer on the assurance that neither Great Britain nor France would keep its pledge.

Germany had a formidable war machine which had been in the making ever since Hitler gained power in 1933. Poland was overwhelmingly outnumbered. The fire-power ratio, for instance, was 72 to 1 in favor of Germany. As Warsaw correctly reported: "It was the largest army of invasion which had at any time in history been hurled on the first day of war against an attacked country.... Seventy-four German divisions and two Slovak divisions were definitely identified as engaged on the Polish front, with ten divisions held in reserve and twenty more holding the Siegfried Line on the western front of Germany."

Records further reveal that Germany had over 2,000,000 motor vehicles, of which half a million were motor trucks. They had 1,900,000 motorcycles, whereas Poland had approximately only 60,000 motor vehicles of all types including motorcycles. The Polish cavalary consisted of eleven brigades against which the Germans threw into the fray sixteen armored and motorized units. Each of these had more "horse power" in its motors than the entire Polish cavalry had in its horseflesh, not to mention the fact that the German motorized units were able to move with far greater speed. A German division had artillery which could fire twenty-seven tons of projectiles per minute, whereas a Polish division's artillery was able to fire only seventeen tons.

At 5:50 on the morning of September 1—one hour after the arrival of the first waves of bombers over Poland—the German battleship *Schleswig-Holstein,* on a "courtesy visit" to the Free City of Danzig, opened fire without warning on the Polish munitions base at Westerplatte on the bay. This the Polish Government declared to be "a wanton attack upon a garrison under the international protection of the League of Nations." Germany's naval power at this time was about seventy-five ships with swarms of submarines, while Poland possessed but four destroyers, five submarines, eight mine sweepers, and one mine layer.

At dawn on this first day of the war, German land forces commanded by General Walther von Brauchitsch invaded Poland from the north, the west, and the south. The long-planned attack was made by land, sea, and air. Said Sir Nevile Henderson, former British Ambassador to Berlin: "Never can there have been or ever be a case of more deliberate and carefully planned aggression."

The Luftwaffe proceeded to bomb the cities of Warsaw, Cracow, Lodz, Lwow, Czestochowa, Katowice, Gdynia, and twenty-three other cities and villages. Even such small towns as Krosno, Zambrow, Radomsko, and Trzebinia did not escape as German troops in blitzkrieg rolled into Poland. The Polish Army, in a heroic resistance against infinitely stronger forces, fought every step of the way. The plan of the Polish Command was to fall back toward the east, thus "lengthening the enemy's lines of communication and gaining the protection of a difficult terrain in the Carpathians and the Polish marshes, where a decisive battle was to take place."

On the seventeenth day of the sanguinary fighting another bombshell struck Poland. The Russians, in what they called "armed intervention," entered the war "to protect their own frontiers." On September 17 Soviet Armies moved into Poland from the east. Poland declared this to be "in open violation of the Polish-Russian non-aggression pact which was still fully binding." The Soviets, fully aware of Germany's intention of invading their territory next, apparently had decided to jump the gun.

Through a strange paradox of "bedfellows" in war and politics, the Russians were temporarily, for the sake of expediency, "playing the game of wits" with the Germans. Although Hitler in many former speeches had viciously attacked Communism, Berlin and Moscow now issued a joint statement to the effect that they were pooling their efforts "to liquidate the war between Germany on the one side and Great Britain and France on the other side."

Within two days the Soviet troops, meeting no resistance, crossed with lightning speed nearly half of Poland, cutting off Hitler from the rich oil wells of Galicia and blocking his direct road to Rumania. Passing quickly to Lwow and reaching Brest-Litovsk, the Soviets took their stand on the Russian border of 1918. They had thus warned Berlin that "Nazi designs upon the Baltic States and upon the Ukraine must come to a dead stop."

While we are considering the plight of Poland, caught between two powerful war machines, we must not forget the three little border countries of agricultural people which were trapped in the same wedge: Lithuania, Latvia, and Estonia. They are typical of the little people of the world who love freedom and who are trampled upon when the rights of small nations are forgotten. Lithuania, with less than 3,000,000 inhabitants, is about the size of West Virginia. Latvia, with about 2,000,000 people, is approximately as large as Indiana. Estonia, with less than 1,200,000 population, covers about the same amount of territory as New Hampshire and Vermont together. All are ancient countries with traditions and cultural institutions which they treasure.

Forty days after the attack on Poland and the outbreak of World War II, Lithuania signed a mutual assistance pact with Russia. It was dated October 10, 1939, and was to continue for fifteen years with a ten-year extension. It granted the Soviets the right to establish army and naval bases for the protection of the frontier. The Soviet Union in reciprocation ceded to Lithuania the city of Vilna, its ancient capital, with the surrounding territory. During the following year the Russians took Lithuania "under protection" and incorporated it into the Union of Soviet Socialist Republics, later expelling the Germans from the country. Latvia and Estonia met with almost identical experiences. They became allied with the fighting forces of the United Nations when Russia aligned its power with the Allies in 1941.

The three-week defense of Warsaw, "a city without fortifications and with a relatively small garrison ... was an epic which had seldom been equaled before or since." The official records state: "The first German motorized detachments on September 8 penetrated as far as the suburbs of Warsaw. In addition to the infantry, two armored divisions, two air armies, and the combined artillery of four German Armies totaling 2,500 guns were used to lay siege to Poland's capital. Warsaw was occupied by the Germans on September 29, after all possibilities for further resistance had been exhausted because of lack of ammunition, the disruption of the sewer and water supply systems, and the failure of the food supply."

Poland had faced alone the mightiest armies the world had yet known. Great Britain and France found it impossible to reach her in time to give aid. Arthur Greenwood exclaimed in the House of Commons: "Poland stood alone at civilization's gate, defending us and all the free peoples ... with unexampled bravery and epic heroism.... We salute her as a comrade whom we shall not desert."

United States Senator James M. Mead later paid this tribute as he spoke before Polish-Americans assembled in Buffalo, New York: "Outnumbered, overwhelmed by the superior mechanized equipment and air forces, the valiant Poles carried on for five bloody weeks—weeks that perhaps decided the fate of the whole world. Those were the precious weeks that gave England the priceless time in which to prepare, weeks that kept the Nazi war machine engaged, weeks that kept Hitler faced in the East when he might have been roaring to the West."

Even the Nazis were impressed by Poland's valiant defense. General

Kleeberg at Kutno was permitted to march his troops with their arms and under command of their own officers, "while their captors rendered military honors to the Poles marching into captivity."

The surrender of Warsaw to General von Blaskowitz took place in a railway car on September 27, 1939. The defenders along the Vistula, entrenched behind the fortress of Modlin, stood their ground for two more days. Along the Hel Peninsula the shell batteries held out until October 2. The last battle on a major scale was fought on October 5, at Kock, near Lublin.

The conquest of Poland had taken thirty-five days. The Germans were later to conquer three countries—France, the Netherlands, and Belgium—in but two days more. Poland had cost the Germans over 91,000 killed and over 98,000 wounded. The German air force over Poland lost over 1,000 planes, while the armored troops lost approximately 1,400 tanks completely destroyed, plus 2,600 tanks rendered unfit for use. Polish losses in prisoners, missing, wounded, and killed were 831,000. The Germans claimed they had taken almost 700,000 prisoners; the Russians claimed that they had captured 10,000 officers and 181,000 men.

The fourth partition of Poland now took place. Germany seized 72,500 square miles with approximately 23,000,000 people; Russia held 78,000 square miles with a population of about 12,000,000. Ten months later, after Germany had attacked Russia, the Soviets declared the treaty of partition abrogated and liberated their Polish area.

The Polish Government-in-exile was formed in Paris on September 30, with Wladyslaw Raczkiewicz as President and General Sikorski as Prime Minister.

General Sikorski became Commander in Chief of Polish forces continuing to fight with the Allied armies. His Polish Army in France exceeded 70,000 men by May, 1940. Some of the men had escaped from internment camps in Hungary, Rumania, Lithuania, and Latvia; others had been recruited from Polish inhabitants of France, Belgium, and Holland; still others had escaped from Poland under the occupation of the Germans and the Russians.

The great Sikorski directed the battle against Germany on all fronts. From the hour the Polish flag was hauled down from Warsaw's city hall to the day it was raised over the ancient monastery of Monte Cassino in Italy, Poland fought on. With the largest army—over 200,000 strong—in support of the United Nations from any of the occupied countries, the Poles continued to march under banners bearing the motto of their forefathers: "For Your Freedom and Ours!" They were among the first to go to the aid of Norway; they fought gallantly in the Battle of France. Just before the French capitulation General Sikorski flew to London to offer the services of Poland to the British.

As the war progressed the Poles took their stand in defense of England and more than 8,000 Polish airmen gave invaluable aid to the Royal Air Force in the Battle of Britain. His Majesty King George VI later visited the Polish squadrons to shake the hand of each flier in gratitude for the gallant part he had played. Poles fought under General Eisenhower in Tunisia, Sicily, and in Italy. They took part in the liberation of France and in the invasion of Germany. They fought in the Libyan campaign under General Montgomery; on the eastern front with the Russians; on ships in the battles of the seven seas. There were tens of thousands of Poles in the United States armies and fleets on all fronts. There were Poles with General MacArthur and Admiral Nimitz in the Pacific, Poles on the road to Tokyo, and Poles on the road to Berlin.

Inside Poland the Home Army was fighting underground under command of the mysterious "General Bor." More than 500,000 were conducting sabotage raids while waiting for the "grand uprising" and the liberation of their homeland. Polish women had joined the ranks with an auxiliary known as the *Pomocnicza Sluzba Wojskowa Kobiet*, nicknamed the Pestki. The first regiments were formed in Russia when the Soviet authorities released Polish women from prison and labor camps. The records state: "Hundreds of thousands streamed southward to Buzuluk where the Polish Army was forming. Women arrived dressed in men's clothes, their feet wrapped in rags, their bodies swollen with hunger, and covered with wounds from scurvy...A part of the regular army, they have since gone through 'thick and thin' with the Polish soldiers in Iraq, Iran, Palestine, Egypt, Great Britain, and Italy."

On July 4, 1943—General Sikorski was flying from the Middle East to London. The plane circled over Gibraltar and somehow it crashed on the landing field. The great Polish patriot, Commander in Chief of the forces and Prime Minister of the Government-in-exile, was instantly killed.

Prime Minister Churchill, standing in the House of Commons on the following day, informed the members that the cause of the United Nations had suffered a great loss. Said Churchill: "From the dark days of the Polish catastrophe and the brutal triumph of the Germans' war machine until the moment of his death, General Sikorski was the symbol and the embodiment of that spirit which has borne the Polish nation through centuries of sorrow and is unquenchable by agony."

President Raczkiewicz in London appointed as Sikorski's successor General Kazimierz Sosnkowski, who had distinguished himself in the Polish campaign in 1939 and had escaped from Poland after its occupation by the Germans.

DENMARK FALLS INTO CAPTIVITY

BLITZKRIEG, which was to engulf all Europe in flames, struck its first blow on the Western front on April 9, 1940, against the Scandinavians. Hitler, in lightning conquest, invaded both Denmark and Norway.

The Danes, who a thousand years ago had built a line of fortifications across Jutland to hold back the Teutonic tribes, fell at last into German captivity. They were awakened at five o'clock on this April morning to find Nazi hordes crossing the Danish borders. Denmark, with less than 4,000,000 people, was being invaded by a neighbor with 80,000,000.

In the First World War the little nation, eager to stay out of the conflict, had succeeded in remaining neutral. The Danish Government mobilized an emergency army of 70,000 men and pursued a policy of confidence and integrity which was respected by the belligerents on both sides. At the armistice these Danish troops were quickly demobilized, again showing the good faith of the Danish people. When Denmark became a member of the League of Nations, a law was passed abolishing the land defense of Copenhagen.

The Treaty of Versailles provided for a plebiscite in the disputed areas. A new frontier was established, and Denmark was given possession of a strip of land where even under German rule the south Jutlanders had never surrendered their Danish nationality. Their language, songs, customs, and culture had remained Danish. True to prophecy, King Christian rode into Danish Schleswig on a white horse.

It was partly due to the Schleswig-Holstein Question that Denmark, though an ancient country and a homogeneous nation, had a constitution that was but twenty-five years old when World War II began. It gives joint legislative power to the King and the Diet (*Rigsdag*). The King has no right to declare war or to sign peace without consent of the *Rigsdag*. He exercises his authority through his cabinet and one cannot function without the other. Because of this inter-relationship between crown and government, the Germans were caught in a dilemma after their invasion in 1940. Their efforts to establish a Danish puppet régime under Nazi rule were doomed to failure.

When Hitler came to power, the Nazis made no issue of the Schleswig territory returned to Denmark, and seemed satisfied with the treatment of German minorities there. However, Denmark realized that she was geographically, if not ethnologically, situated in the *Lebensraum* sphere of the Third Reich. Fearing for her future, she now decided to triple her rearmament program, which by March, 1940, provided for only an expenditure of $25,000,000 to $30,000,000 for two new air squadrons, antiaircraft guns, and fast motor boats. The army, in the form of a national militia, called annually 6,800 men for training. The navy comprised the fleet and the coast defense forces—"toy units" as compared with the strength of even the smaller nations such as Norway, Holland, and Belgium. This military display was hardly sufficient to defend the country.

The Parliament in Copenhagen, on January 19, 1940, backed the country's absolute neutrality by a vote of 135 to 0. Moreover, Denmark was a member of the Oslo group, and a few weeks later united with Norway and Sweden to forestall violations of international law that might involve them in war. To secure friendly relationship with her mighty neighbor to the south, Denmark had also signed, on May 31, 1939, a ten-year non-aggression pact in Berlin, where the agreement was regarded as "another proof of Germany's policy of peaceful relations with neighbor states."

Article I of the pact provided that both countries "will under no circumstances resort to war or any form of violence against each other." A provision was made that Denmark, in the event of a conflict between Britain and Germany, would be able to continue exports of agricultural products to both sides as she had during World War I. Special importance was attached to this clause since England and Germany accounted for two thirds of Denmark's exports in foodstuffs.

Yet despite this pact, and utterly disregarding the rights of a small, defenseless, neutral nation, Nazi Germany once more sidestepped international law and decency by attacking a civilized people whose sovereignty she did not respect and whose democratic ideals she was unable to share.

President Roosevelt a few days later lifted his voice against this betrayal of an honorable and peaceful people:

"Force and military aggression are once more on the march against small nations, in this instance through the invasion of Denmark and Norway," the President declared in Washington on April 13. "These two nations have won and maintained during a period of many generations the respect and regard, not only of the American people, but of all peoples, because of their observance of the highest standards of national and international conduct.... If civilization is to survive, the rights of the smaller nations to independence, to their territorial integrity, and to the unimpeded opportunity for self-government must be respected by their more powerful neighbors."

Just fifteen minutes before the Germans crossed the Jutland border, the German envoy in Copenhagen, Doctor von Renthe-Fink, handed to the Danish Foreign Minister a "memorandum" announcing that on the assumption that Danish military resources were not sufficient to repulse projected Allied attempts against the country's sovereignty, Germany had seen fit to proceed with the occupation of certain strategically important points on Danish territory.

Confronted with overwhelming strength, the Danes realized the futility of resistance. Yet Danish border guards had been put in the highest state of preparedness and the Danish Government at first decided to resist the invasion. Faced with a German one-hour ultimatum, demanding withdrawal of resistance, the Cabinet changed its mind. The alternative was the merciless bombing of Copenhagen and other important cities.

Prime Minister Thorvald and Foreign Minister Dr. Peter Munch hurried to the palace to see the King. Outside, the German envoy waited, watch in hand. The King and his ministers had conferred for fifty-five minutes when the envoy warned that the ultimatum was about to expire. The King sent word that he would withdraw opposition. The dramatic incident was closed.

As far as German strategy was concerned the Danish invasion plan of the Wehrmacht was a mere test case. It was carried out with clockwork precision. For some hours before the Reich forces crossed the Danish border, reports had circulated in Copenhagen that the Germans of South Jutland were expecting Nazi troop trains, carrying 45,000 men, to arrive at the town of Flensburg during the night. It was a convenient starting point for shipping troops northward. In addition, the invaders chose two other ferry points on the Great Belt, Nyborg and Korsoer. At the same hour troops landed a large scale force at Middelfart, where three German cruisers had already arrived, and occupied the town. The last ferry crossing the Baltic Sea from Warnemuende to Gedser carried an armored train instead of the regular international *wagon lits.*

German troops moved into all parts of the country, especially along the Jutland coast facing England. Their motorized columns covered more than 200 miles in some cases on the first day. The nation surrendered to Germany. King Christian and Premier Stauning, calling upon the army and the people to yield, issued a proclamation:

"German troops tonight crossed the Danish border. Some German troops will debark at various points in Denmark.... It is the duty of the people to refrain from every resistance to these troops. The Danish Government will endeavor to insure the security of the people and of the Danish land in face of disastrous consequences resulting from the state of war, and consequently asks the population to maintain a calm, thoughtful attitude. May peace and order reign in the country."

As the German troops crossed the Jutland border and speeded northward through hamlets, villages, and towns, they saw the Danish flag drooping at half-staff. The people were stunned. Boys and girls too young to realize what was happening, watched, curiously, along the roads where troop trains passed and Nazi columns marched.

The entrance of the Germans into Copenhagen, the first time foreign troops had ever occupied the capital, was met with mental anguish and sullen silence. In the gray dawn of April 9, three ships were steered through the mine fields outside Copenhagen by a Danish pilot, who had no idea of the nature of the cargo, and tied up at Lange Linie, Copenhagen's favorite summer promenade. Few persons saw the 1,000 German soldiers debark. Those who did see ran to the radio station and police headquarters. They could secure no help, for the Government order not to resist had come through.

Where this order was not received, a few shots were fired. The most dramatic incident occurred at Amalienborg Castle, the King's residence. The guard, in their picturesque uniforms, opened fire when the Germans approached. King Christian was still in conference with his ministers in the palace. Hearing the shots on the street below, he sent his adjutant to stop the fighting. The Danish officer received the order, rose from behind his barricade, and gave the signal to cease firing. His pistol, still in hand, he walked toward the Germans. Informing the commanding Nazi officer of the order, he turned abruptly and marched away. The King's guard had lost two men in the skirmish.

At the military airport fourteen Danish planes were lined up outside the hangars to await the Germans. The pilots had been ordered to offer no resistance. When the Nazi planes appeared one pilot disobeyed the order. Going up with his machine gunner, he challenged them to fight. His plane was instantly shot down. The knight of the skies and his gunner crashed, and both were killed.

The occupation of Denmark was carried out with speed and thoroughness. German propaganda fully exploited the feat. General Leonhard Kaupisch, German commander of the occupation forces, had established his headquarters in the Hotel d'Angleterre.

Denmark was to have a special place in Germany's "New Order." She was singled out to become Hitler's "Model Protectorate." The experience turned out to be neither a "model" nor did the measures employed by the Nazis "protect." The "show window of the blessings of Nazism"—Denmark by implication—was smashed when the invaders dropped their masks and dealt with the Danes as they had dealt with all other conquered countries.

Denmark, with the exception of little Luxembourg later, was the only country where the Nazi Juggernaut had not met armed resistance. And the Germans probably thought that the bloodless surrender of the Danes would furnish them with a basis for "friendly coöperation." Moreover, they needed economic and industrial products of the country, which was to "sell" food to the Reich in exchange for coal. Coal, in turn, was needed in Denmark to keep her industries moving. Besides, Denmark was a thoroughfare for Nazi troop movements to the north, one more reason that a peaceful Denmark was essential.

King Christian set an example in showing his subjects that Denmark was still a country in her own right. It had been his habit to ride his horse every morning through the streets of Copenhagen, and he continued these daily canters. On October 19, 1942, his mount shied and he was thrown over the horse's head. It was more than an accident. Crowds gathered before the Royal Palace. Expressing their feelings for the then seventy-two-year-old monarch, they showed what he meant to them. The democratic sovereign was hailed as their stalwart leader who had stiffened the national spirit. It was a demonstration of loyalty, reassurance, hope—and warning.

But it was not long before the German mask revealed what was hidden beneath it. The country was being economically wrecked. Before the war Denmark was the largest supplier of bacon, butter, and eggs in the international markets. She furnished 50 per cent of the world's exports of bacon and ham, about 30 per cent of the world's total butter exports, and about 15 per cent of all exports of eggs.

Under the "New Order" Denmark's entire economy, based on world trade, met with terrifying results. Her lifeblood was being systematically drained. For the bacon, fatted hogs, and beef which she was forced to send to Germany, the Danes received a large, unusable balance of credits in German marks. No longer could the Danish farmers obtain the food they had formerly imported. They were compelled now to slaughter their livestock. The cost of living soared and wages could no longer be adjusted to the cost-of-living index. Unemployment mounted and offices were opened for recruiting Danish workers for Germany.

The looting of Denmark was well under way. Merchants, mills, and industries were ordered to begin an immediate inventory of cereals. Feeding of cereals to stock was forbidden. House owners were forced to build dugouts and bombproof cellars. Gasoline became more closely rationed and later was no longer available for civilians. Many foodstuffs, such as cocoa, tea, and coffee disappeared entirely. Other shortages caused undernourishment and endangered the nation's health. Traffic was limited. These were fateful prohibitions that cut deep into the private life of the populace. Though the country had been spared the horrors of warfare, it was being "bled white" by the Germans. Like all Nazi-subjugated nations Denmark was being incorporated into the "Nazi orbit"—a new name for plunder.

The Germans brazenly broke all their pledges. Their interference in Danish civic affairs grew constantly. Increasing their demands upon the Government, Premier Thorvald Stauning had to yield to Nazi pressure in order to maintain authority. Whenever the Nazis thought they had the Danes cornered, they sidestepped by making a minor concession, issuing proclamations to stop sabotage, and appealing to "reason."

After German demands for changes in the Copenhagen Government had been successfully countered by King Christian, the Germans seized ten Danish torpedo boats in February, 1941, in violation of their pledge to respect the independence of the Danish Army and fleet. This infringement upon Danish authority aroused strong feeling against the Nazis. It meant that the nation's neutral status, of which the Danes had been assured by the Germans, had been violated, as these torpedo boats could be used against the Allies. The Germans, foreseeing trouble, had first suggested that the ships be transferred to them as a sign of German-Danish friendship. The Danes indignantly rejected the demand. They likewise refused a suggestion that the ships be loaned for the duration of the war. Finally a threatening note came from Berlin, stating that the refusal to hand over the ships would have serious consequences. The Danes yielded under protest.

Later it became known that, as a means of stronger protest, abdication of the King was seriously considered. It would have thrown the country into chaos, however, and the plan was abandoned. When the ten torpedo boats were surrendered, their flags were lowered to halfmast as a sign of protest and mourning. As the Germans had been guarding them for weeks, their officers and men had had no chance to damage or scuttle them.

When the Danes realized that their German masters were robbing them and that they had no legal means of protecting their sovereignty, they began to offer resistance that promised to be more effective than "protests." Sabotage set in systematically. Carried out where it hurt the Nazis most, it was directed chiefly against the German transit system. Workers in factories made tools useless and dumped carloads of precious nails into the sea. Textiles were damaged by acid and machinery wrecked with sand.

Saboteurs, who first acted individually, soon became organized and worked together. This developed into an Underground movement on a large scale. Patriots turned saboteurs. They worked in groups in which all were members of a secret organization. These units became so proficient that their leaders, in a jocular mood, bestowed "academic degrees" on their "graduates." According to the acts they performed they received a B.S. (Bachelor of Sabotage) or M.S. (Master of Sabotage). In introducing themselves they often mentioned their calling as well as their names.

Before a certain radio factory was blown up, ten men gathered at the gate. The factory guard opened it and one of the group said, "Pardon me, are you the factory guard?" "Yes." Whereupon the group leader said, "Good evening, I'm Saboteur Jensen." To prove it he produced a revolver. The ten men filed in.

Sabotage to railway bridges, railroad lines, and rolling stock finally became so serious that it hampered the Nazi communication system. Strikes of railway workers crippled transportation and German troop movements. A showdown was at hand. The Germans demanded the right to shoot Danish saboteurs. The Danes had to choose whether to hand over patriot citizens or take the consequences.

The Copenhagen Cabinet by this time was headed by Erik Scavenius, a pro-Nazi, who, as Foreign Minister in the preceding Buhl Government, had signed the Anti-Comintern Pact in Berlin. The Danish Government received word from Dr. Werner Best, the Nazi civilian representative in 1943, that all saboteurs must be tried by German law and punished in Germany. This meant death for them. The Danes refused and Scavenius offered to resign. The Germans wished to keep him in office and waived their demands.

More acts of sabotage and protest strikes occurred. All work stopped in Esbjerg harbor. Strikes were called in Aalborg and Odense. In the latter town street fighting broke out and a state of siege was declared by the Germans. On the night of August 19, sixty factories were blown up. Political leaders of Parliament met and the Cabinet, seeking once more to sidestep German pressure, warned the people of Nazi revenge.

More riots occurred. Acts of sabotage increased by the hundreds. A stage of siege was declared in seven Danish cities. Fifty thousand Nazi troops rolled into Copenhagen in a desperate effort to subdue a people's revolt. Machine guns were set up at strategic points. The huge Forum Hall was blown up. A volley of shots was fired in a crowded market place. Yet the wave of strikes spread.

When Danish-German discussions reached a stalemate Doctor Best was called to Berlin to report. He returned with a list of eight demands that included declaration of a state of siege throughout Denmark; creation of a special tribunal to sentence Danish saboteurs to death; a curfew from 8:30 P.M. to 6:30 A.M.; and a fine of 1,000,000 kroner on the population of Odense for starting the wave of unrest. The Danish Government replied that no more concessions would be made.

The climax was at hand. At 4:10 on the morning of August 29, 1943, the Nazis applied martial law to the country. Danes, opposing a German attempt to seize the navy yard at Copenhagen, scuttled part of the fleet. Other navy units fled to Sweden rather than submit to the Nazis. A battle raged near the docks where the Danes blew up ammunition dumps. The capital, blacked out for three years, was for the first time brightly illuminated so that the Germans could see where they were shooting. Fighting took place at the Rosenberg barracks and at Amalienborg palace where dramatic incidents occurred. When the King ordered his troops to stop firing, they broke their rifles before surrendering them.

The Danish Navy had ceased to exist. The Germans deposed the Cabinet, arrested its members, and assumed all civilian power. Taking the law into their own hands they announced death penalties for strikes and sabotage. The King and Queen were taken from their summer residence at Sorgenfri to Amalienborg Castle where they were interned with the rest of the royal family.

General strikes paralyzed every kind of business. Mass arrests began. They included prominent men from all walks of life, labor leaders, politicians, professors, and the chief editors of major newspapers. Gestapo agents occupied all Copenhagen police stations after Danish police had refused to swear loyalty to the German commander. All Danish officers were interned. A round-up of Jews began.

The Danish Minister to Sweden, Johan C. W. Kruse, severed diplomatic ties with his homeland, declaring that a constitutional government had ceased to exist with the advent of German military dictatorship. In Washington, Dr. Henrik de Kauffmann, the Danish envoy, renewed his pledge to fight for the liberation of his country. Ever since the invasion this diplomat had disregarded a "recall" by his Government after the Greenland agreement which he had concluded with the State Department. Upon direction of President Roosevelt, he continued to be recognized as Danish Minister to the United States.

Secretary of State Hull made a statement declaring: "Events in Denmark are an eloquent reminder that German rule in any circumstances is intolerable to a free and democratic people. . . . The resistance of the Danish King and people to German domination will give new heart and encouragement to all peoples of Nazi-subjugated Europe."

King Christian, giving the ingenious reason that as a prisoner of war he could not accept the resignation of the old government, resisted Nazi pressure and refused to form a new one.

So the Germans sought to rule Denmark by an "Administrative Council," like the one they had set up in Norway in 1940. It consisted of three German "Directors General" and fifteen Danish heads of departments who agreed, under force, to carry on their work for the time being.

While sabotage against German production and transport continued at an undiminished pace, the Germans were unable to bring about a pro-Nazi government. General Kurt Daluege, ruthless Gestapo troubleshooter for Heinrich Himmler, had meanwhile taken over military dictatorship from General von Hanneken and demanded that Parliament be disbanded. He insisted upon formation of a puppet government. A committee representing the five big political parties in Denmark refused the proposal.

This put Denmark in the unique position of having no Government at all, neither at home nor abroad. The Nazis had miscalculated the effects of their "benevolent" occupation. They had permitted elections in Denmark in 1943, hoping that Dr. Fritz Clausen's Danish Nazi Party would gain a sweeping victory. But they were under a delusion. The party rule of this Quisling-to-be proved a fiasco.

The Danish people, smarting under the Nazi yoke, gave a smashing demonstration for democracy. The five dominant parties, united on a platform for national unity, polled 362,000 more votes than in 1939. It was a blow to German prestige. Doctor Clausen, when last heard from, was arrested by the Germans on the charge of having diverted to himself 100,000 kroner instead of using them for a Danish Free Press Service. He was given the choice between prison and the Russian front. He chose the Russian front.

Under Daluege's "protectorship" the Nazi reign of terror continued. Jews, needless to say, became the scapegoats of reckless persecution. In Copenhagen, where all but 300 of the 6,000 Danish Jews lived, their mass arrests and deportations were begun by the Gestapo. These Jews' patriotic record had been excellent. There was no "Jewish Question" till the Nazis created one. The Jews offered to surrender themselves to save the country and as a possible price for more Nazi tolerance. But the Danes refused. The King, siding with his Jewish subjects, declared that he, too, would display the Yellow Star should the Jews be forced to wear it. "We have no Jewish problem in Denmark," he said before he was a Nazi prisoner.

The Danish Church stood firm against Nazi interference. "I would rather die with the Jews than live with the Nazis," said Pastor Ivar Lange of the Frederiksborg Church in Copenhagen.

Clergymen protested vigorously. Expressions of sympathy with suffering Norwegian parsons were frequent. Bishop Fuglsang-Damgaard, Primate of the Danish Lutheran State Church, was under house-arrest. Most tragic was the case of Dr. Kaj Munk, outstanding spiritual leader, author, and clergyman, who was found murdered on January 4, 1944, in a park near the Jutland city of Silkeborg. The Gestapo had taken him from his parsonage for questioning after his New Year's Day sermon.

Himmler firing squads were kept busy. Arrests, mounting to 19,000 in 1942, continued at such a terrific pace that the Danish police, numbering 3,250 in 1939, had to be increased to 8,021 in 1943. Prisons soon became too few for those condemned for political crimes, so schools and public buildings were turned into jails.

Concentration camps were opened. The most notorious was in Horserod where about 1,000 persons were held and tortured. Others, whose numbers cannot now be estimated, were deported for forced labor in the Reich. Their families were dispossessed of their homes and properties. Their ranks included peoples from all walks of life.

But the Danes, formerly regarded as the most light-hearted of the Scandinavian people, bore up valiantly under Nazi rule. It was significant that the King once remarked, "I'm happy to hear our dear Danish language still spoken in old Denmark." It crystallized the Danish feeling in a few words. The Danes turned into a "nation of icicles," ignoring the existence of the Herrenvolk and disdainfully showed their would-be masters the cold shoulder. They developed what they called a "neo-Danish style"—a chilliness calculated to show the Germans what they thought of them. It was one way of bolstering their morale, and wearing down the morale of the conquerer. Another weapon used was scathing Danish humor. Sarcasm became a sword in the silent struggle of the home front. In countless stories keen wit was turned against the Nazis and hit a vulnerable spot in German mentality.

A Copenhagen bookseller displayed in his shop window a photograph of Hitler and one of Mussolini. Between the two pictures he placed a copy of Victor Hugo's *Les Miserables*. Also this story of the King, noted for his wit, who one day was held up at a street crossing in his capital by a red traffic light. People around him doffed their hats. "Put on your hats, my friends," the King said, "it'll be some time before we get the green light."

Nazi censorship brought the Underground press into existence. There were thirty underground newspapers in Denmark by 1943.

Outside the country Danes all over the world pledged themselves to work for the freedom of their homeland.

Danish seamen sailed in British convoys. Danish volunteers in the R.A.F. were assured that they were Allies in all but name. Tribute was paid to the 203 Danish ships in the British merchant navy and the 53 Danish ships sailing with the Americans. More than 70 Danish fishing vessels brought to England catches valued at a million pounds sterling. Danes suffered great casualties both in men and ships while aiding the cause of the democracies. The Danish merchant fleet had lost, in 1944, more than 180 ships since the outbreak of the war.

The attitude of the Danes, expressing the greatness of a small people and their undaunted spirit, is reflected by two anecdotes that filtered out of the conquered nation. When the German commander in chief, at the beginning of the invasion, complimented the Mayor of Copenhagen for the good discipline of the people, the Mayor said, simply, "You are mistaken. It isn't discipline—it's culture."

On another occasion a speaker in Copenhagen declared: "If it had been the intention of the Lord that the Germans should run the world, He would have given them enough brains to do it."

14

NORWAY UNDER IRON HEEL OF INVADERS

THE struggle of the Norwegians under subjugation by a ruthless power is a thrilling modern Scandinavian saga. On the same fateful morning, April 9, 1940, that the Danes were taken into captivity, Norway, with less than 3,000,000 people, was attacked by the Germans, a nation nearly thirty times stronger.

For 126 years Norway had been a free nation. Her sturdy folk lived together in peace in a rapidly expanding modern nation whose constitution and independence dated from 1814. Her constitution had been modified at various times in over a century, but it never ceased to vest the legislative power of the realm in the Storting, a parliament representative of a democratic people.

King Haakon VII was a symbol of democracy, and he guided his nation until it became one of the most progressive in the world. Through the difficult years of the First World War, the Norse people stood united and independent of the conflict. The Scandinavian countries proclaimed strict neutrality and agreed to abstain from all hostile action. The spirit of these Scandinavian nations was expressed by their manifesto: "The present crisis (World War I) will come to an end some day ... then the belligerents will surely not be sorry to find still in force some of the principles which were dear to them. ..."

It is, indeed, historical irony that, with the exception of Sweden, none of the signers of the Oslo Protocol was able to stay out of World War II. One of the last meetings of the Oslo nations was held in Brussels shortly before the outbreak of the conflict. It broke up hastily when the appeal for peace was overshadowed by war clouds; yet they believed their neutrality would be respected, even while the Nazi octopus was reaching out its tentacles.

The Norwegians proceeded cautiously and reluctantly. They found it difficult to equip even a small defense army of 60,000 men. The navy, designed for coast-defense duty only, numbered about 10,000 men. The country in a desperate effort for self-defense enlarged her army by calling up two thirds instead of the former one third of the annual contingent of conscripts, and she lengthened her training period to 120 days. She expanded her small navy by arming whaling ships and trawlers to guard her coast.

World War II had already come close to her shores in November, 1939, when the American merchantman *City of Flint* became the object of a heated diplomatic duel between the Reich and Norway. In February, 1940, the British invaded a Norwegian fjord in a daring raid on the German prison ship *Altmark*. The presence of a German submarine in Norway's territorial waters in March was another shock to that nation, which saw herself involved in a European conflict.

When King Haakon opened the Storting on January 12, 1940, which was to be the last before the Nazi attack, he pledged every effort to maintain his nation's neutrality. The country's armed forces, he said, would be increased only as a precaution. Foreign Minister Halvdan Koht, in one of his last addresses before Parliament on April 6, 1940, stressed that Norway was not interested in aiding any belligerent and that she would fight only for her own liberty and independence.

Three days later, the Norsemen—descendants of the Vikings—were involved in the bloodiest struggle in history. German troops invaded Denmark and Norway. Washington received word of this startling action at one o'clock that morning, whereupon the State Department issued the following communiqué: "The American Minister to Oslo, Mrs. J. Borden Harriman, telegraphed the Department tonight that the (Norwegian) Foreign Minister had informed her that the Norwegians had fired on four German warships coming up Oslo Fjord and that Norway was at war with Germany."

At 5:30 A.M. Mrs. Harriman reported that Norwegian shore batteries were still engaged in battle with four invading German warships which were trying to force entry into Oslo Fjord. A Reuter dispatch from Paris, via London, reported the Oslo radio broadcast that German troops had entered Norwegian ports.

These grave developments were preceded by announcements of the British and French Governments that three areas off the Norwegian coast had been mined in an Allied move to deny to the Reich use of territorial waters for the shipment of vital Scandinavian iron ore to Germany. The areas mined were off Stadtlandet, Peninsula, Bud and West Fjord. As justification for the laying of mines in neutral waters, the Allies held that German submarine and airplane attacks on neutral and British shipping were "pure terrorism" and were carried out in "defiance of recognized rules of war." Thus they were forced to establish British blockade. This action heightened a tense situation already aggravated by the torpedoing of a Norwegian steamer by a German submarine and the sinking of the German troopship *Rio de Janeiro* by a British U-boat on the south coast of Norway.

At 4:30 A.M. on April 9, several hours after German forces had already attacked Norway, the German Minister in Oslo, Dr. Curt Braeuer, called on Foreign Minister Koht and presented a number of demands from his Government. These not only included capitulation of the Norwegian Army and the hoisting of the white flag all over the country, but such details as handing over all lightships to the Nazis and stopping broadcasts of weather reports. The demands were as follows:

(1) To issue a proclamation asking the people not to resist German troops; (2) Order Norwegian officers to contact German invaders and hoist a white flag alongside the Norwegian flag; (3) Turn over undamaged all military establishments and fortifications; (4) Disclose the exact position of all Norwegian mines; (5) Blackout the country immediately; (6) Turn over all means of communication; (7) Prohibit all ships and planes from leaving the country; (8) Guide German troopships into narrow Norwegian fjords; (9) Ban all external mail and maintain meteorological service for German troops; (10) Submit immediately to German censorship; (11) Hand over all radio stations; (12) Halt export trade in goods required at home; (13) Cease using codes known to the British and French.

Doctor Braeuer warned that unless all this was accepted, "all resistance would be defeated." The demands were refused, and hostilities, already under way, continued. The Reich Government made a belated war declaration on Norway in a radio announcement on April 26, seventeen days after the start of the invasion.

Immediate reports on the morning of April 9 were alarming. A German armada of 125 armed ships, including a 10,000-ton battleship, several heavy cruisers and destroyers, was approaching Norwegian shores. Oslo, the Norwegian capital, was bombarded from the air. The Government ordered it abandoned by the civilian population within two days. Kristiansand, on the southern Norwegian coast, was bombed by German planes in the early hours of the morning. Coastal batteries near Oskarsberg were shelling German warships.

This is what happened during the first twenty-four hours of the invasion: Nazi forces marched into the capital at 4:00 P.M. on April 9, after German transports had run the gauntlet of Norwegian shore defenses and landed men at two points. They bombed Oslo's East Station twice during the day, and fierce air battles continued to rage over the outskirts of the city. Within the capital the population watched silently as German soldiers marched down the central street. Oslo was quiet that night. Narvik was captured after two German destroyers had torpedoed two Norwegian destroyers in that port, causing a loss of 540 lives. Then the Germans landed 1,500 men from the destroyers and forty minutes later occupied the town. Meanwhile, the Nazis had occupied Trondheim and Bergen.

The courageous King Haakon assured the world of Norway's determination to resist the Germans and rejected Nazi demands for recognition of a puppet government under the traitor Major Vidkun Quisling. The King, after calling a state council, issued the following proclamation: "I fully adhere to the Government's appeal, and I am convinced that the whole population is with me in the decision taken."

Thus Norway took her stand with the democracies and continued her struggle against Germany. On April 11, the Norwegians recaptured Hamar, the first seat to which their Government had fled after the Nazi occupation of Oslo. That same day British warships were reported ready to shell the Germans out of the capital and were engaging German men-of-war in the biggest naval battle since Jutland. They had forced their way through the Skagerrak down into the Kattegat strait and had served an ultimatum on the invaders to give up the capital. There were scenes of panic when Oslo was evacuated.

The Norwegians held the invaders on land in a battle at Elverum "all along the line." They fought fiercely in defense of their Government and newly established capital. Over the North Sea and the Norwegian fjords, British and German aircraft had come to grips, indicating the extent of the far-flung battle. Bergen and Trondheim were recaptured by the Allies. British destroyers smashed into Narvik Fjord, the Grand Fleet's most spectacular feat so far. They sank two Nazi destroyers; destroyed all German merchantmen in the port and withdrew with one of their own destroyers badly and one slightly damaged. Other Allied naval successes included the sinking of the German cruiser *Karlsruhe* at Kristiansand and the cruiser *Bluecher* off Oslo. Thus German's cruiser strength was reduced to a new, very low level.

Altogether, six ships of three nations, England, Germany, and Norway, totaling 27,177 tons had been sunk in two days of naval and air action off the Norwegian coast. The Germans had lost 16,000 tons of men-of-war, the Norwegians 8,332, and the British 2,845, the destroyers *Hardy* and *Hunter*.

Winston Churchill, who had spent almost all night in the operations room of the Admiralty, told the House of Commons that, while no miracles had been performed, the fleet had lived up to its traditions. He considered the German fleet had been "crippled in important respects" with four of the enemy's cruisers destroyed, nearly half of the German strength in cruisers, and several destroyers and a number of U-boats sunk. In addition, a dozen large Nazi ships carrying supplies and invading forces were sunk or captured. Mr. Churchill argued that Hitler's recklessness in undertaking an invasion of Norway made it suspected that the adventure was "only a prelude to far larger events on land."

On Tuesday, April 9, the British ships were cruising on a level with Bergen, when the German planes dived down and a 1,000-pound bomb struck the *Rodney*. Her heavy deck armament stood up and she remained undamaged. The same day, far to the north, the great battle cruiser *Renown,* one of the five heaviest and fastest ships then engaged in the war, plunged through snow squalls and sighted the 26,000-ton

Scharnhorst and the 10,000-ton *Admiral Hipper,* two prides of the Nazi fleet. The *Renown* opened fire at 18,000 yards. Hits on the forward structure of the *Scharnhorst* were observed. The latter stopped firing, then fled. The *Renown* took up the chase at twenty-four knots, firing intermittently. She finally stopped when the Germans were last seen nearly eighteen miles away.

The struggle for Norway unfolded when more sea, air, and land battles raged during the next days and Allied forces made desperate efforts to dislocate the invaders. The fierce battle within the Skagerrak appeared to have ended with the dispersal of a German convoy of troopships. Many German transports went down, either sunk by shellfire or by mines. Hundreds of Germans were seen struggling in the water, and the bodies washed up on shore indicated the extent of loss of life. The action had virtually severed the German line of communication between Denmark and Norway where the Nazi troops were temporarily left isolated.

To make up for the reverses they had suffered, the Germans rushed troops to Norway from Denmark by transport planes. It was disclosed that Bergen and Trondheim were still, or again, in German hands. The Nazis advanced some seventy miles inland along the fjord, occupying the Norwegian military training center of Innaroa and virtually cutting the country in two as far as Hel, only twelve miles from the frontier. At Bergen, which the Norwegians claimed to have captured, eight German troopships arrived with several regiments of soldiers and large quantities of war material.

Norwegian resistance hardened as the Nazis seemed to have established two fronts: the first running along the Oslo Fjord where some coastal fortifications were still holding out, stretching from Frederickstad northward to Elverum; the second extending from Trondheim and centering on Roeros where heavy Norwegian forces were concentrated for attack. They blew up roads and bridges leading into the southern part of the country. There was heavy fighting on the southern front around Lake Mjosa, Loatan Forest, and Mysen.

The Nazis rushed to Elverum in an effort to capture King Haakon. The monarch's whereabouts were unknown, but the Government was reported isolated east of Kale Mjosa. Crown Prince Olav remained with the King. Crown Princess Martha and her three children had succeeded in safely crossing the Norwegian frontier into Sweden before the onslaught.

On Saturday, April 13, the Norwegian High Command issued the first communiqué since the invasion. It was declared that the 26,000-ton German battleship *Gneisenau* and the 5,400-ton cruiser *Emden* had been sunk in Oslo Fjord. Other reports indicated that there were seven German warships in Oslo harbor, bottled up by British Naval forces, and that the Nazis were landing 4,000 soldiers in Norway every day by the use of 200 transport planes.

England, meanwhile, announced the biggest mining operations in naval history: a mine field extending 420 miles from the Netherlands coast near Terschelling to a point sixty miles southwest of Bergen in Norway, blocking the Skagerrak and Kattegat and cutting the North Sea in two. The Germans termed this a "defensive measure."

The British Admiralty reported that a striking force of the British Navy had forced its way into Narvik Harbor at noon where seven German destroyers were shattered and sunk. The action was under the command of Vice Admiral W. J. Whitworth whose flag flew from the battleship *Warspite*. General Nikolaus von Falkenhorst, commander of the German Army in Norway, faced with continuous resistance of the population, broadcast an ultimatum to the Norwegian King and the people, threatening to impose the death penalty on everyone who would resist the invasion or obey the mobilization order of the Government of Premier Nygaardsvold. The King replied with a proclamation in which he ignored all German efforts at negotiations with him, and called upon the Norwegian people: "Stand firm and continue the fight for the country's freedom and independence."

The next phase in the German struggle for the mastery of Norway developed near Oslo. The defenders had thrown a semicircular ring around the city's eastern outskirts, extending from Romerike in the north to Holen in the south. The Germans advanced against this circle on April 14, and their offensive led to substantial successes. They pushed the Norwegians, who were assisted by hurriedly assembled guerrilla volunteers, as far back as Honefoss and Jevnaker in the north, seized Eidsvoll in the northeast, and drove the defenders beyond the Vormen River. They took, in heavy fighting on the eastern side of Oslo Fjord near the Swedish border, the towns of Moss, Sarpsborg, Frederickstad, and Halden. On the western side of Oslo Fjord, they occupied Kongsberg and then struck to the Skagerrak coast with the capture of Larvik.

The picture changed on April 15, when the British disclosed that their troops had landed at several points along the Norwegian coast and had captured Narvik. Berlin conceded the loss of the port, minimizing its importance. Coöperation between the Allies and the Norwegians was increasing rapidly, but the Nazis never lost their foothold around Oslo where they consolidated their positions and pushed down to the Swedish border. A bloody battle was fought at Kongsvinger which the Nazis took. In the north, by a ruse, they rode on a train from east of Trondheim past a Norwegian fortress and across the country to the Swedish border, thereby establishing contact with the Swedish iron-ore fields.

The Royal Navy answered an urgent call for help from the invaded country by racing close to Stavanger where the German-occupied airport was bombarded on April 18. But the Nazis retaliated with attacks on units of the British fleet from their newly won airports and claimed to have hit seven vessels. With the invaders firmly established on Oslo Fjord, they bolstered their lines from Trondheim where the British had made contact with the Norwegians and the first real battle between the opposing forces developed.

British forces had landed near Namsos. Driving south from there, they defeated a "death battalion" of Germans in their first engagement on Norwegian soil. The Nazis rushed reinforcements with howitzers, automatic guns, and machine guns north to the vicinity of Trondheim but, at least for the moment, their advance was checked there. In Narvik, where the Germans were beleaguered, the British also held the initiative. The landing forces were estimated at three divisions; two British, including Canadians, and one French, altogether approximately 50,000 men, about the equal of the estimated German force in the country.

Unfortunately, the British failed to reach their ultimate goal. According to the War Office in London they "achieved considerable success" and surprised the Germans by their swift advance. But the Nazis repeated their performance of the Polish campaign and applied to their Norwegian invasion aërial blitzkrieg methods which destroyed important strategic points and disrupted Allied communications. With the outcome very much in doubt, two major battles developed: one in the neighborhood of Trondheim, the other north of Oslo. Berlin, for the first time, conceded on April 23 that there was fighting between German and Allied forces in Norway.

A crucial battle was fought in a rectangle formed by Lillehammer, Rena, Elverum, and Hamar. The Allies, moving down east of Lake Mjosa, reached Moelv while the Nazis, moving up west of the lake, claimed Lillehammer. Depending on their strength, there was danger on either side of being cut off in this region.

During the next twenty-four hours there was a deadlock in this sector where the Allies had concentrated some 17,000 troops but were unable to meet German air supremacy. They could not establish a sufficiently strong air base and for this reason suffered a major setback. North of Trondheim the Nazis inflicted a defeat on the British at Steinkjer, and after they had bombed the railway between Andalsnes and Dombaas, they advanced rapidly toward Roeros.

In a swift surprise move, after having been stopped north of Roeros by a blown-up bridge, the Germans turned westward and in a daring thrust menaced the Allied positions before Trondheim. To achieve this, they had used snow-covered mountain passes and undefended trails.

Their flanking move after two days of fierce fighting developed into a five-pronged attack for the control of the railroad and highways between Stoeren in the north and Dombaas in the south.

Against this line the Allies still stood firm on April 29, but the next day the important railway junction at Dombaas fell to the Germans. The Nazi High Command announced that a German column, smashing south from Trondheim to a point southwest of Stoeren had united the Reich's forces in the Trondheim and Oslo zones. It was a decisive German victory. In a jubilant proclamation Chancellor Hitler said: "Inexorable advance of German troops has conclusively nullified the Allies' efforts to beat Germany to her knees on the Scandinavian battlefront." General von Falkenhorst, Nazi commander in Norway, was awarded one of Germany's highest orders, the Chevalier's Cross of the Iron Cross.

The Allied forces had been thrown back to their original landing places which were severely bombed by the Luftwaffe. Smashing their beachheads and holding the Allied navy at a distance, the Nazis followed on the heels of the retreating troops. This ended any chance of an Allied offensive not only against Trondheim but also against Oslo. Namsos was bombed by German planes for ten hours.

The critical position of the Allied forces in Norway brought suggestions from London and Paris regarding the advisability of giving up the fight in southern Norway, and instead, concentrating on Narvik and cutting off Germany's iron ore from that port. Parallels were drawn with the failure to land on Gallipoli and force the Dardenelles in the First World War. Moreover, it was feared that the Allies had failed to demonstrate to the world, especially to Italy and the Balkans, that they were prepared to give quick help to an attacked country.

The blitzkrieg phase of the Norwegian campaign came to an end on May 2. The Allies bowed to their defeat and surrendered all of central and southern Norway to the Germans. They evacuated Andalsnes and other southern landing bases south of Steinkjer, thereby leaving to the victor the bulk and heart of the country, its most important towns, railroad, and industrial centers, and most of its population. Evacuation of Namsos followed on May 3, when Allied forces which had landed there three weeks before withdrew.

Despite this defeat, the Norwegian Government issued a communiqué to the effect that the fighting spirit of the Norwegian people had not been weakened and that the war would go on. Surrender of the Troendelag section had opened another stretch of the country to the Germans, who extended their hold up to Mosjoeen, Mo, and Bodoe. But northward of Bodoe a natural barrier blocked the German advance, and in that area, which can be reached only by air or sea, the King and his Government found refuge. From there they directed, with Allied help, the final phase of Norway's resistance to Nazi conquest.

The Allies were determined to drive the Germans out of Narvik. British fleet units engaged in the bombardment of the stronghold on May 4, and the Battle of Narvik lasted for another thirty-eight days. Reinforcements were rushed north by both sides on or about May 10, and the Nazis started their attack on the Lowlands. Allied forces were reported closing in on Narvik on May 16, and the fall of the German garrison was expected momentarily. The Germans had been pushed back into the mountains. Their shore batteries, guarding the port, were destroyed by British naval guns, but the Nazis had sworn to hold their positions to the last man in the defense of their Norwegian "Alcazar." Over the mountains from Bodoe they sent a detachment of ski troops; parachute landings were out of the question. General Otto Ruge was in command of the Norwegian forces still in action.

Narvik fell when Norwegian, British, French, and Polish troops, supported by Allied warships, launched a double offensive against the town from both the north and the south. Norwegian troops crossed Rombaks Fjord and Polish units forced their way across Beis Fjord. Seven German troop transports were sunk in Narvik waters, and 4,000 Allied troops were engaged in the battle that lasted twenty-four hours. The Nazis admitted the port's loss.

The Germans, however, had fortified themselves in seven mountain tunnels above Narvik, and the struggle continued unabatingly. The Allies started an offensive against the main German forces that had concentrated inland and, at the same time, tried to cut off the retreat of the Nazis who had been driven out of the town.

On Sunday, June 2, eleven German bombers swooped down on Narvik and destroyed it by fire after a terrific air bombardment. Five days later, Allied and Norwegian forces reported new gains along the Narvik railway—their last.

Hardly twelve hours later the war in the north ended abruptly. The Nazis had completed their conquest of Norway. The Norwegian Government stated on June 10 that Allied forces had been withdrawn from the Narvik area. King Haakon, Crown Prince Olav, and the Norwegian Government had left the country to carry on the war on other fronts. Norwegian negotiators were on their way to German headquarters to work out an armistice agreement for the surrender of the remaining Norwegian troops. A Norwegian declaration stated: "Necessity of the war forced the Allies to gather all their forces on other fronts where all soldiers and all materials are necessary." Two months from the day Germany had started her treacherous invasion of Norway that country was in her grasp.

The British Admiralty admitted that five British Naval vessels, including two destroyers and the 22,500-ton aircraft carrier *Glorious*, were sunk during the final evacuation of Allied troops from Narvik which was carried out with "the full knowledge and understanding of King Haakon."

In the evening of June 10, at five minutes to ten, a tall, melancholy figure stepped from a train at Euston Station into a dim, blacked-out London. It was King Haakon, then in his sixty-eighth year. He was accompanied by his son, Crown Prince Olav. Ever since the Nazi occupation of Oslo, the King had been hunted across his country by the invaders. Silently King Haakon shook hands with his nephew, King George of England, who was there to greet the royal refugees and offer them a temporary home in Buckingham Palace, where already another European monarch, Queen Wilhelmina of the Netherlands, had taken refuge.

The Norwegian King immediately signed a Government proclamation to his people, stating that since the Government must be maintained free and independent under all conditions, the Storting had decided on Friday, June 7, that it should be moved outside the country. Norway's British, French, and Polish allies, it was asserted, had rendered "generous help" to Norway, but had been forced to remove their help because of "the hard necessity of the war elsewhere."

Immediately after their invasion, the Nazis had set to work to establish a new Norwegian government dominated by Berlin. Their efforts failed miserably. The German attempt to introduce Nazi doctrines to a free, proud, and independent nation was rejected by the vast majority of Norwegians. The traitors in their own ranks were branded by the patriotic people as the country's arch-enemies. The name of Norway's puppet leader, Quisling, became synonymous with treachery, ignominy, and insult throughout the world. "Quislingism" stands for the rule of political gangsters.

Vidkun Abraham Lauritz Quisling, who was to be the tool of the Nazi experiment in Norway, was born in 1887, in a remote parish in southern Norway, the son of a minister. When Hitler had come to power in Germany, Quisling founded the Nasjonal Samling, the Union Party, copied meticulously after the Nazi pattern. In his newspaper *Fritt Folk* (Free People), supposed to be "an organ for Norway's working folk," he took up Hitler's slogans and doctrines, but in the elections of 1933 and 1936 he could not obtain even two per cent of the votes and had no representatives in the Storting. After the outbreak of World War II, Quisling became very active, however. He visited Germany, became acquainted with the Nazi inner circle, became a friend of Alfred Rosenberg, and had interviews with Hitler.

A self-confessed traitor, Quisling admitted that the attack on Norway had been prepared beforehand. He was a party to the Nazi attack and helped prepare its plans during his visit to Germany in December, 1939. His almost forgotten party suddenly came to the fore again, and *Fritt Folk,* previously a single sheet and published only spasmodically, appeared as a full-size daily paper in March, 1940. It was established that Quisling visited Hitler three days before the invasion.

During the night of the invasion Quisling had awaited the Germans in the Hotel Continental in Oslo where the Nazis later installed their general headquarters. There, too, were Albert Viljam Hagelin, later to become Quisling's Minister for the Interior, Birger Oivind Meidell, afterward his Minister for Social Affairs, others of his followers, and a few dozens of the Hird, Quislings Storm Troopers. In the course of the day, as soon as the King and his Government had left the capital, Quisling proclaimed himself Prime Minister. He declared the Nygaardsvold Government dissolved and canceled the mobilization order.

The formation of a Quisling government had a devastating effect upon the population. Received with hatred and humiliation, it created chaos in the civil administration. The people were stunned, and business became paralyzed and trade came to a standstill. The Germans were embarrassed, and the German High Command faced a peculiar situation, a Norwegian government that had no influence whatsoever with the people. Berlin insisted that Quisling must be recognized as Prime Minister. Four days later his prestige was shattered. When he dismissed the head of the Oslo police on April 12, the Germans merely informed the latter to disregard the order. Another three days and the German High Command threw Quisling, his cabinet, and his Storm Troopers out of the Hotel Continental. So abruptly was he dismissed that once more his political career seemed ended. He continued, though, with the obscure title of "Commissioner for Demobilization."

Berlin on April 24 announced "unrestricted German control" over the occupied areas of Norway. A system similar to that in conquered Poland was proclaimed. Hitler appointed Josef Terboven, forty-two-year-old *Gauleiter* (district leader) of Essen and publisher of Field Marshal Goering's *Essener National Zeitung, Reichskommissar* for the Norwegian occupied territories. It was the Reich's scheme for complete Nazi domination, as Terboven's appointment carried supreme authority of government. He was assisted by a German administrative staff, the *Reichskommissariat.* All forms of Norwegian administration, the Administrative Council, public organizations, the Bank of Norway, and other groups were forced to work under German rule.

Hitler demanded on June 13 that the Storting be summoned to depose the King and Government and that a new "constitutional" government be formed. The German ultimatum was followed by threats that all Norwegians of military age would be conscripted for military service or sent to prison camps in Germany. The ultimatum was rejected. Five days later the Germans forced the Norwegian representatives to sign an appeal to King Haakon to abdicate and to his Government to resign. King and Government refused to comply.

Suddenly, Terboven dropped all negotiations. In accordance with Nazi usage, he applied the dictatorial method to solve the riddle of Norway's "government." In a radio speech to the Norwegian people on September 25, he dissolved all parties except Quisling's own, dethroned the King, deposed the Nygaardsvold Government, dismissed the Administrative Council, and proclaimed establishment of a "Quisling Cabinet," consisting of thirteen "acting Councillors of State," each nominally in charge of his respective government department.

Quisling himself was not included in this "cabinet," presumably because this would have been too much of a challenge to public opinion in Norway. But he remained the head of his party which, by another Terboven decree issued the same day, became the "State Party" for whose benefit all other political parties had to surrender their funds and properties.

Thus, by a stroke of the pen, the invaders had invested all power in an obscure political party of traitors which Quisling himself, before the invasion, had estimated at only 15,000 members, a liberal figure that included the entire family of any one member. Of these but ten per cent had followed the call of the "leader," a clear indication that they did not know what was going on.

Terboven, by forcing upon the country the *Diktat* of the conquerors, was figuratively sitting on a keg of dynamite. A united populace was ready to leash a régime of terror against the oppressors. Quisling discovered that his own bayonets were too "hot to sit upon," so in January, 1941, he appealed to the Germans, because opposition to the Nasjonal Samling had become so strong that there was the risk of complete collapse of the Quisling Party without active German support. Thereupon Terboven declared that the German police and armed forces would help the Quislings to crush the opposition of the people. The commissioner for the Reich promised to his Norwegian henchmen arms, protection of their meetings, and personal safety.

Quisling's political career reached a climax on February 1, 1942, when Terboven, in a sudden move, proclaimed him Premier of Norway. The new title did not change his status as a puppet. The ceremony at which Terboven spoke was symbolical. It took place in the sixteenth-century Akershus fort of Oslo which the Germans had been using as a military headquarters and on the ramparts of which they were executing Norwegians sentenced by Nazi court-martial. "On behalf of the Norwegian people," Quisling thanked Reichsfuehrer Hitler and Terboven for "the understanding they have shown for the deepest desire of the Norwegian people."

But Quisling's rule continued to be an empty shell. Acts of sabotage increased and were followed by new methods of terror. It was evident that the "New Order" in Norway would break down the minute the Germans removed their armed guard around it. In October, 1942, the Nazi puppet premier was reported to have told Chancellor Hitler that he would be unable to continue in office unless the excesses of the Gestapo torture and execution squads were checked immediately.

The Norwegian Government-in-exile made Major Vidkun Quisling its World Enemy No. 1. Heading a list of 1,000 names, he was charged with, among other things, selling out his country and preparing the groundwork for the Nazi invasion. This was followed by a decree of January 5, 1943, that deprived 30,000 Axis collaborators in Norway of their citizenship and the right to carry on a trade, business, or profession after the war. Known as the Loss of Public Trust Act, it applied in particular to all members of the Quisling Party.

Disregarding law and justice upon which Norway's existence was founded, brushing aside the cultural standard of the Norse people, an entire nation, practically overnight, was subjugated to tortures as only vandals could apply them.

Terboven, in a speech in Oslo's University Square on October 4, 1941, on the occasion of the harvest thanksgiving, said that it was a matter of complete indifference to him "if some thousands or perhaps tens of thousands" of Norwegian men, women, and children starved or froze to death.

Norwegians continued to defy Nazi domination. As public demonstrations were forbidden by the Gestapo, one way of expressing the people's feelings was by "silent" opposition. On the anniversaries of the invasion, "silence" strikes were arranged throughout the country. The day before the strike, thousands of leaflets appeared, especially in Oslo, asking the people to stay home between 2:00 and 3:00 P.M. and show themselves as little as possible in public on that day. Consequently, the bewildered Nazis and Quislings had the streets to themselves.

Active opposition ran from acts of sabotage, prompted by engendered hatred, to actual killings brought about by the grim experience of the Nazi attack upon the country. Both measures became sanctified in the eyes of Norwegians.

The greatest sabotage deed occurred on the night of November 25-26, 1940, when the hills and mountains in western Norway began to slide at the same hour. These landslides were part of a secret plan to defy the Germans. Rains and snowfalls had melted the ground sufficiently to cause disaster; only slight charges of dynamite were necessary to make it effective. The Oslo-Bergen railway was disrupted in ten places; a week was required to repair it. The Riks highway along the Hardanger and Eids Fjords was completely destroyed.

Similar ingenious acts brought about a wave of terrorism in the German occupation. They reached a climax on two occasions: in September, 1941, when Oslo was placed under martial law, and in October, 1942, when a state of emergency was proclaimed in Trondheim. In the first instance of German revenge half a million Norwegians became virtual prisoners.

The terror at Trondheim was an orgy of blood. Prominent and innocent Norwegians were taken as hostages and executed. All their property was confiscated. The murders climaxed a steadily growing tension between the Germans and the Quisling Storm Troopers on the one side and the Norwegian population on the other.

The Nazis took to new measures in 1943 which were even more diabolical than anything experienced heretofore. One of the schemes provided for the arrest and deportation to war prison camps in Germany of all Norwegian officers who had been "out on parole" since May 10, 1940. Their round-up began immediately. Some 1,500 officers were deported.

Higher police officials in Oslo were dismissed. Gunnar Ailifsen, police chief of an Oslo suburb, was executed when he refused to participate in the arrest of Norwegian women failing to report for Nazi slave duty in the Reich's war industries. Jonas Lie, Police Minister of the Quislings, bluntly informed the police force of the execution, declaring: "The same fate will overtake every policeman disloyal to the occupation power."

Imprisonment in jails and concentration camps became the "order of the day." The number of prisoners in Norwegian jails, which amounted roughly to 1,000 before the invasion, was estimated at about 7,000 at the height of terror. There were in addition, thousands who were deported to internment camps and forced labor camps in Germany and Poland. Among these was the sixty-year-old Rector of Oslo University, Doctor Seip. Intellectuals were arrested and sent for forced manual labor to the far north of Norway. Six hundred and fifty Norwegian teachers who had opposed the Nazi régime of terror were deported as dock laborers to Kirkenes on the Finnish frontier. Many brave Norwegians died in concentration camps because of tortures and maltreatment to which they were subjugated. No announcement of these deaths was made by the Nazis until long afterward, and all cases were falsely attributed to "natural causes."

Cruel methods of punishment were adopted by the Nazis in Norway. After the first Allied raid on the Lofoten Islands, the homes of seventy islanders were burned to the ground and their occupants were forced to stand in the snow and watch their houses burn. All houses were destroyed in the village of Televaag on the island of Sotra near Bergen, after the shooting of two Gestapo men in a gun battle with Norwegian patriots. The entire population of the village was rounded up. Male members were deported to German concentration camps. Women and children were interned in a school at Bergen. Although there were only 1,400 "full" Jews in pre-war Norway, the property of all Norwegian Jews, including so-called "half" and "quarter" Jews, was confiscated. All "full" Jews were arrested and deported to Poland.

The Norwegian Church, in October, 1940, had established a "Christian Council for Joint Deliberation" under the leadership of the seven bishops in Norway. The bishops issued a pastoral letter in February, 1941, condemning the Nazi attacks on the church. This, despite a Nazi ban, was widely read and distributed by "chain letters" throughout the country.

The ensuing fight of the clergy culminated in a struggle between Quisling and the church. In March, 1942, an official in Quisling's Church Ministry declared at a lecture in Oslo University that infamous Quisling was Norway's "first bishop." He sacrilegiously proclaimed that Quisling was planning the creation of a "new Norwegian Christianity based on race and *Lebensraum*."

While the "Quisling clergy" continued to function under Gestapo supervision, loyal churchmen formed the Interim Church Council to handle the affairs of the Norwegian State Church independently.

Nazi attack on education and public schools was equally iniquitous. The Hitlerian creed made education a crime to be stamped out. Ninety per cent of all Norwegian school teachers went on strike in February, 1941, as a protest against interference with teachings and educational methods. A decree was issued compelling all children from ten to eighteen years to enter the Nazi youth movement for physical training, labor service, and training for membership in the Quisling Party— 12,000 of the 14,000 teachers of the country refused to coöperate.

Quisling decreed that the rebellious teachers would lose pay and pensions and be sent to compulsory labor camps in the Arctic Circle. The schoolmasters stood fast and the schools were closed. Mass arrests of teachers followed and many were sent to camps and forced to work for the occupation authorities. Thirteen thousand teachers had already been imprisoned when Terboven announced that he would break the schoolmasters' resistance. Seven hundred more were shipped to camps, but they managed to smuggle out circulars begging parents to stand fast. Appeals by the clergy were ignored. Very few of the country's 400,000 children could return to school for there were either no teachers or the Nazis had turned schools into barracks and hospitals.

The University of Oslo was closed in December, 1943, after the Germans had arrested 1,200 professors and students, men and women alike, and deported them to Reich concentration camps. The Norwegian Government protested to Berlin, but received a brusque answer from

Foreign Minister von Ribbentrop. In the first year of Nazi occupation the Norwegian Supreme Court resigned, its members refusing to bow to a Quisling decree which could arbitrarily appoint and dismiss judges. Practically all Norwegian judges and the Norwegian Law Society supported this resignation. Quisling judges took over the Supreme Court. A so-called "People's Court" was set up to pass sentence on political prisoners. In February, 1942, the Nasjonal Samling established an independent court for trying its own members.

Press and radio were brought under strict Nazi censorship, as in other countries held in captivity. Many Norwegian journalists and editors were arrested. By February, 1941, the country's 350 newspapers had been reduced to 280. This Nazi-sponsored press deliberately distorted all news, or suppressed it. It was the Underground press that kept the people informed. The number of such secret sheets circulating throughout Norway was estimated at 300.

The Norwegian Government in London placed at the disposal of the Allies whatever it could muster in the way of merchantmen, fighting ships, and sailors—6,000 officers and men and a largely increased naval force that took part in convoying, patroling, and mine-sweeping. Norsemen, who escaped their homeland by the thousands, were trained in Scotland and participated in every large Commando raid. The Norwegian Air Force had two squadrons serving with the R.A.F. and another in Iceland. Hundreds of fliers trained at "Little Norway," a base near Toronto, Canada.

In the Battle of the Atlantic, Free Norwegians played their greatest part. In a ceaseless effort to supply Britain and the other Allied theaters of war, 25,000 Norse sailors did their duty regardless of the risks. A 4,000,000-ton fleet carried food, oil, airplanes, weapons, and ammunition wherever they were needed. The Norwegian tanker fleet was rebuilt and became one of the fastest and most modern in the world. It brought daily nearly half of Britain's total supplies in oil and gasoline to England. The British stated that this tanker fleet was worth more to democracy than an army of 1,000,000 men.

When Premier Johan Nygaardsvold visited the United States in 1942, the parliamentarian, who was then sixty-three years old, estimated that of the 2,900,000 Norwegians remaining at the home front, 95 per cent actively supported the Allies; 3 per cent were passive; and 2 per cent were Quislings. Three facts, he said, had inspired him and his Government-in-exile to carry on the fight against the Nazis: first, the unbreakable will of the British to see this struggle through to the bitter end; second, the firm attitude of the United States and President Roosevelt to challenge the Nazi attempt at world domination; and, third, the unyielding courage with which the Norwegians on the home front stood up against their oppressors.

15

BELGIUM IN PATH OF THE BLITZKRIEG

THIRTY days after the Germans invaded Denmark and Norway the Juggernaut rolled into Belgium, Holland, and Luxembourg on the road to France. On May 10, 1940, little Belgium, not much larger than New Hampshire but the most densely populated country in Europe, was ground under the wheels of the conquerors.

On the direct road between Berlin and Paris, the 8,500,000 Belgians were in the path of the invaders. Three times in the course of seventy years they had been the victims of aggression. It was here, too, 125 years before, that Napoleon met defeat at Waterloo. Where his conquest of Europe ended, Hitler's attempted conquest of the world was in its beginning.

The roar of guns and the crash of bombs shattered the serenity of the spring morning in these blossoming garden lands. Great fleets of German planes sowed death over these peace-loving countries, unloading their cargoes of bombs and parachutists.

Germany's pledges were once more brushed aside as the "scraps of paper" they had been termed in World War I. The Treaty of Versailles gave Belgium a free hand to direct her foreign policy. In the interest of self-protection she had concluded a defensive alliance with France. The Locarno Pact acknowledged abrogation of the treaties for Belgium's neutralization. France, England, and Belgium had confirmed this in an agreement signed at Paris. Her international status, moreover, was explicitly defined in the Covenant of the League of Nations and the Kellogg Pact.

Belgium felt the first repercussions of Nazism at the time of the Saar plebiscite in 1935, when German agitators urged the return of Eupen and Malmedy (assigned to Belgium by the League of Nations in 1925) to the Reich. Her anxiety grew when Hitler denounced the Locarno Pact and the Reichswehr occupied the Rhineland. Following that crisis, Britain, France, and Belgium, for the first time since 1914, held staff conferences in London in the spring of 1936.

However, three years before World War II, Belgium abandoned her post-war position and returned to her old policy of neutrality. It meant the end of the Franco-Belgian alliance and withdrew Belgium from collective action and any new Locarno Pact that was to be concluded. "Alliances, even defensive ones," declared King Leopold in announcing the new policy, "would not serve us because, prompt as we may be, aid could not reach us before the first shock of the invader, which might be overpowering and against which we must be prepared to fight alone."

On August 26, 1939, a few days before the Nazis launched their attack on Poland, Vicco von Buelow-Schwante, German Ambassador to Brussels, was received by King Leopold. Stressing the validity of the German note of October 13, 1937, the German envoy reassured the monarch that in the event of war the Reich would respect Belgian neutrality. The King believed him. He put his trust in Germany only to become a victim of his own sincerity.

War came without warning before dawn on May 10, 1940, simultaneously with the German attack on Holland and Luxembourg. The invaders crossed the Belgian frontier at four points. German planes flew over Brussels and bombed the airport and damaged the airfield at Antwerp. Parachute troops landed at Hasselt in eastern Belgium and at Nivelles and Saint Trond in the vicinity of the capital. Antiaircraft batteries went into action immediately and kept up a steady barrage.

London, that day, was in the midst of a Cabinet crisis with Prime Minister Neville Chamberlain, seventy-one-year-old chief exponent of appeasement, likely to fall. For a moment, it looked as if the Nazi blow in the Low Countries would save him. The German onslaught, however, delayed his resignation only for twenty-four hours.

While it was obvious that Adolf Hitler took advantage of the British Cabinet crisis, there was little evidence to indicate that the attack would occur that very day. Linked to the political situation was the desire of the Nazi Government to finish the war before the end of 1940 even at the risk of a gamble. The Germans knew that they had superiority in men and machines. They knew, too, that the only way to win this war, if at all, was by blitzkrieg. They were convinced that they were able to hold France at bay behind her own Maginot Line, which it was folly to assume could be broken by a frontal attack despite Hitler's declaration that he was ready to sacrifice 1,000,000 men to achieve this.

With the Lowlands safely in the hands of the Germans, France would be outflanked. With their armies solidified in Holland and Belgium, the Germans could decide on either of two things: turn against Britain, blockade her and starve her into submission; or eliminate England from the continental battlefield and turn with all their armored might against a trembling France.

Hitler's immediate aim was France, where Paul Reynaud executed power without a working majority. The French Premier summoned his Cabinet Ministers to an early conference while Parisians and the rest of France were still unaware of the immediate danger. The same situation prevailed in London, where Admiral Sir Dudley Pound, leaving 10 Downing Street, remarked to a policeman: "Well, the war has started now."

Next day Churchill took over. And Allied armies once more rushed across Belgium in a life-and-death struggle with the invading Germans. Hitler had made it clear that it was not up to neutral nations to decide their destiny; that people within striking range of Nazi power were no longer able to remain neutral even if they had scrupulously observed the rules of neutrality; and that one by one they had to expect the fate of Denmark, Norway, Czechoslovakia, and Poland.

The German attack was planned on the largest possible scale. The Fuehrer went to his headquarters on the Western Front whence the first Nazi communiqué on the drive was issued on May 10. It revealed that Hitler was to direct the attack personally.

What the Wehrmacht was facing in Belgium was a maximum of 700,000 to 850,000 trained Belgian troops (roughly twenty-one divisions), a country weak in the air and with fortifications designed to retard an invader rather than halt him.

The line of the river Meuse, anchored at two strong points, Liége and Namur, was planned as the country's main defense line against an invasion from the east. Strong pillboxes protected the Hervé Plateau and the terrain of the Ardennes Forest in the southeast. Antitank fences and all sorts of tank obstacles were built to obstruct the roads and protect principal strategical parts of the frontiers.

Against this set-up the Germans put into operation the so-called von Epp plan, a modification of the Schlieffen plan that foresaw disposing of the Netherlands in twenty-four hours. They had twenty-nine divisions on the march. They left no doubt that they were marching "nach Paris," flanking the Maginot Line to attack the Allied armies from the rear.

The French realized the danger. They knew that this was France's battle for which they had waited eight months. Though the Belgians and Dutch in observing their neutrality had declined to hold staff conferences with the Allies, French Army leaders were preparing for this eventuality. General Maurice Gustave Gamelin became supreme commander of military operations. He gave the keynote to all troops in his general order:

"The attack which we have been anticipating since October was launched this morning. Germany has engaged against us in a struggle to the death. The watchword for France and all her allies is: Courage, energy, confidence!"

Little Belgium overnight became part of the Allied war machine. King Leopold assumed command of the Belgian Armies and directed resistance to the invading forces. The Belgian Government issued an appeal to the population to preserve calm and to spot sabotage. Full mobilization took place. Bridges and roads were blown up to prevent the first German advance, and the country's flood system of sluices was put into operation.

Declaring that "Belgium is innocent and with the help of God shall triumph," King Leopold issued a proclamation that read in part: "For the second time in a quarter of a century Belgium, an honest neutral in her conduct, has been attacked by the German Reich, which treats with contempt the most solemn pledges.... The Belgian people are peace-loving and have done all they can to avoid this fate. But when it is a question of sacrifice or dishonor, the Belgian in 1940 will hesitate no more than his father did in 1914."

After the first day of battle the Belgians reported that the Nazis were halted. Defense Minister Lieutenant General Henri Denis told a cheering House of Deputies that "traps, barricades, blown-up bridges and roads" had stopped the Nazi invasion army. French and British liaison officers arrived at Brussels, which was severely bombed from the air. Heavily equipped British and French troops crossed the Belgian border and were enthusiastically received on their way to undisclosed destinations. Luxembourg, unable to put up any resistance, was quickly overrun by the Nazis. Their motorized columns made for the French frontier.

The German offensive quickly developed in two directions: the invaders breached the Albert Canal defenses between Hasselt and Maastricht on May 12, and their advance forces penetrated as far as Waremme, thirteen miles past Liége. In the south, Belgian troops were forced to withdraw from their first lines of resistance. Nazi units that had crossed Luxembourg approached Neufchateau, aiming for the Montmedy bridgehead. But the Belgians counterattacked in the Maastricht region and violent battles raged along the strongly fortified Albert Canal.

Meanwhile, French troops had reached the front lines. Their armored columns counterattacked brilliantly north of Liége where they met the Nazis in a clash of 1,500 tanks. More forts of that citadel fell to the invaders and savage fighting raged all along the front. While the main bodies of the German and Allied forces had not come to grips on the fifth day of the Nazi offensive, the preliminaries for a full-scale battle were completed with the front line running in the shape of a huge L between Luxembourg, France, and Belgium. Its base was south of the border, its angle at the French towns of Mezieres and Charleville. From there the line ran northward into Belgium along Dinant and Namur.

A new Battle of the Meuse was developing on a 150-mile front. It extended on Belgian and French soil and engulfed cities and towns laid waste by the Imperial German Army in its push toward Paris in the early stages of World War I. As compared with then, Hitler's forces, in striking at Namur, were eleven days ahead of the Kaiser's schedule. In 1914, it took the Germans sixteen days to reach Namur.

Brussels was threatened again. So was Antwerp. The Germans pushed on with amazing speed, blasting a path for their motorized units by employing 6,000 to 7,000 planes. Under their unprecedented mass bombings civilians tried to flee from Belgium into France, as the Dutch population along the Belgian border had tried to escape into Belgium before the Netherlands were cut off by the German advance.

A mass migration set in that was likewise unprecedented in the history of modern warfare. It choked the roads to the battlefronts, hampering communications, delaying advances of troops and interfering generally with strategic plans. Moreover, these fleeing masses offered welcome targets for low-flying, reckless German machine gunners. It all aggravated the military situation which, though confused, presented itself on May 14, as follows:

According to a strategic French plan, Sedan was abandoned to massed Nazi land and air forces smashing across the border. The French met the assault east of Sedan in the Longwy-Moselle sector where fierce fighting raged inside and around Longwy. They also stopped the attackers in the Forbach sector below the Saar and in the Wissembourg sector to the east of the turn of the Rhine.

Striking southwest of Liége the Germans had reached the Meuse between Namur and Dinant. They then swung southward in a wide arc south of Charleroi and broke into France north of Verdun. Twenty miles south of Namur, above Charleville and Mezieres, they attacked in force the Belgian forts, some of which had fallen the previous day, and obtained a hold at Givet, the French salient jutting into Belgium.

Farther north, the historic city of Louvain was threatened, as motorized Nazi units had broken through the Albert Canal defenses into the Tuenhout sector. This constituted an immediate danger to Brussels, seventeen miles to the west, as well as to Antwerp, thirty miles to the northwest.

The Allies were concentrating their positions west of the Meuse. "The enemy is making a momentous effort with furious obstinacy and at the cost of heavy casualties" read the communiqué of the Allied High Command, forecasting the gravity of the impending battle, the Battle of Flanders, one of the fiercest in history. The Germans had set the stage for it. Their bid for victory, so far, had been successful, but the issue was still in doubt.

A great battle fluctuated on a sixty-mile front along the river Meuse from Namur to Sedan on May 16. German might struck terrific blows, but they were met by fierce Allied resistance. By nightfall the Nazis had crossed the Meuse River at three points and penetrated Allied positions on the left bank. Their most spectacular gain was south of Sedan, where they advanced into the outer fortifications of the Maginot Line on a four-mile front. The French rushed reserves into the pocket and in heavy counterattacks were able to reduce its size.

To meet the onslaught of the *Panzerdivisionen,* they abandoned the war of position for a campaign of swift movement. Thus the battle spread over the western part of the Flanders plain. Its speed slowed down the next day and fighting was chiefly confined to the air when the Germans brought up reinforcements while the R.A.F. and French planes bombed them again and again. Both sides consolidated their positions, but despite these reports, not unfavorable to the Allies, Premier Reynaud told the French the situation was serious. Paris and its environs were declared a military area.

The Germans struck along the whole western front from the Netherlands border to the northern anchor of the Maginot Line at the Luxembourg corner on May 17. They penetrated against British and Belgian troops to the outlying forts of Antwerp, and occupied Malines and Louvain. Their advance units had reached Brussels. In the south they had broken through the French fortifications along the French-Belgian border and dashed into France as far as Le Cateau, La Capelle, and Rethal on a sixty-two-mile front.

German tactics followed the pattern of the Polish campaign. The Nazis launched giant tank attacks. The British, in a desperate attempt to stem the advance, did likewise. But inferior in strength, they were forced to retreat to positions west of Brussels.

The fall of Brussels was not only a strategic loss but a severe moral blow. Though laid to "obvious necessity" it forced the Belgian Government to make the decision to remove the capital to Ostend.

On the ninth day of their offensive the Germans had overrun half of Belgium. Their drive partly checked by the French, they now advanced at a slower rate and their gains were reduced to only seven miles. Their aim was to reach the Channel at all costs and as quickly as possible—to cut off the Belgian and British forces from the French.

The 2,500 to 3,000 tanks of the heaviest, eighty-ton type which the Nazis used were estimated as half of their armored force. Because of this strength they were able to widen the Sedan bulge which now extended on a sixty-two-mile front north to Maubeuge, reached the Aisne and approached Laon. To meet the German steel monsters the French moved up thousands of their famous 75's, which were used for point-blank fire.

In Belgium, German troops entered Antwerp from whose Town Hall the Reich's war flag flew, as it did in 1914. Fortifications at Namur and Liége held out and remained islands of resistance in the rear of the German advance.

In France Premier Reynaud took over the direction of the war, reorganized his cabinet, and exchanged places with Edouard Daladier who became Foreign Minister. Marshal Pétain, then in his eighty-fourth year, became Vice President of the Council with the special task of advising the new War Minister. Seventy-three-year-old General Maxime Weygand was appointed chief of the General Staff and Commander in Chief of all theaters of operations in the grave emergency. He replaced General Gamelin.

In their drive toward the Channel the Germans reached Charleroi and Tournai in northwestern Belgium, and threatened to trap 300,000 British troops in a "sack" that was being formed on both sides of the Franco-Belgian border west of the Sambre River. Farther north that day the front ran along the Scheldt Valley to the North Sea, and there the British Air Force made every effort to disrupt German communication lines and to destroy armored columns. Belgian resistance in the encircled forts of Liége and Namur was not yet entirely crushed, and French and Belgian forces struck at the German left flank to gain a sortie from Valenciennes and Maubeuge toward the south.

Military observers were amazed at the gigantic German offensive. A neutral officer in the Allied camp described it as "more ruthless than fire and flood." The tidal wave carried them to the Channel on May 22. It was the day Premier Reynaud told a chilly Senate that "France can't die." The Nazis had crossed the Aisne, reached Amiens, and with fighting still raging around Arras, had raced down the Somme River valley to Abbeville. By driving a spearhead to the English Channel they had succeeded in cutting off the Allied troops in Belgium and the northwest tip of France from the main body of the French Army. The Germans estimated that between 500,000 and 1,000,000 men had been trapped. A major disaster seemed imminent. The Nazi Juggernaut had broken the hinge on which the whole left wing of the Allied armies swung.

The Germans paused to refuel their armored divisions. The Allies, with shorter lines of communication, took advantage of it. They stiffened their defenses. Everything was being done to save France, but not much could be done to help the encircled force in the north. There light mobile German units swung north from Abbeville toward Montreuil, and from Amiens toward St. Pol. The entrapped troops pushed south in a desperate effort to broaden the spearhead, but their drive lacked strength. A thirty-mile gap remained open to the Allies between Amiens and Arras, as did a corridor along the shore. Meanwhile, the last resisting fort of the Liége fortifications, Batice, had fallen to Nazi dive bombers and big guns.

Berlin admitted desperate resistance in the Flanders pocket where the Allies smashed down from the vicinity of Douai to the outskirts of Cambrai. In a countermove, the Germans drove farther north from Arras toward Calais and from Abbeville into Boulogne. The Battle of Flanders was at its height on May 25. Driving south from Bapaume and Cambrai and north from Amiens and Peronne, Allied troops reduced to twenty miles the gap through which the German flying columns were streaming toward the Channel ports.

The last phase of the Battle of Flanders was being fought. The Germans announced on May 26 that they had bottled up the Allied forces, trapped north of the spearhead to the Channel. Britons and Belgians, fighting virtually with their backs to the sea, still held their ground. The breach was even narrower that day, but remained unfilled. Through that gap the Germans still poured reinforcements. Their objective was to cut the trapped forces into small detachments and dispose piecemeal of the entire Belgian Army, a large part of the British Expeditionary Force, and the First and Seventh as well as remnants of the Ninth French armies, upward of 1,000,000 men.

Some 3,000,000 civilians were similarly trapped, and 2,000,000 refugees from occupied Belgian provinces. Hourly, their situation became more desperate. The French admitted loss of Boulogne, first important Channel port to fall to the enemy, who also claimed the capture of Calais. The Germans had suffered heavy losses, but their pressure in Flanders had not ceased.

After eighteen days of resistance the Belgian Army capitulated on orders of King Leopold. The monarch had ordered the Belgian Army to lay down its arms, without consulting the French or British Governments. Premier Reynaud broke the news of the Belgian surrender in an early morning broadcast on May 28. His speech lasted less than five minutes but termed the capitulation a "grave event" and branded the surrender as "brusque." The Belgian Government, he added, would continue to function in opposition to the King's order and would raise a new army.

It was a defeat of the first order, the first severe blow to the Allies. At the time of the Belgian surrender the trap in Flanders was tightening but not as yet closed. In the triangular salient extending from Calais down to the Arras-Cambrai area and back up to the Netherlands border, the encircled troops were pressed harder than ever. Yet the British counterattacked at Aire, and French Senegalese troops held the enemy near Lens. The Allies still occupied a considerable part of the coast line, from Gravelines to Hoofplaat on the south shore of the Scheldt estuary, the only piece of Dutch territory still in Allied hands.

A terrific price was paid by the Germans for this battle. A letter from a soldier on the Belgian front told the story: "The Germans have to climb over their dead to get at us—but they still come on." The defenders were hard-pressed, but they were not yet defeated. The surrounded troops made a last, desperate stand. The final chapter of this historic battle in the narrow Flanders pocket was still to be written when the Belgian capitulation went into effect at three o'clock Greenwich Meridian time on Tuesday, May 28. The surrender of King Leopold placed the encircled twenty divisions in an impossible position.

The Nazis compressed the pocket from three sides, from Ghent, Valenciennes, and Bethune. The Allies, on this blackest of the past eighteen days, continued to fight. The Belgian newspaper, the *Meuse,* published in Paris that day, came out with the headline: "Belgium Betrayed by Her King." The Belgian Cabinet, regarding the King's action as "illegal and unconstitutional," decided to continue the struggle. Premier Pierlot and Foreign Minister Spaak placed a wreath at the foot of the statue of King Albert I in Paris. It had no inscription, just a band of crepe as if to mourn the memory of King Leopold's father, the sovereign who never yielded to the Germans.

As far as Allied strategy was concerned, the Battle of Flanders was over. No help could be given the trapped men who fought "desperately but not despairingly" in the ever-tightening pocket. On May 29, the Germans drove a wedge into the sack, cutting it in two. Forces south of Lille were completely surrounded in a square-shaped area whose sides measured only nine to twelve miles. The pocket above Lille was greatly reduced by German attacks on Ypres, Dixmude, and Ostend. On May 30, General Rene-Jacques-Adolphe Prioux, commander of the First French Army, and his staff surrendered. What remained of the Allied forces in the Flanders pockets had lost all contact.

The German High Command declared on May 31 that 330,000 prisoners had been taken. The troops in the pockets had been either captured or destroyed. Only isolated groups still offered resistance. But Dunkirk held out. And there the almost unbelievable evacuation of the remnants of Allied troops was under way. The House of Commons received the report on the "colossal military disaster" in Flanders.

The Belgian Government in London gave the first official account on the Nazi invasion, Belgium's policy of coöperation with the Allies and her preparations against aggression. According to this report the Belgians seized a secret German document on January 10, 1940, which revealed clearly that the Nazis were planning to attack the country and that their offensive would also involve the Netherlands, France, and England. The Belgian Cabinet immediately informed the respective military authorities of these nations.

Belgium was "discreetly advised" to seek French-British aid without awaiting an act of aggression. She did not accept this advice. Regarding it as incompatible with the attitude she intended loyally to maintain, she also feared that "preventive intervention by France and Britain was just what the Germans secretly were hoping for." She was given to understand, however, that the two guarantor powers would be in action on the third day after the invasion. They were.

For the first time, the capitulation of the Belgian Army, for which heretofore King Leopold's decision was chiefly blamed, was viewed from a different angle. His supporters explained: "The capitulation was not the result of a free decision. It occurred at the last extremity under the inexorable pressure of events.... By his (King Leopold's) dignified attitude in the captivity to which he has contented himself and by his refusal to recognize the accomplished fact he has shown himself to be the incarnation of a people that will not accept servitude."

The same attitude regarding the King was taken by the Belgian-American Educational Foundation of New York under the chairmanship of Herbert Hoover. They claimed that in the light of memoranda and documents examined by them, the monarch's surrender was the only thing he could do under the circumstances. This was substantiated by the King's letter to the Pope in which he gave the Pontiff the reasons for the Belgian capitulation, stating that surrender was inevitable since the Belgians struggled "gallantly against hopeless odds." Legality of the King's action had already been attested by a group of prominent Belgian jurists in exile who, in the summer of 1940, published a legal opinion regarding the constitutional aspect of the surrender.

The King, a prisoner of war in Laeken Castle since May, 1940, refused to enter into political negotiations with the Germans throughout his captivity. His firm stand was contrary to Nazi interests and indicative of the state of war that continued to exist between Germany and Belgium.

When Belgium took stock of her war scars, a picture of vast damage and devastation was presented to the world. Eighteen days of blitzkrieg left behind it this record: 34,000 houses had been severely damaged or destroyed; an additional 116,000 had suffered to a lesser degree. Only one fifth of Belgium's numerous towns and villages escaped injury. Destruction of communications and approximately 6,000 miles of highway reduced some districts almost to the level of feudal times. One hundred railway depots had been demolished; 1,455 bridges and tunnels had been blown up.

Major cities, such as Brussels, Antwerp, and Liége suffered only slightly; medium-sized towns such as Louvain, Nivelles, and Ostend were hardest hit. Centuries-old historic landmarks were wiped out. In Tournai, world-famous as the "royal city," numerous monuments, the Town Hall, library, museum, Cloth Hall, and the ancient cathedral were virtually destroyed. The Louvain Library, which Whitney Warren had rebuilt with American funds in the seventeenth-century style of Brabant, was completely demolished by fire. Its 700,000 volumes were lost.

For the second time within a quarter of a century the Germans took over the administration of the country. Lieutenant General Baron Alexander von Falkenhausen was appointed military commander of Belgium and northern France. Toward the end of 1943, he was succeeded by General Richard Jungklaus of the Elite Guard, a close friend of Heinrich Himmler. Secretaries-General, civil servants in the various ministerial departments in Brussels, were replaced by Nazi appointees. Needless to say, only such individuals were chosen who could be trusted to serve the Nazi cause. In violation of the Hague Convention, forbidding occupation authorities to change the laws of occupied countries, administrative decrees were altered and new ones issued. It has been estimated that such decrees, issued in four years of the Nazi occupation, filled over 8,000 pages. A new penal law enabled the conquerors to inflict fines as they saw fit and for measures which the Germans themselves had taken.

The Belgians paid the price for the Nazi conquest. A general contribution of 3,000,000,000 Belgian francs ($100,000,000 at the pre-invasion rate) was imposed upon the country immediately. Fines, termed "individual contributions," varying from 1,000,000 to 10,000,000 francs, were no exception later on. The purchasing power of the occupation marks, *Reichskredit Kassenscheine,* was fixed at ten times the Belgian franc on May 10, 1940, and two months later raised to twelve and a half times. (Some of these notes in circulation had been printed as early as May, 1935.) All banks were placed under German control and a bank of issue was set up in Brussels with power to issue bank notes in franc denominations. The Germans then gradually withdrew the marks and replaced them with Belgian notes. The result was inflation.

The Germans started immediately their systematic robbery with the requisitioning of supplies for their army and the homeland. They appropriated every month 8,000 cattle and 4,000 pigs; in certain coal mines they took up to 70 per cent of the production; requisitioned 45,000 railroad cars and demanded from the Belgian National Railways a monthly war indemnity of thirty million francs. Most of the horses were taken away and plowing had to be done with oxen and cows. The textile industry had to hand over 80 per cent of its production, the leather industry 84 per cent, and the tanning industry 75 per cent.

Nazi "penetration" began in earnest and followed a pattern applied elsewhere. It started with the German attempt to Nazify Belgian educational institutions. Regimentation of boys and girls was modeled after the Hitler Youth organizations. This kind of "education" failed, as did the forced distribution of literature on Nazi ideology and Pan-German policy. Publications opposing such doctrines were taken from public libraries, and textbooks were revised according to the German requirements. Schools were closed if they did not fall in line with German teachings or refused to obey a decree that provided for German as the first language. The free University of Brussels resisted the German attempt to replace Belgium professors with curators from German universities, whereupon the Nazis ordered its closing on the grounds of "subversive political activities."

There were famine and undernourishment. Children, because of physical weakness, fainted. Begging in the streets became a necessity. Black markets were the only way to obtain food. Shoes were available for only 4 per cent of the inhabitants, and rationing of clothes was even extended to babies' wear.

Again, as always, the Nazis resorted to racial persecution. Belgian Jewish refugees were forbidden to return to the country. In cities with large Jewish populations, as in Antwerp, the Nazis decreed that all Jews had to wear armbands with the Star of David. When thousands of Gentiles in that city started to show the yellow brassards, the Nazis had to cancel the order. Whole Jewish districts were surrounded, the inhabitants entrained in batches of 500 to 1,000 and shipped, like cattle, to Eastern Europe.

But the Catholic Church in Belgium suffered to no lesser degree than the Jewish population. In a predominantly Catholic country the clergy were outspoken in denunciation of racial and religious persecutions. Cardinal Van Roey, Archbishop of Malines and Primate of Belgium, ordered the reading in all Belgian churches of a pastoral letter that set forth a line of conduct for Catholics. Likewise a letter from the Pope to the Cardinal was read, in which the Pontiff referred to the "appalling state into which the horrors of war have plunged this noble country." All Belgian bishops took up these instructions and acted in conformity with the principles outlined therein. The entire clergy of the nation opposed extremist movements, and refused Holy Communion to members who consorted with the persecutors.

In an attempt to break down this patriotism of the priests, the Nazis increased their pressure on the church. Catholic welfare organizations were dissolved and Catholic charity groups suspended. Catholic schools were supervised in their educational programs. Heavy fines were imposed on the clergy, and twice on Cardinal Van Roey himself, who became the chief target of Nazi intolerance. In Liége the German military authorities forbade the presence of Belgian flags at religious services. Sermons and addresses were restricted to religious subjects. Services in memory of executed patriots were forbidden.

Belgian prisons were soon too small to hold the great number of men and women condemned for political crimes. More than 10,000 persons had been herded into them by the end of 1942; 1,500 prisoners were in St. Gilles alone, where Edith Cavell was held in the First World War. Additional concentration camps were opened at Huy and Breendonck. The latter became a replica of Dachau and was placed under the sole control of the brutal Gestapo. At Breendonck it has been estimated that 30 out of every 400 prisoners died monthly.

Compulsory labor, or slave gangs, became the first "secret weapon" of the Nazis. About a month after the occupation, an appeal was made to unemployed Belgian labor to volunteer for work in Germany. Working conditions there were described as "excellent" and high wages were promised. When the Belgians did not respond to the offer, registration for employment in the Reich became compulsory. Dole cards were taken away from Belgian workers. After medical examinations, if pronounced physically fit, they were sent to Germany at the rate of 1,500 to 2,000 a week. Belgian women were routed to employment offices in Germany and placed in households and factories.

The Belgians not only resisted the Germans but opposed the Quislings in their midst. The Nazis used these Belgian "leaders" as their instruments but met with little success, for the would-be Hitlers were branded as traitors by their own countrymen. Many Belgian Quislings met the fate of traitors. The first was Teugels, German-appointed Burgomaster of Charleroi; the second was Dr. Charles Henault, local leader of the Rexists and Burgomaster of Ver Eviers, who was shot down in front of his house; and the third, Jules Jasar, Quisling Burgomaster of Sart Les Spa, was riddled with tommy-gun bullets.

A well-organized Underground and systematic sabotage confronted the Nazi reign of terror. Sabotage was divided in two kinds: one highly organized with central headquarters from which instructions were sent out; the other a spontaneous movement in which countless Belgians acted and, risking their lives, did everything in their power against the Germans. They disrupted German communication systems, blew up factories, and slowed down enemy war production. Despite the increase of mine workers, the coal output was reduced; sabotage in the coal mines of the Campine district and the Meuse and Sambre valleys went on day and night.

Municipalities resisted the invaders to such an extent that a German decree ordered the dissolution of the municipal councils. Individual burgomasters and aldermen were substituted. Active sabotage was increased by passive resistance. With the anti-German tide rising, the invaders resorted to terrible methods of vengeance, the shooting of hostages and the infliction of the death penalty. A long list, a "Roll of Honor," contained the names of those whose executions the Nazis themselves made public. When completed, with the names of those who were shot or hanged without trial, tried in secret, or given slow death by cruel treatment in concentration camps, it will be the record of "Murder, Incorporated."

The list will be large, for not fewer than two hundred Underground papers, the largest secret press in any Nazi-subjugated country, were circulated in occupied Belgium.

After the fall of France the Belgian Ministers found refuge in London and became a government-in-exile, but M. Pierlot, Prime Minister, and M. Spaak, Foreign Minister, could not get there till October, 1940. They had escaped from France into Spain where they were detained, but finally reached England via Portugal. Of the Cabinet list as it represented itself in May, 1943, two members had fled Belgium as late as September, 1942. They were Antoine Delfosse, Minister of Justice and Information; and Gustave Joassart, Under Secretary for Refugees, Labor and Social Welfare. With ten portfolios altogether, the Belgian Government-in-exile set immediately to work to deal with the enormous task confronting it.

Belgium's foreign policy had to be shaped. Italy on June 10, 1940, had broken off diplomatic relations with Belgium. But after the torpedoing of the steamship *Kabalo* by an Italian submarine, the Belgian Government announced on November 29, 1940, that it considered itself at war with Italy. Belgium ended relations with Rumania on February 12, 1941, and declared war on Japan on December 20, 1941. Diplomatic relations were also broken with Bulgaria, Hungary, and Finland, and friendly relations established with the provisional Czechoslovak Government under Doctor Benes. Equally friendly relations were entertained with the *Comité National Français* headed by General de Gaulle, and Belgium became a signatory to the Grand Alliance in Washington. Her friendly relations with the Chinese Government, the British Dominions, and all South American countries had never ceased.

Belgium was bent but not broken. The Belgians not only continued the war as members of the United Nations but played a vital part in it after their homeland was conquered. The country actually remained an active belligerent by recruiting 100,000 troops in the Belgian Congo; they constituted an important contingent in the African campaign. They coöperated effectively in Italian East Africa, distinguished themselves in the conquest of Asoa and Gambella and in the Galla Sidamo region, and assisted the British in strengthening the front in Libya.

A Belgian Army, composed of men who were outside Belgium at the time of collapse or who escaped later, operated in Britain where a great number of Belgian pilots joined the R.A.F. Almost the entire Belgian merchant marine escaped from Belgium and was employed in convoy work across the Atlantic. About 40 percent of it was destroyed by enemy action. While all these men were awaiting the final day of reckoning with the invader, stickers appeared on many walls in occupied Belgium, showing the silhouette of a black hand and bearing the inscription: *L'Heure Approche*—The Hour Is Near!

GERMAN INVASION OF THE NETHERLANDS

HOLLAND, for the first time since the Napoleonic wars, became the victim of aggression on May 10, 1940, when Germany violated her neutrality and ravaged the country. Her 8,700,000 people were taken into captivity, and her towns and cities were ransacked by the Nazi invaders. The traditional land of dikes and windmills and fields of tulips was drenched in blood.

Chancellor Hitler in an order to his troops bombastically asserted: "The fight beginning today decides the fate of the German nation for the next 1,000 years."

In Holland the Germans followed the precedent they had set in Poland, the merciless bombing of civilian population in great cities. The destruction of Rotterdam, like that of Warsaw, set the pattern of Nazi warfare. When, in retaliation, the Nazis were given powerful "doses of their own medicine" they whined for mercy and branded it a "crime."

Always in a dangerous position because of the conflicting interests, Holland, through her policy of strict neutrality, went through crucial years during the First World War without having been drawn into the conflict. That this small country, in contrast to neutral Belgium and Luxembourg, was spared the hardships of that war was due not to the sympathies of the Imperial German High Command, but to a change of operation plans. Had the Kaiser's general staff followed the Schlieffen plan, Holland would have shared Belgium's fate. As it happened, von Moltke decided otherwise, probably because the Dutch had chosen to fortify the mouths of the country's rivers and remodeled their land defense systems.

During the crises that preceded World War II the Dutch were not blind to the dangers at their gates, and they took stern measures against perils from within. Twice, prior to her invasion, the country was in a state of siege. First in September, 1939, when military mobilization was prompted by Holland's desire to maintain strictest neutrality. And again in April, 1940, when the Dutch Government, determining to pursue absolute neutrality, stressed that there was no possibility of secret talks with either belligerent. This was in line with a previous drastic warning that all violations of Dutch neutrality would be met with force regardless of their source.

Proof of Holland's resolute stand took form in the publication of an *Orange Book* on November 5, 1939, containing official documents relative to the war. Its chapters included accounts of the offer of good offices by Queen Wilhelmina, her neutrality proclamation, protests against violation of Netherlands territory by planes, detention of ships, and censorship of mail bound for Holland. The book also disclosed that Holland took a firm stand on the question of British contraband control.

It was all of no avail. Six months later Germany invaded the Netherlands. An official proclamation was issued at Amsterdam on May 10: "Since 3:00 A.M. German troops have crossed the Netherlands frontier and German planes have tried to attack airports. Inundations are effective according to plans. The army antiaircraft batteries were found prepared. So far as is known, six German planes have been shot down."

In a statement on the Nazi attack Queen Wilhelmina said: "I and my Government will do our duty." Her declaration, addressed to "My People," read in part: "After our country, with scrupulous conscientiousness, had observed strict neutrality during all these months, and while Holland had no other plan than to maintain strictly this attitude, Germany last night made a sudden attack on our territory without any warning. This was done notwithstanding a solemn promise that the neutrality of our country would be respected as long as we ourselves maintained that neutrality.

"I herewith direct a flaming protest against this unprecedented violation of good faith and violation of all that is decent in relations between cultured States. Do your duty everywhere and under all circumstances. And let every one go to the post to which he has been appointed and, with the utmost vigilance and with that inner calm and sincerity which comes from clear conscience, do his work."

The German version of the invasion was the usual subterfuge. Foreign Minister Joachim von Ribbentrop announced in Berlin that Reich forces had launched military operations against Holland, Belgium, and Luxembourg to "protect their neutrality." Von Ribbentrop fabricated the charges that Germany had received "unimpeachable proof" that the Allies were engineering an imminent attack through the Lowlands into the German Ruhr district, wherefore the Germans were compelled to take corresponding measures. The German Foreign Minister told the world that Germany had decided to settle all accounts with the Allies.

Holland, together with Belgium, appealed for help to the French and British Governments. London and Paris were prompt in their replies. The invaded countries received assurances that they would give all the help the Allies could muster. A cabinet meeting was called at 10 Downing Street immediately, and was in session with Prime

Remember Pearl Harbor!
The Atlantic Charter!
The Battle of the Coral Sea!
1941-1942

The late President Roosevelt and Prime Minister Churchill engage in an informal chat on the H.M.S. Prince of Wales at the historic Atlantic Charter meeting.

The Day of Infamy

The USS Arizona, at anchor in Pearl Harbor, was the target of many bombs during Japanese attack on December 7, 1941. *At right:* Hirohito reviews his troops. *Below:* Hawaii surprise attack force about to take off.

OFFICIAL U. S. NAVY PHOTOGRAPHS

Helpless at Pearl Harbor

Above: The USS Helena suffers torpedo wounds, but her antiaircraft guns shot down six Jap planes. *At right:* Destroyers Downes and Gassin with flagship USS Pennsylvania in rear. *Below:* Sent to neutral countries for propaganda purposes, this aerial photograph shows Hickam Field aflame in the distance.

Defense of Leningrad

Women of Russia's second city plying spades to erect barricades and dig trenches for the defense of Leningrad.

INTERNATIONAL NEWS PHOTO

BRITISH OFFICIAL PHOTOGRAPH

German Bases Raided

British forces land on coast of Norway, and assisted by Norwegian troops, capture German headquarters.

OFFICIAL U. S. NAVY PHOTOGRAPH

The War in Iceland

Gray watchdogs of the U. S. Fleet guard Reykjavik Harbor, as viewed through barbed wire entanglements.

OFFICIAL U. S. NAVY PHOTOGRAPH

History Reverses Itself!

On December 24, 1941, the Japs made this photograph of General Homma stepping ashore on Luzon. By a historic turnabout U. S. forces turn the wheel of war full-circle, as they land on practically the same spot on January 9, 1945.

OFFICIAL U. S. NAVY PHOTOGRAPHS

The Battle of the Coral Sea

Above: "Abandon ship," is ordered aboard the USS Lexington, and the men slide down ropes and are picked up by small boats. Explosion on board same ship (*at right*). *Below:* The USS Saratoga and the USS Lexington anchored off Diamondhead.

U. S. NAVY PHOTO FROM INTERNATIONAL NEWS

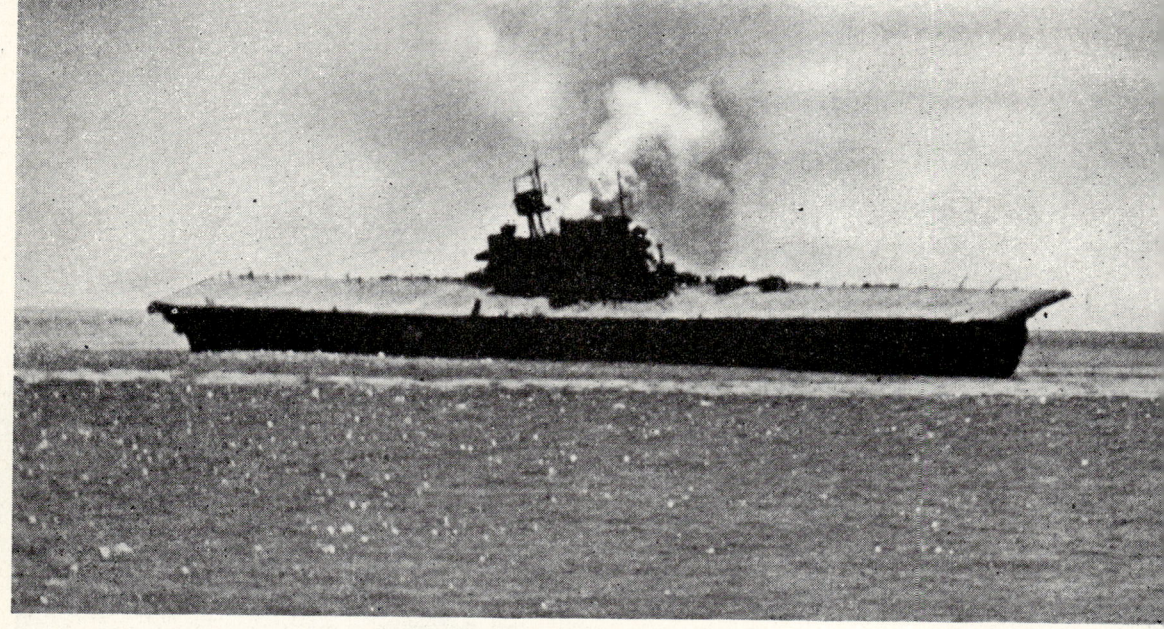

The U. S. S. Yorktown

This 19,900 ton aircraft carrier took terrific punishment in the Midway battle, and is shown listing badly after a bomb attack.

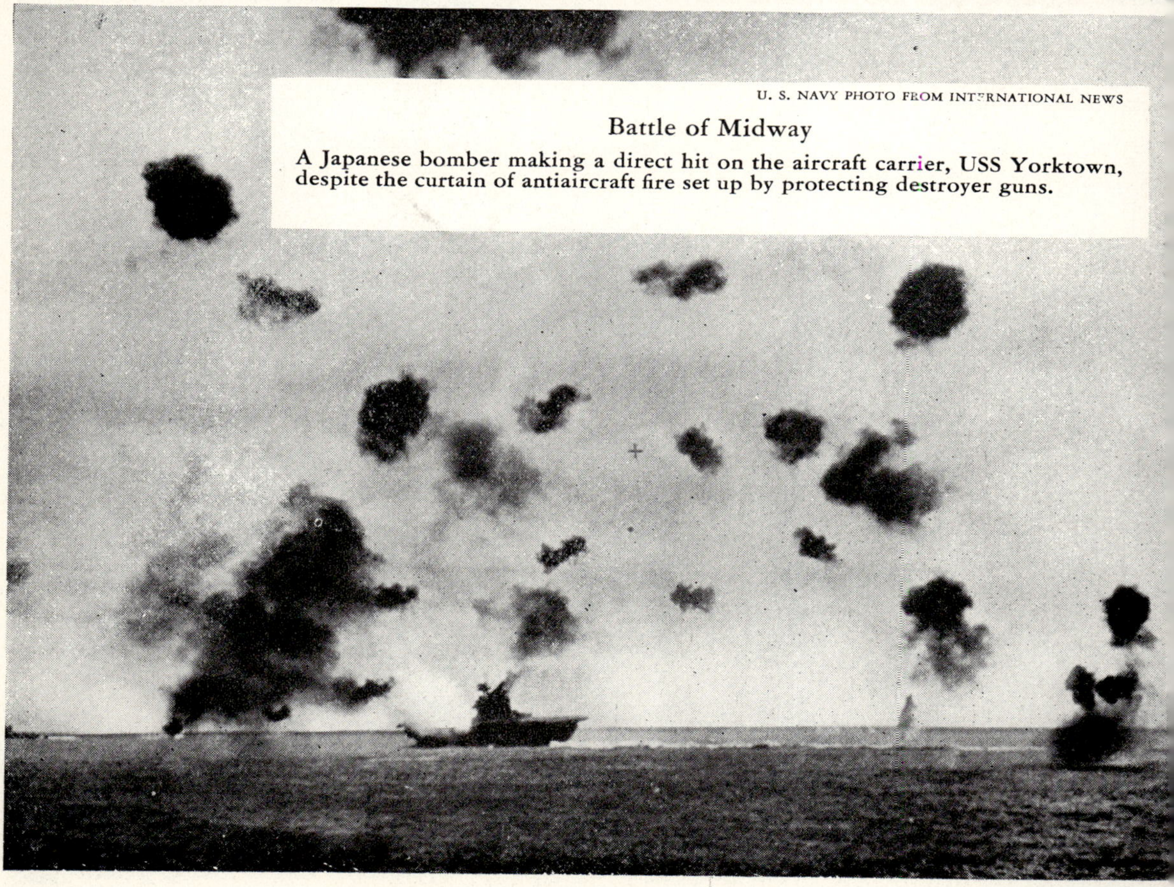

U. S. NAVY PHOTO FROM INTERNATIONAL NEWS

Battle of Midway

A Japanese bomber making a direct hit on the aircraft carrier, USS Yorktown, despite the curtain of antiaircraft fire set up by protecting destroyer guns.

SIGNAL CORPS PHOTO
INTERNATIONAL NEWS PHOTO

A "Flying Tiger"
One of the strangely decorated and famous planes used in the campaign in China and Burma. *Below:* The late President Roosevelt awarding the Congressional Medal to Brig. Gen. "Jimmy" Doolittle for leading the raid on Tokyo.

In the South Pacific

Above: The deck of an airplane carrier abustle with activity during raid on Gilbert and Marshall Islands. *At right:* MacArthur and Wainwright chat for a moment. *Below:* General Douglas MacArthur addressing the officers of a U. S. division in Australia orders every soldier to "get a Jap."

INTERNATIONAL NEWS PHOTO

U. S. Troops Reach New Guinea

Toting barracks bags, personal equipment, and ammunition, American soldiers arrive at Port Moresby.

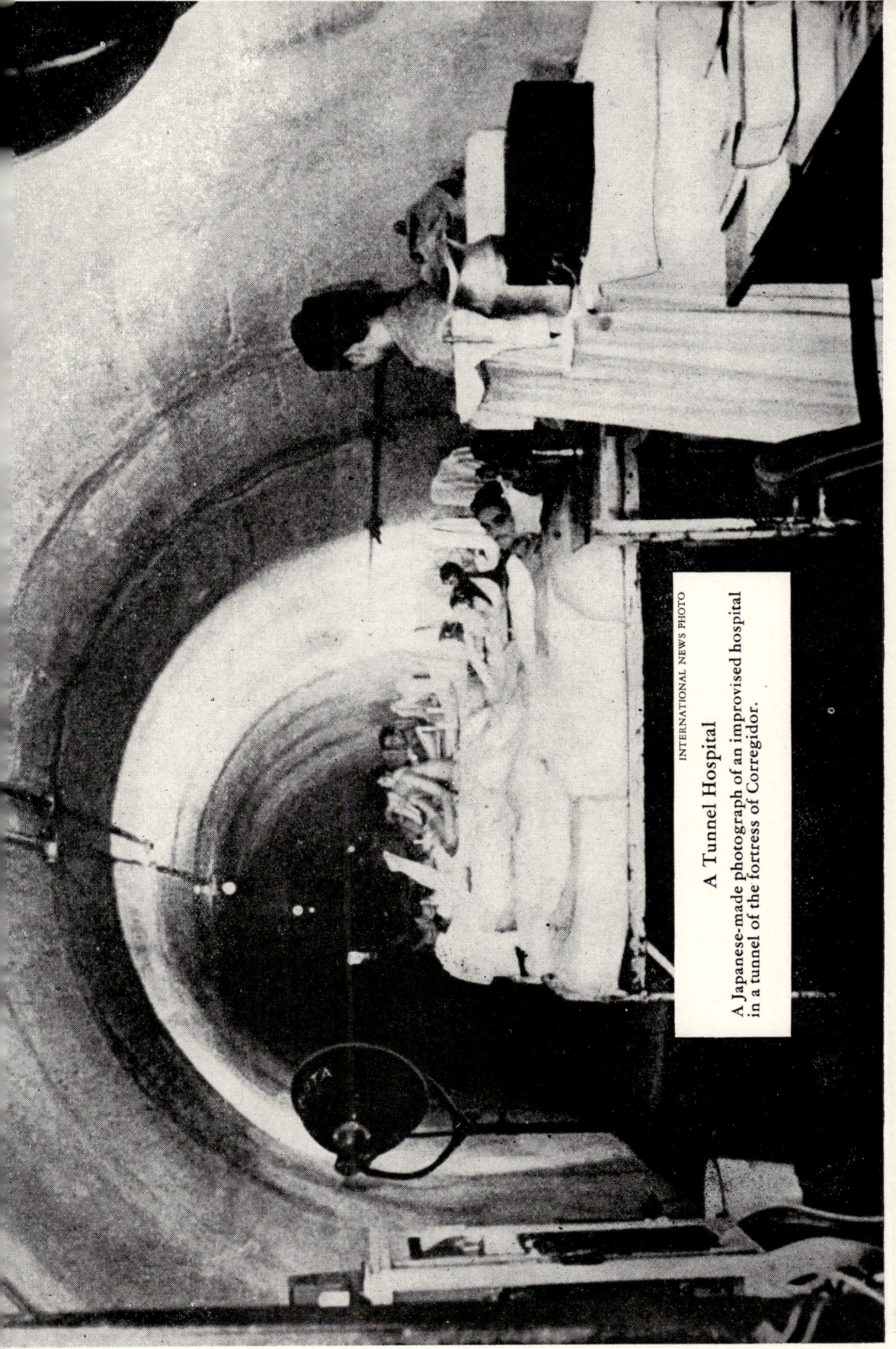

A Tunnel Hospital

A Japanese-made photograph of an improvised hospital in a tunnel of the fortress of Corregidor.

INTERNATIONAL NEWS PHOTO

INTERNATIONAL NEWS PHOTO

The Fall of Corregidor
With the white flag of surrender held high, the Americans walk out to the victors with hands raised.

INTERNATIONAL NEWS PHOTO

After Japs Took Corregidor
A Japanese photograph showing lines of prisoners marching through the bomb-pocked terrain of Corregidor.

OFFICIAL U. S. MARINE CORPS PHOTO FROM INTERNATIONAL NEWS

Last Photo from Bataan
The barbed wire entanglements enabled U. S. Marines to hold off Jap landings for many weeks.

A Nipponese Calling Card
Jap bombers wreaked havoc on this Army hospital on Corregidor.

INTERNATIONAL NEWS PHOTO

U. S. Troops Arrive in Casablanca

Guarded by U. S. Naval units, huge U. S. troop transports arrive in this North African port.

BRITISH OFFICIAL PHOTO

Watching the battle from the turret of a Grant tank in which he traveled—Lt. Gen. Bernard L. Montgomery of the British Eighth Army.

INTERNATIONAL NEWS PHOTO

Yanks Arrive in Algiers

American soldiers, with American flags stuck under the camouflage netting on their helmets, arrive in the thriving Algerian town of Oran.

Minister Neville Chamberlain within a few minutes after receipt of official news of the invasion.

American indignation was aroused by the wanton attack upon neutral countries. President Roosevelt ordered the freezing of all credits held by Belgium, the Netherlands, and Luxembourg in the United States and pictured the Nazi invasion as a definite threat to the security of the Americas.

Pope Pius XII, in a message addressed to the rulers of the three invaded countries on May 11, condemned the German invasion and pledged moral support of the Holy See against the Nazis.

The Hollanders themselves put faith in their defenses which had been steadily increased. Army leaves had been canceled and every possible precaution had been taken against a blitzkrieg. First, second, and third lines of defenses had been designed both in Belgium and Holland. The Dutch defenses were built on the assumption that Belgium in self-defense would permit passage of Allied relief troops from northern France. Dikes, trenches, block houses, and mined canals were designed to delay the invading Nazi army. Although the first lines were by no means believed impregnable, the second and third lines were far more formidable, and with their water defenses, swamps, and other prepared barriers were expected to hold the enemy for a considerable length of time.

On the first day of the attack, Holland resisted. Antiaircraft batteries and fighter planes engaged swarms of German aircraft which appeared simultaneously over Dutch cities. German troops first crossed the Netherlands frontier near Roermond, eight miles north of the Belgian border. Nazi parachute troops were landed at strategic points near Rotterdam, The Hague, Amsterdam, and other large cities. A number of them were reported to be dressed in Dutch military uniforms. Considerable numbers of other German units crossed the Maas River in rubber boats.

Schiphol Airdrome, outside Amsterdam, the country's largest airport, was heavily bombed by German Heinkels between 5:15 and 5:30 A.M. Fifty Nazi planes were over Nijmegen, sixty miles southeast of Amsterdam. Parachute troops were landed at Sliedrecht, Delft, Dordrecht, and Hoogezwaluwe, whose big bridge forms the major communicating link between the northern and southern parts of the country. Other Nazi troops in great numbers landed at Leiden and Waalhaven, major airport of Rotterdam, where a score of enemy planes appeared at 5:50 A.M.

German headquarters revealed little of the results of the first twenty-four hours of the invasion, but it was obvious that the procedure used in the Polish campaign was now employed in the Netherlands. A superblitzkrieg was in progress, aiming at enemy airfields and communications systems and opening the way for motorized infantry and artillery units by tank attacks.

The lightning invasion presented, at first, no connected battlefronts, but concentrated attacks on scattered points. Main objects of attack were at Delfzijl and along the Yssel and Maas rivers, with a struggle raging in the city of Rotterdam. Waves of German bombers raided Amsterdam for twenty-five minutes and dropped three hundred bombs on Schiphol airdrome. At The Hague the Germans dropped leaflets asserting that the city was surrounded.

The Netherlands fought back with both fire and water. Sluices in the main water line running south from the Zuider Zee were opened to complete the shallow, flood-water defenses intended to save the western part of the country and its rich cities from Nazi hordes approaching by land. Farther east, strategic points in the first defense line above and below the Rhine had been already flooded, and Netherland troops blew up bridges across the Maas and Yssel rivers. The position of the German troops was given as somewhere in the vicinity of Arnhem, in the east-central Netherlands, and southward in Limburg Province.

In a determined drive against the Hague and Rotterdam, the Germans landed thousands of parachutists behind the fighting lines and succeeded in crossing the Yssel River south of Arnhem. Rotterdam was attacked from the right bank of the Maas River. Tremendous fires blazed in the city, and the people were without drinking water.

Motorized units, supported by aircraft, had smashed their way from the border to the sea, covering a distance of eighty miles in about forty-eight hours. The German blitzkrieg was well under way. The High Command admitted that the Germans had crossed the Maas and Yssel rivers "at various points" and that the defenders had withdrawn 20,000 British troops landed from transports.

With Groningen Province in their possession, the Nazis pushed south, threatening Amsterdam and other large cities. Already the Grebbe Line, running eastward from Amersfoort, and the Peel Line farther south, had been dented. Moreover, new parachute troops by the thousands had been dropped behind the lines, and Fifth Columnists were at work aiding them and expanding their activities in acts of sabotage. They disrupted the air-raid siren systems and cut what was left of Amsterdam's water supply.

While the Dutch were forced to yield the north, they fought in the center and the interior, mopping up "Trojan horse" traitors and parachutists. French troops made contact with the enemy in East Brabant to the south. Britishers, reaching the front lines, helped the Dutch to flood their water defenses. The Netherlands High Command remarked: "The Germans do not seem to be able to fight in Holland unless they can use Dutch soldiers or civilians as a shield."

Traitorous German Hollanders in The Hague tried to seize a police station but failed. Sniping from housetops at Dutch soldiers, they attempted to march to the center of the city, but detachments of Netherland troops drove them back to the Suez Kade, the lower bank of the Afvoer Canal in the southern part. There they lodged themselves in a house which was shelled by Dutch armored cars.

Holland's combined armed forces, estimated at about 400,000 men, were hardly able to stem the Nazi mass attacks of armored columns and airplanes. The large-scale offensive split the Netherlands in two. This was achieved on the fourth day by taking Moerdyk Bridge across Hollandsch Diep, one of the outlets of the Maas River. This bridge, the largest in Europe, was the main artery for motor and rail traffic between north and south Holland. Consequently, the defending troops in the north were forced to withdraw to the main water defenses protecting the country's main cities, Amsterdam, Rotterdam and The Hague.

With the Germans fifteen miles from Rotterdam and within thirty miles of the Netherlands capital, Queen Wilhelmina with her daughter, Princess Juliana, the latter's consort, Prince Bernhard zu Lippe-Biesterfeld, and their two daughters, Princesses Beatrix and Irene, decided to take refuge in England. The Queen arrived there on May 13 aboard a British warship. She was met at Liverpool Street Station in London by King George VI and her daughter and son-in-law, who had arrived earlier in the day. Prince Bernhard, however, returned immediately to the battlefront in Zeeland. It became known later that the British destroyer on which the Crown Princess, her consort, and children had fled was attacked on its way to England by German mine layers and had a narrow escape. The Princess later took up residence in Ottawa, Canada, where her third daughter was born.

Queen Wilhelmina had been urged to go to Zeeland Province, but when she and members of the Government boarded a ship, word was received that her destination already seemed known to the Germans. A bombardment was going on and it was feared that parachute troops might be dropped. Then the quick decision was made to accept temporarily the hospitality of the King and Queen of England. Queen Wilhelmina visited America in the summer of 1942, and told a joint session of Congress in Washington that the motto of her Government and people was: *"No surrender!"*

On the eve of May 14, General Winkelman, the Dutch Commander in Chief, called upon his troops to lay down their arms "to prevent further bloodshed and annihilation." In view of the fact that the Nazis had thrown a barrier across the country from the German border to the North Sea, further resistance seemed useless. The invaders had overrun the Netherlands in only five days. Adolf Hitler proclaimed on May 15, that it was a "unique achievement whose military importance the future will prove."

General Winkelman, strong man of the nation after the flight of the royal family and the Government to London, spoke to the people over the radio. "It is very likely that a large part of Holland," he said, "will have to be given up to the enemy." Then his voice choked with emotion as he continued: "The Netherlands will be herself again after this war. Long live Her Majesty the Queen! Long live the Netherlands!"

At this hour came the rape of Rotterdam, one of the grimmest lessons of World War II. This system of warfare initiated by the Germans was finally to be brought home to them with stern reality. When the Nazis began the bombing of densely populated cities, they started something that was soon to devour them. German psychology again proved itself a "noose with which to hang itself." They believed that by creating a reign of terror in Rotterdam they were frightening Paris and London into demoralization. Events proved that they strengthened instead of weakened the determination of the British people.

Rotterdam, on the fifth and last day of the Battle for Holland, waited resignedly for the German troops to march in. Dutch military strength was exhausted. General Winkelman, the Dutch commander, set off the red flares that by agreement with the German enemy meant surrender. Its population of nearly 600,000 waited, its Government fled, its sons dead in the meadows, its homeland gone.

The sun shone from a clear blue sky as it had throughout the five days of Dutch resistance. People milled about the city, waiting for the inevitable. Suddenly, without provocation or warning, horror broke loose from the skies. Thirty German planes rose from the Rotterdam airdrome, which the Nazis had captured the night of the invasion. Flying over the heart of the city in orderly formation at an altitude of 4,500 feet, they shuttled slowly and deliberately back and forth, never once breaking formation. No shot was fired at them from the ground. No Dutch fighter went aloft to meet them. No resistance of any kind was offered.

General Winkelman's red flares of surrender were blazing but the Germans ignored them. Deadly cargoes of bombs fell upon the densely filled streets into the heart of Rotterdam. Ton after ton of delayed action and incendiary bombs hurtled down onto a stunned people. Blown to pieces where they stood, or buried in the ruins of buildings to which they fled, or roasted alive in their homes or places of employment, Rotterdam became an inferno.

Homes, schools, hospitals, churches, became flaming furnaces. A department store was set ablaze by incendiary bombs. Its saleswomen were roasted to death in smoldering ruins. A newspaper plant was smashed into wreckage, its employees crushed by the presses crashing through the building.

For two and one-half hours the German rapine continued. From twelve o'clock noon until two-thirty a relentless rain of death poured from the skies. The Great Church crumbled; the Town Hall fell; the library collapsed; the post office was reduced to ruins; the central railroad station was leveled. Binnenstad, center of the business section, and Coolsingel, with its markets and shops, were devastated.

At 2:30 all was over. The sun shone on a scorched earth. More than 26,000 buildings lay in the wreckage. Nearly 25,000 men, women, and children lay dead in the streets or buried under the masses of rubble. In the harbor the great ship *Statendam* was burning. The canal was blocked by sunken ships. Throughout the city broken sewer pipes, water mains, and broken canals poured out a foul flood. Blood mingled with sewage as the German Army finally marched in.

Eyewitnesses who escaped from Rotterdam reported that even after streets had been cleared of their heaps of dead, there was still an average of 1,800 bodies a day being dragged from the ruins for a period of seven days. That the Germans were trying to wash the blood stains of guilt from their hands was proved by the tight censorship they placed on the graveyard city. Pictures smuggled out, or taken from R.A.F. reconnaissance from the air, showed huge blocks of leveled debris and gutted apartment houses filled at the time of the bombing with housewives and their children.

The green-clad Dutch troops, who had stood throughout the bombardment with their feeble rifles pointed at the skies, wept as they surrendered.

Rotterdam was not alone in its terror and devastation on that fateful Tuesday afternoon. Flushing, to the south, also lay shattered and defenseless. The great port of Den Helder was "obliterated," while other cities had fallen under the holocaust. Amsterdam, The Hague, later Antwerp, were bombed. But it was Rotterdam that lay a funeral pyre, the "great monumental ruins" of savage Nazi destruction. It was estimated that it would take fifteen years to rebuild the city.

By ordering his troops to cease defending the key cities, General Winkelman hoped to save Rotterdam and Utretcht from annihilation. The Commander in Chief appealed to the population to maintain a calm and worthy attitude: "Your attitude has been above praise," he said. "You have been fighting against heavy odds and against a very strongly equipped army, but your attitude is worthy of a Netherlander. Maintain this attitude and never forget that you are Netherlanders."

Formal capitulation of the Netherlands armed forces took place on May 15 in the village of Rijsoord, a suburb of Rotterdam. General Winkelman arrived by automobile about 10:15 A.M., accompanied by three staff officers. This meeting with the German commanding general took place around a horseshoe table in the village school. The German general read the conditions of capitulation to General Winkelman. The terms were discussed and finally determined. General Winkelman thereupon left at 11:45 A.M. for Rotterdam. Part of the Netherlands Navy had escaped and remained in the war to defend the country's colonies in both hemispheres.

The decision of the Netherlands to capitulate had been taken after consultation with the Allies. Military experts considered the strategic situation so hopeless that the Allied High Command preferred to withdraw reinforcements into Belgium rather than waste the lives of Netherlanders and the remainder of the Dutch Army. The final casualty list of the Dutch Army was: 2,890 killed, 6,889 wounded, and 29 missing. The Royal Guard alone lost 80 per cent of its strenth. Rotterdam suffered 25,000 casualties. The looting of Holland proceeded according to the customs of Nazi banditry. Bullion valued at 26,000,000 English pounds, forty shipyards, warships under construction, 100,000 tons of oil, and from 2,000 to 3,000 tons of tin were among the spoils filched by the conqueror. Fortunately, shortly before the invasion, bullion worth 117,000,000 pounds had been sent abroad, chiefly to the United States. Most of Holland's 330,000 tons of oil on hand at the time of the attack was destroyed before the surrender. Either the Dutch set the stores on fire or they were damaged by German bombs. Diamonds worth millions of pounds had been taken out of the country. Thousands of head of cattle were drowned when the flood defenses were opened; but enough precious stones and livestock, with great quantities of vegetable and whale oil and margarine, fell into the hands of the invaders.

Although the Netherlands had surrendered, the country juridically remained at war with the Reich. Moreover, the Dutch Foreign Minister, E. N. van Kleffens, who had escaped to France, issued a proclamation in Paris on May 15, declaring: "The Dutch people have not surrendered.... The struggle for the common cause will continue till victory is won."

The peoples in the Dutch East Indies, reckoning with the possibility of a Japanese attack, pledged their loyalty to the mother country. Native rulers remained true to the Queen who, in a radio address to the British Empire from London, saw the spirit of the Netherlands unbroken because our "conscience is clear, and the Dutch will never give up their faith in the cause of freedom and justice."

Netherlands rule was set up in London with the arrival of all eleven members of the Dutch Cabinet. Together with 200 refugees they had crossed to England on a British warship. Soon after their arrival Queen Wilhelmina, declaring that the seat of the Dutch Government was

London, issued a proclamation asserting the intention to reëstablish the régime in the Netherlands as soon as possible.

The Germans took over the administration of the conquered country. It was stressed in Berlin that surrender of the Netherlands did not end the state of war between the two nations; consequently, administration of the country would remain in the hands of the German military authorities. Furthermore, it was warned that if and when a civil administration was inaugurated in the Netherlands, it would be more severe than that accorded to the Danes. There were indications that Germany was determined to wipe out the last remnants of the Treaty of Westphalia of 1648, which confirmed the independence of the Netherlands after the Thirty Years War.

Under Nazi rule all organs of public information in the Netherlands, such as the press and the radio were suppressed. German newspapermen were placed in the offices of leading Dutch journals. They were allowed to print official German news agency reports only. Officials from the press section of the German Foreign Office and Propaganda Ministry set up headquarters in the country to direct the dissemination of news. Listening to foreign radio stations was forbidden.

Gradually the Germans tightened their grip on the subjugated country. Reich Minister Dr. Arthur Seyss-Inquart, who assumed the highest civil powers, in a carefully staged ceremony in Amsterdam's Ridderzaal on May 30, gave his solemn pledge: "Dutch laws hitherto observed shall remain in force as far as possible. Dutch officials are to be the instruments of power in the new administration. The independence of legal jurisdiction is to be preserved." He promised the Hollanders no further living discomforts, and pledged reconstruction of all damage caused by the war. He asserted that the German Army would rather have entered the country "with its arms raised up in friendly salute than with weapons in hand."

These pledges, guaranteed by "German honor," were but steel traps to ensnare the Dutch. German penetration became more systematic and drastic in Holland than in any other of the Nazi-dominated nations. The country, one of the richest in continental Europe, was thoroughly looted. The Dutch were deprived of their natural resources to such an extent that within one year of Nazi occupation not even cheese, of which the Dutch annually manufactured 124,000 tons, was available to the population. Vegetables became scarce in a country that was famed for its truck gardens. Factories specializing in the drying of vegetables worked night and day to ship their products to Germany. All cream, clothing, textile, and leather products were also sent to Germany.

The Dutch paid dearly, for Holland had to finance not only her own defeat and reconstruction, but also that part of German war production which had been transferred to her factories. The invaders took the bulk of the country's products without giving anything in return. Its treasury was compelled to pay the excess of Dutch exports to Germany over German exports to Holland. The Dutch debt increased at the rate of $80,000,000 a month.

German "honor" turned a land of good living conditions and comfortable habits into one of scarcity, slim rations, high prices, and suffering. As a consequence of their conduct and methods, the Dutch took to sabotage despite harsh Nazi measures. Mysterious fires broke out in German-controlled factories; explosions occurred in Nazi ammunition dumps. German military materials were damaged and telegraph lines were cut. Resistance became more widespread and better organized with the launching of the "V for Victory" campaign.

German revenge followed the established Nazi pattern. German authorities ordered the round-up of Jews in Amsterdam's section of 50,000 Jewish inhabitants. Collective fines were levied on whole communities. Wherever labor strikes broke out, mass arrests took place. Summary courts, empowered to impose death penalties for violation of special decrees issued by Dr. Seyss-Inquart, were set up. Drastic restrictions were clamped down on the population and martial law was declared when tension reached the breaking point.

On the third anniversary of the Nazi invasion the Germans decreed that all able-bodied Dutchmen between eighteen and thirty-five must register for what was believed to be a preliminary to conscription for enforced slave labor service. Thousands of Netherlanders had already been deported to concentration camps. Close to half a million Hollanders had been sent to Germany to work in armament factories.

Hitler sent his Gestapo chief, Heinrich Himmler, to the Netherlands in May, 1942. The "friendly" Germans executed ninety-six Dutchmen, re-arrested all former Dutch officers and cadets, and seized 460 prominent Netherlanders as hostages. Indications were that a puppet Nazi administration would be established in Holland, headed by Anton Mussert, chief of the Netherlands Nazi Party and would-be "Little Fuehrer." Mussert, fifty-year-old son of a village schoolmaster, and himself an engineer, had gained notoriety by marrying an aunt eighteen years his senior.

The Netherland patriots, who considered Mussert as their country's arch-Quisling, learned that as a reward for his aid to the invaders he had been appointed by Chancellor Hitler as the "leader of the Dutch people." Mussert set up a "Secretariat of State" and soon thereafter appointed his "personal cabinet." Within the first two weeks of February, 1943, four of his leading cohorts became victims of the well-organized Underground known as "The Black Hand," who had pledged to wipe out the entire Mussert "government." Lieutenant General Hendrik Alexander Seyffardt, a lone traitor among the Netherlands generals, who had just been appointed by Mussert to raise a Dutch army for service on the Russian front, was shot. Dr. H. Raydon, Nazi-sponsored Propaganda Minister, and his wife were killed. Mussert's Secretary for Social Affairs, C. van Ravenzwaai, was assassinated. The name of the fourth victim was not known, but it was reported that he had been nominated for Attorney General.

The Nazi-controlled German press was quick in proclaiming that the Mussert shadow cabinet had no governing authority and would be consulted only in administrative questions relating to Holland's domestic affairs. In the face of so much opposition, Mussert himself was forced to declare that "between the NSB (his own Nazy Party which before the invasion was estimated at 50,000 male and female members) and the Dutch people lies a deep chasm which drives me to despair." This earned him the nickname "Lord Despair."

The day of reckoning was nearing. The underground war was becoming better organized as time went on. It guided the subjugated people intellectually and morally. They found encouragement by listening, risking their lives in doing so, to BBC reports and broadcasts of Radio Orange, the station of the Dutch Government-in-exile, both of which originated in London. The underground press expanded.

Underground orders were given and carried out. Industrial workers were urged not to go to Germany. Farmers were shown how to hide their crops from the Germans. Refugees, Jewish and Gentile, were guided to safety. Suggestions of the Government-in-exile were transcribed. Stipulations were made for the underground war by publications that specialized in "manuals," guides for effective sabotage and proper behavior in case of Gestapo visits. Papers, such as *Virj Nederland, Het Parool, De Oranjebode, De Oranjekrant,* and the students' sheet, *De Geus,* appeared with clockwork regularity and were quickly and mysteriously distributed, to provide, as one of their mastheads read: "Intolerable reading matter for Huns and Traitors."

Copies of these editions, smuggled out of the country, gave valuable information on the inside situation. It was thus revealed that of approximately 1,500 Christian denominational schools, 1,398 joined in a protest to the Nazified Department of Education against a decree to appoint Dutch Nazis as teachers in Christian schools. Almost all the farmers refused to join the Netherlands counterpart of the German food producers' organization. Only 17,500 of the 525,000 organized industrial workers had joined the Netherlands labor front.

Dutch spirit, Dutch integrity, the indomitable will of the Dutchmen could not be intimated. Fostering a united front against the unscrupulous invaders, these fearless documents never failed to encourage their readers. Their watchword was *"Bijltjes Dag,"* the Day of the Little Hatches, the day of final reckoning and liberation.

WHY THE BRITISH ENTERED WORLD WAR II

GREAT BRITAIN, with her Commonwealth of Nations, stood like an impregnable rock in the path of Hitler's scheme for world domination. Through centuries of discovery and exploration she had built an empire which had taken its place in the forefront of progress.

Diplomatic history will require many volumes to record the documents which indict Adolf Hitler. His own official proclamations are self-confessions. They show how he first attempted to enlist British support with cajolery and flattery. Wholly devoid of conscience or principles, he was utterly incapable of understanding the Anglo-Saxon character. Failing in every approach, he resorted to perfidy to entice Great Britain into a "hands-off" policy with guarantees of friendship.

Germany had one ulterior motive—the complete destruction of the British and French empires, with the eventual destruction of democracy throughout the world. And she was suiting the action to the word with a dazzling sleight of hand that Europe had not seen paralleled since the rise of Napoleon. Hitler, from the day he ascended to power in Germany, could think only in terms of the incredible holocaust. The outstanding problem after the armistice of 1918 was the creation of a world molded to endure in peace. "The war to end war" meant what it said. The slogan was not an abstract but an aspiration of the hearts of the world—as unmistakable as the love of life and the fear of death.

The British, imbued with these ideals of world peace, sought to counteract the emergence of any predominant Power in Europe by giving support to other European nations threatened by force. France, for her part, regarded herself as perpetually in danger from German rivalry, and, in accordance with her historic procedure, put her reliance on strong defensive alliances. Vigorously opposed to all this, was the Pan-German cult standing for a German-controlled State called Mittel-Europa. This became a grandiose *Lebensraum* in Herr Hitler's rhetoric with dreams of vast possessions at the expense of its European neighbors. The refrain throughout was that might was right, that by annexation after annexation, Germany's destiny was the ultimate conquest of Europe. As he spoke, so he acted. The measures taken by Chancellor Hitler on achieving power—rearmament, remilitarization of the Rhineland, the absorption of Austria, the subjugation of

Czechoslovakia, Poland, Rumania—were merely the translation of aspiration into actuality.

In the decade prior to the outbreak of the war in 1939, successive British governments had sought to improve relations between Germany and Great Britain. British officials continued to rebut the German charge of a policy of encirclement and restriction of trade. They pointed for example to the Anglo-German Payments Agreement, by which a supply of free exchange had been made available for the purchase of raw materials.

The guiding principle in foreign politics of Prime Minister Chamberlain had been appeasement, and the desire to establish Anglo-German relations on the basis of mutual recognition of the needs of both countries, having regard to the rights of other nations. It was with this object also that the Anglo-German Naval Agreement had been drawn up and signed in 1935.

Herr Hitler's practice of breaking agreements, promises, and declarations made with the British and other governments had indeed gathered momentum by 1939. Within six months after solemn pledges made with Prime Minister Chamberlain at Munich, he marched into Czechoslovakia and issued a proclamation in Prague, annexing Bohemia and Moravia.

Only a week after the occupation of Prague the German Government presented demands to the Polish Government that Danzig should return as a Free State into the framework of the German Reich, and that Germany should receive a route and railway with extra-territorial status through the Corridor. In exchange Herr Hitler offered Poland a twenty-five-year non-aggression pact, and a pledge that Germany would regard the existing boundaries between Germany and Poland as ultimate.

In reply the Polish Government proposed a joint guarantee by Poland and Germany of the separate character of the Free City of Danzig on the assurance of respect for Polish rights, and expressed itself as prepared to examine any further simplifications for persons in transit, as well as railway and motor transit, between the German Reich and East Prussia.

In view of these proceedings Prime Minister Chamberlain, on March 31, made clear to the House of Commons the position of His Majesty's Government: "I now have to inform the House that during that period, in the event of any action which clearly threatened Polish independence, and which the Polish Government accordingly considered it vital to resist with their national forces, His Majesty's Government would feel themselves bound at once to lend the Polish Government all the support in their power. They have given the Polish Government an assurance to this effect.... The French Government have authorized me to make plain that they stand in the same position in this matter as do His Majesty's Government."

A week later an Anglo-Polish communiqué told the world that the two countries would enter into an agreement of a permanent and reciprocal character to replace the prevailing temporary and unilateral assurance given by the British Government to the Polish Government. "Pending the completion of the permanent agreement," the communiqué went on, "M. Beck gave His Majesty's Government an assurance that the Polish Government would consider themselves under an obligation to render assistance to His Majesty's Government under the same conditions as those contained in the temporary assurance already given by His Majesty's Government to Poland."

Germany's first objectives, apart from the domination of Czechoslovakia, were Danzig and Memel. The democracies, it was assumed, were so averse to war that they would accept any step, once it had been taken. With this scheme in view Lithuania was intimidated into surrendering Memel. Warsaw turned out to be of harder metal. Negotiations had been going on from the date of the Munich Agreement for a settlement of the Danzig and the Corridor imbroglio. Following the entry into Prague, the German Government felt brazenly confident. Von Ribbentrop dictated new terms to the Polish Ambassador. The Polish Government mobilized its forces and the British guarantee to Poland was given at the end of March. The Anglo-Polish guarantee was followed by unilateral guarantees by the British Government to Greece and Rumania, as well as by inconclusive negotiations on the part of the British, French, and Russian Governments.

The British Prime Minister on March 23, 1939, made it plain in the House of Commons that while the British Government had no desire to stand in the way of expansion of German export trade it was resolved to oppose the subjection by coercion of independent States into yielding their independence. Two months later on May 23, the British Ambassador in Berlin warned Field Marshal Goering that Great Britain and France would become involved in war with Germany if the Reich attempted to settle German-Polish difficulties by unilateral action such as would compel the Poles to resort to arms to safeguard their independence.

In the face of British and French warnings Hitler proceeded with his system of pressure and browbeating. In his Reichstag speech he revealed the terms he had put before the Polish Government, declaring them to represent the minimum demanded by Germany. At the same time he set forth the claim that the German-Polish Agreement, made back in 1934, had proved itself incompatible with Anglo-Polish promises of mutual assistance against Germany, and as a result had become no longer binding on the Reich.

The German Reich, the Polish minister declared, had taken the mere fact of the Polish-British understanding as a motive for denouncing the pact of 1934. The Reich Government, as had appeared from the text of the German memorandum, had made its decision on the strength of press reports, without consulting the views of either the British or the Polish Government. M. Beck made known that immediately on his return from London he had expressed his readiness to receive the German Ambassador, who had not availed himself of the opportunity of consultation.

The Free City of Danzig, the minister pointed out, had not been invented by the Treaty of Versailles. It had existed for many centuries as the result of the positive interplay of Polish and German interests. The German merchants of Danzig had aided in the development and prosperity of that city, thanks to the overseas trade of Poland. Not only the development, but the very *raison d'être* of the city had been due to the formerly decisive fact of its situation at the mouth of the only great Polish river, and today to its position on the main waterway and railway line connecting interior Poland with the Baltic.

The Polish Minister for Foreign Affairs told Sir H. Kennard, British Ambassador at Warsaw, on June 27, that a *Freicorps* was being formed at Danzig, whereupon the British Consul-General in Danzig reported upon military preparations in the city. A *Freicorps* had been constituted, consisting of 4,000 men, of whom 2,000 were being quartered in barracks in Danzig and 2,000 in new buildings which were being constructed in Praust. Arms for their use were being surreptitiously introduced into the Free City from East Prussia. SA men began preparing the defenses around the Free City. The Polish Feast of the Seas was to be celebrated on June 27. Nearly a thousand SS officers from Germany arrived on June 25, obstensibly for sporting contests with the local SS.

In a speech on that day, Herr Forster, leader of the local Nazis, announced: "Before us lies a new era and for Germany a great epoch. During recent weeks our Danzig has become the centre of political events. We are all aware that we are in the final throes of our fight for freedom... Today everyone knows that the Free State will soon come to an end, and we also know how it will end."

The Danzig situation grew critical. Prime Minister Chamberlain, on July 10, defined the British attitude to the House of Commons. He outlined how the Vistula was Poland's only waterway to the Baltic, and the port at its mouth was therefore of vital importance to her. Another Power established at Danzig could block Poland's access to the sea and exert a stranglehold on her. Those who had been responsible for framing the prevailing Statute of the Free City had held these facts in mind and did their best to make some provision accordingly. There was no question of oppression of the German population of Danzig. The administration of the Free City was in German hands and the only restrictions were not of a kind to curtail the liberty of its citizens. The maintenance of the status quo had in fact been guaranteed by the German Chancellor himself up to 1944 by the ten-year treaty which he had concluded with Marshal Pilsudski.

A month later, in the middle of August, Sir Nevile Henderson discussed with Baron von Weizsäcker the dangers in the Danzig situation. The German State Secretary admitted them to be "even worse than last year."

Momentous news followed immediately—von Ribbentrop's visit to Moscow to sign a non-aggression pact with the USSR. The British Prime Minister sent a personal letter to Chancellor Hitler stating: "Whatever may prove to be the nature of the German-Soviet Agreement, it cannot alter Great Britain's obligations." He went on to say that it had been alleged if His Majesty's Government had made their position more clear in 1914, that great catastrophe might have been avoided.

The following day Sir Nevile Henderson reported his first interview with Herr Hitler: "I told him that we had guaranteed Poland against attack and that we would keep our word." He reported that Chancellor Hitler was excitable and uncompromising. His language was violent and exaggerated, both as regards England and Poland. Herr Hitler declared that Germany had nothing to lose, and Great Britain much. He was convinced that he had obtained the whip hand in European affairs. With what he believed to be a potentially omnipotent Russia at his back his advantage was plain. Hitler was at times incoherent. He proclaimed admiration of the British with envy of their achievements and hatred of their opposition to German aspirations.

Henderson made a brilliant analysis of Hitler's "Jekyll and Hyde" character: "He (Hitler) assiduously courted Great Britain, both as representing the aristocracy and most successful of the Nordic races, and as constituting the only seriously dangerous obstacle to his own far-reaching plan of German domination of Europe... Herr Hitler is a mixture of long-headed calculation and violent and arrogant impulse. The former drove him to seek Britain's friendship and the latter finally into war with her. He failed to realize why his military-cum-police tyranny should be repugnant to British ideals of individual and national freedom, or why he should not be allowed a free hand in Central and Eastern Europe to subjugate smaller, and, as he regards them, inferior peoples to superior German rule and culture. He believed he could buy British acquiescence in his own far-reaching schemes by offers of alliance with and guarantees for the British Empire. His great mistake was his complete failure to understand the inherent

British sense of morality, humanity and freedom. The good intentions of His Majesty's Government were, in fact, patently clear, and had Herr Hitler honestly desired or preferred a pacific settlement, all arrangements to that end seemed to be in full swing."

Hitler had started—but for a few days seemed hesitant. It looked as though Sir Nevile Henderson's visit to Berchtesgaden on August 23 did in fact have the effect of postponing the invasion of Poland—for one week. "I have reason to believe that the order for the German Army to advance into Poland was actually issued for the night of the 25th-26th August," he declared. Henderson established these historical facts: "In the afternoon of the 25th August all telephone communication between Berlin and London and Paris was unexpectedly cut for several hours. Celebrations at Tannenberg (the scene of Hindenburg's great victory over the Russians in 1914) were canceled on the 26th and the Party Rally at Nuremberg on the 27th August. All Naval, Military, and Air Attachés at Berlin were refused permission to leave the city without prior authority being obtained from the Ministry of War. All German airports were closed from that date, and the whole of Germany became a prohibited zone for all aircraft except the regular civil lines. All internal German air services were also suspended. Moreover, as from the 27th a system for the rationing of foodstuffs and other commodities throughout Germany came into force." This last extreme and depressing measure could hardly be explained except on the assumption that war should actually have been counted as breaking out on August 26.

The British statesman made the inference clear that Chancellor Hitler, as a consequence of Prime Minister Chamberlain's letter, had a last hesitation and countermanded the orders to his army, while the other arrangements had been permitted to be put in force. However, he observed, it could not have been any anticipation of the horrors of war that had deterred the Chancellor. He had unlimited confidence in the unrivaled army and air forces which he had created and he was certainly not averse to putting them to the test as far as Poland was concerned. In two months, he had assured the British Ambassador, the war in the East would be ended. He would then hurl a hundred and sixty divisions against the Western Front if England turned out to be so unwise as to oppose his plans. His hesitation would appear to have been due rather to one final effort to detach Britain from Poland.

At 12:45 P.M. on the 25th August, Sir Nevile Henderson received a message to the effect that Herr Hitler wished to receive him at the Chancellory at 1:30 that same afternoon. Of that meeting Sir Nevile Henderson writes: "He made me a verbal communication. Briefly put, Herr Hitler's proposals therein dealt with two groups of questions:

(a) the immediate necessity of a settlement of the dispute between Germany and Poland; and (b) an eventual offer of friendship or alliance between Germany and Great Britain. My interview with Herr Hitler, at which Herr von Ribbentrop and Doctor Schmidt were also present, lasted on this occasion over an hour.... He described his proposals as a last effort, for conscience' sake, to secure good relations with Great Britain, and he suggested that I should fly to London myself with them. I told His Excellency that, while I was fully prepared to consider this course, I felt it my duty to tell him quite clearly that my country could not possibly go back on its word to Poland, and that, however anxious we were for a better understanding with Germany, we could never reach one except on the basis of a negotiated settlement with Poland."

Hitler remained quite calm and never raised his voice once. The conversation lasted from twenty minutes to half an hour, but produced little that was new, except that the Chancellor was far more categoric than in the written reply as to his determination to attack Poland, if "another German were ill-treated in Poland."

"I spoke of the tragedy of war and of his immense responsibility, but his answer was that it would be all England's fault," reported the British envoy. "I refuted this, only to learn from him that England was determined to destroy and exterminate Germany. He was, he said, fifty years old; he preferred war now to when he would be fifty-five or sixty. I told him that it was absurd to talk of extermination. Nations could not be exterminated and a peaceful and prosperous Germany was a British interest. His answer was that it was England who was fighting for lesser races whereas he was fighting only for Germany; the Germans would this time fight to the last man; it would have been different in 1914 if he had been Chancellor then... In referring to the Russian Non-Aggression Pact, he observed that it was England which had forced him into agreement with Russia. He did not seem enthusiastic over it, but added that once he made agreement it would be for a long period."

Hitler's whole attitude was that of a guilty man seeking to throw the blame on everybody else. Meanwhile, toward the end of August, Herr Forster was declared by decree of the Danzig Senate to be Head of the State of the Free City. The Polish Government protested, and sought to establish contact with the German Government. The Polish envoy in Berlin found himself unable to secure an interview with the State Secretary, but saw Field Marshal Goering, who merely regretted that "the German policy of seeking to maintain friendly relations with Poland should have come to naught." He suggested that it would be to Poland's interest to abandon her alliance with England.

Again Britain interceded in a last effort to avert war. Sir Nevile

Henderson, on August 28, presented to Chancellor Hitler a British note, suggesting direct discussion between the German and Polish Governments. The note declared that His Majesty's Government had already received a definite assurance from the Polish Government that they were prepared to enter into discussion and that if such direct discussion led to agreement the way would be open to the negotiation of that wider and more complete understanding between Great Britain and Germany which both countries desired.

Hitler declared that his army was ready and eager for battle. The next day, August 29, the British envoy received from the Chancellor an answer to the effect that the German Government was prepared to accept the British proposal for direct German-Polish negotiations. The German reply said: "The British Government attach importance to two considerations: (1) that the existing danger of an imminent explosion should be eliminated as much as possible by direct negotiation; and (2) that the existence of the Polish State, in the form in which it would then continue to exist, should be adequately safeguarded in the economic and political sphere by means of international guarantees... The German Government desire in this way to give to the British Government and the British nation a proof of the sincerity of Germany's intentions to enter into a lasting friendship with Great Britain. The German Government accordingly, in these circumstances, agree to accept the British Government's offer of their good offices in securing the despatch to Berlin of a Polish Emissary with full powers."

This note proved to be designed duplicity. It was tendered with a gloved hand concealing a mailed fist. The Germans demanded what they knew to be the impossible. The Polish plenipotentiary must arrive the next day. It was a transparent trick. When this was realized, at 4 P.M. on August 30, Sir Nevile Henderson, on instructions from Downing Street, informed the German Government that it would be unreasonable to expect the British Government to produce a Polish representative in Berlin on that peremptory demand without sufficient time. At midnight the British envoy had an interview with Herr von Ribbentrop and handed over to him the British note to the effect that the method of contact and arrangements for discussion must obviously be agreed upon with all urgency by the German and Polish Governments. Sir Nevile Henderson suggested, in lieu of short notice, that normal procedure be adopted and that when the German proposals were ready the Polish Ambassador should be invited to call and receive them for transmission to his Government.

It was in this midnight interview that the fateful policy in the minds of Chancellor Hitler and his colleagues began to be revealed. Herr von Ribbentrop produced a lengthy document which "he read out in German aloud at top speed." When Sir Nevile Henderson asked for the text of the proposals in the document, Ribbentrop informed him that it was "too late," inasmuch as a Polish representative had not arrived in Berlin within the time limit. The British envoy responded by describing the procedure as an ultimatum. He asked why Herr von Ribbentrop could not adopt the normal procedure, give him a copy of the German proposals, and ask the Polish Ambassador to call on him to receive them. Ribbentrop responded "in the most violent terms," Sir Nevile Henderson reported. He swore he would never ask the Polish Ambassador to visit him.

On the evening of August 31, after a number of efforts to get in touch with responsible ministers, M. Lipski, the Polish representative, called at the German Foreign Office and received a copy of the German Government's demands. Here and now the trap was sprung. M. Lipski was unable to get through to his own Government by telephone.

At dawn on September 1, 1939, German forces invaded Poland. And yet, in spite of the onrush of events, the British Government at the eleventh hour made a last effort for peace. This again failed. The British envoy was instructed to inform Berlin that unless the German Government suspended all aggressive action in Poland and promptly withdrew their forces from Polish territory, the United Kingdom would without hesitation fulfill their obligations to Poland.

The British envoy reported during the night of September 1-2 that he had made the required communication to Herr von Ribbentrop and had asked for an immediate answer. Herr von Ribbentrop had replied that he would submit the communication to Chancellor Hitler. Contemporaneously, the Polish Government announced to the British Government that, although the Polish Ambassador in Berlin had seen Herr von Ribbentrop on August 31, and had expressed the willingness of the Polish Government to enter into direct negotiations, Polish territory had been invaded.

Efforts in the direction of peace made by the British Government were seconded by numerous other governments. The whole world by this time had been shocked by the imminence of war. His Holiness the Pope had intervened. Signor Mussolini, the King of the Belgians, Queen Wilhelmina of the Netherlands, and President Roosevelt had proffered their good offices. But Chancellor Hitler and his ministers had made up their minds and every conciliatory approach had been contemptuously rejected.

Prime Minister Chamberlain in the House of Commons on September 2, met a grave assembly of statesmen. They listened patiently as he spoke: "Sir Nevile Henderson was received by Herr von Ribbentrop at half-past nine last night, and he delivered the warning message which was read to the House yesterday. Herr von Ribbentrop replied that he would have to submit the communication to the German Chancellor. Our Ambassador declared his readiness to receive the Chancellor's reply. Up to the present no reply has been received. It may be that the delay is caused by consideration of a proposal which, meanwhile, had been put forward by the Italian Government, that hostilities should cease and that there should be immediately a conference between the Five Powers—Great Britain, France, Poland, Germany, and Italy. While appreciating the efforts of the Italian Government, His Majesty's Government, for their part, would find it impossible to take part in a conference while Poland is being subjected to invasion; her towns are under bombardment, and Danzig is being made the subject of a unilateral settlement by force."

Chamberlain, betrayed by Hitler at Munich, was in no mood to trust him again. He grimly declared: "His Majesty's Government will, as stated yesterday, be bound to taken action unless the German forces are withdrawn from Polish territory. They are in communication with the French Government as to the limit of the time within which it would be necessary for the British and French Governments to know whether the German Government was prepared to effect such a withdrawal. If the German Government should agree to withdraw their forces, then His Majesty's Government would be willing to regard the position as being the same as it was before the German forces crossed the Polish frontier. That is to say, the way would be open to discussion between the German and Polish Governments on the matters at issue between them, on the understanding that the settlement arrived at was one that safeguarded the vital interests of Poland and was secured by an international guarantee."

The Hitlerian method, however, was rapidly revealing itself. The Prime Minister announced that Herr Forster, who, on August 23, had in contravention of the Danzig constitution become the head of the State, had decreed the incorporation of Danzig in the Reich and the dissolution of the constitution. At the meeting of the Reichstag, the day before, a law had been passed for the reunion of Danzig with the Reich. Thus they had repudiated and defied the international status of Danzig as a Free City.

Great Britain was greatly disturbed by the course events had taken. Another world war was being precipitated. The Leader of the Labor Party in the House of Commons gave expression to the feeling of the entire country. "This is indeed a grave moment," Mr Greenwood said. "I believe the whole House is perturbed by the right honorable gentleman's statement.... Hours went by and news came in of bombing operations and news today of an intensification of it, and I wonder how long we are prepared to vacillate at a time when Britain, and all that Britain stands for, and human civilization are in peril. It is not for me to arouse suspicion, but if we must wait upon our allies I should have preferred the Prime Minister to say tonight definitely: 'It is either peace or war.' Tomorrow we meet at twelve—I hope the Prime Minister then will be in a position to make some further statement. Every minute's delay means loss of life, imperilling our national interests. The moment we look like weakening, on that moment dictatorship knows we are beaten. We are not beaten—we shall not be beaten."

The next day, Sunday, Prime Minister Chamberlain replied with an account of what had been going forward since German forces had crossed the Polish border and the fateful consequences as far as Great Britain was concerned: "The statement which I have to make this morning will show that there were no grounds for doubt. We were in consultation all day yesterday with the French Government, and we felt that the intensified action which the Germans were taking against Poland allowed no delay in making our position clear. Accordingly, we decided to send to our Ambassador in Berlin instructions which he was to hand at nine o'clock this morning to the German Foreign Secretary and which read as follows:

" 'Sir, in the communication which I had the honor to make to you on September 1, I informed you, on the instructions of His Majesty's Principal Secretary of State for Foreign Affairs, that unless the German Government were prepared to give His Majesty's Government in the United Kingdom satisfactory assurances that the German Government had suspended all aggressive action against Poland and were prepared promptly to withdraw their forces from Polish territory, His Majesty's Government in the United Kingdom would, without hesitation, fulfil their obligations to Poland.' "

The disillusioned old statesman hesitated. "Although this communication was made more than twenty-four hours ago no reply has been received, and German attacks upon Poland have been continued and intensified. I have accordingly the honor to inform you that unless, not later than 11 A.M. British Summer Time, today, September 3, satisfactory assurances to the above effect have been given by the German Government, and have reached His Majesty's Government in London, a state of war will exist between the two countries as from that hour."

Chamberlain's haggard face was pale. His hands trembled but his voice was firm: "That was the final note. No such undertaking was received by the time stipulated and consequently this country is at war with Germany. I am in a position to inform the House that, according to arrangements made between the British and French Governments, the French Ambassador in Berlin is at this moment making a similar demarche, accompanied also with a definite time limit..."

"We are ready. This is a sad day for all of us—and to none is it sadder than to me. Everything I have worked for, everything that I have hoped for, everything that I have believed in during my public life, has crashed into ruins. There is only one thing left for me to do, and that is to devote what strength and powers I have to forwarding the victory of the cause for which we have to sacrifice so much. I cannot tell what part I may be allowed to play myself. I trust I may live to see the day when Hitlerism has been destroyed and a liberated Europe has been re-established."

That evening in Buckingham Palace, King George, with Queen Elizabeth beside him, spoke to a waiting world. His voice over the radio reached the remotest outposts of the British Empire: "In this grave hour, perhaps the most fateful in our history, I send to every household of my peoples, both at home and overseas, this message, spoken with the same depth of feeling for each of you as if I were able to cross your threshold and speak to you myself. For the second time in the lives of most of us we are at war. Over and over again we have tried to find a peaceful way out of the differences between ourselves and those who are now our enemies. But it has been in vain.

"We have been called into a conflict. For we are called, with our allies, to meet the challenge of a principle which, if it were to prevail, would be fatal to any civilized order in the world. It is the principle which permits a State, in the selfish pursuit of power, to disregard its treaties and its solemn pledges; which sanctions the use of force, or threat of force, against the sovereignty and independence of other States. Such a principle, stripped of all disguises, is surely the mere primitive doctrine that might is right; and if this principle were established throughout the world, the freedom of our own country and of the whole British Commonwealth of Nations would be in danger. But far more than this—the peoples of the world would be kept in the fear of bondage, and all hopes of settled peace ended.

"This is the ultimate issue which confronts us. For the sake of all that we ourselves hold dear, and of the world's order and peace, it is unthinkable that we should refuse to meet the challenge. It is to this high purpose that I now call my people at home and my peoples across the seas, who will make our cause their own. I ask them to stand calm, firm and united in this time of trial. The task will be hard. There may be dark days ahead, and war can no longer be confined to the battlefield. But we can only do the right as we see the right and reverently commit our cause to God. If, one and all, we keep resolutely faithful to it, ready for whatever service or sacrifice it may demand, then, with God's help, we shall prevail. May He bless and keep us all."

Hardly had the King's voice ceased speaking when London was aroused by the first air-raid warning. It was announced later that the

Donaldson liner, *Athenia,* with fourteen hundred passengers, including over three hundred Americans, had been torpedoed west of the Hebrides. Most of the passengers and crew were saved.

The world was stunned by the shocking news. It could hardly believe that again it was to be plunged into war by the power-lust clique in Berlin. The British Commonwealth of Nations rose to the defense of the empire. Within less than twenty-four hours Australia and New Zealand declared war on Germany. Canada pledged support. England formed a cabinet of nine members, including Winston Churchill as First Lord of the Admiralty, the post he had held at outbreak of the First World War.

Germany, while conducting diplomatic relations as a smoke screen of deception, had become a war arsenal, building the most powerful war machine the world had yet known. The democracies, keeping their pledges with the League of Nations, were depending on the machinery of peace rather than war.

France, incredulous of German protestations of friendship, was maintaining a defensive attitude. Out of this mood of doubt, growing with the events in Germany, the Maginot Line had been built. This system of defense works matured in the mind of André Maginot, when he was Minister of War between 1927 and 1935, and spread out along the Franco-German frontier.

After Hitler came to power, Germany had erected its Siegfried Line. Designed by Dr. Fritz Todt, it ran from Holland to Switzerland. It was asserted on the German side in 1938 that hundreds of thousands of workmen, in addition to a hundred and twenty thousand members of the Labor Front and many regular soldiers, had succeeded in closing the frontier in five months. The works were not yet completed in 1938. There was work still to be done at the outbreak of hostilities, in spite of the fact that this vast army of men had toiled from fifteen to sixteen hours a day. According to Doctor Ley, at the head of the Nazi Labor Front, these "Men of the Frontier Wall" had won a victory over themselves for many of them had been Christian Socialists, Marxists, Centre Party men. In building Germany's massive fortification they were united. Todt's system was without the strength and intricacy of the Maginot Line, but was publicized as equally impregnable.

At the outbreak of war the British Army in Britain totaled but 1,000,000 men, including Reserves, Territorials, Militia; compulsory military service having been introduced in the preceding April. The ocean and the Royal Navy constituted of course Great Britain's Maginot and Siegfried Line. This against a powerful German Navy and an army estimated to set into motion over 12,000,000 men.

The German propaganda mill distorted history in a desperate attempt to remove the stain of guilt from their bloody hands. In an "out, damned spot" world-wide campaign they viciously attacked Great Britain and the United States. The usually scientific German mind erupted into a volcano of abuse. They pointed at the British Empire as "built by aggression" and misinterpreted all the fundamental facts of history, deliberately confusing the eras of discovery and exploration in blazing the trail for civilization with their own designs to conduct a war of aggression in the modern world.

They completely ignored the truths that the British Empire came into being as the natural result of centuries of exploration in the creation of an integrated world; that it was a civilizing force in human progress; that it liberated peoples of the earth from dark isolation and through processes of time extended freedom and self-government until it became a Commonwealth of free nations. All German plots to disrupt the unity of the U. S. and England were futile. Attempts to play one liberty-loving nation against the other proved boomerangs.

The Germans were suddenly seized with indignation over India. The fact was ignored that the British had been working for years to find some solution whereby they could grant India its independence without creating bloody civil war and chaos among its conflicting states, castes, and religions, and leaving them to become the prey of Japan or some other aggressor nation in possible collusion with Germany herself. So the Nazis rose in hypocritical rage when they instigated World War II and found that only because of British protection the Axis could not take possession. Future India, free and independent will be ever grateful to the Allied liberators for saving her from falling under the Japanese yoke.

Foiled in this conspiracy the Germans, again ignoring historical truths by neglecting to hold events in juxtaposition with time, and conditions and principles, accused the American people of being an aggressor nation. It did not reveal that in the discovery and exploration of our own continent, laying the foundations for "life, liberty and the pursuit of happiness" on the principles that "all men are created equal," internal uprisings in pioneering days in the wilderness must again be judged in relation to their times, their "sphere of history." And that our civil strifes were for the extension of freedom and our foreign wars in every instance were for the liberation of oppressed peoples, or in defense of our rights—never to impose despotism or tyranny, or to subjugate another nation under iron rule.

Thus, through German machinations, we see how World War II broke upon nations which did not believe it could happen, upon a world unprepared.

18

FRANCE MEETS THE CRISIS IN DEFENSE OF LIBERTY

THE FRENCH people, true to their priceless heritage of *liberté, égalité, fraternité*, prepared to meet the impact of impending events. For the third time in seventy years, German hordes turned France into a bloody battleground. The nation that had thrown off the shackles of tyranny in the French Revolution, and the first to extend aid to the American Revolution, now took its place with the democracies in World War II, as it had done in the First World War.

France had passed through many crises during the centuries, but its inherent love for liberty had never faltered. Again it was to be tested in the crucible of fire. Political intrigues, military debacles, defeat, capitulations, and captivity were to confront the French people, but the soul of France was never to surrender.

At 8:30 on that Sunday night of September 3, 1939, after three days of incredible suspense while the Germans thundered into Poland and their planes roared above that helpless country, millions of men and women waited. At eleven o'clock that morning the tired, sorrowful voice of Neville Chamberlain had proclaimed the existence of a state of war between the British Empire and Germany. None who heard Chamberlain speak that day, as he painfully enunciated each syllable, would ever forget the words or the tone.

More than nine tense hours later, Edouard Daladier, baker's son and Premier of France, ranged his country beside its old ally of a quarter of a century before against the same enemy, the foe who had changed only his banner, never his nature or his purpose—*the conquest of the world*.

Daladier spoke from a capital prepared for the worst. Many Parisians left the city when the first word came of the Russian-German pact of August, 1939.

That night, the last before the war, the lights went out in Paris; the city passed into the long darkness that it could not have dreamed awaited it. Civilians who still remained were ordered to leave by whatever means they could, for the trains were barred to them. Many found themselves compelled to walk as much as fifty miles to their appointed place of refuge. The air was heavy with war, but the people went, under orders. As they trudged along the choked roadways, they asked one another, "Is America going to help us this time?"

Deputies listened intently as Daladier cited the forces working for peace: the determination of the Western Powers to exhaust every avenue of peace before resorting to force; the great desire of the neutral democracies in Europe and the West to avert another holocaust. Then arose the bravest of modern French statesmen, the wise Herriot, who spoke for his country: "France is ready to meet this peril head high and conscience clear... *sans peur et sans reproche.*"

At five o'clock on Sunday afternoon the last French ultimatum to the Germans expired, and the state of war came automatically into being. At that hour the rôle of Robert Coulondre, the French Ambassador in Berlin, ended. The army took over the nation. George Bonnet, one of the engineers of Munich, was still Foreign Minister, but the fate of the country lay now with the Commander in Chief, General Maurice Gustave Gamelin, and his colleagues. The rôle of Gamelin was not to be long; those of some of his associates were to be clouded. The Commander in Chief of the French Navy was Admiral Jean-François Darlan.

Warfare between France and Germany was considered by military experts an impossibility, for each country had supposedly sealed itself behind an impregnable line of the most modern and ingenious fortifications. The Maginot Line was an intricate and continuous chain of fortresses from the Swiss to the Belgian borders. Below the Swiss border, the experts believed, no such protection was necessary, because nature had provided sufficient defense. Above the Belgian border none could be built because of the opposition of the Belgian Government, which emphasized repeatedly its neutrality toward all the countries of Europe and its firm desire to avoid war.

Between the French-German borders, ran the fabulous subterranean defense works to protect the millions who lived behind it. The casual traveler along its route could never have guessed that beneath the trees and barns, among which this road wound, there lay hidden great guns that could hurl tons of steel against an advancing army. Nor could they know that below these guns there were barracks for the thousands of men who served them—a great defensive army to counter any attacker who, by some miracle, might effect a penetration somewhere along this "impregnable" fortress. The ultimate strength and weakness of this magnificent engineering conception would be revealed by time.

Across the Rhine the Germans were behind their Siegfried Line; this was not a continuous line, but broken here and there. The Germans, less considerate of the feelings of their neighbors, had run their fortifications all the way to the North Sea. Between the two defense systems there lay no man's land.

On the second night of the war sirens shrieked in Paris. Residents extinguished the lights they had already carefully shielded by putting blue or yellow paint or paper over every window. Some, but by no means all, for there was a generation of Parisians who had never seen an air raid, went to the designated *abris* in the cellars and organized friendly card games in the shelters. The alarm, though the people did not know it then, was false. As they waited for the all-clear to sound, they talked about this new war.

Frenchmen hoped—and many of them allowed themselves to believe it, since war is an irrational thing—that this would be a short conflict with a reasonable ending. Their Government took a more realistic view. As if in anticipation of the possibility of a long war, it added a protocol to its treaty of alliance with Poland. In this new document, each country pledged itself not to make peace without the consent of the other. This obligation had already been assumed by Poland and Great Britain.

On the third day of the war, September 6, French troops crossed the French-German border. This incursion, symbolic though it was in its contrast to the early days of the First World War, was mere patrol activity. At first the Germans ignored it; then they launched counterthrusts. The French shifted their operations to the area between the Saar and the foothills of the Vosges. In less than a week, their troops entered the outskirts of the industrial city of Saarbruecken. British troops arrived in France and moved up toward the front to the accompaniment of cheers from every French town through which they passed.

Indicative of the solidity of the Anglo-French alliance, was the first meeting of the Supreme War Council. This session, held on French soil, was attended by Prime Minister Chamberlain, Premier Daladier, and their respective aides. The Allies reiterated their resolution to prosecute the war to ultimate victory.

Military activity in the Saar area grew more lively. The Germans counterattacked again and claimed the recapture of the town of Birnberg, southeast of Saarbruecken. However, the French sprang back quickly, again advanced in this sector, despite the fire of German artillery and the presence of land mines. The fighting seesawed back and forth and spread laterally until the entire 125-mile front between Switzerland and Luxembourg was in action. It was in the Saar area that the major clashes occurred. There the first French soldier to be killed in this war fell, a twenty-nine-year-old sergeant, Clément Sarantyn. Artillery bore the brunt of the battle, each side shelling the rear areas behind its opponents' main lines.

Shocked by the Russian-German pact and the subsequent partition of Poland, the French Government outlawed the Communist Party and all its subsidiary groups, despite its undoubted strength in industrial areas, particularly those around Paris. Its seventy-two representatives in the Chamber and the two in the Senate were not unseated, however, although they were warned that, if they violated the new decree in any way, they would be prosecuted as private citizens.

Insidious German propaganda was "firing" on the home front. A renegade Frenchman, known as the traitor of Stuttgart, spoke every night on the German radio, warning his compatriots to get out of the war, criticizing them for standing by the British, and insinuating to the men at the front that their fellows at home were exploiting their absence. German officials declared that "England was going to fight to the last Frenchman."

In a broadcast to the Germans when the war was hardly a month old, Hitler once more gave the Allies the choice between war to destruction or peace on his terms. But Daladier, like Chamberlain, had learned the lesson of accepting German terms; they had learned it together at Munich. The French Premier, like the British Prime Minister, again refused to accept the German's word; he recalled the record of broken pledges and the almost unbroken sequence of outrages that had marked the history of the Third Reich.

It was at this time that Britain and France entered into a treaty of alliance with Turkey, Germany's old partner in World War I. Under this alliance Turkey pledged herself to render military assistance to the Allies if, being attacked in the Mediterranean area, they called on her to do so. This treaty was greeted with much acclaim in both France and England.

Then came the mysterious news from Germany that the French had left all the German territory they had occupied earlier. The Germans gave two versions: one said that the French had evacuated on the orders of their own High Command without the exertion of any German pressure; the other asserted that the Germans had pushed the French out of Germany. In either case, German soil was once more free of French troops. For a long time thereafter, the Germans contented themselves with long-range artillery shelling of France.

By sea and air German arms directed increasing blows at Britain. They began to proclaim that their real enemy was Britain, and that they desired only to live on the most peaceful terms with France. Foreign Minister von Ribbentrop made a turgid speech in an attempt to destroy the Anglo-French alliance and to achieve a separate peace with France. Resorting to diabolical treachery, ostensibly addressing Nazi Party veterans in Danzig, he audaciously told the French that they had been forced into war by "unparalleled cunning, cynicism, and brutality on the part of Britain and her henchmen in Paris and in the French Government." Frenchmen, however, scoffed at this as a desperate plot to sow dissension and lure them into a trap.

The British dug in on the so-called Western Front, prepared to spend the winter there with the French troops. At this point the Germans began to initiate their "war of nerves." Having regained all their briefly occupied territory, they deployed a vast body of troops on a

650-mile front that extended from the North Sea to Switzerland, facing the Low Countries, France, and Switzerland. Continued patrol activities and accelerated artillery bombardments led to the belief that this was the prelude to an imminent general offensive.

But the offensive did not materialize. Western Europe settled back to endure its first winter of the Second World War, the inception of that phase that was first so incredulously and falsely dubbed *le drôle de guerre*—the phony war—and that was finally to flame into a conflagration that was to sweep the world.

At irregular intervals some sensational event occurred to startle the world. On November 8, 1939, a bomb explosion destroyed part of the famous Munich beer hall where Hitler had launched his *Putsch* in 1923. The German Chancellor was addressing a reunion of his old comrades in the old drinking place. Barely a half-hour after his departure, a time bomb burst inside the hall, killing several persons and wounding many others. German propaganda attributed the explosion to the customary scapegoats—"British agents, Jews, and Bolsheviks. These were accused of an attempt on the sacred person of the Fuehrer.

The world viewed the matter with skepticism. One dominant group ascribed the explosion to anti-Hitler elements within Germany and argued that the Nazis' grip on their compatriots was weakening. The major theorists proceeded from the same premise to the conclusion that the explosion had been arranged by the Nazis themselves in order to rally fresh popular support to their leader and the war that he had begun.

The British, however, were awakening to the intrigues and machinations of the Nazi mentality. Through the confusion of events they began to decipher the handwriting on the wall. Britain formed an economic alliance with France for the more efficient prosecution of the war. The French merchant fleet was placed under British control for the duration. The joint economic council thus set up was headed by a Frenchman, Jean Monnet, who was destined to serve his country in a similar rôle, though of far greater scope, a few years later. At the same time, France adopted the British policy of confiscating German exports found on ships running the Allied blockade, in which the French Navy was playing its full part.

The rulers of Belgium and the Netherlands, appalled at the possibilities of a full-scale modern war, made an appeal to the belligerents to seek an immediate peaceful solution. The proposal was carefully examined and as carefully and deliberately rejected. France knew now that in this war of nerves she was fighting for her life against a Germany that had lost even the few shreds of honor in which the Hohenzollern régime had tried to cloak itself. She knew that no treaty could be made with this unscrupulous enemy.

Early in the war France had imposed tight restrictions on her border with Italy, despite Rome's declaration of neutrality—a neutrality that obviously favored Germany. France and Italy had not interrupted their economic relations, but from time to time Italy voiced demands, addressed to no named nation, for greater advantages in the Mediterranean. In an effort to hold Italy's friendship, France relaxed the regulations on her Italian border and, in reassuring response, Italy released 300,000 soldiers for "indefinite leaves!" For the moment it appeared that there was no danger from the Italian neighbors.

The suddenness of the crisis in eastern Europe, followed by the unexpected Russian invasion of Finland, left France as stunned and bewildered as it did the rest of the world. Few realized what lay behind that move. This new turn distracted attention from the Western Front for a while. Soon, however, it was to receive a rude awakening. Hitler was waiting for the psychological moment to strike.

A few days before Christmas, the French Government issued its Yellow Book on the causes of the war. Setting forth the Government's consistent efforts to maintain peace, it reviewed the record of German duplicity and aggression since the Munich Accord of September, 1938. It revealed that, as early as December of that year, Britain and France had been warned of the possibility of the realization of that perennial dream of the German General Staff—an alliance between Germany and Russia.

When Christmas came in 1939, four months after the declaration of war, French soil had not yet been bombed from the air. Many Frenchmen believed that the reason was M. Daladier's firm warning to the Germans that any such attack would bring bomb-for-bomb reprisal. Others, supported by neutral observers, attributed the lack of bombing rather to continued German efforts to split the Allies.

Edouard Daladier addressed the Senate of France in the holiday week, imbued with a vision that the Europe of the future must be a united Europe, with national differences and rivalries sunk forever. The new year was marked by an atmosphere of confidence.

Despite the intermittent alarms and the steady invasion of German troops on the borders of the Low Countries, the front between France and Germany remained unchanged. The Germans were engaged in a war of words, dire threats, and intimidations. Supplementing the placards they had used in the First World War, they brought up amplifiers to broadcast to the *poilus* their appeals for "reason," for fraternization, and for peace. Introduced by a blare of music, these messages invariably reiterated the theme that the Germans had no quarrel with the French. This developed into a war of lies in a conspiracy to drive France out of the war. French troops at the front, which was often no wider than the Rhine itself, were bombarded with wild tales of what was happening to their home folk. These "bombs of scandal" were a last resort to arouse uprisings against their British brothers.

Overnight it became a war of broadcasting systems. The French countered by erecting their own amplifiers on their side of the front. Their most powerful weapon was the dissemination of truthful news, not only from home but from all over the world.

After the Chamber of Deputies had debated the problems of censorship, Premier Daladier announced on February 27 that liberty of political discussion would thereafter be permitted to the press. To facilitate the dissemination of news to the people, a Cabinet post for information and propaganda would be inaugurated.

Daladier's ship of state was broken on the rocks of the Finnish policy. The French Senate reaffirmed its confidence in the Premier, but, when the question was put to the Chamber, three hundred Deputies deliberately abstained from voting. The result was technically a vote of confidence, but its margin was so small and the proposition of abstention was so great that the Premier was in effect compelled to submit his resignation. On March 20 Daladier was replaced as Premier by his Finance Minister, Paul Reynaud, who immediately took his predecessor into the Cabinet as Minister of War.

It was now taken for granted that the war would go on for some time. Premier Reynaud submitted the list of his ministers to the Chamber which approved it by a margin of one vote. Support quickly rallied to the new Cabinet, for its leader was not stigmatized in the public eye with the Munich appeasement and vacillation on Finland.

Monsieur Reynaud immediately undertook to revitalize the war effort in France. The paramount question on every Frenchman's lips was: "Will America come to our aid as it did in World War I?"

The French and British people had full faith in President Roosevelt. Their only fear was that he might be betrayed by men in his own Senate as Woodrow Wilson had been betrayed after World War I. This, they believed, was one of the fundamental causes of World War II. Aroused to the spirit of the old French Revolution, Premier Reynaud broadcast their decision to the United States, the traditional ally of France. He assured America that the French people would never tolerate a compromise peace and declared: "France will fight Germany to complete defeat."

Ten days later, the "phony war" was over. German subterfuges ceased. While engaged in "softening up" processes and attempts to create disunion between France and Great Britain, the Germans struck their blow under the delusion that they could win the war before America could be aroused to action. How far their miscalculations carried them, and how little they understood the American spirit and the power of democracy, was eventually to stagger the German mind.

GERMAN JUGGERNAUT HURLS ITS POWER AT FRANCE

MILLIONS of Germans stood poised to pour into France as soon as her eastern wall of steel and flesh was weakened. The French and British remained equally tensed to meet the first blow. At sea the German raiders, surface and submarine, were desperately attempting to keep the British and French Navies from establishing a steady flow of arms, men, and supplies.

Five days after the Scandinavian invasion, the Germans made their first attempt to cross the Rhine. Their forces launched an attack on a casemate forming part of the Maginot Line. The men of the underground forts, no longer bored by a winter of inaction but keyed to a taut alertness, threw back the invading forces. Dawn might bring on France the bloody day that had broken over Norway. Yet, six days after this German attack, thousands of *poilus* were marching through the streets of Aandalsnes, a town in Norway of which, a week before, probably none of them had ever heard.

Fifty thousand strong, Frenchmen and Britons had sailed to keep their given word, and were now on the threshold of the battle—united in the "fusion" that their two countries had so boldly proclaimed and which they had so firmly embraced for the liberation of Europe from the German peril.

The departure of so many trained French soldiers to so distant a front was a signal to a gathering enemy. Italy, which had begun cautiously to renew her reiterations of her claims on France, spurned Premier Reynaud's offer of an amicable discussion looking toward the settlement of the issues dividing the two countries. "Work and arm!" the Italian dictator cried to his people. Frenchmen began to look apprehensively toward another potential front.

The French were fighting bravely in Norway, as they have always fought everywhere, but the terrain was strange and difficult, even for the Alpine Chasseurs who had long been schooled in mountain fighting. German planes were the unchallenged masters of the Norwegian skies. Mercilessly they bombed the Allies' communications routes and marching men, setting ablaze the few ports through which the French and British could receive fresh supplies.

French troops fighting beside Canadians pushed the Germans back and threatened to seize Narvik. Other Frenchmen, comrades of English troops, isolated the German garrison in the port of Trondheim. But inevitably the Germans reinforced their threatened troops and broke the Allies' lines.

Twelve days after the first French troops had landed in Norway, they were forced to evacuate the central and southern parts of the country. The forces in the Narvik area, being better established and farther from the enemy's major bases, stood their ground.

The Norwegian campaign was obviously going to prove a failure; the Germans would conquer the country. Suspicious activities in Italy foreshadowed treachery.

There was grave apprehension in Paris. Who would be next? M. Reynaud's accounting, first to the Senate and then to the Chamber of Deputies, was secret. The debates that followed were behind closed doors. The Senators dispensed with the formality of a vote, but it was obvious that this statesman of France, who bound himself to no slavery to doctrine or party, had won the confidence of the upper house. And in the Chamber, which had begun his administration by giving him a margin of but a single vote, the man who had always succeeded in any venture he undertook emerged with the resounding approval of every one of the 515 Deputies who voted—and only 16 abstained.

Reinforced in his judgments, Premier Reynaud joined in the decision of the Supreme War Council to strengthen the Allies' guard in the Middle East. A combined French and British fleet steamed for the Levant and took up its station at Alexandria, Egypt, where the French ships were to lie idle for three crucial years.

While the British and French thus diverted their forces, with strong contingents still striving to drive the Germains out of Narvik, the Italian war lord seized his opportunity. Proclaiming the Mediterranean to be his sea, he roared a warning that his country would repulse any attacks made on it.

The Norwegian campaign was, for practical purposes, settled. A wave of fear spread simultaneously over all Europe; a dread that a new German blow would come at once. There were ominous gestures towards the Balkans.

The Netherlands Government, on May 8, suddenly canceled all leaves for the armed forces and silenced the wires that gave Holland contact with other countries. Rigid secrecy as to the reason for the unexpected move was maintained. An equally dramatic crisis was just ending in Britain, where Prime Minister Chamberlain had been compelled to defend himself against bitter attacks on the conduct of his Government in prosecuting the war. A good part of the western world went to bed on the night of May 9, 1940, wondering who was to be the next leader of the British Empire.

Friday, May 10, had not dawned, when the roar of German guns and the crash of German bombs shocked the civilized world. Without warning, without even the attempt at a pretext, the Huns had repeated the crime of 1914, smashing into Belgium—and magnified the outrage against their neighbors by simultaneous attacks on Holland and Luxembourg. Great fleets of planes roared over the three countries, unloading bombs and parachutists—those new-style soldiers at which all the Allies' authorities had mocked. These airborne vandals landed wearing or carrying the uniforms of the country they were violating.

Again the pledge given by Britain and France was to be honored. Two hours after the first bomb had fallen on Brussels, French and British soldiers rolled over the imaginary line that separated France from Belgium.

That day of the tenth of May was one of terror and bewilderment. Incessantly the Germans blared their claims of fantastic successes. No one, in the invaded countries or in the capitals of their allies, could have any certainty of the way the battle was going. But everyone knew that brave little Belgium and Holland were not military nations with great establishments and vast forges for the production of arms. These peaceful peoples were being murdered to clear the roadway to France.

All day the sirens shrieked in Nancy, though the city itself was never bombed. Lyon was struck, and many towns in Lorraine and the Rhône Valley. While the objectives were claimed to be military targets, airfields, communications and factories, it was a reign of terror—the long-boasted blitzkrieg. Screams of those on whom it fell muted the announcement that in London the greatest friend France had among Britons was now at the head of the Government: Winston Churchill.

The scenes along roadways leading into France were indescribable. Tens of thousands of men, women, and children were fleeing in panic from Rotterdam and The Hague, Antwerp and Brussels and Namur—the rich, the comfortable, the shopkeepers, the poor—forced, at the muzzles of German guns into a comradeship of suffering. These were the "enemy" against whom the Germans were waging war. They packed the roads that might lead anywhere as long as it was beyond the fields of carnage.

Into the French border cities streamed the hunted and the hurt, the hungry and the weary. The roads of France were now as red as the roads of Belgium and Holland—red with blood.

Soon the French in the bordering villages were joining the refugees in flight from the oncoming Germans.

Their fears had been heightened by the migrants who poured past their houses, begging a bit of bread or wine and stopping only long enough to describe the litter of bodies that was left on every road after the German fliers had passed over. Every vehicle had been pressed into service to carry the fugitives and what they could take with them. Those who could find no vehicle just walked blindly on.

Thousands of men and women plodding the highway, were carrying terror-stricken children. Blocking this mass of humanity were hundreds of automobiles and trucks, wagons and dogcarts and wheelbarrows. An old laborer would slow his own flight to spare a wearied woman by pushing the barrow in which he made her ride. Here a father, when a bullet killed the horse taken from the farm, put himself between the shafts of the heavy wagon in which his children rode. Every highway, it seemed, was black with the trudging thousands.

These were the same roads that were vital to the great convoys of brown trucks and guns that must roll up into Belgium to keep the Germans out of France; and to the thousands of French *poilus* and khaki-clad soldiers of the British Empire who must man the guns and stop the German bullets. But the fugitives had got to the roads first; everywhere their long lines had to be halted and disbanded to let the troops by. The Germans, who knew that every minute they delayed the Allied soldiers was precious to them, deliberately created the confusion to block the highways.

No one who fled from a peaceful home in Belgium or the Netherlands could say with certainty how many times in any given day he had heard the awful war song of the Heinkels and the Junkers and the Messerschmitts sprinkling the refugee lines with machine guns. At regular intervals, the great dark machines plunged almost to the earth, only to straighten and lunge straight ahead, bombs tumbling endlessly from their bellies while a dozen mouths spat steel into the terrified travelers. Each time, like animals driven by blind instinct, people dived for a ditch or a bush, or threw themselves under a wrecked vehicle.

When the last plane followed its leader down the line, the survivors would pick themselves up and give what aid they could to the victims.

Paris, to every foreigner the symbol of luxury and gaiety, became a city of refuge in which no one could find shelter. Every hotel, every pension was crowded; the streets were blocked with automobiles whose plates called the roll of all the violated soil to the north and east. Disorganized as the city was, the Cabinet was still there, though preparations had been made against an eventual removal.

M. Reynaud, in an appeal to the sentiment of national unity, enlarged his Government, including in it the extremists of the left and of the right. In the War Ministry he put an Under-Secretary, a young general whose name he had good reason to know and on whose military theories he knew he must count—Charles de Gaulle. In the interlude between the two wars, De Gaulle had been the storm center. Old time military men called him a fanatic whose preoccupation was tanks and motorized forces—a preposterous dreamer—a visionary who spoke of using cumbrous metal monsters like cavalry and even forming whole divisions of mechanized troops, warriors in mobile fortresses.

Only five years before, the then Colonel de Gaulle had found but one man, a civilian unversed in military matters, who listened to him and found merit in what he had to say—one M. Reynaud, a Deputy. Impressed by the arguments of De Gaulle, he introduced into the Chamber a bill for the creation of ten corps of technicians to develop what has become known as the armor of the modern army and enable France to wage, if the need arose, a war of smashing attack. For this M. Reynaud was put into the same category as the officer. A Marshal of France scoffed at the theorizing and, when the bill was put to the Chamber, it received only one vote—it's sponsors.

But now the tanks of Germany were smashing their way across the Low Countries and against the walls of France; and their commander had paid public tribute to the book of Colonel de Gaulle for having taught him the mastery of the tools with which he was even now smashing into the country of its author.

French tanks—what there were of them—had already gone into battle against German armor in Belgium. They had proved puny against the mightier machines of the invaders and the latter's superior skill in handling them. De Gaulle's book had been ignored by the French General Staff, which, having reluctantly enough allowed some tanks to be incorporated into the army, had little or no idea how to employ them and coördinate them with the other arms.

But they had been drawn from the point where the Germans feared that they might be, and a gap, though the Allies were not aware of it, had been left. The Maginot Line, whose impregnability was axiomatic to so many, ended at the Luxembourg border; beyond, there was a series of hastily constructed defenses, neither so strong nor so deep as the Maginot Line itself, and not, like it, connected one with another. The Germans had apparently shown no desire, thus far, to take any route into France but the historic road through Belgium and an auxiliary line that ran to the north. To meet both these drives the British and French had rushed the bulk of their forces, men and weapons, leaving the sector between them and the Maginot Line defended relatively lightly.

Five days after they had first struck, the Germans had burned and butchered their way through Holland to augment their own troops in Belgium.

It was believed that the Germans who had entered the lower part of Belgium would unite with the force to the north, and so the Allies had massed to meet them on the Meuse. But the Germans, masters for centuries in the science of war, swung suddenly south and lanced through Belgium past the French border, stabbing directly into Sedan. The shrewd German General Erwin Rommel sent his low-flying black planes out ahead of his light armor, augmented with the fearsome dive bomber that plummeted almost like the missile it finally released.

Before these new tactics the weak defenses crumbled. The Germans gained a new triumph at Sedan, a five-day victory.

At an outpost of the Allies in the far north, the British and French were still sending supplies to the small forces in the Narvik area in Norway. But, for all the world—and for Frenchmen in particular—the was was now being fought entirely in a little triangle of land that ran through three countries. The Allies were massing in a giant L. Its base ran west, from a point just south of the junction of the French, Belgian, and Luxembourg borders, to Meizieres and Charleville; thence the upright pierced deep into Belgium along a line through Dinant and Namur. The names that had earned undying fame a quarter-century before were already emerging into the pitiless glare of bomb-flare again.

As the Germans pushed through the Ardennes, all three Allied armies counterattacked wherever they could. Paris was aflame with rumors. The Germans were at Arras! They had taken Rheims! Laon and Compiègne had fallen! No one knew whom to trust among all these bearers of evil tidings. Premier Reynaud went before a microphone to calm the capital and the nation, to scotch the fearful rumors.

He proclaimed the capital a military area and transferred its rule to the army. He emphasized the reports sent from the front by General Henri-Honoré Giraud, who had distinguished himself so well in the First World War, and General Charles Huntziger: they claimed to have somewhat stabilized the situation. As far as could be determined, no real assault had been launched against the Maginot Line, though an influx of German troops to the enemy's positions near the Swiss border was promptly met by similar reinforcement on the French side.

The Battle of the Meuse screamed and pounded to its climax on May 15. German tanks and planes again led the way; behind came the field-gray hordes, cutting into the often-martyred soil of northern France. They smashed as much as forty-five miles into France and cut out a pocket that ran from Rethel on the south, to the Sambre River on the north.

The generalissimo of the French armies, Maurice-Gustave Gamelin, who must have known that already his command was crumbling beneath him, called on his troops to "conquer or die"—to give no more ground to the invader. For a day the Germans relaxed their pressure in this area, having penetrated the outer works of the "little Maginot" around Sedan and, as the French themselves admitted, driven deeply to the rear. The enemy suddenly pressed his ground effort on a line from Brussels to Antwerp, where British troops were aiding the Belgians. In the air, the onslaught never relaxed over any area.

Premier Reynaud, who had intimated that the war might demand the introduction of "new methods and new men," reorganized his Cabinet once again. He relieved his predecessor, Edouard Daladier, of the War Ministry, assuming it himself with full responsibility for the conduct of the war. As a civilian, he found it necessary to appoint a Vice-Premier whose special task it would be to advise him in his capacity as War Minister. The man he named was the aged Marshal of France, Henri-Philippe Pétain.

When the war began, Marshal Pétain was the French Ambassador to Madrid. Throughout the world he was generally esteemed as a man of honor and gallantry. The name of "hero of Verdun" came automatically to the mind when he was mentioned. Few knew what old Papa Joffre knew, a quarter-century before, that Pétain had wanted to surrender at Verdun: to give up not only the battle but the war itself, and bow to Germany. Joffre had been sent to replace the defeatist Pétain so that the battle might be won.

The presence of Marshal Pétain and young General de Gaulle in the same Cabinet—though De Gaulle was in the field now—was indicative of the basic confusion that prevailed in the attempt at unity in the Government.

Pétain was a confirmed believer in defensive warfare and expressed himself as utterly confident in the ability of the Maginot Line to win the war for France. General de Gaulle believed in vigorous attack—and then more attack—in never being put on the defensive.

Both men were devout Catholics. Both were the sons of good, upper-middle-class French families—De Gaulle, indeed, was of the old petty nobility. Both were conservatives in politics in so far as they concerned themselves with politics. Primarily, their interests were military. But all through the interlude between the wars, Pétain had urged amity with Germany and confidence and trust in any government that was in power there. De Gaulle had warned that France's mortal peril lay always across the Rhine—he knew the Germans.

Marshal Pétain, during his diplomatic mission in Madrid, did not hesitate to remain on the most friendly terms with the German Ambassador there, even after September 3, 1939; their intimacy, in fact, continued until the Marshal returned to Paris to become Vice-Premier. On one occasion, in March of 1940, when the "phony war" was drawing to its end, the Marshal came home to make a routine report. Before he entrained again for Madrid, he told his closest friends, in effect: "You may expect me again about the middle of May. I think I shall be needed then."

There was another change made in the Cabinet. Georges Mandel, who had been Minister of Colonies, became Minister of the Interior—a change that may have cost him his life. M. Mandel was known for his executive ability and his firm hand. As Minister of the Interior, it was his duty to insure the execution of the decrees just promulgated under which all enemy aliens were interned. This order applied to all persons of German nationality and to those who were now stateless but whose last previous nationality had been German: in other words, to the many German refugees, Jewish and Christian, who had congregated in Paris and elsewhere. M. Mandel, as certain pro-Fascist elements, still vociferous, pointed out at once, was Jewish; but M. Mandel was a Frenchman, and in wartime, at least, a good Frenchman's religion is France. He proceeded at once to the performance of his duties: and every German refugee had to submit to the law.

The refugees of the Allied nations were also thronging France. But they were paying well, of their own volition, for what France gave them: they were offering her their lives. The Poles had formed their armies. The Belgian Government, which had already fled from Brussels to Ostende and was soon to seek new refuge in France, had instructed those Belgians—civilians, soldiers and airmen—who had fled or retreated into France, to rejoin their units or offer their services to the French. Thousands of other foreigners who were not refugees but Frenchmen by adoption had already put on the uniform of France.

The Germans, on May 17, had launched a violent blow along the whole front. They had broken through the fortifications of the Belgian-French border for a distance of sixty-two miles on a line running from a point just south of Maubeuge to Carignan, south of Sedan, besides having penetrated to a point north of Rethel.

Primarily, it seemed, the Germans intended to strike for the Channel coast somewhere far to the rear of the main body of the Allied forces and thus to bottle them up with their backs to the sea. Presumably the Germans expected an easy surrender or a mass slaughter.

Berlin insisted that its troops were already within sixty miles of Paris in a thrust down the line of the Aisne River; the French said that the Germans' extreme vanguard was still ninety miles away. The Germans did not emphasize their progress from the northern end of the bulge, but already they were only eighty-five miles from Abbeville.

As the Germans widened the wound they had gashed into the side of France, they plunged deeper along a corridor sixty miles broad. Its course was so set that from it either of two possibilities—or both—was open to them: a blow northward toward the coast or a lunge to the south and Paris. From hour to hour, no one knew what the enemy would choose in this area of the three rivers: the Sambre and the Aisne, which formed the walls of the corridor, and the Oise, which lay ahead. In Belgium, where the battle was hopeless, British and Belgian troops were retreating toward France.

It was during these crucial hours, as Belgium's fate became apparent and the fate of France was hanging in the hands of the Germans, General Gamelin yielded the command of the Allied armies to General Maxime Weygand. Immediately the sanguine grew more sanguine, for Weygand had been the right-hand man of Marshal Foch in wresting final victory out of the First World War.

General Gamelin, almost twenty years younger than Marshal Pétain, was aware of the technical developments of his time and of the march of international events. That another war between France and Germany had been inevitable he accepted as a first truth; he was prepared to fight it with mechanized forces, though small in strength. Gamelin was a disciple of the war of movement, but only for defense: he shunned the attack. A man thoroughly aware of his own abilities if not of his own limitations, Gamelin was a career officer who found politics anathema. He refused offers of a Ministry, to remain purely a military man.

On the other hand, Gamelin had long believed in a military alliance with Russia. He admired its army in many respects, not the least of which were its armor and its aviation, as well as its chief officers. In his years at the War College in Paris, after his graduation from St. Cyr, the West Point of France, and tours of duty in Africa, he studied under Foch; in the First World War he was the intimate of Joffre. Throughout his career he was known for his willingness to learn from his subordinates. He had a scholarly, analytical mind, but he could and did lead campaigns in the field.

Weygand, on the other hand, was a general who had not altogether held aloof from civilian life. Born in Brussels, he never revealed anything of his early life or his origins. When he entered St. Cyr, he became a French citizen and, when the First World War began, he had become a colonel of cavalry. Early in that war he became a general and thereafter served as Chief of Staff to Marshal Foch. This war was, for Weygand, a desk war: he fought it from a parapet of maps.

Having served on the Inter-Allied Supreme War Council, Weygand became Chief of Staff of the Inter-Allied Military Committee after the war. But, when the Russians marched into Poland in 1920, he left Paris as the Committee's representative with the Poles. Marshal Pilsudski had demanded that the Allies send Marshal Foch to his assistance; but the Committee delegated the man whom the Marshal had called his "spiritual son." When Weygand reached Poland the Polish Army was in full rout; after an hour's study of the maps he issued his orders and the Poles turned. The campaign that he evolved drove the Russians out of Poland in rapid retreat.

General Weygand subsequently served as High Commissioner for Syria in 1923 and 1924. On his return to France he became Chief of Staff of the army and was elected to the Academy. In 1931 he was made inspector general of the army and Vice President of the Supreme War Council. Immediately the leftist elements of France raised a protest. Afraid that he was a "political general," they raised the specter of a military dictatorship. Their alarms were not eased by the fact that extreme nationalists continually pointed out that he was always to be found at his post, extremely strong and extremely able.

Weygand ignored his assailants and confined himself to the business of building up the French Army, working with equal harmony among ministers of all parties. It was this ability to function smoothly among colleagues of all beliefs, as well as his undoubted talents as a planner of campaigns, that made him the choice to replace Gamelin. A man who had proved himself so reliable in the most drastic emergencies, as the Poles had found him to be, was urgently needed now.

The new Commander in Chief assumed his post in the midst of threatening developments on both military and political fronts. The Germans had been driving ahead at a rate of thirty miles a day. Their tanks and light armor were sweeping out in an attempt to form a bag in which to tie the 300,000 British troops in Belgium and thus isolate the French forces. The area forming this bag had its bottom at Charleroi, while the mouth gaped open between Cambrai in France and Tournai, just across the Belgian border.

Early on the morning of May 21, the Germans occupied Amiens and Arras. Premier Reynaud told the Senate of France that the Allies were paying the price of their own tragic mistakes. Lack of preparation and miscalculation were the paramount errors he emphasized.

But the outstanding fact in the Premier's speech was the capture of Amiens. The city lay south of the Somme, twenty-five miles beyond Péronne, at which, according to latest reports, the French were still holding the enemy in a violent battle. More important: Amiens was less than thirty miles from Abbeville and the English Channel. Though M. Reynaud did not say it, it was obvious that the Germans were determined to drive for the Channel at Abbeville and close a giant trap on all the Allied forces in northern France so that escape would be impossible. The success of this attempt would mean a disaster impossible to comprehend.

A few hours later the fear was fact. On the evening of May 21, a spokesman for the War Ministry admitted sorrowfully that the Germans had penetrated to Abbeville. German motorcycle units, he said, had thrust ahead from Amiens to the coastal town, aided by aerial bombardment and machine-gunning of the refugee-packed roads.

On every sector of the French and rapidly dwindling Belgian front the Germans were equally active and equally successful. The Channel ports from which any attempt at escape would have to be made were under constant and merciless aërial attack; many were in flames.

As the French and British troops, with the remnants of the Dutch and Belgian Armies, fell back everywhere, Allied planes battered at the attackers. But their efforts were puny in contrast to the task that confronted them. At isolated points they halted, temporarily, the enemy's forward drive, but in the main the Germans were almost uninterrupted. Far behind the line of the new sweep to the Channel, German parachutists and motorcycle squads were sowing panic and destruction, firing everything combustible.

Around Montmédy, far to the east of the main German attack, new thrusts were launched against the outer works of the Maginot fortifications. Here occurred the first of the many situations in this war that would challenge the imagination of a dramatist. General Henri-Honoré Giraud walked into his own headquarters—right into the arms of the Germans, the men who had made a mockery of the words that Giraud had uttered a little more than a year before: "We can resist as long as we want to behind the Maginot Line."

Now the forces that had overrun Abbeville were sweeping back, to tighten the net on the hundreds of thousands of Britons, Belgians and Frenchmen cut off in French Flanders. Imprisoned as they were, isolated from the main French forces in the south and west, they struck out with almost their last strength in an attempt to break the ring that held them at Cambrai and Valenciennes. From the other side of the barrier at its distant edge, the French drove north between Amiens and St. Quentin. Both efforts were successful at first; but the Germans closed their ranks and broke the attacks. And, still racing back along the coast, other Germans took Calais—Calais that looked across the Channel to the white cliffs of Dover.

Almost half a million men were caught within that narrowing ring of steel and fire. They were not going to get out if the Germans could prevent it. The invaders, having secured their prey, sought now to slice it and devour it piecemeal. From Vimy Ridge—a name that many of those soldiers had heard their fathers speak—the Germans thrust all the way to the coast, along the heights to Lillers and St. Omer and to the shore at Gravelines, between Dunkirk and Calais.

Other Allied units were cut off in France, near the Belgian border. To complete their isolation, the Germans drove north from Vimy Ridge and south from Courtrai, intending to doom all the troops within the area bounded by Arras, Cambrai, Valenciennes, Courtrai, Roubaix and Lille. Meanwhile, as if to insure that no possible avenue remain open, the bombings of the three escape ports that the Germans had not captured—Zeebrugge and Ostende in Belgium and Dunkirk in France—continued unabated.

From a Paris that was stunned by the events, Premier Reynaud flew to London to confer with the British Prime Minister. The debacle in France was not their sole danger: Italy had renewed and increased her outcries and was charging now that her nationals were being persecuted in French Morocco. Every report from Rome said that

Italy would surely strike between June 10 and June 20: the period, obviously, when the Germans expected to conclude the slaughter.

While the French Premier was conferring with Mr. Churchill in London; the superb German war machine was intensifying its destruction of the Allied armies. A seventy-five-mile stretch of the Channel coast, from Abbeville almost to Dunkirk, was firmly in the enemy's hands. His artillery was beginning to pound to rubble what his planes had left standing in Dunkirk. It was obvious that this port was the only gate left for the escape of the Allied troops, trapped along the coast. Zeebrugge and Ostende were too far from Britain, and ships attempting to ply between these harbors and the British coast would be too exposed to aerial attack.

While British, French, and Belgian troops fought as one army to break the German lines that held them from the coast and the last hope of safety; while the two major Allies were concentrating all their strength on the salvage of what could be saved, Leopold III, King of the Belgians, announced on May 28 that he had given up the fight.

The son of the great King Albert who fought on undaunted through four years of enemy occupation of his country in World War I had not spoken to his Allies of the plan that was in his mind. When General Weygand visited the King's headquarters behind the lines in Belgium a few hours before the stunning blow fell, even to him young King Leopold had not disclosed his conviction that he must surrender to save his country.

To a mystified France that had seen her supposedly incomparable army already half shattered in what seemed to be less than the flickering of an eyelid, this abandonment by an ally to whom she was bound by so many ties of language, blood and common heritage was staggering.

King Leopold's Cabinet was in England when, over its opposition the surrender came Immediately the Belgian Prime Minister, Hubert Pierlot, convened the other Ministers on the afternoon of that same tragic 28th of May. He announced that the legal Government of Belgium had not abandoned the fight. In the name of the country whose chief of state he remained, he commanded the officers and soldiers of the Belgian Army to fight on.

In Paris, where many of the Belgian Deputies and Senators had already fled, the Belgian Parliament convened in a rump session to indorse the Cabinet's action. It declared the country's solidarity with its Allies. Denouncing their King who had disgraced his throne, the Belgians voted solemnly and sadly to unseat him as unworthy.

The surrender of the Belgain King threw new power and weight into the German attacks against the fleeing troops in Belgium and those who stood so firmly in the approaches to Dunkirk. Like an incredible tidal wave, mass after mass of German might threw itself against the wall of men guarding the last gate. Often that wave was shattered, but always there was another to surge more strongly where it had broken. The air of northeast France was black with steel and rent with the shriek of shells, the eerie howling of the plummeting bombs, the unending rhythmless roar of the German airplane motors. Thousands of anguished eyes looked up almost in prayer to search the sky for a single familiar silhouette that they knew would be emblazoned—invisibly to them—with the Tricolor or the concentric circles of the RAF. But almost never was the prayer of those weary eyes answered.

But the Allied air commanders, French and British, knew what they were doing. They were engaged in one of the greatest strategical feats in history. If they sent no planes over Cambrai or Artois or Courtrai, it was because the bombers were out behind the German lines, seeking to starve the invader by smashing the lines of supply that fed his monstrous machines. It was because the fighters were being saved for the greater task of providing an impermeable roof for the armada that was to crowd the Channel between Dunkirk and the coast of England.

One day after the surrender of Leopold there began that epic week unsurpassed in the annals of war: Dunkirk. The burning port, under constant bombardment by cannon and plane, was crammed by May 29, 1940, with Allied soldiers. Its quays and the roadstead were black with every craft that could keep afloat and make its own headway. The majority of these ships were British, for the majority of the men to be taken off were Britons; but no ship inquired the nationality of the men who stumbled aboard and fell exhausted on the decks.

For seven days and nights that were almost indistinguishable—days black with the smoke of countless fires that raged not only in that doomed city but all along the coast; nights livid with the flashes of explosions and flares and searchlights—uncounted thousands of men proved themselves capable of a heroism to which no words can pay tribute and lived through one of the world's great epics of valor.

Soldiers held their ranks in the streets and at the burning piers, marching without a break to the designated ship when the order was given. Others stood patiently, without complaint, on the bare sand—targets for German bombs and bullets, could any have penetrated the sheet of armor that Britain's fliers kept taut in that great expanse of air—waiting to wade out into the sea and clamber aboard one of the innumerable small boats of every description that had come to their rescue from England. Yachts, cabin cruisers, sport boats, trawlers, fighting boats, tubs whose owners had brought them here to save their fellow countrymen from impending disaster—twelve hundred of these vessels shuttled unendingly back and forth across the Channel between Britain and France. The British sent nine hundred craft. France stood nobly behind her ally: three hundred French ships of the navy and the merchant marine ran back and forth beside the British. Every one of those twelve hundred ships raised anchor only when she was loaded to a weight that would have driven her builders mad with fear.

Endlessly above them roared the protecting planes. Occasionally a German machine would break through the cover, twisting and veering, racing to discharge its missiles. But almost none of those black planes saw base again; those which struck a blow at all were but a minuscule proportion of the horde that tried and failed, smashed and routed by the RAF. The measure of its protection may be gauged by the fact that, of the nine hundred British ships engaged in rescue work all that week, six destroyers and twenty-three miscellaneous small vessels were all that Britain lost. Of the three hundred French vessels that sailed beside them, exactly eight were sunk.

Outside Dunkirk the roads were still clogged with troops moving down to the port. Beyond, the Germans were battering relentlessly to storm the city and capture the thousands of Allied soldiers whose one aim was to make the harbor; to escape the hell of Flanders only in order to renew their arms and their strength and return to smash the conquerors. To keep the port safe for them, to keep as open as possible the roads they must take to the sea, other thousands deliberately gave their lives.

So, in a wide arc whose center was Dunkirk, the men of three nations stood together, fighting on against a vastly outnumbering enemy to assure the safety not of themselves, but of their compatriots and comrades. Belgian soldiers, who had scorned their King's order to cease fire, stood with Frenchmen and with Britons, fired with them, counterattacked with them, and flung themselves to the ground with them when the black planes swept down. Some hint of what they must have endured, of the sublime courage that must have inspired them to stand and give their lives for others whom they did not know, always realizing that for them there was no hope, may be found in the epic of Calais, no less a saga than that of Dunkirk.

Calais, when the Germans struck, was defended by a combined French and British force of but four thousand men. Most of the garrison was French. The British contingent was landed when the German pincers drive threatened to isolate the Allied armies in France from the evacuation ports. Only two orders were given to these four thousand men: keep contact with the British and French forces to the north, and—*hold Calais!*

The Germans took Calais at last; but it did not fall quickly, nor was the victory anything but the hardest. The Germans ranged their long-distance guns against the four thousand, and earthquakes seemed to rock the city. They held out. The Germans brought up tanks, almost to the places where those Frenchmen and Britons stood, and poured cannon and machine-gun fire into every square inch. They held out. The Germans sent planes to bomb and burn them. They held out.

A huge German armored force cut between the city and the army to the north; it was too strong for the defenders to counterattack.

The Germans cut off the Calais garrison's last lines of supply by land. They could not be supplied by sea: every available ship was on Dunkirk run that week. Only by air could they get occasional food for themselves and their guns; and most of the fliers who brought it paid for the gift with their lives.

The men of Calais held off two German armored divisions—an aggregate of four times their numbers, with infinitely more and better weapons; not only held them out of Calais but prevented them from overwhelming that last port open, just a few miles up the coast.

During the four days of battle, the garrison had kept in communication with other Allied forces. After those days, there was silence. A Royal Navy vessel risked its hull and its crew to look for survivors. The navy found the survivors and took them safely out; all that were left of four thousand men—thirty exhausted soldiers.

20

THE BATTLE OF FRANCE—
"VIVE LA REPUBLIQUE"

THE huge German Armies, holding the ground they had gained in northern France, were gathering and grouping for some new bold blow; perhaps an invasion of Britain, or a lunge in the direction of Paris.

Throughout the miracle and the inferno of Dunkirk, the war had gone on at an unslackened pace on the rest of the French front. Even as that evacuation began, a fresh British Army had landed in France to unite with the French forces on the Maginot Line and in the west. A new and stronger line of defense was drawn. On the left flank running from Abbeville up the Somme were the new British troops and the French; beyond, the line followed the Aisne and the Chiers to the border of what had been Luxembourg, and then joined the Maginot.

In the north and west French tanks had rumbled into action and were attacking the Germans along the Somme. In all these counter-thrusts by French tanks to break the attack that might be aimed at Paris, and to drive to the relief of Dunkirk, only one succeeded. It was led by General de Gaulle who, besides being unofficial adviser to Premier Reynaud, was commanding the Fourth Armored Division in the field.

This one French victory in mechanized warfare occurred in the Abbeville area after the Germans had established their bridgehead on the Somme. It was, of course, not enough to turn the tide of the war, this isolated triumph, but with it General de Gaulle was able to prove the validity of all that he had thought and written and practiced. The story may best be told in the citation that the General won a few days later from the Allied Commander in Chief, General Weygand:

"Admirable leader, full of pluck and energy. Attacked, with his division, the Abbeville bridgehead, very firmly held by the enemy. Broke the German resistance and progressed fourteen kilometers through the enemy lines, taking hundreds of prisoners and capturing considerable matériel."

It was this proved military ability that led M. Reynaud to elevate the General formally to the position of Under Secretary for National Defense within the week, when he was reorganizing his Cabinet. It was recalled then that, in the First World War, General de Gaulle had won even higher tribute from General Pétain. The latter had described him as an "officer noted for his high intellectual and moral value," after he had been seriously wounded and captured in a desperate hand-to-hand conflict in the battle of Verdun.

Early in June, while more than 1,500,000 Italians were under arms, the Italian press announced plainly that the country was about to strike at France and Britain alike. The French border was manned as fully as France dared: no man could be withdrawn from any other front.

Meanwhile, their minds still harried by the hell of their escape, the veterans of Dunkirk were going back to war. Their journey was more circuitous now; the Channel coast was almost entirely in the hands of the Germans, and the western port of Le Havre was badly damaged. So the troopships, French and British, sailed around into the Atlantic and down the west coast of France to St. Nazaire and Bordeaux to disembark soldiers of both nations. The French were preceded by their commander in the brief but bitter battle of Flanders, General Georges-Maurice-Jean Blanchard. With his staff, he flew from London to Paris, there to be decorated and to leave at once for a new front-line command.

While the Allied commanders were pondering the probable date and strength of the blow that would be struck from the south, the north blazed into flame again. At 4:00 A.M. on June 5, action started along the Somme as German dive bombers and tanks attacked the French and British. The objective was obvious—Paris.

Forty-five German divisions opened this new offensive. Their advance guard was composed of 1,000 dive bombers, 2,250 tanks, 15,000 motorized vehicles. There were three main points of attack: Amiens, where the Germans already had a bridgehead on the south bank of the Somme: Péronne, thirty miles east of Amiens; and the little Ailette River, forty-five miles beyond Péronne. The Germans, flushed with their unbroken success, were sure of the infallibility of their technique.

In the threatened capital Premier Reynaud met at once this new threat, not neglecting the growing menace at France's back in the south. He revised his Cabinet once again; this time his predecessor, Edouard Daladier, who was now his Foreign Minister, was eliminated. The Premier assumed the Foreign Ministry as earlier he had taken over from Daladier the War Ministry. M. Reynaud openly confirmed his confidence in the Colonel in whom he had so long believed and who, less than two weeks before, had proved himself a worthy general: the Premier appointed as his first assistant in the Ministry the newly promoted General Charles de Gaulle, whose name was shortly to become the symbol of France.

M. Reynaud made a last appeal to the despot of Rome. Knowing as he spoke that the Germans on the Somme were pressing relentlessly against the Allies' line and that at one point the enemy was within eighty miles of Paris, he offered to Mussolini a peaceful settlement of all the grievances, real and fancied, which the Italians could conjure up. He told the world that France was fighting for the creation of a Europe governed by international peace and international prosperity; that the alternative was slavery.

Portentous events were impending. Below Abbeville and at the other end of the line near Soissons, the Germans were advancing steadily, despite French counterattacks in the latter region. Official reports said that as yet there had been no important break-through such as had occurred in the Battle of the Meuse; in effect, the significance of what was happening along those 120 miles of human sacrifice was lost on the capital reading the communiqués and the optimistic analyses of official commentators.

At the end of the third day of the Somme offensive, there seemed to be nothing in the night communiqué to indicate any great increase in the danger. True, it admitted that Allied advance guards had withdrawn all along the line, even east of Soissons; but that, the communiqué made plain, had been done only after these units had "fulfilled their missions" against enemy tanks. The only disquieting note was the appearance of place names that showed the Germans were now only seventy miles from Paris.

Still, seventy miles seemed a long way to Parisians, who knew that after all the main body of their army was still intact and had been reinforced not only with a new British Expeditionary Force but with tanks, planes, and guns from across the Atlantic. These were arriving almost daily at Bordeaux and St. Nazaire; it was said that they were being unloaded faster than they could be uncrated and assembled.

In the outskirts of Paris the barricades went up to bar the strategic gateways. In the beloved Champs-Elysées, the summer green was marred with innumerable ugly steel posts, hastily erected to stop any German tank that might somehow, incredibly, penetrate into the city. Garbage trucks vanished from the streets, to reappear briefly rolling toward the suburbs like caricatures of tanks, each loaded with troops and mounting a single machine gun.

The Nazis plunged twenty fresh divisions into the Somme offensive—now it was almost irresistible. The whole Allied line fell beneath it. West of Abbeville, the Germans were lunging almost unhampered toward Le Havre and Cherbourg; to the south, hundreds of German tanks smashed their way across the Bresle River and pounded into Forges-les-Eaux; a mere fifty-eight miles from the capital itself. In the center of the line the invader was no less ruthlessly successful. All along that line-within-a-line, his tanks and planes battered the *poilus* inexorably backward—five miles, then ten, fifteen, twenty. And, to the right, the Germans crossed the Aisne.

The fifth day brought a new shock. Paris was attacked from the other side, the east, by 600,000 German soldiers. Behind 3,500 of their best tanks, they were driving for the Marne Valley on the road to the capital, while their comrades came down the Seine. As the new battle roared and raged on a thirty-mile front through the Argonne, the advance in the west went on without a halt. The Germans entered Rouen, crossed the Aisne on either side of Soissons, not troubling to take the town, and stood now barely thirty-five miles from the capital.

Paris needed no persuasion to believe the words of General Weygand: "The enemy has suffered considerable losses. Soon he will reach the end of his effort. This is the last quarter-hour. Hold fast." It was indeed the last quarter-hour, but no one understood. No one could foresee how long and terrible that quarter-hour was to be. General Weygand made his prophecy on June 9. One day later the last blow fell—from the rear. Italy declared war on France and Britain.

That day, June 10, was the last for many years to see Paris the capital of France. In a fog of unfounded rumors of Italian assaults on French Somaliland, Tunisia, Corsica, the French Government left its historic capital to establish itself temporarily in Tours, almost in the center of France. The departure of the Government seemed the signal for a fresh exodus of those civilians who had not left before or who, having fled once, had returned. Now they were on the roads again.

From every side the Germans were rushing toward Paris. South of Beauvais, they were thirty miles away. In a dozen places they stormed across the Seine to envelope the city. Reaching the Ourcq Valley, they threatened to flank Rheims. On the east, where the newest onslaught had been launched, the battle reached new peaks of fury. The French fell back to the Marne, where twice before in the First World War, they had rallied and held against German might.

Under crushing pressure by German tanks, planes, artillery, and infantry south of Rethel, the French retreated to the Retourne River, a tributary of the Aisne. Their troops fought with desperation in this area, for they knew their failure would mean the destruction of the hinge that held the Maginot Line to the fluid front running from Montmédy to the Channel. Let that hinge burst, and the Maginot Line was doomed. Should it be turned it had no defense against an attack from the rear.

The environs of Paris had been forced by the Germans! A pall hung over the evacuated city. It was a pall of smoke from the fires set by German bombs in the suburbs, and a pall of grief from a million hearts. Yet official spokesmen erected a brave façade of words that was soon enough to crumble. Paris, they declared with voices that were kept firm only by an effort, might be destroyed but she would never be surrendered. As they were speaking, the streets of the city were being studded with barricades. They were already packed with fugitives.

Despite the apparent imminence of German invasion across the Channel and the North Sea, Britain kept her pledged word of alliance. Not only did British ships risk destruction to shell the German lines near the French coast; not only did British airmen roar gallantly low over the Germans inland to bomb and strafe them; Britain, oblivious of her own danger and awed by the courage of the French troops, sent into the country of her ally every man and every machine available in a desperate effort to repeat the miracle of 1914.

The sacrifice, however gallant, was bound to fail. From Tours the French Government admitted that the Germans had reached what it called the "outworks of Paris."

They were in Persan and Beaumont, only twelve and a half miles north of the city's boundary. They were in Senlis, on the northwest. They had made more crossings of the Seine to the west. In the east they had crossed the Marne between Meaux and Château-Thierry.

Three days after Italy's declaration of war, France revealed that her Premier had sent to President Roosevelt a despairing cry for "clouds of planes" from across the Atlantic. The President's reply was disclosed almost at the same time: America was doing everything possible.

He explained that the United States could not enter the war without action by Congress. Through another American, M. Reynaud made a final effort to spare his beloved Paris. At his request, the American Ambassador, William C. Bullitt, advised the Germans that Paris was an open city and would not be defended.

A few hours later, Ambassador Bullitt informed his Government that the German Army was "within the gates." On every sector the German drive was rolling ahead irresistibly. Deploying a force estimated by the French at 120 divisions, the Germans narrowed the ring their main forces were drawing around Paris, despite the arrival of British troops on the Seine front—many of them hurriedly snatched from vital home-defense positions. The Germans overwhelmed Châlons-sur-Marne and the fate of the Maginot Line became apparent.

In the face of all this, Italy struck her first blow—air attacks on Toulon, in metropolitan France, and Bizerte, in Tunisia.

On June 14, 1940, the German Army in force took Paris. Emphasizing the triumph, the Boches flaunted before the remaining residents of the capital the might that had overwhelmed the armies of France. For the first time in almost seventy years, German troops paraded down the Champs-Elysées. Between the lines of tense-faced Parisians, filled with an anger and a grief that choked them into silence, the dusty tanks clanked savagely. Behind them came the motorized divisions and after them the grey-clad infantry with their pompous goose-step. German bands blared.

On June 14 began the living death of Paris. What other things happened to France that day were hardly noticed. The German drive along the Channel coast reached Le Havre. The invaders in the east swept through Montmédy; they threatened Verdun, where they had been smashed a generation before. The Government of France, in flight like those it governed, left Tours for Bordeaux.

Bordeaux was already a city out of a horrible fantasy. Refugees from the north, from the east, from the capital, from Belgium and Holland, had poured into the city. None had time now to listen to another's story of having been bombed or machine-gunned as he fled. It was always the same. Where it had been the road out of Brussels or Arras, it was now the road out of Paris. Some of the streets of Bordeaux were filled with the automobiles, trucks, and wagons of those who, unable to find even one room in which to sleep, made their homes in vehicles that had brought them here.

Still the fight went on. In the south, the timorous Italians, as if still uncertain that France was really bleeding to death, probed into Savoy and into the Maritime Alps, just north of Nice. Both areas were immediately reinforced by French troops from the Mediterranean coast.

In smashing attacks from front and rear, the Germans shattered the myth of the Maginot Line. The forces that had taken Montmédy had merely turned the line and attacked it from behind, where it was defenseless; but from the front they had actually crashed it in. Verdun fell, almost unnoticed. All through eastern and central France the Allies were in full retreat, pursued without respite.

The French Cabinet met as the Germans were cutting through almost the last remnants of the Maginot Line and French troops were fleeing headlong for the Loire; as German planes poured tons of bombs on the fugitives who still clogged Tours. Premier Reynaud found himself the head of a government divided within itself. He had promised Prime Minister Churchill that he would yield his office before he would take France out of the fight she had pledged to carry on; but he could no longer lead a nation in war when his ministers were deserting him. Rather than join them in their cowardice, and break the word that he had solemnly given, he resigned the Premiership of France.

The aged Marshal Pétain, through appeals to his love of country, was persuaded to assume the responsibilities of the Premiership. Surrounded by sinister forces led by the traitor, Laval, the pathetic end of the old warrior was to become one of the tragedies of history. A virtual prisoner and puppet of Hitler, he was to be used as von Hindenburg had been used—to enslave France as Germany had been enslaved.

In this moment, too, while the future of France was swinging in the balance, one of the most portentous moves in history was made. Prime Minister Churchill of England, in the greatest demonstration at once of statesmanship and of humanity that our century has seen, proposed the union of the French and British Empires in a common single empire. Every citizen of each would become a citizen of the new nation, which would have one government with "joint organs of defense, foreign, financial and economic policies," with a single war cabinet and a single Parliament welded from the legislative bodies of both Empires.

The magnitude of this proposal delivered through the British Ambassador in Bordeaux to Premier Pétain startled the diplomatic world. It would merge into a tremendous unity the two historic leaders of western civilization, the two traditional repositories of western culture. It would unite the richest and most powerful empires in the world.

A few hours later the new French Government announced—not that it would give consideration to the greatest fusion of nations the world had ever imagined—but that it had besought of the Germans and Italians the terms they would set for the conclusion of an armistice. The western world was astounded. It was true that half of France had been overrun, that her army was shattered and her soil ravished; but the other half was untouched, still well-garrisoned; her fleet, one of the mightiest in Europe, was intact, and her empire stood ready to supply her with all that she might need, in men and goods. Her merchant fleet was still bringing arms from the United States. Yet, with all this, with the awesome grandeur of the future opened by the British proposal, she elected—or her leaders imposed upon her—the disgrace of capitulation when she was still unbeaten.

Every radio in France carried Marshal Pétain's plea. Why should they fight on when their rulers were already seeking peace? The courage of their despair turned into numbness and resignation; they threw down their guns and flouted the orders of officers.

Britain, whose confidence had been violated, and whose survival was at stake as the result, watched apprehensively. Her main concern, when she saw that Pétain was irrevocably committed to surrender, was the French fleet which, in enemy hands, might prove her own undoing.

While the Bordeaux Cabinet awaited Germany's reply to their proposal of surrender, Pétain warned the French soldiers that no order to cease firing had yet been issued and they must continue the fight. He spoke in vain; the troops knew that nothing now could rally the country. They waited, too, while the greedy Italian and the rapacious German dictators conferred in Munich. Almost without resistance the Germans pushed on to Cherbourg, at the tip of Normandy, and 105 miles to the south occupied the city of Rennes—on the road to England.

The roads of southern France were thronged with fugitives. Charles Pomaret, new Minister of the Interior, ordered all to return to their homes. Those who had overflowed Bordeaux were fleeing again, spurred by a sudden German bombing of the temporary capital. This bombing followed closely on a similar attack upon loaded British transports lying off St. Nazaire in the estuary of the Loire. Fugitives who had battled and bribed the funtionaries of consulates into giving them entrance visas for South America, Spain, or Portugal were streaming toward the Spanish border. All these thousands would have to cross the border at Hendaye, on the rushing Bidassoa River, over which a narrow bridge would take them after interminable delays into Spain.

The British Prime Minister appealed directly to the people of France. Convinced of the character of the Cabinet that was leading France into slavery, he went over the head of that Government because of "our sense of comradeship with the French people." He told them plainly that their Government, if it accepted the terms of Germany and defaulted in its solemn treaty obligations to Britain, would be throwing away their future.

The future, however, was being fixed at Munich. Foreseeing the impending disaster, the last of the British troops in France were reluctantly being ordered home, for Britain had already bled herself white and could sacrifice no more vainly. The British were sailing from the west coast of France, from St. Nazaire, and Bordeaux. British ships weighed anchor with hundreds of French soldiers aboard: Frenchmen whose sense of honor would not let them remain in an army that was going to leave France to its invaders. They were going to fight on with Britain; many of their officers were already in London.

With the utmost secrecy, Hitler and Mussolini, having concluded their triumphant parley in Munich, transmitted their terms to Pétain.

While Pétain was awaiting the terms set by the conquerors, the voice of the real France spoke on June 18 for the first time in many desolate days. General de Gaulle stepped before a microphone of the BBC in London to speak to his countrymen, whose kinsmen in uniform were already disembarking with the B. E. F. in England. General de Gaulle's first speech was brief. He advocated the French-British Empire that Mr. Churchill had proposed and demanded that his countrymen continue in arms. He concluded with words of indomitable hope that were to inspire brave Frenchmen throughout the world: *"La France a perdu une bataille; elle n'a pas perdu la guerre."* ("France has lost a battle, she has not lost the war.")

The response of the Government in Bordeaux was an order, issued by Pomaret, demanding that General de Gaulle return to France. He ignored it. The scene was being set for the final betrayal of France. It was announced that the emissaries of the French Government would formally begin the negotiations for the armistice on June 21, at Compiègne, in the railway car that had become a national shrine when, on November 11, 1918, Marshal Foch had sat at the head of the table to which Germans had come as suppliants.

To increase the humiliation, Rome announced that it had received, as it had demanded, a separate French appeal for an armistice. Like Berlin, it made it clear that France would never be permitted to rise again. As if to underline the point, German troops occupied Brest while others in the southeast reached out to take Lyons. Between them, still other German units drove across the Loire and plunged south, and a spearhead lanced up the Rhône Valley toward Geneva.

On the afternoon of June 21, General Charles Huntziger, who had shared the command on the Maginot sector when the Germans first broke through at Sedan, led his fellow emissaries into the historic railway car in the forest of Compiègne. Behind him came Admiral Maurice Leluc, Léon Noël, and General Jean-Marie-Joseph Bergeret of the air force. The Germans rose to meet them. When the whole party sat down, General Huntziger found himself facing Adolf Hitler.

The ceremony was brief. General Wilhelm Keitel, head of the German Supreme Command, read in German the preamble to the thirty-page document. This was next read in French. Herr Hitler, who had said nothing during the proceedings, then left. The others remained to study the terms. Near the railway car was a large army tent for the use of the French delegation; it contained teletype machines and telephones linked directly to Bordeaux.

Twenty-seven hours later, in the early evening of June 22, General Keitel and General Huntziger signed the armistice for their respective countries. Its contents were still unannounced, but, before he wrote his name, General Huntziger, his voice choked, made a vain protest against its severity. The French Government, he said, had ordered him to sign.

But this did not end the battle of France. The fighting was to stop only six hours after the Italian Government should have notified the German High Command that an armistice between France and Italy had been signed. And so the four Frenchmen, having left Compiègne, flew to Rome.

Early on Sunday, June 23, one week after his offer of union had been rejected, Prime Minister Churchill voiced the grief and amazement with which he had learned of the ceremony in Compiègne. He indorsed completely the appeal that had been made by General de Gaulle, who, using the facilities of the BBC once more to reach his fellow Frenchmen, had urged again that they reject the armistice signed by a Government that had not the right to surrender.

General de Gaulle appealed to the honor of France to keep the country loyal to her vows. Having given her word, he argued, she would be eternally disgraced by thus dishonoring it. Citing the material reasons for his stand, he emphasized the strength and the resources of Britain, the aid of the United States and the fate of France. What new courage the General forged for his fellow countrymen in that night of degradation, when he laid the foundation for the resurgence of France, was wrought in simple words that will live forever in the history of France:

"For the honor of the country, I demand that all free Frenchmen continue to fight wherever they are and by whatever means they can.... I invite all Frenchmen of the land armies, the naval forces, the air forces, the engineers and the specialists and the workmen of the armament industry who may be in British territory or who can come there, to join me for this purpose.... I invite the leaders, the soldiers, the sailors and the airmen,... to get in touch with me.... Long live France, free in honor and in independence!"

Stung by the denunciation, Premier Pétain replied the next day. Quavering on the radio—already his age was being made much of by his apologists—he ostensibly devoted most of his brief talk to criticizing Mr. Churchill for having passed judgment on France. Only obliquely did he allude to General de Gaulle.

Pétain's claim that his nation was united was a mockery—it was already divided. General de Gaulle, in London, moved to form what he called a French National Committee to administer the affairs of Frenchmen who insisted on remaining free. The Bordeaux Government retaliated in the only way possible: it deprived him of his rank.

The British Ministry of Information, while the French armistice delegation was still conferring in Rome, told the terms that had been accepted from Germany: The occupation of more than half the country, including a wide strip along the whole length of the Atlantic coast.... The demobilization of all military, naval, and air forces except police troops.... The surrender of the arms of the forces in the occupied area and the granting to the Germans of the right to demand all arms and implements of war in the occupied area.... The recall to specified ports, to be placed under German and Italian control, of all naval units except a few that were to be left guarding the empire; against this, Germany's "solemn declaration that it will not use the French fleet against Britain."

Simultaneously with the disclosure of these terms, Britain announced that it could no longer recognize the French Government that had delivered their republic to Germany. France had been betrayed by collaborationists with Hitler.

At 6:15 P.M. on June 23, General Huntziger signed the terms put forward by Italy. Six hours later, the fighting was to cease. Meanwhile, as the shadow war drew rapidly to its end, the Germans had occupied St. Nazaire and pushed on until they were within eighty miles of Bordeaux. As soon as the French had signed the Italian armistice, word of their action was flashed to Bordeaux and to Berlin.

At 12:35 A.M. on June 24, 1940, the Battle of France became history. But the spirit of the French people was to rise again.

THE BATTLE OF BRITAIN—
FORTITUDE OF A GREAT PEOPLE

THE first great war in the air in the world's history was fought over England in 1940. In cataclysmic combats, the British and Germans made the skies a flaming battleground. This was but the beginning of aërial warfare that was to rage in many parts of the world during the next five years.

This was but another prelude to what was to happen to Berlin and the great cities of Germany when retribution set in. What they did to London and Britain was to be visited upon them a thousandfold. The capital of the British Empire was to stand; the capital of Germany was to go down in ruins.

Flushed by an unparalleled chain of victories over Poland, Denmark, Norway, Belgium, the Low Countries, and France, the German dispatched the first solid token of their full intention toward Great Britain on June 18, 1940—following the miracle of Dunkirk. That night over a hundred German aircraft suddenly roared over England's coasts and dropped heavy bombs on selected targets throughout eastern and southeastern areas.

The collapse of France left Britain in a critical position. The British Expeditionary Force of ten divisions had been rendered a nullity because of loss of heavy equipment. It was foreseen that the interval would be protracted before the disbanded troops could be fitted to meet the enemy again. The coast of Europe from the Arctic to the Pyrenees was in German control. German shipping losses had been recovered through capture of war and merchant vessels in Norway, Holland, Belgium, and France. German invasion loomed as a specter whose shadow enveloped the land. The hoarse warwhoops of the German Fuehrer were promising that he would annihilate the British and conquer their islands.

Face to face with peril, Britain summoned all her resources, moral and material, and turned herself into a fortress almost overnight. Public utilities of every kind, harbors, airfields, beaches, roads, and bridges were fortified and heavily guarded. A great army of citizen soldiers was formed into a home guard. Aircraft production was put under the control of Lord Beaverbrook and began to reach for new levels. In addition, help arrived from abroad. United States shipments of World War equipment—2,200 75-mm. field guns, 83,000 machine guns, 900,000 Enfield rifles—aided in rearming British troops.

The victorious German Army in France was busily occupied in preparing advance bases for the invasion of Britain. The Luftwaffe was moving forward for the occupation of airfields that had been the home grounds of the French Air Force and the R.A.F. Guns from the Maginot Line and from the naval arsenals of France were being mounted along the European coast and pointed in the direction of Britain.

War in the air was to be the "softening process." German strategy was to bomb the English people to their knees and then send in the Nazi Armies to complete the conquest. In the four weeks that followed this first bombing, there were 336 civilians killed and 476 seriously injured, while the figures for July amounted to 258 killed and 321 injured. The first German attacks were concentrated on ports and coastal shipping.

The weight of the German attack increased in August. On August 8 over 400 aircraft, in the main dive bombers, with escorts of Messerschmitt fighters, attempted to attack convoys in the narrow waters. They were engaged by Hurricanes and Spitfires in a series of encounters that seesawed from 9 o'clock in the morning until 5 o'clock in the evening. The Royal Air Force destroyed thirty-six of the German fighters and twenty-four bombers. Three days later the Luftwaffe made a mass attack on Portland and Weymouth and a number of small attacks elsewhere. The Germans lost sixty-five aircraft, five of them to the guns of warships. The British lost twenty-six fighters.

Events in the air were rising to a crescendo. It was manifestly the German plan to drive by sheer weight a path into British defenses in the air and on the ground. Hitler declared the British Air Force was to be annihilated, its bases demolished, the sky over England to be cleared for the hosts of the all-conquering Luftwaffe. The theory of mass attack was to be exploited to the full.

Spitfires and Hurricanes, attacking astern, shot the Luftwaffe formations to bits, and harried and hunted the survivors back to their bases. Over Southampton and around Britain's coasts on August 13 and 14 seventy-eight and thirty-one aircraft respectively were brought down. All this was a mere preliminary. In the signal triumph of August 15 all preceding German losses were thrown into the shade. On that day more than a thousand German aircraft raided harbors and airdromes along the southeast coast; 600 of them were heavy bombers. Hurricanes and Spitfires rose to greet them and brought down 180; this was a shattering defeat, but bigger disasters were to come.

Britain had never lost sight of the military axiom that the offensive is the best defense. British machines began the regular raiding of the interior of Germany before Germany attempted to penetrate the interior of Britain. But there was a difference. British raids were directed against military objectives; German attacks were directed against the civilian population. The R.A.F. bombed petrol tanks at

Hamburg and Bremen and Hannover. Thenceforward British raids on Germany were continuous. Railways, roads, bridges, junctions, and marshaling yards in the Rhineland and the Ruhr were attacked; marked attention was paid to oil storage tanks and refining plants.

British bombers worked their way deeper into Germany. Toward the end of August they succeeded in setting up a mark that was a presage of events to follow. On the night of August 25 the R.A.F. for the first time carried the war to Berlin. London had been raided the night before. The attack on Berlin had been directed against military objectives in the environs of the capital of the Reich. The R.A.F. returned to wreak a heavy attack on Berlin on the night of August 29. It was raided again the following night. On September 1 bombers and Spitfires paid their respects to Munich, the birthplace of Nazism.

The Luftwaffe was now feeling its way toward the heart and metropolis of the British Empire. Hit by hit it was making progress toward its goal. On the night of August 22 bombs were dropped over the outskirts of London, and a movie theater and other buildings were demolished. Then on the night of August 24, curtain raiser to the British retaliatory mass attack on the environs of Berlin, German bombs began to fall in central London. It was on that night that the first casualties, the consequence of air raids, occurred in London. It had been preceded by a day of hard fighting over the county of Kent. That day the Nazi attacks had been directed against the airdrome outside Margate. There was a simultaneous attack on Dover and Portsmouth. During August 1,075 persons were killed in Britain and 1,261 injured.

It was on the evening of September 7 that the enemy at long last succeeded in hurling his way through London's powerful defenses and setting off explosions and fires throughout the core of the city. This opened the most compelling trial by fire.

What they like to call the blitzkrieg is dated differently by Londoners, but most of them look on September 7 as its beginning, since it was on that day that the Nazi air attacks, powerful and sustained, first got actually under way. For England as a whole, Hitler's lightning war had been shooting its bolts long before. Cities and centers like Liverpool, Birmingham, Bristol, Coventry, Manchester, and Sheffield had felt almost its full impact.

Then London became subjected to the fiery ordeal that war in the air brings. On that momentous day, beginning at 4:30 in the afternoon, a strong attack, the third since early morning, was launched by powerful bombing formations, escorted by fighters, below the Thames Estuary and the eastern districts of the metropolis. Fires blazed above industrial targets. Grave injury was done to lighting, communications, and similar public services. Heavy raids were made on docks and shipping. London was ringed with air battles for over an hour that evening. From airdromes on every side Spitfires and Hurricanes flew to challenge the first big Nazi raid on London and the docks.

The bright red glow that appeared in the clouds above the East End that night is a vivid memory to Londoners. Speculation became rife as to what would happen when darkness fell and the glowing sky began to serve as a beacon to the marauders. The crisis that all had feared was at hand. The overflowing raid was lapping round the fringes of the city's defense system. Squadrons of the R.A.F. did all that was possible for human bravery to accomplish, but bigger forces overwhelmed them.

That night and the nights that followed, huge formations of Dornier and Heinkel bombers, with an entourage of Messerschmitt fighters, streamed forward in waves that looked endless. "There are oceans of them," declared a squadron leader. Britain's fighter pilots threw themselves into the midst of the waves again and again. Heroism of the airmen was rivaled by the gunners on the ground. Warehouses along the Thames had been set on fire. Great areas were flaming beacons, inviting targets for the massed raids that were to follow.

The second night the havoc was serious. The major weight of the enemy's offensive was concentrated on both banks of the Thames, east of the city, especially on the riverside where three extensive fires were caused. Utility plants, barges, warehouses, schools, houses were demolished. A large fire raged in oil installations on the lower Thames. Fires were blazing in central London. By this time larger and stronger air-raid shelters had been provided, and the population had been drilled in making immediate use of them. The casualties might have run into thousands, but as it turned out the figures were 306 killed and 1,337 seriously injured.

On Sunday night bombs again were dropped over wide areas, and fires sprang up in Thames districts and other quarters of London. Private houses, public and business buildings, served as targets.

Fires broke out in the immediate vicinity of St. Paul's Cathedral and the Guildhall. Bombs fell on a large maternity hospital that was twice attacked, on a poor law institution for the aged, on an L.C.C. housing estate, on large numbers of workmen's cottages, especially in the East End of London, which was heavily and repeatedly attacked, and in the residential districts of west and north London. An elementary school in the East End, which was affording temporary shelter to families whose homes had been destroyed, was hit and collapsed.

The depth of the tragedy that was being enacted in the bodies and souls of the inhabitants of the once peaceful city was incalculable. Heavy as might be the martyrdom of the innocent, it was not only to continue but to increase. The ferocity of one night was to be outdone by the ferocity of the night that followed.

The defense system and antiaircraft barrage around the metropolis had been greatly strengthened. On the night of September 11 the German airmen were met by curtains of artillery fire that appeared to surprise and stagger them. Flying to higher levels, where it was more difficult for searchlight crews and gunners to locate and hit them, they dropped their bombs at random. There was no effort to confine themselves to military objectives. Prime Minister Churchill stated in the House of Commons on September 17 that in the first half of September 2,000 civilians had been killed and 8,000 wounded; three-fourths of these losses were in London. It was estimated that 1,054 German aircraft were destroyed in September. Their loss of trained airmen was at least 3,000.

"In the month of September, between Saturday, September 7, and Sunday, September 15, Hitler took London and didn't know it," was the verdict of an American commentator on the ground. The hyperbole, at once rebuffed, spoke at least of the extremity to which the metropolis had been driven. The situation had grown desperate up to the battle of September 15. It is also clear that the effects of the warfare that night marked a turning point in which the national confidence was renewed. The raids continued, but the people were learning to outwit them. On October 15, a thousand enemy planes, carrying a thousand tons of bombs, raided London. The Germans claimed that "the night was the most terrible for London since the outbreak of the war." Londoners replied that the raid was not so destructive as the early raids of September. The thousand machines streaking across the sky had not equal psychological effect. Public and private refuges had become deeper and stronger. People found safety a hundred feet under the earth, with walls proof against all explosion, in the heart of London. Human resiliency was coming through all its tests triumphantly. "The mind is its own place and can make a heaven of hell, a hell of heaven," the East End had been saying to the West End.

When day dawned the people looked around to observe the effects. Where there had once been dwellings, retail stores, hospitals, theaters, churches, and mercantile buildings, there were now gaping walls and heaps of rubble. The city was still on fire, its transportation disrupted, its streets full of glass and bricks, its water system disrupted. Ruin had been brought to buildings of no military importance, public and private property, which the laws of war had hitherto held in respect. The Ministry of Information issued a list of targets in the London area that had been bombed during the preceding nine weeks. They included five great hospitals—Great Ormond Street, the London, Queen Mary's, St. Bartholomew's, and St. Thomas's; twenty-four churches, including Westminster Abbey, St. Paul's, St. Margaret's in Westminster, St. Martin's-in-the-Fields, and St. Clement Danes; four palaces, including Buckingham Palace, which had been attacked more than once; and a number of art collections and historic buildings, such as the British Museum, the Tate Gallery, the Wallace Collection, Burlington House, the Temple, the Royal Hospital, Chelsea, and Holland House. Destruction that could not by any stretch of the imagination be made to serve any purpose but a return to the stone age.

Up to the end of October, 14,000 civilians had been killed and 20,000 seriously injured. Three-fourths of these casualties occurred in London. Birmingham, Liverpool, Coventry, Bristol, and Southampton were later under heavy bombardment by the Nazis. The Germans made their purpose plain. A new chapter in the Battle of Britain had begun, the Berlin *Rundfunk* informed the world. The strategy was intended to confuse the British population so that no one would be able to foresee where the next blow would fall. This was expected to have a fatal effect on the island's morale.

"Die Englander can be absolutely assured that blow after blow is coming. And all the time the Luftwaffe will keep pounding away at London, scientifically and without mercy," said the message from Adolf Hitler. He promised that all the large cities of England would be laid in ruins as complete as if they had actually been occupied by German troops.

Massed raids on the industrial towns of the country still resulted in numerous casualties, but the rate of death and injury was gradually being reduced. During November 4,588 people were killed in Great Britain and 6,202 were injured and detained in hospitals.

London was heavily raided on December 8. The Royal Air Force had visited Berlin two days previously. British airmen had let loose a great number of bombs on airdromes around Berlin and the coast—airdromes from which it was well known that German bombers set out on their expeditions to Great Britain. The Germans were anxious to demonstrate to the world that, despite the British operations, they were still able to launch large-scale assaults.

A climax was reached in the heavy concentrated attack on London during the night of Sunday, December 29. This raid was directed principally against the historic square mile of the city proper, the London of Ludgate Hill and St. Paul's, which went back even to the time of Julius Caesar. A deluge of incendiary bombs was dropped. Famous edifices burst into flames. The Guildhall and eight Wren churches were destroyed or damaged. The view from St. Paul's in the direction of Old Bailey showed a city in ruins. During the night of terror hundreds of fires illuminated the sky. Here and there the dark figures of heroic firemen with their apparatus were silhouetted against the background of flame.

There were heavy raids on Southampton, Bristol, Portsmouth,

Birmingham, Sheffield, Liverpool, Manchester. Extensive destruction was wreaked on these industrial and commercial centers. During December 3,793 persons were killed and 5,044 injured, which were fewer than in November. That the people were succeeding in acquiring the strategy of defense is shown by their words and attitude. "I can declare on my honor," wrote a commentator in a London weekly, "that since the new phase began (the shifting of attack from London to the provincial towns) a considerable number of people of all classes and types have said to me: 'I wish they'd go on bombing us. We can stand it.'"

If further evidence were needed that Britain could take it, the proof was supplied by the result of the voting in the House of Commons on December 5. The members of the Independent Labor Party in Parliament had made a motion to the effect that a conference be called to consider peace proposals. The motion was defeated by 341 to 4.

Speaking for the great mass of the civilian population, J. M. Spaight reported: "It is a commonplace that today we are all in the front line. The era of absenteeism in war-waging is dead and gone. Not only the men of the fire services, the demolition and rescue parties, the police and the first-aid squads, but the whole of our urban population have helped to defeat the attempt to bludgeon us into submission. London's triumph has been a triumph of London's common folk. The great city has emerged from the struggle with head bloody but unbowed. Never in all its long history has its glory been greater than it is today; and London is but the type of many a great city of our land which has come undaunted through the ordeal of battle."

Bristol, Coventry, and Plymouth were also blitz centers. An American war correspondent graphically described these blitzes: "A blitz is when an armada of four or five hundred planes come over. Great four-engined Focke-Wulfs and Junkers, Stuka dive bombers, flying low—sometimes hardly over housetops—dropping high-explosive bombs, detonation land mines, clusters of dynamite in Molotov breadbaskets, great black globes of steel of the size of a buoy in the sea—hours on hours at a time. This is what happened to Bristol, Coventry, Plymouth, and London. This is all life smashed and torn, all walls and every upright thing crushed into a strange, heavy dust for miles of city blocks. The people gone, blown fully from the earth. This is death and destruction by madmen. This is the blitz."

The direct damage to war production in the Battle of Britain was less a matter of spectacular destruction than of slow attrition. The fires set in the great warehouse districts near the East End docks destroyed food and other imports. "None of the services upon which the life of our great cities depends—water, fuel, electricity, gas, sewerage—not one of them has broken down," said Prime Minister Churchill. Yet many had been interrupted when power stations or gasworks were hit or cables or mains were broken. Labor as well as materials and machines had to be taken into account. Every time a worker took shelter, production suffered. Beyond this was the impairment that resulted from the dislocation of normal living. Thus the civilians also were in the front line. Air-raid wardens and the fire-fighting services engaged in tasks of danger. The bulk of the population was exposed to terrifying perils.

London had to go underground. There was lack of ventilation and lavatory accommodation, there was lack of heat, and there was menace of disease. "Unless effective measures are promptly taken, we can foresee with the approach of winter a state of affairs in respect of contagious and infectious diseases which may prove more devastating than the blitzkrieg," stated the *British Medical Journal*. Yet the notable thing was the patience of the mass of the people under the unprecedented strain. The morale of the British people was not broken. Instead, there were unfathomable resources of fortitude. It was this spirit, as much as her physical resources, on which the survival of Britain continued to rest.

Fighting in the air battles alongside the British were men of many nations. Prominent among the fliers were the Poles, survivors of the Polish Air Force that was caught unawares and overwhelmed by the Luftwaffe on the opening day of the war. Their squadrons won a quick reputation for dare-devil courage. Polish fighter squadrons were credited with bringing down more than 300 enemy aircraft in the Battle of Britain at the end of December 1940. "They introduced their own technique in air fighting," said a Canadian pilot who served with them. "They sailed right into the enemy, holding their fire to the very last moment. That was how they saved ammunition and how they got so many enemies down in each sortie."

The record of the Czechs was as fine as that of the Poles. They had flown with the French Air Force, riding Dewoitine and Curtiss fighters, and were credited with bringing down more than a hundred enemy craft in the Battle of France. Sergeant Franzek, the most successful of the Czech fighter pilots, served with the Poles; he had brought down twenty-eight aircraft, seventeen of them in the Battle of Britain, before he was killed. Dutch airmen with the Royal Air Force showed a preference for flying their own original craft, Fokker T.8 W seaplanes, which did useful service in the Coastal Command.

The brunt of the fighting was borne by men of the British Empire from home and overseas. They came from every part of the empire to defend the motherland. The Canadians were in the van; the Australians not far behind, although their chief theater had been the broad waters of the western seas. A squadron of New Zealanders served in the Bomber Command. Many Americans had also volunteered and were fighting in the Battle of Britain.

The war had come when the Royal Air Force was still in the earlier stages of a revolution in design. The losses in the Battle of France appeared to make its chances look hopeless indeed. And yet in the Battle of Britain men and machines inflicted on Hitler the first decisive defeat of the war. The Royal Air Force, a separate service, worked in close coöperation with the Army and Royal Navy, but always through its own command. Under the Chief of Air Staff, the R.A.F. was subdivided into seven commands, each with well-defined duties, each under an Air Officer Commander in Chief or an Air Officer commanding.

In the Battle of Britain the Fighter Command lost 375 pilots killed, 358 wounded. It became the rule for the pilots of the Fighter Command to wear the top button of their tunics unfastened to distinguish them as pilots in the battle. The attacks of the German Air Force, the stubborn defenses of the British, and the unprecedented warfare in the air, represented far more than a spectacle or contest, ending up with ruined men and machines. They were intended as means to an end. The primary purpose of the Germans was to achieve mastery of the sky over the southeast triangle of England, and under cover of vast air armadas, to launch an invasion by sea and land. The troop-carrying planes, the Junkers 52's, converted air liners, which had played chief rôle in the invasion of Norway, had also been poised for the invasion of Britain, although the main invasion would have been by sea. Had it been possible to interrupt the communications between London and the coast, had chaos been created in Britain's coastal defenses, the first long step would have been taken.

Great Britain's reply to the German threat took the form of a systematic battering of the invasion ports in France and Belgium from the air. The R.A.F. kept a constant watch on all German sea bases from Narvik in the north to Bordeaux in the south, a distance of about 2,000 miles. Their vigilance and harassing tactics interfered greatly with the enemy's plan. Great concentrations of men and ships became more and more imposing at Antwerp, Calais, Dunkirk, Ostend, Nieuport, and Le Havre—ready for the invasion of Britain. From the air, barges were daily reported to be moving slowly from one canal to another. Small warships were also moored near the barges, which were self-propelled, over 150 feet in length and each capable of carrying about two trainloads of men or materials.

Germany had commandeered every available barge of over 500 tons. Armies of workmen were employed in the shipyards, altering the bows of these vessels to enable tanks and guns to be more easily carried and disembarked. In addition to this concentration of barges, there were also submarines in many harbors, some of them of ocean-going type, large motor vessels, tugs, and merchant ships. Forty-five large merchant ships were reported at Le Havre. New aircraft shelters were being built inland on the many airdromes from which it was expected that the enemy aircraft would play their part in the invasion. It was noted, too, that the railways were exceedingly busy between Germany and the Low Countries.

Thus the R.A.F. fliers were the eyes of England. Hourly they reported the vast preparations for the invasion of Britain. In daring raids they broke up concentrations. Attacks followed both by day and night on large buildings at Dunkirk, and the Calais quayside buildings were burned out. Damage was inflicted on the shore buildings at Lorient. Casualties were caused among German troops, barracks bombed, and ships sunk outside the harbor by mines laid at night. Extensive damage was wreaked on ports in Belgium and Holland. These raids were directed against the "potential invasion spearheads—French, Belgian, and Dutch Channel coasts, ships, barges, docks, harbors, and gun emplacements," the Air Ministry announced.

The Battle of Britain continued. Mr. Churchill warned that invasion was possible at any time and added that gas might be used. "We must recognize that the enemy is making preparations for the invasion of Britain even before the springtime comes; invasion by land and sea, but principally in the air," Lord Beaverbrook warned. If the Battle of Britain had been lost instead of won, if the terror of the time had turned to jelly the resolution of the people, if the Luftwaffe had been able to strike fear in the strong young hearts that ran the R.A.F., the history of the war might have turned into another crossroad at that critical time.

Hitler, flushed with his easy triumph on the Continent and confident of his ability to reduce Britain at his pleasure, waited too long. In the few months of relative respite that followed the fall of France, the British had time to develop the Royal Air Force with truly amazing speed. The aërial superiority that it had maintained over the exodus from Dunkirk was doubled and tripled. When the German blitz began, the enemy knew at once that in the air he had met his master. Britain could not be conquered by bombing.

By mid-August it was obvious that the Germans intended to storm the British coast. Behind the shores of France and Belgium great concentrations of materials were being gathered and troop detachments were growing larger each day. But by now the British were ready. They had no appreciably greater army than the one that they had so perilously pulled out of the Germans' jaws in France, but their courage and their ingenuity were never greater.

22

OCCUPATION OF FRANCE BY NAZIS— A STORY OF INFAMY

FROM the day of Adolf Hitler's triumphant entry into Paris, his Nazi legions marching under the Arc d' Triomphe erected by Napoleon, down the beautiful Champs Élysées and through the *grand boulevardes,* it was a carnival of loot, plunder, and desecrations.

The "peace of honor" that Marshal Pétain had accepted for his devastated country stunned his compatriots and the world when the Germans and the Italians announced the full terms of their armistices. Each of the conquerors, even the lately arrived Italy, was to occupy a portion of the vanquished country at the expense of the defeated. The Germans took a full half of France, the half without which the rest could not live.

Dividing France into an occupied and an unoccupied zone, the Germans drew their line of demarcation from a point on the French-Swiss border opposite Geneva northwest to Dôle, southwest to Chalons-sur-Saône, then generally northwest to a point twelve miles east of Tours and from there almost due south to the Pyrenees at Saint-Jean-Pied-de-Port. Thus the Germans acquired all the industrial north, all the Channel ports, and all the great harbors on the Atlantic coast. Paris was, of course, included in this area, as was all Alsace and Lorraine.

The Italians, for their meager rôle in the war, were to occupy the area between their frontier and the most advanced positions reached by their troops before the armistice took effect. This amounted to a strip of eastern France that extended from the Swiss border at Geneva south and southeast to a point on the Mediterranean coast just west of Nice. Although the armistice made no mention of Corsica, it was later to be occupied by Italian troops.

Hitler, whose railings against what he called the "Versailles *Diktat*" had won so many greedy Germans to his ranks, imposed on his defeated enemy an armistice—both the Germans and the Italians stipulated that these documents were only armistices, not final treaties of peace—that had practically taken the French nation under his dictatorship and enslaved its people.

The Germans were thorough and precise in their terms. The northern and western zone was to be occupied for the duration, and France was to pay all the costs of this occupation on a basis to be determined by Germany. The French Government received the choice of setting up its capital in Paris, well within this occupied zone, or in any part of the unoccupied zone that it chose; it ultimately selected Vichy. All the armed forces, except the skeleton necessary to maintain order in the unoccupied or "free" zone and to protect the overseas empire, were to be demobilized and disarmed.

All heavy equipment and all military installations in the occupied zone were likewise to be handed over to the Germans. The fleet and the merchant marine were to report to such French ports as the Germans and Italians might designate. France agreed to permit no armed hostilities by any of her nationals against the Axis and to prevent the flight of Frenchmen to other countries in order to join an Allied army or navy. The use of aircraft was forbidden, save with German permission. All transport facilities were to be placed at the disposition of the Germans.

The French Government bound itself also to return to their homes in the occupied zone all refugees who were in "free" territory and to allow no transfers of property to the "free" zone. It pledged itself to surrender to the Germans any German nationals or former German nationals, in other words German refugees, at the German Government's demand. All German prisoners of war were to be repatriated, but Frenchmen captured by the Germans were to remain prisoners "until the conclusion of a peace."

The final articles provided for the creation of an armistice commission to which the French might send a delegate in order to express their wishes, receive the orders of Germany and transmit these to his Government, and for the right in Germany to a unilateral termination of the armistice if Germany found the French wanting in their performance of its terms. What this meant, in effect, as events were to prove, was that Germany retained the right to occupy the whole of France when she found it expedient. Meanwhile, in the region that was admittedly to be occupied, Germany claimed all the rights of an occupying power.

The Italian terms were no less despicable. In metropolitan France, an area extending thirty miles beyond the line of occupation was to be entirely demilitarized; in French North Africa, a broad strip 125 miles deep was to be similarly treated wherever French and Italian territory were contiguous; in other words, all the Tunisian border and a good part of the Algerian frontier. These terms applied also to the coast of French Somaliland in East Africa. Italy received the right to the free use of the port of Djibouti and all its facilities and of the French section of the Djibouti-Addis Ababa railroad. All military equipment in all these demilitarized zones was to be surrendered to the Italians; fixed fortifications were to be rendered unusable. The exact limits of the zones, of course, were to be determined by the Italians, and their armistice commission was to supervise the execution of the terms of the armistice.

These were the ruthless terms imposed on France, their execution to prove even more cruel. France had suffered most from the war in the north and west. It was there that the Germans had loosed their bombs on the cities most heavily; it was there that their troops and tanks had smashed through countryside and city alike and their shells had crumbled much of the wealth of France.

The great wine country was desolate and would starve for years to come. Factories producing military and civilian goods alike had been damaged and in many cases destroyed. The Germans, to augment their own war and civilian production and to provide a subsistence level for the subject population that would keep it just strong enough to work for them, would have to repair or rebuild these plants. Such an expenditure was a part of the costs of occupation that the French were to bear.

The unoccupied zone, which was soon to be known simply as Vichy France, was ordinarily dependent for much of its manufactured goods on northern France. It found itself now cut off by a line of demarcation more jealously defended than a foreign border; and also it was burdened with a horde of refugees, not only from the north but from all the countries Germany had conquered on her way to France. Not all of these unfortunates could be returned whence they had come.

The roads from Bordeaux to Spain, when the armistices took effect, were still clogged with these refugees. Every head was always half turned to look backward in dread as feet dragged on, for the German armies were pounding relentlessly down the coast in their determination to stand as soon as possible on the Spanish frontier. The international bridge above the Bidassoa seethed with hopeless and more helpless masses, trying to escape the hunter. The bridge was still choked with cars and pedestrians on that last day when the French authorities closed it forever—forever as far as these doomed fugitives were concerned, for well they knew that the Germans would never open it to them.

Within France, there was greater tragedy. In the mad haste to escape the German onrush, parents had become separated from their children, perhaps in a packed railway station, perhaps in some roadside panic when the German planes swooped down, or in the maddening crush of a city in its death throes, like Bordeaux.

Now, when the Pétain Government began to comply with its obligation to the Germans to return these people to their homes, it acted with a speed born of dread of a tyrannical master. There was no time to seek for a missing child or a father not heard from. Everyone who could be shipped back to the place whence he had come was loaded like an animal into a train and packed off to his destination.

For months the newspapers of both zones of France were to contain the heart-rending appeals of parents describing the children whom they had lost and the area where they had last seen them. Almost more difficult to bear were those notices inserted by kind-hearted Frenchmen who had found a weeping child beside a country road or sleeping exhausted in a field, and who sought now to return it to the mother for whom it begged in dry, hard sobs.

These seemed to be the symbols of France under German rule: the homeless on the roads, and bewildered soldiers who no longer had a country to fight for or, in many cases, homes to which they could return. Certainly those Frenchmen whose homes were now in occupied territory, under the harsh military rule of a dreaded invader, were numbed with shock and fear. In the south there was still a flicker of hope. For there, at least, was still the ghost of a French Government headed by a man who was still, in the average mind, a symbol of French greatness. And, though they did not know what he meant, they were eager to seize on Marshal Pétain's pledge that a new order would arise in France.

To assist him in erecting this new order, the Premier had chosen a cabinet under the rigorous scrutiny of the German masters. General Weygand remained as Minister of National Defense; the Vice Premier was Camille Chautemps, whose name had more than once been linked to the right-wing appeasers of Germany and opponents of democracy. The Minister for the Navy and the Merchant Marine was Admiral Darlan, who had openly declared his hatred and distrust of the British. The Foreign Minister, Baudouin, was a man of whom little was known. M. Pomaret yielded the Ministry of Interior to Adrien Marquet, Mayor of Bordeaux and friend of Germany.

Marshal Pétain repeated the strict orders that the Germans had issued to the army, the navy, and the air force. They could not believe that the "hero of Verdun" would betray France; but they could not shut their ears to the impassioned appeals of General de Gaulle that they come to Britain, re-form their ranks, and rejoin the battle as Free Frenchmen. Admiral Darlan, too, ordered French ships to make for metropolitan ports; Vice Admiral Emile-Henri Muselier demanded that they sail for British ports and there join the real France. In their indecision, and their unwillingness to turn over their ships to the Germans, many commanders followed neither course, but took their ships instead to Casablanca, in French Morocco.

The British Government saw the issue clearly from the first. Although they hesitated to sever relations with the Pétain Government, they did not hesitate to extend to De Gaulle's new French National Committee every facility to strengthen it. Britain assumed the responsibility for billeting and training the thousands of Frenchmen all over the world who were cabling their allegiance to this Frenchman who had dared to stand alone, when all the rest were cringing.

The Free French Army on June 20, 1940, consisted of two men: General de Gaulle and a Lieutenant de Courcel; there was no Free French Navy or Air Force. But now recruits were flocking in at the risk of their lives, for Bordeaux declared that any man who rallied to De Gaulle was convicted of treason. Although General Mittelhauser, in Syria, had apparently reconsidered his first impulsive pledge to carry on the fight and had now accepted the armistice, thousands of his troops and officers were streaming into Palestine to join the British and eventually their own colors in London.

From the forgotten far Pacific, New Caledonia declared its adherence to the men who represented the real France, who would not lay down their arms while their own compatriots were being held as prisoners of the Germans on French soil. French sailors and their officers, waiting in Casablanca, felt their courage being reborn. General Charles Noguès, the Resident General of French Morocco, contrary to their hopes, had offered his loyalty to Bordeaux. Betrayed, the sailors could only keep silent now, for to do otherwise meant death.

The Germans, meanwhile, entered Bordeaux, and the French Government prepared to leave for the little town of Clermont-Ferrand, the home of one of its newest and most sinister members. Pierre Laval, who had won the world's contempt when he was Premier of France at the time of the Ethiopian War, had entered the Cabinet as a Minister of State, that is, without a specific portfolio.

Laval was the son of a peasant. He had studied law, practiced successfully, and entered politics early, becoming a deputy. His professional advancement, like his political rise, was steady because it was unhampered by scruples. Laval's only principle was that he must advance his fortunes; to this all else was subordinate. When Italian Fascism was in the ascendant, he was the intimate of Mussolini. When German Nazism began to show promise of growing powerful, he aspired to be the intimate of Adolf Hitler.

Laval knew no loyalty to France; his only allegiance was to Laval. He saw Fascism as his own creed and his own salvation.

At the end of June, Pétain's Government moved to Vichy, a name that was to become the synonym for treachery and cowardice. Laval was daily gaining in power, although he still held no portfolio. Alarm was growing in Britain. French ships were still too close to German control; in German hands they might mean the end of Britain. French possessions and mandates were an equal menace. Britain issued a warning that she would not let the Germans or the Italians enter Syria, for that would threaten the life line to the east. Ominously for France, Britain made mention of her own fleet and of its strength and warned that she was no longer bound by the treaty France had violated; she would act now according to military necessity.

The Germans were already demonstrating the nature of their occupation in northern France by decreeing the death penalty for any Frenchman who possessed arms or radio-transmission apparatus, even of the crudest amateur nature.

Ignoring the orders of the Government, defying the power of the Germans, the little Fort de l'Ecluse in the Rhône Valley held out bitterly. In this "Gibraltar of France" three hundred men rejected the almost daily German demands for their surrender. For ten days they were cut off from all communications with the rest of France but they were Frenchmen fighting for their country and her honor. Only when the angry Germans brought up tanks and field guns and a superior force, was the Tricolor lowered from this last bastion.

Early on the morning of July 3, a British fleet detachment steamed up into the waters of Algeria. Standing off the naval base of Oran, its commander ordered the French ships lying there to join them. The French commander chose to give battle. All day the British warships blasted at their allies of a few weeks before; all day the French ships answered with their own salvos. When it was over, the battleship *Bretagne* was a wreck—the *Dunkerque,* one of the world's finest fighting vessels, was beached and blazing; and other lesser ships were sorely wounded.

On the same day British boarding parties went over the sides of all French ships in British harbors that had not put themselves at the disposal of the French National Committee. In most cases the British were greeted almost with relief, though on some craft there was resistance.

Also on the third day of July, Premier Pétain drove a knife into the liberty, equality, and fraternity that had been the soul of France for 150 years. He appointed the cunning and treacherous Laval to draft a new constitution for France, a charter that was to be no charter but an indenture. He summoned a "national assembly" to meet in Vichy to accept the document that would terminate its existence. This was the end of the Third Republic.

When Laval and his colleagues put together the legal phrases that would destroy their country, they were playing the conquerors' game. The Entente Cordiale that had subsisted for thirty-six years and that had carried France and Britain to a common victory against the same enemy less than a quarter of a century before was denounced by the régime that now ruled what was left of France.

Foreign Minister Baudouin added the final touch to his own betrayal by announcing that France was prepared to defend herself by sea and by air against any British in the Mediterranean, with the "consent" of Germany and Italy. Premier Pétain had already denounced his old allies.

The American Government, afraid lest it be engulfed in war before it was fully prepared, was anxiously watching the degradation of France, the first of its allies when it was an infant nation and the oldest of its friends among the countries of the world. The French Empire had outposts in Central America and in the Caribbean that, if they were in German hands, would threaten the safety of the United States. This was particularly true of the island of Martinique, where several French warships lay at the time of the armistices. Among them was the aircraft carrier *Bearn,* her hangars and deck filled with new American planes. Other American aircraft, recently purchased for the war against Germany, stood on the airdrome of the island. These ships and planes in the hands of an insatiable enemy like Germany might deal almost mortal blows to a virtually unarmed country.

As soon as the news of Pétain's plea for an armistice had become known, President Roosevelt had frozen all French assets in the United States. While the armistice negotiations were in progress, America, through the secrecy of her diplomatic connections with the Bordeaux Government, was making every effort possible to strengthen the French to resist German and Italian efforts to obtain possession of the French fleet. America announced to all the world that she would recognize no change in the sovereignty of French possessions in the Western Hemisphere effected by force or duress.

While neutral America was doing all that her position in the war would permit her to do, British ships in the Atlantic were speeding toward Martinique. The island's High Commissioner, Admiral Georges Robert, was an old friend of Premier Pétain, and it was obvious that he would choose to remain loyal to him rather than to swing to General de Gaulle. The Royal Navy, therefore, could afford no risk, however slight. Its elements were on their way to blockade the French island in order that no German vessel might enter its major port of Fort de France and, even more, that no French man-of-war or merchantman might slip out to fall into enemy's hands. The British established their patrol. The United States, under the duties imposed by its status as a neutral, sent its own destroyers to watch the potential combatants, lest an act of war occur within the waters of the American hemisphere.

When Italy entered the war, several French warships had been patrolling the eastern Mediterranean with British vessels, and had put into the harbor at Alexandria, Egypt, where they were targets for Italian bombs after France and Italy had concluded an armistice. To their commander, Rear Admiral René-Emile Godefroy, the British offered two choices: to carry the Tricolor back to sea with the addition of the two-barred Cross of Lorraine that General de Gaulle had made the symbol of the Free French forces, or to accept the immobilization and partial decommissioning of his vessels.

After some negotiations, Admiral Godefroy took the second choice. The British undertook to repatriate such officers and members of his crews as elected to return to France, to allow those who wanted to enlist in either the British or the Free French Navy to do so, and to continue to pay the others who elected to remain in Alexandria. Britain made no commitments as to the duration of this virtual internment of the ships, but she insisted that the vital parts of their guns be removed and stored ashore under her control. Admiral Godefroy accepted all the terms offered to him, and the ships were duly demilitarized, to be ultimately preserved to fight for France again. For three years the Admiral was to remain aboard his flagship in the harbor, something of an enigma to his compatriots and to the world, never revealing where his loyalties lay until he finally acted.

But the infamy of Vichy was only beginning. As if in rage at the surrender of Godefroy, as well as in retaliation for the attack at Oran, the Admiral's accord with the British was succeeded only a day later by an air attack on the great British naval base at Gibraltar. German, Italian, and French fliers roared in side by side. The disarmed French Air Force, Vichy explained, had received the consent of the conquerors to rearm and to join them in this treacherous blow.

The French at Vichy had issued a statement that threw on Britain the full blame for the fall of France. As if the words had been directed by their conquerors, it was charged the ally had been delinquent in furnishing troops and munitions to the sectors where they were most needed and had favored her own troops, besides going counter to previously accepted joint plans. This Britain vigorously denied, replying that her officers had not been made parties to some plans, that she had weakened her own sectors to assist the French, and that when the British troops executed an attack from Douai and Valenciennes, in which the French were to have joined, they had to carry on unassisted because the French were still unprepared to put the plan into action.

Britain's words were followed by action; she was now convinced that Vichy was under dictatorship of Munich through the puppet Laval. At the moment when London was setting the record straight on these matters, a British motorboat slipped under the cover of night into the harbor of Dakar.

The harbor of Dakar, in French West Africa opposite Brazil, had seemed a safe refuge in those last hectic days when France appeared to be in flight by land and sea. Several units of the navy had crowded on steam to make the port. Among them was the new 35,000-ton battleship *Richelieu*. Now she lay in apparent security from former enemy and former ally alike, until the motor boat stole in under the cover of darkness.

The water of Dakar Harbor was black and thick with oil when the sun rose. The motorboat had dropped depth charges under the *Richelieu*'s stern, wrecking her steering gear. The R.A.F. had struck with bombs that assured the crippling of the ship. The great ship was paralyzed, and was to remain so for the more than two years in which she was to fire her guns twice more in battles against a former ally.

The sun that rose over the wounded *Richelieu* was to set on the death anguish of the Third Republic. For on that day reports were pouring out of Zurich and Berlin, and Vichy itself, which made it more than obvious that the new régime was determined to destroy democracy.

On July 9, 1940, the Senate and the Chamber of Deputies met to vote themselves out of existence. Under the new constitution drawn by Laval, there was to be nothing but a shadow parliament, with only advisory functions. The Senate was to be appointed by the Government; the lower house was to resemble Italy's Chamber of Fasces and Corporations, composed of representatives of trade groups, industry, agriculture, and other economic sections of the nation.

The last legislative act of both chambers was to vote to the Government full power to establish a new constitution, which, the following day, they were to ratify, sitting jointly as a "national assembly." The Deputies were polled first, and granted the power by a count of 395 to 3. In the Senate, only one man cast a negative vote.

When the assembly met on the following day, unexpected opposition developed. Some of the former Senators and Deputies who now found themselves to be assemblymen without rights had reconsidered the extraordinary document for which they had voted approval. They had begun to recognize the ominous implications that its few words contained. After some debate, they won one concession from the Government: it agreed to insert in the resolution a provision for a national referendum. With this amendment, 569 of the assemblymen solemnly cast their votes for its acceptance. Only 80 voices dared to speak for the preservation of democracy in France.

Charles Corbin, the French Ambassador in London, resigned his post in shame at his Government's betrayals. The Embassy was thus put in charge of Roger Cambon as *chargé d'affaires*. M. Cambon's first and last major task was to convey to the British Government the protests of Vichy on the Oran attack. M. Cambon performed his duty; then he too gave up his post as a representative of Vichy. In Syria, General Mittelhauser, who had vacillated from Free France to Vichy, now sought to redeem himself by resigning the command he had continued to hold under Pétain.

The Vichy Government and its leader were quick to show even more openly than before what course they had resolved to follow. The new constitution provided for the appointment of a "Chief of State" instead of a President, who would have the power to designate his successor. This was the "new order" that Marshal Pétain had promised to his country. In furtherance of it, he appointed himself Chief of State in a decree that began with a presumption of royalty: "We, Philippe Pétain, Chief of the French State..." As his heir, the Chief of State appointed Pierre Laval, Vice President of the Council of Ministers—Vice Premier, in other words. The new government contained no Premier. Second only to Laval was General Weygand, as Minister of Defense, and Adrien Marquet, who remained Minister of the Interior. These three men, in effect, were to rule France or the truncated area that now bore that name.

The two waves of occupation that had swept over southwestern France, the refugees and the Germans, had left the area almost bare. The most vital foods, such as meat, potatoes, milk, and coffee, were growing rapidly more scarce. Minor officials left in power appealed to the Germans for relief. In the north the Germans requisitioned all food stocks in the hands of wholesalers and retailers, explaining that this was not expropriation, but the first step toward the assurance of an equitable distribution of available supplies.

In the free zone food rationing was instituted immediately, and the regulations were severe. Both this and the occupied zone were now subject to the British blockade. Britain issued a warning that she would prevent all French ships from making ports in either area. Furthermore, French ships bearing exports would be intercepted even if their cargoes were known to have originated in the unoccupied zone, lest the cash or credit proceeds of the sale of such goods find their way into German hands.

The men who did not love liberty, the renegades of France, had not yet completed their vengeance on those whom they had succeeded in office. Vichy needed manpower, and families were demanding the return of their men, for they could see no further reason for their detention in Germany. To appease both needs, Vichy had begun to make representations to Berlin for the return of the 1,500,000 captured Frenchmen. Pehaps in its eagerness to please the Germans and thus further its cause, Vichy ordered a judicial investigation of the responsibility of Daladier and other ministers for the country's military defeat.

When no one knew whether France would fight on or yield, Daladier, Mandel, and more than twenty other prominent Frenchmen had left Europe and gone to French North Africa, prepared to carry on the war from there if the Government so decided. When they learned of the two armistices, they remained in Africa, for there was no longer a France to which they could return. The African authorities, still loyal to Pétain, were ordered to seize them all. Former premier, former ministers, all were shamefully loaded aboard a ship and carried back to Marseilles, where they were kept in custody.

Before any formal charges had been lodged against them, Vichy stripped them of their nationality and their fortunes. The new Minister of the Interior, Marquet, urged in the strongest terms fullest coöperation with the Germans and declared that the Government would severely punish "the men who threw our country into war when they knew that we were not ready to fight." This subterfuge was followed by a constant changing of the list of defendants. Some of those arrested in Africa were freed because they had acted on orders of superiors, while others who had not fled France found themselves suddenly under arrest as offenders against the state.

The roster was a surprising document of Nazi-inspired charges. Prominent on it was General Gamelin, who had been relieved as Generalissimo of the Allied armies. He was included with Daladier, who was accused of having thrown France into war. M. Mandel was charged with having committed treason in having negotiated with a British cabinet minister and a British general in Africa while the armistices were pending, and with having plotted to go to London to aid General de Gaulle in forming a French Government in exile.

M. Reynaud was likewise indicted and arrested, as were César Campinchi, a former Minister of the Navy; Léon Blum, who was Premier almost three years before the war but who had ardently opposed the Munich agreement; Yvon Delbos, once Minister of Education; Pierre Mendès-France, a former Under Secretary of the Treasury; and two former Ministers of Air, Guy La Chambre and Pierre Cot. The two latter had both escaped French jurisdiction; M. La Chambre was in America and M. Cot was in England.

A Supreme Court of Justice was created by decree. Its chief justice was the presiding judge of the criminal court. Five associates, with two alternates, were to be selected from members of the judiciary, army generals, members of council of the Order of the Legion of Honor, and members or former members of "constituted state bodies."

It was cruelly apparent that France was in chains, enslaved to a conqueror who would let her go only when his grip had been broken by the utmost force. As "ambassador" Germany sent to Paris Otto Abetz, her notorious saboteur of morale. The southern half of France, over which Marshal Pétain pretended to rule as Chief of State, was in a far more tragic plight. From time to time even Pétain was outraged by German demands on his Government and by German insolence in exposing the hollowness of his régime; even he made occasional gestures of protest and revolt. For all his repetitious insistence on his rôle as the guardian of France, he matched the Germans in his repression of everything that the world had accepted as the essence of France. He was not above appointing an "ambassador" to represent his France in Paris, the heart of the real France where now the Germans ruthlessly ruled.

The tragic irony of the years that followed was that France was to exist in her essence, in honor and dignity, only on soil that was completely alien. General de Gaulle's headquarters were in the capital of the British Empire; the territories of the French Empire that were to remain true to its traditions were not truly French soil. Yet a happy paradox was to be the constant parallel of this anomaly: the knowledge of that really free France outside France—symbolized by an English house in Carlton Gardens in London, where the Tricolor flew and the only language heard was French—that was to provide between the two zones of the divided motherland a bond that no line of demarcation and no foreign interdict could infringe.

General de Gaulle stood, with the thousands who risked their lives to rally to his standard, for a homeland that could no longer be home. Other thousands, who were to grow to millions, became in their own lifetime a legend to inspire these who could not escape but must endure. On the other side, against De Gaulle, stood the few who had sold themselves and bartered their very being as Frenchmen for a little pretense of power, for luxury, and for eternal ignominy. These were the men of Vichy and their satellites in the provinces, the traitors of Paris, the Déats and the Doriots and all the little demagogues and prostitutes of principle. This was the only rupture among all who called themselves Frenchmen.

When the Germans had occupied other countries—Norway, the Netherlands, Belgium, and before them Czechoslovakia and Poland—they had sought to preserve the shadow of legality in clearly conquered territory by concluding agreements with native renegades of their own choosing, whom they set up in nominal governments to do their bidding. But in France it was to be only in that area which they did not occupy that they were to have a traitor régime.

In the zone that they openly occupied, they made no effort to erect such a flimsy façade; instead, they were content to rule undisguised. They accepted the help of those traitors who offered themselves, whether politicians or industrialists or financiers or labor leaders, but the Germans kept their own iron hand obvious at all times. They dared not take the risk of allowing this occupied enemy country to have the illusion of any self-government.

The Germans' intention was to use the occupied zone of France as a vast military base and arsenal for the invasion of Britain. Northern France and the Low Countries were springboards from which such an attack would have to be made. France, since it was closest to Britain, had to be under strict army control.

The Germans erected what amounted to a wall of artillery and troops along the Channel coast from Dunkirk to Boulogne, a distance of seventy-five miles. The guns were there to cover any German embarkation against Britain.

Civilian postal, telegraph, and telephone facilities were suspended for a while throughout occupied France to give the Germans a complete monopoly over them. Travel across the line of demarcation between the two zones was forbidden except with special authorization from the German Kommandatur in Paris.

Mines, factories, and railways were operating at the greatest capacity the Germans could get from them. The Nazis confidently boasted that the British Empire would not last out the summer.

Speech and the press were no less shackled. The Germans had put their own henchmen in the editorial and managerial chairs of the principal newspapers in Paris. Through them they dictated the views that the journals would publish. In Vichy, the censor of the "government" exercised a control that was not less diligent.

The zone ruled by Vichy was a weaker replica of the occupied area. In the latter, the German decrees against Jews and Masons were already being applied; in free France a magnanimous exception was being urged for those Jews who could prove that they had fought for France.

A military tribunal was sitting in Clermont-Ferrand. Before it De Gaulle was tried, convicted, and condemned *in absentia*. A court-martial had already sentenced the General to four years' imprisonment and demotion in rank on relatively minor charges. Now it would complete its infamy. Solemnly the court heard the charges read: General Charles de Gaulle was a deserter who had fled to a foreign country in war time; he had engaged in propaganda against France; he had had dealings with a foreign country with a view to favoring action against France; he had incited French soldiers to enter service with a foreign country, and he had committed acts of a nature that would expose his country to the danger of reprisals.

These were what his Vichy accusers charged against this officer of the French Army who was so imbued with its traditions that he had been wounded and captured in one war because of his reckless disregard of his own safety, who had made five attempts to escape, who, after peace returned, had devoted all his efforts to the creation of a new army that would keep his country free, and who now, virtually alone, was giving his life to the redemption of a country that his accusers had betrayed.

De Gaulle was found "guilty" and was convicted on every charge.

The military court pronounced its sentence: The General was to be stripped of his rank, his property was to be confiscated, and he was duly condemned to death. Fortunately for France, the last part of the sentence was mere rhetoric, impossible of execution.

The same day General de Gaulle was convicted and doomed, the "government" announced the convening of a "war guilt" court, to be held in Riom on August 8. Riom was a little town in the foothills of the Aubergne Mountains and had a long history of revolutionary trials. In Riom the puppet régime proposed to bring to book the men who had tried, in varying degree, to keep their country on the road of honor, faithful to its traditions: Blum, Daladier, Reynaud, Mandel, Gamelin.

The régime was already aware of the risks it would run in steering a course too close to that of the Germans. Grumbling had been heard that in both zones of France heavy and light industry were already back at work, producing not for France but for the war machine of her conqueror. Vichy's Minister of Industrial Production and Labor, René Belin, found it necessary to make a public denial of these reports. In order not to offend the Germans by his inept diplomatic lie, he struck a blow against the labor unions that had grown so strong in France. These, he conceded, would be allowed to remain in existence, but henceforth they would function only as craft guilds, forbidden to engage in political activity and kept under strict government control. This control, he added, would be applied equally to employers.

The Vichy régime was still eager to establish itself in Paris, the traditional seat of any French Government. The Germans refused to withdraw their troops from the capital until, Pétain told his countrymen, "certain material conditions" had been realized. In effect this meant "until Britain has been defeated." It had its choice of either returning to Paris and accepting the new shame of pretending to govern from a capital garrisoned by an occupying Power or of remaining where it was. It still had enough pride left to take the latter course. But in other matters it was again subservient to the Germans. Though it was returning refugees to their homes in the occupied zone at an average rate of 45,000 a day, it readily enforced on its own side of the line of demarcation the German ban on the return of Jews, Negroes, and persons of mixed blood.

France was subjected to a "blood bath" and was to live through a reign of terror in which free men were deported for slave labor, women and children cowered under constant threat, homes were looted, and the resources of the country dissipated. All this was a planned conspiracy between rapacious Germans and French traitors to crush the French spirit of liberty, destroy democracy and enslave it under the Nazi-Fascist yoke—a fate that awaited every nation conquered by the Germans.

DE GAULLE RALLIES FREE FRENCH UNDER THE TRICOLOR

DISGRACE after disgrace was being heaped on his homeland by the Germans while General Charles de Gaulle in exile steadfastly worked for its liberation. He had behind him the moral and material support of the British Government which did not hesitate to finance the recruiting, arming, training, and maintaining of the fighting forces under De Gaulle's command.

General de Gaulle and the British Government signed a formal agreement on August 7, 1940, in which Britain undertook these obligations, including payment of pensions to dependents of any men killed or wounded in the service of the French National Committee.

Britain agreed also to release to the Free French, as General de Gaulle's forces were already known, the French ships that she had seized and to man them, wherever possible, with complete French crews. Where this was not possible, Britain was to man the ships with her own crews and operate them. All the ships manned by Frenchmen under the nominal direction of the British Admiralty were to remain the property of France. And already grateful French troops were training to bear their part in defending Britain against invasion. Besides these material obligations, the British Government pledged itself to use its best endeavors on the conclusion of peace to help the French volunteers regain any rights, including national status, of which they might have been deprived as a result of their participation in the struggle.

"I would like to take this opportunity of stating," the Prime Minister declared, "that it is the determination of His Majesty's Government, when victory has been gained by Allied arms, to secure the full restoration of the independence and the greatness of France."

In its eagerness to imitate its German masters, Vichy was directing its attacks now on the nation's intellectual and social life. It announced that hereafter French women would, in effect, be reduced to the status in which the German put his woman: a thing of amusement and usefulness. France, Vichy said, wanted more and better babies and more farmers; to that end it would so revise the education of its youth that French girls would learn more about rearing children and less about Latin, more of domestic duties and less of mathematics. It was going to translate *"Kinder, Kuche und Kirche"* into French.

Vichy had created far greater obstacles to the restoration of France, however; obstacles that grew out of the very nature of its rule. In the Orient that Vichy seemed to have forgotten, Japan was keenly observing the weakness of what had once been a great European Power, a Power that still owned territory coveted by the Japanese. Premier Konoye's Government stated brashly that it intended to incorporate into that "Greater East Asia Co-prosperity Sphere" French Indo-China.

Elsewhere in the Orient, however, there were Frenchmen of another kind. Their spokesman was Henri Sautot, Resident Commissioner of the South Pacific possession of New Hebrides. M. Sautot spoke for the first part of the French Empire to declare its formal, unqualified allegiance to General de Gaulle as the representative of France, and to the Allies' cause.

Other parts of the French Empire were in less fortunate position. Like Indo-China in the Far East, French Somaliland, on the east coast of Africa, was almost cut off from metropolitan France. Its vital port, Djibouti, had been made virtually an Italian possession by the armistice with Italy. The colony could do nothing, therefore, when the Italians deployed troops throughout its small area, using it as a base for their campaign against the British in that region.

The United States watched with concern French territory in Asia being overrun by an ally of the Germans; watched, too, Indo-China increasingly menaced by an ever-stronger Japan. Washington saw the trend of events but was not yet prepared to do more than protest. Europe, rather than the Far East, was of supreme concern to the American Government. Relations with the Vichy Government had been maintained, and Marshal Pétain had expressed his gratitude for American help to civilian victims of the war in France. Two "listening posts" were set up: one on the islands of St. Pierre and Miquelon, off the Canadian coast, where America could watch the Atlantic that was so vital to her and to the transport of implements of war to Britain; and one at Dakar, where French West Africa jutted into the Atlantic.

On Assumption Day, ironically enough, it was revealed by the press of the "free zone" that German control officers were arriving at Dakar to supervise the conduct of the Government and make sure that France was adhering to the conditions of the armistice. These officers, who were appointed by the armistice commission sitting in Wiesbaden, came cloaked in a kind of portable extraterritoriality as if to give weight to Marshal Pétain's statement in Vichy: "I do not pretend that this Government is free.... The Germans hold the rope and twist it whenever they consider that the accord is not being carried out."

Further evidence of the course of collaboration was produced by General de Gaulle, to whom Frenchmen under Vichy's rule were already sending information clandestinely, from the Continent and from North Africa. In French Morocco, Free French sentiment was stronger than in any part of the empire still professing fealty to Vichy.

In the United States, in Canada, in all the British Empire, and in many South American countries, French residents and newly arrived émigrés were forming groups to aid the Free French fight.

In the French Empire, the ancient spirit was beginning to reassert itself. Deep in Africa, the Governor of the Lake Chad Territory declared that he could not accept the disgrace of the surrender and the Vichy régime. He pledged his territory's resources to the Free French and the Allies.

This action was followed almost immediately by a similar step in the Cameroons and in French Equatorial Africa. It, too, was to bear real fruit for the Allies, for it gave them a base from which to stand guard over the suspect Governor-General of French West Africa, Pierre Boisson, and his intrigues with the Germans.

The Vichy régime was preparing, under Nazi pressure, its case against the men whom it had accused of responsibility for the war. Preliminary investigations were being held daily, and each of the defendants found himself called as a witness against all the others as well as against himself. Some, such as Mandel, Mendès-France, and Jean Zay, who had been Minister of Education under Léon Blum, were Jews. This fact seemed not unconnected with the régime's abrogation of one of the latest laws of the Third Republic: the act forbidding hostile criticism of any section of the French population on racial or religious grounds.

Over on the other side of the world, Japan sent to the Governor of Indo-China a demand, amounting to an ultimatum, for the cession of a military base in the country and the right of passage for Japanese troops. The French immediately closed their port of Haiphong.

To the undoubted surprise of the Japanese the Indo-China authorities rejected the Tokyo ultimatum. Immediately the American Secretary of State informed the Japanese in plain language that his Government might react strongly to any change in the status of the French possession. Tokyo, therefore, reconsidered and submitted a "modified" document to the French, withdrawing the original demands for virtually unrestricted use of the territory. This second request, submitted to Vichy, was accepted without apparent scruple even though it meant that the French Empire was to permit the use of its territory for hostile action against a friendly power. The Japanese planned to exploit Indo-China as a base for an attack on Yunnan Province in southern China.

Foreshadowing his imminent declaration that parliamentary government was undemocratic, Marshal Pétain once more revised his Cabinet. This time he eliminated every minister who had held a seat in a French Parliament; every minister, that is, except one: the indestructible Laval, the most articulate champion of full collaboration and coöperation with Germany. The Chief of State could be sure of counting on his "heir's" endorsement of his forthcoming announcement that liberalism, capitalism, and socialism would be forever barred from the "strong, free" France that he professed to be building.

Though Vichy had approved the second set of demands presented by Tokyo, Admiral Jean Decoux who represented Vichy in Hanoi, was far less disposed to allow Indo-China to be so cavalierly violated. In this he had the support of the population, the majority of which was staunchly behind the French National Committee. But Admiral Decoux faced not only the strongest pressure from his Government at home but the far more suasive Japanese Navy so much nearer.

At 2:15 P.M. of September 23, 1940, a British fleet appeared off the harbor of Dakar, West Africa. Governor-General Pierre Boisson of French West Africa without hesitation refused to permit, as the British demanded, the landing of a force of soldiers of General de Gaulle at Dakar. British guns blazed out at the harbor and the ships in it.

The first day of the battle was shrouded with fog. For eight hours the British (who Vichy claimed had brought in two battleships, four cruisers, several destroyers, and four transports filled with Free French fighting men) poured their shells into the targets and stood up against the return fire. One of the French ships that answered the attack was the huge *Richelieu,* which still lay immobile after the British motor-boat attack several weeks before. Though she could not move, her guns could speak—and on the orders of Marshal Pétain they did speak.

On September 24 the battle was resumed. Six times the Free French troops under General de Gaulle attempted to land; each effort was repulsed. Once more the British Admiral commanding the fleet sent to Governor-General Boisson an ultimatum for the immediate surrender of Dakar. Boisson replied briefly: "I will defend it to the end." The battle was resumed. Frenchmen found themselves battling Frenchmen in civil war.

Vichy acted quickly to retaliate against both Britain and Free France. At ten-minute intervals, waves of French planes swept over Gibraltar and pounded the ancient British stronghold in the fiercest aërial bombardment it had yet endured. Against the De Gaullists, Vichy took savage revenge. A Court of Summary Jurisdiction was created in the midst of the battle off Africa; its sole purpose was to try—and, of course, to condemn to death—all Free Frenchmen in Vichy's jurisdiction, within forty-eight hours of their arrest.

On the third day, the frustrated attempt to save Dakar for France and the Allies was abandoned. The British withdrew their ships and the planes that had supported them, and the Free Frenchmen watched disconsolately from the decks of their transports as the African coast faded out of sight.

General de Gaulle had believed, on the basis of reports from his intelligence service, that the population of West Africa would rise to support him—this had proved false.

The Cross of Lorraine and the Union Jack did not fly over Dakar; but the Rising Sun was being carried, by force of arms, ever deeper into Indo-China throughout the three-day battle in the Atlantic. It was on the very eve of that fight that the first Japanese troops invaded Indo-China—despite the fact that Tokyo's negotiators had just received from the French all the concessions they had demanded. The farther the Japanese pushed into Indo-China, the greater the resistance they met. For a while, in some areas, French arms triumphed; Dong Dang was recaptured. The sirens shrieked in Hanoi; they had hardly stilled when the Japanese announced that, at dawn of September 24, they would bombard Haiphong, the capital's port. They had already resumed their thrust at Langson.

Vichy was strangely silent on this invasion in the Far East. The only comment came from the new French Ambassador in Washington, Gaston Henry-Haye, who said that despite the complete lack of outside assistance, the French would continue to oppose with force any infringement of the Indo-China accord. What force the French could muster, however, was bound to be pitifully inadequate against the overwhelming strength of the Japanese in men and equipment and their advantage of shorter lines of supply. The push against Langson compelled a French withdrawal, and heavy fighting followed on a fifty-mile front. In the face of this announcement from the Indo-Chinese capital, Vichy pretended to the world that the fighting had almost ended and that the Japanese were withdrawing. The Japanese had in effect won the whole colony without having actually invaded half of it.

Emboldened by the Japanese success, and egged on by the Japanese agents, the Government of Thailand had the temerity now to demand territorial concessions from the invaded French possessions. The French rejected the Thai demands, but Bangkok maintained its pressure.

Meanwhile, the Vichy régime was beset from other sides. The Italians demanded the cession of military and naval bases in Syria and Lebanon, which Vichy was determined not to grant. General de Gaulle made his first effort to win Madagascar for the Allies by serving an ultimatum on the Governor of that great island lying off Africa in the Indian Ocean. The alternatives were: yield or be subjected to a complete blockade by the British. The Governor informed his superiors in Vichy that he had rejected the ultimatum "with disdain."

The French Empire was in the gravest danger everywhere. The Japanese sent a new general to Hanoi to discuss "larger issues" arising out of the agreement Decoux had made which permitted the Japanese to use Indo-China against China. Both the Germans and the Italians were also emphasizing their demands for more bases. Vichy announced that it was going to strengthen the defenses of every part of the empire remaining in its jurisdiction, including the islands of Martinique and Guadeloupe in the West Indies.

The announcement was followed almost immediately by a conference between President Roosevelt and M. Henry-Haye, at which the President made it clear that this country would disapprove of any such action. This information the Ambassador relayed to his Government. A week later he advised Sumner Welles that Vichy had no intention of fortifying or reinforcing its West Indies possessions.

The influence exerted by the United States must have disappointed one group in the Vichy régime. Headed by the Foreign Minister Baudouin, most of the Cabinet had for some time been trying to persuade Marshal Pétain to take France back into the war on the side of Germany and Italy. A much smaller number of ministers, supported by an ever increasing part of the population—which was swinging more and more to General de Gaulle—wanted the Chief of State to revive France's declarations of war against the conquerors. To both, Pétain was adamant. To Britain, he was equally firm in insisting that his country, or what was left of it, must be regarded as completely neutral. He could not rejoin the Allies without being immediately overthrown by an invading German army; he could not take Vichy France back to war as an Axis partner without making all her remaining resources subject to requisition; and the struggle to meet the costs of the occupation of the other half of France was already draining her. This figure, set by the Germans, was 144,000,000,000 francs a year, more than double the 1939 budget for all France.

The triumphant Germans in Paris had begun to reveal their true character. The very "correct" attitude they had maintained in the first weeks of the occupation of northern France had completely failed to win them the friendly reception they had hoped it would gain among the people. The Nazis reverted to type, to what was normal to them. They began a reign of loot and plunder. They took what they wanted wherever they found it and trampled whoever stood in their way. All private automobiles and trucks were seized at once. Even bicycles and horse-drawn vehicles were taken without hesitation. They aggravated the food shortages by deliberately holding back supplies and delaying the long queues that lined up daily outside food stores; often the people had to stand so long in hunger and desperation that they fought among themselves for places nearer the door. The Germans threw all Jews out of Alsace and Lorraine into the Unoccupied Zone.

They abused the Catholic clergy and sought to degrade and defame the priests and prelates as they had tried to do in Germany. They searched church property on "security" grounds and accused priests of immoralities. Property was seized without compunction.

The worst weapon in the German economic arsenal, however, was currency. They produced an intentional inflation that had only one aim: to destroy the economy of the area they had occupied. They printed special banknotes—occupation marks—which German soldiers could use only in Occupied France, and which all French tradesmen and workers were forced to accept. To one German mark they assigned the arbitrary exchange value of twenty French francs, and two such marks were issued each day to every German soldier. There was absolutely nothing to back up this currency; it was simply another means of stripping the country quickly and thoroughly.

The most elemental rights of private ownership, even for citizens of neutral countries, were not respected. The contents of safe-deposit boxes were made inaccessible to the owners except by the consent of the Germans and in the presence of German officials. When, after having met these requirements, the owner opened his box, the Germans took every security that could be marketed in foreign currency and every item of jewelry and precious metal. No receipt was given; this was not a temporary seizure. This, it was explained, was the first step toward making absolutely certain that, when the peace terms with France were finally settled, at least the down payment of the indemnity imposed on her would be paid in full.

In northern France, where everyone knew at first hand what Nazism meant, Frenchmen knew the vast gulf that lay between French tradition and modern Germanism. It was hardly to be wondered that the Frenchmen of the north turned in disgust from Vichy and looked to London and General de Gaulle for succor and salvation. De Gaulle, in his utterances and his acts, was the direct antithesis of Pétain. In each part of the Empire that joined his colors all the decrees of Vichy were nullified at once and all the laws of the Third Republic reinstated; legislatures resumed their former power; political prisoners of the Vichy régime were released.

Early in October, General de Gaulle paid a visit to the steaming jungle colony of the Cameroons, which had been one of the first to secede from Vichy. He was welcomed when he landed at the port of Duala by a young army officer who called himself Jacques LeClerc. His true name was a closely guarded secret, for his family still lived in the Occupied Zone of France.

This mysterious LeClerc had been a captain during the Battle of France. Captured after being slightly wounded, he had been taken to a château that—though the Germans did not know it—belonged to one of his close friends. With the connivance of the butler, he had obtained civilian clothes and escaped across the closely guarded line of demarcation into Unoccupied France. There he had stayed no longer than was absolutely necessary for he was on his way to rejoin his colors.

Colonel LeClerc was now Governor-General of the Cameroons. Later, as a brigadier general, he was to lead a valiant band of French and native troops across 2,000 miles of jungle, mountain, and desert to Tripoli and Tunis—finally to reappear with De Gaulle in the liberation of France.

On the same day that General de Gaulle arrived in Duala, Vichy revealed that the British fleet was carrying out the ultimatum issued by De Gaulle; it had begun what Vichy called a "starvation" blockade of Madagascar, to force the island to repudiate Pétain.

Frenchmen at home were not altogether ignorant of such things; they were disturbed by them and by something more puzzling: the delay in the start of the "war guilt" trials at Riom that had been so loudly heralded. The régime seemed to have lost much of its taste for beginning the proceedings proper, though the preliminary investigations had been held. As much to stop the embarrassing questions that were beginning to be asked, as to distract attention from the disturbing events abroad, Vichy at last took another step toward the inception of the actual trials. The public prosecutor formally petitioned the special court to indict Léon Blum, Paul Reynaud, and Georges Mandel.

The charges laid against former Premier Blum were summed up as the "betrayal of the duties of his post." It was alleged that he had been ready in 1936 when his Popular Front régime held power to involve France in a war to defend his personal beliefs; that his social policies, emphasizing leisure rather than labor, had impaired arms production, and that his Minister of Finance, Vincent Auriol, had diverted funds appropriated for defense.

Former Premier Reynaud amazingly was accused of "embezzlement of public funds." No political charge was made; but the prosecutor said M. Reynaud had intended to flee to Spain after his resignation and had sent two of his former aides ahead of him with millions of francs of public funds to be held in his name.

The case of Mandel caused some embarrassment. Months earlier, although the Vichy Government had concealed the fact as long as it could, a court-martial in Meknes, Morocco, had acquitted the former Minister of the Interior of the charge of treason. This "treason" had consisted in "plotting" with high British officials to carry on the war from the French Empire overseas. But M. Mandel, who had been Minister for Colonies under Daladier, could hardly have acted traitorously in so doing, for he knew more than any man in France of the potential military power of the empire; it was he who had created the colonial armies. The utmost that could be done now was to accuse him of "corruption and speculation on the value of the national currency."

The charges were lodged—and again nothing happened for a long period. The accused remained in detention and no word as to the probable date of their trial was heard.

It was at this time that Prime Minister Churchill made a new appeal to France. Knowing the trend of the Vichy Government toward increasingly greater collaboration with Germany, the Prime Minister broadcast to the people of both zones a plea that the common enemy of France and Britain be prevented from coming between them. Mr. Churchill assured his listeners who heard him—though the broadcast was on the forbidden list, there were millions—that his country wanted nothing that belonged to France. Britain knew, he added, that France could not help actively in the war at that moment; but, he said, her weight might later help materially in the accomplishment of final victory. He pledged his country not to waver but to drive Nazism out of Europe.

Out of that one-day meeting in a railway car came, not a peace treaty, but a "temporary agreement" in which Vichy agreed to full collaboration with the Axis. What this agreement entailed was the cession of Alsace and Lorraine to Germany and of part of the French Riviera to Italy, the use of French air bases in Africa, and the disposition of French forces in Africa and Syria in such a way as to protect the Italian flanks in Italy's drive on Egypt and the Suez Canal. In return, Germany pretended to make some economic concessions to France, carrying out the fiction that she would be a partner in the reconstruction of Europe: to release war prisoners, to revise the line of demarcation, and to give the Vichy régime a corridor to Bordeaux and control of the port.

When Vichy announced the agreement it revealed also that Laval was taking over the Foreign Ministry, a development dangerous to Britain and the United States. Both countries acted at once. King George sent a personal message to Pétain expressing his sympathy for France in her travail and promising that she would share in the ultimate Allied victory. The purpose of the note was to encourage any members of the Vichy Cabinet who might still be opposing military collaboration with Germany and Italy.

The American Government, though not at war, went further. The French Ambassador Henry-Haye was told that if his Government collaborated with Germany in the war the United States might be compelled for its own protection to occupy all French territories in the Western Hemisphere. The warning to the Ambassador was explicit in its condemnation of any action that France might take to aid her conqueror against her former ally. The plea of duress, President Roosevelt told M. Henry-Haye, could never justify such a betrayal. The message recalled the solemn assurances Pétain's Government had given to the

United States in the first days of its rule that the fleet would never be surrendered. It warned that if the French now permitted their ships to be used by the Germans against the British they would be guilty of a "flagrant and deliberate breach of faith with the United States."

Once again a startling contrast to the pusillanimity of Vichy was furnished from London: General de Gaulle, whose naval aides were being tried and condemned, as he had been, *in absentia* by the Vichy régime, announced the creation of a War Cabinet to fight for France and proceeded to strike another blow to liberate French territory.

These strong men were to guide the military destinies of Free France for some time to come. Their first task was to effect the liberation of Gabon, the African colony that had earlier declared its loyalty to De Gaulle but had been held in the grip of Vichy.

The Gabon campaign was brief. The inland garrison town of Lambarene was the first to fall to the forces under De Larminat. The next objective, the colony's main port of Libreville, resisted and the Free French found themselves compelled to assault patriots who feared to disobey the orders of their officers. After both sides had suffered casualties, De Larminat offered the resisting garrison a day of armistice in which to accept his terms for surrender. When the offer was rejected, he had no alternative but to resume the attack. It was not long before the city was overwhelmed and Free French warships were riding at anchor in the harbor. Only one Equatorial port, Port Gentil, remained loyal to Vichy; and a week later it was in the hands of the Allies, surrendering without a battle.

Defection of Vichy's representatives abroad was further testimony of the true French spirit. Diplomats and consuls, growing daily more ashamed of what they now had to represent, resigned their posts. With almost no exceptions, they turned at once to De Gaulle. Many went to London to put themselves at his disposal; others went simply to the nearest Free French organization in the countries where they were to enroll under its banner. These organizations spread throughout the Americas and in every neutral country in Europe except Spain and Portugal. Many times, however, this split among Frenchmen had to be aired on foreign soil when a Vichy-minded consul found himself in open conflict with a subordinate who refused to resign but instead claimed the consulate for Free France.

The bitterness of such conflicts was aggravated by a new utterance from Vice Premier Laval, who was once more consorting in Paris with his Nazi friends. In the former capital that was now no more than an outpost of Berlin, Laval proclaimed to all the world his contempt for democracy as a hopeless corpse. France's future, he said, had been staked by him on his policy of collaboration with the Axis. He had not hesitated to admit the purpose of his trip to Paris—the discussion of economic and colonial questions with both the civil and the military leaders of the conqueror. He and his German masters agreed that no peace treaty could be made until Britain had been defeated.

But the French Ambassador in Washington gave the lie to M. Laval in the first phase of a cleavage within the Vichy régime that was to result in a series of irregularly spaced climaxes. Henry-Haye, who admired Pétain but secretly considered Laval a usurper of the Marshal's power, denied that either peace negotiations or possible cessions of French territory had been discussed in Paris. But the United States Government, so long the devoted friend of France, could not rest here and Secretary Hull summoned M. Henry-Haye to the State Department. Mr. Hull did not disguise his country's apprehension over the warmth of high French officials toward Germany and the régime's growing antipathy to the United States. He frankly classified it with the Governments of Rome, Berlin, and Tokyo in its indisposition to be either honest or amicable.

Secretary Hull pointed out repeatedly the tendency of the Vichy régime to exceed the armistice terms in actively assisting Germany in her conquests and aggressions, and vigorously declared this country's determination to do all that it could to thwart such proclivities. He cited specifically, as a danger to the American continent, the island of Martinique where many French warships still lay, and urged on the Ambassador that they be immobilized by the removal of vital parts of the engines and armaments, and that American naval officers be allowed to inspect the island's installations and the hoard of French gold that had been taken there. With all this the French Ambassador professed complete agreement. Subsequently an American admiral paid a visit to Admiral Georges Robert, the High Commissioner of the island, and, though none of the steps that Mr. Hull had recommended had been taken, the United States freed certain French credits to permit the island to make purchases in America.

It must be conceded, in the light of events, that the Allies gained inestimably from the American maintenance of diplomatic and consular listening-posts in areas close to the enemy and intimately linked with those regions the Allies needed for the ultimate destruction of Germany.

Vichy's policy and goals were questions that were suddenly becoming unanswerable because of the growing split within the régime. In mid-November two surprising developments occurred on the same day. The French fleet sailed from Toulon for a destination that was not announced; and Vichy disclosed that all French inhabitants of Lorraine were being evacuated by the Germans, who gave them the choice of being sent to Unoccupied France or to Poland.

Vichy's disclosure was couched in language so strong as to lead many observers to believe that the régime was about to rebel; but such a theory was immediately countered by the sailing of the warships. In Berne, the neutral listening-post of the Second World War, all comment inclined to only one conclusion: that Marshal Pétain now faced an open fight for power with Laval and Admiral Darlan. Against Laval's constant urging of the utmost revenge on Britain and his hatred of both England and America, the Marshal had stood firm.

While Pétain wanted to see no more Frenchmen uprooted, and feared the anger of the United States, his rule of the occupied region continued to be as autocratic as before. He assumed the complete control of the budget and continued the "war guilt" trials at Riom. But the only defendants whose cases actually came before the special court were subordinates of those who were to be the major scapegoats. Two minor aides of M. Reynaud were convicted—*in absentia* once more—of desertion, for having carried diplomatic messages and funds into Spain.

But Reynaud himself and Georges Mandel were still not being brought to trial; instead, while the court imposed ten-year sentences and other penalties on men whom it could not reach, it merely changed the detention place of those who were within its grasp and whom it apparently feared even more than it hated.

Pétain and his Cabinet displayed the same authoritarian tendencies in dealing with the economic problems that confronted them as they indulged in dealing with finances and "war criminals." Subsidies to encourage large families were ordered; food rationing was made more severe; employers' associations and labor unions were dissolved.

Toward the growing menace of Free France two opposite courses were simultaneously adopted. In proclamations addressed to the 35,000 soldiers, 1,000 airmen, and crews of twenty warships now serving under the Cross of Lorraine, the Vichy régime wooed them as softly as it could, coaxing them to return to France on the promise that no action would be taken against them—only their leaders were regarded as criminals.

Vichy was beginning to find that some powerful forces of Gaullism existed within France. Too large a proportion of the population, its spokesmen admitted sadly, did not yet understand the meaning of the new order or the necessity for France to help the Axis exploit Africa for the general advantage of Europe. Day after day, Vichy's Official Journal published decrees removing mayors, prefects, whole municipal councils that insisted on living in ignorance of the benefits of collaboration and consequently had to be replaced with more coöperative officials. Many of those ousted were interned. They were joined daily by private citizens who found themselves suddenly ordered into "administrative internment" for no reason other than that their liberty was considered dangerous to the state.

In Syria, which Vichy had counted on most fully among all the overseas territories, and where German and Italian agents had begun their work almost before the signing of the armistices, there was another problem. The High Commissioner, Gabriel Puaux, was becoming more and more outspokenly critical of his Government. He encouraged, or at least tolerated, pro-British sentiment and made no secret of his own hostility toward the Italian armistice commission that had installed itself in Beirut, the capital of Lebanon; nor did he interfere with the enmity shown by both the French community and the native population. Vichy ordered him relieved and replaced by Jean Chiappe, who had made himself notorious when as Prefect of Police he had ordered the Paris gendarmes to smash popular demonstrations.

Chiappe left for Syria by plane and Vichy ordered Puaux to return to France. The régime was fated to have two disappointments: Puaux was to become a De Gaullist and Chiappe's plane was shot down somewhere over the Mediterranean.

More trouble was facing Vichy in the farther reaches of the empire. Emulating the action of her infinitely stronger Oriental colleague Thailand resorted to arms and sent some of her few planes to bomb Indo-China in what she described as "retaliatory" attacks, alleging that French planes had raided a Thai town. From the air the battle quickly spread to the land and the sea. All along the border there was heavy fighting. Thailand charged the French with an amphibious attempt to seize the Thai province of Trad by landing troops from two warships. This effort, the Thai Government said, had failed.

While this war in miniature raged in the Orient, Vichy was shaken from top to bottom by the first great crisis of its history as the capital of France, a crisis that so nearly destroyed the shadow government of Pétain as to awaken in every part of the world the simultaneous hope that France was about to rise in invincible wrath. In an unscheduled broadcast to the country, the Chief of State proclaimed that the man whom he himself had designated as his political heir—the Vice Premier, Foreign Minister, and chief of the information and propaganda services —was no longer a member of the Cabinet: Marshal Pétain announced the removal of Pierre Laval from the Government of Vichy France, the abolition of the office of Vice Premier, and the appointment of Pierre-Etienne Flandin as Foreign Minister.

These ruses, however, were largely blinds to confuse the French people and mislead the British and the United States. The strings which manipulated the mannikins were all pulled from Berlin. Laval was a Nazi agent behind the scenes and Pétain was an impotent puppet. This was the condition in France as the Germans reached out for new conquests designed to bring all Europe within their grasp.

24

BLITZ IN THE BALKANS—"COCKPIT OF EUROPE"

"MITTELEUROPE," the road from Berlin to Baghdad, had long been the dream of the Germans. To accomplish this was the Kaiser's ambition in the First World War, but it met with dismal defeat. Hitler declared he would make the dream come true in World War II.

The Balkans were the key to the fantastic conception of creating a Teutonic Empire from the North Sea and the Baltic, through the heart of Europe, to the Bosporus and on to Baghdad and the gates of the fabulously rich Orient.

Hitler approached the "cockpit of Europe" by the logical route, via Austria, Czechoslovakia, and Hungary. With Bulgaria as his partner, he planned to take over Rumania and Yugoslavia. These Balkan countries, deriving their name from the Turkish word meaning "mountain," were turbulent peoples with a diversity of races whose enmities had seethed for generations. They would become easy prey to intrigues. Hitler stirred up and aggravated the rivalries between the Serbs, Bulgars, Rumanians, and Greeks. He touched the match to the powder keg. The explosion shook Central Europe.

The Balkan Wars of 1912-1913 were only the forerunners of World War I, which actually started in Serbia when the shot that killed the Austrian Archduke, Francis Ferdinand, in Sarajevo, on June 28, 1914, was "heard around the world." It exploded into a European conflagration. The post-war period brought neither peace nor unification to the Balkans. To the contrary, between World War I and World War II it became the laboratory of dictatorial experiments, resulting in such eruptions as the assassination of King Alexander of Yugoslavia and the revolution of the Venizelists in Greece.

Generally speaking, there were between the two World Wars three political phases in the Balkans. The first led to the rise of Hitler's Third Reich in 1933; the second, marked by Franco-British efforts to create a Danubian Confederation, attempted to counteract Axis influence in southeastern Europe; the third, beginning with the Munich Pact of October 1, 1938, gave Hitler a free hand to pursue his *"Drang nach Osten"* policy.

There had been three diplomatic obstacles on Hitler's road to the East: the League of Nations, the Little Entente, and the Balkan Entente. These were removed before Hitler reached there. The League, unable to cope with Axis aggression, became a mere phantom as the protector of small nations, in particular the Balkan states. The Little Entente, strengthened by French influence, was reduced to a shadow when Czechoslovakia fell and the aid of France ceased. The pact which Greece, Turkey, Rumania, and Yugoslavia concluded in 1934 was anything but a "Balkan Entente"; it was a loose bond, partial, incomplete, and defective. The Balkans' last hope of survival vanished with the disintegration of collective security.

Bulgaria was a simple task for Hitler's nefarious scheme. That tempestuous Balkan nation of more than 6,500,000 people failed to learn from her mistakes. Her foreign policy had been a sequence of miscalculations for which she paid dearly. She fought the First World War as Germany's ally and was the first to surrender. She bet on the wrong horse again in World War II when she became Hitler's satellite. In the first war it was Czar Ferdinand who paid for the defeat with his crown. In the second struggle it was his son, King Boris III, who paid for the same mistake with his life.

Ferdinand's son, Boris, for twenty-five years (1918-1943), reigned in the shadow of his father's misfortune over a chaotic nation, of which 47 per cent were illiterate. Sometimes called "the most cunning diplomat in Europe," the King wholeheartedly approved of a Fascist régime for the Bulgarians, generally Slavic in their sympathies and descent. He claimed that "my people are pro-Russian, my Government is pro-Axis, and I am pro-British," but his acts betrayed his personal conception of England and democracy. His attitude may be explained by his family background for he was born with a foot in both camps of World War II. A member of the House of Saxe-Coburg, he was, on his mother's side, a descendant of Louis Philippe of France. His wife was a daughter of King Victor Emmanuel of Italy, thus linking him to Fascism.

When Boris became king at the age of twenty-four, he saw the fruits of his father's autocratic methods, but did nothing to wipe out the mistakes of the past. A semi-dictatorship under Stambulisky ended in revolt and the Premier's assassination. In the next three years Bulgaria was on the verge of civil war with continuous Komitadji warfare on the frontier. Four attempts on the King's life were made. Bulgaria turned Fascist by a *coup d'état* in 1934. The Constitution was suspended and all political parties were dissolved. Under the government of Khimon Gheorghieff, the King was a virtual prisoner for eight months. When he was rid of the Premier, Boris assumed dictatorial powers himself. Subsequent Parliaments of 1938, 1939, and 1940 had practically no legislative powers, cabinets being completely under the influence of the King who at bayonet's point had ousted the officers' cliques. The country was ruled from the royal palace in Sofia.

Nazi Germany, despite Bulgarian affirmation of strict neutrality and in the face of a recent Soviet-Bulgarian trade agreement, was ready to bait the trap. Hitler's economic emissaries succeeded in concluding a Bulgarian trade accord, by which the Reich took 70 per cent of Bulgaria's exports and secured such quantities of her raw materials as the kingdom was unable to barter with other countries for urgently desired goods. She had thereby sold out entirely to Germany where her frozen credits, by the end of 1939, amounted to 6,000,000,000 *leva*.

Economically in Hitler's hands, Bulgaria drifted closer to the Axis camp politically, and strengthened her military position by receiving large quantities of arms from Germany. It was estimated that in the spring of 1940 she had 150,000 men under arms and was ready to mobilize 700,000.

Whatever Premier Philoff uttered thereafter about Bulgarian neutrality was a lie. When Churchill charged, in February, 1941, that German ground forces in considerable numbers had penetrated Bulgaria, Philoff denied this. The facts were that thousands of them had already occupied Bulgarian airfields and that many more German "tourists and business men" had infiltrated the country. Finally, on February 13, Sofia authorities admitted that the Nazis were all ready to march through the kingdom to the Greek frontier to support Italy's unsuccessful venture against the Hellenes. When German staff officers arrived in the Bulgarian capital on February 24, the British Legation began to destroy its confidential records. On March 5, London severed diplomatic relations with Bulgaria.

Hitler was on the march! Bulgaria's move in joining the Axis was neatly timed. It not only came when Hitler was ready to strike against the Balkans, but was meant as a counterstroke against Britain, since it coincided with Anthony Eden's negotiations with the Turks in Ankara. His conferences there, though veiled in secrecy, had to do with English strategy in the eastern Mediterranean. London was confronted by the choice of either continuing the war against the hapless Italians in Libya or moving large army contingents from the Nile to the Balkans in order to support the Greek drive. Once again, Hitler struck first.

The German Army and Air Force occupied all strategic bases in Bulgaria and entered Bulgarian Black Sea ports—the eleventh sovereign state they had overrun. The Commerce Department in Washington froze Bulgaria's gold reserves amounting to $24,000,000 in this country. Russia's belated reproach to Bulgaria came when there were 300,000 Nazi troops in the country and German strategy on a new battlefront became a matter of speculation. Would Hitler concentrate on Greece? Or would he move against Turkey and the Dardanelles? And would he eventually force his way across the Black Sea and into the oil fields of Iran? England was uneasy and Russia restive. Turkey, which had concluded with Bulgaria a treaty of friendship and non-aggression on February 17, did not carry out her threat to break with Sofia and enter the war as Britain's ally.

Bulgarian troops began to march into Grecian Thrace by April 16, and occupied the region from Alexandropolis to the Struma River. Within another three days, according to German war bulletins, they had "occupied some Bulgarian regions liberated by German troops in order to maintain order and calm among the population." What the Bulgarians had actually taken was Greek and Yugoslav Macedonia, where local governments of the occupation forces were set up immediately. Later they took over from the Germans the Greek districts of Florina and Kastoria and the islands of Samothrace and Thasos. Bulgaria was breaking all her commitments under the Yugoslav-Bulgarian pact. This done, she declared, on April 24, that a state of war existed with Yugoslavia and Greece.

As a result of German military triumphs, she had gained access to the Aegean Sea and controlled the mouth of the Danube. The Nazis had delivered the goods and were sure to ask the Bulgarians to pay the price for them. When they were ready to attack the Soviet Union, they urged Bulgaria to fight in Russia and used pressure for the delivery of a Bulgarian contingent on the eastern front. The Hungarians and the Rumanians obeyed, but the Bulgarians refused.

The situation became critical when Moscow, on September 11, handed a note to Bulgaria accusing her of acting as a full-scale base for German-Italian land, sea, and air attacks upon the Soviet Union. It strongly intimated that Russian reprisals would be swift and stern. Sofia rejected the protest. A week later she asked permission from Turkey to move thirteen Bulgarian warships through the Dardanelles into the Black Sea. The demands revived the rumor that Italian warships had been handed over to Bulgaria for this purpose. Ankara turned down the request. Russo-Bulgarian relations had reached a breaking point. On September 22, Germany confronted Bulgaria with a virtual ultimatum demanding prompt entry into the war against Russia. A few days later a last warning was delivered to Sofia that the German Army would occupy the whole kingdom unless 150,000 men were sent against Russia.

The Bulgarian Government, however, refused stubbornly to yield. In fear of anti-Axis uprisings in the country a state of emergency was declared and measures were taken against "Communists and saboteurs." To end the spreading revolt within the kingdom, Boris granted an amnesty to political prisoners, freeing three hundred. Yet the wave of mass arrests and executions continued. In an effort to appease the Axis, the Sofia Government renewed the Tripartite Pact for another five years, and on December 13 declared war on the United States and

1943! Casablanca! Guadalcanal! Sicily!

French Leaders Meet

General Henri Giraud, high commissioner of French Africa, and General Charles de Gaulle, leader of "fighting France," meet at Casablanca.

U. S. NAVY PHOTO FROM OFFICE OF WAR INFORMATION

At Casablanca

President Roosevelt and Prime Minister Churchill quietly read their communique against a background of Army and Navy officials.

Guadalcanal Front Line
Supplies for the Army being hauled in the front line at Grassy Knoll on Guadalcanal Island.

Defense of Guadalcanal
A Marine Corps gunner, behind his 50 caliber antiaircraft machine gun, mans the island against possible Jap raids.

OFFICIAL PHOTO, U. S. A. A. F.

The Waterfront at Tripoli

The damaged buildings along this north African port show that the heavy bombers of the U. S. and the R. A. F. found their targets.

INTERNATIONAL NEWS PHOTO

The First WACS Go Overseas

The first detachment of the Wacs leave for overseas service, to be attached to General Eisenhower's staff.

OFFICIAL U. S. NAVY PHOTOGRAPH

Calm Before the Battle

U. S. Naval officers look out upon the serene harbor of a North African port shortly before the "greatest armada in history" descended upon Sicily.

OFFICIAL U. S. NAVY PHOTOGRAPH

"Old Glory" Unfurled on Sicily

Coming ashore from an LST, Americans plant the flag atop a knoll overlooking the landing operation.

OFFICIAL U.S. NAVY PHOTOGRAPH

A Triumphal Surge

American troops advance inland through the narrow streets of Scoglitti in Sicily.

PRESS ASSOCIATION, INC.

A Hysterical Welcome

A Naples street, crowded with civilians, cheer men of the Allied Fifth Army.

In the Wake of the Tide

The incoming tide, in Makin, Gilbert Island group, caught some equipment being unloaded from the LST's.

OFFICIAL PHOTO, U. S. A. A. F.

INTERNATIONAL NEWS PHOTO

Quebec Conference

On the terrace of the Citadel the heads of the American, British, and Canadian governments meet in a historic conference.

INTERNATIONAL NEWS PHOTO

Women at War

Underneath the palms at a U. S. Pacific hospital base two Army nurses walk down the trim path between rows of "ward" tents.

INTERNATIONAL NEWS PHOTO

End of the Saga

Survivors of the Burma plane crash and their heroic rescuers, as they emerged after a twenty-six day march through the jungle.

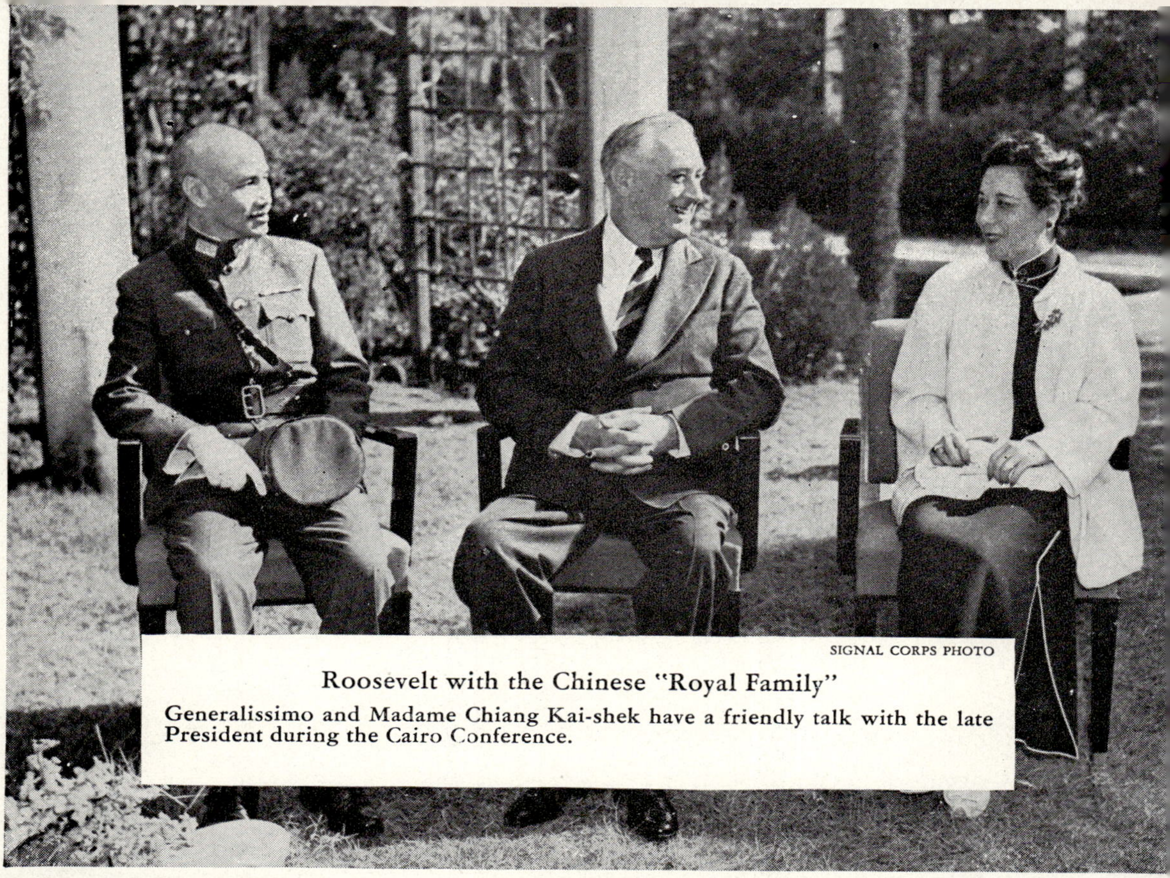

SIGNAL CORPS PHOTO

Roosevelt with the Chinese "Royal Family"

Generalissimo and Madame Chiang Kai-shek have a friendly talk with the late President during the Cairo Conference.

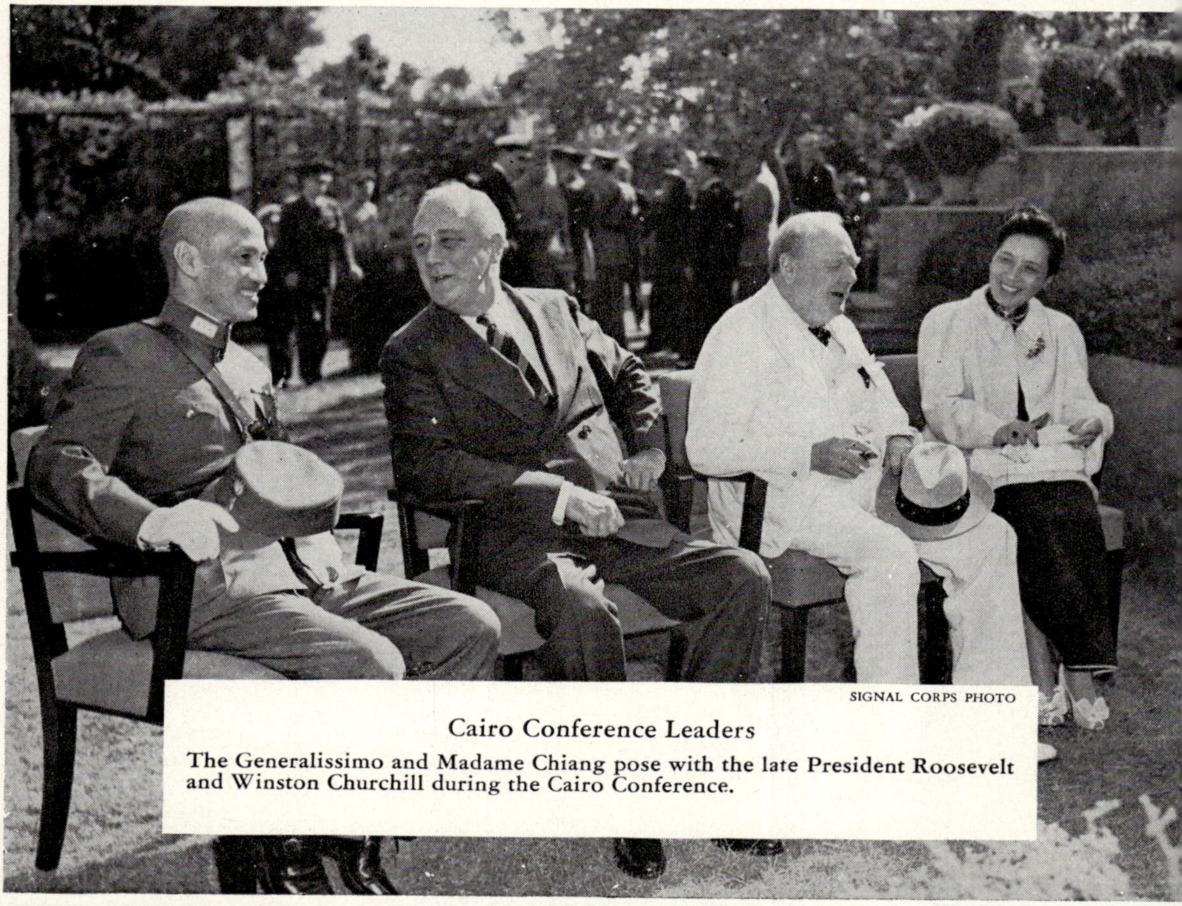

SIGNAL CORPS PHOTO

Cairo Conference Leaders

The Generalissimo and Madame Chiang pose with the late President Roosevelt and Winston Churchill during the Cairo Conference.

At the Moscow Conference

Smiles touch the faces of Secretary of State Hull, Commissar Molotov, and Foreign Minister Eden as they sign the tripartite agreement.

PRESS ASSOCIATION, INC.

INTERNATIONAL NEWS PHOTO

The "Big Three" at Teheran

Premier Josef Stalin, President Roosevelt, and Prime Minister Winston Churchill, pose during the four-day conference at Teheran.

SIGNAL CORPS PHOTO

Roosevelt Jokes with Churchill

The Generalissimo smiles, as his conferees joke with each other at the Teheran Conference.

INTERNATIONAL NEWS PHOTO

China's Generalissimo

Chiang Kai-shek, the famous leader of the Chinese military, in a favorite photograph.

INTERNATIONAL NEWS PHOTO

Happy Air Warriors

Major General James H. Doolittle and a group of his Air Force men at an advanced zone in Tunisia.

OFFICIAL COAST GUARD PHOTO

"Dogs at War"

Pinned down by heavy Japanese fire an American fighter and his dog seek shelter in a foxhole on Philippine beach.

SIGNAL CORPS PHOTO

First American Flag Over Attu

When the Yanks gained their foothold on this island in the Aleutians in 1943, they erected Old Glory on the deck of an abandoned Japanese landing boat.

Great Britain. The act was resented by the Bulgarian people. George H. Earle, 3rd, United States Minister to Sofia, declared: "This was none of the Bulgarians' doing. It is just the influence of a gangster playing with a little nation." Upon recommendation by President Roosevelt, Congress passed a formal declaration of war against Bulgaria, Rumania, and Hungary on June 3-4, 1942.

Bulgaria, which had expected a German triumph, did not profit from the fruits of her "victory," but suffered from the burdens of Nazi occupation. A Gestapo organization had been created in the kingdom, and the German Army controlled everything that the Gestapo did not lay hands on.

The masses of the people aided the Allied cause by the perpetration of sabotage. Fires and explosions occurred frequently in the ports of Varna and Burgas. The Gestapo hunted scapegoats in a vain effort to check widespread derailment of trains, cutting of telephone wires, and other damage. German propagandists in the country had a hard time to explain the Nazi reverses on the Russian front.

While the population continued to suffer from the shortage of all foodstuffs, acts of sabotage increased. Army stores and warehouses were set afire. On December 5, martial law was proclaimed in the capital. Doubt gripped Sofia at the possibilities of a Nazi victory. However, King Boris renewed his pledge of Bulgaria's allegiance to the Axis powers and said: "In this decisive period in history, the political policy of Bulgaria is definitely fixed. It rests on earnest coöperation and friendship with the Axis powers and their allies and loyal adherence to the Tripartite and Anti-Comintern Pacts."

On orders of the King, Parliament was closed in March, 1942. The Philoff Cabinet resigned in April, refusing to approve Hitler's program for the Balkan nations. The Premier, however, formed a new government that retained its pro-Axis policy to "safeguard Bulgarian liberty and independence."

In this state of confusion, with the country moving rapidly from one crisis to another, Boris paid another visit to Hitler in Berchtesgaden on March 31, 1943. When he returned to Sofia, he assumed the *de facto* charge of foreign affairs, demoting Premier Philoff's Foreign Ministership to the post of Under Secretary. The situation became more tense in April when the army was called to suppress demonstrations of students against the régime. Sotir Janeff, rabidly pro-German President of the Sobranje Foreign Affairs Commission and personal adviser to the King, was shot dead in the capital. A few weeks later Colonel Athenas Panteff, former chief of the Bulgarian State Police and responsible for political assassinations, was killed.

Hitler's strong-arm specialist, Gestapo Chief Heinrich Himmler, had been sent to Sofia at the urgent call of the King to help keep the people in line. Sometime later several members of the Liberty Front were killed in northwestern Bulgaria. Another member of the Sobranje, and an outspoken supporter of pro-Axis foreign policy, fell from terrorists' bullets. He was the 110th Bulgarian functionary to become the victim of political opponents. A panic gripped Sofia.

Boris returned from Hitler's headquarters on August 24. At a small railway station outside the capital he was shot. Four days later he died, the Premier announcing "after a brief but grave illness." Had he survived he would have had three days to answer Hitler on three demands: (1) Immediate and total military and economic mobilization of Bulgaria for the furtherance of the war; (2) The creation of a second line along the Turkish frontier that would be manned by German forces and "technicians"; (3) The granting of "full powers" to German political police in Bulgaria to repress further acts.

The Germans sent a delegation to the King's funeral, the mission of the "mourners" being to see to it that the Regency problem was solved immediately. Bulgaria was on the eve of becoming a Balkan "Denmark." In an attempt to save the situation, Philoff asked for a political truce. He resigned as Premier to become one of the three Regents of Sofia in behalf of six-year-old King Simeon II, Boris' son. The two others were the King's brother, Prince Cyril, who until Boris' death had played no part in politics, but was so strongly pro-German that he was considered a German in a Bulgarian uniform. The third Regent was General Kikola Michoff, former War Minister and past commander of the Sofia Army Corps. Dobri Boshiloff became Premier and head of a new pro-German cabinet.

Toward the end of the eventful year 1943, Secretary of State Cordell Hull warned the Governments of Bulgaria, Hungary, and Rumania to quit the war or "share the consequences of terrible defeat." American planes struck hard blows at Sofia which Berlin reported in the process of evacuation. Dispatches from Cairo indicated that Bulgaria had officially communicated peace feelers to the Allied Governments, since both her own régime and the population realized they had lost the war. The only response they received at Sofia was continued Anglo-American bombings and the reiteration that the sole terms that would be considered were "unconditional surrender."

There were signs that the Communist Party membership in Bulgaria had swelled and that the Nazi overlords and the Germanophile government in Sofia were powerless to control a spreading tendency in the country toward a new Slav federation. This was certainly not due to a metamorphosis of the Regency which had lapsed more and more into insignificance. It was rather the result of the successes of the Red Army in the Southern Ukraine and the victories that brought the Russians to the gates of the Balkans. Bulgaria was to meet disastrous defeat.

25

RUMANIA—THE BATTLEGROUND FOR OIL

RUMANIA, with her 13,300,000 people, held the key position to the turbulent affairs in the Balkans in World War II. In this modern mechanized warfare her rich oil fields were needed as the margin between defeat and victory. She became the "battleground for oil." Her rich resources had long been coveted by the nations who wanted her oil, wheat, and grain. French and English influence vied with German, Italian, and Russian efforts, and their interests clashed as they tried to bring the kingdom into the economic fold of either side.

While Rumania's wealth made her the cynosure of the world, it likewise placed her in the least enviable position of any Balkan state. Because she was surrounded by nations from whom she had won her territorial gains, her neighbors were her enemies.

Greater Rumania came into being after the Rumanian Army defeated Bela Kun's Hungarian troops and occupied Budapest in 1919. Through the addition of Bessarabia, Bucovina, Transylvania, the Banat, and other border regions, United Rumania extended her territory of 53,000 square miles to 122,000 square miles. The treaties of St. Germain, 1919, and Petit Trianon, 1920, recognized these gains which created a nation of almost 20,000,000 people.

But this populace only increased the ethnic mosaic of the kingdom and added to its already large mixture of races. There were great percentages of polygot minorities, such as Magyars, Jews, Germans, Ruthenians, Russians, and Ukranians, Bulgarians, Turks, and gypsies. They accounted for one-third of the population.

From the time of Carol's succession to the throne, the National Liberal party opposed him. Carol definitely planned to direct both his country's internal affairs and its foreign policies. Titulescu's ministership proved to be a serious hindrance, so the King conspired with Premier Tatarescu, and a new cabinet was formed without Titulescu. That master mind of diplomacy was replaced by Victor Antonescu who, in fact, was nothing more than Carol's agent. Meanwhile, the King had expelled his brother, Prince Nicholas, from Rumania. This act created bad feeling and resulted in the open opposition of the Iron Guards, who demanded the exile of Carol's mistress, Madame Lupescu.

The four-year term of Parliament ended, and it was dissolved in 1937. Tatarescu resigned and was followed by the anti-Semitic Goga-Cuza Cabinet, giving the country the rare aspect of two anti-Jewish movements, that of the Goga brand and that of the Iron Guards. The Goga government met the opposition of Britain because of the Premier's pro-Axis declarations. Party strife took such dangerous forms that Carol, fearing civil war, finally dismissed Goga and proclaimed a virtual dictatorship.

The international political horizon became more and more clouded as Carol sought personal contact with foreign leaders. He visited Kemal Ataturk and went to London, Paris, and Berlin. Not being able to obtain a British loan, he went to Germany, but Hitler and Goering received him coolly. Upon his return to Bucharest, the plan of killing the Iron Guard leader Codreanu and eleven other Iron Guardists was carried out.

Two weeks later, Carol decreed the foundation of the "National Renaissance Front," its "Roman salute" becoming official and compulsory. By this gesture the ruler played a double game. While flirting with the Axis, he tried to "appease" London by appointing as Foreign Minister the pro-British Grigore Gafencu. When the European war broke out, King Carol declared full neutrality.

It soon became evident that Carol was unable to uphold Rumania's position as a neutral. In March, 1939, Hitler demanded trade control of Rumania and got it. The famous Schacht scheme of barter agreements made for Germany's economic predominance in the Near East had worked out a plan by which Rumania's entire exports of grain, oil, lumber, cattle, and foodstuffs were to go exclusively to Germany. In return, Hitler was ready to guarantee Rumanian territorial integrity and the independence of the Rumanian people. Rumania yielded to the German plan presented in the form of an ultimatum.

Rumania had gained a respite—the respite did not last long. Weighing her might, the kingdom, at the beginning of 1940 had 800,000 men under arms, and at the maximum was able to mobilize 2,000,000. Only four divisions were stationed in Bessarabia in case Russia should impose demands for its return; three divisions were moved west of the Pruth River; six or seven divisions were in Transylvania to face the possibility of a Hungarian attack or to hold off any German menace through Hungary, Eastern Slovakia, or Russian Poland. Some remaining six divisions were near the Bulgarian border.

Rumania knew that she was facing a grim menace, for caught between Germany and the democracies, Britain and France used pressure on her. To bring Bucharest to terms, both countries had tightened their blockade and prevented essential goods from reaching the kingdom. Rumanian industry felt the pinch, and at last the Rumanians gave in. They assured London that shipments of gasoline to Germany had been stopped and that oil sales to the Reich would not be increased. The foreign ministers of the Balkan Entente met at Belgrade in a last effort to bring Hungary and Bulgaria into accord. Turkey declared that she would enter the war the day a foreign power marched into the Balkans.

Events followed swiftly. German military successes in western Europe had impressed the smaller nations on the Continent, especially those who had to settle an account with Rumania. The Allies had lost their last Rumanian friend when Gafencu resigned as Foreign Minister on June 1, 1940, while the Reich gained one by the appointment of Ion Gigurtu, a leading pro-German industrialist, who took his place. The Balkans, Europe's powder keg, exploded when the long-feared Russian ultimatum demanded on June 26 cession of Bessarabia and Bucovina.

Long one of Europe's danger spots, Bessarabia had been Russian for more than a century before the powers recognized Rumania's coup in the confusion of World War I.

Rumania was in no position to resist the Russian claim. Germany and Italy urged Rumanian submission while Russian troops rolled across the frontier. On June 28, details of the transfer were completed.

While the pitiful exodus of Rumanians from Bessarabia took place, the Council of Ministers in Bucharest renounced the Franco-British guarantee of 1939. The last vestige of Allied political prestige thus disappeared with a corresponding increase in German prestige. Rumania was ready to swing in line with the new Nazi-established order.

The season for territorial hunting was on. Hungary and Bulgaria took full advantage of the Rumanian turmoil to satisfy their respective claims in Transylvania and the southern Dobruja. Not only was Rumania too weak to offer resistance, but she had lost faith in her military strength and preferred to rely on a diplomatic settlement, hoping against hope that she would be able to ease her lot by arbitration.

When arbitration reached a stalemate, Foreign Ministers von Ribbentrop and Count Ciano stepped in and gave Hungary approximately half of Rumania's Transylvania territory.

As a result of her territorial cessions, Rumania's area within a few weeks was reduced from 114,000 square miles to about 88,000 and her population from an estimated 20,000,000 to about 13,000,000. Almost half of the population lost in these territorial transfers was Rumanian born.

Carol in desperation made a last attempt to stave off a Guardist coup. He called on General Ion Antonescu, a favorite of the Guardists. Three days earlier, Antonescu had been in prison for "prohibited political activities." To win the General's support, the King surrendered most of his power, dissolved Parliament, suspended the Constitution, and made Antonescu a virtual dictator.

Carol's gesture came too late, for Antonescu, his greatest personal enemy, wanted not only absolute power but a new régime. The General wrote a letter to Carol, on September 5, demanding his abdication as the only means of keeping the country from civil war. At five o'clock the next morning, the King signed an act of abdication in favor of his son. This youth, it appeared, would be as much a puppet as he had been when he wore the crown as a child. Carol went into exile, first to Switzerland, then to Spain, Portugal, and Mexico. He carried with him his personal fortune. And with him, too, as she had gone before, went Madame Lupescu.

While Antonescu tightened his hold on the country, the Russians massed troops on the northern Bucovina frontier and the Nazis marched into Rumania. English diplomats in Bucharest, asking information about the extent of German control, were treated coolly. Washington took the view that Rumania was virtually a German conquest, and the State Department forbade the removal of Rumanian funds, about $100,000,000, held in American banks.

On November 23, 1943, Rumania "formally" pledged her allegiance to the Berlin-Rome-Tokyo pact. Antonescu signed in the German capital a declaration which he called a "state act historically important for the life and development of the Rumanian people." On February 10, 1941, England severed diplomatic relations with Bucharest.

On March 5, 1941, the Premier met Marshal Goering in Vienna and gave the Axis a free hand in all Rumanian economic dealings. The chief topic of conversation of these two, however, was not of an economic but of a military nature.

When, on June 21, 1941, Hitler attacked Russia, the Russo-Rumanian border German troops and newly mobilized Rumanian units launched a surprise attack on the Soviets. Antonescu assumed power as a generalissimo. Relinquishing his civil rôle of Premier to his nephew Mihail Antonescu, minister without portfolio in the Bucharest Cabinet, he claimed a "holy war" to bring "old Bessarabia and the woods of Bucovina back into the Fatherland."

Flames swept Rumania. Bucharest and other cities suffered from Russian air attacks. Bombs set conflagrations in Rumanian oil wells. Soviet land forces had been withdrawn from Bessarabia to a defense line farther inland and closer to the old Russo-Rumanian boundary.

Rumanian troops had fought willingly. But they apparently considered their territorial ambitions satisfied with an advance to the Bug River, from fifty to one hundred miles beyond their 1939 frontier at the Dniester. The Germans used "pressure and persuasion" to keep them in fighting spirit and promised Rumanian annexation of Odessa. After the fall of that city to the Axis, Rumanian officers said the Russian war was over for them.

The Germans, however, had no intention of letting Rumania drop out of the war. They demanded more Rumanian troops to replace their own heavy losses on the Russian front and for service in the

Balkans. These ultimatums were based on the Anti-Comintern Pact which Rumania had renewed for another five years.

The Antonescu Government, after Pearl Harbor, followed Hitler's example and together with Hungary and Bulgaria declared war on the United States on December 12. It seemed incredible that these three small nations who had no quarrel with us should have been forced into this crisis. America and Americans were respected in the Balkan countries whose sons came to our shores as immigrants. Our relief and scientific missions had established bonds of friendship. These countries declared war "not in response to the wishes of their own people, but as instruments of Hitler," as President Roosevelt said in his message to Congress on June 2, 1942.

Eight days later the United States struck its first blow against the Axis Balkan States when a fleet of fifteen American bombers carried out an attack on Rumania's oil fields. Enormous fires were set at Ploesti. This surprised the Rumanians and their German overseers who had only light defenses in the rich oil region. Late in 1942, the Rumanians suffered their first defeat at the hands of the Russians. It happened before Stalingrad. Their troops in a small segment of the line faced "the greatest military disaster in their modern history."

Antonescu, heading a delegation, rushed to Hitler's headquarters to secure a Nazi guarantee against Hungarian threats to invade southern Transylvania, but he did not get it. Instead, Hitler demanded more Rumanian oil, production of which had steadily declined from a 1936 peak of 8,700,000 tons to 5,500,000 tons in 1943. The Fuehrer asked, too, for more Rumanian troops. An estimated loss of 400,000 casualties had already swelled the tide of Rumanian defeatism, and Antonescu was forced to keep twenty-two divisions in the country to meet emergencies on the home front.

By the end of 1943, the Rumanians had seventeen divisions left in Russia. Half of them were trapped in the Crimea, the rest reliably reported to have been withdrawn in view of the swift advance of the Russians who then stood 150 miles from the Rumanian border. Unrest swept Rumania. In fear of bombing raids the Antonescu government decided to evacuate Bucharest, Ploesti, Constanta, and other centers.

With the Red Army drawing closer to Bessarabia, the Nazis established a "state within a state" in Rumania. It was of the Hitler order—ruled by the Gestapo. Authorized Rumanian emissaries arrived in Turkey to find a way out of the impending crisis, but could not contact a Russian ready to listen to their peace proposals. Moscow obviously had but one aim: to let Rumania, as the first of the Axis satellites, pay very dearly for her mistake of climbing on Hitler's bandwagon.

26

BATTLE OF YUGOSLAVIA—
"CRADLE OF THE SLAVS"

YUGOSLAVIA—"cradle of the Slavs"—became a boiling cauldron. Its 16,200,000 people—peasants, mountaineers and city folks alike—were tested by fire. Fathers and sons, even little children, joined the guerrilla bands and defied the Nazis.

This new nation, which sprang out of the First World War, was the fulfilment of an age-old dream to liberate and unify the "Serb, Croat, and Slovene brethren" into a united nation. This dream was realized with the collapse of the old Austro-Hungarian Empire. The Croats and Slovenes strove toward a union with Serbia and, together with Montenegro, declared their independence.

The Kingdom of the Serbs, Croats, and Slovenes came into being, not as the result of bargaining at the Versailles Peace Conference, but as the final outcome of historical developments. For the southern Slavs struggled long to attain this aim. Though divided among themselves into three groups with a mixture of races, dialects, and customs, they are kinsmen whose ideal of a "Greater Serbia" is historically justified.

A forward step toward internal unifications was made in 1939 when a new accord was reached with the Croats. Premier Dragisha Cvetkovitch formed a new Cabinet in February, that included Croats, Slovenes, Serbs, and Mohammedans. In August of that year an autonomous Croat province was created with 25,000 square miles and 4,400,000 inhabitants. It had its own Parliament to deal with administrative, cultural, economic, and financial problems of the Croats. Simultaneously, free elections with secret balloting and freedom of the press were granted.

At this moment Hitler stepped in. He opened his diplomatic Balkan campaign to force the Peninsula to fall in line, politically and economically, with the Nazi "New Order." German agents became active in the parts of northern Yugoslavia inhabited by a German-speaking population of over 400,000. Reports were current of a plan for repatriating the German minorities of southeastern Europe. The scheme created uneasiness. While these groups considered themselves Germans, they had been there for centuries and were by no means pro-Nazi.

This was but the opening shot. It furnished the pretext for Hitler's true intentions: to seize the region's agricultural products and raw materials. The Nazis had already signed a trade agreement with Yugoslavia that instituted a system of direct barter. They agreed to supply Yugoslavia with one hundred Messerschmitt war planes in exchange for copper and other materials. But when German economic experts arrived in Belgrade and demanded that deliveries of Yugoslav goods be increased immediately, the Belgrade Government refused. Thereupon Doctor Goebbels set his propaganda machine into motion and, joined by Rome, gave the Yugoslavs a perfect example of Axis technique in psychological warfare.

Yugoslavia regretted this dangerous "war of nerves" game. She had established excellent relations with Italy since 1937 when both countries agreed to bury their quarrels dating back to World War I. But the Italians, adopting the Nazi scheme of fraudulent charges, claimed to have seized some obscure leaflets in Ljubljana, urging the reconquest of the northern Adriatic coast from Italy. The Fascist press warned the Serbs against pro-Allied influence. There were "Spontaneous" anti-Yugoslav demonstrations in Florence, staged, of course, by the Fascist régime. Hitler's *Voelkischer Beobachter* opened fire by accusing the Yugoslavs of ill-treatment of German minorities. Anti-Yugoslav leaflets from the Reich were circulated in Belgrade. Symptoms of anxiety, however, disappeared when the permanent council of the Balkan Entente met in Belgrade in an effort to preserve peace.

London reminded Italy that the Allies would not "remain inactive in face of an assault upon the integrity or independence of any Balkan nation." This suggested more than a suspicion that some Axis adventure against Yugoslavia was impending. The country was ready for an invader. The Yugoslav army had always been the strongest and best-equipped in the Balkans.

Its maximum wartime effectiveness was estimated at 950,000 men, but the troops were deficient in planes, antiaircraft, antitank guns and mechanized forces. Her naval defenses were likewise considered inadequate. As it was said, she shared the Adriatic by courtesy of Italy. Faced by a double frontal threat from Germany and Italy, plus the possibility of a Bulgarian attack from the back, the nation had only one natural asset for her defense: the mountainous terrain in the north. But how long would even the tough Yugoslav soldiers be able to hold out against a German attack down the Danube Valley?

Yugoslavia in her position of "guarded neutrality" was a stabilizing force in the Balkans, trying to maintain trade relations with nations at war, neutrals and non-belligerents. But her situation was changed with Italy's entrance into the war, first as an aggressor of France and second as the aggressor of Greece. Still, when the Fascist legions attacked the Greeks, Yugoslavia as a friend of both Italy and Greece, regretted the conflict between them and stated her attitude by declaring that her interests would not be menaced "from any side by the development of events in the Balkans." She sat tight and remained deaf to Axis overtures until the end of 1940, when it was clear that Bulgaria was ready to join the Tripartite Pact. Fortunately, Greek victories over the Italians delayed any decision of the Belgrade Government. The Germans and Italians threatened to support actively the separatist movement in Croatia as a means of coercing Yugoslavia into the Axis camp.

Premier Cvetkovitch and his Foreign Minister, Dr. Alexander Cincar-Markovitch, on February 14, 1941, heeded Hitler's call and met him at Berchtesgaden. Four major questions were discussed "in the spirit of the traditional relations between the two nations": First, Yugoslavia's signature to the Axis pact; second, her position in the event of German occupation of Bulgaria and an attack on Greece; third, railroad right of way across Yugoslav territory for German troops and war material; and fourth, increase of Yugoslav exports to the Reich.

Developments were swift. Within four weeks the Balkan powder keg exploded. World War II spread to the region where World War I had started. On February 22, Nazi staff officers in civilian clothes, their black military boots shining under their raincoats, began establishing themselves in Sofia.

Prince Paul was faced by a strong memorandum of Yugoslav opposition leaders, assailing the Government for its failure to inform the people of "the fateful events of the present time." A Cabinet crisis was at hand. The Regent sought a compromise with Hitler by suggesting a non-aggression pact as the substitute for an Axis alliance.

What the Yugoslavs were expected to sign was a three-power agreement with Berlin "limited to political and economic provisions." The puzzle was as confusing as ever when the Yugoslav Premier put off several times his trip to Berlin where he was to seal the document. What were the reasons for the delay? There was a deadlock but it was unlikely to last long as intensive German pressure forced the Belgrade Government into a position where a modified form of the Tripartite Pact was the only peaceful solution.

Popular uprisings indicated that any surrender would be inconceivable for Yugoslavia's hard-won independence. Belgrade still wavered. Dr. Matchek, powerful Croat leader, refused the Premiership. American, British, Turkish, and Greek diplomats in Belgrade used their influence against the Axis. Finally, on March 24, the Cabinet, filled with minor politicians, decided to yield to Hitler's "final demands" and the Premier and Foreign Minister left for Vienna.

The Fuehrer attended the ceremony at which Yugoslavia, on March 25, signed a protocol of adherence to the Tripartite Pact. The document was identical with those previously signed by Rumania, Bulgaria, and Hungary. The Axis pledged to "respect the sovereignty and territorial integrity of Yugoslavia at all times" and "during this war not to direct a demand to Yugoslavia to permit the march or transportation of troops through her territory." It was later revealed that the Yugoslav Government also received a "secret assurance" that the kingdom would obtain "within the framework of a new European order an outlet to the Aegean Sea," namely the town and harbor of Salonika.

Yugoslavia's Government thought that the nation's interests were with the Axis, but the people decided otherwise. There is an old Serbian proverb, "A grave ever; a slave never." The hardy Slav peasants, backbone of the kingdom, clung to this adage now as they had clung to it through centuries of struggle against the Turkish sultans and the Hapsburg emperors.

The people demanded expulsion of "the traitorous Cvetkovitch Government" and formation of a national régime. The Serbian Patriarch, son of a Komitaji leader, when asked whether he approved of the nation-wide demonstrations, said: "Approve of them? I place myself at the head of them." Priests and monks, whose ancestors had fought with the peasants against oppressors and invaders for nearly two hundred years, appeared in the streets and called upon the people to revolt.

At two o'clock in the morning of March 27, General Dusan Simovitch and the Yugoslav Army overthrew the Regency in a lightning coup. At sunrise, King Peter II ascended to the throne of the fighting Karsgeorgevitch dynasty. The blow came so suddenly that the Cvetkovitch Cabinet resigned within sixty minutes. All its members were arrested. Prince Paul left the country. General Simovitch, the liberator, became Premier. He formed a government strong enough to confront a bewildered and outraged Germany. The Yugoslav people wildly hailed their new King. There were scenes of joy and thanksgiving in the streets of the capital.

"Sprenite! Sprenite! Chetnice!" was the fighting chorus that rose from the crowds. Abroad, reaction to the sensational coup was no less spontaneous. In America it was called "a lightning flash illuminating a dark landscape." Demands were made to give the Yugoslavs "every ounce of aid that we can give them" and to send it with all possible speed. In London, Mr. Churchill told a Conservative Party meeting that "Yugoslavia has found her soul." He promised "all the aid we can give these who are fighting to defend their freedom and their native land."

Hitler, who for the first time in his Continental experience had dealt with a government, now felt the will of a people determined to uphold their liberty and to decide their own future.

The Yugoslav drama moved quickly toward a climax. On March 31, the German Minister, Victor von Hoeren, left Belgrade and the country was put on a complete war footing. Nazi anger over Yugoslavia's stubborn resistance prompted Berlin to declare that the situation was "hopeless." Italy made a last desperate move to halt a German-Yugoslav conflict. It found the Yugoslav nation united. Doctor Matchek rejoined the Government as First Vice-President while a powerful German Army moved into position along the kingdom's frontiers.

It was on Palm Sunday, April 6, 1941. At 3:25 in the morning the air-raid sirens in Belgrade awakened the people. This was the first indication for Yugoslavia that the nation was at war. An hour later German forces attacked. In Berlin foreign press correspondents were summoned at dawn to hear a statement by Foreign Minister von Ribbentrop, presenting the German "excuses for military actions against Yugoslavia and Greece." It was aimed at Britain. "The German Armies," von Ribbentrop declared, "will make it clear once and for all to Churchill and his notorious warmongering, intriguing allies that Great Britain has no chance in Europe."

In Washington, Secretary of State Hull, speaking for the United States Government after consultations with the President, denounced the "barbaric invasion" of Yugoslavia as another chapter in "attempted world conquest." He assured the besieged nation that this country was proceeding with all possible speed to support it with military and other supplies. In New York, the 40,000 Serbs, Croats, and Slovenes voiced the united determination of their people to "fight to the last man against the aggressor." A committee for Yugoslav Relief was formed. Word came from Belgrade that Ruth Mitchell, sister of the late American champion of air preparedness, General William L. ("Billy") Mitchell, had been sworn in as the first foreign woman ever to join the revolutionary death-defying *komitaji*.

In Yugoslavia during a week of dramatic intensity all classes prepared for the crucial test. But Nazi conquest of the kingdom was but a matter of twelve days. The German forces struck terrific blows by land and air. During the first twenty-four hours of the attack all Yugoslav airfields were bombed. Fires raged in the capital. The Yugoslavs fought bravely against the onslaught that came from five different areas: first, across the northern plains toward Ljubljana, Zagreb, and Maribor; second, from Szeged, Hungary; third, from Rumania toward Belgrade; fourth, from northern Bulgaria toward Nish; and fifth, from southern Bulgaria down the Struma Valley and toward Kavalla. By April 9, the Germans had taken Veles and Tetvo and cut the Serbs off from all land communications with Greece and their allies. Three days later the heavy columns of the *Wehrmacht* that had pushed down the Sava and Drava valleys from the Austro-Italian frontier, and down the valley of the Mur from Graz, arrived at the outskirts of the devastated capital, with another column moving westward from Virset at the Rumanian border.

The German High Command announced on April 10, the capture of 20,000 Yugoslav prisoners. Berlin falsely declared that the Serb Army had already been "wiped out." It further stated in a special bulletin that the forces of the *Wehrmacht* which had swept across south Serbia had joined hands with the Italian Army north of Lake Ochrida. Yugoslav resistance continued north of Zagreb, south of Nish, in the region near the Rumania frontier and in the mountains northwest of Tevoto. The defenders took a heavy toll for every foot of ground they were forced to yield, especially in the region which Hungarian troops began to occupy on April 12. This was the triangle of Yugoslav territory formed by the Danube and Tisza rivers and the Hungarian frontier, an area of about 8,000 square miles with a population of over 1,000,000.

The German blitzkrieg was slowed down somewhat because of stiffer Yugoslav resistance in south Serbia. The Serbs fought heroically against great odds and destroyed nearly 300 Nazi planes over that territory. But on April 17, twenty-four hours after the surrender of the Second Yugoslav Army at Sarajevo, the rest of the kingdom's forces capitulated to the invaders. The German High Command declared that fighting had stopped on all Yugoslav fronts; that negotiations for the Yugoslavs to lay down their arms were made exclusively with Serb military authorities; and that, since in effect no Yugoslav Government existed and Croatia had declared her independence, capitulation of the army was also regarded as the end of the kingdom.

Within thirty-six hours after the Nazi attack, traitors had cut almost every important telephone and telegraph wire in south Serbia. The Croat revolt allowed the Germans to cut into Sarajevo. Due to Nazi espionage tactics the defenders fled from Bitolj Pass before the Germans were there.

From people who had managed to escape, came stories which made it clear that the Yugoslav debacle was unavoidable. They told of the ferocity of the German onslaught that spread death and destruction. It was generally agreed that mobilization was too late and time too short to prepare detailed armed resistance. Last but not least the fact was revealed that Ante Pavelitch, paid Italian agent and one of the murderers of King Alexander, entered Croatia under the protection of German troops. This treachery by which Croatia fell into Axis hands was one of the reasons why the rest of the country was unable to prolong its defense.

King Peter, who had refused to leave Belgrade during the Nazi bombardment, fled to Athens, thence to Jerusalem. He narrowly escaped death when his plane was attacked by a German warplane.

The fight continued as the eighteen-year-old King had pledged it would. A Yugoslav Government-in-exile was first established in Cairo and after the fall of Crete moved to London in mid-June. The Cabinet was reorganized. Dr. Juarj Krnjevich replaced Doctor Matchek for the Croats; Miho Krek represented the Slovenes; and Vice Premier Slovdan Jovanovich continued to represent the Serbs. The new Government was recognized by the Allied Powers as a member of the United Nations.

Dismemberment of Yugoslavia by her conquerors was completed. Northwestern Slovenia was divided between the two Axis partners, and Italy annexed Dalmatia, several islands off the Dalmatian coast, and a slice of land near Fiume. Albania received her share from eastern Yugoslavia; Hungary the districts of Batchka and Banat; and Bulgaria the Serbian section of Macedonia. In Belgrade a puppet régime was established under General Milan Neditch as Premier.

Rome announced the restoration of a monarchy in Croatia, on May 15. The Duke of Spoleto was proclaimed King, but never set foot there. Ante Pavelitch ruled as dictator and issued a decree fixing the borders between Croatia and Serbia. Subsequent treaties between Italy and Croatia, and Germany and Croatia, regulated the new border lines with the Axis Powers. Croatia joined the Three-Power Pact. The Yugoslav Government protested against the dismemberment of Croatia. Washington, voicing officially its indignation against the nation's mutilation, acknowledged the Yugoslav protest.

The invaders looted the country. The German army of occupation conducted a systematic campaign against private property, homes, and apartments. They sacked whatever they could lay hands on, from furniture and clothing to the last piece of bread and the last potato. From Belgrade shops German officers and men stole all sorts of goods: jewelry and watches, stockings and revolvers, cameras and fountain pens, canned goods and fresh foodstuffs, even cash registers.

Rule of the invaders threw the country into a state of chaos, increased by the people's resistance and sabotage. Confusion and disorder grew as German bureaucracy attempted to restore order. Four Nazi administrations rose and fell, besides the Neditch Government. They included the German military governor, the Gestapo, the Volksdeutsche Buero with a maze of *gauleiters*. And the Civil administrator —the notorious Franz Neuhausen. The latter, a fat, thick-necked Nazi, was the prototype of a German *Uebermensch* (superman) and looked like the caricature in a political cartoon. A businessman, indicted for fraud in Bulgaria and sentenced to prison *in absentia,* he was Berlin's espionage and barter chief in Yugoslavia. He had the title of Consul General and offices at the German Tourist Bureau in Belgrade.

He milked the country dry. He saw to it that crops were sent to the Reich. He conducted thieving shipments of meat, lumber, and grain, and made lead, zinc, and copper mines work overtime. For all goods he set up a dual price system: one for the population and one that enabled the Germans to confiscate all sorts of merchandise. Quantities available for the Serbs were reduced to such a low level that the people had to relie on the black markets for foodstuffs. Consequently, there was starvation. A quart of milk cost 50 dinars as compared to 3 before the war. A pound of fat which had been 7 dinars rose to 150; meat sold at 110 to 140 dinars instead of the regular price of 6 to 10.

The Germans paid in occupation marks at a fixed rate of 20 dinars to the mark. The pre-war rate was 14 to 1. When payments in marks ceased and payment in dinars were resumed, the Neditch Government was obliged to redeem all occupation marks held by the population at a cost of more than 40,000,000 dinars. Neuhausen refused to take back the marks held by the Serbian National Bank in Belgrade.

A memorandum of the Yugoslav Government-in-exile to the United States charged in May, 1942, that Axis occupation forces had executed more than 465,000 persons in the kingdom. It dealt principally with Hungarian atrocities in the Banat and Batchka regions where 100,000 had been killed.

Some 800 Serbs were arrested in Belgrade and 500 killed as "accomplices in conspiracies" in October, 1942. Things in Croatia went from bad to worse. German occupation troops were increased because of the failure of the puppet Chief of State, Pavelitch, to enforce order. The Gestapo chief for Croatia, a Major Helm, was assassinated in a street in Zagreb in July, 1942. His bodyguard, running amuck with revolvers and handgrenades, murdered 700 persons in the crowd.

While the struggle against their conquerors continued, there emerged from that dismembered land the most amazing story of two Underground movements whose conspicuous hostility against each other divided and handicapped their activities. The first symptom of Serb revolt was passive resistance which quickly developed into open hostility and acts of sabotage. General Draja Mikhailovitch's guerrilla armies harassed the Axis forces. He and his Chetniks, supported by the Yugoslav émigré government and the British, performed acts of extreme heroism against the enemy.

After Germany's attack on the Soviet Union, well-organized Communist cells were formed within Serbia and from them emerged the units that grew to army status and called themselves "The Yugoslav People's Army of Liberation." They became commonly known as the Partisans under the leadership of Josip Broz, the fabulous Marshal Tito. Around both leaders and their bands epic legends grew.

Mikhailovitch, a colonel and the youngest officer on the Serb

General Staff, was raised to the rank of general and named Minister of War in the reorganized Yugoslav Government-in-exile, toward the end of 1941. He had fought with the Serbian Army in the First World War and his service with the Chetniks had been long and distinguished. Warfare was in his blood and he knew the country well. Descended from peasant stock, he also knew his countrymen and fellow fighters. When German infiltration of the country and the Balkans began he submitted a memorandum to the Belgrade Government. But Neditch, then Minister of War and later puppet Premier, ignored his demand for action and had him transferred to Herzegovina for "disloyalty." There Mikhailovitch renewed his alliance with the Chetniks and was ready for action when the Germans smashed through.

He led his guerrilla armies into the mountains. After nine weeks of preparation, he launched his war against the invaders in a relentless campaign that ranged through the length and breadth of Yugoslavia. What he and his warriors accomplished will go down as one of the most remarkable achievements in World War II. In his raid on the Kragujevach arsenal in June, 1942, he led 1,500 picked men who killed more than 2,000 Germans and captured all the arms he needed, with which he later wiped out more than 2,000 Nazis west of Visegrad.

Guerrillas, under Mikhailovitch, governed a region with 6,000,000 inhabitants who established small munitions factories and supplied bullets and powder for some 100,000 Chetniks. They picked off isolated Axis forces and disrupted enemy communications. By February, 1943, the General reported to London that he was prepared to mobilize an army of 200,000 in the occupied country.

The Chetnik leader, a supporter of the Serbian Karageorgevitch dynasty, fighting for the restoration of the pre-war Kingdom of Yugoslavia, had the moral support of Soviet Russia till midsummer of 1941. He and Tito were said to have met several times and even collaborated for a period in joint operations. Unfortunately, political dogmas and strategic conceptions clashed. The rivalry between the two leaders (Tito refusing to yield to Mikhailovitch's supreme command) led to an open rift. The Tito forces gained strength in Montenegro, Dalmatia, Bosnia, Croatia, and Slovenia; the Chetniks in Serbia, Macedonia, Sanjak, and eastern Montenegro.

Tito was the "mystery man of the Balkans." Till the end of 1943, he never expressed himself for or against the dynasty, but because of his close relationship with the Soviets his movement was Leftist. Strangely enough, nobody knew who Tito was until he rose to prominence. To the world he was a legendary figure on whose head the Germans placed a reward of 100,000 gold marks. Actually, he was known to his co-workers and followers as a Croatian Communist and trades union leader. Under King Alexander he had been held many months in prison. A political offshot of the Partisan movement, he was head of the Anti-Fascist Committee for the People's Liberation and signed his decrees and orders as "Supreme Commander of the People's Army of Liberation."

Tito's guerrillas were estimated at close to 200,000. They held down Axis forces sometimes numbering twenty to thirty divisions. They captured in October, 1943, the important German-held stronghold of Trnyi, near Rakek on the Ljubljana-Trieste railroad. They held at one time Fiume and the entire Dalmation coast, despite land and air attacks by German, Bulgarian, and Croatian forces. Capturing the steel city of Vares Majdan after a twelve-hour battle, they drove the Nazis from the last center they held in central Yugoslavia.

Tito and Mikhailovitch fought not only the Germans and traitorous collaborationists within their own country, but unfortunately they also fought each other in a civil war somewhat traditional of Balkan bitterness. They accused each other of rendering aid to the enemy and their rivalry led to open hostility. There was a sensational development in October, 1943, when seventeen Mikhailovitch supporters were tried and executed by a Partisan people's court.

The line of division widened when Tito set up a temporary government under his own presidency, and his régime was assailed by King Peter as the work of "impostors." Whereupon the Tito party denied the King's rights, and urged the Allies to repudiate the monarch. On December 18, 1943, Tito formally requested the Allies to acknowledge the Partisans' newly created Yugoslav Government as the sole representative of sovereignty among the southern Slav peoples. Peter departed from Cairo to London to secure British help and to strengthen his and his Government's position. In February, 1944, Captain Randolph Churchill, the Prime Minister's thirty-two-year-old son, conferred with Tito at his headquarters in Yugoslavia.

As the Prime Minister admitted, "the situation was somewhat complicated." Said the Prime Minister: "These (Tito) forces are at this moment holding in check no fewer than fourteen out of twenty German divisions in the Balkan Peninsula.... What then is the position of King Peter and the Royal Yugoslav Government?"

This, obviously, put the British in a precarious position. Downing Street could not dissassociate itself from Peter. On the other hand, a Yugoslavia that continued to fight and was supported by the Allies made it impossible for Hitler to take over that country.

Regrettable as the Tito-Mikhailovitch feud was, the Serbs did not wait to be liberated. They chose to take the struggle for their liberation into their own hands. Their determination was, after all, a sign of national strength.

MODERN ILIAD OF THE HEROIC GREEKS

TRAGEDY, with stark realism, fell upon the Greeks in 1940. It was to hold them in its grip for five years. From the hour when the perfidy of Mussolini drove a dagger into the heart of Greece, until the day of their liberation, the Greeks, with sublime courage, stood true to their ancient heritage.

The Hellenic world was created by men whose thought and actions were close to our own codes and standards. We inherited our share from Greek philosophy, art, and science, and we owe to the Greeks the framework of our social and political structure.

Many words in the English language are derived from the Greek. It is significant that "democracy" not only means "power of the people," but infers the Greek synonym *demokratia* (a composite of *Demos* —the people; *Kratein*—to rule; and *kratos*—authority).

The total area of the country today is 50,147 square miles, including the Greek Islands, or about the size of New York State. Before the invasion Greece had a population of slightly over 7,000,000. The background of these people gives us an insight into the events which culminated in World War II.

During World War I King Constantine was forced to abdicate, and Venizelos formally declared war against Germany, Turkey, and Bulgaria. By July, 1918, a Greek army of 250,000 men had been equipped with the help of the Allies. This force took part in the Macedonian offensive that succeeded in bringing about the surrender of Bulgaria. The Treaty of Sèvres gave Thrace and the Smyrna hinterland to Greece.

After the First World War, Greece again was isolated when Venizelos was defeated at the polls and King Constantine returned. The Greco-Turkish War ended with the disaster of Smyrna in 1922 and the King's final abdication. The revolutionary Government was faced with the problem of settling 1,400,000 refugees while attempting to form a constitutional government. George II, who had succeeded his father to the throne, left the country voluntarily during the plebiscite of 1924 which favored the republic. There followed violent outbursts under the dictatorship of General Pangalos. Feuds persisted, but Greece, with one brief interval, continued to be a republic till 1935, when King George returned and the monarchy was restored.

The *coup d'état* of August 4, 1936 brought General Metaxas into power. He was Prime Minister, but with Parliament dissolved and certain articles of the Constitution suspended, he ruled as his country's virtual dictator until his death in January, 1941.

Italy long had had designs on Greece. It was largely due to the consistency of Metaxas' policy and diplomatic skill that Greco-Italian relations continued as they did. Historically, Greek and Roman interests had clashed in the Ionian and Adriatic seas for centuries. In modern times, history repeated itself in the disputes between the two countries over the Dodecanese Islands and the territories of Northern and Southern Epirus. In both instances Italy took advantage of her position as a world power; Greece as a smaller nation was forced to yield to this greater power.

On Good Friday, 1939, Mussolini seized Albania. This was the initial step toward Fascism's attack on Greece. The Italo-Greek Friendship Pact was still in force. Mussolini assured Metaxas that the Albanian intervention was of a "merely provisional" character; that Greece had nothing to fear; and that the good relations between Rome and Athens would remain "the basis of Italian policy in the future."

Fascist Italy played the double game of intrigue for which the Axis was notorious. Mussolini sent Metaxas a document in September, 1939, in which he declared "solemnly" that no military action would be taken against Greece in the event of a European war. Renewal of the Friendship Pact was discussed in a friendly atmosphere.

In May, 1940, the Greek Government was informed that "should Italy be involved in war against Great Britain, she would not attack Greece, provided the latter was not converted into a British base." Obviously, Italy was looking for trouble. If Mussolini had no reason to strike he would surely find a pretext. And he did. Immediately the Rome Propaganda Ministry launched a campaign that followed the familiar Hitler pattern. Its charge that Greek ports were being used by the British fleet was constantly repeated, and a "war of nerves" set in. Hidden Fascist imperialism came out into the open. Mussolini's propaganda was aimed at the border populations and attacked the Greek "minorities" just as the Nazis had constructed their "case" against the Sudeten Germans in Czechoslovakia.

Metaxas was still determined to keep the peace if possible, and so renewed his declaration of neutrality. But the tension grew so rapidly that emergency measures were decreed in Athens. Greece hurried partial mobilization to meet the threat of a possible Axis move.

Finally, the Italian Minister in Athens, Emmanuele Grazzi, presented a note to the Greek Government on October 28, 1940, accusing Greece of coöperating with Great Britain against Italy. In it the Fascist accusations of "provocative activities against the Albanian nation" were repeated. Mussolini demanded as a "guarantee of security" permission to occupy several strategic points in Greek territory for the duration of "the present conflict with Great Britain." An answer to this ultimatum was demanded within three hours.

Metaxas' reply was an emphatic "NO!" He considered the communication as a declaration of war. Half an hour before the ultimatum expired, the Italian Army crossed the Greek-Albanian frontier.

Greece became the tenth victim of Axis aggression when Italian troops, on the morning of October 28, 1940, attacked her by land, sea, and air. Fascist soldiers who had made armed thrusts into foreign soil in France and Egypt crossed the Greek-Albanian frontier at 5:30 A.M.

Against Rome's military might the Greeks could muster nothing that was equal in strength and equipment. The normal Greek Army in time of peace was estimated at between 50,000 to 80,000 men. Since the outbreak of the European war it had been expanded to probably 140,000, and the small nation had reserves of about 600,000. Because of lack of arms it was doubtful that she could maintain more than 300,000 in the field. The army, organized in four army corps with thirteen infantry divisions, had virtually no mechanized forces and no motorized columns. The navy was pitifully inadequate to defend the country's long coast lines. The air force, a separate fighting arm, was negligible. There were about 120 planes in all, many of them obsolescent.

The Italians attacked on October 28 with 2,000 planes and five infantry divisions, on a 100 mile front composed of the Epirus sector in the south, the Pindus sector in the center, and the Florina sector in the north. Italians at home were completely unaware of the fact that they were at war with Greece. No official statement was made until the next day, when the Rome radio reported that Italian troops had penetrated forty miles into Greek territory. Another twenty-four hours and it was apparent that the Italians were making but slow progress in the mountain territory. Greek outposts had fallen back from the Albanian frontier and fought delaying actions with the invaders struggling through the mountain passes. British marines meanwhile had landed on certain Greek islands, while the British fleet laid mines along the coast.

In smashing attacks the Italians captured the Greek highway town of Breznica in an eastward drive in the direction of Salonika, but they had difficulty in advancing from nearby Koritza. Nor could they gain against stubborn Greek resistance on the coast.

The Greeks launched their first counterattack on November 2, in the north where General Papagos was in command. There, in a flanking movement that threatened the Italian rear and barred their path to Salonika, the Greeks fought their way into Albania and toward the Italian base of Koritza in terrific bayonet charges.

On November 11, the Greeks announced their first victory. They captured the bulk of a reinforced division of Alpine troops in the gorges of the River Aoos in the northern sector. It was the end of the initial Pindus offensive of the Fascist Army. The rest of the Alpine troops were forced into panic retreat up the canyon. This marked the beginning of a general advance of the Greek Army. Fighting in Italian territory on four fifths of the front, they smashed another Italian division and repulsed three localized Fascist attacks. To avoid disaster from their badly exposed eastern flank, the invaders fled all along the line, and only at the Kalamas River still stood on Greek soil.

For the first time, the small Greek air force had come into prominence as an offensive element by bombing Koritza and Argyrokastron. With a loss of 20,000 mountaineer troops, the standards of Rome were back where they had come from—in the mountains of the Albanian border. Two thousand Greeks had accomplished a miracle.

General Ubaldo Soddu, Italian Under Secretary of War, was sent to Albania to replace General Sebastiano Prasca as commander of the broken Fascist forces. He rushed new reinforcements into the region south of Lake Ochrida and Lake Presba to repel Greek attacks.

Before 1940 came to a close, more Italians had been debarked at the port of Durazzo and were moved to the defense line that ran from the Mokra Mountains in the north to the port of Khimara in the south. The latter was only twenty-seven miles from Valona which the Greeks and British had bombed so extensively that it was unusable as a debarkation port for Italian troops. President Roosevelt's denunciation of the Axis Powers and his recognition of the Greek struggle was hailed by wildly cheering crowds in Athens. With confidence in final victory, heroic Greece saluted a fateful year—1941.

As the new year dawned, the Greeks held the whole of eastern Albania. They did not give the Fascists a respite that would have enabled them to reorganize and regroup their forces. Klisura fell. It cost General Soddu his job. For the third time within ten weeks the Italian Army had a new commander, this time in no less a person than General Cavallero, recently appointed Chief of Staff. The state of confusion in the Italian High Command apparently had reached a climax. Things had gone from bad to worse.

Tragedy came: On January 29 John Metaxas died. It was a great shock and a severe loss for Greece, engaged as she was in a struggle for her existence. The General was the great leader and military genius largely responsible for the successes against Italy. As his country's dictator, the "Little Moltke" was not an extremely popular figure, but his call to unity and duty in the hour of danger commanded the people's respect. At the age of seventy he had fought four wars when the fifth, long threatened, found the kingdom at the mercy of the Axis.

But the Balkan scene at that point shifted from the military to the political stage. Italy's failure in the Greek campaign ran counter to

Axis prestige. It threatened Germany's designs in the Balkans where the Reich's satellite, Bulgaria, was waiting for the Nazi legions to march across her territory into Greece. The Bulgarian-Turkish accord was anything but reassuring. Rumania was in the Axis camp.

At the end of the fourth month of the Italo-Greek conflict the military situation was extremely favorable for the Greeks. With over 30,000 Italian prisoners in their hands, they prepared for a spring offensive. General Wavell had been in Athens to discuss further British aid. Mussolini and Hitler met to discuss "questions of military importance," and Il Duce staked everything on Nazi might. Yugoslavia, meanwhile, had temporarily yielded to German demands, and Berlin announced that Belgrade would "not hinder the Axis Powers in any action they may have to take to preserve peace in the Balkans."

What these actions would be became clear on February 28, when Bulgaria admitted the presence of Nazi troops in her territory after she had become the seventh signatory to the Three-Power Pact. They amounted to forty-five German divisions, about 450,000 men. Bulgaria was definitely controlled by the Germans. Mussolini had pleaded for this help to avert his own disaster. A few days after the Tripartite Pact was signed by Bulgaria he went to Albania to assume personal direction of the Italian troops on the front.

Mussolini stayed for eighteen days without being able to inspire his men by his presence. On March 15, Field Marshal Alexander Papagos, Chief of Staff of the Greek Army, announced that Il Duce's great spring offensive had been broken. Heroic Evzones had hurled back the Fascist aggressors all along the line and achieved one of Greece's greatest military triumphs.

Greece celebrated the 120th anniversary of her national independence in a festive mood. The King of the Hellenes received a telegram from President Roosevelt expressing confidence in a Greek victory. The same day, Yugoslavia signed on the dotted Nazi line. While she refrained from sending troops against Greece, she accepted, according to Berlin, "all the implications of the Tripartite Pact" and gave Germany permission to occupy her territory. Hardly was the ink dry when army leaders overthrew the government, tore up the pact with the Axis, and defied Hitler and his legions. "If German troops enter our country we will fight," they said. Attempts to preserve peaceable relations with the two countries failed, and on April 6 the German Government announced a state of war with Yugoslavia. At the same time war was declared on Greece.

For the second time in six months this small nation was attacked by a great Power. For the second time she refused to give in. There were scenes of extraordinary emotion in the streets of Athens. People embraced each other. Crowds, singing patriotic songs, shouted, "Down with Germany!" Marching to the British and American legations, they thundered cheers for Churchill and Roosevelt.

Hitler accomplished what Mussolini had failed to accomplish—a "Salonika front." Calling the fighting of the first day "one of the greatest epics in Greek history," a spokesman in Athens said: "German forces attacking us have left bodies piled high before our defenders without being able to advance." Yet the Germans did advance, slowly but steadily. After the first resistance was broken, they progressed systematically on a plan that had been prearranged to the last detail. Their assault was violent. Their main drive was directed down the Struma River Valley. Nazi troops also crossed the Rhodope Mountains on the Greek-Bulgarian frontier in a push through the Mestra Valley toward Kavala on the Aegean Sea. Anticipating such moves, the Greeks had prepared to abandon Thrace, eastern Macedonia, including the Metaxas Line, and Salonika.

London, for the first time, confirmed that British troops had landed in Greece. They comprised units from Great Britain, Australia, and New Zealand and constituted a fully equipped expeditionary force.

On the fourth day of the Nazi attack Salonika was in German hands. Greece was split. The entire Greek Eastern Army, while resisting vigorously, was isolated. The German drive down the Vardar Valley had cut off the strong Greek fortress defenses along the Bulgarian border at Rupel Pass and east of there on the Neurokopi plateau. On April 12, the Germans, coming through a gap near Monastir, reached the Greek lines in the Florina section. The German tide surged on. The Greeks hurled back the invaders at several points and wiped out considerable numbers.

First indications of Allied retreats came on April 15, when the British announced that they had withdrawn to new positions. The Germans were quick in reporting that the English were starting to prepare a "Greek Dunkirk." But the British were able to establish a new defense line running from the Gulf of Salonika to the Adriatic.

The bulk of the Greek Army was still in Albania, and the newly established lines in the north central mountain ranges were not sufficiently strong in men and armor to resist the powerful German drives. Under continuous pressure the Greeks withdrew farther south, reorganizing their positions and shortening their lines. What they had won in six months of hard fighting was lost. The Italians moved toward the Greek border from Albania. On April 19, German Alpine troops hoisted the Nazi war flag on the pinnacle of Mount Olympus.

At this moment of national crisis Premier Korizis committed suicide. He took his life, bitterly depressed by the sufferings that war had brought to his country. The King assumed personal command of state and army. He called in General Alexander Mazarakis, a brilliant strategist and liberal, as his chief deputy. The new Government headed by the monarch was proclaimed as one of "National Victory." It was a dramatic move that had the elements of tragedy. Three days after the King was in control, the Greek Army in the Epirus and Macedonia was forced to lay down its arms. The surrender convention, consisting of ten articles, was signed in Salonika on April 23, by Generals Jodl and Ferrero for the Axis, and by General Tsolakoglu for the Greeks. The King abandoned Athens under "the hard destinies of war" and transferred the capital to Crete.

With the British standing at Thermopylae, the final phase of the Battle of Greece was on. The "Dunkirk of the Aegean" was in full progress. Greeks and British stood shoulder-to-shoulder on a forty-mile front between Thermopylae and the Gulf of Corinth. It was their last desperate stand. Great waves of German bombers smashed at Greek ports and caused damage in Piraeus, Salamis, and Megara. The Germans failed in their first attempt to storm the historic pass of Thermopylae, eighty miles north of Athens, and brought up their heaviest artillery. Then the pass fell on April 24.

(This was the fourth defense of the historic pass. The first was attempted by Leonidas, King of Sparta, against the Persians under Xerxes in 490 B.C. The second was in 279 B.C., when Calippus headed a Greek army and met the invading Gauls under Brennus. Antiochus of Syria, in command of the Greek Army, defended the pass again in 191 B.C. against the Romans under Manius Acilius Glabrio.)

Fierce fighting continued north of Athens. It preceded the fall of the capital. On the slopes of Mount Gerania, Australian troops stood off German Panzer divisions; the British were clinging to Mount Cithaeron. On Sunday at 9:30 A.M. German motorcyclists entered the capital. Athens waited quietly. Past the temples of Athenian glory Nazi armored columns drove in a victory parade through the city. There was no more resistance. The last British troops had gone. The battle-worn defenders had made their final stand on the historic plains of Marathon where the Greeks smashed the Persian invaders in 490 B.C. The peoples of Athens displayed a proud calm. They met the Nazis with a stoic smile upon their lips, showing greatness in defeat, knowing that every phase in history passes.

Three weeks after Hitler began his Balkan blitzkrieg, the Nazi hordes marched into the cradle of culture, the very city of Socrates and Plato, of Pericles and Demosthenes, where flowered the first democracy of which we know. It was the fate of ancient Greece to become the fourteenth state to fall to the Third Reich. Under a blue sky on a sunny spring morning the Nazi swastika was hoisted over the crumbling columns of the Acropolis. No finer epilog could be written to this tragedy in Grecian history than to recall the story told of the

Greek soldier who was ordered to lower the blue and white colors from Athens' citadel. Winding the flag around his body, he hurled himself over the parapet and plunged to his death three hundred feet below.

The Germans had won another victory, but they had not yet won the war. The Greeks had suffered a military defeat, but had gained a moral triumph together with their British Allies who succeeded in withdrawing 80 per cent of the B.E.F. As the original British force was 60,000 men, this meant that 48,000 got out of the Peloponnesus safely.

The Battle of Crete lasted for twelve days. There the Greeks, numbering 15,000 men, gave the last example of their indomitable courage. Together with their British allies and under the command of Major General B. C. Freyberg, they wrote into history another chapter of heroic resistance. On May 21, the Germans launched an airborne attack against the island. Parachutes, gliders, and troop carriers were used and 10,000 Nazi troops were landed.

The swift conquest of Crete convinced the Germans that there was no "unconquerable island" for the Luftwaffe.

King George and the Greek Government found refuge in Cairo. Greek officers and men, several thousands all told, escaped to the Near East in fishing boats and smacks. They formed the nucleus of a new Greek Army ready to fight on the side of the Allies for the glory that was Greece. There were many other aspects to the lost battle of Crete. Without Crete's holding out after the fall of the Greek mainland, the British could not have triumphed in Iraq. Syria might have been in Axis hands by then, and the situation in the Middle East could have had unfavorable consequences in Iran and Turkey.

At the crossroads between East and West, Greece has been a highway of history throughout the ages. Persians, Romans, Goths, Slavs, Moslems, and Venetians crossed her territory from one part of the world to the other. Germans and Italians now penetrated the land of the Hellenes and devastated it deliberately. Fascists and Nazis, who professed so ardently their admiration for Greek culture, committed acts of barbarism unprecedented in modern history. No country, except Poland perhaps, was ever reduced to such bitter destitution by its conquerors.

Nazis and Fascists divided the spoils among themselves. The Bulgarians received their share. They cut the country into three zones: Bulgaria annexed the richest regions in the north, eastern Macedonia, and Thrace, a territory of 16,000 square kilometers that includes the provinces of Serrai, Drama, Cavella, and Rhodope. Almost 600,000 Greeks thereby came under Bulgarian rule and faced ruthless extermination. Italians occupied the Ionian Islands including Corfu, bringing 230,000 Greeks under their domination. Fascist Albanians seized an area of 7,800 square kilometers with a population of 300,000 in the provinces of Janina, Thesprotia, and Preveza. The Germans occupied Central Macedonia with Salonika, the Aegean Islands, and Crete. In the torso on the Greek mainland, Thessaly and the Peloponnesus, they held captive a population of 3,500,000 people, exactly half of the Greek populace before the invasion.

Hardly had the Nazis set foot on Greek soil when the invaders, whose army was supplied with food for the campaign only, began to live off the land. Regardless of the hunger of the population, they seized whatever they could lay hands on and stripped the shops like hordes of locusts. They looted the country systematically and flooded it with cheap occupation marks (*Reichskassenscheine*).

Scarcity of goods was nation-wide. At one time not even wood was obtainable in Athens for coffins to bury the thousands dying of starvation. Factories closed down because of lack of raw materials.

The German administration of Salonika and in the Aegean decreed all males between sixteen and fifty years of age be forced to work for the conquerors, regardless of skill and wages. If they did not comply, they had one other choice: to be put in a concentration camp. As this method did not produce a sufficient number of "volunteers," a civilian draft was ordered. The number of Greeks forced to work in factories in Germany and Nazi-dominated lands has been estimated at 20,000.

Financial ruin was only one side of German economic administration. Barbarian rule had its devastating effects on the nation's soul and body as a result of German terroristic methods. Greek villages were wiped out; homes sacked and entire populations deported. Six thousand Greeks were driven from Thrace and Macedonia into Bulgaria, and Bulgarians were sent into the occupied regions to take over their homes.

Mass executions took place. German columns that entered the town of Kalambaka on October 18, 1943, executed all prominent Greek leaders and left their bodies lying unburied in a ditch. By the end of 1943, the number of Greeks who had been made homeless by the Nazi and Bulgarian terror was estimated at more than 100,000.

The Germans set up such a reign of terror that the situation became a nightmare. There were towns in Livadia where the Nazis were hanging leaders of the community from the windows of public buildings, leaving the bodies hanging for forty-eight hours. When they raided Kalamata they arrested all males between the ages of eighteen and sixty years, a total of four thousand. Hundreds were shot forthwith. Others, ill-shod and ill-clad, were marched to Athens.

A constant struggle went on between Greek guerrillas and the invaders. The Greek Underground waged a heroic struggle with acts of sabotage against the Nazi defense system. A German-controlled railroad, leading from Greece toward the Russian frontier, was disrupted by Greek guerrillas, striking from strongholds in the Rhodope

Mountains. Special groups operated against the so-called Bulgarian "Rural Pursuit Police" in Macedonia. A wave of sabotage swept Athens, Piraeus, Salonika, and Salamis Island. Guerrilla resistance on Crete continued. Something new was added to European warfare when "sea guerrillas" started to operate in the Aegean Sea a flotilla of some thirty ships which they had recaptured from the Germans and Italians.

During this heroic fight of the Greek Underground civil strife raged in Greece among three rival guerrilla bands. It broke out in the late fall of 1943 and took on the aspects of a small-size civil war. It had its parallel in the differences between the Yugoslav Partisans and the forces of General Draja Mikhailovitch.

King George of Greece and his Government-in-exile, which moved from Cairo to London, pledged themselves to "continue the fight till the last enemy is driven from our land." Their pledge was supported by Greeks in the homeland whose spirit remained unbroken under the Nazi yoke. Thousands of Greek soldiers and sailors, who escaped from Greece and Crete, continued the struggle for the liberation of their country and fought in the ranks of the Allied armies and navies.

The first Hellenic Commando, known as the Sacred Company and consisting of 250 Greek officers and soldiers under the leadership of a white-bearded colonel, Christo Tsigantes, fought in the Tunisian campaign at the side of Britishers and New Zealanders. It was the first Allied unit to push forward ahead of the French in the initial move to outflank the Mareth Line. The Greeks were the first to enter Gabès.

What survived of the Greek Navy and escaped from Greece was put on duty again after necessary repairs were made. A new fighting unit emerged which became stronger than before the war and took its place in patrol and convoy duty. Composed of thirty-three ships, submarines, destroyers, and antisubmarine craft, and manned by 5,400 men, this new fleet also operated during the Tunisian campaign and thereafter extended its activities far beyond the Mediterranean.

The Greek merchant marine engaged in supplying food and war material to England and to the war fronts. It supplied the Allied bases at Tobruk and Singapore and suffered a heavy toll of life on the seven seas. It is estimated that up to October, 1942, 4,000 Greek seamen had lost their lives. The Greek Air Force was reorganized in the Middle East. Equipped with British fighter planes it attacked the enemy on the El Alamein front. Its strength was increased to three squadrons, and their excellent work was recognized by Air Marshal Tedder in a message to the Greek King.

President Roosevelt paid high tribute to Greece, declaring on the second anniversary of its resistance to the Axis: "She set an example that every one of us must follow until the despoilers of freedom everywhere have been brought to their just doom."

28

BEHIND VEIL OF JAPANESE TREACHERY

JAPAN'S partnership with Nazi Germany and Fascist Italy formed a despotic triumvirate for world control. Secret documents indicate their plans to set up a reign of terror and throw civilization back into medieval barbarism. When they conspired to turn back the clock of human progress, they failed to reckon, however, with the power of the democracies when once roused to action. They failed, too, to comprehend the inherent instinct in the human race for freedom.

A brief flashback of Japanese history is necessary in order to know the people whose treacherous thrust at Pearl Harbor drove the United States into World War II. The fanaticism which our sons were forced to combat in the battles of the Pacific, and the various events of the war as they occurred will then be clear.

The Japanese Empire, with its medieval structure, comprises more than 105,000,000 people in a territory of 260,770 square miles—about the size of the state of Texas.

A Japanese is not a Japanese by mere accident of birth. He is the sublimation of mythological, historical, religious, hereditary, and political power designed through the centuries to impress upon him the unalterable conviction that as a descendant of the Sun Goddess, he is born to rule the earth. This he declares to be the "way of the gods."

The Mikado's realm throughout its history has struck first and declared war later, if it felt such a formality were necessary at all. Actually, wars begin long before the first shot has been fired. Economic rivalries, inordinate ambition for wider dominion, and sordid court intrigue have all sown the seeds of war.

In the case of Japan it is possible to argue plausibly that foundations for the war were laid as far back as 2,500 years ago. There is a measure of truth in the argument that when, according to the Japanese legend, Izanago and Izanami, the male and female gods of desire (Kami), thrust their spear into chaos and created the eight islands of Nippon, Japan's entry into world conquest became inevitable.

It is equally possible to find the roots of Japanese lust for conquest in the story of its first ruler, Hikoho no Ninigi (Rice-Ears-of-Ruddy-Plenty) who became "the heavenly sovereign" sometime between 800-850 B.C. The perpetuation of Japan's mythological origin has been impregnated into the people for centuries—the divine descent of the Mikado and the heavenly kinship of all his subjects in the cult of Shintoism; the stout and martial defense of all that Shinto represented by *monobe,* the warrior families (*uji*) who were the progenitors of the *bushi* and their *bushido*. These, with the development and tenacious power of the *samurai,* all played a part in bringing Japan into World War II.

For every practical purpose Japan's part in World War II can be said to have started on September 18, 1931, when Toyko declared that Chinese soldiers had blown up the South Manchurian Railway track five miles north of Shenyang (Mukden). This was the famous "Mukden Incident." It was a trial balloon sent up by aggressor nations to test the reactions of the rest of the world. When these reactions proved to be nothing more than words—diplomatic notes, statements, resolutions of protest—Japan, Germany, and Italy saw they had nothing to fear. Mukden went unpunished.

Four months later, Japanese marines landed at Chapei in Changhai, setting alight flames that were to devour China. Then Italy dared to invade Ethiopia; in quick succession followed the Saar "plebiscite"; the Franco revolution in Spain; Hitler's defiance of the Versailles Treaty, Locarno Pact, and League of Nations by reoccupation of the Rhineland; annexation of Austria by Germany; seizure of Albania by Mussolini; and the other steps leading through the Sudetenland and Munich to the invasion of Poland on September 1, 1939. Japan's "sneak attack" on Pearl Harbor, December 7, 1941 was a logical climax to the alleged bombing of a railroad track in Mukden ten years and a few months before.

The history of Japan, in its broad outline, is a determined effort to keep the nation with its face toward *Amaterasu-o-mi-Kami* (the Sun Goddess), its soul consecrated to *Kami-no-michi,* and its feet dedicated to conquest of the world for the greater glory of the Mikado. The Japanese thus have been deluded for some 2,500 years, and it is too much to expect that the crushing defeat suffered in World War II will, of itself, eradicate the influence of two and one-half millenniums. We must understand these influences to follow the course of the war in the Pacific and as a guide to help prevent a next war.

American Ambassador Joseph C. Grew, in a remarkable dispatch to Secretary of State Cordell Hull, dated December 27, 1934, described the Japanese national psychology as the "ultra-sensitiveness of the Japanese, arising out of a marked inferiority complex which manifests itself in the garb of an equally marked superiority complex, with all its attendant bluster, chauvinism, zenophobia, and organized national propaganda."

Ambassador Grew saw through the delicate poetry, entrancing paintings, and charming manners that have always cloaked the true nature of the Japanese. The bloodiest warriors wrote dainty verses on sublime subjects. Everything the Occidental world considered the requisite basis of all human relationships the Japanese repudiated. Outside the family or immediate circle they practiced cruelty, trickery, defiance.

Treachery seems to have been the outstanding quality of the *kami* in the Japanese Valhalla. Another important trait was cruelty and destruction. From the earliest beginnings Nippon and her creators have been dominated by the concept of expediency—that the end justifies the means. This doctrine guided not only the *kami* and the early rulers of Japan but determined every important decision down to and through World War II.

It would be easy to dismiss the legends of the gods as merely typical of apocryphal saga in all parts of the world, were it not for the fact that they have been incorporated into Japan's living history, and kept alive as literal truth by the *bushi* and *samurai* warrior caste. This is the basis and virtually the sole reason for the existence of Shintoism, the country's closest approximation to a religion. It has been officially pounded into the minds and spirits of the Japanese through the state-controlled educational system.

Shinto has no supreme being. It has no sacred law, such as the Bible or the Koran. It has no code of morals, such as the Ten Commandments. It has no founder. Shinto has been described as the spontaneous expression of the spirit of Japan, of *kokutai,* the "national genius." Based upon the legends of prehistoric Nippon it became a comparatively simple matter to weave the religious and the temporal into a single, closely integrated fabric in which Amaterasu became the supreme figure and her grandson the Emperor became the supreme ruler. Shinto thereby was established as a cult of loyalty and a religion of patriotism deeply ingrained in the hearts and minds of Japanese of all generations. Its roots were deep in ancestor worship.

When Buddhism was introduced into Japan in A.D. 552, with its canon that Buddha alone directed and controlled man's destiny, the traditional faith in the divine authority of the "son of heaven" received its first shock. The prestige of the crown began to ebb and the Shinto priests watched new temples rise to a new idol. At the same time the power of the great families, the *uji,* grew until it transcended that of the throne, and ministers and councillors began to rule the country. They acted, of course, through the emperor, a fiction maintained, with occasional lapses, through World War II.

The ethical concepts of Confucianism had found their way into Japan at a much earlier date through the commercial intercourse with Korea and China. For a long time there was a struggle to reconcile the obvious differences between Confucianism, Buddhism, and Shinto until about A.D. 700 a "revelation" was worked out making Amaterasu an incarnation of Buddha. In other words, the Shinto *kami* were avatars of the Buddha. Shinto's sphere was said to be the origin of human beings, Confucianism dealt with present-day affairs, and Buddhism concerned itself with things to come. Such a liaison robbed all three of their purity and vitality but it did establish Buddhism in Japan.

The significance of this strange blending has been felt ever since in Japan. Confucianism and Buddhism reached the shores of the Dragon-fly Island as the result of friendly relations with other countries, in those days Korea and China. Contact with abroad was encouraged by the civil branches of court circles and whenever the influence of the ministers grew strong there was much interchange of travelers and ideas.

The *monobe,* or warrior class, were interested in foreign lands only from the standpoint of conquest. The Shinto priests, seeing their power undermined by the importation of Confucianism and Buddhism, grew hostile to contact with the outside world. And so, nearly 1,500 years ago, the doctrine of the "closed door" was first enunciated. From that day to this, the history of Japan has presented a series of intrigues and battles within court circles between those who saw commercial and cultural value in international activity and the warrior-priest combination opposed to the importation of any foreign ideas. First one group would be in the ascendant and then another, but the significant fact lay in the *bushido-Shinto* (warrior-priest) alliance that elevated dying in battle for Japan to a religious as well as a patriotic duty.

The last such struggle between the court groups began when the American Commodore Matthew C. Perry sailed into Japanese waters with four United States warships and 560 men. Japan was then forced to open her doors to the world for the first time. They were to remain open until the warrior-priest combine, by patient manipulation and persistent assassination, gained the upper hand once again. This time they did not slam the door shut; they attempted to put in a one-way door barring the rest of the world not only from Japan but from the entire Orient and permitting Japan to rule the "Greater East Asia Co-Prosperity Sphere."

The power of the *samurai* is another factor that must be fully comprehended. One of the *kami* sent along from heaven with Ninigi was charged with the duty of administering the army and another with overseeing the palace guards. They founded families whose existence continues to the present time. The first warrior families (*uji*) were the *monobe,* dating from about A.D. 300. Later they were called *monono-fu,* or *bushi,* from which derives the term *bushido* representing their code of honor. Subsequently the warriors were known as *samurai*. Although abolished with the passing of the feudal system in 1868, they never passed out of existence.

Poems dating back as far as the sixth century set forth the tenets of *bushido*. The warrior believed he had inherited the sacred duty of dying for his sovereign if necessary. His loyalty to the throne knew no limitations of time or space. He must prefer death in battle or by suicide (*hara-kiri*) to surrender. He must overcome all obstacles and hardships, and rest not until vengeance was enacted. His sword was an object of deepest veneration. His word was sacred and irrevocable and, inasmuch as he had received his body from his family, the dictates of filial piety compelled him not to dishonor that family by failing in the strictest observance of *bushido*. In short, he was convinced that his country's fate and the life of the Mikado depended entirely upon him.

Bushido is a vast unwritten body of rules and precepts governing knightly and chivalrous conduct. It has been handed down from generation to generation by word of mouth and ritual for centuries. When compulsory universal military service was introduced into Japan in 1873, it scandalized the *samurai* into subsequent rebellion. The conscripts, however, did such a good job of defeating the traditional warriors that it soon became apparent that warlike qualities were not the private property of a particular class but were characteristic of the entire nation. *Bushido* became the code of the Japanese Army and every able-bodied male of military age became a *samurai* in fact if not in name. The history of the Pacific war shows how stoutly they fought, how fanatically they died, how *samurai*-like they committed *hara-kiri*, and how few surrendered.

May third was the one day in the year most looked forward to by Japanese lads. It was *Tango no sekku*—boy's festival. The purpose of the celebration was frankly to inspire the youngsters with warlike propensities. The boys received gifts of figurines of great heroes. The day was the occasion for passing down from one generation to another the family military heirlooms of swords, bows and arrows, spears, etc. The boys carried inflated paper flags shaped like carp because that fish symbolized indomitable courage and tenacity of purpose in war. Latter-day Japan moved to seal any loopholes there might be in the *samurai shinto* indoctrination of the young. Just in case the mothers or playmates might have failed to make a lasting impression, the Government decided to put the schools to work. In its earlier years compulsory universal education was based on American and European lines with friendly advice from missionaries. But in 1890 the Imperial Rescript on Education was promulgated, and western influence minimized. The chief aim of elementary school education developed into the inculcation of dedicating their lives to the Emperor and the Empire. Spartan *samurai* discipline and "national spirit" were pounded into the young bodies, souls, and minds. After that the youngsters might absorb education in the accustomed sense of the word.

Japan started them young, six years of age, when children are uncritical and susceptible. The majority of those who finished the sixth grade continued their patriotic learning outside of schools—at home, in places of work, through radio programs, magazines, and newspapers, in the theaters, in cultural organizations, and so on down the long list. The secondary school curriculum was more vocational in character and even more patriotic in content. Instead of simple gymnastics, high-school boys now learned physical education par excellence—fencing and judo. Military training in Japanese high schools had been part of the curriculum since 1886. Since 1925 it had been greatly intensified by the appointment of military officers to take charge of this branch of instruction. Advanced military training in universities and colleges had been put on a compulsory basis since 1938; three years of it were required of all male undergraduates. The entire educational system of Japan became the incarnation of military-Fascist ideology.

Even Japanese art, despite its elegance and delicacy of execution, perpetuated the heroes, horrors, and the superstitions of all Nippon. Those superstitions, linked so closely to ancestor worship, were powerful enough to influence their military leaders.

Japan can be understood only by watching her cunning machinations through the years. Japan had lived behind closed doors for generations, during which time the *shoguns* ruled supreme and the Emperor was a virtual prisoner in his palace. Feudalism flourished and the *samurai* loyally fought and died for their feudal chiefs. Government, with all its intrigues, corruption, and selfishness, was the concern of but a handful. The millions of Japanese people just went on scraping a meager existence out of the land or dragging a bare pittance from the sea, satisfying their ego by repeating the tales of divine origin, and deriving spiritual comfort from the observance of ancestor worship.

As the story of the years from Perry's visit to the First World War unfolds, Japan's hatred for the "white world" becomes evident. "New Japan" emerged in 1868 with the opening of the *Meiji* (Enlightened Government) Era. Emperor Mutsuhito had succeeded to the throne upon the death of his father, Komei, the year before. Mutsuhito immediately declared the separation of Buddhism and Shintoism and proclaimed the equality of the four classes of Japanese society—*samurai,* farmer, artisan, and merchants. Feudalism was abolished in 1871, the ancient topknot headdress of the men was altered to the western style of haircut, and the Gregorian calendar was adopted. In 1874 the first political party was formed.

These internal reforms were revolutionary and accomplished quickly in the light of Japan's devotion to tradition. But the Government did not have an easy time of it. Nippon had always coveted Korea, its closest neighbor, and for a time had actually ruled that country as a vassal state. Ever since Toyotomi Hideyoshi had conquered Korea in 1593, that country had sent ambassadors bearing gifts to felicitate the accession of each *shogun*. But in 1873 the custom not only was summarily abandoned, Korea sent a message declaring her intention to cease all relations with a "renegade Oriental civilization."

The *samurai* were all for starting another invasion and teaching Korea a lesson. Although the Emperor prevented a warlike demonstration, Japan was furious. The *samurai*, chafing under the irritation of seeing their powers taken away in the modernization of the country, staged minor rebellions. The Government found a way out of the dilemma by giving the *samurai* something to do. On the pretext that China had mistreated castaways from Ryukyu thrown up on the shores of Formosa, Japan sent an expedition which quickly landed on Formosa. Japan settled for the Ryukyus for a small indemnity and, in return, recognized that Formosa was part of China's Middle Kingdom.

This episode has importance in two respects. First, it showed the little islands offshore that Japan was able to protect them. Second, it was a forerunner of the acquisition of Formosa twenty years later as the result of the Sino-Japanese War. When, in 1874, a Korean fort fired upon a Japanese warship, Japan marshaled a fleet off Korea's shores and, without firing a gun, won a treaty of amity and friendship. While the *samurai* did not like this bloodless victory, it did let Japan into Korea, from which country she never withdrew until her defeat in World War II.

Russia had come into the picture by virtue of Siberian expansion, so China and Japan signed the Treaty of Tientsin in 1885. Both countries recognized the independence of Korea and agreed to withdraw their troops. There was the additional, important proviso that if a third nation put troops into Korea, the two signatories would give each other written notice of intention to reënter the country. In the spring of 1894 the Tonghak rebellion, an uprising of some importance, brought large bodies of troops from both China and Japan.

Matters came to a head in 1894 when both countries declared war. In 230 days the great continental power of China was defeated by the little island country of Japan, and the Treaty of Shimonoseki was signed. It recognized the independence of Korea, ceded to Japan the Liaotung Peninsula of Manchuria (Kwantung) and the islands of Formosa and the Pescadores, opened four new Chinese ports to foreign trade and navigation, provided for a Sino-Japanese treaty of commerce and amity, and imposed an indemnity of 200,000,000 taels upon China.

Then occurred one of the most unusual events in history. Russia, Germany, and France, sent a joint note to Japan six days after the Treaty of Shimonoseki had been signed, advising the Emperor to "renounce the definite possession of the Peninsula of Liaotung." The effect among the people was profound.

The liberals lost their international liberalism and were thrown into the arms of the nationalists. From then on a liberal statesman in Japan was unable to do more than fight the excesses of jingoism.

Russia had pushed the Trans-Siberian Railroad across to the Pacific and had started another line farther south, skirting Manchuria by a circuitous route. France was allied to Russia. But the participation of Germany amazed the Japanese. The new Constitutional system was being patterned after the German. Berlin had sent military and civil teachers to Tokyo. The only possible explanation was that Germany thought it would be well to embroil Czarist Russia in Pacific problems, thus clearing the European field for the Kaiser and the Junkers. Russia entered into a treaty of defensive alliance with China against Japan and in return won the right to build her railway to Vladivostok through northern Manchuria, shortening the distance by hundreds of miles. Russia and France also provided China with the money with which to pay the indemnity to Japan.

Three years later, two German missionaries were murdered in China's Shantung Province. Germany demanded and obtained as compensation a ninety-nine-year lease on Kiaochow with the right to build railways and work the mines in Shantung. Russia obtained a twenty-five-year lease from China on Port Arthur and Talienwan, and the right to build a north-south branch of the Trans-Siberian Railway from Harbin through Manchuria (Mukden) to the two ports. France got a lease and concessions south of Kwangohow Bay (French Indo-China). Later the British leased Weihaewei on the Shantung Peninsula. Washington reiterated its stand for the "open door" and equal opportunity.

In the summer of 1900, the Boxer Rebellion broke out in China and the Powers were brought together for the first time. The attack on the legation quarters at Peking quickly convinced the rest of the world that no adequate defense could be put up by the small garrisons maintained by Russia, France, Great Britain, Germany, the United States, and lesser nations. Only Japan was near enough to send reinforcements. But she did nothing until the others requested her to act when she dispatched 20,000 troops. Russia increased materially her forces in Manchuria, only to withdraw some of them in the face of another historic event, the Anglo-Japanese Alliance.

Great Britain signed her first treaty of alliance with an Oriental nation in 1902. England and Japan declared that they were moved solely by a desire to preserve the *status quo* and general peace in the Far East. To this end they desired to maintain the independence and territorial integrity of both China and Korea with equal opportunities for all nations in those countries. The two signatories recognized the mutual right to counter aggressive action there by any other power and to protect their interests in event of internal disturbances. In such event the other country would remain neutral and would try to prevent any third power from joining hostilities against the ally. Finally, Great Britain and Japan contracted to come to one another's assistance and make common cause against any such third power.

Only the existence of China and Korea, effectively answering the purpose of buffer states, had prevented Japan and Russia from coming to grips before they finally did in 1904. Developments in Primorsk Province were speeded. This territory lay east of the Amur, a river that has been the scene of bloody fighting before and during World War II, and next to Korea. This development increased the importance of Vladivostok. Tokyo felt herself strong enough to bring matters to a head. Construction of the Trans-Siberian line to Vladivostok and the spur down the Liaotung Peninsula to the ice-free ports of Dairen (Dalny) and Port Arthur was jealously watched by Japan. Tokyo reached for Manchuria's mineral resources and both nations pushed their influence in Korea. Tokyo broke relations with St. Petersburg and war was declared in both capitals on February 10, 1904, but not until after Japanese destroyers, on the night of February 8-9 had hit two Russian battleships and a cruiser with torpedoes at Port Arthur. Admiral Togo had hit three more in a long-range action the next day. At Chemulpo, the port of the Korean capital, Seoul, the Russians lost a cruiser, a gunboat, and a transport. The similarity between the sequence of events in the Russo-Japanese War and the entry of Japan into World War II is striking.

This Russo-Japanese War is important as a prelude to events culminating in World War II. It was bitter and bloody. The initial blows at Port Arthur and Chemulpo gave Japan sufficient freedom of the neighboring seas to transport her forces to the mainland. The Vladivostok fleet that had finally put to sea was virtually annihilated on August 14. On New Year's Day, 1905, General Anatol Mikhailovitch Stoessel surrendered Port Arthur to the Japanese. Mukden fell on March 10 after a terrific struggle of three weeks. On May 27, Admiral Togo destroyed the Russian Baltic Fleet in the Battle of Tsushima Strait, and for all practical purposes the war was over.

President Theodore Roosevelt, foreseeing the dangers, instructed the American Ambassador in St. Petersburg and the American Minister in Tokyo to hand identical notes to the Russian and Japanese Governments urging them to end the war by direct approach. The offer was accepted by both countries the next day. Two months later, on August 10, the peace envoys met at Portsmouth, New Hampshire, where the treaty was signed on September 5, 1905.

The Treaty of Portsmouth, provided for no general indemnity, merely for $20,000,000 to compensate Japan for the cost of maintaining Russian war prisoners, less the moneys paid out by the latter on account of Japanese prisoners of war. Opinion at home had been whipped up to expect that Russia would buy back the island of Sakhalin, long a moot point between the two countries, for $580,000,000. When not a penny changed hands, the *samurai-Shinto* combination seized on this to attack the rest of the world and to call the Treaty a betrayal of Japan by the Occident.

As a matter of fact, Japan gained so much by the Treaty of Portsmouth that she might well have been willing to pay $580,000,000 out of her own depleted treasury for what she did get. In the first place Russia admitted Japan's over-lordship of Korea. In Manchuria both countries pledged complete and simultaneous evacuation of the land and restoration of full sovereignty to China, except for Liaochow Peninsula. Russia turned over to Japan her twenty-five-year lease on the Peninsula together with the southern section of the railway to Port Arthur, her mines, and every other privilege she had in Manchuria. Furthermore, the Russians promised to obtain China's consent to all this and the final stamp of approval was placed on the deal in the Treaty of Peking, signed in 1905 by Russia, Japan, and China.

There were other provisions in that Treaty relating to commerce, friendship, etc. But the real significance of the document signed in a New England seaport lay in the fact that by patiently waiting for time to take its course and arming herself in the meantime, Japan finally obtained everything she had wanted. September 5, 1905, marked the effective date of the Japanese Empire; for Tokyo possessed Ryukyu, Formosa and half of Sakhalin. Her dominant position in Korea was recognized, and she obtained the right to exploit part of Manchuria.

After World War I she obtained the German possessions in the Far East and was awarded the mandate over the countless islands whose names became familiar in World War II. When Hitler conquered France in 1940, Japan walked into French Indo-China and continued down into British Burma, Malaya, and the Netherlands Indies. She captured the Philippines and held a strangle-hold on China's coast. The Pacific had become the Empire of Japan.

Less than a month before the Treaty of Portsmouth was signed, Japan won another victory. The original accord with England still had a year and a half to run when it was superseded by another agreement concluded in London in 1905. Great Britain recognized Japan's preferred position in Korea in words identical with those agreed to by Russia twenty-four days later. Japan reciprocated by recognizing Great Britain's preferred position "in the proximity of" the Indian frontier. Both pledged the "independence and integrity of the Chinese Empire" and all three considerations were linked in the Treaty's preamble to "the consolidation and maintenance of the general peace in the regions of Eastern Asia and China."

This treaty, although not due to expire until 1915, was renewed in 1911, and that is how Japan got into World War I, the Versailles Peace Conference, and the Marshalls, the Carolinas, the Marianas, and other islands of the Pacific. But Japan did not enter the First World War until she had compelled Great Britain to promise full support to all Japanese demands at Versailles. Against the opposition of her dominions, Australia and New Zealand, and over the vigorous protest of President Woodrow Wilson, who wanted all the Pacific Islands mandated to Australia, Japan won such places as Truk, Yap, Ponape, Eniwetok, and Kwajalein. She now set out to take the final steps for consolidation of her Asiatic supremacy. Europe and America withdrew their legations from Seoul in accordance with the changed status of Korea, and thereafter dealt through Tokyo. Japan had formally annexed Korea in 1910, ending the independent existence of a nation that had endured for more than 4,000 years and the rule of a dynasty that had reigned for more than 500 years.

Revolution broke out in China, and in 1912 Dr. SunYat-sen set up the Republican Government at Nanking, with himself the provisional president. The Manchu Emperor abdicated, the final act of a dynasty that had governed China for 268 years.

Step by step the clutching claws of Japan reveal themselves. The *samurai-Shinto* combination, having the upper hand at the moment, seized the German rights in Shantung, Tsingtao, and Kiachow in 1914 as soon as Japan entered World War I. A few months later, she presented to China her famous "Twenty-one Demands" containing a secret clause not published until sometime later. Its full significance did not dawn upon the world for many years. They soon revealed themselves as an extensive scheme to legitimize Japanese penetration into Shantung, Fukien, the Yangtze River Valley, and to extend Tokyo's "rights" in Manchuria and Mongolia. Had the secret clause been known at the outset it is probable that the Occidental Powers might have protested. But the Japanese Government was then headed by Marquis Shigenobu Okuma, who had begun his career as a progressive, and the rest of the world had no reason for suspicion. Those "Twenty-one Demands" would have reduced China to a state of vassalage, for the secret fifth group, ingeniously labeled "miscellaneous" demanded that China:

Employ influential Japanese as political, financial, and military advisers;
Permit Japanese police to function alongside Chinese constabulary;
Be dependent upon Japan for financing her mines, industries, railways, and harbor developments;
Give Japan the right to send her missionaries to carry on propaganda inside China by means of churches, schools, and hospitals;

Permit Japan to build an extensive system of railways within the country, and finally;

Purchase at least 50 per cent of her munitions from Japan or in lieu thereof, a joint arsenal be established, employing Japanese material and technical experts.

China rejected the secret provisions in the usual Oriental manner of failing to reply to them, but three years later Japan succeeded in obtaining an agreement for common military and naval defense, purportedly for the purpose of keeping Russia in her place. Common defense against the Central Powers was another excuse for this alliance which was supposed to terminate with the end of hostilities. But Japan never withdrew her forces from China.

In the meantime Tokyo had begun to blackjack the United States. When the United States declared war on Germany in 1917, Japan refused to accept this country wholeheartedly as an ally unless certain conditions were met. Secretary of State Robert Lansing and Viscount Ishii signed an agreement in which the United States met those conditions by conceding Japan's paramount interests in China, a violation of our traditional "open-door" policy. World War I gave Japan the opportunity to force the rest of the world to accept her overlordship in Asia, to gain mastery over China's coast and the shipping lanes in that section of the world, and to obtain a foothold on the continent itself.

From the time Japan entered the First World War she became a recognized World Power sharing her position with Great Britain, the United States, and France. She was a full partner at the Versailles Peace Conference although her contribution to the war effort had been far less than that of the other nations, except to the extent to which she employed the war to fortify her own position. She became a full member of the League of Nations and its various councils.

The ensuing years were crammed with conferences and treaties. Occidental statesmen were trying desperately to attain the joint aim of establishing peaceful, international relationships and reducing armaments. Japanese statesmen were trying to satisfy the minimum requirements of such a program and, at the same time, to prevent the *samurai-Shinto* combination at home from taking things in their own hands and creating another international conflict.

Through the years leading up to World War II, Japan was slyly laying her plans. Her chicanery and cunning were outwitting other nations.

The army moved suddenly to make it independent of the rest of the government and responsible to the Emperor alone. The military forces were in a position to prevent the creation of any cabinet they could not control, or to overthrow any cabinet or parliament which proved "unruly." The foreign office had no control over the war lords and found itself many times in the position of having its promises and understandings violated by direct action of the army and navy.

The rest of the world was too busy fighting Germany, Austria, and the other Central Powers to do more than gasp when Japan pounced upon the German possessions in China and elsewhere in the Pacific. They were too engrossed to make effective protest against Tokyo's refusal to grant China's request for permission to join in battling Germany in Asia. When the First World War ended, Japan had mobilized 800,000 men and had suffered only 300 killed in action, 907 wounded.

With this virtually bloodless conquest, Japan, only two generations removed from her traditional feudal state, reverted to her earlier convictions fostered through the centuries. All the old arrogance, conceit, brutality, and chauvinism burst through the thin veneer of hastily acquired civilizing influences. The Japanese confronted the rest of the world with demands and remained intransigent in the face of all appeals for just a little compromise and coöperation. They nearly wrecked the Versailles Peace Conference with their demands, beat all opposition into the ground, and came out with a "blessing" on their hold of Shantung Province and more than six hundred Pacific islands over which they had been given a mandate. The United States did not consent to these concessions at Versailles. The Senate, in ratifying the Treaty, specifically exempted the Shantung provisions from the general approval.

All the world, except Japan, was war-weary when President Warren G. Harding announced in 1921 a conference on the limitation of armaments and a general discussion of Far Eastern problems. Japan was the last nation to agree. It was not until August 11 that Secretary of State Charles Evans Hughes was able to issue the official call for a conference to open in Washington on Armistice Day. Japan instantly raised a number of objections. She feared she was going to be called to account before the rest of the world for her seizures of Shantung, the "Twenty-one Demands," her control over Yap, and the manner in which she had wrung from the United States recognition of her "special interests" in China. The tactics of *fait accompli* appealed especially to the Japanese; once an incident was closed it could not be reopened. Premier Takashi Hara told the leaders of his Seiyukai Party in Tokyo that such accomplished facts as Shantung and Yap would not be included in the discussions.

Before the Japanese delegation sailed for Washington, army and navy authorities in Tokyo conferred with officials of the foreign office, at which time the latter were informed just what the military expected them to do: "The powers concerned shall not establish any naval base or make any arrangement to serve as naval bases for their navies in the

Pacific," thus giving Japan virtually a free hand. The informal agenda sent out included a call for discussion at the Washington Conference of restoration of China's full and practical independence, return of Shantung to China, radical modification of Japanese control of the former German island of Yap, settlement of Japan's military occupation of parts of Siberia and other Far Eastern matters. But Japan would not participate if those questions were to come up.

The Washington Conference lasted until February 6, 1922. It got absolutely nowhere on the Siberian matter, and scarcely any distance on China or the mandated islands. Japan did not withdraw but merely agreed not to press the secret clauses of the "Twenty-one Demands." She refused to discuss her leases on Liaotung Peninsula or elsewhere. She promised to withdraw from Shantung when China had a "stable government," and the Lansing-Ishii agreement was canceled. Baron Kijuro Shidehara, Tokyo's Ambassador to the United States, told the Conference in a closing speech: "To say that Japan has special interests in China is simply to state a plain and actual fact."

It had been agreed that all decisions of the Conference were to be unanimous, thus the "dissenting opinion became the prevailing opinion." Japan effectively controlled all decisions reached on the Pacific and Far East because she knew that the other nations would rather yield to her than admit the Conference had proved a failure. The inconsequential results were solemnized in such instruments as the "Shantung Agreement" returning Shantung to China but gaining other concessions for Japan; the "Nine-Power Treaty" reaffirming the integrity of China; the "Four-Power Treaty" terminating the old Anglo-Japanese Alliance and the "Five-Power Naval Treaty." The world soon forgot everything but the last because Japan, having had her way on the other points, immediately set out to bring about a revision of the naval agreement either by joint action or by secretly ignoring the terms.

The best-known feature of the naval treaty was the so-called 5-5-3 provision calling off all capital ship-building programs and saying: "The total capital ship replacement tonnage of each of the contracting Powers shall not exceed in standard displacement, for the United States, 525,000 tons; for the British Empire, 525,000 tons ... for Japan, 315,000 tons." But the 5-5-3 ratio applied only to capital ships and airplane carriers. So Japan concentrated upon building cruisers, destroyers, submarines, and auxiliary vessels, much as Nazi Germany did on "pocket battleships." Only the United States and Britain destroyed their naval protection and cut their new construction to fit the specifications.

In return for a seeming acceptance of the 5-5-3 program, Japan won two highly significant strategic victories which were to strike back at the United States in World War II. In the first place, by agreeing to settle amicably the controversy over cable rights on the little island of

Yap, she finally obtained the approval of the United States for her mandates over all the Pacific islands as set forth at Versailles. Great Britain and the United States agreed to maintain with her the status quo "with regard to fortifications and naval bases" in the Aleutians, all American islands west of Hawaii, and at Hongkong and other British possessions east of 110 degrees east longitude, except off the Dominions. The status quo was defined: "No new fortifications or naval bases shall be established in the territories and possessions specified; that no measures shall be taken to increase the existing naval facilities for the repair and maintenance of naval forces, and that no increase shall be made in the coast defenses of the territories and possessions above specified."

In other words, the United States was forbidden to fortify Guam or build up the defenses of Manila and the Philippines. That is why Japan was able to walk quickly into both those places and into Wake Island and the Gilberts at the outset of the Pacific War.

The "Tanaka Memorial" exploded on a startled world late in 1927. General Baron Giichi Tanaka, Japan's chief exponent of the "positive policy" resting on the ultimate use of military force against China, was Premier at the head of a thoroughly chauvinist Tokyo Government. He called a conference in Mukden of the civil and military chiefs from Mongolia and Manchuria where, for eleven days from June 27 to July 7, were laid "plans for the colonization of the Far East and the development of our new continental empire." The results of that conference were embodied in a Memorial presented to the Emperor, a startling exposition of Japan's position and intentions. It was one of the Empire's most closely guarded secrets. When published by the Chinese some months later it was officially denied by Tokyo.

Baron Tanaka launched into a bitter denunciation of the Nine-Power Treaty signed at Washington. He laid the entire blame upon the United States. At this moment, fourteen years before Pearl Harbor, Baron Tanaka enunciated a policy of "Blood and Iron" and a willingness to fight the United States in a formal declaration of advice to his Emperor that set forth Japan's subsequent war aims more clearly than any of his successors has since done. He wrote: "In the future if we want to control China we must first control the United States just as in the past we had to fight in the Russo-Japanese War. But in order to conquer China we must first conquer Manchuria and Mongolia. In order to conquer the world we must first conquer China. If we succeed in conquering China the rest of the Asiatic countries and the South Sea countries will fear us and surrender to us. Then the world will realize that Eastern Asia is ours and will not dare to violate our rights."

The Memorial is remarkable, also, for the manner in which it revealed the strategy and tactics to be followed out by the Japanese High Command. Baron Tanaka advised using Manchuria and Mongolia "as a base, and under the picture of trade and commerce penetrate the rest of China." He urged that British and American capital be invited to share in building railroads, to allay suspicion, and thus make these two countries contribute toward their own downfall. He laid down fourteen specific proposals for unrestricted Japanese political and economic exploitation of China. He detailed infiltration of disguised military men—the first "tourists" of the new Fifth Column—while China and Russia were too busy with their domestic reorganizations to pay much attention.

Baron Tanaka declared: "For the sake of self-preservation and of giving warning to China and the rest of the world, we must fight America some time. The American Asiatic Squadron stationed in the Philippines is but within a stone's throw from Tsushima and Suichima (straits off Japan)." The Baron conveniently ignored the Japanese victory at Washington when Article XIX stopped the United States from further fortifying the naval facilities of the Philippines.

This is the blueprint of the Japanese plot to conquer China, destroy the United States fleet at Pearl Harbor, establish rule over the islands of the Pacific and the Asiatic continent, and strike at the western coast of the United States. These are the events which led up to the notorious "Manchurian Incident," and Japan's undeclared war on China that was merged into World War II, when Japan threatened to take into captivity more than half the population of the world.

29

HOW AMERICA WAS DRAWN INTO VORTEX OF WORLD WAR II

WORLD WAR II had been raging for two years and three months, or some 828 days, when the United States was precipitated into the conflict—forced to declare war against Japan on December 8, 1941, and against Germany and Italy on December 11, after valiant efforts to restore peace.

Throughout this period it had been the constant victim of Nazi plots to undermine it. There were continuous conspiracies to cause dissension at home, with our neighbors in Central and South America, and with Great Britain, France, and Russia. State documents and the records of the FBI (Federal Bureau of Investigation) unfold the damning evidence against the Axis conspirators at home and abroad. These intrigues would require volumes in themselves; the accumulated evidence runs into millions of words of irrefutable testimony.

At what moment the Hitler plot to destroy the democracies would explode in America, it was impossible to calculate. That it was inevitable every intelligent person knew. There was no escape from the combination of circumstances which were impelling us toward war in self-defense. The very existence of our nation was at stake.

When it came it was like a bolt of lightning hitting every home in the United States. More than 12,000,000 from these homes were to leave pursuits of peace and take up arms in protection of human freedom—to hold off the Axis Powers from making our own homeland a battleground. Fighting the conflagration in all parts of the world, they were stamping out the flames before they could reach America—to save our 135,000,000 people from the terrors that were being inflicted on the women and children of nations invaded by the Axis hordes.

It was not until Sunday, December 7, that the American people were awakened to the full realization of the danger which confronted them. It was a typical Sabbath Day, with millions in their homes and churches, still somewhat complacent with their aloofness from the horrors being enacted in distant countries. The newspapers and radio commentators were commending President Roosevelt's fortitude and patience, while warning us of crucial events. Headlines informed us of "Roosevelt's Appeals to Hirohito after New Threat in Indo-China—Direct Appeal to Tokyo Not to Precipitate a Conflict."

Suddenly through all the loud-speakers in the United States, and throughout the world, came this astounding announcement: "We interrupt this broadcast to bring you a special news bulletin—*Pearl Harbor has been attacked by the Japanese!*"

The country was stunned. As the details began to come over the air into our homes the truth was born in the consciousness of every man, woman, and child. The hour of trial was here. Newspaper headlines on December 8 proclaimed: *"Japan Wars on United States and Britain—Makes Sudden Attack on Hawaii—Heavy Fighting at Sea."*

During the night hours something had happened to the people of the United States. Every sign of division, every internal conflict had disappeared. The nation faced the dawn with determination—America United. Instantly they stood steadfast together. The spirit of the American people asserted itself. The spirit of democracy which Hitler had said was "incapable of working together"—too impotent to meet a crisis. He had sneered at the Americans as a nation of "cowards" in the "last gasp of a decaying civilization." He jeered at human freedom as a fool's dream in its death throes.

It was in this setting that the United States Senate and the House of Representatives met in historic joint session in the nation's Capitol at 12:25 P.M. on Monday, December 8, 1941. At 12:30 President Roosevelt, his face grave, stood before the august assemblage of the elected representatives of a free people. Before him sat the members of the United States Supreme Court. Galleries were crowded with diplomats of all friendly nations; spectators were tense.

Here was the inspiring figure of the statesman who had fought resolutely to preserve peace. His vision had penetrated far deeper than that of most of his countrymen. Were it not for his sagacity we would have been caught entirely unprepared. Through his wisdom we had been taking steps to meet whatever emergency might arise within our limits of neutrality. His voice was solemn as he spoke:

"Yesterday, December 7, 1941—a date which will live in infamy—the United States of America was suddenly and deliberately attacked by naval and air forces of the Empire of Japan.

"The United States was at peace with that Nation and, at the solicitation of Japan, was still in conversation with its Government and its Emperor looking toward the maintenance of peace in the Pacific. Indeed, one hour after Japanese air squadrons had commenced bombing in Oahu, the Japanese Ambassador to the United States and his colleague delivered to the Secretary of State a formal reply to a recent American message. While this reply stated that it seemed useless to continue the existing diplomatic negotiations, it contained no threat or hint of war or armed attack.

"It will be recorded that the distance of Hawaii from Japan makes it obvious that the attack was deliberately planned many days or even weeks ago. During the intervening time the Japanese Government has deliberately sought to deceive the United States by false statements and expressions of hope for continued peace.

"The attack yesterday on the Hawaiian Islands has caused severe damage to American naval and military forces. Very many American lives have been lost. In addition, American ships have been reported torpedoed on the high seas between San Francisco and Honolulu.

"Yesterday the Japanese Government also launched an attack against Malaya.

"Last night Japanese forces attacked Hongkong.

"Last night Japanese forces attacked Guam.

"Last night Japanese forces attacked the Philippine Islands.

"Last night the Japanese attacked Wake Island.

"This morning the Japanese attacked Midway Island.

"Japan has, therefore, undertaken a surprise offensive extending throughout the Pacific area. The facts of yesterday speak for themselves. The people of the United States have already formed their opinions and well understand the implications to the very life and safety of our Nation.

"As Commander in Chief of the Army and Navy I have directed that all measures be taken for our defense.

"Always will we remember the character of the onslaught against us.

"No matter how long it may take us to overcome this premeditated invasion, the American people in their righteous might will win through to absolute victory.

"I believe I interpret the will of the Congress and of the people when I assert that we will not only defend ourselves to the uttermost but will make certain that this form of treachery shall never endanger us again.

"Hostilities exist. There is no blinking at the fact that our people, our territory, and our interests are in grave danger.

"With confidence in our armed forces—with the unbounded determination of our people—we will gain the inevitable triumph—so help us God.

"I ask that the Congress declare that since the unprovoked and dastardly attack by Japan on Sunday, December 7, a state of war has existed between the United States and the Japanese Empire."

It was 12:38 when the President ceased speaking. At 12:40 the Joint Session was dissolved and the Senate returned to its own Chamber at the other end of the Capitol. At 1:00 P.M., twenty minutes later, the Senate unanimously adopted a resolution declaring a state of war with Japan. At 1:10 the House of Representatives, with only the dissenting voice of isolationist Congresswoman Jeannette Rankin of Montana, adopted the resolution. At 4:10 P.M. President Roosevelt signed the declaration. The United States was formally at war with Japan three and one-half hours after the Commander in Chief had asked the Congress to declare war.

It is interesting to note that at 4:00 P.M. Washington time on December 7—twenty-hours before the President's signature—the Japanese Imperial Headquarters announced that war had begun as of "dawn" on that date, hours before the first bombs hit Pearl Harbor.

Ambassador Grew had been held incommunicado under house arrest in Tokyo since that "dawn" and the State Department had been unable to contact him. During the night of December 9-10 Secretary Hull received this telegram from the Ministry of Foreign Affairs, Tokyo, dated December 8 (December 7 in Washington) and bearing the signature "Grew": "There has arisen a state of war between Your Excellency's country and Japan beginning today."

American newspapers of December 9, 1941, carried this headline:

U. S. DECLARES WAR; PACIFIC BATTLE WIDENS; MANILA AREA BOMBED
1,500 DEAD IN HAWAII

And the headlines of December 10, 1941, read:

ROOSEVELT PREDICTS A LONG WORLD-WIDE WAR; JAPANESE INVADE LUZON;
FIGHT IN MALAYA; 2 BIG BRITISH WARSHIPS SUNK, TOKYO SAYS

German treachery was clearly evident behind Japan's violent action, abetted by Italy as an Axis partner. This was all the original design of the aggressors. There was no mistaking Hitler's sinister hand. He believed that he was knocking Russia out of the war and now he and Japan could wage war against the United States. On December 11, 1941, Germany and Italy, simultaneously with the United States, declared a state of war, the declaration in Washington timed with that from Berlin.

The American people were now joint partners with the Allies in the death struggle between tyranny and human freedom. Later we were to declare war against the Axis satellites, Bulgaria, Hungary, and Rumania. The strength and will of the American people were to be decisive factors in crushing the powers of despotism. American manpower and American industry were to perform a modern miracle in organization and production.

Before traversing the battlefields some background is necessary of the diplomatic war we waged to preserve peace through the years before the outbreak. President Roosevelt, with his able Secretary of State, Cordell Hull, and Secretary of War, Henry L. Stimson, waged a continuous war against war from the time they took office in 1933. In fact, Mr. Stimson, who had been Secretary of State under President Herbert Hoover, had long been utilizing his knowledge of diplomacy to keep the storm from brewing. President Hoover, too, a vigorous exponent of peace, had tried to avert disaster.

During the ten years leading to Pearl Harbor the American people, with the rest of the world, had been fighting a war against an economic depression which was the direct result of the costs of the First World War—for all wars must be paid for. Hundreds of billions of dollars cannot be squandered in destruction without meeting the losses. "Pay Day" cannot be long postponed. Ultimately it must be met out of the pockets of the people. They pay first in lives, then in taxation, depression, and unemployment.

It was during this period of world depression that Hitler found his opportunity to arouse the spirit of revolution in the German people, and Japan laid her plans to overthrow the economically depressed democracies.

Democracies, by virtue of a free press which resists any attempt to control it, do not indulge in the device of inflaming public opinion against other nations. But the Government of Japan controlled the Japanese press and Ambassador Grew warned the Tokyo Foreign Office (in a report to our State Department) against "deliberately" pouring fuel "on the temporarily quiescent flames of public animosity against the United States ... to build up a public war psychology." There was no effective weapon with which the United States Government could strike back at Japan's psychological warfare.

Nelson T. Johnson, our Minister to China at the time of the Mukden Incident, telegraphed to Secretary Stimson from Peiping on September 22, 1931, that the whole Manchurian affair was "an aggressive act by Japan, apparently long planned, and when decided upon most carefully and systematically put into effect. I find no evidence that these events were the result of accident nor were they the acts of minor and irresponsible officials."

Mr. Stimson, then in the Hoover cabinet, appealed to both China and Japan to resort to peaceful means, knowing that Japan would continue to profess no plan of conquest and would go right on doing what she had been doing for years. But he had other plans in mind. He hoped to present a solid front of the other signatories to the Nine-Power Treaty in protest against Japan's action and in the threat of economic sanctions.

But the ghost of 1919 and 1920, when the "wilful few" in the United States Senate had prevented America's joining the League of Nations, rose to plague Mr. Stimson's plan. Had the United States been a member of the League the story of the world from 1931 on might well have been different. When Mr. Stimson presented his proposal for joint action under the Nine-Power Treaty to Sir John Simon, British Foreign Minister, the latter, while approving the general purpose, felt constrained to hold back in order not to interfere with the League of

Nations and its program. In the meantime, Japan had staged the "Shanghai Affair."

The net result was that the Stimson plan for quick joint action never went through, as he had no voice in the League of Nations which had been repudiated by the United States Senate. The League adopted the Lytton Report on February 24, 1933. By that time Japan was firmly intrenched and her only reaction was to withdraw from the League. Mr. Stimson set forth his country's position in a letter to the Senate Committee on Foreign Relations. Japan had been confronted with nothing more serious than a report and a letter.

In one of his last meetings as Secretary of State, Mr. Stimson had a frank talk with Japanese Ambassador Katsuji Debuchi. Mr. Stimson's own memorandum of the conversation on January 5, 1933, said in part: "He (Debuchi) said that in any event Japan had no territorial ambition south of the Great Wall. I reminded the Ambassador that a year ago he had told me Japan had no territorial ambitions in Manchuria. He became flustered and said that that was so but the situation had changed greatly...."

When Secretary Hull took office a record had been established of straight talk to Japan. Although we might be in no position to do more than register moral indignation, our officials had let Tokyo know that their intentions were plain to us and that their actions spoke much more forcibly than their words. Japan changed its ambassadors with amazing frequency, but each newcomer was immediately informed in definite terms what the position of the United States was on Far Eastern matters. Each succeeding ambassador brought with him assurances of Japan's peaceful intentions and desire for the friendship of the United States. But these assurances invariably stood against a background of overt military action or chauvinistic utterances.

The outspoken Ambassador Grew told Japan's Foreign Minister Koki Hirato in Tokyo on April 25, 1934: "The Government and people of the United States would be less impressed by statements of policy than by more concrete evidence." In defiance of this, Japan extended her sphere of "special interest" from Manchuria and China to all "East Asia." Secretary Hull asked the newly arrived Ambassador Hirosi Saito "whether this phrase of formula had ulterior or ultimate implications partaking of the nature of an overlordship of the Orient." Mr. Saito emphatically denied such implications. Subsequent events proved Mr. Hull's interpretation to be correct.

Matters had reached such a state that Ambassador Grew sent a report dated "Tokyo, December 27, 1934," to the State Department fully explaining the situation.

Mr. Grew's dispatch warned that the Japanese Navy contemplated seizing Guam in order not to lose too much face as the result of the army's conquests in Manchuria and Asia. He complained bitterly over the lack of American awareness of "the real potential risks and dangers." Unless, he went on, we were prepared to "subscribe to a 'Pax Japonica' in the Far East...we should rapidly build up our navy to treaty strength."

The Ambassador concluded by declaring: "It would be criminally shortsighted" to discard the possibilities of eventual war from our calculations, and urged, as the only language the Japanese would understand, a complete preparedness for that eventuality. The responsibility was thus squarely placed on the shoulders of Congress. Despite this full and frank exposition the State Department was unable to awaken Congress to the realization of the conditions which threatened.

Fortified by this attitude, Japan made its first serious attempt to set up a puppet régime in northern China. It met with instantaneous rebuke from the State Department. Saburo Kurusu retorted to E. R. Dickover, First Secretary of the United States Embassy in Tokyo, on December 22, 1935: "Japan is destined to be the leader of the Oriental civilization and will in course of time be the 'boss' of a group comprising China, India, the Netherlands East Indies...." Mr. Kurusu, at that time Chief of the Bureau of Commercial Affairs, Japanese Foreign Office, prided himself upon the use of colloquial English. He attempted to soften his statement of Japan's "destiny" by saying that the United States would be "boss" in the Americas and Great Britain would be "boss" in Europe, Africa, and Australia.

Events in China grew worse until they culminated in Japan's undeclared war in the fall of 1937. Secretary Hull wired Ambassador Grew: "In view of the methods employed by the Japanese military forces...it may be doubted that the elements actually controlling Japan's policies and actions value appreciably the friendship of other nations or efforts made by the United States and other governments to cultivate good will, confidence, and stability in general."

Time was running short and the pace of events was quickening. Mr. Hull told Sir Herbert Marler, Canadian Minister to the United States, on September 21, 1938, that "since August a year ago (1937) I have proceeded here on the theory that Japan definitely contemplates securing domination over as many hundreds of millions of people as possible in eastern Asia, and gradually extending her control through the Pacific islands to the Dutch East Indies and elsewhere, thereby dominating in practical effect that one-half of the world."

It was not until December 12, 1937, when Japanese planes wantonly bombed and destroyed the United States gunboat *Panay* and three American merchantmen in the Yangtze River, that the United States suddenly awoke to the fact that something of vital significance had been going on for years.

Beginning in June, 1938, the Government was able to translate into action the growing American resentment against Japanese aggressions in China, by making it exceedingly difficult for airplane manufacturers to accept orders from the Japanese Government. Moral and limited economic embargoes were placed on shipments to the Asiatic aggressor. On December 15, 1938, the United States granted China its first $25,000,000 commercial credit. A week later Premier Prince Fumimaro Konoye retaliated by announcing Japan's determination to create a "new order in East Asia." The United States firmly rejected the "new order" as "unjust and unwarranted ... counter to the provisions of several binding international agreements voluntarily entered into."

Japanese chicanery played its cunning hand. While conniving with Hitler in Berlin, it sent Kensuke Horinouchi to Washington, fifty-two days before the outbreak of World War II, under pretenses of peace. Foreign Minister Arita had suggested that the United States join with Japan to try to avoid war in Europe. Secretary Hull replied that the United States was always ready to "work in a friendly spirit with every peaceful nation to promote and preserve peace" but that "we draw the line between honest, law-abiding, peaceful countries ... and those who are flouting law and order and officially threatening military conquest without limit as to time or extent...."

Secretary Hull reminded Ambassador Horinouchi: "For six years we have been earnestly pleading with and urging upon your Government the view that there is enough room on this planet for fifteen or eighteen great nations like yours and mine." He allowed him to know that we were fully aware of Japan's intentions to seize all China and the Pacific islands skirting it. Two weeks later, on July 26, Japan was officially informed that the trade agreement (Treaty of Commerce and Navigation) signed more than a quarter of a century before, on February 21, 1911, would be terminated at the end of six months. The economic isolation of Japan had been begun.

Horinouchi saw Mr. Hull again on August 26. A new tone had entered into the voice of Japan's representatives in the United States. The logic of events had reduced them to only expressions of pious hope that something might be done to improve Japanese-American relations.

Mr. Hull told Mr. Horinouchi: "It should be evident to Japan that there is something wrong with policies and practices on the part of one nation which arouse antagonism on the part of almost all other nations.... The future of American-Japanese relations lies largely in the hands of Japan. American policy is a policy of friendliness and fair dealing toward all nations. It will not change."

Six days later Hitler invaded Poland. The situation in the Pacific grew even more complicated. The fate of French Indo-China, the

Netherlands East Indies, and Singapore gave the United States grave concern. Japan moved slowly, and not until Hitler's "blitzkrieg" gave every apparent indication of quickly subjugating France and the Netherlands and Britain, did Tokyo reach out for further prizes. In furtherance of her aggression in East Asia, Japan revived the absurd distortion that she was merely applying the Monroe Doctrine to her neighborhood. On April 20, 1940, Ambassador Horinouchi called upon Secretary Hull. Here is Mr. Hull's memorandum of the conversation:

"I proceeded to say to the Ambassador that I wished I could get over to him and his Government the fact that there is no more resemblance between our Monroe Doctrine, as we have interpreted and applied it uniformly since 1823, and the so-called Monroe Doctrine of Japan than there is between black and white."

Ambassador Grew sent another penetrating appraisal of the situation, giving the State Department the benefit of his first-hand observation on September 12, 1940. The German victories, he said, had gone like strong wine to the heads of the chauvinist elements in Japan who saw a "golden opportunity to carry their dreams of expansion into effect."

The dreary months under which the State Department suffered in silence the adverse criticism of its policy were justified by subsequent events when it finally became possible to publish the facts underlying that policy. In the shaping and pursuance of that policy the United States Government in August, 1940, refused to grant licenses for the export to Japan of aviation gasoline and most types of machine tools, and announced in September that, beginning October 16, no more iron or scrap steel might be shipped to Japan.

Tokyo was enraged over the embargoes. It ordered Ambassador Horinouchi to tell Mr. Hull in no uncertain terms that the steel embargo was an "unfriendly act," "discriminatory," and might lead to "unpredictable results." The Secretary of State found it "really amazing for the Government of Japan, which has been violating in the most aggravating manner valuable American rights and interests" in China to question the propriety of the embargoes, and added: "That of all the countries with which I have had to deal during the past eight years the Government of Japan has the least occasion or excuse to accuse this Government of an unfriendly act."

Japan's indignation was sheer hypocrisy. She had for many years been building a navy and army to strike at the United States with the very materials she was getting in the States—to shoot them back at us when her plans for war against us were completed. Her protests were at least ironic. The diabolical plot had been discovered—this she resented. Confidential reports proved that Germany, Italy, and Japan were soon to admit their Axis partnership for world conquest.

When the Tripartite Pact was actually signed on September 28, 1940,

Mr. Hull issued a statement to the effect that it had been known to exist for several years. On September 30 Mr. Hull assured Lord Lothian that our special desire was now to see Great Britain win her war with Hitler, and that our action in the Pacific "would be more or less affected as to time and extent by the question of what course would, on the part of this Government, most effectively and legitimately aid Great Britain in winning the war."

During 1940 the United States extended two additional commercial credits to China, and in 1941 China came under the provisions of the Lend-Lease Act, signed by President Roosevelt on March 11. In all their public and private utterances the President and Secretary Hull made it ever more clear that they considered Japan and Germany equally responsible, equally reprehensible. They left no doubt that the two aggressor nations were in constant communication and carrying out a common plan.

President Roosevelt felt that he was at last able to speak out boldly. At the dinner of the White House Correspondents' Association in Washington on March 15, 1941, he said: "Let not dictators of Europe and Asia doubt our unanimity now.... The big news story of this week is: The world has been told that we, as a united nation, realize the danger which confronts us—and that to meet that danger our democracy has gone into action." He was referring to passage of the Lend-Lease Act. "There is no longer the slightest question or doubt that the American people recognize the extreme seriousness of the present situation. That is why they have demanded, and got, a policy of unqualified, immediate, all-out aid for Britain, Greece, China, and for all the Governments-in-exile whose homelands are temporarily occupied by the aggressors.... China likewise expresses the magnificent will of millions of plain people to resist the dismemberment of their nation. China, through the Generalissimo, Chiang Kai-shek, asks our help. America has said that China shall have our help. Our country is going to be what our people have proclaimed it must be—the arsenal of democracy."

The United States still clung to the tenuous hope that it might be possible for the non-chauvinist elements to gain control of Japan before it was too late. Despite the overwhelming weight of evidence to the contrary, there was some basis for this hope. Japan had developed a fairly strong labor and liberal movement. Many of the statesmen were internationally minded and truly desirous of world coöperation. But they were confronted with a government at home cowed into submission by an uncompromising military caste. Time after time Secretary Hull noted in his records that one Japanese Ambassador after another had frankly admitted he was in a difficult position. Many Japanese statesmen had already been assassinated by the terrorists in the employ of the militarist group which held that constitutional government had broken down in Japan.

A quick glance at the record covering eight years will demonstrate clearly the risks run by any Japanese statesman who believed in international accord and harmony. Premier Yuko Hamaguchi was shot in a Tokyo railroad station by a member of the "Love of Country Association." The Premier was accused of having betrayed Japan by agreeing to the London Naval Treaty. This almost duplicated the events when the then Premier Takashi Hara, a leader in the movement to establish civilian supremacy over the military, was shot in the same station while about to depart for the Washington Disarmament Conference. Former Finance Minister Junnosuke Inouye was shot by a member of "Siesanto" an off-shoot of "Kokuryukai," the notorious "Black Dragon Society." His crime consisted of being a liberal, opposing military force in Manchuria and being conciliatory toward China. Baron Takuma Dan was shot by the "Blood Brotherhood," the members of which had subscribed to their oath of fidelity in their own blood. The leader was Nissho Inouye, a priest of the Nichiren sect, the same sect to which belonged the missionaries in China whose alleged murder contributed to the causes of the "China Affair." An attempt on the life of Premier Wakatsuki a few days earlier had failed. Premier Ki Inukai was shot. An attempt was made upon the life of Minister of War Sadao Araki.

The murder list grew with the pre-war years. Matsutaro Shoriki, publisher of *Yomiuri Shimbun,* Tokyo's third largest newspaper, was shot by a member of the "Warlike Gods' Society" for having sponsored the good-will tour of Babe Ruth and an American All-Star baseball team. Good will between Japan and the United States was not wanted by the jingos. Lieutenant General Tesuzan Nagata, Director of Military Affairs in the War Office, was stabbed through the heart by a fellow officer. The General and War Minister Senjuro Hayashi had been purging the Japanese Army of political agitators, demoting many high jingo officers in the process.

The army had been dissatisfied with civilian officials who were attempting to restrain them in Asia. (It was at that period that Mr. Kurusu was telling our Embassy in Tokyo that Japan was going to be "boss" of Asia.) The London Conference at which Japan was demanding naval parity was also under way. The object lesson was emphatic and clear. An attempt was made to assassinate Premier Koki Hirota. Premier Senjuro Hayashi moved into an "assassination-proof" house. Nine conspirators were arrested for plotting the assassination of older and conservative statesmen believed to be "too pro-British." Vice-Premier Kiichiro Hiranuma (former Premier) was shot. He was the first Japanese to be called a Fascist, but later modified his views and urged moderation in China. Whereupon he was shot.

The foregoing incomplete recital indicates how thorough and ruthless were the Japanese militarists. It shows the difficulties confronting moderate statesmen who virtually signed their death warrants in accepting office. It explains the patience and understanding of the United States Government in trying to encourage the moderate leaders.

The man behind most of the assassinations and violence was Mitsuru Toyama, a sinister figure who traveled with the mightiest and who was immune from interference. He was so feared that Japanese newspapers never printed his name, using asterisks to indicate whom they meant. Officially, he headed only the "Black Dragon Society," the most reactionary, pseudo-patriotic outfit in Japan. Actually, he inspired the creation of many other similar organizations. He was Japan's "Little Caesar."

One month before Lend-Lease was signed, the last in Japan's parade of ambassadors arrived in Washington. Admiral Kichisaburo Nomura had been appointed to succeed Mr. Horinouchi. He reached the American capital on Lincoln's Birthday, February 12, 1941. At his first press conference on the 19th he spoke through an interpreter, although he knew English well. He refused to be quoted directly but stated "there would be no war between the United States and Japan, provided the United States did not take the initiative in the fighting." This was true to the pattern of Japanese deceit and trickery—an attempt to throw us off guard. Six feet tall and weighing 180 pounds, Nomura did not at all resemble the popular conception of an unctuous, diminutive Japanese statesman with a stage-property smile hiding unknown feelings. He was no stranger in this country, having graduated from the United States Naval Academy at Annapolis when a young man. He returned to be naval attaché at the Japanese Embassy during World War I, and again as an aide to the representatives of his nation at the Washington Conference. He had taken a training squadron of two Japanese cruisers and more than 1,500 men through the Pacific to Hawaii, through the Panama Canal and to various East Coast ports in 1929. He came back once again three years later on another "good will mission" to explain Manchuria and Manchukuo to the United States.

Kichisaburo Nomura had been called upon to prepare the way for much of Japan's aggression. He led his country's naval force into Shanghai at the outbreak of trouble there, and immediately established a record for breaking his word. He gave his guarantee that there would be no more flying by his war planes over the territory of the International Settlement. At nine o'clock the next morning two Japanese pursuit planes flew over the Settlement for an hour and bombed Chapei. When a Korean threw a bomb at the speaker's platform of a Shanghai meeting celebrating the birthday of the Japanese Emperor, Admiral Nomura was wounded and subsequently lost one eye.

While Admiral Nomura was crossing the Pacific on his last mission to America, Ambassador Grew sent the following telegram to Secretary Hull: "Tokyo, January 27, 1941—6:00 P.M. A member of the Embassy was told by my ——— colleague that from many quarters, including a Japanese one, he had heard that a surprise mass attack on Pearl Harbor was planned by the Japanese military forces, in case of 'trouble' between Japan and the United States; that the attack would involve the use of all the Japanese military facilities...."

This first specific mention of Pearl Harbor caused considerable activity within the President's Cabinet. Decisions of policy had been arrived at when Ambassador Nomura presented his credentials to President Roosevelt. On March 8 Mr. Hull told the Admiral that certain groups in Japan had appealed to the United States to do something to halt the militarists but that this country could deal only through the established Government. Ambassador Nomura was plainly embarrassed and ill at ease and his discomfiture increased at every meeting.

Exploratory conversations proceeded with no change in the situation until on May 12 the wily Admiral revealed what was up his sleeve. The Japanese Government presented a draft proposal for an agreement with the United States. It was plainly a brazen stall. Tokyo sought to obtain the signature of the United States to a treaty sanctioning everything Japan had done. This country was to guarantee to "discontinue her assistance to the Chiang Kai-shek régime" should China refuse to agree to a negotiated peace. To top off everything, the United States was to concede that "Japanese expansion in the direction of the southwestern Pacific area" was "of peaceful nature" and was to promise full economic coöperation.

When Mr. Roosevelt returned from his first conference with Prime Minister Churchill—at which the Atlantic Charter was drawn—the President asked Ambassador Nomura to call upon him and on August 17 handed the Admiral two statements. One briefly summarized the state of affairs between the two countries. The other concluded: "If the Japanese Government takes any further steps in pursuance of a policy or program of military domination by force or threat of force of neighboring countries, the Government of the United States will be compelled to take immediately any and all steps which it may deem necessary toward safeguarding the legitimate rights and interests of the United States and American nationals and toward insuring the safety and security of the United States."

Ambassador Grew continued to send warnings of the increasing imminence of war. Tokyo dramatically rang up the curtain on the final act of the conspiracy to keep the United States off guard. It suddenly announced that it was sending Saburo Kurusu to Washington as a special Ambassador to assist Admiral Nomura in improving relations between the two countries. Kurusu left Japan by plane on November 6, 1941, and arrived in Washington on the 15th. Before this event, Premier Konoye had been overthrown and the fire-eating Admiral Hideki Tojo had become Japan's war Premier. Kurusu was the exact antithesis of Admiral Nomura in every respect. He was small, sharp, precise, and suave. He was a career diplomat who had spent many years as consul in Chicago where he acquired his familiarity with American slang and where he married an American woman. He then became consul general at Manila, and when he left that post he assured us that the United States should keep control of the Philippines because "Independence of the Philippines unprotected would be just one more disturbing element in the Far Eastern situation."

The three weeks from November 15 to December 7, 1941 were the most dramatic in the history of diplomacy. There was real tragedy behind the farce being played by the Japanese under a mask of politeness and protocol. Coincident with the departure of Kurusu from Japan, Secretary Hull had told a Cabinet meeting in the White House on November 7—exactly one month before Pearl Harbor—that relations between Japan and the United States were extremely critical; there was "imminent possibility" Japan might at any time start a conquest by force.

Ambassador Grew sent another warning that the Japanese were about to exploit "every possible tactical advantage, such as surprise and initiative." The time and place were still unknown. Mr. Kurusu and Ambassador Nomura called on President Roosevelt on November 17 —the date of Mr. Grew's alarm—"a courtesy call." The next day they saw Secretary Hull. Mr. Kurusu thought that after the Sino-Japanese conflict it might be possible to improve relations between the United States and Japan. Ambassador Nomura, more and more uncomfortable and with less and less to say, emphasized that the situation was very pressing and remarked that "big ships cannot turn around too quickly." He may have been referring to ships of state or, perhaps, to warships already under orders.

These sly Nipponese tricksters were playing the diplomatic game with a marked deck and five aces up their sleeves. On November 20 they presented a new proposal differing in no important respect from those advanced previously, except to make the geographical boundaries conform to Japan's new conquests. When, on November 26, Secretary Hull presented this country's reply Mr. Kurusu sneered at it and said it was a "reiteration of the Stimson doctrine." Tokyo's official reply was not to be received until after Pearl Harbor had been laid in ruins.

This last proposal for peace from the United States provided for: (1) A multi-lateral non-aggression pact among the British Empire, China, Japan, the Netherlands, the Soviet Union, Thailand, and the United States. (2) A multi-lateral agreement to respect the territorial integrity of French Indo-China. (3) The Government of Japan will withdraw all military, naval, air, and police forces from China and from Indo-China. (4) The Government of the United States and the Government of Japan will not support—militarily, politically, economically—any government or régime in China other than the National Government of the Republic of China with capital temporarily at Chungking. (5) Both Governments to give up all extra-territorial rights in China and to attempt to induce other governments to do the same. (6-10) Elimination of trade and commercial restrictions, other economic provisions and guarantees for the establishment and preservation of peace throughout the Pacific area.

Mr. Kurusu immediately rejected points 3 and 4 and said the United States could not "expect that Japan was to take off its hat to Chiang Kai-shek." After many more fruitless interviews during which Secretary Hull reminded the Japanese envoys that while they were apparently talking peace in Washington, their Government and Government-controlled press in Tokyo were talking and acting war. Ambassador Nomura and Mr. Kurusu called again at the State Department on December 5—while the Japanese fleet was on its way. Ambassador Nomura, who had been doing little talking since Mr. Kurusu arrived, reminded Mr. Hull that "offense is the best defense." A little later he muttered under his breath in Japanese the equivalent of "this isn't getting us anywhere."

President Roosevelt in a final effort to avoid catastrophe took the unprecedented step of sending a message directly to Emperor Hirohito. Under date of December 6, Mr. Roosevelt telegraphed to the effect that after almost a century of peace and friendship matters had come to such a pass that "I address to Your Majesty messages on matters of State." After reviewing quickly the movement of Japanese troops on the Continent of Asia, the President concluded: "I address myself to Your Majesty at this moment in the fervent hope that Your Majesty may, as I am doing, give thought in this definite emergency to ways of dispelling the dark clouds. I am confident that both of us, for the sake of the peoples not only of our own great countries but for the sake of humanity in neighboring territories, have a sacred duty to restore traditional amity and prevent further death and destruction in the world."

The secret Japanese armada was on its way at this moment to strike at America's outposts. Little Mr. Kurusu and big Admiral Nomura were still playing their game, smiling and bowing, and proffering their felicitations and assurances of devotion to the American people.

Sunday had always been a diplomatic day of rest in Washington. But the Japanese Ambassadors telephoned for an appointment to see Secretary Hull at 1:00 P.M. The bulky, now glum Admiral Nomura and his colleague, the ingratiating Kurusu, had the reply of their Government to the United States' proposal of eleven days ago. Mr. Hull, kindly, gentlemanly, and upright in every move, graciously agreed to meet the Japanese diplomats. Here is the official State Department text on that meeting: "December 7, 1941. The Japanese Ambassador asked for an appointment to see the Secretary at 1:00 P.M., but later telephoned and asked that the appointment be postponed to 1:45 as the Ambassador was not quite ready. The Ambassador and Mr. Kurusu arrived at the Department at 2:05 P.M. and were received by the Secretary at 2:20. The Japanese Ambassador stated that he had been instructed to deliver at 1:00 P.M. the document which he handed the Secretary, but that he was sorry he had been delayed an hour owing to the need of more time to decode the message. The Secretary asked why he had specified one o'clock. The Ambassador replied that he did not know but that that was his instructions.... After the Secretary had read two or three pages he asked the Ambassador whether this document was presented under instructions of the Japanese Government. The Ambassador replied that it was. The Secretary as soon as he had finished reading the document turned to the Ambassador and said:

"'I must say that in all my conversations with you (the Japanese Ambassador) during the last nine months I have never uttered one word of untruth. This is borne out absolutely by the record. In all my fifty years of public service I have never seen a document that was more crowded with infamous falsehoods and distortions—infamous falsehoods and distortions on a scale so huge that I never imagined until today that any government on this planet was capable of uttering them.'"

Ambassador Nomura and Mr. Kurusu then took their leave without making any comment. Their poker faces were now grim and blank. Secretary Hull's sense of justice, honesty, and humanity had been outraged. For he knew as he spoke to the Japanese diplomats that the attack on Pearl Harbor had begun at 1:20 Washington time.

The treachery had been consummated. Every tenet of truth and honor had been violated. War had finally come to the United States. The long, patient, tedious, disappointing diplomatic battle had been lost. While Pearl Harbor, Hickam Field, and the surrounding country were going up in flame in the Pacific, the Japanese began to send up in smoke at their Embassy grounds all papers and records not supposed to fall into enemy hands.

Ambassador Nomura and Mr. Kurusu were later to be given their passports and returned to Tokyo, according to diplomatic procedure. Ambassador Grew was to come home to Washington to reveal the hazardous experiences through which he had passed as the Japanese war lords kept him under constant surveillance.

"DAY OF INFAMY"—STABBED IN THE BACK AT PEARL HARBOR

THREE minutes were to change the entire course of world history on Sunday morning, December 7, 1941. When Japan attacked America at Pearl Harbor she started a chain of events which nearly four years later were to force her to commit hara-kiri.

This sunlit morning on the Hawaiian Islands, the crossroads of the Pacific, will always be known as the "Day of Infamy" to Americans.

It was 6:30 on this momentous December 7 when the U.S.S. *Antares*, an auxiliary ship used for target service, sighted a suspicious object protruding from the glistening waters in the early morning light. Immediately she notified the U.S.S. *Ward*, the destroyer on patrol duty. At 6:45 the *Ward*'s patrol reported sighting a periscope in the channel. Lieutenant Commander W. W. Outerbridge gave the order to let go with the No. 3 gun. The shell was a little high. The *Ward* closed in on the elusive target without ever losing sight of it, and at 6:40, when only fifty yards away, fired a second shot that scored a direct hit. The target proved to be a Japanese midget submarine. The *Ward* dumped some depth charges that destroyed the invading craft.

The first shot of the American-Japanese War had been fired. Neither the commanding officer of the twenty-three-year-old destroyer nor the gun crew knew it at the time. Lieutenant Commander Outerbridge sent a report of the action which reached the naval base watch officer at 7:12 A.M. and the Chief of Staff a few minutes later. The "ready destroyer" was sent to investigate, but no alarm was sounded nor was the base put on the alert. Nor was the torpedo net protecting the harbor checked. It had been opened at 4:58 that morning to let in two mine sweepers and had not been closed. The net remained open until 8:40—two hours after the *Ward* had gone into action.

At one of the mobile aircraft detection units somewhere on Oahu Island (containing both Honolulu and Pearl Harbor) Private Joseph L. Lockard looked at his watch and saw that it was 6:58 A.M. The young Williamsport, Pennsylvania, soldier—he was only twenty years old—had been assigned to man the instrument and teach an assistant during the routine duty. This was the only watch maintained at the recording devices from 4:00 A.M.-7:00 A.M. He asked his sergeant for permission to remain after seven o'clock because he "was interested."

It was 7:02 A.M. Detecting evidence of a large flight of planes heading for Oahu from slightly east of north, he estimated their distance at 130 miles. Checking his readings again and again, Private Lockard removed all doubts from his mind. He reported at 7:20 to a lieutenant on duty at the Army's General Information Center who had been detailed to that post to become familiar with the operations of the system. This young officer had been told that some American planes might be expected in the vicinity at about the same time, so he assumed that the aircraft Private Lockard had recorded were those friendly planes.

A half-hour later hell broke loose over Pearl Harbor. The Japanese had struck their first treacherous blow. Every move followed a split-second time-table. Every plane had its place and its target. Every pilot had a detailed map of Oahu showing what ship was supposed to be at each berth, how many planes were supposed to be lined up at each field. Every ship and every plane was where it was supposed to be—with one exception. The mine layer *Oglala* was tied up to the pier where the battle fleet's flagship *Pennsylvania* had been until unexpectedly moved to a drydock. Enemy espionage had been so efficient that nothing was left to chance.

At 7:55 A.M. small squadrons of Japanese dive bombers appeared almost simultaneously over the army air base at Wheeler Field, the Kaneohe naval air base, and the still uncompleted Marine base at Ewa close by Pearl Harbor. They flew in low without detection and without interference. Hundreds of American planes were lined up in orderly rows; seconds later they were burning piles of wreckage. The enemy's first objective was to clip the wings of the defense—it took less than a minute. Machine-gun bullets and incendiary shells ripped and burned Flying Fortresses, Liberators, Corsairs, and Lightnings into impotence. The few undamaged planes could not take off because of the debris-blocked runways.

On the tail of the first wave of destruction rode the Japanese pilots whose charts showed the hangars to be bombed. By that time the first planes over had time to turn around and strafe the American soldiers, sailors, and Marines rushing to their battle stations. Machine guns were hoisted out of wrecked planes or carried from buildings and fired from the shoulder. Mustard-colored planes with the rising sun on their wings began to fall. In those same seconds Hickam Field, so close to Pearl Harbor as to be part of it, received its baptism of fire. Torpedo planes leveled off over the waters of the Naval Basin to drop their tin fish.

For half an hour the Japanese shuttled back and forth over their targets and the civilian areas of Honolulu and the rest of Oahu. The damage had been done in the first two or three minutes. The short swift blow had virtually deprived the billion-dollar base of air protection and inflicted heavier damage on the United States Navy than had been suffered in all of World War I.

When the first phase of the attack subsided at 8:25 A.M. Pearl Harbor and its surrounding airfields were a scene of wreckage. Of 202 navy planes at Kaneohe and the Marine base eighty had been destroyed and seventy damaged; only a few of the remaining fifty-two were able to take off through the wreckage. Of 273 army planes at Hickam and Wheeler Fields ninety-three, including twenty-three bombers and sixty-six fighters, had been destroyed with nearly as many more damaged.

Every battleship, and all but an insignificantly few vessels of the eighty-eight naval craft in Pearl Harbor, had been hit. The battleships *Arizona* and *California* had been sunk as had the *Utah,* converted into a target ship; the *Nevada* had been beached, a burning pyre; the *Oklahoma* had capsized, the *Tennessee,* the *Pennsylvania,* and the *West Virginia* had been damaged. The cruisers *Helena, Honolulu,* and *Raleigh* had been damaged. The destroyers *Downes* and *Cassin* were a total loss and the *Shaw* had its bow blown away. The mine layer *Oglala,* mistaken for the *Pennsylvania,* had been sunk; the seaplane tender *Curtiss* and repair ship *Vestal* had been badly hurt, and a large floating drydock had been wrecked.

Nineteen ships, representing hundreds of millions of dollars, had been sunk or badly damaged; $25,000,000 worth of planes and at least an equal amount of ammunition, buildings, and supplies had been destroyed; 2,383 men had been killed; 1,842—some of whom later died—had been wounded; 960 more were missing.

That was the toll of three minutes' work by Japanese planes. The American losses would have been greater had it not been for the fact that two large task forces were at sea on assigned missions; two others, having completed their operations, were safe in home ports and not at Pearl Harbor. There was not a single aircraft carrier at Oahu.

The Japanese sent over between 150 and 200 planes, most of them dive bombers, a somewhat smaller number of horizontal, high-flying bombers, and a lesser number of torpedo planes. More than twenty-eight of these were shot down by naval antiaircraft fire and more than a score of others by army pursuit planes that managed to take off; also by some of the eighteen navy scouts returning from their task force carrier during the height of the attack.

There was a comparative lull from 8:25 to 8:40 interrupted by sporadic dive and vertical bombing. Then the high-flying Japanese bombers, safe from any effective fighter opposition because of the devastation wrought at the airfields by the first attack, crossed and recrossed their targets at will, adding further to the damage. Dive bombers returned to strafe the wounded and the rescue and repair crews for half an hour. At 9:45 all enemy aircraft retired, leaving Pearl Harbor to lick its wounds and count its losses.

Never in all history have so many instances of epic heroism by civilian and military personnel been recorded in so short a time as in those first 110 minutes of World War II. One Japanese bomb fell squarely on Schofield Barracks at Wheeler Field, the largest single United States Army post. Soldiers, from fully clad to nude, rushed out and made straight for the nearest gun or fire-fighting equipment. Two young lieutenants at the Officers' Club leaped into a car and sped to a near-by field where their planes had been parked. They rose quickly to do battle with their small .30-caliber machine guns against more than a dozen battle planes. Each shot down a dive bomber before returning to Wheeler Field for more fuel and ammunition.

Lieutenant Harry Brown rushed to the aid of his friend, Lieutenant Robert Rogers, who was being attacked by two Japanese, and blew one of the enemy planes out of the sky. Other pilots staged dogfights all over Oahu, thrilling thousands who forgot their own dash for safety from Japanese strafing to cheer the American fighters.

Lieutenant Stephen G. Saltzman and Sergeant Lowell V. Klatt left the shelter of their communications tower to shoot down with rifles one of two enemy planes strafing from an altitude of only 100 yards.

Lieutenant George R. Bickell was eating breakfast with his wife when one of the enemy planes crashed outside their home. Jumping into their car, with a neighboring pilot, his wife, and three-year-old child, Lieutenant Bickell raced ten miles through fire from low-flying Japanese strafers to Heleiwa Field, leaped into his plane and, at 1,000 feet, sailed into a formation of a dozen enemy planes with his machine guns open. A moment later there were only ten Japanese planes. As he was returning to Wheeler Field for fuel, fifteen enemy ships came in low. Three made for him but he managed to take off, only to be shot down 200 yards from shore. While his wife watched breathlessly he swam ashore, got himself another plane, shot down an invader attacking his friend from the rear, and then chased his fourth victim five miles out to sea before delivering the *coup de grace*. Lieutenant Bickell was later promoted to Major and placed in command of the fighters in the Eighth Air Force in Britain. Still later, as Lieutenant Colonel, he led a Mustang group over Berlin in the first attack on that city.

Over at Hickam Field soldiers leaped into burning planes to fire at the enemy from the mounted machine guns. Others braved the flames to remove the precious engines from their moorings and drag them to safety. Hickam Field received its worst blows during the second attack. Ambulances, trucks, buses, station wagons, pressed into service to remove the wounded and to rush supplies, were mercilessly strafed. Kitchen details grabbed what weapons they could and fired back at the attackers. In the midst of the assault a group of unarmed bombers arrived from the United States. Instead of putting down at Hickam they dispersed and landed wherever they could, damning the ill-fortune that brought them into the middle of the attack without a gun or a bullet. Lieutenant Anne G. Fox, head nurse at Hickam Field, received a Purple Heart for bravery under fire, the first American woman ever to be awarded an army medal.

At Ford Field naval personnel were as fearless as their army brothers. Gun crews rushed to salvage their weapons from burning planes and fired at the enemy either from the shoulder or from such temporary mounts as a garbage can. Marines at Ewa lived up to the glory of their tradition, plunging into the maelstrom and continuing to shoot when surrounded by flaming gasoline.

Two cruiser scout planes that happened to be in the air picked on an attacking pursuit ship with three times the speed and destroyed it. Lieutenant Clarence E. Dickinson had left his returning carrier on the way back from Wake Island about 200 miles from Oahu, and flew right into the battle. His plane was hit and his gunner killed but he continued fighting until, when only 700 feet from the ground, he parachuted safely to a mountain road. Hitch-hiking to the airfield he took a plane and went hunting, bagging one Zero before being shot down himself. On the way back to the air station he saw civilian automobiles being strafed and, as he said, "I got mad." Lieutenant Dickinson took to the air again on a 175-mile search flight.

Then there was Lieutenant James W. Robb who grabbed a rifle, jumped into an amphibian plane and went looking for Japanese. He was so angry he did not realize he had no protection whatsoever until he had flown more than 100 miles. Most of these examples of courage related here took place in the few minutes before the major attack was launched against the Naval Basin.

With the loss of Admiral King and Captain van Valkenburgh, forty-two-year-old Lieutenant Commander Samuel G. Fuqua found himself in command of the 32,000-ton wrecked *Arizona*. He had been knocked unconscious by the force of the explosions but quickly regained his senses. Fighting his way through the rain of bombs and bullets to the quarterdeck, he directed fire-fighting operations and the removal of dead and wounded. His calmness and coolness inspired all the men and he was the last person to leave the *Arizona*.

Dorris Miller, negro mess attendant second class, had never fired a gun in his life until he came out of the *Arizona*'s galley. Scornful of the explosions, the fires, the bombs, and everything else, he calmly manned an antiaircraft gun all by himself and kept shooting until the ammunition had been used up. The *Utah*, lying where a carrier was supposed to be—and had been—was the object of special attack. She capsized under the weight of bombs and the blows of torpedoes.

Captain Mervyn S. Bennion, in command of the *West Virginia*, was on the bridge of his battleship from the first moment of the attack.

In that comparative lull following the initial blow a single plane flew over and dropped a bomb that struck the bridge squarely. A fragment ripped open Captain Bennion's abdomen and he fell mortally wounded. As the flames began to mount, as explosions shook the ship, and as the vessel listed over against the *Tennessee,* Captain Bennion, as had Captain Van Valkenburgh on the *Arizona,* refused to be moved and ordered his subordinate officers to save the men and themselves.

Captain Francis W. Scanland managed to maneuver his battleship *Nevada* to a spit of land where he beached her and prevented her from capsizing and blocking the channel. While this was going on, Ensign Thomas H. Taylor assumed command of an antiaircraft battery. Flames began to creep nearer the ammunition boxes. He grabbed a hose and played a stream steadily against the fire, preventing an explosion and saving the lives of his men.

The *Oklahoma* capsized at her moorings and suffered terrific punishment. Seaman James Richards, trapped with his mates in a gun turret in pitch-blackness when the lighting failed, and under water, held a flashlight so the other men of the crew might escape through the emergency exit. There was no one to hold the light for him.

The mine layer *Oglala,* at the *Pennsylvania*'s usual berth, was under command of Rear Admiral William R. Furlong, the man who subsequently salvaged and restored to duty all but three of the ships wrecked during that day. He saw the first bomb hit a seaplane ramp on Ford Island and sounded general quarters. Then three aërial torpedoes flashed toward the ship. One struck and sent the *Oglala* to the bottom. The crew went over the sides and, like the crews of so many other ships, swam to safety through waters covered with flaming oil. The devil and the deep sea had come together in Pearl Harbor.

The vortex of all the excitement was around the floating drydock. The *Pennsylvania,* the destroyers *Shaw, Downes,* and *Cassin,* the repair ship *Vestal* and the seaplane tender *Curtiss* were grouped there. A heavy bomb dropped from high altitude like the armor-piercing bombs that had hit the *Arizona,* had sunk the drydock. The *Shaw* was cut in two, the *Downes* fell off her blocks, the *Cassin* was set on fire, and the *Pennsylvania* suffered damage.

What happened on the *Vestal* was typical of every ship in Pearl Harbor that December 7. When the *Arizona*'s magazines and boilers exploded, the force of the blast blew Commander Cassin Young of the *Vestal* off the bridge into the flaming oil-covered waters between the two ships. His ship had been hit, set afire in several places, and was taking on list. Swimming back to his ship, he climbed aboard and calmly moved her to a safer anchorage.

About the time the *Vestal* had reached its new position, Commander Young noticed the shadow of a two-man midget submarine within a few yards. He immediately opened fire on the intruder. His busy antiaircraft crews had winged an enemy plane that came crashing down on the ship's deck. A passing destroyer finished off the submarine while the *Vestal*'s crew fought the fire from the wrecked plane. Almost immediately a second Japanese bomber attacked the ship and the *Vestal*'s gunners brought it crashing down.

Commander Young saw that the only way to save the *Vestal* was to beach her. While he was steering the ship into shallow water, Warrant Officer Donald K. Ross was in the forward dynamo room which was rapidly filling with smoke, steam, and heat. Young Ross forced his men to leave the room and carried on alone until he was blinded and unconscious. Pharmacist's Mate Lionel S. Baker, although suffering from shrapnel wounds himself, continued to take care of the injured on board until all had been removed.

Marine Sergeant Thomas E. Bailey helped rescue his mates from a sunken ship and, without previous training, successfully operated an antiaircraft gun. Later, clothed only in his underwear, he went up in a search plane on a special mission.

Navy physicians and nurses took care of 960 casualties in sixteen hours, most of them horrible burns. Ten civilian employees of the Supply Department were cited for getting supplies through to Pearl Harbor despite the attack. Vera N. Jones, chief telephone operator at the Naval Base, and most of her girls remained at their boards for twenty-four hours without relief.

The citizens of Honolulu and the rest of Oahu responded gloriously. Their homes were bombed, their children were killed, their cars were strafed. But they mobilized nursing and medical supplies, transportation and other facilities quickly and competently. When an emergency call went out for blood donors, thousands stood in line for hours. They came by families, by factories, and by farms.

Pearl Harbor was the apex of the Pacific defense triangle from Dutch Harbor in Alaska to the Panama Canal. The Canal was considered the military "Achilles' heel" and Pearl Harbor the spearhead. The island of Oahu had been converted into a 598-square-mile fortress at the cost of more than $1,000,000,000. A $2,000,000 ammunition depot, drilled into the rocks, held $20,000,000 worth of shells, bullets, bombs, and torpedoes. Pearl Harbor was a naval base with ten square miles of water, in the center of which stood Ford Island with its naval air station. Midway on the main island was Schofield Barracks with Wheeler Field, and near by was the most modern and one of the largest military airfields in the world—Hickam Field.

Immediately following the attack, Secretary of the Navy Knox flew to Hawaii to obtain first-hand information. He returned to Washington on December 15, and said: "The United States services were not on the

"Day of Infamy" 331

alert against the surprise attack on Hawaii. This fact calls for a formal investigation. . . . My investigation made clear that after the attack the defense of both services was conducted skilfully and bravely."

The investigation was started immediately by a five-man inquiry board appointed by President Roosevelt. It was headed by Associate Justice Owen J. Roberts of the Supreme Court. Hearings were held in Washington and Hawaii and the final report consisted of 1,187 typewritten pages of testimony with more than 3,000 printed pages of documents.

"Specific plans for the protection of the Hawaiian area against every contingency had been prepared," the report said, "setting up a system of coördination calling for 'mutual coöperation' between the responsible army and navy commanders." On December 7, 1941, they were Admiral Husband E. Kimmel, Commander in Chief of the Pacific Fleet, his subordinate Rear Admiral Claude C. Bloch, Commandant of the Fourteenth Naval District, and Lieutenant General Walter C. Short, Commanding General, Hawaiian Department. They had prepared a "Joint Coastal Defense Plan" in which the fleet had been charged with responsibility for the defense of the outlying islands and interception of any hostile craft, while responsibility for the defense of Pearl Harbor lay with the army.

Although military installations had not been completed the report said: "Presupposing timely disposition by the army and navy commands in Hawaii, the forces available to them were adequate to frustrate a surprise air attack or greatly to mitigate its effectiveness." The Board then disclosed a long series of urgent messages from Washington. The War and Navy Departments had urged great caution and close coöperation between the two forces of the service. The last message was a telegram filed in Washington at noon, December 7 (that was 6:30 in the morning in Honolulu, indicating that an immediate break with Japan was to be expected, but the message never got through until after the attack.

"The responsible commanders of the Hawaiian area were aware," the report said, "that previous Japanese actions and demonstrated Axis methods indicated that hostile action might be expected prior to a declaration of war." But every chief officer, without exception, ruled out the possibility of an air attack while the fleet was in Pearl Harbor. Both Admiral Kimmel and General Short testified they had never jointly discussed "means or measures for Hawaiian defense." Each took his own separate action, assumed that the other was doing the same thing and never exchanged information or found out what was being done. General Short put in a 4:00 A.M.-7:00 A.M. air-raid alert and warning system and took special precautions against sabotage. Admiral Kimmel made certain dispositions of his forces and ordered immediate attack on any submarines. Admiral Bloch warned destroyer commanders to be ready for instant action. No inshore airplane patrol was carried out on Sunday and long-distance reconnaissance flights were made only during drills and maneuvers.

"In the summer of 1941," the report declared, "there were more than two hundred consular agents acting under the Japanese consul who was stationed in Hawaii.... It is now apparent that through their intelligence service the Japanese had complete information. They evidently knew that no task force of the United States Navy was anywhere in the sector northeast, north, and northwest of the Hawaiian Islands. They evidently knew that up to December 6 no plane reconnaissance was maintained in any sector. They evidently knew that up to December 6 no inshore patrol was being maintained around the periphery of Oahu." The Japanese consulate was the center of spy activity and messages to Tokyo over the commercial cables had been increasing rapidly in number.

The investigation quickly disposed of rumors that Saturday night passes to enlisted men had left the ships and posts inadequately manned. When the attack began 88.8 per cent of army men and officers were on duty; 96 per cent of the ships' crews; and 60 per cent of the navy officers were at their posts. The report paid a fine tribute to the fighting men: "Officers and enlisted men in defending against the attack demonstrated excellent training and high morale.... Junior officers and enlisted men on their own initiative procured from storage every possible automatic weapon. These weapons continued in action during and in spite of low-level strafing and dive bombing which have been known to demoralize even seasoned troops."

Turning to the question of responsibility, Justice Roberts and his associates found: The commanders were working independently rather than in coöperation. Their first duty was "conference and consultation" and for at least ten days preceding the attack they had held no conferences. Despite the warnings from Washington, "there had been among the responsible commanders and their subordinates, without exception, a conviction which persisted up to December 7, 1941, that Japan had no intention of making any such raid."

The report concluded: "In the light of the warnings and directions to take appropriate action, transmitted to both commanders ... it was a dereliction of duty on the part of each of them not to consult and confer with each other ... a lack of appreciation of the responsibilities vested in them and inherent in their positions as Commander in Chief of the Pacific Fleet and Commanding General, Hawaiian Department. ... Subordinate commanders executed their superiors' orders without question. They were not responsible for the state of readiness prescribed."

"Day of Infamy"

On December 17 Lieutenant General Delos C. Emmons succeeded General Short; Vice Admiral William S. Pye took over temporary command of the Pacific Fleet from Admiral Kimmel until Admiral Chester W. Nimitz could assume the post; and Brigadier General C. L. Tinker relieved Major General Frederick D. Martin as Commander of the Army Air Forces. Admiral Bloch was retained at his same post.

Details of the losses suffered at Pearl Harbor were withheld for one very good reason: Had the Japanese known the extent of their success they would have returned almost immediately and, perhaps, have seized the island. Just as Hitler made his great blunder in not invading Britain immediately after the fall of France, so Tojo threw away all chance of victory by failing to occupy Oahu and send his main forces right across the Pacific to the United States mainland. It was not until a year later, December 5, 1942, that the navy disclosed the full extent of the damage at Pearl Harbor.

The recovery from that blow constitutes another glowing chapter in American history. Destroyed facilities were repaired within a few hours after the last enemy plane had left. All the destroyed and damaged aircraft were replaced within a few days. The battleships *Nevada, California,* and *West Virginia* were lifted from the channel mud, reconstructed, and sent to sea again. Instead of the semi-obsolete battleships they had been, they were the most efficient fighting craft of their size and weight in the world. The *Arizona* remained a total loss, but the *Oklahoma* was righted and modernized in 1944—thirty years after she had been laid down. The *Pennsylvania, Maryland,* and *Tennessee* were quickly healed of their wounds and back in service. Eight battleships out of action; only one lost.

The cruisers *Helena, Honolulu,* and *Raleigh* were back in fighting service in less than a year—three hit, three saved. The destroyer *Shaw* was fighting again in six months—three hit, one saved. Remember the names of these four boats; they figure prominently in the naval actions to follow. Even the old, discarded *Utah,* converted from a battleship to a target ship, was salvaged; and the auxiliary vessels were all back in service.

Heroic efforts of salvage crews, navy yard, and war-plant workers had put all but five of the ships back in service by May 11, 1943—only seventeen months after the sneak attack.

Some 1,300 miles northwest of Hawaii a small garrison of American Marines was located on the little group of islands that has made the name of Midway historic—but five miles long and five miles wide. A cable station and a refueling base for trans-Pacific commercial planes were located on this oldest insular possession of the United States, a trophy of the Spanish-American War. But Midway was not too tiny to be ignored by the Japanese. A pair of destroyers or light cruisers and a flock of planes bombed and strafed the pitiful cluster of houses and whatever installations were on the island.

Twelve hundred miles southwest of Midway, and 2,300 miles from Pearl Harbor, lay a still smaller group of islands only four and one-half miles long and a mile and one-half across. The three islets—Peale, Wilkes, and Wake—go under the name of Wake Island which the United States also possessed as a result of the Spanish-American War. A cable relay station and an airplane stop were the main activities on Wake, but Japanese ships and planes struck there, too, on December 7, 1941. The small Marine garrison answered gallantly with what fire it could muster.

The Philippine Clipper, on a regular commercial flight from San Francisco to Singapore, had arrived at Treasury Island from Wake and was gaining altitude for the hop to Guam when the commandant at Wake Island radioed that hostilities had been begun and advised the plane to return immediately. Twenty minutes later the big aircraft settled in the protected waters of Wake Island. With no planes of his own to help, the Commandant asked the Clipper pilot to make a patrol flight to see what might be approaching. After his return the pilot reported what he had been able to discover, and while walking from that conference to his plane, ducked behind a large water pipe as nine Japanese fighting planes in close formation swept in at 1,500 feet. One squadron strafed the construction camp and the other circled the islands dropping 150-pound bombs for five minutes. The Pan-American building and dock were set afire and the Clipper bore decorations in the form of sixteen holes from machine-gun bullets.

The pilot rounded up the Pan-American personnel and left immediately for Midway. When forty miles off that island he saw two Japanese warships heading for Wake, after having shelled Midway. The latter island was completely blacked out when the Clipper landed amid the wreckage of the little harbor.

Slightly more than 1,500 miles to the southwest of Wake, and about halfway to the Philippines, was another isolated American possession completely surrounded by Japanese-mandated islands—Guam. Here was a relatively large island, thirty miles long and from four to eight and one-half wide. The navy had maintained it as an important station for the Asiatic Fleet, and there was a powerful radio station on the island. Guam had always been a thorn in Japan's side.

Guam was the only island of the Marianas, or Ladrones, not under Japanese mandate. The important enemy base of Saipan was only 128 miles to the north. Rota was sixty-three miles away. Truk, the powerful key-base built up by the Japs in the west-central Pacific, was 635 miles to the southeast and Yap was less than 500 miles southwest. Guam was literally besieged even before the first shot had been fired. At 8:45 on the morning of December 7 eighteen land-based bombers swooped down upon Guam and immediately wrecked the radio station. Then they went after harbor installations and other military targets. The mine-sweeper *Penguin* was sunk. Warships appeared offshore and opened a bombardment. At 4:45 in the afternoon six more planes came over to pick out objectives that might have escaped. Guam was cut off from the rest of the world at the outset but had not surrendered.

Sixteen hundred miles to the west lay the Philippine Islands, now bursting into flames. Nineteen hundred miles southwest of Manila stood Singapore, Great Britain's bastion in the Pacific. Five days before Japan struck, a squadron of British warships headed by the 35,000-ton *Prince of Wales,* the newest and mightiest battleship afloat, and the 32,000-ton *Repulse* had steamed into the naval base at the tip of the Malayan Peninsula.

On December 7 hundreds of Japanese were gathered to celebrate at riotous drinking parties in the geisha houses and hotels of Singapore. A few hours later two flights of Japanese bombers swooped in suddenly over the city and the fortifications and let loose their loads of destruction before the alarm could be sounded. Antiaircraft fire hit the invaders hard. By midnight all the Japanese celebraters had been rounded up and interned. Their advance information of what was coming had not been shared with the British colonial officials.

The day before all this happened the State Department in Washington had disclosed that despite her assurances not to reinforce her garrisons in French Indo-China, Japan had massed 82,000 soldiers in the south and 25,000 in the north. Eighteen thousand men were aboard transports in Cam Ranh Bay and two large convoys had been sighted off Point Camau steaming into the Gulf of Siam. Why they had been there and where they were going was revealed the next day. On December 7 the Japanese invaded Thailand from Indo-China on the south. After a brief resistance the greatly outnumbered Thai forces surrendered and the invaders entered Bangkok, the capital. From there they rushed through the country toward Malaya and Burma.

At the gates of China, seven hundred miles northwest of the Philippines and twice as far north of Singapore, lay the British Crown Colony of Hongkong in Kowloon Harbor, China. Ten Japanese planes came over on the morning of December 7 and smashed the docks at Kowloon. A second flight hit Hongkong in the afternoon. Still farther north, and on the mainland, the Japanese quickly occupied the waterfront at Shanghai and the International Settlement. A British gunboat was sunk by enemy planes, and a United States gunboat was seized. The "China Incident" Japan had started in 1931 became merged with the war in the Pacific and World War II.

WAR IN THE PACIFIC—ITS MAGNITUDE AND PROBLEMS

THE arena in which the Pacific War was fought is so vast that it challenges the imagination. The distances to be traversed by ships, planes, and armies challenged, too, the genius of naval and army commanders and home front to keep them supplied.

The war front on which the destiny of half the population of the earth was to be decided covered half the globe. The Pacific Ocean itself, which was one vast battlefield, has an estimated area of about 70,000,000 square miles and the Indian Ocean about 30,000,000, a total water area of 100,000,000 square miles. This is more than twice the extent of the continents of Europe, Asia, Africa, North and South America combined. The entire United States, with its 3,000,000 square miles, could be dropped into the Pacific, which would hold twenty-three countries its size.

The struggle in the Pacific, like that in Europe but over far more extended areas, was a one-front war with many widely separated but closely integrated sectors. Every battle was another step on the long road to Tokyo. Every man in this great crusade for human freedom was fighting to keep the Japs from the doors to his homeland, for Japanese war documents revealed that they planned to strike at the western coast of the United States in a plotted invasion. These plans were timed with Hitler's grandiose scheme to sink the American and British Navies in the Atlantic in submarine warfare, and to bombard New York and the cities of the eastern coast while the Japs bombarded San Francisco and the western coast cities.

The plans of both Germany and Japan were to force the United States into a two-front war and keep it so engaged that Hitler could send armies from Dakar, in Africa, to land on the coast of South America, thus creating a third front on the south. Under this pressure from three sides, he believed that democracy in the United States would crumble and crash. For this purpose he had further created a formidable "Fifth Column" to undermine faith and confidence in the Government, to rise up at the appointed time in a reign of terror and sabotage.

The vast extent of Japan's simultaneous activities was the final proof that she had planned long and carefully for her multiple strokes. On that fateful December 7, 1941, she had thrown into action well over 1,000 vessels of war: battleships, carriers, submarines, mine layers, and auxiliary craft. Hundreds of transports were crowded with hundreds of thousands of troops, accompanied by hosts of supply ships proceeding to designated points on a meticulously worked-out time-table.

This secret armada was spreading out over the Pacific with such startling precision that it devoured everything before it. Like a huge spider web it stretched for thousands of miles and gathered islands and nations into its net.

America and all its outposts were in peril. The heavy responsibility of protecting this country from a direful fate fell upon the shoulders of admirals and generals at their posts. As we have seen at the attack on Pearl Harbor our Hawaiian Islands outpost was under command of Lieutenant General Short, who had entered the army in 1902 as a second lieutenant. He had served in the Philippines and in Mexico and made an excellent record in World War I in the battles of the Aisne-Marne, St. Mihiel, and the Meuse-Argonne, with the First Division of the A.E.F. After having held several intervening commands, he was placed in charge of the Hawaiian Command on February 8, 1941.

General Short, as has been noted, was removed from active service after Pearl Harbor and succeeded by Lieutenant General Delos C. Emmons, one of the army's most air-minded officers. General Emmons lacked only a month of having reached his fifty-fourth birthday when he took over the Hawaiian Command. He was graduated from West Point in 1907 and entered the air force in 1917, passing through the aviation section of the signal corps and serving at various airfields. In 1934, after having completed his work at the army's Command and General Staff School, he was sent to Hawaii as commanding officer of the Eighteenth Composite Wing and Air Officer of the Hawaiian Department with headquarters at Fort Shafter. In March, 1939, he was promoted to Commanding General of the General Headquarters Air Force at Langley Field, and on June 20, 1941, became Chief of the Air Force Combat Command.

Rear Admiral Kimmel had held important posts with the navy prior to taking command of the Pacific Fleet on February 1, 1941, when he was promoted to full admiral. Among his earlier assignments was special duty with Franklin D. Roosevelt in 1915, when the man who became war President was Assistant Secretary of the Navy. Admiral Kimmel's chief aide on December 7 was Rear Admiral Claude C. Bloch who had fought through the Spanish-American War, and during World War I, when he ran the transport *Plattsburg* safely through the German U-boat and mine blockade on four trips. Various command posts were filled by Admiral Bloch before he became Commander in Chief of the United States Fleet on January 29, 1938, after which he was named Commandant of the Fourteenth Naval District at Hawaii. He was exonerated of all responsibility for the events at Pearl Harbor on December 7 and retained his post until April 13, 1942, when he was replaced by Admiral David W. Bagley, until Admiral Chester W. Nimitz could take over command. Admiral Bloch returned to Washington as special adviser to Navy Secretary Knox, and later in the year was appointed to the reorganized General Board of the Navy.

In the Philippines three of the most stalwart warriors in the military and naval history of the United States stood guard over American interests: Admiral Thomas C. Hart, Commander in Chief of the Asiatic Fleet; General Douglas MacArthur, Commander of the Philippine Department; and Major General Jonathan M. Wainwright, commanding ground forces.

Admiral Hart was graduated from Annapolis in 1897, just in time to get into the Spanish-American War. Most of his experience was in the Pacific, fitting him perfectly for the test that came to him in his sixty-fifth year. During World War I, he was called to the Atlantic and placed at the head of the submarine and tender forces in European waters. Later he received other important assignments, mainly with submarine forces, and for three years served as Superintendent of the Naval Academy at Annapolis. On July 25, 1939, he became Commander in Chief of the Pacific Fleet.

General Jonathan M. Wainwright, one of the most brilliant tacticians in the United States Army, was born to both the army and the Philippines. His father had commanded a squadron of the First Cavalry at the battle of Santiago and had died in the Philippines uprising of 1901. General Wainwright was graduated from West Point in 1906 and commissioned a second lieutenant in the cavalry. He was assigned to his father's old First Cavalry and first saw action against the Moros in Jolo, during the 1909 troubles in the Philippines.

When World War I broke out, General Wainwright was sent to Plattsburg to help organize the Seventy-sixth Division, and then went to France where, as a lieutenant colonel with the Eighty-second Division, he fought brilliantly in the St. Mihiel and Meuse-Argonne offensives. In 1940 he returned to the Philippines to whip the modern Thirty-first Infantry into fighting trim, after which he served as instructor in the Philippine Army Command and Staff School. Ordered to organize a new infantry division in Luzon, he was given the temporary rank of major general. He was thus engaged on December 7.

During the first weeks and months the tidal wave swept everything before it. Premier Tojo was repeating on land and by sea his Pacific version of Hitler's blitzkriegs in Poland, western Europe, and Russia. Defeat followed defeat for the staggered United Nations. Our occasional tactical victories won at the cost of precious lives served neither to hinder nor to halt the strategical advances by the Japanese.

During the first week of the war the enemy took full advantage of the element of surprise. Previously deployed forces moved with clock-like precision toward their objectives. Some two hundred United States Marines at Tientsin and Peiping in China were quickly disarmed and interned. The Japanese Army that had moved into Thailand, pressed right on into Malaya, and toward Burma. Hongkong was raided by hostile planes and the Philippines were subjected to heavy bombings. All this took place on December 8. On the Allied side Britain declared war on Japan. China, ending the fiction of the "Chinese Incident," also declared war on Japan and ranged herself at the side of the United Nations by declaring war also on Germany and Italy.

December 10 brought Japan a victory only slightly less complete than the one at Pearl Harbor. Admiral Sir Tom Spencer Vaughan Phillips, Commander of the British Far East Fleet, signaled from his flagship the 35,000-ton *Prince of Wales* to the battleship *Repulse* and other vessels, steaming out of Singapore on December 9:

"We are out looking for trouble and no doubt we shall find it. We hope to surprise the enemy transports tomorrow and we expect to meet the Japanese battleship *Kongo*. I am sure everyone will give a good account of himself."

The British had set out to annihilate the immense Japanese armada sailing up the Gulf of Siam and scheduled to land on Malaya to conquer the Peninsula. But an enemy reconnaissance plane spotted the British battleships during the day. The warships changed their course during the night and the tack seemed to have worked until, at eleven o'clock in the morning of December 10, eight Japanese planes were spotted flying at 15,000 feet. The battle was promptly joined. A torrent of bombs straddled both the *Prince of Wales* and the *Repulse*. Massed antiaircraft batteries opened up simultaneously. One 15-inch armor-piercing shell dropped from a high-flying bomber stabbed the catapult deck of the *Repulse*, penetrated the Marines' mess deck and started a fire.

The first high-level attack was followed by a swarm of torpedo planes. Dropping down from all directions, they skimmed close over the sea's surface discharging hundreds of lethal "tin fish." The *Repulse* dodged nineteen torpedoes, but one caught the *Prince of Wales* in the stern at 11:40, putting the rear armament out of action and cutting down the battleship's speed. A second attack was launched from on high by thirty-five bombers. Both ships escaped with near misses. Then the final assault began, reaching a fury never before equalled in intensity. The thirty-five vertical bombers had been rejoined by fifty or more torpedo bombers. Reckless Japanese pilots swooped and zoomed from all points in the compass, barely avoiding crashing into one another. The sight of both warships burning seemed to spur the enemy to frenzy.

In one hour and a half the only two capital ships the Allies had in the Pacific were sent to the bottom of the ocean. The quick seizure by the Japanese of the Malayan airfields had deprived the battleships of air support, leaving them vulnerable to and unprotected against the kind of slaughter to which they had been subjected. Neither ship blew up, thus enabling more than 2,000 men to be saved by destroyers and British aircraft that finally reached the scene from distant fields after the battle was over. An explosion would have killed most of the crew floundering through the water so thick with oil that progress was almost impossible. Nearly 600 British sailors and marines lost their lives.

By sinking the *Repulse* and the *Prince of Wales*—the latter ship the scene of the Roosevelt-Churchill meeting only a few months earlier at which the Atlantic Charter was drawn up—the Japanese succeeded in accomplishing in three days of war what Germany had not been able to do in more than two years.

Additional dark touches to this black day included heavy Japanese landings on northern Malaya. The Japanese also put some small detachments ashore on Luzon below Manila in the Philippines; an attempt was made to invade Hongkong; the Japanese occupied three American islands in the Gilberts and attacked Nauru and Ocean Islands a little to the south. Cavite naval base at Manila was bombed. The message was received from Guam: "Last attack centered at Agana. Civilians machine-gunned in streets. Two native wards of hospital and hospital compound machine-gunned. Building in which Japanese nationals are confined bombed."

That was the last direct word from the 400 Navy men and 155 Marines garrisoning the outpost. Guam had been mercilessly attacked for three days. On December 8, twenty-four Japanese planes had come over in two waves, sinking the mine sweeper *Penguin*. Construction workers on projects laid down their tools and manned machine guns. During the short hopeless struggle the Americans made the enemy pay heavily, sinking seven naval craft and downing a number of airplanes.

Out of the gloom in the Philippines burst suddenly a bright ray. A Japanese battleship had been sunk off the coast. Captain Colin P. Kelly, Jr., a twenty-six-year-old West Point graduate, had flown his bomber over the 29,000-ton *Haruna*. His bombardier, Corporal Meyer Levin, had planted a bomb squarely on the ship, leaving it in flames and sinking. The plane was on a mission off Aparri, the north coast of Luzon, when the enemy craft was sighted. Captain Kelly, scorning the heavy antiaircraft fire, held the plane on a straight course over the ship. One of the bombs fell just to port of the target, another just to starboard, the third struck amidships.

Captain Kelly went on to complete his observation mission and was the last of his squadron to return home. As his plane was nearing Clark Field, it was set upon by two Zeros which had been hiding behind a cloud. They attacked from the rear. Cannon and machine-gun bursts rattled all through the ship. Staff Sergeant William J. Delehanty, the flight engineer, was killed at one of the machine guns. The oxygen system caught fire. The ship burst into flames. Captain Kelly ordered all men to bail out. Before he, himself, could get away the plane exploded and America's first World War II hero perished.

By the end of the first week of the Pacific War the Japanese had landed in force on Malaya and brought one-man tanks into the steaming jungles to help crush the British defenders. The British had abandoned Kowloon on the mainland and had retired to the island fortress of Hongkong. The Japanese had landed strong forces on the Philippines and begun a pincers movement toward Manila.

With control of the sea and superiority or control of the air the Japanese pushed their landing barges through, regardless of casualties. The enemy did not make the mistake of trying to land in overwhelming strength at a single point where he would be met by the full force of the defense. He established beachheads at numerous widely scattered points, compelling the defenders to spread their meager resources over a wide area, weak everywhere and strong nowhere. Inasmuch as reinforcements for Malaya or the Philippines were out of the question, it was a simple matter for the Japanese to build up the necessary numerical superiority wherever they desired.

During this first week United States bombers sunk, besides the *Haruna,* at least four transports off northern Luzon and damaged three others. Dutch submarines had sent four more troop-laden transports to the bottom off Thailand. The campaign of attrition against Japanese manpower and shipping had got off to a good start.

The tempo of the Japanese advance grew faster during the second week. Having knocked out sea and air opposition from Malaya, the enemy was able to concentrate upon overwhelming the heavily outnumbered British, Australian, and Indian soldiers. Pushing forward with amazing rapidity through the jungles and swamps infested by tigers, rhinoceroses, vampires, and serpents, the Japanese were halfway down the Malay Peninsula to Singapore. Penang had been evacuated, the southern tip of Burma had been yielded to the enemy, and the Japanese had landed on north Borneo and Sarawak. To counter these latter advances, Australian and Dutch troops occupied Portuguese Timor to keep the Axis out. Farther to the south the Australian Government ordered civilian evacuation of Papua and New Guinea.

The Japanese had been able to make little progress in the Philippines until the end of the second week when they landed in force on the southern end of Luzon. Fierce fighting was going on around Davao, on Mindanao, where the Japanese were trying desperately to establish an air base for use against Luzon and for protection of transports and warships.

On December 16 the Japanese reappeared in Hawaiian waters for the first time when the docks at Kahului on Maui, one hundred miles from Honolulu, and installations on Johnston Island were shelled. Later during the week submarines appeared off the California coast, sinking a few ships and coming to within twenty miles of land. One American tanker, after being fired on, turned to ram the Japanese raider.

The bright streaks in the second week of the war included the cheering messages from Wake Island: 378 Marines and seven medical officers were holding off attacks by sea, air, and land with only light weapons and twelve fighter planes. No more than four were in operation at any one time. There was no fort or protected quarters on the little island. The only armament consisted of six 5-inch guns, two 3-inch antiaircraft guns; eighteen 50-caliber and thirty 30-caliber machine guns plus rifles and side arms. Most of the planes had been destroyed or damaged during four sea and air attacks on December 9, but the defenders sank a light cruiser and a destroyer. On December 14-15 forty-one Japanese bombers destroyed the airfield and other installations. The next day submarines joined the attack. A constant battle was waged until the twenty-first. The garrison had lost the island's power plant and all but one battery of guns. Yet in response to a query from Washington if anything was needed, Wake Island radioed back: "Send us more Japs."

Lieutenant Boyd D. Wagner, of Johnstown, Pennsylvania, known to his men as "Buzz," made air history during that second week. He had already won acclaim by his heroism on December 8, when over Aparri, northern Luzon, he attacked five Japanese pursuit ships all by himself, shot two out of the sky, machine-gunned a dozen more on the ground, and then reported: "My gas was running low so I returned home." All this despite wounds received when an enemy shell struck the canopy of his plane and fragments showered into his eyes and face.

Ten days later Lieutenant Wagner led a raid on the new Japanese airfield at Vigan, blasting a nest of twenty-six enemy planes and removing, for the moment, a threat to Manila. During the first two weeks of the war he had shot down a total of five planes and ruined a score or more on the ground. The first pursuit pilot to win the Distinguished Service Cross and America's first "ace" of the war, his career came to a sudden end when a year later a single-engine plane he was flying on a routine trip crashed back home in Florida.

During the second week United States submarines sank another Japanese destroyer and a transport, and Netherlands fliers got three more troopships and three warships. MacArthur in the Philippines was elevated to full general, the first field commander to receive four-star rank in World War II.

Three weeks after Pearl Harbor, Prime Minister Churchill arrived unexpectedly in Washington, on December 22, for the first of a series of war conferences that were to demonstrate the solidarity of the anti-

Axis nations. He conferred for several days with President Roosevelt and highest military officers. Agreement was reached that Hitler was to be considered the first menace to be removed, on the sound premise that, with Germany out of the war, Japan could not long threaten the rest of the world. Conversely, the Reich would not be seriously affected by a defeat of Japan. However, Mr. Churchill and President Roosevelt agreed on joint action in the Pacific and laid down the broad outlines of Allied strategy in that theater. The Prime Minister addressed a joint session of Congress and gave solemn assurance that Britain would fight at the side of the United States until Japan had been so thoroughly defeated she never again would be able to upset the peace.

A few days later, on Christmas Day, Generalissimo Chiang Kai-shek called a meeting in Chungking to create a Pacific War Council. General Sir Archibald P. Wavell, hero of Britain's drive in Libya, and Major General George H. Brett, Chief of the United States Army Air Corps attended. It was announced on January 2 that General Wavell had been placed in Supreme Command of the Southwest Pacific. General Brett would be his deputy and in command of air activities. Admiral Hart would direct naval operations. Generalissimo Chiang was Supreme Commander for China.

While these Allied conferences were preparing for eventual offensive action, Japan pushed forward during the third week of the war for some of her most important victories. On December 22, the day after they had asked for "more Japs," the defenders on Wake Island were subjected to fierce assaults. The enemy attempted to land, but all sallies were repelled and two destroyers were sunk. Pressure was increased the next day and the Japanese managed to land a number of men. On December 24 more than two hundred enemy planes hit the island and thousands of Japanese troops poured ashore. Wake Island sent out its last message: "The issue is still in doubt."

For more than sixteen days the gallant band on Wake Island, under Major James P. S. Devereux, U.S.M.C., had stood off the best the enemy could offer. His few guns and the planes under Major Paul A. Putnam had sunk seven Japanese warships, damaged two more, and shot down at least a dozen enemy planes.

The next day was Christmas. The sixteen-day siege of Hongkong ended. The British Government instructed Governor Sir Mark Young to stop the hopeless slaughter. The Japanese Navy, under Vice Admiral Masaichi Niimi, had set a blockade around the port on the first day of the war. Lieutenant General Takashi Sakai had launched his first heavy attack on December 9 and never removed the pressure until the surrender. The ill-fated British garrison consisted of about 12,000 men from Scotland, England, Canada, and India. It was under the command of Brigadier J. K. Lawson, of London, Ontario, who only six weeks before had proudly taken command of the Royal Rifles of Quebec and the Winnipeg Grenadiers, and set sail for Hongkong. There were some 2,000 men in the Canadian contingent.

Twice during those sixteen days Brigadier Lawson scornfully rejected demands for surrender. During the last eight days, following withdrawal to the island from Kowloon, Hongkong suffered forty-five air attacks. For the last seven days it was under constant artillery fire from the shore, from navy guns at sea, and eventually from batteries on the heights of Hongkong itself. For the last five days the garrison was cut off from communication with the rest of the world. For the last three days it had no water or lights. The defense was as stalwart as it was brilliant. Tokyo paid its respects to the bravery of the garrison. On December 22, a shell burst and killed Brigadier Lawson and his senior staff officer Colonel Patrick Hennessey. Colonel W. J. Horne of the Quebec Royal Rifles assumed command. In the final phases of the struggle, when casualties were so severe that guns remained unmanned, Americans in Hongkong took over the vacant positions. When surrender finally came, the Japanese were within a few hundred yards of the headquarters.

The very thought of losing Singapore shook the British Empire more profoundly than the actual defeats already suffered. To calm public feeling already aroused over the loss of the *Prince of Wales* and the *Repulse,* and in an effort to delay the Japanese until new naval and air units might reach the Singapore area, the Government named Lieutenant General Sir Henry Pownall as Commander in Chief in the Far East, to replace Air Chief Marshal Sir Robert Brooke-Popham.

On Christmas Day General MacArthur in the Philippines proclaimed Manila an open city. He wished to spare the 625,000 inhabitants the torture of air attacks. But the Japanese had no more regard for Philippine civilians than they had shown for Chinese non-combatants. Their bombers and strafers flew over the defenseless city day after day.

When the third week opened, a Japanese flotilla of eighty transports appeared off Luzon between Lingayan and Agoo, about 110 miles northwest of Manila. About the same time another flotilla of forty transports approached 135 miles southeast of the city. By the end of the week there were 200,000 enemy troops ashore with artillery, tanks, and planes. Manila had been ringed by the enemy. At one point, Lamon Bay to the southeast, the enemy was within fifty-five miles of the city. Heavy fighting was in progress on the Lingayan front. General MacArthur took the field to direct operations in the hour of crisis.

The "Flying Tigers" had made their first appearance far across the China Sea when they shot down four Japanese bombers raiding Kunming near the Burma Road on December 20. Five days later, another Christmas episode, 108 Japanese planes, equally divided between bombers and fighters, came suddenly down upon Rangoon in Burma. Three "Flying Tigers" managed to get off the ground before the raiders were over the target, and the trio of modern musketeers sailed into the enemy. Despite the ridiculous odds of thirty-six to one against them, the Americans held off the invaders until the R.A.F. reached the scene. At least thirty-one Japanese planes were destroyed.

The boys in the Philippines maintained the daredevil pace of the preceding fortnight. There is space here for only a fraction of their daring exploits. Navy Lieutenant C. A. Keller, of Wichita, Kansas, sighted the enemy battleship *Kongo* off northwest Luzon. Despite heavy antiaircraft fire, he kept the ship in sight until the other planes of his squadron arrived under command of Lieutenant Commander J. V. Peterson. The attack was pressed and hits were scored, leaving the ship definitely out of control and seriously damaged. Navy Lieutenant H. T. Utter attacked three Japanese planes single-handed. After one had been shot down, the other two fled. Lieutenant Utter landed his damaged plane at sea, taxied to shore, repaired the plane, and then flew back to base the next day. Lieutenant Jack C. K. Dale, of Willoughby, Ohio, almost broke up one heavy landing when he attacked a group of transports off the Philippines, silenced their antiaircraft guns and then swept down to strafe the landing barges. Lieutenant Samuel H. Merett, leading a squadron against enemy transports trying to land on Luzon, set two afire and then, when his plane was damaged beyond control, dove it into a third where he and his comrades perished in the resulting explosion that wrecked the transport.

The honor roll grew with each hour. Lieutenant Joseph H. Moore led a group through machine-gun fire to their grounded planes and took off after the raiders. When one American airplane was hit, the Japanese started to machine-gun the pilot who bailed out. Lieutenant Moore dove into the center of the group of five, downed two and distracted the others until the falling pilot had made good his landing. Captain Hewitt T. Wheless, of Menard, Texas, was on a bombing mission against two transports when he was attacked by eighteen Japanese planes near Legaspi, southern Luzon. In the ensuing battle the bomber's gun crew shot down seven enemy planes and capsized the transports. Private William C. Killin, the radio operator, was killed at his gun in the belly turret. Corporal William W. Williams took his place and was shot through the leg. Sergeant John M. Gootee, at one side gun, operated both weapons. When he was shot in the wrist, he tied up the wound with his handkerchief and kept on shooting. Lieutenant William F. Neenagh, the navigator, alternated with the other gunners as did Lieutenant Taborek, the co-pilot, and Sergeant Albert H. Cellette, the bombardier, after he had got away 4,800 pounds of bombs.

The Japs followed Captain Wheless until they ran out of ammunition. Two of his four engines had been shot out, the radio was not working, the oxygen system had been wrecked, only four of eleven cables operating the plane were left. The big bomber was punctured with 1,500 bullet holes. But Captain Wheless held true to his course and landed safely on his home field despite the barricades.

The United Nations drank deep from the cup of defeat in the fourth week of the war. At the moment that President Roosevelt, in Washington, was pledging that freedom of the Philippines would be redeemed and the Commonwealth's independence established, the Japanese were bombing the unprotected city of Manila for two hours and forty-five minutes, leaving it a mass of flaming wreckage. The enemy was only forty-five miles from the city. General MacArthur shortened his lines in preparation for the final stand on Bataan Peninsula. On December 30, Manuel Quezon, President of the Philippines, and Vice President Sergio Osmeña appeared in an underground refuge near General MacArthur's field headquarters. There, in the presence of the General, they were inaugurated for a second term.

While the brief ceremony was taking place, American and Filipino forces were retreating on both the north and south fronts. Japanese dive-bombers controlled the roads, and enemy tanks and armored equipment pushed hard on the heels of the retreating defenders. The invaders were only thirty miles south of Manila and sixty miles north. The next day saw the Japs landing on Luzon in large numbers, while the defenders held a semicircular line about two hundred miles long around Manila.

In far-off Malaya the enemy was pushing closer to coveted Singapore day by day. The famous British base was under constant aërial bombardment. Martial law had been proclaimed. Sarawak, the British protectorate on the north coast of Borneo, fell to the Japs on December 31.

32

MacARTHUR LEADS THE FIGHT TO SAVE THE PHILIPPINES—THE FALL OF MANILA

FOUR hours after Japan had delivered her treacherous attack at Pearl Harbor she struck at the Philippines. This was at noon on December 7, 1941. At that moment there began the first great epic of America in World War II. It also brought instantly to the front a name that was to resound around the world as a symbol of American courage, character, and power—MacArthur.

Tested in the crucible of war—leading his forces against crushing odds on the first battlegrounds of the war in the Pacific—this stalwart American was to rise from defeat into epoch-making victory. We shall meet him frequently in this history—the redoubtable General who was to administer retributive justice to the Japanese.

The Philippines, which MacArthur himself calls "the key that unlocks the door to the Pacific," comprise an archipelago of 7,083 islands of which only 2,441 have been explored and named. The riches in over 73,000,000 acres of virgin forest, sugar cane plantations, coconut groves, fields of hemp, and untapped mountain mines, are beyond calculation. This potential wealth was coveted by Japan.

The Filipinos are an intelligent, industrious people who were making tremendous progress under their own constitution. This provided for a republic with its own powers as a free government, its own National Assembly and judicial system, its own highly developed educational system, and its own Bill of Rights granting freedom of press, speech, and religion. Its people had elected the patriot Manuel Quezon as their President and Sergio Osmeña as Vice President. The United States High Commissioner was Francis B. Sayre, son-in-law of Woodrow Wilson. Complete Philippine independence, as proclaimed in 1935, was to become finally effective in 1946. General MacArthur was building an army to establish the security of the islands when they should take their place as an independent nation.

The Japs struck at the Philippines five years before General MacArthur could complete his plans to make the islands impregnable. At midday on December 7, they came in waves of aërial bombers over Clark Field, sixty-five miles from Manila. In perfect formation, fifty-two bombers flying at 20,000 feet altitude dropped their bombs in a straight line across Clark Field. It was like the sudden break of a thunderstorm with lightning striking everywhere at once. The soldiers had just finished their lunch. A mess truck driving across the field was blown to bits, and two drivers were instantly killed. From every direction at once, crisscrossing each other, Japanese pursuit planes dove in over the field. American planes took off instantly and the first dog fights of the Pacific war were in full swing.

The Japs were feeling their way while large invasion fleets bearing tens of thousands of men stood out at sea, waiting for the signal to come in. The United States Asiatic Fleet had its headquarters at Cavite near Manila on the principal island of Luzon. The United States Army had a sizable force of regulars assisted by a national army known as the Philippine Scouts and a new constabulary organized only seven months before by General MacArthur. The Philippines were defended by an efficient air force and protected by coastal batteries. Munitions chambers were well stocked. Manila Bay was almost landlocked, with Cavite on the south, Bataan Peninsula on the north, and the fortress island of Corregidor in the narrow channel.

Here was a choice target for the wily Japanese in their lust for conquest. Fleets of bombers attacked central Luzon, Tarlac, seventy miles north of Manila, and Apassi, chief port of northern Luzon. They blasted Camp Ord, one hundred miles north of Manila, and Camp John Hay at the summer capital, Baguio, still farther north. Other aircraft concentrated on Davao and on the southwestern portion of Mindanao, the island south of Luzon which is only slightly smaller. The fleet, under orders of Admiral Thomas C. Hart, was out patrolling adjacent waters and never was in danger from the bombing attacks. The Army, under General MacArthur, was on the alert.

These first attacks obviously were not intended to paralyze the Philippines in the same way in which Pearl Harbor had been laid low. The islands were sufficiently well within the orbit of Japanese sea, air, and land power to be handled in other ways. They were, however, far enough from the United States—nearly 8,000 miles—to render prompt and adequate aid almost impossible. The enemy was satisfied to create what damage he could while reconnoitering for the latest information. The attacks also served to stir the active Japanese Fifth Column groups. These immediately set to work planting lights and other markings.

In the first hours of attack the United States 1,500 ton-destroyer *Preston* was sunk and the aircraft carrier *Langley* was damaged.

On the first night the Japs came back under cover of darkness and bombed Nichols Field in Manila, setting fire to gasoline supplies which flamed up in the night skies. On Manila Bay, one of the finest harbors in the East, with its 770 square miles where ships from all parts of the world found shelter, the naval drydock and repair shops were blasted.

The first bombs fell on Corregidor; and during this fight, Captain Colin Kelly, Jr., piloting an American bomber, roared out to sea and sank the mighty battleship *Haruna,* the first Japanese major loss.

Fall of Manila

On the second day of the war, Lieutenant Boyd Wagner, of Johnstown, Pennsylvania, known to his men as "Buzz," added to the glory of MacArthur's men. He, too, was scouting over Aparri when he attacked five Japanese pursuit planes all by himself. He shot two out of the sky, machine-gunned a dozen more on the ground, and then reported: "My gas was running low so I returned home." Wagner did not complain of the wounds he had received when an enemy shell struck the canopy of his plane.

As the Japanese penetrated the islands from many points and Manila braced itself to meet the crisis, women and children, with fathers and sons, crowded the churches and knelt in prayer. Soon many of these churches, with their schools, hospitals, and colleges, were to fall in ruins. Swarms of Japanese bombers were to hurl tons of bombs on the defenseless capital. This was to be but one more lesson in Japanese treachery.

President Manuel Quezon, beloved first President of the Philippines, walked through the streets of Manila to give his people courage. They knelt at his feet, kissing his hand and crying: "Long live Quezon! God bless Quezon!" As the President entered the cathedral, tears rolled down his cheeks. Little did he realize that soon he would be fleeing to America, never to see his homeland again. Manuel Quezon, tired, worn-out, broken-hearted, was to die in the United States just before the great day of deliverance came to his country.

General MacArthur sat in his headquarters, issuing orders to his troops holding back the enemy hordes on the way to the capital. An officer remarked: "General, the American flag flying from your headquarters makes a fine target for the bombers."

Looking up from the maps on his desk, MacArthur replied quietly: "Take every normal precaution, sir—but we'll keep the flag flying."

General MacArthur comes from a family of famous fighters, born defenders of their country. He has been under fire in five wars. His father, General Arthur MacArthur, also fought in five wars and many Indian campaigns on the American frontiers. His brother, Captain Arthur MacArthur, Jr., of the United States Navy, had fought in every war on the seas in which his country was engaged during his lifetime, when death overtook him and ended a remarkable career. Douglas MacArthur is the son of a Virginia mother, a daughter of the Confederacy, while his father, formerly a colonel in the Union Army, came from Wisconsin. Thus are the North and the South united in the person of a national hero.

Here began one of the most notable father-and-son stories in history. Douglas was born at an army post in Little Rock, Arkansas, on January 26, 1880, and grew up to the whirr of Indian arrows on the plains and the ping of Army bullets on the camp range. The older MacArthur later became Military Governor of the Philippines and, after graduating from West Point at the head of his class and breaking all records with the highest scholastic standing in twenty-five years, the son found himself a second lieutenant in the army of his father, fighting against the murderous Moros.

During the difficulties with Mexico in 1914, the bullets from guerrilla mausers whined past him. Less than four years later he faced the thunderous barrages laid down by the Germans on the Western Front in Europe. Returning from France with the Rainbow Division, the recipient of frequent citations for heroism, MacArthur became Superintendent of the United States Military Academy at West Point. Six years later he was the youngest active major general in the army, and five years after that the youngest full general and chief of staff. In 1935 he was permitted to give up his post in Washington at the request of Manuel Quezon, the newly elected President of the Commonwealth of the Philippines, to become Chief of Staff of the Philippine Army and military adviser to the Government.

As we see General MacArthur at his headquarters in the Philippines, he has gathered about him one of the ablest military staffs that ever faced a crisis. His right arm was Major General Jonathan M. Wainwright. A veteran cavalryman and infantryman, known as "Skinny" at West Point, he commanded the northern front. MacArthur's left arm was Brigadier General Albert M. Jones, fifty-one-year-old Yankee from Massachusetts, graduate of the Army War College and in command of the southern front. In command at Fort Mills on Corregidor Island was Major General George F. Moore, a fifty-five-year-old Texan artillery expert.

In the group of highest-caliber men surrounding MacArthur, we find Major General George M. Parker, Jr., a fifty-three-year-old fighting Iowan; Major General Richard Sutherland, fifty-nine-year-old Marylander, graduate of many military schools, including the École Supérieure de Guerre in Paris; Brigadier General Edward P. King, a last-ditch fighting Georgian; Brigadier General William Brougher, fifty-three-year-old tank expert from Mississippi; Brigadier General William Sharp, fifty-seven-year-old Dakotan, artillery and chemical warfare expert; Brigadier General Hugh G. Casey, Brooklyn-born army engineer; Brigadier General William F. Marquat, coast artilleryman from Seattle; Brigadier General Harold H. George, advanced from colonel by MacArthur for bravery under fire; Brigadier General James Weaver, fifty-three-year-old Ohioan, expert in tank and chemical warfare; Brigadier General Bradford G. Cynoweth, fifty-two-year-old engineer and tank expert, infantry officer from Wyoming; Brigadier General Carl Seals, fifty-nine-year-old infantry specialist from Texas;

Brigadier General Clifford Bluemel, fifty-eight-year-old West Pointer from New Jersey; and a staff of colonels and majors many of whom MacArthur promoted for bravery in action.

Within five months many of these great generals and other officers were to be taken prisoners of war and held incommunicado for more than three years in Japanese prison camps. Trying to outwit MacArthur was Japan's foremost warrior, fifty-seven-year-old General Tomayuki Yamashita, brought in to replace the wily General Homma. The Jap war cry was: "Get MacArthur! Force him to surrender—or kill him!"

Now let us meet General Jonathan M. Wainwright who at a spectacular moment a few weeks later was to be left in command by MacArthur to make the last stand at Bataan and Corregidor. Wainwright, one of the most brilliant tacticians in the United States Army, was a stanch friend of the Philippines. His father had commanded a squadron of the 1st Cavalry at the battle of Santiago and had died in the Philippines uprising of 1901. General Wainwright graduated from West Point in 1906 and was commissioned a second lieutenant in the cavalry. He was assigned to his father's old 1st Cavalry and first saw action against the Moros in Jolo during 1909.

When World War I broke out General Wainwright was sent to Plattsburg to help organize the 76th Division, and then went to France where, as a lieutenant colonel with the 82nd Division, he fought brilliantly in the St. Mihiel and Meuse-Argonne offensives. In 1940 he returned to the Philippines to whip the modern 31st Infantry into fighting trim, after which he served as instructor in the Philippine Army Command and Staff School. Ordered to organize a new infantry division in Luzon, he was given the temporary rank of Major General.

On Christmas Day, 1941, General MacArthur, in his desire to save the 625,000 inhabitants and the historic buildings of Manila from bombing, proclaimed it an "open city." But the Japanese had no more regard for Philippine women and children than they had shown for noncombatants in China. Bombers and strafers flew over the defenseless city day after day, sowing death and ruin.

When General MacArthur pulled his lines back into the hills northwest of Manila, he indicated for the first time his intention to retire to Bataan Peninsula instead of following the example of the old Filipino insurgent Aguinaldo who in 1898 fell back into the mountains and fought a guerrilla war for years.

The Asiatic Fleet had withdrawn to the south leaving the islands to be defended by ground troops, the forts and a few PT (Patrol Torpedo)-boats, and miscellaneous small craft. The fortifications had been in the process of being strengthened and new air fields were being built when the war broke out, but these were far from complete. Our troops fought under a skilful tactical policy designed to husband their manpower and munitions for a final stand while retarding the enemy's advances through the mountains and along the shores.

Even while the enemy pincers closed about Manila, no attempt was made by General MacArthur or General Wainwright to hold it. The capital had never been blacked out despite persistent Japanese bombings of the "open city." When the enemy entered Manila, the old community, originally built as a fortress in the 16th century by the Spanish Conquistadores, was little more than a wreck. Six thousand flimsy homes had been smashed or burned out. The business center was mainly a pile of rubble and charred timbers. The Pasig River was blocked by the hulks of bombed ships. Docks were in ruins. Besides the old church of Santo Domingo, the splendid cathedral of the Immaculate Conception and the college of San Juan Lateran, with its priceless historical manuscripts, were among the public and religious buildings which had been gutted.

Manila had been in enemy hands only two days when the reign of terror began under the Japanese lash. Brutality and murder became the order of the day. The people were cruelly mistreated. Prisoners, both American and Filipino, were subjected to horrible ordeals and thrown into prisons and concentration camps. The world was shocked by the revelations of savagery when, three years later, the prisoners of Manila were liberated.

33

RUSSO-FINNISH CONFLICT—ITS CAUSES AND RESULTS

LITTLE Finland was one of the war's first tragedies. A republic smaller in area than the State of Montana and with a population only about equal to Missouri, it was crushed between the millstones of combating powers. First it was forced to meet alone the giant Russia, a nation of over 182,000,000 people as opposed to less than 3,888,000 in Finland. Then it was to be linked with Nazi Germany in a second struggle with Russia.

Through that fateful autumn the thunderheads over Finland mounted dangerously. Then, on November 30, 1939, the lightning struck. Russian bombers darkened the sky over Helsinki and began the destruction that was to lay waste a large part of the nation. Red Army troops crossed the Karelian border above Leningrad and started their stoutly contested march on Viborg. Other Soviet forces speared in from the eastern and northern frontiers. The outnumbered Finnish Army, already mobilized, deployed to parry the attack.

Thus was launched one of the biggest little wars in history. It was a war that by its bizarre features and stirring surprises eclipsed for a time Hitler's dramatics on the Continent.

Conflict was a logical sequence in Finland's history. Originally a migrated Mongol-like race ethnologically related to the Magyars, the Finns were first conquered by the Swedes in 1157. Charles XII and Peter the Great partitioned the country, but in 1809 Finland was united to the Russian Empire as an autonomous grand duchy with a parliament of its own. When the First World War came, a clamor for complete independence arose. In December, 1917, after the Germans had defeated the Russians, the Finnish House of Representatives proclaimed Finland an independent and sovereign state. The declaration of independence was confirmed by the treaty of Brest-Litovsk between Germany and Russia, March 3, 1918.

Joined with Russia by the narrow Karelian Isthmus, which points a troublesome finger toward the vital Leningrad region, Finland was drawn between her own tendency toward the democracies and the influence of near-by Russian Communism. The Finns' traditional attitude of semi-truculent defiance toward Russia had its corollary in a position of vigilant suspicion on the part of the Soviet Union.

Then came the German invasion of Poland, and with it Russia's disconcerting treaty of friendship with the Reich. Soviet Russia, advancing into Poland after the conquest of that distressed country by Germany, extended her influence into the Baltic states, Estonia, Latvia, and Lithuania, and made certain demands on Finland to which the Finnish Government refused to accede.

For a few days the Russian march up the Karelian Isthmus progressed methodically, though it met determined resistance, which exacted considerable losses on both sides. Along the two railroads and several highways of the region just beyond the frontier, the Red Army's mass force, augmented by planes and tanks, prevailed over the Finns' guerrilla-like tactics. But when the defenders, fighting backward step by step, finally retired behind their Mannerheim Line, the contending forces began to equalize.

The Mannerheim Line was not a continuous rampart, but a series of individual fortifications scattered across the isthmus in formidable depth. Taking advantage of the region's forbidding terrain—a wild complex of lakes, forests, and marshes—it consisted of interlocking steel-and-concrete and earth-and-timber pillboxes and gun positions which afforded fields of deadly cross fire to isolate every approach.

Here was elemental warfare in the midst of the modern military world. Delayed accounts filtering back to western civilization caught at once the imagination of the people everywhere. It was a saga out of the ages: long winter Arctic nights—temperatures far below zero. Across snowy wastes and through demoniac forests, white-robed warriors flashed like wraiths on skis, battling with tommy guns or closing in death combat with long knives. Here was a form of battle in which the forest-bred Finns and Laplanders were on even terms with their heavily armed adversaries. Striking with stealth and cunning, the Finnish "ski cavalry" lashed like bull-whips at the Russians' flanks and rear. In this weird warfare the Russians' northern lines swayed. Aided by blizzards and an extraordinarily cold winter, and by the Russians' ill adaptation to such severe battle conditions, the Finns notched their guns with a string of stunning successes.

The almost legendary valor of the Finns appealed to the heart of the world. In the United States, France, Great Britain, and Scandinavia the people strongly favored the Finns' cause. Finland had won high regard in America by paying cash regularly on her debt from World War I long after other nations had defaulted. Her integrity was unimpeachable. She had captivated millions as a small nation of big accomplishments. Her native industry and thrift, her progressive social and economic legislation, her leadership in modern architecture and artisanship, her rapidly expanding cultural background—these were factors that gained admiration.

Sympathy in the United States, where Finns have become stalwart American citizens, had been demonstrated many times before the conflict. President Roosevelt's move in removing the embargo on the shipment of arms to favored belligerents, despite the American policy of neutrality, had brought a response of protest from the Kremlin. When the Finno-Russian negotiations reached their crisis, Secretary of State Cordell Hull, after consultation with Mr. Roosevelt, offered Washington's good offices in the effort to reach an amicable settlement. The note reached Moscow a few hours before hostilities began.

Soon after the fighting started, Congress and other governmental agencies sought means of sending financial help to Finland, including the diversion of war-debt payments. Public reaction was expressed in the opening of a Finnish relief organization in New York under the chairmanship of former President Hoover. Volunteers enrolled to go to Helsinki, some for ambulance duty, others for combat service.

Britain almost immediately sent arms, ammunition, and gasoline. France debated a declaration of war against Russia and proposed sending troops to Finland. Italy, interested in husbanding her interests in the Balkans by keeping Russia engaged in the north, sent planes and pilots, transported by way of Germany. Sweden and her Scandinavian neighbors, prudently resolved to keep their powder dry, remained in neutral coalition and banned the transport of arms or troops over their territory, but permitted considerable numbers of volunteers to join the Finnish forces.

Spurred on by these promises of practical help, the Finns redoubled their military effort. But the help that actually arrived was too scant to alter the situation and the seesaw battles continued with the power of the Red Army's fighting machine gradually rising.

Almost from the start of the war, the Finns continued to seek a settlement with Russia. But their pleas for an armistice and for the resumption of negotiations went unheeded. Responding to an inflamed public opinion, President Roosevelt and other nations' leaders declared Russia to be an aggressor. The League of Nations, then in its declining days in Geneva, took up the issue.

On December 11, just after Italy had ceased to be a member, the League telegraphed to Moscow, requesting that the Soviet Union halt the war against Finland and submit its demands to negotiation. The proposal had been made by Sweden, supported by Britain. At Britain's suggestion, twenty-four hours were given for an answer. Premier Molotov promptly replied, declining League arbitration on the ground that Russia was not technically at war with Finland.

A committee of the League's Assembly comdemned Russia as an aggressor and urged the Assembly to act. The report was drafted by delegates of Britain, France, Sweden, Portugal, and Bolivia. On December 14 the Assembly adopted the report and further resolved that the USSR had placed itself outside the League of Nations. There was no formal vote of expulsion and no Russian delegate was present. Assenting members of the Council were France, Britain, Bolivia, Belgium, and the Dominican Republic, as well as two new members, South Africa and Egypt.

As the year ended, ushering in the decade of the forties, the weather in the north put an icy clamp on all but the most desultory fighting. In temperatures 25° below zero, motor equipment froze solid, crankcase oils refused to flow, metals snapped like glass, rubber disintegrated. Men slain in battle froze in the grotesque attitudes in which they fell, and even the slightly wounded died of the cold. Only the hardiest of native troops ventured abroad on skis and sleds.

In this weird element the Finns gained world acclaim as snow fighters. The encircling maneuver, one of the oldest principles of warfare, a tactic classically exemplified by the American Indian, became the bane of the cold-benumbed Russian forces. Taking full advantage of their knowledge of the country, the skiing Finns appeared as out of nowhere to stab swiftly at their foe's formations, cut off their columns, surround their remnants and force them into action to their disadvantage.

Finnish planes, darting over Leningrad, dropped leaflets with pictures of poorly equipped Russian troops frozen in Finland and of Russian prisoners sitting before steaming food and smilingly smoking cigarettes. Other leaflets said simply: "This might have been a bomb." Russian bombers over Finland, far more numerous, dropped not leaflets but bombs and returned again and again to Helsinki and other principal southern cities, as well as to strategic junctions and supply points throughout the nation.

But the Russian steamroller, stalled in the snowy cold of the north, still was making only inch-by-inch progress on the Karelian Isthmus and it became plain that Moscow was impatient. Late in December the original commander, General Kyrill A. Meretskoff, was superseded by General Gregory M. Stern, who had become a popular hero in 1938 in the Soviet's Changkufeng "vest-pocket war" in the Far East. With him came General Leonid A. Govoroff, regarded as a preeminent exponent of a Russian military specialty, hurricane artillery fire. Decisive events were brewing before the Mannerheim Line.

The closing week of January, 1940, witnessed what was perhaps the heaviest assault on fixed military positions that had been made in the war up to that time. Tremendous masses of artillery were wheeled up to the Russian line, spanning the isthmus.

Among the novelties introduced by the Russians were armored sleds on which gunners, grenadiers, and infantry pushed across no man's land for close-up assaults on individual pillboxes and gun emplacements. Some of these were towed by tanks as a tentative forerunner to the later use of tank-borne infantry. A variation was a propeller-driven sled, powered by an airplane motor, that swished over the snow at high speed, bearing machine gunners and automatic-rifle men.

Russian gunfire, after blasting in vain at the forts' above-ground structure, was pulled back to points just short of the bastions' front bases. Gradually the earth and stone were blown away until the big shells were exploding deep under the very foundations of the heavy structures. Little by little the forts were lifted from their anchorage in the earth, raising the gun positions above so that the heavy cannons' muzzles were deflected upward and their range destroyed. Thus, one by one, the Finnish guns, which had been proof against destruction or capture, were made impotent by a stratagem.

The turning point was reached about January 26, when the Russians broke the Mannerheim Line's strongest defenses at the town of Summa.

The Red Army moved up the isthmus. Other forces advanced across the ice of the Gulf of Finland and Viborg Bay and captured piecemeal the islands off shore. Having mopped up the shores of Viborg Bay, their forces crossed the ice of the northeastern arm of the Gulf of Finland and won a foothold on the coastal road of the southern Finnish mainland, posing a serious threat to Kotka, Helsinki, and the other principal cities. The progress of Red Army units that had driven in from the eastern frontier above Lake Ladoga accentuated the seriousness of the situation.

At a meeting of the Allied War Council in Paris, on February 6, Premier Edouard Daladier reported that a French and a Polish division were ready to go to Finland. He proposed that Britain supply a Canadian division and that the expedition be sent by way of Sweden; otherwise in British ships to northern Finland or Russia. British Prime Minister Chamberlain, after consulting with his war chiefs in London, rejected the plan. Sweden had refused to let Allied troops cross her territory and the British Admiralty reported that the Russians had mined their waters near Murmansk and set up shore batteries around Petsamo to repel any attack. Later Sweden also rejected the Finns' appeal for military help.

Military phases of the war were approaching their dénouement. Diplomatic activity aimed toward peace began to develop in Stockholm. Reports that peace offers had been made by Moscow through Sweden were soon followed by the announcement that armistice negotiations had been arranged. A Finnish delegation, headed by Premier Ryti, went to Stockholm and was taken to Moscow in a Soviet airliner. The delegates of defeated Finland were received in the Kremlin by Premier Molotov.

Fighting around Viborg and elsewhere went on for four more days while the armistice conference was under way. The treaty of peace was signed on March 12, 1940, at 11:00 P.M. Hostilities ceased the next day —104 days after they had begun. The Russians captured Viborg just before the armistice. The peace treaty was ratified by the Finnish Parliament on March 15 and by the Soviet Presidium on March 20.

The treaty called for the cession to Russia of the entire Karelian Isthmus, including Viborg, the area of Viborg Bay and the shores of Lake Ladoga; certain islands in the Gulf of Finland, already captured; a large strip of north-central Finland around Salla, and part of the Rybachi and Sredni peninsulas on the Arctic coast. Finland further agreed to lease to Russia for thirty years, for use as a naval base, the town of Hangoe and its surrounding waters and islands.

The Soviet Union agreed to give back the occupied Petsamo district, but stipulated that the Finns should not maintain any but the lightest warships on the Arctic coast, and no submarines or planes. The Finns also were obligated to construct a railway from Kandalaksha, on the Russians' Murmansk-Leningrad line, to Kemijaervi, the terminus of a Finnish line leading to the Gulf of Bothnia and Sweden. Russians were to have free transit over this line, and similar privileges in crossing the Petsamo district to Norway. Each nation likewise pledged itself not to join any alliance or coalition directed against the other.

The Finns' mood at the end of the war was indicated by Foreign Minister Tanner: "All that can be said against us is that as a nation we are too small.... Peace has returned to Finland. But what a peace!" Marshal Mannerheim, in his final order of the day, revealed that 15,000 Finns had been killed in action and added: "We have paid to the very last penny any debt we may have owed to the west."

Further events of the World War proved that the Russo-Finnish peace was indeed only an armistice. Not many months later they were to be plunged into another ordeal of bloodshed, destruction, and economic stagnation by entering the global conflict as an ally of Germany.

34

RISING POWER OF RUSSIA IN WORLD ARENA

THE emergence of Russia as a world Power was one of the epoch-making developments in World War II. Here were more than 182,000,000 people, occupying about one-sixth of the earth's land area, who as an aftermath of the First World War had thrown off the shackles of centuries of serfdom and created a new economic and social system under which to live.

How would they react to the cataclysm of events in the outside world? Which side would they take in determining the future of the human race? Would they ally themselves with the Western democracies? Or would they join forces with the rising power of Nazism and Fascism? Building their own Soviet Republics on the foundations of state socialism rather than free enterprise, would they be lured by Germany's declared intentions of destroying the capitalistic countries? Or would they tear off Hitler's disguise and expose him as an impostor and fraud?

Russia was the world's question mark. In her isolation from the rest of the world while engaged in the herculean task of building her own nation on principles which were opposed by her fellow nations, no one knew her strength, resources, and fortitude. She was the enigma of the times. Behind her closed doors, vast economic and social transformations were taking place. Events were to reveal the magnitude of their accomplishment. A people 95 per cent illiterate were in a generation transformed into a people 95 per cent literate, thus reversing the conditions. The barriers of class distinctions had been broken down. Peasantry was giving place to collective farming. Great state-controlled industries were being built in a country where industry had hardly existed.

This was being achieved by what was called "communism," or collective security for the masses directed under rigid discipline by edicts from the Government. There is no doubt that this unparalleled development faced many crucial problems. To weld itself together in so short a time it required compulsory methods with heavy penalties for transgressions. Strictest rules of conformance to plans and policies promulgated by those in power were mandatory. Those who refused to abide by the new order felt the heavy hand of authority.

America, Great Britain, and the nations built on individual initiative and free enterprise, were astounded by this iron rule of a central committee from the proletariat. Lenin, the founder of this system, and his successor, Joseph Stalin, were declared "dictators" in the enforcement of their commands. We, who had achieved our purposes under our own system of human freedom, protested vigorously with honest indignation. We, in the United States, who had performed a constructive miracle under our Constitution and its Bill of Rights with equal opportunity for all, foundations upon which we had built the greatest and freest nation the world had ever known, instinctively and intuitively rejected the new Russian system. It was entirely contrary to all our conceptions of self-government and the rights of man.

This conviction was challenged by Communistic propaganda and groups in our own country whose declared purpose was to overthrow our established Government and impose the "new order" upon us. There was no need in our highly developed nation for such an upheaval. The conditions which engendered it did not exist in our democracy. All attempts to undermine us aroused the American people against this psychological aggression. We were willing that Russians should live under whatever form of government they desired in meeting the exigencies that confronted them, but we demanded the same right to live and work in America under the system which best fulfilled our ideals and aspirations and which had laid the solid foundations upon which our structure of "government of, for, and by the people" had been erected.

This was the situation when World War II broke out. And there never was any equivocation. We remained stolid when Russia first allied herself with Germany. We wholeheartedly extended the hand of brotherhood when she was betrayed by Hitler and allied herself with the forces of democracy. Russia became our brother-in-arms and together with our allies we worked out the plans to carry us to victory.

The progressive steps of this stupendous achievement are herein briefly related. Let us glance for a moment at the magnitude of Russia as she stood on the threshold of decision. The Soviet Republics alone covered a territory nearly four times larger than all Europe and almost equal to the whole North American continent.

In his *Mein Kampf*, Hitler declared that the Reich's destiny lay eastward in European expansion at the expense of the Russians. More than a decade later, while he was climbing his way up the first rungs of his ladder of power, Hitler constantly restated his thesis. At a Nazi Party congress in Nuremberg three years before the war, he said: "If the Urals, with their immeasuable treasure of raw materials, Siberia, with its rich forests, and the Ukraine, with its limitless grain fields, were to lie in Germany, this country under National Socialist leadership would swim in plenty."

The "Bolshevist menace," like the mythical machinations of the Jews and the sins of the western "plutocracies," was set up as a bogy to feed the strife on which Nazism thrived. The burning of the Reichstag building in Berlin in 1933 was attributed to the Communists, and "Reds" became hunted outlaws throughout the Reich. The Germans' enmity toward the Russians was fanned to a frenzied flame in preparation for the battles to come. While this wedge was being driven between the Russian and German peoples, the Soviet Union was launching a new era of friendship with the western Powers, Germany's other potential enemies. Foreign Commissar Maxim Litvinoff went to Washington in November of 1933 and, after his conference with the President, the United States renewed its diplomatic relations with Moscow.

There was widespread resentment and criticism in the west during the Soviet régime's stern liquidation of opposition to its collective farm program, and during the Moscow trials and purges that followed. Similarly, it was a common belief before the war that Russia lacked capacity for industrial enterprise, that Russia's supposedly chaotic transportation system made an effective war effort impossible and that *mujiks* in the mass never would make good soldiers. Berlin's sly propaganda fostered this belief, and Moscow did little to combat it.

The western democracies, still confused by the German-fostered fear of the "Bolshevist menace," remained aloof and diffident toward Russia. When Prime Minister Chamberlain went to Munich to deal with Hitler, he reflected this state of mind by ignoring Moscow, despite Russia's obvious major interest in any European settlement. That Moscow's foreign policy was radically altered at this period was indicated when Litvinoff retired as Commissar of Foreign Affairs in May, 1939, and Premier Vyacheslaff M. Molotov took over his portfolio.

Belatedly, Britain and France sent missions to Moscow in an effort to patch up their delicate relations with Russia. They were eclipsed by German power diplomacy, for Berlin had been quick to seize its opportunity. The Allied envoys were figuratively cooling their heels in an antechamber of the Kremlin when two huge German planes descended on the Moscow Airport on August 23. Out stepped Foreign Minister Joachim von Ribbentrop and thirty-two assistants. A few hours later the Soviet Union signed its ten-year non-aggression treaty with Germany.

Hitler invaded Poland on September 1, with Russia as a passive ally. Within two days Britain and France declared war. Two weeks later Soviet troops joined in the occupation of Polish territory. In October, Lithuania, Latvia, and Estonia yielded naval and air bases to Russia. On November 30 the Red Army invaded Finland. The Russo-Finnish War ended on March 13, 1940. Further relations between Germany and Russia, allies in name but enemies in spirit, became strained.

The blitzkrieg then swept down through Europe. Germany, Italy, and Japan signed a ten-year treaty of alliance in Berlin on September

27, 1940. Just after President Roosevelt was reëlected for his third term in November, Premier Molotov made a ceremonial visit to Berlin. The communiqués pictured an atmosphere of "mutual trust," but the world was sceptical about it. The German friendship for Russia was plainly *ersatz*.

Joseph Stalin announced on New Year's Day, 1941, that Russia was totally mobilized. On January 10, Germany and Russia signed a new pact of friendship, extending their trade agreements. In February the Soviet Union revealed that one-third of its huge budget was earmarked for defense, 24 per cent more than the expenditure of 1940. Foreign Minister Matsuoka of Japan visited Moscow late in March on his way to Berlin to confer with Hitler. He stopped off again on the return trip and signed a Russo-Japanese neutrality pact. When the Nazis attacked Yugoslavia on April 6, Moscow signed a friendship pact with the Yugoslavs.

The Soviet Union's official May Day slogan that year was: "Preparedness." Moscow reported laconically that Germany was sending troops to Finland. Stalin on May 6 succeeded Molotov as Premier, symbolizing his leadership for the first time with an official title. Reports of Russian military movements began to circulate. Foreign diplomats in Russia were forbidden to visit the frontier zones. Rudolf Hess, Deputy Reichsfuehrer and third man in Germany, landed by parachute in Scotland. He had brought a German offer of peace to Britain with the proviso that Hitler receive a free hand, or even help, to destroy the "Bolshevist menace" to the east.

How long the United States could stay out of the war had become more problematical than ever. American ships were taking matériel to Britain and U-boats were attacking them. President Roosevelt accepted the challenge. "Unless the advance of Hitlerism is forcibly checked now," he said, "the Western Hemisphere will be within range of the Nazi weapons of destruction.... We shall give every possible assistance to Britain and to all those who, with Britain, are resisting Hitlerism.... We in the Americas will decide whether and when and where our American interests are attacked and our security threatened. We are placing our armed forces in strategic military position. We will not accept a Hitler-dominated world."

Hitler retorted that "convoy means war."

When Hitler revealed his real intent—the invasion of Russia—he explained his action only by typical rambling sophistries about aggravations that had outworn his patience. "For weeks," he complained, "the Russians have been committing frontier violations. Russian planes have been crossing the frontier again and again to prove that they are the masters.... The march of the German Armies has no precedent. ... The task is to safeguard Europe and thus save all. I have therefore today decided to give the fate of the German people and the Reich and of Europe again into the hands of our soldiers."

On Sunday, June 22, 1941, Molotov announced the attack to the Russian people in these words: "Today at 4:00 A.M., without any claims having been presented to the Soviet Union, without a declaration of war, German troops attacked our country, attacked our borders at many points and bombed our cities.... This war has been forced upon us, not by the German people, not by the German workers, peasants, and intellectuals, whose suffering we well understand, but by the clique of bloodthirsty Fascist rulers who have enslaved Frenchmen, Czechs, Poles, Serbians, Norway, Belgium, Denmark, Holland, Greece, and other nations....

"This is not the first time our people have had to deal with an attack of an arrogant foe. At the time of Napoleon's invasion of Russia our people's reply was war for the fatherland, and Napoleon suffered defeat and met his doom. It will be the same with Hitler, who in his arrogance has proclaimed a new crusade against our country. The Red Army and our whole people will again wage a victorious war for the fatherland, for our country, for honor, for liberty."

All the world was asking the question: "How strong is the Red Army?" No one, except the Russians themselves, believed that the Soviet Union, even with its unlimited manpower and enormous potential resources, could stand up long against the onslaught that Hitler was unleashing. Many qualified observers predicted the war would be over in a few weeks, with Russia at Hitler's mercy.

Strong defense had been a major keynote of every Soviet program, and its requirements were dovetailed into provisions for the nation's other Spartan needs. Consistent with the other aspects of the people's régime, the defense establishment was emphatically a people's army. The people's labor and privations made it. It was composed of the best of their manhood.

Russian might was to stagger the imagination of the world. Joseph Stalin, the iron man of Europe, was to prove himself one of the world's great statesmen. After the trial balloons with Germany, the adventure into Finland, and the first shock of the German impact against Russia, Stalin was to straighten his course and stand an impenetrable wall of indomitable will and courage. Russian manhood was to write new epics of glory. Russian valor was to assert its power. Russian genius was to gain the world's admiration. Backed by financial and industrial aid from the United States, Russia was to earn its place, through blood and sacrifice, in the brotherhood of nations.

GERMANY PITS HER MIGHT AGAINST RUSSIA

THE skies of eastern Europe were streaked with the blood red of dawn on Sunday, June 22, 1941, when Adolf Hitler unleashed his war-hungry legions on the 2,000-mile Russian frontier, from the White to the Black Sea. Dwarfing man's prior conception of war, the victory-drunk Reichsfuehrer hurled the full power of his military machine against massive Russia, gambling on a swift surge of conquest to make the Soviet Union his serf, destroy the threat to his eastern flank, and fatten his empire for domination of Europe.

The German debacle in Russia is the epic story of the Red Army. It is the saga of millions of men and women who, though faced with the engulfing might of a reputedly unconquerable war machine, pitted the naked courage of their zeal against the fanatical crusading fury of a self-anointed "super-race." Outnumbered at first, outgunned, outweighed in armor and overwhelmed in the air, outmaneuvered and outfought, the Soviet's stalwart defenders were thrown back from their borders.

Strategy of the Red Army's Supreme Command was charted to cut its own losses to a minimum while inflicting as heavy losses as possible on the enemy. With typical Russian stoical realism, the situation was accepted at face value. There was no immediate alternative to extended retreat. The objective was to retard the retreat as much as possible and make the Germans pay an extortionate price for it, at the same time building up a sufficient counterforce behind the lines to wrest the initiative from the foe at the strategic moment.

Blitzkrieg of Nazism rampant burst upon western Russia in a titanic crescendo of destructive terror. From Finland to Rumania, countless fleets of bombers ranged forth to rain havoc on key Russian cities, on every observable troop concentration, on rail and road junction points, on vital supply centers and the arteries of military movement. Clouds of fighter planes streaked across the skies to sweep opposition from the air. On every strategic highway the motorized Wehrmacht, tanks, armored cars, troop carriers, artillery, and supply columns, roared eastward in a fog of dust, fumes, and battle smoke.

Infantry and special-service troops fanned out into the countryside to mop up the islands of opposition left behind by the quick cleavage of the armored columns. With a momentum that rapidly rolled over all resistance, the endless streams of men and armament, the product of years of preparation, were aimed in deadly precision at the Soviet Union's heart and vitals.

All Germany was breathlessly looking on. Herded to their radios by diligent *gauleiters,* the home folk listened to minute descriptions of battle scenes broadcast from the spot by well-schooled propagandists. It was their duty to inflate the pride of the German people.

Major German thrusts were designed to yield a maximum of quick and damaging conquest on one hand and of the prestige of spectacular victory on the other. They stabbed at Russia's richest regions and greatest cities: (1) from northern and eastern Finland, on an intermittent front stretching from Petsamo to Lake Ladoga, into the Murmansk district and the Karelian Republic, with the object of severing Russia's supply lines from the Arctic, a supplementary drive being launched down the Karelian Isthmus toward Leningrad from Viborg, which the Russians had held since the War with Finland; (2) across the Baltic belt from East Prussia, aiming to overrun Lithuania, Latvia, and Estonia and eventually take Leningrad in conjunction with the southward assault from Finland; (3) through Sovietized Poland on the road to Moscow, by way of Bialystok, Minsk, Vitebsk and Smolensk; (4) into the rich northern Ukraine, Russia's breadbasket, with Kiev, the Dnieper River, and Kharkov as primary objectives; (5) from Rumania along the north shore of the Black Sea to take Odessa, the Dnieper Delta, the Crimea, and the teeming mining and manufacturing region of the Donets Basin.

Hitler intrusted his Russian field operations, under his general command, to four leading field marshals of that time: Sigmund List, Fedor von Bock, Walther von Reichenau, and Karl Gerd von Rundstedt. The initial Russian field commanders were Marshals Klementy E. Voroshiloff, Semyon Timoshenko, and Semyon Budenny.

Within two days the Germans had recorded a 120-mile advance into the Ukraine and the occupation of a large part of Bessarabia, which had been ceded to the Soviet Union by Rumania only a few months before. Rumania and Italy had joined the Reich in declaring war against Russia; Hungary and Finland followed within a few days.

Berlin marked the close of the first week of the war with claims of enormous advances. It said Minsk had been taken; that fast-moving troops were headed for Kiev to the southeast with the Black Sea as their objective; that Lithuania, part of Latvia, and most of Poland had been overrun, with the capture of Grodno, Lwow, Dubno, Kaunas, and Dvinsk. At the end of June Hitler boasted that his legions were halfway to Moscow.

In Moscow state authority was vested in a Defense Committee, with Joseph Stalin as its chairman. Premier Vyacheslaff M. Molotov was vice chairman; other members included Marshal Voroshiloff, as the chairman of the Defense Council, and L. P. Beria, Commissar of State Security. The first regenerative steps in the final development of the Soviet Union's great war machine were thus taken.

Up to this point the German operations had been a staggering demonstration of the Hitlerian conception of "war of movement." Still painfully aware that the limitations of a "war of position" had been an important factor in their defeat in 1914-18, the Germans believed they had eliminated this obstacle by making their forces so mobile and so powerful that battles could be kept fluid and virtually any fixed enemy positions overcome. Yet before the war in Russia was three weeks old, the Germans had learned that even their brand of blitzkrieg must pause, at least momentarily, for the consolidation of positions and preparations for new assaults.

At least two of the German spearheads made swifter progress in Russia than they had in their conquest of western Europe. According to German communiqués, one thrust toward Leningrad through the Baltic states averaged twenty miles a day for eleven days; another, aimed at Moscow, twenty-seven miles a day for the first nine days.

Britain and Russia had just signed a treaty of mutual assistance in Moscow, and there was speculation in the western world whether help could reach the Russians before it would be too late. Soviet Government services began to pack up and leave the capital. Rationing of food and manufactured goods was imposed in Moscow, and later in Leningrad. The Red Army's political commissars, who had been shelved after the Finnish war, were restored as war commissars. Stalin took over the post of defense commissar.

The Germans reached Smolensk on July 16, 230 miles from Moscow and junction point of some of western Russia's most important railroads. They drove on and in a few days had reduced the distance from Moscow to 200 miles. The Stalin Line now was sixty miles behind them. On July 21 the Germans began to bomb Moscow.

First strong opposition to the German advance developed after the fall of Smolensk. The Russians had concentrated reserve troops and matériel in the Smolensk region in the hope of at least delaying the invaders' onslaught.

Meanwhile, developments behind the lines helped to bolster the Russians' hopes. The British sent naval planes to bomb the Germans at Petsamo and R.A.F. night raiders left a "volcano of fires" in Berlin. Harry Hopkins arrived in Moscow with a note from President Roosevelt for Stalin. A few days later Roosevelt and Churchill held their historic conference at sea and drew up the Atlantic Charter. Another result of the meeting was a proposal that British and American emissaries meet with Russian officials in Moscow to work out the Red Army's supply problem. Stalin accepted with gratitude, and the foundation was laid for the tremendous flow of Allied help that eventually became one of the major factors in the Germans' defeat.

Leningrad's peril was becoming increasingly acute. On August 19 the Russians announced their retirement from Kingisepp, seventy-five miles southwest of the northern metropolis. On the next day they admitted their forces farther south had fallen back fifty miles to the Novgorod region. The Germans claimed Novgorod, about seventy miles south of Leningrad, on August 21. The people of the great city of the north took up arms to defend their homes. Barricades were erected in the streets. The German advance continued inexorably, and soon Berlin proclaimed that a "ring of steel" was being forced around the city. The Leningrad-Moscow railway was cut on August 28.

Blasting of the Dnieper dam was a dramatic climax in the Soviet's Union's "scorched earth" program in the Ukraine. The rich Ukraine's resources for war purposes were part of the German design. Stalin ordered that everything possible be moved or destroyed before the Red Army retreated. Thus the Germans again were cheated of the real fruit of their conquest. Hard on their army's heels, German experts and technicians rushed into the Ukraine in droves to start the expected flow of food and supplies back to Germany. They found wheat fields burned, factories dismantled or destroyed; virtually no usable industrial machinery, transport equipment, or public utility equipment.

But the scorching of the lost Ukraine was far more than a program of destruction. Russian ingenuity was winning a battle of wits. Long before the Germans arrived, Russian men, women, and children labored night and day dismantling machinery, moving farm equipment and livestock, loading all available railroad rolling stock with everything that could be moved. All this saved equipment, and material was transported eastward in the greatest mass migration of modern times. Some of it went to relatively near regions considered safe from the invaders for the moment. More important war plants were taken almost in entirety, except for their buildings, to the distant Urals and beyond, in the heart of central Russia. There they were set up anew, usually close to abundant raw materials, and put in expanded production again.

A further factor in insuring the Russians' supply potential developed late in August when Soviet troops collaborated with the British in driving German trouble-makers out of Iran.

Although the Russians and British went into Iran with the avowed purpose of safeguarding the Near Eastern flank, the development of a supply route from the Persian Gulf became the ultimate objective. The project, eventually developed and manned by American personnel, was to become one of the Soviet Union's lifelines, supplementing the flow of supplies over the Arctic route through Murmansk.

Hitler and Premier Mussolini, after a conference and an inspection tour of the Eastern Front, issued a joint declaration late in August, pledging to "thwart United States' aid in the east and west and achieve a victory that will destroy Bolshevism and plutocratic exploitation." On the same day President Roosevelt announced that he was sending a mission to Moscow to study Russia's supply needs. It was headed by W. Averell Harriman, who had been Lend-Lease expediter in London.

Germany was awakening to the fact that its "quick conquest" was being disrupted.

Marshal Budenny's armies in the Ukraine were making a strong bid for the initiative, recrossing the Dnieper at some places and slashing out in destructive counterattacks at several points. Hitler, now taciturn in his communiqués, seemed to have only a wavering chance of breaking through to Moscow. Then the tide turned in his favor in other directions. On September 12 the Russians lost Chernigov, south of Gomel, heightening the threat to Kiev, but the Germans' attempt to crash through to Bryansk, 220 miles southwest of Moscow, was hurled back with punishing losses. On September 20 the Nazis raised the swastika over Kiev, Russia's oldest and third largest city.

Russia's southern line of resistance was shattered. A series of German columns swept victoriously through the Ukraine, some reaching the Sea of Azov and cutting off the Crimea. Berlin called this history's greatest "battle of destruction." It claimed that fifty of Budenny's divisions had been cut to pieces and 380,000 prisoners taken.

The people of the Soviet Union were keenly aware of the danger that confronted them. It soon became apparent that the collapse of the Ukraine front was a major disaster. Through great and widening gaps the alien brown tide was pouring into the basins of the Dnieper and the Donets and threatening the Don at the gateway to the Caucasus. Marshal Budenny, venerated as a hero of the civil war and as the teacher of some of Russia's best commanders, was removed to make way for younger though less famed generals.

The frontal attack on Moscow was halted. The invaders held at bay around Smolensk probed ceaselessly for an opening and were poised for a fatal thrust at the first opportunity. Moreover, the German forces that had swung around Kiev to the southeast were striking northeast toward Bryansk and Tula with a good chance of outflanking the Smolensk bastion. In the north Leningrad was battling for its life as the besiegers hammered at its gates. The Finno-German forces bore down from the Karelian Isthmus.

The armies of the Reich, Hitler announced, were poised for a paralyzing blow. The most gigantic development of the Russian war was about to be unfolded. On October 7 the Germans launched a two-pronged offensive against Moscow from the north and west with the avowed object of capturing the capital before winter.

BATTLE FOR MOSCOW—RUSSIAN CITIES AFLAME

"THE military decision has already fallen. The rest of the operations will take the course we wish them to. For all military purposes, Soviet Russia is done with. The British dream of a two-front war is dead."

Thus spoke Dr. Otto Dietrich, the German press spokesman, when he returned to Berlin on October 9, 1941, from a conference with Hitler at the front. He gloated that the last complete Russian Armies, those of Timoshenko before Moscow, were hemmed into two circles, sixty to seventy divisions of Voroshiloff's army were locked in Leningrad; Budenny's southern armies were routed.

The next day Berlin announced that German forces were pouring through a breach more than 300 miles wide between Vyazma and Orel. They had forged a path to a point 105 miles south of Moscow and were turning north to cut off the city from the rear. A new encirclement of Russian divisions was reported north of the Sea of Azov, where the ports of Mariupol and Ossipenko had been claimed a few days before. The Germans declared their objective was to complete the "inexorable annihilation" of the Russian Armies.

London was frankly alarmed, aware that the fate of Russia depended on the quality of the Soviet Armies' defense. Washington said its help to Russia would continue on the assumption that the Soviet Union would win. Moscow acknowledged the fall of Orel, 200 miles southwest of Moscow, and admitted German pressure was heavy. Moscow revealed on October 12 that women and children were being evacuated from the capital. German strategy was developing a double threat to Moscow in the form of huge sweeping arcs that reached out for the capital like great pincers: from the south in the Orel region toward Tula and in the north toward Rzhev and Kalinin on Moscow's western perimeter.

Capture of Odessa by German and Rumanian troops was proclaimed by Hitler on October 16. The historic port had long been under siege, cut off except for a precarious water route across the Black Sea. Impatient at the upset of his time-table for the quick conquest of Moscow, the key to his plans for German glory and Russian humiliation, Hitler now ordered an all-out frontal attack.

Moscow stripped for the crucial battle. The diplomatic corps and virtually all Government offices except the defense establishment moved to Kuibyshev, 550 miles to the southeast. Stalin, declaring a state of siege for the city and its environs, called on the people to gird for a finish fight. Fresh Russian reserves poured in from the eastern reservoirs, and 4,500,000 citizens, including women, labored day and night, digging tank traps and building barricades in concentric semi-circles from the city outward.

While the battle for Moscow was at its height the supreme command of this zone had been transferred to General Gregory K. Zhukoff, Chief of the General Staff. Timoshenko, whom he replaced, was sent to command the southern front, relieving Budenny.

The defense of Moscow, which served as a symbol of the defense of the whole Russian motherland, called forth the full limits of the Russian people's heroism. Front-line valor abounded in instances of epic self-sacrifice. At one stage of the battle fifty German tanks broke through to the station of Dubosekovo, dangerously close to Moscow. There stood an officer of the Panfilov Division with twenty-seven determined comrades. "Russia is vast," said the officer, "but there is no place to retreat—behind us is Moscow!" All twenty-eight men died in the path of the tanks, but the tanks did not pass.

Countless evidences of Russian courage, and its reflection in the stone-wall quality of the Red Army's defense, amazed the rank-and-file Germans. They had been taught to expect little from what Hitler called the "Bolshevist scum." Even Berlin now gave grudging tribute to the resoluteness of the Soviet people's stand. The western world was electrified by the stirring news from Moscow. The public clamored for increased assistance to the Russians.

The stalemate before Moscow was evident. German attention was shifted momentarily to the southern front. After a breathing spell to consolidate its advanced forces in the Ukraine, the German Command resumed its march on Kharkov, heart of the industrial Donets Basin, and Rostov, gateway to the oil-rich Caucasus. By October 26 Axis armies had swept into Kharkov and near-by Belgorod. The entire Ukraine was engulfed and most of the Donbas area was threatened by spearheads that wound through lightly protected valleys toward the Don.

The Crimea, cut off by the German sweep across the south Ukraine, was staunchly defended at Russian barriers across the narrow neck of the Perekop Isthmus, between the western arm of the Black Sea and the Sea of Azov. Not until October 30, after a ten-day battle, were the Germans able to crack the Perekop wall and stream down through the Crimea toward Kerch, opposite the Caucasus, and Sevastopol, a main base of the Red Navy in the Black Sea.

The menace of the potential German drive into the Caucasus loomed as half of a pincer operation against Suez in combination with the Axis campaign in Africa. Britain and Russia completed joint defense plans for a protective link stretching from Syria to India.

Stimulated official rapprochement between Moscow and Washington was evidenced on November 7 when Maxim Litvinoff was appointed as Soviet Ambassador to the United States. Probably the most western-minded of Russian officials, Litvinoff had long been a figurehead of Soviet collaboration with the democracies. He was appointed at the same time to serve as Deputy Commissar of Foreign Affairs.

In the south, the Germans took Stalino, important steel city of the Donbas, on October 22, and drove on toward Voroshilovgrad. Kursk, a Russian anchor position between Orel and Kharkov, held out until November 3. The Red Army withdrew from Taganrog, on the southern coast, falling back toward Rostov.

The battle for the Crimea was turning in the Germans' favor. Simferopol, the capital, fell on November 2, and Theodosia, a southeastern port, on November 4. The strong defense of Kerch, separated from the Caucasus only by a narrow strait, compelled German and Rumanian forces to besiege it for two weeks more with all available infantry, tank, and air forces. Berlin claimed it on November 16.

The Germans' basic aim in the north was to win prestige for the Wehrmacht and to humble the Soviet Union by planting the swastika in Moscow and strangling the heart of Russia. In the south the objective was territory and loot—the wheat, mines, and factories of the Ukraine and the Donbas and the oil of the Caucasus. Mounting simultaneously two gigantic offensives to achieve this double aim, the German Command believed it could force the Red Army to spread its strength so thin that resistance would become ineffective.

Mortal danger from both German offensives was ominously acute. In the horseshoe of last-ditch defenses around Moscow, Zhukoff was straining every resource to check the invading hordes' tremendous blows. In the south, German Field Marshal General Karl Gerd von Rundstedt, in general command, was driving his easternmost salient downward toward the Caucasus. He sent a powerful army under Colonel General Paul Ludwig von Kleist, supported by a force of Panzers and infantry under General Schwoedler, pounding for Rostov.

Unknown to the Germans, the secret transfer of Timoshenko to the southern front had begun to bear fruit. He had already taken the Wehrmacht's measure in the first Russian tactical victory of the war by stopping von Bock's first big push for Moscow in August and September, when he outmaneuvered the advance Nazi force that had speared east of Smolensk. Now he was preparing the ground for a similar operation to checkmate von Kleist.

Von Kleist first lashed out in a tentative frontal attack across the Donbas steppes. Timoshenko threw him back with heavy losses. The

German strategist regrouped his force and struck out anew northwest and north of Rostov. During the first week of November he crossed the northern Donets at several points and pushed toward Shakhty, intending to cut down from the north through Novocherkassk; thus he planned to outflank the main Rostov force and attack the city from the northeast. Timoshenko met him with Major General Fedor M. Kharitonoff's Ninth Army, which threw the Axis troops out of Novochaktinsk about November 10 with heavy German, Italian, and Hungarian casualties. But von Kleist was persistent. With a strong, highly mobile armored force at his command, he regrouped again and overwhelmed the Russians by sheer weight. He entered Rostov on November 22.

At dawn on November 29, seven days after the Germans' triumphal entry, the Russians rolled back into Rostov. Troops under General Remizoff, with other units led by Generals Kharitonoff and Lopatin, drove the Nazis westward through the streets. The city was ablaze and littered with wreckage from both German and Russian bombing and shelling. Von Kleist put up a fierce rear-guard action to cover his retreat. For two days every yard of ground was contested in close fighting. When the surviving residents emerged from their hiding places, they showed the Red Army the gallows that the Germans had erected in the public squares and newspaper kiosks that had served as machine-gun nests to enforce a reign of terror.

The forty-mile road between Rostov and Taganrog was cleared of the enemy by December 1. Three days later the Russians stormed through Taganrog and on toward Mariupol. Other Red Army columns thrust forty miles to the north and reached the suburbs of Stalino. The Germans, laboring feverishly to throw up a bulwark before Mariupol, finally stabilized their positions on the Mius River.

It was undeniably a Soviet victory of the first caliber. It was the Red Army's first positive triumph of this war, an indication of the shape of future events. The Hitlerian legend of German invincibility was shattered. Timoshenko had shown what could be done with a determined will and even moderate means.

While the battle for Rostov was under way, the equally crucial struggle for Moscow was proceeding with intermittent success on both sides. After a short deadlock, the Germans had launched a revitalized offensive to extend the pincers groping toward the capital from north and south. They had broken into Tula, 110 miles southwest of Moscow.

The Germans occupied Tolstoy's birthplace, which all Russia revered as a cultural shrine, near Tula, at Yasnaya Polyana. Reports seeped out that the Nazis had thrown the master's priceless manuscripts out into the snow and chopped up the furniture for firewood. A similar fate befell Tschaikovsky's home near Klin, northwest of Moscow, where the *Sixth Symphony* was written.

The prospect of sizable American help was becoming an important factor in the Russian outlook. An exchange of letters between President Roosevelt and Stalin revealed a pledge of $1,000,000,000 in Lend-Lease aid. The United States granted the loan without interest, to be repaid in a ten-year period beginning five years after the war. The United States also decided to arm ships carrying war materials to friendly belligerents. Washington likewise attempted to use its influence to take Finland out of the war against Russia. The Baltic ally of Hitler was warned that her operations against Russia were endangering American friendship. Helsinki rejected the overture, contending that the Finns were not a full Axis partner but were kept in the struggle by the fact that Russia still held areas deemed vital to Finnish security.

Weather was playing a strategic rôle in the northern warfare. Having expected a swift autumn victory, the Germans were unprepared for the terrible rigors of a Russian winter. First the autumn rains turned the countryside into mud, then freezing nights and howling blizzards tortured the inadequately clad German soldiers. A German broadcast of the period gave this lugubrious picture: "Gray is the country, gray the sky, everything gray and empty. With its aspect of forlornness, the whole country is frightening. The road to Moscow resembles one vast, soaked sponge, along which men, horses, and lorries slog painfully and strenuously. Slowly they move, dragging themselves step by step. Time after time they are bogged down. This is Russia."

The battle of Moscow reached its crisis on December 4. The Germans had been able to punch holes repeatedly in the city's outer defenses by massing tremendous armored "fists" at selected points. Every attempt to widen a penetration into a sizable breach was frustrated by the frenzy of the Russians. Literally hurling themselves in the tanks' paths, they interposed human walls when other barriers were broken, until the spearheads spent their strength or their penetrations were sealed off.

Hitler had boasted that he would be in Moscow in six weeks; it took him more than five months, at terrible cost, to learn that he would never take the Russian capital.

With the timing that marked the Red Army's notable feats, Zhukoff was ready for the moment of the siege flood's ebb. Carefully calculated Russian plans for a decisive counterattack were set in motion on December 4. Heavy reserves had been drawn into the city from the east, together with a large quota of new tanks, other armored vehicles and guns. Pools of aircraft of all types had been mobilized at strategically situated fields.

The temperature stood at 13° below zero in Moscow. The Germans, benumbed with cold and debilitated by the fatigue of their long effort, were in poor condition to meet the Russians' thundering blows. Turning their backs on Moscow, the humiliated Germans plodded westward in Napoleon's very footsteps, fighting a desultory rear-guard action to cover their retreat.

Ultimate defeat of Hitler was looming on the horizon. While his retreat from Moscow was under way the world was shaken by a tremendous explosion. The United States was drawn into the war on December 7. It was no longer a struggle for European power; it was all-out global war. Hitler's scheming to avoid a two-front war had come to naught. The Axis now was facing not a depleted Britain and an untried Russia, but the unlimited potential resources of the nascent United Nations coalition.

The extent of the German reverse was manifested to the world on December 21 when Hitler took over supreme command of the German Armies, removing Field Marshal General Walther von Brauchitsch. There were reports of a sharp clash between the Nazi Army clique and the old-line generals. Hitler, it was understood, had undertaken his attack on Russia over the objections of many of his ablest strategists.

Just before Christmas, Prime Minister Churchill and Lord Beaverbrook arrived in Washington for new conversations with President Roosevelt and his military advisers on the implications of the spreading war. The basis was laid for an inter-Allied war council and Russia's growingly hopeful fight figured prominently in the new calculations.

In the last days of December the Red Army, with the help of Red fleet marines, struck back into the eastern Crimea in a bold amphibious operation and recaptured Kerch and Theodosia, relieving the pressure on Sevastopol and menacing the Germans' grip on the whole region.

Before the Russians paused on their now wide-stretched Moscow perimeter, they crumpled the Germans' southern flank in a smash across the Oka River that swept up broad stretches of territory and many populated points. At the year's end their lines west of Moscow were some thirty miles from Rzhev.

Hitler sang a new tune when he made his customary New Year's speech at the outset of 1942. He no longer promised easy victories and quick conquests. He served notice on the sobered Reich that it faced "still harder battles if we are to circumscribe the powerful foe that confronts us."

What really awaited him his dull wits were little able to comprehend. The invincible power of the democracies was rising. His dreams were to be blasted after four more years of nightmare. The inexorable fate of tyrants was to hang over his head—the sword of the modern Damocles.

BATTLE OF STALINGRAD—
GATE TO THE EAST

THE 164-day-battle of Stalingrad was one of the decisive battles in history. Here on the Volga River leading to the Caspian Sea and the Kingdom of Iran, thus virtually starting on the road to India, the destiny of the Orient was at stake.

This historic battle began with the German tanks crossing the Don River loop on August 22, 1942, and closed with the capitulation of the last remnant of two beaten Axis armies in the ruins of Stalingrad on February 2, 1943. Between these terminal events, Hitler witnessed the doom of his dreams of extending the borders of Germany to Asia.

Stalingrad became the first of Hitler's Waterloos as a result of two salient blunders: his overwhelming ambition to gloat from the banks of the Volga, and his vainglorious underestimation of the strength and resourcefulness of his Russian adversary. In a sense, the issue at Stalingrad was decided at Voronezh; Voronezh was the vital hinge of the whole southeastern front. The Reichsfuehrer's military chiefs advised that it be reduced before proceeding eastward. Hitler, cocksure of his ability to force any decision at will, overruled them and swept past the bastion of the upper Don. Voronezh did not fall and the Russians, in their own good time, used it as a fulcrum to crack the German front.

The Germans pushed mighty armored wedges in the form of pincers some one hundred miles apart, from Kletskaya on the north and Kotelnikov on the south. There was no subtlety in the Axis operation. It was a simple double assault, aiming by sheer weight of men and armor to smash through to the Volga north and south of Stalingrad and invest the city by encirclement along the river's bank.

Within forty miles of the city on both north and south, the Germans claimed positions on August 25. Admitting tenacious Russian resistance and strong counterattacks, they reported that these were being overcome by their numerically superior forces. Losses on both sides were cumulatively heavy. With a force estimated at 1,000 planes, the German air arm repeated the destructive story of Warsaw, Rotterdam, and Coventry, with major amplifications. Hundreds of high-level bombers and countless squadrons of dive bombers poured explosives and incendiaries on the city with unceasing regularity. Skyscrapers in the center of the modern town, huge industrial plants along the Volga, workers' districts surrounding them, and rows of stately apartment houses in residential areas offered shining targets for the Germans' lust for destruction. Tremendous conflagrations were raging in Stalingrad, fed and blasted around the clock by pattern bombing designed to leave only rubble for the Russian garrison to defend.

Press Association, Inc.

The battle for Stalingrad grew more critical as German troops maintained a bridgehead forty miles from Stalingrad.

The Red Air Force rose to meet the attackers, and the sky above the city became an auxiliary field of battle. The Luftwaffe, at terrific cost of planes and pilots, hurled new squadrons into the conflict so profligately that the Russian fliers, hard-pressed to support their ground troops as well as defend the city, could not stay them. The Germans extended their air attacks to gun positions and supply points east of the Volga, as well as to river traffic and rail and highway supply routes. On September 10 the Germans claimed to have reached the Volga south of the city. Moscow said that more than 1,000,000 men now were locked in battle for Stalingrad. The conflict for the city proper began on September 14, when the German Sixth Army engaged the Russian Sixty-second Army in the outskirts.

Battle of Stalingrad

The next day Berlin reported street fighting in Stalingrad and claimed the capture of the central railway station. Describing hand-to-hand battles, Moscow said: "The city, built by the toil of the young nation and the skill of foreign engineers, from which machines to cultivate the Russian harvests were poured out, now is a vast cauldron in which two armies with burning hate grapple for a decision."

Formerly Tzaritsyn and renamed for Stalin after his leadership of its defense in the battles of 1918, the city straggles for twenty miles along the broad Volga. One of Russia's greatest industrial centers, its modern sections had been built in the previous twenty years, largely with the help of American technicians. It processed ores from the Donbas and oil from the Caucasus. Its huge new factories had turned out tractors and other farm machinery for peace—and tanks, planes and guns for war. The mile-wide Volga, flowing under steep cliffs on the western bank, was so busy an artery of commerce that it was sometimes called "Russia's Main Street."

Since mid-August the thunder of guns to the west had mingled with the sounds of Stalingrad's teeming industry.

As the Golden Horde of the Tartars had borne down on the ancient Volga colonies from the east, the brown flood of Nazism was now sweeping from the west. Stalingrad, pride of modern Russia, was at bay, pounded by wave after wave of men and machines. Warplanes, dominating the sky, battered the city unceasingly. Rail routes to the north and south had been cut. Only the precarious Volga remained as a supply link with the hinterland. Russians stood with their backs to the Volga, sheer cliffs dropping to the water from their heels, as tanks bore down on them. With antitank rifles, automatic weapons, and grenades, they stood their ground. As at Moscow, they said, "Russia is vast behind us, but there is no place to retreat."

The city was a shambles of chaotic wreckage. No building remained intact; only the walls of the sturdiest structures were still standing. Streets were choked with a tangle of charred timbers and crushed masonry. Buried in the débris were the remains of destroyed tanks, smashed guns, and abandoned equipment.

Stalin had ordered: "Stalingrad is not to be yielded so long as there is a man left to defend it." The Supreme Soviet Command had prepared its precise, crafty plans to catch the investing armies in a huge trap. As usual, the Stavka's strategy was coldly realistic. Recognizing the futility of attempting to stem the initial major assault, it was predicated on the Napoleonic formula of circumspect defense followed by rapid, audacious attack. The first phase was carried out by containing the siege as firmly as possible, permitting the foe to extend his communications and use up his strength while waiting for the moment when the counterattack would have maximum promise of success.

That moment, meticulously gauged by the Soviet Command, arrived at the end of October. Moscow announced that a Soviet counterattack in the southern outskirts of Stalingrad had ejected the Germans from a belt of machine-gun posts, blockhouses, and dugouts. The Red Army at the peak of its might pitted enormous fresh forces against the considerable but battle-weary Axis formations.

Details of the complex offensive reveal the care with which the Russian Supreme Command had prepared its coup and exemplify the subtlety of the new Soviet strategy. They clarify what Stalin meant when he said that the Red Army had been schooled in the war's early phases to "smite the enemy unerringly, taking into consideration his weak and strong sides, as required by modern military science ... having discarded the foolish and harmful linear tactics and having firmly adopted the tactics of maneuvering."

The German Sixth Army at Stalingrad might have escaped by breaking away to the west during the early stages of the counter-offensive. But, as the Soviet command had calculated, the German strategists failed to comprehend the strength or significance of the great Russian move and defiantly clung to what remained of their positions, ripe for destruction. The Sixth Army was inextricably ringed by November 25.

Russian forces, now arrayed in a huge ring around Stalingrad and constantly reinforced, proceeded to widen the belt separating the Sixth Army from other Axis forces to the west. The German Command was forced to supply its surrounded troops by air, and the steady battle of attrition included an ever-growing destruction of Axis transport planes by Russian fighters waiting to pounce upon them.

The Red Army was beginning to demonstrate the full effectiveness of its tank tactics, now brought to perfection by the large-scale production of the Soviet Union's war plants and the arrival of machines from Britain and the United States. Even before the war, Soviet generals had conceived of tank units as a prime striking force, employed with the integrated support of infantry and other arms. These tactics, involving the astute use of antitank units, tank-riding infantry, cavalry wings, and other features, were to play a decisive part in the later stages of the war. On the Don-Stalingrad front the Germans, long considered masters of mobile warfare built around Panzer units, began to take lessons from the Russians in their former specialty.

Collapse of von Mannstein's relief expedition placed the hopelessness of the Sixth Army's position beyond all doubt. The ever-widening Russian belt around Stalingrad rapidly spread westward as the enormous Russian forces swept the rest of the German armies back toward Rostov. Rigors of the Russian winter, at their worst in this virtually unbroken steppe country, further confounded the Germans.

Colonel General Konstantin K. Rokossovsky's armies of the Don front had been brought into position to begin the extermination of the German Sixth Army. Reluctant to undertake needlessly such one-sided slaughter, Rokossovsky and Colonel General Nikolai N. Voronoff, in supreme command, sent an ultimatum to Colonel General Friedrich von Paulus, the Sixth Army's commander. The hopelessness of further resistance was explained and surrender terms specified. The first emissaries sent with the offer were fired upon. The next day they were sent again and this time were received. Von Paulus curtly rejected the terms.

The battle of extermination began on January 10, 1943. Rokossovsky first massed his forces west of the encirclement and gradually developed a series of pincer and crisscross attacks that hacked off a bit here and there and slashed the remaining positions into isolated groups. The Germans, well-schooled in defensive tactics, were determined to die fighting. Still well-armed and supplied, they stubbornly dug in.

Withering artillery barrage, coupled with infantry assaults and mass air attacks, broke the Sixth Army into two parts; one in the northern section of the city, the other in the south. Rokossovsky's men, advancing from the west, then joined with the divisions in Stalingrad. The southern German group was liquidated first, but the northern group, defending von Paulus' command post, fought on. After the first stages of the attack the closely ringed Germans began to surrender in large numbers. Others, ill, half frozen, and famished, were swept up in the net each day.

By the afternoon of February 2 all fighting had ceased. The formalities of surrender had been completed. Distraught and disheveled, many of them ill, some 91,000 Germans and Rumanians were herded out of their hiding places. The prisoners included twenty-four generals and more than 2,500 other officers. Altogether, the Axis troops killed or captured at Stalingrad totaled 330,000. When the Russians recovered control of the city they found its destruction almost complete. Some idea of the extent of the gigantic battleground is conveyed by the recorded fact that in their clean-up task the Russians found and buried the bodies of 147,200 Axis troops and 46,700 Soviet soldiers.

"The Hitlerites sowed death copiously and reaped it just as copiously," said a laconic Russian comment.

Stalingrad marked the close of the epoch of German triumph and ushered in the start of the period of Russian victory. It demonstrated to the world the indomitable will of the Russian people to win, and it unveiled the Red Army at its best. The war up to that point had been but a prolog. The Red Army and the Russian people, the front and the rear, had now been totally mobilized and completely welded into the full potentiality of their fighting power.

38

THE RED ARMY STRIKES BACK—
• 141 CRUCIAL DAYS

THE tide of Hitler's fortunes in Russia reached the crest and the Red Army struck back in 1943. It had become apparent—even to the German High Command who had permitted the Fuehrer's "intuition" to eclipse their military judgment—that the Axis had overreached itself. The decline and fall of the German military empire was under way.

We are now to witness 141 days of terrific battles. When the Russians seized the initiative, the Germans had lost most of the advantages with which they started the war. The first of these advantages had been surprise attack, with numerical superiority in tanks, planes, guns, and battle-trained divisions. This was lost after seventeen months of war. The Soviet Union had attained a status so close to parity that Nazi supremacy was no longer decisive.

Another advantage had been the professional German generals' traditional adroitness in strategy and maneuver. This had been sacrificed by Hitler's meddlesome bungling. They now were challenged by the Red Army's rapidly maturing mastery of the science of war. Germany started with the advantage of a strongly mobilized home front, with industries geared to production of implements for war. The Russians had faced the urgent necessity of coördination of front and rear with tremendous expansion of industries, supplemented by the enormous production power of America and Great Britain.

Let us inspect for a moment the Russian forces and their leaders: At the start, the Red Army was divided into three fronts, the northwestern, western, and southwestern, commanded respectively by Marshals Voroshiloff, Timoshenko, and Budenny. As events showed, these were large, unwieldy organizations, lacking elasticity and difficult to control. The reorganized set-up consisted of twelve fronts, each small enough to be readily manageable in any situation and to be fitted into the complex over-all program.

The twelve fronts, from north to south, were the Karelian, Leningrad, Volkhov, northwestern, Kalinin, central, Bryansk, Veronezh; southwestern, Don, Stalingrad and Caucasian. The skilled, seasoned generals who commanded them included Leonid Govoroff, of Leningrad; Kyrill A. Meretzkoff, of Volkhov; Semyon K. Timoshenko, of the northwestern; Filip Golikoff, of Voronezh; Nikolai F. Vatutin, of the southwestern; Konstantin K. Rokossovsky, of the Don; Andrey

Yeremenko, of Stalingrad, and Fedor I. Tolbukhin, of the Caucasian. Other field commanders who came into prominence during later operations included Generals Ivan S. Koneff, Ivan Bagramyan, M. M. Popoff, and Rodion Y. Malinovsky. The Supreme Command, or Stavka, which coördinated the operations of the various fronts, was under the general direction of Stalin as Commander in Chief of the Armed Forces, with the assistance of Marshals Klementy E. Voroshiloff, Gregory K. Zhukoff, Nikolai N. Voronoff, Alexander M. Vasilevsky, and Semyon Budenny.

A further factor in the growing strength of the Red Army was the mass production of key weapons of particular effectiveness. Automatic rifles, antitank and antiaircraft guns were being turned out in great quantity by the Soviet war industries. The newly organized, well-trained divisions were abundantly equipped. The tank and tractor plants of peace time had been rapidly expanded with the arrival of additional machines from the United States and Britain. Redoubtable Soviet tank armies were going into action. The best-known and most widely used tank was the KV, a forty-six-ton monster, conceived in the Putiloff works in Leningrad and named for Marshal Klementy Voroshiloff. Many a German line was broken through its mass use.

Among the many types of Red Army guns, the Katiusha, operating on the mortar principle and endearingly named for the heroine of a popular love song, became the most famous. Invented by Andrey Kostikoff, an army engineer, it was a strong element in the defense of Stalingrad. British and American planes flowed into Russia in large numbers.

Misrepresenting Stalingrad as firmly in German hands, Hitler hinted at his impending defensive strategy of retreat by saying it was not worth the price to make new Verduns of other Russian strongholds. This was translated into action when General Franz Halder was removed as Chief of the German General Staff and General Kurt Zeitzler put in his place. General Hans Jesschonnek became Chief of Staff of the Luftwaffe and Admiral Fricke Chief of the Naval General Staff.

Berlin's tone changed from one of continuous triumph to bald admissions of strenuous defensive fighting. Geographical details usually were vague or lacking. Increasingly heavy losses were being inflicted on the Germans in the region west of Rzhev. The fall of Velikiye Luki, close to the important Leningrad-Vitebsk rail artery, was reported by Moscow on New Year's Day, 1943. Attention was focused on the last stages of the Stalingrad battle and the correlated operations in the Don loop, which were beating the Axis back toward Rostov.

The successful double drive to break the blockade of Leningrad was launched in January, 1943. For seventeen months the Germans had been at the near approaches to the former capital. Capture of the city had been an important item in Hitler's war plans. Besides coveting its economic and cultural riches, the Nazi Command had hoped to drive north to Murmansk and Archangel, sever the communication lines uniting the Soviet Union with its allies, and open the way for another offensive against Moscow and the hinterland from the north. Hitler had ordered that Leningrad be taken in September, 1941. An Axis army of more than 300,000 men attempted to storm the fortress city from the south and southeast, while Finnish troops pressed down from the north.

Failing to take Leningrad by storm, Hitler set out to strangle the city by hunger. The blockade only raised the beleaguered people's determination to new heights. On short rations, they labored indefatigably in war plants and formed volunteer battalions to reinforce the outnumbered garrison. A new German drive to take the city was undertaken in September, 1942. In a preliminary move, the Finns tried to capture the island of Sukho, a key communications point, but were disastrously repulsed. The entire German plan collapsed.

The Russian offensive to break the blockade had been meticulously and laboriously prepared with specially trained troops. It consisted of simultaneous drives from the Leningrad and Volkhov fronts. Attacks began on January 12, 1943—eastward from the west bank of the Neva River southwest of Schluesselburg, and westward from a point south of Lake Ladoga. Forcing the Neva and breaching strong German fortifications to a depth of nine miles, the Russians overwhelmed a series of strong points, including Schluesselburg and Sinyavino.

The battle, in which the Axis troops were pinned between two fronts closing like a vise, raged for seven days. It reached its climax in a workers' village, where the Germans, after bringing up reinforcements, chose to make their last-ditch stand. Ten thousand Germans were killed at this point alone. The invaders were driven out of the settlement and the two fronts were joined. Thus a corridor was won from Leningrad to the east and the siege ring was broken. This victorious operation was commanded by Generals Govoroff and Meretskoff under the coördinating direction of Marshals Zhukoff and Voroshiloff, representing the Supreme Command.

While the Trans-Caucasus forces were smashing their way up the Caucasian isthmus from the south, other Red Army divisions were bearing down on Rostov from two sides—the Voronezh offensive from the north and another drive across the Kalmuck steppes from the east, below the lower Don.

Berlin announced the German evacuation of Voronezh on January 25. The city, through which both armies had swept repeatedly during the six months that the lines fluctuated, was a shambles of destruction. Some 11,000 Axis prisoners were taken in the final attack, but the futile German attempt to maintain an anchor in the city had cost many times that number in killed and wounded.

Demoralized Axis armies were thrown into such headlong flight that Berlin vied with Moscow in describing the fury of the Russian onslaught. Tank-paced Soviet columns drove westward from Voronezh on a front nearly fifty miles wide. More than seven Axis divisions were trapped by the swift thrust, some 12,000 enemy troops were killed and nearly 15,000 more captured. Stary Oskol and Izyum fell into the Russian bag at opposite ends of the Kharkov front on February 5. The virtually continuous offensive line now extended from a point north of Rostov almost to Bryansk. At the same time the northern Caucasus forces broke through to Yeisk, on the southeastern shore of the Sea of Azov, extending the southern arm of the arc closing on Rostov. Also, the northern wing of the offensive had cut the road between Orel and Kursk, further complicating the German supply situation around Kharkov.

The Germans were driven out of Rostov for the second time on February 14. Berlin announced the evacuation as a "strategic withdrawal" after the destruction of important military installations—but the speed with which the Germans were driven westward along the shore of the Sea of Azov made it plain that the movement was part of the Axis rout.

Reconquest of Kharkov by the Russians was a heavy blow to the Germans. The Red Army entered triumphantly on February 16. This was the most important rail junction in Russia, after Moscow, and the commercial and industrial center of the Ukraine had been a rich prize of the Germans since October, 1941. Blasted out of their strong positions in and around Kharkov, the Axis armies were driven westward.

The Germans, using twenty-five divisions of some 275,000 men, swept back toward Kharkov, forcing the Russians to retreat hastily from unconsolidated positions in the region of their swift conquest. Fresh and well-supplied Axis armies brought their lines back as much as eighty miles on the Kharkov-Dnieper-Donets front.

A violent battle raged for days in the outskirts of Kharkov. The strength of the German initiative eventually prevailed. Berlin announced the recapture of the city on March 14.

The later stages of the winter operations gave ample demonstration of the value of the Russians' small independent and self-contained fronts. While the Kharkov offensive was under way, the other fronts undertook initiatives of their own. When the advance beyond Kharkov was reversed, the adjoining fronts were able to lend support by increasing the pressure on the Germans in their sectors. Late in February a large-scale Russian attack was spearing into the Axis lines in the Lake Ilmen area, 120 miles south of Leningrad. The Black Sea Fleet was assisting in amphibious operations against Novorossiisk, landing troops in the rear of the Axis bridgehead in the Caucasus while the Red Army of the Caucasus hemmed in the constricted enemy garrison from the east.

It was revealed early in March that Marshal Timoshenko had achieved a sizable success south of Lake Ilmen, recapturing more than 300 localities, liberating some 900 square miles of territory and killing or capturing 11,000 Axis troops. The invaders were forced out of Demyansk, a formidable *place d'armes* that had served as a bastion to prevent the liquidation of an encirclement at Staraya Russa during the previous winter. Another resounding Russian victory was the recapture of Rzhev, on March 3, one of the strongest anchor positions on the central front. This had supported the salient that remained as a lingering threat to Moscow after the invaders had been driven back from the capital. At the same time the Rzhev-Velikiye Luki railway was cleared, paving the way for a multi-pronged drive toward the major German base at Smolensk.

It was the Russian Juggernaut now in action with the Germans reeling under its momentum. Gzhatsk, secondary strong point in the Rzhev salient, fell to the Russians on March 6 as they swiftly erased a large part of the long German-held area in their sweep southwestward. Vyazma, a five-way rail junction and the strongest base protecting Smolensk, was the next objective. As one Red Army force advanced toward it from the east, another pushed southward from the Rzhev-Velikiye Luki rail line against the Moscow-Vyazma-Smolensk line. Sychevka, a main point on the Rzhev-Vyazma railroad, fell on March 8 in another fierce battle. The Germans exerted counter-pressure against Orel, but it failed in its aim of weakening the drive for Vyazma and Smolensk.

The 141-days' winter campaign was ended. Russia was on the march! Moscow announced on March 31, 1943, the statistical summary of its achievements: liberation of 185,328 square miles of territory; westward gains of as much as 435 miles; the killing of 856,000 Axis troops and the capture of 343,525 prisoners; the capture or destruction of 5,000 Axis planes, 9,190 tanks, and 20,369 guns.

During the spring lull in ground action, the Red Air Force made heavy raids on German supply and communications centers, aiming mainly to disrupt the preparations for the summer campaign. Königsberg, capital of East Prussia, was bombed constantly. Warsaw, Danzig, Tilsit, Rostok, and Insterburg were being "softened up."

Importance of American and British war supplies as a factor in the Soviet victories was being widely discussed. Admiral William H.

Standley, American Ambassador in Moscow, expressed his personal opinion that the extent of the help arriving from abroad was not sufficiently recognized. Accounts of the extent and value of the supplies received from the United States and Britain began to appear in the Soviet press. The Ambassador had been an outspoken critic of the Russian policy of limiting the information given to foreign diplomats and military missions. Some time afterward, Admiral Standley returned to the United States and asked to be relieved of his post. He was succeeded by W. Averell Harriman, who had been in close and cordial contact with Russian officials through his duties as Lend-Lease expediter in London.

Moscow severed diplomatic relations with the Polish Government-in-exile in London, on April 25, charging that the Poles had connived with the Germans in spreading false stories that the Russians had massacred 10,000 Polish officers and men in the Smolensk region prior to the German occupation of the area in 1941. The Soviet Foreign Office formally declared that the Poles had acted under the influence of pro-Hitler elements and that some of the Polish representatives then in London had engaged in espionage in Russia. The actual facts, according to Moscow, were that some Polish prisoners of war had been kept in prison camps near the Katyn Forest west of Smolensk and had been abandoned there when the Red Army was forced to retreat during the German invasion. Moscow charged that these prisoners had been killed by the Germans to dispose of enemies and to swell the Russian casualty figures; that these and other Poles killed elsewhere had been buried in the Katyn Forest by the Germans.

The incident had the effect of disrupting relations between Moscow and the accredited Polish representatives and of causing some temporary friction between Moscow and British officials, the nominal hosts and sponsors of the Polish Government. Another result was that Moscow withdrew its affiliation with the Polish military forces originally organized and partly trained in the Soviet Union, but later transferred to the Near East. Instead, new Polish units, made up of Poles living in Russia, were formed and trained as a part of the Red Army.

Prime Minister Churchill arrived in Washington for his fifth war conference with President Roosevelt in May, 1943. On the historic occasion when he addressed Congress during his visit, he argued for the continued concentration of the major Allied effort against Germany and in support of Russia. "While the defeat of Japan would not mean the defeat of Germany," he said, "the defeat of Germany would infallibly mean the ruin of Japan."

His reference to the opening of a "second front" touched an issue on which Moscow was becoming more and more importunate. Though confident of the Red Army's ability to drive the Axis forces out of

Russia, Soviet leaders were aware that this would be a costly and protracted undertaking unless the Germans were engaged simultaneously with a full-scale invasion of Europe in the west. When President Roosevelt sent American greetings to Stalin on the occasion of the second anniversary of Russia's war with Germany, the Soviet Premier replied by reminding the President of the United Nations' pledge of an invasion from the west, and declared: "Victory will come all the sooner, the sooner we strike our united blows against the enemy."

This was the tense situation when, on June 1, 1943, the Germans launched a prelude to the summer campaign with a mass air attack on the junction of Kursk, employing 500 planes, aimed at disrupting supply lines for the coming offensive. Russian air and ground defenses downed 123 of the planes at a cost of thirty Soviet aircraft. Three nights later the Red Air Force responded by bombing German communications at Orel with 520 planes and followed this up the next night with attacks on German supply trains at Bryansk and Karachev, junction points for the central and southern fronts. In the week from May 30 to June 5, Russian pilots and ground gunners accounted for 752 Axis planes and their announced toll for five weeks was 2,821 planes. The Red Air Force persistently attacked the main points of the now evident German preparations for a large-scale offensive. The Russians opened their third year of war by attacking or reconnoitering in five key sectors. Big and decisive battles were brewing. Both sides were girded for far greater combats than the world had yet seen.

RUSSIA'S FATE ON THE RIVERS OF DESTINY

WAR and peace, as stark as a Tolstoian novel, rode the rivers of Russia in the summer of 1943. Rivers that had played vital rôles for centuries were now stained red with blood. Never had the famous song of the Volga boatmen rung with deeper import: "Pull, lad, pull with all your might. Pull together—pull once more. In the east the sun is setting fast—one more day, our toil will soon be past."

The Volga and the Terek had served as high-water marks of Nazi conquest in 1942; the Donets and the Mius delineated the extent of the Wehrmacht's retreat in early 1943; and the Dnieper was the goal for which the Red Army fought in the latter half of 1943.

During the three-month lull in the spring of 1943, the Germans in the south labored to strengthen their positions guarding the industrial regions of the Donbas and the mineral and agricultural resources of the Ukraine. Their line stretched northward along the Mius River from the Black Sea east to Taganrog; slanted northwestward along the Donets near Voroshilovsk, Lisichansk, and Izyum, and curved eastward around Kharkov to Belgorod. Belgorod was the Germans' anchor-point at the southern extremity of the Kursk-Orel double salient, the focal area of the fierce summer battles to come.

On the Russian lines their Kursk salient represented an ominous threat aimed directly at Kiev and the middle reaches of the Dnieper. The Germans menaced this Russian position on both of its flanks from their fortresses of Kharkov and Orel.

The Germans struck first, on the morning of July 5. The orthodox strategy of Field Marshal General Guenther von Kluge might have been predicted from the nature of his positions. Attacking simultaneously from both Belgorod and Orel, he counted on the sheer power of his armor, especially the new Mark VI Tiger tanks, to break through the Russian lines. His objective was to pinch off the Kursk salient by merging his forces west of Voronezh and then proceed to recapture that city. Thereupon the implied German plan was to cross the upper Don, engage the Red Army's massed reserves in the hinterland and eventually recoup the defeats of the previous winter by outflanking Moscow from the south or by driving a new wedge to the Volga.

Von Kluge's grandiloquent program never materialized. Its successful antidote was the new "blitz-grinding," or active-defense, tactics of the rejuvenated and expanded Red Army, as brought into play by the young Soviet commanders who had risen to eminence at Stalingrad. One of the chief architects of the defensive victory, which soon was developed into an offensive of decisive scope, was General Konstantin K. Rokossovsky. He had attained top military stature while in his middle forties by helping to nullify the sting of the hitherto deadly Stuka-Panzer weapon. Chief among his numerous collaborators in the field was General Nikolai F. Vatutin, victor of Voronezh and a leading exemplar of the new school of Russian tactics.

Their strategy was a product and a concomitant of the metamorphosis of the Soviet military machine. Under the personal direction of Stalin, the increasingly brilliant work of the Supreme Command reflected dynamically the revamping of the Red Army's high council. After the retirement of Marshal Boris Shaposhnikoff, the emergence of such younger minds as Marshals Gregory K. Zhukoff and Alexander M. Vasilevsky were to revitalize Russia. Active in laying out the broader aspects of the Red Army's program, and especially in mobilizing and training its tremendous reserves, were the men who had directed the opening phases of the conflict, Marshals Klementy E. Voroshiloff, Semyon K. Timoshenko, and Semyon Budenny.

The Russians had tamed the Nazis' new Tiger tank by permitting it to pass their ambushes and then coolly firing into its vulnerable rear with their ubiquitous antitank rifle—another symbol of the maturity of the Soviet military machine. Lacking a corresponding stratagem, the Germans could not effectively stop the monster Soviet KV tank. They dug their own tanks into the ground to serve suicidally as fixed forts; the Russians simply swirled around them and mopped them up at will. In the second fortnight of July the Red Army did what the Wehrmacht had failed to do: pierced the enemy's tough fortified belt and debouched in the less strongly defended operational spaces to the rear.

The essence of Soviet strategy was an endless train of bewildering surprises. Steeped in the tradition of orthodox maneuver on classical lines, the Germans were continually lured into situations for which they were tactically and emotionally unequipped. Where they looked for a conventional operation the Russians unfolded something audaciously novel. The next time, when the chastened Nazis prepared diligently for all possible surprises, the Soviet Command would confound them again by falling back on the obvious.

Orel fell to the Russians on August 5. With it toppled Belgorod, 170 miles to the south, the other anchor of the German arc protecting Kiev and the Dnieper. The double victory, the first great triumph of the summer campaign and a portent of still greater ones to come, had the effect of releasing the brakes on the Soviet line in the Ukraine. Both wings swept forward with new momentum. The first phase of the gigantic operation was completed, but the offensive, instead of pausing, was redoubled in power.

This rapid widening of the front was accomplished without loss of stride in the all-important Ukraine push. After capturing Orel and Belgorod, the Red Army was thirty miles from Bryansk and sixteen miles from Kharkov. The advance against strong and resourceful opposition continued daily. By August 8 the Russians had slashed the rail line between Sumy and Kharkov, cutting off the defenses of the latter city from supply sources to the northwest. Thereupon Kharkov was invested from three sides. Meanwhile the northern wing was marching frontally on Bryansk.

Political aspects of the Russian war were stimulated by a Moscow announcement on August 21 that Maxim Litvinoff, Soviet Ambassador to the United States, had been relieved and would be succeeded by Andrei A. Gromyko. Since Mr. Litvinoff had been a traditional symbol of Russian collaboration with the western Powers, it was feared that his recall might portend a new direction in Soviet diplomacy. Events revealed the true significance of the transfer: the popular western-minded Ambassador had been chosen for a post of greater importance in the Kremlin's inner councils—he became a deputy commissar for foreign affairs. Soviet policy, far from turning away from the west, was committed more staunchly than ever before to thorough-going collaboration.

The long and hard-fought battle for Kharkov culminated on August 23. The Russians, who had been storming toward it by short stages, at last drove the Germans from the metropolis of the Ukraine. It was the fourth time in the war that Russia's third city, its handsome modern buildings now badly battered, had changed hands. As it fell, the German line south of it also collapsed.

Storming into Stalino on September 8, the Red Army completed the liberation of the Donbas. Berlin, again employing its familiar propaganda line, announced: "In conformity with our elastic fighting tactics, the town of Stalino was evacuated according to plan to shorten the front after the destruction of all militarily important establishments."

The forces in western Russia, fighting for every inch of ground against concentrated German units in strong defense positions, had brought Bryansk within artillery range. The Russians had crossed the Desna River and begun the direct siege of the city. Faced with insuperable pressure, the Germans started to abandon Bryansk, which they had held nearly two years. They taunted that they were destroying all military installations and that the arriving Russians would "put their hands into an empty pocket." The Red Army occupied the ruined city, together with its twin town of Rezhitsa, on September 17. On the same day the Russians in the far south took the Sea of Azov port of

Ossipenko, placing them roughly halfway between Rostov and the neck of the Crimea.

While this advance along the Azov coast was under way, the Russian Caucasus army, aided by the Black Sea fleet and its marines, had been hacking persistently at the German bridgehead in the Kuban. Here the Wehrmacht, augmented by Rumanian units, was determinedly trying to hold the Crimea from a flank assault across the Kerch strait. The Black Sea port and naval base of Novorossiisk, long a no man's land because hovering Russians guns denied its use to the Germans, finally fell to the Red Army when landing parties of Red fleet marines took it on September 16. Its fall undermined the Germans' last foothold in the Caucasus and raised the prospect of an early pincers action against the Crimea.

The Red Army swept into Smolensk on September 25, engulfing the entire surrounding region. On the same day they captured Roslavl, another junction seventy miles to the southeast on the Bryansk railroad.

This was the route of Napoleon's march to Moscow—and of his disastrous retreat. The path of Hitler's emulative conquest, it had now become for him, too, a hard and galling road back, strewn with battles fought no longer for conquest, but to escape retributive destruction.

The Germans, after they had been thrown back from the Donets, drew a new defense line that ran southward from Smolensk, through Kiev and along the curve of the Dnieper to Kherson. This line was already unhinged at the north with the loss of Smolensk and the entire Dnieper position was in grave peril. Hitler rushed to the Dnieper front and again took command, declaring that the river was the natural frontier and exclaiming: "Here I am and here I shall remain."

But, as usual, the Fuehrer's blatant arrogance did not conform with the position and capabilities of his armies. German propaganda drew an ominous picture of the size and might of the Russian offensive. "In one sector," said a Berlin broadcast, "the Russians are so massed that there is a soldier every yard, a grenade-thrower every seven yards, a field gun every fifteen yards, and a multi-barreled gun every forty yards."

The Red Army's constantly expanding battle line, more than 1,000 miles long, stretched from the northern tip of White Russia down to the Black Sea shore of the Caucasus by the end of September.

While the Ukraine armies were driving to the Dnieper, clearing the east bank of the river and preparing to storm across, the Soviet forces in the Caucasus were battling to eliminate the Germans' Kuban bridgehead so that the advance along the Black Sea might proceed in concert with the rapid gains farther north.

The Black Sea port of Anapa fell on September 22. The remaining Axis troops fell back on the fortress of Temryuk, the last important defensive position in the northwestern corner of the Caucasus jutting toward the Crimea between the Sea of Azov and the Black Sea. Driven out of Temryuk on September 27, the Germans began ferrying their forces across the strait to Kerch. Planes and small naval craft of the Black Sea fleet took a heavy toll of Axis transports and barges engaged in the evacuation. Moscow announced on October 7 that the Caucasus had finally been cleared of the enemy.

The Red Army on October 13 pierced the Germans' "Crimea Line" in the southern Ukraine below the Dnieper elbow and entered the fortress of Melitopol. Street fighting raged with savage intensity for eleven days. The Russians captured Zaporozhye, the last east-bank Dnieper stronghold on October 14. The Germans evacuated Zaporozhye after dynamiting the famous Dnieper dam, a pride of the Soviet Union's pre-war industrial era. The Russians had damaged the dam when the region was overrun by the Germans.

The battle in Melitopol ended in Soviet victory on October 23. Its cost to the Germans—20,000 killed, or the equivalent of two divisions—indicated the importance the Wehrmacht attached to the city. It not only covered the withdrawal of the remaining Axis troops and matériel east and south of the Dnieper, but protected the lower reaches of the river and the entrance to the Crimea.

During these summer and autumn victories of 1943, the effective cohesion of the United Nations was steadily being advanced by diplomatic gains that kept pace with the military achievements. Churchill had warned Parliament that "the bloodiest portion of this war lies ahead." Stalin had sent a message to the American people, acknowledging their share in the credit for the dawning victory and praising the workers who had built the tanks, planes, and other matériel poured into Russia.

United States Secretary of State Cordell Hull and British Foreign Secretary Anthony Eden arrived in Moscow on October 18 to open with Foreign Commissar Molotov the conversations foreshadowed in the prior British-American conference in Quebec. A product of these talks was the European Advisory Commission, which was to sit in London and make recommendations to the Allied Governments. China was represented at some of the Moscow talks. The four leading powers agreed to carry their coöperation and collaboration beyond the period of hostilities and laid down principles for a broad system of international coöperation and security to include all peace-loving nations.

About the same time the United States, British, and Canadian Governments signed in London the third agreement with the Soviet Union for Lend-Lease relations, assuring that the flow of military supplies into Russia would continue without interruption.

RED ARMY'S MIGHTY SURGE DRIVES GERMANS FROM SOIL OF RUSSIA

RUSSIAN resurgence rolled like a tidal wave against the Germans in 1944-45. Hitler's "supermen" were driven from Russian soil by the raging torrents of Stalin's powerful armies. The young Soviet Republics proved their strength in mighty thrusts which forced the old Prussian militarists and their Nazi hordes to fall back toward their last lines of defense on their own borders.

Countries which had been occupied by the Germans were wrested from them. The Red armies flooded into Latvia, Estonia, Lithuania, Finland, Poland, Hungary, Bulgaria, Rumania, Czechoslovakia, Austria.

Capture of Kiev in the first snows of the winter of 1943-44 was the signal for a continuation of the embattled march across the rest of the Ukraine. The Kursk-Orel triumph had cracked the keystone of the Germans' strong positions in the Donbas; the spectacular toppling of Kiev broke the Nazis' grip upon the Dnieper.

In the scourging of the German forces in the east an outstanding quartet of the Red Army's brilliant military leaders became known as "the Four Horsemen of the German Apocalypse." These bearers of a lion's share in the growing victory were Generals Konstantin K. Rokossovsky, Ivan S. Koneff, Rodion Y. Malinovsky, and Fedor I. Tolbukhin. In this climactic phase of the war another miracle-working tactician, who obviously also carried a marshal's baton in his knapsack, met death during a crucial campaign and was deprived of his deserved place among the destroyers of German might. This was General Nikolai F. Vatutin, who had marched from Voronezh to the Dnieper at the head of the First Ukrainian Army.

When the winter campaign started, Vatutin's forces were deployed from a point above Kiev southward to the region of Cherkassy; Koneff was on his left flank in a sector that spread down to Dniepropetrovsk; still farther south, Malinovsky was besieging the lower Dnieper. North of this theater, Rokossovsky was poised in White Russia for the lunge that was to take him into Poland. On the Black Sea front, Tolbukhin was laying the groundwork for his famous collaboration with Malinovsky by preparing to leap from the Caucasus into the Crimea.

Staggering surprises awaited the Germans. Vatutin's dazzling envelopment of Kiev was one of them. Kiev stands on the high western bank of the Dnieper, from which the Germans' guns commanded the low eastern bank and the river's islands. While a token Russian force

INTERNATIONAL NEWS PHOTO

1944 — D-Day!

En Route to Invasion

Lieut. General Mark W. Clark peering eagerly ahead from a PT boat that carried him to the Anzio beachhead.

OFFICIAL U. S. NAVY PHOTO

The Palm Tree Stands for War
Although palm leaves are often used as the symbol of peace, these palm trees proved valuable as fortification bulwarks at Tarawa.

OFFICIAL U. S. MARINE CORPS PHOTO

Tarawa Beach Scene
Marines on the littered beach camouflage their ammunition and other gear in case the Japs tried an air attack.

OFFICIAL U. S. NAVY PHOTOGRAPH

The Light That Failed

Put out of commission by accurate U. S. fire, this giant Japanese searchlight was one of the many war devices which the Japs had set up on Tarawa.

SIGNAL CORPS PHOTO

Occupation of Rome

The day after Allied troops of the Fifth Army occupied Rome, Pope Pius XII addressed the people.

Invasion Beachhead

While hundreds of others move toward the beach in landing craft, American assault troops with full equipment, move onto a beachhead in northern France.

SIGNAL CORPS PHOTO

SIGNAL CORPS PHOTO

Awaiting "Sailing Orders"

American men and equipment on a loading dock in England, await orders to join the ever-increasing stream of men and matériel pouring into France.

SIGNAL CORPS PHOTO

Barge to Beachhead

Vehicles being unloaded onto a beachhead in France from a barge. In the foreground is a captured German anti-tank gun.

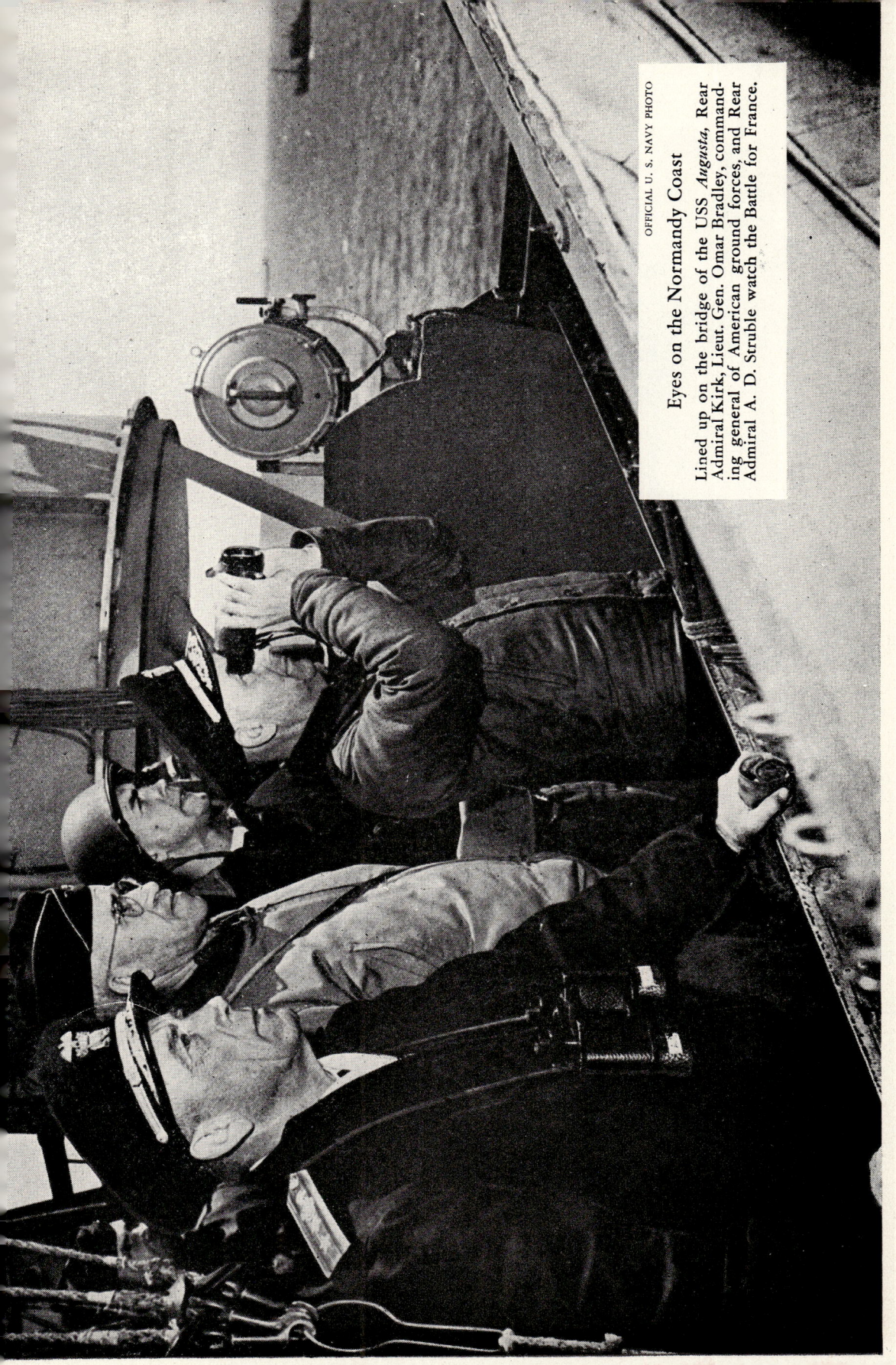

OFFICIAL U. S. NAVY PHOTO

Eyes on the Normandy Coast

Lined up on the bridge of the USS *Augusta*, Rear Admiral Kirk, Lieut. Gen. Omar Bradley, commanding general of American ground forces, and Rear Admiral A. D. Struble watch the Battle for France.

OFFICIAL U. S. NAVY PHOTOGRAPH

Eyes Alert
Navy men aboard a landing craft, while awaiting the order to dash for the French invasion coast.

OFFICIAL U. S. NAVY PHOTO

An LST "Welcome Mat"
Army men rehearse rolling out the steel matting in beaching operations.

Activity on the Cliffs

An American command post in France hurrying German prisoners down the cliff side to waiting ships in the harbor.

SIGNAL CORPS PHOTO

SIGNAL CORPS PHOTO

German "Supermen"

German soldiers, most of whom were abandoned by their officers at Cherbourg, are marched through the city after its liberation by American forces.

Generals Smile Too
General Eisenhower and Lieut. General Patton enter 3rd Army Headquarters to review the Guard of Honor.

SIGNAL CORPS PHOTO

OFFICIAL U. S. NAVY PHOTO

For the Saipan Front
Marine reinforcements move toward the front along a road being widened by a bulldozer.

OFFICIAL PHOTO U. S. A. A. F.

En Route to Saipan
A 7th A. A. F. Aviation Engineers' gun crew maintains quarters next to the gun it operates from the deck of their landing craft.

Part of "Operation Uppercut"

Parachutes fill the air over the coast of southern France, somewhere between Nice and Marseilles.

OFFICIAL PHOTO U. S. A. A. F.

OFFICIAL PHOTO U. S. A. A. F.

Smoke from Rumanian Oil Refineries

B-17 Flying Fortresses of the 15th A.A.F. come off the target during the heavy bomber attack at Ploesti.

Hengyang Airfield

Clouds of smoke spread over this airfield in China after General Chennault's Headquarters had issued orders to abandon the U. S. Army 14th Air Force base.

OFFICIAL PHOTO U. S. AIR FORCES

SIGNAL CORPS PHOTO

Time Out for a Chat
General Eisenhower, chatting with Lieut. Gen. Bradley and Major Gen. J. Lawton Collins, during a tour in France.

SIGNAL CORPS PHOTO

"Monty" and "Ike"
General Montgomery and General Eisenhower in Normandy shortly after D-Day.

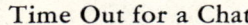

SIGNAL CORPS PHOTO

Yank Infantry
The infantry moves through another town in France abandoned by the Germans, as civilians line the curb to watch.

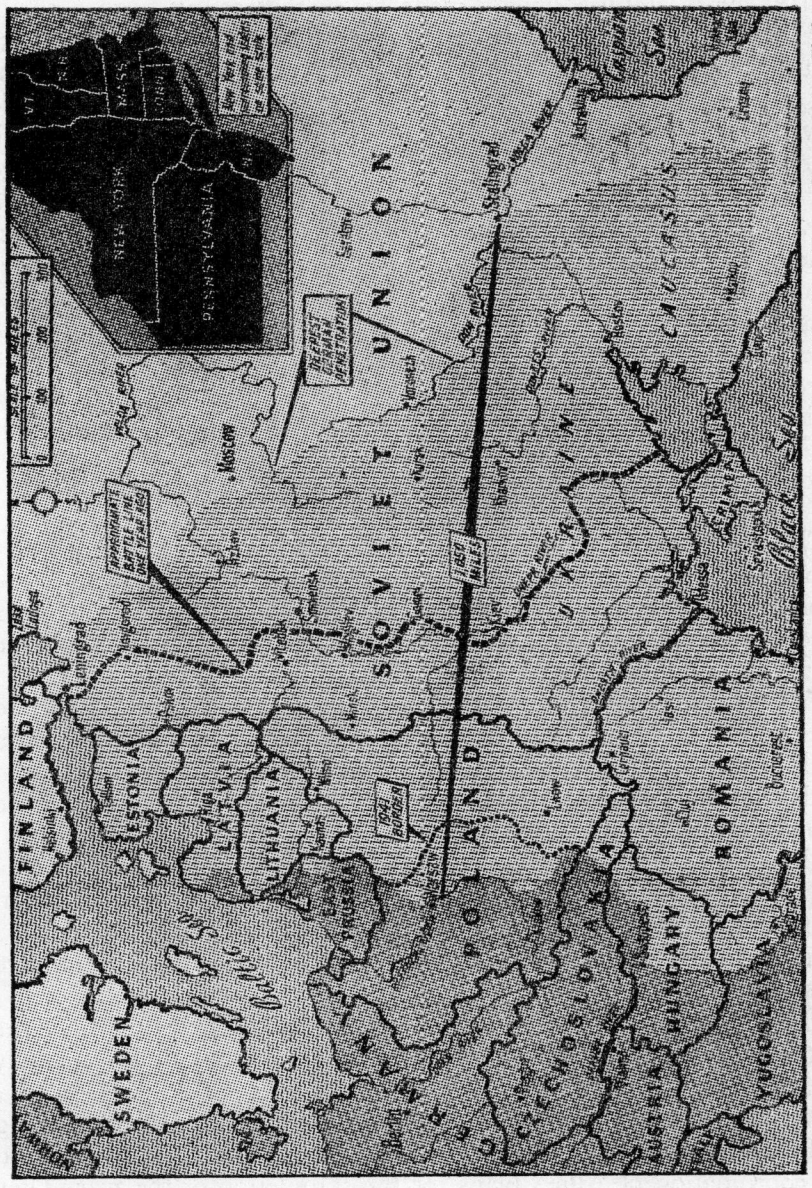

A chart of Russia's military feat after November, 1942, when the Nazis were in the streets of Stalingrad. The vertical shading indicates the territory out of which the Germans were driven—a land area at least five times the combined area of the states in the inset map.

NEW YORK HERALD TRIBUNE *map*—Fleck

conspicuously attempted crossings opposite the city and occupied some of the islands, Vatutin quietly made his main crossing further north and assembled his principal force above Kiev. On November 4-5, Vatutin's men drove southward to the west of the city, by-passing it and cutting its supply connections with Korosten, Zhitomir, and Berdichev. With the city thus neatly boxed in, Vatutin swung around and attacked it from the south. The dumfounded Germans were overpowered without a prolonged struggle on November 6. They lost at Kiev, according to Russian accounts, 15,000 killed and 6,200 prisoners.

Recapture of Kiev meant far more than the fall of just another city. Historically clothed in the aura of holy Russia, it was a symbol of old Russia as Stalingrad is of the Soviet era. It stood in the traditions of eastern Orthodoxy as Rome stands in the Roman Catholic world. It was, moreover, one of Russia's "mother towns," seat of the first czars and of ancient cathedrals. Its captivity and desecration had caused anguish throughout Russia; its liberation epitomized for the nation the promise of total victory. Kiev's fall marked the end of the battle of the Dnieper and the beginning of the battle of the Western Ukraine.

The stage was set to strangle the Axis garrison in the Crimea and to proceed with a characteristic hammer-and-sickle sweep against the disorganized Germans crowded into the western Ukraine. With ample reason, Moscow was in a carnival mood for its celebration of the twenty-sixth anniversary of the Red Revolution.

Vatutin at once struck out westward from Kiev in a spreading arc to threaten the Germans' only remaining north-south railroad. Within a week he cut this lifeline at Zhitomir, seventy miles west of Kiev. Hundreds of additional populated places were liberated. The Germans were stung by the bewildering series of strategic and tactical defeats. Alarmed by the acute threat to their entire southern position, they struck sharply at Rokossovsky's southern flank in White Russia, at Rechitsa, in an effort to draw off Russian strength from the south. Then they launched a strong frontal counterattack toward Kiev, recapturing Zhitomir five days after its fall.

The Red Army was forced to give ground for the first time since the start of the summer offensive in July, and Vatutin fell back slowly toward Kiev.

While this battle was at its height, Premier Stalin was conferring in Teheran with President Roosevelt and Prime Minister Churchill on the coördination of Allied plans for the completion of the war. They announced on December 1: "We have shaped and confirmed our common policy" for the destruction of the German forces and for a peace that would "banish the scourge and terror of war for generations."

Late in December, Vatutin struck out anew west of Kiev in the direction of Zhitomir, along the southern flank of the German bulge. Scattering some twenty-two German divisions—about 300,000 men—he made a 200-mile breach in the enemy lines, captured the fortified rail center of Zhitomir and sped on beyond it toward the 1939 Russian-Polish frontier at a point south of the Pripet Marshes.

Moscow announced on January 10, 1944, that the Soviet Union was prepared to guarantee a strong and independent Poland provided the Polish Government, then in exile in London, would agree to abandon its demands for territory east of the Curzon Line. Stalin rejected as unjust the Treaty of Riga, which had ended the Russian-Polish war in 1921 and created the pre-1939 boundary. Thus Russia called for a frontier that would classify as Russian territory the broad eastern zone including such cities as Vilna, Pinsk, and Rovno.

On this basis Moscow invited Poland to join the Russian-Czech treaty of alliance, mutual assistance, and postwar collaboration. Rejecting this offer, the Polish régime in London asked the United States and Britain to join in a four-power conference to adjudicate a "fair border." This proposal in turn was rejected by Moscow and the dispute remained an unsettled point for the remaining months of the war.

General Leonid N. Govoroff, commander of the long-stalemated Leningrad front, launched a surprise offensive on January 18 that quickly broke through the strong German defenses hemming in the battered, blockaded former capital. A complementary offensive was started on the Volkhov front, immediately south of Leningrad, commanded by General Kirill A. Meretskoff.

The tidal wave of the Red Army spread like a flood along the coast of the Gulf of Finland and down the railroad toward Narva.

The Russians were exploiting a virtually continuous battle line from the Gulf of Finland to the Black Sea by February 1. Again the Germans were taking lessons from the Red Army in what they had once considered a Wehrmacht specialty—lightning war of movement. The Russians would strike first at one point and then without warning at another one far distant.

The Leningrad offensive cut off Finland from her German ally, hastening the day of reckoning for that unfortunate country which had been impressed into the Nazi camp. The United States sternly counseled Finland on February 8 to make peace with Russia and get out of the war or take the consequences. Although popular sentiment in Finland appeared to favor this course, the Germans retained their military grip upon the country and forced Helsinki to hold out. It eventually was necessary for Russia to compel Finland's capitulation by force of arms.

The reckless desperation with which the Germans clung to the southwest Ukraine—apparently at one of Hitler's capricious orders—brought about their undoing. Their Dnieper bridgehead at Nikopol was the keystone of their position; to lose it meant a retreat to the Bug River, beyond which lay Odessa, Rumania, and the Danube. Nikopol garrison was ordered to hold to the last man. Malinovsky's Third Ukrainian Army stormed into and through the city foot by foot. The Russians captured it on February 8 after a four-day battle that cost the Germans 15,000 or more killed and 2,000 prisoners. With its fall the last German was cleared from the east bank of the lower Dnieper. The valuable manganese-producing center was returned to Russian hands.

The great story of that winter's warfare was the intricate interrelation of a series of widely separated drives that pried the Germans away from the Dnieper. Focal event in this interplay of episodes was the operation that made Koneff the first of the "Four Horsemen" to win his marshal's star. That red-letter achievement finds its place in history as the battle of the Korsun pocket.

While the Germans were busy dealing with the First Ukrainian Army's second attack from Kiev, in January, Koneff's Second Ukrainian Army set in motion a series of complicated maneuvers whose significance apparently escaped the German command. What happened was that Koneff, using swift cavalry and tank-borne infantry, thrust spearheads against the sides of the German salient near its bases on separate routes. When the Nazis awoke to their peril, the salient had been neatly cut off by lightning-like double encirclement. The area thus isolated centered near Korsun and consisted of a large part of the region bounded by Kanyev, Boguslav, Gorodishche, and Smyela.

This pocket was closed about February 3. For the next two weeks a terrific battle raged. The Germans tried to escape from the trap. Koneff's men held the ring tight and destroyed its occupants bit by bit. Trapped troops threshed in vain against the Red Army's steel vise and thereby assisted the Russians' purpose of wearing them down. A blockade by the Red Air Force prevented any considerable reinforcement from the air. Koneff cut the pocket into segments with new spearheads and proceeded to strangle each one with a narrowing circle of fire. Soldiers reported later that they had sickened from the grim monotony of the daily slaughter.

Premier Stalin, in an order of the day on February 17, announced: "Koneff's Army after a fourteen-day fight completed an operation aimed at the annihilation of ten German divisions and one brigade encircled in the Dnieper bend. The Germans left on the battlefield 52,000 killed, and 11,000 surrendered."

Koneff's success at Korsun greatly facilitated the rapid reduction of Nikopol, Shepetovka, and Krivoi Rog, which, taken together, meant the bursting of the last remnants of resistance in the Dnieper bend and a resumption of the advance toward the Bug and Dniester Rivers.

It was revealed that Vatutin had been forced by illness to yield his command at the height of his success. He died a few weeks later after an operation. His place was taken by Marshal Gregory K. Zhukoff.

Zhukoff and Koneff had forced a crossing of the Dniester and speared into Bucovina by March 20.

Farther south the highly mobile forces of Malinovsky were still rolling on, unleashing powerful blows against Odessa, Tiraspol, and the lower Dniester. His infantry and motorized cavalry swept into Odessa on April 10 after a four-day battle on the outskirts, to find that a large part of the German-Rumanian garrison had been withdrawn by sea.

Early in April, Tolbukhin built up his offensive to full force in the Crimea. Germans and Rumanians were driven from the Kerch Peninsula. As he advanced, his forces joined at Dzhankoi with those of General Yeremenko, which had broken through the Perekop Isthmus on the north. Simferopol, the capital, and the secondary ports of Evpatoriya and Feodosiya, fell to them in a grand surge on April 13. There they were joined by Marshal Alexander M. Vasilevsky.

After a twenty-four-day siege under Vasilevsky's direction, the Fourth Ukrainian Army, with major assistance from elements of the fleet and the Red Air Force, completed the capture of the Sevastopol Fortress on May 9. The complete reconquest of the Crimea was consummated.

Russia's offensive up the Karelian Isthmus was a magnified duplicate of the Red Army's war against Finland in 1939. The Mannerheim Line, which had proved a difficult obstacle for the Russians nearly five years earlier, now hindered the Soviet forces only momentarily. The Finns made a fighting retreat northward, with scant German help.

Timed with the Allied second-front landing in Normandy on June 6, 1944, the Red Army contributed to the grand attack a brilliant offensive in White Russia. Rokossovsky delivered sudden, simultaneous thrusts from several directions that surrounded Vitebsk. The Dvina stronghold fell on June 27 with 10,000 prisoners. Central German "bolt positions" at Bobruisk and Mogilev were toppled soon afterward, undermining the dam that had penned up the Soviet flood. White Russian Armies swept forward in one of the most spectacular advances of the war, descending on Minsk from the northeast and southeast. Minsk was captured on July 3 in such a lightning stroke that large German forces east of the city were enveloped. In one day a typical bag of 6,000 prisoners was tallied. By July 13 the advance had surged past Vilna, where 5,000 more Germans were captured. Scope of the Russian triumph was epitomized on July 17 when some 60,000 German prisoners from White Russia were marched through the streets of Moscow.

The on-sweeping Red Army approached the German frontiers and threatened to engulf all Poland and the Baltic States. In August, 1944, they were tightening the noose along the Vistula River and converging on Warsaw. Here a great people were waiting for liberation.

RAPE AND RAPINE IN WAKE OF NAZI ARMIES

"WAR is hell!" This has long been the expression of the civilized world. But it remained for the Axis powers to reveal its full significance. Destruction and devastation are inevitable results of battle. In modernized warfare they rise to their highest crescendo with bombing and annihilation of cities. It was the Axis, however, that was to defy all provisions of international law, resort to savagery and barbarism, and create an inferno on earth.

Documented evidence began to accumulate in the conquered countries early in World War II, condemning the inhuman treatment of prisoners and women and children. The ravages and outrages of Axis armies developed into a reign of terror and wholesale murder. Sworn testimony and mutilated bodies were the unimpeachable witnesses of the ghastly carnival of torture and horror, rape and rapine, loot and plunder, with the desecration of homes, churches, schools. As the Red Army liberated conquered territory the gruesome story unfolded in the wake of the German Armies and their satellites. When the invaders were driven back from Moscow in 1941-42 and from the Don, the Caucasus, the Donets Basin, and the Ukraine in 1942-43, the extent of Nazi cruelty left its irrefutable records.

As early as November 25, 1941, Foreign Commissar Molotov addressed to the ambassadors and ministers of all countries with which Russia maintained diplomatic relations a formal note: "The Soviet Government is in possession of numerous facts testifying to systematic atrocities and outrages perpetrated by German authorities against captured Red Army men and commanders... revealing the German soldiery and the German Government as a band of extortioners disregarding all provisions of international law and all human morality. ... The Soviet military command has established many instances in which the captured... were brutally tortured, tormented, and murdered by the German military command and by German Army units ... with red-hot irons, their eyes gouged out, their legs, arms, ears, and noses cut off, their fingers hacked off and their stomachs ripped open. They have been tied to tanks and ripped apart.

"A number of cases have been recorded in which the German Command drove captive Red Army men before advancing German columns during an attack, threatening them with shooting. In particular, such cases were recorded near the Vybory State Farm in the Leningrad region, near Yelna in the Smolensk region of the White Russian Republic, in the Poltava region of the Ukraine and in a number of other places.... There are innumerable instances of defenseless sick and wounded Red Army men in hospitals being bayoneted or shot.... In the small town of Rudnya, in the Smolensk region, Nazi units which captured a Soviet field hospital shot and wounded Red Army stretcher-bearers and nurses.

"In German camps for war prisoners, sick and wounded Red Army men get no medical assistance and are doomed to death from typhus, dysentery, pneumonia, and other diseases. An arbitrary and extremely brutal discipline is imposed.... In the Porkhov Camp captive Red Army men are kept in the open day and night, despite cold weather. Early in the morning they are awakened by blows with sticks and clubs and driven to work without regard for their physical condition. During their work the guards—German and Finnish soldiers—drive them on incessantly with whips. Sick and weakened Red Army men are beaten to death with clubs.

"Looting is rampant among soldiers and officers of Hitler's army. With the advent of winter, looting has taken on a mass character. In their rush to get warm clothes the Nazi bandits stop at nothing. They not only strip dead Red Army men of warm clothing and footwear, but take literally all warm things from the wounded, felt boots, socks, sweaters, warm jackets and caps, stripping them naked and even donning women's clothing taken from dead and wounded nurses.

"Captive Red Army men are starved and kept for weeks without food or on miserable rations of rotten bread or rotten potatoes. Refusing to supply war prisoners with food, the Nazis force them to search garbage cans and look for remnants of food thrown away by German soldiers or, as happened in several camps including the camp at Korma in White Russia, dead horses' carcasses are thrown over the wire fence to the prisoners.

"Striving for mass extermination... German authorities and the German Government instituted a bestial régime in prison camps. The German High Command and the Ministry of Food and Agriculture issued a decree... to doom Soviet war prisoners to excruciating death by starvation... which violates the most elementary norms of human morals. The Soviet Government places the whole responsibility for these inhuman actions on the German military and civil authorities."

On January 2, 1942, Molotov sent another documentary letter to the foreign envoys in Moscow relating to the civilian population in occupied territory. Here are some of the charges: "Voluminous documentary data... testify to the fact that the plunder and ruin of the population, accompanied by brutal outrages and wholesale murder, are the rule in all districts which have fallen under the heel of the

German invaders. Indisputable facts testify that this régime of despoliation and bloody terror against the peaceful population of occupied towns and villages is not a matter of excesses by individual, undisciplined military units, nor by individual German officers and soldiers, but is a definite system worked out in advance and encouraged by the German Government and the German Command....

"Every step of the German-Fascist Army and its allies on captured Soviet territory in the Ukraine, Moldavia, White Russia, Lithuania, Latvia, Estonia, Karelian-Finnish territory and Russian districts and regions spells destruction and ruin for untold material and cultural values of our people.... The Soviet Government and its organs are keeping a detailed account of all these heinous crimes committed by the Hitlerite army.... The German invaders... have wrecked and even burned to the ground scores of cities and thousands of towns and villages in the temporarily occupied districts of the USSR. Numerous examples have been recorded of the vandalism of German troops, the devastation and destruction of municipal buildings, factories, and other structures, and entire city blocks, as happened in Minsk, Kiev, Novgorod, Kharkov, Kalinin, and other cities.

"The German invaders wiped from the face of the earth hundreds of towns and villages in the Ukraine and White Russia and in the Moscow, Leningrad, Tula, and other regions.

"An ordered issued in the 512th German Infantry Regiment, signed by Colonel Schittnig, which was intercepted recently near the town of Verkhovye in the Orel region, brazenly stated: 'The zone subject to evacuation must look like a desert after the withdrawal of our troops. ... In places where total destruction is to be effected, all houses must be burned. For this purpose, the houses should be stuffed with straw beforehand, particularly brick houses, and all existing brick structures should be blown up, special care being taken to destroy all cellars. Measures for devastating a zone must be prepared and executed ruthlessly and thoroughly....' They blow up and burn public buildings, factories, mills, schools, libraries, hospitals, and churches. In villages occupied by the German authorities the peaceful peasant population is subjected to unrestrained pillage and violence. The peasants are robbed of possessions acquired by decades of hard work; they are deprived of their houses, cattle, grain, clothing, everything down to the last baby's shirt, down to the last handful of grain.

"In the village of Golubovka, Voroshilovgrad region, the population, already robbed of its stocks of food, was again plundered by the Germans, who took away from the women and children whatever food remained and all the household goods, clothing, pillows, blankets, and kitchenware they could carry. The marauders accompanied this pillaging with bloody reprisals. In Orel, for example, the Germans put up a gallows in the center of the city and publicly hanged an old man who had protested against the looting. Besides him they hanged several citizens who had refused to assist the Hitlerites in robbing the population of clothing and linen. In Rostov-on-Don, the Germans looted all shops; stripped passersby in the streets of their clothing, footwear, watches, and valuables; pillaged private houses one after another, indiscriminately destroying everything they could not carry away with them.

"The German authorities have legalized marauding by their army and encourage this looting and violence. The German Government regards this as a realization of the bandit 'principle' they have proclaimed, according to which every German soldier must have a 'personal, material interest in the war.' Order No. 24220, issued by the chief of the Fourteenth Rumanian Division, Colonel Nikolaescu, states: 'Grain, cattle, sheep, goats, and poultry must be requisitioned from the population for the army. Thorough search must be made in every house, and everything taken away.... The slightest resistance must be punished by summary shooting, and burning of the house.'

"With increasing frequency one encounters on the Soviet-German front, and particularly on the approaches to Moscow, officers and soldiers wearing plundered clothing, their pockets bulging with stolen articles, carrying in their tunics women's and children's clothing, footwear and underwear stripped from their victims.... The facts testify to the utter moral degradation and corruption of Hitler's army, which for its looting, thievery, and marauding has earned the wrathful condemnation and scorn of the whole Soviet people.

"The occupationists have introduced a régime of forced hard labor for the peaceful population, which is ruined and deprived of all means of subsistence. Disregarding their age and the state of their health, the Hitlerites throw many Soviet citizens into concentration camps after occupying or destroying their houses, and force them under threat of torture, shooting, and starvation to perform without pay various hard tasks, including work of a military nature. On many occasions after civilians have been used for some kind of military work all of them have been shot to preserve secrecy.

"A number of documents of the German Command, intercepted by Red Army units during the offensive at Rostov, prove that the exploitation of the local population for particularly dangerous military work is provided for in special instructions. For example, in an order dated October 11, issued for the 76th German Infantry Division, Article 6, dealing with the cleaning up of mine fields, states: 'It is necessary to use prisoners of war and individuals from the local population for work entailing danger to life.'... It has been established that the peasants and other peaceful citizens drafted for forced labor are automatically classed in German staff reports as 'prisoners of war,' thus artificially and illegitimately swelling the number of war prisoners.

"In Kharkov the occupationists made a special point of abusing the local Ukrainian intellectuals. On November 5 all actors were ordered to report for registration at the Shevchenko Theater. When the actors gathered they were surrounded by German soldiers, who harnessed them to carts and drove them along the main streets to the river to haul water. In all the occupied regions the German Government has appointed as the local Fascist rulers all kinds of scoundrels from the Hitlerite party, who totally ignore the civil rights and national customs of the population, attempt to Germanize everything and exterminate recalcitrants.

Listing other instances of "base violence, abominable outrage of the honor of women, and the wholesale slaughter of Soviet citizens," the document continued: "On June 30 the Hitlerite bandits entered Lwow, and on the very next day staged an orgy of murder under the slogan: 'Kill the Jews and Poles.' Having murdered hundreds of people, the Hitlerite bandits held an 'exhibition' of the corpses in the city arcade. Prominently displayed were the bodies of a mother and child impaled on the same bayonet. In many cases Hitlerites have used Soviet children as targets for shooting practice. In the village of Bely Rast, in the Krasnaya Polyana district, a group of drunken German soldiers stood twelve-year-old Volodya Tkachev on the doorstep of a house and opened fire at him from automatic rifles.... In the township of Voskresenskoye, Dubinin district, the Hitlerites used a three-year-old boy as a target for setting the range for their machine guns. In the village of Volovo, a district center of the Kursk region, where the Germans spent four hours, an officer dashed the head of the two-year-old child of Boikova against a wall and killed it because it was crying.

"The occupation of towns and villages usually begins with the erection of a gallows, on which the German hangmen execute the first civilians who happen to cross their path. Moreover, the Fascists leave the corpses hanging on the gallows for days on end, and even for several weeks. They also leave untouched for many days the bodies of those whom they shoot in the streets of towns and villages. In the Ukrainian village of Voronki the Germans placed forty wounded Red Army men, war prisoners, and Red Cross nurses in a former hospital. They took from the medical personnel all dressing materials, medicines, food, and other supplies. The nurses were raped and shot. Guards placed beside the wounded allowed no one to approach them for four days. Some of the wounded died and the rest were later thrown into the river. The local population was forbidden to remove the bodies.

"Near the town of Borisov in White Russia, seventy-five women and girls who fled before the troops fell into the hands of the Hitlerites.

The Germans raped and brutally murdered thirty-six women and girls. On orders of German Officer Hummer, the soldiers took sixteen-year-old L. I. Melchukova into the forest and raped her. Later other women taken into the forest saw Melchukova impaled with bayonets to boards propped against a tree. Before the eyes of these other women, V. I. Alferenko and V. M. Bereznikova, the Germans hacked off the dying girl's breasts.

"Horrible massacres and pogroms were perpetrated by the German invaders in the Ukrainian capital, Kiev. Within a few days the Germans killed and tortured to death 52,000 men, women, old folk, and children, dealing mercilessly with all Ukrainians, Russians, and Jews who in any way displayed their loyalty to the Soviet Government. Soviet citizens who managed to escape from Kiev gave an agonizing account of one of these mass executions. A large number of Jews, including women and children of all ages, was gathered in the Jewish cemetery. Before they were shot all of them were stripped naked and beaten. The first persons selected for shooting were forced to lie face down at the bottom of a ditch and were shot with automatic rifles. Then the Germans shoveled a little earth over their bodies. The next group of people awaiting execution was forced to lie on top of them and was shot in the same way.

"Many mass murders were also committed by the German occupationists in other Ukrainian towns. These bloody executions were especially directed against unarmed and defenseless Jewish working people. According to incomplete figures, no less than 6,000 persons were shot in Lwow, over 8,000 in Odessa, nearly 8,500 killed or hanged in Kamenets-Podolsk, more than 10,500 persons shot down with machine guns in Dniepropetrovsk, and over 3,000 local inhabitants shot in Mariupol, including many old men, women, and children, all of whom were robbed and stripped naked before execution. According to preliminary figures, about 7,000 persons were killed by the German-Fascist butchers in Kerch.

On April 27, 1942, and May 11, 1943, Molotov sent additional notes to the foreign envoys in Moscow detailing further voluminous data collected on the Germans' looting of the Russian population, the institution of a régime of serfdom and slavery in the occupied districts and the abduction of the civil population to captivity. He charged that captured German documents showed that the Germans had carefully charted their program before the invasion and had designed it to ruin, subjugate, and enslave the civilian population in occupied districts on one hand, and to exploit these regions to provision the German troops and supply petroleum and foodstuffs for Germany on the other hand.

As far back as November 7, 1941, Reich Marshal Hermann Goering, at a secret conference in Berlin, gave instructions for the utilization of

Russian people in forced labor in Germany, according to the documents quoted. These said: "Russian workers have proved their ability in building a colossal Russian industry. Now they are able to be used for Germany.... This is a task for the appropriate authorities and the secret police...." The dragooned Russians were to be used "chiefly for road construction, construction of railways and in harvesting, for the clearing of mine fields and for building airdromes.... German construction battalions should be disbanded. Skilled German workers must work in war industry; they should not dig earth and break stones, for these purposes exists the Russian."

On March 21, 1942, Hitler appointed Gauleiter Fritz Sauckel as "Chief Commissioner for the Utilization of Labor Power." A month later, according to the documents, the new commissioner issued a secret order embodying his program: "Along with the war prisoners already available in the occupied regions, it is chiefly necessary to mobilize skilled civilian workers, men and women above fifteen years of age, and to utilize them for work in Germany.... To alleviate the work of the extremely occupied German peasant woman the Fuehrer charged me with the task of delivering to Germany 400,000 to 500,000 picked sound and strong girls from the eastern regions.

"There is literally not a single town, not a single village, not a single populated place on Soviet territory that had been seized by the Germans from which the German-Fascist bandits did not drive a considerable part of the population to slavery," Molotov reported. "In some large towns this amounted to tens of thousands of men, women, adolescents, and children."

According to the assertion of the Hitlerite satrap Erich Koch, Reichskommissar of the Ukraine, published in the newspaper *Deutsche Ukraine Zeitung* in January, 1943: "710,000 Ukrainians have been sent to Germany." According to a statement issued by the administration, headed by Sauckel and published in the *Minsker Zeitung* on January 14, 1943: "In 1942 about 2,000,000 persons were dispatched to Germany from the occupied regions in the east."

With the sadistic cruelty inherent in the Hitlerites, when driving the people to slavery they broke up families, separated parents from children, brothers from sisters, wives from husbands. Whole towns and districts have been depopulated as a result of organized kidnapping.

Numerous materials depict the inhuman conditions of the forcible dispatch of peaceful people to Germany in boarded-up cars guarded by soldiers or police. Day and night trains with slaves rolled to Germany from the occupied districts of the Ukraine, White Russia, and Russia. The people were loaded into cars like cattle, sixty to seventy to each boxcar. Exhausted and sick people were thrown out of the cars down embankments and the roads to the west were littered with bodies.

On October 14, 1942, the Soviet Government, with the collaboration of the exiled governments of the European countries occupied by the Germans, issued a formal statement solemnly warning the German leaders of their responsibility for the crimes committed in the occupied countries. On November 2, 1942, the Soviet Government formed "an extraordinary state committee for the ascertaining and investigation of crimes committed by the German-Fascist invaders and their associates and damage caused by them to citizens, collective farms, public bodies, state enterprises, and institutions of the USSR."

After investigations this committee issued a series of statements with documented instances of German outrages and, in most cases, naming the German officers and civil officials held responsible for them. At the end of these lists the committee declared: "History has never witnessed such mass extermination of human beings as that perpetrated by the German-Fascist invaders. Sentiments of pity and mercy are unknown to them. With monstrous cruelty they outrage helpless old people. Neither mothers' tears nor children's outstretched hands imploring for help stop them. The German Army brought up by Hitler torments and murders all those whom the Germans do not need, while those who can work for them they carry like cattle to slave markets in Germany."

The indictments presented by the committee included charges that high German officials, on orders from Berlin, destroyed ancient relics, looted museums and other repositories of cultural treasures, and plundered scientific institutions and libraries, sending their booty to Germany; that patients in psychiatric hospitals and in sanatoria for the tubercular, as well as others chronically ill, were exterminated wholesale; that large massacres had been carried out in other districts to rid the regions of unwanted elements of the population; that people in certain regions were systematically poisoned and others subjected to various forms of sudden death.

One instrument of mass extermination was the so-called "murderess-van." This was a large boxcar-like body mounted on a motor truck, lined inside with metal and hermetically sealed, with locked doors at the back. The committee declared that victims were stacked in the van like cord wood and locked in, after which the motor's fumes were injected through a hose between the exhaust and a grating on the bottom of the van. The vehicle would be driven from its loading place to some remote region and the bodies there would be thrown into ravines.

"It has been established," the committee reported, "that before retreating from the town of Georgievsk on January 9 and 10, 1943, on the order of the chief of the German hospitals, Chief Physician Baron von Haimann, alcohol and drinking soda were sold in the town market by German soldiers to poison the Soviet people. The alcohol proved to be methylated spirit and the 'soda' to be oxalic acid. Mass poisoning of citizens of the town took place."

A member of the committee, Alexei Tolstoy, gives this impression of some of the evidence he helped to collect: "Half my life was spent during those years when European civilization flourished under the sun of almost half a century of peace. Unafraid, I stayed at German hotels, and slept there without locking my door, for no one ever stole my baggage in Germany. I believed implicitly that every drop of my blood belonged to me, and that no German had the right to let it flow out through a little hole plugged by a bullet or made by a knife. I'm of the older generation. I fail to understand the Germans of today...."

Tolstoy reports: "In all the towns and villages of the north Caucasus and Kuban regions and republics the Germans blew up or burned down without exception: all schools, theaters, cinemas, hotels, libraries together with the books, hospitals, sanatoria, young pioneer clubs, and public buildings. In those places where, because of their hurried retreat, their demolition squads did not arrive in time, German soldiers dashed around with crowbars and pickaxes, smashing windows, bathtubs, lavatory basins, and even ventilation grids, peppered sculptured and modeled panels with submachine-gun bullets, ripped off upholstery, broke furniture, and gashed the zinc roofing metal with their bayonets."

He relates how in Zheleznovodsk, a resort unmatched in Europe for its medical equipment and comfort, the Germans set up a meat-smoking establishment: "In the magnificent sanatoria, where the rooms were paneled in costly hardwoods and marble, they put up smoke ovens. For five months the smoke of fat and bacon came through the broken windows of these palaces. And in January, fleeing from Zheleznovodsk, they dynamited what they had defouled.... Everything I describe I saw with my own eyes. But I have seen still more ghastly sights. In the north Caucasus the Germans massacred the whole Jewish population, most of whom had been evacuated during the war from Leningrad, Odessa, the Ukraine, and the Crimea. The Germans began their preparation for mass murder in the very first days of their occupation. ... At last, 'settlement day' was announced. The Jews assembled at the places named. At one o'clock in the afternoon a train, bearing about 1,800 people, steamed past Mineralnye Vodi station and stopped in a field. The German officers accompanying the train began studying the lay of the land through their field-glasses, but they were not satisfied. The train was backed into Mineralnye Vodi again, where the German convoys bawled: 'Out with you! Come on, jump out!' ... Then came the order to hand over all valuables. Earrings, rings, and watches were quickly removed and dropped into the field-service caps of the German sentries. Ten minutes or so passed. A German staff machine drove up with Welben, the chief of the Gestapo, and the Commandant Paul. Then came the command: 'Strip to the skin!'

"All this was told me by the only survivor, an old man by the name of Fingerut; he hid in the grass between the wheels of a car on a distant siding. When the people were ordered to strip, they understood this to be the end. They started shrieking and dashing to and fro. Cars were driven along the fringe of the throng, shooting down those who tried to escape. It is no easy thing to massacre 1,800 people. The shooting went on till evening."

The mark of the German was left in the hearts of the Russian people as a boiling anger crying for retribution. It was left more visibly in the befouled ruins of ancient and stately cities. Aërial photographs of the once proud, modern Stalingrad, taken after the Germans were driven out, give an impression of ruins as gaunt and desolate as those of Pompeii. Leningrad, though the invaders never entered it, bore irremediable scars of the siege shelling after the Axis retreat. Its cultural and sentimental loss was as great as that of many cities that knew the fury of demolition squads. Leningrad's greatest treasures, the architectural masterpieces of the city's outlying area—at Peterhof, Pushkin, Pavlovsk, and Gatchina—fell into the Germans' hands and suffered accordingly.

In the museum palaces in this cluster of towns around Leningrad were embodied the creative genius of not only the greatest Russian architects, sculptors, painters, and masters of the applied arts, but of eminent western Europeans as well. The Grand Palace of Peterhof was destroyed in the early days of the occupation. The Germans left only its collapsing, charred walls.

Ancient Novgorod, too, became an example of the Germans' mania for destruction. It was the cradle of Russian culture and statehood, with so many remarkable monuments that had come down through the ages that 60,000 publications on the city had been catalogued. In their hatred for everything Russian and Slavic, the Germans demolished the ancient monuments, ransacked the museums, and sent the most valuable exhibits to Germany. The Novgorod Kremlin castle, a center of political and cultural life since the ninth century, was badly mutilated. A hole had been blasted in one of its many old towers, a latrine made over it and the bottom turned into a cesspool.

Destruction of another sort was visited upon the industrial cities of the Donets Basin. The Germans evidently had expected to remain in possession of these centers in perpetuity and they had proceeded to destroy what they did not want as a phase in the cities' Germanization. When the Red Army approached, the Germans did their best to complete the task of destruction before fleeing. In Stalino, for example, not a single large building remained in the principal street. At Krivoi

Rog, one of pre-war Russia's largest industrial and iron-mining centers, the Axis occupants tried to wipe the city from the earth. The iron and steel works were destroyed, the blast furnaces blown up, central heating and power plants wrecked, and the mines made unworkable. About a million and a half tons of the mines' ore had been shipped to Germany. All metal parts in the plants and all mining equipment were blown up or broken in pieces and taken away as scrap. Workers' homes, hospitals, schools, commercial establishments, and water mains were blown up or burned. The damage to the coal industry in the Donbas was estimated at more than two billion rubles.

A partial measure of the vandalism is provided by the steps taken for the restoration of liberated regions. In the last four months of 1943, while the war was still at its height, 326,461 new dwellings sprang up among the ashes and ruins of town and countryside. Nearly 2,000,000 persons who had been living in dugouts acquired homes. Twenty-five factories were erected for the construction of building materials, and sawmills started to provide housing for 800 families a month. The rebuilding and repair program included 122 railway station buildings and large numbers of schools, hospitals, and libraries. The Soviet budget for 1944 provided sixteen billion rubles for the economic rehabilitation of the liberated districts. In the Moscow region alone the damage caused by the Germans exceeded seven billion rubles. In the Smolensk region the invaders destroyed thirty cities and 2,000 villages.

Many stories are told of Russian shrewdness in defending themselves from the invaders. When members of the Red Partisan collective farm were ordered by a German commandant to drive their cattle to the west, they mapped out a special route and drove the cattle for thirteen days through ravines in a circle around the village. On the fourteenth day the Red Army arrived and chased out the Germans. Many of the farms saved their seed grain by distributing it in secure hiding places. The Russian peasant came out of the war with small regard for the intelligence of the would-be German overlord.

Soviet planners made a virtue of necessity and planned their reconstructed living and working centers as improvements on the old. The nation's architects had been working in coördination before the war on the replanning of old cities, the creation of new ones, and the construction of huge industrial and transport undertakings. This work was projected scarcely without interruption, but on a greatly expanded scale. Women and young girls worked heroically to rebuild their homeland. They labored as masons, carpenters, engineers, and technicians.

Nazi-Germany followed the pattern established by the Prussian military caste when a half century ago, Count von Gesler lined up his troops in the city square of Metz and expounded to them this program: "Our civilization must inevitably be built on mountains of corpses, on oceans of tears, on the death rattle of countless numbers of people." After Hitler had come along, his collaborator in Nazism, Alfred Rosenberg, offered a companion doctrine: "Pity is a disease grafted upon the Aryan soul. This plague comes from the Jew Christ and the Russian Tolstoy, from the British Dickens and the French Victor Hugo."

How it feels to have been a victim of such a program and its progenitors has been recorded for history by Ilya Ehrenburg: "I shall bless the day when we forget about the Germans. That will indeed be a wonderful day. I should like to be thinking about other things— about love and labor, about art; about the woods outside Moscow, and about gay Paris. But I see a ditch filled with children's corpses. I see ashes. I see the faces of mothers twisted with anguish and all the woe of our land. And my thoughts always turn to that ruffian, tall or squat, pop-eyed, stupid, and soulless, who marched hundreds of miles only to trample the life out of an infant in some Russian village...."

"There have been blood-drenched periods in history before. There were the fires of the Inquisition. St. Bartholomew's Night has become a legend. The Old Believers were burned in their houses. But awful and repulsive as these crimes were, even they were illumined by a certain faith.... But for the sake of what did Hitler's soldiers slaughter millions of innocents? If you ask a German this he will grin, or cry like a coward. He has nothing to say. He has neither ideas nor faith. He slew because he was told.... He slew becaue that was his mission, his justification, his whole life.

"That is the most terrible thing about the atrocities of the Germans: they slaughtered millions of fine people for nothing at all—simply out of greed, stupidity, inborn ferocity. They were told, 'When you cross the frontiers of the Reich, everything is permitted. There you'll find only subhumans and you are superhuman!' And among the millions of Germans there was not to be found a handful of men of conscience to cry 'Halt!' Among these 'supermen' there was not a single man.... They have perfected the art of murder, invented the 'murder van,' built barracks for asphyxiation with gases, manufactured poisonous liquids with which they anoint the lips of infants. They ... jot down in notebooks the number of children killed and where.

"What people of all the ages have deemed a terrible sin, they have converted into an immense industry.... The Germans will come forward with studied speeches in their own defense and with sham tears; they have loopholes all ready when the fatal hour comes for them; they will betray their Fuehrer ... while they retire to the background and dig themselves in; they will try to fool the world with penitential speeches, anathemas, and greetings."

42

INVADERS STOPPED AT GATES TO EGYPT —1,750-MILE RETREAT ACROSS DESERT

"ON TO Egypt" became the battle cry of the Axis in 1940. They believed that the road to Suez through Libya was wide open, and from there on through Iraq and Iran to the conquest of India. These illusions were to be blasted after two years in the African deserts, with constantly changing tides of battle, until they ended in the Axis rout and retreat across 1,750 miles of sand.

Mussolini pledged Hitler that he could control the Mediterranean, create an African empire, and break the British life line through the Suez Canal. This grandiose campaign started from Italian Libya on September 13, 1940, with Marshal Graziani in command of the Italian forces. General Sir Archibald Wavell in Egypt and Admiral Sir Andrew Cunningham in command in the Mediterranean defended the British front at the outbreak of this assault.

Graziani crossed the Egyptian frontier in great force, his troops far outnumbering the British patrols. At Sidi Barrani he stood three months building up the strength of his army. Wavell, who had been reinforced with Australian, New Zealand, and Indian troops, took the offensive on December 9 with his armored and motorized forces. In sixty-two days of classical desert warfare he drove the Italians out of Egypt and Cyrenaica—500 miles through the deserts, back to the place where they had started. He seized all their strongholds and virtually destroyed the Italian army. With but 30,000 men Wavell captured more than 133,000 Italian prisoners, including nineteen generals and one admiral, together with 1,300 guns, tanks, and large stores of supplies.

With the British decision to send troops to help the beleaguered Greeks, Wavell faced critical problems. The Germans, stunned by the severe Italian defeat in the Egyptian adventure, hurried strong forces through Sicily and on to Libya under command of Marshal Erwin Rommel, in a desperate effort to resume the drive for the Suez Canal.

Wavell was soon to be menaced by a huge new Axis army in front of him and the additional danger of the heavy Italian forces in Ethiopia at his rear. He took immediate precautions by striking at the Italian stronghold of Eritrea on January 19, 1941. To do this he used his 4th Indian Division detached from the western desert to the Sudan and based at Khartoum. Another force based at Nairobi struck against Italian Somaliland and the two closed like pincers around Ethiopia. After two months of fighting, the capital, Addis Ababa, fell to the British, who had covered 1,725 miles in fifty-three days. Thus, on April 6, 1941, ended Mussolini's dream of conquest.

In Libya Rommel, with his famous Afrika Korps, brought to Tripoli and protected by the Luftwaffe, started his drive where Graziani had so ignobly failed. Wavell's strength had been drained by the necessity of sending 60,000 troops to the aid of Greece. Rommel's offensive took the British off balance. In an "all-out" blitzkrieg he drove Wavell's depleted forces back to Egypt. Behind the German lines the British, with the aid of their navy, held out at Tobruk.

Two events now stalled both armies. The Germans were hard-pressed for more men on their Russian front; the Japanese drives in the Pacific demanded that the British withdraw forces from Africa to send to the defense of Australia and India. General Wavell was transferred to India and was succeeded by General Sir Claude Auchinleck. The latter opened his drive to relieve Tobruk from its seven months' siege, recaptured Benghazi, and was stopped at El Agheila on January 7, 1942. Rommel in a counteroffensive drove him back to El Gazala.

Meanwhile, from Greece and from Sicily, in spite of having to run the gamut of the R.A.F. and the Royal Navy's submarines, the enemy was shipping materials much faster by the port of Benghazi. Thus the battle of supply was as real as any engagement on the field. Rommel was ready first because of his much shorter lines. On May 26 he attacked in full strength, establishing a half-mile gap in the British lines.

Tobruk, which the British had hoped to hold, fell after a fierce twenty-six-hour attack. General Auchinleck lost almost 23,000 men as prisoners. The remains of the Eighth Army had to retreat rapidly to the frontier, back to El Alamein. There the Eighth Army made a stand. This was the last defensive position from which to hold Alexandria and the Nile Delta against the Axis.

On June 30 Rommel flung the tanks of his Italian Littorio Division against the Eighth Army stronghold and was driven back with heavy losses. The next day he threw his infantry into the teeth of the South African division holding the north end of the line. Rommel announced that he was pursuing "the beaten British into the Nile valley." But what began as a retreat wound up as a counterattack. This time Rommel backed off.

The Germans were now at the last barrier. Only seventy miles away was Alexandria, the British naval base which protected the entrance to the Suez Canal and Cairo, the capital of Egypt. One more breakthrough and they would be on the road to India. The situation looked like a black day for the British Empire and for the world.

It was at this moment that General Sir Harold Alexander stepped in. With him was General Bernard L. Montgomery (later knighted) who was to out-fox the "Desert Fox." Moreover, great things were happening. American bombers, including the first Flying Fortresses, with General Lewis H. Brereton in command, were hurrying to the support of the Eighth Army. Great supplies were coming from the United States around the Cape of Good Hope and up to the Persian Gulf. These included the new American tank, the General Sherman.

"Thus far and no farther," was General Alexander's command. He was waiting for the moment to strike. It came at exactly 9:30 P.M. on Friday, October 23, 1943, when the actual Battle of Egypt began.

As the British artillery let loose its combined power, Royal Air Force bombers took to the air and dived over the German positions, tearing up communications and ripping supply lines into chaos. Rommel was surprised and outwitted. British units were moving forward; first the sappers, locating the land mines with their detectors and making the ground safe for the tanks and infantry. Paths were laid out in white tape in the wake of these heroic men; following the tape came the infantry, advancing steadily through the desert night to the music of the Scottish bagpipes. By 6 o'clock the following morning they had advanced four miles along the entire front.

On the night of October 25 Australians on the northern end of the front and Highlanders on the southern sector widened the salient until it was near the edge of the dangerous mined area. Numerous enemy counterattacks were beaten off during the next six days.

On the night of November 1-2 the break-through was accomplished in the "Hell's Kitchen" sector near Kidney Ridge by units of the 50th and the 51st Divisions and the New Zealanders on a front four miles long. The first phase of the Battle of Egypt was finished. Italian and German forces in the south were in full retreat along the impassable Qattara Depression, while in the north the Germans began to retreat along the coast.

German air reconnaissance during the initial stage of the battle flew over the British lines each day and saw what appeared to be the 10th Tank Corps still training. What they actually saw was a sham encampment, realistic enough from the air but consisting of fake tanks, dummy tents, and other camouflaged equipment.

Thus, on the very morning that his air reconnaissance was reporting to Rommel that the British tanks were still a safe distance of forty-five miles away in the Nile Delta, those very tanks—British Crusaders, American Shermans and Grants—were roaring forward through the gap cut by the infantry. During the previous seesaw campaigns one of the Eighth Army's major shortcomings had been the lack of heavy tanks, but now they were a full match for the Germans' heaviest armor.

Rommel counterattacked wildly as the infantry advanced. He was forced to send his 21st Armored Division to the rescue. This in turn was reinforced by the Italian Ariete Armored Divison from the central sector. The forces met on the burning sand under the blistering sun. All through the day guns boomed.

Approximately three hundred enemy tanks were destroyed in the battle which lasted for nine hours. Thus the second phase was victoriously concluded.

Montgomery's next move was to order the New Zealand Infantry to swerve to the southern end of the line. The original break-through on the northern end had left thirty-four miles of the Qattara Depression comparatively deserted. The New Zealanders began to round up Italians by thousands. They had been deserted by the fleeing Rommel without food, water, or motorized equipment. Roaming the desert in thick-tongued agony, they were only too glad to surrender.

Rommel began his long and arduous retreat along the coast, leaving behind 8,000 Germans, including General Ritter von Thoma, field commander of the Afrika Korps; Major Burkhart, leader of German paratroops; Italian Generals Masina, Brunetti, and Bignami. The total cost to the Axis in the Battle for Egypt was: 75,000 men killed, captured, or wounded; 500 tanks knocked out; 1,000 guns blasted into wreckage; and 800 aircraft destroyed either in the air or on the ground. The German dream of expansion through Egypt to the Suez Canal was smashed. Rommel, the Desert Fox, was on the run, destined to flee across the burning sands until he was finally trapped on Cap Bon. Axis power had been broken in the ten days from October 23 to November 2 and the first two phases of the war in North Africa were over. The third phase—a record-breaking pursuit—was about to begin.

The harrowing scenes on the trail of Rommel's retreat are described by an American eyewitness, Major Rowan T. Thomas, who was with the 513th Bombardment Squadron under the command of British Air Marshal Sir Arthur Tedder and the American General Brereton. From Flying Fortresses the "round-the-world" squadron bombed the path ahead of Montgomery. Major Thomas, in his *Born In Battle,* written from notes taken in his Flying Fortress, *The Judge's Jury,* records:

"I have never seen such a spectacle of ruin in my life. Burned-out cars, trucks, and armored vehicles, tanks and storehouses with thousands of tons of war materials lay abandoned all along the way. Messerschmitts, Junkers, Macchis, and many British planes were lying where they had crashed. Wrecked fortifications and pocked defenses told the story of the ferocity with which the battle had raged. Lifeless bodies were strewn over the desert ... tattered, shattered men; heads, arms, legs blown off, stark still in death with horror on their lacerated faces. ... Many of these bodies covered with blowing sand were those of British, Scots, Canadians, Australians, Irish, and American volunteers. The Nazi loss was so great that Rommel burned and buried them quickly to destroy the evidence. When the British tried to bury the remaining Germans and Italians they found that mines had been wired to their bodies, so that many burying parties were obliterated."

By November 13 the British had advanced 325 miles to Tobruk. Still the "Desert Fox" made no stand and Allied air forces swept out day and night to strafe and bomb his motorized columns. After the fall of Tobruk the next destination was Benghazi, 525 miles from El Alamein. Benghazi fell on November 20, a ruined city.

When Tripoli was reached it became obvious that Rommel was to make his long awaited stand at Homs, a little town not far removed from the city. General Montgomery ordered the armored divisions and the New Zealand Infantry to do what Rommel considered the impossible. This involved the splitting of Montgomery's forces, one-half proceeding along the coastal road and the other swerving south, the strategy being to attack Tripoli on the coast by a left hook from below. This ground was by far the worst terrain ever encountered in the campaign—rocky, sandy, and generally impassable.

Many an old desert veteran in the group thought the plan suicidal—but it succeeded. Rommel found himself outflanked and on the run again. The hook swerved up through the town of Tarhuna, a few miles south of Tripoli, and drove at him from the side, while the coastal forces engaged him in a frontal attack. He was forced to withdraw or be cut off. On January 23, 1944, the British entered Tripoli after a stubbornly fought battle at Tarhuna. This event marked the end of the Italian Empire in Africa.

After the fall of Tripoli Rommel again withdrew—this time to a final stand at the Mareth Line. The trail of blood then led through Gabès, Sfax, Sousse, Tunis, to Bizerte. One by one these cities fell to the Allies as Rommel fled through them, leaving a path of destruction behind him. Final catastrophe awaited him. The American-British forces under General Dwight D. Eisenhower had landed on the western side of North Africa and were soon to face him in Tunisia. Rommel was fleeing into disaster, with Montgomery lashing at his back all the way and Eisenhower waiting for him. Altogether Rommel had fled 1,750 miles across the grueling sands of the desert in eighty-two days. It was the longest sustained retreat in history.

COMMANDO RAID ON DIEPPE—
TEST TUBE FOR INVASION OF EUROPE

WHEN and where will the first great Allied invasion of Europe take place? This was the question that kept the Axis under tension in 1942. Germany, who expected the Allies to strike across the English Channel at France or Belgium, was frantically building an "impenetrable wall" along the coast, manned by huge armies and heavy defenses.

On August 19, 1942, the Allies decided to make a daring test of German strength. The test tube was Dieppe, on the coast of northern France, which through the centuries had been a battle port from the days of the Norman conquests. This trial probe was assigned to the adventurous Commandos, which had been organized in England in the early days of World War II.

Although it was strategical, largely designed to throw the Germans off guard for an all-out invasion to come eighty days later at a far distant point, it was believed by the Axis and the entire world to be a bona fide attempt at invasion revealing the point of the coming thrust at the Continent. In this it was a brilliant and costly feat.

The almost legendary Commandos were commanded by Admiral Mountbatten. Mountbatten was related by blood to the royal family of Britain and the Hohenzollerns of Germany (the family name had been changed from Battenberg during the First World War). He was a fearless soldier and a sound tactician. Before he took over the special force that was to play such a large part in so many invasions, he had commanded three destroyers in the Royal Navy and had seen each in succession sunk under him. His mettle had been proved.

The force under Lord Mountbatten was as exceptional as he was. Its members were chosen especially for their strength, their ability, their intelligence, and their will power. Their training consisted of the toughest obstacle courses, the surest and quietest techniques of killing, the quickest way of getting from any given place to any other, and the art of living off a foreign countryside. Many of them were parachutists as well as infantrymen; all knew how to handle perfectly a half-dozen different weapons, from knife to tommy gun. Most of these men had at least a rudimentary knowledge of several languages.

The majority of these troops were British subjects, many of them Canadians. In addition, many a European who had escaped from German domination had joined their ranks. American Rangers had trained with them in Britain; other Rangers had received the same type of training at home in the United States. All of them, regardless of nationality, had learned the hard way how to slip up on an enemy unseen and unheard, by day or night, before he ever knew of their presence. Their creed was to get their man.

For a year before their grand début in action, small forces of them had harried the Germans with dozens of landings on the shore of Europe from the Channel coast to St. Nazaire. Sometimes they had only to destroy a German radio station or plane detector; sometimes they were under orders to wreck a port. Whatever the task, the Commando forces had specialists trained for that job.

Admiral Mountbatten and his men objected to the use of the word "Commando" as the name for their force. Its official title was the Combined Operations Command; its units were called Commandos after the term used by the South Africans in the Boer War. However, the popular use of that word to designate both the whole force and its individual members soon overrode the stiff official title.

In the year before the assault on Dieppe, the Commandos had been rigorously trained in maneuvers and in small lightning operations against the enemy for the major tasks that lay ahead. It was at Dieppe that they were to undergo their first real test. For weeks before the scheduled landing date—August 19, 1942, a time chosen as much on the basis of weather conditions in the Channel as on that of the troops' readiness—Canadians, Fighting Frenchmen, Belgians, Dutchmen, Poles, Britons, and Americans practiced to the last detail all the operations of the planned assault. Minutely exact replicas of the coast and the town of Dieppe were constructed for the men and their officers to study until they knew the terrain as well as if they had spent their lives there.

The embarkation for Dieppe began on the night of August 18. From a half-dozen ports in the south of England, clusters of landing craft laden with tanks, guns, and men moved out into the dark Channel, escorted by destroyers and patrol craft. Aboard the varied fleet were such men as Major General J. H. Roberts of Canada, who commanded his country's men. At operational headquarters the offices were filled with other men who were to play major rôles in the war: Brigadier General Frank Hunter, of the United States Army Air Forces; Air Marshal Trafford Leigh-Mallory; Major General H. D. G. Crerar of Canada.

Daylight was breaking when the landing craft approached the French shore. Six beaches around Dieppe had been chosen for the assault. A more strongly defended region could not have been selected at that time. The Allies knew this before the operation started. Extensive aërial reconnaissance and earlier Commando raids, besides the reports of correspondents from Americans still in France who had inspected the defenses, had supplied almost complete data on the obstacles that the Allies would meet.

This area had been designated for the landing partly because it would provide a test of the Germans' defenses, and partly because it would permit the destruction of a radio location center that played a vital part in enabling the Germans to play havoc with Channel shipping. When the attack came, it was described by the Combined Operations headquarters as a "reconnaissance in force"; by the Germans it was called, in another vainglorious propaganda boast, a vain attempt to invade Europe and open that "second front" for which the Russians had so vociferously called.

In the Dieppe sector the Germans had emplaced artillery batteries in hillside caves and on the crests of heights so that a withering cross fire could sweep the entire beach area. All the guns were within range of one another. Behind and before them were machine-gun nests at frequent intervals, with intricate barbed-wire barricades. Where the streets of Dieppe ended at the beach were formidable tank barriers. As the defenses deepened, the caliber of their guns increased in direct ratio. Every house in the shore-front area of the town was a bristling strong point. Every man in the Commando assault force knew his part in the great operation and the objective that would be his; hardly a rifle pit had been omitted from the carefully studied models.

The Commandos had hoped to make their way into the beach itself without observation. If this could have been accomplished, the whole result of the attack might have been different. But this, unfortunately, was not to be. The invaluable element of surprise was destroyed before the shore of Europe was in sight. One group of landing craft was approaching Berneval when it was sighted by a German patrol boat that immediately flashed a signal for help. E-boats rushed to the enemy scout's assistance and the alarm was spread along the whole French coast. Out of this ill fated squadron of landing craft, few returned; many of the men aboard were slaughtered in the sea.

When the E-boats opened fire and the word was sent to the rest of the raiding force, there was a second of indecision while the commanders debated the advisability of carrying out the attack now that it would no longer be a surprise. The enemy was fully alert and the cost of the dangerous venture, unfortunately, was bound to be many times multiplied.

There could be no turning back. The boats sailed on. As they nosed in toward the sloping beach, the air was suddenly rent with a giant drumming of thousands of planes—the attackers' own. From that moment on, through the nine hours of the Dieppe fighting and for hours after that, the sky was black with fighters and bombers of all the

Allied air forces—American, British, Canadian, Polish, Belgian, Dutch, French.

The operation was upset by the inestimable factor of that chance German patrol boat that gave the alarm. The R.A.F., the R.C.A.F., and most of the other Allied air forces were plastering Dieppe and its defenses with bombs. Fighter craft augmented by large detachments of Americans were mercilessly strafing the German ground troops and killing off the German aircraft that attempted to frustrate the landings. The United States Eighth Air Force's Flying Fortresses were paralyzing the centers inland from which the Germans might have deployed reinforcements for the coastal defenses and neutralizing the enemy's airfields. At the same time, the British destroyers that had shepherded the troops to the shore were lying off the coast and lobbing shell after shell into the fortifications on the land.

Every precaution had been taken to leave the French themselves in no doubt as to the purpose of the attack. Lest they swarm into the line of fire and lose their lives, the BBC was endlessly reiterating from the moment of the first landings the warning that this was not the long-awaited invasion. The French were urged to keep behind the battle area and off the roads, for the hour of their liberation was still far off. Nonetheless, French men and women and children could not sit in their houses while the roar of guns was making the air tremble and the flashing wings of hundreds upon hundreds of planes were spitting fire or hurling bombs upon the enemy.

The American objectives were the airfields of Rouen and Abbeville and the adjacent communications facilities. The sky was clear and the Fortresses, almost at their ceiling, were able to pin-point their targets with the greatest accuracy through their secret bombsights. From almost six miles in the air, they loosed their bombs with breath-taking accuracy on the German fighters ranked on the airfields. Fuel tanks and dispersal areas and administration buildings were reduced to shapeless rubble.

In the raid on Rouen the Fortresses had an escort of British Spitfires whose pilots were astounded at what they saw. Flying in perfect formation, the big bombers—the biggest of their time—laid their "eggs" with utter precision on the complex railway system of the city and then proceeded to blast factory after factory into wreckage. British fighter pilots fought off the German planes that attacked them and more than once penetrated within range of the bombers' own defensive guns. These two smashing assaults, on Rouen and Abbeville, effectively isolated the German defenders of Dieppe and the immediately adjacent areas from any large-scale help from the interior.

The first Commando troops had begun to scramble up the Dieppe beaches even before the sun was up. Behind them, a heavy smoke screen laid down by the destroyers shielded the waves of attackers that followed, while overhead the R.A.F. and all its components fought furiously to provide an impenetrable armor against the German bombers roaring and diving in to destroy the assault forces. In the midst of this savage clash of aërial machines, the first official word of the landing was carried back to Britain by a pigeon released by an officer with the first men to land. Yet the reason was sound, for complete radio silence had to be maintained in the first hours.

Initial successes of the landing forces varied from beach to beach. At Berneval, where the first alarm had been given while the soldiers were still at sea, the slaughter was the greatest. The larger part of what was officially described as Commando No. 3 was prevented from landing, but a handful did get ashore. With skilful mortar fire, these Canadians were able to divert a major part of the German artillery fire on the beaches of Dieppe proper.

Dieppe lay about five or six miles southeast of Berneval, at the mouth of the Arques River. The Germans had constructed a strong seawall there, and headlands on either side had been fortified and armed to repel any assault. Here the main force attacked. About five miles west of Dieppe, at Varengeville, another strong Commando force was to land and wipe out the enemy's coastal batteries. Still other troops were destined for Pourville and Puys, respectively two to three miles east and west of Dieppe.

It was at Varengeville that the American Rangers were most strongly represented, although their numbers were still few. By far the biggest group was the Canadians, about 5,000 strong. They had been chosen from the Second Division, augmented by a battalion from the First Tank Brigade. None of these troops had seen any large-scale action against the Germans, for they were still in training at home while the heroic Canadian First Division was battling in vain to save Belgium and later France in 1940. In addition, there were detachments of the Third and Fourth Royal Marines made up predominately of Britons, with a sprinkling of assorted Europeans. Some were Fighting French troops fighting almost within sight of their homes and families.

On all the beaches a fierce cross fire greeted the onrushing Commandos. As they had been trained to do, they dropped on their bellies almost as one man and wormed their way along. Inch by inch they made their way to German rifle pits and slew the troops who manned them. Indomitably they continued to the machine-gun posts.

The Royal Regiment of Canada was detailed to land at Puits, seize a heavy coast-defense battery, and capture the headland that dominated Dieppe from the east. Pourville was the objective of the South Saskatchewan Regiment, which was then to take a similar headland to the west of the town. Thereafter the Queen's Own Cameron Highlanders were to pass through it, down the valley of the Scie, to the St. Aubin Airfield. The main assault was aimed at Dieppe itself, to be made by the Essex Scottish Regiment on the eastern half of the beach and the Royal Hamilton Light Infantry on the west. The Fusiliers Mont-Royal were waiting at sea as a floating reserve.

Most of those who got ashore at Berneval were members of No. 3 Commando. When they attempted to reach and scale a cleft in a cliff in broad daylight, they were confronted by an aroused enemy who poured down withering fire. The British senior officers were cut down almost at once and Lieutenant E. D. Loustalot of the American Rangers took over. He displayed exceptional skill and courage until he too was killed. No. 3 Commando kept on fighting, even though it could not gain a yard. Eventually it had to surrender with most of its surviving complement wounded.

At Belleville-Sur-Mer, near Berneval, another unit of No. 3 Commando had better luck, although it consisted of only one landing craft load of men with comparatively little armament. Barely a score of troops and officers piled ashore before dawn and set out to assault a battery, which they knew was held by more than 200 Germans. This battery stood atop a cliff that could be reached only by way of a steep gully choked with wire. Although there were neither Bangalore torpedoes nor wire cutters in the attackers' arsenal, they were not daunted. They were unable to destroy the wire, but they exploited it by stretching it taut and using it as a kind of stairway.

It took the Commandos nearly an hour to climb to the top of the cliff. Then they entered the village of Berneval and advanced through fields on the rear of the German battery, which was pounding the ships in the Channel. As the Commandos sniped carefully at one gunner after another, the fire of this battery soon became spotty. The Germans finally turned one of their guns around, but they could not lower its muzzle sufficiently to hit the British. These Commandos remained for several hours, until their ammunition was practically exhausted. Their job well done, they went back as they had come and reëmbarked from the beach.

Ten miles southwest, near Varengeville, No. 4 Commando was doing a similar job. Its objective was a six-gun battery with a range that imperiled any ship within five miles of Dieppe. No. 4 Commando, many of whose men had dozed on the cross-Channel trip as peacefully as if they had been off for a week-end, landed 250 strong under the command of Lieutenant Colonel Lovat. It was split into two forces about a mile apart. The party that landed at Vasterival was three minutes behind zero-hour in landing. It destroyed the barbed-wire barriers with its special torpedoes. Their noise, coupled with a simultaneous cannon-strafing by fighters, so confused the Germans that the attackers had little difficulty in scrambling to the top of the cliff and a wooded position so close to the battery that they could hear the Germans.

The Commandos opened up with small-arms fire and then loosed a mortar bomb that fell on the enemy's ammunition dump. This one explosion wrecked the battery. From a point behind the battery, a smoke bomb rose, an indication that Lord Lovat was ready to begin his attack from the rear. The first unit thereupon rested, lest it fire on its comrades. Lovat's men had landed near the mouth of the Saâne River and subdued a pillbox. They proceeded inland along the river for about a mile and then turned left into a wood directly behind the battery, cutting telephone and telegraph wires as they went. Two advance scouts astonished thirty-five German assault troops forming for a counterblow at the frontal attackers and mowed down the whole formation with two tommy guns.

The Commandos were now preparing to charge the battery. Among them were a number of Rangers, including Corporal Koons, the first American soldier to kill a German in European combat. Koons was detailed to a farm stable for sniping and got twenty of the enemy while his fellows advanced. From this vantage point he could see the battery smashed by mortar bombs and, a second later, cannon-firing Spitfires.

Charging across 250 yards of open country, where both their chief officers fell before the battery was reached, the Commandos stormed on as they crossed a belt of barbed wire over the bodies of their dead and wounded fellows. In a few moments, the entire German garrison was dead, shot, or bayoneted, except four prisoners. Then the Commandos withdrew toward the beach at Vasterival, after demolishing the guns and laying their dead comrades beside the ruins.

At 7:30 A.M. the attackers began to reëmbark, wading out neck-deep in fast ebbing tide to reach their boats, while the wounded were ferried out in a rubber rowboat. By 9 o'clock every survivor of the unit was aboard ship and under way. Although the casualties numbered about fifty and the raid was minuscule in proportion to what was to come, the official report declared that it "was carried out strictly according to plan and may well become a model for future operations of this kind."

The two inner landings flanking Dieppe were more hazardous. The Royal Regiment of Canada was detailed to take Puits, east of Dieppe, capture a coast-defense battery like that at Berneval and then seize the eastern headland that overlooked the site of the main assault. The enemy was completely alerted behind the low but strong sea wall at Puits. A withering fire met the first wave of attacking troops, storming ashore in the gray daylight. The Canadians rushed forward to the dubious shelter of the wall. Here they were swept by fire from the flank and most of their officers were among the first casualties.

The sea wall was crowned with jagged barbed wire, which the officers strove desperately to clear with Bangalore torpedoes. Near by was a pillbox; a lieutenant rushed it alone and tossed a grenade through its firing slit. The grenade killed every man in the pillbox but the young officer was riddled with bullets from other posts. Two other companies had landed to the west of the sea wall despite equally heavy fire. Here the attackers were able at last to cut a path through the barbed-wire barricades and begin to hack their way up the cliff. Quickly, a few of them reached the top and cleared the Germans out of the houses. But they could neither return to their comrades nor be reinforced by them. The Germans had sealed off their path with machine-gun fire.

The isolated men atop the cliff began to strike westward, hoping that the Essex Scottish Regiment had been able to penetrate Dieppe and they would be able to establish contact with it. Strong enemy patrols were on the watch for them, and they had to hide out in a woods. There they remained all day. Help never reached them; they had no choice but to surrender. The hoped-for sea support could not have helped these men. The officer, who was to have directed it, could not communicate with the destroyer assigned to aid them. He made every effort from his post with the land troops to indicate the worst resistance areas of the Germans, but his signals could not be made out from the sea.

The attack at Puits met with failure. It remained only to take off as many men as possible. It was now full daylight. The brilliant sunlight of mid-August had dispelled the early-morning mists. The operation had to be executed without the slightest protection by way of concealment. Landing craft ran in almost to the beach under direct and heavy fire that supporting aircraft succeeded only partly in cutting down. The Royal Regiment's men clambered aboard or swam out to farther boats while shells and bullets peppered the water around them. Surprisingly, only one of the boats was lost. It capsized. All aboard clung to its upturned hull until other light craft rescued every man.

Meanwhile, the Saskatchewan Regiment had stormed the beach of Pourville, west of Dieppe. Its task was to capture Pourville and move on to a place known as Four Winds Farm, where it was to establish a defensive position to cover the main landing. Toward this end, too, the Saskatchewans were supposed to capture the western headland overlooking the beach. The actual landing operation encountered little opposition until the men were ashore where, as at Puits, a sea wall divided the beaches. This the Commandos scaled with ladders, cleaned up a couple of pillboxes, and started to move inland under a smoke screen. About 6:00 A.M., they encountered a road block, and a fierce skirmish ensued.

Other Commando companies, which landed on either side of the first group, had battled their way into the town of Pourville itself. They had wiped out antiaircraft batteries and a radio-detector station on the way. Established in the village, they marched through until they had come to the bridge over the Scie River, where heavy mortar and machine-gun fire held them up. Many men made their way across the bridge, while others swam the little stream or improvised rafts.

Despite the heavy fire, their commander provided them with an example of gallantry that no man in his command could ignore. Lieutenant C. C. I. Merritt strode on to the span bareheaded, swinging his steel helmet in his hand. "See," he told his troops, "there's no danger here." Four times he made a return trip across the bridge. With such leadership the men pressed on to the edge of Four Winds Farm and overwhelmed its pillboxes. A Canadian private named Fenner was the hero of this action. Undeterred by German resistance, he walked into the enemy's positions and calmly fired his Bren gun from the hip.

The landing of the South Saskatchewans was closely followed by the Queen's Own Cameron Highlanders of Canada. They swept to the beach in broad daylight to the accompaniment of their own piper's playing of "The Hundred Pipers," an air that he kept repeating again and again until every man was ashore. The Saskatchewans had absorbed most of the enemy's resistance here and the Camerons advanced rapidly, one company soon reinforcing their predecessors east of Pourville. The remainder headed for the St. Aubin airfield, following the Scie River to avoid enemy fire. Nowhere in this area had the Canadians met any tanks. This was regarded with apprehension because it indicated that something had gone wrong in the laboriously careful calculations that had preceded the attack. All the evidence had indicated that tanks should have been encountered.

There was good reason. C Company of the Saskatchewans had captured the headland overlooking the Dieppe beach according to plan, but then the Germans had counterattacked. The enemy far outnumbered the Canadians and had soon recaptured the height. Now the Germans held a position that dominated not only the Dieppe sands but the beach from which the attackers of Pourville would have to be reëmbarked. Wounded men were already being carried back to the beach for reëmbarkation. At 10:45 A.M., when the landing craft came back to take them away, the boats met heavy fire. Only one of them was sunk. The rest had to lie fairly well offshore while those men who could do so swam out across 150 to 200 yards of open water after crossing an equal stretch of unprotected beach.

During the reëmbarkation, which took more than three hours, Colonel Merritt and his men attacked the machine-gun post scourging their beach from the west and silenced them. They then formed an improvised rear guard to defend a perimeter behind which all the wounded and other survivors of the Saskatchewans could safely embark. Their defense continued to the last man. They surrendered about 3:00 P.M. when all their ammunition was gone.

The men at sea had their hands full, throughout the land fighting. Shore batteries started to bang away at the little boats in the channel. Assault craft and destroyers replied gallantly and tirelessly, while from the skies Spitfires and Hurricanes roared down to bomb and cannonade and machine gun everything in sight. The naval men were forced to stay fairly well out to sea. A few German planes managed to slip through the seemingly impenetrable cover of the R.A.F.'s machines and loose their bombs on the tiny cockleshells below.

The main assault on Dieppe was to be delivered by the Royal Hamilton Light Infantry and the Essex Scottish Regiment. The site chosen for their landing was a 1,700-foot beach that stretched westward from the breakwater and ended near the cliffs topped by the Casino. Beyond the beach, from which it was divided by a sea wall, ran the Boulevard Marechal Foch on one side of a garden stretching inland to the Boulevard de Verdun. The boulevards were lined with houses and hotels that the Germans had strongly fortified. The infantry's task was to seize the beach, neutralize the enemy defenses, and permit the Allied tanks to come ashore and into the town. The infantry was then to move in, hold Dieppe, while other forces carried out important demolitions.

Two regiments went in together, the Essex Scots on the eastern flank and the Hamiltons on the western. Just before they hit the beach, there was a brief but intense bombardment from their accompanying destroyers. As the roar of their guns rolled away, a flight of Spitfires and Hurricanes swooped down on the fortified houses and riddled them with cannon fire. Once the infantry regiments were ashore, they plunged ahead. Like their comrades at Puits, they immediately met heavy frontal and flanking fire. The defenses in the houses behind the water front had been mauled, but they were still strong. These opened up on the Canadians. German guns on the headland to the east had been rendered temporarily impotent by a heavy smoke screen laid by low-flying British Blenheims. As the wind carried this away, the attackers were exposed to fire from still another quarter—weapons mounted on the sides and top of the cliff.

The Essex Regiment was nearer to them than the Hamiltons. The former suffered more heavily and was held up at the sea wall, which was topped by barbed wire. The Hamiltons, however, stormed as far as the Casino and captured it. Here they were joined by a party of Royal Canadian Engineers. The infantrymen blew up near-by pillboxes while the engineers wiped up the remaining resistance in the Casino and destroyed a four-inch gun that threatened the beach. The two groups then pressed on together into the town but, having no support, they were soon stopped at a church.

While the foot soldiers were battling their way into the outer defenses and the town itself, the tank-landing-craft were approaching the beach. There were six of these carrying not only the big machines but parties of engineers and landing troops. The engineers were under orders to destroy the enemy's tank obstacles that blocked the streets.

Every one of the landing craft was hit by the Germans' shore fire. One sank; another ran aground, flaming, and remained beached. In spite of these mishaps, only two of the tanks carried across the Channel were not landed. Barely a half-hour later, a second wave of tank-landing-craft hit the shore, only to meet even worse fire from the inland and flanking defenses. One craft was sunk, another lost her entire naval complement and was taken over by a sergeant of the Royal Marines. He managed to get one of his three tanks ashore and then had to pull away, for his craft was in imminent danger of being sunk. As he tried to land the other two tanks at another point along the beach, enemy fire was even heavier and in a few minutes there were more than twenty holes in the boat. The attempt to land the tanks had to be abandoned.

Nevertheless, twenty-eight tanks were put ashore. Several of them never got beyond the beach, for the Germans' fire was accurate and had destroyed their treads so they could not move. But the rest moved along; some of them managed to get past the sea wall and onto the open ground beyond. There they divided, one group heading westward to knock out the enemy's defenses and the other group heading directly into Dieppe.

The losses of the Engineers had been so severe from the moment of their landing that none of them had been able to get through the barriers in the small streets. However, one tank smashed right through a house near the beach and thus continued into the town; two more followed it. The rest of the undamaged tanks confined themselves to patrolling the broad boulevard that paralleled the water front and fired into the German defenses. By the time the tanks had exhausted their ammunition they had inflicted considerable injury to the enemy and silenced a few of his positions; but beyond that they could do nothing.

The force commanders at sea could not know every last-minute detail, for communications could not be maintained on an up-to-the-minute basis under such circumstances. They did know that the tanks got ashore, but not that they had been able to achieve so little. Intent on accomplishing as much damage as possible, the commanders decided to throw in their reserves, the Fusiliers Mont-Royal.

The Fusiliers landed at 7:00 A.M. As soon as they were ashore they ran into undiminished German resistance and had to break for cover. Some found shelter in the lee of wrecked tanks, while others had to rely on the scattered dunes and hollows of the beach. More than half the force was carried west of Casino by a sudden shift in the tide Their landing place was not the main beach but a small stony strip beneath high cliffs that they could not scale. Wherever they turned, they met heavy enemy fire. They could not return it because it came from high positions that they could not see. They held out for several hours, but not before they had suffered heavy losses.

Two other groups of Fusiliers landed virtually in front of the Casino. By the time they reached it, it was securely held by the Allies. The two parties of Fusiliers pushed on, one heading for an attack on the houses along the Boulevard de Verdun, the other striking deep into the town for the Bassin du Canada, the inner harbor. This outfit had to hack its way street by street. It fought on until it had passed the last substantial German force. This triumph, however, dissolved in irony; they had no ammunition left and had to surrender to the first armed party that they met.

The Fusiliers soon showed that they were worthy comrades of the Commandos. Their captors forced them to strip to their underwear and face a wall, lined up side by side. Only one German was left to guard them. As a Canadian soldier distracted his attention, his comrades fell on him. In a flash the guard was dead, killed by bare hands. The Canadians dashed off through the town in their jerseys and shorts, determined to reach the beach and eventually England. A good many lost their way in the town and were eventually recaptured, but a considerable number arrived at their destination.

General Roberts decided to throw in new reinforcements. This time he chose the Royal Marine Commandos. Unfortunately, the command ship could receive only fragmentary reports from the battle area. Because of the smoke screens and the haze of battle, little could be observed. Therefore, no one aboard knew at this time of the tanks' defeat.

The clear sky was clouded only with Spitfires as the Marines moved inshore under a blazing-hot sun. The sea was calm. As the landing boats sailed in they passed a British destroyer, a cluster of assault craft, landing craft, R-boats, motor launches, and motor gunboats.

A smoke screen was soon laid down to cover the Marine Commandos' landing. The boats entered it, necessarily as blinded as they hoped the enemy would be. As the first craft penetrated the onshore edge of the screen, every enemy gun within range, from the lightest antiaircraft to rifles, opened up full blast. The Marines replied with Bren guns, recklessly shooting at every target from the unprotected decks. Men struggled ashore after having swum from their wrecked boats; others waded in from the ramps of their vessels. The fire was merciless. To quote the official report of the action, the Marines went in "with a courage terrible to see."

Few survived unhurt. The beach was swept by a concentrated enemy fire. The officer in charge of the landing forces, Lieutenant Colonel J. P. Phillips, decided to halt the landing if it were still possible. His own craft was close to the beach. He pulled white gloves over his hands to make them more easily visible, then ran to the forward deck and started to signal to the other boats to turn back. Their officers saw the movement of his hands and immediately took in the situation. As the boats turned in obedience to his command, Colonel Phillips fell to the deck with a mortal wound. His own life had saved two hundred.

Throughout these operations the aërial cover was constantly maintained, and the Germans rarely penetrated it. From time to time, however, they scored several damaging near-misses. Their luck was greatest when it was combined with accident. They sank the destroyer *Berkeley* by the sheerest mischance. The bomb that hit her was one of several that a Junkers-88 had been compelled to jettison after a Spitfire had crippled the enemy plane. Bombs were dropped at random, and the destroyer just happened to be beneath one of them. It tore away her bridge, where Lieutenant Colonel L. B. Hillsinger of the U. S. Army Air Forces had been standing with a British officer.

Colonel Hillsinger was another of the hundreds of heroes of that heroic day. He was flung into the water and began to swim for the nearest craft, hardly aware of the pain or the nature of the wound that the bomb had inflicted on him. As he swam, he saw a foot float past, clad in a brand-new brown shoe. Suddenly he realized that foot and shoe were his own. In sheer rage, he tore off his other shoe and flung it after the first. When taken aboard a motor gunboat, he refused to leave the deck. While medical corps men tried to aid him, he lay flat and directed the craft's antiaircraft fire to prevent further losses.

As the day wore on, the rôle of the Allied aircraft changed from that of an arm of an offensive to that of cover for a defensive operation. The withdrawal from the main beaches was scheduled to begin at 11:00 A.M.; from then on, the planes would have to protect the retiring raiders from German assaults. Promptly at the set hour, R.A.F. Bostons roared over the eastern headland that flanked the Dieppe harbor and dropped a dense smoke screen that covered the entire area between the two headlands. Enemy antiaircraft guns were murderously active, but the smoke-laying planes flew through their fire unheeding.

Under this shroud of smoke the Royal Hamilton Light Infantry began to move back toward the shore and to enter the craft drawn up to await it. Many of its men, with others from the Fusiliers, had held the Casino until the last possible moment and withdrawn only when imperative orders were issued. By 12:20 P.M. most of the survivors who had escaped capture or death had been taken off the beach; others were still hoping for transport homeward. Among them were many doctors and orderlies of the medical corps, who had done perhaps the most heroic job of all. Unarmed, defenseless, and unprotected, they labored throughout the battle to ease the wounded and comfort the dying. One by one they saw other units taken off the beach and out to sea and England; yet they stuck uncomplainingly to their tasks until there were no more wounded to tend or boats to carry them away.

It was almost 1:00 P.M. when the British naval forces made one final effort to save the few remaining men on the beaches. The Allies themselves were now hampered by their own smoke screen as they tried to close on the shore. Through the darkness the enemy was maintaining terrific fire. The destroyers risked everything by going so close to the German posts on the Dieppe breakwater that they were within easy range of the enemy's machine guns.

Those few men remaining ashore were not to be taken off. At 1:08 P.M. the ships received their last signal from the shore, where Brigadier Southan of the Canadian infantry was about to surrender. It was hopeless for his men to try to reach the sea. Reluctantly but inevitably, the order was given for the ships to start on the voyage back to England.

Few of the major objectives of the raid had been achieved and a fantastic price had been paid for these. The Canadian troops engaged in the operation—virtually the entire force—had numbered 5,000 when they left the coast of England. In seven hours of fighting on a hostile shore, more than two-thirds of that number had become casualties: 593 killed, 1,901 captured, and 287 unaccounted for, while those wounded numbered 591.

What price glory? Valorous men had gone down that day. Two years later their lives were to be redeemed. Their deaths had given the Allies their first tragic lesson on the dangers of invasion. The enemy had lost nearly two hundred first-line planes, bombers, and fighters in a single day. The nature of his defenses had been subjected at last to the ultimate test, and they had been proved something less than impregnable. Above all, from one end of Europe to the other, the Germans had been thrown into a momentary panic: they had not known that this was only a reconnaissance in force but had taken it for the already long-feared invasion from the west.

The Dieppe raid proved conclusively that the Allies were mastering that intangible and elusive key to every great military victory—"perfect synchronization." The Germans knew that on a bigger scale it would be perfected. Where and when that assault would be made was now their constant fear. Time after time they were to believe that the final blow was being struck, but it was to be nearly two years before all the lessons of Dieppe and all that followed were to reach fruition.

44

COURAGEOUS CHINA'S LONG DEFENSE OF HER HOMELAND

AFTER ten years of patient suffering, China declared war against the invader Japan and her cohorts, Germany and Italy, at midnight on December 9, 1941. The 400,000,000 people in this ancient civilization had found their traditional tranquillity broken when the Japanese war machine swept over their homeland, leaving millions lying lifeless in its wake. There is no more tragic story in fact or in legend than the story of almost superhuman endurance, inexhaustible patience, and strong resoluteness of the besieged Chinese people.

Henry L. Stimson, Secretary of State in President Hoover's cabinet, was sitting in his office in Washington on September 17, 1931, when the Japanese Ambassador, Katsuji Debuchi, called to make his adieus before returning to Tokyo on his triennial leave. The next day Mr. Debuchi canceled his return because "a bridge in a section of the Japanese-owned South Manchuria Railway, near Liutiaokou on the outskirts of Mukden, had been blown up."

It is from such apparently insignificant "incidents" that wars start. While the Japanese were undoubtedly the incendiaries, they concocted this tale: At 10:30 P.M. on September 18 some three hundred Chinese regulars were detected by Japanese railway guards trying to blow up the tracks. When discovered, the Chinese opened fire, to which Japanese reinforcements (who had mysteriously arrived) replied. The Chinese barracks were besieged at 11:20 and completely occupied by 1:25 A.M., September 19. An hour and a half later the walled city of Mukden had been entered. By 11 o'clock that morning Japanese troops had captured several other towns. Communities fell in rapid succession; the strategic railway city of Kirin was occupied September 21.

China denied the entire "incident" and declared it to be a diabolically conceived Japanese plot to instigate an invasion. She instructed her troops to offer no resistance but to withdraw everywhere. That this was done is attested by neutral accounts and Tokyo's own casualty reports, which boasted of hundreds of killed and captured Chinese and then listed Japanese losses as only "two killed, thirteen wounded, at Mukden; twenty killed and forty wounded at Changchun." How the Japanese engaged in simultaneous military operations at this point, 175 miles north of the scene of the Mukden "incident," was not explained. Tokyo further admitted that in a few hours every city along the 693 miles of the South Manchuria Railway had been seized by the Japanese.

Tokyo did not reveal, however, what orders had been issued by General Honjo to his new command three days before the alleged bombing. It did not reveal the tests that were carried out, or how, when, and why Japanese troops began their march in advance of the bombing. The quick seizure of communications centers over thousands of square miles might explain everything. The fraud is transparent.

The Japanese Cabinet met in Tokyo on October 9. Although they deplored the "incident," they made it clear that Japan would hold on to Manchuria until a friendly régime had been established. This set the stage for the creation of the puppet state of Manchukuo and the installation of Henry Pu-yi as chief executive on March 9, 1932.

Tokyo, proceeding on the theory that Japan was the overlord of all East Asia, including China, ignored treaties, promises, armistices, threats, rebukes. An incident was created at Shanghai on January 25, 1932, following closely the pattern of Mukden. This was called the "Shanghai Affair" and here, again, the versions differ. Tokyo said that a local newspaper had printed an article "disrespectful of the Imperial family of Japan" and that, shortly after, two Japanese Buddhist priests and three of their followers were assaulted "by a mob of workers of the Sanyu Business Company, manufacturers of towels." The Buddhists undoubtedly had entered as a result of the "Twenty-one Demands." Eventually the Japanese issued an ultimatum that was ignored and then sent troops to the Chapei section of Shanghai, which resulted in a clash.

The Chinese declared that Japan had staged the whole affair in order (1) to turn Chapei into a Japanese concession, and (2) to find an excuse for the seizure of Jehol Province to round out the borders of her puppet state of Manchukuo. When one truce after another had been broken, the Japanese sent an expeditionary force ashore and seized numerous strategic localities. After all objectives had been gained the Japanese on March 3 ordered hostilities suspended. The commander of the Japanese fleet was Vice Admiral Kichisaburo Nomura who arrived in the United States as Tokyo's ambassador nine months before Pearl Harbor.

Japan was ready to break with the rest of the world now that Manchuria, as Manchukuo, was firmly in her grasp and her forces were deployed within China. China had appealed to the League of Nations. That body found that Japan had broken her pledge not to employ force against another member of the League; she had also violated her "frank renunciation of war as an instrument of national policy" and her agreement to settle "all disputes or conflicts of whatever nature ... by pacific means." Japan had also broken every pledge to which she had subscribed when, in 1928, she accepted the Pact of Paris, better known as the Kellogg-Briand Treaty.

On March 17, 1932, fourteen days after she had stopped shooting in China and eight days after Henry Pu-yi took over "Manchukuo" for her, Japan repudiated the League of Nations and withdrew from that body. Thus, by the end of the first quarter of 1932, Japan had: (1) set the wheels of World War II in motion at Mukden; (2) set the example for bombing civilians from the air; (3) set the example of conquest to be followed by Mussolini in Ethiopia and Albania and by Hitler in Europe generally; (4) set the first "Quisling" in power in the person of Henry Pu-yi; and (5) set the fashion for aggressors to leave the League of Nations and persist in their aggressions.

The world was still hopeful, however. It could not envisage another international holocaust. Despite the continued depredations of Japan in China and the mounting Russo-Japanese tension, a naval conference had been held in London in 1930 which turned out to be another diplomatic triumph for the Tokyo war lords. Two treaties were signed in London. Great Britain, the United States, and Japan were joined by Italy and France in declaring a holiday in naval construction, in scrapping certain warships, and in agreeing to limit naval armaments and practices. The three first-named powers signed another treaty modifying the Washington Five-Power Naval Treaty. This established ratios for other than capital warships and airplane carriers. The net result was to raise Japan from a 5-5-3 basis to a 10-10-7 basis. This gave her parity with the United States and Great Britain in the number of submarines. In the classification of cruiser types the United States accepted the Japanese dividing line of 6.1-inch guns instead of her own 8-inch guns—another Japanese victory.

The final scenes leading up to World War II began to crowd one another more quickly. On October 14, 1933, Germany followed Japan out of the League of Nations. On December 29, 1934, Tokyo notified the United States of her intention to terminate the Washington Naval Treaty under which she had pledged no further fortification of the Pacific islands under her control. Our Government was in possession of evidence that tended "to show the existence of unusually close and friendly relations between Germany and Japan, even to the extent of a possible secret alliance."

The perfidy of Japan now revealed its plot. On November 25, 1936, Ambassador Joachim von Ribbentrop and Ambassador Viscount Kimitomo Mushakoji signed for their respective countries a five-year "Anti-Comintern Pact." Ostensibly an alliance solely to combat Communism, it was obviously aimed at Russia in an effort to prevent interference with Japan's plans in China. Germany guaranteed Japan's possession of Borneo, the Celebes, and Netherlands New Guinea, while Japan, in return, guaranteed Germany's possession of Sumatra, Java, and the rest of the Netherlands East Indies. Japan, through her puppet state Manchukuo, had been having trouble with Russia along the border.

The night of July 7, 1937—ten years to the day after Baron Tanaka's

Mukden conference—found Japan with her decks cleared for action. What actually started the shooting at Marco Polo Bridge, southwest of Peiping, is another mystery. Those shots started the war in the Pacific and made certain the eventual conflict between the United States and Japan. The best authenticated version of the affair is as follows: The Japanese were engaged in maneuvers in the vicinity of Lukouchiao and Lungwangmiao. The Chinese said that the Japanese, under the pretext of seeking one of their missing men, started a row. Japan was ready at Lukouchiao in exactly the same manner as she had been prepared at the time of the "Mukden Incident." Her forces seized strategic points and closed the military noose that she had been drawing about Peiping.

The issue was drawn ten days later when Generalissimo Chiang Kai-shek declared that everything, even Chinese patience, must come to an end, that any settlement of the Lukouchiao affair must "not infringe upon the sovereignty and territorial integrity of China," and that under no conditions would the Central Government consent to external pressure in domestic affairs.

Japanese forces had been poised to strike for some time, and they moved quickly. Two Japanese marines were shot on August 9 while trying to force their way into the Hungjao Military Airfield at Shanghai. The fact that the Japanese were moving on many fronts did not constitute justification for the shooting in Tokyo's eyes. The battle of Shanghai was begun four days after the airfield incident. It lasted from August 13 to November 11, when the Chinese evacuated the city. On November 20, 1937, they set up their capital at Chungking. A month later, Nanking, the seat of the Central Government, fell.

After each major Japanese advance the Chinese heroically counter-attacked and regained virtually all the lost territory. This process was repeated year after year in sector after sector. Japan was able to show little net gain anywhere after her initial thrusts in 1937-39. She lost more than a million of her finest soldiers, either killed or so seriously wounded that they could not return to duty. Her chief victories were political. The breach between the Communists and Chunking was reopened. This deprived China of the full use of her armed forces and enabled Japan to keep only token forces on certain vital fronts.

Japan had only 10,000 troops when the battle of Shanghai was begun on August 13, 1937, five weeks after the Marco Polo Bridge incident. But Tokyo's war lords had been so well prepared that in approximately forty days there were 200,000 troops in action. The total number of Japanese troops in China rose sharply to more than 1,000,000.

Shanghai fell on November 12, 1937. One month later, Japanese naval planes, under the pretense that they were chasing fleeing Chinese, bombed, machine-gunned, and sank the United States gunboat *Panay* and three of our merchantmen in the Yangtze River.

Just before Christmas of that year China electrified the world with an example of heroic self-sacrifice, adopted subsequently in Russia on a wide scale—the "scorched earth" policy. Whatever could not be removed was burned—homes, factories, food, clothing—so that the enemy could not live off his conquests. Still the retreat continued as the Japanese tried vainly to encircle and annihilate the Chinese Army. Then suddenly the Chinese won a victory.

The battle raged until April 6-8. For the first time in their history the soldiers of "New Japan" were forced to flee. The myth of Japanese "invincibility" had been shattered, just as that of the Germans was to be exploded at El Alamein and Stalingrad a few years later, against the heroic fighting of the British and Russians.

The most important lesson learned at Taierhchwang was this: The Japanese soldier had been taught that he could not lose a battle. He now found that the spirits of his warrior ancestors would not help him. Further, believing that if he died in battle he in turn would join the spirits of those ancestors and return to the struggle to help his comrades, he often plunged headlong to his death. When American soldiers and Marines later clashed with the Japanese on the islands of the Pacific, they knew from the lesson of Taierhchwang the wisdom of letting the enemy throw himself into the murderous fire of our machine guns. The fact that the Japanese subsequently did capture Hsuchow merely emphasized the lesson, for Japan would have "lost face" had she not either taken the objective or gone down trying.

There were four major battles fought in the first period of the Sino-Japanese War, all ending with Japanese occupation of the objective: Shanghai, Sinkow, Hsuchow, and Hankow. Hsuchow was evacuated by the Chinese on May 19, 1938, Hankow on October 25, 1938. Then the second period of the war set in, and things became more difficult for Japan. The Chinese had an opportunity to build up some sort of defensive position. Their army was fully mobilized, if not properly equipped.

Mounting tension in Europe was not unnoticed by Japan. She knew that the outbreak of European hostilities would have a Pacific reaction, as in World War I. On February 10, 1939, therefore, Tokyo moved to increase her blockade of the South China coast and at the same time to dominate French Indo-China by seizing the island of Hainan. Then she took another step which effectively sealed the South China Sea and the Chinese coast—the annexation of the Spratly Islands. The full significance of this action appeared first when Japan spread her conquests to the gates of Australia and later when the tide turned and the Allies began to hem in the Japanese homeland.

The slow progress of the Chinese invasion set Japan on a still more cruel and desperate course. She began her extended air raids on

Chungking, making that city the most frequently and heavily bombed community in the world up to that time.

One reason why the attacks failed and finally were discontinued was that Generalissimo Chiang Kai-shek, following the outbreak of the First World War, had put three Americans on his staff in charge of building up an adequate air force for China. One of these was Claire L. Chennault, an associate of Brigadier General William ("Billy") Mitchell during the days of the bitter struggle for a strong United States air force. The Generalissimo appointed Chennault as a Lieutenant Colonel and subsequently placed him in command of all air activities.

In the fall of 1939 Japan decided to end the "China Incident"; it was becoming too expensive, and there were bigger things in the offing. General Toshizo Nishio was made commander in chief in China, with Lieutenant General Seishiro Itagaki his chief of staff.

In Europe, Hitler had overrun France. On June 20, 1940, Tokyo wrung from the tottering Pétain's new French Government an agreement to close the Indo-China route for the transport of war material and supplies into China. On September 22 the Franco-Japanese Agreement was signed. This permitted the Japanese to use French Indo-China as a military and naval base. The following day Tokyo's troops moved in. Japan followed up her success with France in tightening the blockade on China by pursuing the advantages gained by the aggressors in western Europe. She next turned the screws on Great Britain. Almost coincident with her heroism at Dunkirk, Britain yielded to Japan's pressure and agreed to close the Burma Road for three months from July 18, 1940. It was over this route that China was receiving the small quantities of supplies that were reaching her from the outside world. Burma was a British possession, and the English were in no position to withstand a Japanese thrust from French Indo-China should Tokyo's demand be refused. When that agreement expired on October 17, 1940, the Burma Road was reopened, but during those ninety days China suffered grievously.

The scene shifted again to Berlin. There, on September 27, 1940, the "Tripartite Pact" was signed. This was a ten-year political, economic, and military alliance entered into by Berlin, Rome, and Tokyo. Foreign Minister Joachim von Ribbentrop signed for Germany; Mussolini's subsequently executed son-in-law, Foreign Minister Count Galeazzo Ciano, signed for Italy. The man who signed for Japan was Ambassador Saburo Kurusu who, with Admiral Nomura, was to appear in Washington the following year, presumably to arrive at harmonious relations with the United States.

The "Tripartite Pact" recognized Europe as the sphere of Germany and Italy, allotted Asia as the sphere of Japan, and agreed that the three nations would act as one if any of them was attacked by a "Power not at present involved in the European war or in the Chinese-Japanese conflict." Russia was specifically exempted from any of the provisions of the Pact; obviously, therefore, the document was aimed solely at the United States. Specifically it declared: "Germany and Italy recognize and respect the leadership of Japan in the establishment of a new order in Greater East Asia."

The final diplomatic bulwark erected by Japan was the ten-year "Russo-Japanese Non-Aggression Treaty," signed on April 13, 1941, two months before Hitler repudiated his similar agreement with the Soviets and struck suddenly at Russia. With the ostensible purpose of retaining "peaceful and friendly relations" and the promise to "mutually respect the territorial integrity and inviolability of the other," the Treaty declared: "Should one of the contracting parties become the object of hostilities on the part of one or several of the third Powers, the other contracting party will observe neutrality throughout the duration of the conflict."

This provision cut several ways. It assured Japan against an attack from Russia if war broke out with the United States. It assured Russia against an attack in Siberia from Japan if Germany should strike.

While these diplomatic battles were being waged, the fighting in China had reached a comparative stalemate. Chiang Kai-shek's generals had worked out a way to stop the enemy. Japan struck with speed, numbers, and power in three columns, occasionally four, toward a particular objective. Chinese tactics consisted in first clipping one wing of the three-prong drive, then the other, and finally launching a fierce counterattack against the center, which had been permitted to flow into a pocket. This device was used time and again. The Japanese countered it with poison gas. By this method they made desperate attempts to take the baffling city of Changsha, only to meet defeat. The Chinese reoccupied Ichang, but poison gas drove them out two days later. On November 1, 1941, they regained Chengchow and were nibbling off more of the conquered province when, thirty-seven days later, the Japanese struck at Pearl Harbor and the Philippines.

We now have a clear picture of the events leading up to that "Day of Infamy" from which we can gauge the action that was to follow. Now long-suffering China had companions in misery. The enemy whom she had been battling for five long years had, in the space of almost the same number of weeks, been able to overrun vast areas of American, British, and Netherlands territory.

On December 8 the people of China aligned themselves with the United States and Great Britain in a formal declaration of war against the Rome-Berlin-Tokyo Axis.

On New Year's Day, 1942, Generalissimo Chiang Kai-shek sent this message: "I believe that when a certain stage has been reached the

Allies will find themselves in a position to inflict overwhelming defeat on the enemy on the sea and in the air as a preliminary to a decisive rout of his forces on land.... The Japanese, suffering from an insatiable thirst for conquest, have drunk deep from what they were perfectly aware was poison, a poison that will eventually kill them."

The United States, always the friend of China, brought cheer to the besieged republic in April, 1942, when announcement was made of the appointment by Generalissimo Chiang Kai-shek, upon President Roosevelt's recommendation, of General Joseph W. Stilwell as commander of the Chinese Fifth and Sixth Armies in Burma. Before going to China to become chief of staff to the Generalissimo, "Vinegar Joe" was promoted to the rank of lieutenant general by Mr. Roosevelt. Shortly after he had assumed the China-Burma command "Uncle Joe" became "head man" for all American forces in that theater.

Jungle and mountain fighting were nothing new to this tall, wiry fighter who had been quarterback on the West Point football team. He had learned it as a young officer in fighting the Moros of Mindanao in the years immediately following the Spanish-American War. He also knew China well. After serving as a lieutenant colonel in the First World War, he had reverted to the peacetime rank of captain. At his own request he had joined the Chinese language detail and had gone to China as a student, returning to the United States to go through the Infantry, Command, and General Staff Schools. In 1928-29 he was chief of staff of American forces in China and six years later returned to become military attaché in China and Siam, a post he held until 1939. Stilwell was loved and trusted by his men, American and Chinese alike. Together they had a bitter hatred for the Japanese and an immense determination to bring them down in defeat.

45

INDIA, GOAL OF THE AXIS—BURMA, MALAYA, AND FALL OF SINGAPORE

MOTHER INDIA, which cradled early civilization some five thousand years ago, with her population of more than 400,000,000, was the goal of the Axis in World War II. Here the war lords of Japan expected to join forces with the Germans under Hitler in their blue print for world conquest.

The Allies, with full realization of this Axis plan to clasp hands with the Japs, established strong forces in India early in the war. While the British were holding their defense lines, the Americans were on the way early in 1942. American Air Forces under General Lewis H. Brereton were bombing the approaching Japs as the Flying Tigers under General Chennault in China were creating havoc along the routes from the north. Brereton was Commander of United States Air Forces in India, later commander of all our Air Forces in the Middle East. Finally he was to be in command of the famous Ninth Air Force to spearhead invasion forces in the liberation of Europe.

Iran, a gateway to India, was occupied by the British and Russians on August 25, 1941—104 days before the United States entered the war. It ended relations with Italy, Bulgaria, Hungary, and Rumania, on September 16, with Japan and Vichy France in the following year, and with Germany a year later. Iraq declared war on Japan, Germany, and Italy the same year. India declared war on Hungary, Rumania, and Finland the day the United States was catapulted into the war.

India was one of the richest goals. Its defense by the Allies created many problems. Protected by the British from the Jap invaders, the strength of the Indian Army in the first year of the war was about 1,000,000; a year later it exceeded 2,000,000, all of them volunteers.

There were strong political divisions in India—the groups who immediately joined the cause of the Allies; the groups who demanded Indian independence before taking action; and the pacifist groups who followed the leadership of Gandhi. To grant independence and withdraw in wartime would be fatal to both India and the Allies. It would immediately create internal warfare among the 45 races, speaking 200 languages, with their 2,400 castes and tribes and 700 feudatory states. In this chaos the Japs would march on to complete conquest of India.

To avert this crisis, the British, Americans, and their Allies stood strong in the defense of India against every conspiracy by the Axis partners to create dissension and confusion. At the outbreak of the war the British Governor Viceroy and Governor General was the Marquess of Linlithgow, later to be succeeded by Field Marshal Sir Archibald Percival Wavell, who was to gain fame during the war.

Two years before the outbreak of the war Burma had been detached from British India, and made a crown colony with a constitution of her own. American and British supplies were steadily rolling into China over the famous Burma Road. The early invasion of Burma by the Japs was a severe blow. They set up Dr. Ba Maw as their puppet premier, a year later made fake pretentions of granting Burma its independence, and under this disguise immediately declared Burma at war against the United States and Great Britain.

British Malaya, the Straits Settlements, with Singapore as capital and chief port, was the great water highway between India and China. Singapore—with a polyglot population of over 600,000, more than 80 per cent Chinese—was the port of more than 30,000 ships annually. Its strategic importance was increased by the fact that more than three-fourths of the tin and three-fifths of the rubber used in the United States, essential to warfare, came from British Malaya.

The battle for Malaya, Burma, and India, therefore created many crises. As American Flying Fortresses and Allied bombers were "jumping the hump" over the Himalayas, highest mountains in the world, to carry aid to China, other squadrons constantly bombed the Burma Road and the Japanese Armies on their way through Burma.

The long-prepared plans of the Japanese to conquer Asia were made evident from the day they struck at the Philippines. Within twenty-eight days, with lightning thrusts, they were on the Perak River line north of Singapore and succeeded in making a landing behind the defending lines. The enemy seized an airfield 190 miles and only one hour's flight from Singapore.

India was no better garrisoned than was Malaya, and the country was in political turmoil. Should the Japanese reach India, they could drive across the vast country toward a planned junction with the Germans who, at the time, gave every indication of smashing through Egypt and joining their Asiatic partner in Iran or Afghanistan.

If the Axis could accomplish this, Russia would be isolated; China would be surrounded; Australia would be invaded; England would be forced to stand alone on her little island—after which Germany, Japan, and Italy would concentrate on a still partially armed United States.

When January, 1942, bowed out, the Japanese were in possession of Moulmein and were driving fast upon Rangoon. They had lost more than one hundred planes and thousands of soldiers during the eighth week of the war, but more men and supplies came in daily.

The fighting in Malaya had entered its final stage. On January 26 the British abandoned Batu Pahat, western anchor of the line north of Johore Strait. Singapore was under constant aërial bombardment, and field artillery soon brought the city under fire.

On January 31 Lieutenant General Arthur Ernest Percival gave the order to abandon the mainland and retire to the island. The British, Australian, and Indian troops crossed under cover of darkness the Johore causeway over the half-mile strip of water that separated Singapore from the rest of Malaya. When the last man had completed his trip, the causeway was blown up.

February and March, 1942, were bleak months for the United Nations in the Pacific. In the first eight weeks of the war the Japanese had overrun more than 350 miles of the jungles and mountains of Malaya in one of the most rapid military advances in history. They had managed, in that short time, to overcome the most difficult obstacles of terrain that nature could provide and to bring under siege the mighty bastion of Singapore, on which Great Britain had spent more than $400,000,000 over a period of twenty years.

The storming of Singapore began during the night of February 7-8, 1942. As the first step, the Japanese went after Ubin Island, a small but strategically vital bit of land in Johore Strait about a half-mile off the northeast coast of Singapore Island. A terrific barrage preceded the landing parties, which were able quickly to seize Ubin and stock it with artillery, ammunition, and materials required for the further operations.

Twenty-four hours later the Japanese got ashore on Singapore Island and were soon in possession of sufficient waterfront to be able to land tanks. Furious fighting raged during the day and the next night. The defenders wiped out the Japanese beachhead time and again, but the enemy with his seemingly endless supply of men and barges kept pouring new troops ashore until the tired British were compelled to withdraw. A line was then drawn along a ten-mile front in West Singapore. The Japanese had no sooner intrenched themselves before they made a formal demand for surrender. This was refused immediately. Warships and merchantmen speeded the evacuation of women and children under a hail of bombs and shells. Many refugee ships were sunk in the harbor, but the majority made good their escape.

The most bitter fighting of the entire Malayan campaign came on February 13-14. On the former day the defenders counterattacked four times in desperate efforts to restore a semblance of balance between the contending forces. The Japanese, however, had repaired the causeway over Johore Strait and were rushing over new men and tanks faster than the garrison could knock them out.

During the night the enemy succeeded in capturing the waterworks. The defenders' massed batteries poured shells into the Japanese ranks without appreciably affecting the hostile action. On the 14th three Japanese columns advanced on the city. The central column, having completed occupation of the reservoirs, reached the northern outskirts. Another column by-passed the waterworks, crossed the Kalang River, and cut the road from the city to the airport. The third column reached Alexandria road in the western part of the city. During the night General Percival sent a message to General Wavell that due to heavy losses in men and equipment and shortage of water, gasoline, oil, ammunition, and food, it would be impossible to continue the struggle. At 10:30 A.M. on February 15, 1942, four years and one day after Great Britain's mighty naval base, second only to Gibraltar, had been formally dedicated, General Percival met General Yamashita in the Ford Motor Plant building and signed terms of unconditional surrender.

At 8:00 A.M. the next day a Japanese tank detachment led the conquerors into Singapore. General Percival, Sir Shenton Thomas, Governor of the Straits Settlement, and more than sixty thousand soldiers were made prisoners. Although the main installations had been destroyed before the surrender, a vast amount of equipment and supplies fell to the enemy.

The loss of Singapore stunned Great Britain. The darkest moment of the war had come.

That same day all men of the United States between the ages of eighteen and sixty-five were registering under the terms of the Selective Service Act.

Japan did not wait for the actual fall of Singapore before intensifying her efforts in Burma and against the Netherlands Indies. The Burma campaign was essentially a repetition of the drive through Malaya. At the beginning of February the British had withdrawn to the Salween River and had stabilized the front there. The Japanese employed devious primitive devices in a strange mixture with modern motorized warfare to speed their advance. Firecrackers would suddenly pop in an effort to draw British fire and thus reveal defending positions. The Japanese would dress in the uniforms of British prisoners and advance boldly until in position to open fire. These ruses were employed throughout the war. Natives were forced to carry supplies for the invaders, so that a Japanese column presented a strange agglomeration of a native safari with elephants, a military train with mules, and a sightseeing excursion of civilians on folding bicycles. The fall of Singapore released some 200,000 Japanese troops for use in Burma and the progressing drive against Java.

After crossing the Salween, the pace of invasion was stepped up. A second, third, and fourth crossing of the Salween were quickly effected by the Japanese, and the attack on Rangoon developed in conjunction with the enemy forces proceeding up the coast of Lower Burma.

The Rangoon-Lashio Railroad was cut on the 28th and large Jap-

India, Goal of the Axis

anese reinforcements began to arrive at the front. The days of Rangoon were numbered. Japanese airplanes lashed without mercy. The road to Prome had been cut by the Japanese twenty-five miles north of Rangoon. The main body of British troops managed to break out of the trap and reach a point eighty miles above the doomed city to prepare for the defense of India.

On March 7 Lieutenant General Harold R. L. G. Alexander, later to become famous for his masterful work in North Africa and in Europe, took over command of British Forces in Burma from Lieutenant General Thomas J. Hutton. Two days later, shortly after noon, all the oil refineries, port installations, munitions, and other dumps at Rangoon blew up with a roar that shook the country for a hundred miles. The demolition switch had been thrown at two o'clock. A little later Rangoon was occupied by the Japanese.

The Japanese carried the war to India at the close of February. They bombed Port Blair, capital of the Andaman Islands in the Bay of Bengal. It was advance warning that they intended to try to seize the strategic islands. The enemy followed a stereotyped tactical approach that served him well in the early days of the war but helped to hasten his undoing as Allied strength increased. This approach was carried out by sending out a small flight of bombers against their next objective some two to four weeks before the real assault was undertaken. The Andaman Islands lie at the eastern side of the Bay of Bengal close to Burma. The 1,000,000 square miles of water constituting the bay separate Burma from India. This body of water, almost as large as the Mediterranean Sea, controls the approaches to the Indian Ocean and the shipping routes from Britain and the United States to India. Possession of the Andamans would provide a base from which to strike toward Ceylon and raid Allied shipping. It might also serve to cover an amphibious attack on the shores of India.

There was little economic value for the Japanese in possessing these islands. Their hilly, jungle-covered terrain was poor and undeveloped. The people were the relics of a pygmy race. On March 24, when a Japanese invasion flotilla appeared off the shores of Port Blair, they found the British had evacuated sometime before and the Andaman Islands were occupied without opposition. The menace to India grew graver.

JAPS SWEEP THROUGH THE ISLANDS OF THE PACIFIC

WAR swept like a typhoon through the Pacific. In ninety days after Pearl Harbor the Japanese controlled the South China Sea, the Sulu Sea, the Celebes Sea, the Java Sea, the Flores Sea, the Banda Sea, and the Arafura Sea. She controlled the Strait of Malacca and was soon to control the Bay of Bengal dominating India, and the Bismarck Sea with its main islands of New Guinea, New Britain, and New Ireland, and the Solomons Sea—still nearer Australia.

American ships and men were hurried to the battlefronts. Within a few weeks they were forming a bridge of ships across the Pacific and were later to bridge the Atlantic and encircle the globe. More than 600,000 men, with virtually the entire bomber force, floated into the Pacific area with record speed in the early months of the war. The great triangle from Dutch Harbor in Alaska, down the American west coast to the Panama Canal, and then thrusting out to Hawaii, was finally on the alert.

Twenty-four days after our Declaration of War, Admiral Chester W. Nimitz walked into the office at the Submarine Base at Pearl Harbor and assumed active command of the Pacific Fleet. This brilliant strategist immediately made his presence felt. He had been skipped over twenty-eight senior officers when he was named to succeed Admiral Kimmel. At fifty-seven years of age he left his post at Washington as Chief of the Bureau of Navigation to go into action. Nimitz always craved action. After being graduated from Annapolis he had commanded submarines. He was in command of the gunboat *Panay,* sunk by the Japanese early in the "China Incident." During the First World War he served as Chief of Staff to the Commander of the Submarine Force in the Atlantic and then in the office of Chief of Naval Operations. Before becoming Chief of the Bureau of Navigation he had commanded Battleship Division 1.

During his first weeks at Pearl Harbor Admiral Nimitz was plied with questions about future operations, about the return of the Fleet to offensive action, about pushing the enemy back to Japan. To all of these he gave the placid answer: "Time will take care of that." Unfailingly courteous to all men, he was always fair in his treatment of enlisted men and officers alike. While being rescued from a plane crash in the Pacific the Admiral stood up in the small rescue launch. "Sit down, you!" the coxswain bellowed, not recognizing his passenger. Suddenly seeing the four gold stars on Admiral Nimitz's blouse, the coxswain became confused and started to stammer an apology. "Stick to your guns, sailor," the Admiral advised. "You were right!"

Vice Admiral William F. Halsey, Jr., was in command of the carrier task force that was not in Pearl Harbor on December 7. He was two and one-half years older than Admiral Nimitz. The two men had much in common but in other ways differed greatly. Halsey was a salty sailor, with a picturesque tongue not made for a drawing room but perfectly at home on the deck of a ship in battle.

After going through World War I in command of a destroyer squadron hunting down U-boats, and safely escorting troopships to the other side, Halsey served as naval attaché at Berlin and other European capitals and then returned to sea again with his destroyers. By that time he had become convinced of the rôle aviation was to play in future military operations and, when fifty-two years old, qualified as a pilot and flew his own plane. The next year he was named Commandant at the Pensacola Naval Air Station and in charge of the carrier *Saratoga*.

Nimitz and Halsey complemented each other perfectly, and it was just one month to the day after Admiral Nimitz had taken command at Pearl Harbor that the team first went into action.

Since no military move can be undertaken without some time elapsing for the concentration and disposition of forces, it is evident that Admiral Nimitz had established the broad lines of his strategy before he reached Hawaii. The essentials of that strategy were: (1) Japan could not be stopped until she had reached a certain line; (2) The United Nations must prepare to prevent the enemy from progressing beyond that line; (3) Japan must not be permitted to intrench herself in new positions and build up powerful defenses against the day the United Nations were able to assume the offensive and drive the enemy back to her home islands; (4) With the United States Navy stripped of capital ships and no substantial naval help in sight from the Allies the immediate job was to keep Japan off-balance in her new possessions.

Only a few days after the defensive Battle of Macassar Strait, the United States Navy went into offensive action for the first time on January 31, 1942. Admiral Halsey appeared "from nowhere" with his task force off the Marshall and Gilbert Islands.

Admiral Halsey's force consisted of the carriers *Enterprise* and *Yorktown*, the heavy cruisers *Chester, Louisville, Northampton,* and *Salt Lake City,* the light cruiser *St. Louis,* and ten destroyers. It had been at sea under a blanket of radio silence for days. The commander, instead of leaving his carrier a hundred or more miles away from the target, led it so close under the enemy's nose he could not see it. Japanese scout planes and bombers searched far and wide but never saw the Admiral's ship which was almost within range of shore batteries all the time.

Seven of the nine ships in the harbor of Wotje were sent to the bottom, the entire shore establishment including two hangars, antiaircraft batteries, coastal guns, and large supplies of fuel and oil were wrecked. The new airfield at Taroa was plowed up like a farm field in the spring, all fuel dumps, two hangars, and several industrial buildings were demolished, and twenty-three enemy planes were destroyed. One American bomber was lost, and the *Chester,* the only naval vessel to be struck, suffered a minor bomb hit in which four men were injured. Some shell fragments spattered over the *Enterprise.*

The immediate effect of the blow was to prevent the Japanese from building up air and naval bases at points closest to Hawaii and the United States.

Admiral Nimitz characterized Halsey—known in the navy as "Fighting Bill," "Wild Bill," and "Slugger" thus: "Aggressive, audacious, yes; but not reckless. He has an uncanny ability to feel out the enemy."

The "Slugger" was on the loose and the Japanese did not know where he would strike next. On February 24 he took the *Enterprise,* two cruisers, and seven destroyers on a trip to Wake Island where he succeeded in catching the enemy by complete surprise. Two patrol boats and three large seaplanes riding peacefully at anchor were sunk, the new airfield and installations, upon which the Japanese had been feverishly working since they had captured the island, were demolished. Antiaircraft and coastal batteries were wrecked.

A week later, on March 4, Admiral Halsey's task force showed up at Marcus Island, 769 miles north-northwest of Wake and less than 1,000 miles from Yokohama. The "Slugger" sailed deep into enemy waters and in a pre-dawn blow, during which the targets were illuminated by flares, leveled hangars and installations and chopped up the airfield. There were no enemy ships or aircraft present. One American plane was lost at Wake Island and one at Marcus. After this attack a task force centered around the *Lexington* was sent under Vice Admiral Wilson Brown into the Bismarck Sea-Solomons area. A combined sea and air attack was planned against Rabaul, just captured by the Japanese on New Britain.

It was Admiral Brown's force, approaching for the attack, which was sighted on February 19 by two Mitsubishi 96 twin-motored bombers off Bougainville. The enemy aircraft were promptly disposed of but not before they had had time to flash to their base the fact that hostile craft were headed toward Rabaul and to give their positions. The elements of surprise having been lost, the planned attack was put aside, but another battle not anticipated soon developed.

Late in the afternoon nine more Mitsubishis appeared in V formation. Only three survived the defense sent up by American fighter planes, and massed antiaircraft fire, long enough to reach the release point over the *Lexington* from which to drop their bombs. The Jap squadron leader was hit. He sent his plane into a suicide dive straight for the carrier. The plane exploded when only 100 yards from the flight deck and skilful navigation kept any of the wreckage from striking the ship. A half hour later a second wave of nine enemy planes attacked. All the American fighters, except two, were back on the carrier for more fuel. It was here that Lieutenant (j.g.) Edward H. O'Hare, an Annapolis graduate from St. Louis, Missouri, made fame. The attacking V formation was sighted a dozen miles from the ships at 12,000 feet. The two Americans started to attack. Then Lieutenant O'Hare noticed that his partner's guns had jammed and were unable to fire. He sailed into the nine Mitsubishis, first passing down the left side, then up the right and repeating the process five times. Five of the bombers reached the release point over the carrier, when Lieutenant O'Hare followed the enemy through his own antiaircraft fire. The whole engagement lasted about four minutes. When it was over the score showed that Lieutenant O'Hare—"Butch" to his mates—had destroyed five of the nine planes and had wounded a sixth so badly that it was counted lost. Eighteen of the twenty planes that had attacked the *Lexington* during the day had been destroyed. Two United States planes were shot down, but the pilot of one was saved.

President Roosevelt, in awarding the first Congressional Medal of Honor to go to the navy in the war, said Lieutenant O'Hare's feat was the "most daring single action in the history of combat aviation." It was the first time one aviator had destroyed so many enemy planes in one battle. Lieutenant O'Hare was promoted several grades to Lieutenant Commander and remained a terror in the Pacific for almost two years, when he was shot down during a terrific night battle off Tarawa not very far from the scene of his heroic accomplishments.

The conquests of Malaya and southern Burma in no way interfered with the campaigns which were simultaneously being waged against the Netherland Indies and beyond toward Australia. Java, with its 40,000,000 population was preparing for invasion. The situation at Amboina was critical. Twenty-six escorted Japanese bombers struck a powerful blow at Surabaya, and the enemy had sufficient planes to raid Port Moresby on New Guinea, across the Coral Sea from Australia, two days in a row. The attack on Surabaya was disastrous. Two-thirds of the defenders' fighter planes were destroyed or so badly damaged they were of no immediate use.

During the fifth week a United States submarine slipped into a Javanese port and one of the men to step out of the conning tower was gray-haired Admiral Hart. He had successfully moved his entire fleet, including the "fleet train" of supply vessels, from Cavite to safe waters. During the time he had been in the cramped quarters of the submarine, dodging enemy warships and planes, the sixty-four-year-old veteran had been named Supreme Naval Commander for the United Nations in the Southwest Pacific, in addition to his duties as Commander in Chief of the United States Asiatic Fleet.

Before the month of January was out Admiral Hart demonstrated how fortunate the escape of himself and the fleet was for the United Nations' cause. The Asiatic Fleet included the heavy cruiser *Houston*, the light cruiser *Marblehead*, thirteen over-age destroyers, twenty-nine submarines, and two squadrons of ponderous Catalina patrol bombers comprising Patrol Wing Ten. There were a few gunboats and auxiliaries not included among combat vessels. The light cruiser *Boise* happened to be in Asiatic waters when it became apparent that Japan would go to war, so she was added to Admiral Hart's Fleet. Just before the attack on Pearl Harbor the *Marblehead* and eight destroyers had been sent to Borneo, while the *Houston, Boise,* and the destroyer tender *Black Hawk* had been dispatched to other southern waters. Before the evacuation of Cavite could be completed, the submarine *Sea Lion* and destroyer *Peary* were hit. But Admiral Hart saved the entire 200,000 tons of Allied shipping, much of it with valuable cargo, except for the *Sea Lion* which was destroyed to prevent her capture by the Japanese. When Admiral Hart moved to Java he left Rear Admiral F. W. Rockwell in command of the local Philippine naval defense forces.

The sea prong of the attack on the Netherlands Indies was matched by the steady advance on land through the Malayan jungles. The Japanese drive gained momentum with each day. Small reinforcements in men and planes had been sent to the British from Australia.

Over one hundred Japanese bombers heavily attacked Rabaul, Australia's main base and the chief port of New Britain, on January 20. New Britain, a large island, with the still larger island of New Guinea, lies athwart the direct sea route from the Netherlands Indies to Australia. The Japanese were so certain of success that they pushed down through the Bismarck Archipelago before conquering the Celebes and Java Seas.

This major effort toward Australia did not diminish the force of the enemy's blows in other areas; in fact, the power was increased.

On January 23, Netherlands bombers, from secret fields hastily prepared to escape enemy air detection, spotted a convoy of more than one hundred ships heading down the Strait of Macassar between Borneo and Celebes. In a stirring battle they hit four warships, including a battleship, and four transports. That encounter was the signal for the Battle of Macassar Strait that raged on sea and in the air for five days. Admiral Hart sent out his men with the following orders: "Submarines and surface ships will attack the enemy and no naval vessel will leave the scene of action until it is sunk or all its ammunition exhausted."

At dusk the same day the American destroyers *John D. Ford, Paul Jones, Parrot,* and *Pope,* under Commander P. H. Talbot, sighted a Japanese cruiser sailing south near the Borneo coast. Closing in they discovered three destroyers, then two more. On the shore side were a large number of troop-laden transports and supply ships shepherded by a second cruiser. Undeterred by this display of might the four American craft charged into the middle of the line as darkness fell. They broke through, firing every gun as they got between the escort and transport vessels, and raced at full speed in the direction opposite to that which the convoy was taking. The Americans accomplished their first purpose when the enemy warships left their convoy and started in pursuit of the rash destroyers. This chase kept up until a heavy rainstorm finally broke, making visibility bad. The American ships silently and slyly turned around and the four destroyers were sent plowing back after the unprotected convoy. The enemy did not see this maneuver and continued speeding north. The destroyers sank several transports and returned to their base with scarcely a scratch. The only casualties were four men wounded. With the break of day Allied fliers returned to the scene, capsized one large transport and damaged another and a destroyer.

When the battle ended, the Japanese had lost fully a third of the hundred ships which had entered the Strait of Macassar on January 23. Fifteen vessels had been sunk outright. More than 30,000 Japanese soldiers and sailors had perished. Ignoring these heavy losses, the enemy exploited his numerical superiority to push on to land men from the surviving ships at Balikpapan. Having obtained rubber in Malaya, the Japanese were determined to obtain the oil and other raw materials of the Netherlands Indies—and they were prepared to pay the price.

The situation on Malaya grew worse during the seventh week. The defenders held a perilous line across the Peninsula running from sixty to seventy-five miles above Singapore. In seven weeks, by skilful blending of flanking amphibious attacks and infiltrations through the marshy jungles, the Japanese had advanced more than three hundred miles from the Thai border to their objective at the tip of Malaya.

Across the more than 1,000-mile front of the Indies the Japanese victories continued to pile up. A fifth foothold had been gained on Borneo at Pemangket, some 500 miles from Java. The enemy landed on Amboina, where the Dutch had an important naval base, but the defenders had demolished all installations before they were overcome.

In the middle of the Pacific Ocean, Wake and Guam had been captured; but the land oasis of Midway in the midst of the sea was still holding out. The Japanese had launched their first assault by moonlight at 9:30 on the night of December 7 on an outlying island of the Midway group. At 9:50 a Japanese cruiser and destroyer moved within range of shore batteries. The enemy was surprised by the simultaneous appearance of powerful searchlights silhouetting the warships and shells falling on the decks. Midway was equipped with only 5-inch guns and 50-caliber machine guns. Three of the heavy shells struck the lead ship, and two the others. After a brief engagement the enemy turned and fled.

Damage to installations had been negligible. Among the few casualties was Lieutenant George H. Cannon, U.S.M.C. of Ann Arbor, Michigan. He was directing fire from the command post when an enemy shell shattered the lower part of his body. He continued to lead his men until he died from loss of blood. Corporal Harold R. Hazelwood, of Stark City, Missouri, was operating the switchboard under Lieutenant Cannon's orders. The same shell that killed the officer, broke Corporal Hazelwood's leg. Ignoring his injuries the Corporal set up the board again and restored communications making it possible to direct accurate fire against the attacking ships.

The next word from Midway came in a brief cable message: "All okay" on December 14. Three days later Medical Officer Francis Fishburn, of the navy, cabled: "'Still intact, morale high." Harold Leonberger, Pan-American Airways engineer, wrote his wife: "We are all well and the time is flying fast. Just don't worry, as we can take care of ourselves." The Navy Department issued a communiqué saying that Midway was "countering the blows of the enemy" and on Christmas Day a cabled message from the brave defenders of Midway read: "We are still here. Merry Christmas!" Douglass Grummond sent his mother a New Year's greeting the same day that Tokyo announced the deaths of General Yamagata and Colonel Ishii at Midway. On January 27 a navy spokesman said: "Midway is still holding, and that's that!"

During the eight weeks the Japanese had made several half-hearted forays against Midway but never pushed through. Submarines surfacing to shell the island quickly submerged after being fired upon. One of the mysteries of the war is why Japan did not take Midway. There were no means of getting American reinforcements to the small garrison and a persistent attack would soon have exhausted the meager supply of ammunition. This failure to capture Midway eventually developed into a blunder ranking in significance with Japan's failure to capitalize fully on the destruction at Pearl Harbor.

Amboina fell on February 7. The Japanese considered it a cheap victory despite loss of a cruiser and damage to a submarine and a second cruiser. Surabaya, Sumatra, and Banda Island off New Guinea, were attacked the same day. There seemed no limit to the enemy's ability to hit hard at all points simultaneously. In another forty-eight hours the pincers on Java began to develop with a landing near Macassar on southwest Celebes, five hundred miles from Surabaya, and an advance through Borneo. The occupation of New Britain was strengthened by a

Japanese landing at Gasmata, about midway on the southern coast. Balikpapan was also in enemy hands.

Against these advances the United Nations were in a position to interpose only paper counteractions. President Roosevelt announced in Washington on February 6, the creation of a Pacific War Council and a Combined Chiefs of Staff Group to handle all matters of strategy in the beleaguered zones. General Wavell was placed in charge of tactical details. Rear Admiral William A. Glassford, Jr., was put in command of American naval forces in this area, and Vice Admiral Herbert F. Leary was placed at the head of American naval forces in the Australia-New Zealand area, subsequently to be called the South Pacific Fleet.

Admiral Hart was called to Washington on a special assignment for Secretary of the Navy Knox. Subsequently Admiral Hart was appointed to the enlarged Navy General Board and two years later the nature of his special assignment was revealed. He was charged with collecting evidence bearing upon the responsibility for the disaster at Pearl Harbor. Vice Admiral C. E. L. Helfrich, Commander of the Netherlands Indies Navy, replaced Admiral Hart at the head of the combined United Nations warships in Indies waters.

Announcement from Washington at about the same time emphasized the interrelationship of all Pacific Zones and the fact that the United Nations were proceeding carefully and deliberately along a well-charted strategical path. It was disclosed that the United States had landed and established garrisons on a number of islands between Honolulu and New Zealand to protect the long supply line to the military base and staging area into which Australia was being converted.

Japan intensified her activities in an effort to win irrevocable victories before the United Nations could muster enough strength in the Pacific to stop her. On February 9, a direct attack was launched on Macassar. The next few days saw the Netherlands garrison fighting a bitter battle to save that city, capital of the Celebes. The defenders at the Borneo capital of Banjermassin were putting up a last-ditch stand there.

Australian and United States reinforcements, in small number, began to reach Java, but it was a Pacific version of "too little and too late." Banjermassin and Palembang fell in rapid succession, but not before everything that would burn or could be wrecked had been demolished. Installations producing half the oil on Java and Sumatra were smashed beyond possibility of restoration. The fate of Java was sealed on February 19 when the Japanese landed on the peaceful island of Bali. The peacetime "Garden of Eden" was overrun in twenty-four hours—only one mile of open water separated the enemy from the shore of Java. At the other end there were only fourteen miles of water between Sumatra, now almost overrun, and the Netherlands' chief Indies island. Batavia, its capital, had been under almost constant aërial bombardment.

On the evening of February 23, President Roosevelt was scheduled to deliver a radio address to the people. It was to be his first "fireside talk" since Pearl Harbor. At the time Japan was fighting on a front 3,000 miles deep and 7,500 miles broad. Malaya had been conquered, Burma was being overrun, the Netherlands Indies were about to fall, the advance on Australia was unchecked. Toyko was so cocky that her leaders were talking about attacking Russia.

Just as President Roosevelt started to speak a Japanese submarine surfaced off the California coast some twelve miles from Santa Barbara. It was an unusually large underwater craft. At 7:05 P.M. (Pacific Coast Time) she fired the first of twelve or fifteen shells at the oil field on the old Elwood Cooper Ranch. For twenty minutes this desultory shelling continued. When it was over minor damage had been done to a pumping unit at one derrick by a single hit. All the other shells had fallen harmlessly into fields or ditches. There was no fire, there were no casualties, there was no interruption to production. But enemy shells had fallen on continental United States.

Five nights after the spectacular but unimportant shelling of the Elwood oil fields a large tanker was fired upon without warning by a Japanese submarine only thirty miles off San Francisco. The tanker, the *Will H. Berg,* owned by the Standard Oil Company, manned her guns and forced the raider to submerge and retire.

Back in the Netherlands Indies the Japanese were massed for the final assault on Java.

The Battle of Java Sea was a courageous but costly venture. On March 2 the Japanese had landed 85,000 men on Java and another large invasion fleet was offshore. Dynamite and the torch were applied to Batavia. The capital of the Netherlands Indies fell on March 5—Governor-General A. W. L. Tjarda van Starkenborg Stachouwer surrendered to Lieutenant General Hitoshi Imamura. Among the 90,000 military prisoners were 5,000 American and British soldiers. The Netherlands had lost her Pacific Empire.

The remaining defenders in Java were engaged in a hopeless last-ditch stand. After taking Batavia, the Japanese pushed on to complete their conquest. They were already behind their schedule as the result of the heroic delaying tactics and were in no mood to lose any more time. Subang and several other key places were captured and the railroad lines and highways to Surabaya were quickly cut. Allied forces, exhausted from almost continuous fighting, managed to summon enough energy to launch a fierce counterattack around the edges of the narrow strip in central Java into which they had been pushed.

On March 7 the Bandung radio at 7:55 A.M. New York time, concluded its program with these words: "We are now shutting down. Good-by 'til better times. God save the Queen!"

It took the Japanese just one week to conquer this richest jewel in the Netherlands Indies necklace. A little larger than the State of New York, it was the most thickly populated region on earth with 821 persons to the square mile. Despite this fact Java had only a dozen cities of more than 50,000, but the mountains rising to 10,000 feet and the red-soiled valleys were dotted with countless thatched-hut native villages. The Japanese coveted not only the country's oil but the carefully irrigated rice *sahwehs* which made Java the granary of the Malay archipelago. Cinchona bark, providing most of the world's quinine, rubber plantations, teakwood forests, and tin mines added to the country's strategic importance as a source of raw materials.

The Japanese at Java gave the world a lesson in amphibious operations. There had been nothing like it before. The enemy landed along the 620-mile northern coast at more than a dozen places after having won control of Bali and Sumatra. In a few days, despite heavy losses at sea, they put some 150,000 fully equipped men ashore, together with tanks and artillery. With precision, speed, and thorough coördination the Japanese pushed through to their coastal objectives and then overran all land resistance. There were not more than 80,000 fighting men on Java to defend the island. Lieutenant General George H. Brett, in paying tribute to American fliers who had participated in the bitter battle, pictured the kind of struggle the out-numbered Allied forces waged. He said that American heavy bombers were removed from Java only after it was found impossible to give any assurance that there would be an airfield upon which a bomber could land after returning from a mission. The main airdromes had been destroyed or captured by the enemy; the emergency fields were surrounded.

The American bomber crews flew until they were so exhausted that medical officers would not permit them to reënter the planes. They took off from water-logged fields with heavy loads in all kinds of weather, and sometimes spent from 6:00 A.M. to 2:00 P.M. trying to find a hole out of the storm area. Those who did get into combat ran up a record of better than three to one over the enemy, despite the latter's great preponderance in numbers and the total lack of fighter protection for the bombers.

In the first three months the Japanese dragon, like a fabulous winged monster breathing fire, swallowed greedily everything within its reach. It gorged itself with quick victories on which it soon was to strangle. The "Son of Heaven" was preparing for himself a severe case of cramps —and our generals and admirals were ready to administer the antidote.

LAST STAND AT BATAAN–CORREGIDOR SURRENDER AND MARCH OF DEATH

WHEN Manila fell the long Battle of Bataan began. The first 124 days of 1942 witnessed startling events in the Pacific. The Japanese were still rolling on to victory. The Tokyo war lords demanded the capture of the Philippines "at all cost."

These islands stood as a barrier on the road from Japan to the Netherlands Indies, Australia, and India. Their possession was vital to the conquest of Asia. Of equal importance was the fact that the Philippines possessed immense economic value in the conduct of the war as a source of raw materials and foodstuffs.

The Japanese, while regrouping their forces and continuing to land reinforcements, concentrated upon bombing Corregidor and undefended towns. The Bataan line ran from Subic Bay on the west across the Peninsula to Manila Bay on the east, just ahead of the towns of Olongapo and Hermosa respectively. The capture of Olongapo was the first step in an attempt to turn General MacArthur's left flank. At the same time the Japanese applied pressure to the right flank but were held back by the exceptional artillery fire of American gunners.

On Bataan the heavy artillery fire drove the Japanese back. On January 13, after a twenty-four-hour duel between the big guns, our cannoneers silenced eleven enemy batteries and shattered several tank and armored units. This action could not avert the inevitable, but it did win time. And now the United States learned for the first time about her PT-boats and Lieutenant John D. Bulkeley.

PT-boats derived their designation from the first letters of their class: Patrol Torpedo-boats. They were high-speed, shallow-draft craft loaded to the gunwales with death and destruction. Heavily armed but only thinly armored, they carried four 50-caliber machine guns in two compressed-air-driven turrets and four 18-inch torpedo tubes. Their three engines developed 4,200 horsepower which drove the craft at a maximum speed of eighty miles an hour. At fifty miles they could cruise far and wide, stalking targets as long as their fuel held out. The original models were seventy feet long. Seven feet were added later to make room for more instruments of destruction and to add maneuverability. They cost $250,000 each, due to their double mahogany hulls and expensive high-speed equipment. But the one officer and eight men comprising the crew wrought so much havoc upon the enemy that the investment turned out to be a relatively small one.

Corregidor Surrender

Lieutenant Bulkeley arrived in the Philippines in the fall of 1941 as commander of MTB Squadron 3 at Cavite. His junior officers were Lieutenant Robert B. Kelly and Ensign George Cox.

The pattern of fighting on the Philippines was unchanged. American planes continued to blast the enemy out of the skies and off the sea. Having won Subic Bay, the Japanese landed heavy artillery and backed it up with warships to bombard General MacArthur's positions on Bataan. Moron, on the China Sea coast back of the defenders' lines, fell to the enemy on January 23, bending back our left flank. Another withdrawal was ordered with towering Mount Natib, 4,225 feet high, in the center of the line. Fierce American and Filipino counterattacks prevented the enemy from exploiting the withdrawal.

As the week came to a close General MacArthur prepared to retire to his second line of defense running from Balanga on the west to Pilar on the east and behind Mount Natib in the center. The enemy attempted to accomplish with leaflets what he had been unable to do with bullets and bombs, namely, to prevail upon the Americans and Filipinos to surrender. The defenders replied by opening up on a concentration of troopships at the port of Ternate on the south side of Manila Bay which was preparing to attempt a mass invasion of Corregidor and Bataan. The big guns of Port Hughes on Corregidor and of Forts Drum and Frank on the mainland fired across ten miles of water to sink scores of troop-laden barges.

The struggle was replete with deeds of heroism. Second Lieutenant Alexander R. Nininger, Jr., of the 57th Infantry (Philippine Scouts) found himself in the midst of heavy going at Abucay, near Bataan, on January 12. Although this twenty-three-year-old officer was assigned to a company not in combat at the moment, he voluntarily joined Company K of his regiment while it was under attack from heavily superior enemy forces. Japanese snipers in trees and foxholes were picking off defenders by the dozen. In hand-to-hand fighting Lieutenant Nininger frequently forced his way into enemy positions, destroying several groups of Japanese wtih rifle fire and hand grenades. Severely wounded, he kept on fighting until, alone, he pushed into an enemy position and was killed. When his body was recovered a dead Japanese officer and two soldiers were found under him. Lieutenant Nininger was awarded the Congressional Medal of Honor posthumously and was the first soldier to receive his country's highest military honor in World War II.

Sergeant José Calugas, a Philippine Scout, was the second to receive the Congressional Medal and the first enlisted man to be so honored. He, too, was a hero of Bataan. Young Calugas was a mess sergeant of Battery B of the 84th Field Artillery and ordinarily he would not have been in combat. On January 16 he saw the gun of another battery standing cold. The position had been blasted by the Japanese and the previous cannoneers had been killed or wounded. Sergeant Calugas organized a volunteer squad, dashed 1,000 yards across shell-swept fields, put the gun back into action, and blasted the enemy as long as the ammunition held out.

The Japanese launched a heavy frontal attack against General MacArthur's lines during the first days of February, but suffered such heavy losses that the action was suspended.

A new phase was introduced into the bitter struggle when the Japanese resurrected from obscurity the seventy-two-year-old Emilio Aguinaldo who had led an unsuccessful revolt during the Spanish-American War. When the Philippines were not granted immediate independence, Aguinaldo led an insurrection which caused considerable disturbance until he was captured by Brigadier General Frederick Funston. The Japanese brought Aguinaldo out of his retirement and placed him before a radio microphone to urge General MacArthur to surrender immediately and avoid useless bloodshed in a hopeless cause. This appeal went unanswered.

The forts guarding the entrance to Manila Bay were brought under heavy air attack and a concerted land and air assault was opened upon Bataan. For three days the shelling and bombing continued, but the American ranks held firm. On February 11 the Japanese began regrouping for a new attack. For five days they replaced battle-worn troops with those freshly arrived and added to their superiority in men and guns along the short front.

Colonel George S. Clark had planted extensive mine fields in front of the positions held by his 57th Philippine Scout Regiment. Japanese suicide squads were sent to "de-mine" the area. Each enemy soldier stood erect, shouted "Banzai!" and flung himself upon the buried charge to explode it.

It was at this point that the "One-Man-Army" went into action. He was Captain Arthur W. Wermuth, of Traverse City, Michigan, an officer in a Marine unit successfully evacuated from Cavite. With a brace of pistols at his hips and a Garand rifle under his arm, Captain Wermuth, now attached to the 57th Filipino Scouts, went out on scouting and raiding missions. For two weeks he stalked behind the enemy lines obtaining valuable information which enabled the defenders to forestall developing attacks. From time to time he would appear in the no-man's land between the two forces and pick snipers out of trees or from under a rock. When he finally returned to his regiment he had killed 116 of the enemy in his own private guerrilla war. Captain Wermuth had been wounded three times during his adventures, each time administering first aid to himself and crudely dressing the injuries.

After the Japanese had completed their regroupings they opened a heavy artillery barrage against General MacArthur's lines and began to apply steadily increasing pressure. Just as they were about to launch their main blow in full force, MacArthur unleashed a sudden, furious counterattack which caught the enemy completely by surprise. The defenders advanced along the entire line, in some places to a depth of five miles. By suddenly assuming the initiative the American commander on February 25 threw the enemy's plans completely out of line. The Japanese after their withdrawal were compelled to start preparations all over again. General MacArthur had thus gained more time.

The Battle of Bataan raged on as the outnumbered defenders took heavy blows and returned them in full measure, slowly falling back according to strategy to the last barricade at Corregidor. The American-Filipino troops were going through their "Valley Forge" and their "Winter of Misery" with deeds of valor worthy of their great traditions. We can give but a few typical citations from General MacArthur himself. In again citing Captain Jesus Villamor, Filipino airman, the General says: "Several of our P-40 fighters were escorting a slow biplane trainer on a photographic mission over Cavite Province when they encountered six enemy fighter planes. The ensuing combat was one of the most spectacular that has been waged in the Philippine campaign. Captain Villamor ... recently was awarded the Distinguished Service Cross with Oak Leaf Cluster for repeated acts of extraordinary heroism."

General MacArthur relates this story about Sergeant Leroy C. Anderson of Milwaukee, Wisconsin, who received the Distinguished Service Cross: "On February 3, 1942, a counterattack of one of our units, to reestablish its lines on Bataan Peninsula, was held up by heavy machine-gun fire. Sergeant Anderson, in command of a small group of tanks in reserve, eagerly requested permission to use his unit against the enemy's machine-gun nests.... He moved his tanks through the rough and difficult terrain against the hostile resistance. With skill and determination he destroyed the enemy guns and their crews. Fighting his way through the thick jungles, Anderson located more hostile guns and destroyed them. After his own tank had been put out of commission by enemy fire, Sergeant Anderson and his crew left the tank and continued the fight with rifles and hand grenades. By this gallant action, Sergeant Anderson and his men enabled our infantry to advance and regain the lost positions." Anderson was wounded.

And so go the stories of the heroism of Lieutenant Willibald C. Bianchi, of Minnesota, wounded three times; Major Emmet O'Donnell, of New York, who, in a gallant air battle with overwhelming forces, downed four enemy planes; Private Robert Enders, who made seven trips during a severe bombing raid to carry wounded in an army truck to a hospital; Lieutenant Boyd ("Buzz") Wagner, who shot two planes out of the air and machine-gunned twelve more on the ground, leaving five burning. Stories of bravery and courage such as these mounted into thousands.

General MacArthur gave high praise to his Igorot native infantry. Without flinching or thought of retreat, a whole company died to a man in fighting from their foxholes, while exacting a tremendous toll from the Japanese.

On Washington's Birthday, General MacArthur decorated two of his staff officers, Major General Richard K. Sutherland, Chief of Staff, and Brigadier General Richard J. Marshall, Deputy Chief of Staff, who occupied key positions in mapping the defenses of Bataan. "Cool and resourceful, courageous and determined, resolute and devoted," said MacArthur, "they are deserving of this immediate award of these well-earned decorations. Tomorrow they might well be casualties, too late to know of a nation's military honor to them."

The war in the Pacific had now reached a stage where the Allies must organize on a vast scale, with defense lines moved farther down into the Southwest Pacific. There a base for grand strategy could be erected. General MacArthur was the man who had been selected for this prodigious achievement. Leaving General Wainwright in full command in the Philippines, he left on a secret mission in order to perfect these plans.

General Wainwright took command while the Battle of Bataan was entering its final stages and Jap naval guns were blasting strategic points on Mindanao.

On March 21 the Japs started to hammer Corregidor with heavy shells. A preliminary thrust on Bataan was easily repulsed and in some incredible manner the American and Filipino troops were able to spring a surprise raid on the northern part of Mindanao. On this day Japan addressed an ultimatum to Major General Wainwright.

"Your Excellency: We have the honor to address you in accordance with the humanitarian principles of Bushido—the code of the Japanese warrior. It will be remembered that, some time ago, a note advising honorable surrender was sent to the commander in chief of your fighting forces. To this no reply has yet been received. Since our arrival in the Philippines with the Imperial Japanese Expeditionary Forces, already three months have elapsed during which, despite the defeat of your allies, Britain and the Netherlands East Indies, and in the face of innumerable difficulties, the American and Filipino forces under your command have fought with much gallantry. We are, however, now in a position to state that, with men and supplies which surpass both numerically and qualitatively those under your leadership, we are entirely free either to attack and put to rout your forces or await the inevitable starvation of your troops within the narrow confines of the Bataan Peninsula.

"Your Excellency must be well aware of the future prospects of the Filipino and American forces under your command. To waste the valuable lives of these men in an utterly meaningless and hopeless struggle would be directly opposed to the principles of humanity. And, furthermore, such a course would sully the honor of a fighting man.

"Your Excellency: You have already fought to the best of your ability. What dishonor is there in following the example of Hongkong, Singapore, and the Netherlands East Indies in the acceptance of an honorable defeat?

"Your Excellency: Your duty has been performed. Accept our sincere advice and save the lives of those officers and men under your command. International law would be strictly adhered to by the Imperial Japanese Forces, and Your Excellency and those officers and men under your command would be treated accordingly, to the joy and happiness of those whose lives will be saved, and the delight and relief of their dear ones and families would be beyond the expression of words. We call upon you to consider this proposition with due thought. If a reply to this advisory note is not received from Your Excellency through a special messenger by noon, March 22, 1942, we shall consider ourselves at liberty to take any action whatsoever. (Signed) Commander in Chief of the Imperial Japanese Army and Navy."

General Wainwright, reporting to the War Department, said: "No reply was necessary and none was made."

The Japanese assault began on March 24 with heavy air raids, particularly on Corregidor. This consisted of heavy bombing and shelling almost continuously.

Warships sailed in close to land and added their devastating fire to that of the artillery. This kept up until April 2 when the Japanese launched a terrific smash at the left center of the defenders' line. Several breaches were made and it required almost superhuman effort to close the gaps in time. Three days later the weight of the enemy attack was shifted to the right center. By April 6 the end was in sight for the twenty to thirty thousand men on the tip of Bataan. The next day the Japanese threw in fresh reserves. That night General Wainwright drew his men back to their last line. The War Department communiqué on April 8 said:

"The present Japanese attack is the longest sustained drive of the enemy since operations began on Bataan. Waves of shock troops have attacked almost continuously, without regard to casualties, which have been heavy on both sides. American and Filipino troops, including naval and Marine contingents, have stubbornly resisted every advance. Repeated efforts of the enemy to land behind our lines have been frustrated by our beach defenses, manned largely by naval and Marine personnel."

Then, at 5:15 on the morning of April 9, the War Department issued this communiqué: "A message from General Wainwright at Fort Mills (on Corregidor) just received at the War Department states that the Japanese attack on Bataan Peninsula succeeded in enveloping the right flank of our lines, in the position held by the Second Corps. An attack by the First Corps, ordered to relieve the situation, failed due to complete physical exhaustion of the troops.... This situation indicates the probability that the defenders on Bataan have been overcome."

Those brave defenders—numbering 36,853 starved, diseased, exhausted, crippled, wounded men—came from the following contingents: the 31st Infantry Regiment, called "Manila's Own," part of America's foreign legion, with headquarters in the Philippines since its formation in 1916, which had served in Siberia from 1918-1920, and in Shanghai in 1932; the Philippine Division, the "Scouts," numbering about 10,000; the 4th Marine Division, transferred from Shanghai before Pearl Harbor; a battalion of bluejackets; units scraped up from air personnel and ground crews who had lost their planes and fields; and units of the Philippine Army, drafted Filipinos, and some National Guard units.

President Roosevelt sent a message to General Wainwright commending the latter's courage, skill, and determination, and saying that the Commander in Chief was fully aware of the tremendous difficulties under which the Philippine campaign had been waged. General Wainwright received full authority to surrender or to fight on at Corregidor. He chose to do the latter.

Before withdrawing from Bataan—the greatest single loss in the history of the United States Army—every bit of ammunition was blown up, every ship and drydock was destroyed. About 3,500 fighters and nurses braved the shark-infested waters separating Bataan from Corregidor to reach the protection of "The Rock." As they swam or crowded into rowboats, Japanese planes maintained a steady bombing and machine-gunned the narrow strip of water. The survivors reached their haven stunned, dazed, unaware of their surroundings.

When General MacArthur received the tragic news he said: "The Bataan force went out as it would have wished, fighting to the end of its flickering, forlorn hope. No army has ever done so much with so little. Nothing became it more than its last hour of trial and agony. To the weeping mothers of its dead I can only say that the sacrifice and halo of Jesus of Nazareth has descended upon their sons and God will take them unto Himself."

Major General Edward P. King, Jr., made the actual surrender, refusing to the end to give up Corregidor with Bataan. The Japanese captured, in addition to the troops, some 25,000 civilians. What happened to these men was not known until nearly three years later when the world was shocked by the revelation of the "March of Death"—the gruesome story of a barbaric orgy. Nothing like it had ever occurred in the history of modern warfare. When the march was over more than 5,200 Americans and many times that number of Filipinos had been tortured to death. A wave of revulsion swept the world.

The War and Navy Departments, in a carefully documented joint statement, made public the agonizing chronicle of that Philippine Calvary. The official statement was based upon reports brought back by three American officers who had managed to escape from the Japanese after nearly a year in captivity. The officers were: Commander Melvin H. McCoy, of the United States Navy; Lieutenant Colonel S. M. Mellnik, of the Army Coast Artillery Corps, and Lieutenant Colonel (then captain) William E. Dyess, of the Army Air Corps.

The "March of Death" began at daylight on April 10 when thousands of prisoners, after their surrender, were herded together at Mariveles Airfield on Bataan. Neither Americans nor Filipinos were permitted to eat any food they had with them. They were searched and stripped of all personal belongings. Those men found to possess Japanese tokens or money were forthwith beheaded. In groups of 500 to 1,000 the prisoners were marched along the National Road of Bataan toward San Fernando in Pampanga Province. During this march they were subjected to further searches and the seizure of any personal belongings that had escaped the first looters.

"The Japanese slapped and beat them with sticks as they marched along without food or water on a scorchingly hot day," the official report stated, and then quoted Colonel Dyess: "A Japanese soldier took my canteen, gave the water to a horse, and threw the canteen away. We passed a Filipino prisoner of war who had been bayoneted. Men recently killed were lying along the roadside; many had been run over and flattened by Japanese trucks. Patients bombed out of a near-by hospital, half dazed and wandering about in pajamas and slippers, were thrown into our marching column of prisoners. What their fate was I do not know. At 10 o'clock that night we were forced to retrace our march for two hours, for no apparent reason. At midnight we were crowded into an enclosure too narrow to lie down in. An officer asked permission to get water and a Japanese guard beat him with a rifle butt. Finally a Japanese officer permitted us to drink water from a near-by carabao wallow."

Thus ended the first day in captivity for the soldiers who had been promised by General Yamashita treatment befitting warriors and in accordance with the principles of international law. Before daylight the next morning the march was resumed as a Japanese soldier in a passing truck used his rifle stock as a club on the heads of the passing prisoners. Through dust and blistering heat they marched all day without food, but they were granted the privilege of drinking dirty water from a roadside stream. Three officers were taken from the column, thrown into an automobile and never heard from again. "Our guards repeatedly promised us food but never produced it," continued the account of Colonel Dyess. "The night of the 11th we again were searched and then the march resumed. Totally done in, American and Filipino prisoners fell out frequently and threw themselves moaning beside the road. The stronger were not permitted to help the weaker. We then would hear shots behind us."

At 3 o'clock the next morning, after having marched all day, a column of 1,200 men were herded into a barbed-wire bull pen big enough to hold 200. There was "no room to lie down; human filth and maggots were everywhere." April 12 will never be forgotten by the survivors of that march. The Japanese, who had expressed much tender regard for human considerations, introduced a refinement in a form of torture which came to be known as the "sun treatment."

"We were made to sit in the broiling sun all day long without cover," the official report said. "We had very little water; our thirst was intense. Many of us went crazy and several died. The Japanese dragged out the sick and delirious. Three Filipino and three American soldiers were buried while still alive." The next day they received their first food—a mess kit of soggy rice. All day long they sat again in the broiling sun, resuming the march at night until daylight. Sometimes the sick, starving, exhausted men were paced by Japanese on bicycles; at other times they were forced to a slow shuffle. Each step was an agony. Filipino civilians who tried to help by throwing food or offering water were mercilessly beaten by the Japanese guards.

Six Filipino soldiers, half-crazed with thirst, were brutally slaughtered when they made a dash for a roadside artesian well. A little farther down the road the gutted body of another soldier was found hanging on barbed wire. That night, the 14th, the prisoners were again herded into a tiny bull pen. The Japanese guards amused themselves by charging with their bayonets into the crowded compound. Before daylight 115 men were crammed into a diminutive box car not large enough to hold forty, on the narrow-gauge railway. In the words of the report: "The doors were closed and locked. Movement was impossible. Many of the prisoners were suffering from diarrhea and dysentery. The heat and stench were unbearable."

After that ordeal they were subjected to another three-hour sun treatment and then marched off to Camp O'Donnell, a prison camp under construction. On this last leg of the march the Japanese permitted the stronger to carry the weaker. Colonel Dyess said: "I made that march of about eighty-five miles in six days on one mess kit of rice. Other Americans made the 'March of Death' in twelve days without any food whatever. Much of the time, of course, we were given the sun treatment along the way." At Camp O'Donnell prisoners stood in line for six to ten hours to get a sip of water. The principal food was rough, dirty rice, with an inch-square meat ration twice in two months. Even at that, there was sufficient for only one-fourth of the prisoners at one time. "Camotes," a species of sweet potato, were so rotten that the men had to post their own guards to keep their starving companions from eating them from the refuse pile.

"After the prisoners had been at Camp O'Donnell for one week," the report continued, "the death rate among American soldiers was twenty a day, and among Filipino soldiers 150 a day. After two weeks the death rate had increased to fifty a day among Americans and 500 a day among Filipinos. To find men strong enough to dig graves was a problem. Shallow trenches were dug to hold ten bodies each. Men shrank from 200 pounds to ninety. They had no buttocks. They were human skeletons. It was plain and simple starvation."

Medicine was never supplied. Drugs and food sent from the United States through the American Red Cross were not delivered for many months. The men were forced into labor battalions. By May 1 only twenty men out of every company of 200 were strong enough or well enough to go on work detail. The officer commanding Camp O'Donnell gave the key to the official Japanese attitude when, in a speech to the survivors of the Death March from Bataan, he told the starved, exhausted, dazed men "that they were not prisoners of war and would not be treated as such, but were captives without rights or privileges."

During these tragic days General Wainwright was holding the fort at Corregidor, under terrific bombardment. It was only a question of hours. He radioed a brave, defiant message to Washington on April 10: "Our flag on this beleaguered island fortress still flies." But it flew under incessant blows from artillery, ship batteries, airplane bombs, and machine guns. During the first week after Bataan it was attacked from the air sixty-five times. On the 17th "our flag on Corregidor was a casualty for a few minutes," the War Department announced. "Normally the United States flag flies from a 100-foot pole at the highest point on the besieged island fortress. During an intense bombardment from an enemy battery in Bataan a shell fragment struck the pole and cut the halyard. Slowly the flag began its descent. However, before it reached the ground, Captain Brewster G. Gallup, of Cornell, California, Technical Sergeant Ezra R. Smith, of Summer, Illinois, and Honorio Punongbayen, Philippine Islands, rushed up and gathered the colors in their arms. Not content with saving their country's flag from touching the ground, the group of soldiers immediately set about repairing the pole and the severed halyard. Amid the bursting shells the repairs were completed and the flag was soon waving proudly and defiantly at the top of the island.

The flag was hit again on May 2—this time by dive bombers. Again it was hoisted to the top of the pole. The situation on Corregidor grew more desperate. The Japanese had brought 240-mm. (9½-inch) guns to bear upon Forts Hughes, Drum, Mills, and Frank. During one heavy bombardment from these guns, punctuated by five bombing attacks, Brigadier General Charles C. Drake, of Brockton, Massachusetts, gathered the Massachusetts men and women around him and observed Patriot's Day. This typical New England demonstration was reported in a dispatch sent out from Corregidor. A war correspondent, leaving "The Rock," said to General Wainwright: "You should be leaving; not I." To which the Commanding Officer replied: "I have been one of the 'battling bastards of Bataan' and I'll play the same rôle on The Rock as long as it is humanly possible."

It seemed almost incredible that the fury and concentration of the Japanese assault could increase. Fort Drum, shaped like a battleship, turrets and all, and Fort Mills, containing the army post, were the chief targets. The enemy sought to knock out all guns, barbed wire and other defenses against landing parties. The two most bombed places in the world—Malta and Corregidor—exchanged radio greetings of praise for the defenders and hope for the future.

The final attack was in full fury by May 2. The Japanese had placed their heavy guns in the mountains of Mariveles on Bataan, overlooking Corregidor. These heavy pieces, and others from Cavite, fired continuously at almost point-blank range. Lack of food had reduced the defenders to virtual starvation. Lack of ammunition and serviceable guns had rendered them practically defenseless.

About midnight on May 5 Japanese started to land on the shattered, undefended shores of Corregidor. Earlier that day President Roosevelt, speaking not only as Commander in Chief but for all the American people, had sent General Wainwright a message saying: "During recent weeks we have been following with growing admiration the day-by-day accounts of your heroic stand against the mounting intensity of bombardment by enemy planes and heavy siege guns. In spite of the handicap of complete isolation, lack of food, and ammunition, you have given the world a shining example of patriotic fortitude and self-sacrifice. The American people ask no finer example of tenacity, resourcefulness, and steadfast courage. The calm determination of your leadership in a desperate situation sets a standard of duty for our soldiers throughout the world. In every camp and on every naval vessel soldiers, sailors, and Marines are inspired by the gallant struggle of their comrades in the Philippines. The workmen in our shipyards and munitions plants redouble their efforts because of you and your example. You and your devoted followers have become the living symbols of our war aims and the guarantee of victory."

A short silence was broken by the simple dispatch: "General Wainwright has surrendered Corregidor and the other fortified islands in Manila Harbor." His message a few hours before had disclosed that for the fourth consecutive day Corregidor had been bombed from the air in thirteen separate attacks. The shelling never let up.

Between the fall of Bataan and the surrender of Corregidor isolated American and Filipino forces had been fighting and harassing the enemy on the other islands of the Philippine group. Guerrillas were active there as well as on Luzon. The Japanese had launched a number of attacks on Panay, Cebu, and Mindanao but their supplies were constantly cut and their garrisons harried by the small defending parties.

General Yamashita refused to accept General Wainwright's surrender of Corregidor unless all fighting everywhere in the Philippines ceased. Wainwright demurred until Yamashita threatened to slaughter all prisoners in Japanese hands. Under such a threat General Wainwright reluctantly broadcast an order for all resistance in the Philippines to cease forthwith.

Corregidor proved as empty a capture, from the material standpoint, as had Bataan. Most of the negotiable wealth, including several tons of gold, silver, and securities removed from Manila, had been taken away from the rock vaults of Corregidor in the final days by a daring United States submarine. This underwater craft, commanded by Commander Frank W. Fenno, picked its way through the mine-strewn waters of Manila Bay right under the noses of scores of Japanese naval vessels and hundreds of pieces of shore artillery. For their heroic accomplishment the War Department awarded Commander Fenno the Distinguished Service Cross and an Army Star was given to every member of the crew.

The Corregidor garrison, at last official count, consisted of 2,275 naval personnel under Captain Kenneth M. Hoeffel; 1,570 Marines under Colonel Samuel L. Howard (for the most part the Fourth Marine Regiment transferred from Shanghai); 3,734 American troops; 1,280 Philippine Scouts; 1,446 Philippine Commonwealth Army men; and 1,269 civilians—a total of 11,574.

The approximately 7,000 American and 5,000 Filipino soldiers were herded into the garage area of Kindley Field, by that time only a square of concrete of about 100 yards on each of three sides, with the waters of Manila Bay on the fourth side. The 12,000 prisoners, including all the wounded who were able to walk, were kept on this concrete floor without food for a week. There was one water spigot for the 12,000 men and a twelve-hour wait to fill a canteen was the rule. After seven days the men received their first rations—one mess kit of rice and a can of sardines.

The Corregidor prisoners were forced to march through Manila on May 23, 1942, having previously been forced, while still a hundred yards from the beach, to jump out of the barges which had brought them over from the island. Two officers, Colonel Mellnik and Commander McCoy, who later escaped from imprisonment, reported: "We were marched through Manila presenting the worst appearance possible—wet, bedraggled, hungry, thirsty, and many so weak from illness they could hardly stand.... All during the march through Manila the heat was terrific. The weaker ones in our ranks began to stumble during the first mile. They were cuffed back into the line and made to march until they dropped. If no guards were in the immediate vicinity, the Filipinos along the route tried to revive the prisoners with ices, water, and fruit. These Filipinos were severely beaten if caught."

The March of Death was an indication of what lay in store for the soldiers fated to spend the rest of the war in Japanese prison camps—not as prisoners of war, but as captives. Most of the 50,000 survivors of Bataan and Corregidor were murdered in one way or another, either on the march, while at work, or in camp, under the studied Japanese cruelty which constantly devised new methods of torture.

General Wainwright and his staff were secretly taken to a "destination unknown." There were rumors that they were held for a time in the Philippines, then taken to Japan. Messages purporting to bear their names came occasionally from the Japanese. These merely stated that the Americans were being "well treated." Among such messages was one from Major Robert Chambers, Jr., son of the famous novelist—then came long years of silence. The Philippines were lost under a shroud of darkness.

48

AUSTRALIA—LAND WHERE THE TIDE WAS TURNED BACK

THE island continent "down under" the Equator, with its 7,300,000 stalwart people, was the bulwark against which the Japanese tidal wave of aggression beat in vain. Australia, with the Pacific Ocean on the north and the Indian Ocean on the west, was to stand as an impregnable fortress against the invaders.

With an area nearly as large as the continental United States, but with a population only one-seventeenth that of its American ally, it marshaled nearly 1,000,000 men and 50,000 women in defense of its freedom. Out of its manhood seven of every ten men between the ages of 18 and 35 years served in the armed forces. Some 500,000 of these volunteered to serve in any war theater. Australians fought gallantly on every battlefront in the world. With 40 per cent of all men and women of working age in armed services or war production, the remaining 60 per cent provided food and necessities for the Allied forces and their own civilian population. Australian war plants produced tanks, field guns, aircraft, and ammunition. With the aid of Lend-Lease it provided 90 per cent of the food for American forces in the South Pacific fighting zones.

Australia and her gallant neighbor New Zealand were the first members of the British Commonwealth of Nations to rise to the support of the motherland and declare war on Germany. This took place on September 3, 1939—the very day on which Great Britain entered the war. Simultaneously with Britain they declared war on Italy on June 11, 1940. Again in unison with Britain, and also with the United States, Australia and New Zealand declared war on Japan on December 8, 1941. Working at all times in complete coöperation, they stood strong in every crisis.

New Zealand, with a population of less than 1,700,000, sent more than 55,000 of her sons to battlefronts overseas, about 45,000 to aid in the pending liberation of Europe, while some 60,000 more defended the homeland.

The Pacific War was but forty-six days old when the entire Bismarck Sea in Australian territory was under powerful attack. Eleven Japanese warships with strong air protection were sighted on January 22, 1942. Thirty minutes later the Australian radio station went dead. Before the day was over the enemy landed on New Britain, New Guinea, and the Solomon Islands. In a little more than twenty-four hours thousands of square miles were conquered by Japan. The situation of Australia was critical. Shipping lines from the United States were imperiled. Convoy routes were changed and in some instances lengthened more than a thousand miles.

Shortly after the Japanese invasions began, the headquarters of the American South Pacific Fleet were moved from the Netherlands Indies to Port Darwin, Australia. The Japanese, expecting to destroy this fleet, bombed Darwin twice on February 9, 1942, but the fleet had been secretly moved again to a safer base. Airport, docks, warehouses, and virtually every ship left in the harbor, including the United States destroyer *Peary,* were destroyed.

Just before the fall of Batavia, Java, Darwin was raided for the third and fourth times. On March 8 the Japanese moved still closer by landing at Salamaua and Lae, only 150 miles from Port Moresby in Papua and 400 miles from the Australian mainland.

Two days after the Salamaua and Lae landings the Japanese occupied Finschhafen to the northeast. These three points gave the enemy a strong hold on a compact and highly important coastal area. Australia reacted quickly. The Government issued orders that, in the event of invasion, all livestock and other supplies of value along the northern coast that could not be removed should be completely destroyed. That this was no imaginary peril was evidenced by the increased weight of attacks on Port Moresby, the Papuan city facing Australia.

In addition, there was a great invasion fleet assembling at Rabaul, Salamaua, and Lae. The Australian airmen had been pounding the first of these for days and inflicting heavy damage, but the Japanese seemed to have an inexhaustible number of new transports and supply ships to replace those sunk or crippled. On March 12 a combined American-Australian air fleet descended upon Salamaua and Lae in the fiercest battle yet seen in the South Pacific. Allied fliers wrecked the airfields and sank or damaged thirteen enemy transports and warships. Still the Japanese came on, and for the next few days convoys were reported at sea off Buka in the Solomons and elsewhere.

On March 15 the War Department announced: "General Douglas MacArthur arrived in Australia by plane today. He was accompanied by Mrs. MacArthur and their son and by his Chief of Staff, Major General Richard K. Sutherland, Brigadier General Harold H. George of the air corps, and several other staff officers. He will be the supreme commander in that region, including the Philippine Islands, in accordance with the request of the Australian Government. On February 22 the President directed General MacArthur to transfer his headquarters from the Philippines to Australia as soon as the necessary arrangements could be made. General MacArthur requested that he be permitted to delay in carrying out the order until he could perfect arrangements within his command in the Philippines. This delay was authorized by the President."

The entire anti-Axis world rejoiced. Australia called it "the best single piece of news since the outbreak of the Pacific War." President Roosevelt stated that General MacArthur would command all sea, land, and air forces east of Singapore in the Southwest Pacific, thus straightening out several confusing situations resulting from overlapping commands.

The General's loyalty both to the Philippines and to his soldiers was so strong that he was unable to disguise his feelings. He was not the type of commander to seek personal safety; he knew that his men were doomed to defeat. As a general he knew, too, that the surest way to save the Philippines was to take the higher command to which he had been assigned. He did not leave Bataan before giving solemn assurance that he would return and drive the Japanese out. With that pledge he joined Mrs. MacArthur and their four-year-old son Arthur on the trip to Australia to become the Supreme Commander of forces in the Southwest Pacific.

When General MacArthur had accepted the Philippine invitation to build up the Commonwealth's defenses, the great number of islands and narrow, shallow straits comprising the archipelago convinced him that a score of small, speedy, powerful, armed patrol boats were worth more than a battleship. He even returned to Washington to argue with admirals in favor of what came to be known as PT (Patrol Torpedo)-boats. Tentative approval of the plan was obtained shortly before the outbreak of the Pacific War. Lieutenant John D. Bulkeley appeared in Philippine waters with his squadron of six little ships.

Early in March General MacArthur called in Lieutenant Bulkeley and began to draw up plans for his departure from Bataan. Over the protests of his staff officers, who considered the risks from enemy submarines, warships, and planes too great, the General, committed to the orders from his Commander in Chief, replied: "We will go with the full of the moon; we will go during the Ides of March."

So it was that on the night of March 11 General MacArthur and his personal and official family, including Rear Admiral Francis W. Rockwell, navy commander, stepped into four PT-boats. With Lieutenant Bulkeley at the wheel of the leading craft, they roared in close formation through the blacked-out waters, in an attempt to break through the Japanese blockade.

In the darkness the boats became separated. When the rendezvous was reached the next morning only one of the boats was at the designated point at the selected hour. The others pressed on alone through the dawn, easy targets for enemy ships and planes, until they were able to reach the shelter of some friendly island.

All four PT-boats finally came together, but one had to be abandoned to continue the trip alone later. Submarines had been ordered to the rendezvous to rescue the party if marooned. It was almost agreed to wait for one of these when General MacArthur and Lieutenant Bulkeley decided to distribute the members of the party in the remaining boats and proceed. The two leading boats arrived at their destination on the island of Mindanao—partly occupied by the Japanese—shortly after daylight. The third boat, miles away, made the perilous voyage under bright sun and reached the rendezvous at noon.

It was planned that the rest of the trip was to be made by airplanes specially flown from Australia. But the aircraft had not arrived when the party disembarked and reassembled inland. For three days and three nights the harried group waited, expecting any moment that enemy bombers would come over. How could a secret of such strategic importance be guarded so long? Finally, on the third night two Flying Fortresses landed on the diminutive airfield after the long, perilous hop. Three planes had been expected but no more time could be lost, so it was decided to discard arms and equipment. With little more than the clothes on their backs the party was crowded into the two B-17's and took off about midnight on March 16.

Before leaving Bataan General MacArthur did two things: He turned over his command to General Wainwright, elevated on March 19 to Lieutenant General, and gave to United States High Commissioner Francis B. Sayre a token for President Roosevelt. It was the saber of a dead Japanese officer, part of the handle trimming of which had been shot away by shrapnel from the shell that had killed him.

After a few days' rest General MacArthur went to Melbourne to receive the official welcome of Australia. At Adelaide, before boarding the train, he said: "The President of the United States ordered me to break through the Japanese lines and proceed from Corregidor to Australia for the purpose, as I understand it, of organizing the American offensive against Japan. A primary purpose of this is relief of the Philippines. I came through and I shall return."

On the day that General MacArthur arrived in Australia, Secretary of War Stimson, in Washington, pulled out of the nation's famous fish bowl the number 3,485 to start the first wartime draft. It was the third recent drawing but the first since Pearl Harbor. The earlier drawings had been made on October 29, 1940, and July 17, 1941, when the United States was building up its "defense" army under the terms of the Selective Service Act. When the new Allied Commander in Chief reached Australia he found that the country was rapidly being turned into a United States camp. Ever since the end of December giant convoys had been pouring in men and matériel—not enough, but a fine beginning. Army headquarters had been functioning since early in

January and the American Expeditionary Force had fanned out over hundreds of square miles.

One of the first things decided upon after Pearl Harbor was to establish bases with which to protect the convoy route to Australia. In addition to some scattered islands under the British or the American flag, there were French possessions for which arrangements were made with the "Fighting French." Efate, Espiritu Santo, some of the Fiji Islands, and New Caledonia were selected as advance bases and developed.

The first convoy that zigzagged its way across the 10,000-mile route from the United States to Australia did not have the full benefit of protection from these bases. As the Japanese closed in on the Marshalls, the Carolines, New Britain, and New Guinea those island bases proved the wisdom of the military and naval planners.

In that first convoy, as in all the others, there were remodeled liners, fast freighters, and naval vessels. Cargoes traveled in slower convoys. Antisubmarine protection was perfect. Communication between ships was by flag and dim-spot blinkers. Garbage was disposed of only at twilight so that when daylight came the ocean currents would have spoiled any possible trackage and the convoy would be far away. All bottles were smashed and every tin punctured before being thrown overboard. Not a speck of paper was sent over the sides. The enemy was given no clue to follow. This first, record-breaking trip, the longest nonstop voyage ever made by a United State convoy, took twenty-four days.

Convoys kept arriving in ever-increasing size and frequency. But the task confronting General MacArthur was so great that whatever he received was not enough. Here was the situation confronting him: The Japanese had occupied the Netherlands Indies, Rabaul, Lae, Salamaua, and some of the Solomon Islands. Except for the continuing battle of Bataan and Corregidor and that in Burma, the Japanese had realized their first objectives. They were consolidating their newly-won positions and preparing to push on to the next objective, an invasion of Australia. To meet such an invasion MacArthur had the beginnings of a United States Army, Australian Militia, veterans just beginning to return from the North African campaigns, and a few warships and planes. It had been decided before General MacArthur arrived to fall back from the northern part of Australia if necessary and fight to hold a line that ran just north of the most populous southerly area of the country.

But General MacArthur had other plans. He was determined to get back to the Philippines. The only way to do that was by offensive action. The prospect of abandoning northern Australia did not appeal to him; instead, he decided to base his defense upon that very section of the sub-continent plus the islands immediately to the north. Northern Australia was quickly converted into an unsinkable aircraft carrier with a vast chain of airfields. Port Moresby was strengthened and became a powerful base. Bombers and troops were stationed on the new airfields as fast as they became serviceable. When the Japanese finally were ready to launch their full strength at Australia a formidable line had been built and manned.

The basis of the reasoning behind that strategy was simple. No further retreat was possible, such as there had been from Malaya, the Netherlands Indies, and the islands in the Bismarck Archipelago. Australia was the last foothold. Furthermore, a long, indecisive, defensive campaign in that country could not win the war. The Japanese could apply there the same stranglehold they had on China, merely by occupying and holding the coastal area and communications lines.

Under his plan of action General MacArthur would be able to start what was at first an "island-hopping" drive back over the line of earlier retreat, to deliver a smashing flank attack on any Japanese thrust into the Indian Ocean-Middle East area, or to strike from the rear should the enemy decide to go to war in Siberia against an already sorely pressed Soviet Russia.

American submarines had entered the war in the Pacific and were cutting heavily into Japanese shipping. The figures were a closely guarded secret in order to keep Japan worried. These daring craft carried the war to the enemy's front doorstep, torpedoing his ships almost within sight of the lookouts at the principal home ports, and in the face of fierce depth-charge attacks. Submarines left their bases regularly on long, perilous voyages during which they were cut off from all communications with the outside world. In their cramped, uncomfortable craft the crews risked the combined total of all the hazards of war. Rescue from a submarine is rare.

When President Roosevelt decided to establish General MacArthur in Australia he made significant changes in the military and naval organization. The air arm of the army was finally given recognition, due largely to the lessons learned in the Pacific where the Japanese had won their quick victories primarily through control of the skies. The old air corps was "promoted" to the title of United States Army Air Forces. Lieutenant General Henry H. Arnold was made commander. The army hierachy was stripped of its peacetime encumbrances and all the ground forces were placed under the single command of Lieutenant General Leslie J. McNair. In a parallel move in the navy, the post of Chief of Naval Operations was combined with that of Commander in Chief of the United States Fleet. Admiral Ernest J. King, serving in the latter capacity, relieved Admiral Harold R. Stark in the former to assume the dual command. These were the men who stood behind General MacArthur in Australia as he built up his forces in order to strike back at Japan and start on his long, long road to victory.

49

MacARTHUR STARTS BACK—FIGHTING THROUGH JUNGLES OF NEW GUINEA

MacARTHUR, in Australia, reached his momentous decision in July, 1942. He was ready to strike back, to start back on the long road to liberate the Philippines and "on to Tokyo." What might be called D-Day in the Pacific came nearly two years before it did in the Atlantic.

When MacArthur's own troops started on their first offensive, taking their positions at Port Moresby, which was but one hundred miles from the Japs at Buna on the island of New Guinea, the forces of the "Rising Sun" were still trying desperately to break through to Australia, after their first defeat in the Battle of the Coral Sea.

MacArthur's drive from Australia was so closely coördinated with naval actions during the last six months of 1942 that the battle on New Guinea, on Guadalcanal and the Solomon Islands, and the great sea battles were all integral parts of the whole.

The United States Marine Corps had begun to arrive and from this time on the fighting Marines were to play a leading part in the advance toward the homeland of Japan. The U.S.S. *Wakefield*, formerly the United States Lines' flagship *Manhattan*, sailed out of the Norfolk naval base during the night of May 19-20, 1942, with the advance echelon of the First Marine Division which, under Major General A. A. Vandegrift, was to make history in the Pacific, starting at Guadalcanal. The ship, with its vanguard of men and ranking Marine officers, was under heavy escort as it sailed down the Atlantic, through the Caribbean and the Panama Canal into the Pacific, arriving finally at Wellington, New Zealand, on June 15.

The First Division was scheduled to take over defense of the beaches against the threatening Japanese invasion and at the same time perfect itself in its primary task, that of amphibious operations. It was to be the spearhead of the United Nations' drive on the Pacific through the southern waters to the Philippines, and then farther north to the empire of Japan itself.

Port Moresby had to be held at all costs. With that gone there would be no more land outposts to protect Australia. During the weeks in which the weather delayed troop movements, the defenses of that bastion were strengthened and the airfields supplied with all the planes, supplies, and antiaircraft guns MacArthur could muster. Then the enemy issued an ultimatum to the effect that unless the Australians and the Americans evacuated Port Moresby by May 25 they would be bombed off the face of the earth.

That ultimatum was ignored. The Japanese bombers came over and ran into the surprise of their lives. For the first time, they found themselves blinded by a battery of glaring searchlights. The bombs fell wild —but the Japanese kept coming time and again. They lost heavily in planes but succeeded in doing considerable damage to our small force.

The first Allied land attack since the Japanese had established themselves in the South Pacific was delivered on the night of June 28. Commandos suddenly swooped down upon Salamaua, the largest invasion base. Under cover of darkness, they killed or wounded sixty of the surprised Japanese, captured as much equipment as they could carry away, and destroyed the rest. Our casualties were two wounded.

American troops, mainly Negro, landed at Port Moresby. Air duels continued. On July 22, the Japanese landed at Gona Mission, near Buna, and started up the track to Kokoda. Gona was the eastern terminus of the trail through the Owen Stanleys to Port Moresby, 120 miles away.

The Gona landing and the push toward Kokoda was the first Japanese offensive action since the Battle of the Coral Sea. There was no Allied garrison at Kokoda, and the situation looked black as advance elements of the enemy's 2,500 troops started inland.

One week after the Gona landing, Allied patrols contacted the Japanese forces near Oivi, just east of Kokoda, fifty-five miles inland and halfway to Port Moresby. Land forces met for their first encounter a few days later. The enemy was pushed back from his advance positions for his first setback. A week of skirmishing continued until the Kokoda airfield fell. Heavy fighting raged between the light units for several days and the field changed hands, finally resting with the Japanese.

The developments in Papua, coupled with the increased tempo of the Japanese build-up of staging bases and advanced positions in the Solomons, made it clear that the Allies must move quickly or not at all. Vice Admiral R. L. Ghormley, who in April had assumed command of the South Pacific Force, called a conference at Auckland with General Vandegrift and Rear Admiral R. K. Turner. On the next day the Amphibious Force, South Pacific Area, was formed with Admiral Turner in command. That Force consisted of the First Marine Division, reinforced by the Second Marine Regiment, the First Raider Battalion, and the Third Defense Battalion, supported by three major units of the Navy, two of which were under Admiral Fletcher and the third under Rear Admiral John S. McCain.

Admiral Fletcher's group consisted of an air support force under Rear Admiral Leigh Noyes who had three carriers, one new battleship, five heavy cruisers, one antiaircraft light cruiser, and a number of destroyers; Admiral Turner's amphibious force consisted of six heavy cruisers, two of them Australian, a single Australian light cruiser, some destroyers, and twenty-three transports. Admiral McCain had no ships, but he did have a handful of planes of various types based in New Caledonia, the Fijis, and Samoa. This roster of vessels represents the entire naval strength which the United Nations were able to muster in the South Pacific on the very eve of battles upon which the fate of the war depended—to face virtually the entire Japanese Navy. The situation was almost the same in the air, with the enemy outnumbering our planes ten or more to one and with plenty of replacements easily and quickly available. On land our only troops were in Papua, some two or three thousand; we had twenty-three transports, the enemy had hundreds.

We did not have nearly enough, either in men or matériel, with which to start an offensive. Our leaders knew it and so did the Japanese. We had to take the chance and we were going to do it. On the morning of July 22 the First Marines' convoy left Wellington harbor, rendezvousing four days later at sea with the warships and later with the transports carrying the Second Marines, reinforced, under Colonel J. M. Arthur, the Third Defense Battalion under Colonel R. H. Pepper, and Colonel Merritt A. Edson's First Raider Battalion. On the twenty-eighth the small armada appeared off Koro Island, New Caledonia, where for four days practice invasions were held.

Late in the afternoon of July 31 the ships turned their prows toward the Solomons. D-Day was tentatively set for August 7, with joint landings west of the Ilu River, four miles east of the Guadalcanal airfield, and across Sealark Channel at Tulagi, off Florida Island. General Vandegrift took over direct command of the Guadalcanal operations, Brigadier General William H. Rupertus of the Tulagi-Gavutu area.

Early in the morning of August 7 the amphibious force passed between Savo and Guadalcanal. The Marines had been summoned about 2:00 A.M. from their crowded shelters, given their last good meal for many months, and stood waiting for H-Hour. The destroyer *McCawley,* flagship of the amphibious force, led the way through the channel. The *Quincy* fired the first gun to bring down the Japanese radio mast on the northern tip of Florida Island before the enemy could flash a warning. With the *Astoria,* the *Vincennes,* and the Australian *Canberra,* she then headed for Guadalcanal while the *Australia,* with Vice Admiral V. A. C. Crutchley, the *Hobart,* and other ships moved toward Tulagi.

At 6:15 A.M. the warships opened their devastating barrage, raking Japanese positions around the airfield. Then navy dive bombers and fighters pounded the enemy along the landing area, concentrating upon Kukum, northwest of Lunga Point. Seaplanes at known positions on Tulagi were also given rough treatment. The first Marine units hit the beach at 9:10 and found no opposition. The landings proceeded smoothly and quickly, with supplies piling up on the narrow beaches as patrols pushed through the jungle on the coral ridges which rose almost directly from the water's edge.

The first enemy reaction came at 3:30 in the afternoon when a flight of Japanese planes, ignoring the troops on Guadalcanal, attacked the ships. They scored no hits, but dive bombers a half hour later knocked out the aft gun of the *Jarvis*. By the afternoon of August 8 the airfield and its approaches were in the hands of the Marines.

It was evident that our landings had taken the Japanese by complete surprise, and they had fled to the safety of the hills. Food was on tables. The airfield was in perfect condition. Ammunition and gasoline dumps, antiaircraft guns, radios, trucks, refrigerating equipment, concrete mixers, and the electric plant were undamaged. The field, with its 3,778-foot runway, lacked only 197 feet of concrete for completion. Crews were put to work to make the field ready for our own planes to use.

But on Tulagi, Gavutu, and Tanambogo, there was another story: The Japanese there had nowhere to retreat. Barricading themselves into powerfully defended dugouts, caves, and other natural defenses, they fought off the Marines for three days before being wiped out. This was our first experience with the fanatical to-the-death resistance that was to become common in all operations on the long trek back north in the Pacific. Our losses were heavy before the Tulagi islands were secured and the delay so upset the invasion time-table that our ships, as well as the Guadalcanal force, were exposed to danger longer than had been anticipated.

The battling on Tulagi was ferocious. The Japanese counterattacked at night shouting, "American, you die!"—and many did. The defenders used knives, grenades, tommy guns—anything they could lay their hands on. There were many heroes on our side, but the back of the enemy defenses was not broken until Captain Harry L. Torgerson, of the First Parachutists, devised a method of closing up the hillside caves into which the enemy retreated during the day. It was impossible to enter the narrow passages or to blast the foe out even with the heaviest weapons. Captain Torgerson tied TNT charges to boards, and thrust them into the cave openings with such short fuses that there was not time for the trapped Japanese to throw them away.

Control of the area was so effective by noon of August 8 that General Vandegrift set up his headquarters on shore alongside the airfield. The immediate objectives had been attained at the cost of one transport sunk, one destroyer damaged and subsequently sunk, another destroyer damaged, the loss of twenty-one fighter planes in widespread operations including battling the enemy raiders, and Marine casualties, mostly wounded. The Japanese had lost Tulagi, Gavutu, and Tanambogo as well as the airfield on Guadalcanal, and scores of planes.

The night of August 8-9 was one never to be forgotten by the Marines on Guadalcanal. A drizzle set in shortly after dark and turned quickly into a downpour that soaked the men and their equipment mercilessly. Tents had not come ashore. The men lay out on the ground under the protection only of the tall coconut palms. Vicious thunder and the rattle of rain sounded suspiciously like enemy movements.

Before 2:00 A.M. another sound reached the ears of the drenched, tired, sleepless men. It was that of a plane and marked the first appearance of "Louie the Louse" who was to plague the existence of the Marines during their entire stay. He buzzed over the airfield, but neither fired guns nor dropped bombs. Instead, this cruiser-catapulted craft dropped flares that always signaled a bombardment or action.

In the small hours of August 9 these flares were followed by flashes and terrific explosions at sea. The Marines forgot their own troubles and followed the distant spectacle with awe. They soon realized that a naval battle was being fought off Savo Island—and the sounds told them that ships had been hit and mortally wounded. With supreme confidence in their navy they cheered, certain that the enemy had been sunk. It was a long time before they learned the truth of the First Battle of Savo.

Lack of fuel, the presence of a horde of Japanese submarines, and the enemy's early air strength had combined to force the withdrawal of the American carriers from their covering position. The men on shore, the cargo ships, and the light warships were left with virtually no air support. During the afternoon a reconnaissance plane had reported a Japanese task force bound for the Solomons, including a battleship, two seaplane tenders, and lighter craft. That night Admiral Crutchley disposed his screening forces to protect Guadalcanal and Florida Islands and the channel on either side of Savo Island that was to become known as "Iron Bottom Bay." This was in recognition of the vast tonnage of warships which found their final resting place under its waters.

The heavy cruisers *Vincennes, Quincy,* and *Astoria,* screened by the destroyers *Helm* and *Wilson,* covered the northern area; the heavy cruisers *Canberra* and *Chicago,* with the destroyers *Patterson* and *Bagley,* were stationed to the south; the destroyers *Ralph Talbot* and *Blue* lay off Savo Island. Admiral Turner's flagship, *McCawley,* ranged the troubled waters. About 1:45 in the morning, a hitherto undiscovered Japanese force of three cruisers and seven destroyers slipped speedily through the dark. Aided by the flares so suddenly dropped by "Louie the Louse," they opened fire with guns and torpedoes.

Our lookouts did not have time to flash a warning. The *Astoria* was crumpled; the *Vincennes,* hit through the hangar, burst into flames;

the *Canberra*'s guns were put out of action by the first bursts as three torpedoes rammed home; the *Quincy* blew up. All this happened within the space of three minutes. The *Canberra,* dead in the water and swinging aimlessly, fired all her remaining guns into the blackness hoping that some shells might strike. The action ceased at 2:15 and, perhaps because they did not know the extent of their victory or because they feared Allied reinforcements were being rushed up, the Japanese rounded Savo Island and fled for home.

During that half hour the *Quincy,* the *Vincennes,* the *Astoria,* and the *Canberra* were so severely damaged that they subsequently sank; the *Chicago,* the *Ralph Talbot,* and the *Patterson* were much damaged. The Allies had left only six heavy cruisers, two light cruisers, and a depleted destroyer flotilla for action in the Solomons. The three carriers and the battleship had been removed to distant waters.

Admiral King, in a frank analysis of this first naval defeat suffered by the Allies, said: "The surprise, which was the immediate cause of the defeat, was the result of a combination of circumstances.... Certain communication failures made a bad situation worse. Fatigue was a contributing factor in the degree of alertness maintained.... Needless to say, the lessons learned were fully taken into account. The immediate consequence of this cruiser battle was the retirement of the enemy force, without any attack made on our transports which were unloading men and supplies on the beaches of Guadalcanal. The loss of the four cruisers, however, and the subsequent loss of two aircraft carriers, left us inferior in strength for several months. The Japanese did not take advantage of this opportunity to engage in a fleet battle with the balance of power on their side, probably because they did not know how severe our losses were."

Dawn came to end the first of the "purple nights" that did so much to make Guadalcanal a veritable hell. All that the Marines on Guadalcanal and Tulagi knew was that there had been a furious, if short, naval engagement in the dead of the night.

The Marines thought that we had won the First Battle of Savo Island, thereby assuring them of steady supplies and reinforcements. Unfortunately, that was not the case, but they did not know it until some days later, when the men and ammunition failed to arrive.

Food became scarce. Stocks of captured rice, canned meats, and other articles were quickly depleted and iron rations became the order of the day. On August 12 the men were reduced to two scanty meals a day. The next day a survey disclosed there was food for only another week and a half. Malaria began to claim its victims. Japanese patrols kept probing and denying sleep or rest to the Marines clinging to their tenuous hold on the airfield and its approaches. Enemy bombing raked the ground positions and made the waters untenable for transports, cargo ships, and our few warships during daylight. At night Japanese cruisers and destroyers continued to bombard installations almost at will.

This was the situation on August 12 when General Vandegrift decided upon heroic action. It was essential to drive the enemy troops on the island back from the coast before reinforcements could reach them. The main Japanese position was along the coast west of the Matanikau River, about eight miles from the airfield, with the central position in the village of Kokumbona, some three miles beyond. Despite the fact that he did not have enough men safely to weaken his own defenses, plus the additional fact that there were not sufficient landing boats to carry a force strong enough to do a real job, General Vandegrift had to go through with the attempt.

The Japanese had concentrated their 2,000 workers in naval construction battalions and 500 naval personnel into the area when our attack started. In the first encounter a reconnaissance patrol under Colonel Frank B. Goettge, Division Intelligence Officer, was fired upon within twenty-five feet of its hastily established defense line on the beach at Point Cruz. Colonel Goettge fell at the first shot. Other American elements attacked from inland positions. Matanikau and Kokumbona were captured, but only seventy-five Japanese had been killed. The rest escaped into the hills.

Clashes went on in the same manner for another week, with each side feeling out and annoying the other, but without any action of consequence. In the meantime, work was continued on the airfield, completing the runways and other installations, and adding new features to handle American planes most expeditiously. The field was named Henderson Field, in honor of Major Lofton R. Henderson, the Marine Corps flier who had so heroically gone to his death on June 4 at Midway. On August 20 the doughty Marines ducked for their foxholes when a huge flight of planes appeared over the newly christened Henderson Field. But they soon came out shouting with joy when nineteen Grumman Wildcats and twelve Douglas Dauntless dive bombers circled the field to make the first mass landing.

On August 19 a Marine patrol along the beach beyond Koli point, to the east of the Tenaru River, suddenly flushed a detachment of thirty-five Japanese. The enemy naval personnel had landed from rubber boats, carrying a heavy supply of radio equipment. In the engagement that followed the enemy lost all four officers and eighteen men killed; we had three dead and three wounded.

The presence of such a detachment where the Japanese had not been expected could mean only one thing—impending action. At dawn that morning Japanese warships heavily shelled our positions and cruiser-borne aircraft kept up a day-long strafing. Something big was afoot.

50

UNITED STATES BECOMES "ARSENAL OF DEMOCRACY"—A NATION IN ACTION

AMERICA girded itself for war as it entered the world struggle in the third year. The transformation of 135,000,000 peaceful people into one of the greatest fighting forces the world had ever known proved the power of democracy.

With their country's existence as a free nation threatened, some 13,000,000 men and women entered the armed services. More than 60,000,000 more took their places in the production line on the home front. These, with many among the remaining millions, poured their life savings into war bonds to help provide a war chest of nearly $200,000,000,000. Here was a might never before equalled—the spirit and resources of a free people.

Washington became not only a world capital, but the heart of humanity. Through Lend-Lease, which had begun in March, 1941, sums reaching $60,000,000,000 were appropriated in the next three years, with more billions to follow, to extend aid to the Allied Nations in helping to provide the sinews of war and eventually to reconstruct a devastated world.

The United States of America, founded on the principles of the equality of man and the "unalienable rights of life, liberty, and the pursuit of happiness," demonstrated that all races, nationalities, and creeds can work together in unity for a common cause. Its forty-eight States, a virtual United Nations in themselves, with nearly 35,000,000 foreign-born or of foreign or mixed parentage, and 100,000,000 of native parentage, presented a united front in defense of human freedom. The dissidents, still clinging to alien ties, were fractional.

This vast home front of loyal Americans, with its few exceptions, included over 5,000,000 Germans, and nearly 5,000,000 Italians. There were 1,300,000 from Austria, 700,000 from Hungary, 250,000 from Rumania, and nearly 136,000 Japanese under the American flag. From the Allied countries, sons and daughters living in the United States were approximately 2,000,000 from England, 3,000,000 from Canada, 1,250,000 from Scotland, Wales, and Northern Ireland, and 27,000 from Australia.

These were augmented by nearly 2,700,000 from Russia, nearly 3,000,000 from Poland, nearly 1,000,000 from Czechoslovakia, and nearly another 1,000,000 from Norway. There were 450,000 from Denmark, 373,000 from the Netherlands, 350,000 from France, and 327,000 from

Greece. Also 384,000 from Yugoslavia, more than 715,000 from Lithuania, Latvia, Esthonia, and Finland, and over 131,000 from Belgium.

Americans from the neutral countries included 2,500,000 from the Irish Free State, nearly 1,400,000 from Sweden, nearly 300,000 from Switzerland, 177,000 from Portugal, and 110,000 from Spain. Nearly 350,000 came from Near East and Asiatic countries, 1,200,000 from Mexico, and an estimated 250,000 from Cuba, the West Indies, Central and South America, and the Azores. Lesser groups hailed from all the countries of the world, including 5,000,000 loyal Jewish-Americans.

It was from this brotherhood of races in the United States—the home of some seventy nationalities—that our armed forces rallied under the American flag. The names on the rolls of honor which constitute our United States Army, Navy, Marine Corps, Coast Guard, and Air Force, came from all the peoples of the earth. They nobly represented the high traits in courage and character—a united family of races and creeds. And to this memorial must be added the sons from the homes of our 13,000,000 Negroes who did valiant service for America.

Tremendous responsibilities rested upon the War Cabinet which surrounded President Franklin Delano Roosevelt when the United States entered the conflict. Vice President Henry A. Wallace presided over the Senate. Cordell Hull, as Secretary of State, was in command of the diplomatic front with its world-wide organization of ambassadors, ministers, and special emissaries in negotiations with foreign nations. The burden of financing the nation with the additional necessity of providing enormous funds for conducting the war, fell upon Henry Morgenthau, Jr., as Secretary of the Treasury. The duty of directing the greatest war organization in history was in the able hands of Henry L. Stimson, as Secretary of War, and Frank Knox as Secretary of the Navy.

Agricultural and food demands to support the nation and the armed services were directed by Claude R. Wickard as Secretary of Agriculture. Internal problems were under the management of Harold L. Ickes as Secretary of the Interior. The tremendous task of industrial organization was placed on the experienced shoulders of Jesse H. Jones as Secretary of Commerce. Legal problems with their complexities centered in the office of Attorney General Francis Biddle. The only woman in the cabinet was Frances Perkins, Secretary of Labor, the focal point of unity between organized labor and industrial production. In charge of the vast postal system, with its increasing necessity of maintaining mail communications with millions of service men in all parts of the world, was Frank C. Walker. There were changes as the war progressed and a gigantic structure of special war bureaus was created to meet the expanding emergencies.

The direct responsibility for the conduct of the war fell upon

President Roosevelt, Commander in Chief of the Army and Navy as prescribed by the Constitution. It may be said that President Roosevelt fortunately had two right hands: General George C. Marshall, Chief of Staff of the United States Army, and Admiral Ernest J. King, Chief of Naval Operations. The achievements of these military geniuses would require extended biographies. General Marshall, a Pennsylvanian who was graduated from the Virginia Military Institute, commanded the great staff of army organizers and field generals. Admiral King, born in Ohio and graduated from the United States Naval Academy, commanded the largest navy and the greatest naval operations in history.

The complete list of these war staffs is given in official records in this history, and their achievements will appear in the development of the war as the armies and navies go into action in decisive battles. We call especial attention here, however, to General Henry H. Arnold (Pennsylvania), who, in command of all our army air forces, directed the first great aërial war in history; Generals Leslie J. McNair (Minnesota) and Ben Lear (Canada) who commanded the army ground forces; General Brehon B. Somervell (Arkansas) who supplied the army service forces; and General Alexander A. Vandegrift, Commandant of the United States Marine Corps, and his predecessor, General Thomas Holcomb.

President Roosevelt, foreseeing the impending dangers, had constantly appealed to the nation to be ready for every emergency. The mobilization of the manpower of the nation as a defense measure had begun with the passage by Congress of the Selective Training and Service Act on September 14, 1940, and had been set in operation two days later by the signature of the President. This was the first compulsory peace-time military training law in the history of the country. Its first director was Dr. Clarence A. Dykstra, President of the University of Wisconsin, who was succeeded nine months later by Brigadier General (later Major General) Lewis B. Hershey.

This system, expanded to meet the exigencies of war, developed into a vast manpower organization through which more than 13,000,000 of America's manhood entered the army and the navy with their various branches of the service. During its operations every male in the United States, between the ages of 18 and 65 years, was registered; and of those under 45 service selections were made. At its fullest expansion it comprised a staff of 220,000 with 54 State organizations, 515 appeal boards, 6443 local boards.

The stupendous task of building an army and navy required some 1,200 training fields, camps, posts, schools, etc., in which "boys from home" became soldiers, airmen, naval men, and Marines.

American womanhood rallied to the defense of its country. For the first time in history women were allowed to volunteer for service. The first organization of its kind was the Women's Army Auxiliary Corps, authorized by Congress on May 14, 1942, which became the Women's Army Corps (WACS), a component part of the United States Army on July 1, 1943. Nearly 90,000 women soldiers served during the war. Some 12,000 went overseas to fifteen foreign countries and every theater of operations, while their comrades served in 400 military installations in the United States. Their duties included those of radio and telephone operators, motor vehicle drivers and airplane mechanics, medical and laboratory technicians, supply clerks, interpreters, army office administrators, and many other diversified positions according to military needs. Many of these women performed acts of bravery which brought them medals and decorations, including the Purple Heart, Legion of Merit, and Soldier's Medal. This Women's Army was under command of a Texas officer, Colonel (Mrs.) Ovieta Culp Hobby, U.S.A.

More than 85,000 American women enlisted in the WAVES, the development of the Women's Reserve in the United States Naval Reserve, under direction of Captain Mildred H. McAfee, U.S.N.R. Organized in July, 1942, for continental service, it was extended in September, 1944, to shore stations in Hawaii and Alaska, and the Western Hemisphere. It derived its name from its classification as "Women Accepted for Volunteer Emergency Service." An arm of the United States Navy, with rank and rating according to qualifications and service performed, it became an important adjunct at naval bases.

Women Marines—18,000 strong—became a valued branch of the United States Marine Corps on February 13, 1943. This was the second war in which American women had served with the Marines; they had made an excellent record in the First World War. Under Colonel Ruth Cheney Streeter, in World War II they were assigned to more than 50 bases in the United States and hemispheric duties covering more than 125 types, including parachute riggers, gunnery instructors, trainer operators, celestial navigators, machinists, and radio operators. As full members of the Marine Corps, they were granted ranks and pay as men. The Women Marines acquired no nickname but held proudly to the title, MARINES.

Another women's organization known as the SPARS, over 10,000 strong, was attached to the Coast Guard Reserve, under Lieutenant Commander Dorothy C. Stratton. Organized in November, 1942, it was given its name from the Coast Guard motto: "Semper Paratus" (Always Ready). The duty of these women was to replace men eligible for sea duty by taking posts as yeomen, seamen, radio operators, and storekeepers. Most of them served in the Western Hemisphere, with some 300 in Alaska, and over 200 based in Hawaii.

The largest war service organization—with nearly 30,000,000 senior members and 18,000,000 junior members—was the American Red Cross. With a record of 62 years as a humanitarian body in every war and disaster, it entered World War II under the chairmanship of Norman H. Davis and secretarial direction of Mabel T. Boardman, with Basil O'Connor appointed on July 13, 1944, to succeed Mr. Davis, who died during the war.

The Red Cross recruited some 60,000 war nurses for active service in the Army and Navy Nurse Corps. They expended more than $200,-000,000 in services performed. Their Red Cross Blood Donors Service became the largest achievement in medical history—10,000,000 blood donations from men and women who volunteered throughout the country. The Red Cross conducted first aid courses in which nearly 300,000 persons received instruction. Since establishing this course in the First World War, the Red Cross has awarded approximately 2,500,-000 certificates. In one year of World War II they issued nearly 762,000 first aid certificates; 233,000 swimming, 92,000 life saving, and 42,000 water saving and functional swimming certificates. They operated 2,382 first aid stations and 11,479 mobile first aid units.

The services rendered by the Red Cross included a Volunteer Special Services Corps of 3,000,000 women for home-front duties in hospitals, canteens, recreation, etc., and as nurses' aides. In a single year nearly 938,000,000 surgical dressings were shipped to the army, and over 2,000,000 to the navy, with 619,000 for civilian use abroad. Over 30,-000,000 people in thirty foreign countries were supplied with food, clothing, medicine, and other necessities after the outbreak of the war. Some 15,000,000 food parcels, largely packed by volunteers, and containing produce valued at nearly $74,000,000, were sent to American and United Nations prisoners of war. The Red Cross Information Service was often the only direct means of communication between prisoners in all parts of the world and their kin at home.

The first great battle was fought on the home front—the Battle of Production—and it won the greatest victory in industrial history. Approximately 200,000 American industries "went to war." On their production front was an army of workers larger than that on all the battle fronts combined. Management and labor under our free enterprise system performed modern miracles, supplying tanks, planes, guns, ships, munitions, and all the necessities to support the armed forces, while supplying the needs of the homes throughout the nation. More than 6,000,000 farms joined this battle to supply foods "to win the war" and "feed the homefolks." Organization and distribution of these vast quantities of products centered in executive boards in Washington, under the Administration of National Defense.

The story of these record-breaking achievements would require many volumes. We can indicate but a few of the administrative bodies here:

The Office of Production Management (OPM) headed by W. S. Knudsen, was merged into the War Production Board (WPB) under Donald M. Nelson (who was later succeeded by James A. Krug), to mobilize the nation's industrial strength. The War Labor Board (WLB) was set up with William H. Davis as chairman, to arbitrate labor disputes without strikes. The War Manpower Commission, with Paul V. McNutt as chairman, was created to mobilize the nation's manpower for war. The War Shipping Administration, with Rear Admiral Emory S. Land as administrator, was established to provide the tremendous tonnage of shipping necessary for the successful prosecution of the war.

Washington soon found itself administering the greatest business enterprises in the world. The ablest leaders in the country coöperated with this unparalleled undertaking and directed it to a successful conclusion—a triumph of the unlimited capacity, ability, and integrity of American business.

The system of executive boards expanded until it covered every phase of the nation's existence. Among them were the Office of Economic Stabilization (OES), directed by Fred M. Vinson, to preserve the domestic economic structure and prevent inflation and dislocation; the Foreign Economic Administration (FEA), with Leo T. Crowley as administrator, to consolidate and unify governmental activities in foreign economic affairs; Office of Price Administration (OPA), administered by Chester Bowles, to ration foods and commodities, stabilize prices on living costs and prevent speculation and inflation; Office of War Mobilization and Reconversion (OWM), James F. Byrnes, director, to unify activities on the home front, develop wartime policies, and plan for peacetime reconversion and reëmployment, with a unit headed by Bernard M. Baruch and John Hancock to adjust war and postwar problems; and War Food Administration (WFA), headed by Marvin Jones, to protect essential war and civilian needs with adequate supply and efficient distribution of foods.

The three vital "M's" in warfare are men—money—munitions. To these should be added two more "M's"—mechanization and manufacture. The Munitions Assignment Board (MAB) was under the chairmanship of Harry L. Hopkins, a power in Lend-Lease and a personal emissary of President Roosevelt. This board was invested with the important decisions in making assignments of war materials to the United States, Great Britain, and the United Nations. The Combined Chiefs of Staff (CCS) was established with Admiral William D. Leahy, Chief of Staff to the Commander in Chief of the United States Army and Navy, to provide for full collaboration of the United States, Great Britain and all the United Nations. The Combined War Materials Board (CWM), with William M. Batt as United States member, planned development and expansion of raw material resources. Mr.

Batt also headed the Material Coördinating Committee (MCC) and the Joint War Production Committee (JWP) between the United States and Canada. The Permanent Joint Board of Defense (JBD) for protection of the North American Continent operated with Fiorello H. LaGuardia as chairman of the United States section.

The diversified experiences of American leaders in all lines of activity were utilized in support of the Government. Jesse H. Jones, banker, exerted vast powers with the Reconstruction Finance Corporation (RFC), the Federal Loan Agency (FLA) and as member of many war boards. Leon Henderson, economist, served on the Advisory Committee to the Council of National Defense, as first administrator of the OPA, and as director of Civilian Supply on the OPM and the WPB.

Nelson A. Rockefeller was coördinator on Inter-American Affairs between the nations of the Western Hemisphere. Joseph E. Davies was chairman of the President's War Relief Control Board. Former Governor Herbert H. Lehman of New York became director of the United States Relief and Rehabilitation Administration in devastated countries. Charles B. Henderson served as chairman of the Reconstruction Finance Corporation. Claude B. Wickard was chairman of the Combined Food Board to coördinate the food resources of the United Nations.

War and national defense, as we have stated, became the "world's biggest business." The Federal Communications Commission and the War Communications Board operated under the chairmanship of James L. Fly; the Petroleum Administration for War was administered by Harold L. Ickes; the War Relocation Authority with Dillon S. Myer as director; the National Housing Agency with James B. Blandford, Jr. as administrator; the Committee of War Employment Practice with Malcolm Ross as chairman; the Office of Alien Property Custodian with James E. Markham as custodian; the Office of Civilian Defense with William N. Haskell as director; the Office of Defense Transportation with Colonel J. M. Johnson as director; the Office of Scientific Research and Development with Dr. Vannevar Bush as director; the Federal Works Agency with Major General Philip B. Fleming as administrator; the Office of War Information (OWI) with Elmer Davis as director; the Office of Censorship with Byron Price as director; and many other groups.

Organized labor, through its leaders, William Green of the American Federation of Labor and Philip Murray of the Congress of Industrial Organizations, pledged as a war measure that labor would sacrifice its right to strike. They supported the Nelson plan for joint labor-management boards for increased production. Sidney Hillman, head of the Garment Workers' Union, represented labor in OPM. Charles E. Wilson, president of the General Electric Company, representing industry, joined the War Production Board as production vice chairman under

Donald Nelson. The able group surrounding Nelson included William M. Jeffers, Lemuel W. Boulware, J. A. Krug, Donald D. Davis, Clinton S. Golden, Joseph D. Keenan, Arthur H. Bunker, William L. Batt, Albert M. Carter, and Arthur D. Whiteside, president of Dun and Bradstreet. While serious disputes did occur between labor and management, the net results in production broke all world records. The nation is deeply indebted to the millions of workers who stood loyally by their country in every crisis.

The power of a free press asserted itself immediately when the United States entered the war. The full strength of nearly 1,900 daily newspapers, with nearly 47,000,000 circulation, presented a solid front in defense of our country. This was reinforced by more than 10,000 weekly, semi-weekly, and tri-weekly home newspapers, and national monthly magazines, thereby binding the entire nation in a common cause. This united action of a free press was one of the strongest forces in support of the fighting fronts.

Never before in history has the press performed a public service of such magnitude. With the great news-collecting organizations augmented by war correspondents on all fighting fronts in every part of the world the people were kept well informed. It is estimated that some 150,000,000 words on the war's progress passed through these great clearing houses of world information, which, if printed in book form, would require 1,500 volumes. Supplementing this were thousands of volumes from our book publishing houses.

Radio entered its first great war 60,000,000 sets strong, bringing the war into the homes of the nation. For the first time in history, the home front was kept constantly in touch with the war fronts. The sound of battle, the voices of soldiers, the latest dispatches and analyses came instantly into our homes through the miracle of this new science. Radio "went to war." It became one of the most valued arms of modern warfare. Battles and campaigns were fought by means of radio communication. The Allied nations were held together as a coördinated force through the air waves. Ships at sea and planes in the air worked together and with the armies by radio contact. Generals, admirals, heads of nations, were in continuous conference through the new power of communication.

The giant young industry with its vast system of broadcasting networks went all out immediately after Pearl Harbor. It placed its engineering resources, electronic devices, and full production at the service of the armed forces and the Government, with more than 300,000 employees—some 225,000 of them women by 1945. The broadcasting networks volunteered their services and became "liaison officers" between governments, armies, navies, and the home front. With official communiqués and commentators they interpreted the war to the home-folk, took leadership in bond drives and home defense measures, and remained on constant duty to deliver Government orders. In maintaining morale the broadcasting systems performed one of their most important war services, flooding the air waves with music, entertainment, and information, while keeping the armed forces in all parts of the world in direct communication with their folks at home.

Motion pictures also "went to war." The $2,000,000,000 industry in the United States offered its services to the Government. It sent its camera men, many of whom lost their lives, to the battle fronts and recorded the war for posterity. Historic events and great personalities were brought to the screens of more than 12,000 theaters in our country alone, and in this way practically all the people at home witnessed the war in action. The industry became a war service which produced documentary films in support of war loan drives, training films for military camps and industrial plants, approximating more than 15,000 features and 20,000 short subjects. It is estimated that an average of 630,000 overseas men saw motion pictures each night.

More than 8,000 motion picture men were inducted into the armed forces. Leading stars, male and female, went by land, sea, and air to entertain the troops at home and abroad. They faced danger from air bombardments behind the battle fronts in Africa, Italy, France, Germany, England, China, India, Australia, and the islands of the Pacific. The industry not only proved its valor but played an important part in stimulating morale and keeping the people visually informed—essential factors in winning the war.

Thus the American people mobilized for war and stood loyally behind the fighting forces until the last battle was won.

REBIRTH OF AMERICAN SEA POWER INTO WORLD'S GREATEST NAVY

WAR in the Pacific quickly proved that it could be won only by superhuman efforts. The manpower of America, with its great industrial resources, must build the mightiest navy the world had ever known—and back it with the largest air force and ground troop concentrations. Only by rapid coördination on land, on sea, and in the air could total victory be attained.

It is useless to deny that at the outbreak of war, despite the continuous warnings of President Roosevelt, the United States was unprepared to meet the crisis. The nation must start from the smallest beginnings and perform a modern miracle. When the blow fell on Pearl Harbor we finally realized the full import of the situation facing us. Fortunately, our seven large airplane carriers were at sea and escaped destruction or damage in the Japanese sneak attack, but four of them were soon to be lost in action. Aside from them, the navy had little other than Admiral Hart's Asiatic Fleet. The entire United States Pacific Fleet had been reduced to the dimensions of a task force.

The first appearance in this war of a task force on our side was on January 24, 1942, when Admiral Hart decided upon a night torpedo attack against the advancing Japanese. Collecting the few American ships available for battle—all the British and Netherlands warships being engaged in convoy duty in Malaya—he set off for the Battle of Macassar Strait already described. A little later, Rear Admiral Doorman, Netherlands Navy chief who succeeded Admiral Hart, gathered four cruisers and seven destroyers, about equally divided between his own and American ships, for the disastrous Battle of the Java Sea. The plan of Admiral Doorman was sound in its conception but, unfortunately, the Allied ships were unable to escape detection by the omnipresent Japanese Air Force.

Those two battles deep in the Netherlands East Indies were the result of the improvisation to which the Allied commanders had been driven by necessity. But they provided the initial lessons in a development that was to restore naval and air mastery of the Pacific to the United Nations. On February 20, 1942, a task force built around the carrier *Lexington* and commanded by Vice Admiral Wilson Brown, attempted a combination air and surface attack on Rabaul. This, too, was detected and, having lost the element of surprise, was not pressed.

However, on February 24, Admiral Halsey took the *Enterprise*, two cruisers, and seven destroyers to Wake Island, far to the north. There he caught the Japanese completely by surprise, inflicting terrific damage at the cost of only one plane. On March 4 he did the same thing to Marcus Island. The basis of successful task-force technique had been laid and the development flourished until it culminated in the gigantic Task Force 58, of which we shall soon hear more.

"Paradoxical as it may sound," Vice Admiral F. J. Horne, Vice Chief of Naval Operations, told a Congress committee in April, 1943, "the fleet as such no longer exists; that is, as an operational unit. Missions in modern warfare are generally accomplished by task forces. In these the cruiser plays an essential part. The ideal task force is one built around the aircraft carrier, and, since the carrier is relatively inferior in armament, it is necessary that someone run interference for her. The cruiser is the ideal type for flexibility, speed, and armament."

Task forces are rarely the same in any two missions. The ships are shuffled and redealt to meet each specific task. Even the entire navy may be used as a task force if the mission is of major importance. Bearing in mind the fact that flexibility is the keynote of the task force setup, it is easy to understand that such a force may run from a single carrier with a few destroyers and a cruiser or two to one involving dozens of carriers supported by a large number of battleships and a horde of destroyers and cruisers. Services of submarines were utilized and army land-based planes coöperated with the naval task force. In its later development the task force carried along its own transport, repair, and supply ships, so that it was a self-contained, self-sufficient fighting unit, able to remain at sea indefinitely without having to return to base for other than major repairs.

The development of the task force marked the rebirth of American sea power in the Pacific and dates from May 30, 1943, when the *Essex*, the first carrier of its class, steamed into Pearl Harbor ready for action. This 25,000-ton flat-top with an 850-foot flight deck was the last word in naval efficiency, built out of the experiences of war and the achievements of science. The various navy and shipbuilding yards were turning out *Essex*-type craft (known as CV's) so quickly that a score of the new ships were added to the navy within a year. At the same time, smaller carriers of the *Independence* class (known as CVL's) joined the fleet. They were much smaller, of 10,000-ton rating, but were fast and had a wide range. They suffered only from the fact that they sacrificed armor and armament for weight and speed and consequently were more vulnerable to enemy attack. In addition to these two mainstays were the CVE's, known as "baby flat-tops," mainly converted from tanker or cargo hulls. They were a great deal slower, carried a much smaller number of planes, and were easy targets for the enemy. But they did a marvelous job of escorting convoys of troops and supplies.

Late—1944! Leyte! Paris! Berlin!

Nazi Dejection at Its Best

Captured near Fismes, France, this German general looks dejected, while the M. P. grins happily.

A Trio of Generals

Lieut. General Courtney Hodges, First U. S. Army, Lieut. General Omar N. Bradley, 12th Army Group, and Lieut. General George S. Patton, Jr., Third U. S. Army.

OFFICIAL PHOTO U.S. A.A.F.

A Shower of Parachutes

Paratroopers were brought to this dropping zone by transports of the 12th Air Force Troop Carrier Air Division. The scene is somewhere in Southern France.

INTERNATIONAL NEWS PHOTO

The Sign of Surrender

High-ranking German officers taken prisoner during the liberation of Paris raise their hands in surrender as they are marched through the streets.

BRITISH OFFICIAL PHOTO

British Airborne Forces in Holland

Glider-borne British troops group around a lone sunflower, as they listen to radio instructions before going into action in Holland.

The big carriers were the home bases for the F6F Grumman Hellcat fighters with a speed of 400 miles an hour. These planes had six 50-caliber machine guns in their wings and were powerfully armored. They were able to outfight the Japanese Zeros at from ten to twenty to one. The Grumman Avenger torpedo plane, the Douglas Dauntless dive bomber, and the Curtiss Helldiver were the mainstays of the task force striking power.

To handle this new explosive force the navy was fortunately in a position to call upon men both air-minded and experienced in sea warfare. There were Admirals Halsey and Fletcher, already familiar names, Vice Admiral Marc A. Mitscher, Vice Admiral John H. Towers, the oldest naval aviator in point of service, Admiral Raymond A. Spruance, Rear Admiral Frederick C. Sherman, Rear Admiral C. A. Pownall, Rear Admiral Alfred E. Montgomery, and Rear Admiral Arthur W. Radford. There were, of course, many other officers, commanders of task groups—subdivisions of task forces—and of individual ships, who contributed their full share to the success of the naval war.

It fell upon the shoulders of Rear Admiral Charles Alan Pownall to try out the new naval-air weapon for the first time. This operation was at Marcus Island on September 1, 1943. Admiral Pownall had served with distinction in World War I and had been later designated a naval aviator. He completed a postgraduate course in mechanical engineering and was assigned to the Bureau of Aëronautics. As chief of the Engine Section in the Bureau, he carried on a series of experiments which resulted in eliminating carbon monoxide poisoning as a lethal menace to naval air pilots. In 1942 he became Commander of Fleet Aircraft, West Coast. After the successful blow at Marcus he was appointed Commander of Air Forces, Pacific Fleet, holding that post until he was brought back to shore to become Chief of Naval Air Training at Pensacola, Florida.

Rear Admiral Alfred E. Montgomery led the next strike, at Wake Island, on October 5, 1943. He, too, had established a fine record in World War I and later qualified as a naval aviator. After two years as Commander of the Naval Air Station at Seattle, he was appointed aviation officer on the staff of the Commander of Cruiser Divisions, Scouting Force, from which he went to the Bureau of Aëronautics, remaining until he was placed in command of the carrier *Bangor*. In 1942 Admiral Montgomery was one of the seven career naval aviators, including Rear Admiral John H. Towers, who were recommended by President Roosevelt in a wholesale breaking of seniority rules for promotion to Vice Admiral.

The first full-scale task force assault was that against Rabaul and was directed by Rear Admiral Frederick Carl Sherman. On October 1, 1943, he struck at the Buka-Bonis area of Bougainville. On the 5th he was dispatched to Rabaul and made another strike on the 11th.

Rear Admiral Arthur W. Radford was one of the Annapolis class, graduated in 1915, which gave an unusually large number of aviation leaders to the navy. He conceived and developed the entire program of pre-flight training in which athletics and realistic personal encounters were emphasized. He was advanced from Chief of Training in the Bureau of Aëronautics to become Acting Deputy Chief of Naval Operations for Air when Vice Admiral McCain was given a new assignment. Admiral Radford held that post until he appeared in the front line of the Pacific encounters.

The rapidity of the growth of naval aviation was such that the man who was Commander of the Air Force, Pacific Fleet, when the *Essex* sailed into Pearl Harbor was Vice Admiral John H. Towers, the second man ever to become a navy flier. To the naval aviators, however, he was always the Number One Flier. Three years before World War I the navy bought three planes. Towers was placed in one and the other was entrusted to Lieutenant Eugene Ellyson, the navy's first flier in point of fact, but who was later to die in an accident while a commander. Young Towers had early become an air enthusiast and had taken lessons in flying from Glenn Curtiss, the inventor and manufacturer. His subsequent activities included two terms of service with the United States Embassy in London, acting as assistant director of naval aviation in World War I and then as commander of the spectacular flight of the navy's NC-4 boats across the Atlantic in 1919. He was Assistant Chief of the Bureau of Aëronautics; commanding officer of the first carrier *Langley* and then of the *Saratoga;* and subsequently Chief of the Bureau of Aëronautics. This post he held until called up to head the navy's Pacific Fleet air arm. Later Admiral Towers became Admiral Nimitz's Deputy Commander in Chief, Pacific Fleet. In 1942, off Guadalcanal, he was on his flagship, the carrier *Wasp,* when it was torpedoed and sunk on September 15. Because he had so consistently urged upon his superiors, with all the vigor at his command, the necessity of building planes and carriers, Admiral Towers is considered the father of the modern task force built around carriers.

Among the men who flew Admiral Towers' NC-boats across the Atlantic was Marc A. Mitscher, who had won his wings as a naval aviator only four years before. This short, bald, vigorous man was to become the first "boss" of the most powerful and destructive unit in the history of sea warfare—Task Force 58. He, too, passed through various stages in the development of a naval officer. He supervised the construction of the *Saratoga,* the first carrier specially built for that purpose by the United States Navy, and landed the first plane on her new flight deck. In 1941 he commissioned the carrier *Hornet,* not knowing that a half year later he would command the vessel under the alias "Shangri-la" for General Doolittle's visit to Tokyo. Admiral Mitscher was on the *Hornet* at the Battle of Midway and then took over as commander of all air forces—army, navy, and Marine—at Guadalcanal, where he taught the Japanese many a lesson in aërial warfare. He was then put in charge of a carrier force, subsequently taking over Task Force 58, to relinquish it in October, 1944, to Vice Admiral McCain.

The top fighting man in the Pacific was Admiral Raymond A. Spruance who, at fifty-seven, became the youngest four-star admiral in naval history. His brilliant action at Midway was rewarded with command of the newly created Fifth Fleet, which included Task Force 58 and the other task forces. The Fifth Fleet had been known as the Central Pacific Force until it grew to a size larger than the entire navy had been. A great tactician, calm and cool in planning before battle—in which he is a recognized master—as well as in actual combat, Admiral Spruance was a true fighting man. He willingly took chances, but never went beyond the limits of calculated risk.

During the summer of 1943 Admiral Nimitz and his staff decided that the time had come to use the new armament placed at his disposal. Three new carriers—the *Yorktown,* the *Essex,* and the *Independence*—were riding at anchor. They were the only new carriers in the navy. Admiral Pownall, in command of one of them, was handed sealed orders and immediately he steamed out of Pearl Harbor with his destroyer escort. The next morning he was joined by the other two carriers, a battleship, two cruisers, some destroyers, and a tanker. After several days at sea the orders were opened. The air personnel learned that the show—the real thing—was to start at dawn on September 1.

Ever since Admiral Halsey's startling attack on March 4, 1942, a year and a half before, Marcus Island had been leading a sheltered existence under Japanese control and under its Japanese name, Minamitori Shima. Nearly 1,200 miles southeast of Tokyo and 875 miles northwest of Wake, it was too deep in enemy waters and too strongly defended to risk attack by the depleted American forces. The original equipment built up on this closely guarded island had been greatly increased. It was a key stepping-stone on the way from Japan to the Gilberts and Marshalls and to the naval air base at Truk.

Lights were burning on Marcus a little after five o'clock on this September morning. Japanese officers in the airfield's control tower were undisturbed when they heard the sound of approaching planes and saw aircraft with running lights on. Of course they must be friendly planes! A few seconds later the crash of 2,000-pound bombs and the glare of incendiary missiles shattered the enemy's complacency. The new offensive in the Central Pacific had begun.

Everything worked to perfection in this try-out. The American force was undetected all the way in and the weather, for a change, favored

Admiral Pownall's ships. The morning was solidly dark when the planes took off from Captain J. J. ("Jocko") Clark's *Yorktown* and from the *Essex* and the *Independence*. Lieutenant Commander Richard Upson first spotted Marcus from his TBF (torpedo-bomber) and fired the opening shot of a campaign that was to surge and swell until it had engulfed the enemy.

"There it is, boys! There it is!" he shouted into his radio. Seeing the lights burning in buildings on the island, he conceived the idea of having the attacking planes switch on their own running lights to make the surprise complete. The TBF's and SBD's (dive bombers), taking off for the first time from carrier decks with bombs weighing a ton apiece, soon had the island ablaze. By 7 o'clock a third of the vital enemy base had been damaged. The Hellcats came in on the wake of the bombers for their baptism under fire, but found little to do beyond strafing because not an enemy plane got into the air.

The assault on Marcus lasted for nine hours. When it was over, eighty per cent of the installations, which had been increased 400 per cent since Admiral Halsey's visit to the 740-acre island, had been laid in ruins. A smoke cloud hung 8,000 feet overhead. Antiaircraft positions had been progressively knocked out so that later attacks were carried on without any interference.

The task force had met its first test perfectly. A pattern for future action had been set. Three new carriers had arrived at Hawaii—the *Lexington,* the *Princeton,* and the *Belleau Wood*. Admiral Pownall was instructed to proceed to the Gilberts, 2,000 miles southeast of Marcus. This was to be an experiment in the joint operation of land-based and carrier aircraft.

On the night of September 17-18, twenty-five planes from the United States Army Air Force took off from the newly acquired base at Nanumea in the Ellice Islands. During the spring of 1943 Marines had occupied Funafuti, 275 miles to the southeast, and Seabees had converted it into an advanced air base. On September 4 the Marines made an unopposed landing on Nanumea, only 525 miles southeast; in little over a week land-based planes were using it as a forward base. Their initial blow was aimed at Tarawa, its neighboring islands of Makin and Abemama (Apamama), and Nauru, to the west.

Tarawa, also called Knox Island or Cook Island, is the largest and most important of the Gilberts. It had been built up as the principal Japanese air base in that area. It is a twenty-two-mile atoll, with nine large islands, numerous small ones, and a large lagoon with but a single entrance. Makin lay directly north and Abemama a little to the southeast. Nauru is a single, almost circular island whose seven square miles contain deposits of phosphate rock and were providing Japan at the time with a large share of the vital mineral. Nauru, with neither lagoon nor harbor but fringed with coral reefs, is about 500 miles from the Gilberts in the general direction of the Solomons.

For three days the selected islands were blasted from the air. After the opening attack by army Liberators, 190 carrier planes bombed and strafed from low level, heavily damaging the airfield on Tarawa and destroying twelve enemy aircraft. *Princeton* fighters got three more at Makin. Abemama was badly cut up and Nauru's installations were smashed. The shooting ended with another visit by the army planes. Pictures taken at that time were carefully studied for use in the near future, and seemed to show Tarawa left almost helpless. Unfortunately, that was not the case. The Japanese had performed a marvelous job of camouflage which was to prove a costly surprise.

Wake Island, like Marcus, had been without serious molestation since Admiral Halsey's visit on February 24, 1942. The little island so heroically defended by the Marines in December, 1941, had its subsequent calm rudely shattered when the (then) "greatest carrier task force ever assembled" struck it heavily. This time there were six flat-tops: the *Essex,* the *Yorktown,* and the *Lexington* of the largest class, and the *Independence,* the *Belleau Wood,* and the *Cowpens.*

Surprise at Wake was missing. Twenty-seven Japanese fighters and seven bombers were in the sky as a reception committee. Heavy antiaircraft defenses were fully manned. Cruisers stood offshore and did much on the first day of the attack to neutralize the antiaircraft guns. Land-based Liberators, operated by naval personnel, added their weight to that of the gigantic force of carrier planes.

When the attack was called off on October 6, Wake had been deprived of most of its military value. Fuel, water, and ammunition dumps had been wrecked. From the tactical angle the main point proved at Wake was the value of the F6F Hellcat. It had its first real test and conclusively established its worth.

Between the Tarawa and Wake raids Admiral Halsey came in from the waters of the Pacific to headquarters at Pearl Harbor. Admiral King came over from Washington. Admiral Nimitz was waiting for them and for several days they conferred.

General MacArthur had captured Finschhafen and was on the way to Madang. The New Guinea base of Wewak had been knocked out and the same process in the case of Rabaul and New Britain had been begun. Amphibious forces were closing in on Bougainville, the last Japanese foothold in the Solomons.

The Allied time-table called for the invasion of Bougainville on November 1. On that day, and for several days and nights thereafter, shooting was fast, furious, and continuous on land, on sea, and in the air. First word of the new operations came in General MacArthur's communiqué of November 2, when he said: "Exploiting to the full our recent comprehensive air sweeps at Rabaul and in the Solomons, our right wing under Admiral Halsey was thrown forward approximately 200 miles into central Bougainville on the morning of November 1. In a combined ground, water, and air movement our forces seized and occupied the Empress Augusta Bay on the western coast. ... We are now in the rear of the enemy's position at Buin, in the Shortlands, and are athwart his line of supply to that area."

Again surprise had worked, but it was soon followed by a stubborn, persistent opposition that would have made occupation a serious, costly proposition. However, the Allied command never intended to conquer the island. The same results could be obtained by neutralization—complete blockade preventing reinforcements, supply, or withdrawal, and the pinning down of 30,000 or more Japanese troops on the island.

United States Marines, led by Lieutenant General Vandergrift and back in action after having turned Guadalcanal over to the army, stormed smoothly ashore on the mountainous jungle island, somewhat larger than Guadalcanal. After a heavy naval bombardment and air assault, the landing was made in the Torokina area, about fifty miles northwest of the bases at Buin and Kahili and directly across the island from Kieta. Buka and Bonis were farther to the north. The Japanese had expected that we would land at one or more of these heavily defended bases, instead of which the Americans achieved their vital surprise by selecting the lightly held Empress Augusta Bay.

The surrounding airfields had been subjected to heavy and persistent attacks for weeks, and their planes were in no position to offer serious opposition to the sizable armada of warships and transports standing off Bougainville. Bearing in mind the strength of Rabaul and its ability to send reinforcements and support to the closer airfields, Admiral Halsey sent Admiral Sherman with the *Saratoga* and the *Princeton* to blast Buka and Bonis, whose airfields flanked Buka Passage on the north of Bougainville.

During the night of November 1-2 the Japanese sent a flotilla of four cruisers and eight destroyers steaming out of Rabaul to relieve Bougainville. Intercepted about forty miles from Empress Augusta Bay, they turned tail after a ninety-minute battle and fled from the area, leaving behind a cruiser and four destroyers sunk and two cruisers and a pair of destroyers holed. Sixty-seven planes attacked our ships and seventeen were shot down. Despite the fury and length of the engagement, not an Allied ship was hit.

The next morning General MacArthur, anticipating that the Japanese would attempt a counterattack from Rabaul upon the infant beachhead at Empress Augusta Bay, sent General Kenney's bombers into that port. They found Simpson Harbor jammed with traffic and the air full of protecting planes. Antiaircraft opened up as it never had before.

"Our fight cover engaged his attacking planes" (of which there were about 150), General MacArthur reported, "and our mediums went in at masthead height. The harbor was swept practically clean, nearly every ship there being heavily hit or sunk by 1,000-pound bombs."

Japan's seaborne power had suffered its worst defeat at Rabaul.

The moment Admiral Halsey heard the news of the encounter he realized that Rabaul would become the scene of further activity. His scouts confirmed his surmise that the Japanese would start pouring cruisers, destroyers, transports, and cargo ships into Rabaul from Truk. Replacement planes were already on the way. It was imperative that Rabaul's stature be kept permanently reduced. That is why he called Admiral Sherman back from Buka and Bonis.

The *Saratoga* and the *Princeton* were in position to strike on the morning of November 5. All the planes, numbering nearly 100, left early, to be met over the target by enemy fighters and violent antiaircraft. Since the MacArthur assault the Japanese had rushed down from Truk more planes than had ever settled on the five airfields.

Simpson Harbor was again alive with ships. Some thirty men-of-war and a host of noncombatant vessels were zigzagging frantically for the exit from the enclosed waters in an effort to gain the open sea. Two Japanese cruisers were sunk and five cruisers and the pair of destroyers were so badly battered that they were out of action for months, if not forever. Half of the enemy planes, numbering nearly 100, were shot down and half of the remainder badly damaged.

Meanwhile, Admiral Halsey was maintaining support of the operations on Bougainville, landing a large force of army troops without opposition to reinforce the Marines who were extending their Torokina beachhead at Empress Augusta Bay.

Rabaul still loomed as an important objective. Admiral Halsey moved quickly and with daring to keep up his attack. A tremendous force was being assembled in the central Pacific for an operation of immense magnitude, from which three carriers under Admiral Montgomery were temporarily detached and rushed to augment Admiral Sherman's pair of flat-tops. The *Essex,* the *Bunker Hill,* and the *Independence* made the rendezvous in time to deliver a concerted attack on November 11.

As the approaching planes were detected offshore the Japanese hurried their fighters into the air and their warships out of the harbor. When the American carrier craft emerged from under the low-hanging rain clouds they found twenty-two enemy warships scurrying about Simpson Harbor with a sizable grouping of tankers, merchantmen, and transports. In the wildest of mêlées, with planes of both sides ignoring antiaircraft and machine-gun bullets that literally showered everything, the United States Navy fliers sank a cruiser and two destroyers, and heavily damaged three cruisers and eight destroyers.

As the last men began to return to their ships, the early crews having already landed, the tables suddenly were turned. More than 125 Japanese planes attacked the force in the heaviest assault yet launched against carriers. Our own planes took off in the midst of the attack, flying through their own antiaircraft to reach the enemy. Japanese fighters and bombers were blasted from the sky every few seconds. Eleven burning planes fell through the air simultaneously. The Japanese attacked with Aichi 99 dive bombers in three waves for an hour, starting at 1:30 P.M. At the end of the fray more than 100 of the enemy planes had been shot down. Fighting was so thick and fast that an accurate tally was impossible, but less than ten of the Japanese were believed to have retired in one piece. The famous "Fighting Nine" Squadron of the *Essex* alone shot down forty-one planes which, added to the fourteen downed over Rabaul, gave it a record of fifty-five in one day. We lost but three planes and the carriers escaped damage.

The Gilbert Islands, a group of sixteen coral atolls lying athwart the equator, had been under persistent air attack by army and navy bombers for more than two months. Major General Willis H. Hale's Seventh Army Air Force was carrying the major load. The Gilberts had been held by the British up to the outbreak of the war. Seized by the Japanese, they were woven into a web of defenses in Micronesia and integrated with the Marshall Islands to the northwest into a powerful screen protecting the Japanese Empire. Their capture was an essential part of any serious thrust toward Tokyo. Carrier and land-based air blows had served to soften the defenses for the assault about to be launched by the great collection of ships recently placed under command of Admiral Spruance.

It is from these beginnings—these first sea fights—that we may trace the rise of American naval power. Its force was steadily augmented until, together with expanding air power and land forces, it fought the great battles near Luzon in the Philippines, along the coast of China, around Iwo Jima and Okinawa, and up to the coasts of Japan itself.

52

"SHANGRI-LA"—FIRST RAID ON TOKYO —CRISIS ON CONTINENT OF ASIA

AMERICA'S future was inextricably interwoven with that of both Europe and Asia as the war expanded. Within six months after the United States entered the conflict we were entrenched in key positions on all fronts.

General MacArthur from his base in Australia and Admiral Nimitz in Hawaii held the destiny of the Pacific in their hands. General Stilwell and General Chennault in China, with General Brereton in India, were the advance guards of America's rising power which was to come to the liberation of Asia.

It was during these critical days in 1942 that daring exploits began to awaken the American people to world-consciousness. The adventures of "Jimmy" Doolittle's boys in the first bombing of Tokyo were of historic import—the first warning to the Japanese of the mighty forces that some three years later would lay the cities of Japan in ruins.

Doolittle's boys were the Paul Reveres of World War II in a revised and reversed version. They were riding the clouds on steeds of steel as their bombs sounded the warning: "The Yanks are coming!" This famous ride to Tokyo was historically timed. It occurred on April 18, 1942—the 167th anniversary of Paul Revere's ride in the first hours of the American Revolution. But this time it was not to arouse fellow countrymen to impending danger but to warn the enemies of what was awaiting them.

The news of the first bombing attacks on Japan startled the American people as much as it did the Japanese. How and where that raid came from remained shrouded in mystery for exactly a year. All that President Roosevelt would reveal was that the warplanes had come from "Shangri-La."

This much was known: A squadron of B-25 medium land-based bombers swooped suddenly upon Tokyo, Yokohama, Nagoya, Kobe, and Osaka. Bombs were dropped on carefully selected targets among armament plants, dockyards, railroad yards, and oil refineries. The raid was commanded by Colonel James H. Doolittle, a veteran of the First World War. For this exploit over Japan he was rewarded with a promotion to Brigadier General.

It was not until April 20, 1943, that the historic facts about the first bombing of Japan were released by the War Department. Shangri-La was revealed to have been the airplane carrier *Hornet*. It had been equipped with special apparatus to permit large land-based bombers to take off from its short flight deck. Never before had such an undertaking been attempted.

The *Hornet,* escorted by the carrier *Enterprise* and a powerful force of destroyers and cruisers, bore the army fliers to within eight hundred miles of Tokyo, when a small Japanese boat suddenly bobbed up before the armada. It was sunk within a few minutes but there was no way of knowing if she had been able to flash a radio warning before going down. It had been the original intention to sail to within four hundred miles of Japan and take off on Sunday evening. The unexpected encounter forced a last-minute switch. It was decided to risk running short of gas and take off Saturday morning from eight hundred miles out. In the words of the War Department statement:

"The American planes were to have sought specified landing fields in China. Because of a combination of circumstances (one being the earlier take-off) the planes were unable to reach their assigned landing fields. One came down in Soviet Russian territory. The others made forced or crash landings in China—some in Japanese-occupied territory—or in waters off the Chinese coast. All these planes were wrecked."

Fifteen out of the sixteen planes that had left the *Hornet* were lost. "Five of the eighty participants in the historic raid," the statement went on, "are interned in Russia. Eight are prisoners, or are presumed to be prisoners, of the Japanese Government. Two are missing. One was killed. Although several were long delayed, the other sixty-four participants made their way to the camps of our Chinese allies and then back to American authority. Seven of those who escaped in this manner were injured, but survived."

The story as given out by the War Department continued: "The planes were not spotted until they had almost reached their targets. The Japanese were taken entirely by surprise. Each plane went directly for its specified target and when the shooting was over, parts of five Japanese cities were in flaming ruins. There was little enemy fighter opposition and that did not develop until too late to be effective. Antiaircraft fire was as erratic and panicky as were the defending fighter planes. By order of General Doolittle, no attack was made on the Japanese Emperor's palace, although it was in sight of the fliers. It was not a military objective. It was upon leaving Japan that the most hazardous part of the venture was reached. The scattered airplanes ran into a storm. Their already depleted gasoline reserves were drained further as they bucked the winds. There were no light beacons or landing flares. Unable to go farther, there in the darkness 6,000 to 10,000 feet above a strange land, the great majority of the men bailed out."

The tales of heroism and narrow escape were thrilling. The *Ruptured*

Duck, with a Donald Duck insignia, crash-landed in the China Sea two hundred feet from shore. The crew of the *Whirling Dervish* bailed out over the Chinese mountains in the dark of night. *The Tokyo Express* and the *TNT* had similar experiences. A gunner landed in a tree and and lit a cigarette. As he threw the glowing butt away he saw it drop down a great cliff. He remained in the tree until daylight when he cautiously crawled down to safety.

Captain Ted W. Lawson's plane landed on the sea with such force that he was thrown through his windshield and suffered a broken leg. Corporal David J. Thatcher, although badly cut and momentarily knocked unconscious, swam back to the sinking plane and saved the medical kit. Subsequently they met Lieutenant J. R. Wright, flight surgeon of another plane, who carefully nursed Lawson's gangrenous leg.

The *Hornet* carried on for another six months until lost in the Battle of Santa Cruz on October 26. She was replaced by a new carrier of greater size and increased power which, in response to the unanimous demand of the American people, was named *Shangri-La.*

Within twenty-four hours the jubilation over the smash at Japan's leading cities gave way to indignation. President Roosevelt disclosed that the Japanese had executed some of the eight captured fliers and had sentenced others to prison terms. Tokyo declared that the men had been executed because non-military objects had been bombed and citizens had been deliberately fired upon. Returning participants of the attacks, and Americans later repatriated from Japan, unanimously testified that no civilian building had been hit and that panicky Japanese fighter pilots, frantically trying to keep away from the fire of the American planes, had swooped low over the streets and mowed down men, women, and children with erratic machine-gun bullets.

The first news that American soldiers had been treated like common criminals instead of as prisoners of war came in a Japanese broadcast on October 19, 1942, reporting the capture, trial, and severe punishment of the captured fliers. Not until five months later, March 12, 1943, was the United States successful in obtaining official confirmation that the Americans had been placed on trial and sentenced to death, with the executions carried out in some cases but commuted in others.

Frequent reports of the Japanese action had caused the State Department to intensify its efforts, through the Swiss Minister in Tokyo who was handling affairs for the United States, to find out the fate of the two bomber crews who had landed within Japanese lines. In a note dated February 17, but not handed to the Swiss Minister until weeks later, the Japanese refused all details. They would divulge no names nor the nature of the sentences imposed. They refused to permit the Swiss Minister to see the prisoners and further declined to treat those still living as prisoners of war.

The State Department lodged an official protest on April 12, knowing in advance it would have little effect upon the enemy. That protest made for the purpose of record declared, "The American Government will visit upon the officers of the Japanese Government responsible for such uncivilized and inhumane acts the punishment they deserve."

Of the eight men from the two bombers these five were known to be prisoners: 1st Lieutenant William G. Farrow, Washington, D. C.— 1st Lieutenant Robert L. Hite, Earth, Texas—1st Lieutenant Robert J. Meder, Lakewood, Ohio—1st Lieutenant Chase J. Nielson, Hyrum, Utah—2nd Lieutenant George Parr, Madison, Wisconsin. The three believed to be prisoners were: 1st Lieutenant Dean E. Hallmark, Dallas, Texas—Sergeant Harold A. Spatz, Lebo, Kansas—Corporal Jacob D. Deshazer, Madras, Oregon. This was the roll of honor of the martyrs of the first raid on Japan.

The American Government appealed to Japan in the name of honor and humanity. Tokyo's defiant reply was: "This same policy (murder of captured prisoners) will continue to be enforced in the future." It concluded with this diabolical thrust over the radio: "And, by the way, don't forget, America—make sure that every flier that comes here has a special pass to hell. And rest assured it's strictly a one-way ticket."

In the Southwest Pacific the Japanese continued to expand their holdings and to creep closer to Australia. General MacArthur was making full use of his Australia-based planes to inflict heavy damage upon enemy shipping and installations but he did not have enough force to do more than delay the Japanese.

Disaster continued to stalk the Allied forces in Burma. The country teemed with Fifth Columnists, for the Japanese skilfully exploited racial and religious differences and political animosities.

General Sir Harold R. L. G. Alexander, shortly after assuming command of the British forces in Burma, summed up the situation by saying: "The local population as a whole appears actively in support of the enemy." After the Allies had been driven from Burma and the Japanese had impressed forced labor, starvation, and indignities upon them, the "local population" came to realize that British colonial administrators were gentle ministrators of benevolence compared to the cruelties of the Japanese. When the United Nations, two years later, began their reconquest of Burma, they were welcomed and offered wholehearted aid from that same "local population."

The Japanese military campaign was swift and relentless. After the capture of Prome the enemy, safely ensconced on Singapore and Sumatra, took over command of the Bay of Bengal and the Indian Ocean. While the Japanese Navy, including battleships, patrolled the waters, planes raided Ceylon early in April, 1942, and the airfield at Colombo. This was but a prelude to the disastrous blow at the naval base at Trincomalee a few days later when the destruction that was wrought upon Pearl Harbor was duplicated in India. Virtually every British aircraft was demolished and the harbor was littered with sunken ships.

Almost simultaneously other planes sank the 10,000-ton British cruiser *Cornwall* and the 9,975-ton *Dorsetshire*. Dive bombers caught the 10,850-ton aircraft carrier *Hermes* alone and sent it to the bottom. Allied naval power in the Indian Ocean was virtually wiped out.

On land the Japanese kept climbing up the Irrawaddy River, and when the second week of April opened, the British were holding a thin line about sixty miles from Magwe, entrance to Burma's precious oil fields. The Japanese staked everything on an effort to clean up the campaign before the monsoons set in.

The next few weeks were a repetition of the early months in Burma—retreat, destruction of vital installations, courageous but futile counter-attacks. General Stilwell, in a brilliant march, sent his Chinese troops to reinforce the British. The only possible result was to delay the Japanese push for a few days on the British side and to weaken the defenses of the Burma Road. The American Volunteer Group continued to raise havoc by bombing and strafing the Japanese although they now had no bases for their planes.

Shifting the weight of their punches from one side to another the Japanese captured Magwe on April 18, Pyinmana on the 23rd, Loikaw on the 24th and Lashio, terminal for the Burma Road, on the 29th. Mandalay was captured on May 1; three days later the Japanese entered China at Wangting. The Chinese here had been destroyed as a fighting force and were carrying on guerrilla warfare. Akyab, on Burma's west coast, fell during the first week of May. The Chinese rallied and drove the Japanese back in Yunan, but the enemy advance to India continued unchecked. After a last desperate stand on the Chindwin River at Kalewa, the British remnants in a masterful retreat reached the India frontier on May 15 and the Japanese had completed their conquest of Burma. Tengyueh, a vital center along the Burma Road in China, was captured the same day. China had been completely cut off from land reinforcement and supply from the Allied bases in India.

That Burma campaign will always remain an inspiring example of courage and determination in a doomed cause. When Rangoon fell, it became impossible to hold the country; but for four months a handful of British Imperials, who had never been trained in jungle warfare, and a few under-manned, ill-equipped Chinese divisions battled a great military machine. For hundreds of miles they fought, withdrew, and fought again until there was hardly anyone left to fight.

There was one small ray of consolation after the loss of Burma and that came with dramatic suddenness. On May 25, General Stilwell appeared in New Delhi, India. He had led the surviving members of his force over the mountains, through the jungles and across the swollen streams of Burma to safety.

"The Japs ran us out. We were licked. We've got to find out why, go back, and do something about it."

China was brought into Lend-Lease by President Roosevelt, but with the Burma Road gone the practical result was small although the moral effect was great.

To add to all these military woes Mahatma Gandhi chose the moment of Britain's greatest military and political weakness to renew his demands for India's independence. With the rest of Asia gone, and Australia in danger of invasion, it became of paramount importance that India be retained as the main Asiatic base for the United Nations.

Prime Minister Churchill recalled Sir Stafford Cripps from his post as Ambassador to Soviet Russia and sent this liberal on a momentous journey. Generalissimo Chiang Kai-shek, after a visit with Gandhi and Pandit Jawaharlal Nehru in India, appealed to Britain to give "real political power" to the Indians. Sir Stafford left London for India early in March and reached New Delhi later in the month. The entire world had high hopes that success would attend the mission. After a long series of conferences with the leaders, the All-India Congress, under the urging of Gandhi, rejected the offer proposed by Sir Stafford.

The proposals made public on March 29, read in part: "The object is the creation of a new Indian Union which shall constitute a dominion associated with the United Kingdom and other dominions by a common allegiance to the Crown but equal to them in every respect, in no way subordinate in any aspect of its domestic and external affairs. His Majesty's Government, therefore, make the following declaration: (*a*) Immediately upon cessation of hostilities, steps will be taken to set up in India... an elected body charged with the task of framing a new constitution for India. (*b*) Provision shall be made... for participation of Indian States in the constitution-making body."

Each state received the right to join the proposed union, to remain independent, or to join subsequently. Britain was prepared to sign a treaty with the constitution-making body covering matters "arising out of the complete transfer of responsibility from British to Indian hands ...in accordance with... protection of racial and religious minorities."

When the proposal was rejected by the India Congress, it was immediately withdrawn and Sir Stafford returned to England. Britain took the position that the subject could not be reopened until the war was over. London reorganized the Government of India, giving to the Indians a large majority of the Viceroy's Council and naming three to the War Cabinet. Gandhi promised that his organization would do nothing to hamper the war effort, but this promise was not kept. However, except for some temporary difficulties, no serious injury developed.

BATTLE OF CORAL SEA

THE battle of Coral Sea, May 8, 1942, was the first turning point in the War in the Pacific. Here the Japanese, sweeping through the Pacific, were stopped at the gate to Australia. And from here they were to be driven back island by island in the fiercest jungle fighting in the annals of mankind.

In these few crucial hours the clock of destiny was to begin to tick the minutes which presaged their doom. Their attempt to turn time back to the Middle Ages was frustrated. Their expectations of taking possession of the rich continent of Australia were blasted by American bombs.

When the Philippines, the Netherlands East Indies, and the islands of the Bismarck Archipelago—principally New Ireland, New Britain, and New Guinea—were written off by the Allies it became evident that crucial struggles would have to be fought out in the waters around the Solomon Islands. A further advance by the Japanese would make the defense of Australia, New Zealand, and New South Wales almost impossible. Beyond that, it would make almost equally impossible the execution of any plans the Allies had prepared for building up bases and strength with which to push the enemy back north in the Pacific.

United States forces landed on New Caledonia, the fourth largest island in the Pacific, about March 17, 1942. It was French territory and, following the fall of France in 1940, had staged its own three-months struggle in which the Fighting French forces seized the island. The Vichy governor managed to escape aboard an armed sloop and later 750 of his supporters were deported. When the Americans, under Major General Alexander McM. Patch reached New Caledonia, the local authorities coöperated fully in all plans of defense and offense.

New Caledonia lies 800 miles east of Australia and is strategically situated on a direct line from San Francisco to Australia, the convoy and supply route to General MacArthur's base, and from New Zealand to the Netherlands Indies, the route of attack to be followed in regaining the territory Japan had conquered.

Fortresses based on New Caledonia played an important part in future decisive actions in the Solomons-Bismarcks area. The fact that our landing operations were accomplished almost a month before the Japanese became aware of what was going on added to the mounting evidence that it was a complete surprise to the enemy.

For some time the Japanese had been concentrating transports and warships in the ports of Salamaua and Lae on New Guinea despite punishing blows by Allied planes.

Army reconnaissance planes reported during April a new heavy concentration of Japanese transports and supporting elements, including aircraft from carriers and shore bases. Early in May the advance actually began. One of the last advanced bases to be seized by the Japanese was the little strip of land two miles long and half a mile wide called Florida Island, the northeast end of Guadalcanal. It had one small port, Tulagi; the rest of the island was wooded, with hills and plateaus.

Tulagi was the last invasion base in the Japanese plan for the conquest of Australia. Its western counterpart was at De Boyne Island which, with adjacent Misima Island, controlled the Jomard Passage between the Louisiades and the southeastern tip of New Guinea. It was necessary for the enemy to secure this tip and Port Moresby in order to protect his flanks during the attack on Australia.

The island naval base at Truk, far to the north, was the center of Japanese invasion activities. Constant ship movement was indulged in to deceive the Allies, but the Allied commanders were not to be fooled. They knew that two invasion fleets with their escorting warships had reached their bases. They knew, also, that two other fleets, including battleships and carriers, had been sent straight down from Truk as additional protection. One, consisting of two carriers, five cruisers, and twelve destroyers, went for the Jomard Passage to account for General MacArthur's bombers. The other swept around the Solomons to the east to handle any naval force in the area and was supposed to join the first fleet at the southern end of the Jomard Passage.

This was the picture on May 3 when eight Zeros, always an indication of Japanese carriers, appeared over Port Moresby. General MacArthur immediately sent out his bombers to make the first contact with the enemy fleet. They got only one ship, but they brought back a wealth of information which was flashed to Rear Admiral Frank J. Fletcher who was cruising in the Coral Sea with the carrier *Yorktown*, the cruisers *Astoria, Chester,* and *Portland,* and six destroyers. At about the same time a scout plane from the carrier *Lexington,* under command of Captain Frank C. Sherman, reported a concentration of shipping in Tulagi harbor.

Admiral Fletcher lost no time getting into action. Convinced that the Japanese were completely unaware of his presence, he boldly slipped into position one hundred miles southwest of Guadalcanal and sent his planes at tree-top level for the mass of ships in the harbor. The engagement was furious and devastating. When it was over twelve of the fifteen Japanese ships had been sunk. The remaining three, damaged, fled to the open sea through Sealark Channel.

Tulagi was knocked out promptly and completely, but it was obvious that the shooting had only just begun. The enemy now knew that there were carriers in the neighborhood. The conclusive battle had to come up. That night Admiral Fletcher pushed southwest for a rendezvous with tankers and other supply ships. He then joined other Allied units under Rear Admirals Thomas C. Kinkaid, Aubrey W. Fitch, and William W. Smith. Among the ships were the carrier *Lexington,* the heavy cruisers *Minneapolis, New Orleans,* and *Chicago,* and eleven destroyers. There were also the Australian heavy cruiser *Australia* and light cruiser *Hobart,* forming part of a unit commanded by Rear Admiral J. G. Grace, of the Royal Navy. Enemy scout planes kept appearing over the ships but were shot down as quickly as they appeared.

During the next two days Admiral Fletcher moved into position and deployed his forces. He was so heavily outnumbered that combat seemed foolhardy. But the situation was so desperate that an attempt had to be made. By the afternoon of May 6 the Japanese had consolidated their forces sufficiently to indicate that the amphibious operation against Port Moresby was about to start. The Allied squadron had been speeding northwest toward Tulagi. Admiral Fletcher, knowing that enemy forces would have to round New Guinea to attack Port Moresby, detached three cruisers—two Australian and one American—to the mouth of the Jomard Passage with orders to hold it against the Japanese force numbering probably twenty-five warships and as many transports. The two American carriers and their escorting vessels continued toward Tulagi.

Before dawn on May 7, Admiral Fletcher had decided to ignore the invasion fleet and to attack the fighting fleet. Scouts left the decks of the *Yorktown* and *Lexington* before sunrise. Hours passed without word coming back, but a Japanese flying boat picked up our ships and was able to send off his report before being downed. At eight o'clock a scout sent in the first word: a carrier, three cruisers, and six destroyers were north of Misima Island driving southeast. The Japanese, following their usual custom, had split their force into two bodies. General MacArthur's bombers ran into one; this was the other.

By 8:15 o'clock seventy-six American planes were in the air: twenty-four carrying torpedoes, thirty-six scout or dive bombers, and sixteen fighters. They plowed down upon the big new Japanese carrier *Ryukaku* which was turning into the wind to launch her planes. Why the enemy should have been surprised by our attack puzzled the fliers, but they went right to work and planted fifteen bombs on the *Ryukaku*'s deck and fifteen torpedoes in her hull—all in less than two minutes. A few minutes later the *Ryukaku* slid under the water with all her planes and 1,800 men.

Commander Bob Dixon opened his radio long enough to flash back the exultant and famed message: "Scratch one flat-top!" The pilot of a lone bomber, in the midst of his dive, saw the carrier go under. He shifted enough to catch a cruiser on the fantail and send it down. During that day twenty-five Japanese planes were shot down. The Americans lost six.

We had other casualties that day, but not off Misima Island. The tanker *Neosha,* after having refueled the carriers on the night of May 4, had headed east to round the Solomons on her way back home. She was being escorted by the destroyer *Sims* when Japanese bombers trying to pick up the main Allied ships reported by their scouts came upon the two vessels. The *Sims,* trying to defend the relatively helpless tanker, was sunk during the attack that afternoon. The *Neosho,* though crippled, was able to get away but subsequently sank as a result of the damage. Most of both crews were saved.

This, however, proved expensive for the enemy. Admiral Fletcher had had no knowledge of the battle fleet swinging around the Solomons until word of the attack on the *Sims* and *Neosho* was received. His planes had just administered a beating to the only enemy carrier force he had known about definitely, and that was in the Louisiades. The attack off the Solomons must have come from another such force.

During the night everything was made ready for what all knew would be a terrific day. At 8:30 on the morning of May 8 an American scout found a lucky break in a heavy cloud belt and spotted two carriers, at least four cruisers, and a covey of destroyers 175 miles northeast of the *Lexington* and *Yorktown.* In another hour all reports had been received and seventy-three planes took to the air: twenty-one torpedo and thirty-seven dive bombers.

Barely had the planes left their carriers when an enemy scout picked up the American ships and escaped to report their exact position. The Japanese attack would not be long in coming. Both carriers were placed on Condition A, with watertight doors closed and all ventilation cut off. Men at power and control stations suffocated and sweated until 11 o'clock, when the opposing planes filled the skies. Five minutes later 108 Jap planes, half of them attacking each carrier, swooped down. The *Lexington* dodged nine out of eleven torpedoes launched at her within as many seconds. A 1,000-pound bomb wrecked her port forward 5-inch battery, killing the whole crew. Another hit and several near misses caused further damage. The *Yorktown* took a bomb square through the deck, blowing out a compartment and killing forty-four men, the only ones she lost in the engagement.

The Battle of Coral Sea ended. Japanese losses as officially stated were: Sunk—fifteen warships, including a new carrier, four heavy and three light cruisers, two destroyers, four transports, and four gunboats; Probably sunk—one cruiser and one destroyer; Damaged—one carrier, one heavy cruiser, one light cruiser, three destroyers, two seaplane tenders, two transports, and ten miscellaneous vessels; a total of thirty-five sunk or damaged.

Several hours after the battle, and with all her planes on board, a terrific internal explosion rocked the *Lexington* while she was steaming at a reduced speed of twenty knots. Gasoline fumes escaping from ruptured lines in closed compartments below decks had become ignited.

Finally, with all machinery disabled, the ship stopped. Flames enveloped nearly her entire length. Captain Sherman gave the order: "Abandon ship!" Men slid down lines from the carrier's sloping deck to boats from other ships, or crawled aboard life rafts and rubber boats. Captain Sherman, with his ten-year-old cocker spaniel Wags in his arms, was the last to leave the *Lexington*. While he was sliding down the rope to safety the torpedo warhead locker exploded. With a final detonation that shook near-by ships, the *Lexington* sank under the waters of Coral Sea. Ninety-two per cent of the ship's complement had been saved.

The *Yorktown*, under Captain Elliott Buckmaster, put back into a South Seas harbor to inspect her damage. After emergency repairs she returned to Pearl Harbor to be made ready for further heroic encounters. Against the staggering losses incurred by the Japanese we lost three ships: the *Lexington*, the *Sims*, and the *Neosho*, and sixty-six planes. Personnel casualties totaled 543.

The Battle of Coral Sea marked the first major engagement in naval history in which surface ships never exchanged a shot. It was fought entirely by planes. Other similar battles were to follow. The great significance of Coral Sea lay in the fact that the Japanese had been stopped—definitely and finally. Australia was saved from the threat of invasion.

The Allies, taking quick advantage of the Coral Sea victory, went over to the offensive and held to it until the very end.

The weeks following Coral Sea were relatively quiet. The enemy withdrew to the safety of his ports and the base at Truk to count his losses and to revise his plans. The power of Allied naval and air strength in the lower Pacific was a surprising revelation to Tokyo. Fortunately, the Japanese High Command did not know that our forces at that time were actually very weak, too weak to withstand a determined attack. Had the Japanese naval commanders assumed the offensive after the second day at Coral Sea instead of being content with the one blow at the *Lexington* and *Yorktown* they might have wiped out Admiral Fletcher's small task force—and the way to Port Moresby and Australia would have been left open.

The Japanese withdrawal immediately after hitting the two carriers was proof that they believed other strong units of Allied warships were still in the neighborhood. As a matter of fact, Admiral Nimitz, correctly reading the mental operations of Admiral Yamamoto, shifted Allied naval strength to the north, setting the stage for another surprise for the enemy.

During the remaining weeks in May, General MacArthur's planes continued their punishing blows upon Salamaua, Lae, Rabaul, and other enemy staging areas. Allied bombs and torpedoes continued to exact a heavy toll of Japanese shipping and warships. But the enemy persisted in attempting to build up strength at the advanced bases and sent his submarines scouting off Australia. Early in June, midget submarines entered Sydney Harbor. They did little damage. Three were destroyed within the harbor and a fourth outside. The diminutive craft were raised, taken to shore and carefully studied, so that the net result of this foray was to reveal Japanese naval secrets and show what little advance had been made over the midget boats that had hit at Pearl Harbor six months earlier.

Even before the Battle of Coral Sea had ended, American naval commanders were looking ahead to what was to follow.

"Our immediate problem," Admiral King reported, "was to anticipate as nearly as we could what the next move of the enemy would be, as we had lost touch with the heavy Japanese forces which had participated in the Coral Sea action. It was clear that the Japanese would not long remain inactive."

During the lull following Coral Sea the various "eyes of the navy" —shore-based reconnaissance planes, submarines, patrol boats—reported a general withdrawal of enemy units from the Southwest Pacific toward Japan. Concentrations made it apparent that large-scale offensive operations were planned by the enemy.

Where, and when? Admiral King said the answers were arrived at on this basis: "Naturally enough, our various important outposts would be good targets, with Dutch Harbor and Midway offering them (the Japanese) the best chance of success, either in the nature of a raid or of an invasion. Furthermore, an operation directed against these points would permit the enemy to retire without too great loss, or complete annihilation, in case their plans did not work out. At the same time, we had to consider the possibility that they might renew actions in the Coral Sea. It was a plain case of calculating the risk involved in stationing our forces. A mistake at that point would have proved costly. Considering the chance that the enemy knew little concerning the location of those of our ships which had not participated in the Coral Sea engagement, but certainly was aware that most of our available carrier and cruiser strength was then in southern waters, it seemed reasonable to expect that the Japanese would make the most of the opportunity to strike us in the central and/or northern Pacific. Such an attack was likely because of the prospect of success in the immediate operation, and because if successful the advance to Australia and the islands in the South Pacific could be accomplished in due course with comparative ease, once the enemy had cut our lines of communication."

With that analysis of the situation the navy went to work. Scouts and patrols were set well to the west of Midway Island and, just in case, along the approaches to the Panama Canal. All other warships that could be assembled were dispatched at once to the probable area of combat. The *Yorktown,* temporarily patched up, was rushed more than 5,000 miles from the Coral Sea up and around Hawaii to join the *Enterprise* and the *Hornet.* These three carriers, seven heavy cruisers, one light cruiser, fourteen destroyers, and about twenty submarines represented the total naval strength we could then assemble in the central Pacific. The ships were divided into two task forces—the beginning of that inspired organization that eventually swept the Japanese from the ocean—one under command of Rear Admiral Raymond A. Spruance, with the cruisers under Rear Admiral Kinkaid; the other under Admiral Fletcher who also had Rear Admiral W. W. Smith. Bases in the outlying islands and in Alaska were hurriedly reinforced by long-range, shore-based aircraft—a precaution soon to reap big dividends.

The Japs were now to strike at Midway and also far north at the Aleutian Islands to set up a base for their planned invasion of the North American continent.

BATTLE OF MIDWAY—AND THE ALEUTIANS

THE first Japanese warnings of their ambitious plans to break through to the American continent came on June 3, 1942. The first enemy air attack on North America took place when Japanese bombers raided the United States Naval and Air Base at Dutch Harbor, Unalaska, one of the American Aleutian Islands.

These volcanic islands extend from the coast of Alaska over a thousand miles toward Kamchatka and the mainland of Asia and Japan. Bleak, barren, inhabited by fishermen of Eskimo origin as a whaling and sealing center, they became key outposts in the Pacific War.

The Japs were striking at American defense lines in an attempt to make a break-through. Early on the morning of June 3, naval patrol planes reported a strong force of enemy ships proceeding east. Five waves of three planes each, launched from Japanese carriers to the south, appeared over Dutch Harbor on Unalaska, an island of matted grass and a few trees. It was a small island, but of vital strategic consequences as the northern apex of our Pacific defenses from Dutch Harbor, to Pearl Harbor, and the Panama Canal.

The first enemy bombs ever to fall on North America did little damage. Six hours later the Japanese sent over reconnaissance craft which did not attempt an attack. About 5 o'clock the next afternoon, eighteen bombers and sixteen fighters came over again, delivering an attack at the same time on the army post at Fort Glenn on Unimak Island seventy miles to the west. Nine fighters attacked Fort Glenn. Two were shot down so quickly that the other seven beat a hasty retreat.

Under cover of the Dutch Harbor raids the Japanese landed a small force on Attu, at the western end of the Aleutians, and hovered off Kiska, in the Rat group of islands 275 miles southeast of Attu and 550 miles from Dutch Harbor. Occupation of Attu and Kiska gave the enemy his first North American observation posts from which to watch Allied movements, and deprived our forces of the weather station maintained at Kiska. It also constituted a threat of further movement toward the mainland. The atrocious weather constantly shrouding the Aleutians precluded their use as major bases.

In order to obtain freedom of action and to remove this pin-prick the Allies set out at once to keep the Japanese from building up strength. Army and navy planes, light naval craft, and submarines opened up a harassing campaign that was maintained during every favorable break in the weather. Three Japanese cruisers, a gunboat, and a transport were damaged during the enemy's first attempts to land.

Some 1,900 miles to the southwest these raids were followed up on the American Midway Islands, about one third of the way between Pearl Harbor and Tokyo, on June 4-5-6, with a combined air and warship attack on the American Wake Island—all of which developed into a general conflict over a wide area.

Down in the Midway area there was little time to do other than note the attack on Dutch Harbor. Ensign Jewell Reid, flying the navy patrol bomber that first picked up the enemy, reported that there were eleven big ships in the water beneath him. Admiral Spruance took stock. The enemy was far beyond the range of carrier bombers, but among the reinforcements that had been rushed to Midway were a few fast B-26 mediums to strengthen the two Marine dive bomber formations stationed there and the navy torpedo planes comprising the reserve of the *Hornet*'s famous squadron "Torpedo 8." In addition there were some big, slow navy PBY scout planes. The only fighter defense for the island consisted of twenty-five out-dated Brewsters in "Fighting 221." Flying Fortresses from Hawaii had been hastily flown out to give Midway the strangest assortment of ancient and modern aircraft ever assembled at a critical point.

Lieutenant Colonel Walter Sweeney, Jr., was ordered to take off with nine Flying Fortresses, to intercept the enemy and to attack. They found five columns of Japanese ships, picked out the largest concentration of big vessels and came down. A cruiser and a transport were badly damaged and left burning, while several other ships were in trouble from near misses.

The attack by land-based Flying Fortresses, the biggest and most powerful weapons in the American aërial arsenal, was more of a shock to the Japanese than the loss of the ships. Where did they come from? What did it mean? Before they had a chance to find the answers they were hit by another surprise blow. About midnight four of the slow, ponderous PBY's, hastily rigged out with improvised gadgets with which to release torpedoes from under their wings—a thing never before attempted—set out under Lieutenant William Richards. Attacking suddenly and fiercely, they hit two big cargo vessels, one of which was sunk. We lost one plane that ran out of gas, but the crew was rescued.

Our bombers were off again before dawn, but so were the Japanese. Lieutenant William A. Chase, patrolling beyond Midway, sighted more than one hundred enemy bombers, heavily escorted, flying in tight formation. They could have but one objective. Lieutenant Chase immediately flashed a warning to Midway. Lieutenant Colonel Ira L. Kimes, in charge of Marine Aviation at the island, and Captain Logan Ramsey, Chief of Naval Operations, ordered every plane into the air. Heroic

"Fighting 221," all twenty-five of them, flashed out to meet the overwhelmingly superior enemy. They met twenty-five miles out, and then began one of the most furious battles of the war. There were not enough American planes in the air to keep all the bombers off and some got through, but not enough of these to wreck the island. Antiaircraft fire kept the attackers from getting into position. Laborers working on the installations picked up guns and manned defenses.

When the battle was over forty-three Japanese planes had been blown to bits. Thirteen of our fighters, more than half of the number that had gone up to do battle, had been lost. Some of our pilots had been machine-gunned as they parachuted from their burning craft. But the airfield had not been put out of commission.

While this was going on, our bombers were doing their own jobs. The reserve of "Torpedo 8," with six machines, had been the first away, followed by the sixteen Flying Fortresses. Next to take off were four army B-26's, rigged up with torpedoes in the same manner as the PBY's had been during the night. Sixteen of the Marines' "Scouting 241" under Major Lofton B. Henderson and eleven under Major Benjamin W. Norris were last away. They were loaded with bombs.

The six torpedo bombers first off made the first contact with the main enemy. The air was swarming with Zeros. Without hesitation the planes dashed through the screen of protecting fighters and solid curtains of antiaircraft fire to score a smashing hit on a carrier. Only one of the six planes returned to its base. The torpedo-rigged B-26's came upon the scene during the height of the first attack. Some of the Zeros went straight for the medium bombers which roared in and down upon the carrier *Akagi*. Two of the four American planes were lost. Major Henderson's dive bombers came in a few minutes later and swooped down upon the carrier *Soryu*. The leader's plane was hit as he went into his dive. Major Henderson held the burning ship true to its course until, with its half-ton bomb, it crashed into the *Soryu*'s "island" superstructure. Three more bombs hit the enemy carrier. Major Norris's echelon came upon the scene and smashed two bombs into the fantail of a battleship. Only half of our sixteen planes that went out returned.

The Japanese split their striking force into two groups, with the *Kaga* and *Akagi* in one and the *Hiryu* and *Soryu* in the other. Supporting ships moved to defend the main body. The Fortresses, which had started off to attack the transports, received new orders as word came in of the hits scored on the carriers, and were sent into that battle area. They found the Japanese regrouped into a long battle line with destroyers outside, then cruisers, battleships, and the carriers far to the rear. Colonel Sweeney decided to go for the carriers. Two of these, a battleship, and a cruiser were left burning and in sorry condition. One Fortress crashed into the water, but only one man was lost.

It was not until the morning of June 4 that Admiral Spruance's scouts found the enemy in position, with at least four carriers each nesting fourteen torpedo planes, thirty-six dive bombers, and a heavy fighter escort—a total of close to three hundred planes.

Lieutenant Commander John C. Waldron, who led the *Hornet's* "Torpedo Squadron 8," having lost contact with the other planes of his command, correctly estimated the enemy's intentions when, shortly after 11:00 A.M., he found his quarry spread out on the Pacific below him. Short of gas, he requested permission to return and refuel, but Admiral Spruance, fearful that the Japanese would slip away again, ordered Commander Waldron to attack immediately the four carriers in close formation below him and the other ships in the force. Just as the lone plane started into its dive the other fourteen bombers of Commander Waldron's flight came upon the scene.

What actually happened probably never will be known. All fifteen planes were lost. The sole survivor among the thirty officers and men in that heroic "Torpedo Squadron 8" was Ensign George Gay. He scored a square hit on one of the carriers, and was hit himself. His plane crashed into the sea. He came up from under water, grabbed a floating cushion from one of the seats and witnessed the most spectacular encounters human eyes had ever seen. He has reported that the enemy line was strung back for ten miles, with the air full of Zeros and tremendous antiaircraft fire.

Ensign Gay took hold of the life-saving cushion just as Lieutenant Commander Clarence McCluskey of "Bombing 6" and "Scouting 6" hove in sight with fighter cover. The torpedo planes kept the enemy's fighters and antiaircraft so busy that the dive bombers were able to drop bomb after bomb. First the carrier *Kaga,* trying to get off her refueled Zeros, was pounded with bombs until she finally blew up. Hit after hit struck the decks of the *Akagi* and a torpedo rammed into her side. The *Soryu,* hit by "Bombing 3" was afire. Gasoline from wrecked planes on all three carriers spread fires around the ships. Two battleships were hit and burning; at least one destroyer was sunk. When the American planes turned for home the whole horizon was filled with burning and damaged ships. The carrier *Hiryu* escaped.

Meanwhile, our carriers turned to get away from any possible attack the Japanese might launch with their battleships. The *Hornet, Enterprise,* and *Yorktown,* stripped almost entirely of their fighter protection and without sufficient naval cover to cope with the heavy, long-range guns comprising a battleship's armament, turned toward the southwest —but not in time. Thirty-six enemy planes from the undamaged *Hiryu* found our ships about 2:00 P.M. Eleven of the eighteen bombers were shot down before they could get their loads away. Seven managed to get through our fighter protection. One of these was blown to bits by antiaircraft fire; a second dropped its bombs wildly and crashed into the sea; a third was ripped into shreds by machine guns from fighter planes. The other four scored three hits on the *Yorktown* and escaped.

The big carrier was badly damaged. Several large fires were brought under control, but the engine room had been crippled. For a time the ship lay dead in the water. Emergency repairs soon made it possible to work up fifteen or twenty knots an hour. At 5:00 P.M. she was attacked again by more than a dozen torpedo bombers escorted by fighters. About half of the enemy's bombers were destroyed by our weary fighters and three more succumbed to antiaircraft fire. Five got through and launched their torpedoes. The crippled *Yorktown* managed to evade all but two of the missiles. Those lodged in her vitals. The big ship was put out of action. She listed so badly that the flight deck was useless, so her planes operated from the *Hornet* and the *Enterprise*. Captain Buckmaster gave the order to "abandon ship."

Exactly as the *Lexington*'s planes crippled the Japanese at Coral Sea while their own ship was under attack, so, at Midway, were the *Yorktown*'s bombers blistering the enemy. Lieutenant Sam Adams, in a scout plane, discovered the *Hiryu*'s position. He described the composition of the armada and its course so precisely that our pilots and bombadiers were able to be briefed thoroughly before taking off from their ships at 2:30.

The Japanese had suffered such heavy losses that when the *Yorktown* and *Enterprise* bombers came upon the scene, fighter opposition was scant although antiaircraft continued strong. The *Hiryu* was hit repeatedly and left blazing from stem to stern; she sank the next morning. Both battleships in the formation were severely pounded, and a cruiser and destroyer were blasted and set afire. The carrier planes, having done a thorough job, went back home—to be followed shortly before sunset by a flight of Fortresses from Oahu, more than 1,000 miles away. By that time there were no more Zeros to take the air.

Both fleets continued to steam away from each other during the night. Early in the morning a Japanese submarine that evidently had not heard what had been going on surfaced off Midway, pumped a few shells harmlessly into the sands and then withdrew under our concentrated attack. Our own scouts reported they had picked up the Japanese occupation force of transports, supply ships, and escort vessels that had managed to escape from the attacks on the fighting forces. Admiral Spruance turned his carriers around. The weather was so thick that the ships' planes could not spot the Japanese ships.

Undismayed by his failure to locate the enemy, Admiral Spruance pushed his ships after the Japanese all through the night of June 5-6. Early in the morning two enemy groups were picked up by the scouts and between 9:30 and 10:00 A.M. the carrier craft opened an attack.

Instead of finding an unhurt carrier and a battleship, as they had expected, they discovered an even juicier plum, for among the vessels were the "cheat cruisers" *Mikuma* and *Mogami*. The London Naval Conference had limited light cruisers to 8,500 tons. Japan announced the *Mikuma* and *Mogami* as light cruisers, but they were actually 13,000 tonners—heavies in the fullest sense of the word.

Both ships became the concentrated target for assault. They were peppered and riddled. Twenty planes hit the *Mikuma* at once and she went down. The *Mogami* was so badly smashed that she, too, probably followed to her watery grave, but as no one actually saw her sink the navy never claimed her as a total loss.

At about the time the carrier planes left for the attack, the list of the *Yorktown* had been so reduced that a salvage party was placed on board and she was taken in tow to start her slow trip back to Pearl Harbor for repairs. The destroyer *Hamman* was escorting the carrier when, shortly after noon, an enemy submarine got off four torpedoes—two into the *Yorktown* and two into the *Hamman*. The carrier was mortally wounded, but remained afloat for another twelve hours. The *Hamman* sank almost immediately, most of her crew being rescued. Captain Buckmaster, the last to leave the *Yorktown,* called down on the intercommunicating telephone to some men trapped in a compartment below decks by the blast of the torpedoes. "How are you doing?" he asked. Then came the startling reply: "We've got a hell of a good aceydeucey game going down here." Major General Clarence L. Tinker, leading a group of Army medium bombers, was killed when his plane was forced down at sea. General Tinker was in command of the army air corps operating from Hawaii.

The Battle of Midway, lasting more than three days and nights, was a series of complex and widespread actions involving a number of engagements. Every officer and every man who participated is entitled to unstinted praise. Great credit goes to Admiral Nimitz whose strategic handling of the forces involved was as masterly as anything in all naval or military history. Here, as at Coral Sea, not a shot had been exchanged between ships. Planes fought it out entirely, except for the two blows struck by submarines—one American, the other Japanese.

Admiral Kirk summed up the significance of the encounter in these words: "The Battle of Midway was the first decisive defeat suffered by the Japanese Navy in 450 years when the Korean Admiral Yi-sun administered a resounding defeat to the Japanese Admiral Hideyoshi (so-called father of the Japanese Navy) in 1592 off the Korean Coast. Furthermore, it put an end to the long period of Japanese offensive action and restored the balance of naval power in the Pacific. The threat to Hawaii and the West Coast was automatically removed, and except for operations in the Aleutians area, where the Japanese had landed on the islands of Kiska and Attu, enemy operations were confined to the South Pacific.

In exactly six months from the disastrous blow to our naval strength suffered at Pearl Harbor the balance of power in the Pacific had been restored. This had been achieved through a combination of daring and brilliance on the part of the American leaders who exploited with their limited forces every enemy weakness, and the inability of the Japanese to follow through when things looked desperate. The only thing that had stood between the Japanese and capture of Midway was the spirit and courage implicit in the statement of that island's Marine commander, Colonel Harold D. Shannon: "The Marines will hold it until hell freezes over."

For all practical purposes the limit of Japanese expansion had been reached. In the six months from Pearl Harbor the enemy had conquered the Philippines, Malaya, Burma, the Netherlands Indies, and most of the Bismarcks-Solomons area. He was to make a few more futile efforts to extend his gains to the south. In the Central Pacific he never overcame his first great mistake of not having taken Midway during the early weeks of the war. In the North Pacific he had landed on Attu, Kiska, and Agattu, but those barren, cruel rocks were to mean only the high tide of Japanese invasion toward North America.

During the last week of June, President Roosevelt, taking advantage of Prime Minister Churchill's presence in the United States, summoned a special session of the Pacific War Council. The two leaders explained how, in the light of the decision to make the defeat of Germany and Hitler the first strategic aim, the Pacific War would have to go on at reduced speed while naval and military strength were being built up. The offensive-defensive would, necessarily, proceed slowly and build up gradually to the point of becoming an overpowering offensive in fact as well as in name.

55

BATTLES OF GUADALCANAL AND THE SOLOMONS—LAND, SEA, AND AIR

GUADALCANAL was becoming a hellhole while our navy was trying to save it by cutting off Japanese reinforcements, and MacArthur was blasting his way through the jungles of New Guinea on the other side of the sea.

About 10:30 on the night of August 20, a white flare rose from the woods east of the Tenaru River. About two o'clock on the following morning shadowy figures dashed from the eastern bank toward the sandbar separating the river from the sea. American machine guns immediately opened up, mowing down the Japanese who charged with fixed bayonets at the gunners. Two platoons of Marines held off the charge and kept the enemy from reaching the sandbar. Tanks were thrown into action. By five o'clock that afternoon almost the entire force of 1,000 Japanese was annihilated.

Although we had won the Tenaru battle, our commanders were well aware that the attempted landing was but the first step in a well-laid plan of action designed to be decisive. The enemy had been concentrating his forces in the Rabaul area ever since Savo. On the morning of August 23, planes from Henderson Field sighted a strong Japanese naval force heading for Guadalcanal. It included carriers, battleships, cruisers, destroyers, and a host of transports.

Admiral Ghormley had concentrated two task forces southeast of Guadalcanal, built around the carriers *Saratoga* and *Enterprise*, and including the battleship *North Carolina*, the cruisers *Minneapolis, Portland, New Orleans,* and *Atlanta,* and eleven destroyers.

During the night the combined force moved north and established contact with the enemy on the morning of the twenty-fourth. That day and the next witnessed the maddest scramble of naval-air fighting the war had seen. Planes from the *Saratoga* found the small carrier *Ruyijo* and knocked her out of action. They also damaged a cruiser and a destroyer. The *Enterprise* sent her planes against other enemy warships. Army bombers from Noumea, as well as the Marine aircraft from Guadalcanal, poured more destruction and ruin upon the Japanese.

In the Battle of the Eastern Solomons, the War and Navy Departments, in their usual cautious manner, listed the results as follows: Japanese losses: one carrier sunk and another heavily damaged; one battleship, several cruisers, and two or three destroyers damaged; one transport sunk, four damaged. Our only loss was the damage to the *Enterprise*. In addition, the enemy lost more than 100 planes.

The Japanese, virtually stripped of their carrier support, had broken off the fight although their powerful surface forces were largely intact. For our part, we were still too weak to run the risk of chasing the retreating enemy close to the protection of his land-based planes. The most important result of the Battle of the Eastern Solomons was that the enemy's first substantial attempt to invade Guadalcanal had been turned back long before the island's shores could be sighted. But the destroyers that had, on the night of the twenty-fourth, shelled Guadalcanal and roused our Henderson Field fliers into action, had succeeded in landing a large body of troops at Cape Esperance.

Although the Japanese were unable to rout our naval protection and, as far as they knew, halt the flow of reinforcements, they took advantage of their shorter lines and well-established staging areas to rush supplies and reinforcements at night to their harried garrison by speedy destroyers which were capable of the additional job of firing hot lead on the Marine positions. The enemy was greatly aided in this sort of operation by the fact that we had no long-distance bombers to take off after the destroyers had started on their homeward journey.

Most of the Japanese troops, however, were ferried by transport from Rabaul, Lae, and Salamaua to the Shortland Islands and then transferred to ocean-going landing boats or large barges. They crossed to Santa Isabel Island at night, then hugged the shore closely to the southern end of the island and finally dashed across to Cape Esperance on Guadalcanal during another night.

While the Battle of the Eastern Solomons was raging, the Japanese, who still retained the strategic initiative, appeared suddenly with a small convoy off Milne Bay, New Guinea, and, on August 25 sent a landing party ashore. General Brett's air scouts spotted the ships so that the enemy was stripped of the advantage of surprise. Bombers from Port Moresby immediately attacked.

Japanese landing boats were heavily strafed and a good part of the invading force was killed before it could reach shore. The survivors immediately headed for the airfield where United States engineers were working. Australian scouts held off the enemy until the Americans had time to drop their shovels and pick up guns. They saved the airfield.

It was at Milne Bay that English-speaking Japanese first used the trick, to become common in other battle areas, of suddenly shouting: "Hey Bill! Is the corporal there?" When the unsuspecting Australian or American raised his head to look for "Bill," he was promptly picked off by a Japanese sniper.

The enemy convoy had come down through the Trobriand Islands to the northeast and the d'Entrecasteaux Islands that lay to the east. There were only three medium transports with their escort ships which appeared in Milne Bay, a fine expanse of water about twenty miles in each direction.

The fact that the Allies were not surprised by the attempted invasion made it possible to dispose of the enemy in short order. By September 9, the ground forces were wiped out, except for some isolated stragglers who were hunted from tree to tree for another month.

The main result was that for the first time a vast amount of equipment fell into Allied hands undamaged. The weapons and ammunition were taken to Australia and the United States for minute examination, enabling the Allies to perfect protection and countermeasures. The Japanese had few secrets left after Milne Bay.

Japanese reinforcements continued to arrive on Guadalcanal via the "Tokyo Express," an endless stream of destroyers and landing barges. The Buin-Faisi area on Bougainville Island, about midway between Rabaul and Guadalcanal, was the main junction stop on the run. By September 13, the enemy had been able to land a full division of men, more than replacing his casualties.

Japanese submarines, soon discovering that our carriers were woefully deficient in destroyer protection, boldly attacked the big ships. The *Hornet,* for instance, dodged twenty-two torpedoes from underwater craft within a few days. Our dive bombers, substituting for the destroyers, sank many enemy submarines, but they continued to attack.

The virtually unprotected carrier *Wasp,* shepherding a big convoy with the Seventh Marines and stores toward Guadalcanal, was due at the island on September 13. At 3:09 that afternoon, with her decks crammed with returned planes being refueled, the *Wasp* was flushed in the periscope of a Japanese submarine. Two torpedoes caught her amidships; a third struck a little abaft. The *Wasp*'s magazines exploded. Gas lines trailed flames over and around the entire ship. The destroyer *O'Brien* took a torpedo and made port only to break up and sink. The *Wasp* was abandoned and went to the bottom. Most of the crew had been taken off safely. The convoy finally reached Guadalcanal on the eighteenth.

From September 9 on, the Japanese sent over twenty-six bombers escorted by Zero fighters every day, attacking shipping, ground positions, and Henderson Field. They lost heavily, but continued to come until the 12th, when they destroyed the base radio station, some very precious stocks of gasoline, and three grounded dive bombers. The night before, Henderson Field had received reinforcements of twenty-four fighters and three dive bombers.

Defending positions were strengthened. One of these was along the low Lunga Ridge, running from about a mile south of the main runway on Henderson Field about 1,000 yards southward toward the mountains. Coral hills, cut into a maze by ravines and jungle growth, made it a difficult position to hold with the limited forces at General Vandegrift's disposal. The defense was entrusted largely to Edson's Raiders, the First Raider and First Parachute Battalions, which had had no rest since the day the invasion started.

At 9:00 P.M. on September 12, an enemy plane dropped flares over Henderson Field. Half an hour later cruisers and destroyers opened their shelling. Through the noise of the bombardment could be heard the chugging of landing craft as the Japanese threw men ashore. The Marines had intended to open the attack themselves the next morning, but the enemy moved first. As soon as the bombardment ended, strong Japanese groups started pushing through the lines along the Ridge. Groups infiltrated and opened fire on the Marines from the rear. Then the Japanese launched a frontal attack which overran some of the advanced positions and cut off many of our men.

On the morning of the thirteenth only 400 men held the Marine line of about 1,800 yards, and there were unprotected spaces of 100 yards separating platoon strong points.

At about 10:30 at night, nearly 2,000 Japanese assaulted the 300 Marines holding the center of the Ridge. The situation was exceedingly black as enemy warships added their fire to that of the mortars pounding the thin Marine line. Then our artillery swung its full weight against the Japanese. Batteries of 75-mm. pack howitzers and 105's had been brought into position and laid down a powerful curtain of steel that barely passed over the Americans' heads into the enemy.

Colonel Edson re-formed his lines under the protection of the barrage, and at 2:30 on the morning of the fourteenth the enemy stopped fighting. The Japanese employed the pause to push patrols around the Marine flanks and into the rear from which at 4:30 they laid down mortar and machine-gun fire. The defenders held firm. At 5:15 the enemy pressure was broken.

The only real offensive action started by the enemy against the Marines during the entire Guadalcanal campaign had failed.

In a little more than a month of valorous defense three Marine pilots had become aces and two squadron leaders had been awarded the Medal of Honor. On September 22 all fighters from the three services were placed under the single command of Colonel William J. Wallace and all bombers under Lieutenant Colonel Cooley. By the end of the month Henderson Field planes had shot down 171 enemy aircraft, a record never equaled in any theater by so small a force fighting under such adverse conditions.

Operations were resumed against the Matanikau area. Marine commanders learned that the enemy not only had much greater strength

For the Job Ahead

An armada of LST's pours Army equipment ashore on Leyte Island. Note the causeways leading from the beach to the ships.

OFFICIAL U. S. NAVY PHOTOGRAPH

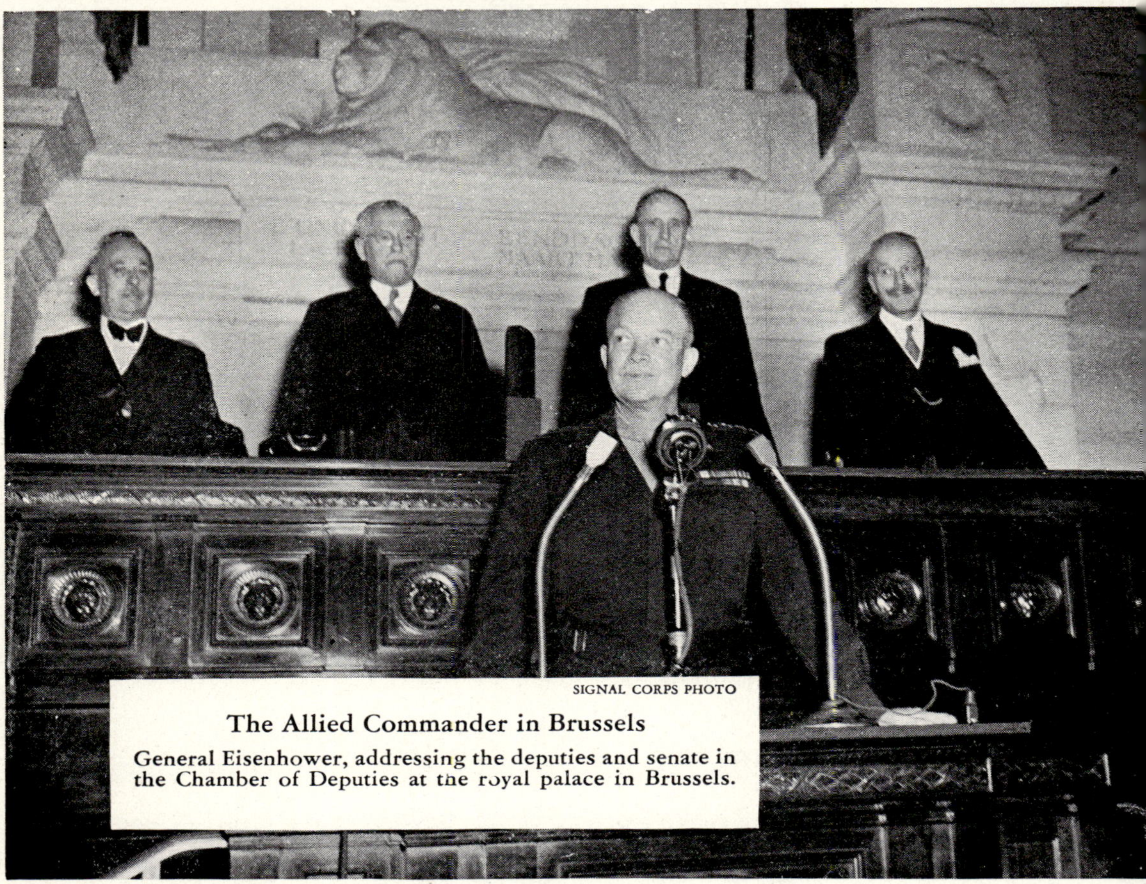

SIGNAL CORPS PHOTO

The Allied Commander in Brussels

General Eisenhower, addressing the deputies and senate in the Chamber of Deputies at the royal palace in Brussels.

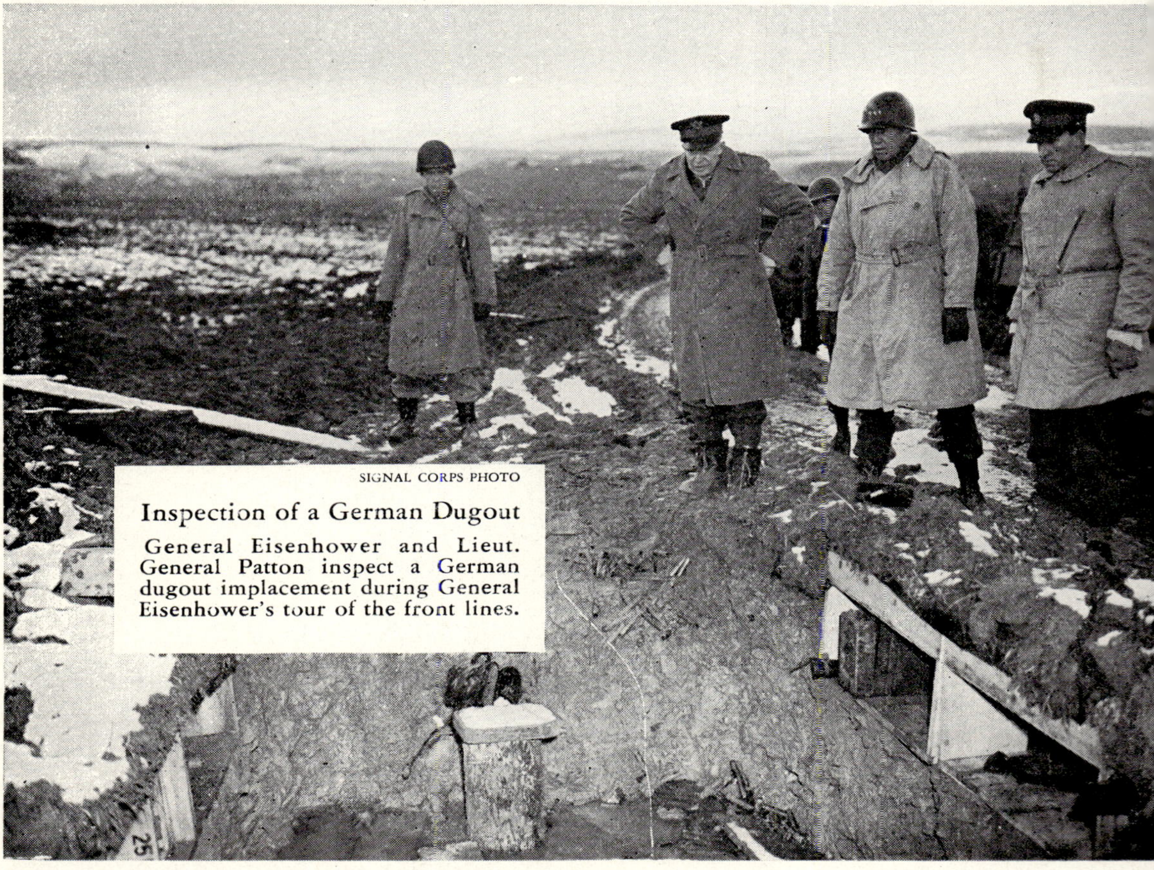

SIGNAL CORPS PHOTO

Inspection of a German Dugout

General Eisenhower and Lieut. General Patton inspect a German dugout implacement during General Eisenhower's tour of the front lines.

BRITISH OFFICIAL PHOTO

British Force Enters Salonika

Partisan troops of E. L. A. S. marching with Allied flags to greet the British troops landing in Salonika harbor.

PRESS ASSOCIATION, INC.

The Long March

German prisoners, captured by British and Canadian troops in northwestern France, are marched along to a prisoner-of-war camp under escort of jeep riding troopers.

Hitler Sadly Surveys Ravages of War
This German film captured by the U. S. Army Signal Corps on the Western front shows the Nazi leader looking at the damage done to his homeland.

there but that he was trying to secure positions on the east bank of the Matanikau River for artillery with which to shell Henderson Field.

Air raids continued by day and landing of enemy reinforcements kept up through the nights. There was no longer possibility of delay if the Matanikau situation were to be cleaned up. On October 7, strong detachments of Marines went into position for a three-day battle that raged on the eigth, ninth, and tenth. Fierce, wild fighting, in jungle thickness and dark of night, was incessant. Both sides had elements behind the other's front. When the scramble was over the Marines had wiped out the enemy's bridgehead on the east bank of the Matanikau.

Just after noon on October 11 in a wide-circling air battle over Henderson Field, some of our planes spotted an enemy force of two light cruisers and six destroyers 200 miles out—headed for Guadalcanal.

Admiral Ghormley had regrouped his naval strength and disposed his ships in three formations. One was built around the carrier *Hornet*, west of Guadalcanal; a second, including the new battleship *Washington*, was east of Malaita Island (itself east of Florida Island); and the third, under Rear Admiral Norman Scott, was held in readiness south of Guadalcanal. This force had the heavy cruisers *San Francisco* and *Salt Lake City*, the light cruisers *Boise* and *Helena*, and the destroyers *Buchanan, Duncan, Farenholt, Laffey*, and *McCalla*.

As soon as Admiral Scott received the flash that the enemy forces were in the "slot" between Choiseul and the New Georgia group of islands, he headed north at full speed and rounded Cape Esperance, at the northern tip of Guadalcanal, about 10:00 P.M. Just before midnight the enemy nosed into range. The American ships opened up with all guns. The Japanese were so surprised that they did not return the fire for nearly ten minutes. In less than five minutes four enemy ships had been blown out of the water and two more put out of action by the *Helena* and the *Boise*, while the *Farenholt*, the *Duncan*, and the *Buchanan* each drove torpedoes into enemy cruisers. The *Buchanan* also had wrecked an enemy destroyer by gun fire and set an unidentified ship, probably a transport, ablaze.

The Japanese finally opened fire. The *Boise*, one of our light ships, found herself battling it out with a heavy cruiser which soon burst into flames. The *Boise* took an enemy 8-incher amidships but was still very much in action. The *Salt Lake City* ripped an enemy auxiliary vessel and destroyer. Admiral Scott, finding no more targets within sight, halted firing to rectify his formation.

The heavy cruisers and the *Helena* then reopened the engagement. They were soon joined by the *Boise* which had brought her fires under control. But the *Boise* was hit again and had to retire. The *Salt Lake City* and the *San Francisco* concentrated upon a Japanese heavy cruiser until the enemy broke off the engagement. In this purely naval engagement, fought between Savo Island and Guadalcanal, our defeat in the first battle two months before was thoroughly avenged. Four Japanese cruisers and four destroyers were sunk, another destroyer probably sunk, and four cruisers damaged. Other enemy ships were also hit, some so badly that they subsequently went to the bottom. The destroyer *Duncan* sank off the island in the morning, our only ship to fall to enemy fire in that stirring battle of Cape Esperance. When daylight came on the morning of October 12, Henderson Field dive bombers took off after the enemy cripples and sent a cruiser to the bottom, leaving another cruiser and a destroyer in dire straits. At noon on the thirteenth the Japanese attacked Henderson Field in revenge.

The thirteenth of October brought us good news: two American transports under heavy convoy came in with reinforcements. These were the 164th United States Infantry under Colonel B. E. Moore, the first Army troops to reach Guadalcanal. The men were mainly National Guard units from North Dakota and several states in the midwestern area who had been mustered into the regular army. Immediately, they took up positions in the defense perimeter, relieving Marine contingents who were rushed to the Matanikau sector.

A new threat now loomed. Six enemy transports, escorted by eight destroyers, had picked up their supporting force of one battleship, three cruisers, and four more destroyers on the run to Guadalcanal. At 4:00 P.M. the enemy was only 180 miles away. Our few planes made the long run, braved fierce antiaircraft fire, harried the approaching ships and scored several hits, but they were too few for so many. At two o'clock on the morning of the fifteenth, five of the transports started to unload between Kokumbona and Cape Esperance while the warships bombarded the American positions.

Lieutenant William L. Woodruff, in charge of maintenance for the scout bombers, worked with his ground crews for seventy-two hours without rest, under shelling and bombing, to recondition the damaged planes and hour by hour put more aircraft into action. Every plane that could leave the ground, even General Vandegrift's slow, ponderous Catalina flying boat, was sent after the enemy. Flying Fortresses from Espiritu Santo arrived at noon in response to pleas for immediate assistance, and six new dive bombers landed on Henderson Field during the afternoon. This tragically small, heterogeneous group of American planes sank all the enemy transports, but not until after the men had been landed. Then the aircraft turned their attention to strafing the Japanese beach positions.

When the day ended, there was no more aviation gas on Henderson Field. A few hidden drums were retrieved, the tanks of damaged planes were drained dry, two hundred drums were ferried under cover of night from Tulagi. The destroyer *MacFarland* came in the next day, October 16, with several thousand gallons, but before she could get more than a few hundred drums ashore was attacked by Japanese bombers, damaged, and towed to safety in Tulagi Harbor. A shuttle service was established between Guadalcanal and other American bases, each plane ferrying in a few drums. The destroyer *Meredith* was sunk at sea while towing a barge loaded with gasoline. Other destroyers ran the gantlet with their decks crammed with gas drums.

The lack of naval support proved puzzling to the Marines, who began to feel that they had been more or less deserted. But there were good reasons why our warships were not in evidence for about two weeks after the Battle of Cape Esperance. Enemy submarines and aircraft poured increased pressure upon our ships at sea simultaneously with the stepped-up attacks on Henderson Field. In addition to the loss of the *Meredith,* the heavy cruiser *Chester* was put out of action by a submarine torpedo. Behind the fighting areas reinforcements were added. The damaged *Enterprise* had been restored to combat efficiency and the new battleship *South Dakota* was added to the fleet. The enlarged force was divided into two parts: one was built around the battleship *Washington,* with Rear Admiral W. A. Lee, Jr., in command; the other, consisting of two carriers, one battleship, three heavy cruisers, three antiaircraft light cruisers, and fourteen destroyers, was under Rear Admiral T. C. Kinkaid. The entire fleet, on October 18, was placed under the command of Admiral Halsey, the hero of the Gilberts-Marshalls raid in the previous spring. Admiral Halsey replaced Admiral Ghormley.

On October 23 the Japanese opened their terrific battle for the recapture of Henderson Field. The enemy started his campaign by launching a holding attack along the coast to the west, with the main effort designed as a wide enveloping movement against the southern sector. The Japanese had planned well. They had cut trails through the jungle west and south of the Marine positions, over which the reinforcements landed during the previous weeks were pushed into their posts. Lieutenant General Maruyama commanded the Sendai, or Second Division, a force of Imperial Japanese Army veterans who had never known defeat in China, Malaya, the Philippines, and Java. It was the cream of the enemy crop that was sent against the small group of Marine-Army defenders. General Vandegrift left for South Pacific Headquarters that morning for conferences, and the command was turned over to Brigadier General William H. Rupertus.

Big guns concentrated on the Marine positions forced abandonment of the naval operating base at Kukum, but Marine artillery laid down 6,000 rounds upon enemy infantry behind the tanks near Point Cruz, killing more than 600 Japanese soldiers who had tried vainly to form into attacking groups. The enemy attempt to cross the Matanikau and to roll back the coastal positions failed.

Sunday, October 25, was a hard day on Guadalcanal. Japanese planes came over in such frequent waves that the men were in their shelters most of the day, giving it the name of "Dugout Sunday." Heavy rain since the opening of the Japanese attack had made Henderson Field a quagmire from which it was well-nigh impossible to take off. Japanese destroyers sailed boldly into Guadalcanal waters, sank several small ships, and pounded shore positions. Another enemy convoy, with several warships and transports, was speedily approaching the battle area. Only a dozen Avenger dive bombers were in operating condition on Henderson Field and General Brett was able to dig up only three more, plus seven fighters, as reinforcements. Nevertheless, when the day was over that dauntless little American air force had shot down seventeen Zeros and five Japanese bombers besides having scored heavy hits on two cruisers in the convoy. Two of our Wildcats were lost.

That night the fighting broke out again around Henderson Field. Despite the ferocity of the Japanese attacks all lines held. After a day of comparative quiet the battle was resumed on the night of the twenty-sixth. But the enemy charges were unmistakably weaker. When daylight came the battle was over except for some sporadic outbursts during the following night. The famous Sendai Division had suffered its first defeat. Henderson Field had been retained and the Japanese were never again able to launch a serious attack against the airfield.

The Battle for Henderson Field was a grim, bloody struggle characterized by hand-to-hand fighting and deeds of individual and platoon valor that will live in Marine Corps and army history.

NAVAL BATTLES AT THE "DEAD END" IN THE SOUTHWEST PACIFIC

THE American Navy, with its air fleets and Marines, carried the brunt of the war in the Southwest Pacific until the arrival of the invading armies. It was a titanic task to build armies figuratively overnight and to transport them overseas to battle zones.

While the struggle was being waged on Guadalcanal, along the Solomons, and in New Guinea, the navy was scoring victories in daring sea battles. On the morning of October 26, 1942, another conflict was shaping off Santa Cruz Island where Japanese ships were standing as "watch dogs" to stop any transports on their way from America to Australia. Patrol planes of Admiral Halsey's fleet spotted three enemy forces north of Santa Cruz. While our carrier planes were pursuing the enemy, 135 Japanese aircraft swooped down on the American ships. The *South Dakota* and the *Washington* and several destroyers covered the *Enterprise,* while the antiaircraft cruisers *Atlanta* and *Juneau* teamed with the remaining cruisers to protect the *Hornet*—the "Shangri-la" from which the Doolittle raiders had attacked Tokyo.

One bomb caught the *Hornet* in a vulnerable spot, and she was soon afire. A Japanese "suicide bomber" pilot drove his burning plane into the carrier's stack, exploding his unreleased bombs over the signal bridge. Torpedo planes attacked at the same time. The blazing, crippled carrier dodged fourteen of the missiles, but two of them entered her vitals, stopping all power and communications. Three more high-altitude bombs crashed on the *Hornet's* deck, and a second "suicide bomber" smashed into the helpless craft. The attack lasted eleven minutes. All but seven of the Japanese planes had been destroyed—but the *Hornet,* listing heavily, lay dead in the water, fires raging on board. Wounded personnel were quickly removed by destroyers, the fires were extinguished in half an hour, and the *Hornet* was taken in tow by the *Northampton.* But the Japs revenged the first bombing of Tokyo. That afternoon they caught up with the *Hornet* again. Abandoned and sunk by our own fire, the *Hornet* went down.

When the Battle of the Santa Cruz Islands ended, the score stood—Japanese: a battleship of the *Kongo* class, three carriers and five cruisers damaged, some so severely that they probably never made shore; at least 150 planes destroyed; American: the *Hornet* and the *Porter* sunk, the *Smith* badly damaged, and superficial damage done to the *Enterprise* and the *South Dakota.* Four Japanese air groups had been cut to pieces. While our carrier strength was again dangerously low, the strategic result was another victory for the United States Navy.

So precarious was the American hold on Guadalcanal that there was no time to lose in resting the men who had been under fire, attack, and mental punishment for nearly three months.

The First Marine Division, reinforced, had suffered severely under strain of bombing, shelling, and battle, plus the heavy toll of disease. There was also a serious shortage of ammunition. General Vandegrift decided that even under these handicaps the "calculated risk" made it imperative to renew the Matanikau drive in order to remove Henderson Field from enemy artillery range and the threat of a new assault.

The Marine offensive began at dawn on November 1 and progressed according to plan except at Point Cruz where skilfully emplaced machine and antitank guns delayed the advance. This Japanese strong point was by-passed, to be encircled and eliminated later. For two days the Marines advanced, inflicting heavy casualties upon the Japanese, overrunning enemy positions and capturing a large amount of equipment, including medium artillery.

Just as the campaign was beginning to gain real momentum, a new crisis arose. A Marine detachment had been sent out on the first of November as a precautionary move toward Koli Point to prevent any landing the Japanese might attempt east of the airfield. At 10:30 that night a Japanese cruiser, a destroyer, and a small troopship pulled into the bay between the Malimbiu and Metapona rivers below Koli Point and began to disgorge troops.

At dawn on the morning of November 3, a Japanese patrol stumbled upon a Marine outpost. The firing disclosed to the Japanese for the first time that a reception committee was waiting. Lieutenant Colonel H. H. Hanneken, in command of the Second Marine Battalion, laid down a heavy barrage from his 81-mm. mortars upon the Japanese beachhead. A breakdown of the radio prevented Colonel Hanneken from notifying the Command Post of the new landing so that he was left alone with his few men to hold off an overwhelmingly superior enemy force backed up by naval guns.

It was not until 2:45 that afternoon that Headquarters knew the enemy had landed; the field radio had finally been repaired. Henderson Field immediately went into action. Two Marine and two Army battalions were dispatched to the Malimbiu, with General Rupertus in command of the Eastern Front. Artillery was moved into position. In the middle of this crisis word was received that a large American convoy would arrive the next day. Men were needed to help unload the ships; these were the same men who were so desperately required at the front. The convoy sailed in and immediately landed the Eighth Marines under Colonel R. H. Jeschke.

Encirclement of the enemy's new beachhead was carried out efficiently and expeditiously. General Rupertus was so ill with a tropical fever that he had to be returned to Headquarters, and Brigadier General E. D. Sebree, of the Army, took command. The final push began on November 10. Within twenty-four hours the beach was cleared of all Japanese except several hundred dead. About as many more had filtered through the jungle to become a source of annoyance until exterminated by Carlson's Raiders some time later. Our casualties were forty dead and 120 wounded.

Another large-scale Japanese move against Guadalcanal seemed so imminent that during the afternoon of November 11 the western lines were withdrawn again to the east bank of the Matanikau.

Daylight raiders appeared over Henderson Field for the first time in a week on November 11, Armistice Day. They also attacked supply ships unloading off Lunga Lagoon, the transport *Zeilin* being damaged. The enemy lost seventeen planes; we lost seven. Rear Admiral Norman Scott withdrew with the escort vessels to Indispensable Strait for the night. The next day Rear Admirals R. K. Turner and D. J. Callaghan shepherded another convoy into Guadalcanal, unloading two army battalions and a Marine contingent.

During November 12, scout planes located three strong enemy naval groups descending upon Guadalcanal from the northwest. Admiral Turner withdrew with the transports and cargo vessels after having assigned two heavy, one light, and two antiaircraft cruisers and eight destroyers to Admiral Callaghan. His purpose was to fight a delaying action until Admiral Kinkaid could intercept the Japanese landing forces with his heavy ships.

Admiral Callaghan, who, before returning to active service at his own request, had been President Roosevelt's naval aide, escorted the transport group clear of the impending battle area and then returned shortly after midnight through Lengo Channel to start a search of the Savo Island area. His ships were stretched out in a single column, four destroyers in the van, four more at the rear, and the five cruisers in the center. Plowing through the pitch-black night the American ships almost ran into four Japanese naval groups. At 1:30 on the morning of November 13, "Louis the Louse"' had droned over Henderson Field and had dropped a flare.

When that flare burst, the American ships opened fire. The enemy then switched its searchlights to Admiral Callaghan's ships, and for fifteen minutes a furious, confused battle raged in which it was frequently impossible to distinguish friend from foe. First results were distinctly favorable to the Americans. In less than a minute one enemy ship at the right was blown out of the water; two enemy cruisers on the left burst into flames. Other Japanese ships quickly took fire. The

Atlanta sank a destroyer crossing her path. Although slightly damaged herself, the *Atlanta* concentrated upon an enemy cruiser until a torpedo jammed her rudder and cut off all power. While circling aimlessly in the midst of bursting ammunition, she was battered by a heavy cruiser; one shell killed Admiral Scott and many of the men.

A few minutes later Admiral Callaghan's cruiser *San Francisco* was fighting it out with a battleship of the *Kongo* class in the center of the enemy group. The destroyers *Laffey* and *Cushing* rushed to the aid of the *San Francisco* and pumped torpedoes into the Japanese battleship. The *Laffey*, hit by a torpedo, blew up. Gunfire put the *Cushing* out of action. The destroyer *Barton* was sent to the bottom before she could launch her torpedoes, but the *O'Bannon* closed with the battleship and scored several topedo hits. The cruiser *Portland,* although carrying an enemy torpedo herself, wrecked a destroyer. The *Juneau,* having lost all fire control, retired from the action.

Admiral Callaghan radioed: "We want the big ones!" While waiting for the *South Dakota* and the *Washington* to arrive, he concentrated his fire with that of the *Portland* on the Jap battleship. An enemy cruiser rushed in on the *San Francisco* and was taken under fire by the *Helena*—but not until after a Japanese shell had burst on the *San Francisco*'s bridge where Admiral Callaghan was standing. He was killed instantly. With him at that moment was Captain Cassin Young, the ship's commanding officer, to whom also death came, as well as to many other officers and men. The ship's guns continued to fire. Before the *San Francisco* was put out of action, she sank another destroyer.

At the end of those fifteen minutes only the destroyers *Aaron Ward, Monssen,* and *Fletcher* remained. The *Laffey* and the *Barton* were gone; the *Cushing* was dead in the water; the *Sterrett* and the *O'Bannon* were damaged; the *Atlanta* was burning; the *San Francisco* and the *Portland* were badly holed; the *Juneau* had been forced to retire, and the *Helena* had received some minor damage.

The three undamaged destroyers continued the unequal struggle for nine minutes longer, scoring shell and torpedo hits on Jap cruisers and destroyers. Then the *Monssen* was damaged and had to be abandoned. The *Sterrett,* badly crippled by gunfire, was compelled to retire. That left the *Fletcher* alone. She fired a torpedo into an enemy cruiser and scurried from the scene. The Japanese continued to fire upon their own men in the dark.

When the damaged American ships met in the morning, the *Portland* saw a Japanese battleship circling slowly northwest of Savo Island with a cruiser standing by. The *Enterprise* launched a flight of torpedo-bombers which sent three missiles into the injured battleship. All day long land-based planes from Henderson Field and Espiritu Santo maintained the attack, shooting down a dozen Zeros which were trying to

Naval Battles in Southwest Pacific

protect the battleship, and pounding the destroyers that were attempting to screen the injured craft. Fifteen bombs and torpedoes left the Japanese battleship a helpless hulk at dusk, abandoned by her crew.

The *Portland,* still turning in circles, caught sight of an enemy destroyer and sank her. The *Cushing* and the *Monssen* finally went down, and during the afternoon the *Atlanta* was abandoned and sunk. A short time later a Japanese submarine caught the *Juneau* with two torpedoes, sinking it almost immediately, with heavy losses.

At 10:30 A.M., on November 14, a Japanese invasion force was spotted moving down from New Georgia and Santa Isabel islands. A battleship, two heavy cruisers, and four destroyers were less than 150 miles from Guadalcanal. Later six more destroyers and twelve transports and cargo ships joined the battle fleet; 140 miles to the west was another column of two light cruisers and five destroyers. Planes shuttled to and from Henderson Field with orders to "hit the transports." The transports were hit, picked off with deadly precision one after another. The escorting Jap warships fled to save their own hulls. When the last flight was made in the failing twilight, five of the transports had been sunk, three were burning and dead in the water, two of the remaining four were nursing bomb wounds. The invasion force had been routed in one of the most notable victories that was ever scored by land-based planes.

Admiral Lee had been unable to bring his heavy naval force, built around the battleships *Washington* and *South Dakota* and the limping carrier *Enterprise,* into the battle area before early evening on the fourteenth. He ordered an immediate search for the enemy with the intention of intercepting and destroying its warships and transports. Contact was made shortly after midnight with an enemy force north of Savo Island and headed east. The *Washington* immediately sent salvos into the lead ship. The *South Dakota* pursued the third. Both targets quickly disappeared into the Pacific Ocean. Simultaneously, four of our destroyers plowed into a group of about ten enemy ships which also came under fire of the battleships' medium guns after the original targets had been sunk. The *Preston* was sunk by gunfire; the *Walke* was abandoned and sank after taking torpedoes and shells; the *Benham* was crippled by a torpedo, and the *Gwin* suffered so much damage that she was compelled to retire.

The Battle of Guadalcanal came to a close when *Enterprise* fighters from Henderson Field wiped out a flight of twelve Zeros. The hard-fought American victory was the greatest in the war up to this time. The Japanese had lost twenty-eight ships which had been sunk, and eight damaged: two battleships, eight cruisers, six destroyers, eight transports, and four cargo ships. Two of our light cruisers and seven destroyers had been sunk, several were damaged, but subsequently repaired and restored to action. Over 5,000 Japanese troops were drowned, never to reach Guadalcanal.

The crisis on Guadalcanal was over. Our own strength began to increase so that danger never again could threaten seriously.

The tide had turned on New Guinea also. The heavily outnumbered Australian units, after having stopped the Japanese at Ioribaiwa Ridge, thirty-two miles from Port Moresby, started to push the enemy back. Early in October the bush soldiers scrambled up the precipitous 1,200-foot rise to advance six miles to Efogi, the entrance to the passes through the Owen Stanley Mountains, and Myola Lakes.

While the Australians were pushing the Japanese back, the 2nd Battalion of the 126th Infantry Regiment of the United States' 32nd Division was engaged in one of the greatest marches in military history. The men had been flown and ferried to Port Moresby during September when the Japanese advance was at its height. The road to Kapa Kapa, along the south coast of Papua, was improved. The battalion, commanded by Lieutenant Colonel Henry A. Geerds, was moved there and ordered to Juare in the mountains to protect the Australian right flank. A little later orders came to traverse the entire width of New Guinea by foot to the Buna-Gona area.

On October 14 the 2nd Battalion, consisting of 849 men, stripped to bare essentials, had started its march. They wore herringbone fatigue suits dyed a mottled jungle green, and the army's "fisherman's hats," and they carried head nets for protection against mosquitoes and poisonous insects. They wore no underwear; their only protection against the mountain cold was a woolen shirt or field jacket. Mess kits consisted of a single spoon with which to eat their iron rations and whatever else they might snare. They carried spare woolen socks, vitamin tablets, quinine, salt pills, foot powder, iodine, adhesive tape, axes, machetes, one blanket each, and two shelter halves with a mosquito bar for every three men. The only weapons the men carried were sidearms and a few tommy guns. It was only 103 miles by air to Buna, but over the mountains and through the jungles it was nearly 300 miles. Native carriers had cached some supplies along the trail.

The wild trail was so narrow that the men had to walk single file. Incessant rains made the mud knee-deep and the ravines raging torrents, so that eight miles forward became a hard day's march. Men quickly developed sore feet, bruises, serious injuries, and fever. Malnutrition began to claim its victims. Some of the sick and injured were evacuated, but others had to be carried and many died. By October 23, advance patrols reached nine miles south of Wairope, on the flank of the retreating Japanese; by November 3, the day the Australians recaptured Kokoda, the battalion came into Juare. It was a haggard-looking outfit, for fatigue suits were torn and muddy, and faces were gaunt and bearded. Blankets, raincoats, mosquito bars had been discarded to lighten weight. Poisonous plants and leeches had covered the men with painful sores.

Three days later the battalion had advanced a few more miles and reached Natunga, a squalid native village where the men rested for ten days. The march was then resumed to Bofu, where the 2nd Battalion joined the rest of the 126th Regiment in mid-November, while the Battle of Guadalcanal was raging, and prepared to go into the joint Australian-American campaign against Buna and Gona.

By November 14, the Japs had been pushed back to the coast, and four days later the joint Australian-American operation, in which the 2nd Battalion participated, had pinned the Japanese down in a fifteen-mile strip between Buna and Gona. This was followed by a slow process of systematic extermination.

Back on Guadalcanal sporadic action continued after the disastrous Japanese defeat on November 13-15. The 2nd Raider Battalion, under Lieutenant Colonel Evans F. Carlson, which had become famous as "Carlson's Raiders," had landed at Aola on November 4.

The exploits of "Carlson's Raiders" read like fiction. Tramping 150 miles through the jungle in a month, with only their light arms, they killed more than 500 Japanese, destroyed or captured large stores of food, drugs, and ammunition, and cleared a vast area of enemy soldiers. The "Raiders" lost seventeen killed, with an equal number wounded. Other patrols turned in equally one-sided scores whenever they went out. Aside from these expeditions, Guadalcanal was relatively quiet.

On November 30, while crossing Savo sound, the Americans ran into seven enemy ships in Lengo Channel, off the north coast of Guadalcanal. The *Minneapolis,* Admiral Wright's flagship, which was commanded by Captain Charles E. Rosendahl, was to the rear of four destroyers; then followed the other cruisers and the two remaining destroyers. For twenty minutes the fight raged furiously, with a hitherto undetected force of Japanese closing in behind the Americans from Cape Esperance. When the shooting was over, the Japanese had lost two large cruisers, four destroyers, two transports, and a cargo ship—nine more vessels under the waters of Iron Bottom Bay. The *Northampton* was torpedoed, and was so badly damaged that she sank after being abandoned. The *Minneapolis,* the *New Orleans,* and the *Pensacola* were also badly crippled.

The effect of the engagement, known as the Battle of Tassafaronga or the Battle of Lunga Point, was to break up a Japanese reinforcement attempt—the last one ever made. Our losses were severe, but the results were of great importance. After losing the fifth round of the fight in Guadalcanal waters, the Japanese threw the "Tokyo Express" into reverse and began evacuating their forces.

On December 9, the Marines reëmbarked and left Guadalcanal in the firm possession of United States Army troops. General Vandegrift relinquished his command to Major General Alexander M. Patch who was to appear in Europe less than two years later at the head of a United Nations force invading southern France.

The Marines had spent the record time of five months without relief on Guadalcanal and, when they left, only 4,000 Japanese remained on the island. When the army completed its work, there were none. The enemy had lost 40,000 men in a desperate, futile attempt to regain Guadalcanal, for the Japanese commanders well knew that the fate of the war in the Pacific hung in the balance. Guadalcanal natives, in two months, built a chapel of thatch and native wood as a memorial to the fallen Americans. In that chapel rest 1,600 American boys.

Henderson Field planes began to lay bombs heavily upon Japanese bases on surrounding islands: Buin, on Bougainville; Munda, on New Georgia; Lae and Salamaua, on New Guinea (as well as Buna and Gona); and Rabaul, on New Britain.

The fighting on New Guinea reached a climax at about the same time the Marines left Guadalcanal. General MacArthur arrived in the Buna-Gona area to direct the campaign in person. At Gona the Australians caught the Japanese making a sudden rush and mowed them down with machine-gun fire. Mixing with the enemy in hand-to-hand fighting, they worked their way into the enemy positions where they annihilated the Japanese. Gona fell on December 9, 1942.

The enemy was much more cautious at Buna, and remained on the defensive; so the Americans pressed in on both flanks, launched a drive through the center, dividing the Japanese in half. This breach was widened, and on December 14 Buna Village was captured in the first American Army victory since MacArthur had opened his land offensive.

After the fall of the village, the enemy still held Buna Mission and its two clearings used by the Japanese as airfields. The Japanese, fighting with that fanaticism so characteristic of the Mikado's troops, had to be routed from every point of land, from under every log-covered dugout. It was a slow process of strangulation during which the enemy was pushed into a nest of bunkers and foxholes running a mile along the coast and inland only about 600 yards. The Japs struggled desperately against our tanks, infantry, flame-throwers, and grenades, causing heavy American casualties before the ruins of Buna Mission fell into our hands on January 2.

The only point now left in enemy hands was Sanananda Point, three and one-half miles northwest of Buna on the way to Gona.

The crucial six months ended with Guadalcanal a United Nations base; Port Moresby firmly held; and Australia relieved of the threat of invasion.

AMERICANS LAND IN NORTH AFRICA—FIRST GREAT ALLIED OFFENSIVE

DAWN of November 8, 1942, broke upon a mighty spectacle. Eight hundred and fifty ships passed through the Strait of Gibraltar into the Mediterranean. The Americans landed during the night in North Africa.

For the first time in this war it was the Allies who were on the offensive. They had swung at last into the attack. Ships, guns, and huge armies of the United States and the British Empire, commanded by a staff of brilliant minds of both countries, were working in complete coördination. Within seventy-six hours they had won 1,300 miles of the coasts of North Africa, advancing from Algiers and Morocco. Eisenhower, aided by the British, had outwitted Hitler and Mussolini.

Great as was this military and naval feat, it was but the beginning of greater invasions to come. The Axis was taken by complete surprise. It had expected the first attack to come from across the English Channel and strike directly at the European continent.

At their June conference in the White House, Mr. Churchill and President Roosevelt were shocked, on a Sunday morning, to learn that the now-surrounded and outnumbered garrison of Tobruk on the Libyan coast had at last fallen to the Germans and Italians sweeping down once more to overrun the delta of the Nile. What the President and the Prime Minister heard that Sunday morning served only to strengthen their own conviction, shared and encouraged by their military and diplomatic advisers, that the Allies' first real blow in the European theater must be struck at French North Africa. That decision had already been reached. The disaster in Libya served to confirm it.

An invasion in force there would end the threat to South America from Dakar, whose excellent port facilities, still nominally in the hands of the Vichy Government, might be seized by the Germans and Italians at any time. Further, it would reopen the Mediterranean to Allied warships and merchantmen, which now had to reach Egypt and the Middle East by the long voyage around the Cape of Good Hope, through the Indian Ocean, and up the Red Sea. It would end any threat to Gibraltar from the south.

Should the German drive into Egypt triumph, the Allies would lose their last hold on the Mediterranean. The Suez Canal would be lost. All the Middle East, so vital strategically and economically to the prosecution of the war, would be at the mercy of the Germans and the Italians. And beyond the Middle East lay India—to the north, Russia, which would be in mortal danger of a new invasion from the rear. A successful Allied invasion of North Africa would put an end to all these perils.

Some of the safeguards for this grand invasion that was worked out to the last detail in June of 1942 had been made, quite fortuitously, long before. One of these was the establishment of the American consular "listening-post" in Dakar in 1940, when America was very far indeed from an active rôle in the war. The step had been taken to keep America out of war; it now contributed enormously to her success when she was a belligerent.

In maintaining diplomatic relations with Vichy, the United States had been enabled to act for the United Nations by keeping in France itself not only an Ambassador and consuls but military and naval attachés. These officials could quite honorably and openly learn much of the French strength and its disposition; the diplomats could cautiously sound out the Vichy régime on the possibility of its coöperating with an Allied force invading Africa. Above all, they could, as the representatives of a friendly Power, move more or less freely within Vichy's territory, which included North Africa. Thus it was possible, long before the Washington parley, for Robert D. Murphy, the counselor of the American Embassy in Vichy, to make visits to North Africa without exciting the slightest suspicion in either the French or the Germans and Italians. Some time before the joint Anglo-American blow was struck, Murphy removed permanently to North Africa and began the cautious probing that resulted in the fullest coöperation of many Frenchmen with the invading forces. It was shortly after this that General Mark W. Clark cramped his long body into a British submarine and traveled under the sea into Algerian waters. On the night agreed, the submarine surfaced at a point previously set. Its officers watched anxiously for the little light that was supposed to shine for them from the coast.

The Commandos stayed with the rubber rafts. The General and his party made their way up the beach in the darkness until they were met by the man who was waiting for them. Identities established, he conducted them to a country house where the French officers and officials with whom the General was to confer were waiting. One of these was Charles Brunel, the De Gaullist Mayor of Algiers; others were civilians and army officers.

The Americans and the Frenchmen talked all night, perfecting their plans, differing on details, forecasting the probable reaction of this or that official, the potential resistance to be expected from this or that regiment. Throughout the talks shades were drawn so no light would shine from this lonely house on the shore to excite the suspicion of sentries or curious Germans or Italians. On the return trip the rubber raft nearly capsized, and General Clark, when the wall of water swept over him, lost his trousers. With them went $18,000 that he was carrying for emergency use in Algeria. But the loss was inconsequential compared to what he had achieved in that dark house.

A submarine put into Gibraltar during these tense days after an even more dramatic and mysterious voyage. This was British, but, for the one trip, she was under the command of an American naval officer, Captain Jerrauld Wright, of Washington. Her prize was a French general with five stars: General Henri-Honoré Giraud.

General Giraud had been captured soon after the German breakthrough in the Sedan area. He had been confined for almost two years in the supposedly impregnable fortress of Koenigstein, well within Germany. Eventually, as he had done in the First World War, he had escaped, assisted by friends in France—and, some whispered, in high places in Germany. In any case, the General made his way into Switzerland and then France, where he went to report to Marshal Pétain.

The Germans demanded that he be returned; the Marshal refused. The General himself received the offer of liberty if he would pledge himself not to fight again against Germany; he refused, but he remained free. His only commitment was a promise to Marshal Pétain not to engage in any hostile act against France. American agents had made contact with General Giraud and proposed that he join the Allies in the invasion of North Africa. After innumerable arguments and demands and reversals, they won his consent. At first he insisted that he must be the supreme commander of all the forces engaged.

General Giraud withdrew, temporarily at least, this demand; but he refused to leave France on a British ship; it must be an American vessel that took him out of his country. No American submarine was immediately available and there was too little time to summon one from another area; speed was essential. At last, after hours of argument, General Giraud compromised: he would go aboard a British vessel provided that it was under American command.

General Eisenhower received the Frenchman with friendship and deference—at this time Eisenhower was still a lieutenant general, outranked by many of his British colleagues. The generals plunged at once into discussion of the great task before them. Once again it seemed as if the Frenchman were going to refuse at the last moment to lend his aid. At last Giraud yielded, receiving the promise that when the French in Africa had joined the Allies he would command all the French forces there.

Out in the Atlantic, the hugest convoy of the war up to this time was racing south, crammed with American and British soldiers who had not the faintest idea where they were bound for, but who knew, and were glad to know, that they were going to see action. Around them steamed a moving wall of warships; above them roared an unending stream of planes. Behind, on a hundred airfields in Britain, the Allies' biggest bombers were being rolled out to take off for flight direct to action. Troop-carrying gliders were being made ready for the biggest airborne operation yet known in history.

As the first American soldiers, Marines, and Rangers rushed from the open prows of their landing-craft onto the shores of French North Africa at a half-dozen points, the voice of President Roosevelt was heard over the radio from the United States. He told his own people that we were landing in Africa to forestall an enemy invasion of those territories. He assured the French that the Allies had absolutely no territorial aspirations but rather pledged themselves to maintain the integrity of French Africa and restore it, liberated, to the Empire.

General Eisenhower broadcast from Gibraltar. He made two proclamations. The first, addressed to the French forces in North Africa, told of his orders forbidding offensive action against them on condition that they refrained from resistance. He urged them in sign of their accord to fly two Tricolors, or a Tricolor and an American flag, by day—and by night to direct a searchlight vertically toward the sky. He ordered all French naval and merchant units to refrain from scuttling their ships and all aviation units not to take off. Disobedience, he warned, would be construed as proof of hostile intent.

The magnitude of the blow paralyzed resistance in the first hours. American landing-craft disgorged division after division. Inland, behind the coast, American bombers and American transports and gliders were swarming down on French airfields, and landing American troops and fliers.

Marshal Pétain immediately sent President Roosevelt a message denouncing "the aggression of your troops against North Africa." A puppet of Hitler, under duress, he ordered his commanders to fight against the Americans. The army and navy commanders in chief under orders from Vichy were General Alphonse-Pierre Juin and Admiral Jean-Francois Darlan.

Admiral Darlan, who had engaged in a triangular rivalry with Marshal Pétain and Pierre Laval for the supreme power in the Vichy régime, was a rabid enemy of Britain and a close friend of Germany, with personal and financial interests in collaborationist circles. His presence in Algiers at the moment of the invasion has never been satisfactorily explained. The pretext was a visit to his son, who was suffering from infantile paralysis, but his supporters have contended that he was in reality coöperating with the Allies.

Algiers was the first city to surrender to the invaders. On November 9, the French troops returned to their garrisons and American patrols took over the city. Outside the great harbor of Casablanca, Allied warships were blazing away in a deadly combat with shore defenses and the guns of the uncompleted battleship *Jean Bart,* lying in the harbor. At Oran, Port Lyautey, and Fedhala the French were fighting fiercely. Two appeals were made for them to join the Allies. One was broadcast from Africa by General Giraud, who had arrived at the advanced headquarters General Eisenhower had already set up in French territory; the other came from London, from General de Gaulle, the leader of the Fighting French. Admiral Darlan, who claimed to be the sole representative of the legal French Government in Africa, was taken prisoner by the Allies.

But Oran was proving a major operation, exceeded only by the battles in Morocco. The harbor defenses refused to yield. The Allies' plan was to land two motorized infantry columns on beaches east and west of the naval base in order later to converge on the city.

Six hundred American soldiers attempted a landing in the harbor. Two American Coast Guard cutters, manned by American and British sailors, steamed in at full speed to crash the harbor and seize the docks for a mass landing by other troops in ships lying outside the range of the defenders' guns. Every weapon in the harbor focused its fire on the two heroic little boats. Shore batteries, a light cruiser, and destroyers poured steel into them at point-blank range and drove them back with heavy casualties.

The main American assault column landed twenty-five miles northeast of its objective, at Arzeu, where the French had a seaplane base. Naval units there offered the feeble resistance of machine guns to the large invading forces, which battled their way ashore and pushed on inland against the streams of tracer bullets.

The battle for Oran was in full swing. Infantry marched ahead toward the village of St. Cloud. Five miles outside the town the columns were stopped by heavy firing from French 75's, machine guns, and well dispersed snipers.

Meanwhile, the American artillery had come up with the troops. Early the next morning it opened a bombardment of the French forces on a hill outside the town. French 75's responded mightily, but the Americans' fire was irresistible. By the middle of the morning American infantrymen were within the village. Their advance was costly. Artillery, mortars, heavy machine guns, and snipers beset them from every side and they had to fight their way from house to house. At midday they were withdrawn to allow their artillery to bombard the village. The bombardment order, however, was canceled and the troops were commanded to by-pass St. Cloud in darkness and capture Oran the following day.

The infantry had split its forces to advance along three converging roads heavily defended by artillery and machine guns. An armored flying column that had worked up behind Oran struck the city.

Two other armored columns pushed northward to a road junction just outside the city. There, with some of the American infantry, they were met by a determined French battalion that offered brief resistance. It was only after many Americans had lost their lives in the African sand that the French gave ground.

This was the last serious opposition to save Oran. At 12:30 P.M. on Tuesday, November 10—the third day of the North African invasion—the air-raid sirens in the naval base wailed the "all clear." Oran was ours! Its people were ecstatic at the Americans' entry. Theirs was to prove only the first and the smallest of the many demonstrations of French loyalty to the Allies that the victorious troops were to meet.

The battle for Morocco was being waged at Port Lyautey, the site of an important airdrome. It was defended by Foreign Legion troops and crack rifle and cavalry battalions of native troops. Americans had landed south of Port Lyautey, near a ridge ten miles from the town that served as a natural fortress. Their objective was to isolate the town and the airdrome from the strong forces at Rabat; but their commander had ordered their fire withheld as long as possible. The French opened fire first, with 150-mm. cannon, 75's, and machine guns emplaced on the height. A continuous blanket of gunfire poured down for two days on the invaders. They could not gain an inch. The French at Rabat had sent out a strong force of tanks and infantry to drive the Americans from their beachhead. Trapped by the withering barrage from the ridge the Americans had to call for help.

They got it—from the land, from the sea, and from the sky. American tanks started down from another landing-head to the north, but they could not hope to arrive in time to save the beleaguered force. Off the coast lay aircraft-carriers whose scout planes were the first to spot the advancing French. They rushed back to their ships and in frenzied haste the armorers fitted instantaneous fuses to the depth bombs that the planes carried for their normal task of destroying submarines. Racing back to the Rabat road, they dived down almost "on the deck" to drop their improvised missiles on the leading French tanks. Enough were destroyed and damaged to block the road. Before the French could clear away the obstacles, their exact position had been reported to the big warships lying out to sea. In a few moments great naval guns were lining shells squarely into the concrete of the roadway and the steel of the tanks. The French withdrew and the firing stopped.

Over the ridge that blocked the advance of the infantry, American dive bombers came roaring down. Fighters and torpedo-planes from the carriers had fast established the Americans' mastery of the air in the sector, destroying or damaging all the fifteen de Woitine fighters that were based at Port Lyautey—and these were the best fighters in the French Air Force. After an hour's work by their pilots, no gun spoke from the ridge and the American soldiers could begin their advance. On the third day—the day when Oran capitulated—Port Lyautey fell.

The fall of Oran had ended all resistance in Algeria. After Port Lyautey's capture, Casablanca was the last remaining major objective. Naval resistance there ceased when the Allies took Port Lyautey. On the same day American tanks entered the outskirts of the city.

In surrendered Algiers the captive Admiral Darlan had begun an exchange of confusing messages with Marshal Pétain in Vichy, who had solemnly proclaimed the rupture of diplomatic relations with the United States—a proclamation that evoked from Secretary of State Cordell Hull the comment that, since American recognition of Vichy had now served its purpose, Washington was completely indifferent to Vichy's attitude toward the North African campaign. Admiral Darlan, claiming to be the heir of the Vichy régime in North Africa, advised Marshal Pétain that he was about to surrender Algeria, Morocco, and Tunisia to the Americans and to coöperate with them.

Pétain replied to the Admiral in a message that completely repudiated him and stripped him of his authority.

Darlan claimed to have not only the approval of the American military authorities but the support of General Noguès in the next step that he took: the formation of a French "command" in North Africa and his own assumption of full responsibility for all French interests there. General Noguès, he said, had transferred to him the powers given to the General by Pétain (what these were was not disclosed). Darlan now became what he called High Commissioner for French North Africa. In this capacity, as well as that of Commander in Chief of the French Fleet under the Vichy régime, he now called on the warships at Toulon to sail for North Africa. The Germans had not occupied the great southern French naval base, but they had completely surrounded it and their planes and light naval vessels were on constant patrol above and outside it. Thus the Admiral's appeal, even when it was implemented by a similar call from General Eisenhower, brought no response.

Three specific steps were taken by President Roosevelt to insure the complete coöperation and the maximum of active assistance from both Frenchmen and natives in Morocco, Algeria, and later in Tunisia. First, the army had prepared detailed handbooks for the soldiers that explained to them the importance of their maintaining respect for Arab customs, such as that of not talking to women, and of dealing with Frenchmen always with the recollection of the traditional friendship of their two countries. President Roosevelt demanded, too, that all political prisoners in North Africa who had favored coöperation with the Allies receive unconditional amnesty. This, the French régime of Admiral Darlan, under the control of the Allies' military command, immediately ordered. As a corollary, the Allies began interning high officials in Algeria who were still agitating on behalf of the Axis. But the third step was the most important from not only the military but the psychological point of view. The President ordered the Lend-Lease Administration to furnish weapons and equipment to the armed forces in North Africa and food, clothing, and other needed supplies to both the forces and the civilians.

As the American and British troops neared the Tunisian border, the Allies' supply services worked feverishly to improvise depots at Bone and Philippeville for seaborne men and equipment, with inland bases for their transfer to the advancing armies. General de Gaulle and the Fighting French had refused to deal with the Admiral's régime. President Roosevelt announced that all arrangements permitting Darlan to continue in power were a temporary expedient dictated by military necessity—the recent "heir" of Marshal Pétain won for the Allies the complete adherence of all that part of French West Africa that had not already joined the Fighting French. Thus the menace of Dakar, the elimination of which was one of the primary objectives of the African campaign, was permanently ended.

Admiral Darlan's self-proclaimed authority extended into Tunisia. French troops there, within a week of the first Allied landings in Algeria and Morocco, had staged an abortive attempt to overthrow the German forces in Tunis. On November 14, for the first time, British and American planes bombed the capital of the protectorate. The vanguard of the British and American army had already crossed the frontier on the coast and in the mountains, but they were yet to meet enemy troops.

As the Americans and British marched on, they were joined by French garrisons in their path, while behind them other French troops were being rearmed as rapidly as possible and trained in the use of American and British weapons. Over these, as well as the air forces and the navy, General Giraud received from Admiral Darlan the supreme command that he had demanded.

Now was the time for General Eisenhower to execute the audacious stroke he had been planning. As the British Eighth Army relentlessly pressed the Germans and Italians back in Libya, Tunisia became increasingly vital to both sides: as an escape for the Germans, as a trap if the Allies got there first. So Eisenhower launched his lightning drive for Tunis and Bizerte, the heart of the protectorate.

It was on November 18, 1942, that the Allies first announced both their entry into Tunisia and the beginning of action. The British First Army was not all British. About one-fourth of its number consisted of

Americans commanded by an American, Major General Charles Ryder. The First Army as a whole was under the command of Lieutenant General Kenneth A. N. Anderson of the British Army, a veteran of Dunkirk whom General Eisenhower appointed to the post because of his tested battle experience against the Germans. Many of the officers and men of the First Army had fought in France and Flanders. General Anderson was classified as a task-force commander. He had working behind him and with him, under General Eisenhower, Major General George S. Patton, Jr., and Major General Lloyd R. Fredenhall, both of the American Army. They commanded task forces in Morocco that maintained order in that area and assured the efficient passage of supplies and reinforcements. For support from the sea he could rely on the tight-lipped, shrewd, gallant Scot, Admiral Sir Andrew Browne Cunningham, who commanded all the Allies' naval forces in the North African theater, assisted by Rear Admiral Henry K. Hewitt of the United States Navy; while Brigadier General James H. Doolittle of the United States Army Air Forces, the hero of the bombing of Tokyo, was in command of the Allies' air forces.

General Anderson was the leader of an attack force; he left to others the concern of protecting bases at Bone, Bougie, and Philippeville against the almost daily bombing by the German Air Force. It was their job to defend and to get the supplies through; it was his to carry the supplies into action. Even before his forces crossed into Tunisia, Allied parachute troops were dropping far in the interior to aid the French battling the Germans in and around Tunis. The Allies faced an increasingly superior force that was getting not only men but even light tanks by air over the relatively short line of communications from Italy and Sicily.

The Allies had already begun to learn the lesson of coördination. Far ahead of the land armies ranged the American Flying Fortresses, pounding the airfields that protected Bizerte and Tunis in an effort to render them useless, while British Spitfires kept close to the advancing troops to protect them against the German dive bombers. The first patrols were easily routed and the Allies were only sixty-five miles outside Bizerte—fifty miles from the Algerian border. The Germans were rapidly securing the rest of the protectorate. They overran Gabès and threatened Sfax, two major ports on the eastern Tunisian coast they would badly need if they were driven out of Tunis.

Late in November the First Army, having gathered sufficient forces, threw its men, guns, tanks, and planes against the little railway town of Medjez-el-Bab, thirty-five miles southwest of Tunis. Medjez-el-Bab not only dominated a vital stretch of railway running from the capital to the interior of the protectorate but was one of the toughest strong points in the enemy's line of defenses outside Tunis.

The moon was fading into the dawn of November 25 when the American armor started to roll, sparked by the words of its commander: "We are going into Tunis." That proud promise was not to be fulfilled for almost six months. But the tanks more than accomplished the task set for them. They smashed the Germans in Medjez while enemy dive bombers pounded relentlessly down at them.

Another force of the First Army was advancing on Bizerte. This group had followed the coast road to Tunisia, whereas the divisions now at Tebourba had crossed the border well inland. The northern force had driven through Tabarca and Tamera and was aiming toward the last important railway junction before Bizerte: Mateur, only twenty air miles from the naval base. While it drove ahead, another equally vital junction was stormed and seized by its comrades to the south: Djedeida, barely ten miles out of Tunis.

This was the first American offensive. They were tough and game. Whatever the odds, or the hardships, they took them in their stride and fought on. They seemed to enjoy and to court danger—disturbed only at the thought of the worries that must beset those at home who loved them.

Their advance was so far ahead of the scheduled progress plotted by the commanders in Algiers that not only supplies but the most necessary equipment were of necessity far behind the front lines. Big American tanks were speeding to both groups of the First Army as fast as the terrain would permit through narrow, hairpin-turned cuts through the mountains and in the flatlands' unimproved roads. Rolling up a hundred miles a day despite their bulk, the impossible highways, and their drivers' unfamiliarity with the country, they had to rely entirely on maps. Ahead of them rolled the great army trucks familiar to every American back home, carrying weapons, ammunition, food, and fuel for other vehicles, including the slower tanks.

Our American boys, with their British cousins, had passed valiantly through their first baptisms of fire and blood. They had shown their steel-courage to the world—a preview of what was to be witnessed on all the world's battlefields as the war developed. Here on the Tunisian borders it was now to be challenged by almost insurmountable obstacles. Eisenhower's military strategy was facing its first crucial test.

EISENHOWER STRATEGY AT GATES OF TUNISIA

THE North African campaign had reached a crucial stage. General Eisenhower and General Anderson, in their audacious enterprise, well knew the penalty of failure. They must now gamble against the weather. They must capture Tunis and Bizerte before the downpours of the rainy season.

If Tunis and Bizerte were not taken before New Year's, the Allied commanders knew, the campaign would drag on throughout the winter while the Germans drew daily reinforcements from the Afrika Korps, already beginning to filter into southern Tunisia from Tripolitania.

Behind the lines, meanwhile, political developments of the utmost importance were taking place. When, late in November, the Germans marched into Toulon, most of the French fleet there had been scuttled by its crews rather than yield to the Germans. A few small craft had made good their escape: two of these, submarines, arrived in the harbor of Algiers on November 30 to join the Allies. They were immediately claimed by Admiral Darlan's régime.

The Admiral, who had proclaimed himself High Commissioner for French North and West Africa and had put himself at the head of what he called the Imperial Council, now assumed a new title. He announced that, since the occupation of the Vichy zone of France had made Marshal Pétain a virtual prisoner, he was becoming Chief of State for North and West Africa.

At the same time, the Allies released the final figures on the cost of the landings in Tunisia. Of all the vessels in the invasion armada, only sixteen were lost. The biggest of these was a small British aircraft carrier, and the others were transports, destroyers, gunboats, and the like. Against this, the Allies could point almost daily to the toll that their submarines were taking in the Mediterranean against enemy shipping that sought to reinforce the German and Italian troops in Tunis and Bizerte.

The Germans were fighting with their backs to the hastily built wall of defenses and were determined not to let this barrier be breached. The battles around Djedeida and Mateur were deadly. On both sides tanks were employed; the ungainly monsters rolled ahead in formation, usually behind cover where it existed, and then fired when they had come to a complete halt. The Germans had the advantage of machines with lower silhouettes, so that they could not be so easily seen by the crews of the Allies' machines, which were thus more vulnerable; and the Germans enjoyed superiority in both armor and armament. Nevertheless, the skill and the determination of the Allied gunners were a match for this material superiority, and every battlefield was marked by the heavy smoke of burning German tanks. In another arm the Allies enjoyed a definitive mastery: their artillery was far better, particularly the American 155-mm. cannon that had the added advantage of great mobility. These were hauled into position at night. As soon as it was light enough for scout planes to give them their range, they started pounding a path through the German lines for the tanks and the infantry.

Germany, however, had one gun that had the complete measure of the Allies' tanks. This was the famous 88-mm. antitank gun that was designed specifically against armor but could also be used as an antiaircraft weapon. It was later to be mounted on the giant of all German tanks: the sixty-two-ton Mark VI "Tiger." American artillery concentrated on these in the enemy's positions. The Germans, who seemed to lack long-range artillery, used dive bombers and strafing fighters as they had done in Europe.

The Allied planes were achieving results that far exceeded, in proportion, the facilities available to them. Long-range Fortresses and the medium Mitchells and Marauders were constantly stepping up the frequency and intensity of their attacks on Tunis and Bizerte, as well as the eastern coastal ports. It was not long before they were ranging as far east as Tripoli. Their coöperation with the Royal Air Force units working with the advancing British Eighth Army was complete.

As the first troops of the Afrika Korps began to filter over the border from Tripolitania, French units under General Giraud, who, in turn, was at the command of Allied Headquarters in Algiers, struck out for the south and east. These troops consisted of garrisons already located in central Tunisia and of forces reactivated in Algeria, where all Frenchmen of military age were being called to the colors. Their vanguard was the famed Méharistes, or camel corps, who now were striking toward Sfax and Gabès.

While the Allies were pounding relentlessly at the Tunis-Bizerte defenses, the French were recording steady progress. Pont-du-Fahs, thirty-eight miles south of Djedeida, fell to them early in December; from there they were in a position to strike at the important coastal railway which ran from Tunis to the south. For both sides, transportation was a constant and grave problem, because there were few railways or roads that could accommodate the movements of large groups of men. Whoever held the main roads and the railways had in effect the dominance of great regions. Inland, there was little besides desert trails and poor roads, broken in many places by wide salt marshes. In the western part of the country, there was a large spur of the Atlas Mountains which crossed North Africa all the way from Morocco. Since the Allies held no ports in Tunisia, they could not supply their forces by sea but were compelled to rely on slow land transport. On December 1, the first of the unbelievably huge bombings that were to play such a vital part in this campaign was launched against Bizerte, which was raided steadily for twenty-four hours. These attackers had to come from bases far behind the battle area and could not be accompanied by protecting fighters to ward off the German planes which had so many bases within a few miles of the targets.

The enemy held a temporary mastery of the air. To combat this, the Allies summoned the commander of the United States Army Air Forces in the European theater, Major General Carl A. Spaatz. He had built up the Eighth United States Air Force, based in Britain, to an enviable mark of hard-hitting efficiency in less than a year. It was now his task to overcome the obstacles that beset the Twelfth United States Air Force in North Africa, under General Doolittle.

This assignment, however, was one that required time and materials. The Germans were resolved that they would not give the Allies the time. They launched the first big counterattack of the Tunisian campaign. It was pointed at the American and British lines in the Djedeida-Tebourba area, held by troops from the British Midlands and the American Middle West. Pursuing their old tactics, the Germans opened up with bombing and strafing from low levels and followed this with tanks, supported by infantry.

The next day, heavier German forces attacked again, this time using parachute units in large numbers. Djedeida was the scene of the heaviest fighting. The little village changed hands several times, and the Germans lost much valuable equipment; but at the end of the battle they had succeeded in driving the Allies out. Other German forces swung to the west, passing north of Djedeida, and battled the Allies with equal fury but inferior results at Tebourba. A third force lunged out of Mateur in a vain attempt to dislodge the Allies in front of the town, from which a winding road ran to Bizerte between the two lakes of Ferryville and Bizerte.

From London came two warnings of the stakes in North Africa. Prime Minister Churchill counseled the people of the Allied nations to beware of overconfidence, asserting that "the hard core of Nazi resistance is not yet broken in upon." The fierce counterattacks outside Tunis and Bizerte were more than sufficient evidence of the truth of his remarks. The other warning came from General Georges Catroux, a trusted aide of the Fighting French commander. He urged the Allies to terminate as quickly as possible their "military expedient" of coöperation with Admiral Darlan and gave military reasons for his plea. The Allies' position in Africa, he argued, was potentially far too dangerous to permit the control of their supply lines to remain in the Admiral's hands.

Troops on the battle lines in the meanwhile were facing a renewal of the pounding German thrusts in the triangle formed by Mateur, Tebourba, and Djedeida. Wedging between the two latter towns, the Germans separated the Allies and drove them out of Tebourba in fierce battling in which both sides employed parachute troops extensively. The Allies rallied on the heights behind Tebourba. The Germans, though they had routed the Allies from the town, could not hold it themselves under the withering fire poured down on them.

While the fighting raged in this area, heartening news came from the south, where the French were operating with American parachute and infantry units. Driving toward Sfax, on the coast about two thirds of the way from Tunis to Gabès, they routed German patrols at Sidi bou Zid, about eighty miles below Tunis. Another French-American unit forty miles still farther south plunged on between Gafsa and Gabès, the last eastern port in Tunisia, taking prisoners and pushing the enemy eastward before them.

Action in the north produced the first of those amphibious operations that, on a far vaster scale, were to help the Allies in the subsequent campaigns of Sicily and Italy. Landing secretly behind the German lines at a point very close to Bizerte, British Commandos, American Rangers, and other troops of both nations, including many drawn from such units as tank divisions, made a striking success of this initial "leap-frogging" action. The raiders carried only light arms and worked diversely. Some were assigned to individual tasks, others were allocated to groups for a given operation. This first raid was not intended to have any permanent effect on the battle lines but rather to sow as much havoc and confusion as possible behind the Germans' lines and thus hamper the moving of reinforcements and supplies to the actual front.

The thrust at Tebourba was soon caught in the muck caused by the increasing rains. Official Allied quarters in London explained that the first Allied units to reach the Tunis-Bizerte neighborhood had in reality been little more than spearhead forces, operating so far ahead of schedule that much time was required before the main body of the troops, together with the great mass of supplies needed for a major attack, could catch up to them.

Discontent on the "home front" was aggravated by the paucity of news from North Africa and the delays attendant on the transmission of what did get out. While part of this was the natural result of military censorship, more of the fault was to be found with the régime which had been set up to govern French North Africa. Admiral Darlan and his entourage seemed to be interested more in concealing facts from the Allied public than in helping it to learn what was happening.

First reports of the imminent failure of the Allies' lunge for Tunis and Bizerte were not long in coming. The Germans rushed out against the Allies' stronghold of Medjez-el-Bab, the vital junction recently captured from the enemy. From two sides, north and east, German tanks and infantry poured against the Allied lines. The first attack was followed the next day by a fresh drive at Medjez but halfway between that junction and Mateur. Again both attempts were shattered, but only after the fiercest fighting. It was apparent that the Germans would spare no effort and would disregard every cost to uproot the Allies even before their own reinforcement had been completed.

American Secretary of War, Henry L. Stimson, took occasion to explain the Tunisian campaign and its significance to the American people. The first objective, he said, was the capture of all Tunisia; after that came other, bigger tasks. One was the crushing of the still impressive German and Italian forces in Libya before they could come down from Tunisia to strike from the rear. Above all, there was the vital job of clearing the whole southern coast of the Mediterranean and, in coöperation with the British, holding the sea as a safe and short line of communications with the Middle East.

In furtherance of these objectives, the American Government emphasized to all the United Nations that it was going to take no hand in internal French politics but would concentrate on developing military resources of North Africa. Over 150,000 trained soldiers were available, and 500,000 could eventually be put in the field.

Behind the scenes the undoubted military value of much of the political maneuvering was making itself felt. After much pressure French West Africa finally yielded completely and cast its lot wholly with the Allies.

This meant that the Allies would be able to use not only the trained native troops in the colony but the naval units and the merchantmen tied up in the port of Dakar. And this was a war in which shipping, both transport and naval, played a prime rôle.

French who had already joined the fight were covering themselves with honor in central and southern Tunisia. There were simply not enough modern weapons then available in Africa for the Allies to distribute to the French. Colonial troops under their native officers fought the Germans and Italians with the antiquated equipment at their disposal. In one foray, a handful of guerrillas reached the eastern coast between Sfax and Sousse. They mined the railroad while awaiting the arrival of a scheduled enemy troop train and wheeled up 1,917 machine guns fixed on light armored cars built in France in 1931 when General de Gaulle was beginning to dream of that "army of the future." The train was derailed by the guerrillas' mines. As the enemy troops came rushing out of it, the French manned their guns and calmly cut them down in batches.

As the French troops in Tunisia, commanded by General Giraud, demonstrated their eagerness to coöperate with the Allies, the French régime in Algiers began to "warm up" toward the Americans and British because, perhaps, of the application of Lend-Lease to both North and West Africa. Although it was put on a purely military basis and accords were not made with civilian authorities, the French officials were not perturbed, since all except Boisson and Yves Chatel, the Governor-General of Algeria, were military men; and Chatel was in no position to protest since the "High Commissioner," Admiral Darlan, was in Algiers, too. However, it was to General Giraud that the Allies were looking as the French leader whose exclusive aim was the liberation of France.

Both the Americans and the British were striving to establish themselves as rapidly and firmly as possible in order that there should be a minimum of behind-the-lines interruption of military operations. To release more men for combat duty, the Americans had already begun to bring in members of the Women's Army Auxiliary Corps, as it was then called. These women served primarily in clerical and secretarial posts; but some of them were rapidly being employed as drivers of army vehicles and as radio operators.

As the Christmas letters and packages began to arrive in the lines, the troops turned their attention to the holiday and laid plans for feasts in addition to the army's Christmas dinners. In their free time they would visit the Arabs near their positions, finding them invariably friendly when there was business to be done. Most of the transactions were conducted by barter. An old, worn-out pair of army trousers, for example, could be traded for a turkey and a few dozen eggs. Other deals were made with British troops. The puddings that were part of the British rations were eagerly hoarded by the Americans, who had to part with American cigarettes for such treasures.

While no large-scale action was impending on the northern front, the Allies found it imperative to know the dispositions and the plans of the enemy in that sector. Once again they sent a raiding party far behind the enemy's lines, shipping Commandos by sea to a point five miles west of Bizerte. The Commandos, accompanied by some Americans, encountered extremely strong German positions and well-built machine-gun posts, obviously indicating that the enemy was going to fight hard and long if the Allies launched a new attack.

On all sectors the greater part of the action for some time was of patrol and artillery nature. In northern Tunisia, at this time, it was the Germans who resorted to steady bombardments intended to break up the Allies' positions. The Allies sent patrols fanning out from both Medjez-el-Bab and Pont-du-Fahs, some twenty-five miles to the southeast. There were sharp clashes and losses on both sides, but the relative positions of the opposing armies remained unchanged. While the troops were eager to push on to the capital and felt no qualms at the thought of spending Christmas within the range of German guns, the commanders who directed their activities were cautious. It seemed extremely likely that Marshal Rommel might not make another stand in Tripolitania before the Eighth Army, but would retreat directly to the northeastern triangle of Tunisia to take over the command of the enemy's defenses there. And Rommel was a wise and brilliant soldier.

It was Christmas Eve, 1942, an hour when kinsmen of American troops would be trimming the Christmas tree in the living-room back home. This picture must have been in the minds of our soldiers as they advanced under the roaring of a thousand shells from medium and heavy British and American guns. For twenty-four minutes the thunderous bombardment continued, heedless of the accurate German counterfire that splashed shells all around the Allies' positions. Then there was a sudden silence, more deafening at first than the pounding of the guns from whose fire the low-hanging clouds still glowed red in the rain. As the barrage lifted, the Allied infantry rushed forward. German 88-mm. guns began to bark. Red tracers streamed through the gathering dark as the enemy's machine guns opened fire. A minor renewal of the Allies' artillery action silenced them, and what followed was the grimmest hand-to-hand action. Americans and Britons battled Germans with rifles, with bayonets, with pistols and revolvers.

The Germans gave ground before the sudden onrush up the steep heights. Then they counterattacked and drove the Allies back, fiercely fighting every inch of the way. British Guards units joined the fray and tried again, against withering fire from all the enemy's arms. Again they were dislodged. They tried a third time, and shortly after midnight of that Christmas Eve, the Allies' fighting men saw their own Christmas star rise in the sky over the hill they had captured so dearly.

This was Christmas on the Tunisian battlefield. Hardly less spectacular was the ushering in of Christmas far behind the lines in Algiers, although there it cost only one life. Admiral Jean-François Darlan was in his offices in a closely guarded building in Algiers. Shortly before 3:30 P.M. of the day before Christmas, a twenty-year-old Frenchman presented himself at the doors of the palace and somehow gained admittance not only to the building but to the Admiral's quarters. There he whipped out a revolver and emptied its contents into the Admiral's body. As the assassin turned to leave, he was seized.

Algiers and all North Africa that heard of the assassination was in an uproar.

Neither the French nor the Allies allowed any indication of the assassin's identity to be disclosed. In every capital of the world, Allied, Axis, and neutral, a thousand rumors sprang from nowhere. Some said that the youth was a rabid Fascist who had brooded over Admiral Darlan's betrayal of Vichy and the Germans; some said that he was a De Gaullist fanatic, or a Fighting Frenchman. Germans said that he had been hired by the British; again it was suggested that he was a Royalist. General Giraud hazarded the opinion that the boy might simply have been a madman. Whatever his motive, he had committed an act whose result North African Frenchmen, Fighting Frenchmen, Americans, and Britons united to denounce. They could not condone individual terrorism as an instrumentality for any end.

The day after Christmas, Admiral Darlan was buried. His assassin was executed by a firing squad.

General de Gaulle manifested his willingness to coöperate fully with the North African régime now that General Giraud was at its head.

Operations on the battlefront were becoming fluid. In central Tunisia, the French had gained; Foreign Legion troops now held Sidi bou Zid, eighty-five miles southwest of Sousse.

But a hard blow had been struck against the Americans in the north. The hill over which a rocket had flared like a Christmas star after the night of bloody battling was no longer theirs. The very crest had always remained in German hands; now the enemy was exploiting its superior position and the Allies' troops were compelled to withdraw. Doughboys and Guardsmen fell back along the Tunis road, back into Medjez-el-Bab, but they fought as they retreated and left their scars deep on the enemy while American guns covered their withdrawal. This loss did not change the lines essentially; but it was a psychological blow. Its effect was partly countered by the daring American raid well to the south, that penetrated to Maknassy, only forty miles from the eastern coastal road that linked Tunisia with Tripolitania.

The two great struggles on the Mediterranean littoral were beginning to merge more definitely into a single battle for Africa. Along the borders of Tunisia the year of 1942 went out to the accompaniment of the rumble of the Allies' guns in the rolling hills above Medjez-el-Bab which the enemy now held unchallenged. The first fifty-four days of the first great offensive were over.

GREAT BATTLES IN LIBERATION OF AFRICA

"UNCONDITIONAL surrender!" These words were the trumpet call along the battle fronts of North Africa. With the battle swinging like a pendulum in the early weeks of 1943, they were to rally the Allied forces from disaster to triumph.

Hitler scoffed at them. Mussolini reverted to his old bombast and promised his Fascist henchmen that Italy would surely reconquer her African empire. He boasted that the Mediterranean is "my sea, and I shall drive the Americans and British from my shores."

Mussolini's desperate stand to make good his pledges was in full action within seven days after the Declaration of Casablanca. On the last day of January, two American officers were killed on a reconnaisance mission in Tunisia. Their bodies were recovered and buried that evening. At the brief military funeral their requiem was three artillery salvos, fired, not into the air but into "profitable enemy targets." This grim tribute to the dead was in a sense the spark that touched off the fiercest and most concentrated German-Italian attack of the Tunisian campaign.

The first lunge was made by a strong enemy force against a relatively small French unit defending the narrow mountain gateway of Faïd Pass, on the road between the port of Sfax and the town of Sbeitla, almost one hundred miles inland. Faïd itself was only thirty miles southeast of Sbeitla; there the Germans struck out with artillery, infantry, and their new monster Mark VI tanks. These machines, called Tigers, weighed sixty-two tons and mounted, as their principal armament, the famous 88-mm. gun that the Germans had first employed as an antitank weapon.

The Germans were attempting to throw the Allies out of Tunisia and all French North Africa. The risk of failure was high, but the stakes were immeasurable. In addition to the purely military value of reconquering the strategic territory, there was the profound blow that such a German success would strike to the morale of all the Allied and occupied nations.

Rommel struck as he had struck in France and as other German commanders had struck in Poland. His vanguard was the superb 10th Armored Division, conqueror in Poland and France and seasoned, if momentarily crippled, veterans of Russia. Its losses had been made up by replacements subjected to the training of battle-wise officers and rehearsed in the costly and bloody action on the beaches of Dieppe.

American tanks and infantry sent to assist the French displayed the utmost skill and courage. The Germans, however, were in control of Faïd Pass. Their guns, mounted on the hills on either side of the defile, erected a veritable wall of fire that neither ingenuity nor valor could overcome. It could be eliminated only by superior strength. The Americans were forced to fall back every time they attacked.

Momentarily there was a lull. The Allied commanders knew that the Germans would not rest with the mere possession of Faïd Pass and Maknassy while the Eighth Army's main body was steadily and methodically nearing the Tunisian border.

On February 10, General Sir Harold R. L. G. Alexander, the British Commander in Chief in the Middle East, made an announcement that challenged the enemy's whole schedule. The main body of the British Eighth Army was now in Tunisia, he disclosed, advancing toward the Mareth Line. He declared that this fortification could easily be flanked. Naturally, the General did not go on to disclose the highly important fact that on the southern flank of his advancing Eighth Army a strong force of French troops was pacing its drive with that same object in mind. These troops were the Maharistes of North Africa and the Fighting French armored column from the Lake Chad territory.

In what was rapidly becoming the unrecognized but actual capital of France, General Georges Catroux had arrived to head General de Gaulle's mission to General Giraud. General Catroux was one of those rare men who combined military ability with statesmanship. After a distinguished military career he had been Governor General of French Indo-China. When the Petain régime accepted German rule, he had severed his connections with the shadow government and joined the Fighting French.

In the reorganization of his command, General Eisenhower became the chief of what he himself called "the three stars of the British Empire." General Alexander became deputy Commander in Chief in charge of all British, American, and French land forces in the theater, which was defined as extending from Casablanca to the Tripolitanian-Tunisian border. Alexander, who was known as "the last man off the beach at Dunkirk," had later been the British commander in Burma. Despite the handicap of these two defeats, he had risen to be the victorious strategist of the Libyan campaign, with whom General Montgomery as tactical commander had been able to work in perfect harmony. Air Marshal Sir Arthur William Tedder became the American General's deputy for the air forces of all three nations. It was his task to coördinate the operations of the air forces in Tunisia and Algeria with those of the forces in Egypt and Libya and to direct the aërial strategy of the Allies. His tactical deputy was the American General Spaatz. Admiral Sir Andrew Browne Cunningham was the naval Commander in Chief. Since the Allied naval forces in the Mediterranean were predominantly British, his position was less complicated than those of the other commanders. The United States Navy, as its rôle grew, sent Vice Admiral Henry K. Hewitt to serve under him.

There was a real challenge to Germany's might. The strongly organized Allied forces were to start their new phase under the most ominous conditions. Much of the French force in Tunisia was being withdrawn from the lines for rearmament with modern British and American equipment and training in its use, thus depleting the Allies' numerical strength. The new adventure presented the gravest peril.

It was General Alexander's announcement of his Eighth Army's entry into Tunisia that was the most immediately productive of all these developments. The first result was manifested by Marshal Rommel, who began in the marshy frontier areas of southern Tunisia the strongest delaying action that he had staged since his departure from El Agheila, hundreds of miles to the east in Libya.

For the first time Marshal Rommel recognized that he was in danger of being outflanked from the south, as General Alexander had predicted. The main force of the Eighth Army had crossed the border near the coast.

The French who had entered Tunisia much farther south were soon joined by the Seventh Armored Division of the British Army. Together they constituted a powerful threat to the Germans, who were completely surprised by the fact that the British armor had been able to move so quickly over ground that had been pounded for months by the winter rains. It was vital to Rommel to hold off the advancing British as long as possible while he strove to widen the passage to Tunis and, if possible, knock the Allies out of the protectorate.

From both North Africa and the Middle East, Allied air forces were concentrating on distant enemy bases. Naples was bombed by American Liberators, for much of the heavy material and the reinforcements intended for Tunisia were sent from that port. Smaller Allied planes concentrated on the railroads feeding the lesser ports of southern Italy. Flying Fortresses based on North Africa extended their range to the vital Sicilian harbor of Palermo, a way stop on the run from Naples. It was while the Allies' biggest planes were thus diverted that Marshal Rommel found the time suited best for his grand effort in Tunisia.

The site that he picked was Faïd Pass, which his forces already held. It was the gateway to the Tunisian hinterland and Algeria.

Rommel's 10th Armored and his 21st Divisions converging toward Sbeitla caught the Americans and their French allies by complete surprise. The resistance was incredibly stubborn. The Allies fought with superhuman courage and determination. The first day each of the German columns advanced eighteen miles from its starting point. The 10th which attacked from Faïd Pass, led by fifty tanks and screened by fighters and dive bombers, drove out north of the road from Faïd to Sbeitla, some thirty miles to the northeast. It started at 7:00 A.M.; by 9:00 A.M. it had cut the road to Sidi bou Zid.

The metal monsters slugged it out on the Faïd-Sidi bou Zid road while other tanks were battling with equal ferocity on the road from Sidi bou Zid southwest to Gafsa, more than fifty miles away. Peril now confronted Sbeitla. If the Germans took that vital communications center, the last link between all the Americans in the center of Tunisia and the British First Army in the north would be broken. The wedge thus driven between the two forces might carry irresistibly on into Algeria. The whole Tunisian campaign hung in the balance after this one day of battle.

Americans and Britons alike had fastened all their attention on the fighting in Tunisia. Thrown back eighteen miles from the Sidi bou Zid area, the Americans lost no time in regrouping. The next day they counterattacked with all the strength at their command. A vanguard of medium tanks, their battered brown sides daubed with the names of American girls in towns of a dozen states, rumbled out into the plain west of Sidi bou Zid, where the German armor was waiting. The Americans drove firmly ahead, despite the fact that to get within range for their own guns to be effective they had to brave fire from the superior armament of the German tanks.

The battle of armor raged until dusk, when nothing could be seen of the tanks save the flashes of their guns or the flames of the victims. As the Americans slowly gained the upper hand, artillery and infantry came up to join the battle. The biggest of the American tanks, supported by lighter, faster units, started a series of sharp, short rushes into the plain. Each push gained a little ground, which the infantry quickly occupied.

Throughout the battle the American forces were subjected to the most sustained dive bombings and strafings. Their own aërial support still consisted only of fighters and the lightest attack bombers; the heavies and the mediums were at Tunis and Bizerte and Kairouan. Despite this grievous handicap, the Americans drove the enemy back from the plain and off the highest of the ridges commanding the Faïd-Sbeitla road, until the Germans found themselves fighting within the town of Sidi bou Zid.

When the battle was broken off, the Germans still held Sidi bou Zid, but the Allies commanded all the approaches from the north, west, and south.

Marshal Rommel's southern column, the 21st Armored Division, had turned back after it had cut the Sidi bou Zid-Gafsa road; instead of driving on for Sbeitla, it had lunged into Gafsa. The light American force there had already been withdrawn to Norok to the northwest, and the Germans occupied the town. The whole Allied line in southern Tunisia was in danger of being rolled back.

The Eighth Army was on the march again. American and British hearts leaped at the news, inclined to view the loss of Gafsa and the withdrawal before Faïd as local setbacks. Marshal Rommel proceeded to awaken them to the true danger of their groups' situation. One day after the successful American counterattack in the Sidi bou Zid neighborhood, on February 16, the Germans lunged out of the town with irresistible fury. In the new attack they advanced twenty-two miles and hurled the Americans to the very outskirts of Sbeitla.

The next day the Germans renewed their pounding at Fériana and turned other forces against Kasserine. Guns and tanks occasionally checked the German advance in desperate rear-guard actions to cover the retreat of the American forces and their French comrades. Every step to the rear was with the desire to turn again toward the front. The Americans were now fighting mad. They wanted only one thing—unlimited revenge. They had much to avenge. Since February 14 the Germans had smashed fifty-four miles from Faïd; they overran 4,000 square miles of Tunisia and drove a wedge between the Americans and not only the British First Army but also the Eighth Army advancing in the far south. The Allied line now ran well over the Algerian border from its hinge at Djebel Chambi, not too far within the Tunisian border; and the Germans rested. They had already inflicted terrible damage.

The French abandoned Pichon, some forty miles north of Faïd Pass, in an apparent effort on the part of the Allies to take up stronger defense positions on the western side of the Ousselat Valley that would thwart any German effort to wedge between the Allies in that area. The British Eighth Army in the south continued a limited offensive operation, taking Foum Tatahouine and pushing on to occupy positions to the west, while a Commando force sallied into the Gulf of Gabès to clear the Axis garrison off the Island of Djerba. Thus an approach to that port was opened and virtually the whole southern tip of Tunisia east of the Mareth Line—some two or three thousand square miles—was firmly in Allied hands.

But Rommel, the Fox, was fighting furiously in western Tunisia to drive the Allies from the gateways to Tunis and Bizerte. Here he was staking his last chance. If he could deliver a knockout blow, he might yet save North Africa. If he lost, he must make his escape along the roads to the sea. Here he must choose between another Dunkirk or the surrender of his armies.

CASABLANCA—ROAD TO VICTORY AND "UNCONDITIONAL SURRENDER"

WAR was waged not only by two great Powers—the Allies and the Axis—but it was many wars in one: economic, political, diplomatic, all inextricably interwoven into the military. Allied Governments and General Eisenhower's staff were harassed by problems in which solutions were as decisive as winning battles.

Diplomatic events in Casablanca in January, 1943, were to set the pace that was to pronounce the doom of the Axis. During the preceding weeks, while Eisenhower's armies were fighting mud and torrential rains, the Governments of the United States and Great Britain were fighting to save the people in North Africa from hunger and starvation.

Thousands of tons of civilian necessities, food, clothing, and medicines, were shipped from America and Great Britain.

It was indisputable that Allied prompt and thorough action averted probable revolt. There was another equally deeply rooted threat to the tranquillity of the territories. The Fighting French had long made it one of their basic principles that coöperation with the men of Vichy was impossible. The British were inclined to lend the weight of their influence to the De Gaullists' demands. The Fighting French made it plain, in the beginning of 1943, that before any French unity could be achieved the entire Imperial Council in North Africa would have to be dissolved. In their opinion General Giraud was the only one worthy of the slightest confidence. This stand was not without foundation, for the councilors were all Vichy men and had almost unanimously shared Vichy's bitter hatred of the British.

Conditions in Morocco, where the influence of Vichy and the Germans was even stronger than it had been in Algeria, were politically critical. Profiteering was rampant, and the Government made no effort to control it. The Sultan was little more than a figurehead. Real power was in the hands of the French Resident General; Noguès was using it for the aid and comfort of the enemy.

In Morocco, before the landings of the Allies, the persecution of De Gaullists and pro-Ally sympathizers had been even more far-reaching and more drastic than it had been in Algeria, a part of metropolitan France. Arrests were made on the slightest pretext. Trials were repeatedly postponed while the prisoners, held on what amounted to open charges, were confined in foul, crowded cells or sent to work on roads in the steaming desert. The Vichy-dominated *Légion des Combattants* and its successor, the *Service d'Ordre de la Légion,* were more influential here than in France. A denunciation by their agents was tantamount to a formal prison sentence.

It was obvious that the De Gaullists, whose record was untainted by double-dealing, could not work side by side with such men as Noguès, or General Bergeret. The latter was the air force commander who for a time had been Minister of Air in Vichy and equally frank in his opposition to Britain.

Unity was imperative for the success of Allied military operations. So long as there was dissension, it meant not only impediments behind the lines but the loss of the use of many thousands of well-trained and eager troops. General Giraud moved slowly, with the caution of his years and his admitted lack of knowledge of what had happened in France and the Empire during his two years in the German fortress of Koenigstein. As the Allies had demanded, he declared a general amnesty for political prisoners held on charges of having sympathized with or aided the Allies, but he excluded the twelve men recently arrested on the charges of plotting his and others' deaths. In addition, he revoked the anti-Semitic laws of Vichy and gradually released those Frenchmen who had been put to forced labor on the Trans-Saharan Railroad.

Many of General Giraud's actions brought about violent disputes. He agreed with the Fighting French that the retention of Yves Chatel as Governor-General of Algeria was harmful to both French democracy and the Allies' military operations, and replaced him with the Vichy Ambassador in Buenos Aires, Marcel Peyrouton. Peyrouton had been one of the early Ministers of the Interior in Vichy and was hated by millions of Frenchmen because he had instituted the "racial" laws, tracked down De Gaullists without mercy, and interned thousands of republicans on charges of Communist activities. No appointment could have done more to widen the breach between Frenchmen or to aggravate the suspicions of many Britons and Americans. Yet at the same time Giraud allowed the Americans to arrest Charles Bedaux, financial adventurer, in North Africa, where the French-born industrialist had gone to plot with the Germans against not only his native but his adopted country, for Bedaux was a naturalized American citizen.

General Giraud insisted that he must proceed slowly in weeding out collaborationist subordinates because of the scarcity of trained administrators to replace them. At the same time the General's régime was permitting the most questionable Frenchmen to enter North Africa: men like Pierre-Etienne Flandin, the former Premier who had been so devoted to Fascism. Pierre Pucheu, although he had held the Interior Ministry in Vichy after Peyrouton, was invited by General Giraud to

North Africa and then arrested on his arrival. Hundreds of lesser fry were sent deliberately by Vichy and the Germans to stir dissension and to impede the progress of the Allies in Tunisia.

Many people asked why it had been necessary to bring the founder of the first concentration camp on French soil—Peyrouton had opened the prison in Tunisia in 1936 when he was Resident General—four thousand miles to replace a less offensive personality. Clement R. Attlee, at that time Britain's Deputy Prime Minister, defended political and military leadership and said that both the American and British Governments had but one political objective in Africa—the promotion of the union of all Frenchmen in the war against the Axis.

As 1943 began, in mud that veterans likened to what they had endured at Passchendaele in the First World War, the ground troops in the north saw only spasmodic action, but their comrades of the air scored smashing victories. Great aërial batterings increased on all the Tunisian ports from Bizerte to Gabès.

There were sharp clashes in the central area where earlier the French and Americans had scored such gains. Here the Germans launched their first counterthrusts. At Fondouk, a road junction about sixty miles southwest of Sousse that the Allies had held for some weeks, the Germans opened up with heavy artillery bombardments, followed with tank attacks. Their initial momentum carried them into the Allies' lines, but the French troops, using American tank destroyers and aided by American and British planes, bounced back and threw the enemy on his heels. The Germans regrouped, while the Allied fliers continued to rake their columns and reinforcements poured in through the port of Sousse and the important road and rail town of Kairouan—a holy city to thousands of Moslems.

There was a brief flare-up in the north, where a British regiment, reinforced by Commandos, stormed and seized a height under heavy machine-gun fire. This action occurred fifteen miles west of Mateur, the junction that the Allies had nearly reached in the first lunge for Bizerte. In six hours the height of Djebel Azzag was won. Here, too, the Germans re-formed their lines and launched a counterattack.

The enemy's forces were considerably stronger than the British troops that had scaled the hill. They had not only new blood but a new, and apparently wiser, commander—Colonel General Jurgen von Arnim, a veteran of the First World War. He so employed his forces that they had little difficulty in driving the British back from Djebel Azzag, and the earlier positions were restored. In the center the enemy was less successful, and a new attack on Fondouk was again repelled. In the extreme south the French camel corps that had crossed the Algerian-Tripolitanian border continued its advance and met only the opposition of Italian forces. Ahead of it American Flying Fortresses bombed the

Italian fort at Gadames, opposite the southern anchor of the Mareth Line.

While Frenchmen in London and Algiers were still in bitter dispute over the ways and means of achieving unity, these Méharistes of General Giraud's command effected the first amicable contact of the war with Fighting French troops. Months before, a light motorized column under the mysterious Brigadier General Jacques Leclerc had set out from the Lake Chad area to join the British Eighth Army in Libya. On its way it had stormed a score of Italian strong points, captured their defenders, and taken over whatever equipment could aid in its advance. The full story of that safari over mountains, through jungles, and across barren deserts is another epic in itself. Here it is enough to report that the Fighting Frenchmen joined forces with the North African troops in southern Libya on their way to Tripoli. These two groups fought on together until the end of the Tunisian campaign.

British units in the center had been moved in to back up the French at Pont-du-Fahs, where German tank attacks had gained but little ground. The British held a sector between Goubellat, a few miles south of Medjez-el-Bab, and Bou Arada, about fifteen miles farther south.

The Allied commanders entertained no illusions that their forces could prevent a junction between the Germans in Libya and those in Tunisia. They knew it was inevitable and that it must come in the eastern coastal area. Once the junction had been effected, the Allies would be facing a force of some 160,000 men, all picked troops, for it was Marshal Rommel's fixed rule in his retreats across Libya to save his rabid Nazis and leave the Italians to be captured.

The Germans in central Tunisia were stronger than the Allies. They continued the push against the French until their vanguard was only two miles outside Robaa. The French had been forced back twenty-five miles from Pont-du-Fahs. Two other German forces, both heavily armored, were striking through parallel valleys farther south, toward Djebel Ousselat and the town of Ousseltia. American and British troops were hastily rushed up to help the French, and their counterattacks regained a few miles of the road from Robaa to Pont-du-Fahs.

The troops of the three nations, led by American tanks, guns, infantry, and planes, completely blocked the drive on Ousseltia. The Allies now struck out to dislodge the enemy from the positions that he had strengthened. But the Germans had the advantage of holding heights east of Ousseltia that dominated the road into Kairouan, which they also held; this protected their coastal artery only thirty miles to the east.

The threat to the Allies from the south was growing. Tripoli fell— the greater part of the enemy's Libyan forces was pouring over the border despite daily bombing and strafing by planes from both Tunisia and Libya. It was racing for the temporary protection of the broken string of fortifications known as the Mareth Line, which the French had originally built as a protection against an Italian attack on Tunisia from Tripolitania.

The Germans were now in a position to make their desperate bid to drive the Allies out of Tunisia. The Afrika Korps was well entrenched behind the Mareth Line. The southern end was already threatened by the merged French forces that had met in Tripolitania, but alone they were by no means strong enough to launch an attack. Late in January the first patrols of the British Eighth Army crossed the Tunisian border, but the main body of that army was still in Tripolitania.

Hundreds of miles away from the front, while the troops of both sides had been battling, their whole futures were being reshaped. One of the most dramatic announcements of the war was made by the Allies. A clarion of hope and faith—that was at the same time a crash of doom to the Axis—rang through the air waves of the world for twenty-four hours on January 27, 1943. Without a break, the most powerful transmitters of the British Broadcasting Corporation and of the stations operated by the American Government in the United States and North Africa reiterated the historic news that meant the beginning of the battle of liberation for the victims of Germany, Italy, and Japan.

President Roosevelt and Prime Minister Churchill, with their military and political advisers, had met for ten days at Casablanca—almost within the battle zone of the first major offensive staged by the Allies. There they planned and perfected the attacks against the enemy's vitals. At 2:00 A.M. Greenwich Mean Time, the zero hour arrived to give to the world the historic communiqué that had been kept sealed and locked away in hundreds of newspaper offices since January 24. Nothing can tell more simply the essentials of the dramatic conference than this document, the contents of which were so loyally guarded by thousands of men and women in many countries—military censors, telegraph and cable and wireless operators, office boys, and editors:

The President of the United States and the Prime Minister of Great Britain have been in conference near Casablanca since January 14. They were accompanied by the combined Chiefs of Staff of the two countries, namely—

For the United States: General George C. Marshall, Chief of Staff of the United States Army; Admiral Ernest J. King, Commander in Chief of the United States Navy; Lieutenant General H. H. Arnold, commanding the United States Army Air Forces.

For Great Britain: Admiral of the Fleet Sir Dudley Pound, First Sea Lord; General Sir Alan Brooke, Chief of the Imperial General Staff; and Air Chief Marshal Sir Charles Portal, Chief of the Air Staff.

These were assisted by: Lieutenant General B. B. Somervell, Commanding General of the Services of Supply, United States Army; Field Marshal Sir

Casablanca

John Dill, head of the British Joint Staff Mission in Washington; Vice Admiral Lord Louis Mountbatten, Chief of Combined Operations; Lieutenant General Sir Hastings Ismay, Chief of Staff to the Office of the Minister of Defense, together with a number of staff officers of both countries.

They have received visits from Mr. Murphy and Mr. Macmillan; from Lieutenant General Dwight D. Eisenhower, Commander in Chief of the Allied Expeditionary Force in North Africa; from Admiral of the Fleet Sir Andrew Cunningham, naval commander of the Allied Expeditionary Force in North Africa; from Major General Carl Spaatz, air commander of the Allied Expeditionary Force in North Africa; from Lieutenant General Mark W. Clark, United States Army, and, from Middle East Headquarters, from General Sir Harold Alexander, Air Chief Marshal Sir Arthur Tedder and Lieutenant General F. M. Andrews, United States Army.

The President was accompanied by Harry Hopkins and was joined by W. Averell Harriman. (Mr. Hopkins was then chairman of the British-American Munitions Board and Mr. Harriman was the American Lend-Lease expediter in England.) With the Prime Minister was Lord Leathers, British Minister of Transport.

For ten days the combined staffs have been in constant session, meeting two or three times a day and recording progress at intervals to the President and Prime Minister. The entire field of the war was surveyed theater by theater throughout the world, and all resources were marshaled for a more intense prosecution of the war by sea, land, and air.

Nothing like this prolonged discussion between two allies has ever taken place before. Complete agreement was reached between the leaders of the two countries and their respective staffs upon war plans and enterprises to be undertaken during the campaigns of 1943 against Germany, Italy, and Japan, with a view to drawing the utmost advantage from the markedly favorable turn of events at the close of 1942.

Premier Stalin was cordially invited to meet the President and Prime Minister, in which case the meeting would have been held very much farther to the east. He was unable to leave Russia at this time on account of the great offensive which he himself, as Commander in Chief, is directing.

The President and Prime Minister realized up to the full the enormous weight of the war which Russia is successfully bearing along her whole land front, and their prime object has been to draw as much weight as possible off the Russian Armies by engaging the enemy as heavily as possible at the best selected points. Premier Stalin has been fully informed of the military proposals.

The President and Prime Minister have been in communication with Generalissimo Chiang Kai-shek. They have apprized him of the measures which they are undertaking to assist him in China's magnificent and unrelaxing struggle for the common cause.

The occasion of the meeting between President and Prime Minister made it opportune to invite General Giraud to confer with the combined Chiefs of Staff and to arrange for a meeting between him and General de Gaulle. The two generals have been in close consultation.

The President and the Prime Minister and their combined staffs, having completed their plans for the offensive campaigns of 1943, have now separated in order to put them into active and concerted execution.

The two French generals issued a brief announcement.

"We have met. We have talked. We have registered complete agreement on the end to be achieved, which is the liberation of France and the triumph of human liberties through the total defeat of the enemy. This end will be attained by the union in war of all free Frenchmen fighting side by side with all the Allies."

This, in brief, is what happened during those ten historic days in the suburb of Anfa, a few miles outside Casablanca, French Morocco. In this assemblage of statesmen, military leaders, political and diplomatic observers, the Allies conceived and matured the final conquest of Tunisia and the first attack on the European mainland. There they made their first concrete effort to unite the opposing exiled forces of one of the greatest of the nations that they were fighting to set free. The vastness of the agenda of the conference is indicated by the communiqué: The commanders and their advisers discussed and analyzed every theater of a war that covered the entire world. Although neither Russia nor China—the other two major Allies that with Britain and the United States made up what was to be called the Big Four—was represented at the talks, both were kept advised of their progress and their outcome and both were included in the plans adopted.

All the principals arrived in North Africa by air. Prime Minister Churchill and General de Gaulle flew from Britain in separate bombers. The Prime Minister used the giant Liberator bomber, manned by an American crew, that had taken him to Moscow not long before for talks with Premier Stalin. President Roosevelt left the United States in a giant transatlantic airliner that took him to North Africa, where he transferred to a four-motored bomber for the final flight to Casablanca. It was the first time that a President of the United States had left American soil while the country was engaged in a war.

The greatest secrecy surrounded the ten-day parleys. Days before any of the participants was scheduled to arrive, the area around Anfa was cleared and the seashore resort lay deserted except for the garrisons of Allied soldiers. The tropical villa in which President Roosevelt lived and many of the talks were held was heavily guarded. It stood in the center of a tract of many acres that had been enclosed in two lines of barbed wire hung with tin cans, so that no intruder could have progressed in silence. Every square foot of ground behind this fence work was under the surveillance of alert American infantrymen. There were antiaircraft batteries on the flat-roofed Moroccan buildings. On the tree-shaded walks from which they could see the house where their Commander in Chief was working, guards watched the land and the sea and the sky unremittingly.

President Roosevelt was the chief speaker when the press gathered at the end of the meetings. The President told the correspondents that he and the Prime Minister and their aides had agreed above all on one thing: That the enemy would be battled until the Allies had won *"unconditional surrender."* These were the only terms that any of the Allies would accord to Germany, Italy, or Japan. This, he explained, did not mean the destruction of the peoples of those nations, but the uprooting and casting out of those countries' philosophies of conquest and subjugation of other peoples. In this aim, he said, Russia and China supported Great Britain and the United States.

The President set three goals for the Allies for the year that was just beginning. The first was the maintenance of the initiative, its extension to other theaters of war, and its increase in those where the Allies were already pressing it. The second goal was the dispatch of all possible assistance to the Russians, so that their offensive might be maintained and thus cut down German manpower and resources. The third goal was an increase in Allied help to China, to eliminate forever Japanese domination.

Mr. Churchill corroborated what the President had said of the Allies' determination to impose *"unconditional surrender"* on all their enemies. He concluded with the reminder that behind every step taken by both Great Britain and the United States there lay "design, purpose, and an unconquerable will."

For the first time since the days of Abraham Lincoln, an American President reviewed the nation's troops in a theater of war. Seated in a jeep driven by a drafted soldier almost bursting with pride, preceded and followed by armed guards, President Roosevelt was driven slowly past long columns of armored and infantry divisions.

President Roosevelt paused to decorate a hero of the first landings with the Congressional Medal of Honor, the highest award of the United States. The recipient was Brigadier General William H. Wilbur. As a colonel he had landed with the first waves of assault troops at Fedhala, prepared the plan for making contact with the French commander at Casablanca, and obtained an armistice as bloodlessly as possible. His mission was performed under incessant fire. On his return, he found a hostile battery firing on American troops. Leaving the car that he had commandeered, he took charge of a platoon of tanks and captured the battery. Mr. Churchill, Admiral Mountbatten, General Marshall, and Admiral King watched the presentation.

"The captains and the kings departed" from Anfa and Casablanca to go their separate ways: some home to resume the work that awaited them there, others back to the battlefield. President Roosevelt left by air, but his plane did not head straight for the United States. Instead, it "sat down" somewhere in the waters of Brazil, the largest of our good neighbors in South America. President Roosevelt was taken in a launch to an American destroyer lying in the Potengi River harbor at Natal, the easternmost point of the Western Hemisphere and hence the most exposed to attack. It was to prevent Natal from being the first step of a German invasion of the Americas that the Allies had watched Dakar so anxiously after the fall of France.

The Italians were stunned by the news from Casablanca. They and the Germans tried to distort it by attempting to adduce evidence of division among the Allies. They said this because neither Stalin nor Chiang Kai-shek had been present, ignoring the Allies' statement that both had been kept informed of all that was done at Anfa.

The reaction in the Allied nations, however, was one of triumph and hope. The fulminations of the baffled Germans and Italians were ignored. The people of the democracies hailed the conference for its expressed aims and its implicit meaning, real and symbolic.

The first notes of French harmony began to be heard, curiously, from Algiers. The press there, still heavily censored, carried on its front page pictures of Mr. Roosevelt, Mr. Churchill, General Giraud, and—for the first time—General de Gaulle, with the first praise of the Fighting French Commander that had been permitted since 1940.

Although the Casablanca conference was held primarily to confirm and collate the plans that had begun immediately after the decision in June, 1942, to launch the North African campaign, there was no question that its work had been materially increased by developments that could not have been wholly anticipated. One of these was the extent of the successes on the Russian front and another was the rapidity of the British Eighth Army's rout of Rommel in Libya. All the projects that had been under study in Washington and London now had to be retimed, lest the precious advantages be lost by undue delay in exploiting them. Any hesitation would give the enemy time to regroup his forces and accelerate his war production; therefore new blows must be struck as quickly as possible.

Thus this problem began early to sketch out the solution: the Sicilian and Italian campaigns. Both the civilian and military leaders knew that the invasion of western Europe from England—the real second front that the Russians wanted and that was an inescapable necessity—could not be mounted in 1943. For both military and political reasons, it would be necessary to strike somewhere on the mainland of Europe and to strike hard. Another Dunkirk would be an almost fatal blow to the Allies. Therefore, the next major step was the only logical course open: the immediate invasion of Europe at its weakest point, the south. That meant Italy.

61

BATTLE OF KASSERINE PASS ON THE ROAD TO TUNIS

THE gateway to Tunis, in the conquest of North Africa, was the scene of a battle that reënacted on a modern scale the valor of the ancient Greeks at Thermopylae. The almost impregnable Kasserine Pass was a challenge to strength and courage. Here the Americans and British, aided by French troops, were locked in a death struggle with the might of the Germans and Italians.

General Eisenhower, genius of Allied organization and strategy, matched his power against Rommel, the "Desert Fox," who had been driven across the African desert sands from the gates of Egypt and was now desperately trying to block the Allies from gaining a foothold for the first invasion of Europe.

After ten days of heartbreaking Allied retreats, in which every foot of ground was tenaciously contested, the issue was now to be decided in the cold mud between the jagged cliffs of the pass at Kasserine.

At 3:00 A.M. on February 20, 1943, Rommel's artillery began to fire sporadically into the Allied positions around Kasserine Pass, one of four important gateways through the last chain of peaks in front of the Algerian town of Constantine. For three hours irregular firing continued. Then there were two hours of silence. Suddenly, at 8:00 A.M., German guns hurled into the American lines the fiercest barrage of the campaign.

The American troops had been continuously in their first heavy action without rest; they were tired and exhausted. The high quality of their morale was illustrated by the countless instances of men who, just returned from days of dodging their way through the German lines without food or sleep, demanded immediate assignments to action. Even the combat engineers on the east side of the pass had been fighting constantly for days. The enemy's heavy artillery barrage was soon augmented by strong machine-gun fire and the shells of tanks. Under the combined weight of all this, the worn-out Americans, much of whose heavy equipment had been of necessity abandoned in their retreat, could not long stand up. The enemy broke through the pass. However, at its outlet, he was suddenly stopped.

Kasserine Pass was flanked by two other important defiles, both held by Americans. East of the American line, a merged unit of British and American troops held their position at Sbiba. Now that the Germans had taken Kasserine, the Allies were endangered from the rear.

The first German attempts to probe the Allied positions with tanks and infantry were smashed by American artillery behind Kasserine Pass. A stronger force tried again, reaching almost to Sbiba, to the northeast. However, British Guards units inflicted such severe losses in a short but vicious clash that the enemy withdrew in haste.

The following day the Germans attacked in full force. In a concerted assault, tanks and infantry smashed through the Americans and the British armor that had been moved to their support. Counterattacks by the Allied tanks and infantry poured down from the heights of Djebel Chambi and Djebel Semmama. The Germans drove ahead and once again the Allies were in retreat, leaving the Germans only twelve miles from Algeria. The Allies withdrew toward their next defensive line twenty miles to the northwest, Hainra Pass. Northeast of Kasserine, a German thrust at Sbiba was repulsed by the British Guards. It was obvious that the Germans were now determined to smash Allied resistance in this sector and pour into Algeria. The Allies, outnumbered as they were, still dared not draw further on the reserves of the First Army lest General von Arnim's forces at the head of the Medjerda Valley, in the Medjez-el-Bab area, take advantage of such an action to launch a strong attack there.

Fully aware of the dilemma of the Allies, Marshal Rommel pressed his advantage to the hilt. The day before Washington's Birthday, he lunged out with a crack armored column in what was to be his final daring attempt to split the Allied forces in northern Tunisia. At 3:00 A.M. on February 21, the first of three tank assaults was launched in the direction of Thala, twenty miles north of Kasserine Pass and approximately the same distance west of Sbiba. Two other drives, less powerful, also starting from Kasserine Pass, were directed against Tebessa, not far across the Algerian border, and against Sbiba.

The Tebessa thrust was beaten back by the Americans. It was the German lunge toward Thala that came the nearest to success. On a front that recalled descriptions of Valley Forge in its cold and dampness, forty German tanks hurled themselves against veteran British armored units backed up by American artillery. Behind the enemy tanks came truck after truck carrying grenadier troops of the 10th and 21st Armored Divisions. For more than twenty-four hours the Allies battled the Germans only four miles outside Thala, sixteen miles from the point where the attack had been started.

By 3:00 P.M. of the second day, the British and Americans could report to their commanders that the enemy was "very tired." He had reason to be, for he had battled not only the familiar weapons of the Allies but the new forty-ton British Churchill tanks. These, although lighter than the German Mark VI's, proved themselves their equal in this first action. Profiting at last by the costly lessons of Faïd, the

Allies had kept up a steady flow of air attack against the German tanks.

The Germans faltered at last beneath the aërial bombardment and the uninterrupted barrage laid down by American guns on the hills flanking the road into Thala.

When the moon rose, the rugged hills and the barren plains were strewn with burned-out tanks, broken guns, and the bodies of slain German soldiers. With the faint light that followed the moonrise and the breaking of the clouds, a few tanks and guns of both sides returned to action, opposing armor firing from distances of only a few hundred feet. These intermittent, isolated clashes continued throughout the night, but by morning the strength and spirit of the enemy were broken. His weapons were grotesque ruins; his men were exhausted, battered hulks. The next day the *Herrenvolk* turned tail and streaked for the coast and safety.

Tanks, artillery, and infantry launched the Allied counterattack behind the pass. The Allied commanders recognized that this was not enough. They knew that the only thing that would smash the enemy was what had so devastated their own ranks—superior aërial coördination. Every type of plane available to the Allies in North Africa was summoned to this one sector: Lightning, Airacobra, Hurricane, and Spitfire fighters, British Bisley and Boston light bombers, American Mitchell and Marauder medium bombers, and even the giant Flying Fortresses roared down on the German positions to envelop them in a deadly machine-gun fire and blast them with bombs.

Kasserine Pass became a seething inferno. At last the Germans were powerless to strike back. Allied ground forces pounded forward along the whole line of the German positions in this cauldron trap. German tank wedges were posted to protect the withdrawal of the infantry into the wreck-choked pass, smoking with the fires of scores of ruined vehicles and strewn with dead and wounded.

Allied tanks rolled through this human sepulcher and got into the open plains against the enemy's armor. Our infantry boldly struck cross-country, peppering the Germans with machine-gun fire. Bayonet charges drove the Italians into panic. In Tunisia, as in Libya, the Italians showed no taste for battle. They turned and broke. German infantry could not long withstand the concentrated assault of our infantry, which was backed by tanks, heavy artillery, and the bombs, machine guns, and cannon of our planes. Only the German tank crews maintained the iron discipline for which they were famous; they alone yielded ground yard by yard in perfect order.

General Eisenhower and General Alexander, who were watching the battle, could see the enemy still retreating by the light of the fires of his own trucks, whose wreckage lined the roads as well as the pass. The two Generals had been on the battlefield for several days, directing the plan of the battle with Major General Lloyd R. Fredenhall, who commanded the United States Second Corps, as the American force in Tunisia was known, and the Allied units attached to it.

It was the aërial assault that turned the tide at Kasserine. The pass was jammed with German transport vehicles. The town was already an important enemy supply depot, and the roads were vital arteries of enemy communications. The Allies sent the Flying Fortresses against the town and the road to the pass, while Marauders and Lightnings swept down on the pass and virtually blanketed it with bombs.

No vehicle caught in that infernal traffic jam had a chance of escape. Simultaneously the Allies battered the enemy's gun positions that flanked the pass. Other planes ranged out to the roads that bottlenecked at the gap and sowed bloody havoc among troops and vehicles that were moving up to the battle area.

General von Arnim's task, as German commander in the north, was now one of relieving the pressure on his compatriots in central Tunisia. To achieve this, he opened strong drives in six sectors of mountainous northeastern Tunisia. For once the weather seemed to be on the side of the Allies. Except on the few main roads, the whole countryside was deep in mud, and German tanks were compelled to keep to the highways. Thus they were easy targets for the skilfully concealed antitank guns of the Allies, which scored heavily against them.

The Germans were preoccupied with making good their escape from the Americans while preventing the British on their northern flank from impeding them. The British counterattacked so boldly after they had checked the German drives in the Medjez-el-Bab area that the enemy reeled back. Far to the south, patrols of the Eighth Army were driving ever nearer to the Mareth Line in repeated clashes with the German outer defenses. Over both fronts, with the retreating Germans in the center, the Allies stepped up the power and frequency of their aërial assault. This arm contained elements of the air forces of the United States, Great Britain, Canada, Australia, New Zealand, South Africa, Greece, French Africa, the Fighting French, and Poland. Spitfires flown by men of all these forces swooped in almost "on deck" at ground level to ravage enemy troops and communication lines. And, from the indomitable island of Malta, R.A.F. planes were now sweeping out more and more frequently to harry the enemy's rear bases in Sicily and his communications across the Mediterranean to Tunisia.

As the British forced the enemy back from the hills east of the Medjez-Goubellat road, the heroic Royal Artillerymen fought literally to the last man. When last seen, the lone survivor of one unit was advancing, grenade in hand, against a group of tanks. Credit is equally due to the sheer guts of unsung Americans who had defeated the devil of supply as conclusively as the combat troops had smashed the

Germans at Kasserine Pass. American forces exclusively had tackled this problem and solved it. An ever-increasing stream of equipment and food and reinforcements was kept moving toward the front by truck and multi-gauge, single-track railroad.

New names began to come into the stories of the battle. Far in the interior of Southern Tunisia, the Germans had penetrated to the oases of Kebili and Tozeur, one on the south, the other on the north side of the great Chott Djerid; they were bombed by French planes. In the extreme north a German force had struck out from Mateur to the coastal road and reached Cap Serrat, forty miles west of Bizerte, where they met the *Corps Franc d'Afrique*—The African Free Corps of fierce Moroccan *goumiers,* who were superb fighters in darkness and in close combat. There the Germans had to stop.

The Germans were keeping up their determined battle assaults. The setback suffered in the attempt to take Medjez-el-Bab served only to inflame them. Throughout the northern sector they launched new thrusts that were more savage and revealed unsuspected strength. All the drives failed, and the enemy lost heavily.

Over the battlefronts and in attacks behind the lines, the Allies met heavy antiaircraft fire and strong fighter resistance, but in most of the daily tallies the enemy's losses far exceeded ours. Despite our lack of bases to support any real mass air action, we were slowly achieving numerical mastery in the air by the sheer superiority of our planes, guns, and men. The Allies still faced the necessity, however, of dispersing their air strength rather thinly and could not always have adequate cover for all ground forces at the same time.

Meanwhile, the American pursuit of the Germans in the center was picking up speed. Sbeitla was retaken and with its recapture the Allies regained their control of the network of roads leading south, north, and east. The Americans drove on for Faïd Pass, while another American column to the southwest reëntered Feriana, which the Germans had evacuated. Thirty miles to the south, French troops, coöperating in the gradual reëstablishment of the Allied lines, occupied the road junction of Tamerza, some fifty miles west of Gafsa. A new knot was being slowly tied for the "Desert Fox," who must have known that the thundering artillery barrage being maintained against his positions in the Mareth Line was the sure forerunner of a new blow there.

It was obvious that Marshal Rommel was most anxious for the safety of his Afrika Korps behind these fortifications. The Americans met virtually no opposition; as they drove east from Sbeitla, they reoccupied Sidi bou Zid and neared Faïd Pass. Von Arnim's forces in the north, operating under Rommel's supreme command, lashed out again at the British in the Sedjenane area.

On March 7 General Montgomery issued to his forces at the Mareth

Line one of those famous messages that almost invariably were the prelude to a new grand assault. Rommel, the General said, would be caught like a rat in a trap and the Allies would smash right through him. At that moment the Axis forces were advancing in a desperate defensive attack to prevent the Eighth Army from starting its own assault.

While observers in Algiers feared the disruption of the whole Allied time-table, even including the schedule for the invasion of Europe, by the desperate maneuver of the German Marshal, Montgomery was calm. And Montgomery was right. The "Desert Fox" had indeed become a cornered rat lashing out at any opportunity for an escape. He sent out wave after wave of tanks to smash the British positions before his line. As his vast force of tanks rolled out into the plain, the Eighth Army's artillery stood its ground and poured thousands of rounds into the rolling monsters. Advance British outposts directed small-arms fire against both men and vehicles. The crews that tumbled out fell victims to the gunnery. At no point did the British lines give an inch. The Germans shattered themselves against that wall of steel.

The fury of Rommel's assault was reflected throughout the rest of the Tunisian front. Americans in the center swept to a point within two miles of Gafsa, and met only with Italian opposition. Other American forces swept into Pichon. They held this for twenty-four hours in the face of German artillery on the commanding heights and then retired only a little more than a mile to the west of the town. This constituted a continuing threat to the Germans. In the north the First Army was able to go completely over to the offensive. The enemy's efforts to reinforce all the sectors of his line in Tunisia was now depleting his garrison in Sicily.

Regardless of the utter failure and the heavy cost of the first day of his frantic assault on the Eighth Army's positions, Marshal Rommel renewed it with equal fury on the following morning. British tanks went into action to assist the artillery, while the R.A.F. and American planes operating with the Eighth Army pounded the Germans from above. Before night the Germans abruptly broke off the action.

The Eighth Army now showed its mettle in a daring maneuver by its Fighting French contingent. Unknown to the Germans, these fighters had been sweeping far south of the Mareth Line, unheard from for days. They did not turn north again until they were forty miles west of the axis of the fortifications. Then they struck sharply upward into the desolate country in the rear of the enemy. At Ksar Rhilane they encountered a force of armored cars on a rear-guard patrol.

The numbers and equipment of the French were no match for the Germans, but they were undeterred. As enemy reinforcements arrived, they sent a radio call for air assistance. Australian planes were in the air within ten minutes, having been ordered to stand by for such an emergency. This aërial attack was a complete shock to the Germans, who had only small-arms fire with which to oppose it. The Australians circled over them incessantly, machine-gunning and bombing their armor. The enemy, in his turn, called for reinforcements. The Australians waited to inflict the same treatment on them. In all, forty German vehicles were wrecked. The planes swooped so low that one came home with a tarpaulin wrapped around it and German razor blades embedded in its fuselage.

The battle for Tunisia was moving swiftly toward a new climax. The Mareth Line position became more and more untenable. Before it, however, the Eighth Army was taking its time, wearing the enemy down by trying his nerves to the limit and warily feeling out his weakest spots. The Allies now held the initiative.

Marshal Rommel, nervous at the continued inactivity before his Mareth Line positions, opened up with his artillery on March 14, but it had no appreciable effect; he neither threw the Eighth Army back nor provoked it into any large-scale action. In the north, however, the British struck out in force and made inroads into the German positions around Tamera.

At last the Eighth Army struck again. The British onslaught was preceded by a long and terrific artillery barrage that raked the enemy's front-line positions and communications to the rear. Then, in bright moonlight, the full strength of the Eighth Army fell on the enemy's lines along a wide front. Aërial resistance was kept at a minimum by a strong Allied attack on the fields at Gabès, on which the enemy largely relied.

Marshal Rommel's worst fears were realized. The exploit of the Fighting French at Ksar Rhilane had underscored the constant danger in which his rear lay. He well knew that a far stronger force of Americans, with French-African support, was lurking somewhere behind Gafsa, from which a good highway led almost into his lines. As the Eighth Army pounded into the Mareth fortifications, the Americans behind Rommel lunged down to cut off his retreat. They seized Gafsa in a thirty-mile advance in one day.

If Marshal Rommel had known the name of the new commander of these forces, and his reputation, his fears would have been even greater. On the eve of the attack General Eisenhower had replaced General Fredenhall, who had commanded the Second Corps at Faïd and Kasserine, with Lieutenant General George S. Patton, Jr.

When the Allies landed at Casablanca, Patton had dashed ashore cradling a tommy gun in his arms and leaped immediately into the midst of the worst fighting, remaining there until it was over. A robust man, he had sworn neither to smoke nor to drink until he had entered

Tunis. He was looking forward eagerly to the breaking of his fast. He held a profound admiration for the ordinary buck private "who is out there getting shot at" and made it a point to be out there with him.

Part of Patton's Second Corps was the First Division, composed of troops who matched the commander. In the whole division, which contained men from every state in the Union, there were only six draftees. It was known as "the first team" in the Tunisian campaign, and it had a long and glorious history to which it was determined to live up. In the First World War, a captured German colonel had called it one of our top divisions; it was resolved to keep the rank. The divisional general, Major General Terry Allen, was a man ideally adapted to the division and to his chief. Other officers called him "the wild man" because he liked a good battle and would go anywhere to lead his men in the fiercest combat.

It was with such troops and officers that the Americans launched their all-out onslaught to get their revenge on Marshal Rommel for Faïd Pass. Starting out from Feriana to take Gafsa, which was held entirely by Italians, they accomplished their objective on the first day. As with the Eighth Army, artillery prepared the way into the town for the infantry, which had come up by truck during the night and sat through a three-hour bombardment. Then American planes attacked the town. Fifteen minutes later two combat teams converged on it while a French force was driving up from the south and southwest.

Various German obstacles slowed the advance of the Americans, but they were not enough to stop it. From Gafsa the attackers poured on toward El Guettar, twelve miles farther on the way to Gabès, while a strong section of the force turned due east toward Sened, which the Germans still held. One of the colorful figures of this force in central Tunisia was Brigadier General Theodore Roosevelt, Jr., whose jeep bore the name "Rough Rider" in honor of his famous father. The general was liaison officer between the Americans and the French and also served as a kind of assistant commander and an expert in morale.

It was not only such generals who distinguished themselves, but also anonymous American medical officers. These were to be found within a thousand yards of the front, working night and day to save the lives of wounded American soldiers under all sorts of handicaps. Sometimes their operating rooms were tents; more often they were the tonneaus of half-tracks or the covered bodies of trucks, where everything from the lighting to the anæsthetizing equipment was of the most impromptu kind.

The American captors of El Guettar now found themselves before the soggy Guettaria Pass, a six-mile stretch of rain-soaked terrain between Djebel Berda and Djebel Chemsi. When this dried it would provide a good avenue for an assault on Rommel's flank. It was feared that the Germans might try here, as they had elsewhere, to break out before the Allies could complete the closing of their trap. Von Arnim, in the north, was putting enough pressure on the First Army to cause it to yield Tamera and fall back toward Djebel Abiod. Aërial support for its defense cut into the planes available to the forces in the center and south, although the latter now had the advantage of support from the famous Western Desert Air Force that had traveled with the Eighth Army from El Alamein. This was under the command of Air Vice Marshal Sir Arthur Coningham.

Temporarily, any large-scale land activity by either side was blocked by renewed downpours. While the armies were thus preparing for the next decisive step, political developments behind the Allied lines had reached a new stage of progress that reflected the profound influence of the Allied successes on the minds of neutral and even antagonistic Frenchmen. The most important of these was a step to which General Giraud was practically driven by Allied pressure: the repeal of all legislation enacted since the downfall of the French Republic; the restoration of democratic institutions to North Africa; and General Giraud's promise to the people of France that after their liberation they would once again be the masters of a democratic country.

General de Gaulle again expressed his desire to confer with General Giraud on French soil. At the same time he reiterated his stand that, before coöperation was possible, the men of Vichy would have to go. As if in answer, or in token of the African régime's good faith, General Bergeret resigned his post as General Giraud's deputy. Bergeret had been one of the signers of the 1940 armistice and thereafter was violently anti-British and anti-Fighting French. The National Committee in London announced that General Catroux, having concluded his economic and military mission in Algiers and returned to Syria to wind up his affairs as High Commissioner, would soon return to Algiers as a diplomatic envoy.

Along the fighting fronts big events were brewing. A fast American column, led by tanks and covered by Spitfires and Airacobras, took Sened Station in a surprise assault and drove on toward the important junction of Maknassy. Other American forces streamed east down a road out of the junction beyond El Guettar. Simultaneously, Prime Minister Churchill, broadcasting to the world from London, revealed that he had just received a message from General Montgomery saying that the Eighth Army was "on the move" again. The Germans announced that the Fighting French column at Ksar Rhilane, reinforced by other units, had launched fifty tanks and two thousand truckloads of troops directly northeast toward Gabès to outflank the Mareth Line.

Rommel had been in many tight places and wriggled out. The "Desert Fox" was in a trap, but he was not yet caught.

62

ROMMEL ROUTED ON MARETH LINE

ROMMEL was to hold his troops intrenched behind the fortressed Mareth Line in the spring of 1943. Against the heart of this line the famous British Eighth Army was driving with increasing power. Heavy bombardments by its Western Desert Air Force, supported by American planes, were battering relentlessly against this last Axis stronghold.

Concentrated bombings of Rommel's communications and airfields between Gabès and Sfax were creating havoc. On the plateau of Djebel Tebaga and to Mezzaouna, fifty miles southwest of Sfax, French planes were in action. At the same time, the Allies' planes were not neglecting the important sea lanes from Sicily to Tunisia, along which the Germans were trying constantly to bring in reinforcements. The Allies had inflicted such damage on these convoys that they had exceptionally strong aërial protection, and every attack entailed a fierce air battle.

The ninety-mile gap between the American and British forces in the center and the south was being narrowed daily and the Allies were inflicting severe losses on the Germans. Hundreds of planes continued to bomb the enemy without mercy. The Eighth Army bit deeply into the center of the Mareth Line, capturing hundreds of Italians, and the Americans were within sight of Maknassy, while the African French continued to gain in their drive southeast from Gafsa toward the Fighting French coming up from Ksar Rhilane.

The Eighth Army had attacked on a front that ran six miles roughly north and south with the town of Mareth as its approximate center. Their path was sown with mines. British engineers worked night and day at clearing the mines, eliminating pillboxes, and building new roads and bridges over flooded *wadis* (seasonally dry watercourses) under constant enemy fire. Often some of their number would have to stop their work to return this fire and protect the rest. The most outstanding accomplishment of the Royal Engineers was the bridging of Wadi Zigzau, a deep, rock-walled gulch almost impossible to cross and almost devoid of approaches. To build their roads, the engineers often had to resort to such improvisations as huge bundles of sticks and branches tied together to form a bed, or tarpaulins and sandbags filled with rubble. Much of their material had to be hauled by hand to the places where it was to be set. The engineers, like stealthy poachers, crept up to the enemy's concrete fortifications in miniature that were impervious to anything short of a direct cannon shot and slipped timed explosive charges through the firing-slits which the Germans used. In the finding of mines they became so expert that in one area 900 were removed. The subsequent use of a magnetic detector, called the "carpet-sweeper" because it resembled one of the large circular floor-cleaners used in office buildings, revealed only three machines that the engineers had overlooked. All this work as we have said, was performed under fire and often in the path of German counterattacks. Front-line engineers had ample opportunity to observe the conditions. Germans frequently machine-gunned Italian troops who fought with them to prevent their desertion *en bloc*.

The Americans were driving with amazing speed along three roads toward the sea. One road ran through Maknassy and the others led southeast toward Gabès. The southernmost and best of these, which led to the "Gabès gap," a corridor between the sea and the hills that Rommel could be expected to keep open at all costs, ran past two heights, Djebel Chemsi and Djebel ven Kreir, where trouble was expected. In the first days of their assault, the Americans had sent to the rear, under the customary light guard, 1,400 Italian prisoners.

March 22 was one of the big days of the narrowing pincers assault on the Afrika Korps. Dawn brought the Americans into Maknassy, to the complete amazement of the Germans in the town. Royal Engineers put the finishing touches to their causeway across the Wadi Zigzau, standing knee-deep in water that reflected the bright moonlight and made them an excellent target for enemy artillery.

Behind them, reinforcements were being brought up rapidly; ahead of them, advance posts of infantry were calmly brewing tea after twenty-four hours under the hottest fire while they "picked the lock" of the Germans' defenses. Past them walked almost a thousand prisoners—smiling, relieved Italians and sullen, arrogant Germans. These were the captives of those men brewing tea on the other side of the wadi—men who had spent the hot desert day smashing strong points and beating off repeated enemy thrusts. At the end of the day they radioed hundreds of messages to the waiting armored cars across the wadi, telling them that the road was now open.

At the entry of the first patrol of eighteen Americans into Maknassy the Germans fled precipitately on the last train out for the coast. The Italians surrendered. Opposition came only from German dive bombers that tried to work over the Americans' communications but were driven off by heavy ground fire.

The Mareth Line position was now in the gravest danger. Slugging for two days against its heart, the Eighth Army's infantry pushed through and established a bridgehead on the main road to Gabès while the main body of the Eighth Army drove well within the perimeter of the line. Fighting French on the far left lunged forward in a brilliant flanking maneuver to a point only ten miles southwest of El Hamma and twenty-five miles southwest of Gabès.

Over the whole sector, not only all Tunisia but even Sicily, the Allies were keeping up an incessant bombardment. So intense was the attack that British and American crews were mixed in planes of both nations, and the coöperation was perfect. Airfields, troop concentrations, movements-shipping, and railways were pounded and set ablaze. Enemy tanks in action were left hulks.

While the British and the Fighting French were hacking away at the Mareth Line defenses, the Americans in the Maknassy area continued their drive toward the coast. But the other American force in the center, between Maknassy and the Mareth Line, found itself opposed by elements of one of the finest divisions in the Afrika Korps. Marshal Rommel, anxious to keep open his coastal escape corridor which these Americans now gravely threatened, detached crack armored units he could hardly spare and sent them racing up the road to El Guettar. Their purpose was to smash the American columns and, if possible, to recapture Gafsa. The Germans' armor struck the Americans by surprise, rolling between two American infantry positions southeast of El Guettar. It soon met American artillery fire at only 1,000 yards' range. Four of the attacking tanks were smashed. One-and-a-half hours after their attack, the remainder retired behind two ridges. American artillery and tank destroyers sallied up the heights against the fire of German 88-mm. antitank guns and heavier artillery.

German dive bombers joined the battle. Shells and bombs fell indiscriminately around and among the Americans. These battle-toughened youngsters were determined not to yield. More than once, as the Germans threw in fresh waves of tanks and planes, it looked as if the counterattack would succeed. Then the American planes roared over the battlefield. The fighters took on the German bombers and the enemy interceptors that rose against our bombers, while the latter methodically worked over the enemy's men and guns. By the end of the day the Americans had smashed the enemy's counterthrust.

Another German attack was being waged much farther north. Twenty-three miles northwest of Faïd Pass, at Hadjeb-el-Aiou, the Germans threw back a mixed force of American and French troops. That this part of the line was less strongly held was due in large measure to the fact that the Germans, with consent of the Spanish Government, had kept from the time of our landings in Africa a large force in Spanish Morocco. This force necessarily immobilized an equivalent American force that must keep constant watch for an attack on French Morocco. In the extreme north, the Germans again tasted defeat, for the First Army recaptured Nefsa and increased its guard over Djebel Abiod.

Marshal Rommel in desperation launched a furious counterattack from the Mareth Line itself and against the Fighting French near El Hamma. The first was briefly successful; but the Eighth Army quickly re-formed. Under a sky darkened for a whole day by the incessant flight of Allied planes bombing and strafing the Germans it regained the initiative, threw the Germans back to where they had been before, and then resumed its own drive forward into their positions. By nightfall the British were hammering at the second of the three defense lines the Germans had hastily erected.

The Germans were so preoccupied in the Mareth Line and so sorely battered by the Americans around El Guettar that they attempted nothing farther in that area immediately after their counterattack had failed. As they nursed their wounds, the Americans awaited a favorable opportunity to attack. But in the Maknassy area the American infantry kept going without a let-up.

In four days they advanced more than one hundred miles from their starting-point at Feriana. While their northern flank met virtually no opposition, the men on the south proved themselves more than the equals of the Germans, soldier for soldier. The heroism of the combat troops stopped dead in its tracks the German division that had driven the Canadians off the beaches of Dieppe. Signal and engineer corps men behind the lines strung telephone wires and performed their other duties with the utmost calm while German shells screamed past them. They proved conclusively that, given the numbers and equipment to match the enemy's, they could smash him.

Over all the fronts, the combined air forces, augmented by Liberators from both the R.A.F. and the American Middle East Commands, ranged as masters. In many cases the enemy fliers deliberately avoided giving battle. This aërial onslaught over the battle area, including the north where the First Army was continuing its slow progress, exceeded anything that had been launched against the ports and communications of Tunisia; yet these did not escape. Strong Allied forces were daily pounding every dock and landing strip, railway track, and road that might be of use to the enemy. Shipping in the Mediterranean, ports and railways in Sicily and southern Italy were equally mercilessly pounded with the coöperation of R.A.F. planes from Malta.

It was becoming increasingly evident, as the two-ton "block-busters" that had devastated German cities began falling on the positions of Marshal Rommel's troops, that the Allies were gaining mastery of the air. With the assistance of the planes, the Eighth Army, on the sixth day of the battle for the Mareth Line, was able to inch slightly ahead.

Again, near El Guettar, the Germans attacked, determined to block this threat to their flank since, apparently, they could not smash the French around El Hamma. They were no more successful against the

Americans. Although they seized the southern slope of Djebel Berda, the doughboys retained their iron grip on the peak of the mountain. In the Maknassy area the enemy stiffened and even the Italians attempted to counterattack, but in vain. Then the Americans caught the enemy by surprise. More than one hundred miles north of the central front's uppermost line in the Maknassy sector, they lunged out in a sudden blow for the town of Fondouk, which the enemy held, at the lower end of the Ousselat Valley.

Uncertain of the significance of the new American drive, the Germans in the center, around Maknassy and El Guettar, awaited developments. The Eighth Army continued its inexorable grinding into the Mareth Line. Above it, and its French comrades around El Hamma, planes concentrated their bombs, shells, and bullets on the enemy, striking with force and effectiveness at his armor and artillery.

The German commanders, with their much flaunted military genius, had waited too long. They had indeed little choice, for to counterattack anywhere except perhaps in the far north would have been ultimately suicidal. The "big push" so long feared was now at hand. The Allies struck along all the hundreds of miles of the Tunisian front in a coördinated attack supported by dominant Allied air power.

The First Army in the north advanced farther east of Djebel Abiod. The French took the heights east of the Ousselat Valley and occupied dominating positions northwest of the "holy city" and railway junction of Kairouan. Below them and to the west, the Americans, who had started twenty miles away near Hadjeb-el-Aiou, emerged from one of the deepest passes in central Tunisia to seize Fondouk, a strategic point from which they could threaten the enemy forces already menaced from the Maknassy sector and pose an added peril to Kairouan.

The greatest advances were being scored in the south, due largely to the Western Desert Air Force, whose magnificent achievements in the face of the deadly *Khamsin,* a desert wind that raised thick yellow sandstorms, won special commendation from General Montgomery. His forces, both those driving directly into the Mareth Line and the flanking force far to the west, scored notable successes. The Fighting French, in one of the most brillant and daring strokes of the Eighth Army's whole march across Africa, broke their way into El Hamma.

This audacious flanking drive was to set the pattern that Montgomery was to follow more than once in the future, not only in Tunisia but later in Sicily. It was not only a brilliant military achievement in the tactical sense, it saved innumerable lives and days that would have been sacrificed in a purely frontal assault on the Mareth Line. It was a daring, though coolly deliberate, gamble that involved a high risk of failure.

The Fighting French had been operating in considerable strength to the south of the main body of the Eighth Army. On March 23, large elements of the Eighth Army were sent "out into the blue" to join them and, as far as possible, insure the success of the battle plan. These forces set out at night to escape enemy observation, rolling south through the village of Foum Tatahouine with its almost Biblical aspect of low, domed houses and camel-caravans in the streets. Stinging sand particles almost blinded the men and caused considerable damage to their machines.

Against this almost complete lack of visibility and the constant miring of vehicles in the heavy sand, the column reached the Matmata Hills without the loss of a man or a vehicle. Rolling now with General Leclerc's Frenchmen it turned into a valley flanked by mountains and sown with mines to impede the advance of the column.

When the first column had broken through the wastes into the valley, another followed. Both moved with a speed that was little short of miraculous in view of the conditions they encountered. At last they were discovered, as they knew that eventually they must be. A sizable German force awaiting just such a move, though not anticipating its strength, was amply supplied to give battle. What followed was part of the battle of Ksar Rhilane that has been described, and the advance to El Hamma. That town and the heights around it were taken in fighting as fierce, if not so large in its scale, as that of the Mareth Line itself. For days the Allies' planes battered at the enemy's armor in front of El Hamma, while the ground troops and tanks flung themselves upon it. Gaining slowly but invincibly, they threw back all counterattacks until they had battled their way into El Hamma itself, where they stood less than twenty miles from Gabès and the sea.

This strong and indomitable force at their rear shattered the Germans' tremendous will to resist. Unbreakable thus far, it began to crumble. Led by low-flying Spitfires and light bombers, the Eighth Army's main body, which had reached the Germans' second line of defense, smashed it down and broke into the third and last line. The main forts and the towns of Mareth, Toujane, and Matmata were left behind by British soldiers pouring through the gaps they had cut. The Afrika Korps was streaking up the coastal road for Gabès, hammered incessantly by the Western Desert Air Force as the fleeing troops neared the bottleneck of the Gabès-El Hamma gap. This was growing steadily narrower, for the Allies' columns in El Hamma had lost little time in gathering their strength before pushing ahead, eastward toward the coast.

In the eight days of bitter fighting that preceded the final breakthrough the enemy had lost heavily in men and equipment. With 6,000 of his soldiers already captured and thousands dead, Marshal Rommel was now busy planning the course of his withdrawal with counterattacks along his inland flank to prevent the Americans and French in the center from cutting off his retreat.

The Allies' strategy, too, was planning carefully for the enemy's withdrawal. As his columns raced out of the Mareth Line, a series of Allied attacks was opened from El Guettar to Djebel Abiod. In the Guettar area, the Americans scaled Djebel el Mcheltat under German fire, driving the enemy off the height nine miles east of El Guettar. Their comrades around Maknassy and the French in the Ousselat Valley heights also pushed forward.

As the battered Axis creaked, the Allies continued their advance in every sector. Led by the New Zealanders, Britons, and fierce Maoris commanded by Lieutenant General Sir Bernard C. Freyberg, the Eighth Army marched victoriously into Gabès. The city was hysterical with happiness. In that French port the Allies met the first of a series of wild demonstrations that were to increase incredibly in ardor until they culminated in the reception of the conquerors of Tunis. The entire population went mad with joy. From a thousand houses flew the Tricolor, usually emblazoned with the Cross of Lorraine, the Union Jack, and the Stars and Stripes, flags which had been hopefully concealed for months while the Germans and Italians held the city.

But the Allies could not stay for applause and thanks; they were on the road to battle. Rommel was still in flight ahead of them. The French African troops who had taken Tozeur had rounded the Chott Djerid to occupy Kebili and were now driving toward the sea. Ahead of the Germans other Frenchmen and strong American forces were advancing, all concentrated on the destruction of the enemy before he could reach the relative haven of the Tunis-Bizerte corner.

Along the shore, paralleling the enemy's flight, the Royal Navy swung into action. Its guns sent shells arching in to fall on the troops themselves, on the roads ahead of them, and on their bases. Constantly the Allies' planes kept pace with the retreat, giving the Germans a taste of the punishment to which they had subjected civilian refugees on the roads of France and the Low Countries almost three years earlier. As air and sea attacks and the jamming of the roads forced the Germans into ever larger clusters, they became increasingly better targets. Their own aircraft and their scattered ground fire were impotent to cope with the might of the Allies.

The "invincible" Germans and fellow Italians were definitely on the run. The outcome of the Tunisian campaign was no longer in doubt. The campaign for Tunisia was the last leg of a retreat of 1,430 miles by one of the finest armies in history, a distance covered in the unheard-of time of 158 days. In its latest stand, the Battle of the Mareth Line, the Afrika Korps had lost 8,000 prisoners, besides the men killed and wounded, and vast quantities of most precious equipment. With every additional mile of this unparalleled retreat, more equipment had to be abandoned. Stragglers whose wounds prevented them from keeping up had to be left behind. The great Rommel retreat was one of the most costly in history.

Gabès was found to be a mass of wreckage. There, as in Tripoli and other Libyan harbors and as in more Tunisian cities in the very near future, the Germans destroyed everything that might be of value to the Allies. Harbor and rail and airdrome installations were wrecked. They knew they were beaten. As they fled up the coastal road to the north, they could not even stop in a stagnant desert stream, as the Fighting Frenchmen did on their way into Gabès from El Hamma, grateful for a spot of green oasis and brackish water after days of battle and of endless travel. Through the sand, in vehicles so close one behind the other that the exhaust gases were almost asphyxiating, they plunged on.

The Eighth Army pushed through the narrowest part of the Gabès Gap in hot pursuit of the Germans, while the flanking column that had entered Gabès from El Hamma returned to the west and continued a parallel northward drive fairly well inland. Even defeat was organized with Rommel's characteristic skill. His main body kept out of the way of the British, delaying them with well-fought rear-guard actions along the coastal road. At first the Germans planned to make a stand in the first line of natural defenses seven to nine miles above Gabès, but the British were so close that the enemy abandoned the strong points of Metouia and Oudref to avoid a new battle such a short time after the Mareth Line disaster.

Instead, the "Desert Fox" elected to make his next stopping place Wadi el Akarit, about twelve miles north of Gabès. This was a steep gully running into the sea and protected on the inland side by one of the salt marshes so common in that region, Chott el Fedjadj. Before this position the Germans were laying mines, rapidly and thickly. The same protection was being applied to the inland flank even north of the wadi, for the Americans were not relaxing in their drive to reach the sea and effect a junction with the Eighth Army. Below El Guettar the American troops were finding the enemy mine fields a considerable hindrance, while in the Maknassy and Fondouk areas there were still substantial German forces.

The Allies seemed less intent on trapping Marshal Rommel on the coast than in forcing him to merge with the forces in the north under von Arnim so that the whole campaign might be decided in one final major battle. To this end the Allies were drastically revising their aërial tactics to increase the emphasis on coöperation with the land forces. Strategic bombing, however, was not neglected.

The Allies were resolved that Rommel should not be allowed to stand on African soil. To drive him off, it was necessary to cut off his supplies and reinforcements. It was estimated he was still getting 500 to 1,000 men daily and a minimum of 75 tanks a month from Sardinia and Sicily and Italy by both air and sea. The Allies decided to strike these sources at their heart. The month of April was ushered in by a great attack on the seaport and airdrome of Cagliari in Sardinia. The largest fleet of Flying Fortresses yet assembled for one operation—something less than a hundred planes—went into action. Escorted by the long-range Lightning fighters that had proved themselves so valiantly in Tunisia, the bombers roared in over the city in the midst of a swarm of enemy fighters. In the shrieking, swirling air battle the bombers unloaded their cargoes and sank or damaged twenty-six ships, while their own guns and fighter escort sent seventy-one enemy planes hurtling to the ground. Though the power of the enemy's strong ground fire was directed against them in battle, every one of the American bombers and fighters returned to base.

The whole Allied line was moving forward. The capture of Sedjenane in the north made almost untenable the position of the enemy forces that had taken Cap Serrat on the coast in their earlier drive westward; already First Army patrols were within twelve miles of the promontory in their return along the coastal road. As the Germans in southern Europe rushed frantically to defend their coasts, the Algiers radio put on a special broadcast. To the accompaniment of recordings of the terrific aërial and artillery bombardments, the announcer read a letter written by General Giraud to the arch-traitor Laval: "Listen to the thunder of the guns and planes. Do you hear, M. Laval? They are attacking!... The Eighth Army of General Montgomery, the American divisions of General Eisenhower, the First British Army of General Anderson and the divisions of General Giraud are chasing Rommel.... There are French soldiers attacking, like their comrades of Verdun. Do you hear?... You have lost the right to call yourself a Frenchman."

M. Laval may not have listened to the broadcast; but millions of Frenchmen heard it and rejoiced at every new gain by the armies of liberation, knowing that Tunisia was but a symbol of what waited in Europe.

While General Montgomery gathered his forces for his next crushing blow at the Afrika Korps, other British troops in the north kept battering their way eastward. Dedjenane and Cap Serrat were left behind as the First Army drove for its first objective on the road to Bizerte—the town of Mateur, only twenty miles from the naval base, which the Allies had almost taken in their first gambler's lunge into Tunisia four months before.

While Marshal Pétain, fulminating over a raid by American Flying Fortresses on the industrial Parisian suburb of Billancourt, bitterly denounced the Frenchmen outside France as the authors of the country's anguish, Frenchmen in North Africa were giving their lives to liberate their country. In the north, working with the British, they were steadily forcing the Germans back on Jefna along the road to Mateur. The French people in Tunis were sacrificing to the point of hunger. Bread rations had been reduced to six ounces a day and meat had not been seen since January. In Bizerte the Germans were evacuating the population to points as distant as Mammamet, sixty miles away, in the course of their preparations to defend the base to the last. In both cities, able-bodied civilians were impressed into virtual slavery to clear the débris left by the constant Allied air attacks.

These targets were important as the termini of the enemy's supply routes. One of the most important bases from which these routes ran was Naples, well up on the west coast of Italy. The port had been bombed before from the Middle East. Now the Flying Fortresses of the Northwest African Air Forces turned their fury loose upon it. Almost a hundred of the huge planes cascaded their bombs on the heart of its harbor area, pounding it four times harder than it had ever been hit before. Ships, warehouses, and docks suffered severely; twenty-seven of ninety-six planes on a near-by airfield were left in ruins.

Italians and Germans had not recovered from the shock of this new blow, with all its implications, when their armies in Tunisia reeled again beneath the shattering strokes of a new assault by the indefatigable Eighth Army. In the pre-dawn blackness of April 6, Montgomery's forces threw all their strength against Wadi el Akarit. The enemy was caught completely off guard, for it had expected the British to await a junction with the Americans before striking again.

One thousand planes and hundreds of guns had opened huge holes in the enemy's lines in the preceding day and night. The Eighth Army's tanks and infantry, with Fighting Frenchmen and tough New Zealanders in the van, poured into them. Deep V-shaped antitank ditches were no more effective than the natural defenses of empty wadis and steep heights in holding back this mighty assault. It rolled invincibly forward.

Americans on the Germans' flank were moving forward at the same time. Showers of steel darts were rained on them at night by low-flying German planes. The doughboys held their ground. Then, after their own planes had routed the enemy's flying archers and gone on to break up a tank column to the southeast, they advanced. With the dawn they found their quarry had gone, fleeing apparently toward the coast to rejoin their main body as it came up in retreat from Wadi el Akarit.

While the bulk of the Eighth Army was hammering its way into that position, a patrol force was striking northwest up the Gabès-Gafsa road, the same road on which the Americans, balked of their prey, continued their advance in the opposite direction. Suddenly, in the shadow of the menacing heights the Germans had held only a few days before, the occupants of a yellow British scout car, followed by two armored cars, saw a little procession of dull-green vehicles rolling down the road toward them. It was mid-afternoon and the sun was in the British soldiers' eyes. A sergeant took up his field glasses. Seeing the deep bowl-shaped helmets worn by the men in the green cars, he turned to his driver.

"They're Jerries," he warned. But another occupant of the scout car had also scanned the approaching soldiers through field glasses and his recognition was keener. "No, by God!" he shouted. "They're Yanks!"

The news was passed to the armored cars behind. All three vehicles increased their speed. The Americans, who had had no difficulty identifying the yellow vehicles, "stepped on the gas." As their cars drew nearer to the British, American doughboys slipped onto their running-boards. Then, while the brakes of their vehicles were still bringing down their speed, they leaped off to run to the halted British cars.

This was the historic junction of the two armies, the veterans of a 1,500-mile drive across the worst of Africa and the new graduates of the harsh school of battle who had proved themselves men of equal worth. A few hours later, British liaison officers were strolling through Gafsa, wanting to know whether the Yanks had any beer.

Thus did the desert warriors meet, while the skies were black with their planes striking fiercely and lethally against the enemy wherever he was to be found. German air convoy bound for Tunisia never got there; twenty-five miles off the coast, thirty-one of its planes, including eighteen of the big Junkers' fifty-two transports, were hurled into the sea. A sea convoy was battered. A destroyer was blown up by aërial bombings. Ships it was escorting were left in flames. Docks and airfields in Sicily were left smoking. In Tunisia, the airfields of La Fauconnerie and El Djem, vital to the German defense of Sfax, and of El Aouina near Tunis were battered despite the enemy's efforts to protect them.

The advance elements of the Allies' two armies had met in southern Tunisia; their main forces were not long in joining. Together they forged an arc around the fleeing enemy, 6,000 of whose men had already been taken by the victorious Eighth Army in its newest breakthrough. The astonished British found that almost all Rommel's armor had been used in the vain attempt to hold back the Americans. His remaining tanks were in an untenable position and had to withdraw rapidly to the coastal area.

Prime Minister Churchill appeared that night before a cheering **House of Commons.** Only the day before, the members had been depressed by predictions of political bombasts in both their own country and the United States, that the campaign might last as long as four months and even be lost. Now they laughed in good-humored scorn at the discredited pundits.

Allied Headquarters in Algiers paid a glowing tribute to the Fighting French whose leader was De Gaulle and the other French who acknowledged allegiance to Giraud. The tide of battle had brought the forces together; De Gaullists and Giraudists had joined in Tripolitania and advanced into Tunisia. Together now they were fighting in the ranks of the Eighth Army and beside the Americans on the British left flank. They had, as if by silent accord, ignored the political beliefs that might have caused such severe dissension in their ranks at a crucial moment and had jointly obeyed the orders of the armies to which they were attached.

Both the African French and the Fighting French had found themselves many times opposed by forces that far outweighed them in number and arms, but won many a victory despite these handicaps. The two groups together had never had more than 70,000 men in the field at one time, and most of these had fought with ancient rifles and machine guns that seemed obsolete to the excellently armed Americans and Britons. Most of the time they had to move on foot with horses and mules to haul their equipment. Their casualty rate had been the highest of the three nations. But they had never lost heart. In every crisis they had moved into the gaps in the line; they had held positions for days when Americans and Britons were far away.

General Eisenhower proclaimed that the Allies now held the whip hand in Tunisia. In a message to General Alexander, whose combined land forces, to which the Eighth Army now belonged, were designated as the Eighteenth Army Group, the Commander in Chief expressed his delighted congratulations on the troops' achievements. He declared that the army, navy and air forces were "now in position to exact the full price from the enemy."

The Afrika Korps was still in full retreat. So close were the Allies behind and the Americans on the flank that the enemy had less time to strew his mines as he rushed toward Sfax with his rear guard doing what they could to protect him. In a single day the Eighth Army advanced fifteen miles, gathering huge amounts of abandoned but serviceable matériel. The Americans found the Germans' flank more heavily guarded. So intense was the air support that the more distant strategic targets had to be left to the Middle East and Malta planes, which constantly raked Sicily and southern Italy, as well as striking occasionally but strongly at Naples.

The Americans garnered hosts of prisoners. Like the British, they found the Italians genial at the idea of capture while the Germans kept all their arrogance. Truck after truck, as on the Eighth Army's front, rolled toward the rear loaded with captives. In the arc where the

American and British forces met, the line was pushed forward by Gurkhas, silent, small East Indian troops as adept with the knife as the Moroccan *goumiers*. As the Germans swept northward, the Allies' line came to vibrant life to "get" them. The enemy still held the important railway junction of Kairouan, as well as the towns of Pichon and Fondouk protecting it. As long as this obstacle remained, no Allied troops could reach the coast; so, with infantry, tanks, and massed artillery, American and British forces struck hard at both, while the French in the Ousselat heights to the northeast drove steadily toward the bigger peaks between them and the coast. At Pichon and Fondouk, the enemy relied chiefly on mines, mortars, and antitank artillery in a vain struggle. The Americans, who had held Fondouk once before, took it again. The British threw the enemy out of Pichon. Both Allied forces continued to advance.

Axis leaders were plainly worried. Fearful of an invasion of Europe within the month Hitler summoned Mussolini to his headquarters to study the situation with him. For four days they conferred and planned, while the British Broadcasting Company, to give their people some idea of what the Allies had in store for them, broadcast recordings of the 500-gun barrage that the Eighth Army had hurled at the Mareth Line. The two dictators could offer nothing more than words and false hopes. The Italian leader was so frightened by the imminence of an invasion that he was begging Hitler to draw no more troops from Italy and was threatening to move his capital into the north.

In striking contrast were the pronouncements of the Allies' commanders in the field. General Patton, whose rhetoric was as picturesque as his fighting, paid tribute to his First Division for its victories at El Guettar. He declared that the Americans' task had not been to surround the enemy, but to engage, delay, and destroy his armor to weaken his frontal defenses. This was the simple truth: The American force had never been intended to do more; any such attempt would have resulted in disaster not only to the First Division but to the whole Allied plan of campaign. Patton, praising the troops for their discipline, loyalty, and coöperation, concluded: "Nothing in hell must delay or stop the First Division."

General Montgomery, paying tribute to his own men for their latest victories, recalled what he had told them before the Mareth Line battle: "Deal with the enemy there, burst through the Gabès Gap and drive northwards on Sfax, Sousse, and finally Tunis." The first two objectives had been gained; the third item on his agenda was being executed. Giving full credit to the achievements of the Western Desert Air Force, he said of the troops: "I doubt if our Empire has ever possessed such a magnificent fighting machine as the Eighth Army. You have made its name a household word all over the world."

BATTLES LEADING TO HILL 609 AND TRIUMPH

THIRTY-TWO more days of terrific battles and the Allied conquest of Africa would end in triumph. On April 10, 1943, smashing blows were being struck against the tottering Axis, inflicting grievous wounds in both Tunisia and Sardinia, by air and land. The Eighth Army launched forward. Americans on the flank poured eastward. Flying Fortresses in heavy force swept over the important Italian naval base at La Maddelena in Sardinia. The *Trieste* was sunk at her anchorage; the *Gorizia,* though still afloat, was badly crippled.

The two-day air offensive had other profitable results that bore directly on the success of the land campaign. Under heavy fighter escort, the Germans were now pouring men and matériel, even gasoline, into Tunisia by transport plane, using the slow, cumbersome but capacious Junkers 52. In two days, sixty-one of these and twenty-four of their escorting fighters were shot down into the sea; the Allies lost only three machines in taking this toll. They met for the first time the newest of the German aërial vehicles, the huge, six-motored Merseburg 323. This plane was a so-called power-glider. It was too big and heavy, especially when fully loaded, to take off unassisted, and had to be towed until it was airborne.

While the Allies' fighters were thus smashing the Germans' efforts to reinforce their rapidly dwindling Tunisian bridgehead, other fighters and bombers were lending their full support to the new and powerful land drive that was breaking the back of the enemy's resistance in central Tunisia. The Eighth Army's advance was the most spectacular. It roared through Sfax, which the Germans hardly defended, and on along the coastal road toward Sousse, plunging through La Hencha. In four days, it had gained eighty miles from Wadi el Akarit.

The Americans on the flank were in equally vigorous movement. Joined by the British, who had taken Pichon, they plunged boldly into the "holy city" of Kairouan, which the Germans did not stay to defend. Behind the captors of Kairouan the French moved in to clean up the Pichon area, while the British and Americans hurried on to join the Eighth Army and harry the enemy into his last corner.

Other American forces to the southwest were at last taking their revenge for their defeat of February. Eager to overtake fleeing German rear guards and heedless of exploding mine fields, tanks of the Second United States Corps went crashing into and through Faïd Pass.

In Sfax the Eighth Army found the same demolitions that had marked other German-held cities. The ferocious bombing that the town had endured was reflected in the coolness of the first welcome to the British commander. Montgomery entered the town first in a staff car and proceeded to a reviewing stand past which the victorious soldiers were to parade. Sensible of the people's chill, the General ordered that his Fighting French contingents should precede all other elements of the Eighth Army on parade that day. An hour later the populace was cheering him wildly.

The main body of the First Army in the extreme north was awaiting the opportune time to strike in coördination with all the other Allied forces converging on Tunis and Bizerte. This area, which the enemy had held throughout the campaign, was more thickly mined than any the Allies had encountered. They faced much tough campaigning before they reached it.

Allied planes began now to concentrate on Tunis and Bizerte. Both cities had excellent airdrome and harbor facilities and both could serve as bases for a sea evacuation. While Montgomery had urged his men to make the Germans undergo a "first-class Dunkirk," it was not the Allies' intention that the enemy should match that achievement by bringing off any considerable part of his forces.

The greater part of the Allies' planes was concentrating on Marshal Rommel's probable next stopping-place—a line extending inland from Enfidaville on the coast. Here the road was flanked on the inland side by a series of steep, rugged mountains; a fairly large salt marsh, Sebkret Sidi Kralifa, lay between it and the coast. The position abounded in natural defensive advantages. Montgomery's devil-fighters, as the enemy knew to his cost, were bound in the end to be more than a match for Rommel. Even the official Italian radio described it as "the finest fighting force in the world today." It admitted to its own hearers that the situation was hopeless and lamented bitterly that the Italians had to bear the brunt of all the rear-guard actions against this massive and superb war machine. It did not mention that at one point in his flight, Rommel had stayed in a requisitioned mansion while an Italian general had lived in a tent on the front lawn.

The Eighth Army, however, when it reached the Enfidaville positions, which the Germans had hastily prepared, was brought to an abrupt halt. The bulk of the action shifted again to the air. The Allies returned to the assault on the enemy's supply lines with a massive Flying Fortress attack on two Sicilian airfields at Milo and Castelvetrano—names that were to figure again a few months later.

In the mountains above Kairouan and southwest of the British lines at Enfidaville, American and French troops were taking up their positions in preparation for the next stage of the battle. They had cleaned out the isolated German pockets of resistance in the heights, killing 500 enemy troops, capturing 1,100, and seizing considerable booty. Djebel Mansour, southwest of Pont-du-Fahs, was recaptured by French troops. Far ahead of these operations the Eighth Army's Western Desert Air Force—now far beyond the region that had given it its name—was already ranging over the extremities of Cap Bon, lest the Germans attempt either to flee or to land fresh troops on its beaches. On the northern front, the First Army began to pick up power. Dependent on the free use of the road from Medjez-el-Bab to Tebourba, it rushed over Djebel-el-Ang and Heidous, two heights that dominated the highway, to secure it for the grand assault. With their capture, the British stood only twenty-two miles outside the capital.

As the fatal position of the enemy troops became ever more indisputable, General Eisenhower allowed himself to make one of his rare predictions. Not given to undeliberate speech, he declared that the enemy's defeat was inevitable—that, while Marshal Rommel was indubitably a great general, he was not a superman, and his army, though deserving the highest respect as a fighting machine, was far from invincible. The Germans seemed to share the belief that Rommel was only human, for they put both his and General von Arnim's forces under a new commander, Field Marshal General Albert Kesselring.

The Allies' shipping situation had now improved incredibly. Ten and a half million tons of shipping had entered the North African theater since the first landings; their losses had been less than $2\frac{1}{2}$ per cent. On the east coast, the newly captured harbors of Sousse and Sfax— General Eisenhower wanted Sfax so badly that he had promised to give General Montgomery a Flying Fortress if he captured it—were being made usable by Allied naval parties assisted by the French.

German attempts at reprisal were weak. Almost all failed. A small number of bombers, aided by a bright moon, destroyed a convent in Algiers while the Allies were achieving successful raids against convoys at sea, shipping in harbors, and the important town of Ferryville, about twelve miles southeast of Bizerte. Lying midway between Lake Bizerte and Lake Achkel on a narrow isthmus that separated the two fairly large water barriers, Ferryville was the center of the electric power supply for not only the normal functions but the naval installations in Bizerte. It suffered heavily at the hands of the Allies' planes.

The Allies held undisputed aërial mastery. General Spaatz, in support of this announcement, reported that since the battle of the Mareth Line the enemy had lost 519 planes in aërial combat and 1,000 on the ground, while the Allies had lost only 175—a ratio of almost 10 to 1. One of the most notable achievements of the Royal Air Force was the development of the so-called "tank-buster," known affectionately to the men who flew it as the "can-opener" for its power in destroying tanks.

This was a new modification of the famous British Hurricane fighter, armed with two 40-mm. cannon firing 2½-pound shells either singly or automatically.

This newly won control of the air was put to the test while the ground forces were still preparing for the "big push." Protected by the natural defenses and their own fortifications on the hills before Enfidaville, forming an arc around Tunis and Bizerte, the Germans were organizing the withdrawal of their most valuable personnel in big Junkers transport planes accompanied by fighters. The operation had no sooner begun than it was smashed into costly, bloody failure. American Warhawks and British Spitfires roared out over the Cap Bon Peninsula and the Sicilian Narrows. In one day they destroyed eighty-five enemy planes—fifty-eight of them being lumbering troop carriers—against the fiercest resistance the Germans could offer. Of the eighty-five, the amazing total of seventy-four was shot down.

While the Allies' fighters were concentrating on the enemy's evacuation planes, their bombers were seeing to it that any of these that might escape should have as rough a time as possible in landing. The string of airports along and behind the southern coast of Sicily, and other fields in Sardinia, to which the transports were bound and from which replacements would be sent to Africa, were mercilessly bombed.

On the eve of the birthday of Adolf Hitler the British Army began its celebration early, with the launching of the big drive for Tunis. In bright moonlight, its heavy guns opened up with one of Montgomery's characteristic barrages against the irregular crags and gorges that protected the enemy's forces in their thirty-three-mile-wide defense line. Veterans of the desert, long accustomed to its heat and thirst and grime, had now to learn for the first time a grim and wholly strange type of combat—mountain fighting. The Enfidaville line formed part of the almost unbroken mountain range that curved 120 miles toward the northern coast of Tunisia to protect the capital and the big naval base; behind it lay other heights. But the New Zealanders and the Indians, the Poles and the Greeks and the Frenchmen, the Scots and the Southrons were eager and apt students, however hard the lesson, however high its cost.

Their first objective was Djebel Garci, 1,200 feet high in the line of ridges into which the enemy had strongly dug. Twisting gorges and almost impossibly steep rises were sown with mines. Every gully concealed a machine-gun nest. Every rock mass sheltered German artillery. The Eighth Army battered and clambered and clawed its way up the rises and down the slopes in the face of furious fire. Before dawn of the Fuehrer's birthday his troops had lost Djebel Garci.

Simultaneously with the Eighth Army's new blow, other sectors of the front flared into new activity. Between the Enfidaville sector and the northern battleground, North African French troops were returning to the battle, rested, vengeful, and better armed than ever before. They no longer had to rely on mules to carry their outmoded weapons, or on ancient scout cars with improvised machine guns to withstand the German tanks. These troops—many of them veterans of armor battles in France in 1940—had spent their time behind the lines in learning the use and care of the most modern American weapons. They returned to the front, not on long marches but in speedy six-wheeled trucks, accompanied by General Sherman tanks made in the United States. Other American trucks kept pace, hauling the newest 105- and 155-mm. American artillery to its appointed place.

This was the sector that lay between the Rag-el-Hejij region, where the Fighting French were continuing their advance, and the area around Bou Arada, the southern extremity of the First Army's operational ground. The grand strategic concept envisaged their advance with the Eighth and First Armies in a converging drive on Tunis.

The Eighth Army smashed farther into the Germans' line. Enfidaville itself, the eastern anchor of the defenses, fell on Herr Hitler's birthday when Montgomery split the right wing and sent the two component parts around the town to the east and the west to meet again beyond it. Thus encircled, the town was rapidly taken.

The Allies threw almost all the weight of their air force into attacks against the enemy's airports, from Bizerte to the south fighting line, in a concentrated effort to keep the enemy's planes from attacking the ground troops. The Germans were compelled to put up a much stronger fighter defense than they had offered for some time—and, as a corollary, to abandon for the moment their evacuations, since they could not spare fighters to protect the transports. Many of their fliers shirked every offer of engagement and streaked away.

The First Army, meanwhile, was pressing onward in the north, mauling crack enemy divisions in its path and forcing them into retreat. The Germans, even while they had to withdraw these battered elements, recognized the imminent danger of a major offensive in this area while the Eighth Army was pounding at Rommel. In a desperate effort to prevent it while they screened the retirement of five infantry battalions, they counterattacked suddenly on an eight-mile front below Medjez-el-Bab.

Seventy big tanks, including the giant Mark VI's, were employed to cover the withdrawal after a moonlight attack that could not compare with the nocturnal masterpieces of General Montgomery. The British refused to be deterred. Bringing up their artillery, they proceeded to knock twenty-seven of the tanks, including two of the biggest, out of action. When, at daylight, the enemy attempted to disengage, the British swarmed out of the hills and cut great holes in his fleeing forces.

While the Eighth Army labored and clawed its way deeper into the hills above Enfidaville, the First Army, encouraged by its destruction of the German counterattacks below Medjez, opened the offensive which that costly effort had been intended to stop. On a nine-mile front between Bou Arada and Goubellat, they hurled a strong mass of infantry against three hills whose western slopes occupied seven miles of the front. These heights, Argoub Hamra on the north, Ahrab-el-Mahalla in the center, and Kodiat Sibarka in the south, commanded the entrance to the so-called coastal plain lying before Tunis—virtually all flat country where the Germans would have to stand and fight or run for the sea. North of Medjez-el-Bab, another strong force of the First Army was hurled against Long Stop Hill, after a heavy artillery barrage that overshadowed anything yet seen in the north. Like the hills below Goubellat, Long Stop commanded a vital pass to the coastal plain, the pass from Medjez.

In the face of these assaults and in spite of the pressing need to protect their troops from the air, the Germans tried to stage a reversal of the evacuation by air with fighter support. This time they employed, instead of the Junkers 52's, the even more vulnerable Merseburg 323's—huge, overweight, six-engined power-gliders which the Allies' airmen were to compare to sitting ducks when they attacked them. When the engagement was over, not a German transport was left in the air. Ten of the protecting fighters had joined them beneath the Mediterranean. The transports—so big that their noses could be let down as ramps for tanks or trucks to be driven inside and flown to a battlefield—broke apart in the air, spilling men and gasoline out of their flaming bellies, or disintegrated as they tumbled into the sea.

With dramatic suddenness, the United States Second Corps reëntered the story of the fighting. After the battle of El Guettar, it seemed to have disappeared, and no more was heard of its colorful commander, "Old Blood and Guts" Patton, after he had issued his congratulations on its achievements. But, in all the silence, the Americans had been accomplishing one of the most brilliant non-combat maneuvers of the campaign. From the southern Tunisian front, great masses of troops with all their equipment were ordered to join the First Army's northern wing to launch the final offensive for Bizerte and Tunis. The shift meant moving north over three hundred miles of ground far enough behind the battle lines to keep out of enemy observation.

In a country where there were few roads that could afford quick passage to a large body of men and machines, the move was made without mishap, and, above all, without waking the slightest suspicion in the Germans. So efficiently and speedily was it achieved that it won special commendation from General Alexander. "Senior British officers," he said, "have the fullest admiration for the excellent staff work, particularly for the speed and secrecy in which the move was carried out. They equally praised the excellent march discipline of the United States Army troops on the roads."

When the Second Corps reached the northern front, it found itself under command of Major General Omar N. Bradley, an efficient, skilful handler of men and armor. His men were disposed on either side of the Sedjenane-Mateur road—some six miles to the north, others twelve miles to the south. On their left they had the French Moroccans and some British troops along the northern coast. The whole Allied line from the coast to the Enfidaville area began to roll forward.

The enemy was thrust deeper into the cage that the Allies were forging around him. It became evident that there would be no "Dunkirk" on the Mediterranean. Spokesmen at the Allied headquarters in Algiers declared that the main objective was now the destruction of the Afrika Korps rather than the capture of Tunis and Bizerte, which, they said, would be achieved incidentally. The enemy was frantically building makeshift wharves wherever the beaches of the Cap Bon Peninsula permitted, using planks and beams and whatever material came to hand. General Montgomery had made no secret of his desire to drive the Germans on to those beaches and give them a taste of the hell they had inflicted on the British almost three years before.

The Allies' land armies, with the powerful support of the armadas of the skies, were now launched on an irresistible tide. Never did it halt. From the northern coastal road through the mountains and defiles to the eastern shore, British, American, and French troops were on their victory march.

British and Americans advancing inland met the best that the enemy could offer. American field guns provided magnificent assistance to the infantrymen of the Second Corps, methodically wiping out enemy artillery positions and strong points that held up the advance.

The First Army, meeting the strongest opposition of the whole northern sector, crashed its way into the Medjerda Valley, the historic "road of the conqueror" to Tunis. Here the enemy brought up his newest plane, the Henschel 129—a heavily armed and armored antitank machine that was his answer to the R.A.F.'s "can-opening" Hurricane. But they could not halt the Allies' advance. The British took Sidi Medien, a point farther than any they had reached in the December lunge, and found themselves within twenty-four miles of Tunis. In bloody fighting, they cleared Long Stop Hill, the fiercely defended mountain that they had so nearly mastered on Christmas Eve, and entered a new range of hills leading to Tebourba.

In the drive for Pont-du-Fahs, the French were not able to make rapid progress against the more numerous Germans. The southern wing of the First Army, therefore, thrust out from both shores of the

Kourzia salt marsh to form a pincers drive on Pont-du-Fahs. Here the British were on a plain where they could use their tanks to the best advantage. The enemy, foreseeing this, strengthened his mine fields and his antitank batteries so that the going could not be too fast. Nonetheless, the British armor pushed on doggedly to the very slopes of Djebel Bou Kournine, northwest of Pont-du-Fahs, destroying fourteen enemy tanks in a day-long battle, while the French advanced from the Djebel Mansour area, southwest of the town.

Both North African and Fighting French were still battling their way into the Djebibina sector, almost thirty miles due west of Enfidaville and some twelve miles south of the line of the farthest Eighth Army advance along the coast. The British found that their strongest and most profitable blows were those struck by night, for the darkness enabled them to gain considerable ground. Invariably they had to defend it on the following day against strong counterattacks, but these never succeeded in pushing them back.

The Germans were fighting desperately. Their High Command's awareness of the critical situation was evidenced by the fact that for the first time units of the Élite Guard—the black-shirted Schutzstaffel— were sent outside Europe to fight. These were now among the troops that the enemy still sought to bring into Tunisia by air. Leaders in Germany and in the field at last realized that the Allies had finally learned to get the better of that supposedly unbeatable combination: the tank and the dive bomber.

As the all-front attack gained in momentum the Americans, in the biggest and hardest battle of their limited experience, were literally irresistible. Despite the toughest fighting and the lowest ruses—of which the treacherous use of the white flag to lure them into ambushes was not uncommon—they refused to be halted and hammered inexorably closer to Mateur. It was in this fighting that Lieutenant General Leslie J. McNair, commander of all the United States Army ground forces, was wounded. He was touring forward lines to learn what lessons battle conditions there could offer for the training of troops at home. A shell splinter pierced his steel helmet, penetrating his skull and halting only a quarter-inch from his brain. Other splinters entered his body; nevertheless he walked to a jeep and rode three hours in the jolting vehicle to a base hospital.

The Americans encountered dense mine fields in their path, but from the moment of their junction with the Eighth Army in the south, they had had the inestimable advantage of training by British veterans who had much more experience of the Germans' mining technique. The British gladly imparted their knowledge to the Americans, who used it to good advantage in northern Tunisia, where, under constant artillery fire, engineers ranged far ahead of the infantrymen to reap a harvest of thousands of mines. Many of these were buried in the ground beneath bodies of dead Germans, abandoned by retreating comrades.

The whole of the Allies' advance was accelerated by a marvelously coördinated job of supply and base work—all the way from the battle front back across Tunisia and Algeria to French Morocco. There the Americans had set up assembly lines that in their speed rivaled the automobile factories of Detroit. Equipped with the most modern tools available, they were staffed largely with native labor which had proven remarkably easy to train. All day long they put together the thousands of combat vehicles, planes, and other machines that had been shipped to Africa and started them rolling to their jobs of war. On a smaller scale, the same process was being repeated at smaller Moroccan and Algerian harbors, where, as in the biggest assembly plants, the work was directed by American men of the Army Ordnance Corps, most of whom had been recruited from similar work in civilian life.

Nearer the battle lines, the big American transport planes were pressed into service to fly whole air-base units to new landing grounds in one trip, or to bring up vitally needed goods. But there were parts of the Mateur sector where no plane, truck, or jeep could be of use because of the nature of the wooded heights. Here the American troops had to rely on the old-fashioned mule, which, for all its temperament— and it lived up to its worst traditions—could still carry its two hundred pounds of equipment anywhere, and return bearing wounded soldiers down the rocky declivities.

The Americans barely paused in their bloody advance to mark Easter Sunday, for they could not be sure that the Germans would respect the holy day. In many sectors, brief services were held with improvised altars or pulpits. Soldier congregations sat on their upturned steel helmets with their rifles slung over their shoulders—always on the alert for a surprise blow. This was the irony that marked the celebration of the Resurrection in the midst of wholesale slaughter, where the worshipers could not drop their tommy guns when they knelt to pray.

The enemy's situation was growing more crucial daily. Since January he had lost 66,000 men (36,000 of them prisoners), 1,750 planes, 250 tanks, more than 3,000 other vehicles, and 425 artillery pieces. At sea he had lost 34 war and merchant craft of all types, including 11 submarines, which had been seen to sink or to blow up; 53 more had been seriously damaged. The store of weapons and the roster of men had been steadily depleted. Ground had been steadily cut out from under the enemy and his one reliable means of escape, ships, had been badly mauled. But his troops continued, for the most part, to fight with savage desperation. The Allies tried the experiment of showering leaflets on the Axis lines, telling the enemy that Rommel had fled to Europe and left them to their fate. No one knew whether the recurrent rumor to this effect had any substance. The leaflets bore safe-conduct passes for any who chose to cross the lines and surrender.

As the Allies closed in on Bizerte, General Giraud received an offer of services from Vice Admiral Emile-Henri Muselier, who, until a year before, had commanded the then Free French Navy of General de Gaulle. Muselier was a man of unquestioned integrity and courage who had joined De Gaulle on the signing of the armistice, remaining in France only long enough to snatch highly important secret naval documents out of the Germans' reach. But his seizure of the French islands of St. Pierre and Miquelon and the resulting American official hostility had ultimately caused him to lose his post under De Gaulle, through whom he now offered his services to Giraud—a phenomenon in itself indicative of the growing closeness of the French groups. Giraud gladly accepted, for Muselier was the man who had built the defenses of Bizerte against both land and sea attack. He was the one man who could be invaluable to the Allies in helping them to breach those defenses if the Germans were to man them and force a siege.

The Allies increased their pile-driver blows against every inch of the Germans' line. At last this had to crumble. The line gave way first in the center, roughly from Tebourba to Pont-du-Fahs. British and French troops inflicted staggering blows and were quick to follow them up. The First Army, fighting almost without rest for five days, consolidated its positions on Djebel bou Aoukaz and started down the eastern slopes; while the French battled deeper into Pont-du-Fahs and began the laborious and bloody ascent of Djebel Zaghouan, the 4,250-foot guardian of the town of Zaghouan, one of the highest peaks in Tunisia. Between them, the British and the French had now cleared the enemy from the whole of the Grande Dorsale range.

On either flank the Allies increased their progress at the same time. The Moroccans on the north coast were pressing ever closer to Bizerte; while the Americans, splitting off part of their force from the main road into Mateur, drove north and hacked out a victory on the crest of a hill only eight miles from Lake Achkel—twenty-five miles from Bizerte. Djebel Azzag and Djebel el Ajred—Green Hill and Bald Hill to the Americans—were also captured in tough fighting seemingly far out of proportion to their heights of 1,200 and 1,500 feet. The hills were all heavily fortified. The Americans had to tackle them in a series of sharp, savage rushes, smashing through one line of enemy infantry after another. The Eighth Army, on the extreme south and east, began to score noticeable gains inland on the coastal road.

The Second Corps met some of the worst of the German resistance. Their road into Mateur was flanked by Djebel Anntra and Djebel Tahent, which the Americans called Djebel Devil because of the tenacity of its defenders. This was the famous Hill 609, so denominated on the military maps because of its height in meters, the equivalent of 1,998 feet. It was to go down in the history of American fighting men with the great battles of all their wars. Here they had to weave their way in and out among treacherous rocks amid which the Germans were exceptionally well dug in, armed with mortars and all types of machine guns. Its crest was almost like a mesa; there the Germans could stage an even stronger defense. In repeated charges, the Americans could gain perhaps a half-mile before being driven back under a thicker hail of fire than any they had ever seen. At the end of a whole day of terrific fighting, they found themselves back at its base, their numbers sorely diminished.

But at Hill 609, as everywhere else on the front, the Germans' worst counterattacks could do no more than hold the Allies from advancing; at no point were they forced to yield any of their previous gains. General Eisenhower was at the front during the beginning of the Americans' assault on Hill 609. Unfortunately he could stay to see only their repulse, and not their return to the attack and their final triumph. On the day after the first failures, the Americans brought up their heavy artillery against the mountain and its approaches.

The Germans were under orders to hold Hill 609 for fourteen days. Once the new assault had been launched, they held it for less than fourteen hours. The Arabs had abandoned their village at the foot of the hill, and the Germans had moved into it in force. Tracers from machine guns showed their hiding places there; behind them their artillery boomed. But the American artillerymen soon had the positions "taped." In an incredibly short time the German defenses literally crumbled away, then the infantry moved in.

When the artillery barrage had ceased, the Americans strode warily through the village, wiping out snipers still concealed in the ruins, and began to climb among the wheat fields, followed by their own machine gunners. German machine guns rattled steadily in front of them from the caves and the rock groups. American guns replied with equal volume. The doughboys fired from the hip or the shoulder, or prone where they had thrown themselves to escape the murderous bullets.

It took them all day to fight their way to the top of the hill; there was never a minute that was still. Men saw their comrades fall and had to leave them for the stretcher-bearers to find later. Before dusk they were at the summit, forcing the fiercely fighting Germans slowly back to the eastern edge and eventually down the farther slope

FALL OF TUNIS AND BIZERTE—FIRST GREAT ALLIED VICTORY

THE first Allied campaign came to its victorious conclusion 185 days after the Americans landed in North Africa. The Axis met disastrous defeat, lost one of its greatest armies, lost its African Empire, and began to crumble.

The last ten days, from May 2-12, 1943, were scenes of Axis disintegration and collapse. On the roads to Tunis and Bizerte the Allied armies were sweeping everything before them.

Though he must have known that his fate was unalterable, the enemy was still trying to send men and matériel into Tunisia. Some of the prisoners taken by the British had arrived there only five days before their capture. Many were veterans of the Russian campaign who had been resting and recuperating at home after wounds or illnesses. Others were drawn from garrisons in Italy and her islands, while the rest were younger troops from units that had just completed their training. But this flow of reinforcements had been swiftly cut to little more than a trickle, for the Allies were striking hard and costly blows at the enemy's supply lines.

In one day, as the armies were compressing their grip on Tunis and Bizerte, the Allies' planes destroyed a half-dozen transport ships en route to Tunisia, while British submarines sank ten more. Nor were merchantmen the only victims; Italian cruisers were crippled and German E-boats—the enemy's equivalent of the American PT's and the British MTB's—were sunk or driven ashore. The planes struck too at the few German attempts at aërial transport: one fighter pilot of the R.A.F. destroyed five Junkers 52's in five minutes and went on to find more game. The fliers ranged constantly to the enemy's bases in the Italian islands and also poured bombs and bullets on his makeshift piers and jetties which jutted out of the Cap Bon Peninsula.

At Allied Headquarters in Algiers confidence was now expressed without hesitation. General Giraud, speaking on May 2, predicted that the war in Africa would be over within the month. General Eisenhower had set himself the deadline of May 15. Both, as it turned out, were wrong: they had not been optimistic enough, although Eisenhower came closer to the actual date of the ending of the campaign.

The Americans now took the lead in the Allies' advance. These American boys from farms and cities were worthy allies of the veterans of Dunkirk who were fighting south of them.

The Germans could not tell from which side the climactic breakthrough would come. While they wondered and speculated, the Allies answered the question. From Djebel Hazemat, fifteen miles to the northwest and up the main road from the southwest, the Americans lunged out so suddenly and so irresistibly that before the day ended, they were in full possession of that desirable and highly important junction, Mateur.

From there they could turn north again to Bizerte, or southeast to Tunis. Apparently, to the stunned astonishment of the Germans who had to yield Mateur after a terrific artillery pounding and an irresistible infantry advance, they were going to do both. Mateur was entered by an American half-track, soon followed by a reconnaissance battalion, as the last Germans were evacuating.

The Americans' success seemed to have inspired the whole Allied line. It began to move forward again. The Americans themselves were pounding Ferryville with their artillery, which was also trained on numerous airfields in the Bizerte area, including the most important one at Sidi Ahmed, only five miles from the naval base. American armor and infantry had joined the French north of Lake Achkel and these forces were within thirteen miles of Bizerte. The Americans southeast of Mateur were gaining while the First Army in the Tebourba sector also advanced, both drives being pointed toward Tunis. Northeast of Pont-du-Fahs the French struck out again, gaining slowly against bitter opposition, while the Eighth Army's line around Takrouna hurried forward to straighten the front that the right wing had pushed beyond Sebkret Sidi Kralifa.

The whole tide of the war had turned. In Washington, the Director of the Office of War Information, Elmer Davis, confirmed the Germans' worst fears by predicting that the Continent of Europe would be invaded before the summer was over; but he did not satisfy their curiosity by corroborating their questioning prediction that the Allies would strike at Sicily and then at Italy. Secretary Stimson, while acknowledging the extent of the Allies' gains, warned once more that heavy fighting lay ahead.

His words were strikingly emphasized within twenty-four hours. Out of scores of airdromes, fighters and bombers roared by the hundreds to scourge the enemy from the front lines to his bases in Sicily, returning only to refuel and reload for new attacks. In a single day they made 2,000 sorties—a figure previously unheard of. They had two purposes and they accomplished both: They left the enemy's supply lines strewn with sinking and burning merchantmen and escorts; more important, they blasted out a road for the Allies' land forces through the enemy's defenses.

The gigantic air blow provided the impetus needed to set off the final Allied onslaught. Artillery began to thunder with the first crack in the blackness of the night. Ground forces surged forward along a sixty-mile front from the northern coast to a point below Medjez-el-Bab and sent the enemy reeling.

Americans in the north rushed up Djebel Cheniti and Djebel Achkel, flanking the eastern end of Lake Achkel, giving them a commanding position overlooking Ferryville. These American troops had been toughened and hardened by battle. What they had seen in recaptured towns of German savagery inflicted on helpless civilians had not disposed them to kindliness.

Toward the British, with whom they were fighting the same despised enemy, they felt comradeship of the closest kind, for the men of both countries were sharing the same hardships and striving toward the same goals for the same reasons. The Americans driving down hard on Tebourba did not say that "the British and we" would take the town; they said only "we" and meant by that word all the forces in the action.

The First Army, largely supported by the Allies' unmatched aërial assault, finally broke the back of the Djebel bou Aoukaz defenses. At dawn, the Americans in the north and the British in the south threw every man and tank and gun into the assault. The Americans then stood eight miles outside the naval base of Bizerte, ringed by the strongest defenses in North Africa. The British were ten to fifteen miles outside the capital, the last stronghold of the enemy in Africa. Half a year before, these Germans had stood at the gates of Egypt.

By 4:15 P.M. that day—May 7, Jeanne d'Arc Day to Frenchmen—the Americans were rolling through the streets of Bizerte in flower-decked tanks. Five minutes later the British were being embraced on the streets of Tunis by Frenchmen, heedless of the bullets whining overhead. It was an unbelievable day. At noon the Americans had entered Ferryville, on the road to Bizerte. Without stopping, their vanguard of tanks had rolled on toward Bizerte, crushing German rear-guard resistance and routing snipers from houses in the outskirts. The main German force had begun to scurry from the city even before the capture of Ferryville, streaming down the roads that would lead them past Tunis to what they hoped would be the embarkation point to safety—the Cap Bon Peninsula.

The British had started out along a ten-mile front from Medjez-el-Bab to a point four miles east of Massicault. Infantry stormed up the hills to wipe out the enemy's antitank positions, while the British armor went forward to spearhead the whole advance. It was a day of bitter, bloody battle for the British.

Capture of the two cities—Bizerte and Tunis—overshadowed all the other fronts where the French and the British were still grinding forward slowly. Two divisions of the Eighth Army had been secretly shifted to the First Army's front near Djebel bou Aoukaz. It was Eighth Army armor and infantry, fighting temporarily under General Anderson, that cracked that powerful German defense. The Eighth Army's men marched with the First Army's in the triumphal entry into the long-enslaved city.

Tunis was a madhouse of joy. Frenchmen and Frenchwomen brought out the Tricolors they had hidden for months. An old man stood at a corner to watch the tanks come past. His suit, obviously kept for this day, was immaculate, if old, and he wore the Legion of Honor in his lapel. Proud and erect, his arm at the salute, he stood motionless in the rain, heedless of the tears that poured down his cheeks. Women kissed the embarrassed British soldiers. When the French troops of Giraud's North African Army came in, they embraced them and wept.

Bizerte's welcome to the conquering Americans matched the scenes in Tunis. Flowers and food were thrown to the tankmen. Infantrymen were embraced on the streets by weeping Frenchmen who, like their compatriots in Tunis, braved the fire of German snipers to welcome their deliverers. The whole city was turned over to the Americans.

General Eisenhower proclaimed that the fight must go on until not an armed German remained in all Africa. He underscored his point by presiding at the formal transfer of new American armanent to equip several divisions to the French Army of General Giraud while the pursuit of the enemy's remnants was really only beginning. The French themselves in the central Tunisian area, as the Eighth Army in the east, were not yet to move forward substantially; the Allies' strategy called for both forces to continue only to engage and destroy as much as possible of the enemy's strength in their sectors while the First Army and the Second Corps concentrated on the forces they had driven out of Tunis and Bizerte.

In this endeavor the coöperation of land, sea, and air forces was superb. All functioned together as smoothly as if each were an integrated part of the same perfectly designed machine. Over the Cap Bon Peninsula and the waters around and beyond it, the Allies' planes streamed in a never-ending surge, blasting and burning whatever target came within their range; while the American and British soldiers pressed fast along the land to corral or kill the troops whom the planes had immobilized. The Allies' ships lay off the three coasts of the peninsula to trap any German or Italian who might unaccountably have eluded the pursuit of the other two services. The fliers met almost no opposition.

Prisoners were streaming into the Allies' lines in such numbers that they could hardly be handled. Vast enclosures of barbed wire had been prepared for them, but the Allies could not have anticipated the volume of surrender that awaited them. Germans and Italians alike threw down their arms without resistance in many areas. Many piled into their own trucks and, with one of their number at the wheel, drove straight for the Allies' lines—a white flag streaming from the vehicle and every passenger standing with both hands held high. Even tankmen piloted their great cruel machines, under makeshift flags of truce, into the safety of surrender; only in a few instances did they continue to use surrender signals as a ruse to trap the Allies' troops.

The "advance to the rear" by these swarms of prisoners got almost out of hand before the Allies entered the Cap Bon Peninsula. Even the Germans were no longer conducted to their cages under the heavy guard that had always differentiated them from the Italians in the African campaign; weary M.P.'s of both the British and the American forces merely waved them all back to the reception centers that had been hastily set up to deal with them.

The northeastern corner of Tunisia was the scene of even larger mass surrenders. Five thousand Germans surrendered to the Americans near Bizerte, while the savagely mauled wreckage of the Germans' 15th Armored Division yielded to the 7th Armored Division of the Eighth Army which had pursued Rommel from Egypt to this last battleground just north of Tunis. Throughout that long manhunt the German 15th had screened Rommel's retreat; now at last it could rest, in a British prison cage.

The enemy's makeshift barrier at the entrance to the peninsula was soon crumbled after the first breaches had been made by British armor. American and British troops poured in, impeded as much by the hordes of surrendering enemy troops as by the mine fields that had been planted earlier. The Americans included the 34th Infantry Division, bred to battle in southern Tunisia and destined to win increasing fame in other Mediterranean campaigns.

As the Allies' troops advanced on the Cap Bon Peninsula, the enemy's last foothold of the once vast African empire, the German Air Force gave up the fight. On May 9 not a single enemy plane appeared over any area of the protectorate. The Royal Navy added itself to the potential target list by sending its destroyers off Kelibia, the one port of the peninsula that could be used to bombard its installations. Other destroyers and smaller craft patrolled the waters on every side under orders to "sink, burn, and destroy" whatever they might find. But the enemy, it seemed, had abandoned any idea of a "Dunkirk"; instead, it appeared, it hoped now to emulate the Bataan stand of General Douglas MacArthur's heroic defenders in the Philippines. This effort, too, was doomed to failure.

Enemy units that had been detached to the south and center began to attempt to disengage themselves and gain a respite on the peninsula. But on both sides of their line the Allies launched attacks that threatened to overrun the enemy's hardly begun retreat. The Eighth Army, in the east, began inching slowly up the coastal road, picking up momentum gradually for its final plunge. On the west, the French who had taken Pont-du-Fahs and had begun the assault on Djebel Zaghouan, lashed out in a surprise move that swept the enemy completely from the highest mountain in all Tunisia and carried the French into the heart of the city of Zaghouan itself.

There was drama in the capture of Zaghouan that surpassed even the surrender of 25,000 Germans in the north to the Americans. At Zaghouan's mountain a French officer, representing in his person at that moment, all France and all Frenchmen, avenged all the shame and degradation of that June day three years before when the Germans had desecrated the sacred Armistice car of Compiegne.

A white flag waved in the breeze on Djebel Zaghouan. As it came nearer to a French post, a German helmet could be seen. The wearer, an infantryman, showed his face as he approached, accompanied by an officer of the invincible German Army. His outfit could fight no longer; and he wanted information. Under his white flag, which the French respected without too much trust, always ready for a ruse, he walked to the French officer in command on that hill and put his question, the hardest question for any German to ask:

"What are the French terms for an armistice?"

The answer was quick, brief, and unmistakable: *"Unconditional surrender,"* the French officer snapped, "with all equipment intact."

The German relayed the unwelcome message to his commander, who accepted the ultimatum. No one knows the name of this Frenchman who rendered historic justice against the traditional despoilers of his country and of all the west; but everyone can imagine something of the vast, impersonal pride and satisfaction that must have made his voice ring with a strength of something far greater than himself when he laid down his terms to the enemy.

In the Bizerte area to the north, the Germans sent three officers, representing Major General Fritz Krause, commander of all the artillery of the Afrika Korps, to get the Americans' terms. An armored-force general received them and spoke substantially in much the same manner as his French colleague in the south: "Unconditional surrender —no sabotage—no attempt to evacuate troops by sea. We will kill all who try to get out."

The Germans, with an American escort, returned to their lines twenty-five miles away, near Djebel el Faouar, east of Bizerte. American shells were falling ominously near the place where General Krause and his staff were waiting. The German commander advanced to the Americans' interpreter and saluted him, although the interpreter was a young lieutenant outranked by many of the other Americans. He asked the terms. Lieutenant Albert Klein was the first American who had the honor of repeating to a German general, face to face, the historic declaration of Casablanca. He quoted what his own general had said and added: "You must make up your mind within twenty minutes."

General Krause did not need all that time. He accepted. The Americans radioed his surrender to the armored-force general to whom his emissaries had gone; the general relayed it to the commander, General Bradley, adding almost wistfully: "I can knock hell out of them by dark." But Bradley, laughing, ordered him to accept.

On the third anniversary of the German onslaught against France and the Low Countries, the finest German Army to take the field outside of Russia was a broken, struggling mass of men caught in a trap that was closing too rapidly to permit an escape. It was a fitting date for King George of Britain to send his message of thanks and praise to General Eisenhower. The message was brief; its concluding words must have echoed in every heart in the United Kingdom: *"The debt of Dunkirk is repaid."*

The repayment was to be complete; the account was to be settled without compromise or default. General Bradley had issued a general order to his Americans, saying: "This ends operations for the United States Second Corps in North Africa." But these Americans, on whom once again General Alexander bestowed unstinted adulation, were to fight side by side with the British until the last man of the enemy had been eliminated by capture or death. While this process was going on, President Roosevelt sent his own thanks and tribute to General Eisenhower, to General Giraud, and to all the American, British, and French commanders and troops fighting under them.

On May 11, the last tank battle of the North African campaign was begun and ended. Near Grombalia, close to the base of the Cap Bon Peninsula, what was left of the Germans' 10th Armored Division tried to make a stand and hold off the powerful 6th Armored Division of the British. The effort was gallant and skilful; but it was foredoomed to failure. Battered and broken, the Germans disintegrated. Before the day had ended, the British had thrust to the very tip of the peninsula along both coasts and joined forces at Cap Bon itself, thus cutting off the last German and Italian forces on the peninsula.

On the night of May 12, 1943, the Allied Headquarters in Algiers issued a special communiqué. It was brief but historic, and it said: "Organized resistance, except by isolated pockets of the enemy, has ceased. General von Arnim, commander of the Axis forces in Tunisia, has been captured. It is estimated that the total of prisoners captured since May 5 is about 150,000. Vast quantities of guns and war material of all kinds have been captured, including guns and aircraft in a serviceable condition."

Fall of Tunis and Bizerte

The Eighth Army driving up the coast had swung, by-passing Bou Ficha, to capture the port of Hammamet on the southeast side of the neck of the Cap Bon Peninsula. Within the peninsula itself, British tanks were roaring up and down with infantrymen clinging to their sides on a grim joy ride among the frightened German and Italian troops, who kept cringing out of their hiding places to surrender to the men in and on the British armor.

The French, momentarily delayed north of Zaghouan, had smashed the Germans, blocking their advance, and then swept on, intoxicated at having received the surrender of 25,000 Germans and two major generals. At Ste. Marie-du-Zit, twelve miles northwest of Bou Ficha, they had formally rejoined the First Army to surround the German pocket that the Eighth Army was also attacking. The enemy, crushed on the peninsula and isolated here on the coast, could no longer keep up the pretense of battle. Its commander in this area, the heir of an old Junker family, Major General Graf von Sponeck, had to bow his head and go as a suppliant to Lieutenant General Sir Bernard C. Freyberg, the tough, rugged commander of the Eighth Army's gallant and reckless New Zealanders. The German nobleman asked to know what terms he would receive if he were to end the battle. The New Zealand General gave him the two magic words: "Unconditional surrender."

Characteristically arrogant to the last, the German reported that he would fight to his last bullet. British guns soon settled his German point of honor and he came again to Freyberg; this time to accept.

General von Arnim, who had taken the command of all enemy forces in Tunisia when Marshal Rommel returned to Europe, retained his defiance.

He was captured by Indian troops of the First Army at Ste. Marie-du-Zit and taken to a point behind the lines to await the arrival of General Anderson. The latter accorded to his enemy the honors due to his rank and demanded the unconditional surrender of von Arnim's troops.

Von Arnim refused. Having been captured, he had no choice but to surrender his own person; but he refused to surrender his army. Thus he left his men, caught between the First and Eighth Armies, to be further battered and crushed until, of their own volition, they threw down their arms and begged the British to accept their surrender.

On the day of the official ending of the Tunisian campaign, another general entered a city that the Allies had liberated. With a Spahi guard of honor, Henri-Honore Giraud made his formal entry into Tunis, along streets flanked with French, British, and American flags and lined with cheering thousands who cried their *"Vive Giraud!"* with equal fervor. But the general's patriotic triumph was marred by deep personal grief.

His daughter and her four children had long lived in Tunis, where his son-in-law was stationed as a colonel in the colonial army. Shortly after the General's escape from France, his wife, his three other daughters and the husband of one of them had been interned by the Germans in reprisal for his flight. Of all his family, only his two sons were free; and they were both at the front with the colonial army in Tunisia. So General Giraud must have long looked forward to a reunion with his loved ones in liberated Tunis. The Germans—with Nazi revenge and cruelty—had made certain that the man who had beaten them would be thwarted by them now. Before the Allies had entered the capital, the entire family that General Giraud had hoped to see again, daughter, son-in-law, and grandchildren, had been carried off to Europe. The General was never to see his daughter again; she died in a German prison camp a year later.

Giraud was every inch a soldier. Regardless of personal griefs, he knew his was the task of war. One of his first official acts was to replace Admiral Edmond Derrien, who had commanded the French Navy in Tunisian waters and had transferred units at Bizerte to the Germans, with a man whose loyalty was above suspicion, Vice Admiral M.A.J. Leclerq.

On May 13 both the Allies and the Axis agreed that the ultimate mopping-up in Tunisia had been completed. At 11:45 A.M. the few Axis troops still holding out—the German 90th Light Division, or what was left of it—surrendered immediately after a severe bombing, the last of the whole African campaign. On the night of May 13, the Allies' communiqué could say simply: "No Axis forces remain in North Africa who are not prisoners in our hands."

Thus ended the three-year battle of Africa. The empire that the Germans had thought to overrun, with the dubious help of the Italians, was now a series of prison camps in the Tunisian wheat fields and a string of graves from Egypt to Bizerte and Tunis and Cap Bon. The picked troops of Germany and Italy had lost more than 500,000 men.

The African campaign had accomplished these principal results: It had reopened the Mediterranean to the Allies' shipping. It had eliminated the menace to Gibraltar from the south, and to Egypt. It had served as a proving ground for the Allies' men and materials. It had diverted important numbers of troops and quantities of machines from the Russian front. It had provided the Germans' victims in Europe with new courage to wait and endure and fight from below. It had filled the Allies' troops with the knowledge of their own capacities and of the enemy's mettle, as well as his character. It had laid bare what Mr. Churchill had long called the "soft under-belly of Europe." It has severely damaged the enemy's morale and—above all—deprived him of the initiative. It had driven the Axis out of Africa.

PANORAMA OF 15,000 MILES IN EAST —AND BATTLE OF BISMARCK SEA

JAPAN'S holdings in the Pacific in 1943 represented a circle about 5,000 miles in diameter, with a perimeter of some 15,000 miles. Every place within that perimeter was strongly held in Japanese hands. Every habitable island among the tens of thousands rising out of the Pacific was in their possession.

Several salients into Allied positions were also held by the Japanese. There was the northern salient in the Aleutians, including Kiska and Attu. In mid-Pacific there was the Gilberts salient, extending 600 miles to the southeast from the Marshall Islands. A third was the Solomon salient, running some 500 miles southeast from New Britain. On land the Japanese held a salient in Burma and another in China.

Let us tour the Pacific area quickly: With the fall of Burma and the rise of Japanese naval power in the Indian Ocean, Madagascar, controlled by Vichy France (an Axis collaborator) assumed vital importance. Madagascar, the third largest island in the world, lay athwart the United Nations' main shipping routes, not only from the Cape of Good Hope on Africa to India, but to Egypt and Asia Minor. In enemy hands it would have cut the supply lines to India, to Egypt, Asia Minor, and to Russia, through Iran.

The seizure of Madagascar had been frequently discussed. Marshal Pétain gave assurances that the island would never be handed over to the Japanese. As soon as Pierre Laval took over the active administration the situation changed. Vichy forces on Madagascar began, in April of 1942, to imprison the sizable body of De Gaulle Fighting French sympathizers. Reports were received of Japanese military missions touring the island.

Consequently, on May 5, the British Admiralty and War Office issued a joint communiqué which said: "The United Nations having decided to forestall a Japanese move against the French naval base at Diego Saurez in Madagascar, a combined British naval and military force arrived off the island at dawn this morning. It has been made clear to the French authorities of Madagascar that the United Nations have no intention of interfering with the French status of the territory, which will remain French and continue to be a part of the French Empire."

Diego Saurez fell quickly and the advance was pushed inland at a minimum cost of lives. The island was virtually conquered in less than two weeks. Two months later the British hopped two hundred miles west, toward Africa, to take the French island of Mayotta in the Comoro Group dominating the Mozambique Channel.

The British thrust across the border from India into the Chittagong area, catching the Japanese off guard in the last days of 1942. The push carried down through Arakan to Buthedaung where the enemy stiffened and ended the advance. The British remained in the southwest corner of Burma until May, 1943, when they withdrew after having accomplished their purpose of preventing the Japanese from organizing and pursuing a campaign into India.

Behind this screen of action, General Stilwell began to train Chinese troops which had escaped from Burma with him, and others who managed by tortuous travel to reach India from China.

Military events in China were speeding up. The Japanese started a drive in Chekiang Province designed to gain control of the Nanchang-Hankow Railroad as part of the cherished dream of a Shanghai-Singapore rail line. The enemy, as usual, scored impressive gains at the outset. After a month of retreats the Chinese braced and pushed the invaders back to where they had started. The Japanese also drove for the Chekiang port of Foochow, but lost all they had previously gained.

The A.V.G., the daring "Flying Tigers," became incorporated into the United States Army Air Force in China as part of General Stilwell's command on July 4, 1942. Brigadier General Chennault retained control over the fliers, with Colonel Caleb V. Haynes at the head of the United States Bomber Command and Colonel Robert L. Scott at the head of the Twenty-third United States Pursuit Squadron of fighters. They immediately began their long, amazing career during which they made life intolerable for the Japanese.

Wendell Willkie, Republican 1940 candidate for President, arrived in China as a personal representative of President Roosevelt in the fall of 1942. Shortly after that Madame Chiang Kai-shek went to the United States. These two representatives of great peoples created such good feeling and understanding between the United States and China that nothing was ever able to shake their friendship.

The heaviest blow struck at enemy divisionists tactics came on the eve of the thirty-first anniversary of the Chinese Republic, when the United States and Great Britain simultaneously announced their intention to relinquish all extraterritorial and related rights and privileges which they had enjoyed for nearly a hundred years.

President Roosevelt and Secretary of State Hull had gone on record with the determination to end the treatment of China as an inferior nation at the earliest possible moment. The principle was implicit in the Atlantic Charter. Extraterritoriality finally ended on January 11, 1943, when Dr. Wei Tao-ming, the Chinese Ambassador, and Secretary Hull signed the agreement in Washington, and Dr. T. V. Soong, Chinese Foreign Minister, and Sir Horace James Seymour, British Ambassador, signed in Chungking.

Under the impact of Allied blows events had not been moving too well in Japan, itself. Tokyo finally came to realize that the Pacific War was going to be long, costly, and perhaps disastrous. Premier General Hideki Tojo, leader of the military clique which had formed the war cabinet before Pearl Harbor, decided to merge foreign affairs with the war. Shigenori Togo, who had been a career diplomat for nearly thirty years and had established a reputation as a "moderate" able to placate both the United States and Russia, resigned as Foreign Minister "for personal reasons." General Tojo assumed that post as well as the premiership. He issued a statement enunciating Japan's Greater East Asia Coprosperity Sphere policy, which was a euphemistic way of saying that all Asia must come under Japan's rule.

Following the Battle of Midway operations in the Central Pacific consisted of diversionary, spectacular raids on Japanese-held islands. It will be recalled that Carlson's Raiders played an important part in the Guadalcanal campaign. They had, however, captured the imagination of the American people some months before they appeared in the Solomons. Lieutenant Colonel Evans F. Carlson, who before the United States entered the war had spent come time in China, had long been convinced that Japan would launch an attack; his only mistake was that he had expected it to come six months before it did. While in China he became acquainted with the Communist Eighth Route Army. Shortly after Pearl Harbor this forty-six-year-old retired officer was called back into service and became the organizer of the Second Marine Raider Battalion, to become famous as "Carlson's Raiders."

One thousand men out of more than seven thousand who had volunteered at San Diego were selected on the basis of physical fitness, alertness, and understanding of what the fighting was all about. Officers were chosen from the young men who showed particular qualities of initiative. The Raiders were put through an arduous training for guerrilla warfare—swift marches, living on concentrated dehydrated food in the field for a long time, carrying automatic weapons and compact radio equipment. They made forty-mile marches a day with full packs and fought under every possible kind of adverse conditions.

After three months of this they were ready to go to war. The Raiders had become so thoroughly imbued with the spirit of the Eighth Route Army in China that, although an American Commando outfit, they called themselves the "Gung ho Battalion," adopting the motto of the Chinese coöperatives meaning "work together, work in harmony." "Gung ho" was applied to everything possessed by the Raiders as a unit and personally. About August 15, 1942, units of the Battalion entered the submarines *Nautilus* and *Argonaut* in what became the first instance on record in which undersea craft were used as troop transports.

On the night of August 17-18 they surfaced off the enemy-held island of Makin at the northern tip of the Gilbert Islands, about halfway to the Marshalls.

The Battalion was scheduled to make a blind raid, with no information about the enemy's installations or the disposition of his forces. All the Raiders knew was that there existed on Makin a radio station that had to be destroyed. With their hands and faces painted green, Carlson's men boarded their rubber boats in the dark of the moonless night. Taking advantage of a flood tide, they landed on the beaches a half hour before dawn. They assembled in the darkness, with owl-like vision, and proceeded inland without noise until a Browning automatic rifle accidentally went off.

The enemy was aroused. Japanese sentries strapped high in the trees poured down rifle fire upon the Raiders, who moved quickly toward their objectives, and destroyed two seaplanes at anchor. Enemy planes from neighboring islands came in response to radio appeals, but the Americans so confused the Japanese airmen that their own positions received the full weight of their bombs and strafing.

Fighting ended at 4:00 p.m. the second day. In the forty hours they remained on the island Carlson's Raiders killed every one of the 350 Japanese stationed there, set fire to 1,000 gallons of gasoline as well as the seaplanes used for advanced scouting, destroyed every truck and all the supplies, and left the place no longer fit for military purposes.

Shortly before the Makin raid the army had sent its own surprise package to the enemy in the form of the longest over-water bombing mission ever undertaken by land-based aircraft. Four months after the navy had administered a sea and air attack to Wake Island, Brigadier General Howard Ramey sent a mission of Flying Fortresses on the 4,000-mile round trip from Hawaii to Wake as a follow-up to the Battle of Midway. The bombers appeared in bright moonlight at medium height, plastered the shore installations, and induced the Japanese fighters to keep at a safe distance. All the Flying Fortresses led by Colonel Arthur W. Meehan returned, with only slight damage, after having destroyed most of what the Japanese had been able to build up in the six months they had occupied Wake Island.

Six months later, shortly after midnight of December 23, 1942, and exactly one year after the Japanese had wrested Wake from the heroic Marine defenders, Colonel A. Matheny led another group of Flying Fortresses over Wake. In this biggest assault ever administered up to this time in the Pacific the American planes dropped 75,000 pounds of bombs from low altitude as a birthday-Christmas present. The planes returned without casualties, and this time without damage.

The navy under Admiral Nimitz was active in the Central Pacific. Continuing their prowling and harassing operations—to let the Japanese know that all the Allied strength was not tied up in the Solomons—a naval expedition sailed into the waters below the Carolines late in October, 1942, and raked Tarawa in the Gilberts and the Ellice Islands to the southeast.

These attacks were forerunners of things to come in the Central Pacific. They were a necessary part of the thrust to be made at the Japanese Empire. At the northern end of the vast Pacific battleline a separate war was being waged in the Aleutians against fog, rain, snow, storms, and against the Japanese who had occupied Attu, Agattu, and Kiska.

Bombers and fighters began operating from airfields cut quickly out of the barren, frozen terrain on Adak, in the Andreanof Group. By the middle of September it was possible to inaugurate an aggressive bombing policy against Kiska, and within a few weeks Canada sent in airmen to reinforce the American fliers.

Because of atrocious and frequently changing weather conditions, and preoccupation with other theaters, the only attacks that could be made against the Japanese were the ever mounting bombings, occasional shellings, and the constant inroads by submarines upon enemy shipping.

The United States took another long hop toward the Japanese bases on January 12, 1943, when Major General Simon B. Buckner, Commanding General of the Alaska Defense Command, sent a strong force under Brigadier General Lloyd E. Jones to occupy Amchitka, only seventy miles from Kiska. The enemy, who had reacted to the Adak occupation by sending in more troops and supplies to Kiska and Attu, was taken completely by surprise. He never seemed to be able to anticipate in any part of the Pacific where the United States would try next. Guns, ammunition, and food were all landed during the first day. Bivouac areas were built and defense installations set in place.

Amchitka Island is only five miles wide and the nearest land to Kiska, thus making it an ideal bombing target. The Japanese were unable to interfere effectively with its development although they threw in numerous heavy attacks. By February 16 the air base was in operation, and the first American planes landed on the heels of a powerful enemy attack. Occupation of Amchitka gave us a spearhead into the Japanese positions, interdicted the freedom of enemy operations, and completed the final preparations for the grand assault designed to throw the enemy back from the Western Hemisphere. Kiska was kept under almost daily attack by planes based on Adak and Amchitka. Attu, also, received its full share of attention.

Tokyo reacted quickly to the latest threat against its Aleutian salient and moved to strengthen its positions. Early on the morning of March 26, a unit of the North Pacific Force commanded by Rear Admiral C. H. McMorris discovered through the fog a small, but heavily protected Jap convoy proceeding with supplies and reinforcements toward Attu and Kiska. The enemy cargo ships, covered by heavy and light cruisers and some destroyers, were picked up about sixty-five miles south of the Komandorski Peninsula, halfway between Attu and the Kamchatka Peninsula on Siberia. Our light force of two cruisers, the *Salt Lake City* and the *Richmond,* with its few destroyers, was heavily outnumbered. Admiral McMorris promptly closed for attack.

The engagement developed into a protracted running gunfire duel between our two cruisers and the Japanese cruisers, followed by a concerted torpedo attack launched from our destroyers. Under the visibility conditions surrounding the battle it was impossible to determine just how severe were the losses inflicted upon the enemy. The Japanese broke off the engagement after three and one-half hours, turned tail and set back for Japan.

Plans for an assault upon Attu were nearing completion at the time of the Komandorski engagement. Turbulent weather interfered with scheduled operations, and it was not until April 24 that a detachment of cruisers and destroyers was able to proceed to Attu and place the defenses and shore installations under heavy bombardment. With the effective neutralization of Attu's defenses the weight of the air attacks was shifted to Kiska which, much closer to Alaska, seemed to be the logical objective of any Jap landing attempt. The Japanese had virtually completed a fighter field on Kiska and were rushing to completion a bombing strip on Attu.

Behind this cover of aërial activity Rear Admiral F. W. Rockwell, Commander of Amphibious Forces of the Pacific Fleet, was collecting a powerful force consisting of battleships and an auxiliary aircraft carrier—the first appearance of capital ships in Aleutian waters—destroyers, auxiliaries, and transports. Rear Admiral Robert C. Giffen and Rear Admiral McMorris added their detachments of cruisers and destroyers; Major General William O. Butler concentrated all the army air forces in the area. The sea and air armada appeared off Attu on May 11 with transports laden with troops under command of Lieutenant General John L. DeWitt, of the Western Defense Command.

Attu, a treeless tundra thirty-five by twenty miles in extent, is ringed by reefs and consists almost entirely of formidable, rocky, snow-covered mountains rising 3,000 feet and more. It has only one harbor, Chichagof, although the coast is dotted with coves and bays. Lying west of Kiska it outflanked that island. Capture of Attu would make the Japanese hold on Kiska perilous if not untenable.

Early in the May morning landings were made on the north coast of

Attu and the troops quickly moved inland. In the afternoon the main assault was launched with landings at Blind Cove on Holtz Bay to the northeast of the mountain range, and at Massacre Bay to the southeast. Major General Alfred F. Brown commanded the landing troops during the first five days, after which Major General Eugene M. Landrum took charge.

The Japanese, as had been the case elsewhere in the Pacific, were taken by surprise when Colonel Frank L. Culin, Jr., stormed ashore with his men at Holtz Bay, and Colonel Edward P. Earle's men landed at Massacre Bay. The two forces worked a miniature version of a pincers movement upon the enemy who rallied quickly and offered stubborn resistance from the numerous machine-gun and mortar nests cut in the rocky ridges. Within six days all the high ground between the two American forces had been captured. Colonel Earle, leading his men over a ridge, had been killed by a sniper's bullet. Lieutenant Colonel Glen A. Nelson, succeeding to the command, led a party of men through the enemy fire to recover the body.

On the Holtz Bay side, 210 men of the Seventh Scouts under Captain William H. Willoughby, staged a fight that did much to make the final outcome quickly certain. The Scouts, most of whom had frozen feet and had been without food for three days, attacked the enemy positions, forced back the foe, withstood vicious counterattacks, and finally rooted out the few remaining Japanese who had not been killed. The fighting raged in snow eight to twenty feet deep.

The ground troops had captured one pass after another and herded the Japanese remnants into a pocket where army bombers came over and laid death upon the trapped enemy troops. Final stages of the conquest developed into bitter hand-to-hand fighting in which the Americans, climbing over the bodies of dead Japanese, blasted the enemy from trenches and strong points. The pursuit continued along Lake Cories in the clouds until the final batch of Japanese were exterminated on Fish Hook Ridge.

The airfield, which the Japanese had been unable to complete on Attu, was quickly put into shape by the Americans. From it Kiska was pounded, as well as from the Andreanofs.

On August 15 American and Canadian troops stormed ashore to find Kiska deserted. When Attu fell, the Japanese knew that Kiska could not be held. In a bold, hazardous venture, and probably taking a lesson from the raid on Makin in which submarines carried the battalion to its destination, the Japanese evacuated their troops from Kiska in their own submarines and under the protection of a fog cover.

This was the first captured American territory to be redeemed from the enemy. Japanese penetration into the Western Hemisphere had lasted about one year.

While this was taking place in the North Pacific the Solomons-New Guinea area was in eruption. Before turning back to the Southwest Pacific to the point where we left it after the capture of Guadalcanal, Buna, and Gona, it might be well to become acquainted with two men whose influence over events in the Pacific was to be second only to that of General MacArthur himself.

First is Major General (subsequently Lieutenant General) George Churchill Kenney, a five-foot-six-inch bundle of dynamic fighting man who took over command of the Fifth Air Force in September of 1942 and became Commander of Allied Air Forces in the Southwest Pacific. In that post, and later as Commander of the Far Eastern Air Force into which several units were to be merged, he was to direct some of the most sensational and significant air operations of the war. In the First World War he won the Distinguished Service Cross for extraordinary heroism and came out of the conflict with a scarred face and a captaincy. He was the first man to put guns into the wings of an airplane when, in 1922, he installed a pair of 32-calibre Brownings in an old de Haviland. Six years later he devised the parachute bomb whereby bombers might drop low over their targets for better marksmanship and have time to leave the area before the gently dropping missile struck the mark and exploded.

It was General Kenney who worked out the plan for ferrying American and Australian troops by plane from Australia to New Guinea, thus making possible the successful campaign against Buna and Gona.

General Kenney had a definite idea how the air war in the Pacific should be fought: "The way to fight this war is to concentrate our strength on worthwhile targets—planes and ships. The Japanese never go anywhere without plane cover. If we knock that down, or destroy it before it has a chance to get up, then we've got them exactly where we want them. If we destroy their ships they won't be going anywhere, either."

General Kenney's counterpart on land was Lieutenant General Walter Krueger who, in February, 1943, at General MacArthur's request, was placed in command of the new United States Sixth Army being sent into action in the Southwest Pacific. General Krueger, born in Prussia, came to the United States when eight years old, and enlisted at the outbreak of the Spanish-American War, seeing service in Cuba. When mustered out he reënlisted and went to the Philippines where his commanding officer was General MacArthur's father. Army life suited the close-cropped, pipe-smoking young man who remained in military service with distinction in a total of four wars.

Before going to the Southwest Pacific General Krueger, one of the few general officers to have risen from the ranks without any West Point training, had commanded the Eighth and Third Armies, where his reputation as a tactician was steadily enhanced in an extensive series of maneuvers held in Arkansas, Texas, and Louisiana during 1941, the most ambitious field exercises ever undertaken by the United States Army and involving hundreds of thousands of men. Nearly every United States Division to see service before the middle of 1943 had learned from General Krueger, either because it had served under him or had fought against him in maneuvers.

Back in the Southwest Pacific, the evacuation of Guadalcanal by the Japanese on February 8, 1943, was no indication that the enemy was retiring from the Solomon Islands. In fact, everything tended to show that he was strengthening his positions and preparing to resume his interrupted drive toward Australia and New Zealand.

The islands of the Southwest Pacific were a huge chessboard on which the contestants were making their strategic moves. The Solomons cover some 17,000 square miles of land, culminating on the easterly side in New Britain and New Ireland, with the Admiralty Islands a sort of northern continuation of New Ireland. It is about 1,500 miles from Guadalcanal to the Admiralties. Directly to the west of Guadalcanal, and between the Solomons and New Guinea, lies a host of small islands, the most important of which fall into the Trobriand, d'Entecasteaux, and Woodlark groups. That massive land block in the Pacific called New Guinea stretches its long span west-northwest until it reaches the Netherlands Indies, a vast and irregular grouping of islands in an extent of water so great that it embodies several seas, mainly the Arafura Sea, the Banda Sea, the Molucca Sea, and the Celebes Sea, the last named lying south of the Philippines.

Directly west of the northern tip of Guadalcanal is the little Russell Island, and above that New Georgia, with its satellite islands including Vangunu and Rendova, on the south and west, and Arundel off the northwest. To the east of Arundel and running north is the Kula Gulf, separating New Georgia from Kolombangara. Then, running northwest, lie Vella Lavella, Bougainville, and Buka, the most northerly of the Solomons. The eastern fringe of this important group of islands is made up of two long, narrow islands, Santa Isabel at the southeast and Choiseul to the northwest. From Guadalcanal to Buka is 500 miles and from Buka to New Britain, directly west, about 150 miles.

Within the area thus outlined Japan and the United Nations were to lock horns in a series of desperate encounters. The most important enemy position in the northern Solomons was the airfield the Japanese had constructed at Munda Point on the southwest coast of New Georgia and its secondary base at the mouth of the Vila River on the southern tip of Kolombangara. Both these bases were right in the geographical and strategical center of the area. They lay only about 200 miles from Henderson Field on Guadalcanal so that all through the spring of 1943 they were kept under constant attack by Allied planes and occasional naval bombardment.

Just 203 days after the Marines had landed on Guadalcanal and two weeks after the Japanese had evacuated the remnants of their forces from the island, a sudden move on February 21, 1943, landed American forces on the small cluster of the Russell Islands, eighteen to thirty-seven miles northwest of Guadalcanal. The American landings had been so skilfully executed that Marines were on the island for six days before the Japanese knew about it. Then they pulled out in a hurry; the occupation was completed without bloodshed.

Just one week after the occupation of the Russells, Lieutenant Walter Higgins, of Fort Worth, Texas, was flying with other pilots scouting the waters of the Southwest Pacific. For hours he had been maneuvering his Liberator through tropical storms and heavy clouds. The dense rain was penetrated only by lurid lightning flashes. His gas indicator showed that it was time to return. Just as he started to take his ship back home he saw a small break in the clouds and decided to go down for one final look around. There in the Bismarck Sea was strung out for twenty miles a great Japanese convoy between Wide Bay and Jacquinot Bay off New Britain's southern coast. Lieutenant Robert F. Paviour, of Rochester, New York, the bombardier, Lieutenant George Sellmer, of Indianapolis, the navigator, and co-pilot Second Lieutenant Lyle A. Schoenauer, of Plainview, Nebraska, caught sight of the ships at the same time. Immediately they radioed the information to their base. It was well they did, for had the Japanese not been sighted they would have made port at Lae or Salumaua on New Guinea during the night to try to trap MacArthur.

There were fourteen ships in that convoy, but by the time General MacArthur and General Kenney could get their bombers to the scene eight more enemy ships had joined them, making a total of twelve transports and ten cruisers and destroyers heading through the Bismarck Sea between New Britain and New Guinea. The last-minute signal flashed by the Americans was like lighting the fuse to dynamite. From the early morning of March 1, all through that day and into the night, American bombers attacked the Japanese as no convoy ever had been assailed before.

In that first day's battle the enemy lost thirteen planes and a 10,000-ton transport; an 8,000-ton, 6,000-ton, and medium-sized vessel were left in distress and sinking. The remnants scattered over a wide area northeast of Finschhafen and during the night re-formed. With the first break of dawn the battle was resumed. Enemy air opposition grew weaker and weaker because a total of fifty-five Japanese planes had been shot down and a score more badly damaged. Finally, with the skies all to themselves, the Americans concentrated upon the ships.

SIGNAL CORPS PHOTO

Across the Rhine in Holland

A steady stream of British armor and vehicles pours across the Nijmegen Bridge, following capture of the bridge.

U. S. ARMY AIR FORCES PHOTO

Nazi Maintenance Base Bombed

Liberators of the U. S. Army 8th Air Force did considerable damage to this Nazi base at Kjeller, Norway.

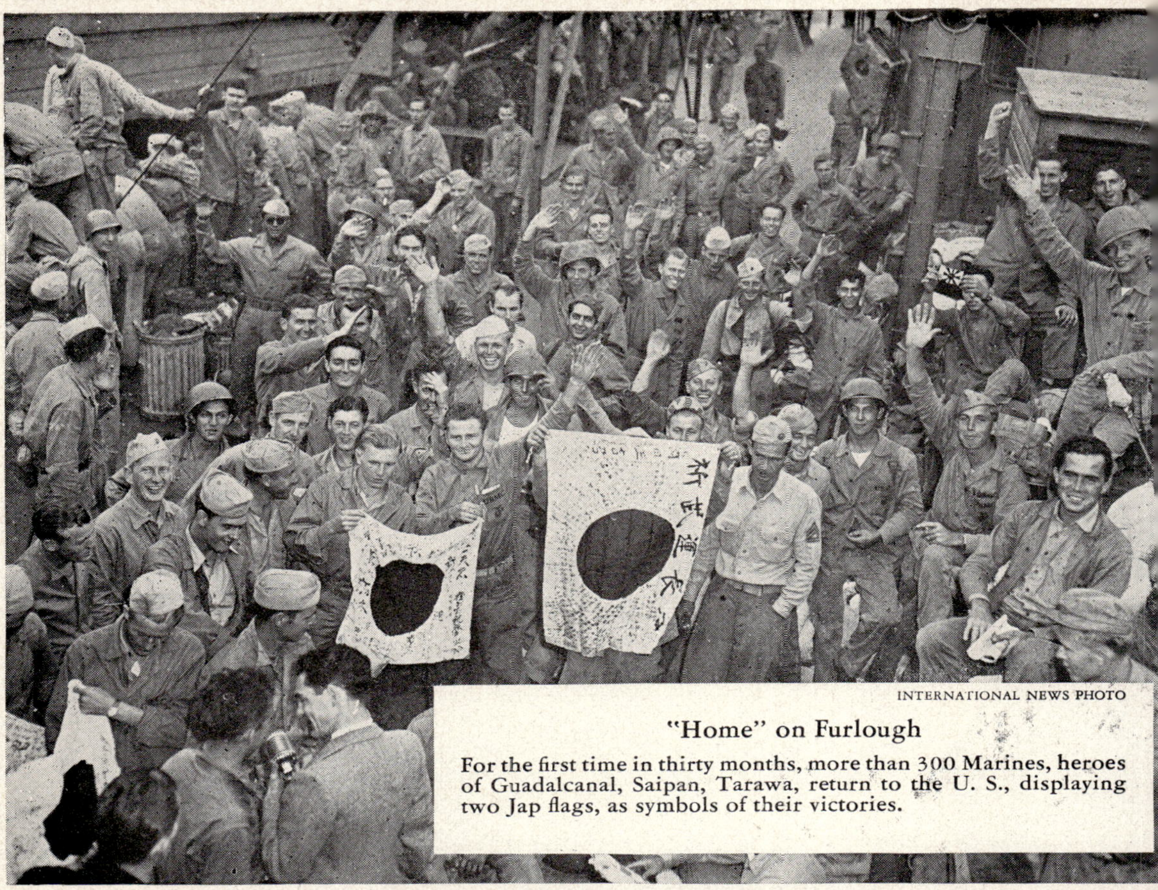

INTERNATIONAL NEWS PHOTO

"Home" on Furlough

For the first time in thirty months, more than 300 Marines, heroes of Guadalcanal, Saipan, Tarawa, return to the U. S., displaying two Jap flags, as symbols of their victories.

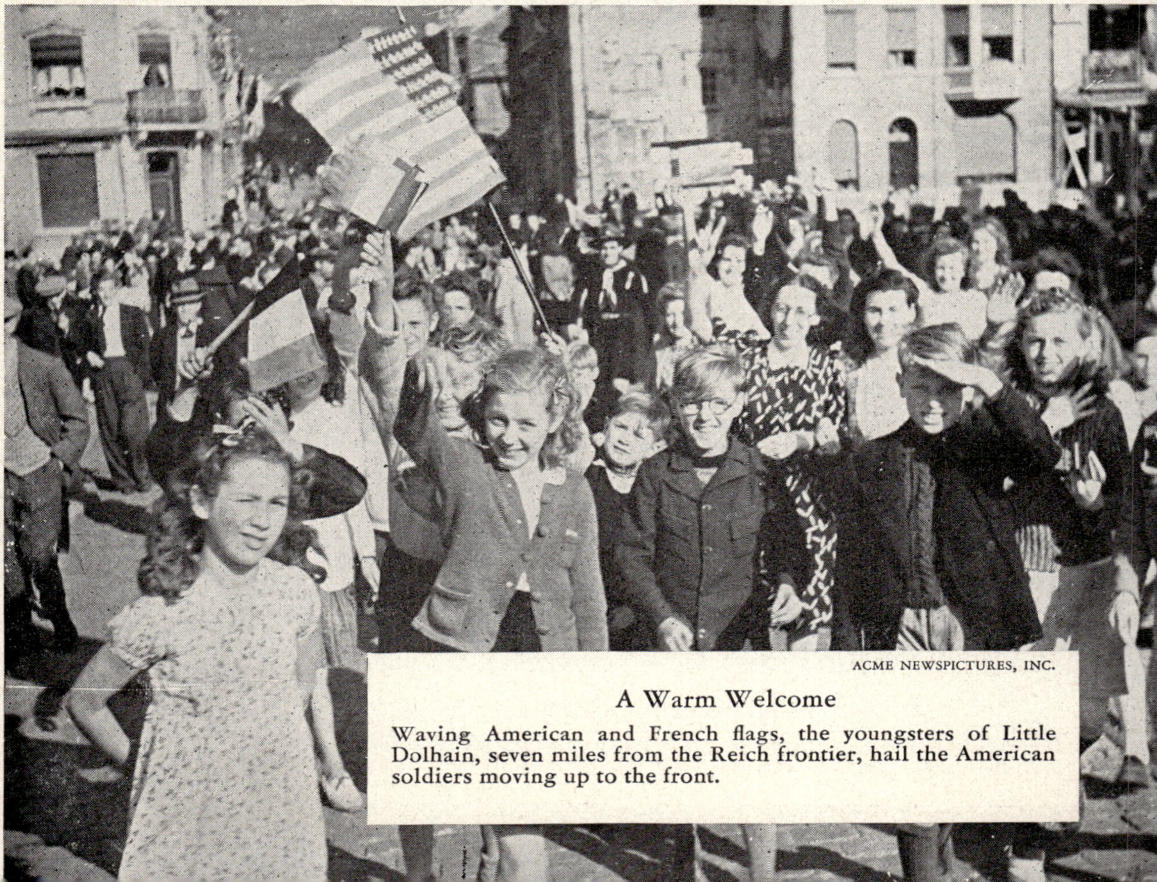

ACME NEWSPICTURES, INC.

A Warm Welcome

Waving American and French flags, the youngsters of Little Dolhain, seven miles from the Reich frontier, hail the American soldiers moving up to the front.

U. S. Troops in Paris

Thousands of American troops march down the Champs Elysees during the liberation celebration.

INTERNATIONAL NEWS PHOTO

Liberators Return to Belgium

Among the British forces that liberated Brussels, was a brigade of Belgians, many of whom are shown here receiving an enthusiastic welcome by the people of Brussels on their return home.

INTERNATIONAL NEWS PHOTO

Yanks Tramp Through Paris

American and French soldiers stand guard against snipers as a United States Infantry Division marches through the Place de la Concorde, en route to the front.

When our fliers turned home late that afternoon not a single Japanese craft of the original twenty-two was afloat.

This was the Battle of Bismarck Sea. General MacArthur, in his communiqué of March 3, said: "Our decisive success cannot fail to have the most important results on the enemy's strategic and tactical plans. His campaign, for the time being at least, is completely dislocated. We have achieved a victory of such completeness as to assume the proportions of a major disaster to the enemy."

Over the vast Pacific area the surging tide was sweeping against the Japanese.

Liberators from Australia flew more than 4,000 miles on June 23 to attack Macassar on Celebes, drop thirty-eight tons of bombs, and hit a Japanese cruiser. The only longer flight was the one made from Hawaii to Wake. A month later the same planes established a record by striking Surabaya on Java, the principal base in the Netherlands Indies; while, at the same time, a single plane went over Macassar again. Day after day, in all weather, this long-distance sparring was maintained.

The Allies were on the offensive in the Central Pacific. Tarawa, in the Gilberts, and Nauru, were under attack. Nauru, also known as Pleasant Island, is a coral formation ten miles in circumference just thirty-two miles south of the Equator. It provided Japan with a large part of the phosphate required for explosives. The Seventh Air Force paid its first visit to Nauru on March 26 and returned a month later. Bombing Nauru became a pleasant occupation for young American crews flying for Major General William H. Hale. The navy, too, sent its Catalinas against both Nauru and Tarawa.

Early in the spring of 1943, Marines landed without opposition, as they had in the Russells, and occupied Funafuti atoll in the Ellice Islands. While the new seizure of this southernmost Central Pacific point advanced the Allies no closer to Tokyo, it was an excellent point from which to protect the convoy line to Australia, New Caledonia, and Guadalcanal, about 1,200 miles to the southwest.

These "curtain raisers" in the drama of the Pacific were setting the stage for the summer of 1943, which was to flame in fury over the Solomons and New Guinea, where MacArthur's men were gaining their foothold for their long drive to victory.

JAPANESE SUN BEGINS TO SET OVER INDIA–BURMA–CHINA

FIRST signs in the zodiac of approaching total eclipse of Japan's military power appeared in 1943. American and British statesmen were charting impending events. American engineers were building that Victory Road from India and Burma over which was to begin the march for the liberation of China. Other mighty American forces were striking from the Pacific.

In far-away Quebec, Canada, and in Cairo, Egypt, plans were being laid which were to explode like bombshells upon the Japanese. President Roosevelt and Prime Minister Churchill came to full agreement in Quebec in August. Two supplementary conferences in November wrote the tentative dates in the Japanese Doomsday Book. Allied military leaders met in Chungking and Generalissimo Chiang Kai-shek met with Roosevelt and Churchill in Cairo. After five days of momentous discussions the three leaders issued the following proclamation:

"The several military missions have agreed upon the future military operations against Japan. The three great Allies expressed their resolve to bring unrelenting pressure against their brutal enemies by sea, land, and air. This pressure is already rising. The three great Allies are fighting this war to restrain and punish the aggression of Japan. They covet no gain for themselves and have no thought of territorial expansion. It is their purpose that Japan shall be stripped of all the islands in the Pacific which she has seized or occupied since the beginning of the First World War in 1914, and that all the territories Japan has stolen from the Chinese, such as Manchuria, Formosa, and the Pescadores, shall be restored to the Republic of China.

"Japan will be expelled from all other territories which she has taken by violence and greed. The aforesaid three Powers, mindful of the enslavement of Korea, are determined that in due course Korea shall become free and independent. With these objects in view, the three Allies, in harmony with those of the United Nations at war with Japan, will continue to persevere in the serious and prolonged operations necessary to procure the unconditional surrender of Japan."

This was the first clear, unalterable expression of war aims in the Pacific. It meant the return of Japan to the borders of 1894, before she started the series of wars, raids, and occupations that brought more than 3,000,000 square miles and 500,000,000 human beings under her control. It meant, also, the loss of the ores, industries, railroads, and other industrial materials of Manchuria and northern China, and of the oil, rubber, rice, and spices of Oceania and Burma. It was an explicit pledge to China to help her regain her lost territories and to Korea for the return of her independence.

War in the Pacific was to be speeded up from every direction. Lord Louis Mountbatten, grandson of Queen Victoria and organizer of Britain's famed Commandos, was sent to India as Allied Commander in Chief in Southeast Asia. He had commanded the aircraft on the carrier *Illustrious,* and during the Battle of Crete had led a flotilla of destroyers until his ship was blown from under him on May 23, 1941.

He had been appointed Chief of Combined Operations for the British in March, 1942, and subsequently was placed in charge of the landings of General Eisenhower's Allied forces in North Africa. He was forty-three years old when named Supreme Allied Commander in Southeast Asia. His appointment was simultaneous with those of General MacArthur as Supreme Commander in the Southwest Pacific and General Eisenhower in North Africa.

Major General Albert C. Wedemeyer, United States Army, was appointed Deputy Chief of Staff by Mountbatten. Wedemeyer was an old "China hand"; he had been sent to Tientsin in 1930 with the 15th Infantry. Two years later he became aide to Major General C. E. Kilbourne at Corregidor, retaining the post when Major General Stanley D. Embick took over Manila's famous "Rock." Three years before World War II Wedemeyer went to Berlin to attend the German War College and, upon returning to the United States, held several significant offices in Washington. He finally became Assistant Chief of Staff of the Operations Division and aide to General Marshall. An expert on tanks, he took that knowledge to Burma in October, 1943, when he joined Lord Louis Mountbatten.

During the monsoons which had been raging in Burma that summer Brigadier General Caleb V. Haynes had kept the United States Tenth Air Force flying against Japanese targets. His work had been so effective that he was able to announce in September that ninety per cent of the enemy's airfields, docks, bridges, railroads, and other facilities in Burma had been pulverized.

Ever since the Japanese had driven the Allies out of Burma in 1942 they had rested, for some inexplicable reason, along the India border. They were "sitting ducks" for the Allied airmen. Toward the end of September, 1943, word leaked out of the Burma mountain jungles that engineers were hacking a new road called by the men the "Tokyo Road." The fighting that followed in Burma was primarily a struggle to push that road through to completion. As details began to filter out of the wilderness, it was learned that the penetration into northern Burma over the mountains had been begun at the end of 1942. Then it was that the decision was made to build what subsequently came to be known as the Ledo Road and then was officially designated the Stilwell Road by a grateful Chiang Kai-shek.

The main purpose of the Ledo Road was to open a land route for supplies to the sorely pressed Chinese troops. Ever since the loss of Rangoon and the Burma Road the blockade of China had been complete. The only supplies to reach that beleaguered country were those flown from India by intrepid fliers over the "hump" of mountains. It is true that by the end of 1943 American planes of the Air Transport Command were delivering more material into China than ever had been carried over the Burma Road. But it was only a trickle in relation to the actual needs. This aërial route required flights over jagged peaks towering more than 20,000 feet, thus limiting the cargo capacity and using gasoline desperately needed in combat operations.

A road had to be opened. It took more than two years to build it, and it cost staggering casualties; but the results justified the cost. The fighting that made the road possible brought with it the liberation of Burma.

The Allies had been pushing a harassing campaign along a 500-mile triangular segment from upper Burma, through the Chin Hills, to the coastal lowlands north of Akyah on the Bay of Bengal.

The entire area soon became known as the "Battle for a Road." The British in Arakan captured the town and port of Maungdaw at the head of the Mayu Peninsula during January; the Chin Hills push showed gains; and General Stilwell's Chinese-American troops were gradually clearing the way for the Ledo Road.

During the dark days of 1942 and 1943 a bearded officer who had just reached the age of forty convinced his superiors that anything was better than inaction. He was Brigadier General Orde C. Wingate of the British Army, a rugged, hard-fighting man. Bible-quoting, onion-munching, a believer in original methods of warfare, he was as colorful a figure as his kinsman, "Lawrence of Arabia." Wingate gathered a mixed force of Lancashiremen, Ghurkas, Kachins, and Burmese. In a few months of training he developed an adventurous group of jungle fighters and started on one of the strangest campaigns in history. He was going to out-Jap the Jap.

"Wingate's Raiders" entered the jungle with a supply train ranging from 1,000 mules to bicycles and elephants. Most of this equipment was soon lost in the hazardous terrain. The men were then compelled to rely upon supplies flown to them in a shuttle service by American planes. Before their three-month mission was over they had eaten most of their remaining mules and horses. Sick, wounded, and injured soldiers were abandoned because there was no means of transporting or evacuating them. But in those three months the Raiders blew up bridges, delayed the Japanese drive against the British in the Chindwin area, took the pressure off the Chinese in the Hukawng Valley, and saved 5,000 loyal Burmese threatened by an enemy force. Wingate's men moved so quickly and struck with such fury that the Japanese, believing it to be a full-fledged army, used most of their own strength in trying to counter the unexpected blows.

General Wingate had established a pattern for the reconquest of Burma. Summoned to North America, he outlined his plans so forcefully to President Roosevelt and Prime Minister Churchill at Quebec that they told him to proceed with the organization of an airborne Commando outfit. Results soon became apparent. The Commandos captured and even built airfields far behind the Japanese lines. Harassing and cutting communications, they tied down large forces by appearing as if from nowhere in sharp, sudden strikes. Wingate had insisted upon only one thing—some means to evacuate casualties, for he was not going to repeat the heart-breaking performance of abandoning his wounded to die. General Henry H. Arnold, commander of all United States Army Air Forces, promised two hundred small liaison planes for the purpose. Colonel Philip G. Cochran, of Erie, Pennsylvania, and Colonel John R. Alison, of New York City, were placed in charge of the new unit. "I want you to go into that country," General Arnold told them, "and take out General Wingate's wounded. I want you to do more than that. I want the United States Army Air Force to spearhead General Wingate's campaign in Burma."

That is just what was done in one of the epic glider invasions of the war. Airborne men and equipment were dropped on raw ground deep in enemy territory. Airfields were quickly constructed. Just how the herculean task was accomplished is evident from this story: A British commander, standing amid the wreckage of gliders on a rock-strewn field, asked Colonel Alison, "Can you build an airfield here?" It seemed an almost impossible task. Colonel Alison asked his engineer officer if it were possible and how long it would take. "Well," replied the American engineer, "will this afternoon be too late?"

On March 24 General Wingate flew from one of these secret airfields 150 miles behind the Japanese lines to return to headquarters. But he never reached it. His Mitchell bomber crashed into a mountain peak in a fierce storm and the colorful leader was killed with all his companions. Major General W. D. A. Lentaigne succeeded to the command.

Shortly before the Quebec Conference Brigadier General Frank D. Merrill, of New Hampshire, had called for volunteers for a "dangerous and hazardous mission." This young officer, who had been rejected five times for sight deficiency before being admitted to West Point, had been assistant military attaché at Tokyo and had spent forty months in China learning the various dialects. He then went to Manila as General MacArthur's intelligence officer and was in Rangoon on a flying mission when the Japanese struck. Remaining there as General Stilwell's aide, he took the "long walk out of Burma into India" at his side.

Merrill was swamped with responses to his call. He welded his volunteers into a long-range penetration group patterned after Wingate's Raiders, and it soon came to be known as "Merrill's Marauders." These first American infantrymen to see action in Asia set out from Ledo in the northwest Indian province of Assam late in February, 1944. They were to make a 100-mile circling march to the rear of the Japanese at Maingkwan. In drenching rains they averaged twenty miles a day through the wild jungles of the Naga Hills and lived on iron rations dropped to them by the United States Tenth Air Force. Cutting the enemy supply lines, they turned the Japanese road block technique against the foe and then went on to capture Walabum. There were but 650 men in this force. They killed over 2,000 Japanese and wounded 2,000 more out of one of the enemy's best divisions. Their own casualties were seven killed, thirty-seven wounded.

The Japanese were finally aroused to their peril in Burma and launched a four-prong drive into India. Their objectives were Imphal, capital of Manipur State; Kohima, to the north; and, above that, the Bengal-Assam rail line that supplied the Allied bases along the Brahmaputra River from which troops and material were sent to Burma and China. Another column swept toward Silchar, west of Imphal, an important town on the strategic railway.

Lord Louis Mountbatten and his staff realized that their outnumbered forces could not wage more than a delaying action in the mountains along the Burma border. They gradually withdrew to the Imphal Plain where Allied tanks and heavy artillery would hold a decided advantage. The Japanese, aided by elements of the "Indian National Army" recruited by their puppet Subhas Chandra Bose, crossed into India for the first time during the last week of March. From then on the battle was furious. The enemy infiltrated into Imphal early in May, and enveloped Kohima. But that was as far as he got. British and Indians waged a stout defense of the two towns. The Japanese tried desperately to hold on until the monsoons, hoping to be able to dig in and resume the offensive in the fall. But Merrill's men and Wingate's men had raised such havoc with their long lines of communications that the Japanese were compelled to retreat. Fighting all the way, even when cut up into isolated bands of stragglers, the last Japanese were not thrown out of India until August 15.

Myitkyina, terminus of the railway from Rangoon, and heart of Japanese activity in north Burma, finally fell on August 4 after a siege that had been begun on May 17. The Japanese, in the last two and one-half months of fighting, lost more than 3,000 killed. Allied casualties also ran high in the hole-to-hole, hand-to-hand struggles.

Meanwhile, the Ledo Road—the "toughest road in the world"—had been pushed steadily forward. Veterans of Guadalcanal had joined the Chinese in the building-fighting operations. A northern spur was started across the mountains to Yunnan Province in China; the southern route was carried to Myitkyina and then east for a junction with the Burma Road near the China-Burma frontier. Malaria, monsoons, and mountains failed to halt its progress.

The "Battle for a Road" was being waged also on another front. On the night of May 10-11, 1944, the Chinese Expeditionary Force in Yunnan Province crossed the Salween River to attack the strongly entrenched Japanese to the west, between them and the Burmese border. The Chinese, under General Wei Li-huang ("One-Hundred-Victory Wei"), and his Chief of Staff General Hsiao I-Hsu, were assisted by officers and technical men from the United States Y-Force Operations Staff and others attached to the military mission to China. General Stilwell was in over-all command of these Chinese troops who had been almost entirely trained and equipped by Americans.

The first crossing of the Salween was made in pneumatic rubber boats by 40,000 men who had flown over the "Hump" after the long Pacific trip from the United States. By the time the campaign was in full swing the total ferried across the Salween had risen to 100,000—the largest Allied ground force to battle the Japanese up to that time. The Salween campaign was designed to throw out the enemy from territory he had occupied for two years and thus open the China end of the Burma-Ledo Road. The terrain lying between the Salween and Shweli rivers is dominated by the Kaolikung Mountains, an awesome range whose peaks rise to 12,000 feet. Only a few primitive trails, some of them always above the clouds, cross the mountains.

This campaign continued throughout 1944 and into 1945, including the monsoon seasons. Fighting was bitter, uncompromising, and costly. By the time the last objective, Wanting, had been occupied on January 20, 1945, Tengyueh, Lungling, Pingka, and some 400 other communities had been liberated.

China had concluded her first successful major offensive in seven years of war. She had liberated Yunnan Province after more than two years of occupation, and had reopened the Burma Road.

While the Salween drive moved to its successful conclusion, the Allied forces pushed slowly ahead in Burma, driving the Japanese toward Mandalay from the north and from the west. The path of the new road was made secure against all enemy attacks from land and from puny forays by remnants of a once proud Japanese air force. The "Battle for a Road" had been won.

Inside China the military situation had remained relatively stagnant during the summer of 1943. The plight of the people and the country, however, continued to grow worse. It was now imperative to regain some territory to feed and equip the troops, and to repair the little stretches of transportation facilities left in Chinese hands. Japan, aware of the strategic value of China's rivers and few rail communications, had early neutralized every road, railroad, and river. Isolated sections held by the Chinese did not lead to the outside world.

Admiral Nimitz said, after the capture of Kwajalein in the Pacific: "My objective is to get ground and air forces into China as soon as possible. I don't believe Japan can be defeated from the sea alone, and the very fact that you will be able to get troops into China implies that their [the enemy's] communications to the south will then be cut off.... I believe Japan can be defeated only from bases in China."

A week later General Stilwell said that Admiral Nimitz's invasion forces would be "supported heavily by an aggressive land and air offensive projected from inside China in spite of the existing blockade." General Chennault declared that his United States Fourteenth Air Force was laying the groundwork for collaboration with Admiral Nimitz, preparing bases, airfields, and other support.

That Tokyo took all these warnings to heart became evident in April, 1944, when the Japanese opened their spring drive. The objective was to gain full possession of the Peiping-Hankow railroad running north and south and the Lung-Hai railroad running east and west.

Fighting raged furiously for months. The Japanese won control of the Peiping-Hankow line, but were unable to hold it in the face of Chinese counterattacks which regained enough of the trackage and surrounding territory to make the railroad useless to the enemy. At the same time another campaign was opened by the enemy from north and south to gain possession of the Canton-Hankow railroad. In this fighting the Japanese captured Changsha on June 19. The capital of Hunan Province, which had been the Waterloo of so many enemy commanders, fell to 50,000 troops powerfully supported by artillery, tanks, and planes.

When the year ended Japan had occupied large stretches of China but had failed in the strategic objective of gaining unrestricted use of the rail lines. China never had been in greater danger from either the military or the economic standpoint. Her heroic soldiers, however, aided by General Chennault's fliers—to which had been added a Chinese-American Composite Wing made up of Chinese pilots—had inflicted a significant defeat upon Tokyo's defensive position in Asia.

TARAWA—CONQUEST OF THE ATOLLS—STEPPING-STONES IN THE PACIFIC

ATOLL warfare in the Pacific in 1943-44 was the beginning of a new test of courage for American fighters. It marked the most savage combats with the highest casualties up to this time.

We are now to see these men of ours in death struggles at Makin, Tarawa, Rabaul, Bougainville, Arawe, Kwajalein,—names that will live in history. With the dawn of November 18, 1943, American carrier planes began a sustained attack that smothered Betio, Makin, Abemama, and the other atolls marked as stepping-stones. The next day Admiral Spruance brought his warships up and covered the island coasts with a layer of shells. On November 20 our landing forces went ashore on Makin and Tarawa.

Major General Ralph C. Smith commanded the Makin assault troops. Major General Julian C. Smith, U.S.M.C., led the Second Marine Division on Tarawa and its principal island of Betio, while Major General Holland McT. Smith, U.S.M.C., was over-all commander of the landing forces. Rear Admiral Richmond K. Turner was in charge of amphibious operations, and Vice Admiral John H. Hoover, commander of aircraft, directed all land-based air activity.

For weeks Admiral Hoover's planes had been smashing the Gilberts, and in the opening phases of the assault carrier aircraft swiftly won air mastery by low-level strafing. More than 100 ships, exclusive of landing craft, were in the armada that operated over a battle area covering thousands of miles of water. They brought with them 800 carrier planes, the greatest number yet assembled for a single attack. Rear Admirals Montgomery and Van H. Ragsdale led the flat-tops off Tarawa; Rear Admirals Radford and Henry M. Mullinix, the latter on the *Liscome Bay,* were off Makin. Other carriers were under Rear Admirals Sherman and Pownall, the latter on the new *Yorktown.*

Makin was the scene of a weird, fanatical suicide attack by the Japanese in which they were annihilated in hand-to-hand struggles by the "Fighting 69th," now the 165th Infantry Regiment of the 3rd "Shamrock" Battalion. Only a few prisoners were taken; the rest of the garrison of 1,000 were killed. We lost sixty-five dead and 121 wounded in a campaign that ended in victory in fifty-four hours. Abemama, south of Makin, was invaded on November 21, and its 200 defenders disposed of in a few hours. American losses were one killed, two wounded.

But Tarawa, with its Betio, was another story. There the fate of the entire invasion hung on a very slender thread. Betio, also known as Betitu, is a flat, elongated stretch about 800 by 5,000 yards with a highly valuable airfield. Nature has surrounded it with a reef from a quarter to a half mile wide. The Japanese improved upon this by sinking barbed-wire underwater defenses compelling ships to steer a tortuous course covered by machine guns, mortars, and other arms on land. Betio's beaches are narrow, only ten or fifteen feet from high water. The enemy had constructed an intricate system of interlocking defenses with pillboxes every twenty yards around the island. These pillboxes, built of concrete, steel, sand, and logs, were of such strength that they were never reduced despite the fact that the rest of the island had been clipped bare by naval fire and aërial bombs. Furthermore, the Japanese had medium tanks on the island and it was studded with cleverly devised tank traps. Photographic reconnaissance had shown that Betio was strong, but it could not pierce the adroit camouflage with which the enemy had concealed the full power of his defenses.

It was into this pit of death that the Second Marines lunged. Here, on the beaches, they were met by withering fire from concealed guns and one- or two-man pillboxes. Covering planes ran into unsuspected antiaircraft fire. In the hulk of a wrecked boat crouched a large Japanese contingent. Letting our landing boats proceed to the beach, they opened fire from the rear upon the Marines as they jumped into the surf. The tide of battle did not turn until noon of the second day when communications finally were established on a firm basis. By noon of November 23 the last organized resistance had been overcome and on the following day American planes were using the airfield.

The Second Marines, in their conquest of Tarawa, wrote with their blood the most brilliant page in the records of their Division. They wiped out 4,500 Japanese, but lost 1,026 of their own killed, and 2,557 wounded: Betio was a graveyard when the battle was over. Dead bodies were strewn over the entire island; Marine corpses hung over the barbed wire offshore; wrecked landing craft littered the waters. Nothing remained whole above ground except the stout Japanese pillboxes which had been taken with flame-throwers, TNT, and burning gasoline thrust through apertures. In the midst of this universal destruction the Seabees performed a record job on the airfield; planes from escort carriers landed amid wreckage and flames on the base that was to become the backbone of defense against Japanese assaults from the Marshalls.

Our naval losses were, under the circumstances, light. An Independence class carrier was damaged by a torpedo plane which sneaked through during the first night, but the most serious loss was that of the escort carrier *Liscome Bay,* the only carrier lost during 1943. After weathering plane attacks for several days off Makin, the *Liscome Bay* took a submarine's torpedo in her middle shortly after 5:00 A.M. on

November 24. She exploded, burst into flame, and went down in twenty-two minutes, a blazing inferno still bursting from internal explosions. Admiral Mullinix, Captain I. D. Wiltsie, the ship's commanding officer, fifty-two other officers and 686 men were lost.

A few nights later the United States lost one of its heroes. During the dark of November 27, Japanese planes appeared in force to attack the carriers off Makin. American planes took the air. One of the fighters was flown by Lieutenant Commander Edward H. "Butch" O'Hare. Fighting was furious and the black sky was pierced with tracer bullets and the flaming ruins of falling Japanese planes. Suddenly, Commander O'Hare's plane turned off and disappeared. His wingman searched for him in vain. Another pilot saw a plane drop into the water. That was all that was ever known. Admiral Radford recommended a second Congressional Medal of Honor for helping to save the carrier formation from certain torpedo hits. The first Medal of Honor had been awarded to Commander O'Hare for his bravery in saving the old *Lexington* in February, 1942.

The entire Gilbert chain of islands had been won in four days. There were still Japanese forces on isolated islands, but they were wiped out later at our leisure.

General MacArthur's land-based planes took over on December 1 and began to flay New Britain's western shore.

This was only part of the New Britain picture. Lesser air blows had been delivered against an area on the south coast some sixty miles southeast of Cape Gloucester. The Japanese considered these to be diversionary attacks and prepared for landings at Cape Gloucester.

On December 15, under a terrific air and sea bombardment, General Krueger's Sixth Army jumped across the seventy-mile water stretch from New Guinea and landed near Arawe, an important Japanese barge base some 270 miles from Rabaul. They hit the beaches in their familiar green camouflaged invasion rig at Cape Merkus and Pilelo Island, using amphibious tanks and rubber boats.

By 7:49 that morning the Americans, in tracked "Alligator" amphibious tanks finally got ashore on the mainland and planted the flag of Texas on the beach beside that of the United States. The entire three-mile Arawe Peninsula was occupied in five hours. The invaders pressed into the interior where they cut communications with Cape Gloucester to the west and Gasmata to the east. The task force under Admiral Daniel E. Berbey, who was to be associated with all of General MacArthur's invasions, kept the entire area under heavy naval fire. Brigadier General Julian W. Cunningham, commanding the landing force, had the benefit of new weapons used for the first time in actual combat. Two of his amphibious "ducks" were equipped with rocket guns which leveled shore opposition in seven minutes at their particular beachhead.

In three days the troops pushed inland six miles, capturing the Arawe airstrip. They sent one force toward Gasmata and the other toward Cape Gloucester. Progress was slow because of the terrible jungle swamps and hills. Flying Fortresses were used for the first time in regular supply service, carrying supplies and food to the Arawe fighters.

The Japanese managed to throw in a heavy counterattack which pushed the United States troops back toward the beaches. American Indians representing twenty tribes were thrown into the battle after having received intensive training as "Bushmasters" in Panama. Carrying a varied assortment of knives as their chief equipment, these men, mainly from New Mexico and Arizona, during the second month of the invasion, sent the Japanese reeling back, captured positions and artillery, inflicted heavy casualties, and seized large amounts of supplies. Part of the 150th Infantry Regiment was also landed to reinforce the Texas First Cavalry Regiment, dismounted, that had first hit the beachhead. This cavalry regiment was destined to see action all along the way to the Philippines, and won numerous brilliant victories.

The ground regained by the Japanese in their Arawe counterattacks was of little comfort to them, for other things were happening on New Britain. At 7:45 on Christmas morning, 1943, Marines, including many Guadalcanal veterans, leaped into the waist-deep waters off the beaches of Cape Gloucester and stormed ashore. The Japanese garrison included the 65th Brigade and 70th Division that had swept through Bataan almost two years earlier. The Marines were determined to avenge that disaster.

Admiral Berbey had moved his warships over from Arawe to cover the Marines under Major General William H. Rupertus who landed just where the enemy did not expect them. One beachhead was at Silimati Point, another at Borgen Bay, both north of Cape Gloucester.

For three days a fierce and unrelenting battle was waged for the capture of the Cape Gloucester airfield. The Japanese were strongly entrenched on Target Hill and held out in one of the most savage battles of the war. The Marines literally "out-furied" the defenders and more than 1,000 Japanese dead were counted. On the fourth day the enemy survivors took to the hills, carrying their thousands of wounded with them. General Krueger, supervising the entire operation, wired to General MacArthur: "I have the honor to present you Cape Gloucester as a New Year's present."

Growing might of Allied power in the Pacific was further evidenced by another amphibious move while the Arawe and Cape Gloucester operations were in their early stages. On Sunday, January 2, 1944, the New Year was inaugurated with a combined land, sea, and air assault that seized Saidor, 110 miles above Finschhafen on New Guinea.

The Japanese were unable to visualize so many rapid, powerful strokes. The harbor and airfield were quickly captured. Chief significance of this landing lay in the fact that the Japanese on the north coast of New Guinea were trapped between Saidor and the advancing Australians, with no source of supply or reinforcement. The beachhead perimeter was quickly expanded as the Americans drove toward Sio for a union with the Australians. The Saidor positions also made possible a two-pronged drive farther up New Guinea against Madang and Astrolabe Bay which were being approached by Australian units.

The Pacific war reached the end of one phase on February 14 when American and New Zealand troops occupied Green, or Nissen, Island, 120 miles east of Rabaul and about twice that distance from Kavieng. Green Island is only forty miles north of Buka. Admiral Halsey was in command of the naval end of the operations. With the capture of Green Island, General MacArthur, in command of the Southwest Pacific and the South Pacific theaters, said: "For all strategic military purposes this completes the campaign for the Solomon Islands."

Green Island was ideal for a big air base and in three weeks Seabees, using 12,000 tons of equipment worth $2,500,000 that had been landed from cargo ships, completed a major airfield.

Once again the spotlight shifts back to the Central Pacific. All through December, 1943, and January, 1944, land-based planes from all three services and carrier aircraft piled blows with increasing intensity upon the Marshall Islands—hundreds of low coral islets, more or less huddled in thirty-two groups of atolls and spread through 70,000 square miles of the Pacific in two roughly parallel chains.

With the Solomons and Gilberts regained by the Allies, the Marshalls provided the last salient in the Japanese protective outer ring. Admiral Nimitz, realizing how important they would be to the United States as its own forward base, decided to capture the islands instead of bypassing them. The Japanese fully expected an assault and prepared for landings on Wotje or Maloelap, nearest Pearl Harbor, or Jaluit and Mili, closest to the recently captured Gilberts. They never suspected that Admiral Nimitz would send his ships and planes and men through the barrier of protecting islands and strike at the heart—Kwajalein.

On the night of January 29-30, 1944, the same line-up of task forces and invasion troops that had taken the Gilberts went into action with only one major change. Admiral Mitscher, on the *Yorktown*, commanded the carriers.

Everything was thrown into that "Spruance Haircut," as it came to be known. Carrier planes were joined by land-based aircraft of the army, navy, and Marine Corps. Everything that could float, from battleships to the smallest boat, hit Kwajalein and its surrounding islands. Fighters even bombed with their belly tanks, dropping them to explode and burst into flame over pillboxes, gun positions, and other targets. Not a tree remained standing on Kwajalein, Roi, or Namur.

When, on February 2, the Army's Seventh Division landed on Kwajalein and the Fourth Marines on Roi and Namur, 75 per cent of the Japanese garrison had been killed. The remainder had been driven out of their minds by the impact of the bombardment.

Japanese air power had been destroyed within four hours of the first carrier strikes. These came as such a surprise that 122 enemy planes were wrecked on the ground. Not a single Japanese aircraft attacked any of the invasion ships during the nine days they remained in the Marshalls' waters.

Roi fell in two days, the first piece of prewar Japanese territory to be wrested from the enemy. The 3,600-foot fighter airstrip and 4,300-foot bomber runway were in American hands. Even before the fighting was over army and navy land-based planes began to use the field and within a week the Seabees had extended it for the accommodation of our heaviest bombers. Namur was captured shortly after the fall of Roi. During this fighting Private First Class James M. Thomas, a 150-pound fighter from Biltmore, North Carolina, killed sixty Japanese himself. Admiral Nimitz personally presented the award of the first Bronze Star Medal in Marine Corps history. On Roi and Namur 129 Marines died, 436 were wounded, and 65 were missing; the Japanese lost 3,472 dead and 91 prisoners.

Fighting on Kwajalein was more protracted and it was impossible to capture the island until Roi and Namur had fallen. But the 7th Division troops of Major General Charles H. Corlett subdued all but scattered sniping opposition on February 4. By the next day the most powerful Japanese stronghold east of Truk was completely in American hands. Army casualties on Kwajalein were 137 dead, 712 wounded and 17 missing; the Japanese lost 4,670 dead and 173 were taken prisoner. Thus the total cost in American casualties for this great operation was 1,516, of which 286 were killed. Against this figure were 8,122 dead Japanese and 264 prisoners.

Less than two weeks later a part of the carrier force, including the *Saratoga*, went for Eniwetok, 350 miles closer to Japan. The invasion followed the pattern so successfully laid down at Kwajalein.

The 106th Infantry, a National Guard unit, and the Twenty-second Marines, led respectively by Colonel Russell G. Ayers and Colonel John T. Walker, went ashore on February 17 following the naval-air preparation. Rear Admiral H. W. Hill commanded the amphibious forces with Brigadier General Thomas E. Watson, U.S.M.C., in over-all command of the assault troops. Eniwetok was cleared quickly, but Parry Island proved more formidable. The Japanese remained hidden in their foxholes without giving any sign of life during the activity on

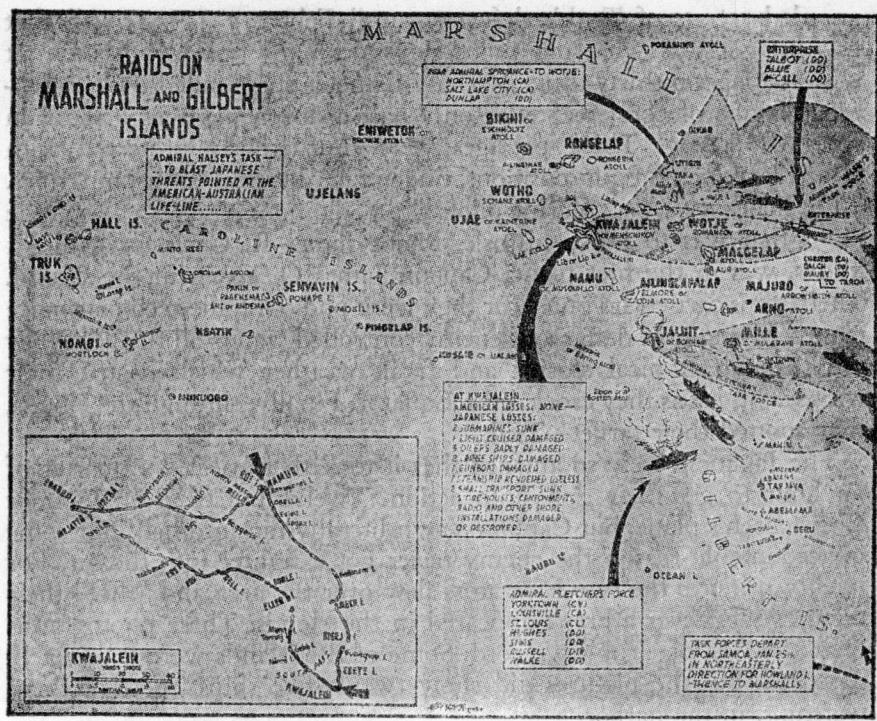

Official U. S. Navy Photograph

Combat action during first six months of the Pacific War.

Eniwetok. When the Marines moved onto the island they met opposition of the most fanatical kind. Parry Island fell at 7:30 P.M., February 22. This completed the conquest of the Marshalls.

With the Marshalls in the hands of the United Nations, the campaign to drive the Japanese out of the Pacific had reached 2,700 miles west of Pearl Harbor. The Allied advanced line was 362 miles from Ponape and 750 from the great base of Truk in the Carolines. Just how important that fact was had been brought home to the Japanese with a double punch. Paradoxically, Truk was both a reality and a myth. Its gigantic naval and air bases, its importance as a shipping and staging area, with its powerful natural and man-made defenses, seemed to combine all the values of Pearl Harbor, Singapore, and Gibraltar. During the Japanese advances through the Netherlands Indies and the Solomons it had proved its value. Its strategic significance had been emphasized again during the terrible months the "Tokyo Express" had run into southern waters. Its supply of reinforcements in the way of planes, men, ships, supplies seemed inexhaustible.

For years past no eye of white man had penetrated the closely guarded secrets of Truk's defenses—until February 4, 1944. All that was known was what old maps showed: many volcanic islands set within a lagoon thirty-three miles in diameter surrounded by a treacherous fringe of coral reef with only half a dozen passages leading in from the ocean. These passages were murderously protected with mines, interlocking gun positions, underwater barriers, and submarines.

On February 4, two Marine pilots left a Solomons base on a 2,000-mile flight that was to prove historic. Major James R. Christensen, flight leader, was in the first plane, Captain James Q. Yawn in the second. Their ships carried no guns, for they were photographic reconnaissance planes. Flying over dangerous enemy-controlled waters all the way, they ran through tropical storms and freak weather which coated their wings with ice as they crossed the Equator. Finally, through the clouds, they spotted their target—Truk.

The Japanese were so amazed that it took them nearly a quarter of an hour to get their guns into action. Twelve bursts greeted Major Christensen's plane, but Captain Yawn literally ran into hell. For some unaccountable reason the enemy never got a fighter into the air. For twenty minutes the two Liberators flew over the area and "shot" their pictures whenever a break appeared in the clouds. These photographs were the first of Truk on record. Some of the islands were completely obscured, but the pictures did show twenty-five ships, most of them warships, in the harbor.

As soon as the pictures had been developed, their significance became apparent. The report was rushed to Admiral Halsay who, despite the presence of numerous Japanese snipers, had gone to Kwajalein to inspect the damage done by his ships and planes, and to perfect final plans for the Eniwetok operation. It took the ranking admirals only a short time to reach a decision. Admiral Spruance stripped the Kwajalein forces down to the bone, leaving only escort carriers to protect the new acquisition. The *Saratoga* and other large carriers were already on their way to Eniwetok. All the other ships, including the newest and fastest battleships and carriers, cruisers, and twenty-eight destroyers headed at once for Truk, nearly 1,000 miles away. Admiral Spruance took with him Admiral Mitscher to direct the carriers. Task Force 58 finally had a target worthy of its mettle.

On February 14, Army Liberators hit Ponape, the strategic outpost between Truk and the Gilbert-Marshall grouping of islands. This bold stroke deep into enemy territory smashed the airfield and its planes, blinding Truk's reconnaissance. Task Force 58 proceeded to its station without observation or interference. The next day General Kenney's bombers caught a convoy bound from Truk to the Bismarck Sea, and almost completely wiped it out.

Early in the morning of February 16, Admiral Mitscher launched his first planes when forty-six minutes flying time from Truk, which was only ten hours from Tokyo. Hellcats came over the island first. Wheeling in from the north, they brazenly circled the whole lagoon in the pale light of early dawn before doing anything else—then a series of fierce battles began. Pilots from "Fighting Nine" alone shot down thirty-six Jap planes. Individual heroes were created by the score. The battle raged for hours and when it was over the Japanese had 204 fewer planes than when it had begun; 127 had been shot out of the air.

American warships were lying sixty miles northeast of Truk when a group of escaping Japanese ships was spotted steaming for the North Pass out of the lagoon. That was the signal for which Admiral Spruance had been waiting—surface action at last. The *Yorktown* sent out planes while Admiral Spruance rushed two battleships, a pair of cruisers, and escorting destroyers toward the target. The planes sank a destroyer and a merchantman and left a cruiser burning; the other ships got away. During the afternoon three warships were discovered hovering around a wounded destroyer; Admiral Spruance sent out more planes to harass them and keep them under observation.

Once on the spot the men-of-war went quickly into action. A damaged mine-layer was sunk first; a crippled *Katori* class cruiser and a destroyer were cornered. An American plane spotted the wake of torpedoes launched by the destroyer in time to signal the battleships which just escaped disaster. The destroyer was sunk as the cruiser got away in the dusk. Admiral Spruance ordered his ships to break out their "victory flags" and then sailed completely around Truk.

When the American planes resumed the attack on the seventeenth, no Japanese fighter rose to challenge them. It was during the night that the first night carrier strike was attempted. Captain William I. Martin, commanding Torpedo Squadron Ten, had always believed that a night carrier blow would be tremendously effective. Admiral Mitscher permitted him to try it at Truk. Captain Martin sent twelve unprotected bombers over the harbor at low altitude to go after the ships in the lagoon. Antiaircraft fire was inaccurate because the planes were not visible in the dark; but later, as flames from burning ships threw off illumination, the defensive fire became heavy. Thirteen direct hits and seven probables were scored by the Americans.

The second day's attack ended at noon. In addition to the 204 Japanese planes destroyed, and havoc wrought on ground defenses and installations, Task Force 58 also sank twenty-three ships, including two cruisers and three destroyers, probably sank six more ships, and damaged seven others. The myth of Truk's invincibility had been shattered.

Admiral Nimitz announced: "The Pacific fleet has returned at Truk the visit made by the Japanese at Pearl Harbor on December 7, 1941, and effected a partial settlement of the debt."

"I SHALL RETURN!" MacARTHUR ON ROAD BACK TO KEEP HIS PLEDGE

MacARTHUR'S strategy had been completely worked out in Australia. During the year 1943 it was being tested in New Guinea and in the Solomon Islands—to be expanded through 1944 until he found himself at last back in the Philippines, his pledge made good.

It was a long, hard road from Australia to the Philippines. It meant first a fight to the finish for the army in New Guinea while the navy and the Marines were stopping the Japs in the Solomons. The decisive steps were Port Moresby, the Owen Stanley Mountains, Milne Bay, and the Buna-Gona area on land, and Guadalcanal from the sea.

Painfully aware of the limited resources in men and matériel at his disposal, MacArthur worked out a plan whereby he could use his planes in mass assaults to overcome his numerical superiority to the enemy. He determined to seize advanced air bases so that his relatively light force of bombers would be able to operate under cover of a limited number of fighter planes. With each such capture MacArthur's base line of attack was pushed farther from Australia and closer to the main Japanese bases. The new base lines furnished not only points from which to attack the enemy but also land-based plane protection for the few naval vessels which the United Nations could send to the Pacific combat area.

As an additional weapon General MacArthur relied upon the skilful use of surprise. It will be seen how he and the other American commanding officers seldom failed to catch the Japanese unaware in the long march up and across the Pacific. General MacArthur disliked frontal assault as too expensive in human life. He therefore developed to a high degree a deceptive cover to all his movements which permitted him to strike suddenly and unexpectedly, first upon one enemy flank and then upon another. As soon as he acquired sufficient forces to do so he engaged in combined maneuvers from several directions and against several points. The first of these expanded operations was soon to break over the Japanese. In the subsequent development of his strategy General MacArthur almost invariably by-passed enemy strong points. These, carefully prepared and powerfully manned by the Japanese, were left to be starved into death or submission through the economical process of neutralization, or to be strangled by cutting their supply lines by air and sea power.

The axis of Japanese power in the Southwest Pacific ran from Rabaul, New Britain, to Wewak, New Guinea. To approach the Philippines and Japan that Rabaul-Wewak axis and all its dependent bases must be smashed.

It was on just such an undertaking that the Allied commanders had been constantly hacking away since Guadalcanal, Buna, and Gona. Building up bases, consolidating positions, and accumulating power with which to carry on an offensive are slow, tedious propositions. On the other hand, their importance is as great as the crucial battle itself.

After Buna and Gona General MacArthur directed Lieutenant General Robert L. Eichelberger, who had so ably led the Americans and Australians to victory at those points, to push on toward Wau and Mubo. Oro Bay, twenty miles south of Buna, was converted into a powerful Allied base.

Wau was a little gold-mining town in the mountains some thirty-five miles southwest of Salamaua. It had a good airfield and thus became doubly desirable as an advanced Allied base. The town and field were quickly captured, and the enemy then began his retreat toward Mubo, twenty miles to the northeast.

Mubo, which is about ten miles inland from Nassau Bay on Huon Gulf, had first come into notice when an Allied Commando force raided Salamaua. The Japanese, infuriated and perplexed, bombed Mubo and several other native villages mercilessly, believing the Papuans to have been responsible. The enemy then moved into Mubo, to be harassed every few weeks by Allied patrols which would dash into the outpost, kill or wound most of the garrison, destroy virtually all supplies, and then retire.

Air attacks on Mubo were preliminary to a ground drive which, by the end of April, had won for the Allies all the positions atop Lababia Ridge overlooking Mubo and its airfield on one side and the Huon Gulf on the other.

The Japanese command was unable to decide definitely just what General MacArthur was up to or to devise a proper defense to meet it. They relied upon the routine expedients of pouring more men and supplies into Lae and Salamaua and lashing out with ground and air attacks wherever an opportunity seemed to present itself.

On June 15 sixty bombers and an equal number of fighters appeared over Guadalcanal. A tremendous Allied convoy was in the surrounding waters and Henderson Field was jammed with planes, oil, and other supplies. But neither the ships nor the planes were sitting ducks on a pond when the enemy came over. About a hundred American and eight New Zealand fighters were in the air as a reception committee. In the furious battles which ensued 107 of the 120 Japanese planes were shot down. The convoy, which had been the main target, was undamaged, and our losses were six fighter planes destroyed, and a cargo ship and an LST (landing ship tank) damaged.

On the night of June 20 Rear Admiral A. S. Merrill bombarded the Vila-Stanmore and Buin-Shortland areas near the southern end of Bougainville. The convoy which had escaped the Japanese plane attack steamed away from Guadalcanal. That same night, two companies of the 103rd Infantry, 43rd Division, and two companies of Marines slipped silently ashore at the mouth of the Viru River on southeast New Georgia, only thirty air miles east of the big enemy air base at Munda. The combined maneuvers were under way.

June 30, 1943, was a great day. Hell popped all over the vast area. Troops, secretly landed at Viru Harbor, attacked and wiped out the Japanese garrison. Thousands of picked infantrymen, Marines, and sailors from all over the United States, but mainly from New England, swarmed over the beaches of Rendova Island singing "Marching Through New Georgia." Then, in succession so rapid as to be almost simultaneous, landings were made on Vanganu and New Georgia; the Woodlark and Trobriand Islands were occupied; and a major amphibious landing was made at Nassau Bay, ten miles below Salamaua.

Blows fell upon the enemy so quickly, from so many directions, and over such a wide area—500 miles from Guadalcanal to Rabaul and 750 miles to Salamaua—that he was stunned and unable to react quickly. To add to Japanese discomfiture, Prime Minister Churchill chose the very moment of the great attack to pledge Great Britain's word that "after the defeat of Hitler every man, every ship, and every airplane that can be moved to the Pacific will be sent and maintained there in action... for as many years as are needed to make the Japanese, in their turn, submit or bite the dust." Britain, moreover, did not wait until Hitler's defeat to fulfil that pledge and send valuable help into the Pacific.

To avoid confusion let us follow the action from the Solomons to New Guinea in geographical rather than chronological sequence, always remembering that the entire area was ablaze. On the morning of that fateful June 30 the two commands into which the Pacific had been organized for purposes of dealing with the tremendous distances went into a series of operations. This was the beginning of coördinated activity between General MacArthur's Southwest Pacific Command and Admiral Halsey's South Pacific Command. Vice Admiral Arthur S. Carpender, commanding the Seventh United States Fleet, sent a sizable task force into the waters west of the Solomons to cover a convoy bearing troops of General Krueger's Sixth Army. The armada appeared with such surprising suddenness off the Woodlark and Trobriand Islands, not far from the southeastern tip of New Guinea, that the objectives were quickly captured.

Rear Admiral Daniel Berbey was in charge of the amphibious forces, Captain H. J. Carter headed the escort vessels, and Commander Homer F. McGee commanded the landing craft which took the troops to the beaches. Lieutenant Commander John Bulkeley had a squadron or two of his redoubtable PT-boats at Trobriand; and General Kenney's Allied airmen provided protection from the skies. The first landings were made on Kiriwina Island in the Trobriands and spread over the entire group which was brought quickly under complete control.

At the same time other combined United States forces stormed ashore on Rendova, to the west of New Georgia and just below Munda. There the Japanese were caught as flat-footed as in the Woodlark-Trobriand assault.

Having speedily cleaned up Rendova, including the enemy garrison, the picked infantry and Marine detachments took to small boats. Under cover of the "Long Toms," naval guns, and planes, they paddled across the water to New Georgia, and landed at Zanana, six miles east of Munda. Here they joined the scouts who had been landed secretly the week before and had worked their way close to the air base.

While all this was taking place in the Solomons another great American amphibious force moved boldly into Huon Gulf. Here other contingents of General Krueger's Sixth Army piled ashore at Nassau Bay, ten miles south of Salamaua. After a skirmish the beachhead was secured and Nassau Bay captured. The Americans immediately started driving inland.

Every move in the gigantic operation launched on June 30 had succeeded. All initial objectives had been seized. The night before the troops went ashore on Rendova the Commanding General sent his men a message which was read on all ships: "You have got what it takes. Your path will not be easy. But your guts will make you carry on. God speed and God bless you."

Far to the southeast the Marines who had landed at Segi on the night of June 20 began to move against Viru Harbor in an attack from the rear. For seven days they had trekked through the jungle from their landing point, constantly harassed by snipers and wiping out occasional machine-gun nests. They had traveled four and one-half hours in rubber boats to the head of the trail leading to Viru. On June 27 they were attacked from the rear by nearly forty Japanese. After eighteen of the enemy had been killed, the Marines stormed a hill to wipe out with grenades an enemy strong point. The two companies were living on their "D" ration of solid chocolate, were without water, and carried their wounded with them.

Courageous exploits of that advanced Marine contingent made it possible for the main landing body to get ashore and capture the highly important Viru Harbor, with total casualties, including wounded and missing, of thirty-three, and virtually no loss of equipment. The port had been one of the enemy's main barge bases for ferrying men and supplies from one Solomon Islands point to another.

The swift-moving action now leaps from Viru, thirty miles below Munda, to the Kula Gulf on the north, across a ten-mile neck of land which thrusts New Georgia Island into the west.

During the night of July 4-5 a task group of United States cruisers and destroyers bombarded enemy positions and gun installations on either side of Kula Gulf to support landings at Rice Anchorage. The destroyer *Strong* was hit by shore batteries and torpedoes and soon went to the bottom.

If their reinforcements were not to give the Japanese overwhelming numerical superiority on New Georgia, the first thing to do was to stop the "Tokyo Express" from reaching Vila. Rear Admiral W. L. Ainsworth was in command of a task force of cruisers and destroyers under orders to "flag the train." Early on the morning of July 6 contact was made with two enemy groups. The first group was landing troops for Munda when the firing was opened. The effect upon the enemy was disastrous. After all the ships had been sunk or left afire, the Americans went after the second group.

The cruiser *Helena,* commanded by Captain Charles P. Cecil, a veteran of many Pacific battles, was in the forefront of the attacks. The ship's main battery fired upon a large enemy vessel and sank it while the secondary battery sent a covering destroyer to the bottom. A second Japanese destroyer, followed by several more, came close to the *Helena* during these exchanges. A concentrated torpedo attack was launched. The *Helena* was mortally wounded and sank in twenty minutes. Some of the 1,000 men in the crew were picked up on the spot, but the majority made their way by one means or another to Vella Lavella, from which they were subsequently rescued. Loss of life was small.

A few days later the enemy attempted another sortie from Vila to New Georgia, but his ships were turned back by alert Allied planes. Then, on July 12, off the mouth of Vella Gulf, Admiral Ainsworth intercepted another run of the "Tokyo Express." Again it was running in two sections. In the engagement fought in the early hours of the 13th the first section was badly shot up, with one enemy cruiser sunk. The second section, however, inflicted heavy damage upon our ships. When the battle was over the Japanese had lost five destroyers besides the cruiser. On our side, the cruisers *St. Louis* and *Honolulu* were badly damaged by torpedoes; the destroyer *Gwin* was set afire, and had to be sunk; the New Zealand cruiser *Leander* was also hit by a torpedo.

Without the heroic support of the navy it is doubtful if the ambitious attempt against the Solomons could have succeeded. General MacArthur's confidence in the devoted naval coöperation here established was fully justified. It formed the foundation upon which all subsequent moves were built.

The fighting on New Georgia was typical of all the actions in the Southwest Pacific and a description of what went on there will serve as a pattern for the action in other places. During the night of the Kula Gulf battle in which the *Helena* was sunk a combat team of the 169th Infantry came ashore near Zanana. After three days of nerve-racking stalking through the jungle with its hordes of mosquitoes, fever-ridden swamps, heavy rains, and terrain more difficult than that of Guadalcanal, the 43rd Division began its slow infiltration move toward Bibolo Hill. By nightfall the troops had gained 1,000 yards. It took two days of Indian fighting to gain the next 1,000 yards, with the 172nd Infantry pushing through the coconut groves along the beach. By July 13, Laiana Plantation had been taken in a total advance of 2,300 yards from the landing point. The 169th was badly cut up in repulsing a night counterattack.

Meanwhile the forces landed at Rice Anchorage in a bold end run under the very guns of Japanese coastal installations were having heavy going. Slogging through swamps and over mountain spurs, they pushed the Japanese back to Enogai. By the end of two weeks Munda had been encircled, and an American airfield had been built and placed in operation in the Viru Harbor area.

This was the slow process of strangulation imposed upon the Japanese by the Americans pushing up from Zanana and Laiana. By July 26 the 161st had by-passed the northern center of enemy resistance. Two days later the 148th Infantry, also from Ohio, infiltrated the slopes of Bibolo Hill, a three-knobbed affair about 250 feet high with each ridge about 200 yards long. Bibolo Hill was the main protection for the Munda airstrip, which had been cut out of a palm grove with trees surrounding it on every side.

The Japanese had prepared for a frontal assault against Bibolo Hill, but the American commanders had other plans. On August 4 American troops reached the water's edge at Kindu, 600 yards north of the airfield and 1,200 yards west of Bibolo, thus severing communications with reinforcements trickling in from Bairoko. The next day Bibolo Hill was overrun, the airfield was seized, and all resistance was overcome. Some of the Japanese escaped in barges to Arundel; others fled to the jungles where they were hunted down. Two days later Allied planes were using the quickly repaired Munda airfield. By August 28 all of New Georgia was wrested from the enemy.

The Japanese had had 5,000 troops at Munda. Before General MacArthur's amphibious forces were able to win their first major triumph they had been compelled to engage in the most savage fighting recorded between two modern armed forces. New Georgia, which fell about a year after the Guadalcanal landings, was the keystone of the entire Japanese defenses in the Solomons. Its capture radically altered the strategic picture.

Now let us see how events were proceeding with MacArthur on New Guinea. Beachheads had been established quickly and consolidated. The type of action fought resembled that on New Georgia, except that the terrain was different in that the mountains came close to the shore line and were cut up by rivers, gullies, and foothills.

The results of the first two weeks of fighting were succinctly summarized in General MacArthur's communiqué of July 15, which said: "The Mubo bastion has been captured. United States forces, after landing and consolidating the beachhead at Nassau Bay, June 30, moved inland up the valley of the Bitoi River, effecting a junction with Australian units at Buigop Creek at dusk, July 10. This move, effected in complete secrecy, operated to cut the enemy's line of communication between Mubo and Salamaua and isolate his garrisons on Observation and Green Hills. Following this enveloping move, in coördination with attacks by elements from the rear areas, Australian forces attacked from Lababia Ridge and Garrison Hill and destroyed the enemy defenses at Observation Hill, the Pimple, and Green Hill. Our ground forces have now cleared the Mubo area of all organized resistance and are pressing on Komiatum. Approximately 950 enemy troops were destroyed. Our losses were light."

The Japanese in New Guinea had been building up their positions for nearly a year. Despite the blockade of Allied naval craft, including PT-boats, the enemy succeeded in running numbers of small boats down the coast from Madang and Wewak and pushing other reinforcements and supplies through the Markham Valley by tedious overland transport. From our standpoint we were farther from our bases than we ever had been. The air ferry system which had supplied the small forces operating during the previous months could not possibly handle the amount of material required by the large army now landed. Virtually everything had to come in from points in Australia or New Zealand after having reached those distant ports from the United States.

During the first weeks the air forces bore the brunt of the attack upon the enemy. Maintaining an incessant pounding of positions, they whittled down the Japanese defenses and neutralized their advantages of position and numerical superiority.

Artillery and more men had been landed and it became possible to push the frontal attack with greater vigor. By the third week of August the Allies had won control of all the high ground in the Bobdubi area.

The Japanese counterattacked time and time again. Sometimes they won the temporary advantage of a little delay. These delays, however, worked to the advantage of the Allies, for General MacArthur's plan anticipated every possible contingency. On the night of August 15-16, without waiting for the actual conclusion of the Salamaua fighting, Allied bombers hopped 340 miles up the New Guinea coast to Wewak, the enemy's most important air base in the southwest Pacific. They found 225 Japanese planes neatly lined up wing-to-wing on the cluster of airfields. Swooping down suddenly, General Kenney's fliers dropped 10,000 explosive and incendiary bombs in twenty minutes. When the bombing was over, 120 enemy planes had been destroyed and fifty more had been damaged; 1,500 Japanese fliers and ground crew men had been killed; dumps had been blown up; and hangars and other installations had been demolished.

"It was a crippling blow at an opportune moment," General MacArthur stated. "Numerically, the opposing forces were about equal in strength, but one was in the air and the other not. Nothing is so helpless as a plane on the ground. In war, surprise is decisive."

The entire Japanese air cover had been wiped out in one bold, masterly stroke. The enemy's ground forces were thus temporarily unprotected. The next day General Kenney's men paid a return visit to the four airfields at Wewak, Borum, But, and Dagua, destroying all but ten of the original 225 planes. The Japanese rushed reinforcements from Rabaul, from Truk, and from bases in the Netherlands Indies. Two days later the Allies went back and shot down twenty-eight of the thirty-five Zeros which rose to intercept them. The following day they went back again to get thirty-three more. By the end of the week more than 300 Japanese planes had been destroyed. The Japanese abandoned Wewak as a base and shifted 200 miles farther up the New Guinea coast to Hollandia, 550 miles from Salamaua.

Destruction of the Japanese planes not only served to protect our ground forces from air attack, but also made it possible for our naval forces to enter the narrow waters between New Guinea and New Britain without fear of sustained attack from above. During the series of raids on Wewak the navy sailed in close and shelled Finschhafen at the outer tip of the Huon Peninsula. This was the chief enemy point for reinforcements for Lae and Salamaua.

While the Japanese were staggering under this rapid succession of blows, a task force of cruisers, destroyers, and smaller craft appeared on September 3 off Nopoi, east of Lae. Here it landed the Australian 9th Division and other troops to cover the enemy's rear. American parachute troops came down on inland fields of tall reeds to set the stage for the complete encirclement of the 20,000 Japanese troops on the Huon Peninsula. Quickly overpowering the few enemy outposts, the paratroopers began swinging their powerful jungle knives like scythes, clearing an area large enough for an airfield upon which Allied planes soon landed with artillery, light tanks, and reinforcements.

The amazing courage and heroism against heavy odds on the part of American boys in all branches of the service never flagged. Seaman First Class Johnnie David Hutchins, U.S.N.R., a Texas sharecropper's son, was posthumously awarded the Congressional Medal of Honor for his heroism. He was stationed on a landing-ship tank when the craft came under a hail of shore fire and attack by dive and torpedo bombers. A torpedo was bearing down upon the ship. In the words of the citation: "In the tense split-second before the helmsman could steer clear of the threatening missile, a bomb struck the pilot house, dislodged him from his station, and left the stricken ship helplessly exposed. Fully aware of the dire peril of the situation, Hutchins, although mortally wounded by the shattering explosion, quickly grasped the wheel and exhausted the last of his strength in maneuvering the vessel clear of the advancing torpedo. Still clinging to the wheel, he eventually succumbed to his injuries, his final thoughts concerned only with the safety of his ship, his final efforts expended toward the security of his mission." In such deeds is the history of the Pacific War written.

The amphibious and parachute landings doomed Japanese resistance around Salamaua. The airfield was invested and captured. In three days of bitter fighting from pillbox to pillbox and yard by yard, this first New Guinea objective was captured on September 11, ten weeks after the landings. Allied fliers then concentrated upon Lae.

The Americans, chasing the fleeing remnants of the beaten Salamaua garrison, were in a race with the Australians driving from the opposite direction upon Lae. A siege was quickly clamped about the fortified town. On September 16, five days after the fall of Salamaua, Lae was captured. The Japanese who escaped fled along three trails into traps previously set by the Americans and Australians.

Finschhafen was now the next objective of the Allied amphibious force. On the morning of September 22 destroyers shepherded landing craft to a beach six miles north of the town and after a brief bombardment left a strong Australian force there. Enemy air attacks were ineffectual and Finschhafen was captured on October 2.

Thus in three months the most ambitious offensive yet undertaken in the Pacific attained its objective. The road up New Guinea was open, the way across to Cape Gloucester, Gasmata, and Rabaul on New Britain was clear. The northern Solomons, consisting mainly of Choiseul and Bougainville, were all that remained of the former Japanese control of the Coral Sea.

FINAL STAGE IN GREAT SWING FROM PIVOT AT NEW GUINEA

TOKYO was so upset by events in the Pacific in 1944 that the Japanese Cabinet was drastically shaken up. The war lords were reading the handwriting on the wall. Field Marshal Sugiyama and Admiral Nagano, in command of the empire's land and sea operations, were "dethroned."

Task Force 58 was definitely on the loose. The taste of blood drawn at Truk whetted the appetite of Admiral Spruance. The whole Pacific was his range, and he meant to go wherever he wished and whenever he wanted to. The Japanese did not have long to wait.

The American armada was on its way to new hunting grounds for its deepest penetration into Japanese-controlled waters—the Marianas. Saipan was the main Japanese base and anchorage in the Marianas. Tinian, just below it, served as a naval base, and held an airfield as large as that at Hickham Field at Pearl Harbor. This island was eleven miles long, not quite so wide, and was characterized by steep shores that rose to a plateau 550 feet above sea level.

During the afternoon of February 21, 1944, a Japanese observation plane spotted the fleet. Admiral Mitscher immediately signaled: "We have been sighted by the enemy. Get ready to fight your way in." About eleven o'clock that night the Japanese attacked. For three and one-half hours they tried relentlessly to bore through our antiaircraft fire that, in the words of one American officer, was "so thick that no darkness could be seen through it." When the enemy finally gave up, without having hit a ship, fourteen of his planes had succumbed to the antiaircraft and five more had been shot down by air patrols. Six of our planes were lost.

The Japanese had eighteen hours' notice of Mitscher's plans and knew the exact location of the carriers, but did not dare to meet the Americans. Saipan and Tinian were hit hard in the morning; in the afternoon the Saipan airfield was shattered and an unscheduled visit was paid to Guam, where a brand new airfield was discovered. More than 125 Japanese planes were destroyed.

On February 29 General MacArthur switched his direction suddenly to the north and landed troops on Los Negros Island in the Admiralties. The original intention was to conduct a reconnaissance in force, determine the strength and disposition of the enemy forces, create as much havoc as possible, and then retire with a minimum of losses.

With this in mind, elements of the First Cavalry, dismounted, under command of Major General Palmer Swift, went ashore on Los Negros with other Sixth Army units, all commanded by Brigadier General William M. Chase. The men were landed directly from destroyers instead of the customary landing craft, to insure the speed essential to a raid and to give the troops the benefit of naval gunfire. Vice Admiral Thomas C. Kinkaid was in command of naval forces; Admiral Berbey headed the amphibious operations, with Rear Admirals Russell S. Berkey and William M. Fechteler; and Major General Ennis C. Whitehead commanded the forward echelons of General Kenney's fliers.

Cavalry troops rode boats ashore instead of horses and then drove tanks on land. This oldest full cavalry division in the United States Army, which included the Seventh Cavalry Regiment that fought with Custer at Little Big Horn—and the Eighth, oldest of all, founded in 1840—speared quickly to Momote airfield and captured it in record time. The ease with which this objective had been gained caused General MacArthur to change his plans quickly and convert what had been intended as a raid into a full-scale invasion.

It was not until three days after the landings that the Japanese decided to react. Then it was too late. Heavy American reinforcements had been put ashore. Imperial Japanese Marines, the same sort of fighters who had defended Tarawa, had been ferried across from Manus and launched a series of vicious attacks on the airfield after dusk on March 3. The battle raged through the night. After daylight General Kenney's planes added the weight of their guns and bombs. Less than a week later Los Negros was cleared of the enemy, the airfield enlarged and put in full operation, and the navy was using the harbor.

The Admiralties campaign lasted eighteen days. All but a few hundred of the 5,000 Japanese on the islands were killed. General MacArthur had pushed his string of air bases deep into the enemy lines. The salient that once had pointed dangerously toward Australia had been inverted and directed toward Truk, the Philippines, and Japan.

The final step in the isolation of Rabaul and Kavieng was taken on March 20 when Marines, including Carlson's Raiders, slammed shut the back door by seizing Emirau Island in the St. Matthias group. While the Marines, under Brigadier General Alfred H. Noble, U.S.M.C., were making a swift conquest of Emirau, 600 miles below Truk, Allied naval units were smashing Kavieng, 75 miles to the southeast to keep the Japanese occupied.

Simultaneously with these operations, progress was being made in the New Britain campaign. On March 6, Marines from Cape Gloucester, in a shore-to-shore hop, landed on Willaumez Peninsula, which juts out like a thumb from New Britain's north coast 110 miles to the east. Landing in Higgins boats during the midmorning five miles northwest of Talasea, they again caught the Japanese off guard. After fierce fighting along the beachhead during the third day, the Talasea airfield was captured, then the town, and the Peninsula was cut in half. It was only a matter of time before the isolated Japanese were killed and the Bismarck Sea was turned into an Allied lake.

Between the Admiralties and the Emirau landings, General MacArthur returned to Australia, where he was guest of honor at a dinner by the Australian Government in Canberra to commemorate the second anniversary of the General's escape from the Philippines. Speaking there, on March 17, 1944, he said: "Two years ago when I landed on your soil I said to the people of the Philippines, whence I came: 'I shall return.' Tonight I repeat those words: 'I shall return.' Nothing is more certain than our ultimate reconquest and liberation from the enemy of those and adjacent islands. One of the great offensives of the war will, at the appropriate time, be launched for that purpose."

The blows reached a climax on March 29. With the two army air forces striking at outlying targets. Admiral Mitscher sailed Task Force 58 into the Palaus for a three-day assault on Yap, Ulithi, Babelthuap, and Woleai. The Palaus, 1,176 miles beyond Truk, are only 500 miles from Davao in the Philippines and New Guinea and had become a refuge for enemy warships after the February attack on Truk.

When Task Force 58 sailed away, every Jap ship at anchorage had been sunk or damaged. The score stood 28 ships sunk by planes and three by naval guns; 18 ships beached or damaged, 214 planes destroyed or damaged; most of the docks, radio, and other installations wiped out. We lost 25 planes and 18 men, but not a single American warship was touched. The Palaus had been put completely out of commission at the very moment they were most dangerous to Allied plans.

The moment arrived on April 22, when Task Force 58 joined hands with General MacArthur in the greatest joint operation yet attempted in the Pacific—the invasion of Netherlands New Guinea at Hollandia. This was so vital in the strategy of the war against Japan that Admiral Nimitz came out from Pearl Harbor to witness the gigantic amphibious operation. Task Force 58 came down from the northeast, while General MacArthur's transports came up from the southeast guarded by American and British warships, including baby flattops. Three separate landings were effected: one at Tanahmera, one at Humboldt Bay, and a third at Aitape. Behind Tanahmera and Humboldt Bay was a short mountain coast line effectively protecting the three airfields at Hollandia, Cyclops, and Sentani.

The gigantic invasion was launched on April 22. Three big forces of cruisers and destroyers raked the landing beaches for an hour, after having feinted for several days at the Palaus to throw the enemy off guard. Dive bombers and fighters took over until rocket boats and landing craft carried the first waves of infantry ashore at Tanahmera Bay and Humboldt Bay on either side of Hollandia, and at Aitape.

Hollandia airfield fell quickly to the troops from Tanahmera Bay, but the Japanese fought like madmen at Sentani. To overcome this opposition and to by-pass the enemy strong points dug into the Cyclops Mountains, the Humboldt Bay force detoured to the mouth of a small river entering the lake. Modern, mechanized creatures of war such as the "Buffaloes," "Ducks," and "Alligators" never seemed more out of place than they did in the waters of the river inhabited by live alligators.

Inland amphibious operations crossed the lake six miles to Nefaar, two miles southeast of Cyclops airfield, overawing the Japanese by their daring and weird appearance. Amphibious tanks fired rockets as they slid in and out of the water, accounting for some measure of the terror that filled the Japanese soldiers. Five days after they had landed, the Americans overran Cyclops and Sentani. Shortly after that all three airfields were housing Allied planes. Patrols pursued the remnants of the fleeing enemy into the hills. The total enemy casualties were 871 killed, 183 prisoners. The American losses were 28 killed and 95 wounded in one of the most important amphibious operations in this phase of the war.

While American casualties were low, there was a great deal of fighting and many feats of heroism. Pvt. Artie Bracknell, of Fort Payne, Alabama, leading a scout platoon, walked into a Japanese machine-gun nest. The Americans, although heavily outnumbered, fought gamely. Private Bracknell, to save his comrades on the opposite bank of a narrow stream, turned and waved to them to stay back. This act of sacrifice to save his mates cost Bracknell his life. Lieutenant John L. Cross, Jr., of New York, was ducking in a foxhole when a Japanese bomb landed directly in a munitions pile. Shells and bullets filled the air, heavy bulldozers were scattered like matches, the beach was a flaming mass of oil and gasoline. Lieutenant Cross jumped from his safe spot to carry a wounded soldier from the scene. Explosions blew him off his feet eight times, but he made the rescue and reached a rear position, where he found no doctor. There he dressed the soldier's wounds himself. Shortly afterwards, although he was a detached cavalry officer assigned to General MacArthur's public relations staff, he gathered 200 men and deployed them to protect the flaming beach from possible invasion.

Aitape village was captured on April 24 in so sudden a dash that only one Japanese was left to be killed, but seventy-five breakfasts were cooking on the mess stove. By May 12, 1,716 Japanese had been killed and 354 captured. American casualties were slight. Australian troops, advancing up the coast, gained 80 miles in 28 days, capturing Hansa Bay, just below Wewak, on June 15. The landings resulted in the liberation of 86 Allied prisoners at Aitape and 621 at Hollandia.

The Hollandia-Aitape invasion proved to be of such significance that the news was broken to the United States not through the usual filing of a communiqué but by a simultaneous broadcast from General MacArthur's Advanced Headquarters over all American networks at 7:30 P.M., April 23, Eastern War Time. As the war progressed, it became evident that Hollandia, with its merging of Task Force 58 and General MacArthur's forces, was a full-scale rehearsal for the Philippines.

After cleaning up, Task Force 58 turned around and headed north for an undertaking of its own—a return engagement at Truk. The ships were constantly followed by enemy "snoopers," most of which were shot down. Eight rescued Japanese visited their hapless base from the deck of the *Yorktown*. That carrier was to concentrate on the seaplane base on Dublon and the important airstrip on Eten. Other carriers were assigned targets on Dublon, Paran, and Moen.

When Admiral Mitscher took his ships away, Truk had been finally eliminated as an important factor in the war. The only job left was to see that it remained paralyzed and neutralized. Notable as was the destruction wrought during this second visit to Truk, the event that stirred the country most was a heroic feat of rescue. The submarine *Tang,* commanded by Lieutenant Commander Richard H. O'Kane, had been stationed off Truk by prearrangement to handle any enemy naval craft that might put in a sudden appearance. The main traffic that Commander O'Kane had with the Japanese was with their shore batteries while he ran a shuttle service rescuing American fliers who had been shot down.

Carrier planes led the *Tang* from one pilot on a raft or in a "Mae West" jacket to another. Lieutenant John A. Burns, of Wynnewood, Pennsylvania, flying a single-seater, picked up some men and overweighted his ship so that he couldn't take off. The *Tang* came along in time to take the men on board. Then Lieutenant Burns picked up more fliers and taxied them to the *Tang*. During the last rescue he had three survivors on each wing and one in the cockpit, virtually in his lap. His plane was so battered by the sea that Commander O'Kane insisted they all come aboard. When Lieutenant Burns had been sent below, the airplane was sunk with gunfire.

The *Tang* kept up its rescue work during the two days of the attack, plowing fearlessly through narrow, shallow waters that were mined and braving fire from coastal defenses. When it finally turned back toward Pearl Harbor, there were twenty-two rescued airmen, most of them injured, trying to find a spot in the cramped quarters of the submarine. Commander O'Kane deposited his precious cargo safely in Pearl Harbor.

On May 17 General MacArthur took his next long stride. United States troops from Australian and American transports landed at Tum and Arara, just below Sarmi. The soldiers reëmbarked in landing craft, after having established a seven-and-one-half-mile beachhead, for the two-mile trip to Wadke, where they quickly seized Insumanai Island, the smaller of the two in the group.

The landing field was won on May 19. The Japanese were compressed into an area only half a mile square, from which they fired upon engineers repairing the runways and hangars. By the end of the third day the enemy garrison of 700 had been wiped out at a cost of 16 Americans killed, 83 wounded, and 2 missing. Insumuar, the air strip, gave the United Nations an air base 350 miles from Manokwari at the western end of New Guinea, and 1,000 miles from the Philippines.

Ten days after the Sarmi-Wadke landings, General MacArthur hopped two hundred miles farther along the New Guinea coast. Infantry and tanks were put on Biak Island in the Schoutens.

In summarizing the Biak landings, General MacArthur said: "For strategic purposes, this means the practical end of the New Guinea campaign. The final stage has also been reached in the offense initiated in this theater on June 29, 1943, by combined forces of the Southwest Pacific and South Pacific areas. It has resulted in reconquest or neutralization of the Solomons, Bismarcks, Admiralties, and New Guinea. From the forward point reached by the Japanese, we have advanced our front approximately 1,800 statute miles westward and approximately 700 miles to the north. Compared with the enemy, our offensive employed only moderate forces and through maximum use of maneuver and surprise has incurred only light losses. These operations have effected strategic penetration of the conquered empire Japan was attempting to consolidate in the Southwest Pacific and have secured bases of departure for the advance to its vital areas in the Philippines and Netherlands East Indies."

The Supreme Commander in Paris

General Eisenhower; Lieut. General Omar N. Bradley; Gen. Joseph Koenig, military commander in Paris; and British Air Marshal Sir Arthur William Tedder, pose at the Arc de Triomphe.

INTERNATIONAL NEWS PHOTO

SIGNAL CORPS PHOTO

Equipment for Philippine Invasion

LST and other ships of the convoy head for the invasion of the Philippine Islands.

OFFICIAL U. S. NAVY PHOTOGRAPH

Ashore at Leyte
U. S. Army troops go ashore from landing craft during operations to liberate the island.

OFFICIAL U. S. NAVY PHOTOGRAPH

A-Day, October 20, 1944
Army troops move to the front on Leyte in the Philippines.

SIGNAL CORPS PHOTO

The Flag Goes Up!
Bos'n Mate 1st Class John E. Brandau hauls up the American flag on Leyte.

70

SMASHING JAP DEFENSES—BATTLES OF SAIPAN AND PHILIPPINE SEA

HARD drives by the Americans were cracking Japanese defenses throughout the Pacific area in the summer of 1944. While on land the Allies were whittling down Japan's hold on Burma, the United States Navy was spreading destruction far and wide over the ocean in anticipation of new strategic moves. Submarines littered the waters of the Pacific with the wrecks of a large part of Japan's prewar merchant fleet, and served as eyes for American naval craft in paving the way for invasions.

Tokyo suffered from a perpetual case of jitters, with Premier Koiso and War Minister Sugiyama warning their people that an invasion of the home islands might come at any time. Every resource—men, women, children, land, wealth, industry—was placed under the control of the armed forces. Japan was literally mobilized into the army. It was announced that Admiral Mineichi Koga, commander of the combined Japanese fleet, had died at his post while directing operations from an airplane. The evidence, however, indicated that he had committed suicide as a result of American victories.

An Allied battle fleet under Admiral Sir James Somerville, commander of Britain's Eastern Fleet, sailed out of the Bay of Bengal on April 19 and closed in on Sumatra. British tonnage dominated the armada, but eighty per cent of the aircraft on the carriers were American. The planes smashed installations at Sabang, on the island of We, and hit airfields on Sumatra itself.

In April, also, the United States Navy changed its organization to meet the new strategic and tactical demands. An Alaskan Sea Frontier was established, including the old Northwest and Alaska areas, and placed under Vice Admiral Fletcher, of Coral Sea fame. Vice Admiral D. W. Bagley took over the new Western Sea Frontier comprising the west coast area.

On the day that Task Force 58 was returning from Hollandia to give Truk its second disastrous blow, the navy lost its civilian chief. The Honorable Frank Knox, who had been Secretary of the Navy since July 11, 1940, died of a heart attack in his Washington home on April 28. He had supervised the growth of the United States Navy from 435 combatant ships of all kinds to nearly 1,000. Under Secretary of the Navy James V. Forrestal succeeded his former chief.

During the month of May, Admirals King, Nimitz, and Halsey

conferred on the next moves from the American line. This line ran in an arc from Attu, 2,300 miles from Tokyo, through Midway, 2,545 miles away, Eniwetok, 2,050 miles, and Hollandia, 2,100 miles. The following week a combined British-American-French carrier force, drawing upon the ships under Admiral Mountbatten, General MacArthur, and Admiral Nimitz, struck with devastating effect at Surabaya, principal Japanese oil refinery center in the Netherlands Indies. It was the first joint operation by the three commands.

Early in June Admiral Spruance assembled his Fifth Fleet, the greatest invasion armada the world had yet seen, for an amphibious operation against the Marianas.

Task Force 58's carriers were assigned to wipe out the enemy's air opposition on the 600-mile chain of islands. Admiral Mitscher's carriers were discovered approaching the Marianas. He put on speed and struck a day earlier, opening an unprecedented four-day pre-invasion battering. Planes launched from far off hit Saipan, Tinian, and Guam. Despite their advance notice the Japanese were again caught by surprise.

Captain William I. Martin, who had devised the night bombing attack on Truk, was forced to parachute on to the reefs near Saipan's Charan Kanoa airfield. While waiting to be rescued he charted the waters and marked the reefs with bits of cloth on sticks, thus making it possible later for invasion craft to avoid disaster.

By the time the planes and warships which had sailed in toward Saipan had finished their preparatory job, every enemy coastal gun had been knocked out; there were no planes to offer opposition and most of the Japanese shipping was at the bottom. On June 14 the 2nd and 4th Marine Divisions, followed by the 27th Infantry Division, went ashore on a two-mile beachhead south of Charan Kanoa at the southwest end of the island.

In the face of heavy mortar fire, Aginigan Point was quickly captured. Then Charan Kanoa was taken in street-by-street fighting, and the adjoining airfield fell into American hands. As the invaders pushed inland, resistance became harder, but after three days the beachhead had been expanded to five and one-half miles in length and two miles in width. The Americans were close to Aslito Airfield and had pushed halfway to Magicienne Bay on the east coast.

For four days the enemy offered only local resistance on Saipan. Then he countered with swarms of planes. The attack forced Admiral Spruance to delay the planned invasion of Guam, but it paid dividends in an unexpected direction. It resulted in the Battle of the Philippine Sea that ended in a tremendous American victory.

Admiral Spruance learned that a large part of the Japanese fleet had been sighted on June 14 steaming north from Tawi Tawi in the Sulu Sea. Despite this, Admiral Mitscher sent two task groups under

Admirals J. J. Clark and W. K. Harrill to hit Iwo, Chichi, Haha, and other islands in the Volcano and Bonin groups 700 miles to the north.

The weather was atrocious and the planes had difficulty in leaving the decks on that first day, June 16. They returned to the attack the following day, pulverizing ground installations and destroying ninety planes, and then headed back for Saipan. On the way Admiral Mitscher learned that a second Japanese force, with battleships and carriers, had been sighted 400 miles east of the Philippines. This second enemy fleet made the picture clear. The Japanese planned to catch Task Force 58 in a vise, sink it and, at the same time, wipe out the Saipan invasion.

But Admirals Spruance and Mitscher decided to hold the fleet near Guam and keep the Marianas airfields neutralized while the small task groups built around the *Yorktown,* the *Essex,* and the *Hornet* sortied to the Bonins and the Volcanoes. Admiral Shigetaro Shimada planned to launch his carrier planes from maximum distance to strike the Americans, and then return to Saipan, Guam, and Rota to refuel and rearm. His grand scheme was to maintain a continuous pounding "until not a United States ship remained afloat."

The flaw in this pretentious reasoning was that there was no serviceable airfield left in the Marianas. Japanese naval planes had no place to land. The Americans were ready for the attack. Land-based planes had been flown out to join the carrier craft. When the air was filled with Zeros and other Japanese planes the slaughter began. The attack started on the morning of June 18 and lasted well into the afternoon. Few of the enemy got through to the American vessels, but one torpedo hit the old battleship *Maryland* which had been damaged at Pearl Harbor and repaired. Two torpedoes straddled Admiral Mitscher's flagship. Japanese planes fell like flaming torches, fifteen burning simultaneously in the sky. Americans were waiting over Guam to slaughter the enemy planes when they returned to Orote airfield out of fuel and ammunition. Admiral Shimada lost more than 400 planes and an equal number of his best Japanese Navy pilots.

The next day Task Force 58 rushed west, bucking gales in an effort to catch the enemy ships. With only two hours of daylight left, Admiral Mitscher turned his carriers around into the wind to launch hundreds of planes at extreme range to chase the foe. At 6:30 the oilers and small craft bringing up the rear of the Japanese train were sighted. Despite low fuel and the knowledge that they stood little chance of making their mother ships, the Americans flew straight on until they sighted six carriers—all with empty decks—four battleships, and six cruisers halfway between the Marianas and the Philippines.

For fifteen minutes the attack was pressed. Twenty-six of the thirty enemy planes in the air were shot down. One large carrier was sunk and another damaged; a cruiser exploded; a battleship, two cruisers, a destroyer, and two light carriers were damaged, and a third was sunk by a submarine. There was no chance to pursue the attack and the Americans turned home. Seventy-five per cent reached a carrier in safety despite the dense blackout and bad weather. More than two thirds of the men forced to land in the water were saved.

The Battle of the Philippine Sea was over. Besides the ships, the Japanese lost 450 or more planes, failed to damage Task Force 58, and did not slow the Saipan operations for one moment. On the contrary, the Americans went on to hit the Bonins and the Marianas again, bringing their two-week total to 757 planes destroyed, thirty ships sunk. The Japanese never made another attempt to reinforce the Marianas.

While the greatest ship-plane battle since Midway was being fought in sky and on sea, the Americans on Saipan went steadily about their grim business. Aslito Airfield was captured and Magicienne Bay was reached, which cut the island in two. The importance of Aslito was to become evident to Tokyo, 1,465 miles to the north, and to Davao in the Philippines, 1,470 miles to the west. In four days American planes began to use the field.

Reinforcements were steadily poured ashore. Attack was begun on Mount Tapotchau, which rises 1,554 feet in the center of the island. The Japanese fought to the death from the caves that honeycomb its slopes, but by the end of June the Americans had scaled its cliffs, and and an eyewitness with the troops wrote: "From the top of Mount Tapotchau the battle area looks like a cradle filled with jagged, broken crockery. Ridges, blind ravines, and sheer cliffs are jumbled crazily. Advances are made over goat paths and down precipitous slopes, through tangled mountain vines hiding sub-machine guns."

Garapan, capital of Saipan, was entered during the last days of June. The process of wearing down the Japanese and breaking their resistance-centers got under way. This second phase of the campaign carried the advance across hills covered with limestone dust. Over sixty per cent of the island had been conquered by July 1, but the casualties had been great—three times those at Tarawa in the first two weeks alone. The Japanese lost heavily, too, in their desperate defense from the caves.

The crisis had been passed on July 4 as the Americans pressed the remaining defenders downhill into a death trap at Marpi Point on the north end of the island. A few days later artillery broke up an attempt by the enemy to escape in barges.

The Battle of Saipan was over on July 10. The island had fallen in twenty-five days. Over 25,000 Japanese had been killed. Those who were left kept up their sniping assaults for more than a year, but the main link in the Japanese defenses had been broken. The Americans lost 2,359 killed in action, 11,481 wounded, and 1,213 missing.

Saipan was an orgy of death. Private George Ruckman, of Grant-town, West Virginia, shot blindly into the undergrowth and in fifty yards killed eighteen Japanese. Sergeant Thomas Baker and Lieutenant Colonel William J. O'Brien, of the 105th Regiment, 27th Division, were posthumously awarded the Congressional Medal of Honor for heroism in the same action. On July 7, while wounded, Sergeant Baker fired at ranges as close as five yards until his ammunition ran out. When comrades tried to carry him to safety he ordered them to let him make his last stand, for he knew they would all be mowed down. Colonel O'Brien, when last seen alive, was firing side-arms with both hands at Japanese who had surrounded him.

Lieutenant General Holland F. Smith was promoted from Commander of the Fifth Amphibious Group to Commanding General of Fleet Marine Forces of the Pacific. This was in recognition of his valiant work in the Saipan campaign, the greatest amphibious victory of the Pacific War to that time.

Saipan was of such importance that Tokyo had sent Vice Admiral Chuichi Nagumo, Commander in Chief for the Central Pacific, to lead the defense. He had commanded the forces that delivered the sneak attack on Pearl Harbor and was in charge of carriers at the Battle of Midway. On Saipan Admiral Nagumo was killed.

The decisive defeat shook Tokyo. Premier Tojo was relieved of his post as active head of the Japanese Army which he held by virtue of his position as Chief of Staff. He was succeeded by General Yoshijiro Umezu, Commander in Chief of the Kwantung Army in Manchuria and Japanese Ambassador to that puppet state. On July 19 Tojo, with his entire cabinet, resigned, and General Kuniaki Koiso succeeded him as premier.

Secretary of the Navy Forrestal gave advance warning of what was to come when he said: "The final occupation of Saipan will enable us to project surface and air operations that will include the mainland of Japan, the Philippines, and a greater part of the Dutch East Indies."

BOMBING 5,000,000 SQUARE MILES IN PACIFIC—GUAM REDEEMED

THE bombing of the island fortresses of the Pacific began to rise toward its crescendo in the last months of 1944. The greatest air show on earth was in progress. Attacks were being made over the 5,000,000 square mile area from the Kuriles to Celebes.

Guam was redeemed. The Marianas were invaded. Marines fought their way to Tinian, Rota, the Volcanoes, the Bonins, the Palaus, Peleliu, and Bloody Nose Ridge. In these battles and in scores of others they added glory to their long record.

The original intention had been to invade Guam within a few days after the landings on Saipan, but the strong resistance on that island and the unexpected opportunity to strike at the Japanese fleet delayed the task of reclaiming from the enemy the first United States possession to fall into his hands. But now the Japanese fleet had been so thoroughly disposed of that we held undisputed control of the air. Big battleships were able to stand offshore with impunity and pour their destruction upon shore installations and other targets.

Admirals Halsey and Mitscher continued with their work. More than 720 tons of bombs fell on Guam in two days. On July 19 the planes delivered 727 tons and 147 rockets in the final strike preparatory to the actual landing. Rear Admiral Richard L. Connolly on July 20 led his amphibious forces to their stations. Major General Roy S. Geiger, U.S.M.C., stormed ashore with the Third Marine Division, the Seventy-seventh Infantry Division, and the First Marine Provisional Brigade, all elements of his Third Amphibious Corps.

The Japanese were well aware they could not long hold out on Guam. They were realizing the truth of the statement by Secretary Forrestal and Admirals King and Halsey: "The Marianas would provide the key which will unlock the door to Japan, the Philippines, and the coast of China." All Tokyo could do was to form a new government under General Kuniaka Koiso, the "Tiger of Korea," member of the "Manchuria Gang" and long an exponent of "expansion." Admiral Mitzumasi Yonai, leader in the "Japanization of Asia" went in as Navy Minister.

Major General Allen H. Turnage's Third Marines, and Brigadier General Lemuel P. Shepherd, Jr.'s Provisional Brigade (including Carlson's Raiders and other similar units) quickly expanded the beachheads which they had established on Guam. They were then joined by Major General A. D. Bruce's Seventy-seventh Infantry. By the end of the fifth day the two landing areas were a solid front. The airfield with its 4,700-foot runway was captured, the Sumay naval base and barracks were seized, and resistance on Orote Peninsula was wiped out.

At 4 o'clock that afternoon, July 28, 1944, the United States flag was raised in the shadow of Mount Alifan, and American rule over Guam was proclaimed once more, after the island's two and one-half years under the Mikado. On August 9, twenty days after the landing, all organized resistance had ended on Guam.

The three-week campaign cost the Americans 1,214 killed, 5,704 wounded, and 329 missing. More than 17,000 Japanese were killed and nearly 500 were taken prisoner.

While Guam was being liberated Major General Harry Schmidt took his Fifth Marine Amphibious Corps ashore on Tinian, separated from the southern end of Saipan by a channel two and one-half miles across. The Second and Fourth Marine Divisions, after only a week's rest on Saipan after capturing that island, undertook the new conquest. Ships of Rear Admiral Harry W. Hill, Commander of Group 2, Amphibious Forces Pacific Fleet, kept pouring shells into the Japanese positions.

During the night of July 31 the Tinian garrison, which probably had not heard of the doings on Saipan, made several equally futile suicide attempts to break out of the trap, and that ended organized resistance—nine days after the invasion.

Rear Admiral Turner announced during August that he had moved the headquarters of the Amphibious Pacific Fleet from Pearl Harbor to Saipan—which was 3,000 miles closer to the Philippines, China, and Japan.

General MacArthur's forces were making slashing air assaults on the Moluccas and Mindanao in the Philippines during the last week in July. At the same time the Allied Eastern Fleet sailed out with battleships and carriers to leave Sabang, on Sumatra, a pile of wreckage. These blows had the long-range objective of whittling down Japanese strength into an ever-decreasing area, and the immediate aim of setting the stage for the next move, on July 30, when the Sixth Army leaped 200 miles from Numfor to seize the Sansapor coastal strip at the northwestern end of New Guinea and the islands of Amsterdam and Middleburg off the coast. The surprised enemy was unable to offer much resistance. General MacArthur pushed his spearhead to within 600 miles of Mindanao.

"Our air bases are now established from Milne Bay [at the southeast tip] along the entire coast of New Guinea," General MacArthur said. "The enemy is no longer able to operate in this area, either by sea or by air, beyond the Halmahera-Philippine line, which is the main defense cover for his conquered empire in the Southwest Pacific. Should this line go, all his conquest south of China will be imperiled."

General Kenney's fliers now poured destruction on Mindanao, particularly the principal city of Davao and its airports. They softened up airfields, coastal defenses, shipping, and industries in Celebes and Lesser Sundas, but saved their heaviest concentrations for the Moluccas.

After conferring with President Roosevelt and Admiral Nimitz at Pearl Harbor, General MacArthur said that the hammering of Halmahera's airfields had left them so weakened that the entire Japanese-conquered empire was menaced, its airfields neutralized, its shipping hampered, its ground forces immobilized. Our navy now had more than sixty flattops and 37,000 planes.

General MacArthur's troops, on September 15, invaded Morotai, northernmost of the Halmaheras, and 500 miles to the northeast Admiral Halsey's Third Fleet carried landing forces to the Palaus.

The Palau invasion, in this double-barreled attack, was a spectacular story. An armada of 2,000,000 tons poured 1,350 tons of shells into Peleliu and Angaur while LCI's launched 9,000 rockets.

The First Marine Division, which two years and five weeks earlier had made the initial landing on Guadalcanal, spearheaded the Palaus invasion. Many of the units fresh from Saipan and Guam swept over the reefs, through barbed wire, to establish a two-mile beachhead along the southwest coast.

Peleliu, which lies at the southern end of the Palaus, was a tough proposition although only twelve square miles in area. The Marines captured the prized airfield the day after landing. Artillery had been put ashore quickly on a thirty-foot ribbon of sand between water and vegetation. This, together with the naval guns, softened the airfield defenses. It was not until tanks had gone into action that the principal airfield in the Palaus, 610 miles from Davao, finally was taken.

Fighting on "Bloody Nose Ridge" was the worst yet encountered in the long history of the First Division, but the airfield was finally made safe from continued enemy artillery fire.

A day after Peleliu was invaded, September 16, the 81st (Wildcat) Infantry Division, commanded by Major General Paul J. Mueller, went into its first engagement of World War II by landing on Angaur Island just to the south.

Organized resistance ended after three days of fighting, with more than 1,200 Japanese killed; but here, as elsewhere, it was months before the last fanatical enemy soldiers had been exterminated. Organized resistance in the Palaus ended. Our casualties on all the islands were 1,022 killed; 6,111 wounded; 250 missing.

The eastern flank of MacArthur's drive on the Philippines was now nailed down. The long road back was nearing its end.

72

AMERICAN NAVY WITH THE AIR FORCES BLAST ROADS FOR MacARTHUR'S ARMY

PERFECT coördination of land, sea, and air forces was the American "secret weapon" in the Pacific. It revealed itself with such power that it remained no longer a secret, but a flaming torch of destruction which almost blinded the Japanese. The Nipponese Navy fled before it—afraid to come out and fight.

MacArthur prepared his campaigns on the basis of "the greatest possible protection" for his forces. The safety of his men, the cost of the campaigns in human lives, was his first concern. With this objective in mind, his campaign for the liberation of the Philippines was planned. Through the magnificent work of the navy and the air forces, roads were blasted for armies.

General MacArthur had started to feel out Japanese defenses in the Philippines in July, 1944. The United States Fifth and Thirteenth Air Forces were merged with Australian, Netherlands, and New Zealand air groups into the Far Eastern Air Force, with General Kenney in full command. The first strike was made on July 23 when a pair of patrol planes sank a Japanese freighter right under the enemy's nose. The Philippines were mentioned as a war front for the first time since the fall of Corregidor, in General MacArthur's communiqué of July 24 from Advanced Headquarters on New Guinea: "Our air patrols sank a coastal vessel seventy miles off the coast of Mindanao."

The pace quickened. September 1 saw the heaviest United States assault of the war on the Philippines. Three Davao airfields were hit, destroying thirty-seven planes on the ground and one in the air. There was heavy antiaircraft fire but only nine enemy fighters rose to challenge the Liberators, all of which came back unhurt. More than 110 tons of bombs fell that day. An equal load was dropped on September 2, when more than fifty Liberators maintained the assault in the longest military flight up to that time. Lasang, Licanan, and Sasa airfields were badly mauled and heavy fires raged through installations.

The navy sent in some Catalinas to look over the situation. The information brought back by the Catalinas so fully confirmed Japanese aërial weakness that Admiral Halsey decided to send his carrier planes out for a real "look-see." Then went out on the morning of September 8 and swept five airfields and three ports in a fast, ferocious assault. The damage wrought amounted to: sixty-eight planes destroyed; eighty-nine ships sunk or damaged, including a convoy of fifty-two wiped out off Hinatauan Bay, north of Davao, after which cruisers and destroyers finished off the cripples. This was the largest bag of shipping ever recorded in a single strike. All the strategic targets—Del Monte, in north-central Mindanao, Valencia in the center, Cagayan on the northwest coast, Buayan on the southeast coast, and Davao—were left in ruins. The extent of Japanese vulnerability was now clear.

A full-scale carrier attack of unparalleled daring stabbed directly into the heart of the Philippines. At dawn on September 11 the Third Fleet sent out its planes on a three-day assault of the Visayas, the central group of the Philippines lying between Luzon and Mindanao. The islands of Leyte, Panay, Cebu, and Negros were thoroughly raked, with diversionary blows at northern Mindanao. As Admiral Halsey brought his big ships deep into the waters presumably controlled by the Japanese, General MacArthur kept the enemy busy with blows at Zamboanga and other targets in southern Mindao.

The Visayas' attack was the most successful the Third Fleet had ever launched. The Japanese lost 156 planes in the air and 277 on the ground; 84 ships and numerous sampans had been sunk or damaged. Since Admiral Halsey opened his campaign with the Mindanao strike on September 8 the enemy had lost 501 planes, and 200 vessels had been sunk or damaged.

This wholesale destruction of Japanese planes and shipping called for an immediate change in Allied plans. The seizure of Ulithi Island had been intended as a prelude to the invasion of Yap, and on September 15 an army corps had embarked at Honolulu for that purpose. The results of the Philippines aërial blows were so startling that it was decided to forget Yap as unimportant. The convoy was ordered to a new rendezvous—with the Philippines the ultimate destination.

At 9 o'clock on the morning of September 21 the Manila radio signed off its "setting-up exercises" and opened a program of American tunes called "music for your morning mood." That mood changed suddenly at 9:29 when the excited announcer broke in: "Attention all listeners. This is an air-raid warning!"

Hundreds of carrier planes that had left their Third Fleet nests from decks that were pitching and rolling in heavy rain squalls, loosed their first bombs at that moment. Americans were over Manila for the first time in nearly two years. This was the pay-off. Nichols Field and Clark Field were attacked with even greater ferocity than that with which the Japanese opened up on December 7, 1941. Shipping in Manila Bay and Subic Bay was lashed unmercifully. Shore installations were pounded to dust. Hell-divers screamed down from 10,000 feet and torpedo planes skimmed over the water's surface.

There was no rest for the enemy. The assault was renewed the next day, with some of the planes flying as far as Aparri, at the northern tip of Luzon. During the two days 103 Japanese ships and 405 planes were destroyed or damaged. We lost fifteen planes, with most of the personnel rescued.

The Japanese Air Force in the southern and central Philippines had been wiped out during the twenty-five days of Admiral Halsey's attacks. 1,101 Japanese planes had been destroyed, probably destroyed, or damaged; nearly 525 ships had been sunk, probably sunk, or damaged. American losses were about fifty planes and an equal number of men.

Secretary of the Navy Forrestal conferred in San Francisco with Admirals King and Nimitz on supply plans for the "forthcoming operations." It was disclosed that from five to ten tons of supplies, including 700,000 items running from surgical thread to locomotives, must be landed for each soldier in an invasion force. This meant a minimum of 1,500,000 tons to put 250,000 men ashore with the bare immediate necessities that must be constantly replaced and enlarged. The magnitude of the supply problem is evident in the fact that the average ship took thirty to forty-five days for the round trip from the West Coast to Hawaii; and from there the round trip was as long or longer to and from the invasion point.

It was on the night of October 9 that hell really broke loose. It continued for the longest period of action yet seen in the Pacific. On that night a cruiser-destroyer group appeared off Marcus Island and administered the heaviest damage that enemy outpost had suffered in a long time; but it was only a diversion force.

For the next five days the attack was pressed without a pause. Admiral Mitscher's carriers embarked upon the heaviest and most sustained carrier assault in history. It penetrated so deeply into Japanese waters that the ships were west of Japan, and planes within 100 miles of the China coast. The first blow fell on the Ryukyus, the 570-mile chain of rugged, partly volcanic islands stretching southward from Japan across the entrance to the East China Sea and making that body of water virtually a Japanese lake. The ships sailed boldly up and down the coast battering targets on shore while the planes leveled selected objectives on land.

General MacArthur added to the enemy's confusion by sending General Kenney's land-based craft not only against Davao and Tacloban on Mindanao, but by extending the range to include Leyte. The Japanese were taken so completely by surprise that little air opposition was encountered over the Ryukyus.

The morning of October 12 brought a strange sight to Formosa and the Pescadores—a sky filled with 1,000 United States carrier planes. The battle that raged in the sky for the greater part of the following five days did much to determine the character of fighting for the next six months. Formosa, an island 250 miles long and 100 wide, was

Japan's main bastion. It was studded with powerful air bases and equipped with numerous major naval bases. The enemy maintained a strong garrison on Formosa which was swollen by troops on their way to and from China, the Philippines and other parts of the stolen empire.

The first day's attack on Formosa and the Pescadores set the pace for the entire campaign. Aviation facilities, factories, warehouses, wharves, and shipping were obliterated and 193 planes were blown out of the sky with 123 more destroyed on the ground. When the attack was called off, the Third Fleet's scoreboard showed: 915 planes destroyed, 565 in the air, 350 on the ground; 80 ships sunk, probably sunk, or damaged; 104 small craft sunk; 80 probably sunk or damaged. Fleet losses were 79 aircraft, 31 pilots and 21 crewmen; a cruiser and a destroyer torpedoed but able to reach port for repairs.

Vice Admiral W. A. Lee, Jr., was second in command to Admiral Halsey of the Third Fleet, and Admiral Mitscher's carrier units were commanded by Admirals McCain, Sherman, R. E. Davison, G. F. Bogan, and H. B. Sallada. The fleet had sailed into what Japan had always considered her own private preserve. Their bold sortie west of Japan was an open challenge to come out and fight, but the enemy ignored it.

The Japanese fleet came out of hiding on the 17th and a showdown naval battle seemed certain. But as soon as the enemy had one look at Admiral Halsey's complement, he turned tail and sped back to the Inland Sea. Not a shot was fired.

Even before the Formosa attacks many transports, "fire support" ships, and escort carriers had been temporarily transferred from Admiral Halsey's command to the Seventh Fleet, under command of Vice Admiral Thomas C. Kinkaid, all under the immediate leadership of General MacArthur. There was a Northern Attack Force, known as the Seventh Amphibious Force, commanded by Admiral Berbey; a Southern Attack Force (the Third Amphibicus Force) under Vice Admiral Wilkinson; surface and air groups, fire support, bombardment, mine sweeping, and supply groups. There were more than 750 ships in the armada. Its job was to land four army divisions in the heart of the Philippines and give them protection and supplies until they were able to take care of themselves.

The task groups left their ports in New Guinea and the Admiralties on October 11, picked up the transports and under difficult weather conditions commenced on October 17 the operations preliminary to invasion. By D-Day, three days later, the islands guarding the eastern entrances to Leyte Gulf were secured.

On the morning of October 20, ships' guns opened a heavy bombardment of the Leyte shore. The invasion of the Philippines had begun —the process of liberation was under way.

"PEOPLE OF THE PHILIPPINES, I HAVE RETURNED!"—MacARTHUR AT LEYTE

ON the morning of October 20, 1944, one of the greatest scenes in history was enacted. The American flag was planted on the shores of Leyte. After 948 days MacArthur was back on the soil of the Philippines. From Australia he had fought his way back, island by island, in one of the world's greatest military achievements. He had fulfilled his promise to return.

In a drenching rain, at the beginning of the typhoon season, he stood on a broken-down Signal Corps truck before a microphone on a muddy beachhead at Leyte. His voice electrified the people of the Philippines, who had waited in captivity for two and one-half long years under the rule of the Mikado:

"*This is the Voice of Freedom,* General MacArthur speaking. People of the Philippines: I have returned! By the grace of Almighty God our forces stand again on Philippine soil—soil consecrated in the blood of our two peoples. We have come, dedicated and committed to the task of destroying every vestige of enemy control over your daily lives, and of restoring, upon a foundation of indestructible strength, the liberties of your people.

"At my side is your President, Sergio Osmeña, worthy successor of that great patriot Manuel Quezon, with members of his Cabinet. The seat of your Government is now, therefore, firmly reëstablished on Philippine soil.

"The hour of your redemption is here. Your patriots have demonstrated an unswerving and resolute devotion to the principles of freedom that challenges the best that is written on the pages of human history. I now call upon your supreme effort, that the enemy may know from the temper of an aroused and outraged people within that he has a force to contend with no less violent than is the force committed from without.

"Rally to me. Let the indomitable spirit of Bataan and Corregidor lead on. As the lines of battle roll forward to bring you within the zone of operations, rise and strike! Strike at every favorable opportunity. For your homes and hearths, strike! For future generations of your sons and daughters, strike! In the name of the sacred dead, strike!

"Let no heart be faint. Let every arm be steeled. The guidance of Divine God points the way. Follow in His Name to the Holy Grail of righteous victory."

At the sound of MacArthur's voice, stilled since the dark days when it had brought daily messages of hope to the Filipinos from a tunnel deep in the heart of the fortress at Corregidor, the inhabitants of the islands went literally wild with joy. After the long months and years of Japanese occupation and brutality, the natives braved naval shells and aërial bombs to line the hills in a spontaneous welcome. When Tacloban, capital of Leyte, was liberated on the third day of the invasion, the citizens told how their Japanese "masters" had compelled them to parade during the previous week in celebration of the "great naval victory" the enemy claimed to have fought and won off Formosa. They told of the indignities heaped upon them since the first Japanese marched in on May 25, 1942—the weekly house-to-house searches, forced labor, wholesale food requisitions, worthless money, starvation.

The annals of war contain no more glowing testimonial to the courage and loyalty of a people. The Filipinos carried on bravely and confidently during the occupation years, preparing themselves for the liberation General MacArthur had promised. Three former employees of a Manila radio station rowed in a small boat all the way to Panay and crept into a mountain hide-out. They fashioned a homemade portable radio set with which they planned to communicate with the Americans. There was no electricity. They took turns all day pedaling a bicycle which generated enough power to permit transmission for fifteen minutes daily. During that brief period they tried to tell the world of the guerrilla movement forming in the Philippines. Month after month they broadcast in vain until one day, late in 1942, a powerful War Department station picked up a few words and relayed them at once to General MacArthur in Australia.

That faint message was a pledge of internal support if the hungry, scattered patriots could be fed, armed, and adequately led. Food, arms, and leadership were promptly supplied by General MacArthur—first in meager fashion and then in increasing amounts as the march up the Pacific progressed and it was possible to dare the Japanese guards. Submarines landed skilled radio operators and equipment for powerful stations secretly located on Luzon. American officers began to build an army, selecting cadres of commissioned and non-commissioned officers from two Filipino regiments trained at Camp Cooke and Camp Beale in California and smuggled into the islands.

The guerrilla movement was consolidated under an American commander responsible only to General MacArthur, and soon began its devastating work of sabotage and intelligence. By October 20, 1944, it was strategically disposed and powerfully equipped throughout the Philippines. On every one of the islands these daring men and women contributed mightily to the overthrow of the Japanese and to the minimizing of American battle losses.

NEW YORK HERALD TRIBUNE map—Fleck

The American flag indicates where the 800-ship American armada went into Lingayen Gulf to reconquer the principal island of the Philippines. The Japanese flags designate the places at which the Japanese invaded Luzon at the beginning of the war.

President Roosevelt sent this radio message to General MacArthur: "The whole American nation exults at the news that the gallant men under your command have landed on Philippine soil."

Among the first troops to go ashore under the command of General Krueger was every able-bodied soldier who had escaped from Corregidor before it surrendered. They actually spearheaded the invasion designed to liberate their imprisoned fellow Americans and the Filipinos. A similar note of poetic justice was struck at sea where two of the "ghost ships" flattened at Pearl Harber on the Day of Infamy appeared to demand payment in kind. The veteran battleships *California* and *Pennsylvania* stood close in to Leyte's shores and poured salvo after salvo of 14-inch and 16-inch shells over the heads of the landing troops and into the Japanese shore positions. The Japanese were taken completely off guard. Only one enemy plane put in a brief appearance before being shot down.

That first historic day can best be described in the words of General MacArthur himself: "In a major amphibious operation we have seized the eastern coast of Leyte Island in the Philippines 600 miles north of Morotai and 2,500 miles from Milne Bay whence our offensive started nearly sixteen months ago. This point of entry in the Visayas is midway between Luzon and Mindanao and at one stroke splits in two the Japanese force in the Philippines. The enemy's anticipation of attack in Mindanao caused him to be caught unawares in Leyte, and beachheads in the Tacloban area were secured with small casualties. The landing was preceded by heavy naval and air bombardments which were devastating in effect. Our ground troops are rapidly extending their positions, and supplies and heavy equipment are already flowing ashore in great volume.

"The troops comprise elements of the Sixth United States Army, to which are attached units from the Central Pacific with supporting elements. The naval forces consist of the Seventh United States Fleet, the Australian Squadron, and supporting elements of the Third United States Fleet. Air support was given by Navy carrier forces, the Far East Air Force, and the Royal Australian Air Force. The Commander in Chief is in personal command of the operation.

"The enemy's forces of an estimated 225,000 include the Fourteenth Army Group, under command of Field Marshal Count Terauchi, of which seven divisions have already been identified: The 16th, 20th, 26th, 100th, 102nd, 103rd, and the 104th."

A day later the 15th Japanese Division which, in the words of General MacArthur, "did the dirty work at Bataan," was identified and became the primary object of vengeance on the part of the Americans.

General MacArthur, as was his custom, gave full credit to his fighting forces in calling this roll of honor: "Lieutenant General Walter Krueger was in command of ground forces, which consist of the 10th Corps commanded by Major General Franklin C. Sibert, and the 24th commanded by Major General John R. Hodge; 3rd Engineers Brigade, Amphibious, commanded by Brigadier General William Seavy, and supporting supply and other troops; 1st Battery Division, Major General Verne B. Hart; 7th Infantry Division, Major General Arnold; 24th Infantry Division, Major General Frederick A. Irving, and 96th Infantry Division, Major General Bradley.

"Vice Admiral Thomas C. Kinkaid, commander of Allied naval forces in the Southwest Pacific, is in command of the Seventh United States Fleet. The Australian Squadron is commanded by Commander John A. Collins. Elements of the Third United States Fleet, commanded by Admiral William F. Halsey, Jr., are providing naval support. Elements supporting the operation include the United States Far Eastern Air Force and Royal Australian Air Force, commanded by Lieutenant General George C. Kenney, commander of Alled air forces in the Southwest Pacific; Third Fleet carrier forces are commanded by Vice Admiral Marc A. Mitscher. Amphibious operations are under command of Rear Admiral Daniel C. Berbey and Rear Admiral Theodore S. Wilkins."

The first troops to go ashore in LCI's, rocket boats, and other craft were greater in number than had ever stormed an enemy-held beach before. In less than a day 125,000 troops were put on land, and within a few more days an invasion force of 250,000 had been landed, with tanks, artillery, and everything else that goes with a full-scale attack.

The element of surprise caught the Japanese unprepared on Leyte, but the fighting was to be severe. One contributing factor to the surprise had been prepared weeks before the invasion force set out from New Guinea. There the radio correspondents, who had been accustomed to broadcast to their networks at regular hours each evening, spent the days before the convoy sailed making recordings. These were put on the air during the time the correspondents were steaming toward Leyte with the troops. American listeners now know why that week of broadcasts contained little that was new or exciting. The ruse fooled the Japanese monitors, who listened daily to everything the Allies put on the air. If the recordings had not been made and there had been no broadcasts, the Japanese would have known that something was afoot.

So complete was the surprise, however, that resistance during the first days was disorganized and the invasion proceeded rapidly during the first week. Tacloban and Dulag airfields were repaired and enlarged. A great base from which to carry on the liberation of the entire Philippines was begun. The strategy of that week was to drive the Japanese away from the Leyte coast and into the inland mountains.

In approximately a week the Americans controlled a sixty-seven-mile front and they had sent amphibious tanks across the one-mile San Juanico Strait to Samar Island. When October went out on the wings of a raging typhoon, nearly 2,000 square miles of Leyte and Samar were firmly in American control, and more than 1,500,000 Filipinos had been liberated. An unbroken coastline of 212 miles was held on Leyte from Carigara, on the northwest coast, to Panaon Island off the southeast. On Samar the Americans had reached the northwestern tip of the island and could look across San Bernardino Strait at Luzon. More than 25,000 Japanese had been killed, while American losses had been 706 killed, 270 missing, and 2,245 wounded.

These great gains had been won before the dreaded typhoon struck. As soon as the Japanese weakness was discovered, the American commanders had decided to face this great hazard of Nature, even though it would undoubtedly be worse than anything the enemy might interpose. The typhoon arrived without notice. A seventy-mile wind drove the rain laterally, blew down tents, disrupted communications, and flooded the unpaved roads with flowing mud. Houses were unroofed. Light fighter planes using the captured airfields were nearly blown from the runways. Fortunately, little material damage was done to the fighting equipment, and every ship weathered the blow. However, the typhoon season delayed full conquest of Leyte for many bloody weeks.

INVASION OF SICILY—DOORSTEP TO CONTINENT OF EUROPE

ON the night of Friday, July 9, 1943, President Roosevelt was host at an official dinner in the White House. The guest of honor was General Henri-Honoré Giraud, commander of the French forces in North Africa. At the table with him were General George C. Marshall, Chief of Staff of the United States Army, and Admiral Ernest K. King, Commander in Chief of the United States Fleet and Chief of Naval Operations.

The discussion included the recent liberation of North Africa and pending events. About nine o'clock the dinner was briefly interrupted when a message was brought to the President. He glanced at it hurriedly and put it in his pocket. Almost an hour later, when the guests were ready to rise, he indicated that he had a few words to say. He spoke quietly and simply: "I have just had word of the first attack against the soft under-belly of Europe."

This was the brief but dramatic announcement that summarized the invasion of Sicily—a vast operation embracing some 2,500 ships, great fleets of airplanes, and hundreds of thousands of men.

Some 4,500 air-miles away from Washington a great soldier was at his post directing gigantic operations. General Eisenhower was standing vigil during the night, carrying the tremendous burden of responsibility from his headquarters in North Africa. As the armada was setting out on one of the greatest missions in history, General Eisenhower with members of his staff drove to the shore, where he stood in silence. He raised his hand in salute as the first formation of Allied planes roared suddenly between him and the moon. The invasion had begun.

Allied strategy, weeks before undertaking the invasion of Sicily, had wreaked destruction on the little volcanic island of Pantelleria which stood in the pathway. Heavy naval and aërial bombardments had forced its unconditional surrender. Three years before the first shot had been fired in the Second World War, Mussolini had built on Pantelleria what he believed to be an impregnable fortress. It was to the Italians what Malta was to the British.

In clearing the roadway the Allies had also delivered knockout blows to the little islands of Lampedusa, Linosa, and Lampione, all stepping-stones to Sicily.

Within a month after the reduction of the island fortresses, the Allies were striking their first blow at Europe with the invasion of Sicily, the doorstep to Italy and the continent of Europe—at one point only two miles across the Strait of Messina.

The initial forces facing each other in Sicily were more than a dozen Italian divisions and about four German divisions—some 250,000 men —against the Allied invasion force of ten divisions or some 160,000 Americans, British, Canadians, and French.

Allied planes throughout and since the North African campaign had been steadily bombing the strongholds in Sicily and southern Italy. The invasion itself was a masterpiece in organization and coördination. The troops of four countries took part. The major participants were the famed British Eighth Army under General Sir Bernard L. Montgomery and the newly activated American Seventh Army, commanded by Lieutenant General George S. Patton, Jr. The Seventh Army consisted largely of the Second United States Corps that had captured Bizerte and shared in the last round-up of scores of thousands of German and Italian soldiers in northeastern Tunisia. It was augmented by divisions that had undergone exhaustive training in French Morocco and in newly liberated Tunisia but had not yet been in battle. These were to be joined by a large Canadian force that left Britain in the greatest secrecy under Lieutenant General Andrew G. L. McNaughton, to fight with the Eighth Army.

The landing-points chosen by the Allied command were on the southeastern coast of Sicily, at Licata, Gela, and Pachino, with supporting landings to be made at unidentified locations along the coast, interspersed among the main objectives. The first two were assigned to the American Seventh Army. The strip of coast winding from Pozzallo around the southeastern tip of the island and up to Avola was given to the British and Canadians. Many of the British were Commandos brought in secrecy from Britain with the Canadian troops.

The first Allied troops rushed ashore on Sicily at 3:00 A.M. on July 10, 1943, preceded five hours by a detachment of airborne Americans whose gliders and parachutes brought them to earth far behind the enemy's lines.

The vast convoy that had to be massed for the invasion was brought together in sections at various African ports and finally assembled as a unit under cover of darkness for the short traverse of the Sicilian Channel. There were no ship movements to offer an indication of the Allies' objective. Finally, to complete as far as possible the disorganization of the enemy's defense, one hundred four-motored Liberators of the Ninth U. S. Air Force, on the day before the invasion, crashed hundreds of tons of bombs into Axis command headquarters at Taormina, that delightful resort on the northeast coast of Sicily.

The 2,500 ships, with their hundreds of escorting warships of every size and a half-dozen Allied navies—including Greek, Polish, and

Dutch—were still gathering out in the channel when the American airborne forces landed out of the mist behind Gela and Licata, twenty miles apart in the center of the south coast. British airborne units were performing a similar operation in the extreme east.

Gliders came in first, landing at 10:10 P.M. while their big towplanes were roaring back to base. The first gliders settled to the ground almost without opposition and the soldiers crowded out of them to carry out their assigned jobs—the rupture of communications, destruction of outposts, and the capture of such objectives of opportunity as they could take with the greatest profit to the seaborne forces. One hour and ten minutes after the gliders had "sat down," there was a roar of motors in the air. A fleet of transport planes streamed through the night. The sky was suddenly pocked with the white blobs of opening parachutes as the Allies rushed in more airborne troops.

The seaborne forces at the eastern end of the line were headed by Canadians and British Marines and Commandos. Flares laid down by the R.A.F. around Gela after the American landings served to guide them, if only indirectly, for Gela was far to the west of their objective. Britons and Canadians dashed out of their landing craft into water that was waist-deep, holding their weapons above their heads as they splashed, shouting, to the shore. But they were disappointed; there was no resisting enemy to be beaten down.

Americans were landing at Licata and Gela, under far different circumstances. On the whole curving one-hundred-mile front embraced in the invasion operation, it was at this western end that the first and fiercest opposition was met.

Storming up the shore, the Americans made contact more quickly than they had expected with some of their own airborne units; for these had been thrown off their proposed course by the heavy wind which prevented them from controlling the direction of their descending parachutes. Thus they had come to earth some miles from their objectives. Having had the opportunity to ascertain the strength of the enemy defenses, their officers had ordered them to fall back toward the beach and join the main force.

With the addition of these soldiers and the landing of heavy guns and tanks, the Americans launched their attack on Gela in spite of the odds against them. Here the severest fighting of the first phase of the invasion took place. The Germans came out of Gela to give battle. The Americans rushed them with the bayonet while their ships, lying offshore, gave the full support of their guns. Finally the Americans fought their way into Gela.

Here the Germans re-formed their lines and threw in troops and tanks they had been holding in reserve. With all their force and all their skill they launched a savage assault on the Americans' foothold in the town.

The attackers-turned-defenders battled back vigorously. Their own tanks were not sufficiently numerous as yet to withstand the enemy's. Heartbreakingly the tide of the battle turned. The Americans were forced out of Gela.

At Licata, however, the Americans were scoring a triumph. Their warships were firing in close support of the landing-forces. No sooner did a gun flare from the shore than a half-dozen shells screamed into it from the sea and it would not be heard again. A little group of parachutists, victims of the treacherous wind, had gathered near the beach; they lost no time in exploiting their fortuitous positions. Smoothly and quickly they captured one gun of an enemy coastal battery and then engaged the crews of the rest. In a few hours every battery and every pillbox was silent. The Americans had taken Licata. The capture of this town, held predominantly by Italians, cost exactly four American lives; 300 to 500 of the defending Italians were captured and sat morosely on a hillside as the American Army streamed past on its way into Europe.

The greatest initial successes were at the eastern end of the long beachhead. There the Canadians landing at Pachino encountered virtually no resistance and pushed rapidly inland through the burning town. Opposition to their advance mounted—though at no time did it approach what the Americans were facing at Gela.

Over the whole land and sea front there was a constant cover of Allied fighter planes on the watch for German bombers. For the first few hours none appeared. Many of the Sicilian airfields had been rendered temporarily useless in the week of Allied bombing that had preceded the invasion. Those that remained were fighter bases; so the enemy had to call on more distant airdromes for bombers. Though the invasion of Sicily had been no surprise to the enemy, it had inevitably produced a temporary shock. At 4:00 P.M., the first enemy bombers appeared over the much-augmented invasion fleet. In both high-level and diving attacks, they sought to break up the armada. But the Allies' fighters and the antiaircraft batteries of the ships themselves destroyed and drove them off.

As the troops fell back from Gela, General Patton was riding in a landing-barge just off the shore, watching the reinforcements come in. Suddenly he saw his own fighting men rolling back on the new arrivals; and then the enemy's troops and tanks came into view. With a shout, the immaculately uniformed commander leaped from his boat into the water and waded ashore, cursing, to take personal command. The sight of their dripping general striding up the sand of Sicily under the enemy's fire did something to those exhausted, battered, yet unbeaten doughboys.

To the American and British warships lying off shore a radio message was sent from the land, reporting the German tanks massing behind Gela. Then came the most superb example of coördination in warfare that had yet been achieved. While infantry and artillery on the shore stood their ground and traded blow for blow with the enemy and the American General shouted orders to his subordinates, the Allied warships "joined the army." Scouts gave them the range and position of the Germans' tank column, rapidly forming to launch a final successful attack. Naval gun crews were at their stations, ready for orders. Warships' turrets became the housings of antitank artillery. The ships poured their shells straight and true into the heart of the enemy's armor miles away. Elevation, range, and direction were exact. When the firing had ended unopposed—for the shore batteries in the area had been knocked out—the German tanks were destroyed.

When the Americans on the beach got word of the ships' feat, it fired their imaginations almost as much as the sight of the General with the six-shooters swinging from his belt. A third time, the Americans—the tired veterans of two days' battling and the freshly landed reinforcements—surged forward again. The Germans broke before them and under them—the beachhead was saved.

The Americans in the west had gained new momentum after having broken the last enemy counterattack at Gela. Once the foe had lost the tanks on which he had relied, he had been driven out of Gela and beyond it, while the Americans' coastal force had swept into Scoglitti, fifteen miles southwest, and then turned inland. With the Canadians and the Eighth Army, which were likewise driving inland, they were converging on the key junction and air base of Ragusa, about forty miles southeast of Gela and thirty miles northwest of Pachino.

As the Allies advanced, they met enthusiastic welcomes. Desperately poor Sicilians, abandoned by their German and Italian defenders, crowded the doors of their wretched houses to hail *"Gli Americani"* and to shout *"Evviva George VI!"* The Algiers radio broadcast an appeal to the people to force their régime to surrender, promising them complete freedom in the choice of any non-Fascist government.

When General Eisenhower went ashore in Sicily on the third day of the invasion, the British were landing just below Catania, almost in the shadow of Mount Etna—fully fifty miles from the first landing-point at Pachino. On that same day, the Americans driving east from Gela and the mixed British and Canadian force driving out of the Cape Passero area effected a junction at Ragusa. This sealed off the whole southeastern end of the island behind a solid, unbroken wall of Allied troops that ran from somewhere west of Licata to a point on the edge of the Catanian plain.

The Germans must have been more deeply impressed by the Allies' perfect swinging together than they cared to admit. Reading the pessimistic secret reports of their military commanders' withdrawals, they were preparing the German nation for the loss of all the Italian islands before the summer's end.

To keep the invasion "safe" was one of the primary aims of the Allied air force, not only in the Mediterranean but in distant Britain. A series of heavy, skilfully placed and timed assaults from Mediterranean bases produced a temporary but complete paralysis in the enemy's supply lines for Sicily.

In the land fighting the toughest job had been put up to the Americans; but the Germans began to shift their entire defensive strength, slowly but unceasingly, back toward Catania in the shadow of Mount Etna. They were determined to prevent the Eighth Army from driving right up the coast to Messina and thus cut off their retreat into Italy and trap them between their own lines and the still distant American and Canadian forces. Progressively, therefore, the Americans were to find the going easier and quicker, while the British were to be held almost motionless for weeks.

These troops had already engulfed the entire 206th Coastal Division of the Italian army and captured its commander, General Achille Davet, in their spreading push northward and westward. Well ahead of their vanguard, the American and British cruisers and destroyers, in mixed squadrons, were systematically shelling every probable obstacle to the advance and lining more hot steel into the enemy's troops concentrated at Porto Empedocle and Agrigento. British motor torpedo boats swept into the narrow Strait of Messina on the east coast to harry the enemy's light forces there and to attack the ponderous railroad ferries on which he depended for his supplies from Italy.

In five days the Allies had captured 12,000 prisoners, most of them Italians. These complained bitterly, as they had done in Africa, that the Germans had used them merely as buffers to take up the shock of the Allies' assaults while the crack German units got away to make another stand. In their headlong rushes in the southeast and in the solid advances that followed the first German counterblows in the Gela sector, huge amounts of booty were taken, abandoned by the fleeing troops. This included such weapons as the giant 240-mm. field guns the Germans had captured from the Russians and transported to Sicily only to lose them there—as they lost the fighter pilots whom they likewise transferred from the Russian front—and an ammunition dump that measured one-and-a-half by two miles.

While the armies were pushing steadily forward, the Allies were throwing their big planes against the targets that were still relatively far from the fighting lines. One of the most frequently bombed was Messina, which was chosen because of its eventual use by the beaten enemy for his evacuation. This city, in repeated blastings, was virtually laid in ruins; yet somehow the enemy continued to improvise shipping facilities that allowed his supplies to come in and, eventually, many of his men to go out.

The city of Agrigento was the next major objective to fall to the Americans. The steep heights around the city were too much for modern mechanized equipment to negotiate and, as in Tunisia, the attackers had to fall back on the use of mules which they requisitioned in the surrounding countryside. These animals carried the Americans' dismantled heavy artillery into the hills and, later, the shells that the big 155-mm. Long Toms were to hurl into the historic citadel.

When the guns had been reassembled and made ready to fire, the American warships were already lying off the coast within easy range of the town. At a given moment, the guns of the cruisers opened up in cadence with the artillery in the hills. Under the withering crossfire thus brought to bear on the beleaguered fortress, the Italian garrison was at last beaten to its knees. After that, the fall of Porto Empedocle was automatic.

The center of the line, meanwhile, continued to advance at a less rapid pace. The whole sector from Canicatti to Grammichele was particularly important to the Germans' defense because it represented a strong barrier before the town of Enna, eighteen miles north of the center of that sector—Enna was the heart of the whole communication system linking the entire interior of Sicily. Its capture would enable the Allies to drive a fatal wedge between the enemy troops in the northwest and their escape outlet at Messina.

As the Allies' advance progressed in the rest of Sicily, their commanders had to face a new task simultaneously with their conduct of the military campaign. This was the administration of the occupied territory. To meet the problem, the Allies conceived the establishment of a combined Anglo-American agency called the Allied Military Government of Occupied Territory (later contracted to Allied Military Government) to follow in the wake of the invading armies and assure the smooth functioning of essential activities behind the lines.

Less than a third of Sicily had been captured when General Sir Harold R. L. G. Alexander, the commander of the Allies' ground forces, was made military governor of the island. Naturally, his authority could extend only to such parts as the Allies had conquered; with the growth of their occupation, his authority would expand. His staff consisted of men long trained and experienced in government work and problems, now serving with the AMG with military rank and under military discipline. Their job, like General Alexander's, was to keep Sicilian economy and civilian life running as smoothly as possible.

While the British were striving to reach Catania, the American and Canadians in the center were advancing in parallel drives; the Americans, led by Major General Terry Allen's First Infantry Division that had borne the brunt of the Gela fighting, wrested Caltanisetta from the enemy. The Canadians drove the Germans and Italians out of Piazza-Armerina. Each of these towns was thirteen miles from Enna. In this sector the enemy's resistance had at last begun to crumble.

The Allies struck at last at the very heart of Italy. The Italians had scorned the ultimate appeals of President Roosevelt and Prime Minister Churchill; it was time that they should know fear in their own sanctuary. In broad daylight, five hundred Allied planes from the Middle East, North Africa, and Sicily dropped the first bombs of the war on Rome. For almost four years the Allies had spared the city, out of deference to its religious significance, in spite of its immense military importance.

The historic attack was not undertaken without the most careful preparations. For months before, the Allies' reconnaissance planes had carefully photographed and mapped every square foot. In the exhaustive "briefing" that preceded the take-off, all the air crews were painstakingly instructed in the absolute necessity for utmost precision in bombing. The targets chosen were the San Lorenzo freight yards, just outside the main railway station in the southeastern part of the city; the Littorio yards on the northern edge of the city, and the Ciampino airfield, four miles southeast of Rome. Every one of these targets was of the highest military importance, for the capital was the center of a vast rail network on which the Germans depended exclusively for the shipment of men and materials of war to southern Italy and Sicily.

Every flier was provided with the finest detailed maps on which the targets were clearly delineated; other warning marks set aside every point that might be of the slightest religious significance. The boundaries of Vatican City were heavily pictured; every shrine was identified beyond the least possibility of error. Because the Allied commanders recognized the necessity for explaining to the world the significance of the attack and the care with which religious monuments would be avoided, seven press correspondents were sent with the fliers to record the events and demonstrate the Allies' punctilious care. For the citizens of Rome, the bombs were accompanied by pamphlets explaining why their city was being bombed. Among the American and British fliers on the mission were many Catholics; all had the opportunity to refuse it without penalty, but none did—and many asked to go. They knew that, with all the other precautions, a final warning had been added: No bombs were to be dropped if clouds offered the slightest impediment to visibility over the target.

The first planes took off at 7:15 A.M. and were over the city at 11. The first bomb was dropped at 11:13; the last was dropped some time after 1:00 P.M. When the first Flying Fortresses roared over the city—Liberators and Marauders also participated—the enemy was taken completely by surprise. Feeble Italian antiaircraft batteries went into action, but scored no hits. German fighters rose to meet the succeeding waves of Allied bombers. Despite the size and duration of the attack, only five planes of all that armada were lost.

Statesmen and religious leaders, with only a few exceptions, paid willing tribute to the forbearance that the Allies had so long shown, the care with which the attack had been planned, and the skill with which it had been carried out. Unfortunately, one church—the Basilica of San Lorenzo fuori le Mura—was slightly damaged; that structure was at the very edge of the San Lorenzo railway yards. That it should have been struck was unavoidable and deplorable. The enemy tried to magnify the fact into a horrendous crime, without saying a word about the dozens of shrines that his own planes had smashed to rubble in Rotterdam, Warsaw, London, Coventry, and other cities.

On the very day of the Rome bombing came word that General Guzzoni, the Italian commander of Sicily, had warned his king of the imminence of defeat. In a message to Victor Emmanuel, General Guzzoni went as far as he dared without exposing himself to disciplinary action by the Fascist Party. He said that he could not guarantee any prolonged resistance on the island. The General spoke with reason. He knew of the phenomenal progress that was being made by the American Seventh Army's 3rd Division in its westward sweep after the capture of Agrigento. This tended to be overshadowed by the joint American-Canadian advance on Enna in the center—fighting in which the 1st and the 45th Divisions of General Patton's army played so large a part—and the bitter battle for Catania on the east coast.

The capture of Enna, on July 20, was achieved by the process of catching the city between two relentless arms of pincers. The Canadians kept pounding up from the south while the Americans, who had taken Santa Caterina on the west, drove northeast until they were directly in the rear of Enna. From there a regiment of American infantry dashed into the beleaguered town, already much battered by constant artillery and aërial bombardment.

With the fall of Enna, General Patton proclaimed that the American Army had outstripped the Germans at their own invention of "blitzkrieg." With due allowance made for the vast difference in terrain, the General said that in the first ten days of the Sicilian campaign the Americans had made greater progress than the Germans had done in their sweep through the Low Countries and France in 1940 or even in their overruning of Poland in the fall of 1939.

In those ten days, with the Americans' westward drive and the American-Canadian pounding in the center, the Allies had already taken half the island of Sicily.

The Allied command deliberately turned the floodlight of news on the hitherto shrouded western drive of the American Seventh Army. In three days that force had covered sixty miles. On July 22 it entered empty Marsala, overrunning on the way the enemy's abandoned airfields at Sciacca and Castelvetrano.

After the capture of Castelvetrano, the main body of the force had swung northeast for the Tyrrhenian Sea and Palermo. In one day the city fell to a three-pronged assault from the southwest, the south, and the east.

But Palermo was a prize of the first order. With its airdrome at Bocca di Falco only 175 miles from Naples and 295 miles from Rome, it represented a tremendous threat to the heart of Italy. Its harbor, which was naturally fine, had been extensively improved by the Italians, with a particular view to employing it as a naval base.

The Americans swept east out of Palermo to take Termini Imerese, twenty miles away, without oppositon. The Germans recognized that their only hope lay in the northeastern mountains. So much did they rely on the assistance of nature there that they were rushing in reinforcements. These came by air, descending in parachutes, and by sea; the latter used the small port of Milazzo, fifteen miles west of Messina, which had been rendered almost useless by repeated Allied bombings. But the parachutists found the terrain as inhospitable to them as their commanders hoped it would be to the Allies; they became lost and could not rejoin their lines. Many of them wandered in to give themselves up to the British and Canadians.

From Italy itself, after the fall of Palermo, there came a sudden spate of unbelievable, wild rumors. Returning soldiers had spread a great pall of fear over the country, telling their families and friends of the holocaust from which they had barely escaped in Sicily—warning them that their own turn in Italy was not far off.

News also came through the wall of censorship—news that disturbed the Germans and the "neutrals" in Spain. There were stories that Mussolini's power was all but gone, that the Fascist régime was about to crash in ruins. Twice Rome announced that King Victor Emmanuel would address the nation; twice the speeches were mysteriously postponed. Then once more, on Saturday, July 24, Rome hinted profusely but mysteriously at an "important pronouncement" that might be expected on the Sunday or Monday following.

On Sunday, July 25, the King did not speak. The Italians and Germans alike were racing eastward across the top of Sicily on that day, while the British, in the dust and heat of the Catanian plain, were pounding their tanks into the enemy's line—opening a new drive against the stubborn port that their ships kept bombarding without a let-up. The day passed and night came without anything to justify the almost melodramatic hints that were pouring out of Rome.

ABDICATION OF MUSSOLINI—AND THE FALL OF SICILY

AT eleven o'clock on the night of July 25, 1943, the Rome radio electrified the world. Victor Emmanuel, King of Italy, had demanded the resignation of Premier Benito Mussolini. Il Duce —dictator of Fascism for twenty-one years—had abdicated.

The historic meeting took place in the regal Palazzo Venezia, where the dictator had long ruled with pomp and ceremony. The Fascist Grand Council had been summoned here to discuss the crisis and to hear Il Duce's report of his meeting with Hitler at Verona.

The grim councilors gathered in a scene of splendor. Il Duce, sitting in state at the head of the table, informed them that he and the Fuehrer of Germany had reached a grave decision. Hitler had refused to send more German troops to protect southern Italy from the impending invasion. The battles in Sicily had convinced him that it could not be saved. It had been agreed, therefore, that the entire lower peninsula be abandoned and the German-Italian defense line be established along the Po River and its historic valley. Mussolini confessed that he had been unable to obtain any other alternative. Therefore, he was compelled to advocate the acceptance of Hitler's demand.

The words fell like a death sentence upon the stupefied councilors. For the first time in his rule, Mussolini was faced with dissension in his own cabinet. Alternately cajoling and pleading with them, he watched their stern faces for some sign of approval. Astutely, he suggested due time for consideration. His own friends were in open rebellion. Mussolini had failed them. He was now attempting to retain himself in power without regard for the fate of Italy. A vote was demanded: nineteen of the twenty-five members of the Grand Council refused to accept Mussolini's craven surrender to Hitler. Only six stood by him.

Events followed rapidly. Mussolini sulked in his palace, refusing to accept the decision of his cabinet. The critical situation was laid before King Emmanuel. Shocked by the proposed sacrifice of more than one-half of what remained of his realm, the head of the ancient House of Savoy, with his guards, confronted Il Duce with an ultimatum. He demanded the resignation of Mussolini and the cabinet in which the Premier held most of the portfolios.

Thus came the fateful announcement of his abdication on that night of July 25th. Twenty minutes after the first cryptic statement, the voice of Marshal Pietro Badoglio, a retired warrior seventy-three years of age, was heard: "I have assumed the military government of the country with full powers. The war will continue.... Whoever believes that he can interrupt the normal progress of events or whoever seeks to disturb internal order will be struck down without mercy."

The Italian people, however, were to answer this challenge. The spirit of Garibaldi still lived. Crowds thronged the streets of Italian cities demanding peace. "Take us out of the war," they shouted. "We want peace!" The throngs that had hailed wildly the imposing figure of Mussolini for a generation now cheered his fall. They had had enough of blind subservience—enough suffering and war.

The first night of his new power, Marshal Badoglio made no effort to curb the demonstrations in the capital. In Milan, in the northern industrial region where the working class was celebrating, German soldiers fired on the demonstrations. While Romans were singing in the streets, their Duce was being unceremoniously hurried from his palace into a waiting ambulance. The darkened car bore him out of the city to a suburban villa, where he was put under the strictest guard. His chief subordinates—such men as Ciano, his Foreign Minister, and Carlo Scorza, the Secretary General of the Fascist Party—were put under house arrest.

It must have been a supreme moment for Badoglio. In 1922, when the Fascists marched on Rome, it was he who had begged the king for one division with which to "disperse that rabble." His demand had been refused. Subsequently Marshal Badoglio had made his peace with the new régime and had distinguished himself in its service. He was the conqueror of Ethiopia, a military achievement by a large army with the most modern equipment against native levies armed with spears and outmoded rifles. The Italian campaign against the Greeks in 1941 had been the Marshal's undoing; its ignominious failure had resulted in his being retired by order of Mussolini. After that he had remained in obscurity until the King called him to guide the nation through this newest crisis. At last the Duke of Addis Ababa—this was the title Mussolini had given him after his victory in Ethiopia—was to reap the reward of his lifelong, fanatical loyalty to his king.

The days and weeks that followed were filled with rumor and punctuated by the crash of bombs on Italian soil; Bologna, Genoa, La Spezia, Leghorn, Rome, Naples, Foggia, San Giovanni, and Reggio Calabria rocked and rocked again. The peace clamor that had risen in Rome was quickly stilled by Marshal Badoglio's military government.

In Sicily the enemy's defense of the Etna line, which was being hurriedly fortified in the north, seemed to depend on the speed of the Americans, who had picked up 7,000 more prisoners. These included six generals and an admiral.

When more Germans attempted to enter the fighting area from Italy by air, twenty-one of their big transports were shot into the sea. The German commanders launched a smashing counterattack against the American and Canadian troops in the center of the line. This Axis counterattack, for all its force, was a failure. It slashed great gaps here and there in the Allied line, but it never bent it back.

General Patton once more took the enemy by surprise. He adapted to his own purposes the tactics that General Montgomery had used with such striking successes at the Mareth Line. Montgomery had flanked the enemy on his left, but Patton had only the sea at his left; so he struck from the right. Instead of plunging frontally against San Stefano, he sent his infantry in a swift thrust against Nicosia, the inland anchor of the subsidiary German line, and took the town by storm. With this one blow he imperiled the whole enemy position in the area. At the same time, the Canadians, after four days of heavy battling, stormed into Agira and threw the enemy into even greater jeopardy.

The Germans who had been driven out of Nicosia were now being gradually forced back into the mountains around Troina, closer and closer to the main Etna line. By constant pounding the Americans were forcing the Germans to take shelter in the town itself and the surrounding heights from which they were to have such a bitter fight to dislodge them.

The Gerbini sector was the last flatland of the Catanian plain. From there on the armies were battling in mountains ranging in height from 4,500 to 5,500 feet. These mountains were far worse than any they had encountered in Tunisia. Cut and crisscrossed by crevices and gullies, they made the use of any motorized equipment impossible. Both the Americans and the Canadians had to levy on the inhabitants of the countryside for the mules and carts that alone could negotiate the treacherous narrow trails and paths. The problem of supply was immeasurably increased. Heavy weapons could be moved only after they had been dismantled; they had to be reassembled before they could be used again.

Bloody Ridge, on the road to San Stefano, an almost perpendicular hill, was held in force by the Germans. Their machine guns projected from every ravine and crevice on all sides of the height. The Americans stormed it one hot summer day. The first assault on the hill was thrown back; so was the second. The third attack, made late in the afternoon, finally forced the Germans off the hill, but at high cost. American soldiers fell in the greatest numbers since the start of the campaign.

A new drive along the whole front seemed destined to roll forward without a halt. In a single day the Americans on the coast advanced nine miles, threatening to turn the Germans' whole flank and throwing them back across the San Stefano-Troina road, while the British in the south made a decisive breach in the Catania line. The front, which had been 125 miles long a few days before, was now less than half this length, and the constant pounding of artillery was reducing it daily.

The enemy was beginning to recognize the full significance of his position. He tried to mass ships in the Strait of Messina to evacuate his picked troops and what booty he could transport out of the island. Allied planes and torpedo boats beat an incessant tattoo against their hulls and decks and left them battered hulks.

With the capture of San Stefano, the Americans concentrated their forces before Troina, after a single combat team had tried to take the town alone. They had been sent reeling back by the greatly superior German force strongly located within the mountain town. The Germans had set up in the town and on the surrounding peaks and slopes strong artillery and machine-gun posts that defied the Americans for six days of almost continuous aërial and land bombardment. When at last the town fell, a half-finished letter left by a fleeing German told the whole story of the victory: "The damned Americans fight all day and all night and shoot all the time."

Advance inland from the west had entailed the capture of Gerbini and its complex chain of airdromes. The enemy had already abandoned most of his intricate defensive positions there and the Gerbini area was taken without much loss of life. The fields had suffered badly, not only from Allied bombings but from German demolitions on the eve of the withdrawal, but the Allies were already landing new ground crews when Montgomery's troops overran them. These ground forces were brought in by sea and included Negro troops from British Basutoland, whose debarkation caused considerable uneasiness among Sicilian idlers around the docks where they landed. One of the Sicilians asked a British soldier who these dark-skinned troops were and received the casual reply that they were Ethiopians. A second later there was not a Sicilian to be seen.

The capture of Catania, after three weeks of furious fighting, gained a fine port only fifty-five miles below the Allied goal at Messina, and the use of a modern city of 250,000. Four-fifths of the population had long before fled to the country under the constant assaults of the Allied planes; the remaining 50,000 had found life miserable between constant attack and German rule.

The battle of Troina, as we have said, was a six-day assault in which there was no let-up. It ended at 3:00 A.M. on August 6, one day after the fall of Catania, when an American patrol crept cautiously forward into the rubble that had been Troina. A half-hour later the patrol returned to report that it had found no life. Apparently contact with the enemy had been lost through his withdrawal, but the American commanders were taking no unnecessary risks. They waited for full daylight; as a last precaution, they sent a final wave of dive bombers against the wreckage of the town to flush out the few remaining snipers.

The last thunderous cascade of shells did the job. From the first lines of defense, masses of Germans rose and stumbled forward, their hands high in sign of surrender to the force that had unleashed such a concentrated and unbroken rain of fire and steel. When the Americans entered Troina, they were amazed to see what they had wrought. Virtually the entire population had remained; there had been no place for the people to go. Fortunately for them—and this in part accounted for the duration of the Germans' stand—the whole town was built of stone hewn from the mountains. The town had withstood incredible punishment while its residents cringed in their cellars and listened to the crump of bombs and the scream and smash of shells that burst overhead.

The liberated people were hysterical when they greeted the Americans. Strangely, they bore no malice for the horrors the guns had inflicted on them. Their anger was reserved exclusively for the Germans, and for Mussolini.

While the Americans were completing the reduction and occupation of Troina, the British captors of Belpasso had pushed out to the west to join the Canadians. Together they knifed far into the enemy's positions and swept him out of Biancaville, Adrano, and Bronte. The latter was the little town that King Ferdinand IV of Naples had granted in fee to Lord Nelson in 1800, with the title of Duke of Bronte, and it had continued in the possession of his heirs until this war. This comprehensive gain and the continuing American advance beyond Troina brought the two armies within ten miles of each other and threatened the enemy's one chance to stabilize his whole line.

The Americans now sprang one of the most daring innovations of the campaign, a maneuver that so startled the enemy as to rob him momentarily of the power to resist—an outflanking movement by sea. The enemy held both San Fratello and, on the coast, Sant' Agata di Militello. A battalion of American infantrymen with mobile weapons embarked from a point near Acquedolci in a fleet of landing craft and "ducks," those amphibious vehicles so useful on water and solid ground alike, and sailed several miles northeast until they were well behind Sant' Agata. This was to be the first of many such leapfrogging ventures that played havoc with the enemy. The first wave of Americans landed unopposed, without a sound, while their comrades waited anxiously on the water. A blinker signaled: "Landing unopposed. Come on in." Cautiously the next wave hit the beach and disembarked from the landing craft or drove the "ducks" up on the shore. The men's confidence was increased by the sight of destroyers looming near them in the dark, ready to blast to pieces the first shore defenses that opened up.

Precisely on schedule, while the Americans were landing, their artillery far to the west opened up.

The Germans now on the alert sent their tanks and artillery into action. American armor and guns and crews were more than a match for them. German tanks were set afire in the streets of the town by well-placed shells, while little Italian tankettes were literally crushed by the American machines.

The net was closing on the Germans. The two-pronged advance on Randazzo—by the Americans from the west and the British and Canadians from the southwest—was impeded by a 4,000-foot mountain that lay close to the apex of the triangle formed by Randazzo, Cesaro, and Bronte. The height was so situated between the two roads leading into the junction that its defenders could dominate both. Both forces had to concentrate a goodly portion of their strength and effort against that peak. While they were engaged in its reduction, their supporting air power continued its deadly blows on the German concentrations within Randazzo.

The Allies maintained their advance on both coasts. In the north the Americans pushed toward Cape Orlando, the northern anchor of the enemy's Etna Line, whose eastern or southern anchor had already been torn up when the British captured Catania. These forces, driving on beyond Acireale, reached the little town of Guardia. With its occupation, a great symbol came before the hard-slugging British troops: from the shore of Sicily, at that point, they could see the coast of Italy, visible sign of the incredible progress that the Allies had made in their still young onslaught for the liberation of Europe. Here at last, for the first time since the disastrous spring of 1941, when Greece and Crete fell, the Continent was within sight of an Allied army. This time the army was not leaving it behind but advancing to storm it.

This same shore loomed almost as large in the eyes of the enemy; for him it represented a temporary refuge. A fleet of light ships and barges was engaged in running the almost continuous Allied bombardment of the narrow Strait of Messina. On both sides of the strait, to counter the bombing and strafing, the Germans had posted more than 500 antiaircraft guns, besides the batteries that many of the evacuation craft mounted. The evacuating troops were under the strictest orders to save not only themselves but all their equipment. "The passport to Italy is a gun," a captured German order declared.

As they had done in Libya and Tunisia, the Germans abandoned the Italians—an act that did not tend to increase the Italian will to resist. The few Germans interspersed among them were fanatical. As at Randazzo, their positions and their armament—largely the deadly 88-mm. guns—were excellent and their courage was indisputable. It was their task to hold off the Allies as long as possible, regardless of the sacrifice, while the Germans used every means of crossing the strait. Landing barges, speedboats, big motorized lighters, and even Siebel ferries, which were nothing but large pontoons joined together and equipped with engines that enabled them to tow other craft, were jammed with fleeing soldiers.

The whole enemy line in Sicily at last crumbled before the massed Allied infantry, armor, artillery, air power, and sea strength. On August 13 the Americans seized Cape Orlando; other Americans, with the British and Canadians, swept the foe out of Randazzo; and the Eighth Army pushed closer to Riposto and Taormina.

While Italy was trembling before the growing specter of invasion, the Americans struck another sharp blow at what morale was left in the peninsula. For the second time during the war—and also the second time within a month—they sent their big bombers again over the heart of the country: Rome.

A few hours after the smashing American air blow at Rome, the enemy declared it an "open city." Under international law, this meant that it had been stripped of all military installations and none of its facilities was being used for any military purposes; that there was no defense anywhere within the city. International law required also that, when a city was declared open, an impartial commission of observers must inspect it to ascertain the genuineness of the declaration. The Allies, knowing that both the Germans and their Italian satellites had little regard for truth, did not propose to delay their campaign while a commission was assembled and sent to Rome to see that the city had been demilitarized. They knew that Nazi and Fascist treachery would strain every muscle to remilitarize it; so the declaration was rejected.

The land battles in Sicily were rapidly nearing their end. Loss of Randazzo had not only broken the enemy's lines completely but demoralized his troops.

Messina and the Italian shore were now a scene of chaotic destruction. Boat after boat broke and sank under the steady pounding of the Allied planes.

It was the Americans who were to have the honor of firing the first Allied land artillery shell into Italy. This event occurred on August 16. The artillery unit that sent the shell screaming into Europe had hoped to do so the previous night, but by then it had advanced only far enough to claim the less glamorous credit of hurling the first shell into Messina. Then the 155-mm. "Long Toms" moved up with the rest of the American line, which advanced eighteen miles that day under a constant barrage from the enemy across the strait.

The "Long Toms" had a range of only about five miles. As the American infantrymen slogged ahead, the commander of the "Long Tom" battery kept reconnoitering to find out whether they had pushed far enough to permit his guns to go into action against Italy. At last the point had been reached, within 25,000 yards of the Italian coast at San Giovanni. The lieutenant found a hollow that suited his purpose. It was well hidden from enemy observation. Walls had to be broken through and trees chopped down before the great machine of destruction could be escorted into its chosen position, toward which its towing tractor plunged and twisted like a tank. Then was begun the business of calculating range and wind direction and velocity. The colonel of the artilley regiment, a veteran of the Sicilian campaign from the first day, was watching; he could not resist the temptation to be there and to be first. It was he who pulled the lanyard, at that historic second; the hissing shell, which the Germans called "whispering death," exploded in San Giovanni. The battle of Europe was on!

The night of August 16 was the last of the Sicilian campaign. All that night, under a full moon, the Americans, British, and Canadians streamed east and north, battering down the last half-hearted resistance along the roads and fanning out into woods and hills between the two coasts to mop up any stragglers.

The night was shot through with the red flashes of the Allied heavy guns. Across the narrowing front, troops of the Allied armies were deploying in force. Along the whole advancing line they encountered heavy demolitions. Bulldozers had to be brought up to clear the way, while the engineers hastily constructed temporary bridges to carry not only the men but their heaviest equipment.

It was a little after dawn when the first troops—Patton's men—entered Messina. They found it virtually abandoned by the enemy; only a few snipers remained.

Three hours after the first Americans had crept into Messina, the British entered the city. Like the Americans before them, they were greeted with rousing cheers by the inhabitants.

Messina was a tragic city. Hardly a building of any size had been left intact. The Allies' thorough bombing and shelling of the harbor and the industrial and commercial area had wreaked ruin, yet few of the residents had been victims. Their joy at the arrival of the Allies was tempered only by regret that so many of the Germans had escaped into Italy—almost three divisions.

The battle of Sicily was over. The enemy had lost 167,000 men to the Allies' 25,000. Of the latter, 7,400 were American casualties. The enemy's loss represented more than half the 300,000 men that he had on the island when the Allies landed.

The Sicilian campaign represented a triumph for Allied strategy. "The American army," said Lieutenant General Leslie J. McNair, "came of age in Sicily."

Sicily was also a victory of supply. A month before the campaign was scheduled to begin, General Eisenhower had everything needed, down to the last bullet and the last K-ration for the last man. He told Prime Minister Churchill that he was supported better than any general in history. At the beginning of the campaign, according to his Chief of Staff, Major General Walter B. Smith, the Allies had been outnumbered by one-third. The conquest over this handicap was attributed to planning, coördination, security, surprise, and battle discipline. These lessons had been learned in Africa. Sicily had planted them more firmly in every man's mind, officer and private alike.

One of the most remarkable aspects of the conquest of Sicily was the masterful job in transportation. Rear Admiral Alan G. Kirk, of the United States Navy, was honored for having landed a whole division in Sicily, after having brought it across the Atlantic from America to North Africa and then to Sicily. Not a ship in Admiral Kirk's convoy was lost, although it was under repeated attacks from the air and the enemy's shore batteries.

More than 2,500 ships had sailed for Sicily on paths that covered 1,000 square miles of the Mediterranean in the actual invasion. A. V. Alexander, First Lord of the Admiralty, declared in London: The entire loss in terms of weight was 85,000 tons.

Another sidelight of the campaign was the care of the wounded. The use of air ambulances, begun in Tunisia, was brought to a much higher stage of development in the conquest of Sicily. The U.S.A.A.F. and the R.A.F. pooled their ambulance equipment. In five weeks they transported 15,000 casualties back to Africa without a single loss.

Not the least of the lessons of the conquest of Sicily was political. The island was a natural staging area for the next big blow by the Allies. To assure its maximum utility in this capacity, the Allies had to be certain of internal tranquillity. The AMG reminded their subordinates constantly that in Sicily and Italy they would not be dealing with an enemy country in the sense that they would in Germany. For example, when 2,000 political prisoners were released in Palermo on General Eisenhower's orders, most of them volunteered to join the American army.

In towns where Fascism had taken a greater hold, there was opposition. But the AMG dealt with this resistance in the only way possible: scrupulously impartial trials, with imprisonments when the prisoners were found guilty. To assure the continued functioning of the island's economy, military currency was introduced. Finally, the AMG revised the legal and judicial system solely to implement the revocation of anti-democratic laws and decrees of the Fascist Government and to introduce, as far as possible, the basic principles of law and order to achieve a greater measure of justice.

The conquest of Sicily had been accomplished in thirty-seven days.

BATTLE OF SALERNO

THE first great battle on Italian soil started on the night of September 8, 1943. More than 700 Allied ships, covering 1,000 square miles of the Tyrrhenian Sea, steamed off the shores of Salerno. In this war fleet were ships of the American, British, Dutch, French, and Polish navies.

On the bridge of the flagship stood Admiral Henry K. Hewitt, in charge of all amphibious operations. General Clark was at the alert with his aides in the army operations room below decks, ready to change his plans at a moment's notice if necessary. Above the ships, protecting fighters circled.

There were only three divisions in this first assault force: one was American—the 45th Infantry—and two were British. The 45th was an outfit that was made up largely of men from the Southwest: Texas, Arizona, New Mexico. They were tall, tough fellows, with more than 1,000 Indians among them. All three divisions had been schooled for months by General Clark in the heat of French Morocco and on the shore. The General had the utmost confidence in these men.

As the ships neared the coast they encountered dense mine fields, where the enemy had sown the water with plastic-skinned explosives to prevent their detection by the ships' equipment. More than one vessel was crippled and lost before the beach was reached. It was not yet light when the first wave hit the shore. Among them was a battalion of Japanese-Americans, born in the United States. Every man in the unit was a volunteer; they had spent most of their training clamoring to be sent overseas. Now they and thousands of others had their chance.

The landing craft were racing inshore when the night was split with fire and thunder as American and British battleships, cruisers, and destroyers poured the full strength of their fire power into the shore defenses. It was a holocaust of steel that was to last for days while the troops were consolidating their bitterly contested beachhead. At point-blank range the ships engaged every shore battery at the enemy's command, hurling shell after shell without respite.

The Germans had expected a landing below Rome, at the mouth of the Tiber, but they had not neglected their defenses elsewhere. Only twelve hours before the Fifth Army swarmed ashore, seasoned German troops had relieved the Italians in the whole invasion area. The Germans had come in armed to the teeth. The very first Allied soldier to touch the beach had to fight his way in right from the water's edge.

The Britons and Americans crouched in the damp sand as flares glowed above them and bombs rained down. Close behind the infantrymen had come the barrage-balloon squads. The sausagelike bags were already floating above the troops to protect them from the German planes that swooped down in ever-increasing numbers.

More troops kept pouring ashore. Far at sea, other convoys were racing in with reinforcements. Meanwhile, the invaders were giving their lives for every inch of sand they took. Soon after daybreak the Germans sent their tanks against them. Thus far the Allies had landed little "heavy stuff"; tanks and tank destroyers alike were sorely needed. At one sector of the American part of the beachhead a gun crew of five men was hauling its piece up a road that led from the shore when they ran into a squad of thirteen German Mark VI tanks. The Americans were alone, and their commander was an eighteen-year-old lieutenant, John Whitaker, of Fort Worth, Texas.

The boy had the courage and the coolness of a seasoned warrior. He deployed his little squad and resolved to hold out to the end. They manned their gun for hours, despite the cannon and machine-gun fire that was poured upon them from the enemy tanks and from enemy positions on every side. Young Whitaker tried to keep his men in check, for they were coldly angry and unheeding of consequences. But one lad, his courage greater than his foresight, rushed out from his shelter to tackle an advancing iron monster with only a tommy gun. He could not have hoped to scratch the giant machine but he was trying to protect his pals. He died trading bullets with the tank.

Whitaker and his men were husbanding their ammunition and strength, hoping that some real antitank strength would come to support them. When they had begun to believe that it would never arrive, it finally came. The reinforcements found that Whitaker's boys had knocked out three German tanks and so badly damaged a number of others that they could not fight off the augmented American force.

On that same first day Sgt. Manuel S. Gonzales, of Fort Davis, Texas, earned his Distinguished Service Cross within an hour after going ashore in Italy. His unit was pinned down almost from the first by artillery, machine guns, and small arms. The nearest enemy post was armed with four machine guns and a mortar. Gonzales slung his Browning automatic rifle over his shoulder, loosening his pistol, and started to crawl toward the German lines. "I had so many hand grenades with me," he said later, "that, as I look back on it, I wonder I could move at all." A German grenade burst beside him as he crawled. Its steel gored his back and his left hand and arm, but he did not stop until he had reached the German position. When he came crawling back to his outfit, the mortars and machine guns were silenced.

The first day of the attack—September 9—the Allies succeeded, despite all opposition, in establishing several disconnected beachheads. The next day, while the big American and British ships poured shell after shell into the enemy land positions, demolishing the last of the coastal defenses, the German troops struck the first of five punishing blows. The Anglo-American lines held; the Germans retired to try again, keeping up a barrage of artillery and mortar fire.

The Germans made four more attempts that day to throw the Allies off the beaches. They failed every time. The Allies, backed up by the heavy guns of the warships, threw the enemy out of Salerno, only to lose the city again. Thus the battle seesawed for several days, until, on September 14, the enemy made his greatest effort.

This effort of the Germans was destined to fail, but it came perilously close to success. Part of the reason for its failure was due to the fact that among the Allies were dauntless men. Typical of these was Corporal Charles Kelly, of Pittsburgh, or, as his comrades and the whole Fifth Army called him after September 13, "Commando Kelly, the one-man army." The twenty-three-year-old corporal was a volunteer in a patrol that set out from a position near Altavilla, about twenty miles southeast of Salerno, to spot and destroy enemy machine-gun posts. In the course of this mission Kelly offered to establish contact with an infantry battalion that was supposed to be on a hill a mile away. But it wasn't there; instead, the hill was occupied by well-organized German troops. Kelly learned this after he had crawled there under constant enemy sniper, mortar, and artillery fire. So "Commando" offered to join another group chasing down machine-gun posts and kept on until he had run out of ammunition. When he went to an ammunition dump to replenish his supplies, he found the Germans attacking.

The Germans far outnumbered the little American garrison, and the sergeant in command ordered the evacuation of the storehouse. Kelly offered to stay behind and cover the flight of the other boys. There he stood, firing a bazooka through another window until every man had left. Then Kelly followed, cautiously. On his way down a hill he spotted an abandoned 37-mm. antitank gun, complete with ammunition. As long as the shells lasted, he lobbed them at the Germans.

On September 14 the Germans made their strongest and last attempt to smash the Fifth Army's invasion. New tank tactics employed by the enemy, who used his metal monsters in small groups assisted by armored-car units, gave the drive an initial impetus that carried it within a mile of the sea in the triangle formed by the junction of the Sele and Calore Rivers northwest of Altavilla. The first assault was mounted at dusk on September 13, and it gained in intensity throughout the night as American and British troops stood shoulder to shoulder in the brilliant moonlight that flooded the battlefield.

As the Germans ground ahead, the Allied naval power entered the battle. Offshore stood the U.S.S. *Boise,* with other cruisers and those two gallant queens of the Royal Navy, the battleships *Warspite* and *Valiant.* Throughout the night their shells added to the pandemonium of noise and carnage while the troops hit back stubbornly at the counterattacking enemy. Confident that they had broken the back of the landings, and their own forces far more shattered by the Allied land, naval, and aërial resistance than the invaders realized, the Germans had exhausted themselves. They had beaten in vain against a wall of British troops and against the American 45th Division that, after having been ground back for a time, had at last taken root and turned immovable. The Thunderbirds (the division's emblem was the totemistic Indian bird) beat the Germans by a combination of grit and wit. The 45th, which was sent inland to relieve the pressure on the flank of the 36th Division, which had been landed later, pushed up between the Sele and Calore Rivers without much trouble, for the Germans had planned a trap. When one regiment of the 45th had reached Persano, the Germans sprang their trap and apparently cut it off.

The 45th's commander then sent another regiment—or what there was of it, amounting to two battalions—up the north bank of the Sele to flank Persano. The Germans did not have the faintest idea of this force's strength; they knew only that another American outfit had been hurled at them. So they retired to gather for a fresh assault. The trapped regiment scurried back to its place in the beachhead line.

The fighting was still fierce at noon of September 14. Suddenly the tall lean figure of General Clark again appeared at the front-line command post, where divisional commanders were directing the battle. "Now there is no falling back," the General said quietly. "If you go back any more, we won't have a beachhead."

The Germans were trumpeting arrogantly from Berlin that they had smashed the beachhead and won the Battle of Salerno. They said it was another Dunkirk. They boasted that the Allies had massed their ships to carry away what was left of the defeated invaders, and the beachhead was no more. This was a tune that the Germans were to change a day later. That great fleet had come not to evacuate the conquered but to land fresh swarms of conquerors.

Salerno was a triumph not only of courage but of skill. The joint Allied command had met the crisis, the worst since the invasion of North Africa nearly a year before, with great efficiency. Army, navy, and air force had worked as one, and the enemy had been powerless to resist their united might. On that critical day of September 14 alone, more than 2,000 sorties were made over the battle area.

Only a day after the crisis, American Army nurses went ashore on the beachhead, their uniforms topped by regulation steel helmets.

At last the American and British troops had time to chuckle. In the height of the battle, Benito Mussolini had been "rescued" by the Germans from his prison north of Rome, to which the Badoglio Government had sent him. It was not much of a prison, for he was kept in the Gran Sasso Hotel at Lake Bracciano, under an armed guard. As in a comic opera, a German plane landed beside the place, soon followed by others. Heavily armed men tumbled out and overpowered the Italian guards, while other Germans floated down in parachutes. In a short time the hotel was surrounded by machine gunners. Two hours later Mussolini was in Rome; the next day he was in Munich.

Salerno itself was now permanently cleared of Germans, and the Fifth Army overran the Sorrentine Peninsula to the northwest, liberating the lovely town of Amalfi and many another beautiful resort on the Tyrrhenian coast. For the first time the Allies had a continuous, unbroken front from one coast of Italy to the other.

The next goal was Naples. Before the reduction of one of Italy's greatest harbors the Allies were determined to reduce the threat to their flank, embodied by the enemy's possession of the Italian island of Sardinia and, just to the north, the French island of Corsica in the Tyrrhenian Sea. Both islands contained a number of extremely good airdromes from which the enemy could harry and materially hamper the Allied advances in Italy, as well as ports from which his surface raiders could cut into the Allies' shipping.

On September 19 the two Italian divisions in Sardinia, aided by units of their fleet and some Allied strength, rose up against the German garrison and drove it from the island.

In Corsica the French population, long chafing against Italian and German rule, had at last received from their Government in Algiers the orders they had so long awaited, and they seized Ajaccio, the island's capital, at the same time the Italians were rising in Sardinia.

The fighting was hardly a week old when General Henri-Honoré Giraud toured the liberated part of the island and returned to Algiers with the optimistic forecast that the island would be completely free within ten days. The Germans were fighting hard to keep their last foothold on Corsica, but the eighty thousand Italian troops on the island had laid down their arms to the French.

Resistance grew more fierce in direct ratio to the Allied gains. On October 5 the liberation of Corsica was officially declared to be complete. The last of the German garrison that had escaped death and capture had fled to the island of Elba and the Italian port of Leghorn.

It was the Corsicans and the Sardinians who helped to break the flank and remove the menace that enabled the Allies to march on into central and northern Italy. With the loss of these islands, and danger removed from their backs, the Allies could now fight their way along the roads from Salerno to Naples.

FALL OF NAPLES—FIERCE FIGHTING ALONG THE VOLTURNO

THE land of the Cæsars was now to become one of the bloodiest battlegrounds in all history. In twenty months nearly 110,000 men in the American Fifth Army alone were killed, wounded, or missing, while the German losses were near 500,000.

The Allies lashed out on a forty-mile front in the second phase of the Battle of Italy, on September 21, 1943, attacking from the tip of the Sorrentine Peninsula to a point well east of Salerno. Artillery preceded the infantry and armored assault, which fanned out east of Mt. Vesuvius, the famous volcano that compressed the Naples-Salerno coastal road into a narrow defile. The first objective was Avellino, an important railway and road junction twenty-five miles east of Naples.

The main obstacle to the Fifth Army's advance was a vicious mountainous terrain. Before the mountains lay a narrow valley that paralleled, on either side, the small Sarno River; there the Germans made an abortive stand while their artillery traded blows with the Allies' big guns.

Eagerness of the American troops to capture Naples was accentuated by refugees who reported that besides sacking the city the Germans were killing its residents in wanton butchery, machine-gunning women and children. Italian soldiers and civilians were being forced into slave-labor battalions to dig defenses, with death as the penalty for refusal.

Ninety miles to the east, the Eighth Army was putting on a sudden burst of speed and strength. Until it was near the outskirts of the great railway junction and airport of Foggia, it had met little opposition aside from mines; but, as the peril to the city grew, the Germans came out and fought. The impetus of the twenty-four-mile thrust that carried the British into Foggia was so great that the relatively small forces left to defend Foggia could not stand before it. On the threshold of one of his most prized possessions in Italy the enemy was overwhelmed. Foggia had a chain of airfields that gave to its possessor a vast aërial circle of domination that included not only Italy and the Mediterranean but Africa, southern France, lower Germany, Austria, and the Balkans.

On the Naples sector, however, the enemy's resistance continued to be fierce. Allied warships moved up into the Gulf to be ready to lend a hand to the army and air force in the final reduction of the city. Aboard one of the ships was Colonel Frank Knox, the American Secretary of the Navy, who utilized his tour of the Mediterranean theater to see for himself how the combined navies of a half-dozen nations were coöperating in the common cause.

On September 28, the American and British troops burst their mountain bonds with a great assault that carried them down to the northern shore of the Sorrentine Peninsula and out into the empty plain of Naples. The Germans' expectation of a flanking movement was fulfilled when the Allies overran Avellino; but they had not altogether reckoned with the danger of a drive up the narrow coastal defile to the west of Vesuvius. American troops and armor rolled along the highway in a steady stream, while even greater numbers swarmed past the volcano on its eastern side. On the ocean side, Sorento and Castellammare di Stabbia—the latter an important naval base—fell to the onrushing Americans, and the inland towns were swiftly captured.

In the harbor of Valletta, as the Fifth and Eighth Armies pounded their way up the Italian peninsula, General Eisenhower was maintaining a temporary headquarters aboard H.M.S. *Nelson,* the great British battleship. There he received Premier Badoglio of Italy, who had set up a temporary capital in Bari, on the Adriatic, after his escape from Rome. Aboard the giant British man-of-war, the Kansan farm boy laid down his plans before the aristocratic Italian field marshal and head of state—not for approval but for obedience.

As American and British troops streamed past on both sides of the grim volcano of Vesuvius, the Germans began to speed their last units from Naples, leaving only rear guards to cover the removal of large bodies of troops with heavy equipment. Roads northward toward Rome were black with big trucks, self-propelled guns, and clanking tanks above which Allied planes streamed endlessly, sowing havoc.

Not the least of the factors accelerating the enemy's evacuation was the sudden upsurge of revolt among the people of the great harbor city. Italian citizenry were storming the Piazza Dante. Though the Germans had ordered the people of Naples to surrender all their arms, few had complied. Instead, they came from outlying districts as if drawn by some lodestone, and unleashed their true feelings toward the Germans.

Hospitals of Naples were crowded with dead and wounded children and adults. The German remnants entrenched themselves solidly in the city and laid down a horrendous fire with tanks, artillery, and machine guns. American and British soldiers rolled in, their entry signaled by the crackle of rifle and machine-gun fire ahead of them, as the Italians were still battling the last of the Germans who remained inside the city.

Neapolitans were hysterical with joy over the arrival of the Allies. The triumphant liberating troops were showered with flowers and fruit and foods that the people could ill afford to give away. Voices of thousands rose in cheer after cheer for President Roosevelt, Prime

Minister Churchill, and King George. Not a few shouted their praise for the Red Army and Marshal Stalin.

The capture of Naples was ahead of the Allies' time-table; they had beaten their schedule by four days. General Clark wrote to his wife that he would give her the capture of the city as a present for her birthday, October 5, adding in the same letter pages of glowing praise for the gallantry and stamina of his troops. Now the birthday present was delivered four days early.

It was a tragic sight the Allies had before them when they surveyed the fruits of their victory, while advance units pushed on beyond the city toward Capua in pursuit of the fleeing enemy. The once-proud harbor was a shambles, augmented by the explosion of a German ammunition ship hit by an American bomb. As if to wreak vengeance on the Italians for their surrender, the Germans had been barbarously wanton in their destruction of places of no military importance, giving evidence once more of their hatred for all culture.

The University of Naples was put to the torch; the famous aquarium was ruined. The San Carlo Opera House was gutted by a deliberately set fire. Hundreds of shrines were pillaged. In the Royal Society of Naples, the Germans methodically destroyed 200,000 books by soaking each one—including many priceless and irreplaceable treasures—in gasoline and then firing the lot with hand grenades. The Royal Palace was destroyed, with the same methodical tactics, and many churches were desecrated.

The task of reconstruction, which awaited the Allied Military Government, was to be augmented by the booby traps which the Germans had hidden in many of the buildings. One gigantic charge, weighing 1,500 pounds, was placed in the very hotel that General Clark chose as his headquarters. This was not a single explosive; it was concealed in a series of packing cases that were wired together, so that the detonation of any one would have immediately discharged all the rest and reduced the hotel to rubble. The slightest touch by an unwarned stranger would have been sufficient to set off the inferno. Italian civilians, who knew of the concealed explosives, warned the Allies in time; and American engineers removed the whole deadly device.

Naples was the biggest problem the AMG had so far encountered. For two days its officials surveyed the difficulties confronting them in this big city now without food, water, or the most elementary facilities of a modern community. They turned their attention first to bringing in food, restoring the water supply, and giving the city the electric power needed to put it in running order again. With the first shipments of food came medicines—not only preventive medicines to forestall the possibility of epidemics, but drugs to cure such diseases as already existed among the underfed inhabitants. Pending investigation, most of the city's Italian officials, except the most flagrant collaborators who had not fled with the Germans, were retained in office under the control of the AMG whose regional commissioner for the Naples area was Lieut. Colonel Charles Poletti, formerly Governor of New York.

On the Adriatic, the British leapfrogged the foe once more, this time to land in Termoli, on a line well to the north of Rome. At the same time, the enemy's defense of Italy was further weakened by a strong thrust by Yugoslav Partisans in the general area of the Italian-Austrian-Yugoslav frontiers, pinning down a considerable force of Marshal Rommel's troops in northern Italy and thus depriving his colleague in the south, Marshal Kesselring, of their strength.

A little more than a week after the fall of Naples, the Fifth Army found itself on the southern bank of the Volturno and plunged into Capua. Here all the scenes of the capture of Naples were repeated; the patriots' battles with the Germans, the enemy's demolitions and pillage, and the jubilant welcome to the liberating soldiers of the west. Stricken with fear, the puppet Italian "government" that the Germans had set up in Rome with Mussolini as its absentee Premier hurriedly shifted its seat far to the north, in Verona.

But in their steady march northward the Allies were fighting nature as much as enemy soldiers. When the rains came, the invaders were compelled to slacken their pace, and the enemy exploited every break in the weather to strengthen a new line of defenses behind the Volturno—the famous Gustav Line that was to have as its hub the fiercely contested town of Cassino.

It was at this time that the Italian Government under Marshal Badoglio took the final step to line itself up beside the Allies; it formally declared war on Germany on October 12, 1943 (Columbus Day) and received from the Allies the status of a cobelligerent. This change was largely a paper one; Italy continued to be ruled by the AMG and the Allied Control Commission set up by the Italian Advisory Council —a group composed of representatives of the United States, Britain, Russia, France, Greece, and Yugoslavia. The Control Commission worked through the Italian Government, which was nominally independent but could do nothing without the Commission's approval.

Throughout the land fighting, the Allies' heaviest bombers were concentrated on the industrial cities of northern Italy and the highways and railroads leading from Germany to the battle areas. In this continuing assault, which was to go on throughout the whole Italian campaign, they had the assistance of the American and British "heavies" based in Britain, which were later to make shuttle flights a regular part of their activity. They would take off from Britain, bomb northern Italy, and land at Foggia or in North Africa to refuel and reload; bomb the cities again on their northward journey and return to Britain.

Known also as the Winter Line, the Gustav fortifications were for some time a subject of ridicule to the Allies' soldiers and officers; and even the omniscient war correspondents scoffed at its existence. But it was real and it was strong, as the lives of many American and British soldiers were to demonstrate. Its long-maintained function of stalemating the Allies was to point up the true significance of the whole Italian campaign. From the Allies' point of view this was primarily a giant holding operation—probably the greatest in the thousands of years that men have waged wars. The invasion of Italy, in other words, was undertaken to immobilize as many German troops as possible and to divert the German High Command's attention to the maximum extent from the Allies' real objective—the invasion of western Europe.

Behind the Gustav Line a strange "ghost army" was haunting the Germans' night. A motley group of unofficial guerrillas living on the land, it was composed of American, British, Australian, and Indian troops who had been captured in Africa, Sicily, and Italy. Imprisoned in northern and central Italy, they had at last escaped and taken refuge in the hills and woods of the Abruzzi. There the fugitives had been brought together by friendly Italian peasants, who had also added many of their own number to their ranks. In addition, there were thousands of Italian officers and soldiers who had deserted the Germans and the "Fascist Republicans." All these forces joined; they stole arms from the Germans, begged old guns from the peasants, and captured fresh weapons from isolated parties of German scouts that they waylaid. Thus equipped, and growing stronger, they engaged in hundreds of hit-and-run forays by night to smash German outposts, sabotage communications, and, in general, harry the foe in every way possible.

The Allied armies before the Gustav Line, however, could expect but little aid from these "ghost armies." The battle-hardened veterans of the Fifth and Eighth Armies faced not only the Gustav Line itself but heavily fortified outposts well in advance of it: the major ones were Venafro in the Fifth Army's sector; Isernia and Alfedena in the center (where the Eighth Army was soon to deploy a considerable portion of its forces) and Atessa, near the Adriatic.

The Eighth Army struck directly for Isernia, attacking across the Apennine peaks and valleys in the pitch-darkness of a November night. Artillery flamed and roared through the inky blackness for hours, covering the indomitable advance of the British troops. At 3 o'clock on the morning of November 4, the vital junction town had fallen. With its capture the British cut the last trans-peninsular road in south-central Italy, thus effectively driving a wedge between the two ends of the Gustav Line, and dominating the main highway to Rome.

On both ends of the front, in the Fifth and Eighth Armies, they stormed onward. On the west, ignoring the Germans flooding the countryside by damming up streams, the Fifth Army reached the Garigliano itself; on the east, the Eighth swept into Vasto and beyond.

Several of the strongest points of the Gustav Line were now in various degrees of peril. In the outskirts of Mignano the Allies threatened to cut the vital Casiline Way—National Highway 6—that led to Rome. At Isernia they had already cut another road.

As the weather held the Allies in their positions, the Germans increased their counterattacks, but even on days when as many as nine blows were launched at the same position the enemy could not dislodge the tenacious fighters. Seized written orders from the German High Command demonstrated how vital the enemy considered the maintenance of his line—it must be held for at least eight weeks.

On the Eighth Army's front the greatest progress continued near the shore of the Adriatic, where the British established a bridgehead across the Sangro River that was to prove the entering wedge to the destruction of the eastern portion of the Gustav Line. Thanksgiving came and in the Fifth Army every doughboy got turkey and all the trimmings, regardless of where he was; but most of them ate their dinners with one hand on a rifle.

The Fifth Army line gradually advanced on both sides of Mignano until only that town remained in the Germans' possession, while the Allies enfolded it on both sides and pushed on. Besides Mignano, the major obstacle to the Fifth Army was the mass of heights formed by Mt. Camino and Mt. Maggiore, contiguous, multiple-peaked mountains ranging to 5,000 feet of almost sheer walls rather than slopes. There was hardly even a path to the top and every move had to be made with infinite caution, not only because of the enemy's guns on higher positions but because of the natural dangers of the terrain.

The Allies attempted to reduce enemy positions by concentrated low-level bombing, but the method was only partly effective. While the explosions often caused landslides that blocked or crushed the Germans' positions, the avalanches as often created new obstacles for the infantry and artillery to overcome. Supply was a major difficulty, for no mechanized vehicle could negotiate the steep, jagged hills. Only mules could carry the burden, and often they were unable to make the full climbs and the troops themselves had to lug disassembled artillery, ammunition, and other materials, under constant fire.

The Americans' first hard-won grip on Mt. Camino was dislodged by a series of determined German counterattacks. Driven back to the lowlands, the Americans regrouped and reorganized, preparing for a new assault. The Eighth Army was driving steadily forward not only on the east but in the center, already formulating a threat to flank the main portion of the Gustav Line. This of necessity diverted the enemy, and the Americans, in a new and skilful lunge, regained Mt. Camino.

Ground troops found their pace slowed as they neared Cassino and Pescara, despite all the aërial assistance at their command. Flame-throwing tanks were hurled against them in such flatland as they encountered between mountains; and, behind the belching monsters, the German infantry and artillery stood like steel that would not flex. On the mountains, the enemy fortified the natural caves and blasted new ones for defense, fighting from them literally to the last man.

In the midst of the mountain fighting the Italian troops, newly activated as "cobelligerents," went into the line for the first time. Eager to redeem themselves, they attacked a German hill position with a complete disregard for safety, fighting with great dash and courage.

Momentarily, the drives on both Pescara and Cassino were stalled by fierce countertattacks. Raiding parties of patrols were unable to do more than destroy an occasional small position, capture a few prisoners for such information as they could or would give, and return to their own lines. In such forays American ingenuity again showed its value. Generally, it was the custom to reduce pillboxes by grenade fire from extremely close range. But some American troops turned to that invaluable antitank weapon, the rocket-launching "bazooka." At a hundred yards it could be depended on for accuracy, so, instead of saving it for tanks, they directed its fire on pillboxes and found that one missile from a bazooka was enough to reduce the strongest. The patrols found, too, that the Germans' worst fear was the Indians of the American 45th Division—who, they were sure, would scalp them alive.

Only the largest-scale maps could show the daily gains of the Fifth Army. The Eighth, making better progress, was soon battling the Germans in the streets of Ortona, a town that was not long in falling to the Allies. Meanwhile the Fifth Army was paying heavily for its little advances, though its ranks were filled with heroes. One of these was a chaplain, the Rev. Stanley J. Kusman of Chaminade College in Clayton, Mo., where he taught psychology, a field in which he had gained a high reputation. In the battle area he acquired new laurels. Hearing that one sector lacked a chaplain and numbers of fallen soldiers could not get decent burial, he volunteered to go out into the no man's land between the lines. Daring constant enemy fire, he brought in on his shoulders the bodies of fifty-seven American and British soldiers, refusing to accept any help.

The Fifth Army was now at the gates of Cassino, that vital town that meant so much to both armies. Its components of Americans, Britons, Frenchmen, and Italians had battled their way against terrific odds and seemingly insuperable natural handicaps. General Eisenhower, visiting the front, declared that the campaign in Italy had given the Allies the invaluable harbor of Naples and the airport of Foggia, from which they could bomb all southern Europe.

ITALY SURRENDERS—
FIRST AXIS POWER TO COLLAPSE

THE collapse of Italy had been imminent since the fall of Sicily and the abdication of Mussolini. After forty days under Prime Minister Badoglio—forty days of Italian uprisings demanding peace—Italy surrendered unconditionally on September 3, 1943.

The first Axis power to be knocked out of the war fell on the day the first Allied troops were landing on the soil of the Italian mainland and the continent of Europe. King Victor Emmanuel and General Badoglio, having lost their African empire and being now face to face with destruction at home, were trying to save the last remnants of former glory.

Three days after the Badoglio cabinet assumed power, Badoglio began to send out peace feelers to American and British diplomats in the neutral territory of Vatican City. It was evident that his intentions were to parley for "honorable capitulation" and avoid "unconditional surrender." Through protracted negotiations, he seemed to be sparring for time to avoid a direct break with the Germans. While this was a natural desire of the Italian Government, it was a dangerous game that was to have its repercussions.

To strengthen his hand, Badoglio ordered the recall of all Italian troops in France, four divisions, and the twenty-two divisions in the Balkans, to bolster up his defenses in Italy; at the same time he proclaimed that he would remain in the war as an ally of Germany. The people demanded that he take them "out of the war immediately." The Germans, anticipating the crisis, poured heavy reinforcements into northern Italy, until there were twenty-six divisions between the Brenner Pass and the Po.

The press began to warn openly of armed revolt unless peace were quickly achieved. While the Allied leaders were meeting in Quebec and the German and Italian Foreign Ministers were conferring in northern Italy (instead of Rome, where they had originally planned to meet), the Allies made their second air attack on the Italian capital. When the Pope toured the bombed areas, the people of Rome crowded the streets to beseech him to bring them peace.

The Allies, massed in Sicily waiting the command to cross the Strait of Messina and invade Italy, sent their warnings to the hesitating Badoglio Government through two of the most famous battleships of the Royal Navy. Accompanied by a cruiser and nine destroyers, H.M.S.

Rodney and *Nelson* steamed almost under the noses of the Italian coastal guns at Reggio Calabria and Cape Pellaro to pour shells into the mainland.

On September 1 and 2 the Allies intensified their harrowing aërial attacks. Planes based in North Africa and Sicily ranged from the southern tip of the peninsula to Bologna, Trento, and Bolzano, a city only thirty-five miles from the historic Brenner Pass.

Great bodies of troops and innumerable landing craft were being massed at and around the beaches north of Messina, where the strait was narrowest. The Allies struck their first direct blow at the continent of Europe from that sandy shore. The date they chose was a historic one: September 3, 1943, the fourth anniversary of the English declaration of war with Germany.

An hour before the peasants of Calabria expected day to break, the sky burst into flame in the west. Almost immediately, from the same direction, the air was split by a roll of thunder that seemed endless.

This was the famous overture to a British Eighth Army attack, a barrage that made the cannonading of El Alamein pale in comparison. The Eighth Army had been chosen to strike the first blow on European soil. For half of its members—Frenchmen, Poles, Greeks—the first step on the soil of Italy was a step toward home and freedom.

The barrage was at its height when hundreds of planes roared out of Sicilian airfields to blanket the narrow strait and the land beyond. Only a few stars gleamed as the guns began to roar and the fires began to glow in Italy, augmented by the bombs that crumped into the hilly country rising beyond the shore. It was still dark when the first troops clambered into their boats and the first "ducks" drove down the Sicilian beaches. As these boats grated on the shore of Italy and these "ducks" touched their wheels to the sands of Italy, dawn began to lighten the peaks of the Calabrian hills.

Machine guns chattered an *aubade* from scattered pillboxes; Bren guns answered briefly; then there was silence on the Italian shore, save when a shell exploded or a bomb burst far inland. The silence lasted only a moment. Men tumbling from the boats and others advancing, guns in hand, farther in on the beach began to shout exultantly. The invasion of Europe was on at last!

Italian soldiers who had been left to man the coastal defenses began to straggle out of their pillboxes, hands in the air and words of surrender on their lips. Not another shot was fired by the invaders or the quondam defenders. The British went to work to establish their beachheads and pour in their supplies.

Those who had landed first were soon outnumbered by a force that poured down from the hills. It was not a hostile force, however; it was the Italian rear guard that had taken refuge in the high ground and was coming down now to surrender to the Allies. On all the beaches where the Eighth Army disembarked the same scenes were repeated. Every town was practically deserted. Cautious troops fired a few bursts here and there, but there was no answering fire.

On the very day of the first landing, Italy signed an armistice with the United Nations. The victors had reserved the right to announce the fact at the moment they judged most favorable to themselves. This time arrived on September 8, in the first hours of dusk, as a new and powerful Allied army was at sea only a few hours off the coast of central Italy to strike the real invasion blow.

At 6:30 P.M. on that day, the Allied Commander in Chief in the Mediterranean Theater, General Eisenhower, stood before a microphone of the powerful United Nations radio in Algiers. He told the Italians, his own troops, and the world that as of that moment hostilities between the Allies and Italy were at an end. The first of the enemy nations had been knocked out of the war!

After General Eisenhower's announcement, the radio sent forth two vital messages. The first, signed by Admiral Sir Andrew Browne Cunningham, the Allied naval commander in the theater, was addressed to the Italian fleet and merchant navy. It directed every unit afloat to steam for the nearest harbor held by the Allies or, if it could not make such safety, at least to thwart the German plans for seizure by taking refuge in a neutral port. Precise instructions were given as to recognition signals, preferred harbors, and so forth. The Italians were assured that the Mediterranean waters were alive with Allied ships waiting to receive them and guard their passage.

The second message from Algiers was directed to the people of Italy. It was equally precise in its instructions: The Italians were ordered to give every assistance to Allied troops and to do nothing to help the Germans. Transport workers were urged to render active aid to the Allies by sabotaging the movement of every German vehicle on land, on the sea, and in the air. The message said: "Italy now has the opportunity of taking vengeance on the German oppressor and of aiding in the expulsion of the internal enemy from Italian soil."

From Cairo, too, stirring words rang over the air as the Allied supreme commander there, Lieutenant General Sir Henry Maitland Wilson, issued orders for the Italian military forces stationed outside Italy —in the Balkans and the Ægean Sea. Every aircraft was directed to an Allied base; every Italian soldier was forbidden from that moment to commit a single act of hostility against the people of the country where he was stationed. Troops whose situation permitted were instructed to return to Italy without laying down their arms to the Germans; those who were in a position to fight, as in the Dodecanese, were ordered to take possession of the territories for the Allies.

In Rome, Marshal Badoglio stepped to a microphone and told his countrymen that he had "yielded to the overwhelming power of the enemy with the object of avoiding further and more grievous harm to the nation." He ordered his troops to cease all hostilities against the Allies, but to "oppose attack from any other quarter." In Rome and Naples the Italian people went wild with joy.

The armistice had actually been signed five days earlier. The Italian Government, after all its pleas for peace, had balked time and again at the Allied terms and refused to sign. General Eisenhower had given Marshal Badoglio a twenty-four-hour ultimatum. This gave the Allies time to launch their attack on Calabria while the Italians were still haggling. Thus it was that Allied troops had been on Italian soil for nearly twelve hours on September 3 when the Italian representative negotiating with the Allies at last put his name to the document.

While Badoglio in Rome pondered and conferred with his king, the Allies were aligned to cross the Strait of Messina. Marshal Badoglio was not long ignorant of this. He must have known, too, that the Allies were on the sea in a giant armada bearing down on the western shore below Naples. He could not fight both the Allies and the Germans. In the end he had to give in; and so, sometime before the ultimatum expired, he sent his complete surrender to General Eisenhower "by secret methods of communication." On the afternoon of the next day, while General Montgomery's men were streaming ashore in his country, General Castellano picked up a pen and signed the document of unconditional surrender.

The final ceremony was simple. In a room of the Allied Headquarters in Sicily, a half dozen men sat or stood: one was Italian, the rest were Americans and Britons. None was of lower rank than brigadier general. The Italian General Castellano, the long tension at an end, signed his name for his country. An American, Major General Walter B. Smith, chief of staff to General Eisenhower, placed his signature on the historic document as the representative of not only his own country but all the Allies: England, Russia, and all the Mediterranean countries that were among the United Nations.

The austere ritual represented the climax of months of mystery-story intrigue and, on the part of Italy, unhappy vacillation. It was from Rome that the first move came through neutral sources. A secret delegation made its way from Rome to Lisbon in neutral Portugal after British representatives in two neutral countries had been approached by Italian diplomats who frankly confessed that the situation at home was "desperate." The British said simply that President Roosevelt's and Prime Minister Churchill's terms of "unconditional surrender" still stood.

When the surrender came, the Italians had seven battleships, three of them new, and one being built. Of the seven, one had been sunk in the British torpedo-plane attack on Taranto in 1940 and, although she had been refloated, she was generally considered useless for warfare. Italy also had a score of light and heavy cruisers, fifty destroyers, and about as many submarines, besides a great number of smaller craft. These ships were variously distributed among bases at Taranto, Pola, and Trieste on the Adriatic, La Spezia and Genoa at the head of the Ligurian Sea, and Sardinia. In various heavy attacks by Allied planes, a number of other cruisers had been sunk or badly crippled. What was left of the fleet now came forth—some units for the first time in a year or more—to surrender to the Allies.

It was eminently fitting that the ceremony of the fleet's surrender should be held in the harbor of Valletta, the capital of the little island of Malta, which had suffered so long and so severely while Italy was still an effective enemy base. As one of the biggest groups of the Italian fleet steamed in, a British destroyer lay in the roadstead. On her bridge stood General Eisenhower and Admiral Cunningham, watching silently but no less triumphantly as the British battleships *Warspite* and *Valiant* led the defeated enemy into port.

The liberation of Italy from the German armies that now held it in their grasp was the stupendous job that confronted the Allies. While the last scenes of the drama of Italy's surrender were being enacted, and while General Eisenhower was announcing to the world the enemy's surrender, the Fifth Army, under Lieutenant General Mark W. Clark, was only a few hours off the beaches of Salerno. The Eighth Army was sweeping ahead unchecked in southern Italy. Montgomery landed another force at Taranto after the surrender and started a drive up the east coast as swift as the main group's drive on the western shore.

Only a few hours before the armistice announcement, Flying Fortresses bombed the Roman suburb of Frascati, destroying the German headquarters, and the Germans were certain that the capital's area would be the next invasion target. Hastily they garrisoned the city and seized control as the King, Premier Badoglio, and most of the Government scurried hastily out of the city and headed south. The Germans' guess was not too far wrong, for General Eisenhower had indeed planned to send an airborne division into Rome when the surrender was announced to seize the capital for the Allies. Reliable reports indicated that the German garrisons not far north of the capital were sufficiently strong to wipe out such a force; a larger one could not then be spared. So the Allied commander concentrated his effort on the twenty-mile strip of beach that centered on Salerno.

At Salerno was to be fought the battle that gave the Allies their first foothold on the Continent.

CRUCIAL BATTLES AT CASSINO AND ANZIO

ON the eve of crucial battles on the Italian front world-stirring events were taking place. President Roosevelt, Prime Minister Churchill, and General Chiang Kai-shek of China, met in conference at Cairo, Egypt, in November, 1943, and then went on to Teheran, Iran (Persia), without the Chinese Generalissimo, on December 3, to meet with Stalin of Russia.

Here epoch-making decisions were reached. On Christmas Eve, while General Eisenhower was visiting his Fifth Army at the doorway to Rome he received a message informing him that he was to return to England immediately to take command of Allied forces for the long-awaited great invasion of Europe from the Western Front. This, the highest honor ever conferred on an American general, was in recognition of his victories in North Africa, his conquest of Sicily, which forced the abdication of Mussolini and the surrender of Italy. He had been appointed Supreme Commander for the greatest test in the war.

Two days later, on December 27, General Eisenhower delivered his farewell speech to his armies and naval forces in Italy and North Africa as they stood facing the most gruelling battles they had yet met, in which he pledged them: "United we shall meet again in the heart of the enemy's continental stronghold." His last words were: "Godspeed and good luck to each of you along with the assurance of my lasting gratitude and admiration."

The Allied forces in Italy were to fight on under new commanders. In his place as Commander in Chief in the Mediterranean came General Sir Henry Maitland Wilson, an able soldier who had done a thoroughly efficient job in the Middle East; his deputy was to be Lieutenant General Jacob L. Devers, the American who had succeeded Eisenhower in the European theater when "Ike" was sent to Africa.

The greatest personal loss was undoubtedly felt by the British Eighth Army, for General Eisenhower announced that he was taking with him to Britain, as his deputy commander for all ground forces in the new invasion, the Eighth's beloved "Monty." General Montgomery's successor was Lieutenant General Sir Oliver Leese.

The strategy for the battle of Cassino began to be apparent. It was primarily one of simultaneous encirclement and frontal attack. North of the town, the French were driving for the road from Colli to Atina, while the Americans were infiltrating into hills closer to Cassino and forming for the direct assault and something of a southern flanking movement. On the Garigliano River itself, down to the coast, the main force was British.

For days the communiqués reported that the front was quiet. It meant only that little or no ground had been gained or lost; for every day the guns roared as they had roared before, and their rending shells tore men's minds and bodies. At the very extreme of the front, courageous American girls were braving enemy fire without flinching, always on hand to treat the wounded in dressing-stations and farther back in field hospitals.

The Eighth Army, when its new commander took over, was well beyond Ortona. The change was not reflected in the army's tactics, for General Leese had served under Montgomery; he had commanded the 30th Corps that had formed part of the vanguard of Monty's lightning push from Egypt to Tusinia. While the British in the East were plugging ahead, the Fifth Army opened a new drive on a front ten miles wide. Like a huge, unwieldy steam roller, slow but irresistible, the assault ground down the Germans.

The main barrier to Cassino itself was a chain of three mountains—La Chiaia, Porchia, and Cedro—that formed a razorback running from a point just below Cervaro to the southern side of the Casiline Way. On each of these heights the Allies attacked in force, winning one position after another, while additional troops drove into the lower ground between them.

One by one Cassino's outposts crumbled. Cervaro was battered into submission by a fierce artillery barrage. Troops went in so close behind it that they had literally to crouch in order to avoid being hit by their own shells; a barrage whose superb markmanship evoked awed tributes from captured Germans. The Germans in the village fought back fiercely and inflicted heavy losses; as at San Pietro, companies lost all their officers. One such was taken over by Sergeant William J. Owen of Centerville, Iowa, who had spent his brief civilian career as a bellhop. Now he was giving orders instead of taking them, and making a brilliant job of it.

In the extreme western sector of the front, the British elements of the Fifth Army were on the move. Three weeks after the reconnaissance stab to the farther side of the Garigliano, they stormed across in force, fighting their way with grim determination.

The French had crossed the Rapido at a point less heavily defended than those the Americans confronted; then they pushed on to take an important peak north of Cassino. They were superb mountain fighters, though their officer loss was high; this was attributed to the French tradition of personal officer leadership in combat. In spite of these losses, the French swept the Germans off more and more peaks in the slow but steadily strengthening drive for Cassino. Where the Germans tried to thrust back the Americans in the Cervaro area they were soundly beaten. But farther south, where the Trocchio ridge blocked the Americans' access to the Casiline Way, the going was far tougher.

With the capture of the ridge, the Americans found a new natural barrier—the Rapido. After the first patrol stab into the enemy's territory on the farther bank, they regrouped to storm the river in force. Its current was almost a torrent and the water was glacial.

The 30th Division attempted a series of frontal assaults on the enemy's line across the stream. They plunged through dense mine fields on their own side of the river, carrying on their backs the heavy equipment vital to the attack and the assault boats in which they were to cross. Many of the boats were riddled by enemy fire and the little river ran red with blood. Hundreds of soldiers, many of them badly wounded, tried to swim through the icy water to the other side and establish a bridgehead in the face of the enemy's guns. Impossible as it seemed, they succeeded.

The Germans had prepared for this onslaught. Flatlands were strewn with the trunks of trees cut down in order to improve their field of fire. A low fog added to the Americans' woes. Hurriedly the troops strove to dig foxholes in the cold, hard soil; and almost as fast, it seemed, they filled with water.

Suddenly the fog dissolved and a clear sunlight left them almost naked to the defenders' fire. English-speaking Germans in a dozen parts of the line shouted to them: "Give up! Give up!" Rocket, mortar, and artillery shells drove home the exhortation. The Americans' casualties were high, but they would not give up. After more than a day of fruitless effort, they finally turned and still under the same heavy fire made their way back to their own side of the river. This time almost everybody swam, for the boats were all but gone. "The boys fought," said Lieutenant Colonel Andrew Price of Fort Worth, "until they did not have a bullet to shoot."

An almost deathly quiet followed the gallant failure at the Rapido. But the Allies had even more daring plans in mind. On January 21, American dive bombers smashed to nothingness a German Air Force headquarters almost next door to the Pope's summer villa in Frascati as the first step of the next assault to be launched south of Rome. Guided by maps as exact as those that enabled them to spare every artistic treasure in Italy, the airmen did not touch the Papal residence.

The next day a shattering blow fell on the enemy—a blow whose full impact was not to be felt for months to come. Backed by American, British, French, Dutch, and Greek warships, fresh American and British troops of the Fifth Army stormed ashore within thirty miles of Rome, at the harbors of Anzio and Nettuno.

They were almost stunned by the utter lack of German resistance to what was potentially the most hazardous operation yet undertaken in the Italian campaign. Not a German soldier appeared, not a gun fired, not an enemy plane flew over the beachhead.

Almost every branch of the services was represented in the landings. There were not only combat troops but medical units, nurses, and AMG units to take over the captured towns at once.

The new invasion was a full day old before the first real opposition developed. Then a hundred German fighter-bombers swept in over the landing stages; fifteen were destroyed by the Allies' protective cover and the rest were ignominiously routed. But some of their missiles found marks—on three hospital ships, one of which was sunk, despite the fact that all were brilliantly illuminated and clearly identified.

The assault forces continued to push inland. It was only after they had advanced several miles that the first real ground resistance appeared, offered by outposts and patrols.

The Germans unleashed a savage counteroffensive along the whole of the Cassino front and progressively stiffened their opposition to the new invasion in a grim effort to prevent any junction between the Allies' two armies; for such an achievement would completely wreck the Gustav Line and lay Rome open to speedy conquest.

But, the varied Fifth Army forces fighting desperately for Cassino had taken the brunt of the newest German counterblow without flinching, and now they were rolling the enemy back on his own lines.

A patrol of fourteen men led by Second Lieutenant Filbert Munoz of Kansas City, Kansas, first penetrated the bitterly contested town. Cautiously they stepped through the outskirts, but no sign of the enemy was to be found. They advanced until they were within four hundred yards of the center of Cassino. There they saw a German sentry give the alarm. In a moment machine guns were chattering at them from buildings. Soon mortars were hurling shells from the nearby hills, but the American patrol withdrew intact.

Allied successes were at this point stirring fresh fears in the enemy, and he gave the order for fiercer resistance in both the north and the south. Ten miles north of Anzio, tanks powered a brutal but futile counterattack near Aprilia while the Garigliano-Gustav front flared anew as the enemy imposed a "stand or die" defense on his troops.

In the Rapido sector, scene of the heaviest and most protracted fighting since Salerno, the enemy himself demanded a truce to allow him to bring in his wounded after three days of hellish combat. The request was granted and the terms were settled by two American emissaries who, under a Red Cross banner, marched across the bloody fields to the Germans' barbed wire with their instructions. The two Americans' names must have hurt the pride of the *Herrenvolk* officers who had to beg a favor of them—Captain David Kaplan of Sioux City and Private Arnold Fleischmann of New York. The private must have had, too, a grim satisfaction in his errand, for he was a refugee from German tyranny, fighting it now under the flag and in the uniform of the United States.

In an effort to break the deadlock on the Cassino front, the Allies adopted a tactic of the Red Army that had served the Russians well. Using tanks and infantry as a team instead of coördinated units, they sent engineers out first to lay log roads where the Germans had diverted streams to flood the low land before and around Cassino. Then the tanks and infantry advanced simultaneously, in many cases the troops rode on the tanks and leaped off to engage German troops that threatened to impede their progress.

Thus the Gustav Line was cracked, and its attackers drove within a mile of Cassino on the north. Often when enemy tanks came out to give battle, American foot soldiers of the 34th Division leaped upon them to hurl grenades inside, blowing themselves to bits with the enemy. On both fronts the action was growing more intense.

Resolved as the Germans were to hold the Anzio beachhead, they were even more determined not to lose Cassino. As the Americans pushed nearer the town, its defenders on the surrounding heights added to their artillery fire huge balls of concrete filled with explosives, rolling them down the steep mountainsides against the oncoming attackers.

Both fronts were raging. The thin German line that had held Cisterna at first was by the fifth day of the battle a solid wall against which the Allies flung themselves time after time to make the slightest crack. Their worst handicap, as happened so often in this campaign, was the weather, which made it impossible for aircraft to assist them.

A strange incident occurred at this time. Though it was generally known that German troops were using the Abbey of Mt. Cassino, behind the town, their own artillery shelled the monastery. This action was for the purpose of accusing the Allies of bombing a monastery. Elsewhere in the sector they were compelling captured Allied soldiers to carry munitions under fire. The Allies' forbearance concerning the abbey was provoking considerable angry discussion in both America and Britain, where many people argued that it was better to destroy even the most precious cultural monuments than to waste the lives of men who could be saved if the monuments were reduced. The Germans were deliberately using sacred shrines as military fortifications.

In Cassino, meanwhile, the Americans were engaged in fierce hand-to-hand battle. In one house, where the Germans still held some rooms, a German-speaking American, Lieutenant Paul M. Koerner of Pontiac, Illinois, picked up a score or more prisoners in the dark by answering the German soldiers' inquiries in their own tongue.

On the morning of February 18, long before dawn, the Germans in Cassino were awakened by a nerve-shattering bombardment of 52,000 shells. The defenders of the hilly outposts quaked with fear. Eerie cries in a tongue they had never heard rent the air around them. The Eighth Army's Indians were attacking!

With large New Zealand detachments the Indians—tough, knife-wielding Gurkhas—had been secretly shifted from the Eighth Army's sector to the Cassino area to augment the Allies' other forces there. Now they were charging the heights in the first pale gray of the cold, dismal, winter dawn. Heedless of shells and bullets, they were eager to get close enough for the in-fighting in which they could wield their tempered knives with such fatal effect.

On the Anzio beachhead, too, the Allies' guns were roaring, smashing the very guts out of still another German counterattack. The enemy outnumbered the Allies now in that area. It was the artillery that finally saved the beachhead for the Allies. Hour after hour the big guns roared, backed up by warships and planes, while cargo ships, landing craft and "ducks" poured reinforcements into Anzio and Nettuno to match the enemy's strength.

Around Cassino, the Japanese-American troops of the Fifth Army distinguished themselves by their valor, endurance, and disregard of casualties. Part of their battalion consisted of pure-blooded Hawaiians and Chinese with whom the Japanese soldiers were always on the best of terms: for these men fighting a common enemy here in Italy, the antagonisms of the Orient did not exist. They had only one aim: to smash the Germans.

Throughout the winter months the battles of Cassino and the Anzio beachhead were a series of spectacular exploits to clear the way for the drive on Rome—they were in fact the back doors to Rome. In the first week of March the Germans brought up their much-touted "secret weapon" that turned out a dismal failure. This was the manless tank, a small tractor-type vehicle controlled from its base by electric cables and, in some cases, by radio. It carried in its nose a 1,000-pound explosive charge somewhat like the war-head of a torpedo. But the "beetles" proved cumbersome and easily vulnerable.

On the Ides of March the Allies unleashed an unheard-of fury against Cassino. In the secrecy of the preceding night, every soldier of the Allied forces was stealthily withdrawn well out of the town. Then, early in the morning of March 15, a tremendous crashing roar went up that momentarily stunned every man who heard it. The Allies' biggest guns had opened up in a barrage 40 per cent heavier than the record bombardment that heralded Montgomery's break-through at El Alamein almost one-and-a-half years before. The first wave of more than 4,000 planes swept in over the city. In that one morning Cassino was crushed to rubble under the heaviest concentrated aërial bombardment that had yet been inflicted on a single target—3,500 tons.

That destruction, ironically, owed much to a young man from East Orange, New Jersey, who had never actually fought in a battle. Captain David Ludlum, before the war, had taught history in a boarding school and amused himself with meteorology as a hobby; but in the army his hobby became his assignment. It was his long, painstaking study of his weather charts that determined the date and time for the gigantic bombardment, officially known as "Operation Ludlum."

The Allies swept into Cassino and through the town to the fiercely defended heights on the other side: Castle Hill and Abbey Hill, where the Germans were still clinging to the shambles that had been the Benedictine monastery. The Allies' armor was crossing the Rapido at a nearby point, and New Zealanders were clearing a path for them into the Liri Valley.

In the midst of the smoke and dust of the battle, the Allies laid down a smoke screen of their own—and almost lost the battle. For the vagrant wind quickly slapped the smoke back into the faces of the men whom it was supposed to shield, making it now a cover for the enemy. And, behind this cover, the Germans rose and clambered out of their cellars and crannies and wreckage, creeping forward silently and steathily while their outposts were reinforced through a multitude of subterranean tunnels, the hidden course of the Gari River and even the sewer system of Cassino. Parachutists, serving as infantry, moved in on the one avenue of supply left to the Germans—Highway 6—entering the town at its southwest extremity, and together all the enemy forces struck out against the Allies.

Relentlessly they inched the Allies back, even recapturing Castle Hill. Then the Allies re-formed and, in the face of incredible mortar and machine-gun fire, stormed back up the hill and into the town.

Then the Germans counterattacked. Throughout a whole day, wave after wave of gray-green men crawled over some obstacles, sprang over others and rushed the ruined houses where the American, British, and other troops stood firmly at their posts. The cost was high, and the wounded had perforce to lie where they fell; but, when dusk came, the Germans had not gained a room of a house or a yard of a rubble-heaped street.

Easter, the festival of the Resurrection, was celebrated in foxholes from one side of Italy to the other. On the Americans' sector, broadcasting apparatus carried the services to the enemy, 400 yards from where the American troops knelt in prayer. Both Protestant and Catholic services were held, lasting almost two hours. During the entire time not a single shell fell in the area.

In the midst of the quiescent battle, the troops found time to maintain contact with home. A shortwave radio station was set up on the Anzio beachhead to provide more direct and speedy communication with home.

Occasional patrols came back without some of the men who had gone out with them—men such as Pfc. William J. Johnston of Colchester, Connecticut, whose buddies had been ordered to leave him when they retreated, for the officers agreed he was dying and could not be saved. Johnston said it was "O. K." and waved to the last of the men who had gone out with him. Then he passed out. Advancing German scouts ignored him as just another corpse. The next day an American outpost saw a man crawling wearily toward the Allies' lines. It was Johnston—torn of foot and too exhausted to walk. He had dragged himself for miles to tell his comrades not only that he was still alive but that where he had fallen an enemy outpost was now established. His information, rushed to officers, enabled the Americans to blast the outpost.

At eleven o'clock on the night of May 11, fifty winding miles of front blazed into furious action. A gigantic artillery barrage opened the battle. The flame seared the night from Cassino to the Tyrrhenian near Gaeta, while, offshore, mighty warships hurtled their heavy missiles.

In every part of the line, the Allies were smashing through; even where momentarily the enemy could counterattack and regain some ground he could not hold it long. French and American troops and armor overran Castelforte, thirteen miles south of Cassino; Santi Cosmo e Damia was abandoned in such haste that German breakfasts were still warm on the tables when the attackers entered the village. Two hundred Germans took refuge in a graveyard that became their own. Cornered by the Americans, they were "shot down like jack rabbits." The French swept far beyond their original objectives, swarming up mountains and into valleys. The Poles and Britons and New Zealanders of the Eighth Army and the French above Cassino all drove on relentlessly, almost ringing the fiercely held town.

In the hilly regions, terraced by generations of farmers, German snipers hid behind every rock and every artificial structure to pick off the attackers. Men crept silently and steathily on one another, lunged with the bayonet or grappled with their bare hands to kill or be killed. The village of Santa Maria Infante took sixty hours of the bitterest conflict to reduce it. Artillery tore its buildings to shreds behind which the Germans still fought on.

On May 18, 1944, seven and a half months after the fall of Naples, the Allies had smashed down the last big barrier to Rome. With the gateway at Cassino battered down, and the hinges of the Gustav Line knocked off, they could now set out on their greatest adventure of the war—the Road to Rome.

LIBERATION OF ROME—ALLIES RESTORE FREEDOM TO THE ETERNAL CITY

TRINITY Sunday, June 4, 1944, was a historic day in Christendom. Rome, the Eternal City and the seat of Christian civilization, was liberated from the modern pagan hordes of Nazism by Allied armies of freedom.

Marching over the roads of the Cæsars, the crusaders for human freedom in World War II stood at the gates of the ancient capital, where in A.D. 312 Constantine had established Christianity as the state religion. In reverence to the sacred day, they waited until Monday to enter.

Day by day the Allies had been closing in on Rome. Part of the Fifth Army had driven up directly through the Alban Hills; other elements had swung east to flank the natural defenses, while the Eighth Army pounded into Frosinone, the guardian of Highway 6. Knowing that they were doomed, the Germans had turned every gun and tank and sniper on the advancing Allies in a desperate attempt to prevent the final break-through. That Rome would soon fall was certain. It had been more doubtful that the Allies would achieve their other major objective—the complete destruction of the German Tenth and Fourteenth Armies. Shattered and crippled as they were, they had yet too many avenues of escape above the capital once they should acknowledge that it was useless to resist longer below it.

That conviction had not taken long to impress itself on the enemy. By a feint, the Fifth Army caught the Germans completely off balance and drove a deep wedge into the defenses of Rome. It appeared at first that a heavy attack was being directed on Valmontone from the rear and flank. The Germans hastily rushed reinforcements into that area. The Americans, however, unexpectedly veered northwest and struck into the heart of the Alban Hills, where they were least expected, overrunning the key peak of Mount Peschio, two and a half miles behind Velletri. The British captors of Frosinone were pounding up Highway 6. German lines were falling away like mist before the two armies. Even as they fled, the enemy troops were firing off great volleys almost at random in an attempt to exhaust their ammunition before the Allies could capture it and fire it into their own ranks.

Only one great obstacle remained between the Allies and Rome—the connected mountain masses of Mount Cavo and Rocca di Papa. On June 3 the Allies had smashed through these heights almost without pause, mowing down whatever Germans still dared to oppose them. On Highway 6 the Eighth Army had joined the Fifth. Together they raced through the ruins of Valmontone as the German rear guards fled in a disorganized retreat.

On June 4 the ancient capital of the Roman Empire was liberated by the Allies. That same day huge Allied fleets and armies in England were waiting for the D-Day command from General Eisenhower to start, forty-eight hours later, on the liberation of France.

It was a cloudless Sunday morning when the first spearhead of deliverance crossed the border of Rome itself: American tanks led the Allies into the Holy City, which through the centuries had seen many come as conquerors, but few as liberators. The first units to enter the city came to protect it from the ravages of the Germans who were in full flight to the northwest. Whether or not demolition squads left behind would lay Rome in ruins, as they had so many other great cities, was not known. Units of the American Fifth and the British Eighth Armies streamed in after them, through and around the capital.

General Clark had insisted the population be given every possible protection. All fire directed against the Germans must be so directed that it would save both Rome and the Romans.

It was on Monday, June 5, that Rome really welcomed the Fifth Army. The capital was up at dawn to hail the ever-growing influx of Anglo-American soldiers. They were young men, but their youth was hidden under beards and deep lines of fatigue; their eyes were old from having looked so long into the face of death.

Throngs cheered and sang and tossed flowers and fruit at their liberators. Roman after Roman broke from the crowded sidewalks to offer bottles of wine and other gifts. Women kissed them; mothers and fathers fell on their knees and wept. The faces of the battle-hardened troops began to soften, slowly and almost with difficulty. They smiled again, and waved back in answer to the greetings that they could not understand but whose meaning needed no translation.

Through the streets of Rome, long lines of jeeps and tanks and half-tracks, grotesque and incongruous in these surroundings, wound their way to a great square in the heart of the ancient city—the Campidoglio, where General Clark stood, in a triumph that had not yet been matched in the annals of the Allied arms in this war.

Except where unavoidable necessity had brought down the Allied bombs, the city was undamaged. There had been few demolitions; few mines or booby traps had been left. The people of Rome started out on a virtual storming of the infamous Regina Coeli prison, but no violence was necessary, for the prison guards were whole-heartedly with the throng. They threw open the gates of the cells of the "politicals" and welcomed their erstwhile charges back to freedom.

American, British, and French flags were flying in the streets of the world's most celebrated city. The sun crowned the dome of St. Peter's, the largest church in the world. Its golden rays emblazoned with glory the Vatican, citadel of Christendom, where His Holiness, Pope Pius XII, knelt in prayer.

Here in Rome crowds cheered when an American doughboy mounted the balcony of the Palazzo Venezia and, in imitation of the pompous Benito, thrust out his chest and delivered a satirical harangue, as the Stars and Stripes of human freedom waved from the balustrade.

That same day, another historic scene was taking place at the royal palace. King Victor Emmanuel III was keeping his pledge. He signed over his royal powers to his son, Crown Prince Humbert, as Lieutenant General of the realm. This declaration was the consummation of his promise that he would give up all power and retain only his title as head of the House of Savoy on the day the Allies liberated Rome.

Premier Badoglio, who had temporarily succeeded Mussolini, offered his resignation. Prince Humbert ordered him to form a new Government. Badoglio, however, was unable to carry out these instructions, and was succeeded by Ivanoe Bonomi, Prime Minister in the pre-Mussolini era. Bonomi gathered about him a cabinet of anti-Fascist patriots representing all of Italy's liberation parties. For the first time in history the new Government took its oath to its country instead of to the king.

Nearly five months later, on October 25, 1944, the free Government of Italy was recognized by the United Nations. Fascism was dead in Rome and southern Italy.

The people of Rome represented a gigantic problem to the Allies that might become a major obstacle to their military progress. The city's normal population of about 1,400,000 had been swollen by the influx of 750,000 refugees from both the north and the south. All these people had to be fed, for the Germans had virtually stripped the capital of food. The AMG was prepared to bring in vast quantities of food to keep to a minimum the danger of outbreaks caused by hunger.

Meanwhile, the Germans were still on the run beyond the city. Berlin used the subterfuge that Rome had been abandoned "to save it from becoming a battleground." At the last moment Marshal Kesselring had tried in vain to persuade the Allies to consider Rome an open city and to permit his troops to evacuate the capital area unmolested. Whatever the enemy's propaganda, his actions laid the truth completely bare: He was in indisputable flight, a rout so headlong, so nearly panicky, that hardly an obstacle was left anywhere in the region of Rome to hamper the Fifth and Eighth Armies.

These two forces divided the pursuit so that the Fifth was to clear up the area west of a line drawn through Rome while the Eighth was to take the region to the east. In this latter sector the German resistance, particularly northeast of Rome, was still fairly strong. But the Fifth Army, sweeping up the coast, overran the ancient port of Ostia at the mouth of the Tiber and swept north.

Even as they were racing after the Germans, there was in the making an event that, with its sequelæ, was to overshadow the rest of the Italian campaign. Only two days after the conquest of Rome, the long-awaited assault on western Europe was launched by the Allies, just after the Pope had publicly thanked both them and the Germans for having spared Rome from the ravages of battle.

The vast import of the invasion to the troops in the lines was to make it more urgent that they occupy the enemy to the full so that he could not withdraw a single man from the southern front to meet the new blow. The armies carried out their obligation to the limit.

From the mouth of the Tiber to the Apennine Mountains—a front seventy miles long—the Fifth and Eighth Armies advanced in a solid phalanx preceded and accompanied by a vast aërial armada whose onslaughts seemed to have no end. The main port of Rome, Civitavecchia, forty miles above the capital, was seized in a lightning drive by the Fifth Army, while the Eighth continued to find the going much tougher in the inland sector.

The island of Elba was well defended by the Germans, who turned their coastal guns on the attacking ships. Under this fire the fleet laid down a smoke screen that was a veritable London fog behind which they could start for the shore. French troops raced up the beaches singing a fierce battle chant. They stormed the outer defenses with a gusto that carried them well inland. A fifth of the island had been won by nightfall of the first day.

In a minor way Elba was important to the Allies. If they possessed it, they could gravely threaten the enemy's sea communication lines to western Italy. This advantage was quickly realized. Two days after the landings on the southern shore of the island, the white flag went up in the last northern outpost.

The Allies were moving steadily ahead on the Italian mainland while Elba was being reduced. The enemy's retreat toward the Gothic Line was maintained at an even pace. Towns such as Assisi, where Saint Francis lived and died, were abandoned without a fight. In others, like Perugia, the Germans withdrew the major part of the garrisons but left defense forces to delay their capture and to engage the Allies for some time afterwards in mopping-up operations.

This was the situation as the Allies, firmly established in Rome, fought their way toward the strongly entrenched Gothic Line in the north of Italy, and the second great invasion from the western front of Europe was on its way to liberate France.

BATTLES FROM ROME TO FLORENCE—PISA—AND THE GOTHIC LINE

SUMMER of 1944 in sunny Italy saw a blood bath in the garden land. Mussolini, a refugee in hiding with Hitler, exhorted his traitorous Fascists to "rule or ruin." Turning against his own nation with violence, he allied himself with the German enemies of Italy as the Allied liberators drove them steadily toward destruction.

The battles from Rome to beautiful Florence and the Leaning Tower of Pisa—to the Gothic Line—were scenes of carnage. German resistance increased as the Allies inexorably drove them northward toward their last strongholds. In fierce sporadic combats the Germans exploited every natural defensive position, even resorting to the use of shrines of art and culture to impede the Allied advance.

The American Fifth Army battled through the hills between Lake Trasimeno, where Hannibal gained his victory over the Romans in 217 B.C., and the Tyrrhenian Sea, toward Perugia with its ancient cathedrals and center of the Umbrian school of painting. The British Eighth Army split into two forces to storm up either side of the lake of enchantment. Towns were captured and lost and recaptured.

In the Allied strategy the next major objectives were still beyond striking distance. The first, on the west, was the fortified seaport town of Leghorn, first built by the tragic Medici family whose wealth once ruled Tuscany. With the possession of this port the important railway city of Pisa, capital of the province, would be vulnerable. Pisa was the birthplace of Galileo, the great Italian who invented the telescope.

Southeast of Leghorn was another major Fifth Army objective, Siena, blocking the way to Florence. On the Adriatic coast, almost even with Leghorn, lay Ancona, a harbor city that the Eighth Army was determined to take.

With the beginning of July the whole Allied line began to accelerate its pace. Gains ranged to five and six miles a day in several sectors, and the Germans' positions had to be abandoned. The Americans were closing on Leghorn, while they and the French troops menaced Siena, and the British Eighth Army's units pressed on along both sides of Lake Trasimeno and all the way east to the Adriatic.

The path of the American Fifth Army led to historic landmarks. Siena, with its ancient walls, gateways, steep streets, and splendid churches and palaces ranked next to Rome, Florence, and Venice in the history of art.

The town of Siena was a shrine of centuries of culture and religious monuments. The Allies refused to loose their artillery against it lest they destroy its priceless relics. One French general remarked that he had warned a divisional commander assigned to capture the city that "if he fired a single shell into Siena itself I wouldn't help him. However, he won't do it. He had read Montluc and you know how delectable Montluc makes Siena."

When, on the next day, the French entered Siena they found the city virtually undamaged. French troops had captured Siena before in the history of Europe, but never as liberators. It was in Siena that the Allies made their first real contact with the Italian patriot groups that had been aiding them constantly behind the enemy's lines in this northern area of Italy. In the heart of the city they were waiting in the streets to greet the liberators, waving their rifles stolen for the most part from the Germans and the Fascists of Mussolini's northern régime, and cheering wildly.

Back in Rome, on July 4, a stirring ceremony took place. Secretary of War Stimson had arrived from Washington and the Stars and Stripes were raised at dawn to mark the Fourth. But it was not just an American flag—it was the same flag that had flown over the Capitol in Washington on December 8, 1941, when the United States declared war on Japan, and again on December 11, when this country went to war against Germany and Italy. Thus, one month after the liberation of the first of the enemy's capitals, it was under the emblem of the United States. That this particular flag should fly over Rome on our Independence Day was the suggestion of President Roosevelt.

Plunging indefatigably up the road to Leghorn, the Fifth Army was pounding its way within fourteen miles of the harbor city despite the most furious artillery defense that the Germans could offer. The Eighth Army in the center of the peninsula had completed its encirclement of Lake Trasimeno, but a new stronghold lay ahead. This was the town of Arezzo, another key in the northern highway system.

Realizing the Allies' endeavor to outflank Leghorn and drive inland, the Germans' resistance grew steadily tougher, but they had neither the men nor the materials to maintain the same intensity of opposition along the whole front. At one point or another the Allies were able to pound their way ahead for substantial gains. Thus the French, while the Americans and British were drawing off large German forces, could hammer their way into Poggibonsi and materially increase the peril to Florence, while the Eighth Army began to fan out around Arezzo.

Among the towns overrun by the Americans in their northward drive was the beautiful medieval remnant called "San Gimignano of the beautiful towers" by Italians and lovers of architectural beauty. The

Americans never fired a shot into the little town. When they arrived at its borders they found it abandoned by the Germans. But, as soon as the Americans moved in, the Germans turned their artillery fire on the town without any attempt to direct it to military objectives. Once more they were demonstrating their inherent hatred for anything that smacked of Western culture. In thirty-six hours all but one of the town's legendary towers had been reduced to rubble.

Suddenly the German defensive emphasis shifted once again: this time to the west coast and Leghorn, for the Eighth Army's sledgehammer blows had demonstrated the futility of trying longer to hold on to Arezzo.

Capture of Arezzo was not only a tactical but a strategic victory, for the town was a key in the Germans' defense system and commanded four major highways to the north. From Arezzo the Eighth Army stormed ahead without a halt and crossed the Arno River.

The Americans, spurred by the British drive, reached the Arno at a point farther west on July 18, one day after the British had crossed the river. They struck the south bank at a point between Florence and Pisa, thus threatening both cities. At the same time, the Eighth Army's easternmost units flung a fresh assault against Ancona and cracked the city's last defenses. Another Eighth Army detachment nearer Arezzo faced an almost insoluble problem. As if in emulation of the defenders of Mt. Cassino, the Germans near Gubbio had carried off 232 Italian civilians, mostly women and children, to a monastery on the crest of Mt. Ingino. When the British urged the Germans in the abbey to surrender, the commander replied: "We will defend this position to the last man and we will see to it that the civilians die with us."

Amazed at the sacrilege, the British commander suggested to the Germans, using an Italian monk as intermediary, that they let the civilians go free and in return his own men would not fire on the monastery. For days he directed his own artillerymen not to fire directly into the grounds of the cloister but to concentrate on such enemy troops as showed themselves elsewhere on the mountains. The terrified Italian hostages knelt daily in prayer for deliverance from their perilous captivity. The Germans were defiant. The British had no alternative—they must reduce the monastery whatever the cost to the innocent victims of the enemy.

July 18 was a new day of triumph in the decelerating Italian campaign. On that day the two most important coastal objectives, one at either extreme of the trans-Italian battle line, fell almost simultaneously: Leghorn to the Americans and Ancona to the British Eighth Army's Polish troops. Leghorn's port facilities were found almost entirely destroyed. What Allied planes had not bombed to bits, the Germans had demolished before they yielded the city. Ancona too had suffered extensively from bombing and demolitions, but its condition was not quite so bad as that of Leghorn.

From Leghorn the Americans plunged on to the Arno against stubbornly defended Pisa. Now, for the first time in history, troops of another American nation were to fight on European soil. A Brazilian Expeditionary Force disembarked in Naples and was soon to join the coastal units of the Fifth Army. Its help was badly needed, for there were indeed times when it was the foe that had the larger force. The Allies, however, could count on sporadic and necessarily limited aid from Italy's Partisans, to whom the Allies were parachuting arms.

Pisa and Florence were now the main objectives of the Fifth Army. As the Fifth moved nearer, the German defense became aggressive. Numerous counterattacks were launched.

The Allies sent three columns against Florence: Americans from the southwest and British from the south and the southeast. Against the attackers the Germans threw in more reinforcements; but the quality of their manpower was by now badly watered down, for the new troops consisted mostly of over-age men and what one captured officer described as "slackers and cripples."

Similar defenses before Pisa, only fifteen miles above Leghorn, could not long hold out when the harbor city had been captured. Four and a half days after the fall of Leghorn the Americans battled their way into the streets of Pisa after an irresistible surge across exceptionally strong fortifications of pillboxes, barbed wire, and mine fields.

The Germans were resolved to defend the main part of Pisa—the section north of the Arno—street by street. With that end in view, they fell back across the river without destroying the bridges. Thus the Americans were able to capture the southern section on the night of their entry, but it was to be many days before the city in its entirety would be theirs. Already joined by the Brazilians, they expanded their activities for a while, clearing the Germans from forty-nine miles of the winding river's south bank. The Germans were using the famous Leaning Tower as an observation post to direct the fire of their artillery and the movements of their tanks. Again the Allies refused to fire on the monument or to bomb it lest even the concussion unsettle it and send it crashing to earth. So the city remained hung, as it were, between the two contending forces. On the Adriatic sector, after the capture of Ancona, the next major goal was the port of Rimini, several score miles beyond Ancona.

In the midst of the slow but furious slugging up the peninsula, the front received a new distinguished visitor—His Majesty George VI of the United Kingdom. The King flew to the front areas as the guest of General Clark, and at the commander's field headquarters he lunched with Archbishop Spellman of New York. While he was dining, there was a tremendous, deafening explosion. Hardly three hundred yards from the table, an American soldier had inadvertently stepped on a mine linked to another and both exploded together. The dignitaries of two nations, the British King, and the American Archbishop, beloved by their peoples, narrowly escaped.

On that same day the King inspected troops of many nationalities—R.A.F. fliers, Americans fresh from the combat areas, and many others. He bestowed on General Clark the medal of an honorary Knight of the British Empire. From this point he went to others on the front, always making friends with the soldiers he met, whatever their country. And the Archbishop went on his long journey to give his blessing and inspiration to the troops of all nations.

Part of the Americans' difficulties in overwhelming resistance at Pisa was the result of a factor they had not yet considered wise to announce. Two of the veteran divisions that had fought their way to northern Italy from the beaches of French Morocco—the 34th Infantry and the 1st Armored—the most seasoned troops, perhaps, in all the American Armies—had been quietly withdrawn from Italy to carry on their grim heroism and add to their glory on the battlefields of France. Troops that replaced them were a mixed group of veterans—though with less experience than the 34th and the 1st—and more or less green soldiers who had never been in an actual battle. Their training, however, both in the United States and in Africa, had been as close to the real thing as training could come and they were no strangers to the whine of real bullets above their heads.

Among the valorous new divisions thrown into the line was the 92nd Infantry, a division of American Negro troops who had fought another and perhaps harder battle before they reached the combat area: the battle against prejudice. When the fighting was over, they knew that they could command the soldierly respect of their white comrades.

Both the Americans and the British were drawing their noose steadily closer around Florence, cutting through the last mountain line below the city without regard for the Germans' artillery and mortar defenses. The New Zealanders in the van knew that if they could battle their way in far enough for hand-to-hand fighting, the Germans would not long stand against the bayonet. It was the one weapon they feared even more than the Allies' soul-shattering artillery barrages.

In one captured house a war correspondent for the British Broadcasting Corporation, entering almost on the heels of the troops, made a startling discovery. In the halls and rooms stood row after row of paintings, stacked against the walls and covered with dust and broken glasses. These canvases so heedlessly left exposed to all the perils of war were from the finest collections of art treasures in Florence, many of them stolen from the city's churches. Among them was Botticelli's famous *Primavera*. In all the urgency of war the Allies could still find time to take them to places of safety from the enemy and the elements alike; for with the combat troops the Allies brought their Fine Arts Division, men trained for just such a contingency as this.

Five German divisions were hurled against the tightening ring around Florence. Allied troops had only one purpose: to hold the line firm and then hurl back the foe. Americans, Britons, Indians, New Zealanders, and South Africans fought together with equal vigor and skill, withstanding the charges of giant Tiger tanks and the pick of the German infantry still left in Italy. The Germans knew that they could not indefinitely withstand the Allies' concentrated drives, any more than they could contain the Americans in the southern part of Pisa for more than a limited time. Their sole object was to delay the Allies as long as their strength permitted, and in the process to inflict the greatest possible loss before they fell back at last to the outskirts above the cities and eventually to the constantly reinforced Gothic Line. Above all, they could not afford to let the Allies break out of Italy into France to join General Eisenhower's mighty invasion army.

The first Allied patrols entered Florence on August 4, just two months after the fall of Rome. Only one of its six historic bridges spanning the Arno had not been destroyed by the Germans in their withdrawal to the northern part of the city. The one bridge spared—the Ponte Vecchio, or Old Bridge—they effectively blocked with skilful demolitions at both ends. This destruction incensed the Allied commanders, for it followed almost on the heels of a German pledge to keep the city open. The pledge, of course, was worthless. German troops were waiting in Florence on the far side of the river that ran between high stone banks forming an exceptionally effective natural barrier to the Allies. It was like a "war in a museum," as Anne O'Hare McCormick wrote in *The New York Times;* for shells screamed down among the most priceless treasures of Renaissance art and architecture as the Germans displayed a cynical contempt for their own promises.

After a week of battle, the situation was still indecisive within the city. The Arno was a fairly clear line of demarcation between the areas held by the attackers and the defenders, but there were constant penetrations from both sides. Both armies had fought hard without any major results and both were weary. As if by tacit common consent, they rested on their arms.

It was at this time that Prime Minister Churchill arrived in Italy to inspect the battle areas, confer with the Allied commanders, and also meet the Yugoslav Partisan leader, Marshal Tito. His visit to the Mediterranean theater immediately provoked a flood of rumors from the

Berlin radio, the majority of which proved, unhappily for the enemy, to be only too true: that the Allies were about to invade southern France. This adventure was so planned as to mean a minimum of weakening of the offensive in Italy itself.

The effectiveness of this planning was proved by the sudden fall of Florence. During the first day of real lull in the city, the Germans decided to take advantage of the Allies' relative inactivity—and they scurried north. But the Eighth Army was not caught napping; it followed on their heels. Liberated Florence was a tragic city—an utterly demoralized, starving city. The AMG rushed in food at once to prevent a wave of looting and crime. Nests of Fascist snipers and guerrillas were left hiding in the town by the Germans. While most of the population greeted the Allies' entry with cheers of a genuineness that could not be doubted, there were hundreds of stealthy cohorts of Mussolini's régime—opportunists and common criminals who united to block the Allies and profit by the disruption of the city. Fascists and Italian patriots battled in the streets as the AMG's relief workers tried to make their way through with vital supplies.

In the Adriatic area the Eighth Army continued to advance, not only along the coast but well inland. Poles and Indians were bearing the brunt of the fighting there. In the center and west, along the Tiber River Valley, other Allied forces were gaining, despite German artillery that shelled not only their advance but the conquered city of Florence. The Germans could not accept the loss of that grand prize without striking back in sheer vengeance. A few days after the Allies had apparently established complete control, several German tanks suddenly sallied into the northern section. Taking up positions of vantage, they swept a great area with random barrages from all their guns, sowing death among civilian Florentines who had taken no part in the war. It was just one more evidence of German savagery.

When these marauders had been driven back—for the Allies swiftly sent pursuers after them—patrols of the Eighth Army began to feel out the enemy's positions above the city in the fringes of the Gothic Line. New Zealanders, who had played so large a part in the capture of Florence, led the way with the South Africans. They found strong defenses in which the Germans were apparently prepared to sit tight until a major attack should be launched. West of Florence, British and American troops were probing carefully forward toward those fortifications, while along the Adriatic the Eighth Army felt its way toward the eastern outposts of the Gothic Line.

The Gothic Line had long been proclaimed "impregnable" in German propaganda—but apparently German commanders in the field thought otherwise. The nearer the Allies came to its outskirts, the fiercer the resistance grew. On the Adriatic, the Poles were within shouting distance of Pesaro, a secondary port only two miles from the much-touted forts. But the Germans were clinging tenaciously to the city even under the guns of British warships. It took a concentrated naval bombardment and all the dash and momentum of a brilliant and reckless Polish charge to dislodge them and win the town.

The Americans in Pisa, no less bravely and certainly at no less cost, were inching their way into and through the northern part of that ancient city, while other Fifth Army units were advancing on both sides of it. Negro troops of the 92nd Division showed themselves in the open country southeast of Pisa the warrior equals of the "Aryan master race" that sought in vain to stop them. General Clark was proud to salute their valor.

Pisa finally fell on the same day the British drove their first great wedge into the Gothic Line, threatening to carry straight on to the Po Valley itself. The Americans, in their abrupt lunge into the last German defenses, carried all before them and plunged on four miles beyond the city to the Serchio River. The Eighth Army, on its part, had executed another of its brilliant and daring maneuvers that had characterized its fighting in the deserts under General Montgomery. His successor, General Leese, had the master's touch too, and he used it with telling skill. Once Florence had fallen, he secretly transferred the bulk of the Eighth Army across the Apennines to the Adriatic sector to smash into Pesaro and across the Foglia. Brilliantly supported by its artillery, the hardened fliers of the Desert Air Force paved the way and kept it clear for the infantry and armor.

The British and their Allies broke the enemy's defenses and surged into the Gothic Line until they had torn a great hole fully twenty miles across. The Gothic Line was the Germans' last hope in Italy. Behind it they had no more prepared lines of defense worthy of note. It had been designedly constructed over the toughest terrain in all the peninsula. Once the Allies could overrun it, they would have before them only the plains until they reached the Alps.

But thus far the line had been breached in only a few points of its 150-mile length. The Germans knew as well as the Allies how vital it was that they continue to hold the rest if they were not to be overwhelmed and attacked from the rear in southern France, in the Balkans, and even in the Reich itself. They had manned the fortress line with the pick of the troops they had been able to salvage from the wreck of their Mediterranean venture. The toughest were those old "Green Devil" veterans of Cassino who had endured more than anyone believed the human body and nervous system could stand—the men of the German First Parachute Division, now holding with what was left of their strength the eastern end of the Gothic Line.

This "Green Devil" sector of the Gothic Line, besides the customary strong points, was sown with dense and deep mine fields and innumerable batteries of 75-mm. and 88-mm. guns. Great antitank ditches and huge concrete emplacements were notched with countless machine-gun slits. Behind all this lay more mine fields. Above the whole was the enemy's biggest artillery. It was to be many weary, costly months before the Allies could destroy all this and the men holding it.

The firmness of the Gothic Line defense was based not only on the ease of transit beyond it but on the industrial and agricultural wealth that it protected for the Germans' exploitation. Some of the most fertile farmlands in all Italy lay in and beyond the Po Valley. Strung across the peninsula behind the Gothic Line were the tremendously productive factory cities of Milan, Turin, Bologna, and others, besides the naval bases of La Spezia, Genoa, and Pola.

Both here and on the Fifth Army's front a new factor began to interpose itself against the Allies. This was the weather. The summer was almost over and the rainy fall was heralded by day-long downpours. Rain hampered the Germans far less than it did the Allies because the Germans, being on the defensive, could be fairly fixed in their positions; while the Allies had always to shift their forces and then send them forward in heavy attacks. The ground began to soften and the Allies' armor had to confine its activities to the main highways.

The Eighth Army in the east had now reached a point some miles north of an east-west line drawn through the Americans' positions above Pisa. Here there was still much mountainous terrain which the Germans were exploiting to the full extent of their skill. Little towns like Lucca and Pistoia, of no great importance in themselves, became tremendous obstacles and many an American lad lost his life before they were reduced. The fighting was intense on both sides.

The Partisans' fighting was closely coördinated with the attacks of the Allied air force. Constant liaison was maintained and enabled the Allies to minimize waste effort in the air and concentrate on the most vital targets. The Partisans kept them informed where the greatest clusters of German road convoys and rail shipments were situated and where they intended to go, and thus they could hurl down tremendous blows against the enemy. These attacks were not limited to movements of men and material on land; they were directed as well to the harbors and naval bases still in the Germans' hands and such sea traffic as the Germans still dared to employ.

General Marshall, having toured the Italian battle areas, had returned to Rome. Before he left there for the United States, he issued a message to the Fifth Army on the first anniversary of its hazardous landings on the Salerno beaches. Congratulating the troops for their achievements during that year, he concluded with the prediction: "The last phase of the German debacle is now at hand."

The Americans and the British were maintaining a constant if almost imperceptible advance into the heart of the Gothic Line. Thus Lucca was taken—not overwhelmed in a single furious assault but painfully wrested from the enemy in days of incessant fighting. The Fifth Army's field of advance was widening and when Pistoia was at last entered it was only one point of a thirteen-mile front rolling irresistibly forward. The Americans were now well into the Gothic Line, and the British at Rimini were counting their steady gains.

On a seventy-mile front from the Ligurian Sea to the area east of the Sieve River, the Fifth Army with its American and British components, together with the French, began at last to roll in the middle of September. German resistance, fierce as it had been, grew even more desperate. For days men fought almost on the same spot, as it seemed to them, only to discover that in little less than a fortnight they had advanced barely 1,000 yards.

Even the outskirts of the Gothic Line were unbelievably strong. There were concrete emplacements for every type of weapon; the structures were defended literally to the death with whatever weapons were at hand. Machine guns and small arms substituted for artillery and mortars; dug-in tank turrets took the rôle of heavy guns—each position had to be destroyed individually. When a defense point had been conquered, the exhausted troops would realize with a sense of frustration that their victory had been no more than a step toward a new battle of at least equal rigor. For the Gothic Line was really a series of lines, one behind another—a defense in depth whose density varied from point to point. Its design was such that every advance by an attacker brought an increase in resistance in direct ratio.

When the assault on the Gothic Line was barely a month old, more than 1,000,000 shells had already been hurled into it by the Allies. The Fifth Army's big offensive began to change the picture. While the initial advances were not large, they did serve to throw the Germans off balance and shatter that psychological poise that every commander and every staff must have for military success.

The result was obvious: The Eighth Army, increasing its pressure in the whole Adriatic sector, found itself rolling forward at greater speed. The 7,000-yard ridge of Coriano and San Savino, southwest of the harbor, was at last wrested in its entirety from the enemy and the Canadians were within a mile of the Rimini Airfield. The Germans overran the tiny independent state of San Marino, neutral for centuries throughout all of Italy's wars, and emplaced their guns in the principality for greater defense against the Allies. Rimini was in the gravest peril; for, as the flanking forces penetrated closer to the city, the other elements attacking frontally were bound to profit. Somehow the Germans were still slipping reinforcements into the area; many of them had already, before San Marino was occupied, violated the little country's neutrality without the semblance of an excuse.

Heavy tanks were hurled in by the Germans to save the eastern anchor of their line. Fighting what was primarily a delaying action, they had by now lost all sense of proportion and were exhausting precious matériel without a thought of its irreplaceability. Nor, apparently, were they dismayed at the constant drain on their reserves of manpower. Despite the enemy's prodigality, the Eighth Army could not be stopped; it could only be impeded. On the airfield outside Rimini the Germans fought like men possessed of demons; but the Canadians, reinforced with Greek troops, would no longer be denied. Every hangar, every revetment was the scene of a major battle in miniature. One by one the German positions were taken, often to be found without a single defender alive.

The Fifth Army was hammering harder and crunching its way slowly into one defense line after another. Even the tremendous initial advantage of holding virtually all the high ground could not avail the Germans long. They were driven from one peak after another. Nor did the Eighth Army slacken on the Rimini Airfield and the area west of the town. Pursuing the fleeing Germans, the British entered San Marino. At their entrance the tiny country's entire army of 900 men, too pitifully minuscule to offer even the slightest token resistance to the well-armed Germans, rose to join the Allies and aid in their own liberation. That was a matter of a single day; less than twenty-four hours after the Allies had crossed the border of San Marino, not a single German was to be found in the entire principality.

The Fifth Army in a sudden surge well north of Florence lunged precipitately into the body of the Gothic Line and cut out a gap six miles wide. At this point it was now in a position to threaten the rich Po Valley from a central spot and to swing northwest over the plains to the naval bases and Milan and Turin, or northeast toward Bologna.

The Fifth Army's gain seemed to instill new vigor into the hard-fighting Eighth Army. On September 21, one day after the new gap had been cut in the center of the Gothic Line, the Greek flag was floating proudly over Rimini.

British units of the Fifth Army, participating with the Americans, French, and Brazilians in the center penetration, had gained a vantage point in the drive toward one of the few breaks in the natural defenses of the Gothic Line: Futa Pass from which major roads split off toward Bologna and Imola. The capture of this pass would mean the doom of the whole central section of the German fortification system. The broad plains of Lombardy would lie open to the Allies.

D-DAY—ALLIED FORCES LAND IN FRANCE —START OF THE WESTERN FRONT

THE great day had come. Through the night hours of June 5 and 6, 1944, the mightiest fleet the world had known was on its way to the liberation of Europe. More than 4,000 ships were en route from England to the coast of France. Aboard were the vanguard of armies that were to swell to more than 4,000,000 men in the world's greatest battles. Above them roared a mighty air armada of more than 3,000 warplanes.

This invincible armada was in direct reverse of the epoch-making event that took place more than eight centuries before when William the Conqueror came from the shores of France with 3,000 sailing vessels and landed his warriors on the coast of England. It had, however, one analogy: Although William's successful invasion changed the course of the history of England, this 1944 invasion was to change the course of the world.

The "Second Front" invasion was one of the greatest feats in history —a masterpiece in organization and coördination. Within a hundred days after General Eisenhower arrived from Italy to take command, it was ready to strike, waiting only for the psychological moment. This came two days after the fall of Rome.

General Eisenhower, surrounded by his able staff of American and British strategists, had welded together the most powerful allied fighting machine of all times. This united front was composed of sons of every nation in the world who had merged their seventy nationalities under British or American citizenship. It was an army of the peoples of the earth under the Stars and Stripes and the Union Jack, later to be joined by the Tricolor of France.

Eisenhower, as Supreme Commander of the Allied forces—land, sea, and air—was invested with the greatest authority ever granted a general. He was now to meet in decisive battles his old foe, Field Marshal Rommel, the brilliant strategist whom he, in coördination with the great General Alexander, had beaten in North Africa.

During his final inspections, Eisenhower had made these prophetic remarks: "If their fighting is as good as their training, God help the Nazis!... Only a self-disciplined army can win battles. We must all work on the basis of mutual respect, consideration, and coöperation, dedicated to the single task of doing our duty in winning this war. We must see that justice prevails.... My deep appreciation to each of you for duty well performed in the past and with best of luck in the future."

To the British he said: "Your nation and mine have found themselves partners in a great war. More than any other time in history, we find the forces of evil ranged against those of decency and self-respect for the human mind. We stand on the side of decency, democracy, and liberty.... Every one of us must not fail to do his duty."

One year to the day after General Eisenhower's arrival in London, he was made a full general to give him equal rank with some of the celebrated soldiers who, although they outranked him, served gladly under him—General Sir Harold R. L. G. Alexander, General Sir Bernard L. Montgomery, General Alphonse-Pierre Juin.

It was not only Eisenhower's outstanding military ability that the Mediterranean campaigns demonstrated; they showed also his extraordinary talent for welding together into a unified force men of many different nationalities and characteristics across the great psychological barriers of custom and usage and even language. His headquarters in Algiers was an amalgam of American, British, Canadian, and French officers. He fused all the officers under him into a perfect whole and won the admiration and affection of all the mixed troops in the field. After Eisenhower was chosen for the task of liberating enslaved Europe and destroying Germany, he appointed three deputy supreme commanders—for land, for air, and for sea. Eisenhower put in command of all the ground forces General Montgomery, whose caliber he had tested in Tunisia, when the British Eighth Army came under his jurisdiction. For the air, he chose Air Chief Marshal Sir Arthur William Tedder, who had worked so closely with Montgomery all across Africa and then added his talents to Eisenhower's staff in Algiers. To command all the naval forces he selected the man who had accomplished the epic feat of the Dunkirk evacuation just four years before the Allies returned to the Continent: Admiral Sir Bertram Home Ramsay.

General Montgomery—later to outrank his chief once again as Field Marshal Montgomery—was the peerless field commander who had saved Egypt, broken the full force of the Germans at El Alamein, and chased Rommel across Africa, out of Sicily, and into the mountains of Italy. He was an Ulster Scotch-Irishman, the son of a bishop and himself a man of almost Puritanical habits. Like Eisenhower, Montgomery had been an unknown only a few years before. He was fifty-five years old and had spent thirty-five years as a soldier after his graduation from Sandhurst, the West Point of Britain. In the First World War he achieved a good combat record, going in as a captain and emerging as a lieutenant colonel. He was wounded twice, decorated by both Britain and France and six times cited in dispatches.

When the Second World War began, Montgomery was sent to

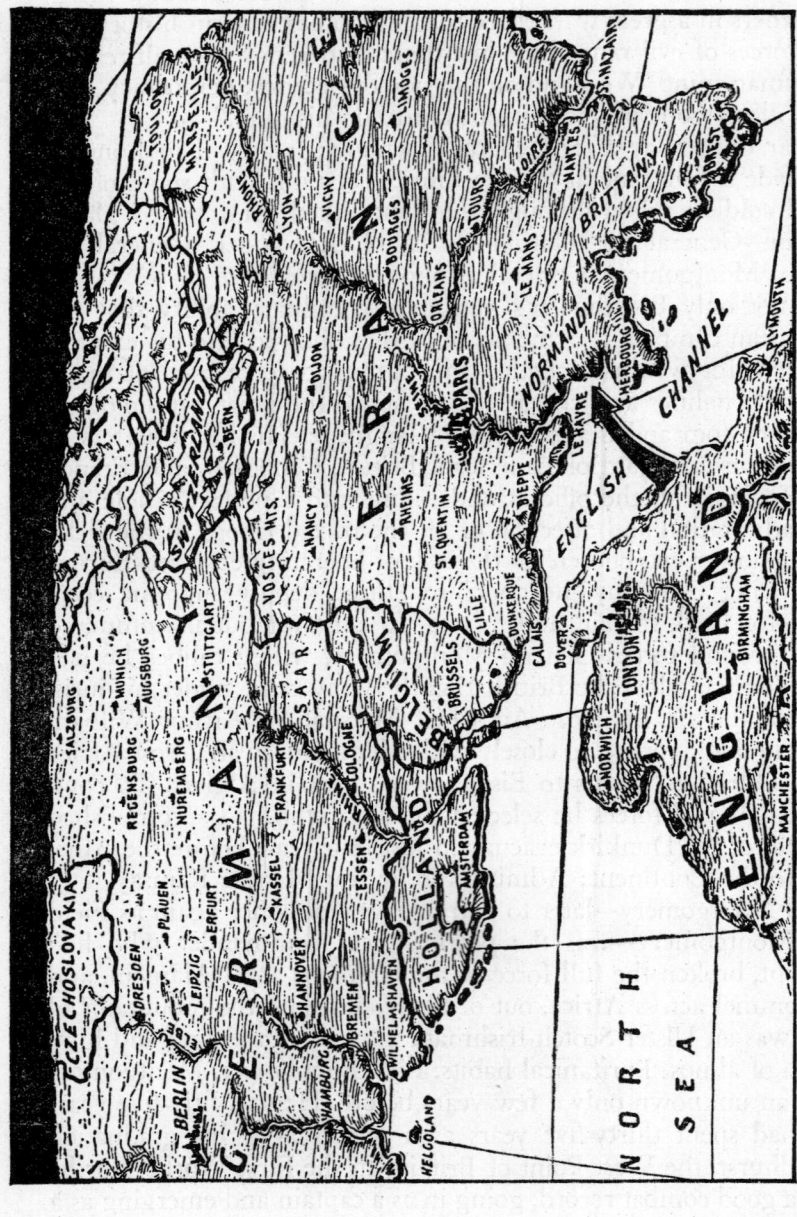

With the coast of England as the starting point, the invasion of June 6, 1944, on the Continent of Europe, is indicated by an arrow.

France as a lieutenant general in command of the Third Division. He commanded his men brilliantly against heavy odds and was one of the last Englishmen to leave the Dunkirk beaches. Then he was put at the head of the Southeastern Command of England—a post that was very important, for it covered the area in which any invasion by the Germans was sure to be made. Monty, as his troops came to call him, resolved at once to build what he called a "Spartan army." He made the men run six miles daily; he insisted on daily calisthenics; he was rigorous in discipline. The result was a tough, synchronized fighting force that was ready for anything. When the Eighth Army had been hurled back almost to Alexandria and the fate of Egypt seemed to be trembling in the balance, he was sent to aid General Alexander. With him went many of the veterans he had saved at Dunkirk.

Air Chief Marshal Sir Arthur William Tedder first won fame during his association with General Montgomery, with whom he worked closely in the African campaign. Tedder was catapulted into the position of commanding the Desert Air Force; because of an accident to the original commander, he was suddenly chosen to replace him. Sir Arthur was a Scot, fifty-four years old, who was graduated from Cambridge in history, played professional football, and became a civil servant in the Fiji Islands before he received a commission in the army. In World War I he was shifted to the Royal Flying Corps, as the R.A.F. was then known; he served in France and later in Egypt, winning acclaim in dispatches. When the R.F.C. became the R.A.F. he remained with it. For a while he was a member of the Royal Naval Staff College, then moved to the Air Ministry, and after that to the R.A.F. Staff College.

From that post Sir Arthur was sent "out East" to command the R.A.F.'s Far Eastern division. A year before World War II broke out, he returned to the Air Ministry as director general of research and development. This quiet man, who had spent most of his life in study and science, was the leader who so dramatically integrated the air arm with the land arm in the victories over Rommel in the desert. His work with Montgomery was primarily in tactical air activity, that is, close support. When Rome was bombed for the first time in a striking example of strategic bombing—the destruction of targets far behind the fronts—it was Tedder who planned the whole operation.

Naval Commander Admiral Ramsay had taken part in one great action with General Montgomery—the evacuation of Dunkirk, which Ramsay had led and planned. By getting the B.E.F. out of France in that operation, he won the nickname that was to stick to him for the rest of his career—"Dynamo," the code word for the Dunkirk evacuation. Sir Bertram was sixty-one years old, the son of an army officer. He entered the Royal Navy at the age of fifteen.

NEW YORK HERALD TRIBUNE map—Fleck

How the Allies drew the ring tighter around Germany. Black areas show territory gained on three fronts after D-Day. Shaded areas show that held by Allies on June 6, 1944.

Each of the three deputy commanders had his own deputies. Under Montgomery were four Americans—Lieutenant General Omar N. Bradley, Lieutenant General Courtney H. Hodges, Lieutenant General George S. Patton, Jr., and Lieutenant General William H. Simpson, each the commander of an American Army in the field. These armies did not all enter the battle together. In the beginning it was only the First and Third, under Hodges and Patton, that formed the American Twelfth Army Group, which was commanded by Bradley. Montgomery was at the head of the Twenty-first Group, which comprised the British Second Army under Lieutenant General Sir Miles C. Dempsey and the Canadian First Army under Lieutenant General Andrew G. L. McNaughton.

Tedder had as his immediate deputy Air Chief Marshal Sir Trafford Leigh-Mallory, commander of the Allied Expeditionary Air Forces, who worked closely with Lieutenant General James H. Doolittle. Sir Trafford was the son of a clergyman. He was only forty-two when he took command of the invasion's air force. In his youth he had intended to practice law, but the First World War had just broken out when he received his degree, so he entered a territorial regiment as a private. In less than two months he had become a second lieutenant; then he was wounded in Ypres. He recovered and returned to active duty, but abandoned the army for the R.F.C. He served honorably in France, winning the Distinguished Service Order in combat. When the R.A.F. was organized after the war he embraced it as his lifework instead of law.

One of Leigh-Mallory's earliest interests in the new career was coöperation between air and ground forces, and he plunged at once into an intensive study of the subject. He became commandant of the School of Army Coöperation and three years later joined the Staff College. Thereafter he served in the Air Ministry and was sent to the Imperial Defense College; later he was put in command of a flight training school. When World War II broke out, he was commander of a fighter group. It was in the Battle of Britain that Sir Trafford distinguished himself. He was a wing commander then and was soon promoted to air vice marshal. He won international acclaim for his feat in keeping up the almost incredible "air umbrella" over the Dieppe raiders in August, 1942.

Little time, however, was to be left to him. The brilliance of his achievements with Eisenhower far outshone even his own previous feats. It was soon decided to lend him for similar purposes to Admiral Mountbatten's Southeast Asia Command, where his talents would be invaluable in India. In the autumn he set out by plane for his new post, but never arrived. His plane crashed before half the journey had been completed. After his death, Marshal Tedder and General Doolittle assumed between them the responsibilities he had brilliantly discharged.

General "Jimmy" Doolittle, the "devil on wings," needs no introduction to us. He gained world fame in the first raid over Tokyo. Before World War II he was an aëronautic engineer, racing pilot, and stunt flier. He won the D.F.C. and the Oak Leaf Cluster for high-speed test flights. He flew over the Andes in South America with both legs in casts. First to fly "blind," he won coveted trophies and was elected President of the Institute of Aëronautical Sciences. Under Eisenhower in North Africa he organized and led the Twelfth Air Force, whose exploits became legendary. They blasted the way for the ground forces with their raids on Tunisia, Sicily, Italy, and were the first to bomb Rome. The consensus of all fliers was: "Jimmy is one of the grandest fellows on earth or in the skies."

Here, too, we meet Lieutenant General Carl A. Spaatz, known as "Tooey" Spaatz, commander of the American Strategic Air Forces in the Western European invasion. He was fifty-two years of age and had commanded, under Eisenhower, the Northwestern Africa Air Force, which became famous as the Anglo-American "Spaatzwaffe." He had made a distinguished record in the First World War and had won the Distinguished Service Cross for heroism in action. One of the fathers of military aviation, he was called to Washington at the outbreak of World War II and made Assistant Executive Officer to General "Hap" Arnold, chief of the Air Forces; then he was sent into the African and European war zones with Eisenhower.

Lieutenant General Omar N. Bradley, fifty-one years old, who was to lead the ground forces under Eisenhower, was a classmate of "Ike" at West Point. He had served at thirty-three army posts up to the time the United States entered World War II. He was in Hawaii when "Ike" was in the Philippines with MacArthur. A master of ground warfare and infantry tactics, he was Eisenhower's field aide in North Africa and then commander of the American Second Corps. It was Bradley and his men who captured Bizerte, the key that unlocked the gates to the conquest of Tunisia, and it was to Bradley that 25,000 Nazi troops surrendered. Bradley admitted at the beginning of the Second Front invasion: "I have but one ambition—to lead my troops straight to Berlin."

We meet also, on this invasion night, a typical Englishman, Sir Arthur T. Harris, known as "Ginger" Harris, fifty-two years old, commander of the British Strategic Air Forces. Although he served under Air Chief Marshal Leigh-Mallory, as did General Spaatz, his job was the destruction of Hitler's war-production centers. He first took charge of the R.A.F Bomber Command in 1942 and began to blast more than fifty German key cities, crippling the power of the Nazis. These gigantic raids, day and night, blazed the path for the invasion armies and terrified the German population.

Eisenhower and his generals had set the zero hour for the early morning of Monday, June 5. That day, however, began with heavy winds and high seas that would have taken too great a toll of the landing forces; so the operation was postponed. All day Monday the Channel was rough. Some assault forces that had already put out to sea had to return to port with their tensed-up hundreds of tough, action-eager troops, while the rest waited impatiently in port. On Monday night the weather gave no indication of any substantial change, although it

D-Day

had moderated somewhat in degree. Generals, admirals, and air marshals debated the momentous decision in their secret trailer GHQ somewhere in a field behind the southern coast of England. Men and ships and planes were ready.

General Eisenhower pressed the button that flashed the signal to hundreds of ports and airdromes that were strung around and across Britain.

Airborne divisions, long alerted and geared, ran across the fields to their gliders and the transport planes that towed them. In the harbors, thousands of vessels from battleships to assault boats and PT's sounded battle stations. With soldiers crowded aboard troopships and landing craft, the fleet nosed out to sea.

The faces of these men reflected every possible facet of human emotion. Most of them were going into battle in a country they had never seen before. Many of them would see action for the first time, although many more were veterans of the tough fighting in Africa, Sicily, and Italy. Dice and card games flourished, with jeep hoods as tables and invasion money as stakes. Other men were singing. Many prayed, while some just stood alone and smoked and thought.

Much of the invasion fleet was still waiting to stand out to sea when the first of the aërial warriors leaped from the open doors of the big transport planes over France. The planes and gliders bore the 82nd and 101st Airborne Divisions, the first American troops to touch French soil in the invasion. The first man out of the first plane was Captain Frank Lillyman, of Syracuse, N. Y.

He was but a forerunner; seconds later the night was full of hardened American veterans of parachute war, falling slowly downward in their harness and their heavy combat gear. Other chutes accompanied them, bearing guns and bicycles and tools and food. Still farther inland the gliders had cut their tows and were nosing downward to touch the soil of France and spill out their cargoes of fighting men and weapons. Gliders carried also another type of soldier—the civil-affairs section, the army's G-5, landed with the first wave of combat troops, getting its baptism of fire preparatory to taking over at once the civil administration of the first towns to be liberated from the Germans.

Airborne troops had to fight from the moment they touched the earth. The Germans had heard the roar of their motors, and enemy observers had seen the thousands of tiny figures plunging into space while the gliders pointed downward for a landing. Enemy garrisons sprang to their posts. Every haystack was a potential trap to the invading Americans. Advancing warily, they followed the maps they had studied so long in Britain, where great replicas of the Norman countryside had been carefully constructed with painstaking accuracy for their rehearsals. Shots rang through the night. Men ran forward or back to cover, some stumbling and crawling, others lying still. The aërial vanguard plunged into the thick of the enemy defenses to ease the task of their comrades still at sea by keeping the foe from rushing troops to the coast.

In the wake of the troop-carrying planes, thousands of the biggest Allied bombers roared across the coast and loosed tons of explosive and fire on the enemy defenses. For miles on either side of the chosen beachheads—on the coast of the Carentan estuary for the Americans, above Caen for the British and the Canadians—and far inland behind and between them, British and American planes rained down thousands of tons of bombs to paralyze the enemy and render him as helpless as possible. Among the bombers and behind them in increasing numbers as the boats neared the shore, the Allied fighter planes raced and zoomed and twisted to beat off German aërial defense and strafe the Germans on the ground.

While the summer night was torn asunder by the dragons of the air, the biggest Allied warships were streaming along the coast, many within range of the enemy shore batteries. The big guns of the ships hurled tons of steel through the air into gun sites and blockhouses and tank concentrations far inland.

All the lessons learned so dearly almost two years before on the blood-soaked beaches of Dieppe were proving their worth. The Channel was black with landing ships and landing craft bearing tanks and men and guns and bulldozers. Ahead and around them raced the American PT-boats to hold off any German craft bold enough to try to oppose the invasion. In the van were men whose task was the most perilous of all—the troops who had to rush the steel-spiked shallows and uproot or destroy the barriers cunningly placed to rip out the bottoms of our boats before they could debark their men—and the sailors of the mine sweepers who cleared the channels for the invasion craft, never knowing when the slightest grazing contact might send their craft in fragments into the air.

More than four thousand seagoing vessels were on the water that night, from battleships to patrol craft. One-third of them was flying the Stars and Stripes and manned by navy sailors and coast guardsmen. Three American battleships were in the van and stayed in the fight for days. Under their wing were the thousand transports and landing boats of every size, all commanded by a veteran of amphibious operations, Rear Admiral Alan G. Kirk. He operated under the supreme naval command of Admiral Ramsay of the Royal Navy. All night the navy worked and fought, almost invulnerable from the air, for our aërial cover was all but impenetrable and few German planes were willing to dare it. However, it was under constant fire from the shore and from scattered light naval units of the enemy that ventured out for what could be no more than harassing nuisance action. The U-boats, strangely enough, stayed away in force.

While the ships were covering the approach of the assault forces and the first wave of landing troops, the planes maintained their ferocious attacks from above. Fighters swooped in at treetop level where the airborne forces were battling German armor and shot it out with the big lumbering tanks, putting a number out of action. Airborne men were battling with automatic rifles, grenade rifles, machine guns, bazookas, flame throwers, TNT charges—everything necessary to the reduction of fortified positions. Blockhouses that were impervious to the aërial bombs were reduced by TNT hurled through their firing slits or hungry tongues of unquenchable flame that licked through the apertures and over every living thing inside.

The Germans were literally caught napping, but telephones and radios all along the coast were soon reverberating with the climactic news. All morning the seemingly endless streams of men and arms poured ashore. Close behind were following the "seagoing harbors" built secretly in British shipyards for use on hostile shores. These were great structures that enabled the Allies to transform empty beaches into makeshift but thoroughly serviceable ports that could serve their needs until they had captured the major harbors of Cherbourg and Le Havre.

It was just two days after the fourth anniversary of the last day of the Dunkirk epic that the Allies landed. Prime Minister Churchill had long planned to land with the doughboys and Tommies in the invasion, but his advisers dissuaded him from doing so. Over the radio, General Eisenhower spoke words of hope and strength to the millions whose liberation was his gigantic task. He warned them to stay off the roads and away from bomb targets. He told them that they would be called on to play a vital rôle in their own liberation. He paid special tribute to the men and women of France whose kinsmen were even then returning to free their country, for there were many French troops among the invaders and more were soon to follow. Above all, he urged the fighters of the various Undergrounds of Europe to pay close attention to the broadcasts that would be directed to them from time to time.

General Eisenhower was followed at the microphone by General de Gaulle, who had arrived in Britain from Algiers only a short time earlier. The French leader who had so long symbolized his nation was now, after four years of exile, almost on its threshold again. He exhorted his compatriots to coöperate fully with the invading troops, to obey the orders of the Supreme Command and his Government. Like King Haakon of Norway and the Dutch and Belgian leaders who spoke later, De Gaulle adjured his countrymen to stay out of the way of the armies, lest they impede the advance into the interior.

The British troops drove for Caen and Bayeux, important junctions, while the Americans drove northwest of their landing place for Cherbourg and northeast for Isigny. The entire operation on land was under command of General Montgomery, who had the Canadian First Army under General Andrew McNaughton and the British Second Army under Lieutenant General Sir Miles C. Dempsey. The Americans comprised the First Army, under General Bradley, and the Third Army, under General Patton, who was acting at the orders of Bradley.

In the area of the Carentan estuary, the Americans battled a tough German division that was not part of the ordinary coastal forces but a crack outfit of the Reich's finest. By the end of the day they had not advanced a hundred yards from the shore, but they refused to give way. Their losses were high and their punishment unceasing; but they held on and threw themselves against what must have seemed an unbreakable wall with such gallantry that Montgomery paid unreserved tribute to them. In the end their gallantry and fighting skill, aided by planes and ships, paid its reward. Fresh troops of a "decadent" country, they overran at last the vaunted troops of a nation of warriors and rolled inland over the bodies of the "supermen."

All day the seaborne troops battled inland and the airborne forces strove to fight their way toward the shore for a junction. The enemy defenses were planned to grow stronger in direct ratio to their distance from the sea.

Throughout the day the Allied naval forces continued to land men and supplies almost unmolested from above. Only the shore batteries could offer any effective opposition, and this was being methodically reduced by air and sea attacks.

Late that night a veritable torrent of help came down upon the Cherbourg Peninsula, continuing well into the day. A sky train fifty miles long landed men and equipment in four great waves as the fighting continued in the dark and the Allies wrested yard after yard of ground from their fiercely fighting opponents. The Allies had the advantage of their initial surprise and were exploiting it to its fullest extent.

It was on the second day of the invasion that the first city of France was liberated, as battle-grimed Britons and Canadians marched into the flower-strewn streets of historic Bayeux.

Dozens of little Norman towns had to be captured before the Allies could enter the old city, but those towns were almost nameless and the city was a symbol. In their own way the little hamlets were symbols too; the people had not left them despite the crumping of shells and bombs and the barking of tank guns along their streets. The people were waiting to thank the strangers who were setting them free, to thank them and to aid them. In every town the FFI members were working frantically to take part in their own liberation.

It was in Bayeux that the invaders were given their first great ovation.

of a liberated city. Men, women, and children thronged the streets, tossed flowers at the troops, ran from the sidewalks to embrace them. They dragged them into their homes to share with them whatever they possessed. Every café became a jovial host. From every aging piano rang out the famous songs of the First World War that Americans and Britons and Frenchmen had sung together nearly thirty years before. "Tipperary" and "Over There" mingled with "Roll Out the Barrel" and "Madelon" as the tall Canadians and the stockier Britons filled the streets, while their tanks clanked through the city and their shells whined in hot pursuit of the fleeing foe. Above the shells was heard the roar of the planes; the sky was black with them.

Bayeux was a first objective. Beyond lay the vital junction of Caen, the key to much of the German's Norman defenses, one of the northern gateways to Paris. That night the Germans struck their first substantial counterblow against the invasion. General Rommel, a skilful warrior, threw in armored units of two German Armies to stem the Allied tide. A withering fire poured on them all night. When day broke, the enemy had to cry quits for the time being. The Britons and Canadians renewed their advance toward Caen.

By the capture of Bayeux, Montgomery had severed the Cherbourg Peninsula's major road and rail link with Paris and all the interior. This gave invaluable assistance to the Americans, who were still being reinforced from the air to meet steadily increasing resistance on the beachhead. Even the pilots of the gliders that brought in the troops joined the battle; one of them, R. B. Fowler, had barely landed when he seized his rifle and a grenade and killed nine Germans in a few minutes. Fowler was knocked unconscious in the skirmish, captured and taken before German officers. His captors, however, had overlooked another grenade in his pocket. When a German colonel drove up, Fowler killed him and his aide with it, seized their weapons and their car, and escaped to the Allied lines.

Allied planes were keeping up a constant curtain of bombing and strafing all over the front and far beyond it. German vehicles would venture into a country road; a few minutes later they were in ruins, their passengers cowering or dying in the ditches and underbrush. Trains and tanks suffered the same swift fate. Relatively few German planes dared to show the black cross and swastika above the ground. The Allies had an air superiority that left even themselves stunned.

On the fourth day of the invasion the chiefs of American armed forces arrived in England to confer with their British colleagues and the invasion command. General Marshall, General Arnold, and Admiral King flew to the British capital for the conferences which preceded their visit to the front lines.

Throughout France the once-secret Underground was emerging into the light, emerging armed and trained. In many sectors where the Allies had been unable to parachute heavy weapons, they had to be content with side arms and whatever they could capture from the Germans. These Underground forces performed innumerable feats that gave them possession of artillery and tanks.

By June 10—the fourth day of the invasion—the invasion forces had fought their way well inland and the beaches were more than secured. However, the phase of combined operations was not yet over. The Germans were counterattacking in the Caen sector with some success. Lest they gain still further and crush the Allied grip on the Caen-Bayeux road, every arm was called into play. While the ground forces were locked in furious combat, and armor and artillery were slugging it out at short and long range, the Allied warships were standing in close to shore as the planes poured death into the enemy lines. Again it was the navy that saved the day, as it had done at Salerno and Anzio. From the Allied inland positions and the reconnaissance planes above the battleground, radios sent the range and plottings back to the ships.

American Rangers and British Commandos were adding their weight to the continuing battle. Their rôle was not limited to spearheading a landing. Usually they struck at night. They would lunge far behind the enemy lines to deal vital blows to his supplies and communications.

While the lines in the Caen sector remained taut, the Americans to the west continued to gain. Well into the Cherbourg Peninsula, they were striking out laterally to cut the railway south from the port city itself and cross to the western shore in a drive to clean up the whole area and isolate the city before attacking it directly. While Carentan remained in the enemy's hands, the Americans pushed northeast toward Isigny, undeterred by the flooding of the valleys in a vain German attempt to halt the advance. Other Americans south of Isigny had driven straight eastward to join the British and Canadian forces at Sully, sixteen miles east of Isigny and two miles northwest of Bayeux. Thus they established a solid front. This line abutted on the beginning of the extremely difficult "bocage" of Normandy, the hedgerow country that in many ways rivaled the jungles of the Pacific islands for danger and toughness.

BATTLES OF NORMANDY

THE battles of Normandy were fought on historic ground. Eisenhower's armies were on the trail of one of the world's decisive battles. Nearly six centuries before, English troops landed in Cherbourg and began the march through Normandy to the decisive Battle of Cressy, which "rang the curfew on the long day of cavalry supremacy."

Here, where the long bow and thrust of the spearhead had proved its supremacy over armor-mounted knighthood, the Allied armies were proving in the summer of 1944 the superiority of tanks, planes, and mechanized warfare in Normandy.

The much-vaunted Atlantic Wall, which Hitler had believed impregnable, was crumbling before them. The beachhead was only five days old when the Allies established their own air bases there, obviating the necessity of bringing planes across the Channel from Britain. British bases were now being used more and more for the strategic bombing of Germany proper, which had never ceased despite the vast demand for planes in the battle area.

The Allies sent record forces from both the beachhead and Britain to smash every German attempt to strengthen their Atlantic Wall. Bombers struck from every level. Fighters swept in "on the deck" to strafe and cannonade and drop delayed-action bombs. The loss ratio continued to be astonishingly low, although many of the fliers returned wounded to their bases. Already the air strips in Europe were being used by giant transport planes that rushed the wounded men of every branch to hospitals in Britain.

German resistance was growing in direct ratio to the Allied successes. It was obvious that Carentan could not be reduced at once. General Bradley did not allow himself to be trapped into throwing his entire force at the defenders of the little town. He had other and bigger game in mind. Bradley continued to branch out in both directions from the town, leaving a substantial contingent, well armed and supplied, to batter at the Germans in Carentan. His troops to the northeast were cleaning up more and more territory south of Isigny, while the force flung into the Cherbourg Peninsula was battling toward Montebourg, sixteen miles below Cherbourg. Another strong body was driving south into the heart of Normandy and heading for the vital German communication center of St. Lô, soon to be the Yanks' first big prize.

Concurrently with this drive, the Americans were attempting

to cut off the Cherbourg Peninsula, an objective that could not be accomplished until Carentan had been reduced. The doughboys attacked it in force on June 11. Battling throughout the night for the town, they charged in the darkness, split by the incessant flashes of a merciless artillery barrage from the defenders, with bayonets outthrust. From the bay, the Allied warships opened fire. The losses were heavy on both sides. As if by tacit consent, both sides virtually stopped firing for a few minutes at irregular intervals to allow the removal of the wounded.

At 8:30 A.M., June 12, the Americans claimed Carentan as theirs. The same day the highest chiefs of the Allied armed forces stepped on the soil of France for the first time in four years. General Marshall, General Arnold, Admiral King, and General Eisenhower toured the beachhead and the front. Eisenhower, stopping for lunch in recently captured Isigny, was amazed when a sergeant drew hot water for him to wash. That day Prime Minister Churchill visited the battle area with Marshal Montgomery and spent hours cruising up and down offshore. With Churchill were Prime Minister Smuts of South Africa and General Sir Alan Brooke, Chief of the Imperial General Staff.

Probably the greatest thrill that the soldiers received that seventh day of the invasion of Europe came from the debarkation of three unknown Americans—the first Red Cross girls to join American troops in France since the First World War. They were assigned to field hospitals to serve as recreation workers with the wounded.

The Allied front in Normandy now stretched eighty-five miles from one end to the other. Both the Americans and the British were determined to lengthen it. British tanks struck the first blow of the next stage of the invasion, lunging out above Caen to envelop Troarn, five miles east of the river city. Caen was now outflanked on both the east and the west. The next move, in order to neutralize its defenses, was to capture the high ground behind it. Other armor, at the point where the American and British sectors joined, plunged deep to Balleroy, thus providing a fitting celebration for the first anniversary of the completion of the Allies' first invasion-plan draft. That draft envisaged the capture of six to seven hundred square miles the first week, which was exactly what happened.

Behind the actual battle area, an event of historic moment took place when the invasion was hardly a week old. Just a few days short of the fourth anniversary of his heroic and seemingly hopeless struggle to keep the good name of France, General de Gaulle set foot on his native soil for the first time in all that period. With a sentence of death proscribed by the traitorous Vichy "government," the standard-bearer of Free Fighting France crossed the Channel from England. He sailed in a French destroyer, the *Combattant,* under the Tricolor.

The Germans were re-forming, preparing to try once more to throw the Allies out of Europe or to hold them off as long as possible while they effected the withdrawal of all the men and arms they could salvage. The Germans struck at night, thrusting the British out of Troarn. Within a quadrilateral bounded by Caumont, Villers-Bocage, Tilly-sur-Seulles, and Balleroy, the largest armored battle in the history of western Europe was being fought.

There was nothing resembling a fixed front. On the contrary, the lines were extremely fluid. Several times in the same day towns and villages would be taken, regained, and taken again.

The whole of France was seething. In a hundred villages and cities patriot forces were rising and striking hard against their oppressors. Unconnected as these blows might seem with the Allies' supreme effort, they were all part of one great battle for the liberation of France and Europe. Every success of the FFI was a gain for the Allies, even though it took place hundreds of miles from the official fronts. In northern France the efforts of the patriots were of necessity far subordinated to the military campaign. The greatest centers of activity in the center and south were around Lyon, Grenoble, Toulouse, Pau, Tarbes. The strongest concentration of all was in the Department of Haute-Savoie, on the Swiss border. In all these places the FFI were cutting German communication lines, waylaying troops, and killing officers. In Haute-Savoie they were already planning the last touches of their daring campaign to free their own province against vastly larger and better-armed forces. These interior forces, despite all the demands made on the Allies' aërial resources by the main military effort, were getting increased help from the sky. Allied planes were even landing on secret air strips to deposit and take off emissaries and leaders.

The Allies were evacuating the worst casualties from the battle area by air as soon as they could be moved. This plan cut deeply into the expected casualty rates. Meanwhile, the American First Army on the Cherbourg Peninsula was taking what must have seemed to the enemy a completely new course. Instead of continuing its northward drive directly to the port itself, Bradley's command struck out westward across the neck of the peninsula to threaten two important towns on the major highway that ran along the western side: St. Sauveur-le-Vicomte and La-Haye-du-Puits, some eight miles to the south.

While the troops fought, their leaders planned. Their rulers, like their people, watched and waited breathlessly. King George VI of Great Britain was the epitome of his people's spirit when he crossed the Channel to see for himself what so many millions wished with all their hearts they could witness. The King, whose human warmth had so endeared him to Britons, would have gone into the lines if his *entourage* had let him. He persuaded Montgomery to take him dangerously close before he bestowed a new decoration on the General, as well as on several of his officers and men. The King had crossed the Channel on one of his cruisers and transferred to a "duck" to go in to the beach. As his craft churned the water, shells from another British cruiser were screaming above his head.

The Americans pressing across the Cherbourg Peninsula were daily diminishing their chances of naval support as they neared the limit of the range of the ships on the eastern coast. To shell the Germans from the west, the Allied ships would have had to come under the guns of deadly coastal batteries that had not yet been silenced.

The lessening of naval assistance did not stop the Americans; it was the Germans who faltered. Caught in this neck of the Cotentin Peninsula, they had been cut off from all reinforcement and supply. They had to live and fight on the reserves they already had, whereas the Americans could constantly augment their forces and weapons.

St. Sauveur was first entered by American parachutists. They had been in action without respite since D-Day. They stormed first into the town to open the way for the main force behind them. The Germans fell back skilfully, fighting at every step, and withdrew only as they inflicted all the loss they could on the Americans.

By June 18, when the invasion was only two weeks old, the Canadians had their First Army in France, the British had their Second Army, and the Americans had the Fifth and the Seventh Corps, each of which comprised three divisions. The components of the Fifth Corps were the 2nd, 5th, and 297th Divisions. The Seventh Corps was made up of the 82nd and 101st Airborne Divisions and the 4th Infantry Division. In addition, the 1st Infantry Division, the 9th, and at least one armored division were in action. More troops were flowing in daily to complement the First and Third Armies.

Among all these units were many men who had never faced an enemy bullet before they landed in France. Their conduct and their achievements under fire won the highest praise from General Marshall, the Chief of Staff. They were the best possible tribute to the "live-ammunition" and other training techniques that the army commanders had developed.

What had been ordinary barren beaches behind the lines were fast becoming great hives of activity. Ports of debarkation, staging areas, assembly plants—all were erected out of almost nothing, immeasurably assisted by the floating harbors towed across the Channel from Britain and put into operation as soon as they arrived in French waters. These alone could make any beach a port within a day or two. By June 20 they were actually within sight of Cherbourg and at the perimeter of its defenses.

The prepared defense positions rimmed the port in a wide radius on all the land sides; its coastal guns were formidable enough to hold out of range all but the biggest of the Allied warships. But, for all the strength of their defenses, the Germans knew that they were fighting a losing battle. They saw at last the inevitability of early defeat and began to demolish the harbor facilities, so that the Allies should have a minimum of gain from them when they took the city.

The city was invested by June 22, but the Germans were hanging on fanatically. On the south and southwest, the Yanks were three to five miles from the port, grimly hacking and battering their way through tangled barbed wire, machine-gun and mortar positions densely sown before the city.

The Americans addressed an ultimatum to the Cherbourg garrison early on the morning of June 22, giving the defenders until 9:00 A.M. that day to yield. The Germans ignored it.

The all-out onslaught against the city began in the afternoon. The first blow was eighty minutes of diabolically concentrated aërial bombardment of the city's defenses, followed by a half hour of big-gun shelling of the same targets. When the barrage lifted, the infantry went forward with the support of tanks.

Fighting valiantly, the Americans cut through to the sea on the eastern coast of the peninsula below the city at St. Pierre-Eglise. Three divisions were making the attack—the 4th, the 9th, and the 79th, all part of the Seventh Army Corps. Their great achievement had cut off Cherbourg from all communication, while French Partisans fighting underground well behind the battle lines effectively paralyzed the German supply lines and blocked the arrival of reinforcements.

By nightfall of June 22 the Americans were firmly established inside the defenses of Cherbourg, but the enemy was not yielding. During the night the R.A.F. went out against the port's defenders and American planes took up the aërial pounding at daylight. The Germans had orders to stand and die: they were obeying them to the letter.

The men storming Cherbourg had their full quota of individual heroes. There were men like Corporal John Kelly, of Grove City, Pennsylvania, who captured single-handed a pillbox with twenty-one Germans in it, despite the withering fire that was pinning down his unit. Kelly wriggled forward on his belly, dragging several long poles tipped with dynamite charges. Under the heaviest fire, he made his way to the pillbox, which was equipped with a periscope for observation by its defenders. Kelly thrust several of his dynamite charges into the aperture that housed the periscope, ignoring the bullets spattering around him. His courage triumphed. As his captain said: "He smoked the Heinies out!"

It was such grim heroism as this, repeated innumerable times, that enabled the Americans, by the morning of June 24, to stand within sight of the docks of Cherbourg, barely one and a half miles from their most advanced position. As enemy resistance was increasing in direct ratio to the American gains, it became more and more apparent that it would be necessary to fight through the streets and destroy the defenses that had been built within the town.

On June 25, a new and fearful element entered the battle against the Germans. Fourteen of the biggest Allied warships—three American battleships, two British heavy cruisers, and several assorted American and British cruisers and destroyers—opened a simultaneous bombardment of the city from the sea. German shore batteries, stronger even than their defenses against a land attack, fired back until they were put out of action. Although they straddled the Allied ships more than once, they inflicted no serious damage. The ships were shielded by a smoke screen and were well out to sea. For three and a half hours, in broad daylight, the doomed city rocked under the explosions of hundreds of shells from 6-inchers to 14-inchers. Their targets were spotted for them by scout planes that flew above the city and radioed the information.

On this day, for the first time, American troops fought their way into Cherbourg proper. A patrol of fifteen men entered the town. Guided by a Frenchman, they flushed hundreds of exhausted German defenders who were fighting automatically and only too glad to have reached the end of their road. From three sides—east, south, and southwest—American infantrymen and tanks stormed into the city. By nightfall they were battling bitterly through the streets.

The capture of Cherbourg was the most important as well as the most dramatic event of the day. The enemy lost four fine divisions. The Allies gained a great port, however badly smashed by the enemy's demolitions and our own bombardments, which would soon be channeling great forces of men and arms into the battle for Europe.

The German prisoners in the fall of Cherbourg passed twenty-five thousand and included the two commanders of the harbor city's defenses, Lieut. General Carl Wilhelm von Schleiben and Rear Admiral Walter Hennecke. It was von Schleiben who had rejected every American ultimatum and thrown away the lives of countless German and American soldiers in the futile defense of Cherbourg.

German placards still disfigured the main square, and snipers' bullets whined across it even as the American commander, Major General Joseph T. Collins—the conqueror of Guadalcanal—formally restored the city to French sovereignty in a solemn ceremony. Resounding cheers arose as he presented to the city a new Tricolor made of red, white, and blue silk from the parachutes in which the airborne invaders had floated down to French soil on D-Day. On the steps of the Hotel de Ville the city's mayor, Paul Reynaud, accepted the token. All through the occupation, the people had somehow managed to secrete French,

INTERNATIONAL NEWS PHOTO

Return to a "Strongpoint"

Civilians return to the rubble-filled street of Houffalize, Belgium. The town was finally recaptured by the American Third Army in the Battle of the Bulge.

EARLY 1945

INTERNATIONAL NEWS PHOTO

Checking Papers on Belgian Front

A precaution to prevent enemy agents from slipping through the Allied lines somewhere on the shrinking German bulge in Belgium.

BATTLE OF THE BULGE

INTERNATIONAL NEWS PHOTO

Rolling Deeper into Belgium

Truck-borne infantry of the American First Army moves through the snowy landscape.

"Snow" Troops in Action

Infantrymen of the Third Army in Luxembourg sector, wearing camouflage for operations in snow.

SIGNAL CORPS PHOTO

OFFICIAL U. S. NAVY PHOTOGRAPH

Midget Sub and P-T Boat Base

This Jap base hidden in one of the sheltered coves of Okinawa was discovered by low-flying carrier-based planes from the U. S. Pacific Fleet.

OFFICIAL U. S. NAVY PHOTOGRAPH

Leyte Landing

General Douglas MacArthur, Lieut. General Richard K. Sutherland, and Captain C. E. Coney, on bridge of USS *Nashville,* observing landing on Leyte Island.

SIGNAL CORPS PHOTO

Bomb Torn Corregidor

Paratroopers of the 503rd Parachute Infantry Regiment, part of MacArthur's forces, land on the bomb-battered terrain of Corregidor.

The Coast Guard in the Philippines

Coast Guardsmen were at the controls of many of the landing barges that swarmed in upon the beaches of Leyte to deliver General MacArthur's liberation forces.

OFFICIAL U. S. COAST GUARD PHOTO

"At Home" in a Rice Paddy
American troops bivouacked in a Burma rice paddy.

A Border Ceremony
T. V. Soong addressing American and Chinese troops at a border ceremony for the first China convoy over the Ledo-Burma Road.

First Convoy Over Ledo-Burma Road

The first convoy to China moves slowly down the side of the Salween River gorge and over the suspension bridge.

SIGNAL CORPS PHOTO

OFFICIAL COAST GUARD PHOTO

Free From the Shackles
Joyous Filipinos swarm over Luzon's beaches to welcome a Coast Guardsman, a few hours after the amphibious landings on Lingayen Gulf beachheads.

SIGNAL CORPS PHOTO

Back in the Philippines
General Douglas MacArthur strides down the main street in Dagupan Luzon Island, following the capture of the town by American forces.

SIGNAL CORPS PHOTO

Visiting the Imprisoned
General MacArthur after visiting the famous Bilibid Prison in Manila, rushed to the equally well-known Santo Tomas Prison.

SIGNAL CORPS PHOTO

Back After Three Years
General MacArthur returned to Clark Field after an absence of three years, and is here shown inspecting wrecked Jap planes.

WAR DEPARTMENT PHOTO

Malta Meeting of Chiefs of Staff

Prime Minister Winston Churchill on board British warship, greeting President Roosevelt on the bridge of a U. S. warship as he passes by.

SIGNAL CORPS PHOTO

Prison Rescue

of the 6th Ranger Bat- crossing a river bed treams, some distance d the Jap lines.

SIGNAL CORPS PHOTO

"Thumbs Up"

Premier Stalin talks with gestures to his Foreign Minister Molotov at the Crimean Conference.

SIGNAL CORPS PHOTO

Manila Burns

ldier watching the city from the beach at naque, Luzon.

SIGNAL CORPS PHOTO

Crimean Conference

Admiral William Leahy, Admiral E. J. King, President Roosevelt and General George C. Marshall have a talk aboard a warship at Malta.

At the Conference Table at Yalta

President Roosevelt, Prime Minister Churchill, and Marshal Stalin at the Crimean Conference at Yalta.

SIGNAL CORPS PHOTO

Beachhead Secured
The first island hit in gigantic assault on Okinawa was Aka Shima.

Foxhole De Luxe
Getting a few winks of sleep between actions, this Marine comes about as close to comfort as possible. His ornate foxhole on Iwo Jima even has a camouflaged roof.

U. S. ARMY AIR FORCES PHOTO

First Glimpse of Iwo Jima
Troops aboard ship inspect their new home of Iwo Jima before disembarking.

U. S. ARMY AIR FORCES PHOTO

At Foot of Suribachi
The scene of the famous flag-raising episode on Iwo Jima forms a background for the equipment of American troops.

OFFICIAL U. S. NAVY PHOTO

Easter on Okinawa
After the ear-shattering pre-landing barrage and the commotion of landing, a strange peace descended on Okinawa.

OFFICIAL U. S. NAVY PHOTO

Ernie Pyle on Okinawa
The famous war correspondent, during his jeep tour of the beachhead, spent Easter on Okinawa.

Eisenhower Honors Airborne Troops

General Eisenhower, Major General Maxwell D. Taylor, and Lieut. General Lewis R. Brereton, saluting during the review of the famous 101st Airborne Division in France.

INTERNATIONAL NEWS PHOTO

The March of the Supermen

A steady stream of German prisoners march through the battered streets of a German town as Americans watch on the sidelines.

INTERNATIONAL NEWS PHOTO

British, and American flags from the Germans. These now decked the square and the streets.

At the other end of the front the British and Canadians were still slugging, aided as before by heavy aërial support and the bombardments of American and British warships standing offshore.

With the completion of the Cherbourg triumph, the Allies could turn their efforts to other sectors of the Normandy front. The British drive below Tilly took on new strength as planes could be diverted from the Cherbourg front to implement it. Ahead of the advancing Tommies and Canadians went special "flail tanks" to clear the deadly mines from their paths. These machines were equipped with steel cylinders, to which were attached long chains. The cylinders revolved as the tank moved, causing the ends of the chains to beat heavily and continuously against the ground and thus detonate the mines *en masse*. Thus the attacking troops and armor were enabled to thrust ahead on a six-and-a-half-mile line and cross the Odon River opposite Tourville.

The combined objective was the destruction of the enemy's communications and the complete isolation of his forces in Normandy from all the rest of France. This result was attained even as Cherbourg was falling. Every railway bridge across the Loire from its estuary in the area of Nantes to Orleans, nearly 250 miles inland, was lying crumbled. Patriot forces were severing telephone lines and wrecking road transport. Railways had been wrecked. Locomotives had been cut off from their fuel depots; rolling stock had been left stranded. It was impossible for the enemy to send either reinforcements or supplies to his forces in northwestern France; they would have to survive on what they had.

Even before the Americans completed the Cherbourg Peninsula clean-up, the enemy launched a big drive for St. Lô. The British in the Tilly sector were still surging ahead unmindful of enemy opposition. In their Second Army, commanded by Lieutenant General Sir Miles C. Dempsey, were two divisions of the old Eighth Army's desert victories—the 7th Armored and the 50th, or Northumbrian—the "desert rats." The forces that crossed the Odon swept on until they were only four and three-quarter miles away from Caen.

While these battles were being fought on the Western Front in Normandy, the mighty Russian forces on the Eastern Front of Europe were driving the Germans back in retreat. The Allied Armies in Italy were closing in on the Germans from the southern front. Hitler, who had feared a two-front war, was now in the giant nutcracker of a three-front war.

It was in this desperation—ten days after the first invasion of Normandy—that Hitler hurled his long-heralded secret weapon at Britain. Jet-propelled robot bombs rocketed over England and fell with thunderous explosions in a last grand attempt to terrorize the British people.

84

CONQUEST OF CAEN BY CANADIANS— AMERICANS CAPTURE ST. LÔ

HEAVIEST blows struck since D-Day landings in France were taking place on the roads to Caen and to St. Lô in July, 1944. As the jaws of Eisenhower's pincers closed around these strongly fortified cities the Germans reacted violently. Hitler had demanded that these key cities be held at all cost. The conquest of Caen and the fall of St. Lô in effect decided the fate of the Germans in France. It was at these points that their main resistance was offered and its back was broken.

Neither the terrain nor the weather was showing much consideration to the Allies. The country was either open fields on which every man was an excellent target, or crowded orchards in which every tree was an obstacle. Clouds had closed in, precluding the exploitation of the Allies' vast aërial superiority in close ground support lest bombs should fall by accident on our own men. But nothing could deter the indomitable Eisenhower from flying over the front lines even as the ground fighting was at its heaviest. For five days in the beginning of July he inspected the entire front, from the Canadian tank battalion slugging it out for Carpiquet, on the approaches to Caen, to the American divisions battling their way to envelop La-Haye-du-Puits on their way to St. Lô.

The Canadians at Caen were led by a fearless general who was a romantic figure to his men. Fifty-five years old, Lieut. General Sir Richard Nugent O'Connor—known behind his back as Rory—had been captured by the Germans in Libya and escaped from an Italian prison camp to rejoin the battle. Under his leadership, the tanks of Lieut. General H. D. G. Crerar's army lunged out fearlessly whatever the odds against them. On the Fourth of July they took the village of Carpiquet, and even seized the city's airfield. This, however, they were forced to yield under terrific German pressure.

The Americans closing in on La-Haye-du-Puits and in the center of the Allied line celebrated the Glorious Fourth in a manner all their own. Every American artillery piece in France was primed for a grand salvo. Promptly at noon on this day that symbolized everything for which the Yanks were fighting, all the thousands of guns roared at once—new "shots heard round the world." General Bradley himself pulled the first lanyard. Within a fraction of a second the entire front roared and trembled with the fearful pounding of the giant guns. Typical of American spirit was another incident of that day in the battle for La Haye. On D-Day, Lieut. Colonel Benjamin H. Vandervoort of Columbus, Ohio, broke his leg; but he would not leave his troops. On July 4, supporting himself on a crutch, he was at the head of his command as it surged to the crest of a bitterly contested hill.

That day seemed to have given even more power to the American columns. On the fifth, they had virtually surrounded La Haye and seized its railroad station, though the Germans in the rest of the town were still giving them a tough fight. To their left, on the road from Carentan to Periers, the Americans were pushing the enemy back.

At the extreme left end of the line the Canadians, having lost part of the Caen airfield, dug in and re-formed their ranks, while the British on the Odon River bridgehead beat off one counterattack after another. The Germans were using tanks in profusion, but even at the front lines they were fueling vehicles with gas made from charcoal—a sure indication of their utter poverty in gasoline and oil.

While the Americans battled inside La Haye, other columns were striking southward on either side of the town. The Germans had made a fort of every house and from each they had to be blasted; there was little surrendering. But the density of their defense here was as nothing to that in the Caen area, where the troop concentrations per mile of front far exceeded that of any battle of the First World War. For all the Allies' advantages in numbers and equipment—Undersecretary of War Robert P. Patterson estimated our firepower at 4 to 1 above the enemy's—the grim tenacity of the Germans and their commanders' recklessness in expending lives made every gain a bitter one.

Meanwhile, the terror of the 1940-41 blitz was being renewed. The robot bombs, pilotless jet-propelled planes fired from hidden launching sites in France and the Low Countries, were falling in ever-increasing numbers on London and the entire southern English countryside. Mr. Churchill warned the people that they faced even worse suffering than that of the blitz year, for the course or landing points of the monsters now falling among them could never be predicted. Fighters and anti-aircraft batteries, however, were learning how to shoot the robots into harmlessness while they were still in the air.

The Germans took the Caen airfield from the Canadians; but Rory's tanks and the infantry were not going to let the matter rest. In darkness and daylight, withering sun and blinding rain, they struck back, fighting hand-to-hand, with small arms, bayonets, clubbed gunbutts, and even fists and knives. They recaptured the airfield and pushed on.

Field Marshal Karl Rudolf Gerd von Rundstedt, that polished old Prussian who had been commanding the Germans in western Europe, could not stop the invaders, however skilfully he planned, however bitterly his men battled. So his master in Berlin ordered him home. The Austrian upstart relied on his famous military "intuition." The enemy commander whose abilities were respected by Eisenhower was removed for Field Marshal Gunther von Kluge, a steady, plodding leader with none of the imagination or the verve of the man he was replacing. This was a victory for the Allies.

Eisenhower put on heavy pressure along the lines with General Bradley in the west and Monty in the east. The campaign proceeded as it had been planned. While the Anglo-Canadian forces were hammering at the gates of Caen, the Americans thrust down from Carentan to reach the Vire River. Their comrades near the Atlantic coast slugged methodically through La Haye as the flanking columns moved south to either side. Above both armies the Allied planes struck constantly. Far behind the lines other bombers were striking—right for the heart of the robot bombs on which the enemy was counting so heavily. The British with their doughty Lancasters, those stolid planes-of-all-work on which the R.A.F. had so long depended, suddenly unleashed six-ton bombs—the heaviest yet known—on the factories where the robots were being made. Nothing made by man could withstand the detonation of those giants of aërial destruction.

The battles for La Haye and Caen were now proceeding almost synchronously. While Monty, in a Norman hayfield that shook with the roar of guns, was pinning high British decorations on almost a dozen American heroes of the initial actions, British troops fought their way into Caen on July 8 and the Yanks were slowly completing their mop-up of La Haye. To the east of this town, another American force was plunging southward parallel to the escape route the Germans were following out of La Haye, while a third American column was striking down from the Carentan area to seek a junction with the others.

On both the American and the British fronts the Allies found the plane invaluable in a new rôle—that of flying-artillery. When the Germans launched their gigantic tank blows to throw the Allies out of the Caen area, rocket-firing Typhoons were sent up to meet the threat—and they smashed it. Flying low to baffle the antiaircraft gunners, they launched their armor-piercing projectiles against the tanks from less than tree-top height and blew up tank after tank with the loss of hardly a plane.

In the drive south of Carentan, the Americans joined forces with the columns plunging southward to the east of La Haye, enveloping St. Jean-de-Daye and posing a direct peril to the enemy's vital communications center of St. Lô, some thirty miles southeast of La Haye. Below this town, the Germans held another good rail and road town, Lessay, commanding the southbound highway to Coutances and thence to the threshold of Brittany.

It was on the day when the first British troops entered the stone city of Caen that Propaganda Minister Goebbels warned his nation for the first time that it must accept the possibility of defeat. As if to emphasize what he had said, British and Canadian troops surged endlessly into Caen, fighting from street to street and from house to house in the inland port. For thirty-six hours the Germans battled like madmen, but never regained an inch. On July 9 they had lost their first great bastion in eastern Normandy. On the same day the Americans wound up their conquest of La Haye.

The Allies' plan of campaign was beginning to unfold. The British and Canadians were going to drive straight across the north of France, sweeping perhaps as far south as Paris, while the Americans cleared the western littoral before turning sharply to cut across France for Germany. The Americans' next objectives were thus Lessay, where the coastal highway to Coutances split off from the inland road to the same town; Periers, another road junction on the highway from Lessay to St. Lô, and St. Lô itself, where roads and railways gave the possessors of the town control over communications well into the interior.

All were heavily defended. Eisenhower planned to minimize losses as much as possible. To accomplish this he used a secret force of the Allied Expeditionary Force of which little was being said. This was a special group of parachutists who were not combat troops in the ordinary sense but rather trained saboteurs whose task it was to work with the French Underground in destroying enemy stores and communications. This group and the Frenchmen with whom it worked had already contributed immeasurably to the speed of the Allied victories. Behind the enemy's lines they were constantly active. Radio and other communication was maintained regularly between them and the armies of which they were the antennæ.

Before the steadily forward-thrusting Americans and Britons, their artillery was laying down massive barrages. In the drive on Periers, for example, artillery of all sizes was active throughout the day and night. The air was so constantly reverberating that men achieved a kind of deafness in which they could not hear the roar of guns. The silence when this stopped was oppressive. Its effect on the Germans was unexpected; more than any other weapon, more even than the bombers and strafing fighters, the artillery smashed the Germans' spirit. In sectors where the artillery was most concentrated, German troops would come forward under the white flag, their trembling hands raised over their heads, begging to surrender that they might escape the nerve-wracking hell of the artillery bombardment. It was the shell-shock of the First World War on an infinitely greater scale.

Such barrages were no less effective on the British front. Because their position was a direct threat to Germany proper, the Germans massed more men and arms there, and progress was necessarily slower. But, once Caen had been taken and mopped up, the British forged ahead through the city and below it, establishing firm bridgeheads on the Odon and the Orne.

Hedgehog defenses surrounded St. Lô. One such hedgehog was the town of Meauffe, which quickly became "Murphy" to the Yanks. Meauffe was held by fanatical German troops determined that the little country village was not going to fall to the Americans while they lived—and not many of them were alive when it fell.

St. Lô, because of its importance to communications, was the most strongly defended of all the American objectives at this point. The town was partly protected by a ring of hills and thick forests that afforded the Germans great natural advantages over any attackers. Here they had concentrated their forces. For days and nights the Americans battled through these woods and up these hills.

Hill 192 was an example of what the Americans had to contend with. This height—whose altitude in meters was indicated by its name—was heavily defended. The Germans had been practicing with it for three years. It was crowned by a clump of trees. At 5:40 one morning, American guns opened up on it. Fifty minutes later, when the guns ceased, the crest of the hill was a huge forest fire. Shells had landed in an ammunition dump somewhere up there and for hours the air was irregularly torn with the explosions of the enemy's arsenal.

Until now the hedgerows, thickset as they were, had seemed invulnerable to armor. But a new technique was tried and it worked. Tanks and infantry went in together, each protecting the other; and along with them went engineers with demolition charges to blow up the natural barriers. When a tank reached a hedge, it would shell the garrison behind it point-blank while the infantrymen cleaned up the flanking hedges. This job done, the engineers blew up the hedges. It was not speedy or spectacular work, but it was effective. Thus the Americans, in seven and a half hours, had won to the blackened crest of Hill 192; four hours later they had fought their way to its base at the other side.

Such fighting, close in as it was, was naturally fraught with losses. Yet there was one loss, in the days of the battle for St. Lô, that hit the army as hard, perhaps, as that of a whole company. That was the death of Brigadier General Theodore Roosevelt. A true Roosevelt, he was no rear-area officer: he died at a divisional command post in Normandy in the thick of battle. And the men felt his loss. He was a man, a soldier's soldier. Every day—as his C.O., Major General R. O. Barton of the Fourth Division, said of him—he rode out where the fighting was thickest, for he sensed how much his inexhaustible energy and enthusiasm meant to the ordinary foot soldiers who were slugging it out up there. He shared their perils and their hardships. General Barton said: "There's not a soldier or an officer in this division who won't feel a personal loss." He was buried in Normandy where he fell—a great son of a great American.

As the guns of liberated Cherbourg roared their Bastille Day salute to still-enslaved France and all the free world, American troops stood within a mile and a half of the waiting German armor at Lessay. The defenses of Periers and St. Lô were being irresistibly shattered under powerful air and artillery blows.

Allied planes were constantly active and one of them caught a big prize. Under von Kluge, wily old Marshal Rommel, the "Desert Fox" of Africa, still enjoyed a field command. In the course of an inspection of his troops by car, he was pounced upon by a fighter that swept down out of the sun with all its guns blazing. The Marshal's car was immediately enveloped in flames. His driver was killed. Rommel, with several of his aides, left a bloody trail as he scrambled for the shelter of the nearest ditch. Eliminated from the war, later to die tragically either from his wounds or by suicide or murder, the "Desert Fox" was gone. Marshal Montgomery was thus denied his cherished hope of one day capturing his long-time adversary.

American might rolled ever closer to Lessay and St. Lô at the ends of the front. Two American forces, striking toward Periers from the northeast and the northwest, united above the town. The front was virtually solidified. Only little gaps existed in the long line winding from the sea to the woods and hills behind and below St. Lô. The town was defended by fiercely fanatical parachutists turned infantrymen, who would rather die than yield, and by other troops whose Élite Guard officers had to threaten to shoot them from behind to compel them to stand up to the Americans' onslaughts. In some sectors, despite his aggregate strength of twenty to twenty-five divisions in Normandy —some 240,000 to 300,000 men—the enemy was impressing cooks, typists, truck drivers, and even slave laborers into front-line duty. "Kitchen Commandos," the Americans called them; and they were usually the first, when their officers were not looking, to surrender.

But the majority of the German troops were standing firm and fighting hard. They had the assistance of a terrain that was far worse than the Argonne of the First World War. Swamps and hedgerows, augmented by skilful German flooding of low-lying areas, made swift maneuvering by the Allies impossible. The doughboys had to fight forward, attacking frontally.

The First Army smashed into Lessay on July 15 and closed in farther on Periers and St. Lô. The important junction town was the center around which a ring was being slowly but irresistibly drawn in preparation for a smashing attack from every side.

This was among the toughest battles in the history of American armies. For almost a week the Americans laid siege to St. Lô. Against them the enemy was using everything at his command. Tanks and self-propelled guns did double duty as regular artillery.

The final entry into the city came from the north, as the Germans on heights were pouring shells into the town and its approaches. The major assault had been held up by the American commanders in the hope of keeping loss of life to a minimum. When almost a week had gone by, with only minuscule gains at great cost, they decided that more lives would be saved by one final smash. This was launched under constant fire and against fierce resistance. Every curve of a road was an ambush. Troops had to crawl on their bellies in ditches along the roads, in advance of the armor, to assure its safe passage.

Other units had been attacking from the east and their fight was equally heroic. The Germans launched the biggest counterattacks they had yet staged. The air was black with flying metal and rent with the screams of shells, the dull booming of explosions, the sharp crackle of rifle and small-arms fire.

Two battalions from the east, fighting down the Bayeux road, were almost lost. There was no real front line when the first, under Major Sidney V. Bingham of Dallas, worked up to the farthest forward position at the village of Le Madel. The Americans fought forward wherever opportunity offered or could be created. The enemy closed ranks behind them and they were cut off. Under constant bombardment, Bingham used his radio sparingly lest he bring down even worse punishment on his troops. Food and ammunition were running short. Wounded men needed care. Just before his radio's battery died, he got word of his plight to his regiment—then he could tell no more.

But another battalion was on the way, bringing not only reinforcements but supplies. Under Major Thomas D. Howie, it fought its way in to Bingham's men and joined them. It had to stay, for behind it the enemy had closed his ranks again. Both battalions were cut off.

The two "lost battalions" were under constant attack from every arm at the Germans' command. Their strength was heavily cut into, but Bingham and Howie rallied their spirits and skilfully deployed them in such a way as to enable them to inflict a maximum of retaliation on the enemy with a minimum of cost to themselves. For thirty-six hours they held out. Then, without rest and on meager rations, they launched their own attack at four o'clock in the July morning. They attacked, however, under only one leader. Howie, who had led them through to the succor of Bingham's men and helped his fellow officer through the thick of the battle, was dead from a German bullet. His men were determined to avenge him.

It was 10:00 A.M. when the Americans entered St. Lô, having made contact with the troops lunging down from the north. Bingham's and Howie's battalions and their reinforcements, lashing out with armored cars and tanks, cracked the last defenses, blazing a path into the town.

Major Howie entered St. Lô, too—in a position of honor, even in death. His body had been placed, at the commander's orders, in a special ambulance. As soon as the tanks and infantry had secured the entrance to the town, the ambulance followed in the place of honor at the head of a special noncombatant section of the task force.

The boys of the First Army, under General Courtney Hodges, made the vital breakthrough to St. Lô, after inching their way on all fours. They had been the first to storm the Normandy beaches—and were to be the first in great victories to come.

Normandy was full of heroes in that eight-day siege of St. Lô. While Wacs were taking up their duties on the original beachhead, hundreds and thousands of Americans were performing deeds that were beyond belief. There was young Sgt. James F. Mathias, who had entered the army from the City College of New York. A teacher of history, a slim, bespectacled Ph.D. from Yale, he found himself pinned down with his company under German fire. Officer after officer fell until only a major was left, too wounded to carry out his duties. Taking charge of what was left of his company, Sgt. Mathias defied the dense German fire from the 88's and got every living man back to safety.

While American troops were battering their way into St. Lô, Monty was striking hard at Caen. His front roared with constant artillery barrages, a sure signal to the Germans that something was brewing. Nor were the signs wrong. On July 16, the British and Canadians broke out on a front six miles wide on either side of Caen.

The British drive was pointed toward Villers-Bocage and Evrecy. Esquay was taken in two hours by an infantry attack, while armor consisting of both American Shermans and British Cromwells was rolling forward for the main objectives. Bretteveille, Gavrus, Bougy, and Cahier were among the towns southeast of Caen that fell quickly. Evrecy, on the left flank, was taken the next day.

Opposed by Élite German units, Montgomery was using the cream of his own army—the 51st Highland Division (the "Ladies from Hell" who had so badly mauled the Germans in the First World War and then smashed them again in Africa, Sicily, and Italy), and crack armored divisions. Overhead he was supported by a great force of bombers of the R.A.F. and the U.S.A.A.F., which poured 7,000 tons of bombs on the enemy's positions and supplies within four hours. The main battlefield had shifted nearer the northern coast, to the area of Banneville-la-Campagne and Emieville.

The Germans were bewildered by Allied strategy. Hitler, in Berlin, raged against his generals. Eisenhower again had outwitted them. Would he strike for Germany—or for Paris—or both? Would he drive across France—or would he swing through Belgium and Holland?

LIBERATION OF FRANCE—VICTORY MARCH INTO PARIS

RESURRECTION of France, after more than four years of captivity, was sounding like a trumpet call throughout the Republic in the summer of 1944. Rainbows flamed in the skies as the Allies drove the Germans steadily back.

As the Allies' triumph began to reap its harvest, the Germans found new difficulties at home. Malcontents among the Junkers took advantage of a secret staff meeting at Hitler's headquarters to attempt the Fuehrer's assassination with a bomb. Many of his staff were killed. Hitler was severely injured. Military leaders in the plot were arrested and eventually hanged. They included two field marshals and some disaffected Nazis. Although wounded, Hitler kept his hands on the conduct of the war. Dissatisfied with his armies' progress under Field Marshal Wilhelm Keitel, who was in over-all command, Hitler replaced him with the man who enjoyed the reputation of undisputed mastery of armored warfare among all the German fighting men—General Heinz Guderian. It was Guderian who, more than ten years before, had immediately sensed the value of De Gaulle's treatise on mechanized warfare and had begun the application of its principles to the German Army; it was Guderian who had conceived and executed the terrible destruction of the Allies' armies that led to the lightning conquest of France and the Low Countries in 1940. Surely he could stop the reversal of that tide of battle.

About this time the Allies lost one of their leaders. General Lesley J. McNair, commander of all the U. S. Army's ground forces, was visiting the Normandy front to observe the results of the training he had ordered for American troops. He was the originator of live-bullet training, in which new soldiers learned the actualities of battle without a real enemy opposing them. During his tour he was struck by a shell fragment that penetrated his steel helmet and entered the brain. Heroic efforts were made to save him. One of the best minds of the American Army was "killed in action."

The British were ironing out their line's kinks and generally straightening the Allies' whole front. In powerful one-two punches, Dempsey's Britons and Crerar's Canadians pounded southward to take May, St. Martin-de-Fontenay, and Verriers. There was fighting in the streets of Tilly-la-Campagne. The Germans lashed back and regained Evrecy, Esquay, and St. Martin, but they were not to hold them long.

The Americans from St. Lô were driving southwest, a spearhead lunged for Coutances and the line opened to a point just east of Periers, where the Germans were still holding. The Americans drove through Marigny, well down the road into Camprond. Another spearhead reached Canisy and then, splitting up, thrust southwest to Cerisy-la-Salle and south to Mesnil-le-Herman. Periers fell and other American forces drove down the third southbound road to Coutances. Staff maps of this area were now like a hand with many fingers all probing deep into the enemy's territory. The thumb of the hand was at Mesnil-le-Herman; the little finger was below Lessay.

By the end of July the Americans had swept through Coutances and were on the road to Brittany. Some twenty-five miles south of Coutances lay Avranches, the entrance to the peninsula. Americans were piling in on it from all sides. The First Army rolled right through Avranches, and the battle for Brittany was on. Rounding the coast, they took famous Mont St. Michel and drove west. Other units following the vanguards were soon spreading across the Breton Peninsula.

But a surprise for the Germans was in an advanced stage of preparation. The British troops beside the Americans at Caumont, with a relatively clear field before them, drove southward and southwest for Vire and Condé and southeast through the woods for Thury-Harcourt to trap the Germans from behind. In Brittany, the Americans were almost at St. Malo on the northern coast, while a spearhead cutting across the peninsula was battering at the gates of Rennes.

The Breton Peninsula was the work of hardly a week. Some ports, such as St. Malo, Brest, Lorient, and St. Nazaire, were very strongly held, with supplies that would last the garrisons for months. The Americans tried at first to overwhelm them, but bigger goals were in view and not too much time or energy could be wasted on what were soon to be isolated outposts. When attacks by sea, land, and air could not quickly reduce the ports, the Americans left naval units to harass, with small but strong forces on land to prevent their breaking out, and passed on to the next objective.

Rennes fell quickly to the Americans; the Germans lost their key to Brittany. This historic city was a vital road and rail center that linked the peninsula with all the rest of France. The main part of the country itself was now in graver peril than ever. As the American forces poured down from Normandy to regroup at Avranches, large bodies began thrusting eastward into the heart of the land, pounding for junction after junction. Artillery was the constant companion of the armor and infantry. Its strength never diminished. For the first time, the Americans found the troops of Hitler's *Schutzstaffel,* crumbling even before they had been hit, surrendering almost before a shot had been fired.

As the Americans entered Mortain, some twenty miles almost due east of Avranches, the British who had taken Vire were executing a parallel movement. Driving east through Condé toward Falaise, they were piling up a solid wall behind the Germans waiting in the woods of Normandy between Falaise and St. Martin-de-Fontenay. The invaders of Brittany, sweeping up everything in their path, freed the entire peninsula with the exception of the few hold-out ports—and the battle for France itself was on.

Guderian, the Germans' new over-all commander, may have been a genius in modern warfare, but he had been tried only in offense. No one could predict how he would acquit himself on the defensive. He was under the handicap of having as his deputy the unimaginative von Kluge, whose mind could not conceive the swift maneuvering and skilful thrust and wheel that had won so many victories for the team of Guderian and the now-dead Rommel.

General Eisenhower was not going to allow Guderian to learn defensive warfare. Now that Rundstedt, the brilliant commander among the Germans, was out of the battle, everything would be much simpler.

From Brittany a whole American army swept inland as the British at the northeast end of the line broke out of their positions like rockets. With perfect coördination of every arm, including the navy in the north, the Allies threw their entire might not only into but through the bulk of the German forces. The retreat became a rout.

Troarn became a memory; British forces were far to the west almost overnight. Along the coast, the lines moved up to the edge of Cabourg; from St. Martin-de-Fontenay, British and Canadian troops poured into Falaise. From Vire the British pressed against the enemy's rear.

The Americans were making the spectacular gains in terms of distance. While one force struck down the coast for Bordeaux, General "Blood-and-Guts" Patton and General Omar Bradley hurled their main strength straight into the body of France. Argentan, southeast of Falaise, fell; Aleçon, ten miles below it, was left far behind. By mid-August the Third Army had swept through Le Mans and, cutting its force in two, was driving for Chartres and Chateaudun. The enemy could not tell which was the main objective: whether the Americans would try to take Chartres and then lunge thirty-odd miles farther for Paris; or whether Chateaudun and the lovely country to the south would be overwhelmed in an effort to form a giant pocket of virtually the entire country.

A scale-model of such a pocket was now unmistakably complete in what was left of Normandy. In a giant vise of American, British, and Canadian troops, almost 250,000 Germans were helplessly pressed within the small area bounded on the north by Sassy and Condé; on the east by Sourdeval and Domfront; on the south by Barentan, Carrouges, and Argentan. The jaws were inching closer together into the narrow gap that was the only possible means of retreat left to the Germans. But this little slit of land—it was barely ten miles wide—was swept by the Allies' artillery, probed by their patrols, and under constant aërial attack.

The Allies were expending vast amounts of fuel to keep their huge mechanized armies and their growing Europe-based air force in constant action. For what they planned, even more oil would be needed. German planes and E-boats—what was left of them—sought in vain through the tossing Channel to cut down the tankers that should have been supplying the Allies' rail and road transport. The Germans marveled at their absence; obviously the gas and the oil were getting where they were intended to go.

That was the Allies' great secret. Long before the first parachutist dropped into Normandy on D-Day, not only the plans but the concrete steps toward the conquest of this supply problem had been taken. Great pumping stations had been set up along the southern coast of England, camouflaged in an amusement park, an ice cream factory, an old fort built to repel the invasion that Napoleon never launched. These stations were linked to Britain's oil pipelines.

From these the Allies thrust out the steel tentacles of what soon came to be known to the men who made it possible as "Operation Pluto"—Pipelines Under the Ocean. That was exactly what they did: They laid great oil lines on the floor of the Channel, reeling out the pipe even in daylight from great floating drums that revolved to pay out pipe in ¾ mile lengths. Twenty such lines were laid—four from the Isle of Wight to Cherbourg and sixteen from Dungeness to Boulogne. The entire idea was the brain child of Lord Louis Mountbatten, the leader of the Commandos. Leading engineers hooted at it, but British and American scientists plugged away at it until they could claim success. By August 12 it was in full operation; by the time the war ended it had pumped 120,000,000 gallons of oil from Britain to Europe. As the Allies took one coastal point after another, the line was hooked up with the existing Continental pipelines to augment the portable lines laid by the Americans as they advanced; so that, before the Germans surrendered, oil was being pumped uninterruptedly, under land and sea and land again from Britain to Frankfort-am-Main, east of the Rhine.

While the Allies were inexorably closing the Falaise pocket and below it threatening Tours, Dreux, Orleans, and striking fear into the hearts of the Germans in Paris, a new blow was being mounted. Early on the morning of August 16, under the leadership of the victor of Guadalcanal, Lieut. General Alexander M. Patch, the American Seventh Army—General Patton's old command in Sicily whose whereabouts had troubled the Germans for almost a year—swarmed into southern France by sea and air. The Americans were the majority of the landing forces; but with them came Frenchmen to fight as an organized regular army once again on their own soil. They were the French First Army of Major General Jean de Lattre de Tassigny.

De Tassigny had stood by his countrymen in their darkest days. He fought through the Battle of France in 1940. When it ended so ingloriously, he withdrew to the Unoccupied Zone and retained his rank in the skeleton police army that the Germans permitted Vichy to retain. Apparently with the régime of Pétain and Laval, he had never been out of touch with the resistance movement within France or with the Fighting French National Committee in London. When, on November 11, 1942, the Germans overran the Unoccupied Zone, De Tassigny rallied his little command and gave battle to the armored might of Germany. He failed, of course, but his conscience was clear. With the occupation of the south his usefulness there had ended. He escaped to North Africa and joined the forces of the French there. General de Gaulle, on his accession to power, assigned De Tassigny to the new French Army that was being formed and sent him into Italy with the Americans for a while; there he devoted himself to preparing for the task of striking a direct blow for the liberation of his own country.

The invaders landed on the Cap Negre Peninsula some twenty miles due east of Toulon by air, and swallowed up the islands of Port Cros and Levant on the way. In a matter of little more than hours they had gained a wide beachhead and driven eight miles inland, aided to the full by the FFI. Cannes and Nice fell quickly. Ahead of the troops, the Allied planes smashed methodically at all the German communications in the south, while behind the enemy the FFI of the Department of Savoie rose as an army. In a fully matured and armed onslaught, they took over the department town by town. Germans near the Swiss border tried to flee across it, but the Swiss soon turned them back to the French, who took few prisoners.

Throughout France the patriots were rising; but elsewhere they had not the strength of the Savoyards. It was fantastic, even so, in Savoie and Haute-Savoie. The Allies had armed the patriots as well as they could, and the men of the resistance movement had stolen arms from the Germans to the best of their ability; then turned to and fabricated their own. Deportations had long since taken off most of the men; those left were few indeed against the mass of the German Army with all its fine modern equipment. The FFI, however, had one thing that the Germans could not match—a real cause. Incredibly, they conquered Grenoble; they won Lyon; Chambery became French again. The Germans fled northward before these ill-armed, un-uniformed civilians.

This was not only gallant and romantic; it was immensely practical, for it assured the Allies in the south that the enemy would not be able to provide any substantial reinforcements to meet their attacks there.

In the other patriot risings, much of the Allies' work was being lightened by the destruction of communication lines, supply depots, and ammunition dumps. The very sinews of war were being stripped from the Germans. Limoges fell to the French. The patriots would not wait for the arrival of their own regulars. For in the north a French division, fully armed and trained, was striking for freedom.

This was the French Second Armored Division. Its history was almost as fantastic as that of the Maquisards who aided it behind the German lines. The division's commander was that heroic French figure who had conquered the jungles and deserts of Africa and stricken terror into Germans and Italians from Tripoli to Tunis—the mysterious Jacques Leclerc, now a major general. After the North African campaign had ended, he had been commissioned to form this division around the nucleus of his own almost guerrilla fighters. Its troops were North African civilians, refugee veterans of the French Underground, Frenchmen who had lived for years abroad. They trained in Africa with the latest American equipment; they trained again in Britain before they landed in Normandy.

Their arrival was a dramatic event in every town through which they passed. For nearly every town was represented in the division's ranks. In every village a tank would stop before a little house, a jeep would pull off the road, a marching man would break ranks under full pack to press a grim yet tender kiss on the wife or the child or the mother whom he had not seen for as much as four years—kinsfolk who thought him dead. But they did not tarry for sentiment; these French fighters had deadly business to finish.

The battle was now in brilliant operation. In north and south alike the Allies could not be stopped. Between them the Underground Army of France was steadily widening its grip until before long it effected a junction with the two invading forces. Their fronts were solidly connected by that of the so-called Maquis in western and central France—sweeping on toward Germany. The one large concentrated German force in France was big, numerically; but paradoxically it was also helpless. It was the bag of the Falaise pocket, whose egress-gap had narrowed to five miles by August 17—the day that for the first time since 1940 the sound of French and Allied guns was once more heard in Paris.

In the extreme west, an American spearhead probing the coast lunged to Nantes and pressed on. The Seventh Army and the French First were meeting relatively light resistance. Town after town fell almost without a fight. The forces fanned out in every direction amid the rejoicing of the French population, who swarmed to feed and house the troops. Only Marseilles and Toulon were to provide any trouble of consequence in southern France.

Northern France was becoming the scene of a gigantic mopping-up operation. Americans joined Canadian troops at Gace and sealed off the last tiny exit from the Falaise pocket; British troops pounded down the road to Lisieux and up the coast through Cabourg on the road that would take them to the great port of Le Havre. The American Third Army's tough warriors spread out west of Paris to cut off the Germans between the Seine and the sea to the north and hack at the capital's outskirts from the south and southwest. Chartres had fallen; Orleans was ours; Fontainebleau was within sight.

Paris, still occupied by the Germans, was a mad city. Unknown to the world and even to the occupants, the Parisian Underground was polishing its last plans for the city to liberate itself. To the vast majority of Parisians this was unknown. They were beside themselves with joy and impatience. Already the more enterprising were selling—at prices that made the worst black-market racketeers of the capital green with envy—seats along the probable route of the Allies' great march of triumph that would follow the rout of the Germans. Already the Allied flags had begun to appear. People sang "Tipperary" and "Over There" on the streets again. They dared to hum the "Marseillaise."

The amazing story of the liberation of Paris is like a chapter from Dumas, a story of intrigue and valor and defiance. The actors were Frenchmen, Germans, neutrals, all compounding a drama of careful planning and almost divine chance. It was carried out without the approval of either General de Gaulle or the Allies' Supreme Command—and almost resulted in the destruction of the city just when the Allies were about to surround it and free it by a master-stroke of strategy.

In August of 1944 one Alexandre Parodi (who is now a member of the French Council of Ministers) was the resistance movement's liaison with the French Committee of National Liberation, whose chairman, General de Gaulle, was still shuttling between London and Algiers. M. Parodi found it impossible to communicate with De Gaulle when, on Monday, August 14, he was informed that one of the three resistance groups within the city's police force had called a strike of the police. Parodi, hearing that the Germans had somehow got a tip on this, urged all three resistance groups to strike at once.

Paris, under the Germans, was then commanded by General Dietrich von Choltitz. He had in the city more than 10,000 regular troops, forty-nine heavy tanks, a few flame-throwers, and some of the so-called robot tanks that had proved so ineffectual in Italy. Near Amiens, eighty miles to the north, another German commander had 150 heavy tanks ready at a moment's notice to move on Paris. And sixty-nine dive bombers stationed at airfields near the city could have bombed it at will, for it no longer had any antiaircraft defenses. The resistance leaders knew all this and fully realized the risks they faced.

The police strike was called. Hardly a man disobeyed. All but 300 of the 20,000 policemen went off duty on August 15. The Germans began to leave at once. Streets were choked with their vehicles. Tanks and trucks hurried north and east in what seemed to be near-panic. The city was vibrant with suspense. Four days the city was without police protection. Late on the night of Friday, August 18, the striking policemen, all armed, assembled in civilian clothes and stormed the Prefecture. By 1:00 A.M. it was in their hands and the German-appointed prefect was their prisoner.

Parodi and the National Council of Resistance—the central directing organization for all the resistance movements in the country—decided to strike the final blow. Some French officers and a British officer were secretly in Paris on missions for the Allies, and tried to dissuade the FFI, but in vain. But during the night the Germans attacked the Prefecture, in which the patriot police had barricaded themselves with their few arms, and surrounded it. At 5:00 A.M. on Sunday, Paris was awakened by a violent thunderstorm. Parodi's first reaction was that the Germans had started to bomb Paris and his plan had failed. The Swedish Consul, Raoul Nordling, had taken a hand. Mediating between the patriots and the Germans, he arranged a truce that suspended the fighting at the Prefecture with both parties in the positions they then held and treated their captives as regular prisoners of war. Thus, in effect, the FFI gained the status of a regular army. The truce was to last throughout Sunday. The French agreed gladly; it was an unexpected opportunity to group their forces and to bring the Americans and Leclerc's armored division nearer to the capital.

Out of nowhere, in this enemy-ruled and German-looted city, cars suddenly poured into Paris. Each was filled to capacity and bore the Cross of Lorraine and the letters FFI on its sides; many carried public-address equipment. It was a strange assortment of vehicles: tiny sports cars, German staff cars stolen long ago and carefully hidden; ancient taxis brought out of storage; trucks and ambulances. They were broadcasting the "cease fire" order.

The Resistance Council reconvened. The truce was to remain in effect throughout the following day but many members of the Council distrusted the Germans. Parodi still feared German bombardment. To his compatriots he made a compromise offer: he pleaded that the truce run for twenty-four hours more. In the interval, Parodi expected the Allies to reach the city. The Council finally voted to accept his plan.

The French resistance movement embraced every possible shade of political opinion and every stratum of society from the Communists to the extreme rightist nationalists. Parodi, the liaison with De Gaulle, was a Socialist; his closest collaborator, who functioned as the secret delegate of the Committee of National Liberation's Commissioner for

Occupied Territories, was an international banker, Alexandre de St. Phalle. While the truce lasted, Parodi learned that the Germans were far less numerous than he had at first believed and that they were fleeing across the Seine. On Tuesday morning, he summoned Colonel Rol, the FFI's chief in Paris, and the military committee of the Council, and told them that the battle should be resumed.

Barricades seemed to spring fully constructed from the pavements. German cars were left wrecked and burning all over Paris; captured cars were immediately equipped with FFI insignia and sent out to serve as cavalry. Each was filled with patriots armed with rifles, revolvers and sub-machine guns blazing from the windows.

The patriots succeeded in capturing five German cannon and set them in place before the Prefecture on the Ile de la Cité. At pistol-point, captured German gunners instructed the Frenchmen in their use. Snipers climbed to the high apartments and rooftops to attack Germans in the streets. Guerrillas slunk along walls and fired into doorways. It was the Revolution of 1789 all over again.

Throughout Wednesday and Thursday the battles raged, diminishing only slightly in fury at night. FFI bands swept through the streets in cars or on bicycles, rounding up Germans who could not flee. Captives were stripped of their arms and sent out of the fighters' way. The Germans, at von Choltitz's orders, burned the Grand Palais. The General threatened to put the entire city to the torch.

French chemists worked with Spanish revolutionaries who had emerged from hiding to manufacture grenades out of bottles filled with stolen gasoline. Incredible amounts of the precious fuel had been stolen during the occupation and hidden away for just this opportunity. Homemade grenades were tossed into German tanks. The heat exploded them. Crews burned to death.

As the fighting raged, women and children risked their lives with a grim, fierce zest to set their beloved city free again. They were fighting not only for their city—they were winning back at long last their own self-respect that a traitor government had stolen from them five years before. At long last they were once more French! They were Parisians again! From building to building the battle raged.

Throughout these tense hours, General Patton, with his gallant Third Army swinging in a wide arc, was at the gates to Paris, waiting for the signal to enter. But he preferred to extend the honors to the French soldiers—a magnificent demonstration of chivalry. The patriots' leaders, meanwhile, got word to General Patton. He sent into the city the first Allied troops to enter it—three tanks from Leclerc's division, which fought their way to the Prefecture, still under siege, on Thursday night. General Billotte of Leclerc's staff sent an ultimatum to von Choltitz as the fighting raged, demanding his surrender.

Nordling carried the message to the German's headquarters in the Hotel Meurice. Von Choltitz rejected the ultimatum but asked the French to accord him the honor of being attacked by them. He also asked them to allow the evacuation of the women of his staff before they attacked. Apparently he reckoned that, if the French launched an assault, he could surrender without sullying his honor, for he did exactly that. The Meurice's telephones had been cut and he had to send an officer into the thick of the fighting to inform his men that the battle of Paris was over—the proud German Army had lost it to an unschooled force of civilians.

While the fighting in Paris was raging, the Allies were steadily nearing the city in force. The Third Army was the closest, and the entry of Leclerc's tanks was soon followed by that of American troops. To the west, the First Army, with the British and Canadians, was cleaning up the Falaise pocket in which 100,000 Germans or more were finally sealed off alive, turning the flank of the German Fifteenth Army. Fourteen enemy divisions and the remnants of four others were being pummeled in pockets west of Argentan.

The Allies were making fresh landings by air and sea in the south. One of these was effected west of the great naval base of Toulon, toward which other units were driving from the east. In only a few places, such as St. Maxime, did the Allies encounter stiff resistance, but it did not long delay them. For the moment they did not attempt any assault on such heavily fortified places as Toulon; instead, they drove northwest behind it to the important road junction of Aix-en-Provence while the other end of their line thrust up as far as Castellane. The capture of Aix gave the Allies dominance over the communications to both Toulon and the important port of Marseilles; there they crashed into Toulon from the north and the west.

The battle in Toulon lasted for days, despite the highly effective assistance of the FFI within the city.

The Americans were far in the lead of the race toward Germany. Lunging southeast of Paris, the Third Army reached Sens, whence a fine road led through Troyes to Germany. Northwest of the capital another force moved down from Mantes. Spearheads had driven around Paris as far as Meaux on the way to the Marne.

The day for the liberation of Paris had come on August 23, 1944. The forces of General de Gaulle and the almost legendary General Leclerc stormed their way in twin drives through German mine fields, artillery barrages, and defenses ringing Paris. The Germans were strongly fortified with tanks in the Place de la Concorde, along the Champs-Élysées, in the Champs-de-Mars and its barracks under the shadow of the Eiffel Tower—a triangle in the heart of the city.

French and American troops entered Paris on August 25 through the gates of the Porte d'Orleans and the Chatillon. Driving their way to the Ile-de-la-Cité in the heart of Paris they joined the Fighting French patriots. The French fought in the Luxembourg Gardens, in front of the French Senate, and along the boulevards to the Chamber of Deputies and Les Invalides, the tomb of Napoleon. The Americans battled around the famous Louvre and the Cathedral of Notre Dame.

The Germans, realizing their doom, began their evacuation. As the Army of Occupation fled on escape routes, the German commander and his staff, who had been surrounded in the Hotel Meurice, offered to accept unconditional surrender. Terms were signed at 6:00 P.M. on August 25, in the baggagemaster's office in the Mont Parnasse railroad station. At an unpainted wooden table in this cubbyhole sat General Dietrich von Choltitz, commander of the Paris garrison. He haughtily splashed his signature as the French Brigadier General Jacques-Philippe Leclerc, with an American corps commander, stood over him.

Within a few hours, the "Provisional Government of France" was established, signed and ratified in London by General Eisenhower, representing the United States; Anthony Eden, representing Great Britain; and French Foreign Commissioner, René Massigli. As the French political leaders moved into Paris to take over the Government on August 26, General Charles de Gaulle entered the liberated city and headed the greatest jubilee procession in history. The Germans, violating their pledges as was their habitual method, dropped bombs into the city as it was officially delivered to Lieutenant General Joseph-Pierre Koenig, as Military Commander of Paris.

General de Gaulle, savior of France, had entered the city in triumph. Never has a returning hero received greater ovation. The stirring song of the *Marseillaise* rang from a million throats. Weaving his way through the exuberant masses he entered the magnificent Cathedral of Notre Dame in thanksgiving and knelt for Mass at its sacred altar.

Then came another day long to be remembered. The Americans had come! The Stars and Stripes gleamed in the sun as the Victory parade marched through the boulevards. The glorious Place de la Concorde was massed with cheering people. As the long line of marching men in American khaki and steel helmets passed up the beautiful Champs-Élysées, bands played the national anthems of the Allies and the voices of the multitude rang out in the "Star-Spangled Banner," the "Marseillaise," and the British "God Save the King."

Under the Arc de Triomphe the lines halted in the August sun to pay tribute to France and her dead. Wreaths were placed on the tomb of the Unknown Soldier with its eternal light.

A few days more and these Yanks were on their way to the Rhine—to the conquest of Germany. And the masses in Paris lifted their voices with one accord: *"On to Germany. On to Berlin!"*

BELGIUM AND NETHERLANDS LIBERATED —ALLIES INVADE GERMAN SOIL

DELIVERANCE Day for the Belgians and the Dutch, after more than five years under the yoke of Nazi tyranny, was now glowing on the horizon. The Allied armies of liberation were at their doors in the autumn and winter of 1944.

At the end of August, 1944, the Canadians overran Rouen and the British took Amiens. The American First Army under General Hodges kept fanning out past Paris to the Belgian border, sweeping up Soissons and Laon and Reims and Chalons in its seemingly irresistible drive. Patton's Third Army kept pace on a parallel line to the south. The Seventh Army under General Patch drove farther into France from the south; Lyon and Nice fell. Western France was for the most part safely in the hands of the French patriots. They had liberated Bordeaux, but the port was immobilized—and was to remain so until almost the end of the war—by the Germans' continued mastery of the Gironde estuary to the northwest. As the French Forces of the Interior formed a linkage of fronts in the west, so the American Third and Seventh were driving closer and closer to a junction in eastern France for the eventual assault on Germany itself.

The First Army, which had made the initial landing in Normandy, was the first of the Allied forces to break out from France. With the British behind it at Abbeville, its troops first crossed the border of Belgium on September 2 at Hirson. Sweeping on to Tournai, after having overrun Mezières, Charleville, and Sedan (where the Germans had broken through in 1940), they crossed the Meuse River. Canadians backed them up, replacing the British in Abbeville, from which Dempsey's men had pushed on to Arras.

Belgium was almost immediately divided. The southern region was the Americans' zone and the British replaced them in Tournai. The Americans entered Mons and Namur, while the British drove from Tournai to the outskirts of Brussels, the capital. Behind the front, Canadian and British troops continued battering at Le Havre, while other units of theirs entered Boulogne and Calais and drove toward the historic harbor of Dunkirk.

The whole Belgian front was fluid. The British, once in the outskirts of Brussels, made short work of the capital. Von Kluge apparently was conserving his main strength for the defense of the homeland. From Brussels the British Second knifed out above Louvain to threaten

How six allied armies battered at the gates of Germany.

Antwerp. American troops, having secured the line from Charleroi to Namur, lunged northeast to Liége.

The Allies' line, by the end of the first week in September, had enveloped the vital Scheldt River port of Antwerp and thrust forward across the Netherlands border, which the British crossed at Breda. But there they were held; they were too close to Germany for the Germans to retreat with the haste they had shown in France and Belgium. Antwerp remained a pocket in which German and Anglo-Canadian hands grappled for the victory. Here the fighting was fierce. Street by street and house by house, the men of Crerar's and Dempsey's armies had to slug their way toward the port section of the city.

Antwerp could not be by-passed as was Brest. The Allies' biggest port on the continent was still Cherbourg; but by now they were hundreds of miles away from it and proposed to go still farther. Speed in supply was vital. The overland truck route created by the Americans could not carry all that was needed with sufficient rapidity to keep the fighting forces' pace unbroken. Another large port and one close to the front was an urgent need.

While the battle for the port raged, other British and Canadian forces were cleansing the Channel coast of the robot-bomb launching sites that had been sowing chaos across all of southeast England in the Second Battle of London.

The outcome of the Battle for the Low Countries was assured, however fiercely the enemy might resist in certain sectors. The British plunged forward from Breda almost to Eindhoven, while Bradley's Americans suddenly hurled themselves out of Belgium and into Luxembourg. The big moment had come. For the first time the Allies were fighting on German soil.

The German border was crossed on September 11, 1944. Not since Napoleon's day had German soil been invaded from the west. Now the war lords of the Reich were to reap the harvest of all their own invasions over so many decades. On this same day Patton's hard-driving Third Army, whose northern extremity had entered Germany with the Yanks of the First, made its long-awaited junction with Patch's Seventh. This was achieved near Somernon, just west of Dijon.

The front was now solid from the Channel to the Mediterranean. The Germans had no way to go but back—back in defeat to their fatherland. The Third and Seventh Armies were forming a pocket of their own west and south of the Belfort Gap, the passage into Germany from France just north of the Swiss border. Here the Germans left a powerful rearguard to cover the withdrawal of their main forces fleeing in panic ahead of both Patton and Patch. Belfort served for a little time as a haven for the Nazi-controlled French Government in flight from Vichy— Pétain, Laval, de Brinon, and the rest, who had been driven by the French Forces of the Interior from their puppet capital.

While the Yanks and the Tommies were freeing the Netherlands, the American Third was leveling the Germans' last defenses in France. The ancient forts of Metz, never attacked since the year 451, were pounded by American guns and planes. Nancy was under siege.

The First Army, as it cleared the enemy's shattered remnants from Luxembourg and widened its hold on lower Belgium, began to have a foretaste of what awaited it in Germany. Thus far the towns freed had been purely Belgian and their people had taken the Yanks to their hearts; but now all this was to be changed. Eupen and Malmédy were part of that area of Belgium which the Germans had annexed. They had driven out the Belgians and had settled their own people there. When the American soldiers entered Eupen they found no flags, no welcoming throngs—nothing but silence and sullen hatred.

While Hodges' First Army took Malmédy, Patton's Third overran Bastogne—two towns with names that were to go down in the bloodiest annals of American fighting men. Spearheads probed into Germany from these strongholds. On September 13 the first German town fell to the Americans. It was a little place called Roetgen, southeast of the vital city of Aachen. By this time Belgium had been virtually cleared and the assault within Germany itself was progressing. The First Army began the siege of Aachen on September 16. The Third Army was still meeting the fiercest opposition in the Metz-Nancy-Strasbourg sector, although Luxembourg, like Belgium, had been liberated. Southwest of Patton's troops Patch's Seventh Army was battling ever closer to Belfort and the gap that led into Germany.

The Netherlands, however, remained almost entirely in the enemy's hands. Here the British Second Army, together with the Canadian First and a Polish division, was bearing the brunt of the struggle. The Canadians took Eecloo, just inside the border from Belgium, near the coast, while the Poles drove on Hulst.

It was now that General Eisenhower tried a new tactic. Emulating the technique that the Germans had used in this same area four years before, the Allies sent a great airborne force into the Netherlands on the night of September 16-17. This was the First Allied Airborne Army. Its members were drawn primarily from the United States and Britain, but also included Canadians, Belgians, Frenchmen, Poles, and men of many other nationalities. By parachute and glider they came down well behind the enemy lines at half a dozen points: on the island of Walcheren in the Scheldt estuary, and at the mouth of the Rhine near Dordrecht, Tilburg, and Eindhoven. Deepest and strongest penetration was made in the area of Arnhem, almost on the Dutch-German border. Simultaneously the Allies launched powerful ground attacks intended to drive a corridor through to the airborne troops at two points: from Boterhoek near the coast, where the Canadians attacked, and around Eindhoven in the British territory.

The Eindhoven drive succeeded; British armor linked up with the airborne troops. The two groups, now merged, smashed northward, their goal the encirclement of the upper extremity of Germany's Siegfried Line and the Hannover plain behind it. Success would mean opening the road to Berlin.

Meanwhile, in the Reich itself, the United States First Army was mopping up in Aachen and pounding on toward Dueren, twenty miles from the vital industrial and communications city of Cologne. Despite the many shattering blows from American and British bombers, Cologne was still an important link in the Germans' defense chain. Below and behind General Hodges, Patton's tanks were rolling on against German counterattacks around Nancy and the town of Pont-á-Mousson; while Patch's Seventh hurried deeper into the Belfort Gap.

The Eindhoven junction, however, was the only one that could be made with the airborne troops in Holland. The attackers of Walcheren were isolated; their only support could come from the Air Forces. American and British troops who had landed at Arnhem found themselves not only isolated but in the midst of strong German defenses.

Tough, indomitable American airborne troops and British tankmen fought side by side in grim resolve, finally wresting the Rhine bridge at Nijmegen from the Germans. They succeeded in taking it intact before the enemy could damage it. Then they struck out almost due north to rescue their comrades trapped in the Arnhem pocket.

The first lunge forced a narrow corridor almost all the way through. As the Allies expanded their base, British armor overran Heeze, Someren, and Soerendonck at its eastern end, and Reusel on the west. The airborne Americans were the only Yanks now in the Netherlands. The main body of their forces was in Germany, approaching the outskirts of the much-vaunted Siegfried Line and fighting farther south in eastern France.

Allied troops in the Netherlands were fighting to develop their footholds to the maximum. British patrols of the American-British spearhead reached toward Arnhem, crossed the Lek River, and made tenuous contact with the Arnhem fighters. Meanwhile the head of the Allies' spear was widened with the capture of Valburg and Elst. American airborne soldiers who had landed in the Nijmegen-Arnhem region battled their way into Germany at the border town of Beek, and stood only seven miles from historic Cleves which was generally assumed to be the northern extremity of the Siegfried Line.

The Germans were beginning to show their real strength in the Netherlands. Elst fell to them; but they could not prevent the British from opening an alternate supply route toward Arnhem by capturing Heesch and Oss on the west side of the salient. The minor value of such gains quickly proved that Arnhem represented not a vantage-point but a liability of the most dangerous character.

On the night of September 26 the Allies began withdrawing their troops from the old Dutch city. Americans and Britons manned the walls of the corridor against attack while 2,000 survivors of many times that number who had plummeted into Arnhem from the sky withdrew to the safety of the stronger lines to the south, bringing their wounded.

Though Arnhem was lost the salient was steadily and painfully widened as the British slugged their way to Gennep and to the Meuse between Wessem and Dislen. West of the salient's base, slow advances had been scored as Crerar's Canadians took Turnhout; their compatriots behind them in France had captured the ancient port of Boulogne and brought the coastal line up to the Dutch border. Much farther behind this advanced front Germans were still holding out in France as September drew to an end. They defended Calais against all attacks by Canadians and Polish troops, while the citizens of the towns cowered in cellars in constant peril, not only from their oppressors but, of necessity, from their liberators as well. Once a twenty-four-hour truce was arranged, solely for the evacuation of such civilians.

The Battle of the Netherlands was far from over. General Eisenhower appealed to slave-laborers inside Germany to revolt against their masters. He warned Germans in areas already occupied by the Allies that he expected absolute and unquestioning obedience to his every order. The Allies, he told the Germans, had "come as conquerors to drive out Nazism and militarism, but not as oppressors."

Gradual liberation of almost all the Channel coast and part of the shore of the North Sea had a great outcome for southern England: it meant the end of the danger of robot bombs. Almost all of these diabolical contrivances had been launched from this general area.

The whole front in Europe was ablaze. The Third Army of the irrepressible Patton had conquered Metz and entered Thionville; the First under Hodges and the Ninth under Simpson had firmly established themselves in Germany. American troops were fighting in the approaches to the Huertgen Forest between them and the Rhine.

The Netherlands sector began to be a gigantic holding operation. Possession of the country was vital to both sides. It meant the fate of the Germans' whole northern flank and their great industrial and maritime cities. Failure of the Allies' bold stroke at Arnhem meant the suspension for months of any major offensive activity in the country, while the Germans could rest on the defensive, merely containing the Allies' bridgehead to the best of their ability.

The first break-through of the Siegfried Line was achieved by the Americans above Aachen. They took Uebach and routed the enemy from Rimburg in Germany in order to begin forging their ring of steel around the city.

Progress of the fighting within Holland was in tremendous contrast to the drives through France and Belgium. Days were spent and lives lost by the hundreds for the capture of little towns that American fighting men's kinsfolk back home had never heard mentioned: Merxplas, Brecht, Hertogenbosch, Westkapelle, Zuid Bevelland. These were heartbreaking and body-breaking days—fighting in the rain and chill of autumn and the first wintry flurries of snow and hail. Cold mud gripped the boots of heavily burdened troopers and clutched at the wheels and tracks of their vehicles. Supporting planes roared low overhead to blacken the already dark days with the smoke and chaos of exploding bombs dropped ahead of the hard-battling ground forces. Canadians and Poles in the western Netherlands faced obstacles that the British and the Americans in the center and the east were fortunate enough to escape—dozens of small streams, and the broad, island-studded estuary of the Scheldt.

Calling on planes and artillery for support, the Canadians employed the leapfrog tactics that had been initiated in North Africa. A strong detachment landed behind the German lines on Walcheren and battled the enemy hand to hand in a bloody struggle to win the island from which a relatively small enemy garrison had wreaked havoc on the mainland advance. Farther inland other Canadian units dammed the canals which veined the landscape. The Germans added to the difficulties of the terrain by blowing up dykes in order to flood the countryside with sea water and thus to trap and ruin the Allied vehicles.

As the cold weather set in the whole front in Europe was of necessity slowed. The enemy seemed to stiffen along the entire length of the line. Before Belfort he held the Seventh Army and forced it to give ground slightly; at Metz he was apparently unshakable; Trier remained German; and the defenders of Aachen held fanatically firm. In the Netherlands American troops gave way to Britons on the east as the Yanks concentrated on their drive into Germany under Hodges.

The Americans were forging tighter their steel girdle around Aachen. General Marshall, Chief of Staff of the United States Army, arrived in Paris to confer with General Eisenhower and his leading advisers. Venomous Goebbels and the coldly ruthless Himmler called on their people to fight a lawless guerrilla warfare behind the American and British lines and to "make every house a fortress."

The Americans entered Aachen on October 12 and found it a city of desolation and ruin after planes and guns had worked over it a second time. A little gap to the northeast served as the passageway for another First Army unit which hurtled into the city and closed the last egress for the remaining German defenders. They fought from house to house for days but Aachen was lost.

The fall of Aachen and the penetrations of the West Wall made it certain that a flanking attack was no longer necessary to assure the destruction of the Siegfried Line. Though the Germans might immobilize a few Allied divisions they could not alter the course or the outcome of the war.

AMERICANS CROSS GERMAN BORDER—ALLIES ON THE RHINE

FIRST American artillery shells to be fired into Germany in the Second World War fell on German soil with ominous detonations on September 10, 1944. One day later Americans of the First Army under General Hodges crossed the border into the fatherland which had boasted through the generations that "no foreign army will ever step foot on German soil."

Germany was first invaded from Luxembourg—the entrance was made above Trier. Within twenty-four hours other forces of Hodges' Army crossed the border from Eupen in Belgium.

The first German civilian reaction to war in their own fatherland was a foretaste of the treachery that was to be met throughout the country. Every civilian—including policemen and municipal officials— denied ever having been a member of the Nazi Party or even having sympathized with it. Highest officeholders unanimously declared they opposed it. Servile, slavishly obedient—and sullen behind the Americans' backs—Germans began to steal and sabotage equipment and take pot shots at American troops. Offenders in these cases ranged from boys of seven to men of seventy. When houses were requisitioned, the German women wept piteously until Americans reminded them how their husbands and sons had taken the quarters they needed at gunpoint, and killed the owners for sport. This civilian and guerrilla opposition, however, was well within the Allies' control.

Simpson's American Ninth Army crossed into the northwestern part of Germany where the First had preceded it, and together the two forces began to take apart the outpost defenses of the Siegfried Line north of Aachen. Attacks launched in force from Heerlen in the Netherlands finally broke the inner crust of the West Wall and carried the Yanks beyond it to Uebach. Here, almost due west of Cologne, as at Stolberg southwest of the cathedral city, the Yanks were about thirty miles from their goal. Far to the south, another Allied army posed an immediate threat to Germany: the French First, which had penetrated deep into the Vosges Mountains and was threatening the Schlucht Pass, gateway to the Rhine valley.

The First Army column that had taken Stolberg thrust out for Cologne along the road that led through Dueren. The Germans were holding hard; gains of a mile a day were counted as good. The weather was growing colder; rain and mud hampered the movement of vehicles

NEW YORK HERALD TRIBUNE map—Fleck

Scene of the Allied advances in the Rhineland. Arrows show the direction of drives by (1) the Canadian First Army; (2) the American Ninth Army; (3) the American First Army; (4) the American Third Army.

and foot-sloggers alike. At the same time, the captors of Uebach struck toward Geilenkirchen to take another highway leading to Cologne.

Then the Americans struck a third blow. Plunging into the Huertgen Forest, one column drove to Germeter and then swung northeast toward the town of Huertgen, while another pushed east of Stolberg to Hastenrath. The Germans struck back hard in the Huertgen sector and scored temporary gains. The doughboys, rolling with the punch, sprang out at them again and in close hand-to-hand fighting regained all the ground that had been lost.

The Third Army now smashed its way into Germany below Luxembourg in a drive obviously aimed at the Saar Basin. It penetrated four miles beyond the border on November 26 to reach Tettingen, a new menace to the fatherland. This meant that Rundstedt had to divert some of the forces with which he had been trying to contain the First and Ninth Armies to the Third Army's front.

At the same time, Patton's men were gradually widening their grip on Reich territory in the face of heavy enemy counterattacks. They struck again, near Saarlautern, north of their earlier point of entry. Troops from the latter area were now within eight miles of Saarbruecken, an important industrial city. The rest of the Third Army and the French First, which linked its lines with those of Patch's, were still in France.

By the end of November the Ninth Army had established a seven-mile front along the Roer River, while below it the First was also attacking the river defenses. At the bridges, particularly, the Germans fought desperately, as if the retention of these spans would prevent the Allies from advancing beyond the water barriers. Other First Army troops were resolutely fighting their way through the Huertgen Forest to bring the whole American line constantly closer to Cologne.

Meanwhile the Third Army was increasing its menace to the Germans. It broke through to the Saar River at Schwemlingen and narrowed the gap separating it from Saarbruecken into which American shells were beginning to pour. Patch's men and the French were now within a few miles of the border at most points on their line. As this menace grew and the Third pressed farther into the Reich, the Yanks found Nieder Limberg, just northwest of Saarlautern, not only abandoned but burned. This was the first instance of Germany's application of the scorched-earth policy to her own soil.

On the northern end of the front the Germans were fighting with increasing desperation. In little towns like Pier, below Juelich, First Army infantrymen had to battle from house to house to take the village. Costs, in relation to the value of the objective, were high. Patton's men on the south crossed the Saar River at a number of places, notably Merzig, northwest of Saarlautern, and the latter city was quickly snapped up by the American fighters. Sarreguemines fell. The Americans were closing in on Saarbruecken, never lowering the intensity of their artillery bombardment of the doomed city.

But the Americans had gained control of Luchem, which, though well to the west of the Roer, gave them mastery of part of one of Hitler's great *Autobahnen*—the marvelous superhighways, eight lanes wide, that led through hills and woods and flat country to his major cities. Built for the acceleration of his onslaughts against his neighbors, these roads were to be turned into the arteries of American and British armored assaults on Germany.

It was at this time that the enemy launched his great effort to turn the tide of the invasion with his break-through in the Ardennes. He split the First and Ninth Armies from the Third (the first two had to be shifted to Montgomery's command for almost a month). Patton had to weaken his own forces to repel the powerful enemy blow. Nevertheless, he was able to push farther into the Saar.

Both ends of the Americans' front in the Reich were thus advancing even as the enemy sought to cut them off by his drive through the center. But after the first four days of that break-through, as we have seen, the tide began slowly to turn, and the peril to the flanks to lessen. At no time did the German attack throw the Allies off balance as the enemy had hoped, nor did it put a halt to our own unremitting push deeper and deeper into Germany. Though the Germans had launched their drive from Monschau, the Ninth Army units southeast of that town continued to drive forward. Capturing Lammersdorf they plunged on toward the road to Euskirchen and Bon. North of Monschau the Ninth Army and the First closed in on Dueren.

The Germans were also in dire straits in the south. They had considerably depleted their forces to mount the Ardennes offensive and now were to pay for it. The Third Army found the defenses of the southern end of the Siegfried Line at Dillingen and gave them no rest. On its extreme right Patch's men finally drove to the German border at Bobenthal, Rechtenbach, Scheibenhardt, and Berg, in what was known as the Karlsruhe corner not far from the Swiss border.

While von Rundstedt fought desperately inside the bulge to expand his wedge between the Allied armies, American forces behind his base line were battling ahead. Ninth Army patrols entered Dueren despite fierce resistance and established a foothold in the town, while to the south the Third cleared Dillingen. Southeast of this town, however, it found the Rheinheim forest strongly defended. Its first blows were roundly repulsed. The Seventh Army too was meeting more resistance. Intensity fluctuated. Towns entered by the Americans, such as Nieder-Schlettenbach, would be regained by the Germans on the following day only to fall again to the Americans a day or so later.

As the campaign went on, the weather in all sectors favored the defending forces more and more. Blinding snow made it more difficult to pick one's way through unfamiliar country. Enemy defenses were ingeniously concealed. Shortening of the days added to the hours of darkness, of which the enemy naturally took full advantage. The freezing cold favored the enemy troops housed in defensive positions, leaving them fresher and stronger than men advancing through snow, ice, and raw, numbing winds.

At this time, too, the Americans found themselves up against perhaps the most ingenious of the enemy's psychological devices. The German secret service sabotage chief, Lieutenant Colonel Otto Skorzeny, who had planned and executed the kidnaping of Mussolini and Horthy, now was plotting to get Eisenhower. Recognizing the Kansas-born General's genius not only as a strategist but as a superpersonnel director, the Germans planned to kill him.

Skorzeny organized a task force of 1,000 men to disrupt the American rear areas during and after the break-through. With 150 specially selected men, ground and air troops who could speak English, he rigorously trained them in American speech. Some were even penned with American prisoners of war for a while. But in more than one case the captives pierced the imposture and taught the German "supermen" what it means in good American fashion to beat the hell out of them.

Skorzeny's men were also drilled with characteristic German thoroughness in American drill tactics and American habits—even in such American ways as the usual fashion of tearing open a package of cigarettes. They, like the eight-hundred-odd others who were to do the dirty work of physical violence, were equipped with forged credentials, properly soiled to make them look genuine, and cards stolen from prisoners. Some had British uniforms and identifications.

The plan blew up almost before it started. One of Skorzeny's men was picked up "because he didn't look quite right" as he walked along a road near Spa. Intensive questioning revealed the plot. There was no way of knowing how far his companions had succeeded. SHAEF in Paris was alerted at once. General Eisenhower's big car with his four stars on the license plate was rolled out and conspicuously driven all over Paris to trap the Germans into betraying themselves; but the General himself was never in it. Lieutenant Colonel Baldwin B. Smith, who looked enough like him to make passers-by do a "double-take" when they saw him, volunteered to impersonate the Supreme Commander even at the risk of being murdered by mistake.

SHAEF doubled its guard not only on Eisenhower but on all the top officers of all the Allied armies. Word went out to all troops to be on the alert for impersonators. Most of them, despite their careful training, betrayed themselves by their accents or by minor defects in their credentials—fresh creases in their "old" cards and the lack of dog-tags around their necks.

The whole plot failed within a week. Of the 150 picked men, about fifty were caught well within the American lines. After trials, they were executed for wearing American uniforms. The rest undoubtedly got mixed up with ordinary prisoners. Similar fates befell most of the 800 men chosen for the routine jobs.

As the failure of the Ardennes attack became more apparent, the Germans in the south tried to set up a diversion with a medium counterattack ostensibly aimed at the recovery of Alsace and Lorraine. It succeeded in driving the Seventh Army out of Germany—but only temporarily. At the southern end of the Third Army's sector, Patton yielded Schaffhausen for a day or two, but regained it quickly. At Geislautern his troops never let the Germans conquer a yard of ground. Instead, once he had retaken Schaffhausen, Patton rallied and hurled the enemy clear across the Saar River. In the face of new German thrusts the Seventh Army, too, rallied its forces and began to hit back. The Germans increased their blows as their forces were pushed back inside the bulge and continued to score some minor successes in the south; but the back of the drive there was broken before mid-January.

On January 16, 1945, the British entered Germany for the first time. They struck from a point north of Sittard to blunt the salient that the enemy was aiming at the Netherlands. Capturing Dieteren, they moved northeast on Echt in a sector mop-up, then doubled back into the Netherlands to meet and eliminate the minor German threat shaping up there. This accomplished, they hammered back into the Reich and swept up a number of towns in a drive that seemed to be pointed at Muenchen-Gladbach and Dusseldorf. Rapidly widening their hold in Germany, they broke into the Siegfried Line after having entered Heinsberg, not far from the northern end of the Americans' lines. The First Army had now returned to Bradley's 12th Army Group and the Ninth was soon to follow suit; but both the 12th and the 21st Army Groups were now working side by side.

The Americans, fully recovered from the effects of the Ardennes break-through, opened up a terrific artillery barrage around Dueren while the whole line began to move forward on the last day of January. Doughboys and the armor advanced under an umbrella of shellfire.

Scottish Highlanders, the dreaded "Ladies from Hell" of the First World War, were swiftly and ruthlessly clearing the enemy out of his positions in the town of Goch. On the south, Patton's men were moving up and in. Patch sent his Seventh Army back into the Reich to threaten Saarbruecken.

Americans and the British firmly established their hold on the entire western border area of Germany. The Ninth crashed through Juelich while the First battled its way painfully through Dueren despite the unwavering opposition of the enemy. With the final fall of Dueren, the First fanned out into the Cologne plain for the final assault on the great cathedral city. The Ninth was close on its heels.

Before the first week of March ended, three Allied armies were within striking distance of the Rhine, the river on which for centuries Germans had pinned their faith in the inviolability of the heart of their country. At Wesel, in front of the Canadians; at Duisburg and Duesseldorf, great inland ports threatened by the Ninth; and at Cologne, toward which the First had thrust seven distinct prongs, the river was bridged by a considerable number of excellent structures.

Capture of these would open the entire interior of Germany to the Allies. Between the cities were other strategic bridges.

The Allies reached the Rhine on March 5, 1945—Americans of the Ninth Army's 84th Division, on the Canadians' right flank, conquered Homberg, facing Duisburg across the river. The 2nd Armored Division swept into the riverbank city of Uerdingen in time to see the bridge there go up in a terrific explosion. Six miles north of Cologne, tanks of the First Army's 3rd Armored Division pocketed enemy forces against the river.

Fighting fiercely to protect the east bank of the river, the Germans retreated from Homberg into Duisburg. They blew up every span there as the 3rd Armored Division reached the Rhine at two more points: Grimlinghausen and Worringen, between Duesseldorf and Cologne. Cologne itself, as bombers pounded at its defenses, was entered from the northwest by the First Army's 3rd Armored Division and from the west by the 8th and 104th Infantry. Meeting desperate last-ditch opposition, they did not falter. The 1st and 9th Infantry, at the same time, were racing for the ancient university city of Bonn, while far to the south Patton sent his men ahead toward another Rhine citadel, Coblenz. North of the major battle area the Canadians, absorbing the bulk of the British Second Army, also reached the Rhine at Wardt.

American troops entered Cologne on March 5. Armor and infantry fought bitterly from street to street and from house to house to reach the river which the city straddled. Above the noises of the battle they could hear the detonations as the Germans blew up the Hohenzollern Bridge; the high Hindenburg Bridge near it had already been destroyed. But the enemy was too pressed to make a good job of the Hohenzollern span; the Americans found it usable for light traffic.

The conquest of Cologne, despite the ferocity of the Germans' resistance, was swift. One day after the Americans entered it, they had cleared the entire western section and reached the Rhine. The 3rd Armored Division sent its tanks and armored cars cruising lethally through the ruined city for the last mopping-up operations against the few remaining enemy pockets, isolated one from another for the most part in temporarily by-passed suburbs. **Cologne was ours—the Allies were at the Rhine.**

SACK OF WARSAW—GERMAN MASSACRE OF THE POLISH PATRIOTS

MARTYRED Poland, the first victim of German aggression in World War II, was now a tragic battleground. The five-year struggle which the Polish people had waged against the brutality of Nazi rule reached its climax.

The Battle of Warsaw—sixty-three days of heroic uprising of the Polish patriots (August 1-October 2, 1944)—stands as an eternal memorial to the courage and sacrifice of the Polish people in the cause of liberty. It is the only instance in the entire war in which a great city conducted such a long and isolated revolution against an army of occupation. The Polish patriots, "by their own means, without heavy equipment, without any considerable help from outside, against an enemy armored with the whole destructive might of modern warfare," fought until lack of food and ammunition made any further resistance impossible.

For the third time during the war the Poles made a noble stand in self-defense. Warsaw, devastated by German bombers and artillery at the beginning of the war in the siege of 1939, ravaged by the Battle of the Ghetto in 1943, rose as if from the grave against the Germans in 1944.

The tragedy of Warsaw, as herein historically recorded, is from official observers and records of the Polish Government. When the Russian Army reached Poland's eastern border in 1944 the people believed that the time for liberation had come. They were ready and waiting to join with the Russians against the Germans. Having been a charter member of the United Nations, the whole population had waited for the day to clasp hands with their allies.

General Rokossovsky's great Red Army had pushed into Praga, across the Vistula River from Warsaw, and sent officers into the Partisan-held sections of the battered Polish capital to spot artillery fire. The Germans, facing imminent disaster, deployed their strength in the west of the city. Polish patriots, who had been operating underground, believed that this was the crucial moment for their long-planned uprising. They were holding in leash a Home Army about 300,000 strong with a garrison of about 35,000 men in Warsaw, under the command of "General Bor," a man of mystery later to be revealed.

Although the Russians were virtually within sight of the city, they were held in check by German counterattacks. Their campaign based on the drive to Berlin was developing vital problems. To strike for the liberation of Warsaw at this moment might endanger their plans for reaching their final objective.

Polish Premier Stanislaw Mikolajczyk described the situation as it existed on July 11, 1944: "The Polish Home Army units, acting under the instructions of the Polish Government and of the Supreme Command of the Polish armed forces, are carrying out orders given to them previously by their commanding officers regarding operations against Germans in case of the approach of the Soviet forces."

Orders were issued to the Polish Underground, which had conducted a long war of sabotage and diversionary activities against the Germans, to "give full collaboration to the Red Army in its fight against Germans without any reservation whatsoever."

Let the Polish Government tell its own story here: Warsaw surged to battle. On July 31, the thunder of Soviet guns shook Warsaw walls. Soviet airmen engaged the Luftwaffe in the skies over Warsaw. The German civilian population left the city. German newspapers ceased to appear. The Gestapo and military authorities ordered the mass evacuation of civilians. German reinforcements began to arrive from the West. On August 1, the Polish Government's Delegation in Warsaw, Chairman of the Polish Underground Parliament, and "General Bor," commander of the Home Army, reported that at 5:00 P.M. the Polish forces had begun an open fight for the liberation of Warsaw.

In the first flush of inspiration and pent-up energy men, women, and children rose to throw the Nazis out of their city. Led by the Home Army terrible struggles ensued. Strong German forces were sent in to "suppress the uprising." The patriots sent out urgent appeals for Russian and Allied help.

The Russians found it precarious to attempt large-scale airborne aid. Volunteer Polish, American, and British fliers from bases in Italy and England parachuted supplies into the city.

"General Bor's" daily communiqués reveal the suffering and valor of the sixty-three tragic days. We record here the official summary from the Polish Government: During the initial twenty-four hours, four districts of the city were occupied by the Poles, among them Ochota and the filter station. After nineteen hours of hand-to-hand fighting the electric power station and the gas works were captured. On the second day the Poles held the center of Warsaw, in which were the General Post Office and the old Town District (*Stare Miasto*) where the heaviest fighting raged. About 40 per cent of the city was in the hands of the Polish Home Army in the first week.

As no help had yet come from the Allies, the Poles had to fight with weapons and munitions seized from the Germans. The Germans threw in bombers, flame throwers, tanks, armored cars, and thousands of machine guns; their antiaircraft guns had been converted into field artillery to be used in Warsaw. Their heavy mortars and gunboats on the Vistula shelled the Polish positions.

The Germans presented an ultimatum for surrender on August 11. The Poles answered by increasing their resistance.

When it seemed likely that the Warsaw fight was doomed—on the day that Warsaw reported: "We have not eaten any bread for ten days" —Soviet help arrived. On September 11, Soviet fighters engaged German planes which had been bombing and strafing the Polish capital for over six weeks. The following night, on the forty-third day of the struggle, Soviet planes dropped food and munitions to the Home Army within Warsaw. Close contact was established between the Polish forces within Warsaw.

The people of Warsaw had endured over two months of constant bombardment and shelling from friend and foe alike. They had endured over two months of fighting for every house, for every street and square. For a whole month they had no bread. They were deprived of electricity, gas, and water, and lived in the cellars of their houses.

Over the Polskie radio from Warsaw on September 27 came this message: "We have a desperate feeling of loneliness and frustration. We are sending this report because we feel that perhaps you do not realize under what conditions we are living and fighting."

On this same day—Mokotow fell. Three days later—Zoliborz fell. Moscow announced that in view of the unsuccessful attempts to force the Vistula from Praga, the capture of Warsaw from the Germans could take place only after an encirclement of the city. On the sixty-third day of the battle of Warsaw—Monday, October 2, 1944—this message came over the Polskie radio from the capital of Poland:

"*Warsaw is no more!* There are only ruins left. Those Poles who are fighting abroad will have to rebuild the capital. A new city will rise in which a new generation will dwell, succeeding those who stood to fight and fought until death. The rising in Warsaw was for this new generation...."

The last communiqué from "General Bor" reached London: "Warsaw has fallen after having exhausted all means of fighting and all food supplies, on the sixty-third day of its heroic struggle against overwhelming superiority of the enemy. On October 2, at 8 P.M., defenders of Warsaw fired the last shots."

Documentary evidence clarifies much of the discussion created by this tragic episode in World War II: the wisdom of its timing, the forlorn hopes, the heart-rending appeals for help, and the political divisions which followed. "General Bor" informed a British airman who had been freed by the Poles from a German prison camp and joined the ranks of the Home Army: "If we had not taken up arms on or about the first of August, we should never have been able to fight at all, because the Germans were beginning to seize our men for digging trenches (against the Russians) or for transference far from Polish soil. Warsaw would have been a deserted city."

"General Bor" also had learned that four new German armored divisions were moving on Warsaw from the west. It was imperative to prevent these divisions from reaching the Eastern Front—they must be stopped in Warsaw to help save the Russian drive toward Berlin. His instructions from London were to use his own judgment on facts ascertainable on the ground as to the "most suitable moment or date of uprising and method of combat."

In Warsaw the Germans were conducting a war of annihilation. The inhabitants were being murdered or carried away to an "unknown destination." This "unknown destination" soon proved to be a large concentration camp near the small town of Pruszkow, ten miles from Warsaw. More than 70,000 men, women, and children were interned in a barbed-wire enclosure in the open. Neither food nor water was given them. The road leading to the camp was strewn with corpses.

Here is a transcript of a message sent to world leaders by Premier Mikolajczyk on September 1, while Warsaw was burning and its people being slaughtered: "Stalin, Roosevelt, and Churchill, leaders of the great Powers, the commanders of the powerful and victorious land and air armies—Warsaw is waiting. The whole Polish nation is waiting. Public opinion throughout the world is waiting. Do all you can to provide the means of further fighting and to liberate this city and the population fighting on her ruins.... !"

The world had not forsaken the Poles—its whole heart was with them as they passed to Calvary. But it was helpless to reach the Polish people in time to save them. President Roosevelt and Prime Minister Churchill made superhuman efforts. The American and British forces were yet too far away. Aërial bombing squads would only have added to the slaughter, as there was no way to distinguish between Poles and Germans in the beleaguered capital.

The valor of "General Bor" and his Home Army, with the Polish people facing extermination before help could reach them, was a calamitous spectacle. The question was asked everywhere: "Who is this General Bor?" The mystery was cleared when he was identified as Lieutenant General Tadeusz Kormorowski who had assumed the name "General Bor" to confuse the Germans. General Sikorski, the great Polish commander, on the eve of his tragic death, on July 3, 1943, had confirmed the appointment of General Bor as commander of the Home Army. More than a year later he was to succeed General Sosnkowski as Commander in Chief of all Polish forces in Poland and abroad.

LAST BATTLES IN ITALY—EXECUTION OF MUSSOLINI—GERMANS SURRENDER

THE LIBERATION of Italy, Greece, Crete, and islands of the Aegean was a spectacle of modern times which rivaled the "Last Days of Pompeii." Inexorable, implacable fate was closing in on the Germans in 1944-45.

The big island of Crete had been held in force by the Germans. The British, who had been driven from the island four years before in the first great airborne operation of modern warfare, had proceeded to erect a virtually impenetrable wall of ships around the island to prevent the escape of the German garrison. Then the Allied Land Forces of the Adriatic—an army composed of British, American, and other troops—landed by air and sea in Albania and struck inland. At the same time, Greece was invaded directly on September 24, 1944, by British troops borne by plane, glider, and ship.

Nowhere in Greece did the Germans offer more than a delaying action. The terrain was even more difficult than that of Italy and it took the British two weeks to cover the few miles to Corinth. The Germans began evacuating even before the arrival of the first invaders. The next great objective after Corinth was Athens, the capital, which the British occupied on October 14 after some skirmishing. Other British forces took the island of Corfu.

It was not long before both Dodecanese and Aegean island groups were swept clear of Germans. In Crete, however, an anomalous situation arose which was to persist until the end of the entire war in Europe. The British had not the men to spare for a thorough clean-up of the island. The German defenders surrendered to such forces as landed and thereafter the two opposing armies lived side by side on the island.

The clearing of Greece, however, did not end the Allies' troubles there. For months to come they were to be plagued by domestic strife in which the British had to take a strong hand to prevent the complete disintegration of the country. The EAM, or National Revolutionary Front, and its military arm, the ELAS, spurred by German agents-provocateurs within its ranks, broke out in armed insurrection against the semi-military Greek régime which had moved in on the heels of the British troops. The latter, in self-defense, had to do battle to protect the governmental authority. In Athens and the provinces the fighting raged for months.

In Italy, meanwhile, the Allies were striving with all their strength for victory over the Germans, solidly dug in behind their Gothic Line. Late in September, American troops crashed through the central and western sectors while the British broke the eastern defenses. The line was crushed except for a small sector west of Futa Pass. This was finally smashed in grim, costly fighting which, proportionately, exacted a toll higher than that of any battle on the Western Front.

In preparation for the spring offensive to come, and also as a result of the death of Field Marshal Sir John Dill, the high comand was changed. General Sir Henry Maitland Wilson, who had succeeded General Eisenhower as supreme commander in the Mediterranean Theater, was shifted to Washington to take Dill's place in the Combined Chiefs of Staff; and General Sir Harold R. L. G. Alexander, promoted to Field Marshal, became supreme commander. Until then this brilliant strategist, who had been Montgomery's over-all commander in the tremendously successful offensive begun two years before at El Alamein, had commanded the 15th Army Group in Italy. This post of responsibility for all the Allied ground forces in the theater went in turn to General Mark W. Clark.

The new year of 1945 opened with a fresh blow by the Fifth Army which recouped all the losses inflicted by the enemy. Carried ahead by the impetus of this success, the Fifth Army renewed its offensive at the extreme left or western end of the front, heading up the coast for the little port of Massa. The spearhead of this drive was the 442nd Infantry Regiment composed entirely of loyal Japanese-Americans, most of whom came from Hawaii and all of whom fought like demons. Their unit suffered proportionately higher casualties than any other in Italy.

While the Fifth Army's Japanese-Americans and Brazilians hacked their way closer to Massa, the fighting in the central sector below Bologna continued to surge back and forth. The Americans lost Mount Belvedere, a vital commanding height, and then recaptured it. The bitter battle was fought step by step up the dizzy, ice-covered crags of the peak and grimly down its slippery sides. Into this sector Clark threw the 10th Mountain Division as a new element of the Fifth Army.

This division had long been trained under special conditions in the United States for just such fighting as this, and it immediately proved the worth of its instruction. In this terrain motor vehicles were virtually useless. Most of the heavy transport work had to be done by mules. There were conditions, however, that even these tough animals could not conquer and men had to take over. Not only did they laboriously disassemble equipment but they had also to lug it up the heights. Then they must reassemble it before putting it into action.

Spring stirred the entire Italian front to action. The Eighth Army moved first and farthest, passing the Senio River in the east and crossing the Po di Primaro River to reach the shore of the Comacchio Lagoon.

Toward the end of March, Field Marshal Albert Kesselring was sent to the Western Front to succeed von Rundstedt. Kesselring turned over his command in Italy to Colonel General Heinrich von Vietinghoff-Scheel, a well-trained and competent officer who, however, was far inferior to Kesselring in imagination and skill.

The Allies proceeded quickly to put von Vietinghoff-Scheel to the test. For more than a year the Italian campaign had not been marked by any of those amphibious "leapfrog" landings which had been so signally successful in the closing stages of both the Tunisian and the Sicilian battles. The new German commander, in fact, had never been faced with one. On April 3 the Eighth Army sprang this almost forgotten technique on the enemy, but added a new twist.

Instead of striking from the sea, the British commander, General McCreery, sent his men out into the Comacchio Lagoon in small assault craft and even rowboats. They disembarked on the southern shore to strike behind the German defenses on the isthmus to the east while, simultaneously, other forces launched a frontal attack on these same positions. The lake-borne forces landed at Smarlaeca and were quickly joined by their comrades fighting up the isthmus itself. By the end of the day half the narrow spit of land had been taken.

On April 16 the long-awaited general offensive in Italy began. On a fifty-mile front the Allies surged ahead. Its path was prepared by two days of unprecedented aërial bombardment which left the Germans dazed and gasping, but still unwilling to yield. Along every foot of the front the enemy's resistance was ferocious. Much of the fighting in the wooded hills was hand to hand. Gun butt and bayonet, knife and fist were as frequently employed as bullets. Yet, however hard they fought, the Germans could not prevent the inexorable closing of the Allied pincers on Bologna. From the southeast, the Eighth Army's tough Polish troops had driven within nine miles of the city; on the south and southwest the Americans were pounding even closer.

The major break-through came on April 19, when the Poles finally crashed through the Argenta Gap west of the Comacchio Lagoon, on the highway and railroad to Ferrara. On the following day the Fifth Army broke out at last into the plains of the Po Valley. That was the beginning of the end for the Germans. On April 21 Bologna was in the hands of the Allies as both Fifth and Eighth Armies crashed through its defenses.

The Germans, having lost Bologna, broke into general retreat. It swiftly approached disorder on the crowded roads as Allied planes strafed and bombed the enemy without mercy or respite. Pounding close behind the aërial spearhead, the Eighth Army swept through Ferrara while the Fifth overran La Spezia. The Allies were at the Po. The Germans had lost northern Italy.

On April 27 the historic cities of Verona and Genoa were taken. On that same day the founder of Fascism fell prisoner to his victims. Benito Mussolini, Il Duce, the modern Caesar—he of all the fanciful titles which he had attributed to himself—had been a hunted man for days. He was in constant flight before the advancing Allies and their Partisan associates, and he dreaded above all else capture by his own countrymen. He hoped to get into Switzerland, although he knew that country had already declared its assent to the Allies' request that it afford no asylum to known war criminals. Mussolini begged the Germans to take him there with his family—and his latest mistress, for he was living with a Roman girl of twenty-five, Clara Petacci. The Germans acceded to his request. Bundled into a car which was part of one of their convoys, Mussolini set out through Como.

The road was under constant and rigid surveillance by Italian Partisans, by now well armed. One of them sighted the convoy. His comrades stopped part of it, including the car which was carrying the fleeing Duce and his mistress. The Partisans seized him and the girl, with a dozen leading members of his entourage. Achille Starace, once the leader of the Blackshirt Militia, was the second prize of that day's bag. They were all hustled off to the hills above Lake Como.

There Mussolini was informed that he would be tried at once as a traitor. He begged. He pleaded. But the trial proceeded. It did not take the court long to determine Mussolini's guilt. When the guards informed him of the verdict his response was characteristic. "Let me go," he whispered. "Help me—and I will give you an empire!"

The fantastic offer evoked no more than ironic grins. Taken out into a field, the trembling, whining Duce was tied to a chair, facing its back. Clara Petacci, crying out her willingness to give her life for his, was bound beside him. The execution squad took its stand behind them.

"Fire!" Mussolini toppled into the dirt; his mistress fell beside him. The bodies were tumbled, with those of the other Fascists captured by the Partisans, into a truck which headed for Milan, the birthplace of Fascism.

Milan was already under the Partisans' control, although little nests of Fascist and German snipers were still harassing them and the first units of the Allies to enter the area.

The arriving Americans were greeted by a gruesome sight in the Piazza Loretto. A dozen bodies, suspended by the heels, were surrounded by a howling, milling crowd which broke ranks innumerable times to spit upon the bedraggled corpses, reviling them even in death. When the bodies were at last cut down, the crowd could not be held back. It surged upon them, kicking, hitting, beating with sticks, defiling, and cursing.

While all this was taking place, Marshal Graziani had been captured by the Americans. And now the British were rushing on Trieste where Italian and Yugoslav Partisans were already mopping up the last Germans.

"The German Army," General Clark announced on April 30, "no longer exists in Italy as a military force."

Graziani, knowing the truth of these words, broadcast an appeal to his troops and the Germans to yield. The Italian Fascists agreed at once. A full German division had already surrendered unconditionally to the Brazilian Expeditionary Force.

On May 1, unknown to the world, von Vietinghoff-Scheel's emissaries met secretly with the Allied chiefs and signed an act of unconditional surrender, effective two days later.

Thus ended the twenty-month battle of Italy. The German surrender turned over 1,000,000 men to the Allies. Thousands had been killed, wounded, and captured. For this victory the Allies had paid a price, but it was not out of proportion to the gains achieved. The American share of this cost, as announced by Secretary of War Henry L. Stimson, was: killed, 21,557; wounded, 77,248; missing, 10,338.

Germany was beaten. Now fighting alone on her own soil she had but one more week to go before her complete collapse—the "unconditional surrender" of her routed armies which had started out on world conquest. Mussolini had met his inexorable fate and Hitler and his Nazi war lords, including many generals and admirals, were soon to meet with retributive justice.

BATTLE OF THE BULGE—GERMANY'S LAST ATTEMPT TO COME BACK

CHRISTMAS 1944 and the New Year 1945 were to be anything but holidays for the soldiers in either the German or the Allied armies. Germany was tottering under the crushing bombardments of the Allied air armadas. Its greatest cities were being reduced to flaming ruins in retributive justice for the terror and destruction which the Germans had meted out to the helpless countries of Europe.

Adolf Hitler, whining in despair, was to be forced to "eat his own poison." He had pulled down the Nazi temple on his own shoulders and with its fall had brought doom upon the German people. They, together with their leader, must pay the full penalty for the building of that monstrous structure. Hitler's first chagrin was in confession of his blunder in penalizing Field Marshal Gerd von Rundstedt, supreme Nazi commander in the west, who had unsuccessfully followed out his Fuehrer's own meddling military orders. It was Hitler's paranoic mania which made him believe himself to be a greater military genius than Napoleon and, hence, vastly superior to his own Prussian generals with all their traditions, training, and experience. In a fit of hysterical anger Hitler had removed his greatest living commander and had replaced him with General von Kluge. When von Kluge in turn failed he was replaced by Marshal Walther von Modl, who fared no better.

Even in the bitterly contested Huertgen Forest German troops could not halt the tough Yanks. In the Low Countries they could not prevent the steady progress of the British and the Canadians. Meanwhile the American First, Third, Seventh, and Ninth Armies were cutting ever deeper into Germany; the West Wall had been breached and the Cologne plain was in peril. At the eastern side of the country the Russians were beating at the gates, and it would not be long before they would smash them to bits. It was time for the Germans to act.

In this crisis they had no recourse but to crawl humbly to the one really brilliant commander at their disposal, the man they had brusquely relieved of his post a few months before—von Rundstedt.

General Eisenhower respected von Rundstedt's ability and was glad to "cross armor" with him again after driving him out of France and out of the German Army. Field Marshal Montgomery had twice beaten the great Rommel and was ready to administer the same knock-out blows to von Rundstedt.

It was December and snow was in the air. The ground was frozen hard. Here, von Rundstedt believed, was a fighting chance for what was left of the once mighty German armor. He swiftly determined to find the invaders' "weakest spot" and make an all-out drive to retake Belgium, drive back into France, and, in his own terms, "rout the Allies." These were his calculations: He would concentrate his remaining power on the Ardennes Forest in order to break through under their cover at what became known as the "Bulge." He counted on the fact that the American Seventh Army and part of the Third Army were being held by grim resistance in France; and the German garrisons were holding out in Le Havre and in the Netherlands.

General Bradley said later that in leaving the Ardennes Forest line so lightly held "we took what is known in military terminology as a 'calculated risk' to strengthen our northern and southern drives." This, he said, was the technique that had brought the Allies to Germany. He also remarked that he had hoped for a German counterattack because of the over-all results it would bring, but he had not expected the movement to be in such force as it was.

Seizing his opportunity, von Rundstedt massed the cream of the German Army for a last-ditch counterattack into which he poured every ounce of strength and brilliance at his command. This was his desperate, final attempt to change the whole course of the war.

The site of this great drive, ironically enough, was that of the mighty German break-through of 1940. Completely unknown to the Allies' intelligence, von Rundstedt aligned his forces south along the fifty miles from Monschau Forest to Trier. As the nucleus of his gamble he rushed in the Sixth Élite Guard Armored Army, which had been held to defend Breslau from the Russians. This was a fanatical force of younger soldiers, toughened in battle and crazed with hyperpatriotism.

On December 16 the Germans struck out mightily. The First Élite Guard of the Adolf Hitler Armored Division lashed westward south of Saint-Vith in Belgium; the Twelfth Élite Guard Hitler Youth Armored Division struck north of the town. Both these groups had a terrific punch. Simultaneously von Rundstedt ordered local attacks along the whole line from Monschau to Trier to divert the Allies' attention from his real blow.

For the first twenty-four hours the Germans met unqualified success. The Allies' defense was thin and the northern enemy spearhead carved out a salient ten miles wide and six miles deep; while his southern column, executing a pincers move northward, penetrated five miles on a five-mile-wide front. One of the diversionary thrusts north of Trier uncovered a soft spot in the American lines which gave ground in the direction of Bastogne. These three gaps were the outlets for the Germans' pressure. On the second day of the offensive the two Hitler

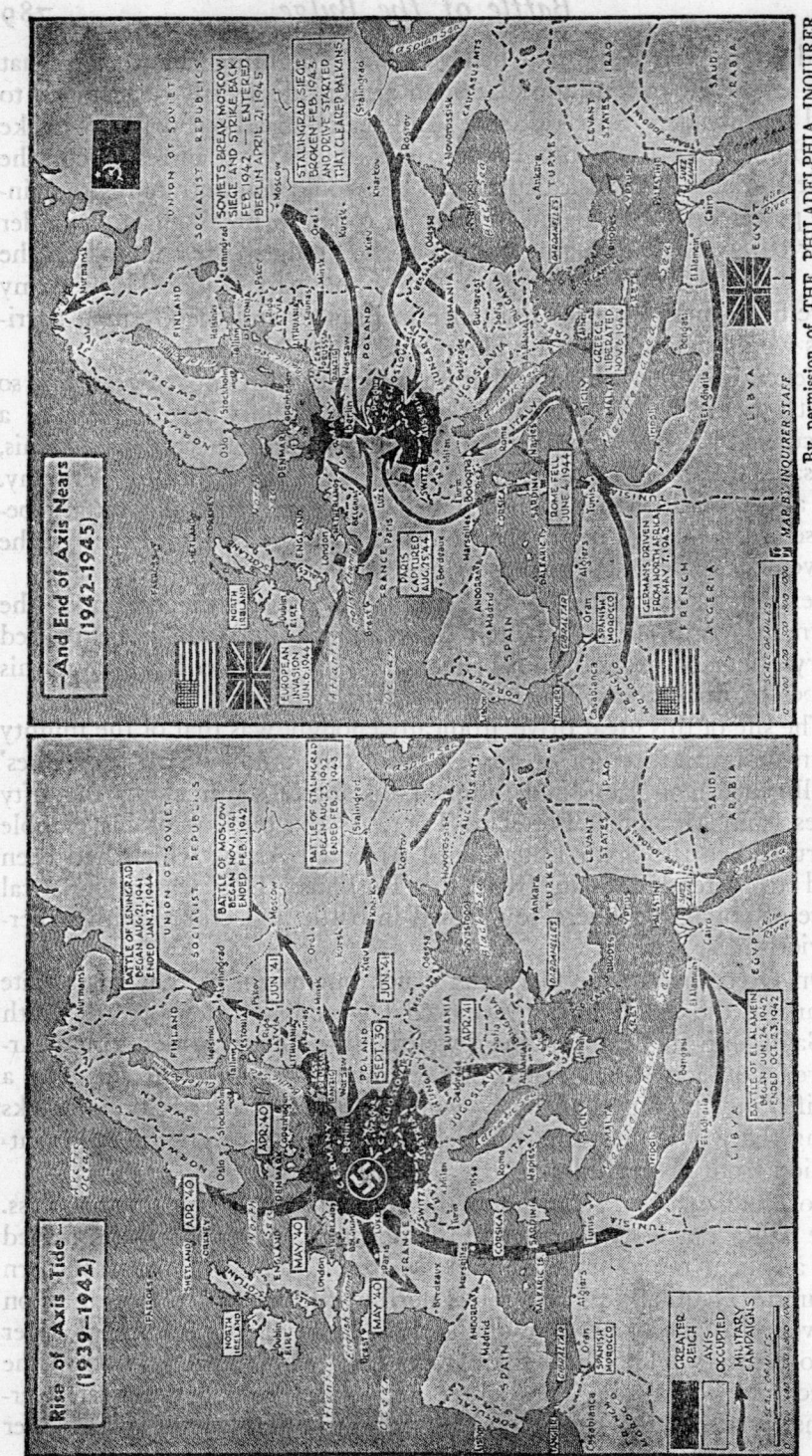

The Greater Reich at the height of its glory, and its diminishing boundaries as V-E Day approached.

Youth divisions effected a junction just east of Saint-Vith, creating a salient twelve miles deep and twenty miles wide.

Saint-Vith, a road junction, was vital to the Germans. They were determined to wrest it from the Allies. But the American and British reacted with lightning speed immediately the peril was apparent.

Field Marshal Montgomery's Twenty-first Army Group—the British and the Canadians—was holding the front in the Netherlands and cleaning up the coast. The canny Briton quickly massed his forces before Antwerp to protect the vital port which, with Liége, was among the major German goals. He well knew that their capture might indeed prolong the war by as much as a year. The German lunge menaced Allied communications with the entire northern flank. To meet this threat General Bradley temporarily committed part of his Twelfth Army Group—the First and Ninth Armies—to Montgomery's command. This left only the Third Army under Bradley. But he and "Monty," working so long under Eisenhower, had thoroughly learned coöperation. Montgomery said:

"When Rundstedt put in his hard blow and parted the American Army, it was automatic that the battle area must be untidy. Therefore, the first thing I did was to busy myself in getting the battle area tidy—getting it sorted out. I got reserves into the right place and got balanced—and you know what happened.... I salute the brave fighting men of America—I never want to fight alongside better soldiers.... I have tried to feel that I am almost an American soldier myself."

Immediate peril pointed at Saint-Vith. In a daring nighttime dash Brigadier General Bruce Clarke led a combat command of the American 7th Armored Division over the frozen roads of Belgium to join the regiments facing annihilation by the powerful German thrust. As a result, the Germans turned north, by-passing Saint-Vith to head for Liége. On the road lay Bollange, and Butgenbach, and Spa. At Spa General Hodges, commander of the American First Army, had his headquarters. Patton, meanwhile, was racing up from the south with every unit he could spare from the heavily engaged Third Army.

The critical phase of the German offensive began on December 18 and threatened to isolate and destroy the First Army and a good part of the Ninth, besides cutting off all the British forces in Europe.

As Harold Denny, who was with Hodges at the time, pointed out in a dispatch to *The New York Times,* von Rundstedt was gambling on the "offensive attitude" in which he found the Americans. This had caused them to bring up almost to the front tremendous stores of supplies, not the least of which were 3,000,000 gallons of gasoline, a tempting prize for the oil-thirsty Germans. This gasoline was stored in five-gallon containers near Malmédy and Spa, as well as at other front-line dumps. The enemy was counting on its capture to fuel his own drive.

But the Americans were too quick for him. As they evacuated threatened areas, gasoline got top priority. Column after column of American trucks rolled out of Spa and Malmédy, each vehicle laden beyond capacity with the precious tins.

Several enemy columns drove on Spa by various roads. General Hodges began evacuating all but the most essential members of his staff. At the end of that day, December 18, there was hardly anyone left besides the General, his intelligence and operations units, and a few service troops.

Then Hodges threw in his last reserves to defend the town of Spa. These headquarters troops, known as the "palace guard" consisted of military police, cooks, clerks, motorized cavalrymen, chemical, and antiaircraft troops, and other miscellaneous personnel. Even the censors went out into the field, battling German tanks with M-1 rifles and screened by engineers. One engineer, as the enemy tanks bore down on the little garrison, rushed out into the road, dragging behind him a "daisy-chain" of mines. He wrecked the first German tank, but his own head was blown off by his mines. It was plain heroism that enabled the "palace guard" to stop the enemy on one road. On another, it was sheer luck: a whole armored column ran out of gasoline at the very edge of town.

"Buzz-bombs" were roaring past—and sometimes dropping down. Liége had long been a favorite target for them because of its supply activities; now the range was being shortened. Bombs were dropping on the Liége-Spa road and on Spa itself. Hodges and his aides stayed at their job without an outward break in their composure, though all knew how close they were to capture and complete defeat.

At 9:30 that night the telephone rang. It was Lieutenant Colonel Robert Evans of the First Division's Intelligence. "We're here," he said, "and we're all set. All we need is fifty copies of the map of this area and we'll teach those SS bastards the lesson of their lives."

Evans got the maps that night. Before dawn the 30th Infantry roared into Spa on its way to the Malmédy gap. News came that Major General Matthew B. Ridgeway's 82nd and 101st Airborne Divisions were tearing out of central France to plug the gap, and that Patton's units were on the move. But Spa was now a dangerous place for a headquarters and Hodges knew it. At 10:30 he left for Chaudefontaine, just east of Liége. He and his aides were the last Americans to go.

As Hodges' First and Simpson's Ninth had been turned over to British command, the Ninth and Twenty-ninth Tactical Air Commands were temporarily placed with Air Marshal Sir Arthur Coningham, chief of the British Second Tactical Air Force. The 7th Armored was still holding much coveted Saint-Vith despite its virtual envelopment by the enemy, whose units turning north were now hammering at Stavelot and Saint-Oumont. Here they encountered more Americans than they had counted on—veteran divisions rushed up at the last minute. Even though fatigued by their journeys, the GI's were in good fighting trim as they tumbled out of their trucks and into the lines.

It was in this drive that the Germans added to their record as the Huns of modern times. The first instance came when an American patrol—a captain, a lieutenant, and four enlisted men—was captured on December 17 in the drive for Bastogne. Forced to surrender, they were stripped of their arms and then cold-bloodedly lined up and shot. Other instances followed on a far greater scale. In the Malmédy sector almost two hundred Americans were forced to form a square in a cold, open field surrounded by tanks. The armored monsters turned their machine guns on the ranks of prisoners and methodically sprayed them again and again until all had fallen. A few who were only wounded feigned death and later made their way to American lines to report the outrage, which was to recur many times.

Every arm the Allies possessed was being thrown into the fight. Until substantial reinforcements could form they had to rely mainly on the air forces. Bombers, fighters, and rocket-firing planes hurled everything they had at the enemy's columns, far outdoing his own fearful dive bombing of 1940. But even this could not stop the drive. The most drastic crippling only slowed it. One German division, for instance—the 2nd Armored Division—entered the battle with 124 tanks. It was unmercifully hacked by the Allies' planes and guns, but it was three weeks before the division admitted it was licked. It then had only three tanks left.

As the days continued the entire Belgian-Luxembourg line was in danger of elimination. In some places the Germans drove fifty miles into Belgium, almost gaining the Meuse between Namur and Dinant. To the south Patton, holding the Luxembourg flank, massed elements of his 4th, 9th, and 10th Armored Divisions and the 4th, 5th, 26th, and 80th Infantry. The Germans were apparently heading north for those precious supply bases.

The most critical day of the entire long-drawn-out battle was December 20. Since there was nothing to stop the Germans in the center of the line they gained the most there; hence the title "Battle of the Bulge." Between Malmédy and Wiltz they pushed out a great blunt wedge that was almost square.

For the first time the Germans' plans went awry. They had timed their attack for an expected spell of bad weather which they hoped would keep the Allies' planes earthbound. Challenging the weather, however, great numbers of Allied planes took to the air. Then the weather broke and they came out in full force. The German Air Force retorted with the greatest effort it had mounted since 1940; but even that was not enough. In five days the German lost 600 planes.

In the initial stages of the battle the 101st Airborne Division had been able to reach Bastogne; but the Germans encircled the little town and swept on. The 101st and the few original troops holding Bastogne were completely surrounded.

The drive to lift their siege began on December 22. Patton's divisions drove up from the south in power. At the same time the 82nd Airborne at Saint-Oumont struck out from its positions and commenced to hammer off the tip of the salient there; while the defenders of Saint-Vith, virtually unreinforced but still in strength, pushed out and started the destruction of the German line in front of them.

Bastogne was now the center of the toughest fighting. The Germans had driven fifteen miles beyond it to the west. The town was held by the 101st, the 9th Armored, and some miscellaneous fighters known to their comrades as Force Snafu. The whole was commanded by Brigadier General Anthony McAuliffe of the 101st, a short, stocky man who was "fighting Irish" to the core. He had lost his only hospital on December 19; his wounded lay wherever they could be sheltered and had the care of a single detachment of surgeons. To them Tony McAuliffe paid the greatest tribute of all: "Every man of them begged to be allowed to leave his stretcher and get back into the battle."

In the midst of his seemingly hopeless defense the Germans sent McAuliffe an ultimatum to surrender. To this he replied with one good American word: *"Nuts!"* The officer charged with delivering the message was asked what it meant; to the Germans it was incomprehensible. To McAuliffe's intense enjoyment, the officer replied: "It means—go to hell!"

For five more days McAuliffe's tiny, battered garrison held its lines without giving an inch. A Piper Cub brought in a surgeon; a few more doctors came by glider.

The final German attack against Bastogne was launched on Christmas morning. The 502nd Regiment halted the main body before it got through. Some tanks eluded the Yanks at first, but since McAuliffe always kept tanks and tank-destroyers in reserve the enemy's few gains were quickly wiped out.

The men of the Third Army were on the way. Patton had sent his 4th Armored and the 4th, 5th, 26th, and 80th Infantry Divisions from Luxembourg to attack the Germans from the rear. Other reinforcements were being prepared for aërial transport to the battleground. Land troops battled for four days before they could break through to relieve McAuliffe's heroes.

On the day after Christmas the Americans passed to the offensive. German spearheads which had taken Celles and Ciney, on either side of Dinant, were driven back. Closer to the base of the enemy's salient, Americans of the First and Ninth Armies on the north and of the Third on the south opened their own counteroffensive and narrowed the neck of the salient to twenty miles. The enemy's failure to seize the great fuel dumps at Spa and elsewhere was beginning to tell on him. Under American pressure and in peril of isolation from lack of gasoline, the Germans began to draw in their horns on the southern flank. Troops sent into Luxembourg headed back for the Siegfried Line.

The Bulge was now a confusing maze of attack and counterattack and counter-counterattack. As the enemy showed the first signs of really faltering the Allies pounced. The heaviest bombers in the European theater—the big Flying Fortresses and Liberators built for long-range strategic bombing—were called into play for close tactical support of the land armies. Allied guns poured out their deadly barrages to cover the thrusts of the ground troops. New divisions, including one composed of "Monty's" Tommies, moved in.

As the New Year, 1945, dawned, von Rundstedt tried again, even more desperately than before, to beat back the Allies. Patton had driven some thirteen miles into the flank of the salient around Bastogne. Against both sides of the American spearhead the Germans threw three divisions that had been rested and to some extent rearmed.

The Yanks, exhilarated by the success of their own counterattacks and mad for revenge on the Germans for their brutal and cowardly massacres of unarmed prisoners, would let nothing stop them. American artillery was raking the enemy mercilessly. At the western extreme of the steadily shrinking spearhead both the First and the Third Armies were steadily blunting it. Rochefort was smashed by Hodges' forces; while Patton's men hammered the Saint-Hubert area.

A blinding snowstorm now enveloped the entire "Bulge" front. Americans and Germans alike had to cut foxholes out of the frozen ground with picks. But neither side faltered. Before the American positions the German dead were piled like cordwood, but German opposition, spurred by the certainty of doom, grew ever stiffer.

Hodges widened and intensified his offensive and gained ground steadily on the northern flank of the "Bulge." South of this battleground von Rundstedt sought once more to trick the Allies with an apparent drive to recover Alsace and Lorraine. Patch's Seventh Army, with the French First and elements of Patton's outfits, had penetrated the Wissembourg Gap, the gateway to the Palatinate, but were compelled to withdraw into France. Temporarily the Germans had the advantage here. This Vosges drive, however, slowed down soon after its inception. The main battleground remained the "Bulge."

By January 6 the American counteroffensive from both sides was well under way. On that day, three weeks from the start of von Rundstedt's onslaught, Supreme Headquarters estimated enemy losses at 80,000 killed and wounded and 20,000 captured, a daily average of 4,760. The First Army, with British support, was striking hard from Hottot at Beffe; the 82nd Airborne had broken out of Saint-Oumont to start its drive on Vielsalm; while the 30th Infantry was breaking out of Stavelot in a series of sharp punches which knocked great gaps in the German lines. At the extreme west other First Army units were driving east from Rochefort in fighting that slowly rounded off the point of the spearhead, while the Third Army from the south kept narrowing the body of the "Bulge." Von Rundstedt was punch-drunk—he no longer had the power to mount a real counteroffensive or to break out of the "Bulge." The most that he could do was to hold it as long as possible at a maximum cost to the Allies. Apparently von Rundstedt intended to group the majority of his forces for a last stand at the base of the salient. The accomplishment of this movement was being rendered daily more difficult by the gains of the First and Third Armies at either side of the waist of the "Bulge," which by January 10 had narrowed to nine miles and was being constantly shelled from either side.

The Allies struck on January 13 to cut off the Germans in the "Bulge" from their armies in the Reich itself. Hodges' First struck along the thirty miles that remained of the northern flank of the Ardennes, and hit the center into which the Germans had retreated.

The initial German break-through, the bitter battles at the climax of the offensive, and the ensuing counteroffensive had cost the Americans 40,000 casualties. Of these 18,000 were listed as missing and most of them subsequently turned up in German prison camps.

It will be remembered that at the height of the offensive the enemy had twenty-four divisions in the thick of the battle. By January 13 the Allies had destroyed twenty of them.

As the distraught Germans concentrated on extricating their last four pitiful divisions still in Belgium, "Monty" was preparing a surprise for them. One month to the day from the opening of the Ardennes offensive the British Second Army under General Dempsey struck the Maeseryck salient in the Netherlands, eighteen miles northwest of Aachen. Disconcerted by this new blow and the failure of their drive in the Vosges Mountains, the Germans were thrown off balance in the almost non-existent "Bulge." The American First Division drove into Ondenval, less than ten miles from the German border, while other First Army outfits entered Houffalize to join the Third Army.

The Ardennes bubble had burst. What remained of the fighting in Belgium was a mopping-up operation. One town after another was methodically cleared by the First, Third, and Ninth Armies. On January 16 the First returned to Bradley's Twelfth Army Group. Saint-Vith was recaptured on January 23. Fleeing German vehicles, under stunning bombing, strafing, and shelling, were being destroyed at the rate of 2,000 to 2,500 a day. Tank and assault-gun losses totaled more than 600; the enemy had lost more than 700 planes. At the very end, when the Germans were staggering along the road within sight of home, the Allies sent 3,000 planes over the remnants of the retreating columns. Bombs and bullets and shells poured into the densely packed roads.

German might was broken. Further effort at counterblows elsewhere could have no more than the most trivial delaying value. On the whole front the Allies were once more on the offensive—this time to keep it unbroken until the final reduction of the enemy. For forty-four days these battles had raged—through the Christmas and New Year season, bringing only "gifts of death" to thousands of boys who had been thinking of the festivities back home.

American troops broke back into Germany from the erstwhile "Bulge" for the first time on January 29, 1945. This was the beginning of the end for the Germans' mad dream of world conquest—only three more months and the war in Europe would be over.

LAST BATTLES IN GERMANY—GREAT CITIES FALL IN RUINS

INEXORABLE fate laid its chastening hand on the German people as the war in Europe drew to its inevitable conclusion. The law of retribution was in action. They had sowed the seed and were now to reap the whirlwind. All the havoc they had wreaked on other countries was to return to them a thousandfold.

Germany had been invaded from both east and west by March, 1945. Their country was a charnel house of flames. Their leaders were cowering in caves—waiting for death by suicide or to be placed before firing squads or hanged as the world's most despised criminals.

More than 4,000,000 troops were fighting in the Allied armies on the Western Front—almost 3,000,000 of these were Americans. The rest were British, Canadians, Irish, Scots, Frenchmen, Poles, Belgians, Czechs, Netherlanders, and sons of all the United Nations. Every race and nation was represented. Among them also were Germans and Austrians, fighting in the armies of the Democracies against the Nazi Fascist scourge.

The Russians were smashing relentlessly toward Berlin along a broad front as the British and American Allies attacked from the west. The Third Army, smashing into the triangle formed by the Rhine, Moselle, and Saar rivers, began to forge a pocket around some 50,000 Germans. The total of prisoners taken in the thirty-five-day drive that had carried the Allies to the Rhine mounted to 100,000. Patton's men were leaping toward Coblenz in giant strides.

The First Army was no less spectacular. Its 9th Armored Division had reached the Rhine at Remagen, between Cologne and Bonn, and found the German bridge across the river there still intact. American tanks stormed into the town with such fury that the Germans were taken by complete surprise and had no time to finish their long preparations for the destruction of the bridge. Ten minutes before they were to have blown it up, the tanks of the 9th had rolled across it into the Rhineland Province and secured its farther end.

It was the first time in 140 years—since the great days of Napoleon—that a hostile invader had crossed the German river. The 1st and 9th Infantry Divisions of Hodges' Army swept up Bad Godesberg. Here, almost seven years before, Neville Chamberlain had meekly flown at Hitler's request to return with the "peace for our time" that had been the fount of the war. Now the Americans were in Bonn itself. Between

NEW YORK HERALD TRIBUNE map—Fleck

Arrows indicate the three regions in which Allied armies poured across the Rhine into the heart of Germany. Top arrow shows where General Montgomery's Twenty-first Army Group crossed the lower Rhine to capture Wesel; middle arrow shows the American First Army's Remagen bridgehead; lower arrow indicates American Third Army crossing. Striped area shows the territory won by the Allied armies after the offensive opened on February 23, 1945.

the First Army in the Remagen-Bonn area and the Third in its lunge for Coblenz another giant trap was forming for the Germans.

A fourth American Army was about to take the field. This was the Fifteenth, under Lieutenant General Leonard T. Gerow.

The navy, too, took a hand in the invasion of Germany. Remagen Bridge was under constant shelling. It could not last much longer and the barrage was still too heavy to permit the erection of a temporary structure to replace it. Yet it was obvious that more and more men and arms must be poured across to the eastern bank of the Rhine. On hurry calls from the front, SHAEF enlisted navy assault-boat crews and loaded them with their craft into trucks and trains for a speedy run to the front. The sailors passed for the moment to army command and wore army battle dress as they got their armed and armored boats into the water some four miles above Remagen and began to ferry the First Army's men and vehicles across the river. Enemy fire on the farther shore was dense; but it was more than answered by the men in the boats. They forced their way ashore. Navy boys leaped out of their boats, guns in hand, to stand in the firing line with the army.

On either side of the growing Remagen bridgehead the Yanks were scoring mighty gains. Patton's 4th Armored Division drove to Guels on the outskirts of Coblenz and cleared the west bank of the Moselle, while the 10th Armored mopped up another big section of the rivershore above Trier. North of Remagen, the Ninth Army at Duesseldorf and Duisburg was calling long-range artillery into play to shell the famed city of Essen, home of the world-renowned Krupp arms works.

As civilians streamed east and south into the heart of the Reich from the Western-Front cities, Hitler pleaded with them by radio: "Stand and fight to the last man." But it was too late. German troops in 1918 had surrendered on foreign soil; German cities had barely been touched by war This was not to be the case again. German leaders themselves knew it. They were beginning to move government offices out of Berlin.

Germany's plight was growing ever more perilous. Its air force was almost completely out of action. Its machines were still strewn over scores of fields, idle for want of men and fuel. Its best commander in the west, von Rundstedt, who had so nearly smashed the entire invasion, had collapsed from nervous exhaustion and he could be replaced only by weakening some other front. The Germans withdrew the tough commander of their forces in Italy, Field Marshal General Albert Kesselring, and rushed him to the west. He arrived in time to face the threat of still another Allied offensive as Montgomery massed the 21st Army Group for still another powerful crossing of the Rhine in the north. To add to German consternation the R.A.F. revealed its newest weapon in a great mass attack—11-ton bombs that annihilated everything within miles of their targets.

The First Army, consolidating its long bridgehead across the Rhine, struck out again, this time for the superhighway to the Ruhr. So furious was the blow that it smashed a counterattack before it could start. The Ninth, acting as advance scout for the British and Canadians, extensively probed the enemy's defenses north of Duisburg; and the southern sector flared up again. Patton cleared all the north bank of the Moselle and smashed into Coblenz. While other units of his Third Army joined with Patch's Seventh for the big drive into the Saar Basin, the French First Army launched a drive for Karlsruhe.

Ten days after the first crossing of the Rhine at Remagen the big Ludendorff Bridge there, weakened by the great weight and volume of the Allies' traffic and the Germans' shelling, collapsed. Fortunately few troops were on the span. American engineers went to work at once to replace it. Amazing even their own officers, they erected the new temporary structure in ten hours.

German losses were mounting faster than they could be calculated. In the Rhine-Saar-Moselle triangle, as the Third and Seventh Armies continued their irresistible advance, more than 40,000 Germans had been killed, wounded, or captured by March 20. Below Mainz American tanks swept east in a long drive as General Eisenhower warned German civilians in the areas of Frankfort-am-Main, Ludwigshafen, and Mannheim to leave the regions entirely, for their own protection and to avoid impeding the Allied advance.

For the moment the spotlight was shifting from the First to the Third Army. Mainz and Worms were cracked wide open by Patton's tough warriors, who were proving themselves as worthy as he of his own nickname, "Old Blood and Guts." They captured Kaiserslautern and raced beyond it. West of the town they formed a junction with Patch's 6th Armored Division to create still another pocket of German troops. The Seventh Army's 70th Infantry cleaned up Saarbruecken as the 3rd and 63rd together drove the Germans out of Zweibruecken.

The north leaped into flame on March 22. Monty threw the British Second Army and the Canadian First into concerted action between Arnhem and Duesseldorf, as Patton's troops were driving into Ludwigshafen and Speyer, and established a new bridgehead across the Rhine at Mainz. But it was the night of the next day that produced the great push destined to carry the whole front beyond the Rhine.

Dempsey's and Crerar's troops stormed over the river near Wesel in the wake of one of those unparalleled artillery devastations that had characterized every Montgomery offensive since El Alamein almost three years before. Ahead of them, carried through the air in the greatest such operation yet attempted, went the Allied First Airborne Army composed of American and British divisions. Fifteen hundred transports and gliders conveyed this huge airborne force to landing areas in the plains of Westphalia, toward which the ground forces rapidly smashed their way to establish a junction in the darkness and the first gray light of day.

Only a little behind them came that indomitable man who had, almost single-handed, brought Britain through her darkest hours: Churchill, cigar in mouth, stood on a landing-raft as it crossed the Rhine and then cruised up and down the historic stream that he had traveled so many years before for pleasure. Not fifty yards from Churchill's raft a German shell burst against the Wesel bridge. It was only by a miracle that the Prime Minister was not killed. Aides begged him to return to the western shore. He calmly continued his cruise.

As the parachutists were landing in Westphalia and beyond, General Eisenhower's warning went out to the Germans. Knowing their temper—civilians and soldiers alike—he warned them sternly that any execution of these regular troops would be punished with extreme penalties. And as if to point up the warning of the ultimate fate of Germany, the Allies in a single day launched more than 12,000 planes against the country to rake it from one end to the other.

Patton's spearheads had stabbed 136 miles within Germany when their commander conferred with Eisenhower, Bradley, and Hodges at the former conference site of Bad Godesberg of such evil memory. Eisenhower was smiling confidently when his aides arrived. He was jubilant as the day progressed. "The German Armies of the west," he declared, "are thoroughly broken and whipped." But he added a caution: the Germans would stand and fight where they could. Eisenhower made it plain to the enemy that there would be no negotiated unconditional surrender; there would be only that imposed by force of arms.

As the British and Canadian Armies advanced, the Ninth paralleled their drive. The Yanks crossed the Rhine between Wesel and Duisburg and swiftly won footholds they lost no time in expanding. There were now seven Allied armies on the western front: the British Second; the Canadian First; the American First, Third, Seventh, and Ninth; and the French First. In the face of this, the German radio in an effort to induce slackness in the attackers began broadcasting to our troops that they had already won the victory. Some German civilians, apparently, already believed this, too, for the residents of Frankfort suddenly rose to disarm the troops defending their city. Only the intervention of the ruthless Élite Guard quelled the rebellion.

For the Allies the battle for Germany was daily gaining momentum. Below the Netherlands border the Ninth Army effected a junction with the British as more airborne troops landed in the Wesel area. The First Army drove steadily forward and the Third was nearing Frankfurt, while the Seventh and the French First periled Karlsruhe. By the end of March both these cities had fallen. The First Army had almost completely isolated the Ruhr, vital to Germany's industrial prosperity and military success, from the rest of the country. The Russians were taking huge strides into eastern Germany and through Czechoslovakia.

The State Department in Washington announced that the armies in their great lunges had captured from enemy officers many documents that demonstrated conclusively the German determination to accept their defeat as inevitable and to renew immediately after it the dissemination of their doctrines and their military efforts at world dominion. "These plans," the State Department said, "have been carefully and skilfully conceived and their execution through neutral countries has already begun."

At the end of March the American Fifteenth Army under General Gerow went into the lines. Emphasizing this reinforcement of the overwhelming Allied might, Eisenhower turned to psychological warfare. He called on individual German soldiers everywhere to surrender to the nearest Allied units as their Government had "ceased to exercise effective control over wide areas of the country." Even before this appeal, the enemy's troops had begun in some areas to surrender in company strength and more.

April began with the encirclement of a great German force in the Ruhr. The British and the American Ninth had started a drive for Muenster; and the junction of the First and Third Armies had completely bottled up the Ruhr defenders between, roughly, Essen and Dortmund on the north and Siegen and Bonn on the south.

Closing of the Ruhr pocket sounded the death knell to the Germans. It was there that their finest forces in the west were almost all grouped. The pitiful Volkssturm that had been hastily thrown together in the cities and the rural areas, composed of all men previously found unfit for the army, was inadequately armed, untrained, and often dispirited before it had begun to fight.

Heinrich Himmler, the butcher-bandit who was more and more assuming Hitler's powers, ordered the creation of the "Werewolves." This was to be an organization of completely lawless and ruthless guerrillas behind the Allies' lines. It was instructed to kill and destroy with abandon, to show no quarter and observe no rules except those of destruction and treachery. Despite the bloodthirsty exhortations, they were to give relatively little trouble. Cowardice and disorganization were their chief characteristics. The "Werewolves" proved to be bluffers and bullies afraid of their own shadows.

An arc of more than a million Eisenhower men was forming east of the Rhine and rolling forward over a 300-mile line into the interior of Germany. Before it German resistance crumbled in some sectors and fanatically increased in others so that the progress of the arc as a whole was never regular. But its eventual triumph was a certainty.

In the United States preparations were under way for the greatest international conference ever held. The forty-six United Nations were to meet in San Francisco, even before the end of the war in Europe, to plan ways and means to prevent the recurrence of another such conflict. In Europe, Himmler's own newspaper was glumly warning the German people that they had "only days or perhaps weeks" before the "absolute collapse" of their country. But Eisenhower was cautious and not to be tricked into overconfidence. Not to be lured by Hitlerian treachery, he drove his forces deeper and deeper in the heart of Germany as his bombers laid the enemy's historic cities in ruins. He intended to carry war to the homes of the German people, to give them a lesson they would never forget.

Germany was being hacked to pieces and laid in crumbling ashes. Her military spirit was being crushed and broken. She must learn to live in peace with other nations—or die. The American Seventh Army drove into Mannheim. A junction between tanks of the First and Ninth Armies sealed the fate of the Ruhr pocket. Canadian and British troops carved new gains in the north in both the Netherlands and Germany. Beyond the pocket, the Third Army speared into Kassel. At their closest points, only 171 miles separated the Allied eastern and the Russian western fronts. Between them and all over Germany American and British bombs rained down in unceasing might. The last of the pocket battleships, the *Admiral Scheer* at Kiel and the *Admiral Luetzow* at Swinemuende, were sunk. The R.A.F. was bombing in support of the Red Army. No German planes went up.

As the Third Army overran the salt-mine town of Merkers, they made a marvelous discovery. Deep in one of the mines was a strongly constructed treasure house in which were concealed, under heavy guard, the treasures of the Reich, stolen from many countries. More than $100,000,000 of pure gold ingots, millions of dollars' worth of German, French, British, and American currency, were found. Priceless artistic and literary masterpieces from all the museums and libraries of eastern, southern, and western Europe, were recovered. Ancient manuscripts, paintings by Vermeer, Rembrandt, Titian, the moderns, were discovered.

But the armies had grim business still to do. The Allies sent parachutists into Groningen, in northern Holland, to cut off the enemy's escape routes, as the Canadians, fanning west and east in the country, periled the defenders still more. British troops smashed ahead to bring Bremen under the fire of their heavy artillery. Farther south, they bypassed Hannover on the north (as the American Ninth did on the south) to reach the Berlin superhighway twenty miles from Brunswick.

Western Germany was tottering on April 9. The Canadians had cut all but one of the enemy's escape routes from the Netherlands. The British drive was now periling Hamburg as well as Bremen. The

Last Battles in Germany

American Ninth Army battled its way into Essen, where the Krupp Works, once employing 200,000 men, was now down to seven employees. Most of the factories had been made hopelessly unusable by years of bombing and more recently by concentrated artillery fire. The Ninth crashed into Hannover the next day, as the British entered the outskirts of Bremen.

On April 11 the Ninth Army made its most sensational drive thus far. It pushed through Meine, north of Brunswick, in which latter city its forces were battling furiously. Then suddenly it stabbed fifty miles to Magdeburg, on the Elbe River, only sixty-three miles from Berlin, while its rear units inflicted still more damage on the Ruhr pocket. The First Army was driving for Leipzig. The city of Coburg surrendered to the Third, while the Seventh entered the important industrial city of Schweinfurt and the French drove to the gates of Essen.

On the tragic day of April 12, as American troops were gaining new triumphs, they and their nation were stunned by a grievous loss. Their Commander in Chief, Franklin D. Roosevelt, died suddenly, "back home." Officers and men alike were startled by the news. They could not believe it when it came over the field radios in the German night. Many of them had seen the President in Casablanca two years before when he reviewed American troops—to all of them, whatever their politics, he was their Commander in Chief.

In tanks and half-tracks, in planes and in foxholes, men bowed their heads. Soldiers wept. They had lost their leader in action; but they had not lost their cause. The war was going on and they would wrest the victory that the fallen leader had so long and carefully planned, even as he had wanted it.

Twenty-four more days and the American troops would erect a memorial to their fallen Commander in Chief which would make his name live through the centuries. All he had worked and died for would become a living reality. It would be engraved on the tablets of history through the ages in seven letters—VICTORY!

RUSSIANS PUSH ON TOWARD BERLIN —FROM THE VISTULA TO THE ODER

BERLIN was doomed. The Russian drive toward the German capital in January, 1945, has no parallel in history for its scale, speed, and the results it achieved. It led to the complete liberation of Poland and much of Czechoslovakia and drove deep salients into the German homeland in Silesia, East Prussia, Pomerania, and Brandenburg. It also established the conditions under which the great final offensives into Berlin and Vienna were launched.

"The Hitlerites," Stalin exclaimed on one occasion, "boasted that for more than one hundred years not a single enemy soldier had been inside Germany—that the German Army had fought and would fight only on foreign territory. Now this German boasting has been brought to an end."

On the twenty-seventh anniversary of the Red Army, Stalin's forces were moving on the 745-mile front from the Baltic to the Carpathians. In their forty-day offensive, the Russians had killed and taken prisoner incredible numbers of the enemy. As many as three thousand German aircraft of various types had been shot down or captured and their bag of captured tanks and self-propelled and other guns ran up into the thousands also. In addition they had taken over a railway network 9,500 miles long.

The Germans had begun the year in strategically strong positions bolstered at their rear with ample facilities for defenses in depth. During the *Wehrmacht's* final show of strength in its Ardennes counter-offensive in the west and its sizable counterblows in Hungary, some military observers felt that enemy resistance might be prolonged from six months to a year.

As subsequent events proved, three transcendent factors made the defeat of Germany inevitable: First, the moral bankruptcy of the Hitler régime, which had been manifest since the generals' abortive revolt in July, 1944; second, the havoc wrought by Allied air ascendency, which was systematically destroying the Reich's production resources and communications; third, the United Nations' decisive superiority in matériel and manpower.

Yet the task facing the Red Army in the east—the breaching of the two great remaining German defense lines—was enormous. The battle line spanned eastern Europe, from the Latvian coast of the Baltic Sea to the Adriatic; at its northern extremity a remnant of the Germans'

Baltic armies was penned up in the Courland Peninsula west of Riga. Another German enclave held out around Memel, at the tip of a Russian salient that had reached the Baltic coast of Lithuania. From there the line bit shallowly into East Prussia and wandered down the Narew River to the Warsaw region, following the Vistula River below Warsaw to Sandomierz, where the Red Army held a bridgehead pointed north of Cracow; from there the armies were arrayed across the eastern tip of Czechoslovakia and the northwestern part of Hungary through Budapest, with a salient jutting to Lake Balaton and the Drava River. Below the Drava the Balkan line, vaguely drawn west of Belgrade, Nish, and Skoplje, was manned largely by the Yugoslav forces of Marshal Tito, with eventual assistance from Rumanian and Bulgarian formations.

In the lull of early winter the Russians were reported to have marshaled some three hundred divisions, with additional armored units, between the Baltic and the Carpathians.

In the redeployment of the Soviet forces for their climactic surge, Marshal Zhukoff replaced Marshal Rokossovsky in command of the First White Russian Army in the Warsaw sector and also served as over-all commander of the front in liaison with the Supreme Command. Rokossovsky took command of the Second White Russian Army above Warsaw, and farther north, General Ivan D. Chernykhovsky led the Third White Russian Army, whose sector included the salient jutting into East Prussia.

Below Warsaw, the First Ukrainian Army of Marshal Ivan S. Koneff operated on Zhukoff's left flank west of Lublin and in the Sandomierz bridgehead opposite Tarnow and Cracow. The Second Ukrainian Army, commanded by Marshal Rodion Y. Malinovsky, was investing Budapest and sweeping through the rest of Hungary. In the extreme south, the Third Ukrainian Army of Marshal Fedor I. Tolbukhin was driving up from liberated Bulgaria to join Malinovsky in southern Hungary.

The eventual strategy also brought into play the First Baltic Army of General Ivan Bagramyan, which completed the clean-up of the northern flank, and the Fourth Ukrainian Army of General A. I. Yeremenko, which broke through the Carpathians between the First and Second Ukrainian Fronts.

The strength of the Germans' position—and the corresponding difficulty of the Russians' assignment—lay in the fact that the main front was anchored to extraordinarily secure flanks: the fortified Masurian Lakes region of East Prussia on the north and the Lake Balaton-Drava River line on the south. This vast front, moreover, was split into two parts by the forbidding Carpathian Range across southern Poland and northeastern Czechoslovakia.

The possibilities of surprise on the Russians' part were minimal: it was obvious to the Germans that the Red Army must canalize its offensive through historic military routes. These were: (1) the main gateway to Berlin, directly westward from Warsaw; (2) the Silesian Gate, between Cracow and Breslau in the direction of Dresden and Leipzig; and (3) the Danube Gateway, through Budapest and Bratislava to Vienna and Linz. There was also the further possibility of bursting through the Moravian Gate from Czechoslovakia to Silesia to nullify the bulwark of the Carpathians. Well aware of these compulsions, the Germans disposed their forces to meet each of the predetermined assaults.

Marshal Koneff opened the offensive on January 12 with a tremendous attack from the Sandomierz bridgehead. Two days later, Zhukoff started a wide, circling sweep around Warsaw. Within a week the greater part of the front between the Baltic and the middle Danube was ablaze.

Though strategic surprise was impossible, the Germans were amazed by the unprecedented weight and power of the multiple Russian attack; by the effective interplay of the Red Army's aircraft and artillery, armor and infantry, engineers and cavalry; by the Soviet command's shrewd choice of successive key objectives in widely separated sectors; by the swift, destructive slashes with which the avenging armies smashed through the strongest defensive walls.

Berlin, with plaintive candor intended to stiffen national resistance, again outdid Moscow in describing the fury of the Russian attack and the appalling accumulation of German disasters. The German radio first pictured the Red Army's surge as a steamroller, then as a landslide, next as an avalanche and finally as a challenging, Apocalyptic "Bolshevist flood."

While Zhukoff invested Warsaw, and Koneff drove an expanding wedge toward Cracow, Rokossovsky and Chernyakhovsky, to the north, put East Prussia in a huge pincers, one arm aiming for Allenstein from the south, the other driving down the Kaunas railway from the east toward Insterburg and Koenigsberg.

Almost immediately the German High Command saw that it would be impossible to hold a connected defense line across the Polish plains. Hitler's defensive strategy was swept away in a flash; the German commanders were now ordered to play desperately for time at their strongest islands of resistance while a new "breakwater" was prepared farther west.

In the small sector of the Sandomierz bridgehead where Koneff touched off the offensive, a little masterpiece of artful deception was carried out for weeks before the attack began. This was along the small but deep Czarne River, one bank of which was held by the

Germans while Soviet troops were drawn up in a dense forest on the opposite side. Here was a well-concealed rendezvous that betrayed few signs of unusual activity to the Germans, but to which men and material were brought up in a constant stream over bridges spanning the Vistula.

In adjacent sectors, however, a noisy show of bustling activity was made daily by small Russian forces. Tractors towed dummy wooden tanks from place to place. Wandering individual guns fired ostentatiously from emplacements where observable wooden guns bristled. Sounds of seemingly purposeful activity were kept up all night in every sector except the chosen one. The Germans spread their forces all along the front and put their strongest concentrations in the wrong places. Three days before the time set for the attack, a battalion was sent across the Czarne on a reconnaissance mission and to win a small bridgehead. Before the appointed hour, Koneff was intimately familiar with every detail of the Germans' defenses and the definite disposition of their forces.

At dawn on January 12, Koneff's offensive started with a shattering half-hour artillery preparation, after which three veteran Guards battalions attacked the enemy positions. The snow had vanished in a midwinter thaw and the terrain was of advantageous sandy ground. Infantrymen and artillery observers pushed into the breaches scooped out by the hurricane of gunfire. Platoons of sub-machine gunners fired on the move. The unceasing artillery fire was extended deeper into the enemy defenses and the infantrymen hurried to keep up with it. In what had been the foremost German positions the Red Army's vanguard found scenes of terrible chaos. The earth was churned up by the intense shellfire and scattered over it were mangled bodies of the German defenders, splintered logs, destroyed weapons, and shredded débris. The few Germans who had survived the storm of fire in dugouts were too stunned to resist; blood streamed from their noses and ears.

The second line of trenches, which ran across a series of hills, was not so easily taken. Heavy machine guns and German tanks buried in the ground established a hard crust of resistance designed to win time while reserves were being brought up. Another heavy artillery assault shortened this delay, dropping thousands of tons of shells on the entire depth of the defenses and silencing antiaircraft guns as well. Following the curtain of artillery fire, Soviet infantrymen seized and strengthened successive positions.

Before the end of the first day, the tactical break-through had become an operational one and tank and motorized infantry formations were brought into play to exploit the advantage. Koneff was on the move.

Like a chain of coördinated explosive charges, the other fronts followed Koneff's into eruption—Zhukoff's around Warsaw, Rokossovsky's farther north, and Chernyakhovsky's above that. Zhukoff burst through his confines on January 14 in a flanking maneuver similar to the one that had surrounded Budapest. In a wide sweep around Warsaw, he forced the Nazi garrison into panicky retreat to escape his trap. The Soviet-equipped First Polish Army under Lieutenant General Poplawski joined him to help break the five-month deadlock and end Warsaw's five-year bondage.

Warsaw fell on January 17. The Polish capital's martyrdom under the Germans' heel had been costly. As part of the Germans' twofold program of slavery for the subjugated people and *Lebensraum* for Nazi families, everything Polish had been marked for destruction. The city was plastered with signs bearings the edict, "For Germans only." Schools, theaters, museums, and cinemas were closed. Polish professors and intellectuals were dragooned as waiters for German night clubs. Native markets were paralyzed. Industrial equipment was shipped to Breslau and Leipzig for German industry. Artistic and cultural treasures were carted off to Germany, and with them went scores of thousands of Warsaw residents as slave labor. Jews were herded into the infamous Warsaw ghetto to die. When the Soviet-Polish forces entered the city, the all but destroyed capital had become a symbol of Nazi military conquest.

Liberation gave new impetus to internal strife among the Poles. The Soviet-fostered régime in Lublin moved its Government to the ruins of Warsaw over the challenge of the exiled Government in London, which renewed its claim to sole legitimacy. The Underground Polish force, or Home Army, which had determinedly and gallantly maintained its Partisan warfare against the Germans throughout the occupation, was split upon this issue and some of its members who opposed the Soviet program for Poland were charged with insurrectionist activities by the Russians.

On January 18, Rokossovsky took the fortress of Modlin, northwest of Warsaw, undermining the left flank of the Germans' defenses on the direct road to Posen and Berlin. The Russians' lightning war, an ironic reversal of the German ideal of 1940, was approaching its apogee.

The pace of victory now was so swift that on January 19, when the offensive was only a week old, Premier Stalin issued five orders of the day to signalize outstanding triumphs. These were for the capture of Cracow, Tarnow, Lodz, Praszka, and Leczyka. The old military tradition of saluting important victories in the capital had been revived by Stalin on August 5, 1943, when salvos were fired to honor the victors of Orel and Belgorod. Each of Stalin's orders of the day, read over state loudspeakers in the public squares of Moscow and the regional capitals, became an occasion for thunderous salutes from Moscow's fixed defense batteries and for the firing of hundreds of colored rockets into the midnight sky. After their long ordeal, their splendid sacrifices, and herculean labors, the Russians tasted the full savor of their cumulative triumph.

Koneff's swift capture of Cracow was second only to the toppling of Warsaw as a decisive blow to the Germans' hopes, both militarily and from the standpoint of morale. Cracow had been the seat of the Polish Government-General set up to rule the Nazis' *Ostland* in the thousand-year new order proclaimed by Hitler for the Reich in 1939. The Cracow area's fortifications were among the strongest on the Vistula.

On the seventh day of Koneff's drive, his infantry, supported by tanks and aircraft and accompanied by artillery, broke through to Cracow from the north and engaged the German garrison just where the Nazis were not expecting a blow. Almost simultaneously, another force approached from the south and closed a pincers on the city. The attacking units curled around the city from the northwest and southwest and overwhelmed its defenses from the rear. The climactic phase of the battle, on the outskirts and in the streets, was fierce but brief.

Zhukoff, with favorable terrain for a mainly straight-line attack, set the pace of the offensive; six days after taking Warsaw he had advanced one hundred and fifty miles, an average of twenty-five miles a day. Koneff, despite the necessity of complicated maneuvers and heavy fighting through strong defenses, averaged eighteen miles a day at the height of his push. Rokossovsky, heading for the southern frontier of East Prussia over fortified terrain of exceptional strength, abounding in natural barriers, advanced at the rate of thirteen miles a day. Chernyakhovsky, who renewed the offensive in East Prussia at Stalluponen on January 15, fought across sixty miles of powerful defenses in the first nine days, an average of six miles a day.

Rokossovsky's sector faced what was believed to be the most powerful segment of the German defenses—the "Blue Line" bulwarking the approaches to East Prussia. Yet these ramparts of the easternmost part of the German homeland—the cradle of Junkerdom—were ripped to pieces in the first four hours of the Second White Russian Army's offensive.

Famous Russian tank units spearheaded the drive, smashing through the German line to fan out in the rear and split the defenders in tight pockets. Steel and concrete fortifications were so formidable that the Russians called the region "the Devil's Threshold." Nevertheless, it was the most direct overland route to Danzig, and Soviet might, carefully calculated to master any obstacle, made good its determination to go through.

Collapse of the extreme German flanks was indicated on January 20 by the fall of Tilsit, on the roof of the salient northeast of Koenigsberg, and of Nowy Sacz, southeast of Cracow on the approaches to Slovakia. Rokossovsky took Tannenberg, the scene of Russia's worst defeat in World War I. President von Hindenburg's remains were taken from the elaborate memorial on the old battlefield before the Russians arrived.

At the same time Zhukoff and Koneff were biting deep into the German soil of Silesia. By January 22 the line had advanced to Insterburg, the last important rail junction before Koenigsberg; Allenstein, a correspondingly important junction in south-central East Prussia, and Gniezno, an outpost of Posen.

The speed and scope of the advance were illustrated by the fact that on January 22 more than 1,750 populated places were taken by the Red Army and on the next day more than 3,500, of which 1,500 were German and 2,000 Polish. Among the latter was Bydgoszcz, at the entrance of the Polish Corridor. On January 24, Koneff added to his trophy-cities Oppeln, capital of Upper Silesia, and Rawicz, 148 miles from Berlin, while Zhukoff was entering Kalicz.

With East Prussia hopelessly pocketed and the primary fortresses of Posen and Breslau immediately threatened, Germany's frank despair rose to new heights.

The German press and radio pleaded with all Germans to take up arms and "work a miracle." Hitler gave Gestapo Chief Heinrich Himmler free rein in East Prussia and Silesia to "make and execute drastic decisions." Berlin acknowledged to the world that its armies were in full retreat on a three-hundred-mile front from central Czechoslovakia to central Poland.

The battles of this period abounded in proof that the German High Command was persisting in the fatal error of trying to meet new situations with the outmoded tactics of 1940. The Nazi commanders attempted to contain the Russian onslaught by drawing a semicircular line through Torun, Posen, and Breslau. As a result, the Red Army simply swept around these strong points, drew tight rings about them and continued its drive westward.

Koneff laid siege to Breslau on January 25 and Zhukoff completed the encirclement of Torun and Posen on the following day. Torun was reduced on February 1, but Posen and Breslau continued to remain stubborn islands of resistance long after the battle lines had swept beyond them.

Stalin was able to announce on January 26 that his troops had plunged to the Baltic coast on Danzig Bay, between Elbing and Koenigsberg, completing the encirclement of East Prussia and cutting off its considerable garrison from Germany. About the same time the long siege of the enclave around Memel was successfully completed, and the eastern phase of the Baltic campaign became a matter of tightening the pocket between the armies of Chernyakhovsky on the north and Rokossovsky on the south and west. The proud Prussian capital of Koenigsberg was now added to the formidably growing list of besieged cities.

The Red Army was streaming into Germany's Baltic province of Pomerania and the Berlin province of Brandenburg, as well as spearing deep into Silesia by February 1.

On the twelfth anniversary of his rise to power, Hitler's only message for his people was that "the horrid fate that is now taking shape in the east will be warded off in the end and mastered by us despite all setbacks and hard trials." Even credulous Nazis found despair implicit in the words with which he declared that not even the Russians could conquer a triumvirate composed of Hitler, God, and the strength of the German people.

As he spoke, terrified refugees by tens of thousands were rushing toward Berlin from the far reaches of his collapsing empire, and Berlin itself was rapidly crumbling to rubble under ceaseless air attacks carried on by the Royal Air Force at night and the American Air Forces by day. The city was in a state of siege, with women manning antiaircraft guns, and children and the aged helping to dig trenches and antitank ditches.

On the second anniversary of the liberation of Stalingrad—February 2—Russian troops stood forty-six miles from Berlin—a march of 1,350 miles from the Volga—and were threatening Frankfort on the Oder, and Kuestrin, twin citadels of the last natural defense line before Berlin. But the *Wehrmacht,* though battered, still was not beaten. The task facing the Red Army before full victory could be claimed remained enormous.

Having reached the Oder, the Germans were better situated defensively than at any time since the Soviet offensive began. The potential strength of their Kuestrin-Frankfort line in front of Berlin was tremendous, and they were close to their main reserves of supplies and manpower. German soldiers and civilians, fighting for what remained of their hearths and homes, had every reason to put their last ounce of strength into the battle.

The Russians, on the other hand, were operating at an increasing disadvantage. Their supply lines were dangerously overextended from their rapid advance on the vast front, although their huge booty of German fuel, weapons, ammunition, food, and vehicles helped to ameliorate this problem to some extent.

The Russians, at this point, had urgent need for reorganization of scattered and weakened units, although the Supreme Command provided regular renewals of fresh troops from the rear. But perhaps the most compelling reason for a pause in the westward advance was the irregular contour of the front.

Observers who wondered whether Zhukoff would push on to Berlin at once might have found their answer in the history of the Red Army's prior major operations. Almost never was a Soviet advantage pursued long at the point of a salient while extended flanks were unable to keep up the pace. And, in early February, although Zhukoff was shouldering against the curve of the Oder below Kuestrin, both wings of his line were beset with difficulty: Chernyakhovsky was temporarily stymied at Koenigsberg; Rokossovsky was still far from Danzig; Koneff's left flank was making necessarily slow progress between Cracow and the Moravian Gap, and Yeremenko was laboring through the tortuous defiles of the towering Carpathians. Moreover, the Germans' desperate grip on encircled Posen and a similar mighty struggle to the death then in progress for Breslau inhibited free access to Poland's network of supply lines.

There were indications that pre-arranged coördination of the Russian operations with the time-table drawn up by the Big Three figured to some degree in the decision to pause at the Oder; but, even if there had been at that time no second front in the west, it seems certain that Zhukoff would not have gone on until his flanks had been secured and advanced.

During a relative lull in the train of spectacular Soviet advances, the Germans unleashed a series of savage tank-led counterattacks. Chernyakhovsky was heavily engaged around Koenigsberg and Rokossovsky had to deal with persistent enemy thrusts northwest of Allenstein.

Heavy tank battles developed in the Frankfort region and Koneff was forced to fight hard to widen his ring around Breslau and to extend his threat to the Moravian Gap. One typical tactic became familiar. This was a boldly executed offensive-defensive maneuver conceived by the Soviet command to meet enemy counterblows, without appreciably slowing up the pace of the general advance. Two echelons of armored forces would go forward to engage the attacking units. The first one would smash directly through the enemy formation and fan out beyond, leaving the second echelon to mop up the scattered and disorganized panzers. Russian superiority in tank power, in both weight and numbers, became a major factor in the mastery achieved over the *Wehrmacht* in the spring of 1945.

The Big Three announced to the world the results of the meeting of President Roosevelt, Prime Minister Churchill, and Premier Stalin at Yalta in the Crimea on February 12.

"Nazi Germany is doomed," their declaration said. "Only when

Nazism and militarism have been extirpated will there be hope for a decent life for Germans and a place for them in the comity of nations."

In announcing their program for the occupation of Germany after victory had been consummated, the Allied leaders left no doubt that the imposition of an unconditional surrender of German arms was a foregone conclusion. To that end they laid their plans for the coördination of even more powerful blows on all fronts to bring the war to an early end.

Having paused east of the middle Oder, Zhukoff started driving northward with the double aim of extending his front toward Stettin and splitting into several pockets the Germans' groupings on the Baltic coast of Pomerania. Meanwhile Rokossovsky was driving down the lower Vistula toward Danzig on the west side of the East Prussian enclave.

One of the war's tragedies most deeply felt in Russia struck the Red Army in mid-February when General Chernyakhovsky was fatally wounded during the heavy fighting for East Prussia. He died on February 18, just when his troops were about to complete the task asigned to them.

A pupil and protége of General Vatutin, Chernyakhovsky had risen rapidly after distinguishing himself in the fighting from Voronezh across the Dnieper and, like Vatutin, he seemed assured of a marshal's star when death snatched him in the midst of battle. The youngest Red Army general, at thirty-seven, he had figured in the spectacular encirclement of Vitebsk and in the capture of Minsk, Vilna, Kaunas, and most of East Prussia.

To replace Chernyakhovsky, Premier Stalin again drew upon his General Staff; command of the Third White Russian Army passed to Marshal Alexander M. Vasilevsky, one of Stalin's close military advisers, who had succeeded Zhukoff as chief of staff in Moscow.

The fall of Elbing and a main German place d'armes at Preussisch Eylau had deprived the *Wehrmacht* of their strongest remaining positions in East Prussia outside of Koenigsberg, and Vasilevsky now concentrated upon the completion of the siege of the provincial capital and the reduction of a pocket to the southwest. This pocket he was successful in swiftly compressing into a narrow strip running along the Baltic coast.

On the opposite flank, Koneff inexorably ground down the strong German positions in the Silesian industrial region north and south of encircled Breslau.

Second only to the Ruhr in industrial importance, Silesia was vital to the continuation of full-scale German warfare, and to counter Koneff's incursion there the Nazi command shifted armored divisions from the Western Front. The district had been shielded by six lines of defenses, built at fifteen- to twenty-mile intervals, the whole comprising a compact network of fortified towns, settlements, and hills. Interlocking fire-nets were only 100 to 150 yards apart and among them wound endless lines of deep trenches, barbed-wire entanglements, and skillfully placed mine fields.

Before the war, Silesia had produced 25 per cent of Germany's coal, 10 per cent of her steel, and 15 per cent of her pig iron. The volume of its production had increased greatly during the war, for many of the industries bombed out of the west had been moved to this region's supposed security. Its industry was so concentrated that its southern part became practically a single city stretching for more than seventy miles. The Germans, manifestly, were in no mood to sell all this cheaply.

Yet Koneff advanced as rapidly as fifteen to twenty miles a day, in heavy fighting, through this bristling fortress. His mobile units attacked fresh reinforcements arriving from the interior, split the defenses, and sped on westward. His line spread from Neisse on the south to Sagan on the north, and from the latter point he started a wheeling movement northwestward toward Berlin.

While Koneff was sweeping through Silesia, Zhukoff and Rokossovsky were proceeding with their methodical chewing up of the remaining German positions in the north. In the Polish Corridor, waves of Red Army troops overran Chojnice, a junction on the Stettin-Danzig rail line, on February 15, and swept through Grudziadz, another key point to the southeast.

In an order of the day marking the twenty-seventh anniversary of the Red Army on February 22, Stalin reviewed his forces' accomplishments on the 745-mile front from the Baltic to the Carpathians.... They had advanced 167 miles from the frontiers of East Prussia to the lower reaches of the Vistula; 353 miles from the Vistula bridgehead south of Warsaw to the lower Oder, and 98 miles from the Sandomierz bridgehead into Silesia. In the forty-day offensive the Red Army had killed at least 800,000 Germans and captured 350,000; destroyed or captured 3,000 German aircraft, 4,500 tanks and self-propelled guns and 12,000 other guns; occupied 300 populous towns, including 100 war plants, and 2,400 railway stations, and taken possession of a railway network more than 9,300 miles long.

The fortress of Posen had been battered into submission by March 1, after a one-month siege and, with the exception of still-resisting Breslau, the only standing German defenses east of the Oder were those that now spread in a relentlessly and rapidly narrowing strip along the Baltic.

Two pockets still remained in East Prussia. One included Koenigsberg and the coastal section of the Samland Peninsula to the northeast, the other stretched along the Frisches Haff from Brandenburg to Braunsberg. Both of these pockets were shrinking daily under Vasilevsky's pressure.

Zhukoff's northward drive reached the Baltic coast at two points, at Kolberg and at Koeslin, on March 4. Thus, in addition to the Germans pinned against the Oder south of Stettin and against the seacoast to the north, two new pockets were created, one in the Belgard region and the other embracing the area between Danzig and Koeslin. The Belgard pocket was mopped up in a few days, after which the operations in the north for the rest of March consisted chiefly of two widely separated drives in opposite directions—Zhukoff moving westward on Wollin and Stettin while Rokossovsky pushed eastward and northward to close his sack on Danzig and Gdynia.

Stalin issued his three hundredth order of the day, on March 13, for the capture of Kuestrin by Zhukoff's troops after a thirty-five-day battle.

Kuestrin, straddling the Oder at its confluence with the Warthe River and guarding the most direct route to Berlin, was, with Frankfort, a twin bastion on which the capital had placed its greatest hopes. Massive artillery emplacements, armored forts designed to withstand the most intense fire, serried ranks of dragon's teeth, antitank pits, and other field fortifications combined to make of one of Germany's oldest and mightiest fortresses a model of German military and engineering skill. Picked divisions manned it to hold the Russians at bay and postpone the assault on Berlin.

After fighting foot by foot across the wide and closely defended approaches to the city, Zhukoff struck at the northern suburb of Neustadt with tanks and infantry, supported by unceasing artillery and mortar fire and also by aircraft. Neustadt was captured the first day. Meanwhile, other units cut all the roads leading to Berlin.

The Germans brought up fresh formations to avoid complete encirclement and the battle grew in scope.

Driving along the Warthe, Soviet units entered Altstadt, the central part of the city, which the Germans in mills and plants had fortified as an island of resistance. Fierce street fighting went on here for days, during which the Russians split the garrison into several isolated groups and drew a tightening noose relentlessly about each one. The Germans made many strong counterattacks, but they were beaten down. In tedious fighting the last knots of resistance finally were liquidated.

During the Kuestrin battle, Zhukoff also was clearing the east bank of the lower Oder as far as Stettin, as well as the shore of Stettin Bay to the north. By March 10 he had taken the river-crossing towns of Alt-Damm and Greifenhagen, southeast of Stettin, and had drawn up his right wing on the coast opposite the island of Wollin.

Rokossovsky's mopping-up operation around Danzig proceeded with such speed that on March 23 he speared to the Bay of Danzig, between Danzig and Gdynia, cutting off the two ports from each other. Twin Red Army forces then pushed into Gdynia and Danzig, and street fighting raged in the two port cities for several days. The capture of Gdynia was completed on March 28. Resistance in Danzig was liquidated on March 30, all but completing the eastern phase of the Baltic campaign.

Soviet troops raised the Polish flag over the former "free city," where the first shots of the war had been fired—a tableau symbolic not only of the virtual liberation of Poland, but of the imminent end of the war in Europe.

Rokossovsky's assignment in the north now was finished, except for processing his thousands of prisoners, burying the dead, and cataloging his vast booty; but, across the Bay of Danzig to the east, Vasilevsky's army fought on to dispose of the last die-hard resistance in East Prussia.

The pocket southwest of Koenigsberg was cleaned out on March 29. The hard-crusted fortress of Koenigsberg, battered to rubble by shell and bomb, kept up the fight until April 9.

Half a century of German work had gone into Koenigsberg and virtually all of the city's eighty square miles was fortified in the grand fashion. A hundred thousand German civilians had been left there to labor further on the defenses.

A line of sixteen forts served as a primary shield. Buildings were interconnected by new underground passages. Brick and steel barricades several yards thick closed the streets. Old castles, palaces, and even cemeteries had been converted into additional forts. Bunkers three stories underground had been amply stored with munitions, provisions, and medical supplies.

The final assault, planned and rehearsed for weeks, began on a clear spring morning. An hour later the sun was blotted out by clouds of dust and smoke.

A maximum artillery concentration, with each gun assigned to a specified target, first divested the forts of their upper cover. Then heavy siege guns blasted away the bastions' steel and concrete. Swarms of Stormoviks and bombers wiped out troop concentrations and pounded other well-plotted objectives.

Picked German divisions, backed by a huge mass of artillery, fought back strongly, but the defense was gradually worn down by the greatly superior Russian forces. Red Army units, under artillery and air cover, moved up with assault bridges, ladders, and explosives. Sappers blew up granite barriers to blaze a way for the Soviet infantry.

The Germans had been forbidden to surrender under pain of death.

Men accused of cowardice or desertion were hanged by the feet in the city's central square.

The garrisons of some forts fought until they were blown up with their casements. Others held out until more than half their personnel had been wiped out in close fighting within the battlements. But during the last two days the Germans gave up in increasing thousands, too battle-shocked to fight longer.

Moscow's figures on the toll taken of the enemy at Koenigsberg were: 92,000 Germans captured, including General Lasch, the Nazi commandant, and three other generals; and 42,000 killed.

Except for wiping up a few thousand additional Germans who had fled to the Samland Peninsula, Vasilevsky had disposed of the last fighting Germans in northern Europe east of Stettin. Zhukoff's rear and flanks were cleared at last.

Below the Carpathians, two mighty Red Armies were storming toward Vienna. Conditions were ripe for Hitler's Wagnerian finale—the assault upon Berlin.

FALL OF BUDAPEST AND VIENNA AS RED ARMY SWEEPS ON

GERMAN usurpation of Hungary, Austria, Rumania, and Bulgaria, came to an abrupt end as the Russians wrested them from the Nazi grip. Hitler's armies fled in panic before the conquering Red Army. The creaking Axis fell apart and left only wreckage behind it. Swastikas were dragged in the streets of the great capitals as the people renounced their allegiance to Hitler and damned him for their disasters.

Budapest was cleared of Germans on February 13, 1945. Vienna was captured on April 13. Into the two-month interval between these red-letter events the Second and Third Ukrainian Armies, commanded by Marshals Malinovsky and Tolbukhin, compressed a campaign that broke the last obstacle to the investment of the fortress of Germany. But the succession of great and complex operations that brought about this achievement rightly goes back to the late summer of 1944, when the sprawling *Wehrmacht* still gripped with its right wing the Black Sea coast near the Rumanian border.

To unclench the last grip that anchored the enemy in southeastern Europe, Malinovsky and Tolbukhin unfolded one of the classic major maneuvers of the war—the Jassy-Kishinev encirclement—in which they surrounded and effected the annihilation of twenty-two German divisions and shattered the *Wehrmacht's* southern strategic flank. Among the immediate results were the elimination of Rumania and Bulgaria from the war, the Soviet occupation of those countries, and the opening of a road into Hungary and toward the Danube.

The Germans, though badly jolted and forced into further retreat, believed their position in the south to be potentially secure because it was bulwarked by the curving fold of the Carpathian Mountains. This mountain wall, the traditional bastion of central Europe against invasion from the east, curves in a nine-hundred-mile question mark from Vienna on the Danube eastward and southward and then westward back to the Danube again. It had balked the Russians in World War I, and the Germans relied upon it to do so again in the fight for Poland and the Balkans.

The gigantic problem facing Malinovsky and Tolbukhin, therefore, was to fight and trick their way up the Danube valley through Budapest and Vienna and thereby outflank the Carpathians—in coördination with Marshal Koneff's corresponding maneuver to the north of the range—by approaching Prague, Dresden, and Berlin from the south in the comparative lowlands east of the Alps.

After consolidating their hold on the Balkans and leaving the campaign in Yugoslavia largely to the Yugoslav forces of Marshal Tito, with some help from Rumanian and Bulgarian troops, the two veteran Ukrainian Armies started northward, Malinovsky across Transylvania into eastern Hungary, and Tolbukhin up the Danube farther west. Meanwhile, the Fourth Ukrainian Army, under General Yeremenko, was beating across the Carpathians into eastern Czechoslovakia.

Tolbukhin stormed across the Danube from its east bank north of the Drava River and spread out in southern Hungary and northern Yugoslavia on November 28. His advance posed a multiple threat to the rich Nagykanizsa oil region southwest of Lake Balaton, the Szekesfehervar communications complex between Lakes Balaton and Valence and the southern and western ramparts of Budapest. Tolbukhin struck swiftly northward along the Danube toward the Hungarian capital. The Germans, alert to the plain indications of another Malinovsky-Tolbukhin pincers, brought up strong armored reinforcements, and stiff tank battles ensued in the Szekesfehervar area.

Driving the Germans out of Szekesfehervar, Tolbukhin continued up the Danube to the southern suburbs of Budapest. Although forced to fend off almost continuous counterattacks from the west, he threw an arm around the city to meet Malinovsky's advance from the northeast. The junction of the two armies was effected on December 26; Budapest was surrounded.

The long, bitter battle for the conquest of the twin city of 1,300,000 persons, the main communications center of southeastern Europe, was reminiscent of Stalingrad and almost as destructive. Loss of Budapest meant the loss of Hungary, which had been a prolific source of war materials and manufactured supplies for the Axis armies. Russian control of the Hungarian plains would mean swift disruption of Berlin's communications with the Italian and Balkan fronts. The Gestapo enforced drastically Hitler's order that no German was to yield an inch.

Malinovsky attacked Pest, the main commercial and governmental part of the city on the east bank of the Danube, while Tolbukhin pushed into ancient Buda, the largely residential section on the high western bank. In both sections the battle was fought street by street and block by block. Buildings had to be taken floor by floor and often the defenders had to be rooted out of dungeons and dugouts several stories underground. Guns roared night and day. In favorable weather air battles and bombing raids were virtually continuous. One day's fighting merged with the next in horrible weeks of the monotony of ceaseless violence and din.

The ancient urban beauty of one of Europe's queen cities soon was transformed into a chaos of ugly ruins darkened by a perpetual pall of smoke and dust. In Pest, the Parliament building, the university, department stores, and banks had been converted into individual strong points by the Germans and connected by deep underground passages. Commercial buildings were emptied of their contents to make room for German guns, munitions, and supplies. Rudolph Avenue was blocked by an incongruous pile of broken pianos that had been hurled from a musical-instrument warehouse. All seven of the stately bridges across the Danube had been mined and blown up.

More than three-fourths of the city's 4,500 blocks had been captured by the two Red Armies by mid-January, 1945. The commander of the German garrison radioed to his superiors, "It is impossible to hold out any longer." But when the Soviet commanders sent an ultimatum for surrender, the Russian emissaries were shot down as they approached the enemy lines.

Pest was finally cleared of Germans by January 18, but the fighting in western Buda went on for almost another month.

Simultaneously with the difficult siege of the city, Malinovsky and Tolbukhin were extending the range of their operations on a growing front to the north and west. Malinovsky was pushing the enemy northward against the Miskolc-Budapest railway, along which ran a German defense line of exceptional strength. The Germans resisted fiercely his attempts to probe into eastern Czechoslovakia from the south. At the same time, Tolbukhin encountered equally strong resistance in his endeavor to drive westward on the northern bank of the Danube above its elbow, from the region of Esztergom. Although he drove a wedge nearly to Komarno in January, German pressure along the south bank of the Danube, northwest of Budapest, forced him back.

The German command made desperate attempts to spear through the line west of Budapest to get relief to the beleaguered capital, but, though Berlin claimed several deep penetrations, the lost communications never were restored. Battle-churned ground all the way from Esztergom to Szekesfehervar changed hands repeatedly.

When the fighting finally was ended in Budapest on February 13 after a fifty-one-day siege, the Russians reckoned that the battle had cost the Germans 49,000 men killed and 110,000 prisoners—a toll approaching that of Stalingrad.

The city's fall theoretically opened the road to Bratislava and Vienna, but such dividends were not immediately cashable. Red Army engineers required time to restore the shattered communications across the Danube and, at any rate, the Germans in western Hungary were in no mood to retreat. Koneff was pounding at the Moravian Gap for a northern access to Czechoslovakia, where Partisans were playing havoc with the German rear. The invaders' position in Yugoslavia and Italy was becoming more and more tenuous. And the western Allies were thrusting deep beyond the Rhine.

Fresh armored divisions, stripped improvidently from other critical fronts, were deployed all the way from the Danube bend to the Drava River to keep the Russians from turning the defenses on both sides of Lake Balaton. The clangor of furious tank battles rebounded again on the Hungarian plains and the relative merits of German and Russian tanks were put to a final decisive test. Here was the outcome of the race between the heavy industries of the Soviet Union and the Reich. Besides overcoming the Germans' early numerical superiority in tanks, Russian designers also eventually outmatched their adversaries in armor strength and fire power. The Soviet medium T-34 and heavy KV tanks bore the brunt of the fighting in the war's decisive months and their performance forced the Germans to produce their Tiger and Panther series, culminating in the King Tiger, Royal Tiger and other mammoth models. But the even heavier Stalin tank, thrown into battle in 1945, gave the Russians an insuperable advantage.

Accounts from the Russian front indicated that the tank battles in Hungary were more a matter of fire power than of maneuver. The favorite Red Army tactic appeared to be the maintenance of a shield of self-propelled guns behind which the tanks deployed, thus protected from enemy guns. One Russian self-propelled gun was reported to approach the caliber of a battleship gun and one Russian tank was said to be equipped with a gun rivaling that of a heavy cruiser. When it was tank against tank, the Russian contender usually outgunned and outarmored its adversary; and if the battle required the matching of self-propelled guns beyond tanks' range, the Russians had here a sizable margin, too.

The broad wheeling movement long under way north of Budapest had brought strong Red Army forces up to the Hron River, which guarded the last fringes of the Carpathians east of the Bratislava plain. The grinding contest between Russian and German armored divisions continued through the first half of March, giving Tank Marshals P. A. Rotmistroff and Y. N. Fedorenko an opportunity to reduce further the reserves of armor available to the German staff for the closing phases of the war. Russian and Rumanian troops captured Zvolen, a main Hron River stronghold, on March 14, breaking the German dam for a further advance to the Nitra River, the strongest remaining barrier on the road to Bratislava.

Malinovsky and Tolbukhin, having completed the regrouping of their armies, resumed their offensive across western Hungary on March 24. Malinovsky's initial blow, directed through the westward sweep of the Danube valley on a sixty-two-mile front, dislodged the Germans from strong positions along the Czechoslovak border. Tolbukhin, on Malinovsky's left wing, swung around the north end of Lake Balaton and stepped up his pressure against the stubborn German line south of the lake. By March 28 the offensive had swept across the Raba River, site of another redoubtable Nazi defense line, and had taken Gyoer, communications hub of northwestern Hungary, and part of Komarno, a Danube stronghold to the northeast. Overcoming stiff counterattacks, Soviet mobile units, followed by infantry, smashed against the Austrian border.

At heavy cost, the Germans had tried to tie down Tolbukhin in the wooded, mountainous country north of Lake Balaton. They clung to every village and height and left ambuscades along the roads and forest lanes, hoping to gain time for their defensive preparations in eastern Austria. But spearheads of tanks and self-propelled guns sped through the enemy lines, leaving secondary groups to surround and mop up the German nests in the hills and woods.

Tolbukhin speared into Austria south of Vienna, and streamed up both sides of Neusiedl Lake on March 30. At the same time he was smashing the Germans' last hold on Hungary in the region south of Lake Balaton. He took Nagykanizsa, the last important oil center in Hungary, on April 2, and completed the liberation of Hungary two days later.

While the drive toward Vienna from the south was gaining momentum, Malinovsky bore down on Bratislava, capital of the Nazis' puppet state of Slovakia. The Second Ukrainian Army, on April 3, quickly overwhelmed the fortress and liberated the city, which had been under the German yoke for seven years. Its capture deprived the Germans of concentrated war industries, chemical, electro-technical, and machine-tool plants, and large German Army stores, as well as the largest power station in Czechoslovakia.

Protected on the west by the small Carpathians and the deep Morava River, on the south by the wide Danube, and on the east by the small Danube, Bratislava was a natural citadel at the meeting point of three countries. All Soviet arms, including the Danube flotilla, took part in the encircling of the city and subsequently in clearing it of fiercely resisting enemy divisions. An avalanche of Cossacks and tanks swept into Bratislava from the north, while artillery-tipped infantry columns engaged the main Nazi forces from the east. The Germans had emplaced machine guns in the windows of the big factories and ringed the streets with guns of all calibers. But Red Army gunners crushed the resistance with massed point-blank fire and the garrison was routed. Its 4,600 survivors were captured.

On the day that Bratislava fell, Tolbukhin drove to within six miles of Vienna on the south, outflanked the capital, and captured Wiener

Neustadt, one of Austria's principal aircraft-manufacturing and railroad centers, twenty miles southwest of Vienna. This split the Balkan front and laid the foundation for the eventual disintegration of the Nazis' positions in Italy and east of the Adriatic.

The crux of the early fighting for Vienna spread along the curve of the Danube southeast of the city. The Russians drove two wedges northward, one west of Neusidl Lake that progressed northwestward toward the Vienna Woods, the other along the eastern shore of the lake, approaching Bratislava from the south. The Nazis fought hard to hold a triangle pointed at the northern tip of Neusidl Lake and stretching from the suburbs of Vienna along the Danube to the outskirts of Bratislava.

The two Soviet forces joined above Neusidl Lake at Bruck, and the German defenders were driven back against the Danube. While Malinovsky fought his way westward along the south bank of the Danube from Bratislava, Tolbukhin continued to widen his wedge south of Vienna.

Tolbukhin's shock troops reached Vienna's southern city limits on April 5 and stormed into the streets against heavy opposition, while his left flank was expanding westward and northward into the elbow of the Danube above the city. By April 10 the Russians had captured all of Vienna west and south of the Danube Canal.

An accomplished administrator as well as a talented tactician, Tolbukhin supplemented his military assault with a political campaign. His fliers scattered over the city leaflets bearing his signature, offering to the Viennese the prospect of restoring their pre-1938 order. He reiterated the pledge of Austrian independence made by the Allied foreign ministers in Moscow in 1943 and called upon the city's people to help the Red Army drive out the Nazis. His overture resulted in the strengthening of the Underground Austrian Freedom Front, and the Soviet troops were welcomed as deliverers.

The crisis in the battle for Vienna came with the storming of the Danube Canal, 125 feet wide and twenty-five feet deep with stone-faced banks, an obstacle that held up the shock troops for several days. Finally, under a cover of gunfire and with further protection from clouds of Soviet planes, Guards riflemen swam across the canal and won footholds on the eastern bank. These were joined, bridges were laid, and the final assault was carried out in the eastern section of the city.

The Austrian flag replaced the swastika on the tower of the Town Hall in Vienna on the day after President Roosevelt's death. More than 130,000 prisoners were taken in the Vienna pocket.

Tolbukhin's westward advance in the Danube valley toward Linz was halted at Gerersdorf. Malinovsky proceeded up the Morava valley along the railway toward Bruenn. Simultaneously, Soviet cavalry lanced across northern Yugoslavia toward the Italian border, in coördination with Tito's clean-up operations along the Adriatic coast.

Malinovsky outflanked Bruenn on April 18 by taking Ivancice, southwest of the important Czechoslovak rail junction. The Germans had been ordered to hold Bruenn at all costs, for the fate of central Czechoslovakia depended on its defense; northwest of it stood the key centers of Jihlava and Prague, and to the northeast were the threatened Carpathian bastions of Olomouc and Moravska Ostrava. The eastern and southern approaches to Bruenn were covered by formidable defense lines set up along the Morava River and running through difficult swampy terrain. Large numbers of tanks and self-propelled guns were concentrated at strategic points. A frontal attack on Bruenn seemed impossible.

Assault groups of the advancing Soviet columns, supported by artillery and planes, overrode the stubborn, dug-in resistance. As in most of the final battles of the war, the Red Army simply brought to bear such a preponderance of all arms that the Nazis, limited in means and numbers and with their thinned ranks filled out by elderly and infirm *Volkssturm* draftees and by convalescent casualties of earlier battles and cadets from military schools, could not stand up against the onslaught. The Red Air Force had full control of the skies and Stormoviks and fighter planes literally hung over the front, attacking every German concentration. Advancing with the infantry and cavalry, Soviet artillerymen leveled point-blank fire at counterattacking mechanized units. Veteran Cossack cavalrymen again distinguished themselves, galloping into villages and slashing down the Nazi troops with their sabers or dismounting to help repel counterblows on open terrain. Caught in a closing vise and paralyzed by a hurricane of gunfire and bombs, the Bruenn garrison was forced to yield.

With the fall of Bruenn, three Red Armies closed in to complete the capture of the rest of Moravia and the eastern Sudetenland. Malinovsky continued to push northward against the bottom of the Germans' easternmost salient; Koneff continued to blast his way through the Moravian Gap, and Yeremenko's Fourth Ukrainian Army advanced through the Carpathian passes from the east. Koneff concentrated his main forces in southern Brandenburg for his impending flanking attack on Berlin. One of Koneff's final operations in southeastern Silesia was the destruction of a German pocket along the Oder between Oppeln and Ratibor, where 15,000 prisoners and rich booty were taken.

In his advance across the eastern appendage of Czechoslovakia, General Yeremenko had the considerable assistance of organized native guerrilla units. Early in the war hundreds of patriots had taken to the hills, sworn to fight until death or liberation. One of the focal units, known as the Stalin Detachment, became famous in central Europe for the terror it spread behind the German lines and among isolated outposts. In towns and villages occupied by the Germans such inscriptions as "To the mountains, brothers!" and "Death to the Fascists, freedom to the people!" appeared on walls. The result was that the Nazis usually hunted in vain for the able-bodied male labor they desired to conscript.

The Germans sent punitive expeditions into the hills to try to surround the guerrilla camps, but the native mountaineers knew their country too well to be caught in traps. The few Partisans captured, including women and girls, were subjected to savage tortures in quest of information, but nearly always lips remained sealed by the guerrilla oath. When the Partisans needed weapons, ammunition, and food, they would raid German outposts, killing sentries silently with knives and using captured weapons to take the rest of the garrison by surprise. When Yeremenko reached the region of Kosice, he found that much of his work had been done for him by the native fighters in the hills. As the Red Army moved westward, many of the Czechoslovak units were incorporated in its ranks.

After the liberation of Kosice, a provisional government was set up there under Russian sanction. Implementing the long-standing fraternal and treaty-bound alliance between Czechoslovaks and Russians, President Eduard Benes returned from exile, stopping in Moscow first to organize a new régime including elements of the Underground.

Similarly, a treaty of friendship, mutual assistance, and post-war collaboration between the Soviet Union and Yugoslavia was signed on April 11, formalizing the alliance already existing between Moscow and the régime of Marshal Tito.

In pursuing an aim of close coördination with Poland, Czechoslovakia, and Yugoslavia, as well as with Rumania and Bulgaria, the Russian Government sought to solidify the union of Slav peoples, destroy the persistent German hope of dismembering Europe, and protect the bloc of Balkan and eastern European states against another European war.

With the Germans' Czechoslovak salient erased, the Soviet Supreme Command at last had a virtually straight line, drawn southward from Stettin, on which to base its final campaign for victory in the east. In late April and early May, Tito continued to carry on his part of this strategy by whittling down the German salient surrounding Zagreb in northern Yugoslavia and cleaning up the Dalmation coast of the Adriatic. The Yugoslav Partisans crossed the Italian frontier on the Istrian

Peninsula on April 25, fought their way through Fiume, and later entered Trieste.

The Russians' train of triumphs in eastern Europe in 1945 left a residue of political contention—the Yugoslavs' disputed claims to part of the Italian province of Venezia Giulia and of the Austrian provinces of Carinthia and Styria; the division of spheres of influence in the rest of Austria; the partitioning of Teschen between Czechoslovakia and Poland; the inclusion of the Carpatho-Ukraine in the Ukrainian Soviet Republic, and the issue in Poland over the drawing of the Russian frontier and the choice of a government acceptable to Moscow.

But the first notes of these minor discords were submerged in the swelling crescendo of the greatest and ultimate battle of the war—the descent upon Berlin—for which Zhukoff, Rokossovsky, and Koneff were eager and prepared.

FALL OF BERLIN—THE PROUD GERMAN CAPITAL LIES IN RUINS

SHAME and disgrace fell upon the Nazi war lords as the grandeur and dignity of the ancient capital of Germany lay in ruins at their feet. Berlin was a graveyard, a city of the dead! This was the destruction which their Fuehrer had brought upon them. The great city which even Hitler had deserted in its moment of peril, surrendered to the Russians on May 2, 1945.

This was the price the Germans paid for following false leadership, false in every promise, betraying them with every word. The disillusioned people of Berlin, numbering some 3,000,000 at the start of the siege, emerged like ghosts from the cellars where they had endured the terrible fury of the final battles, after months of hideous days and nights of death and destruction falling upon them from the skies.

This was the fourth time in history that Berlin had capitulated. But it was the first time a foreign invader had been in the city in 137 years —since the days of Napoleon when the French occupation, following the Battle of Jena, ended in 1808. The first capture had been little more than a raid by Austrian cavalry in 1757; Russian Cossacks, aided by Austrian troops, sacked the city while Frederick the Great was campaigning in Silesia in 1760. Now, in 1945, the Russians of the new Soviet Republics were in possession of proud Berlin.

On April 15, 1945, Marshal Zhukoff, as field commander of the Russian front, had drawn up four armies—some 2,000,000 superbly equipped men—between the Baltic coast at Stettin Bay and the Sudeten range in lower Saxony. Marshal Rokossovsky's Second White Russian Army, reinforced by Marshal Vasilevsky's Third, was deployed on both sides of Stettin and along the Oder River north of Kuestrin. Zhukoff's First White Russian Army was poised before Berlin's main fortress region betwen Kuestrin and Frankfort. Marshal Koneff's First Ukrainian Army formed the southern wing along the Neisse River to the Czechoslovak border. The Second and Third Ukrainian Armies of Marshals Malinovsky and Tolbukhin and the Fourth Ukrainian of General Yeremenko were still engaged in detached operations farther south.

Since the fall of Kuestrin on March 18, the Soviet command had kept its Oder front wrapped in silence during its gigantic preparations for its most crucial offensive. In the interval the German military and propaganda machines had made hysterical preparations to hold off the hovering catastrophe. Every German male, from boys to the aged, regardless of physical condition, was pressed into service. All women were called upon for auxiliary work. Trenches and antitank moats were dug in a continuous arc before the capital. Streets, highways, and fields were mined. Hitler ordered his people to "drown the Russians in a sea of blood and hold Berlin at all costs."

As in the January offensive from the Vistula, Koneff was chosen to strike the first effective blow. Early in April, Koneff started to build up his striking force along the Neisse nearly one hundred miles southeast of Berlin. The Germans countered Koneff's movements by massing armored divisions against his left wing. But the Nazi generals calculated that Koneff would strike toward Dresden for an early link-up with the American First Army, which was driving toward the Elbe from the west. Koneff encouraged this deduction by appearing to make his principal preparations in his southern sector. He permitted German reconnaissance to spot long transport columns moving through the area at night and he built dummy airfields and gun emplacements behind his lines.

Meanwhile he was planning his real break-through farther north, in the elaborately defended terrain of Guben, Forst, and Muskau. This is a region of marshes, forests, and lakes, connected by canals. There were comparatively few roads there and each road or causeway through the marshes could easily be swept by heavy gunfire.

While the Germans' attention was focused on the Goerlitz sector—flat country crisscrossed by numerous roads and favorable to the attacker—Koneff made his surprise assault against the less densely manned defenses around Forst. His artillery preparation, from guns massed 250 to 300 to the kilometer—less than twenty feet apart—swept away all enemy fortifications on the Neisse opposite his positions in the first few minutes. The fire then was lifted to the second, third, and fourth lines of defenses.

Under this arch of shells, Soviet infantry rushed across the river in boats, canoes, and barges. The engineers followed with prefabricated bridges and soon tank formations, emerging from their hiding places in the woods, were rolling over to strike out from the positions taken by the first waves of infantry. On the first day Koneff advanced about six miles, on the second twelve and later, as the armored force grew in the bridgehead, the pace was extended to as much as twenty-eight miles a day.

When Koneff reached the Spree River he encountered another desperate German attempt to stop him. Two powerful forces, with hundreds of tanks and self-propelled guns, were massed on the flanks of his wedge, at Cottbus and Spremberg, with the aim of cutting off the spearhead stabbing into the heart of Germany. Koneff daringly ordered his leading columns to ignore this threat to their flanks and drive on, leaving two battles raging at their rear. His plan worked, for following echelons surrounded and wiped out the German force at Spremberg, taking extensive booty and thousands of prisoners, while his troops on the other flank captured Cottbus in a swift enveloping movement.

This was but the first of a series of bewildering surprises for the Germans. Up to this time, Koneff's advance had been due westward, directed toward Dresden and Leipzig. As the expanding Russian wedge surged on, the Germans hastily regrouped to protect the rich complex of Saxon cities. But Koneff's columns turned sharply north to invest Berlin from the south in coördination with other Red Army maneuvers already unfolding to the north.

After Koneff's initial thrust, Zhukoff opened a massive attack east of Berlin, while Rokossovsky and Vasilevsky struck out around Stettin and along the Baltic coast. Zhukoff's problem was to achieve an element of surprise where none seemed possible, since the Germans had made strong preparations for defense all along the relatively short arc before the capital. To implement his plan of attack, he eventually brought into play some 4,000 tanks, 2,000 guns and mortars, and close to 5,000 planes. Zhukoff's first surprise was an overwhelming artillery barrage, unloosed at night when the Germans least expected it; his second was a tank attack, also launched at night; his third and climactic surprise was the use of a battery of more than 200 huge searchlights, spaced 200 yards apart, which lighted the way for the Red Army tanks and at the same time blinded the bewildered Germans.

Zhukoff made effective use of his bridgehead on the Oder west and northwest of Kuestrin by wheeling through the northern Oderbruch region into a corridor opened between Eberswalde and Wriezen. He thereby served two purposes—outflanking the Germans' massive Oder wall between Kuestrin and Frankfort and developing the northern arm of a pincers to complement the one thrust up from the south by Koneff. His attack, started on April 18, was so sudden and overwhelming that Berlin's outer defenses swiftly crumbled, forcing the German command to throw in reserves that had been earmarked for the defense of the inner city.

The Red Army burst into the rubbled streets of Berlin on April 20. But the most effective action still was taking place outside the city, where multiple columns of wide-ranging Soviet tanks were weaving their intricate patterns of encirclement. Zhukoff's outer columns sped westward through Oranienburg and then wheeled southward. Meanwhile, Koneff's spearheads approached Potsdam southwest of Berlin. Other columns from the north speared through the city's eastern outskirts; on April 24 armored units under Generals Rybalko and Katukoff joined near Bohnsdorf, cutting off Berlin from its defenders farther east. The encirclement of the city was completed the next day when General Lelyushenko's tanks made a junction with General Bogdanoff's forward units north of Potsdam.

Besieged Berlin became a shrinking, isolated citadel, cut off both from the German forces still spread westward to the American Ninth Army's positions on the Elbe and from outflanked defense positions between the capital and the Oder. Moreover, Koneff's maneuvers in the south ring—sixty miles long and thirty wide—enclosed great numbers of confused German units. These were quickly wiped out or added to the enormous bag of prisoners as Zhukoff's left wing pushed in from the Oder, and Koneff's forces tightened the sack from the other side.

By April 25, the Russians had pushed into eastern Berlin as far as the Schlesischer Station and were in control of all of the city east and north of that point. They then proceeded to clamp a vise on the heart of Berlin by driving a wedge toward the lower Wilhelmstrasse; two more from the south, one of which overran the Tempelhof Airfield, and another from the northeast crossed the Hohenzollern Canal and reached the Spree. This drive from the north rapidly joined up with an arm of Koneff's forces that had speared northward through Dahlem, thereby cutting the already constricted Berlin garrison in two.

The western segment, including the Grunewald Forest, Potsdam, and part of the western suburban area, soon vanished, leaving only a ring a few miles in diameter, with the Tiergarten at its center, in which the remaining die-hard Nazis chose to battle without quarter. Here was fought the real battle of Berlin. Here was finally cornered the quarry whom the Red Army men had flushed and hunted and pursued all the way from Stalingrad—the inner core of Nazidom, the Brownshirt potentates and Storm Troop satraps, the rulers of Hitlerite Germany, from Hitler and Goebbels down. There was no haven for them elsewhere in the world and Soviet retribution was at their door.

Every road leading into Berlin was whipped into clouds of dust by the Red Army's endless caravans. In effect, the whole Soviet land was moving in with relish for the kill—men from the Urals and beyond, from the Transcaucasus, from the Donbas, the Ukraine, White Russia, and Moscow. Cannons rumbled over the shell-pocked roads, engines roared in the bumper-to-bumper parade of tanks and jeeps, fuel trucks and field kitchens, tractors and mobile radio stations. Sons of peasants who had been slain on their hearths, husbands and brothers of women and girls who had been transported to slavery, men whose homes and cities had been sacked and burned by the Nazi invaders—such was the Red Army. Perhaps never had a military force moved upon its objective with greater zest for its mission. Soldiers and officers carried in notebooks or in their hearts the names and addresses of individual Germans they would dearly like to meet. With them went the battle banners of Stalingrad, and among them were the war-wise veterans of the whole Baedeker of German defeats.

Zhukoff had set up headquarters in a forest east of Berlin. From there all activity on the teeming fronts was directed. Hundreds of land wires from all directions, as well as countless wireless circuits, had their terminus at this spot. Staff cars hurried to and from it day and night. At a near-by airdrome the drone of planes' motors was constant. There Zhukoff, with his close-knit staff, lived and worked. A man of the people, simple, direct, self-confident, he demanded miracles from the force he had snatched from disaster at Moscow in 1941 and had built into the world's mightiest fighting machine. His miracles were achieved because his men reciprocated the confidence he placed in them, and Zhukoff worked as hard as they did. From before breakfast soon after dawn until late hours at night he worked at his desk, pored over maps and cipher tables, conferred with his specialists and field commanders, laying out the precise details of his precedent-smashing operations. Once, after the painful difficulties of the war with Finland, he had braved the wrath of Stalin by presenting a fearlessly frank critique of the then lumbering Red Army; from that turning point in his career he had been Stalin's right-hand man.

The Red Army carried into Berlin a tradition that went back to the seventeenth century, but with a proficiency that really dated from the accession of the Stalin-Zhukoff team to effective leadership. Its Red Air Force had seen the vaunted Luftwaffe gasp its last breath with the capture of the fields around Berlin; but its mastery of the air had been won in four years of hard uphill battle. Its artillery, a proverbial Russian boast, had given lessons in versatile fire power to the armies of the world—from field guns of frightening proportions to the Red Army men's darling: the secret rocket-firing Katyusha, which had sown fiery terror among the Nazis in countless battles. Its death-dealing, all-defying tanks were streaming over German roads in throbbing legions, hunting the few remaining adversaries they had failed to dispatch. Its infantry had more than made good the boast of one of its pre-Soviet deities, Suvorov: "Where a deer cannot pass, the Russian soldier will get through; where one gets through, a company will pass, and where a company passes, a detachment will follow."

Now the Red Army was living its greatest moment. Under an umbrella of its planes, covered by hurricanes of flaming steel from its artillery, sheathed by battalions of its tanks, and fortified by the expertness of its numerous auxiliary services, Red Army infantry was throttling the enemy in his ultimate lair, carrying out the conclusive directives of Stalin-Zhukoff strategy.

The spirit of the Red Army in Berlin was the spirit of the Soviet Guards. The Soviet Guards were born in the autumn of 1941, when twenty-eight of General Ivan Panfiloff's men stood up against fifty German tanks close to Moscow; all twenty-eight perished, but the tanks were turned back. On a wall in ruined Stalingrad this inscription was found: "Here Rodimtseff's Guardsmen stood to the death." Later, surviving soldiers added to the legend: "They stood—and defeated death." To win the title of Guards became the transcending honor for battle-tested Soviet units, and the brunt of the battle for Berlin was borne by divisions that had been so honored.

The street fighting in Berlin, pressed home on a scale unparalleled in military annals, embraced the whole gamut of every form of fighting known to man. After dozens of columns had moved, like probing fingers, into the city streets from the suburbs, fanning out to consolidate the zones penetrated, they met increasing difficulties amid the wreckage closer to the central district. Streets were blocked by fallen buildings or barricaded with masonry and timbers. German snipers and machine-gunners lurked in unobservable nests in the rubble.

The labyrinth of subways and sewers under the streets became a fantastic secondary battlefield. Storm Troopers crowded into subway trains and rode to stations behind the Russian lines, emerging in suicide attacks to fight until wiped out. Other trains were filled with explosives and detonated under Soviet positions, blasting wide surfaces of pavement in earthquakes of destruction. Red Army men fought their way into subway stations and hunted Germans through the pitch-black tunnels. Artillerymen lowered field pieces into the caverns under the streets and fired shells along the tracks. Soviet sappers, trained in the battle-school of Stalingrad, worked their way through slimy sewers to ferret out Nazis who were poking tommy guns from manholes at unexpected vantage points. Gas mains, burst by shellfire, spouted multicolored flames like volcanos in the streets. Geysers erupted from broken water pipes.

Brownshirt bullies, knowing their era of swaggering braggadocio was over, fought on with the ferocity of doomed men. Those of doubtful fortitude looted homes for civilian clothes and discarded their tell-tale uniforms. Like thieves who had fallen out, the Nazis fought among themselves in sporadic bursts of fratricide. Party officials loaded their persons with money or other valuables and tried to escape. To deprive the rank and file of the same privilege, they forehandedly stripped available automobiles of tires and wheels. Soldiers reluctant to die for their Fuehrer hid in cellars and marched out behind white flags when Russians appeared. Disillusioned German men and women, who had gambled on the perpetuity of Nazi conquest, turned to suicide and a wave of self-destruction swelled further the toll of Berlin's death throes.

Famine and pestilence in time joined the train of horrors. Streets and buildings were filled with dead. The water system was wrecked, reservoirs fouled. Gas and electricity were unavailable. Food for civilians was unprocurable except from looted homes and stores, or when begged from German or Russian Army supplies. Medical services ceased and drugs were lacking. To be ill or wounded in the early days of the battle often was the equivalent of death.

When the Red Army approached Berlin, it was an open question whether Hitler would be found in one of his Bavarian eyries or in his bunker under the Berlin Chancellery. Not until after the Russians were far inside the city was it learned with certainty from German officials captured in the west that the Fuehrer and Goebbels had established themselves in the capital, determined to die there rather than face capture. Yet the remote hope of such a capture remained the ambition of every Soviet soldier fighting toward the hideout. On May 1, the German radio reported that Hitler was dead and that Grand Admiral Karl Doenitz had succeeded him. But the mystery of Hitler's definite fate still was unsolved.

Soviet columns driving into Berlin from the east poured through the Alexanderplatz and down the Unter den Linden to the Brandenburg Gate. Others, from the north, descended upon the Knoenigsplatz from the Stettiner and Lehrter Stations. Units fighting in from the west stormed through the Tiergarten. From the south still others rolled up the Wilhelmstrasse and the streets converging on the Potsdamerplatz.

The battle reached its climax in the fighting for the Reichstag building. The massive pile of ornate German masonry was a symbol of Hitler's power, and rivalry developed among Soviet formations for the honor of raising the red flag over its square tower. The Germans, too, were determined to retain their grip upon this center of their resistance even after the rest of the city had been virtually cleared. The first Soviet troops converged upon the building at a distance of some 150 yards across the Koenigsplatz, but the entire area was swept by fire from all types of weapons. Mortars hurled shells through the avenues of the Tiergarten, machine guns rattled from the roof of the Lessing Theatre, and artillery batteries maintained a barrage from the Unter den Linden.

Through this whirlwind of gunfire four Soviet formations launched a determined attack, supported by hundreds of guns and mortars. Fighting for every yard, they reached the building, but found every door barricaded. The hard-pressed Russians were on the point of falling back to wait for artillery to breach the walls when a unit led by an officer named Zinchenko broke through one of the doors and disappeared in the gloom inside. Other companies followed and Zinchenko set up a command post in the building.

Details of hardy fighters set out for the roof with their flags, but the building was full of Germans and the corridors and attics were bitterly contested. At length a veteran soldier named Gregory Bulatoff reported that his mission had been accomplished. But though the red flag waved over the building the Germans refused to admit defeat. They tried to cut off the Russian forces with a devastating fire on all approaches. Then they asked for a truce and demanded the Russians' surrender, claiming that they outnumbered the Red Army men ten to one. Zinchenko replied that, regardless of numbers, the only possible terms he would consider consisted of an unconditional surrender by the Germans.

Late in the day the Germans began firing incendiary shells and that night the sky of central Berlin was lighted by the flames of the second Reichstag fire, the first having figured in the Nazis' seizure of German power.

Fighting continued through the night, but at dawn groups of Germans began emerging with white flags. More than 1,000 surrendered, in addition to numerous wounded found in a hospital in the basement, and hundreds of men and women civilian attachés. That day, though the battle for the city was not over, the Reichstag roof was agleam with flags carried to it ceremoniously by units that had borne them from the farthest limits of the German invasion.

On May 1, while heavy gunfire still was battering the government district, a delegation from the German command appeared at a Soviet divisional command post with an offer of unconditional surrender. The German group was permitted to return to its lines, accompanied by Major Belousoff and followed by a Soviet signalman with wire to set up a telephone connection. But after the party had entered the German lines, concealed enemy snipers opened fire and wounded Major Belousoff in the head. The Russians, infuriated, renewed and redoubled their attack, sweeping the district with shellfire and deepening their penetration.

On May 2, the fire again ceased at the Germans' request and Artillery General Weidling of the Berlin garrison went to Soviet headquarters to confirm the offer of surrender. He signed an order to his troops to cease fire and the Germans began to lay down their arms. Thousands of the defeated *Wehrmacht's* officers and men moved in columns along the streets from the center of the city to concentration points designated by the Russians.

Before its capture by the Red Army Berlin had been the largest city on the European Continent, and it was the largest center of population ever invested by a military force.

The Russians found Berlin a miserable shell of its former self. The ten-day battering it had undergone from Soviet shells and bombs had wrought terrible damage, but for months before the siege began the city had been scarcely recognizable as a result of the almost incessant bombing carried on by the Royal Air Force and the American Air Forces. In some of the suburbs the havoc was less than complete, but the center of the city was a shambles of razed or burned-out buildings, bomb and shell craters and débris-filled streets.

At the time of the surrender the Tiergarten was still burning and fires smoldered in the ruins of such formerly important edifices as the Reichstag, the Air Ministry, and the Chancellery. The Unter den Linden was closed by barriers made of nine layers of logs covered with sand. The famous Wilhelmstrasse was bisected by the roofless tunnel of the caved-in subway. The towering Brandenburg Gate, symbol of German militarism, surmounted by bronze horses green with age, told a story of battle. The horses had been broken by shellfire; machine-gun embrasures had been built of stone, logs, and sand between the columns, four of which had been shattered, and at the base of the gate was the grave of a Red Army man who had been buried where he fell.

Search of the ruins of the Chancellery, which had been Hitler's Berlin residence, did not solve the mystery of his disappearance. The windows had been blocked with stacks of books with apertures for machine guns. The doors had been barricaded with cases filled with iron crosses and oak leaves. Many burned bodies were found in the building, but few were positively identified. Nazi retainers reported that Goebbels had poisoned his family and killed himself in the catacomb of rooms and offices that formed the Chancellery's many-storied cellar. One report of Hitler's last days was that he had been joined for his Goetterdaemmerung by his protegé and confidante, Eva Braun; that they had been married just before the end, and killed at the last moment by his order. The reporter added that their bodies had been cremated together in a courtyard.

A complete tally of the human toll taken in Berlin was impossible. Thousands had been killed in the Allied air attacks and the Russian siege. Untold numbers of others were reported to have been killed by the Nazis during a series of abortive revolts while the capital was under martial law. The Red Army took more than 70,000 prisoners at the time of the surrender, and Soviet casualty figures indicated that the defense of the city had cost the Germans some 343,000 men, killed or captured.

On the day of Berlin's fall, Premier Stalin announced that the encirclement of German troops southeast of Berlin had wiped out the *Wehrmacht's* Ninth Army, with the capture of 120,000 men and the killing of at least 60,000 more. At the same time he recorded the capture of the Baltic ports of Rostock and Warnemuende by Rokossovsky's Second White Russian Army.

Rokossovsky had taken Stettin on April 27, while the battle in Berlin was at its height. He had crossed the Oder near Schwedt and flanked Stettin from the rear in a drive northward to the coast. A week before, Koneff had made a junction with General Courtney H. Hodges' United States First Army at Torgau, on the Elbe northeast of Leipzig, cutting off the Bohemian-Austrian pocket from the other German forces remaining in northern Europe. Before Berlin fell, Zhukoff's forward spearheads had swept through Brandenburg, west of the capital.

Thus the Russians carried on their share of the task of picking up the few remaining loose ends of the shattered fabric of the Nazi Reich. Reich Marshal Hermann Goering and Foreign Minister Joachim von Ribbentrop had been dropped from the tottering German régime, now nominally headed by Doenitz, who tried through Count Folke Bernadotte of Sweden to arrange a surrender to the western Powers. The maneuver failed and the scattered fighting went on until the German leaders were convinced that there was no possible alternative to a complete unconditional surrender to all the Allied Powers, including Russia.

On May 6, the siege of Breslau, then hundreds of miles to the rear of Koneff's army, ended with the capitulation of the German garrison after eighty-two days of unceasing battle. White flags appeared over the citadel and more than 40,000 surviving troops were taken prisoner.

By May 4, the Russian Armies reducing the Germans' mountain redoubt in Czechoslovakia had cleared all of Slovakia. On May 5, Czechoslovak patriots, anticipating the early arrival of both Russian and American troops, drove the Germans out of Prague and declared the capital liberated. Almost immediately, however, they sent out distressed appeals for help when massed German forces counterattacked and threatened to restore their tyranny over the city. Russian paratroops were sent from Koneff's front to assist the patriots, but fighting continued in the wild surrounding country for another week or more.

On May 6, Rokossovsky completed the destruction of the Germans' last Baltic pocket by capturing the island of Ruegen, site of a seaplane base northeast of Rostock, after taking the port of Swinemuende, northwest of Stettin. He made a junction with the British forces in the Hamburg area while the German surrender formalities were under way in the west. Thereupon all fighting ended except for the campaign in the south to wipe out the last groups of Nazi die-hards in Czechoslovakia and Austria, who refused to recognize the surrender and fought on as outlaws.

Following the signing of the preliminary protocol of surrender with General Eisenhower in Reims on May 7, representatives of the German

High Command certified the final act of capitulation in Berlin on May 8. The document was signed for the Allies by Marshal Zhukoff, as plenipotentiary of the Red Army's Supreme Command, Chief Air Marshal Sir Arthur Tedder, General Carl Spaatz, and General de Lattre de Tassigny. The German signers were Field Marshal General Wilhelm Keitel, General Admiral von Friedeburg, and Colonel General Stumpf.

To signalize the event, Marshal Stalin issued an order of the day declaring that "the great patriotic war waged by the Soviet people against the German-Fascist invaders has been victoriously concluded; Germany is utterly routed."

In a victory address, Stalin added: "The age-long struggle of the Slav peoples for their existence and their independence has ended.... Henceforth, the great banner of freedom of nations and peace among nations will fly over Europe.... The period of the war in Europe is over. The period of peaceful development has begun."

Stalin ordered a victory salute of thirty salvos from one thousand guns fired in Moscow, and the peace-marking thunder of that historic artillery, together with the triumphant cadences of the Premier's words booming from the loudspeakers in Red Square, touched off a celebration in front of the Kremlin that was an epitome of the fruits of Russia's war—of joy tinged with the tragedy of omnipresent bereavement, of satisfaction for the completed tasks of war coupled with the knowledge of the coming burdens of reconstruction, of adulation for the heroic Red Army, of commendation for the supporting war work of the Soviet Union's gargantuan industries.

No demonstration had been announced or prepared. But all work was dropped and the people streamed into the squares—people from every corner of the sprawling Russian Empire. Girls wearing the decorations of their spartan labors danced with soldiers and sailors bemedaled with the orders of imperishable battles. Old ladies smothered officers with kisses. The crowds singled out Red Army men and raised them to their shoulders in a storm of cheers and song. Throngs overflowed the squares and debauched in streets leading to the Allied embassies. Spontaneous tributes under the foreign flags testified to the Russians' consciousness of and gratitude for the Allies' share in this triumph. But the Soviet people—with hardly a family circle left as it had been in 1940—thought, too, of their absent fathers, sons, and brothers. They thought of boyish fliers who had rammed German planes over Moscow, of the numberless victims of the frozen hell of Leningrad, of the heroes of Odessa and Sevastopol, Kiev and Kharkov, Rostov and Grozny, Voronezh and Elista—of the legions who had stood and fallen until the haunted invader turned and fled.

That was Moscow's V-hour. The formal victory review came later, on March 24, when Zhukoff on a white horse and Rokossovsky on a black one led representative units of their valiant men through Red Square, past the tribune on Lenin's tomb, where Stalin took their ceremonial salute. What four years of war had wrought was evident in the massed ranks of stalwart Red Army men—many of whom had gone away as boys—and in the gleaming, massive might of the danger-forged new weapons of the celebrated Soviet armamentarium. Among them the troops bore the battle standards of their famous regiments, and after them came soldiers carrying grimly, face downward, the captured banners of the enemy. The scorpion-like swastikas and grinning skulls of the Nazi insignia, white as death, bobbed amid the mournful black tails of the flags' stained and tattered folds. The Russian crowds stood laconically silent as the soldiers, one by one, cast down their symbolic trophies in a growing, disarrayed pile at Stalin's feet. This was Russia's answer to Hitler's boast that he would one day ride through Red Square.

The most familiar popular question involving Russia that came out of the war was whether the Red Army could have bested the *Wehrmacht* without the help of the western Allies. Although Stalin during the war acknowledged the considerable part played in the course of the struggle by the help from the west, Soviet spokesmen have denied that these supplies were the determining factor in turning the tide. President Truman reported to Congress that from March, 1941, through March, 1945, the United States supplied the Soviet Union with munitions and goods valued at $8,410,000,000. In addition, the Red Army received supplies in smaller amounts from Great Britain, Canada, and Australia.

However, it has been pointed out in Moscow that one Soviet tank-building plant alone produced 35,000 tanks, several times the number supplied by the Allies throughout the war. Soviet artillery units were entirely equipped with guns of Soviet manufacture, and the Red Army's machine guns, automatic rifles, and other infantry weapons were almost exclusively of Russian manufacture. Some 13,000 planes were sent to Russia from the United States—about 5 per cent of the annual American output of aircraft. The Red Air Force was chiefly equipped from Soviet factories with planes designed by Ilyushin, Yakovleff, Polikarpoff, and other eminent Russian aircraft engineers. The rocket-projecting Katyusha, a formidable factor in the Red Army's power, was an entirely Russian product.

In addition to the matériel sent to Russia from the west, the Allied air fleets contributed to the reduction of Germany's war potential by air blockade and bombing. It is considered in Moscow, however, that neither this air activity nor the sending of Allied supplies had any

1945 Moves On!

Air Attack on Berlin

B-17 Flying Fortresses of the U. S. Army 8th Air Force release a cascade of bombs in unison over the Nazi capital.

OFFICIAL U. S. NAVY PHOTOGRAPH

Navy Wings Over Fujiyama

A striking photograph made during the U. S. Navy's attack on Tokyo early in 1945.

OFFICIAL PHOTO U. S. A.A.F.

300 Planes Bomb Tokyo

B-29 Superfortresses struck at Tokyo early in March, 1945, and destroyed over sixteen square miles of the city.

WIDE WORLD PHOTOS

Wings Over the Pacific

Twelve torpedo bombers line up in perfect steplike formation over a Southwest Pacific island base.

OFFICIAL U. S. NAVY PHOTOGRAPH

Target of the Day

The assembled crew and officers of a carrier hear their skipper tell of the coming strike on Tokyo, and the part they will play in the all-important action.

OFFICIAL PHOTO, U. S. A.A.F.

"Waddy's Wagon"

The B-29 men who bombed Tokyo pose to duplicate their caricatures on their plane.

OFFICIAL U. S. NAVY PHOTOGRAPH

Ingredients of a Task Force

Carriers, battleships, transports, and smaller ships form up at a Pacific base.

OFFICIAL U. S. NAVY PHOTOGRAPH

Back Home Safely

A scene aboard an aircraft carrier close to the shores of Japan, showing a fighter plane back for a safe landing during the strike on Tokyo.

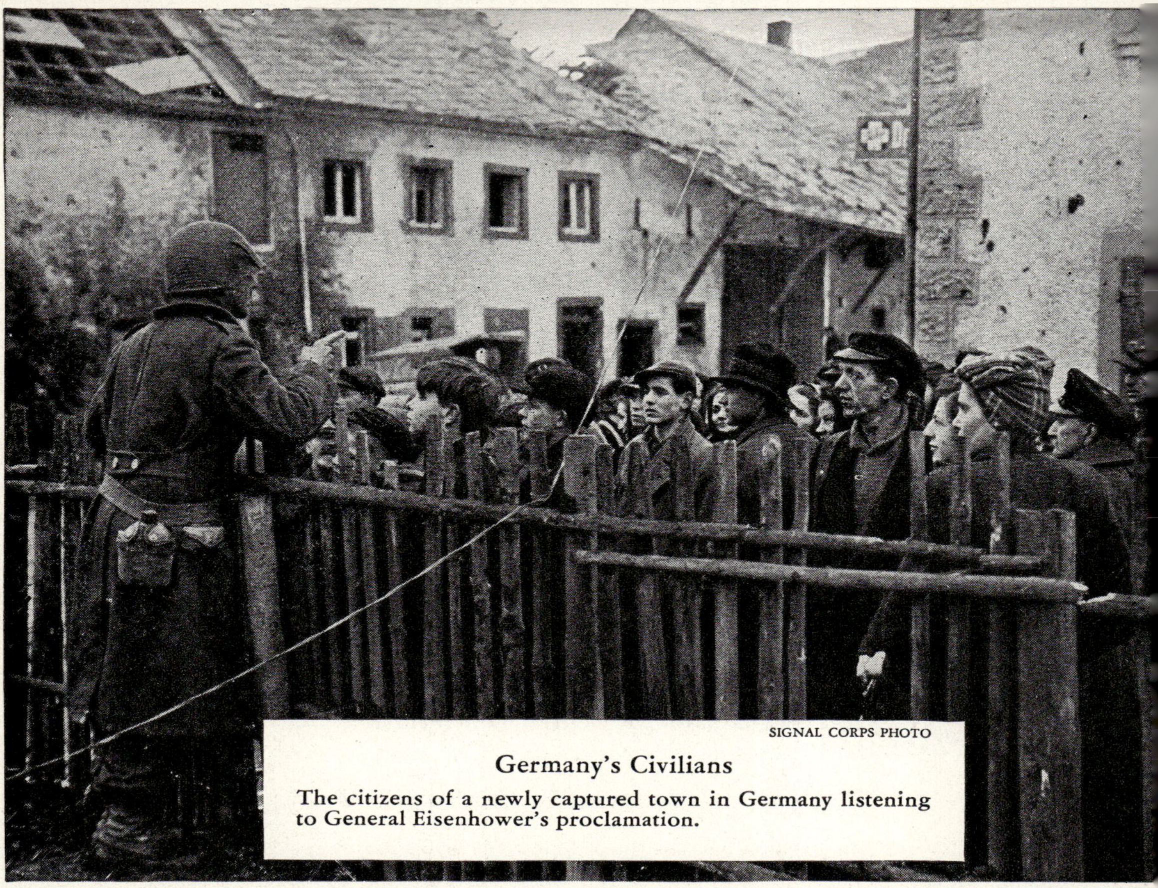

SIGNAL CORPS PHOTO

Germany's Civilians

The citizens of a newly captured town in Germany listening to General Eisenhower's proclamation.

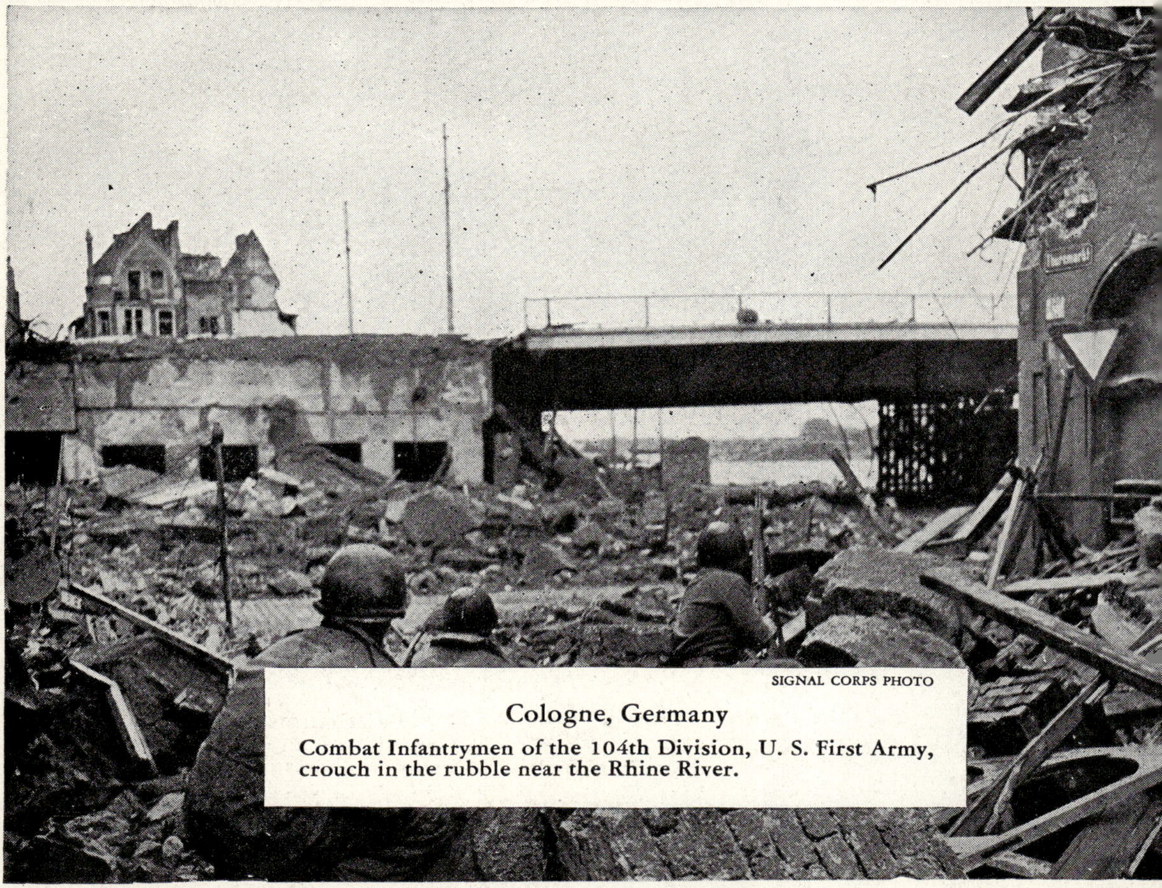

SIGNAL CORPS PHOTO

Cologne, Germany

Combat Infantrymen of the 104th Division, U. S. First Army, crouch in the rubble near the Rhine River.

SIGNAL CORPS PHOTO

Routing a Nazi
An Infantryman of the U. S. Third Army flushing a German soldier from his pillbox in Mainz.

SIGNAL CORPS PHOTO

The Face of Germany
An air-raid shelter in Krefeld, where civilians are packing up to leave. The motto on the wall, translated freely, means "Woman's work helps the war effort."

CROSSING THE RHINE

OFFICIAL U. S. NAVY PHOTOGRAPH
Carrying a Jeep Upstream
A Navy LCVP crew carrying a jeep across the Rhine past fallen Remagen bridge.

OFFICIAL U. S. NAVY PHOTOGRAPH
On the Way to Hitler's Fortress
With once gay and historic Rhine hotels in background, a Navy LCVP crew participate in Rhine crossing.

OFFICIAL U. S. NAVY PHOTOGRAPH
The U. S. Navy Ferry
A Navy LCVP unloading an Army ambulance on the west shore of the Rhine near Remagen bridgehead.

INTERNATIONAL NEWS PHOTO

The Historic Elbe Meeting
U. S. troops reach out to grasp the hands of Russian soldiers on the wrecked bridge at Torgau.

SIGNAL CORPS PHOTO

Surrender of Hersfeld
Two high-ranking German officers drive up to the leading tank of the Third Army to surrender the city.

INTERNATIONAL NEWS PHOTO

"Little Red Schoolhouse"

School at Rheims, France, used as headquarters of the Supreme Allied Command where German representatives signed final surrender.

INTERNATIONAL NEWS PHOTO

A Russian Check-up

Field Marshal Gregori K. Zhukov, Deputy Commander in Chief of all Soviet forces, examines the surrender terms as Air Chief Marshal Sir Arthur Tedder looks on.

INTERNATIONAL NEWS PHOTO

An Accomplished Fact

Lieut. General Walter D. Smith, chief of staff to General Eisenhower, signing Germany's surrender for the Allies.

INTERNATIONAL NEWS PHOTO

Victory Portrait

Ranking leaders of the victorious American forces pose at Bad Wildungen, Germany.

SURRENDER!

INTERNATIONAL NEWS PHOTO
End of Dream of Conquest
General Gustav Jodl, leader of the Nazi delegation, signing unconditional surrender documents.

INTERNATIONAL NEWS PHOTO
At Russian Headquarters
Field Marshal Wilhelm Keitel signing the ratified surrender terms for the German army.

INTERNATIONAL NEWS PHOTO
Germany Capitulates
A formal view of the already famous "unconditional surrender," in the little red schoolhouse at Rheims. The German delegates have their backs to the camera.

Reichmarshal Hermann Goering

The No. 2 man of the Nazi hierarchy as he appeared two days after he surrendered to the U. S. 36th Division.

INTERNATIONAL NEWS PHOTO

The Pens That Were Mightier

Smiling happily, General Eisenhower holds up in the form of a victory "V" the pens used to sign the surrender documents.

VICTORY!

INTERNATIONAL NEWS PHOTO

Victory Congratulations

General Eisenhower shaking hands with Russian General Ivan Susloparoff at General Eisenhower's headquarters in Rheims.

INTERNATIONAL NEWS PHOTO

Paris Cheers

Jubilant Parisians wave flags and cheer following official news of Germany's surrender. The Arc de Triomphe forms a fitting backdrop to the scene.

INTERNATIONAL NEWS PHOTO

A Prayer of Thanksgiving

Wounded soldiers returning from European campaigns bow their heads in prayer as they land at La Guardia Field on V-E Day.

PRESS ASSOCIATION, INC.

Cheers for the King and Queen

Crowds assembled in front of Buckingham Palace cheer the Royal Family on V-E Day.

V-E DAY

INTERNATIONAL NEWS PHOTO

New York joins in V-E Day celebration.

BRITISH OFFICIAL PHOTO FROM ACME

V-E Day in London
Happy Londoners gather in Piccadilly Circus to celebrate the end of the war in Europe.

INTERNATIONAL NEWS PHOTO

President Truman's V-E Day Press Conference
The members of the President's press gather in his office for an advance statement on V-E Day.

Big Ben Glows Again

Lights play on London's famous "Big Ben" as the city celebrates the end of the war.

German U-Boat Surrenders
Once a mighty member of undersea raiding force, Submarine U-858 plows through coastline waters with the American flag flying from its conning tower.

ACME NEWSPICTURES, INC.

INTERNATIONAL NEWS PHOTO

The Surrender of Submarine U-858
The Nazi U-boat captain shown after surrendering his craft off Cape May, New Jersey.

INTERNATIONAL NEWS PHOTO

In Session at San Francisco
The members of the United Nations Executive Committee in session in the War Memorial Opera House.

measurable effect on the war in Russia before 1944-45, and that therefore the turning point brought about by the Red Army's victories at Stalingrad, Kursk, and Orel in 1943 was achieved by the Soviet forces without outside assistance.

Any mathematical apportioning of the credit for victory remains in the realm of speculative academic questions. It is considered in the world at large that the war in Europe was won by the concert of tremendous Allied power and that the absence of either the Red Army or the western Allied forces from that concentration of might would have made the threat of Nazidom more formidable than it was, and would have made its suppression incalculably more difficult. The credit for the greatest victory in human history belongs to the Allied Nations —and the responsibility for preserving peace in the future belongs to the United Nations of the World.

UNCONDITIONAL SURRENDER!
DECISIVE DEFEAT OF GERMANY

DER TAG had come! But it was not the day of triumph that generations of Germans had been promised. It was a day of abject defeat, to be followed by days and years of penance for their evil-doings. The disaster which they had visited upon other nations returned to fell them, figuratively, to their knees in unconditional surrender.

Twenty-five days after Adolf Hitler had gone into delirious tantrums over the death of President Roosevelt, he himself, according to most reports, was a figure of grim tragedy, alternating between displays of diabolic cunning and the ravings of a maniac.

Much of the Netherlands had been liberated by the Anglo-Canadian forces. Former victims of German oppression ran into the streets to strike and club the captured brutes who had so long tortured and robbed them. The Germans were as arrogant as ever in captivity and defeat. "We shall conquer you yet," they sneered, "if not in this war, then in the next!" Officers pointed out grimly that the Germans still held Dunkirk. They also boasted that they still held Saint Nazaire, and the U-boat pens of Lorient.

The enemy also held one last outpost in southwest France—the estuary of the Gironde, dominating the great port city of Bordeaux, long since cleared by the Allies. As a maritime center, however, the city was useless as long as there was no free access to the sea. Thus far the Supreme Command had felt unable to divert forces from the main front to clean up the isolated Germans on the coast, contained by a moderate siege force of FFI and American troops. But by mid-April the war in the interior of Germany had slashed so far into the fatherland that some attention could be paid to the west coast of France, and Leclerc's French Second Armored Division was pulled back.

A mixed naval force of American, British, and French warships laid down a fierce bombardment on April 15 of the main German strong points on opposite sides of the estuary. These were Royan and Pointe de Grave. Heavy bombers of the United States Army Air Forces swarmed overhead to add to the attack. Lighter planes joined in to shower the Germans with a new kind of incendiary—big tanks filled with petroleum jelly and a combustible chemical that ignited on impact with the ground. The combination was a sort of aërial flame thrower.

Under cover of the shelling and bombing, part of the French armored

The last battlefront in Europe at the moment when the Doenitz "unconditional surrender" announcement was flashed.

division drove on Royan from the northeast while another column lunged upward from the southeast. On the western side of the estuary a third column attacked Pointe de Grave from the south. Royan was quickly entered, but the battle in its streets was bloody, for the Germans fought as if the whole war depended on it. However, the French routed them from both Royan and the western shore of the estuary, and finally opened the vital port of Bordeaux to Allied shipping.

In Germany, American armies were scoring many triumphs. Hodges captured the city of Leuna and besieged Leipzig; Patton reached Chemnitz and swept through the famous Bavarian town of Bayreuth, the shrine of Richard Wagner; while the Seventh Army under Patch was menacing Nuremberg. Behind the main front the Allies dealt a crushing blow to the almost-forgotten Ruhr pocket. Elements of the Ninth and First Armies lunged from both sides to slash it in two by joining forces near Wetter, between Essen and Dortmund. Above all these crashing drives Allied planes were sweeping the entire Reich. In one day, April 16, they destroyed 905 enemy planes.

One of the most tragic elements of war is the occasional accident that occurs in the confusion of battle. As in Normandy and before that in Italy, American and British bombers over Germany unwittingly dropped their loads among their own ground forces. Convoys of captured Allied soldiers were occasionally under fire from their own planes. One of these tragedies occurred when several thousand American prisoners were in a train which was unmarked. They broke out and ran into the fields, where they stripped off their shirts and bent from the waist to stand six hours in the hot summer sun, their bare backs spelling out in giant letters: P O W—Prisoners of War. The first fliers let out bursts of their guns before they were close enough to read the letters. Many of the Americans fell, but only one broke position. The fliers quickly understood the message of those scarred, skinny backs. Tipping their wings in a signal of recognition, they dropped notes to indicate that they would direct rescuing ground forces to free the prisoners.

By April 17 the Ninth Army held 150 miles of the western bank of the Elbe, besides numerous bridgeheads on the other side. It was within fifty miles of Berlin at one point. On the other bank of the river the Russians were battling only eighteen miles from the gutted German capital. The Americans withdrew behind the river and the Third Army's drive on Berlin also came to a stop. There were a thousand rumors, virtually none of them correct, including some reporting that scouts had reached the capital's western suburbs and had then withdrawn. The truth was that General Eisenhower had ordered the halt in conformity with the agreements reached at Yalta in February by Roosevelt, Churchill, and Stalin. The Big Three had decided that the Russians would enter Berlin.

With its entry into Nuremberg, Patch's Seventh scored one of the most dramatic victories of the campaign, as this Bavarian city had for years been the shrine of the Nazi party. Following the capture of Nuremberg, Patton's troops drove into Czechoslovakia—into the Sudetenland, that region which had been one of the pretexts for German aggression. This area was German at heart. The Third Army's grimy, unshaven troops, with hands stretched out to share their rations with the populace, were met with stony faces and muttered curses, followed by pot shots from windows and grenades from rooftops. The Yanks met the challenge. If this was enemy country, they knew how to deal with it. Resistance ceased almost immediately.

One of the most spectacular of all the outstanding victories in the reconquest of Europe occurred on April 19—the elimination of the much-diminished Ruhr pocket. Thousands of German troops had died within that solid and ever-narrowing wall of steel and flesh. Thousands more had been wounded. But the bag of prisoners was still more amazing: 317,000 German soldiers laid down their arms and filed back of the Allied lines to the prison cages in a stream so long and so thick that the American receiving facilities were swamped.

The Nazi Fuehrer had shouted long and loud about the "national redoubt" in the Bavarian Alps where his forces would fight the Allies until the last German had perished. However, the Allied reconnaissance discovered no great movements of troops to the south which was now in increasing peril from two American armies—the Third and the Seventh—as well as from the advancing French First. Some government offices had been moved to Munich, the birthplace of Nazism, but most of them had been shifted northwest to Hamburg.

The giant Allied nutcracker was crunching Germany into a shattered shell. Both the Russians and the western Allies were overrunning notorious concentration camps. The most infamous in the west were Belsen, Buchenwald, Luckenwalde, and the dread Dachau. Captured statesmen and soldiers, long-feared dead, were found like men rising from their graves: King Leopold III of Belgium and three former French premiers betrayed to the Germans by Pétain—Leon Blum, Edouard Daladier, and Paul Reynaud—were liberated. Among the many notables found in concentration camps were Kurt Schuschnigg, the last Chancellor of Austria, and Hjalmar Schacht, who had been Germany's financial wizard and now claimed eagerly to have resisted the Nazis throughout their régime.

In many of these camps the Allies discovered incontrovertible evidence of savageries and cruelties which even those who saw the proof could hardly believe possible in the twentieth century. These will be documented in a later chapter. Aghast at what was found, the leaders of the Big Three issued a stern warning to the Germans that individual justice would be imposed on those responsible for these barbarities on captured Allied soldiers. Moving pictures of the tortures were shown to German civilians under compulsion. With a startling unanimity they asserted their ignorance of such things and their lack of any connection with the perpetrators. The German people seemed to be void of all conscience or humanity. Hitler had created not a "super-race," but a race of soul-less robots.

The sprawling front was rapidly becoming a gigantic mopping-up operation. Behind it, in what had been the Ruhr pocket, the Americans battled within Duesseldorf. The defenders of this completely isolated city continued to fight with intense fury. In the Harz Mountains other Yanks began tearing holes in the pocket there with the capture of Wernigerode. Patch's Seventh Army drove to the fabled Danube at Dillingen, where it carved out a bridgehead. With the French, it took the historic city of Ulm, where Napoleon had fought. The Third also reached the Danube and closed in on Regensburg. In the north almost all the Netherlands except the western part had been cleared. The Tommies, with their Canadian comrades, were in the outskirts of Bremen and Hamburg. Augsburg trembled as the Seventh Army drove, with the Third, through the heart of the vaunted "redoubt." The Royal Air Force loosed its six-ton bombs on Hitler's famed mountain hide-out of Berchtesgaden in a ruthless area-saturation bombing. This allegedly impregnable rock fortress, with its luxurious chambers filled with loot from many nations, crumbled into dust as if symbolic of the entire country.

Thousands of miles from the scene of Germany's debacle, the United Nations on April 25 opened their historic conference in San Francisco. On the same day another dramatic illustration of a free world's united stand came on the battlefield itself. The first American and Russian troops met in the heart of Germany. The Americans had long prepared for this junction of Allied forces. Instructions had been issued in minute detail on the recognition of Russian uniforms, arms, and equipment. The official meeting party had been chosen. For a week American soldiers had been listening eagerly to their field radios picking up the conversations of Russian tank units driving toward the rendezvous. The sound of Russian guns could be heard, and German soldiers and civilians were hurtling panic-stricken to the American lines. Their surrenders were accepted until Supreme Headquarters ordered sternly that they were to be turned back to the onrushing army they dreaded —dreaded because they well knew what horrors their own troops had inflicted on the Russian people.

The junction of the American and Russian Armies was a symbolic event of vast import. Second Lieutenant William D. Robertson headed the four-man patrol of the First Army's newest division, the 69th. The official junction was finally made in the city of Torgau on the Elbe. At 4:45 P.M. on April 25 Robertson crawled halfway across a wrecked bridge to be met by a young soldier of Marshal Ivan S. Konev's First Ukrainian Army, Private Nicolai Ivanovitch Andreev.

Robertson and his three privates had been told by people in a town outside Torgau that the Russians were just across the river. He tied a flag to his jeep and set off. Arriving at the bank, he climbed an observation tower and waved his flag toward an armored car which he could see on the other side. *"Tovarich!"* he shouted—the only

Russian word he knew. But he did not know that only a few days before the Germans had done the same thing. The Russians, suspecting a repetition of the ruse, fired two rounds of antitank ammunition into Robertson's tower. The former pre-medical student climbed quickly down and retreated. Among the liberated prisoners in the vicinity he found an English-speaking Russian whom he pressed into service. Taking him back to the tower, Robertson asked the Russian to explain the situation to his compatriots across the river.

The greetings between the armies of East and West were very simple, handicapped as they were by the barrier of language. The four Americans, in the midst of handclasps, back-slappings, and bear hugs, kept shouting *"Tovarich! Tovarich!"* The Russians replied with "Hello! Hello!"

Word of the junction spread swiftly. More and more Russians and Americans, both officers and enlisted men, swarmed to the river. When the higher officers of both sides met, there was a formal marking of the event. Then the formality was forgotten. In the midst of Germany, these men of two widely separated, very different countries, sat down to one of those banquets for which the Russians have become famous. The Americans brought captured—or, rather, "liberated"—French champagne. The Russians supplied vodka and cognac. They lifted their glasses again and again and toasted each others' countries, armies, and leaders. Starting with the chiefs of state and the military commanders, they went down the line to the private soldiers who formed part of the junction parties.

The first junction was quickly followed by many others in greater force, as the eastern and western Allies met in comradeship in the midst of the conquered country. Meanwhile, American and British Armies continued to slash forward in other areas. One day after the junction of the First Army and the Russians, Patton's Third made history. His 11th Armored Division crossed the border in the first invasion of Austria by American troops. At the other extreme of the front the British stormed into the heart of Bremen and made the city theirs.

The disintegration of Germany was obvious everywhere. Rumors of an impending surrender were rife. Hitler was variously reported to be insane and to have fled. Himmler announced that the fat Hermann Goering had been replaced by Field Marshal Robert Ritter von Greim as the head of the nonexistent *Luftwaffe*. General Dittmar, long the Reich's outstanding military commentator, surrendered. He told his captors that Hitler would die in Berlin at the head of his troops, battling the Russians to the end. This, Dittmar said, could be only a matter of days. Hitler's bravery proved to be another false alarm. He was later said to be cowering underground in abject fright.

Count Folke Bernadotte, a member of the royal family of Sweden and married to an American, was acting as intermediary between Himmler and the Allies. Himmler pleaded to be permitted to surrender to Britain and the United States alone, with a promise to let Germany continue the fight against Russia. This offer was firmly rejected by the western Allies. President Truman instructed the Swedish Count to inform Himmler that the utmost concession to the German troops would be unconditional surrender to the Allied commanders in their respective areas.

History, as it so often does, repeated itself with a new twist. The armistice which ended World War I had been prematurely announced in Paris; in World War II there was an equally premature announcement on April 28 by a United States Senator that the war in Europe was over. Senator Tom Connally, chairman of the Senate Foreign Relations Committee, was attending the United Nations Conference in San Francisco when he made this announcement to the press. Crowds surged to Times Square in New York, where for a week the police had been working double shifts in anticipation of the end of the war. President Truman, however, announced that the hour had not yet come.

Soldiers on the battlefronts in Europe heard the German broadcasters telling their people on April 30: "The end may come tomorrow!" Neutral radio stations in Sweden and Switzerland flashed the words: "Himmler has agreed to surrender to all the Allies!" Hitler's voice was silent—it was never again to be heard in World War II. The Fuehrer who had uttered his arrogant threats to the world for so many years was now a man of mystery. The thunderous words "Germany will fight to the last man" were an exploded myth.

Germans in Denmark were beginning to stream along the narrow isthmus and back into the fatherland. Great lines of refugees were fleeing from their devastated cities and taking the road to nowhere. The German people seemed to be completely bewildered without a leader to lash them into line. Their Fuehrer had indeed deserted them.

Meanwhile, the American Seventh Army wiped up Oberammergau, shrine of the famous "Passion Play." Patch's men smashed into the heart of Munich, the birthplace of pagan Nazism. Here, twenty-two years before, Adolf Hitler, the rabble-rouser, had staged his first abortive *Putsch* from a beer cellar.

Patton's Third Army liberated the infamous prison of Dachau. The first Americans to enter the torture camp were almost torn apart by the pathetic inmates, whose dejection and suffering suddenly became the delirium of joy. But German guards, hidden in the towers, turned their machine guns on the prisoners. Inflamed by righteous anger and bitter hatred, the American troops replied with heavy volleys, and many of the prisoners, weak as they were, spread out in search of abandoned German arms with which to wreak the vengeance of years on their torturers. Not a guard who was still in Dachau when the Americans arrived escaped retribution.

May Day, 1945, traditional time for celebration by the working peoples of the world, marked the dawn of the week of liberation from Nazi serfdom. Two more American-Russian junctions were made. French troops cleared Friedrichshafen and entered Austria, while other French units drove across the border from their own country into Italy's Val d'Aosta. Patton's tough Third Army smashed through the little Austrian town of Braunau, the birthplace of the ignorant vagabond whom Germany had enthusiastically taken to its heart and followed through twelve years to this final catastrophe. On this day, when Hitler's birthplace fell, the Hamburg radio with solemn fanfare warned that a vital announcement was to come. After some suspense Grand Admiral Karl Doenitz, the savage U-boat genius who had long since succeeded Grand Admiral Erich Raeder as Commander in Chief of the German Navy, stepped to the microphone to tell the German people and the world that Adolf Hitler was dead.

Doenitz added that Hitler, while dying, had nominated the Admiral to succeed him. Doenitz thereupon proclaimed that he would continue the war because the Allies would not join him in the fight against the Russians. He made hurried changes in the Cabinet, the most notable of which was the replacement of Foreign Minister Joachim von Ribbentrop with Count Ludwig Schwerin von Krosigk. The seat of government was moved to Flensburg, near the Danish border.

German resistance, except in the north, had almost disappeared. From Italy came the announcement of the surrender of all the German forces in that fallen empire of the dead Mussolini. The southern flank of Germany was now utterly bare as the Americans and Russians drove deeper and deeper into the "national redoubt" from the north. The German-occupied country of Denmark was sealed off when the British Second Army under General Dempsey speared to Luebeck at the eastern end of the base of the Schleswig-Holstein peninsula. Even the most fanatical Nazis knew that the end was near when Munitions Minister Albert Speer, speaking from Flensburg, broadcast an open confession of the fact. Yet Doenitz and Himmler would not yield. Negotiations with the Allies through Count Bernadotte continued; with every hour that passed the position of the Allies grew stronger.

Admiral Hans Georg von Friedeburg, who commanded the forces in Denmark, and Colonel General Gustav Jodl, Doenitz's chief of staff, were too realistic to pretend that their situation was anything but hopeless. Yet even they were reluctant to admit the end until events forced them to yield.

On May 4 the Germans surrendered all their forces in Denmark, northern Germany, and the Netherlands.

This northern surrender threw at one fell swoop 500,000 prisoners into the cages of the 21st Army Group, which had already captured as many more in the preceding twenty-four hours of fighting across the top of Germany. However, fighting in the rest of Germany, and in Czechoslovakia and Austria, continued despite its utter hopelessness.

On the same day the American Seventh Army, deep inside Austria, plunged through the Brenner Pass to effect a junction with General Truscott's Fifth Army in Italy. The enemy's doom was reiterated by General Eisenhower, who said that day: "On land, sea, and in the air the Germans are thoroughly whipped." But some Germans apparently did not have sufficient intelligence to know it. Doenitz, in those closing hours of his régime, cunningly declared the Czech capital of Prague, strongly held by German troops, to be a "hospital city." Czech patriots rose in all their strength against the garrison and threw the enemy out. But the Germans counterattacked with armor and a few planes; so the patriots appealed frantically to the Allies for aid.

Although Eisenhower knew the Germans were thoroughly beaten, he insisted that there would be no proclamation of victory while any important enemy pockets remained. These were rapidly dwindling. Besides the relatively insignificant garrison of Dunkirk, there were 100,000 Germans in Lorient and Saint Nazaire in Brittany, and about 200,000 in Norway. These were not included in the surrender accepted by Montgomery. The Germans in Czechoslovakia and about 1,000,000 troops in Austria still held out.

The Allied armies continued their advances. A brief German flare-up in Copenhagen, where German ships were massed, was rapidly quelled. In Berlin and its western environs the Russians were mopping up. But on the eastern wall of the virtually self-formed Czechoslovak-Austrian pocket they were battling hard to relieve Prague and clean out Austria. On the other side Patton drove into the Skoda arms city of Pilsen while the Seventh Army cut farther into Austria.

This was the situation on May 6, 1945. Unknown to the world and to the armies, German leaders and the Allied commanders were in tense contact by radio and courier. Early that evening Jodl and Friedeburg appeared in an advance command post of Supreme Headquarters set up in Reims, grimly prepared to surrender. On May 7 the emissaries of conquered Germany appended their names to the document that confessed their defeat. The war in Europe was officially almost over—hostilities were to end the next day.

Even to the end the Germans were treacherous. Long after their commanders had given the "cease-fire" order, enemy troops bombed and shelled Prague and strove to rout the Czechs. By May 12, however, the last shots in Europe had been fired, both officially and unofficially. Eisenhower and the Russians had declared that the Germans in Czechoslovakia would be treated as outlaws if they continued to resist. After a day or two they recognized the authority behind this declaration and sullenly gave themselves up as prisoners of war.

Thus ended the war in Europe which had lasted five years and eight months. During all this time the very existence of western civilization was at stake. V-E Day was celebrated throughout the civilized world. Millions went to church and thanked God for peace and freedom at last. We have seen General Eisenhower's triumphant ovation in London, Paris, New York, and Washington, and his return to the little home town in Kansas and his eighty-three-year-old mother.

Generals of the army and private soldiers alike were greeted with unbounded enthusiasm as they came home from the war. President Truman called upon the nation to concentrate its resources and manpower on the defeat of Japan. Hundreds of thousands of soldiers remained in Europe to preserve peace, and hundreds of thousands more came home. But ahead of us still lay the final drives to liberate China, Burma, India, the Netherlands Indies, and, finally, to take the war directly to the Japanese homeland and bring about the destruction of the Japanese Empire.

LAST SCENES IN TRAGEDY OF WAR —COLLAPSE OF GERMAN MIGHT

GOTTERDAMMERUNG—the Teutonic conception of a last grand battle in which the world sinks into the sea amid the twilight of the gods—was given a revised version in World War II. The false gods perished, but the world survived.

The last scenes of the war in Europe, amid the devastation of German and Italian cities, were tense human drama. The victorious Allies accepted the unconditional surrender of the German war lords who, in defeat and dishonor, strutted arrogantly from the stage of history.

The first of these historic scenes began on April 28, 1945, in the ancient palace of the kings of Naples in Caserta, Italy, where the Allies had established their Italian headquarters. The Germans had only the slenderest fingerhold left in Italy. Two of their officers, in civilian clothes—looking for all the world as if they had been fitted on Bond Street for a day in the country—arrived by plane and ostentatiously presented their commanders' offer to surrender unconditionally.

The offer was transmitted by radio to the capitals of the three major Allies—Washington, London, Moscow—where the heads of state and the chiefs of staff dictated the outline of the documents to be prepared. At 2:00 P.M. on Sunday, April 29, the documents were ready, and the Germans took copies back to their superiors. Colonel General von Vietinghoff-Scheel, commander of the regular army forces, was represented by a lieutenant colonel who looked like Hollywood's idea of a Prussian officer in mufti. *Obergruppenfuehrer* Karl Wolff, commander of the Elite Guard and Gestapo forces, was represented by a heavy, dark major who also looked his part to perfection despite his lack of a uniform.

Returning to Caserta on April 30, they announced their readiness to sign. On the following day, May 1, Lieutenant General W. D. Morgan, deputy for the British Field Marshal Alexander, signed for the three Allies in a ceremony which lasted exactly twelve minutes. Signatures were placed on five copies of the documents. General Morgan handed three copies to an aide, who turned them over to the Germans. Morgan then said: "Thank you, gentlemen. I now ask you to withdraw." Thus, 1,000,000 German troops, together with all their arms and half the territory of Austria, were yielded up by the fallen "master race."

The second scene took place, symbolically, on the Lueneburg Heath south of battered Hamburg. This is a barren, artificially forested meadow which has served for years as the birthplace and training-ground of German Armies. British Field Marshal Montgomery caused a tent to be struck. Here he received a German delegation headed by Admiral Hans Georg von Friedeburg, who had succeeded Admiral Doenitz as commander in chief of the German Navy after Doenitz' self-proclamation as Fuehrer.

After preliminary negotiations, Admiral Friedeburg, who also bore the title of General of the Army, drove into the British lines on May 3 under a white flag. With him were General Kinsel, chief of staff to Field Marshal Ernst Busch, Major Friede of Kinsel's staff, and Rear Admiral Wagner of Friedeburg's staff. The mighty Montgomery, who had beaten the greatest German generals, turned as he walked slowly to the tent where the Germans were waiting and exclaimed: "This is the moment!" Then, as though he were surprised, his penetrating eyes surveyed the visitors as he brusquely inquired: "What do you want?"

"We come from Field Marshal Busch," Friedeburg replied abruptly, his face impassive, "to ask you to accept the surrender of three German Armies which are now withdrawing in front of the Russians in the Mecklenburg area."

Montgomery refused. These armies, he demanded, must surrender only to the Russians. Stating his views explicitly, he added: "The subject is closed. Are you prepared to surrender the German forces on my northern and western flanks—those forces between Luebeck and Holland and the forces in support of them, such as those in Denmark?"

The Germans tried to dicker. They proposed a complicated withdrawal plan which would have taken months. Montgomery quietly showed them a map of the actual front. They were stunned. Montgomery cut them short and sent them to think things over at luncheon. Friedeburg, as soon as he was out of sight of the Field Marshal, broke into tears and wept throughout the meal. Summoning the Germans once more, Montgomery laid down an ultimatum. They must surrender unconditionally all their forces in the areas designated. He would then be willing to discuss with them the disposition of those troops, occupation plans, and aid for civilians. "Otherwise," he said, "we shall go on with the war.... I will be delighted to do so," he assured the Germans, adding thoughtfully, "all your soldiers and civilians may be killed."

The astounded Germans were speechless for a moment. Then they disclaimed authority to sign such a surrender. Montgomery was adamant. Finally, two of the Germans went back for further orders while the other two remained. On May 4 the two emissaries returned—and this time they brought complete acceptance.

Friedeburg was summoned to Montgomery's trailer for a last-minute conference; the rest of the delegation were left waiting for a time, in a cold rain.

Friedeburg was ushered into a small tent containing only a little table with a blue cloth and a plain inkstand and pen. The haughty Nazi was now the picture of defeat, his face gray and lined.

Shortly afterward Kinsel and the others were also brought in. Montgomery, having let them all wait for a while—to "cool off"—came into the tent, put on his horn-rimmed glasses, and read the terms of the surrender. Led by Friedeburg, the humbled Herrenvolk leaders signed. Montgomery signed last, on behalf of Supreme Commander Eisenhower. This ceremony took five minutes.

The scene shifted to Munich, the birthplace of Nazism, on the following day, May 5. It was an American commander who now took the leading rôle. Army Group G, the German force in southern Germany and western Austria, was hopelessly trapped. This group comprised the First and Nineteenth Armies. Its delegation was headed by Lieutenant General Foertsch, commander of the First. He arrived in a car with some aides at the headquarters of Major General John W. O'Daniel.

Negotiations for the end of the German Army Group G were held in the huge museum of Hitler's favorite sculptor, Professor Joseph Thorak, just outside Munich. The Germans marked on a map the area included in their surrender. Then, one by one, they marched to a table, at whose head was seated General Jacob L. Devers, commander of the American Sixth Army Group. In seven minutes General Devers emerged, shouting: "It's all over on my front!"

The final surrender of the last German Armies took place on May 7 in the magnificent cathedral city of Reims, France, where SHAEF had established an advance command post. Negotiations had begun on May 5, when Friedeburg and Colonel Fritz Poleck of the German High Command arrived in Reims by automobile, after having flown part of the way from Flensburg, Doenitz's capital, via Montgomery's headquarters. The proud Friedeburg had greatly changed since the day before. He was whistling as he washed and changed his collar preparatory to being taken to Lieutenant General Walter Bedell Smith, Eisenhower's chief of staff; Poleck was nervous and ill at ease.

The meeting was held in the École Industrielle, a modern red brick building in the center of the city. There the Germans revealed that they were not really authorized to surrender but only to negotiate. General Smith curtly explained the hopelessness of the German position. Friedeburg countered, as he had done with Montgomery, by asking permission for those Germans menaced by the Russians to surrender to the Americans and the British. Smith spoke decisively, stating that nothing less than an unconditional surrender to all three major Allies would be considered. A Russian representative, Major General Ivan Susloparoff, chief of the Russian mission to France, was present for that purpose.

Friedeburg, stalling for time, complained of the plight of German civilians, an outrageous plea from a nation which had slaughtered millions of civilians.

Friedeburg was left alone in an office, under heavy guard, to study the terms. About eight o'clock that night he asked permission to transmit them to Doenitz. This request was granted. The message went by radio to the British Second Army in code and then by courier to the Admiral. Briefly, the terms were these: Either Friedeburg should be empowered to surrender unconditionally or Doenitz should send the chief of his general staff and the commanders of his army, navy, and air force for the purpose, with complete authority. Unless one or the other alternative were complied with promptly, the new German "government" would be charged with responsibility for continuing the war.

In mid-afternoon of the next day came the long-awaited message: Colonel General Gustaf Jodl, Doenitz's chief of staff, was en route by air with full powers to sign the act of unconditional surrender. He was accompanied by an aide, Major Wilhelm Oxenius, and a British officer, Major General Sir Francis de Guingard, chief of staff of the Twenty-first Army Group. The party reached the Reims airfield at about five P.M.

Jodl was thoroughly arrogant as he strode to the car which was to take him to SHAEF's command post. When Friedeburg saw Jodl he did not salute; he merely said, "Aha!" He looked relieved as they talked, but Jodl was soon pacing up and down. About nine o'clock Jodl made another play for time, trying to avoid a surrender to the Russians. This failed, as earlier efforts had done, and Jodl sent a new message to Doenitz. The Germans in their billets and the Allies in the war room sat up through the night to await the reply. Some time after midnight, big staff cars rolled up.

A little after 2:00 A.M. the conferees gathered in the war room. Supreme Commander Eisenhower was in Reims, but he did not attend. At 2:29 A.M. General Susloparoff, Lieutenant General Sir Frederick E. Morgan, one of Eisenhower's deputies, Admiral Sir Harold Burrough, commander of the Allies' naval forces, General Carl A. Spaatz, Air Marshal Sir James M. Robb, chief of the air staff, and Major General Harold R. Bull, entered the room. Five minutes later, General Smith came in, and they all seated themselves at a long table with a cracked top, under hot, glaring lights. Photographers with still and motion-picture cameras were grouped against the walls, which were covered

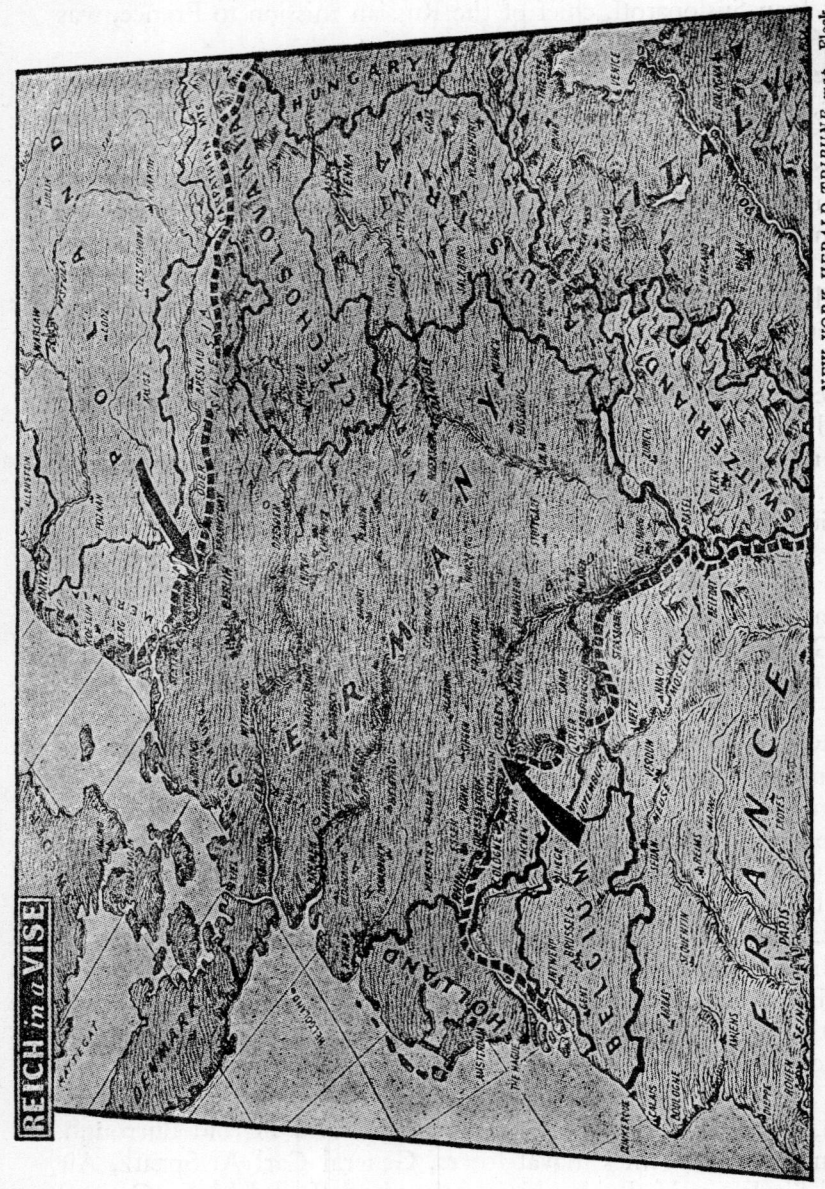

NEW YORK HERALD TRIBUNE map—Fleck

From East and West the United Nations closed on Germany. Arrows show where the Rhine and Oder defense lines were breached.

with detail maps and exhaustive charts of casualties, supplies, and so forth. At 2:34 the Germans entered, glistening with decorations. They stood at attention, then bowed to the assembly.

At each place at the table was a card, a pencil, and a writing tablet. The numerous china ashtrays were never used; no one smoked. No one spoke for a moment. General Smith then asked in a flat voice whether the Germans were prepared to sign the surrender documents placed before them. Jodl nodded. At 2:41 A.M. he took out a gold-capped fountain pen and with a flourish signed each copy, followed by Friedeburg. General Smith signed next, on behalf of General Eisenhower and represented the British as well as the Americans. He was followed by General Susloparoff for the Russians, and by Major General François Sevez, who signed for General Alphonse-Pierre Juin, commander of the French forces under Eisenhower.

Jodl's eyes were glassy from strain but they were still defiant and arrogant. He stood stiffly erect. Turning to Smith, he said in English, "I want to say a word." Then, with characteristic effrontery, he went on in German: "General! With this signature the German people and the German armed forces, for better or for worse, are delivered into the victor's hands. In this war, which has lasted more than five years, both have achieved and suffered more than perhaps any other people in the world. In this hour I can only express hope that the victor will treat them with generosity."

General Smith's inscrutable face was drawn with fatigue. He looked up at Jodl when the words were translated, but he made no reply. A tense silence continued to emphasize the effrontery of a plea for mercy for a people who for almost six years had shown none to any of their helpless victims.

Here is the historic document which marked the downfall of Germany, the nation that had suffered the most complete defeat in history:

(1) We, the undersigned, acting by the authority of the German High Command, hereby surrender unconditionally to the Supreme Commander, Allied Expeditionary Force, and simultaneously to the Soviet High Command, all forces on land, sea, and in the air that are at this date under German control.

(2) The German High Command will at once issue orders to all German military, naval, and air authorities and to all forces under German control to cease active operations at 2301 hours Central European Time on Eight May and to remain in the positions occupied at the time. No ship, vessel or aircraft is to be scuttled, nor is any damage to be done to their hulls, machinery, or equipment.

(3) The German High Command will at once issue to the appropriate commanders, and insure the carrying out of, any further

orders issued by the Supreme Commander, Allied Expeditionary Force, and by the Soviet High Command.

(4) This Act of Military Surrender is without prejudice to, and will be superseded by, any general instrument of surrender imposed by, or on behalf of, the United Nations and applicable to Germany and the German Armed Forces as a whole.

(5) In the event of the German High Command or of any of the forces under their command failing to act in accordance with this Act of Surrender, the Supreme Commander, Allied Expeditionary Force, and the Soviet High Command will take such punitive or other action as they deem appropriate.

Signed at Reims, France, at 0241 hours on the seventh day of May, 1945.

On behalf of the German High Command—JODL

In the presence of:

On behalf of the Supreme Commander Allied Expeditionary Force—W. B. SMITH

On behalf of the Soviet High Command—IVAN SUSLOPAROFF

On behalf of the French—F. SEVEZ

It was only after this document had been signed that the German emissaries were presented to General Eisenhower. With him was Air Chief Marshal Sir Arthur William Tedder, Deputy Supreme Commander. Eisenhower asked the Germans tersely whether they fully understood what they had signed and were prepared to carry out the terms. They said that they did and were, bowed with stiff Prussian dignity, and left the room at 2:55 P.M. to return to their Flensburg headquarters.

At 12:01 A.M. on May 9, 1945, Western European War Time, the fighting ceased, except in the interior of Czechoslovakia.

Only the epilogue remained to be enacted. This was the ultimate German signature in Berlin, the ruined capital of the vanquished. The signing took place at midnight of May 8, one minute before the fighting was to cease.

The ceremony was held in Marshal Gregory K. Zhukoff's headquarters in the large whitewashed hall of an army technical school in the eastern residential suburb of Karlshorst. This was one of the few Berlin buildings that had not been destroyed in aërial or artillery bombardments.

The document differed little from that signed in Reims except for

Collapse of German Might

the signatures. Friedeburg signed again, for the German Navy; Colonel General Hans Juergen Stumpf signed for the Air Force, whose commander, Field Marshal General Robert Ritter von Greim, had been wounded and could not attend; and, finally, that German of Germans, Field Marshal General Wilhelm Keitel, titular head of the vaunted *Oberkommando der Wehrmacht,* the German High Command. This overbearing, contemptuous war lord had been brought to the meeting place in a Russian staff car through the heart of Berlin's ruins.

Marshal Tedder was present to sign for Supreme Commander Eisenhower; he took with him General Spaatz, who signed as an American observer. General Jean de Lattre de Tassigny, commander of the French First Army, arrived independently to sign as a French observer. For several hours before the actual signing took place the British and Russian marshals conferred over the precise wording of the instrument of surrender.

At midnight the German delegates were summoned. In the large hall, glaring under Klieg lights, several tables had been arranged in the shape of an E. Zhukoff, his face stern, took the middle seat; General Spaatz and General de Lattre de Tassigny sat at his left, while Admiral Burrough and Andrei Y. Vishinsky, Assistant People's Soviet Commissar for Foreign Affairs, were on his right. The Germans were to be seated at a separate table near the door. At 12:10 A.M. Keitel led them in, Friedeburg and Stumpf following. The German Marshal was bombastically self-possessed, although his face was flushed. Haughty as if he were the victor, not the vanquished, he slammed his marshal's baton on the table before him. As he waited, however, his composure began to wilt; he moistened a finger on his lips and fidgeted with his stiff collar.

Zhukoff spoke only Russian; therefore it fell to Tedder, speaking English, to open the ceremonies. He rose. His voice was like ice. "I ask you: Have you read this document of unconditional surrender? Are you prepared to sign it?"

The words were duly translated. Keitel then picked his copy off the table before him, rose and, in his harsh Prussian voice, growled: "Yes, I am ready!"

Zhukoff, still silent, motioned with his hand, summoning Keitel to him.

Keitel, with meticulous care, picked up his cap and gloves and thrust his baton under his arm. Slowly he inserted his monocle over his right eye. Then he strode pompously to the Russian Commander's table and took a seat. In a sprawling hand he wrote simply "Keitel" on each of the nine copies.

The German Marshal returned to his table and at Zhukoff's gesture his colleagues advanced to add their signatures. These were followed by the signatures of Zhukoff and Tedder. Spaatz and de Lattre de Tassigny were writing their names as witnesses when Keitel beckoned to the Russian interpreter and demanded that he tell Zhukoff that the surrender left "insufficient time for the Germans to notify all their troops of the cease-fire order."

As the French and American generals signed in their turn, Keitel's guttural voice roared out: "I insist that you go to the Colonel General—I mean Marshal Zhukoff—and tell him I must demand another twenty-four-hour respite."

The interpreter hesitated a moment. Then he consulted one of Zhukoff's aides. The Russian did not even shrug his shoulders. There simply was no reply.

The last signature had been appended. Zhukoff arose and uttered his first words. His voice, like Tedder's, was stern: "I now request the German delegation to leave the room."

Keitel stood up, red with indignation. He snapped closed the folder in which he carried his copy of the instrument of surrender. Glaring at the Russians and the Americans, the British and the French, he did not salute. Jauntily he flipped his baton in their direction, replaced it under his arm, and marched out as if the two officers who followed him had been a victorious army of millions. What feelings lay behind his set stony expression only Keitel himself could know.

Thus the European war, unleashed five and one-half years before by the Germans, came to its formal end. Their last communiqué, dated May 9, 1945, had the defiant ring of 1918: "In the end the Germans succumbed with honor to enormous superiority!"

The cost of the war in terms of money has been calculated in these pages. Its cost in lives—the lives of the millions whom the Germans slaughtered, the millions more whom they tortured, starved, and hounded through Europe on their lust for conquest, may never be known.

It is obvious that there was no humility in these surrenders, no indication of a moral or spiritual regeneration in the refining crucible of war.

While the braggadocio in speech was gone, the swagger and bravado of German militarism and Nazi impudence still remained. Neither was there any evidence of an awakening of the conscience of the German people. They were silent and sullen, evincing no moral comprehension of their disgrace and ignominy in the eyes of the whole world, no expression of desire to live in peace and friendliness with their fellow nations.

The most outstanding social and political aspect of the situation was the German subjugation to the paganistic Nazi doctrines. There was no spirit of revolt against the forces that had held them so long in subjection.

A once great nation seemed to be stupefied by Hitlerian perversion. While most of them in self-defense denied that they had been Nazis, they showed none of the qualities of character which distinguish a people imbued with the spirit of independence. They still seemed to be waiting for "Der Tag"—a day when, in some other guise, perhaps, and under some other banner, they might again venture on the hazardous path of Pan-Germanic conquest.

There may have been some people in Germany with democratic aspirations and a desire for world brotherhood who might later give expression to their ideals. At this time, however, they were silent and leaderless—cautiously awaiting future developments.

TRUTH ABOUT TORTURE CHAMBERS IN AXIS PRISON CAMPS

THE onrushing Allies swept over western and southern Germany before the Axis could hide the evidence which would convict it in the War Crimes Courts. American, British, and Russian troops in their raids on prison camps witnessed with their own eyes the torture chambers of the Nazi war lords. On all battle fronts the Axis brutality exceeded anything ever known in warfare since the savagery of the barbarians.

The confessions of the accused, with the testimony of eyewitnesses, prove beyond any shadow of doubt the gravest charges that have been brought against them. It is positive proof of the moral depravity and degeneracy in the Axis countries which caused World War II. Civilization, with all standards of ethics and human relationships, was trampled under foot in an orgy of blood lust.

General Eisenhower on the European front discovered the fiendish practices of the Nazis as his own soldiers rescued prisoners of war from German camps. General MacArthur witnessed the same perverted practices by the Japs. Under the most inhumane conditions, prisoners of war and captive women and children were taken on death marches, or transported in roofless cattle cars unprotected against the weather, or in sealed-up freight cars devoid of air and light. In neither case did the captives have any sanitary facilities, and many died during their journeys.

As railroad transportation problems grew graver in Germany and there were not enough trains to carry the captives, they were forced to march hundreds of miles on foot in all weathers, prodded by bayonets and bullets. Many who faltered were left to die by the roadside; the rest were beaten, kicked, bayoneted, and shot to death by their captors, in the most callous disregard of the Geneva Convention.

In many cases the convoys, whether afoot or entrained, were not clearly marked as prisoner-of-war groups, and as a result they were inevitably targets for the deadly and accurate strafing of the Allies' fliers, who had no means of knowing that it was their own comrades who were their targets.

The advancing forces found camp after camp filled with men of all the Allied armies, many of them in pitiable states of health. It was far from uncommon for a man to lose as much as forty pounds in three months of imprisonment. Such losses resulted not only from the insufficient prison diet but also from the Germans' deliberate theft or retention of Red Cross prisoner-aid packages which, when they were not stolen and consumed, were apparently withheld for no reason whatever except sheer cruelty.

On July 27, 1945, less than three months after the German surrender, the Red Cross reported that it recovered more than nine million of these packages, representing the deliveries of eight months, which had been stealthily stored away by the Germans—as at the Heppenheim camp in Nuremberg.

The largest prisoner-of-war camp overrun by the Allies was that of Moosburg, some fifteen miles south of Regensberg in Bavaria. It was liberated by the Third Army. Moosburg contained 110,000 war prisoners. In almost every camp, the liberating Allied armies found Americans of note. In one was Lieutenant John G. Winant, Jr., the son of our Ambassador to Britain. Young Lieutenant Winant had been shot down in an air attack on Germany. In another was Lieutenant Jack Hemingway, son of the noted novelist, Ernest Hemingway. Capture of a third camp freed Captain Clyde E. Hering, Jr., son of a Senator from Iowa.

Colonel John K. Waters, General Patton's son-in-law, was held near Hammelburg. Late in March a unit of the American Fourth Armored Division, erroneously informed as to the number of prisoners in the camp and the strength of its guards, attempted to liberate it. In the fighting that followed, Colonel Waters broke out and attempted to reach the rescue party in order to guide it into the heart of the prison. He had been a prisoner since February, 1943, when he was captured at Faïd Pass in Tunisia.

Unfortunately Colonel Waters was caught between the guns of both sides and fell seriously wounded. Another prisoner, a sergeant, crawled out at the risk of his own life to carry him back to the prison hospital. There the 14th Armored Division found him when it succeeded in freeing the camp on April 6.

An officer-companion of Colonel Waters in prison told friends on his arrival in the United States, after his liberation: "We're more concerned with how the people at home feel about the Germans than anything else right now. We hope they realize what has happened; that there must be a hard peace or we'll have another war, sure as shooting. Not many of us believed the atrocity stuff we heard while over there; that is, we didn't until we got a chance to see what the Germans had done."

This officer's attitude was a fair cross-section of the opinion of the men who had spent any time in German prison camps. They had all undergone the same sufferings: being forced to march hundreds of miles while afflicted with trench feet; hearing German doctors refuse to dress their wounds; lying in beds full of lice and bedbugs; subsisting on scanty rations of disgustingly inedible food; under constant threats of death for the slightest complaint. Bread and water twice daily were common fare on the forced marches from one camp to another. Brutal torture was no rarity.

T/4 Stanley Ruzycki of New York, during an 800-mile trek, attempted to trade a bar of soap to a German housewife for a piece of bread. Just as he got his hands on it, a guard who had crept up behind him smashed him in the back with a rifle butt. When Ruzycki asked the guard why he had struck him, the German crashed his fist into the prisoner's nose.

Six American fliers were clubbed to death by a dozen German civilians. These men had parachuted from a crippled plane and been captured. They were being taken, under a loose guard to a prison camp, when the men and women of the mob wrested them from their captors.

The Geneva Convention provides that prisoners, while they may be put to work at wages, must not be employed in war industries. The Germans violated this ban daily, exposing their captives to all the terrors of the Allies' merciless bombings of the German war machine. Other prisoners, spared from the risk of being bombed to death by their countrymen, were forced into slave labor in mines for as much as ten hours every day of every week, on a diet of bread and water—with a sauce of beatings with picks if they faltered at their work. One soldier whose desperate exhaustion forced him to lean on his shovel for a brief moment lost his thumb from the blow of a German worker's pick.

The big prison camp at Barth, on the Baltic, was liberated by the Russians, who found in it six thousand American fliers. Among them were two of the most famous aces of the American Air Forces, Lieutenant Colonel Francis S. Gabreski of Oil City, Pennsylvania, and Colonel Hubert Zemke of Missoula, Montana. Gabreski had thirty-one planes to his credit when he was shot down and captured, and Zemke, a group commander, had thirty and one half. Both corroborated the apparently endless stories of other prisoners who told of German atrocities.

It was impossible to ascribe these atrocities in greater measure to either civilians or soldiers; both groups were equally guilty, and the fliers from the eastern area had as many stories of civilian murders of captives as did those in the west.

About a week after the German surrender thirteen hundred prisoners liberated by their compatriots sailed into New York Harbor. They brought the new password of American prisoners of war: "Six men on a loaf of bread."

One man, who had weighed two hundred and fifty pounds when he was captured, weighed one hundred and fifty on his arrival in the United States. He was swearing as he pulled out a copy of an American magazine distributed aboard the ship that brought him home. It contained a picture of American girls shaking hands with captured Germans at a railway station. The soldier was literally dazed. It was quite unnecessary to ask these men what they thought of fraternization rules.

Another of the men in this detachment had a story of diet under the Germans. Day after day he and his companions had lived on sour soup until they could no longer get it down; finally they were driven by hunger to killing and eating cats. They described battling among themselves over stray potato peelings to accompany their meat. Others told of beatings with rubber hose. All this took place at Bad Orb.

The Germans not only forbade their own doctors to attend the ill or wounded captives but apparently interdicted aid from captured medical men. Despite incredible handicaps, American, British, French, Dutch and other imprisoned doctors and medical corpsmen did all they could to help their comrades. Lieutenant Arthur Wigeland of New York, who spent three months in the Limburg camp, declared that for two of these doctors, Major Henry S. Huber of New York and Captain George Gallup of Los Angeles, there could never be sufficient reward.

Night after night, he said, the two captured medical officers went without sleep to minister to the other prisoners. They were clever and resourceful as well as merciful. From a worn-out rubber tube and a German beer mug they improvised blood-transfusion apparatus. They operated by flashlight when air raids blacked out their impromptu hospital.

Naturally enough, the first concern of every liberated prisoner was to return home. Whenever possible they were flown out of Germany to hospitals and rest centers in France and Britain by heavy bombers, light bombers, and observation planes. Ships waited day and night in European ports to receive and bring them to the United States. Airdromes were crowded with planes to augment the homeward flow of fighting men.

Six men who had never met before the end of the war held a macabre introduction meeting in New York. Each of them had occupied the same cell in a Budapest prison to which, at various times, all had been taken after having been shot down during aërial attacks on the Hungarian capital.

The first man, who had been captured in July of 1944, had scrawled on the wall of the cell: "Meet me in the Plantation Room of the Hotel Dixie in New York at 6:00 P.M. on June 26, 1945." The message bore no salutation: it was addressed to anyone who might follow him in the cell.

Punctually at the appointed time, six fliers—all strangers to one another—met in the hotel. The seventh, who could not make it, was the unknown host—a staff sergeant named Evans who had left the message in the Budapest cell.

The liberation of war-prisoners and concentration camps in Germany resulted in the freeing of many world-renowned personalities. Among them was Mrs. Gemma Gluck, the sister of Mayor LaGuardia of New York, who had married a Hungarian and lived in Berlin until the Germans sent her and, later, her daughter and the latter's infant son also to the infamous concentration camp of Ravensbrueck.

In a raid into Russian-held German territory, the American Ninth Army liberated seventy French generals from the prison fortress of Koenigstein, as well as General H. J. Winkelman, the Commander in Chief of the Netherlands' forces at the time of their defeat. Most of his staff were liberated with him. East of Salzburg, Austria, the Seventh Army freed King Leopold III of Belgium and his family; the Fifth Army, in another area of Austria, struck the chains of bondage from a whole host of European notables including Leon Blum and Edouard Daladier, former Premiers of France. Liberated prisoners included also former Premier Paul Reynaud; General Maurice-Gustave Gamelin, Commander in Chief of the Allied armies in the first months of the war, and Lieutenant General Tadeusz Komorowski, the mysterious "General Bor" who had led the gallant but futile Warsaw uprising for sixty-three days in 1944.

The released prisoners were not all of the same stripe, however. They included on the one hand Michel Clemenceau, a son of "The Tiger" of the First World War, and on the other hand Colonel François de la Rocque, head of the French Fascist group called the *Croix de Feu*. They included also Germans who had incurred the displeasure of their whilom colleagues. Among these men were many well-known names, such as Dr. Hjalmar Schacht, the financial wizard who had headed the Reichsbank, and the Rev. Martin Niemoeller, the far-famed "anti-Nazi" Lutheran pastor.

Others released from this same prison, the Castle of Itter, included a veteran French Labor leader, Leon Jouhaux, for many years head of the General Confederation of Labor; a sister of General de Gaulle; and Dr. Kurt Schuschnigg, the last Chancellor of Austria, with the beautiful wife he had married in prison, Countess Vera Fugger.

The existence of the prison was disclosed by an inmate who escaped to send word of its location to the Allies. Jean Borotra, the French tennis ace, who was soon to find himself back in a cell but this time in Paris. Among his companions in Itter were Lieutenant Viscount George Henry Lascelles, a nephew of King George VI of Britain; Captain Lord John Buller Fullerton-Elphinstone, Queen Elizabeth's nephew; Captain George Alexander, Earl of Haig and son of the brilliant field Marshal of the First World War; Lieutenant Charles William, Earl of Hopetoun and son of the Marquess of Linlithgow; Lieutenant Felix du Hamel, a relative of Prime Minister Churchill, and General Maxime Weygand, who had succeeded Gamelin as Commander in Chief of the Allied armies in 1940 and who was, like Borotra, to return to jail in France in the future.

In Germany, too, the Allies found and freed thousands of the hapless, anonymous civilians whom the Germans had hurled into their mass butcher shops at Dachau, Buchenwald, Belsen, and Luckenwalde. Many of these were Russians whom the Allies liberated at once; but there was nothing to do with them until the Russian Government could arrange for their repatriation.

For a while they were left at liberty, but their random roamings were a constant hazard to military movements and a perpetual source of friction with the German civilians who had so long tortured them. The Allies were finally compelled to set up centers for them almost as if they were prisoners. These "prisoners" said they were receiving food and clothing in generous amounts and their only complaint was that they were not at home.

What the Americans found in the various concentration camps, large and small, sickened even the most calloused fighting man among the liberating troops. None of them had imagined that such brutality on the one hand, and such refinements of exquisite torture on the other, could exist anywhere in the civilized world in the twentieth century. In one camp east of Salzburg, for example, prisoners no longer strong enough to work were picked up from the place where they had fallen exhausted and, screaming feebly, were tossed alive into roaring furnaces.

All the horrors that war prisoners had experienced were mere trivia in the political prisons. The accounts that follow have been vouched for by eyewitnesses who included prominent editors and publishers of the United States, invited by General Eisenhower, with a group of Congressmen, to see the savagery for themselves. They are also vouched for by such generals as Eisenhower, Bradley, Simpson, Patton, and many others.

Army movies taken on the spot are silent witnesses. The Germans themselves professed ignorance of the existence of such camps, even when the stench from their crematories hung over miles of the surrounding countryside.

Belsen, one of the worst of these torture houses, was among the first to be overrun. Soldiers of the British Second Army could not believe the things they saw there, but, having seen them, could not disbelieve the terrible tales they heard from the victims who had survived the holocaust.

Josef Kramer, the Élite Guard commander of the camp, had graduated tortures. Naked men and women were forced to parade for hours in winter rains; other prisoners, fully clothed, were turned into locked compounds with vicious dogs, made half-wild by deliberate starvation. Vivisection on prisoners was common. Women were flogged on their breasts. Men and women alike were lashed on the sensitive soles of their feet. Attractive women were compelled to submit to the lovemaking of their captors.

There were 29,000 living prisoners in the camp at Belsen when the British took it. The number of dead was unknown. The survivors were suffering from typhus, typhoid, tuberculosis, and starvation. Vast mounds of unburied corpses lay everywhere, stripped of their clothing and valuables. In the nearby town, everyone was eating far better than the civilians of France and Britain; in the prison itself there were piles of untouched Red Cross packages that the authorities had deliberately sequestered.

Kramer, the ringmaster of this gruesome circus, had served his apprenticeship at Oswiecim in Poland. In Belsen, Kramer kept an orchestra to play him Viennese music while he watched children torn from their mothers to be burned alive. Gas chambers disposed of thousands of persons daily. Prisoners were starved first as a punishment, then as a sport. SS women under his command would tie a living prisoner to a dead one and chain both to a pyre of slow-burning materials.

When this practice and the cremations were cut short by the lack of fuel, the bodies were piled on the grounds and occasionally buried in huge pits. At Gardelegen the fuel shortage was overcome by the simple expedient of herding a thousand or more prisoners into an old building soaked with gasoline and setting it afire while guards were stationed outside to machine gun any who might succeed in making their escape from the flames.

Buchenwald was also a hellhole of diabolic torture. Soon after its capture, SHAEF sent its own inspectors to report on the German camp. They described it an an "extermination factory." In addition to all the horrors of Belsen, the Buchenwald directorate practiced murder by toxin, using the prisoners for all kinds of chemical experiments. The guinea pigs in these experiments were largely the best brains of Europe —scientists, writers, statesmen, and other leaders from every country of the Continent.

SHAEF's inspectors confirmed the often-published story that SS personnel at Buchenwald kept tanned human skin as souvenirs.

It was known definitely that at least 51,000 people had died in the camp. The "parchment" practice—the collection of tanned skins—was initiated by the twenty-eight-year-old wife of the prison's commander. She was an ardent athlete with a terrible mania for tattoos. Whenever a prisoner with unusual markings was brought in, she ordered the art-work removed from his body. Many of her trophies she had made into lampshades.

A five-hour roll-call starting at 3:00 A.M. was commonplace. Recalcitrant prisoners, on winter mornings, were made to stand under hoses for hours. Or they would be tied naked to stakes and covered with honey and jam before a hive of bees was thrown on them. Bodies and parts of bodies of victims were kept in a museum for the delectation and study of their masters.

The late Harold Denny of *The New York Times* visited the camp shortly after its liberation. A veteran of two wars and a man who had traveled all over the world, Mr. Denny was not given to credulity or naïveté. Yet he found himself compelled to say: "I had not intended to write about Buchenwald, for some correspondents wrote about it when our troops first took it. By nature I am cautious about atrocity stories, and I merely wanted first-hand knowledge so that, if anyone ever asked me about German concentration camps, I could tell him the unexaggerated truth.

"What I saw was so horrible that I would not have believed it if I had not seen it myself.... The world must not forget such things. Here I saw with my own eyes enough to confirm every hideous story I have ever doubted about German concentration camps."

Mr. Denny told of the death house where hangings were conducted. A multiple gibbet faced a rustic settee where the SS boys could sit and sip their wine while they watched the "inferior races" strangle.

There was also a chute down which Jewish prisoners were dumped. At the bottom stood two SS men: one clubbed the victim while the other slipped a noose over his head. Then he was dragged to a large elevator. There were other punishments, said Mr. Denny, "so depraved and so obscene that I could never tell them except to other men in whispers." One thing is certain: the worst savagery of the Japanese has its peer in these German camps.

A British White Paper listed many more practices that combined the ultimate refinements of physical and mental torture. We have not space to list them here, but it was small wonder that so many of the inmates who survived the rigors of Buchenwald will round out their lives in asylums for the insane.

The oldest and best known of the German concentration camps was that of Dachau, near Munich, the birthplace of the Nazi party. It shared the common or basic characteristics of the others mentioned, but it specialized in medical experiments, as the Germans called them—such as injection with viruses of malaria and typhoid.

It experimented with the blood coagulation test, in which veins and arteries were slashed open. There was also the endurance test in which a man was dropped into a salt-filled cistern for a test of his clothing. An iron collar filled with a freezing apparatus held his head immobile and his hands were chained. First the water was gradually chilled to see how long the victim could remain conscious; then the fastest revival techniques would be tested. The victim would be lifted out of the cistern, unconscious, stripped and plunged at once into a tub of hot water. Or he would be left in a room of normal temperature to await revival or death, depending upon his constitution. The long roster of incredible horror continues.

At times the victim was left naked outdoors on a cold night to see how well he stood the ordeal. From this the scientists of Dachau went on to the air-pressure experiments, designed to produce what divers know as the "bends." In these the victim was kept in an iron box in which the air pressure was controlled, sometimes being increased to such a degree that the man would try to pull out his own hair in an effort to relieve the pressure on his head.

As in Buchenwald, human skin was a prized trophy among guards and their wives, many of whom liked manskin gloves and shoes. Castration was also a commonplace among the men of thirty-four nations who lived in the Bavarian prison.

It was small wonder, then, that the inmates turned on the guards when the Americans attacked the prison. The prisoners, of course, had no weapons in the beginning; but, spurred to superhuman efforts by the approach of freedom, they banded together and attacked their keepers with their bare hands, beating them to pulpy death. From these first victims they were able to seize guns and knives and clubs. This was really an accident; for Himmler himself had ordered that, when the Americans approached, every inmate was to be slain because the liberated prisoners of Buchenwald "behaved barbarously to the civil population."

When the battle for the prison ended, the Americans found a railway siding on which were thirty-nine freight cars loaded with the bodies of inmates. They were exposed to the weather and apparently there was no hurry about hauling them off. For once, however, the vaunted and justly praised German efficiency that marked every other aspect of the administration of the German camps and the executions of their intricate tortures, was found wanting. By some mischance, some slip-up in that perfect functioning, one of these carloads of death contained a man who still breathed. Undoubtedly he would not have continued to do so much longer.

The records of the War Crimes Courts will reveal the sworn testimony of thousands of witnesses, and confessions of guilt. These official records will be studied by future generations as evidence of the complete moral bankruptcy of the Axis partners in crime.

WAR IN THE PACIFIC—
DECISIVE BATTLE FOR LEYTE GULF

WAR in the Pacific was rising toward its climax during the final months of the war in Europe. Leyte was the "key to the Philippines" in the brilliant strategical plans of General MacArthur. It was the locked door which he planned to batter down on the road back to Luzon and the recapture of Manila. This strategy was further designed to throw the Japanese lords in Tokyo into confusion.

The far-flung thrusts of the Allied forces on sea, in the air, and on land in the Pacific in the final months of 1944 so confused the Japanese that they were in no position to offer a strong, coördinated defensive at any one point. Their mythical empire was evaporating before their eyes. There was nothing left for them to do but attempt a final stand on their innermost line of defense running down from the home islands through the Ryukyus and Formosa to the Philippines. Even the wily General Yamashita knew that he was being outwitted by MacArthur in the greatest and most daring "comeback" in history.

When General MacArthur led his troops onto the shores of Leyte, the American intention that had been screened by all this "razzle-dazzle" suddenly became crystal clear to the Tokyo leaders. Events have shown that they had a plan to meet the emergency, but its outline was so simple that the American commanders were able to figure it out in advance. When no Japanese submarines or surface craft appeared to challenge the Leyte invasion armada, when air opposition was weak and when the sizable enemy land forces offered only token resistance, there was no longer question that a "surprise" was in store for the Allies. Countermeasures were taken to meet this threat. Ranger infantry units that had seized the islands of Dinagat, Homonbon, and Suluan off Leyte's shores just before the invasion were in a position to keep the Surigao Strait under close observation. Submarines were posted at all strategic approaches to the inner Philippine waters.

The Japanese plan was gigantic in scope. It aimed, at one blow, to annihilate General MacArthur's invasion forces and to wipe out, or at least severely cripple, the United States Navy. The enemy plan of action was a duplicate of that which had worked so well off Savo Island exactly two years earlier. But he forgot that the United States Navy had grown since then, with a Third and a Fifth Fleet in action, either one of which alone was capable of taking on the whole Japanese Navy.

There was also a Seventh Fleet covering the invastion. Admiral Halsey took up a strategic position east of the Philippines, and through the marvel of the Fleet supply train, refueled and restocked without having to leave the scene of any possible action.

Early on the morning of October 23, before daylight, two of our submarine outposts flashed word to the invasion forces that a strong Japanese fleet was headed northeastward from the South China Sea into Philippine waters, between Palawan and the dangerous ground to the west. There were five battleships, ten heavy cruisers, one or two light cruisers, and about fifteen destroyers that greeted the lookouts on the submarines *Darter* and *Dace*. Undeterred by this tremendous show of force, the underwater craft attacked immediately after having sent the warning. Four torpedoes struck each of three heavy cruisers, sinking two and severely damaging the third. These were the first shots in the Battle for Leyte Gulf. The *Darter*, while maneuvering for another attack, grounded on a reef in the middle of the channel and had to be destroyed after her crew had been removed. The enemy forces scattered, to be picked up the next day by carrier planes in the Sulu Sea heading for the Mindanao Sea, between Mindanao, Negros, and Leyte.

During the same day other contacts with the enemy were reported in Mindoro Strait, south of Luzon, and off the mouth of Manila Bay, where the reporting submarine badly damaged a heavy cruiser. These early reports made it clear that at least two enemy naval forces were heading for battle; the Sulu Sea fleet became known as the Southern Force and the Mindoro Strait group, subsequently picked up in the Subuyan Sea, as the Central Force. There was but one exit from the Mindanao Sea into the Pacific for the Southern Force and that was through Surigao Strait, past our Leyte invasion fleet.

This much was known during the early daylight hours of October 24, and if the Japanese had not made the mistake of sending carrier planes to attack the American invasion fleet during that day, Admiral Halsey would not have learned until too late that there was a third enemy fleet, the Northern Force, somewhere in the offing. Neither the Southern nor the Central Force had shown any carriers; Admiral Halsey had to find out where they were. It was not located until so late in the day that nothing could be done in the way of attack upon the most powerful of the enemy forces spotted off Cape Engano, the northeastern tip of Luzon Island.

The battleships *Ise* and *Hyuga*, and four carriers, including one large ship of the Zuikaku class, two heavy and three light cruisers, and six destroyers were in the Northern Force. The battleships were equipped with flight decks. While the threat from this powerful force complicated the already complex problem, its early discovery proved to be the ruin of the Japanese Navy. The battle that was joined with

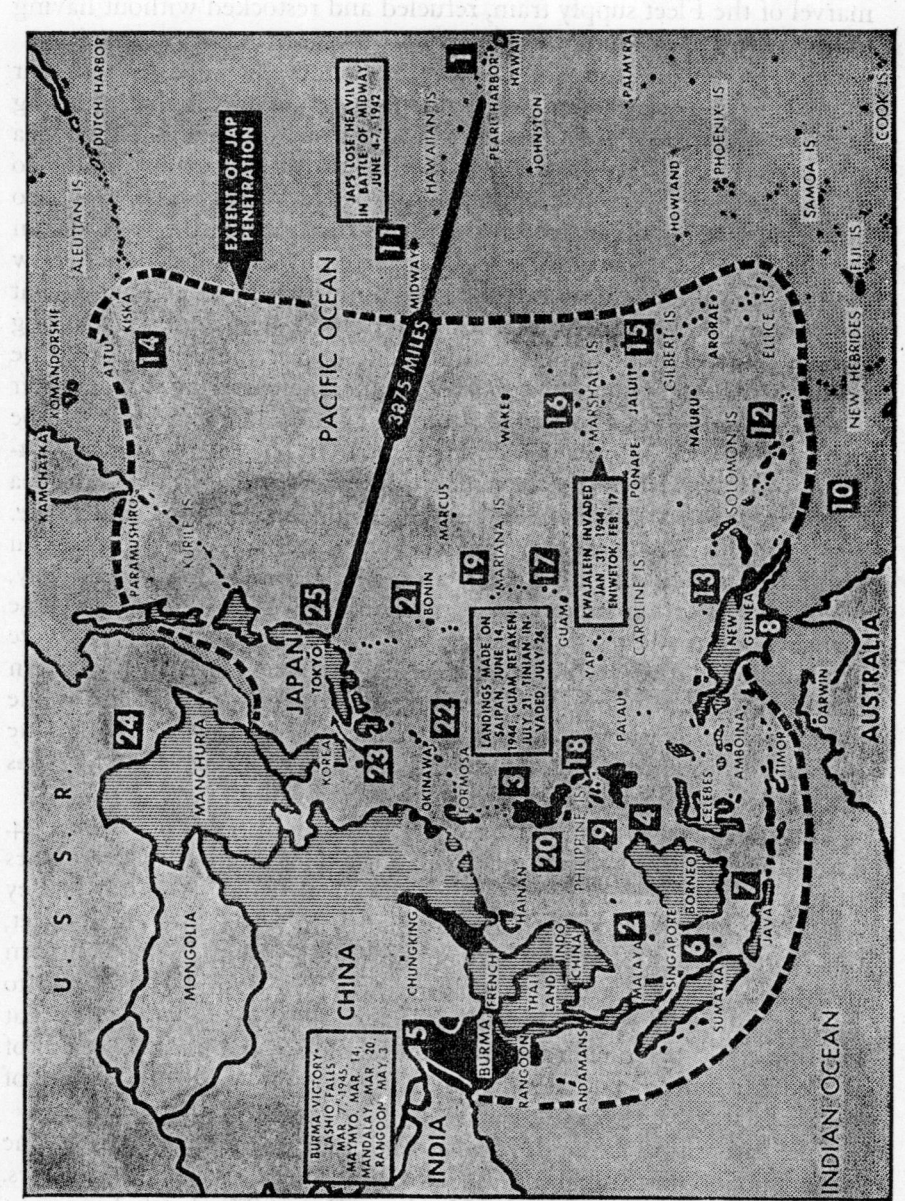

Map, International News

See legend on opposite page.

these three enemy forces approaching Leyte Gulf from three directions was fought in an arena covering 600 miles north and south and 250 east and west. The Navy officially divided the actions into The Battle of Surigao Strait (with the Southern Force), The Battle off Samar (with the Central Force) and The Battle off Cape Engano (with the Northern Force).

While carrier planes were lashing at the enemy's Southern and Central Forces on October 24, the enemy shot out with every land-based plane he could muster from the 100 or more airfields in the Philippines against the invasion ships that cluttered Leyte Gulf. At least 150 of the attacking aircraft were shot down, and, evidently in an attempt to keep the air strength at a maximum, the Japanese made their fatal error of throwing in some carrier planes. The American carrier *Princeton* was hit during the assault. Great fires started which spread to the magazines. Explosions soon wracked the 10,000-ton ship and she had to be abandoned.

Most of the men were saved, but casualties in wounded were heavy. The *Princeton* was the first carrier lost by the United States Navy since the *Hornet* was sunk in the Battle of Santa Cruz on October 26, 1942.

When his scouts reported the enemy's Northern Force about 200 miles off Cape Engano, Admiral Halsey was faced with the most difficult decision of his life. Should he take his Third Fleet north and go after the carriers, thus leaving the Seventh Fleet to its own devices, or remain with Admiral Kinkaid to help repel the Southern and Central Forces? Admiral Halsey decided on the former course, thus escaping being caught in a trap between the three enemy prongs.

Admiral Kinkaid's Seventh Fleet was close inshore in the narrow

---

Legend for opposite page.

TWENTY-FIVE HIGHLIGHTS—WAR WITH JAPAN

1941—(1) Dec. 7, Japanese planes attack Pearl Harbor. (2) Dec. 8, Malay Campaign launched by Japs. (3) Dec. 10, landings on Luzon. (4) Dec. 22, Borneo Invasion. 1942—(5) Jan. 19, conquest of Burma begun. (6) Feb. 15, Singapore falls. (7) Feb. 27, Allies routed in Battle of Java Sea. (8) Mar. 8, first Jap landings in New Guinea. (9) May 6, surrender of Corregidor. (10) May 4-8, Jap defeat, Battle of Coral Sea. (11) June 3-6, Japs turned back, Battle of Midway. (12) Aug. 7, American forces land on Guadalcanal. 1943—(13) Mar. 5, Japs routed in Battle of Bismarck Sea. (14) Aug. 15, Allied forces retake Kiska. (15) Nov. 20-24, Tarawa and Makin Islands recaptured. 1944—(16) Feb. 1, first Jap territory invaded at Kwajalein. (17) June 14, invasion of Marianas begun. (18) Oct. 20-26, landings on Leyte; Battle of Leyte Gulf. (19) Nov. 24, first B-29 raids from Marianas. 1945—(20) Jan. 9, American forces land on Luzon. (21) Feb. 17, landing on Iwo Jima. (22) April 1, invasion of Okinawa. (23) Aug. 6, first atomic bomb on Hiroshima. (24) Aug. 9, Russia invades Manchuria. (25) Aug. 11, Tokyo learns Allied answer to surrender offer.

waters of Leyte Gulf covering the invasion; Admiral Halsey's Third Fleet was farther to the north and standing east of Luzon to take care of any major enemy naval attack and to support the invasion by blows at Japanese airfields or by throwing in support against attacks on the Seventh Fleet.

The Northern Force, whose composition has been described, came down from Formosa and was passing east of Luzon to deliver the final blow—the annihilation of the Third Fleet.

Three enemy forces were approaching Leyte Gulf from three directions. A strong Central Force was driving east through the Sibuyan Sea. It consisted of five battleships: the new *Musashi*, pride of the Japanese Navy, her sister ship the *Yamato,* the *Nagato,* the *Haruna* and the *Kongo;* seven heavy and one light cruiser and from thirteen to fifteen destroyers. This force was supposed to sweep through San Bernardino Strait north of Samar, then turn south to attack the Seventh Fleet. The Japanese figured that Admiral Kinkaid would be too busy covering the invasion and protecting his own heavy old battleships and thin-skinned CVE escort carriers to offer much in the way of opposition.

Altogether, about seventy-five Japanese warships, not counting submarines, were coming to grips with the United States Navy, something that had been sought after for a long time. The enemy had four carriers, nine battleships, eleven to thirteen heavy cruisers, six or seven light cruisers, and about forty destroyers. The stage was set for the showdown.

During the evening of October 24, Rear Admiral Jesse B. Oldendorf deployed his forces for action to meet the Japanese Southern Force, little damaged by air attacks, as it passed from the Mindanao Sea into the narrow Surigao Strait and the Leyte Gulf. At 1:30 A.M. the enemy ran into an ambush of PT-boats which Admiral Oldendorf had stretched across the entrance to the Strait. The speedy little craft let fly with their torpedoes, catching the enemy completely by surprise and heavily damaging three ships before they were picked up by the searchlights of the attacking vessels. The PT's managed to launch two more attacks, although several had been hit, and flash the warning to Admiral Oldendorf who had stationed his ships from Hingatungan to Dinagat Island.

With their typical stubbornness, the Japanese, although they had been detected and no longer could hope to achieve surprise, kept boring straight ahead until they were picked up by destroyers on picket duty. The Japanese were advancing in two columns at about twenty knots to a point only about sixty miles from the Leyte beachhead, where the channel narrows down to a width of twelve miles passing Desolation Point. Rear Admiral Weyler's battleship squadron composed of the five old ships believed by the enemy to have been lost at Pearl Harbor, lay impatiently in the shadows. The rebuilt *West Virginia, Maryland, Tennessee, California,* and *Pennsylvania,* all modernized and more powerful than ever, withheld their fire as the destroyers attacked.

Three destroyer squadrons, first from the left and then from the right, rushed in, launched torpedoes, and then cut back out of the line of fire. The Japanese, unable to see in the darkness and stunned by the sudden ferocity of the assault, made the mistake of firing star shells to throw light on the subject. But the shells served only to illuminate the Japanese ships, making them easy targets for American gunners while their own guns continued to fire into the mysterious darkness, hitting nothing but water.

When the enemy force came to 16,000 yards, the battleships opened up with their 14- and 16-inch guns.

"Every damned salvo landed right on!" Admiral Oldendorf exclaimed.

The Japanese columns slowed down to twelve knots, hesitated, and finally tried to turn about and escape. But in doing so they gave Admiral Oldendorf the opportunity to realize the dream of every admiral: "Crossing the T." As each Japanese ship turned, it became a motionless, broadside target gleaming in the light of star shells and the fires burning on almost all enemy ships. For forty minutes the slaughter continued.

"We really gave them hell on the knuckle," Admiral Oldendorf said the next day in describing the battle.

He pursued the fleeing enemy remnants down the Strait. Of the two battleships, four cruisers, and nineteen destroyers that had sailed into Surigao Strait from the Mindanao Sea, all had been sunk except one battleship, a pair of cruisers, and about half a dozen destroyers. With daylight Rear Admiral Thomas L. Sprague's carrier planes caught the crippled battleship and cruisers and sank them all, adding a few destroyers for good measure. General Kenney's land-based bombers subsequently got more.

In this one-sided and complete victory, American losses were one PT-boat sunk and the destroyer *Albert W. Grant* severely damaged by gunfire. Not another ship was hit.

Quite another kind of story was in preparation to the north, where two factors combined to enable the enemy's Central Force to slip undetected through San Bernardino Strait. In the first place it had gone into retreat and was believed to have left the scene. Secondly, the sudden discovery of the Northern Force off Luzon pulled Admiral Halsey's Third Fleet carriers away, depriving the Sprague ships of much-needed reconnaissance and, more important, leaving them without any protection on sea or in the air beyond their own meager resources.

When the antisubmarine patrol discovered the enemy steaming down Samar's coast on the morning of the twenty-fifth it was too late to run or to receive aid. The escort carriers, with no armor and with 5-inch guns only, were silhouetted against the dawn and were brought under the heavy guns of the Japanese battleships and cruisers. The carriers, converted merchantmen, headed at their top speed into an east wind, launching their planes and attacking the enemy. As the destroyers laid down a smoke screen, the Wildcats braved wind, rain, and blanket antiaircraft fire and the torpedo-bombers pushed their attack in an effort to slow down the enemy. It was only a matter of time before the superior speed of the Japanese would overtake the Americans, and Admiral Kinkaid, receiving word of Admiral Sprague's plight, appealed to Admiral Halsey for immediate aid.

The American planes sank two cruisers and a pair of destroyers. The enemy was slowed, but not enough. By nine o'clock in the morning the first of the American escort carriers went to the bottom. She was the *Gambier Bay*. Twenty minutes later the Japanese were less than 12,000 yards away, pouring 16-, 14-, and 8-inch shells into Admiral Sprague's ships. An hour later swarms of enemy land-based planes joined the battle, and sank the escort carrier *Saint Lo*. The destroyers *Hoel* and *Johnston* and the destroyer escort *Roberts* went down under ships' guns, and the four remaining escort carriers—*Suwanee, Santee, White Plains,* and *Kitkun Bay*—were badly hit.

Then suddenly at noon, when all hope seemed lost, the Japanese, for some unaccountable reason, hauled away, gradually widening the distance and, to the astonishment of the battered Americans, broke off the battle with a final and harmless spread of torpedoes. As the enemy steamed north at high speed, oil trails slicked the waters from hulls that had been pierced. The Japanese admiral must have heard of the destruction of the Southern Force at Surigao Strait and realized that he must get back through San Bernardino Strait or face destruction from the American ships that had virtually annihilated the Japanese Southern Force.

Thirteen ships went into battle for Admiral Sprague; only eight came out, and all of them were much the worse for the experience. The *Hoel, Johnston, Roberts,* and *Gambier Bay* which went down under Japanese guns sacrificed themselves in a hopeless struggle that averted a highly probable disaster to the Seventh Fleet. The American naval forces that had just gone through the Surigao Strait battle were in no position to meet with full power a blow as strong as the Japanese Central Force was able to deliver, even though it had been reduced by more than one third in the successive encounters. No wonder Admiral Kinkaid signaled to Admiral Sprague:

"Your performance was one which could have been expected only from CV's." In other words, the little escort carriers performed a job that only the heavy fleet carriers would have been able to do.

In addition to the ships, the Seventh Fleet lost 105 planes, most of which went down with the carriers. Loss of life was not so great as might have been expected, for despite the harrowing realities of the air-sea battle the surviving ships picked hundreds of men out of the water.

Admiral Halsey had to make his second difficult decision in little more than twenty-four hours, when he received the emergency call to help the escort carriers off Samar.

During the night of October 24-25 the Third Fleet ran to the north and before dawn launched its planes to attack the enemy off Cape Engano. The Japanese were so completely surprised that they never were able to offer effective air opposition. The United States planes had a field day, striking almost at will throughout most of the daylight hours.

The *Zuikaku*-class carrier went down in flames, as did two of the smaller carriers. The remaining one was badly damaged. A cruiser was crippled in the first assault and two destroyers were sunk. While this was going on, Japanese planes came home from their foray, during which the carrier *Princeton* had been sunk and found no place to light. Twenty-one of these were shot down and the others probably plunged into the sea because of the lack of gasoline.

Later in the day American cruisers and destroyers came within range of the enemy, and altogether every single Japanese ship in the Northern Force had been sent to the bottom or was reeling from dangerous wounds, such as the dozen bomb and torpedo hits in the two battleships. In that day's work, which had to be called off before it was finished, the Third Fleet ships did not suffer a scratch; ten planes and eighteen men were lost.

The mopping up in the Battle for Leyte Gulf continued for several days, with land-based planes from the Southwest Pacific and the United States Fourteenth Air Force in China hunting down cripples and sinking many of the destroyers and cruisers that had escaped the main actions.

When the score sheet was finally tallied, it read like this: Japanese: Sunk—four carriers, three battleships, six heavy cruisers, two light cruisers, three light cruisers or large destroyers, six destroyers; believed sunk—three heavy cruisers, two light cruisers, seven destroyers; badly damaged—six battleships, four heavy cruisers, one light cruiser, and ten destroyers. This makes a total of fifty-seven Japanese ships hit, thirty-six of which were sunk or probably went to the bottom.

American: Sunk—one light carrier, two escort carriers, two destroyers, one destroyer escort; damaged—four escort carriers; a destroyer.

The navy, despite the continuing air searches, called the Battle for

Leyte Gulf over by the end of October 26, with the three enemy forces either destroyed or out of range. Admiral Mitscher declared that Japan had been left wide open by reduction of her navy to the status of a fifth-rate power.

After the shooting was over, Admiral Kinkaid declared: "The situation could have been desperate." Actually, it had been so—up to the time the enemy suddenly broke off the Battle off Samar. The Japanese had perfected an ambitious coup that came within a hairbreadth of success, at least to the extent of turning the Leyte invasion into a debacle for the Allies.

Three factors saved the day. The first was that the Japanese had been stripped of the element of surprise before it was too late. In the one instance off Samar where they regained surprise they let victory slip through their fingers. An integral part of the failure to catch the Third and Seventh Fleets unawares was the almost uncanny faculty the American admirals had of refusing to fall into a trap. Admiral Halsey thwarted the major trap by going out after the enemy Northern Force. Admiral Kinkaid refused to be bait in another trap by sending Admiral Oldendorf to Surigao Strait, where the latter turned the tables on the Japanese and caught them in a trap of their own fashioning.

The enemy did not know at the time that the United States had sixteen battleships in the Pacific, including the newest and most powerful *Iowa* and *South Carolina*. There were three of the newest carriers, the *Lexington,* the *Wasp,* and the *Hornet,* all bearing honored names.

Finally, there was the factor of American fighting spirit, a spirit that dared to attack and to die even with all the odds against success. The courageous crews of the little PT-boats in Surigao Strait made it possible for Admiral Oldendorf to bottle up the Japanese there. The daring of Admiral Sprague's men held off the enemy until complete victory, at best, was denied to him.

The Battle for Leyte Gulf was more than a tremendous American victory. It exerted a powerful effect upon Japanese morale. The enemy clearly had planned to permit General MacArthur to commit 250,000 men and vast supplies on Leyte before attempting to wipe him out. Such a stroke would not have averted Japanese defeat, but it would have prolonged the war for many months, if not years. Tokyo had prepared the people for this astounding victory plus a stinging defeat to the American Navy. Instead of the expected triumph, the battle proved to be the elimination of Japan as a naval power, and enabled General MacArthur so to fortify himself on Leyte that the conquest of the Philippines was assured.

The highly emotional Japanese were unable to swallow this double defeat and its disillusionment. A defeatist attitude crept into civilian morale and spread even to high-ranking officials. When the news filtered through to the embattled Japanese garrisons on various island strongholds, doubts began to creep into their minds too. We have seen how the enemy soldiers refused to surrender anywhere, preferring to die in suicide charges or by their own hand. After the Battle for Leyte Gulf this situation began to change, slowly, but clearly, and in six or eight months Japanese soldiers were surrendering not only individually, but in companies and battalions.

Defeat first became a realization to the Japanese with the Battle for Leyte Gulf. The sledge-hammer blows of the oncoming MacArthur had the amazed Yamashita staggering in his tracks. In two months the carrier planes of the Third and Seventh Fleets had sunk 653 Japanese ships in addition to the warships sent down in the Battle for Leyte Gulf, and had shot down over the Philippine area 2,594 enemy planes with damage to 252 more. All this was achieved at a cost of about 300 American aircraft. The most liberal estimate of Japan's plane-building capacity was 1,500 a month, so that the bombers and fighters from the two fleets alone had exacted a toll about equaling the enemy's ability to replace losses. Beyond that, General Kenney's airmen were destroying hundreds more, the Fourteenth Air Force in China, the Tenth in Burma, and antiaircraft gunners on ships contributed still further to the enemy's losses.

Speed was vital. General MacArthur nailed down his hold on most of Leyte during the decisive sea battles, but from the Allied viewpoint it was essential to knock out all Japanese air strength in the area before the show-down fight on land. The enemy was faced with the problem of rushing belatedly reinforcements for the inevitable battle.

Within a week of the Battle for Leyte Gulf the Japanese began to strip their garrisons on Luzon, Mindanao, Cebu, and other islands for action on Leyte. The Americans overwhelmed Carigara on the north coast, held the entire east coast, and captured Baybay on the southwest coast. The only sizable port open to the enemy was Ormoc, at the head of Ormoc Bay, about twenty miles northwest of Baybay. General Yamashita was rapidly withdrawing his troops from the north and east for a final stand. He began to land fresh troops and supplies at Ormoc, putting 35,000 men ashore in less than a week. This enabled General MacArthur to wipe out the enemy piecemeal while bringing about a tremendous reduction of the forces left to defend the other Philippine islands.

The enemy port of Ormoc was being hemmed in, but General Yamashita continued to funnel in more troops. Among them were the notorious First and Eighth Infantry Divisions from Manchuria, powerful units of the Kwangtung Army that had ruled the conquered country with an iron hand. Japanese troops and tanks began to pile up in the narrow Ormoc pocket and the American pincers began to develop. Heavy rains and typhoon winds contributed to the period of pause during which both sides prepared for final action.

Part of the fast carrier force retired to fuel and reprovision at forward bases after the Battle for Leyte Gulf, but the rest remained in the invasion area under Vice Admiral J. S. McCain. By November 2 the enemy was able to launch a strong attack against Third Fleet carriers. Several ships were damaged, but the fighting strength remained unimpaired.

Then the Americans took the initiative back into their own hands. The Third Fleet struck suddenly and savagely at the Manila area on November 5 and 6 to score a new record for damage done. Airfields, harbors, and storage areas were lashed unmercifully, and carrier planes left their targets a mass of wreckage.

During the two days 440 enemy aircraft had been destroyed; 327 had been caught on the ground on the Manila network of airfields—Nichols, Clark, Nielson, Lipa, Tarlac, Bamban, and Mabalacat—and 113 had been shot out of the air. There were not enough Japanese planes left whole after the first day for more than a score to rise on November 6. Hangars were demolished, fuel storage went up in great billows of smoke and flames, nothing was left of runways. Fighters, torpedo planes, and dive bombers sank a cruiser, a destroyer, a destroyer escort, a submarine chaser, an oiler, two transports, and a freighter and so heavily damaged forty-four other ships that most of them probably went to the bottom. Railroads were torn to shreds and rolling stock was demolished.

Plans for future operations combined with considerations of protection for the fleet and the Leyte forces to make it essential that the Luzon and other airfields be laid low once and for all. A carefully integrated schedule had been worked out between General Kenney's land-based planes and those from the carriers to attain this end. The work of the former group seemed mere routine, but it ran up a high record of enemy aircraft destroyed and airfields neutralized. The activities of the Third Fleet were more sensational because of the tremendous power its planes were able to deliver at one stroke as well as the unexpectedness of their furious assaults.

The carrier planes struck Luzon again on November 13 and 14 for another two-day blow, adding the naval installations of Cavite to the usual shipping and airfield targets. Three transports, three destroyers, and three freighters were sunk, a light cruiser and forty-five other ships were badly damaged, a floating dry dock was torpedoed and eighty-four more planes were destroyed. More than one hundred aircraft caught on the ground were severely mauled. Another air attack was launched on Luzon targets on November 19. There was so little air opposition left that only sixteen planes took to the sky, and they were all shot down, but one hundred others were destroyed on the ground. A feeble attempt to retaliate by striking the Fleet cost the enemy eight more planes. Few shipping targets could be located, so that the only damage in this category was a freighter and two small craft sunk and thirteen ships damaged.

Luzon received its fifth carrier strike in three weeks, and the last in support of the Leyte invasion, on November 25. This time twenty ships were sunk, including a light cruiser, a destroyer escort, and a mine layer, and twenty-eight were damaged; 119 Japanese planes were destroyed or damaged, of which twenty-five were shot down over the target, thirty-two were destroyed on the ground and thirty-one more were popped out of the sky when a heavier-than-usual attack was launched against the carriers.

During all these November strikes the Third Fleet carriers sustained a total combat loss of ninety-seven planes.

These Luzon attacks were only part of the tactical picture. The Japanese had suffered an estimated loss of 30,000 of the original 35,000 men on Leyte by the end of the first week in November, but they had been able to land 35,000 more men. General Yamashita, a resourceful, capable, and determined commander, sent his men into attack as quickly as they landed. They were of the fanatical breed that preferred death to surrender, and while the attacks accomplished little more than slowing down of the American advance, they did exact a toll of casualties. Field Marshal Count Juichi Terauchi, Commander in Chief of Japanese forces in the southern regions, which included the Philippines, had led the enemy forces during the first weeks of the Leyte invasion. When they lost the Battle for Leyte Gulf, the Japanese superseded him with General Tomoyuki Yamashita, who had led the enemy drive on Bataan in 1942 and had captured Corregidor. MacArthur and Yamashita were face to face again.

A sudden push brought the American lines so close to Ormoc that it was possible to hold the entire enemy-occupied area under artillery fire, thus setting the scene for the next to the last stage. Ormoc was set afire, causing confusion in the enemy camp, and then the first of a series of hammer strokes began to fall on the trapped enemy.

American planes picked up a Japanese convoy of four transports and fifteen destroyers headed for Ormoc on November 9. The next day army and navy aircraft, together with PT-boats, attacked in force, sinking three of the transports and seven destroyers. The bodies of dead Japanese littered the surface of Ormoc Bay as ships blew up and sank in thirty seconds. The convoy had been able to unload part of its men and cargo before the attack, which was waged under heavy antiaircraft fire and vicious battles in the sky.

All through November the attacks against convoys continued, and the battle of American planes against Japanese ships saw its final big encounter on the twenty-ninth, when thirteen ships, including three destroyers, were sunk. Only two cargo ships in that convoy succeeded in reaching Ormoc. Six convoys, totaling twenty-six transports aggregating 92,750 tons, and seventeen destroyers had been sunk during the month. Nearly 25,000 Japanese troops intended for combat on land were drowned. Yamashita had been denied the strength he so sorely needed.

Determined Americans, slogging through mud that often reached their knees, had compressed the Japanese into what came to be known as the Ormoc pocket. It was at Limon, along the Leyte River in the north, that the enemy intended to make his strongest stand, but after two weeks of preparation in the rain the Americans suddenly lunged forward and turned the northern anchor of the Yamashita Line, virtually wiping out the entire Japanese First Division. The United States Thirty-second Infantry Division then began the hard work of rooting the Japanese out of their pillboxes in the mountains and liquidating enemy snipers in the push down toward Ormoc while the Seventh and Seventy-seventh went to work on the bulge.

Despite his terrific losses, the enemy continued to send reinforcements toward Ormoc. Thunderbolts, operating from repaired airfields on Leyte, skip-bombed another convoy to destruction, raising the Japanese losses in this respect to 26,000 men and 103,750 tons of shipping. American warships steamed into Ormoc Bay to shell that enemy-held port.

While this was going on, the Allied command took time and men to seize, against only light opposition, the Mapia Islands, also known as the St. David Islands, a cluster of small coral atolls off the coast of New Guinea and about 145 miles north of Biak. This capture put out the Japanese eyes for observation of Allied movements and deprived them of a weather and radio station. A few days later an American amphibious operation commanded for the first time by a British naval officer (Captain Lord Ashbourne, a veteran of the Sicily landings in the Mediterranean) further cleaned up the area by occupying the Asia Islands, 130 miles north of Sorong, off New Guinea.

The Japanese opened a series of fruitless suicide attacks on Leyte at the beginning of December, but American tanks that seemed to sail through the ooze, and infantrymen armed with bazookas stopped all attempts to break out of the rapidly closing and ever narrowing trap. Allied naval forces continued to bombard Ormoc, despite a mounting toll of ship losses as the enemy threw in every plane he could muster and the action everywhere grew more furious. The enemy sent about two hundred parachutists behind the American lines at San Pablo near Leyte Gulf in a desperate attempt at diversion. They managed to do some damage by sabotage to airfield installations and communications before they were finally wiped out in a rough and tumble scramble.

The Seventh Division, victors of Attu and Kwajalein, forced the Palana River at two points, one near the sea and the other near Ormoc, to cut the enemy's line.

On December 7, the third anniversary of Pearl Harbor, the United States Navy lifted the Army out of Leyte's mud and, on an end run through Surigao Strait, landed the 77th Division, liberators of Guam, three miles south of Ormoc to split the Japanese forces and to seal off Ormoc Bay. Bitter fighting raged before a beachhead was secured. The landing set off a mighty day-long battle in which the Japanese so heavily damaged the destroyer *Mahan* and the destroyer-transport *Ward* by aërial torpedoes that they had to be sunk. Earlier the enemy had sent the destroyers *Cooper* and *Reid* to the bottom. Nearly seventy-five enemy planes were shot down during the day, but perhaps the juiciest trophy was the annihilation of a thirteen-ship Japanese convoy making for Ormoc, which was so surprised by the American invasion that it sailed right under the guns of Rear Admiral A. D. Struble's warships.

The landings marked the beginning of the end for the Japanese on Leyte. General MacArthur said: "By this maneuver we have seized the center of the Yamashita Line from the rear and have split the enemy's forces in two, isolating those in the valley to the north from those along the coast to the south. Both segments are now caught between our columns, which are pressing in from all fronts."

For several weeks the struggle had been proceeding on Leyte. Desperate as was the Japanese attempt to defeat the Allied intention to seize this cornerstone of the Philippines, it was the weather rather than the enemy that had prolonged the fighting. Mud and rain not only had bogged down the infantry and the tanks but had delayed development of land-based air power so essential to an invading army. Japanese infiltration tactics had been successfully countered by General Krueger, who had ordered his own men to counter-infiltrate the enemy's positions and then follow up with attacks, even if local. Thus, despite all handicaps, the eighth week found the Japanese dug in strongly in a small area, with the end in sight.

After a day of fighting the 77th Division had advanced two miles over rice paddies and was within one mile of Ormoc. Stunned by the suddenness of the bold invasion, the enemy could only react by trying to send in more troops, using barges and other small craft, most of which were sunk. Although the torrential rains continued, the Japanese were pushed steadily back.

On December 10, the fourth day of the invasion, the 77th Division captured Ormoc and provided an anvil against which the 7th Division below it could smash the enemy with hammer strokes. The enemy was caught in a tight trap when the two forces joined and the southern end of the Yamashita Line was broken. The 10th Corps was battering its way down against the northern end of the Line through mountain defiles. The Ormoc garrison had been wiped out to the last man in the most bitter fighting on Leyte.

Still the Japanese sent convoys to Leyte. A furious, two-day sea and air battle on December 11 and 12 sank or damaged twelve more ships, and planes picked off another dozen in separate attacks. The Japanese countered with an air blow at our retiring invasion force from Ormoc, inflicting slight damage but losing more than fifty planes in all encounters. Then the Third Fleet sent its carrier craft over Luzon again, destroying 225 Japanese planes, damaging 100 others, and raising havoc with shipping and ground installations. Every airfield on Luzon had been hit as well as every major port.

A new name began to creep into the communiqués issued by Admiral Nimitz. For several weeks his land-based planes from the Strategic Air Force, Pacific Ocean areas, had been blasting airfields on Iwo Island, in the volcano group between Saipan and Japan.

Another surprise caught the enemy on December 15 when, in his most daring move, General MacArthur by-passed most of the enemy-held Philippines, ignored hostile planes, and landed an invasion force on the island of Mindoro, 155 miles south of Manila. The Japanese, who had been expecting the next invasion to land on Cebu, southwest of Leyte, offered no opposition, and not an American life was lost in establishing the beachhead.

Guerrillas had seized much territory on Mindoro and held many towns and airfields so that the new liberation, which was out of the typhoon belt, meant a great deal in the strategic picture. The Americans landed quickly. Within an hour and a half they drove more than a mile inland and set up artillery and antiaircraft guns. Brigadier General William C. Dunckel led the troops ashore despite the fact that he had been wounded in the head and arm by bomb fragments during a Japanese attack on the ship in which he was sailing to Mindoro.

The Mindoro invasion proceeded rapidly from the landing point at San Jose. At one stroke, General MacArthur said, the Americans had "driven a corridor from east to west through the Philippine Archipelago, which is now definitely cut in two, and will enable us to dominate the sea and air routes which reach the China coast." There was virtually no ground opposition, as the Japanese had stripped the Mindoro garrisons to pour down the funnel on Leyte. In three days the Americans held a strip of the coast eleven miles deep; three days after that, planes were operating from captured airfields that had been improved for defense and for attack on Luzon.

"The Leyte-Samar campaign can now be regarded as closed, except for minor mopping-up operations," General MacArthur said in his communiqué of December 26, adding that General Yamashita had suffered "perhaps the greatest defeat in the military annals of the Japanese Army."

The enemy lost 125,000 men, all but about 500 prisoners killed. American casualties were about 2,750 killed and 8,500 wounded and missing. During the period of the invasion, the Japanese lost close to 3,000 planes, far more than they could replace.

Coincident with the Leyte-Samar victory, word came from Washington that General MacArthur had been promoted to the new rank of General of the Army, entitled to wear five stars arranged in a circle. A Filipino goldsmith hurriedly collected some native gold coins and hammered them into the stars with which the General appeared. At the same time Admiral Nimitz was elevated to the corresponding rank of Fleet Admiral, and he celebrated by sending his ships to shell Iwo for the third time in December.

While the Seventh Fleet was carrying the troops to Mindoro, disaster struck the Third Fleet in the form of a particularly fierce typhoon. How any of the ships caught in the ferocious storm survived will remain a mystery, but the main body of the fleet escaped. The destroyers *Hull, Spence,* and *Monaghan* were lost, on December 17, with heavy casualties.

Americans on Mindoro were experiencing little opposition on land or from the air, but suddenly, on the night of December 26, a Japanese naval task force—consisting of a battleship, a heavy cruiser, and six destroyers—appeared off the beachhead and started to lob shells into the American positions. The battleship was hit with two bombs from a navy Liberator and a destroyer was sunk. PT-boats dashed in and out launching torpedoes. Three more enemy ships were sunk and all they had to show for their efforts when the survivors turned around and went home was a shell furrow across an airfield runway when all the American planes were in the air. That was the last encounter of 1944 in the Philippines, except for the never-ending war in the air, during which one hundred and fifty enemy planes were destroyed on Clark Field alone.

The new year opened with wild Japanese reports of giant American convoys at sea. The Far Eastern Air Forces struck deeply, shooting down Japanese planes and hitting coastal steamers east and south of Formosa. It was the first time that Japanese island stronghold ever appeared in a MacArthur communiqué.

Luzon's west coast was swept by Philippine-based bombers and fighters again on January 1 and 2 and the attack was extended to the Subic Bay area of Manila.

During those first days of January three more landings were made. Store-to-shore hops had carried the Americans to Paluan, on Mindoro's northeast coast, and to another point on the east coast. Then, on the 3rd, General Krueger's Sixth Army swept ashore at Buenavista, on the small island of Marinduque, thirty miles northeast of Mindoro. The island was quickly conquered and the Americans were only ten miles from Luzon, across a narrow stretch of water, and one hundred from Manila.

The climax had now been reached. General MacArthur was about to strike the deathblow to Japanese ambitions.

"HOME AGAIN!" MacARTHUR AT LUZON —ENTERS MANILA IN TRIUMPH

PRESIDENT ROOSEVELT, realizing that the greatest drama in history was moving rapidly to its end, delivered these stirring words to Congress on January 6, 1945: "In the Pacific during the past year we have conducted the fastest-moving offensive in the history of modern warfare. We have driven the enemy back more than 3,000 miles across the central Pacific.

"A year ago, our conquest of Tarawa was a little more than a month old.

"A year ago, we were preparing for our invasion of Kwajalein, the second of our great strides across the central Pacific to the Philippines.

"A year ago, General MacArthur was still fighting in New Guinea, almost 1,500 miles from his present position in the Philippine Islands.

"We now have firmly established bases in the Marianas Islands from which our Superfortresses bomb Tokyo itself—and will continue to blast Japan in ever-increasing numbers.

"Japanese forces in the Philippines have been cut in two.

"The people of this nation have a right to be proud of the courage and fighting ability of the men in the armed forces—on all fronts. They also have a right to be proud of American leadership which has guided their sons into battle. The history of the generalship of this war has been a history of teamwork and coöperation, of skill and daring."

Every successive major landing in the Pacific had become bigger than its predecessor, involving more warships, transports, and troops as well as new techniques learned from the experiences of each landing. As we drew closer to Japan, full-scale psychological warfare was opened against the enemy. Powerful radio transmitters from Hawaii began regular broadcasts during the last week of December designed to whittle down Japanese civilian morale. With each new blow the Emperor's people were reminded that there was no longer any question that they would go down in defeat.

The United States Navy started the year 1945 with 61,045 vessels, including 1,167 warships and 54,206 landing craft. It had become the largest and most powerful navy in the world; during 1944 it had grown by 39,971 ships and 5,457,490 tons to a total of 11,707,000 tons afloat. It had twenty-three battleships, twenty-six large carriers, sixty escort carriers, sixty-three cruisers, 418 destroyers, and 496 destroyer escorts; there were 249 submarines. In addition to all this the navy during the year had acquired 30,070 new aircraft. Great Britain had sent two naval forces into the Pacific: the British Fleet under Admiral Sir Bruce A. Fraser and the East Indies Fleet under Admiral Sir Arthur J. Power.

It had not been an easy march up and across the Pacific. It had cost the Americans about 100,000 casualties. The army alone had suffered more than 15,000 killed, nearly 30,000 missing, and an equal number wounded; some 16,000 had been taken prisoner, most of them on Bataan and at Corregidor.

The mid-December carrier strikes on Manila Bay had led the enemy to expect further landings in that area. The Paluan invasion reinforced that idea.

Admiral McCain sent his Third Fleet carrier planes over Formosa, the Ryukyus, and the China coast on January 3 and 4. There was little airborne opposition as the American planes hit the Asiatic mainland for the first time in the war. Two days later the Manila Bay area was raked for forty-eight hours.

General MacArthur, however, did not oblige the Japanese by landing where they had expected him. Luzon, the largest of the Philippines, with an area roughly the size of Virginia, is generally mountainous, but is cut by two large valleys. The central plain from Lingayen Gulf to Manila Bay is about one hundred miles long and thirty to fifty wide, providing a broad corridor through the major concentrations of population and wealth to Manila; numerous airfields and a network of roads and railways, plus the fact that Lingayen was the most vulnerable part of the central plain, made it the most desirable invasion area.

While the Third Fleet planes were keeping the Japanese guessing, the Luzon Attack Force, commanded by Vice Admiral Kinkaid sailed through the Sulu and China Seas 850 ships strong and headed for Lingayen Gulf, about halfway up Luzon's western coast. This armada was divided into the Lingayen Attack Force under Vice Admiral Wilkinson and the San Fabian Attack Force under Vice Admiral Berbey with reinforcement, bombardment, and covering groups under Admirals Conolly, Oldendorf, Berkey, and C. T. Durgin. The landings were scheduled for January 9, one at Lingayen and the other at San Fabian, farther up the Gulf shore. General Krueger's Sixth Army piled ashore on time because of the courage and the determination of the navy to get the troops to their positions according to plan.

Never was a convoy under more continued or persistent attack. There was no enemy surface opposition on the long trip from Leyte, the one Japanese destroyer that put out from Manila Bay had been sunk before she got well started. But from 11:45 on the night of January 2, when enemy planes first picked up the armada, the ships were under almost constant air attack. Although shadowed day and night, although battling torpedoes, bombs, and machine-gun bullets, the

Americans managed to conceal their destination, feinting in the region of Batangas and other possible landing points on the shore, within sight of which the convoy always remained. The Lingayen Gulf assault caught the Japanese completely by surprise.

It was not until late in the afternoon of January 4, when the battleship *New Mexico* leading the armada was close to Manila Bay, that the enemy opened his attack in full force. What happened to the lead ship was typical of the rest of the journey. Gunners at antiaircraft stations kept most of the Japanese away but some managed to break through to inflict serious damage. The *New Mexico* and several other ships were hit. One bomb fell on the *New Mexico's* forward turret, damaging the bridge and starting fires that threatened to explode the ammunition. The *New Mexico* was scheduled to start bombarding the Lingayen shore the next morning, so all thought of flooding the turrets for protection was out of the question.

Three days before the invasion, on January 6, 1945, the armada steamed through the eighteen-mile entrance into Lingayen Gulf in the wake of mine sweepers and opened up the prodigious bombardment that knocked out coastal defenses and sent the enemy scurrying back into the hills for protection. On the bridge with Captain Robert W. Fleming were Admiral Fraser, watching a Pacific amphibious operation for the first time, and Lieutenant General William Lumsden, Prime Minister Churchill's personal representative.

A lone enemy bomber suddenly streaked through the antiaircraft defenses and let go with a missile that caught the already battered battleship on the starboard side of the flag bridge. Captain Fleming was badly wounded and had to be ejected forcibly from his station by Commander John T. Warren, who took over the ship and directed the work of restricting the damage. General Lumsden was killed outright, and Admiral Fraser barely escaped. Captain Fleming died a short time later. Twenty-nine others on the ship were killed and scores were wounded. But the *New Mexico* kept her place in line, and continued to mete out punishment to the Japanese for five days before turning back to Pearl Harbor for repairs. The cruiser on which General MacArthur and his staff were proceeding barely escaped a pair of aërial torpedoes.

Not a shore battery fired as the hundreds of landing craft brought General Krueger's Sixth Army to four beaches extending fifteen miles north and east from Lingayen. A little mortar fire was quickly silenced, and by the end of the first day the Americans had driven an average of four miles inland to capture Lingayen and its airstrip, Dagupan, railhead of the line to Manila, 105 miles away, Mangaldan, and San Fabian. Little opposition was encountered on land as the troops pushed steadily down toward Manila and started a flanking operation to cut through the Zambales Mountains to Infanta on Dasol Bay at the opposite side of Lingayen Peninsula.

Enemy planes, however, kept up their pounding, midget submarines tried to pick off an occasional American ship, and the Japanese sent suicide swimmers shoving small boxes of TNT in fruitless attempts to sink at least a part of the 2,500,000 tons of shipping in the Gulf. Three days after the landings the enemy sent a forty-six ship convoy into San Fernando, north of the American beachheads, in an attempt to reinforce his garrisons; but light naval craft ever on the alert swooped down, sank or heavily damaged all the ships, shelled the port, and retired without a scratch.

After a week of fighting, with enemy opposition still futile and inept, the situation stood as follows:

On the right wing the Americans had enveloped Alaminos and had established an unbroken line almost thirty-five miles long running southeast beyond Camiling; the other side of the spearhead which had reached to within seventy-five miles of Manila, was at Moncada; the line then wove in and out back to Damortis on the Lingayen Gulf, with every important rail and road line cut one or more times. The only real resistance was encountered on the left flank in the neighborhood of Rosario. The beachhead base had been widened to nearly fifty miles. The captured Lingayen airfield was flying American planes which were pounding Japanese positions ahead of the troops.

The navy continued to throw in supporting blows, and thrust deeply into waters the Japanese had always considered their own. The Third Fleet sailed through 3,800 miles of the South China Sea, striking the coast between Saigon and CamRanh Bay in French Indo-China for the deepest penetration of enemy waters yet made. One enemy convoy was wiped out and two others were badly mauled on January 12. Forty-one ships, including a heavy cruiser, six transports, and several destroyers were sunk and thirty-one more were damaged. One hundred and twelve planes were destroyed, while docks, oil storage and airfield facilities were smashed by the redoubtable carrier planes.

On January 16 the attack was shifted to Formosa, and fighters and search planes went over Amoy, Swatow, Hongkong, and Hainan. The next day the China coast was raked from Hongkong and Canton to Hainan, with considerable damage to docks, shipping, and the Hongkong naval base. Finally, Formosa and the Ryukyus were struck again on the 21st. In all these operations enemy aircraft and airfield facilities were so severely dealt with that the Luzon land forces were able to advance under a steadily decreasing weight of air attacks. Not an American ship was hit during the nine-day sweep.

One reason for the absence of Japanese resistance on Luzon was the effective work by Filipino guerrillas. Four days before the landings they went to work, under instructions that coördinated their efforts with the activities of American planes, to cut roads, destroy bridges, and block defiles, preventing Japanese troop movements. Lieutenant Alex Vraciu, a navy flier with many medals who had been shot down over Luzon, led his own band of 160 guerrillas in raids that seriously hampered the enemy.

The Sixth Army moved relentlessly forward during the second week, splitting the Japanese forces and capturing the major road hub of Tarlac with its two airfields. Without stopping, it continued into Camp O'Donnell, that infamous hell about fifty miles from Manila in which were imprisoned the men who had survived the Death March from Bataan. Clark Field was presented, on January 26, to General MacArthur and General Krueger as a present on their sixty-fifth and sixty-fourth birthdays respectively. The next day the Japanese started to shell the field.

After a siege of two weeks Rosario was captured and the line advanced up the Lingayen Gulf shore and toward the strong center of Baguio. During the battle a Japanese raiding party infiltrated so deeply into American positions near San Fabio that the medical staffs of two hospital units that had just moved in were compelled to hold off the numerically superior enemy until tanks and artillery could be brought into play. An alert sentinel, just before midnight, discovered the ambush. A three-man machine-gun crew fought valiantly until death, but the battle they put up not only thwarted the Japanese surprise but gave the medical men time to remove their precious equipment to safety. Nearer Rosario an American spearhead held out against everything the enemy could throw against it, fighting day and night without food until relieved. But they held the line and protected the position of the entire First Corps.

By the end of January the Fourteenth Corps had captured San Fernando, "Gateway to Manila," and pushed forward to Calampit, crossing the Pampanga River, last major barrier and less than thirty miles from the Philippine capital. The United States Eighth Army stormed ashore between San Felipe and San Antonio at the base of Bataan Peninsula. General MacArthur, for the first time, had two armies headed for a single objective.

General Eichelberger, the most experienced jungle fighter in the Allied armies, led the new army ashore in the San Narciso area northwest of Subic Bay, on January 29. The landing was virtually unopposed, as was the one the next day on Grande Island in the middle of the bay. Units of the 38th Division, made up of Kentucky and Arkansas mountaineers, together with a combat force of the 24th Division, drove inland with record speed, reaching the city of Subic by noon of the morning on which they had landed. The 24th Division had fought with General

Eichelberger during the bloody battles of the dark days at Buna, in 1942.

The General was a "front line fighter." On one occasion, when fired on by Japanese snipers, he grabbed a tommy gun from a soldier and began shooting back. His staff asked him to take the stars off his uniform in order not to give his rank away to snipers, and he replied: "What the devil's the use of being up here if nobody's going to know about it! I want all my boys to know I'm here going through it with them."

"The Japanese doesn't make a bad enemy," he said shortly after landing in Subic Bay, "as we can always expect the worst of him and govern ourselves accordingly. But those Japanese generals must have gone crazy. Where in hell are they going to fight?"

The Eighth Army pushed on to take Olongapo and then cut across the peninsula toward the Sixth Army, which was pressing down on Manila from the north. On the last day of January, elements of the 11th Airborne Division were landed from Admiral Fechteler's ships at Nasugbu, fifteen miles directly south of the entrance to Manila Bay on the eastern shore of that strategic waterway. A parachute landing the next day enabled part of the 11th Airborne to capture Tagaytay, twenty miles inland and less than forty below Manila. General Eichelberger personally led his men from that "1,000-yard-wide, sixty-five-mile long beachhead" on both sides of Manila Bay into the capital city 104 hours after the first troops left their ships.

On the day Tagaytay was captured, the dismounted First Cavalry crashed into the outer limits of Manila from the east and infantrymen broke in from the north. A pincers was closing from three directions about the city in one of the most rapid assaults of the war. The Sixth and Eighth Armies had met on Bataan Peninsula and started their drive toward Mariveles and Corregidor. Fierce hand-to-hand fighting developed in Manila, which had been set afire by the Japanese. Long-planned sabotage wrecked bridges, docks, and the business section. It also claimed non-military objects, leaving the inhabitants homeless and dazed in a city shrouded in acrid smoke and whistling with bullets. Destruction of bridges across the Pasig River held up the American advance until amphibious craft could be brought overland to ferry the troops across and into the Intramuros, the old walled city in which the Japanese made their final, desperate stand.

February 7, 1945 was a great day for the Filipinos—and for General MacArthur. The victorious warrior entered Manila for the first time since he had left it in December, 1941.

"I'm a little late," he said, "but we finally came."

Japanese mortar and artillery fire added a dramatic background to his return. Women and freed prisoners embraced the General. For them it meant not only the advent of their liberator but the release from inhuman suffering and torture. The natives had been forbidden to speak to one another. They had been beaten or tortured for imaginary infractions of undeclared rules. They had been tortured and slain for no apparent reason whatsoever. They had been systematically robbed of their money and their possessions. Their girls and women had been dragooned into the service of the Mikado's soldiers. Their houses had been smashed and burned, and to the Filipinos perhaps more than to any other people, the home is the most sacred of all institutions.

On the night of January 30 green-clad United States Rangers and Filipino guerrillas had rescued 513 gaunt and ragged men, mostly American survivors of the Bataan "death march" and Corregidor, in a bold raid twenty-five miles behind the Japanese lines. It was the first of a series of mass rescues of prisoners and was carried out by 407 picked fighters of the 6th Ranger Battalion and guerrillas who crept noiselessly through the hills of Nuevo Ejica Province and overwhelmed the Japanese guard at the Cabanatuan prison camp.

When the shooting began, the frightened prisoners fell to the floor, expecting the moment of their annihilation had come. Hysterical joy soon replaced their fears when the Rangers, bursting through the barbed-wire enclosed barracks, called out:

"Take it easy, fellows, the Yanks are here! We got this place, pals!"

The men freed, 486 Americans, twenty-three British (some defenders of Singapore), three Netherlanders, and one Norwegian, were all that were left of about 10,000 prisoners who had been held at Cabanatuan. The rest had died from disease, malnutrition, or mistreatment; some had been removed to other camps. Two of the liberated men died on the way to safety; their failing hearts had been unable to withstand the sudden climax of joy to their three years' imprisonment.

A week earlier the infamous Camp O'Donnell, where the Corregidor prisoners had been herded, was captured and found bare. General Wainwright and other high officers had been moved to Formosa, but when Luzon was invaded they were shifted again, this time to Mukden, in Manchuria.

Other prison camps began to yield the physical and psychological wrecks of what had once been fine human specimens. American and Filipino soldiers, in a joint land, sea, and air raid again behind the enemy lines, liberated 2,146 civilians, including 1,589 Americans. Colonel Robert H. Soule led 1,200 11th Airborne infantrymen and 200 guerrillas in an early-morning dash against the Los Banos camp. Entry into Manila opened the doors of Santo Tomas, Bilibid Prison, and other camps.

The stories told by the freed prisoners varied only in detail. Britons related how they had been held in the hold of a freighter for four months without sufficient food or air, with no sanitary provisions; they were forced to bury their own dead secretly in order to dispose of the rotting corpses. An American Marine, rescued on the day before he was to be shot, said he and the other prisoners were compelled to be unwilling spectators at mass beheadings of their comrades. Eleven Baptist missionaries, and the nine-year-old son of one of them, were decapitated at one orgy of blood-letting. Survivors of a Japanese prison ship that had been torpedoed were machine-gunned as they clung to rafts and bits of wreckage hoping for rescue.

The indignities and privations imposed upon the Filipino internees were multiplied for Americans and Europeans, whether prisoners of war or civilians. More than 20,000 had died when their wracked bodies no longer could withstand the degradations and tortures. The Japanese furnished few beds, even for the sick, and diverted Red Cross and other supplies to their own use. The prison officials were absolutely indifferent to the agonies of the sick and dying. Not one of the men and women released was in even passably good health. Many were close to death from beri beri, tropical ulcers, and other epidemic diseases. All were weak physically and broken in spirit.

On February 13 the navy opened the final phase of the Manila assault by bombarding the entrance to Manila Bay and followed this with a shelling of Corregidor Island and southern Bataan Peninsula. On the 15th the 38th Division of the Eleventh Corps went ashore on the southern tip at Mariveles in a surprise landing. The following day parachute troops of the 503d Airborne Regiment dropped on Corregidor, and in less than three hours won command of the island's rocky plateau.

The American flag was raised once more over the "Rock." Manila Bay had been reopened. On March 2, General MacArthur presided over the ceremonies officially of raising the flag. Turning to Colonel George M. Jones, commander of the 503d Regimental Combat Team that had taken the "Rock" and had driven the remaining Japanese deep into the island's tunnels, he said:

"I see that the old flagpole still stands. Have your troops hoist the colors to its peak and let no enemy ever haul them down."

More than a month later, on April 14, in one of the unique operations of the campaign the concrete battleship, old Fort Drum, on El Fraile Island, was blown up. Three thousand gallons of gasoline mixed with fuel oil were pumped into the tunnels and set off with a charge of 600 pounds of TNT. That wiped out the Japanese and all resistance. Corregidor was completely safe.

The battle for full possession of Manila degenerated into a house-to-house combat. It was not until the second week of March that the city was cleared of the enemy. Liberation, however, was so effective that

General MacArthur, on February 27, returned the civil government of the Philippines to President Sergio Osmeña.

"Your country once again is at liberty to pursue its destiny to an honored position in the family of free nations," he said. "Your capital city, severely punished though it be, has regained its rightful place as a symbol of democracy."

There was still much of Luzon to be liberated—the Legaspi Peninsula in the southeast and all of the northern part of the island. This was done in a leisurely, systematic manner. The final battles were fought in the northern Cagayan Valley, but after the capture of Aparri, Tuguegarao, Baguio, and other points, organized resistance came to an end on July 4.

Admiral King explained the ease with which landings were made, giving credit to the mobile naval gunfire which could counteract fixed shore defenses.

"In considerably less than two months from the initial landings at Lingayen Gulf," he said, "General of the Army MacArthur's forces had covered the ground that had required more than four months for the Japanese in 1942. In comparing the methods used by the two invaders for seizing positions controlling the entrance to Manila Bay, it is interesting to note that in both cases the attacking forces had control of the sea and air. The Japanese relied principally on field artillery from Bataan against our guns on Corregidor. Our method employed naval strength as the spearhead of the amphibious assault, thus allowing the ground commander flexibility in selecting the time and place of the attack."

When the issue on Luzon was certain, General MacArthur started against other objectives in the Philippines with dazzling speed and variety of direction. On February 28 the 41st Division of the Eighth Army went ashore on three beaches on the northern shore of Puerto Princesa Bay on Palawan, the westernmost of the Philippine Islands. No opposition was encountered and air bases were quickly developed for the quickening attack against the Netherlands East Indies (Borneo is only 250 miles away), and the China Coast approximately 800 miles to the west.

March 10 saw the 41st Division double far back on its trail and land at Zamboanga, on the southwestern tip of Mindanao. The city and nearby San Roque Airfield were quickly captured. Eight days later the 40th Division carried the invasion into the central Philippines, landing on Panay and capturing the capital Iloilo with its valuable piers intact, on March 20. Here, too, resistance was scattered. The American Division went ashore on Cebu March 26 and on the 29th the 40th Division invaded the large island of Negros, in a shore-to-shore operation from Panay. Bacolod, the provincial capital, was captured the next day. Back on Luzon the Sixth Army landed at and captured Legaspi, completing encirclement of the Japanese there.

On April 1 the tiny islands of Sanga Sanga and Bongao, in the Tawitawi group of the Sulu Archipelago at the southernmost tip of the Philippines, were captured, placing the 41st Division only thirty miles from British North Borneo and 150 from Tarakan, in the heart of the oil refinery country of the Netherlands part of the island. This and the Palawan landing placed a pincers about Borneo. General MacArthur said that "seizure of Tawitawi secured the last link in the chain of blockading airfields which the recapture of the Philippines has made possible along the entire coast, from the northern end of Luzon to the southern tip of the Sulu Archipelago, a distance of more than 1,000 miles." The entire Netherlands East Indies, he added, were now isolated, and the China Sea was under blockading cover by our airplanes.

Masbate, northwest of Leyte, was invaded by the 40th Division on April 3; Jolo, the old capital of the Sulu sultans, was taken by the 41st on April 9, winning complete control of the Sulu Archipelago. The American Division went ashore on Bohol on April 11, and every major Philippine island had been invaded. Two more landings were made on Mindanao on April 18 and the final drive for the capture of Davao and liberation of the island was begun. Progress was rapid, but at times resistance was fierce. Other landings were made during the campaign, cutting the Japanese forces into small groups. It took about a month for the 10th Corps to capture Davao. After that the job was the slow, tedious one of mopping up.

General MacArthur was able to announce, on July 5: "The entire Philippine Islands are now liberated and the Philippine campaigns can be regarded as virtually closed. Some minor isolated action of a guerrilla nature in the practically uninhabited mountain ranges may occasionally persist, but this great land mass of 115,600 square miles, with a population of 17,000,000, is now freed of the invader.

"The enemy during these operations employed twenty-three divisions, all of which were practically annihilated. Our forces comprised seventeen divisions. This was one of the rare instances when, in a long campaign, a ground force superior in numbers was entirely destroyed by a numerically inferior opponent.... The total [Japanese] strength approximated 450,000 men.

"Naval and air forces shared equally with the ground troops in accomplishing the success of the campaign. Naval battles reduced the Japanese Navy to practical impotence and air losses running into many thousands have seriously crippled his air potential. Working in complete unison, the three services inflicted the greatest disaster ever sustained by Japanese arms."

"The objectives of the campaign were as follows:

"1. To penetrate and pierce the enemy's center so as to divide him into north and south—his homeland to the north, his captured Pacific possessions to the south. Each half could then be enveloped and attacked in turn.

"2. The acquisition of a great land, sea, and air base for future operations, both to the north and to the south comparable to the British Islands in its use as a base for Allied operations from the west against Germany.

"3. The establishment of a great strangulating air and sea blockade between Japan and the conquered possessions in the Pacific to the south so as to prevent raw materials being sent to the north and supply or reinforcement to the south.

"4. The liberation of the Philippines with the consequent collapse of the enemy's imperial concept of a Greater East Asia Co-Prosperity Sphere, and the reintroduction of democracy in the Far East.

"5. The liberation of our captured officers and men and our internees held in the Philippines.

"6. A crippling blow to the Japanese Army, Navy, and Air Force.

"All of these purposes were accomplished."

All this had been achieved in little more than eight months since the first landings on Leyte Gulf on October 20, 1944. Only 30,000 of the estimated 450,000 Japanese troops in the Philippines were left alive. This great victory had been accomplished at the cost of about 12,500 American lives, 450 missing, and 45,000 wounded—a total of less than 60,000 casualties.

General MacArthur was "home again"—back in the Philippines with the people he loved, their liberator and savior. He had kept his pledge. Little did he realize at that moment that fifty-seven days later he would be in Tokyo, in supreme command of the Japanese homeland.

FALL OF IWO JIMA—BATTERING DOWN THE INNER DEFENSES OF JAPAN

JAPAN lived under the delusion that she was impregnable. Her people were assured that no power on earth could break through her "impenetrable walls"—that no foreign foot could ever step on the soil of their heavily fortressed homeland. Drugged for generations by this narcotic of inviolability, they were awakened from their age-long stupor when the mighty American naval forces with the intrepid Marines blasted at their inner defenses while huge swarms of Superfortresses laid their great cities in ruins.

Occupation of the Philippines was the most ambitious undertaking in a series of moves designed to close in on Japan. Amphibious operations during 1944 had carried the Allies such great distances across the Pacific that plans for the assault on the inner defenses of the Japanese Empire were ready to be put into effect.

Seizure of Saipan, Tinian, and Guam had established shore-based air forces in positions to attack the Volcano and Bonin Islands and permit long-range bombers to strike Japan.

The next step was to acquire additional bases near Tokyo, from which fighters could rise to escort the B-29's, the Flying Fortresses, and the Liberators.

This made Iwo Island, 750 miles from the Japanese capital, a highly strategic springboard. During the battle for the Philippines, planes under the command of Admiral Nimitz had begun to attack Iwo; this was the first phase of a critical and bloody struggle that reached its climax in February, 1945.

Superfortresses continued to carry the war to Japan. A week after their three-day strike at Formosa, in coöperation with the Third Fleet, they returned to the enemy's home islands on October 25, 1944, leveling a key airplane plant at Omura, on Kyushu, the southernmost island. On November 3 they shifted to Rangoon in Burma, carrying a new record of bombs per plane. Two days later they attacked Singapore and Sumatra. Singapore's immunity from attack since it had been wrested from the British was broken by B-29's which, coming from India, made the longest daylight flight ever undertaken by military planes. Dockyards, repair facilities, and shipping were badly crippled. On Sumatra the aviation gasoline refinery at Pangkalan Brandan was put out of commission. Other India-based planes, in coördinated activity, hit Rangoon and airfields at Vinh, French Indo-China. The wide area covered by all these assaults completely baffled the Japanese defenses.

During the middle of November the B-29's struck Omura, Nanking, and Shanghai. They appeared over Tokyo on reconnaissance flights, completely upsetting the emotional Japanese. The big bombers were able to get in a blow at Iwo, from which the Japanese had been sending fighters and bombers to harass the new American bases in the Marianas. Since June 15, when the B-29's made their first appearance with the attack on Yawata they had struck seventeen times and had hit more than two dozen targets.

A bomb of a different sort fell on Japan when Marshal Stalin, addressing a Moscow throng on the eve of the twenty-seventh anniversary of the Red Revolution, branded Japan as an aggressor nation along with Germany. Tokyo was "surprised and offended," but from that moment Russia's attitude toward Japan stiffened. Defeat of Germany had become certain, and the Red Army finally was free to give some thought to the Asiatic situation. The immediate result was to pin down huge Japanese forces along the Manchuria-Siberia border. The wholesale withdrawal of enemy troops from that area to China, Burma, and the Philippines was no longer possible. Japan, it was estimated, had at least 2,500,000 trained soldiers in Manchuria. With the first signs of deterioration in relations with Russia, this reservoir of reinforcements for other fronts was blocked.

General Arnold declared one day that the time was coming when thousands of American bombers would hit Japan daily. His remarks were punctuated with the appearance of B-29 reconnaissance planes over Tokyo and the Japanese, fearing the worst, ordered evacuation of the main cities forthwith.

On November 24, as the Japanese people were celebrating their two-day harvest festival, the sky over Tokyo suddenly grew dark. The shadows that fell over the city came from 111 Superfortress bombers which—two years, seven months, and six days after Doolittle had swooped over the city from *Shangri-La*—caught the enemy capital as completely by surprise as had the B-25's in April, 1942. The B-29's came from two directions, maneuvered leisurely over the city and poured destruction upon strategic targets. The Nakajima branch of the Musashina Airplane Company, eleven miles northwest of the center of Tokyo, was the main objective; it was left a mass of flaming wreckage.

The attack was the first of the newly activated Twenty-first Bomber Command based on Saipan and commanded by Brigadier General Haywood S. Hansell, Jr. His mounting supply of planes served as bait for the Japanese aircraft on Iwo, and the base was under almost daily air attack. Thirty-eight-year-old Brigadier General Emmett O'Donnell,

Jr., was commander of the Tokyo mission and flew in Major Robert Morgan's lead plane, the *Dauntless Doolittle*.

General Arnold reported to President Roosevelt: "This operation is in no sense a hit-and-run raid. It is a calculated extension of our air power. Combined operations of the navy and the army in the Pacific have won these island bases from which our B-29's now may strike at will into the enemy's homeland. No part of the Japanese Empire is now out of range, no war factory too remote to feel our bombs. The battle for Japan has been joined."

Four days later the Twenty-first Bomber Command paid a return visit to Tokyo, appearing this time by night over the target 1,500 miles from Saipan to bomb the city's congested industrial waterfront area. All the planes returned safely. At the same time, the Twentieth slashed railroads at Bangkok, in Thailand, without loss. On December 3 Tokyo was hit again. The Musashina plant at Nakajima was gutted. One B-29 was lost, making a total of three Superfortresses destroyed in the three attacks.

During the rest of December the B-29's maintained an accelerated pace of blows all the way from Bangkok through China and Manchuria to Japan and out into the Pacific at Iwo. Superfortresses on almost nightly reconnaissance over Tokyo always dropped one or two incendiary bombs, not only to fray the already taut nerves of the residents but also to try out a new type of bomb that, when perfected, was to be used with terrific effect upon the Japanese cities, most of which were highly inflammable. Tinder-box houses were piled close to one another along narrow crooked streets through which flames could eat their devastating way quickly.

The beginning of 1945 saw many vital changes in America's strategic position. In three years the army had grown from 1,600,000 to 8,000,000 and the navy from 430,000 to 3,800,000. War production had increased by 680 per cent. The new strategy of conquest—amphibious operations—had been perfected, largely through extension of the "fleet train" that made it possible to supply an armada of any size with all its requirements for three or four months without returning to base, and to make all repairs, except major battle damage, out in the open ocean. The greatest and most powerful seagoing fighting machine in the world had joined the fleet, the new 45,000-ton battleship *Iowa*. Her nine 16-inch guns could hit an unseen target nineteen miles away, far beyond the horizon, with the heaviest and most destructive missiles ever devised. She carried 149 guns of varied caliber, and was studded with antiaircraft defenses.

There had been many vital changes and improvements since December 7, 1941. Seabees, those heroic constructors of new bases, now went in with assault troops, instead of waiting until some ground had been cleared before starting to work. The men would run bulldozers, wield picks, or operate drills until a sudden call brought them to antiaircraft guns or into hand-to-hand battle with the enemy. After disposing of the Japanese, the Seabees returned to their engineering tasks. Casualties were high among these heroic men who worked while they fought and fought while they worked.

Another group, small in numbers, but equally important, was the Joint Assault Signal Company, known as JASCO. They too went in with assault troops, sometimes even before the landings, to guide and shape the direct support provided to ground forces by naval guns, planes, and whatever artillery might be put ashore. Frequently they operated behind enemy lines in order to direct the fire that would neutralize or knock out positions holding up the American advance or causing unwonted casualties.

Most important of all from the strategic point of view was the development of Guam. It had been invaded on July 21 and was declared secure on August 10. In five months Seabees and others under Major General Henry L. Larsen, U.S.M.C., commanding general of the recovered island, had built a vast, interlocking network of highways through the jungle-covered hills. Bulldozers were carving out a series of giant airfields, some of which were in use. As an incidental part of their work they killed some 6,000 Japanese soldiers who had hidden in the hills, and were tracking down others.

During January Admiral Nimitz moved with his Headquarters, Pacific Ocean Areas, from Pearl Harbor to Guam, 4,000 miles closer to Japan. Shortly after, the island for which Congress before the war would provide no funds for fortifications in order not to offend Japan, was more powerful than Pearl Harbor had ever been. American commanders were confident that no enemy ever could take it. On the 225-square-mile island bastion were 120 miles of Grade A hard-surface road and 240 miles of secondary road. Some of the numerous airfields had runways 8,500 feet long to take care of the B-29's. Hospitals with more than 10,000 beds and the most modern facilities were in operation. In one month the island's gardens produced 1,250,000 pounds of vegetables. The naval base had been extended to a size able to hold the entire United States Navy and to do everything but build new ships. Guam had everything for defense and everything for attack.

All eyes were on Iwo—the next objective on the way to Tokyo. Bitter enemy resistance was anticipated, as the island had been heavily fortified by the enemy over a period of many years, because of the fact that it was the only island in the strategic Volcano-Bonin groups that lent itself to important airfield construction. As the island is only five miles long and less than two miles wide, the entire shore line could be covered with artillery, mortar, and machine-gun fire against any invasion. The defense was made much easier because there were only two beaches on which a landing was possible; so there was no danger of being caught by surprise.

During the last five months of 1944, Iwo had been subjected to air and surface bombardment that increased in frequency and intensity from December on. Attacks by land and carrier planes during the summer and fall had been reinforced with shelling from naval guns, culminating that phase of the preparations with a heavy blow by cruisers and destroyers, under Rear Admiral A. E. Smith, on November 11. In December the Army's Seventh Air Force, as part of the Strategic Air Force, Pacific Ocean Areas, opened up daily attacks on Iwo, with Marine bombers from the Marianas throwing in night assaults against enemy shipping in the area. The fleet, coöperating with the planes, struck twice during December. On January 5 the fleet hit again, this time adding Haha and Chichi Islands in the Bonins to their objectives. On January 24 Rear Admiral O. C. Badger led a powerful force, including battleships, to Iwo and, coördinating his shelling with bombings from every kind of plane from Lightnings to Superfortresses, gave Iwo its heaviest blow.

Almost coincident with this attack came the announcement from Washington that General LeMay had been given command of the Twenty-first Bomber Command in the Marianas, succeeding General Hansell, who was recalled to Washington. The latter's chief of staff, Brigadier General Roger M. Ramey, took over General LeMay's Twentieth Bomber Command based in India and China.

Further to confuse the Japanese, who had to keep their eyes on the Philippines, China, Burma, and other areas, as well as Iwo and the skies over the home islands, the Fifth Fleet sailed close to the shores of Japan, under cover of weather so adverse as to handicap enemy air operations, on the morning of February 16. It launched 1,200 planes against Tokyo, which were undetected until they had reached the city. This was the first time the navy had hit the enemy capital. In the words of Admiral Nimitz's communiqué: "This operation has long been planned, and the opportunity to accomplish it fulfills the deeply cherished desire of every officer and man in the Pacific Fleet."

Never before had an aërial blow been launched from carriers—except for the Doolittle raid—against a great metropolis. For two days the planes kept up their assault, raining unprecedented destruction on the Japanese capital. "Upon completion of the February 17 strike the fast carrier task force retired toward Iwo Jima to give more direct support to the landing operations on Iwo on February 19."

The attack on Tokyo was a decisive victory, Admiral Nimitz said. It had succeeded even beyond navy expectations in proving so complete a diversion that the enemy never suspected that the Iwo landings were approaching their H-hour. It succeeded also because of the unprecedented damage wrought to Japan's industries at so small a cost. "I know that our future operations will hurt the enemy more," Nimitz declared in a message congratulating Task Force 58. The magnitude of the success was made possible by a hard-working group known as Squadron 10, the world's largest mobile base that outfitted the task force within a few hundred miles of Japan. This floating supply and repair base, which Admiral Nimitz called "America's secret weapon," provided the Fifth Fleet as it steamed to attack with enough fuel oil to make a train of 10,000-gallon tank cars 238 miles long, enough gasoline to run 30,700 automobiles for a year, enough food to feed a city the size of Columbus, Ohio, for a month, and enough ammunition and bombs to fill 480 freight cars.

While the Tokyo attack was on, more than 800 naval vessels manned by 220,000 personnel and carrying 60,000 Marines, closed in on Iwo, that volcanic island whose inhospitable shores were covered with volcanic ash so dry and deep that even tanks slithered through the dust, unable to take hold with their treads. The invasion was under command of Admiral Spruance, with Vice Admiral Turner in over-all command of amphibious forces and Lieutenant General Holland M. Smith, U.S.M.C., of the expeditionary forces. Major General Harry Schmidt, U.S.M.C., led the Fifth Amphibious Corps; Major General Clifton B. Cates, U.S.M.C., the Fourth Marine Division; Major General Keller E. Rockey, U.S.M.C., the Fifth; and Major General Graves B. Erskine, U.S.M.C., the Third. Admiral Mitscher once more commanded the carrier task force.

Shortly before 9:00 A.M. on February 19 the battleships *New York, Texas, Nevada, Arkansas, Idaho,* and *Tennessee* led a parade of cruisers and destroyers around the eight square miles of Iwo and poured a devastating load of shells from positions so close that it seemed almost possible to touch shore from the decks. During the preceding seventy-four days the little island that looks like a model of South America had been hit daily by heavy air forces. At about the same time those brave little flat-bottomed boats, the LCI(G)'s—Landing Craft Infantry-Gunboats, originally designed to carry troops ashore in shallow water —moved into the beaches to perform their converted tasks. They pumped small-caliber bullets into the shore positions to clear the way for the Marines who were about to follow. With virtually no armor, drawing only five feet of water, with guns smaller than those available to the enemy, they remained 140-foot sitting ducks for mortar and shell fire. Heavy casualties were suffered, and after the battle the water's edge was strewn with their wreckage, but they did their job.

They did their job so well that two hours after the Marines had hit the beaches on the east coast north of Mount Suribachi, the extinct volcano that dominates the southern end of Iwo, they had established a beachhead 4,500 yards long and generally 500 yards deep. The Fourth Division was assigned the task of cutting across the narrow tip of the island, while the Fifth was to drive for the two main airfields in the center. The Third was held in reserve.

The troops that came ashore encountered an intricate system of defenses as well as some of the most modern weapons the Japanese had yet employed. The garrison, originally estimated at less than 15,000, was discovered to number more than 20,000, and was emplaced in an interlocking system of caves, pillboxes, and blockhouses that totaled almost one per man. There were 100 caves in one area 400 by 600 yards; some were forty feet deep and there were two-story pillboxes sunk into the volcanic sand. More than 115 heavy guns were hidden in concreted positions on Mount Suribachi. The Japanese had added every conceivable device to the formidable fortress created by nature, and the Marine Corps found itself in the toughest fight of its long career. The bombardment from air and sea had knocked out Iwo's air power and had cut down much of the shore defenses, but it could not annihilate all the positions, most of which were skilfully hidden from even the closest observation.

Establishment of the beachhead was the only relatively easy experience of the invasion, but even this was done under a murderous fire from Suribachi's guns and encircling mortars. By the end of the first day the Marines had driven across the island, isolating Suribachi, and had obtained a toehold on the Motoyama No. 1 Airfield. By noon of the second day the entire field was occupied, and the Marines pushed on. The Japanese threw in a heavy counterattack during the early morning hours, but the Twenty-seventh Marine Regiment broke it up after a furious battle.

Desperate fighting continued during the third day, at the end of which 1,800 dead Japanese had been counted and one lone prisoner had been taken. American casualties, too, were heavy, and the Third Division was landed to take positions between the Fourth and Fifth. The depleted enemy air force rose, and sank the escort carrier *Bismarck Sea*. The night of February 21-22 and the whole of the latter day were marked by a series of violent battles with the counterattacking Japanese. All were thrown back; but they did succeed in slowing the American advance and adding to the dead and wounded. Mines strewn over the terrain contributed to the difficulties of the Marines.

February 23 was an important day. The southern part of Motoyama Airfield No. 2 was occupied by the Third and Fourth Divisions, and the Fifth was starting to swing around the western end. On the southern tip of the island, the Twenty-eighth Marine Regiment, including former Raiders and Marines under Colonel Harry "The Horse" B. Liversedge, which had surrounded 554-foot Mount Suribachi, awoke from a disturbed sleep among the seeping steam and sulphur fumes from its volcanic fissures and started to storm the extinct crater. They blasted their way through a complicated system of pillboxes with flame throwers and grenades. Lieutenant Harold C. Schrier, of Richmond, Missouri, tired of the slow progress, rallied a patrol about him and brushed all opposition aside to plant the American flag on top of the extinct crater at 10:35 in the morning. That dramatic flag-raising was photographed by an Associated Press photographer with the patrol, and the picture became the most famous of the war.

Capture of Mount Suribachi eliminated some of the enemy mortar and artillery fire that had poured from behind upon the advancing main body of Marines and had exacted a heavy toll of lives. In the first two days American casualties had been 5,372, of which 385 were killed and 4,168 wounded. Kangoku Rock, a small island to the northwest of Iwo also poured shells on the Marines until the batteries were eliminated by a destroyer.

By February 25 the three divisions, spearheaded by tanks, had captured the southern half of Iwo, including the Number 2 Airfield, and were closing in on the main villages of Higashi and Nishi. By March 8 the Third Division reached cliffs only three hundred yards from the northeastern beaches; on its left the Fifth advanced beyond Nishi on the northwestern shore; on the right the Fourth was being held up between Minami and Higashi.

The beginning of the end came on March 10, when the remaining Japanese were split into three parts, the largest being in a half-mile-square area at Kitano Point, the northernmost tip of Iwo. The Fourth Division finally broke loose and reached Tachiwa Point, the easternmost edge of the island, and had surrounded Higashi. The Japanese finally began to break under the combined land, sea, and air battering. Kangoku Rock and Kama Rock, to the south, were occupied without opposition. By-passed enemy pockets were being wiped out.

Organized resistance ended at 6:00 P.M., March 16. The Marines had lost 4,189 officers and men killed in the twenty-six-day action, 441 were missing, and 15,308 were wounded.

"Capture of Iwo Jima," General Smith said, "an outlying prefecture of Tokyo, was considered essential by those in whose hands the destiny of our nation lies. The cost of winning this objective was no doubt weighed carefully against the importance of having this island as an operating base in speeding the ultimate defeat of Japan. Never in their 168 years' history has their [the Marine Corps] motto 'Semper Fidelis' [Always Faithful] been tried or challenged so greatly as in the capture of Iwo Jima."

Admiral Nimitz, in his communiqué announcing the capture of Iwo, added: "The United States Marines, by their individual and collective courage, have conquered a base which is as necessary to us on our continuing forward movement toward final victory as it was vital to the enemy in staving off defeat.... By their victory the Third, Fourth, and Fifth Marine Divisions and other units of the Fifth Amphibious Corps have made an accounting to their country which only history will be able to value fully. Among the Americans who served on Iwo Island uncommon valor was a common virtue."

The last Japanese gasp on Iwo expired on March 26, when four enemy officers led 196 trapped men from caves and attacked aviation units southeast of Airfield No. 2. They were wiped out, and the Japanese dead mounted to more than 20,000.

During the twenty-six bloody days on Iwo, the Japanese had been taking punishment elsewhere too. Sunday, February 25, saw Admiral Mitscher's carrier planes return to Tokyo, to be followed by more than 200 Superfortresses. The Fleet aircraft smashed airfields, shipping, and other targets, but the B-29's burned out 29,000,000 square feet of Tokyo's industrial heart—the equivalent of 240 New York City blocks. Some of the bombs fell on the grounds of Emperor Hirohito's palace, evoking an apology from the Japanese Cabinet because the Dowager Empress's palace had been hit. The enemy lost 158 planes in the combined action.

The battle of Tokyo was under way. More than 300 B-29's returned to the capital and, in the largest and most intensified assault of the war, dropped the first 1,000-ton load on the city. The bombs were the new type jelly-fire bombs tried out on reconnaissance flights, and they fell on Tokyo for an hour and a half during the early morning hours. The heart of the city was wiped out. Not a building was left intact in an area of fifteen square miles; 1,000,000 people were homeless; vital industrial plants were in ashes. Four times between March 12 and 20 the B-29's struck Japan again, raining more than 10,000 tons of incendiaries on Tokyo, the aircraft center of Nagoya, Japan's second city Osaka, and the great port and shipbuilding center of Kobe.

Japan was turned into a land of chaos. The damage wrought was characterized as the greatest ever inflicted upon any people in a single eight-day period. Flames had wiped out scores of square miles of the leading cities and had wrecked irretrievably thousands of war plants. The ever-tightening sea and air blockade that had been thrown about Japan made the losses even more vital. The enemy had lost more than 10,000 planes in six months and her airplane industry was being shattered, her steel plants were being destroyed, her people rendered homeless and hungry by the millions.

On March 18 Admiral Mitscher's planes raked the southeast coast of Kyushu, some 1,400 aircraft maintaining the assault for eight hours.

The next day they shifted north, finally ending the long hunt for what was left of the Imperial Japanese Navy. They swooped upon the naval base at Kobe and the port of Kure, ripping targets on both sides of the Inland Sea that never before had seen enemy naval weapons.

B-29's maintained their assault on Tokyo and other Japanese targets. By the middle of April Mustangs from the newly won bases on Iwo were also attacking Japan. The new Superfortress tactic of low-level incendiary bombing yielded results, particularly in obliterating the innumerable "shadow factories" surrounding industrial areas. Japan, with its mass population, had converted almost every worker's home into a small piecework factory in which much of the manufacture of small parts was carried on. After the March series of attacks on the major cities, the emphasis of air activity was shifted to the airfields on Kyushu. The reason for this will become clear a little later.

Hell was breaking loose on Japan. American Superfortresses were carrying the messages to the Sons of Heaven that their homeland was to become an inferno—for behind these scenes at this very moment the world's greatest scientists were about to "break down the atom" and unleash the mightiest power the world has ever known—the atomic bomb.

JAPANESE EMPIRE CRUMBLES IN THE PACIFIC AND ON CONTINENT OF ASIA

THE Japanese pagoda of world power was collapsing throughout the Far East in the fateful days of 1945. The pyramidical temple of lust and conquest was crumbling into the dust. The fantastic dream of rule or ruin became a Nipponese nightmare as American air power swept the island like a typhoon and American sea power destroyed the Japanese Navy.

The Japs had lost more than a thousand ships; their navy was a vanishing ghost; their air fleet was but a stalking skeleton. The convulsions during these death throes, however, were fraught with many dangers to the Allies. The Japs still had vast armies, estimated at 5,000,000, with which to strike. In desperation they struck viciously in futile attempts to "save face" and postpone the day of doom.

Let us here witness a few of these crucial moments along the entire Asiatic front when the Japs thrust against American, British, and Chinese forces.

The *Saratoga*, the oldest and largest carrier in the United States Navy, was violently attacked northwest of Iwo on February 21, two days after the landings. Seven bombs blew her hull open, twisted her superstructure into a mass of blackened steel, left a gaping hole in her flight deck, and turned the hangar deck into a sea of flames. One hundred and twenty-three of her men were killed or missing, and one hundred and ninety-two were wounded.

Burning planes and leaking fuel oil blanketed the ship. The enemy maintained concentrated blows against the crippled carrier, but her crew brought the fires under control and sailed her into Puget Sound Navy Yard. Photographs of the damage had been flown to the repair shops so that parts were waiting when the *Saratoga* arrived. She was quickly restored to combat duty and once more resumed her proud place on the battle line.

During the carrier assault on Kure, Kobe, and the Inland Sea in March the new 27,000-ton *Franklin* went through an experience such as no other ship had had and remained afloat to go to war again. Enemy planes managed to break through the defense ring to pick up the *Franklin* after dawn on March 19. The carrier was lying some sixty miles off the shore of Japan, refueling and relaunching her planes as fast as they came in, when the assault began. A lone Japanese dive bomber sped over the ship dropping bombs from stem to stern. Instantly the American planes on deck burst into flames, igniting gasoline drums and ready ammunition strewn over the deck. Damage from the enemy dive bomber was relatively light, but her own exploding ammunition and oil turned the *Franklin* into a literal inferno. Other warships, like the cruiser *Santa Fé* and the destroyers *Hunt, Hickox,* and *Marshall,* quickly tied up alongside to help the stricken carrier.

Death was strewn all over the *Franklin*. Lieutenant Commander Joseph Timothy O'Callahan, a Jesuit priest who was the "Big Ben's" chaplain, alternately administered last rites, consoled the wounded, aided in rescues, and helped stem the fires. Captain Leslie E. Gehres, the *Franklin's* commanding officer, called him "the bravest man I have ever seen." Lieutenant (j.g.) Donald A. Gary, assistant engineering officer, and Lieutenant Commander James L. Fuelling, assistant flight surgeon, rose to heights of heroism. Every man able to walk proved a hero many times over as the big carrier drifted closer and closer to Japan before her machinery was repaired sufficiently to turn her around and steam slowly toward safer waters. The *Franklin* finally came into the Brooklyn Navy Yard under her own power, as scarred and twisted a hull as had ever remained afloat. She had sailed 12,000 miles from the scene of her catastrophe in which 832 men had been killed or were missing and 270 had been wounded. Nearly 200 awards for valor were bestowed in the largest mass decoration in American naval history, to the accompaniment of drills, hammers, and blow torches making the $45,000,000 repairs which sent the *Franklin* back to sea. The *Saratoga* and the *Franklin* were outstanding examples of the spirit, the courage, and the determination of the entire Pacific Fleet.

Meanwhile, things had been happening on the Asiatic Continent. During the end of October, 1944, General Stilwell was relieved of his command and other duties in the Far East as the result of China's inability to assume a more vigorous rôle in the war. There had also been divergences between his views and those of Lord Louis Mountbatten on operations in Burma. The old China-Burma-India theater was split in two and Major General Wedemeyer replaced General Stilwell as commander of United States forces in China, as well as Chief of Staff to Chiang Kai-shek, while Lieutenant General Daniel I. Sultan took over command of American forces in Burma and India.

China's war contribution since Pearl Harbor had been hampered, as it had been during the years before, by internal discord between the Chungking Government and the so-called Chinese Communists in the north, by differences within the general staff, by Chiang Kai-shek's reluctance, and final refusal, to intrust General Stilwell with full command of a unified Chinese war effort. The final break came when General Stilwell, unable longer to stand by and watch the Japanese

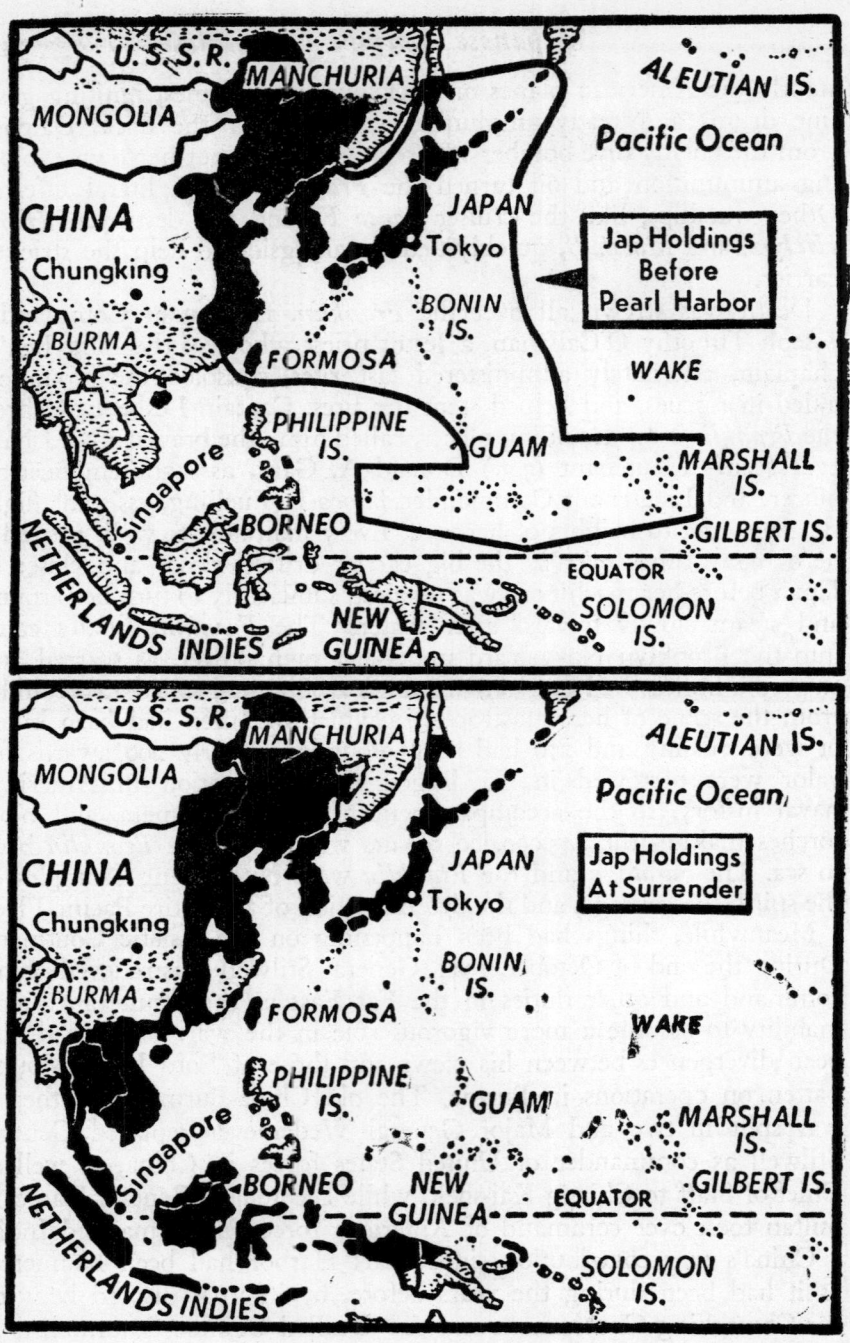

FOUR STAGES IN

The extent of Japanese holdings before they went into war in 1941, their
and the approximate area allowed them under the Potsdam surrender

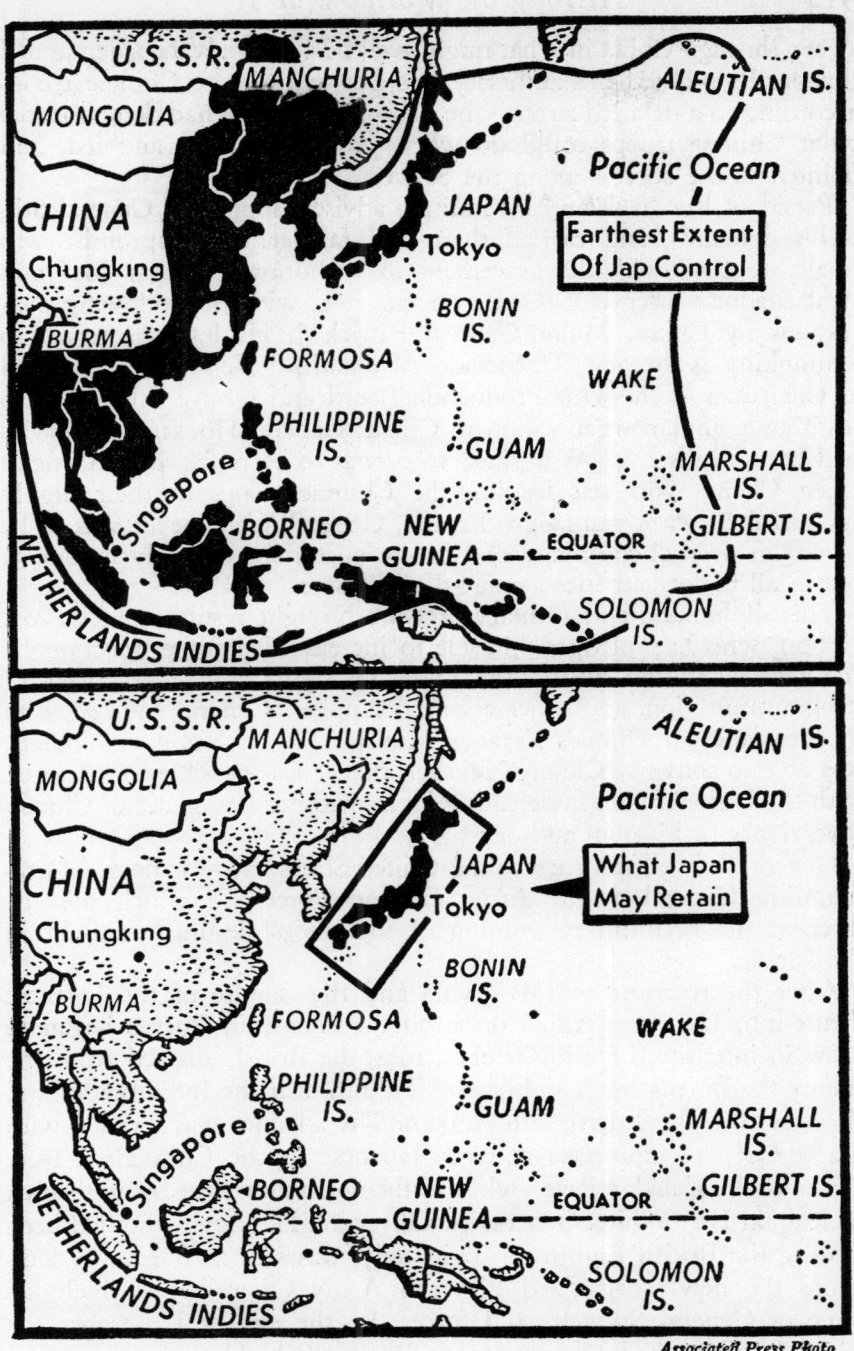

JAP RISE AND FALL

gains during the war, their holdings when surrender negotiations began, terms.

sweep through China in what might well be a fatal advance, demanded that he be granted the authority and power to move Chinese troops according to a detailed strategy he had prepared. He had demonstrated what Chinese troops could do when properly trained and led, and pointed to the success along the Salween.

President Roosevelt and his military advisers supported General Stilwell's demands, and carried them still farther. A compromise was finally reached with the agreement to withdraw "Vinegar Joe" and Ambassador Clarence E. Gauss on our side, with the following concessions by China: Major General Patrick J. Hurley was to go to Chungking as the new Ambassador; Donald M. Nelson was to resign as Chairman of the War Production Board and receive full power to institute a similar organization in China; General Ho Ying-chin, who had been Minister of War since 1930, was to be replaced by General Chen Cheng who was leading the Chinese troops in their highly successful Salween campaign. Finally, General Wedemeyer was to be placed in over-all command of Chinese operations not only in Burma but in all major activities against the Japanese.

This diplomatic and military pressure brought results quickly. Mr. Nelson, who had pledged himself to increase China's production by 100 per cent within six months, raised his sights to a triple output of steel, ammunition, and other essential supplies. General Hurley, with the assistance of China's Finance Minister H. H. Kung and others, was able to convince Chiang Kai-shek that it was possible to coöperate with the United States in defeating Japan without losing any of China's sovereignty or his own authority.

General Stilwell returned to the United States and was named Commanding General of the Army Ground Forces, in which post he directed the preliminary training of the troops destined to fight in the Pacific.

After the recapture of Myitkyina and the repulse of the Japanese thrust into India the Allied drive on the enemy in Burma began to grow in intensity. Late in October, 1944, the British wrested from the enemy the Burma town and base of Tiddim near the India border and also started a third drive into Arakan. The advance was speeded with the end of the monsoons and the Japanese in the Chin Hills were driven to the Kaladan River, while to the north they were being thrown back upon Fort White. General Sir Oliver W. H. Leese, who had been leading the British Eighth Army in Italy, was sent to Burma to command the newly organized Eleventh Army Group which included some of General Stilwell's old forces. By the end of November the Allies, who long had held air superiority, finally had built up numerical superiority on the ground. Kalemyo had been taken and Mandalay was being approached from three sides. The orderly retreat of the enemy toward that city had been covered by suicide squads left to fight rear-guard actions.

The Allied momentum was slowed for a time when Air Chief Marshal Sir Trafford Leigh-Mallory, who had been named Air Commander in Chief in Southeast Asia after a brilliant record as Royal Air Force chief and General Eisenhower's air aide in the African and Italian invasions, was lost on the flight from London to Burma. In the continuing ground actions, however, the Japanese began to abandon their costly hold on northern Burma and to use their troops to better advantage in China, where they were making dangerous progress. The loss of Sir Trafford Leigh-Mallory and the inability to put into immediate effect his plans for coördinated action were overcome by increased activity of the United States Tenth Air Force and the heavy blows added by the Superfortresses which paid particular attention to such rear supply targets as Rangoon and Bangkok.

American combat troops went into action for the first time since the capture of Myitkyina, when the jungle-wise Mars Task Force, after long overland marches, began to spearhead the Allied advance by showing up behind enemy lines and cleaning out concentrations, supply centers, and strong points.

Things began to move with the New Year. Akyab, the last big Japanese naval and air base in western Burma, was captured without a battle by waterborne British and Indian troops on January 4, 1945. By the end of the week Shwebo was captured and the British were less than fifty miles from Mandalay. Back on the coast they landed additional troops on the intricately water-cut Myebon Peninsula to get behind the Japanese retreating from Akyab. Opposition was severe and heavy fighting raged for some time as the enemy tried desperately to prevent annihilation of large numbers of troops. Two weeks later British amphibious forces, aided by naval guns and planes, invaded Ramree Island, more than fifty miles below Akyab, following this successful maneuver with a fourth landing for the month, this time on the mainland near Kangaw, thirty-five miles east of Akyab. Other landings followed quickly and the Japanese were cut into a number of small groups waiting to be wiped out.

The enemy began to rush guns and concentrate troops for defense of Mandalay which was being hemmed in by Lieutenant General Sir William J. Slim's British Fourteenth Army. One column of British and Indian troops slashed across the Irrawaddy River ninety-six miles southwest of the city to capture Pagan after a short, bitter fight. Seizure of this ancient Burmese city, relic of Burma's Golden Age and seat of Buddhist worship and learning for nearly 1,000 years, opened the way to recapture of the big oil towns of Chauk and Yenangyaung. The British did not remain in the city long enough to admire the ancient, historic pagodas but swept right on toward the oilfields. An almost continuous battle line had been forged from Ramree Island to the Irrawaddy south of Burma, and early in March a British motorized and armored column dashed eighty-five miles in eleven days to capture Meiktila, menace Thazi, and trap 30,000 Japanese concentrated to the north for the defense of Mandalay.

On the night of March 8 bearded Punjabi troops of the 19th Indian Division followed a spearhead of tanks to plunge into the heart of fabled Mandalay. They quickly gained control of the northern half of the city which had been overrun by the Japanese in May, 1942. The enemy fought from street to street and house to house until finally cornered in old Fort Dufferin, a fortress a mile square that dominated the city. It took a siege of twelve days before the fort was captured and Sikhs, Punjabis, and Gurkhas were able to enter the burning ruins of the red lacquer palace of the ancient Burmese kings to root out the last desperate Japanese. Mandalay was liberated on March 20 after two years, ten months, and twelve days of brutal Japanese occupation.

With disaster in Burma staring them in the face the Japanese began to strengthen their hold elsewhere. They took over full control of the puppet state of French Indo-China, wiping out the last vestige of French rule. They seized key garrisons, imprisoned the soldiers, and placed strong forces along railroads. The pitifully small band of 30,000 French troops, half European and half native, resisted as well as they could and carried out guerrilla action from the hills where they received meager supplies dropped from time to time by Allied planes.

The advance in Burma continued speedily. The shattered Japanese Fifteenth Army in central Burma was wiped out. Transport planes carried small locomotives to the field enabling the Allies to use the captured railroads and ease the supply problem. Thazi and Taungup were captured in early April, Chauk and Yenangyaung fell shortly after. Thousands of bedraggled Japanese troops were falling back as as best they could on Moulmein, the first port they had seized in the Burma invasion.

British paratroops on May 1 dropped on both sides of the wide mouth of the Rangoon River where it empties into the Gulf of Martaban below the city. The next day a daring amphibious thrust put strong infantry and armored forces ashore. In one day Rangoon, capital of Burma, was captured. The three-years war to liberate Burma was virtually ended on May 3 when the British Fourteenth Army ended its brilliant march through nearly 1,000 miles of steaming jungles and across rugged mountains from the Indian border. The Japanese, whose casualties were officially estimated at 347,000 by Lord Louis Mountbatten in announcing the end of the Burma campaign, were so thoroughly beaten that the port fell, virtually intact. The enemy then began his long, tortuous flight back toward Thailand, with the British maintaining contact all the time. The Chinese drive from the Salween, the American drive from the north, and the British drive from the Indian border had forged an inexorable pincers that inflicted the first major defeat the Japanese had suffered on the Continent of Asia.

In China, however, Allied successes elsewhere had been matched during the fall and winter of 1944 by serious defeats. The Japanese were determined to cut China in half, isolating Chungking and the interior from the coast. They were also determined to push the United States Fourteenth Air Force so far inland that it could no longer be a menace to coastal shipping.

During the summer the Japanese had captured Hengyang and the American air base there. On September 8 they took Lingling, on the 17th Kweilin, a week later Paoking, and on October 1 Tanchuk. Five times the Fourteenth Air Force had to demolish with high explosive charges the bases they had so laboriously built up with improvised material and supplies flown to them over the "hump." The cities had been lost to converging enemy drives, one northwest from Canton and the other southwest from the Yangtze River. After the fall of Tanchuk the Japanese seized Kweiping, threatening Kweilin, capital of Kwangsi Province and site of a large Fourteenth Air Force base. Another drive menaced Liuchow, to the south, so that a corridor of only one hundred miles would separate the two enemy columns. Liuchow was taken in the middle of November after installations, runways, fuel dumps, and hangars had been demolished. The Fourteenth Air Force was virtually driven back to its base at Kunming, in Yunnan Province, four hundred miles from the coast.

The Japanese landed troops northeast of Foochow, on the Fukien Province coast, and by the middle of October had captured the large port. Nothing seemed to stop the enemy drives; in fact, their tempo and power increased. Kweichow Province was almost completely occupied. By the end of November the minor airfield at Nanning which suddenly had assumed such importance was destroyed and abandoned. The United States Embassy urged Americans to leave Kunming as the Japanese drew nearer Kweiyang, the communications and air base between that city and Chungking.

The situation was desperate. China called for landings on her coast by the Americans. Admiral Nimitz obliged to the extent of saying that the China coast was his objective. Chungking frankly admitted that it faced its gravest crisis of the eight-year war and that the next sixty days were critical. If Japan were able to deliver a knockout blow within that time, China would be out of the war.

Then something seemed to happen out of the limitless well of Chinese courage. Early in December the Chinese started a counter-drive that made it impossible for the Japanese to win their final victory. Troops under General Chen Cheng swept quickly through Kweichow Province, virtually clearing it of the enemy and easing the threat to Kweiyang. The Japanese retreated sixty-five miles in five days and gave up Limingkwan, the strategic mountain pass on the Kweichow-Kwangsi border. The seven-month enemy campaign had been stopped and thrown into reverse.

Despite the loss of its forward bases the Fourteenth Air Force and the Chinese-American Composite Wing hurled death and destruction on the retreating enemy with intensified blows that also shattered rear supply areas. The answer to the loss of bases had been found in a self-contained mobile air-transport "task force" able to shift from one place to another and set up its own base wherever it might be. Gasoline, ammunition, and spare parts were smuggled right through enemy lines by a circuitous route involving abandoned railroads, trucks, junks, sampans, and mules. In a final gesture of contempt the Fourteenth, flying for the first time from any base in northern China, began a series of attacks on the Tsinan airfield in Shantung Province on Christmas Eve, destroying scores of planes and throwing a scare into Shanghai.

Nothing ever clouded the work of the gallant Fourteenth Air Force, even with the disheartening conditions under which it was compelled to work. General Chennault declared that during December his fliers had made their best record, destroying, without loss to themselves, 241 Japanese planes, sinking 73,950 tons of shipping and probably sinking or damaging 113,900 tons more.

The tide swung again in January, 1945, with the Japanese resuming their drives along the coast and against the railways. This did not mean that China was out of danger but she had gained enough time to gird up her strength. Artillery and supplies of all sorts were beginning to come over the Stilwell (Ledo) Road. Reinforcements were coming into the central provinces from the Burma front and also from the north where they had been immobilized for years keeping watch over the politically hostile Communist armies who were carrying on their own guerrilla war against the Japanese.

Every mile of that stupendous piece of construction, the 1,044-mile Ledo Road, new lifeline to China, had cost the life of an American soldier; the cost was to be justified.

The Chinese resumed the counteroffensive in February, reopening the seized railroad lines and making other gains. All through March and the first two weeks of April the enemy pushed his attack with increased fury, but never was able to regain the pace and power he had lost earlier in the year. The Japanese were believed to have fifty divisions in China and were trying desperately to widen the inland corridor from Manchuria to Singapore, and strengthen their hold on the coast before it was too late.

Tokyo's war lords did not know it, but the spring of 1945 was already too late. Their armies in China continued to gain on all fronts, but not as easily as before. The havoc wreaked upon their shipping was beginning to show its effect. Fliers and naval vessels had destroyed 5,500,000 tons of merchant shipping since Pearl Harbor.

Against these losses and the consequent weakening of the enemy's power to reinforce and supply his troops in China, the Allies had begun to build up sufficient strength with which to give the invaders a real battle. All plans had been completed for a struggle that was to halt the Japanese, then wrest the initiative from them, and finally drive them back north. It was not until May, however, that General Wedemeyer and General Chen were ready to strike.

A battle was being waged on another front, a front so overshadowed by the more spectacular events elsewhere that it had become virtually forgotten. More than 250,000 Japanese troops, surrounded and cut off from their homeland, were continuing to do battle on the islands of the Central and Southwest Pacific. American Marines and infantry daily killed many and captured a few of the 15,000 in the Marshalls, 5,000 in the Marianas, and 30,000 in the Palaus. Fliers took a constant toll with their explosive and fire-bombs of the 80,000 on Truk and other islands in the Carolines, 4,000 on Ocean and Nauru, 5,000 on Marcus and Wake. Starvation and disease claimed a host of other victims.

There were some 125,000 in the Solomons and New Guinea area; pockets left when Bougainville, New Britain, and New Guinea had been captured and New Ireland and other places by-passed. The campaigns did not end, however, with the advance of the Americans to Morotao, the Philippines, and other points closer to Japan. The task of cleaning-up had been passed to the Australians, who, in the fall of 1944, were able to start their work in earnest. Many of their troops had been brought back from Africa and redeployed to Pacific fronts. The Royal Australian Navy provided the cover for a series of bold amphibious operations that gradually hacked out more ground. In the Spring of 1945 virtually all of New Britain, with the exception of the area immediately surrounding Rabaul, had been safely restored to Australian rule.

On New Guinea on May 14 the Australian 6th Division, veterans of Tobruk, Crete, and Greece, captured Wewak, once the forward base of the Japanese drive on Australia.

These were long, slow, arduous campaigns, fought with insufficient men and inadequate supplies because of the ever-mounting demands of the major drives on Japan. They were marked with the same quality of heroism, determination, and sacrifice that characterized the fighting in the Philippines and elsewhere.

Major Allied strategy again underwent some changes after the capture of Iwo. The speed and success of the Burma campaign indicated that the Pacific front was soon to be shortened and that British warships, men and equipment hitherto committed to that area would be released for use elsewhere. The frantic efforts of the Japanese to increase their hold on China showed clearly that that was soon to become a major front. All Allied leaders seemed agreed that Japan could be defeated only on the mainland, and while it was not certain that the opposing armies would come to final grips on China's soil everything pointed to a series of critical battles there that might lead to the final clashes in Manchuria.

The Allies revised their strategy and their schedules to hasten the reduction of Japan's industrial capacity by more frequent and more powerful sea and air attacks, while placing themselves in a better position to deal telling blows to the enemy forces in China.

Everything that happened in the spring and summer of 1945 followed this strategic pattern. Optimists felt certain that an invasion of Japan was to be expected almost any day. The first move in the revised strategy struck the enemy on Easter Sunday, although he must have known something unpleasant was bound to happen by the ever-increasing attacks on the Ryukyu Islands, the long archipelago that stretches hundreds of miles between the East China Sea and the Pacific Ocean south of the Japanese home islands and northeast of Formosa. A last great battle was brewing on the front doorstep of Japan.

OKINAWA—LAST GREAT BATTLE IN THE PACIFIC—AT DOORWAY TO JAPAN

THE last barrier to the invasion of Japan fell with a mighty crash in the eighty-one days of battle on the bastion of Okinawa. Here, on Easter Sunday, April 1, 1945, the American Marines swarmed ashore on Japanese soil after the navy and air force had blazed the trail. Here they were in a death struggle with the last stand of the suicide Japs when the war ended in Europe on May 7. It was June 21 before they were in possession of this final Japanese stronghold. It was seventy days later when the war ended in the Pacific.

This classic battle of indomitable American courage against medieval fanaticism is the last great epic in World War II. The Philippines were being restored to civilization and freedom. Burma was being cleared, and operations in the East Indies could be undertaken at times and in ways convenient to the broad strategical plan. The South and Central Pacific had been cleared or neutralized with the capture of Iwo, while on the Asiatic Continent Allied commanders felt they could wrest the initiative from the Japanese before summer. The decks were virtually cleared for the invasion of Japanese home territory. There were neither sufficient men nor adequate bases close enough to Japan to warrant immediate invasion of the home islands, but resources were sufficient with which to attack the outlying precincts.

Most tempting of all were the Ryukyu Islands, incorporated by Tokyo as an integral part of Japan itself. A string of lesser islands stretches in a general southwest direction from Kyushu, southernmost island of Japan, toward the Amami group constituting the northern mass of the Ryukyu Archipelago. Below that is the Okinawa group, the largest and most important of all. Every consideration made possession of Okinawa essential. It dominated the entire Ryukyu Archipelago, which served as a bastion protecting the East China and the Yellow Seas. Okinawa in Allied hands would open up the China coast from Foochow to Korea; bring all southern Japan within striking distance of planes; leave Formosa virtually helpless against air and sea attack, and the strangling blockade of the home islands would be drawn even more tightly.

The Okinawa group consists of the main island of Okinawa and fifty-four others of various sizes. Okinawa, some sixty-seven miles long and from three to ten wide, offered many landing beaches, thus giving to the Allies a measure of surprise that was lacking at Iwo. About

500,000 inhabitants were scattered over the island, which is mountainous and rugged in the north but hospitable and fertile in the south. Nearly 70,000 Okinawans lived in the capital city of Naha on the west coast. The Okinawa group had a population of 820,000 and was garrisoned by about 100,000 Japanese troops. The island had been heavily fortified, with thousands of caves and man-made strong points invading even the hitherto sacred precincts of Japanese cemeteries. The enemy developed a series of fine airfields, the principal ones being Naha, Yontan, Yonabaru, and a strip on the island of Ie to the north.

The decision was definitely made—the next and last stepping-stone was Okinawa. The combined chiefs of staff moved quickly to reorganize the command. Lieutenant General Millard F. Harmon had become commander of the Army Air Forces of the Pacific Ocean Areas and deputy commander of the Twentieth Air Force. His plane was lost in early March while flying from Pearl Harbor to an advanced base, and neither he nor his nine companions ever were heard from again. Major General Willis H. Hale, his deputy, succeeded to both commands, assuring continuity of plans already completed.

General MacArthur was placed in full command of all army forces and resources, including planes, in the Pacific theater. Admiral Nimitz received similar supreme authority over all naval resources, including planes. General Arnold retained command of the Twentieth Air Force and its Superfortresses. Over-all strategic direction and coördination was placed in the hands of the joint chiefs of staff consisting of Generals Marshall and Arnold and Admirals King and Leahy. The MacArthur-Nimitz team was announced during the first week of April, but had been decided upon some time before. The stage had been fully set for the Ryukyu invasion.

While all this was going on the Japanese were not idle. Unable to land troops on the American Continent, and with no forward bases from which to launch air blows, the enemy devised a novel weapon of attack that proved ineffective and had only a nuisance value. The fantastic "counteroffensive" consisted of bomb-carrying paper balloons launched from Japan and carried by air currents across the Pacific. A few landed in the United States, one reaching as far east as Michigan. Several American civilians were killed when they innocently picked up the small explosive charges. Five children and a woman on a picnic in Oregon were blown to death when the unknowing youngsters began to play with what looked like a harmless ball. Some of the balloons also fell in Canada.

They were made of five layers of silk paper and when filled with hydrogen expanded to a diameter of thirty-five feet. The bags rose to 25,000 or 35,000 feet where they struck the air currents to carry them east. Automatic devices maintained that altitude by releasing sand bags until a time clock estimated they were over the target, when the bomb was released. This hit-and-miss "attack" was so ineffective that the army did not hesitate to announce the existence of the balloons in order to warn civilians not to touch strange objects on the ground. Tokyo, disappointed, threatened to send over the balloons with pilots.

Much worse were the Kamikaze, or suicide planes, and the Baka bombs launched against ships and men. The Kamikazes—so called after the "Divine Wind" which had once saved Japan from invasion—put in their first appearance at Leyte and did a great deal of damage. The cruiser *Nashville,* which had taken General MacArthur back to the Philippines, was badly damaged by one of the first such planes, and lost 133 men killed and 190 wounded near Mindoro. The Australian cruiser *Australia* suffered 74 killed and 152 wounded at about the same time. Dozens of other warships and cargo vessels were hit. One suicide plane crashed upside down into the battleship *California* off Lingayen, but she kept right on fighting despite fire and 203 casualties. Additional antiaircraft guns were placed aboard the ships and certain alterations were made on deck to counter this blow from planes in which the Japanese pilot was locked and doomed to death, whether he struck his target, crashed into the sea, or was blown to bits by defensive fire. As Admiral Mitscher said: "One thing is certain; there are no experienced Kamikaze pilots."

The Baka bomb was an improvement over the suicide plane. It was a low-wing monoplane with a wing-span of about fifteen feet, launched with its pilot from another plane and propelled at terrific speed by a jet-acceleration device. Every Baka launched, and every pilot of this excellent racing airplane, was doomed. The destroyer *Abele* was hit and sunk by one, losing eighty-one killed and thirty-two wounded. The Baka bomb was a far greater menace than the Kamikaze, but invasion of Okinawa nipped this threat before it could be fully developed.

The white ensign of the Royal Navy joined the Stars and Stripes when Vice Admiral Sir H. Bernard Rawlings led the British Pacific Fleet against the Sakishimas. His flagship was the 35,000-ton battleship *King George V* and his fleet included cruisers and destroyers and a number of carriers, of which the *Illustrious* was the leader.

March 26 saw the first American troops go ashore on Japanese territory. The 77th Division, composed largely of trainees from New York City, northern New Jersey, and Pennsylvania but officered by Major General Andrew D. Bruce and many other southerners, hit the beaches of five islands in the Keruma group, once again taking the Japanese by surprise.

The first man to set foot on Japanese soil was Sergeant Fred A. Myers, of Maybrook, New York, who jumped ashore on the islet of

Aka at 8:04 A.M., beating by a step Lieutenant Robert Berr, of Decatur, Illinois, commanding Company K of the Third Battalion of the 305th Infantry Regiment. Twenty-five hours later Captain Thomas J. Donnelly, of New York, chaplain of the regiment, raised the first United States flag to fly over any part of Japan.

Keruma, the principal island, Zamami, Tokashiki, Hakaji, Yakabi, Amuro, and Kuba were the other islets seized. Small enemy garrisons offered only spotty resistance, but the Japanese had done such a thorough propaganda job that the natives, believing the stories that the Americans would violate their women and slaughter nearly everyone, committed suicide in groups as a lesser fate. When the inhabitants saw they had nothing to fear, they came out of hiding and willingly did what they were told. Word of the American treatment spread quickly and proved helpful to the forces that were to land on Okinawa on Easter Sunday, April 1.

Fifth Fleet guns and planes accelerated their attacks on Okinawa while the Kerumas were being occupied, exacting a heavy toll of enemy planes and ships. The Japanese increased the ferocity of their attacks on Admiral Spruance's vessels, sending over clouds of torpedo and dive bombers as well as suicide planes. Few of the enemy aircraft managed to get through, but those that did claimed many hits. B-29's were added to the American planes that began a concentrated campaign to wipe out the airfields on Kyushu from which the Kamikaze and Baka pilots took off. All through the first half of the Okinawa campaign this desperate struggle went on at a high pitch.

As a final step in preparation for invasion heavy artillery was set up on the captured Keruma Islands to secure safety of the seventeen-mile stretch of water to Okinawa, and on March 31 the islets of Mae and Kamiyama in the channel were seized.

The week that followed was one of the blackest of the war for the enemy, and multiple blows fell on land, on sea, and from the air. At 8:30 A.M. on Easter Sunday, April 1, the United States Tenth Army sent the Twenty-fourth Army Corps and the Marine Corps' Third Amphibious Corps ashore along an eight-mile stretch of Okinawa's west coast. By the end of the first day the Americans expanded their beachhead to a depth of three miles, captured two airfields—Yontan and Katena—and lunged south to within eight miles of Naha. By the end of the week the Marines spread across the island and pushed more than five miles north, and had begun to spread over the Motobu Peninsula. The army also cut across the island to Nakagusuku Bay and pushed closer to Naha. The central third of Okinawa was firmly in American hands.

On April 5, the Soviet Union denounced its non-aggression pact with Japan. "The neutrality pact... was signed April 13, 1941,"

Moscow said, "before Germany attacked the Soviet Union and before the war between Japan on the one side and Britain and the United States of America on the other broke out. Since that time the situation is entirely altered. Germany attacked the Soviet Union, and Japan, an ally of Germany, helps the latter in the war against the USSR. Besides, Japan is fighting against the United States and Britain, who are allies of the Soviet Union. Under these circumstances the neutrality pact between the Soviet Union and Japan has lost its sense and a prolongation of this pact is impossible."

This diplomatic stroke combined with the Okinawa invasion to shake Japan to its roots. Premier Kuniako Koiso and his entire Cabinet were thrown out of office and replaced by seventy-seven-year-old Admiral Baron Kantaro Suzuki, an alleged "moderate," who formed Tokyo's third wartime Government. Suzuki, president of the Privy Council, had been in virtual retirement for years because of his opposition to the army clique.

The same day Japanese planes swarmed over the more than 1,500 naval craft in the Okinawa invasion armada and the newly won American shore positions, and the maddest sea-air battle of the war raged throughout the day. Several Allied destroyers were sunk and many other ships were damaged, but the Japanese lost nearly 400 of their planes without having interfered in any way with the operations.

On the following day, the Fifth Fleet struck back vigorously, catching the Japanese Navy in a sudden sortie in the East China Sea about fifty miles southwest of the home island of Kyushu. For two days the battle went on, and when it was over Japan's great superbattleship the *Yamato* had been sunk with two cruisers and three destroyers; three more destroyers were left burning so fiercely that they probably sank. Only three of these smaller warships survived the contest. In related actions other American planes sank or damaged more than a score of cargo ships and smaller boats. The sortie cost Japan at least one fourth of her remaining major naval forces.

Superfortresses opened a new phase in the aërial warfare against the home islands, striking Tokyo and Nagoya in the first double-blow leveled by the B-29's, and for the first time they were protected by land-based fighters, the giant planes having escort from Iwo.

We follow the conquest of the Ryukyus with Lieutenant General Simon Boliver Buckner, Jr.'s, Tenth Army. General Buckner, known as the "Bull," had last faced the Japanese under entirely different conditions. The noted son of the famous Confederate General of the same name who had surrendered to Grant, went to the United States' most northerly outposts in July, 1940, to command the Alaska Defense Force. In 1943 he was awarded the Distinguished Service Medal for his success in reorganizing the defenses and for having "limited the enemy's encroachment on that territory to footholds of little strategical importance." It was General Buckner who prepared the surprise that thwarted the Japanese when they attacked Dutch Harbor early in 1942. He personally supervised and planned the new bases in that northern territory, driving the enemy back to Kiska and Attu and finally leading the invasion that drove the Japanese back to the Kuriles. General Buckner, a great wrestler and fine hunter, was noted for his physical hardness and his ability to trek with a full pack indefinitely without tiring.

"You've got to march into their country to make them realize their complete defeat," he said in 1943, and the Okinawa assignment was the first step on the march he planned to lead into Japan.

Admiral Spruance was in overall command of the Okinawa invasion as he had been at so many others, with Vice Admiral Turner in command of amphibious landings. Major General John R. Hodges commanded the Twenty-fourth Army Corps and Major General Roy S. Geiger the Marines' Third Amphibious Corps. The first assault forces virtually walked into their shore positions, meeting little or no opposition from the Japanese who were stoutly entrenched in positions facing east, rather than to the west from which direction the Americans came. It was an astounding climax to the mightiest Pacific amphibious operation.

The troops overran undemolished airfields, pushed their lines far forward, transformed the beachheads into vast supply areas, built roads and prepared themselves for a long stay. Except for incessant air attacks there was little evidence that the enemy's home territory had been invaded. Only on the approaches to Naha, where the Japanese took advantage of the terrain, was there any real opposition. The walkover ended on the ninth day, but by that time the Americans held so much of the island and were so firmly entrenched that the final outcome had been shaped. Once again the Japanese were too late in their resistance. All they were able to accomplish was to make Okinawa the most costly loss of the Pacific War.

While the battles in the south grew fiercer each day the Marines in the north maintained a steady advance of about a mile a day. This was the third pleasant surprise for General Buckner who had not counted upon the easy landings and the quick capture of the central third of Okinawa. The north was mountainous, had barely a single serviceable road, and was the most easily defended part of the island.

By April 10 half of Motobu Peninsula had been overrun and barely fifteen miles separated the Third Amphibious Corps from Cape Hedo, the northernmost tip of Okinawa. The Twenty-fourth Army Corps seized Tsukan Island, guarding the eastern approaches to Nakagusuku Bay on April 10, six days later they landed on Ie Island.

The Marines reached Cape Hedo on April 19, cleared Motobu Peninsula the next day, thus making Unten Harbor available for Allied shipping. Three days later, on the 22d the army had completed capture of Ie.

But during those three weeks the Americans had been saddened by the loss of their Commander in Chief. President Roosevelt's sudden death at Warm Springs, Georgia, on April 12, occurred during the Okinawa campaign.

The Japanese decided to make their stand at the first important enemy defense line running from Machinato, five miles north of Naha on the west to Yonabaru on the east coast; each anchor protected an airfield. The Japanese fought ferociously from pillboxes, hillside caves, ravines, and burial vaults. They maintained deadly mortar and artillery fire from impregnable positions cut into the terrain and skilfully camouflaged. On one twenty-minute period 300 mortar shells fell into the American lines, each shell capable of blasting a crater thirty feet in diameter and ten deep. In one day they fired 2,500 rounds of 1,000-pound artillery shells and 500-pound rockets with deadly accuracy. American artillery rolled into position and tanks answered the Japanese fire, opening the greatest duel of big guns seen in the Pacific and comparable to the conflict in Europe.

The battle was growing more costly to both sides. Admiral Nimitz disclosed that up to April 18 the navy had lost 989 killed, 491 missing and 2,220 wounded, mainly to Japanese Kamikaze and Baka planes. Tenth Army casualties had begun to mount to 478 killed, 260 missing and 2,457 wounded. More than 10,000 Japanese had been killed and 400 captured, while nearly 100,000 Okinawa citizens had come under the jurisdiction of the United States Military Government. Between March 18 and April 12 Pacific Fleet gunners alone had shot down 1,277 Japanese planes. The next day they got 118 more during a heavy attack on the Okinawa ships, and in the next four days the Japanese lost 400 more to gunners on land and sea and to American planes.

This sort of warfare kept up for weeks, with the Japanese losing as many as forty planes for every one American plane lost. Damage to ships and casualties to men and officers on board were, however, extremely heavy. While the enemy's suicide air war was a complete failure in so far as its effect upon the invasion or Allied naval strength was concerned it resulted in the heaviest personnel losses in the history of the United States Navy.

The brunt of the southern fighting had been borne by the 7th, 27th and 96th Divisions, but with the end of the northern campaign General Buckner—whose title had been changed to Commander of the Tenth Army and Ryukyus Forces—was able to bring down most welcome reinforcements.

General Buckner's reinforcements were Marines—Major General Pedro A. Vateon's First and Major General Lemuel C. Shepherd, Jr.'s, Sixth. There were also Major General Bruce's 77th Infantry Division which had taken Ie. The 27th Division of Major General George W. Greiner, composed of New York National Guardsmen, was landed and went into action for the first time since Saipan. Major General A. V. Arnold commanded the 7th Division and Major General James L. Bradley led the 96th.

A general offensive was opened on April 20 behind a terrific artillery barrage. Gains of 1,000 yards were made through country studded with fortifications. But the enemy held and there was no sign of a breakthrough. Streams of lead and showers of shells fell upon the three divisions attempting to storm the thick-walled concrete and log bunkers dug deep into the sides of the hills. Admiral Nimitz gave the country an accurate picture of the struggle when he said: "Our troops are now striking at a fortified line which is organized in great depth and developed to exploit the defensive value of the terrain, which is dissected by ravines and terraced by escarpments....They include interlocking trench and pillbox systems, blockhouses, caves, and the conventional Japanese dug-in positions."

B-29's joined the fray, but still the Japanese fought on without yielding and met every American charge with half a dozen counterattacks. Gains were scored in yards, then lost to the enemy and won back again at heavy cost. Carrier planes came over in droves to help the land-based craft already operating from the fields won during the first days, but were unable to break the enemy resistance. It was a war to the death that raged until the end of the month.

By day the Americans advanced in waves with flame-throwing tanks and all the other paraphernalia of modern war. By night the artillery kept the battle going while ground action was limited to patrolling. All attempts to bring back wounded lying between the two contending lines were met by Japanese bayonet charges and machine-gun fire. It was war at its worst.

The gains piled up and by May 1, Machinato and its airfield outside Naha had been taken by the 77th Division, the 7th was starting to outflank Yonabaru and the First Marines, rushing down from the north, moved forward in the center. The second defense line had been reached and held as firmly as had the first.

On May 2 the 7th Division cracked through along the east coast for a gain of 1,400 yards, raising its total advance since the drive had started on April 19 to 2,400—less than a mile and a half in two weeks. American casualties on land and sea, had risen to 16,994, of which nearly 3,000 were killed and more than 2,000 were missing. On the Japanese side, losses were 33,462 dead and 700 prisoners.

The Japanese then went over to the attack in a desperate effort to gain the initiative. Planes sank five American destroyers and other light craft and damaged several others, raising the total of warships lost to the enemy since the Okinawa campaign was started by the navy on March 18 to twenty-four. The enemy also sent out suicide boats and when that helter-skelter action was over 150 Japanese planes and fifteen of the explosive-bearing small craft had been destroyed.

Simultaneously, the Japanese landed troops in small boats at three points behind the American lines. Two were in the vicinity of the Machinato airfield and the other was off the Yonabaru strip which had just been captured. These attacks, which, it turned out were mainly diversionary and designed to sabotage and harass the Americans, were promptly snuffed out, with all the Japanese killed. The 7th and 77th Divisions suddenly found themselves under a fierce assault that enabled the enemy to drive through at some points as much as 1,500 yards before being stopped.

The First Marine Division on the west drove to the outskirts of Dakeshi village about a mile from Naha; the 77th Division in the center advanced behind flame-throwing tanks toward and around the enemy citadel of Shuri, while the 7th Division pressed its encirclement of Yonabaru on the east. It was the last important advance for a time and there the lines stood on May 7, 1945—V-E Day, victory day in Europe.

That great day found the Americans on Okinawa 3,000 miles closer to Japan than they had been at Guadalcanal; they had traversed three fourths of the distance to their goal in less than three years. They had come 4,000 miles across the Central Pacific to Asia. Hard as the battles had been the soldiers tempered their rejoicing with the knowledge that the future victories would be even more costly. It would take plenty of time, they knew, to redeploy their comrades the 14,000 miles from the Rhine and 11,000 through the Indian Ocean from Italy. There were about 1,500,000 British and American troops in the Pacific theater. The Liberty ship that required sixty-five days for a round trip between the United States and Britain needed 120 days for the voyage from San Francisco to Okinawa and return. It was going to be a long time before men and matériel arrived in sufficient number to make much difference. Only planes and their personnel could reach the active front quickly.

So the struggle on Okinawa continued as if nothing had happened in Europe. In the face of casualties which on V-E Day had reached 21,976 the Americans slogged through the Okinawa mud to wrest a few strong points from the enemy.

On May 7, when the fighting in Europe ended, Okinawa became

the locale of the heaviest losses incurred by the Americans in the Pacific, exceeding those of bloody Iwo. The figures were:

Killed: Army, 2,107; Marine Corps, 577; Navy, 1,131.
Missing: Army, 501; Marine Corps, 38; Navy, 1,604.
Wounded: Army, 10,402; Marine Corps, 2,800; Navy, 2,816.

The enemy threw a violent air assault against the invasion fleet as a new offensive was opened on land. For the first time Japanese fliers hit a major warship, damaging the battleship *Nevada*, but they lost 165 of their planes.

The Sixth Marines on May 12 drove over the most bitter kind of opposition into the suburbs of Naha, but the fighting around Shuri was even more savage and of greater strategic importance. The Shuri defense belt was vital to both sides and it was evident that the fate of the invasion hung upon the results there.

General Buckner and Admiral Nimitz confidently expected to take the citadel, which was dominated by an ancient castle fortress and four high radio towers, but not until such heavy losses had been inflicted upon the Japanese that their powers of further strong resistance on the island would have been broken. The Japanese were deeply dug in on the reverse side of slopes that could not be hit by direct fire but from which they were able to lay down a devastating fire upon the Americans battling uphill. Fighting was continuous and without quarter.

To the east stood Conical Hill, a round eminence dominating both Shuri to the southwest and Yonabaru to the east. As long as the enemy held that height it was impossible to use the Yonabaru airfield or to flank Shuri. Conical Hill was taken and lost by the Ninety-sixth several times before finally being nailed down.

A similar struggle went on to the east of Shuri for Chocolate Drop Hill, captured by the 77th after five days of continuous fighting, and for Sugar Loaf Hill near Naha. Seven times that promontory changed hands, but the Sixth Marines at last obtained undisputed possession. All along the front the Japanese used the tombs of their ancestors as pillboxes from which to battle the Americans. Every hill on Okinawa was studded with these ready-made strong points, and the desperation of the Japanese was clearly shown in their willingness to desecrate what, for more than a thousand years, had hitherto been regarded as sacred, untouchable territory. Before the week was over the Sixth Marines had crossed the Asato River and had established themselves inside Naha, the island's capital.

Eight weeks had passed since Easter Sunday. It took three American divisions forty-four days after the early unopposed advance to struggle forward 15,000 yards. In a single night the Japanese poured 10,000 rounds of artillery shells into a 9,000-yard front. American warships had sent 25,000 tons of shells crashing into enemy machines. The enemy had lost more than 2,000 planes and at least six warships in attacking American and British naval forces. The following figures summarize the story:

American casualties were 3,093 soldiers killed or missing and 12,078 wounded to May 18; 1,239 Marines killed or missing and 6,180 wounded to the same date; 3,978 naval personnel killed or missing and 3,958 wounded to May 16—a total of 30,526, of which 8,310 were killed or missing. At the end of May 17 the Japanese had had killed in action 48,103; 139,858 civilians were under the jurisdiction of the United States Miltary Government.

The ninth week of the battle began with the Naha airfield the only one on Okinawa left in Japanese possession. This was so completely dominated by American artillery and warship fire that it was useless to the enemy. Progress along the entire front was slow and painful. Japanese troops, some wearing American uniforms taken from prisoners and from those killed in battle, made a strong but futile counter-attack above Naha.

The 7th Division came back into the line after a rest and joined the 96th to swing through and around the abandoned port of Yonabaru and then edged into the Chinen Peninsula, the southern land arm of Nakagusuku Bay. Naval guns poured heavy fire into the Shuri area to help the First Marines engaged in killing Japanese and sealing caves, but they were still 1,200 yards from the castle. The Sixth Marines again crossed the Asato and tightened their hold in Naha by occupying the city's northeast corner after a particularly fierce battle which was fought in a driving deluge.

The Japanese tried another double counterstroke on May 25, and again failed. An eighteen-hour air assault was launched against American ships, soldiers, and airfields. They landed airborne troops on American-held Yontan Airfield from a dozen transport planes. The Japanese were armed to the teeth and laden with grenades. They intended not only to damage American equipment but to recapture the field.

One enemy plane actually landed on Yontan and poured out its soldiers right on the ground. With no regular troops anywhere near to repel the air invasion so far behind the front, mechanics and other ground personnel, together with fliers awakened from their night's sleep, grabbed guns and whatever other weapons they could find and fought a pitched battle. Seabees joined the melée which raged for hours. The entire enemy force of 150 was wiped out; American casualties were four killed, twenty-five wounded. This strategem failed when tried first on Leyte; it failed again on Okinawa.

Ground positions changed little during the week, but the tenth week brought victories that spelled the end of the Japanese on Okinawa. Premier Suzuki in Tokyo had definitely told the Japanese Cabinet: "Our hopes to win the war are anchored solely on the fighting on Okinawa. The fate of the nation and its people depends on the outcome."

The First Marines captured Shuri on May 30 and at 1:45 in the morning ran up the American flag over the ancient moated castle, replacing the Japanese Rising Sun that had flown from the flagpole since 1871.

The end was finally in sight, but Naha still held out. Resistance began to crumble perceptibly; defense of Shuri and Naha had been too costly. On June 4 Marines swarmed ashore on the tip of Oroku Peninsula after a shore-to-shore amphibious move from Naha. Amphibious tractors and small landing craft rolled up the western beaches against minor opposition and in a few hours half the Naha airfield had been occupied.

At the other end of Okinawa the Seventh Division entered Gushichan, while in between a general advance sped forward. The Japanese lacked manpower, guns, and even spirit to put up a real battle any longer. The Naha airfield was completely occupied on June 6, the Oroku Peninsula was cleared, Naha was virtually captured, and Gushichan were taken the next day.

General Buckner took an unprecedented step. On Sunday, June 10, he sent planes over the enemy lines to drop cannisters containing an ultimatum to the Japanese commander demanding that he surrender. It was the first time in the Pacific war that an American general had specifically asked a Japanese military leader to negotiate an "orderly and honorable cessation of hostilities."

"Like myself," General Buckner wrote, "you are an infantry general long schooled and practiced in infantry warfare. You fully know that no reinforcements can reach you.... The destruction of all Japanese resistance on this island is merely a matter of days that will entail the necessity of my killing the vast majority of your remaining troops."

The enemy commander received thirty-six hours in which to signal his reply. Low-flying American planes searched in vain for the flags that were to mark an answer. The ultimatum had been ignored and the slaughter continued.

The 96th Division scaled the Yaeju Hill on June 14, poured over the escarpment and pursued the enemy toward the sea cliffs a few miles away, while the jaws of the pincers narrowed the escape corridor. Japanese troops began to surrender in groups and later in companies, a new phenomenon in island warfare. Every square yard of terrain was raked by a constant and highly destructive barrage of naval, artillery, and airplane fire.

The Sixth Marines moved back into the line after having cleared Oroku and on the 18th pushed close to the southern tip of the island, which they reached near the town of Uda the next day. There Corporal John C. Corbett of Milwaukee picked up a rock and tossed it into the Pacific, the first man to reach the lower end of Okinawa. He was with the Eighth Regimental Combat Team of the Second Marine Division which, led by Lieutenant David V. Carter, of Kenmore, Pennsylvania, had virtually walked to land's end after overcoming the last natural barrier at the Ibaru-Komesu Ridge.

While the Marines were thus making history by carving out a 1,000-yard beach strip between Mabuni and Cape Ara, tragedy struck the Tenth Army and the Ryukyus Forces. General Buckner had been hit by a Japanese shell fragment that landed squarely in a Marine forward observation post and died ten minutes later from a gaping wound on the left side of his chest.

The General, who liked to go as far forward as possible, was seated on a rock atop a hill overlooking the village of Makabe and the sea beyond. He was talking with Colonel Clarence R. Wallace whose Marine Eighth Regiment troops were even then establishing a foothold on the shore almost within sight of the two officers. Major William Chamberlain of Chicago, General Buckner's operations officer, was with them.

Japanese guns, almost as if they had been given the precise moment and the exact range, suddenly opened up at 1:15 P.M. The first shell from one of the enemy's last artillery pieces, struck the rock on which General Buckner was seated. Shell fragments ripped the leader's left side. He was carried back, smiling, about fifty yards where he received emergency treatment and transfusions, but he died in ten minutes. General Buckner was the highest ranking army officer killed in action during the Pacific war and the first area chief to lose his life in combat within his own sphere of operations. He was buried with simple ceremonies in the red clay soil of Okinawa's American cemetery thousands of miles from home.

Word of the tragedy spread quickly and served to hasten the pace of the final annihilation of the enemy. Admiral Nimitz immediately named General Geiger to succeed General Buckner as commander in chief of the Ryukyus Forces, a navy command, while General MacArthur delayed appointing a successor to the command of the Tenth Army.

There was little left to the Okinawa fighting after that. The Japanese defenses fell apart and the enemy was cut into four relatively small pockets. The wind-up was marked by increasing piles of enemy dead and hordes of surrendering prisoners. For the first time in eighty-one days big guns on land and sea fell silent because the Americans and

Japanese were so close that any shell might claim more American than enemy victims.

The Battle of Okinawa came to an end at 1:00 P.M. June 21, two days after General Buckner had been killed. There was no dramatic, last-stand suicide charge as on Saipan, Tarawa, and other islands. Hundreds of Japanese jumped off the cliffs into the sea, but 1,700 surrendered on the final day.

Lieutenant General Mitsuri Ushijima, Japanese commander in chief on Okinawa, told his cook that morning to prepare an elaborate dinner for a special occasion. It consisted of rice, canned meats, potatoes, fried fish cakes, salmon, bean soup, fresh cabbage, pineapples, tea and *sake* (wine) and was served in a cave at 10:00 P.M., to the general and his chief staff Lieutenant General Isamo Cho.

At 3:45 A.M. the two enemy officers, dressed in full field uniform, highly polished boots and wearing all their medals, walked silently to a narrow ledge outside the cave. They knelt facing the ocean and there, in the presence of their aides and staffs, ceremoniously committed suicide by *hara-kiri*.

It was believed before the invasion that the Japanese garrison was about 75,000 strong. Instead, it was more than 110,000. Of that number about 103,000 were killed and the remainder taken prisoner. Only in the Philippines had the enemy lost more men than he lost in the Okinawa fighting.

The cost to the Americans was also great. Besides General Buckner, the casualties included a great number of high officers, among whom were Brigadier General Claudius M. Easley, assistant commander of the 96th Division, and Colonel Harold C. Roberts, commander of the First Marine's 22nd Regiment. Total American casualties were close to 50,000, of which 12,500 represented killed and missing and 35,500 wounded. The navy, alone, lost 5,000 in the first category and as many wounded.

Most of the navy casualties were due to the Kamikaze and Baka attacks, which the Japanese kept up even after losing Okinawa. One suicide plane dived on the hospital ship *Comfort,* killing twenty-nine and injuring thirty-three patients, nurses, and crew. The destroyer *Longshaw,* caught on a reef off Naha, had been raked by coastal guns until she exploded and sank with more than two-thirds of her crew casualties. The destroyer *Drexler* also went down with heavy losses. Six suicide planes and two bombs hit the destroyer *Laffey,* but she came home to be repaired. The little ships, referred to as "light units" by officers and "cans" by men suffered heavily. Other destroyers hit included the *Hazelwood, Twiggs, William D. Porter,* and the *Newcomb.*

Among the other destroyers lost off Okinawa was the *Halligan*

Photo International News

WHERE LIBERTY AWAITED PRISONERS OF THE JAPS

Following the liberation of Lieutenant General Jonathan Wainright from a prison camp near Mukden, activities of paratrooping rescue parties became a part of the dramatic finale of the war's end in the Pacific. This map shows the location of camps where freedom was just outside the gate.

which had fought gallantly in four major battles. Under young Commander Grace, with Israel Feinstein (a former member of the editorial board of this History of World War II) at the ship's radio, it was mined or torpedoed and went down in a terrific explosion with its fighting crew aboard. The few survivors paid high tribute to the courage and bravery of the men who gave their lives to their country on the fighting *Halligan*.

The old Pearl Harbor "relic" *Nevada* was the only battleship to be damaged, but the "old Maru" repaired her injuries on the spot and she remained in action. Carriers did not fare so well.

The *Bunker Hill,* after having been in continuous action for fifty-eight days and nights was struck by two suicide planes and in thirty seconds was converted into a blazing inferno fed by exploding ammunition. Three hundred and seventy-three of her crew were killed or died of wounds, nineteen more were missing and 264 were wounded, but Captain George A. Seitz, of Rochester, New York, brought her home. It was only because Captain Seitz had skilfully performed a dangerous operation that the carrier was saved.

The decks were literally a sea of flaming oil, and the Captain gave orders to make a sudden turn. This caused the carrier to take a quick, sharp list that succeeded in sweeping the flaming fluid into the sea, accomplishing in a few seconds what fire control never would have been able to do.

The British carriers *Indefatigable, Victorious,* and *Illustrious* weathered somewhat less serious suicide attacks while maintaining the attack on the Sakishima group during the Okinawa campaign. The British Pacific Fleet had sailed 25,000 miles in sixty days to reach the scene of battle on schedule. None of the ships was put out of action by any of the Japanese attacks.

During and after the fighting on Okinawa neighboring islands were seized at leisure. Kume, fifty miles to the west, was occupied without opposition during the last week in June, making available another airfield 300 miles from Formosa, 345 from China, and 370 from Kyushu. Marines had walked in and taken the little island of Iheya, only 310 miles from Japan, on June 3. The small Japanese garrison surrendered without putting up a fight. Six days later, on June 9 Aguni was similarly taken.

During the final weeks of the Okinawa campaign General Stilwell visited General Buckner to find out just what was needed in the way of troops and training. "Vinegar Joe," then commanding general of the Army Ground Forces, went on to Manila to see General MacArthur.

General Buckner was killed while this conference between the two Generals was on and before it had concluded General Stilwell was restored to active duty in the Pacific by being named the new commander of the Tenth Army.

The epoch-making days which followed have been recorded in the opening chapters of this history. Never before has the world been startled by a more astounding series of events in rapid succession. The tragic death of President Roosevelt only fifteen days before the end of the war in Europe—the advent of the atomic bombs which threatened

INTERNATIONAL NEWS PHOTO

Carrier Hit by Suicide Planes Off Okinawa

The U. S. S. *Bunker Hill* becomes an inferno after being hit by Jap suicide planes; but manages to make her way home!

OFFICIAL U. S. NAVY PHOTO

The Beginning of the End

Marines Advance at Okinawa

Marines look for Japanese snipers as they advance across bomb and shell blasted lowlands of island. See burial vaults on ridge.

OFFICIAL U. S. COAST GUARD PHOTOGRAPH

Halftracks Take to the Water

Halftracks loaded with soldiers leave the tank deck of LST off Okinawa for the initial assault waves.

INTERNATIONAL NEWS PHOTO

Hard Going on Okinawa

Heavy rains slowed up mechanized warfare, but infantrymen ploughed on to victory.

INTERNATIONAL NEWS PHOTO

Japanese Prisoners on Okinawa

Prisoners in war enclosure on island await their turn for questioning. Soon they crowded the prison enclosures.

Okinawa

ACME PHOTO

Generals at Okinawa

Marine Major General Lemuel C. Shepherd (with walking stick) and Lieut. General Simon Bolivar Buckner (with camera) watch front line action.

ASSOCIATED PRESS PHOTO

Manila Harbor Activity

Cargo vessels unload Pacific theater of war supplies at newly conditioned pier in Manila Harbor. Note Jap ships sunk in harbor.

SIGNAL CORPS PHOTO

Manila Burns!

Heavy smoke rises from dock area of city, February 7, 1945. Largest fires are in dock area.

OFFICIAL U. S. COAST GUARD PHOTO

A General and His G. I.'s

Just after his assault forces roll onto beaches at Luzon, General MacArthur tours fast-forming American lines. He did return!

INTERNATIONAL NEWS PHOTO

Medical Aid

A Wac in the Army Medical Department aids in care and rehabilitation of veteran.

INTERNATIONAL NEWS PHOTO

First WACS in Central Pacific

Air Wacs boarding Army trucks, en route to overseas stations.

Women at War

INTERNATIONAL NEWS PHOTO

WACS Line Up

Ready for duty in North Africa or anywhere are these well-trained women soldiers.

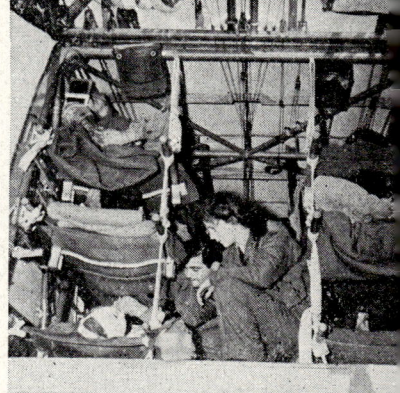

INTERNATIONAL NEWS PHOTO

Flight Nurse Helps Wounded Yanks

Flight nurse prepares wounded for takeoff from Germany to base hospital in glider.

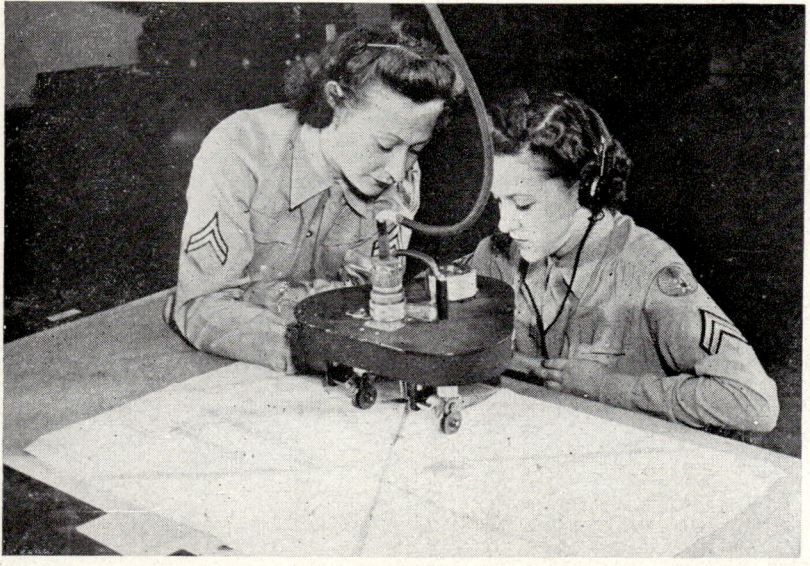

ACME PHOTO

WACS at Work

These WACS are engrossed in observing orientation problems of pilots.

INTERNATIONAL NEWS PHOTO

Spars Marching

Part of the basic training for Spars is intensive drilling. Spars are the women of the Coast Guard.

INTERNATIONAL NEWS PHOTO

Waves Study Aërial Navigation

Future aërial navigators become familiar with an air computer.

INTERNATIONAL NEWS PHOTO

Waves Reviewed by Leader

Lieut. Commander Mildred McAfee reviews Waves during anniversary ceremony of their founding.

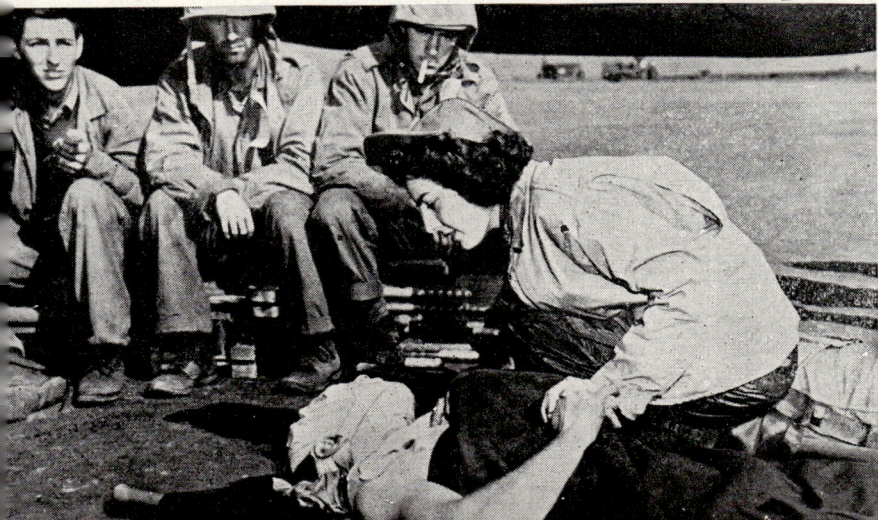

INTERNATIONAL NEWS PHOTO

"Angel of Mercy" on Iwo Jima

The first Navy flight nurse on any battlefield aids wounded Marine.

WIDE WORLD PHOTO

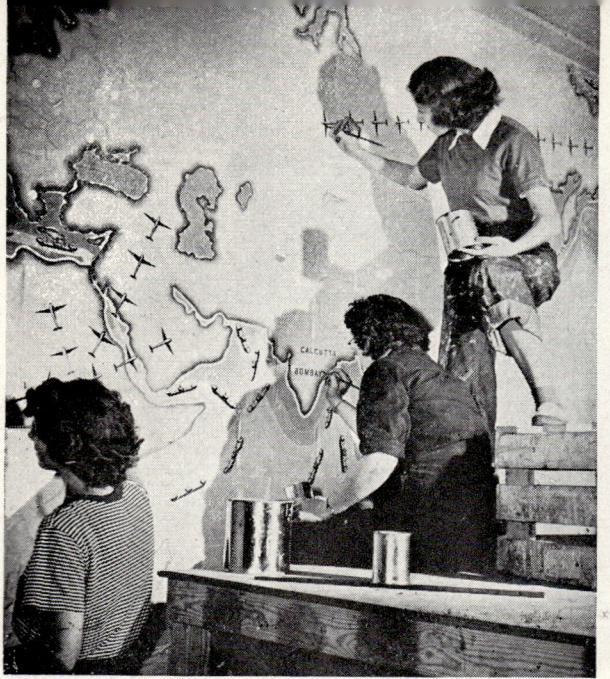

"Brushing Up" Their Geography

Spars executing a map of the world on wall of their mess hall.

WIDE WORLD PHOTO

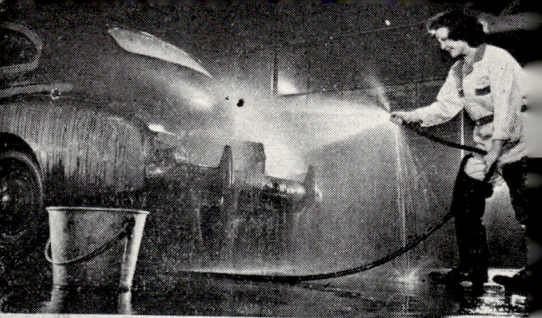

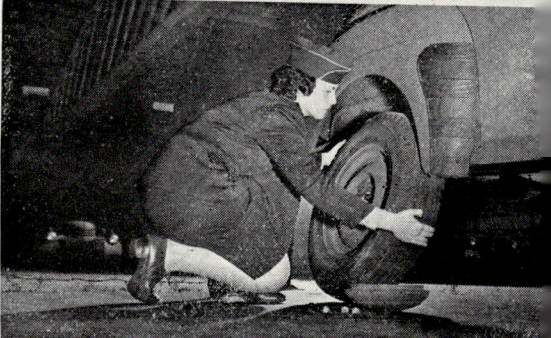

"Home, Jane"—Army Version

Civilian employees of the Army, these women chauffeurs help to maintain the Army's motor fleet.

INTERNATIONAL NEWS PHOTO

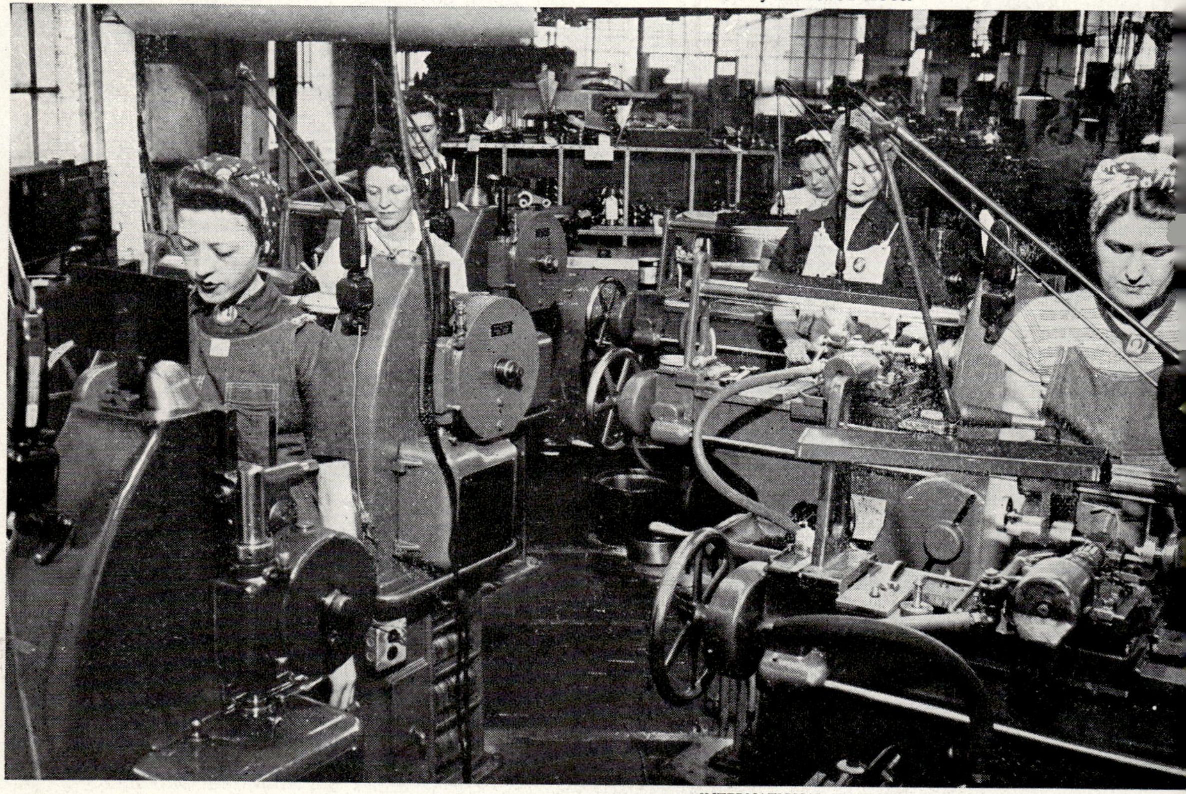

Doing Men's Work

Women answered the call to relieve manpower shortage at Navy Yard in Washington and all over the Nation.

First Women Marine Rifle Team
Women Marines plan to become good shots with pistols and rifles.

Mount Holyoke to Tripoli
Women Marines march across Mount Holyoke campus.

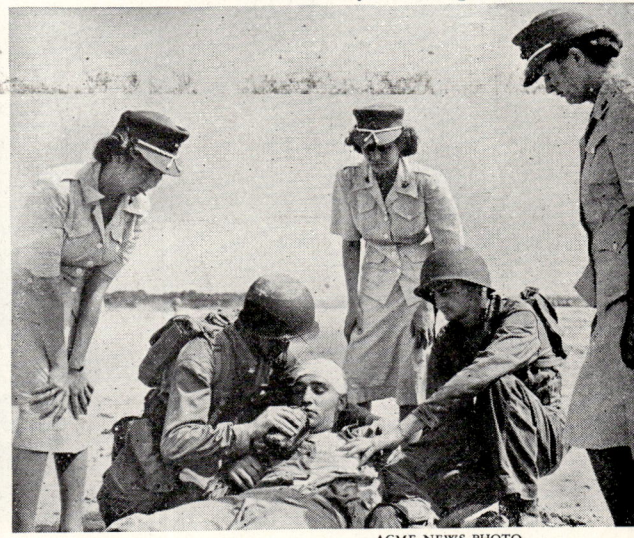

Army Nurses in Rehearsal
Life boat drill on transport taking Army nurses to active duty.

Marine Cadets in Training
Women Marines get a picture of actual battle conditions from Medical Corpsmen.

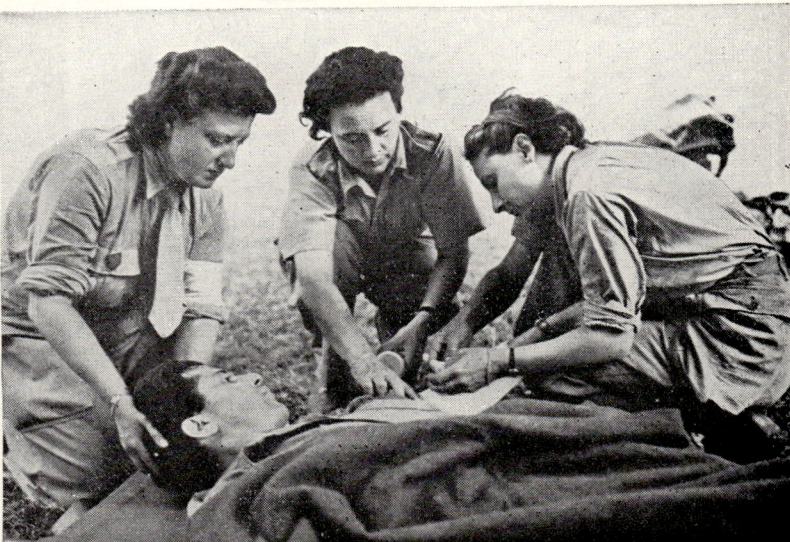

Free French Nurses
French Army Nurses on duty in the front lines care for a wounded soldier near the front lines.

INTERNATIONAL NEWS PHOTO

Here's a New Flattop!

The U. S. S. Lake Champlain starts down the ways at Norfolk.

INTERNATIONAL NEWS PHOTO

The Curtain Goes Down at San Francisco

President Truman congratulates Stettinius, then Secretary of State, on the completion of his great work.

INTERNATIONAL NEWS PHOTO

"Oh, What a Great Day This Can Be in History."

President Truman closes the San Francisco Conference.

INTERNATIONAL NEWS PHOTO

Japanese "Ersatz" Merchant Fleet

Here in a Honshu harbor are the wooden luggers of the dwindling Japanese fleet.

"Japan Takes It"

INTERNATIONAL NEWS PHOTO

Kobe Bombed

Hundreds of incendiary bombs fall on commercial dock area in Kobe.

INTERNATIONAL NEWS PHOTO

Famous Fujiyama

Three B-29 superfortresses are seen in flight over Fujiyama after a raid.

INTERNATIONAL NEWS PHOTO

Balikpapan, Borneo!

Australian troops hit shore in first assault wave on oil-rich Borneo.

Potsdam

INTERNATIONAL NEWS PHOTO

First Conference at Potsdam
Another historic meeting of the United Nations takes place in the suburb of conquered Berlin.

INTERNATIONAL NEWS PHOTO

The "Big Three" in Berlin
Marshal Stalin, President Truman, and Prime Minister Churchill together for the first time before the Potsdam Conference.

ACME RADIOPHOTO

On to Potsdam
Britain's new Prime Minister Clement Attlee and his Foreign Secretary Ernest Bevin leave for Potsdam.

PRESS ASSOCIATION PHOTO

A new "Big Three"
Still at Potsdam, President Truman and Joseph Stalin meet Clement Attlee.

American Negro Troops Overseas
A detachment of crack Negro troops with marching equipment.

Subchaser Commissioned
Colored troops served in every branch of the U. S. Armed Forces.

Ensign Sworn In
Colored Ensign is sworn in as an officer in the Naval Reserve.

Colored Troops on Way Overseas
Gathered for Sabbath services on board a transport, colored troops of a task force are seen on deck.

THE ATOMIC ERA

Where the Atom Was Harnessed

Oak Ridge, Tennessee, one of the three giant production plants for the manufacture of the new atomic bombs.

ACME PHOTO

OFFICIAL U. S. AAF PHOTO

Hiroshima Wiped Out

Smoke billows 20,000 feet above Hiroshima after the first atomic bomb had spread over 10,000 feet on the target.

OFFICIAL U. S. AAF PHOTO

Picture Made at 25,000 Feet

A plane photographed Hiroshima destruction after the atomic bomb burst.

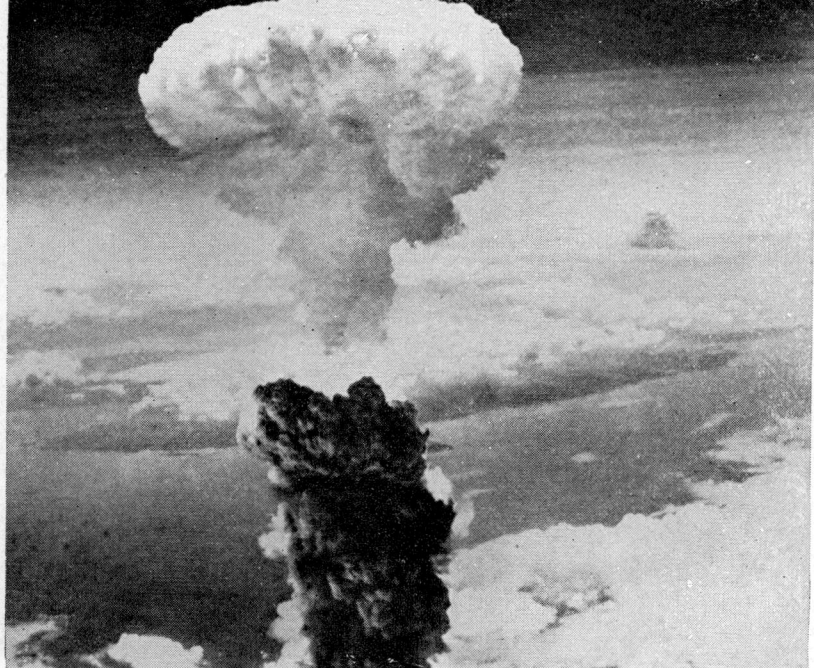

Second Atomic Bomb Lands

Nagasaki—second Japanese city to suffer devastating damage from the new weapon.

INTERNATIONAL NEWS PHOTO

7 P.M.—V-J Day!
A dramatic moment—President Truman announces the end of the war and our final victory.

V-J Day
Los Angeles, typical of all American cities on the day of victory, celebrates riotously.

War Cabinet Turns to Peace
President Truman discusses Japanese surrender with his cabinet.

A Great Moment
Britain's loyal opposition, Eden and Churchill, walk beside Prime Minister Attlee to the Westminster Abbey Thanksgiving Service.

Man of Destiny
First foreign general to enter Japan as a conqueror for over 2,000 years—General Douglas MacArthur.

SURRENDER

SIGNAL CORPS PHOTO

The Jap Surrender Plane

White, with green crosses, the Japanese surrender plane arrives at IE SHIMA.

INTERNATIONAL NEWS PHOTO

Bringing Flowers to IE SHIMA

Two Japanese emissaries leave their plane with bouquets of flowers!

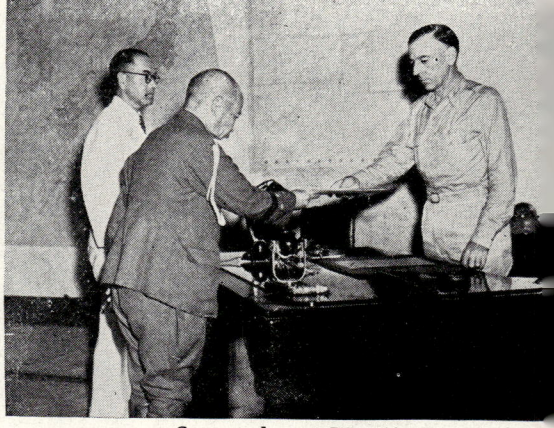

Surrender at Manila

General Takashino Kawake hands his credentials to General Richard Sutherland, Chief of Staff to MacArthur.

INTERNATIONAL NEWS PHOTO

U. S. AAF PHOTO FROM ACME NEWSPICTURES

Grim Japanese Faces

At IE SHIMA the Japanese delegation waits for plane to Manila to receive surrender directions.

MacArthur Signing Surrender Terms

General MacArthur signs as Supreme Allied Commander during formal surrender ceremonies on the U. S. S. Missouri in Tokyo Bay. Behind MacArthur are Lieutenant General Wainwright and Lieutenant General Percival, British Commander.

Pacific Victory

A montage conception of the victory in the Pacific—the ships, the planes, the weapons—but most of all the men, the U. S. soldier, sailor, marine, and seabee who made possible the final victory.

the annihilation of all Japan—the entrance of Russia into the war against Japan as the Soviets with an army of a million men drove the Japs out of Manchuria—the appeal of Emperor Hirohito for peace—the unconditional surrender of Japan on September 2, 1945—the dramatic scenes of the entrance of General MacArthur into Japan as supreme commander and ruler of the ancient empire—the signing of the official documents which ended the greatest war in history—these have all been related in this panoramic vision of World War II.

Signed at TOKYO BAY, JAPAN at 0904 I
on the SECOND day of SEPTEMBER, 1945

重光葵

By Command and in behalf of the Emperor of Japan
and the Japanese Government

梅津美治郎

By Command and in behalf of the Japanese
Imperial General Headquarters.

Accepted at TOKYO BAY, JAPAN at 0908 I
on the SECOND day of SEPTEMBER, 1945,
for the United States, Republic of China, United Kingdom and the
Union of Soviet Socialist Republics, and in the interests of the other
United Nations at war with Japan.

Douglas MacArthur
Supreme Commander for the Allied Powers

C.W. Nimitz
United States Representative

Hsu Yung-chang
Republic of China Representative

Bruce Fraser
United Kingdom Representative

K. Derevyanko
Union of Soviet Socialist Republics
Representative

T.A. Blamey
Commonwealth of Australia Representative

L. Moore Cosgrave
Dominion of Canada Representative

Leclerc
Provisional Government of the French
Republic Representative

C.E.L. Helfrich
Kingdom of the Netherlands Representative

Leonard M. Isitt
Dominion of New Zealand Representative

Surrender document signed on the U.S.S. *Missouri* in Tokyo Bay. It carries twelve names, two of them written in Japanese. The Japanese received one copy of the document, the United States the other.

AUTHORITIES AND OFFICIAL SOURCES

This History of World War II is indebted to official representatives of thirty Governments whose valuable advice is hereby acknowledged. Through their Ambassadors, Ministers, Military Attachés, Consulates, and War Information Services, our historians were enabled to analyze authentic materials from official sources.

We gratefully record our obligation to the Reference Division of the United Nations Information Office, representing the Governments of Great Britain, China, the French National Committee, Australia, the Philippines, India, Belgium, Poland, Greece, Norway, the Danish legation, Czechoslovakia, Yugoslavia, the Netherlands, Luxembourg, New Zealand, South Africa, Canada, and the United States.

The archives of the British Information Services, both in London and the United States, were found to be rich sources for historical material. Similar service rendered by Russian organizations, French and Italian groups, Chinese, Australian, Polish authorities, and the bureaus conducted by individual nations, were of valuable assistance to our analysts.

Among the latter agencies who extended coöperation were the Greek Office of Information, Chinese Ministry of Information, The Netherlands Information Bureau, Belgian Information Center, Australian News and Information Bureau, Polish Information Center, Lithuanian Cultural Institute, French Committee of National Liberation, the Free French organizations, Norwegian Information Service, Wartime Information Board of Canada, Czechoslovak Information Service, and the various associations for the protection of the Jews.

We are further indebted to our own War Administration in Washington and the coöperation of their divisional directors: to the late President Franklin D. Roosevelt for digest of his war addresses; Hon. Henry L. Stimson, Secretary of War, for services rendered by the War Department; to the late Secretary of the Navy, Frank Knox, and his successor, Secretary James Forrestal; to Hon. Cordell Hull, former Secretary of State, for documents from the State Department; to the courtesies extended through the offices of the various departmental officials.

Due credit must be given the great service to history extended by the Office of War Information, the largest institution of the kind in the world, under Director Elmer Davis; to the Committee of Records of War Administration, under direction of Pendleton Herring, established by President Roosevelt to collect and maintain adequate records of war agencies; to the War Archives established by Secretary Stimson; and similar services established for Naval records. The Library of Congress, under direction of its former head, Archibald MacLeash, began to organize what will become the greatest collection of war records in the world.

Other sources for historians include the work being done by the Smithsonian Institution, the American Historical Association, in association with the American Council of Learned Societies, The Carnegie Endowment for International Peace, and the American Library Association through whose members war histories will be made available in public libraries throughout the country.

We desire to make specific record of authorities with whom we have been in communication and express our appreciation for their advice; Lieutenant Colonel F. V. Fitzgerald, Chief War Section Public Relations, War Department; Lieutenant Colonel Douglas Parmentier, Chief Publications Branch, War Department; Colonel Stanley J. Grogan, Deputy Director Bureau of Public Relations; Colonel A. Gibson, Librarian Army War College; Lieutenant Colonel R. B. Hough, Jr., Army War College; Colonel Lloyd Lehrbas, Acting Aide-de-Camp on staff of General MacArthur, Commander in Chief of Southwest Pacific Area; Brigadier General Charles A. Willoughby of MacArthur's intelligence staff.

E. Wilder Spaulding, Acting Chief Division of Research and Publication, Department of State, Washington; Malcolm Morrow, Chief, Division of Public Inquiries, Bureau of Special Services, Office of War Information; David C. Mearns, Director Reference Department, Library of Congress; J. B. Orrick, Head of Reference Division, United States Information Service.

Vladimir S. Hurban, Ambassador of Czechoslovakia; C. Diamantopoulos, Ambassador of Greece; Aurelio F. Concheso, Ambassador of Cuba; Henrik Kauffmann, Minister of Denmark; M. Shayesteh, Minister of Iran; Robert Brennan, Minister Irish Legation; P. Zadeikis, Minister of Lithuania; Dr. Alfred Bilmanis, Minister of Latvia; Hugues LeCallais, Minister of Grand Duchy of Luxembourg; J. Kaiv, Acting Consul General of Legation of Estonia.

Chu Shih-Ming, Major General Military Attaché, Chinese Embassy; Risto Solanko, Counselor Legation of Finland; Ali Foad Toulba, Royal Legation of Egypt; Jonas Budrys, Consul General of Lithuania; Tor Myklebost, Attaché and Historian, Norwegian Embassy; W. Arlet, Counselor of Polish Embassy; Dr. Kazys Pakstas, Director Lithuanian Institute; Prof. Oscar Halecki, Polish Institute of Arts and Sciences.

Count Robert van der Straten-Ponthoz, Ambassador of Belgium; Jan-Albert Goris, Commissioner of Information for Belgium and author of "Belgium in Bondage"; Dr. Bartholomew Landheer, author of valuable collections of historical materials on "The Netherlands," dedicated to Her Majesty, Queen Wilhelmina.

B. C. Thomas, Deputy Controller, British Information Services; J. D. A. Barnicot, Librarian British Information Services; H. Ruth Isaacs, Information Division British Information Services; P. H. Gore-Booth, British Embassy; H. R. L. Henry, Office of Prime Minister of Canada; R. A. Draper, Wartime Information Board, Ottawa, Canada; L. B. Pearson, Minister Counselor Canadian Embassy; David W. Bailey, Director Australian News and Information Bureau.

Dr. Halvdan Koht, former Norwegian Foreign Minister and eminent historian; Vytautas Stasinskas, Vice Consul of Lithuania; Colonel Ilia M. Sarayev, Acting Military Attaché of Union of Soviet Socialist Republics; N. Matveeva, Secretary Embassy of Soviet Republics.

To the aforementioned authorities who have extended courtesies in reply to our inquiries, we give this historical recognition. And to the eminent historians of many nations who have aided our researches, we send our fraternal regards.

CHRONOLOGY OF THE WAR

1939

SEPTEMBER

1 Nazi Germany, under Adolf Hitler, invades Poland.
3 Great Britain and France declare war on Germany.
18 Russian troops occupy eastern Poland.
27 Poland surrenders unconditionally to Germany.

OCTOBER

14 German U-boat sinks British battleship *Royal Oak*.

NOVEMBER

3 U.S. neutrality bill is amended to permit shipment of arms on a cash-and-carry basis.
8 Attempt on Hitler's life is made in Munich beer hall.
30 Russia invades Finland.

DECEMBER

17 German pocket battleship *Graf Spee* is scuttled off Montevideo, after having been crippled by three British cruisers.

1940

JANUARY

19 Norway and Denmark reaffirm their attitude of neutrality.
20 Winston Churchill, British first lord of the admiralty, asks European neutrals for "united action" with the Allies against Germany.

FEBRUARY

1 Russians attack the Finnish Mannerheim Line with bombing planes and armored sleds.
17 British cruisers raid German ship *Altmark* in Norwegian fjord and, after a hand-to-hand battle, free 400 British captives.

MARCH

12 Finnish-Russian war ends. Finland cedes certain territory to Russia.

18 Hitler (German leader) and Mussolini (Italian leader) meet in conference at Brenner Pass.

APRIL

4 Prime Minister Chamberlain affirms his faith in victory, declaring that Hitler "missed the bus."
8 Franco-British allies lay mines in Norwegian waters, to stop ore shipments to Germany. Norway protests.
9 Germany lands troops in Denmark and Norway, startling the world with the suddenness of the invasion. Denmark makes no resistance. Norway fights. Oslo in German hands. The capital is removed to Hamar.
10 Naval battle between British and German fleets reported off Norway.
17 British forces occupy Narvik, northern port of Norway.

May

3 Norwegian Army on the Trondheim front, under Colonel Getz, surrenders. King Haakon escapes to the north and eventually reaches England. Major Quisling, a pro-Nazi Norwegian, is named leader of the state.

10 Germany smashes into Holland, Belgium, and Luxembourg at dawn with air and land attacks. Hundreds of parachutes land armed troops. The blow stuns Britain. Neville Chamberlain resigns. Winston Churchill becomes British Prime Minister.

11 Dutch open their floodgates and check invaders on eastern frontier.

13 Germans take Liége and make lightning advance over flooded areas in Holland. Rotterdam suffers heavy damage. Queen Wilhelmina flees to England.

14 General Winkelman, commanding the Dutch forces, surrenders "to prevent annihilation." Ex-Kaiser Wilhelm II remains at Doorn, under German protection. Nazi offensive carries to Meuse River on 80-mile front, extending from Sedan to Liége, through Namur.

16 Germans cross the Meuse in Sedan sector, piercing the northwestern extension of France's Maginot Line.

17 Belgian Government moves to Ostend. Brussels and Antwerp occupied by Germans. British Expeditionary Force begins strategic withdrawal.

19 France names General Weygand generalissimo of the Allied armies, replacing Gamelin. British bomb Hamburg and Bremen.

20 Laon captured by the Germans, creating a deep thrust into France.

21 German blitzkrieg armies smash their way to the English Channel.

26 Boulogne in German hands, after hard fighting.

28 The Belgian Army surrenders, by order of King Leopold.

29 Allies begin evacuation of troops from the German "pocket" in Flanders.

June

1 The British Navy is given great credit for bringing safely back to England 300,000 troops who narrowly escaped the German pincers at Dunkirk.

5 Dunkirk falls to the Germans.

10 Germans press on, breaking the Weygand line at places, and reach the suburbs of Rouen. Italy declares war on France and Great Britain.

11 French Government in flight from Paris. At Soissons the French retire to positions south of the Marne.

12 Reims and Rouen fall. Enemy troops within 12 miles of Paris.

13 Germans cross the Marne at Chateau-Thierry, the field where American soldiers helped break a German advance in 1918. French Premier broadcasts "final appeal" to President Roosevelt for American help.

14 Paris occupied by German army without fighting, all French troops having been withdrawn. Le Havre falls. German advance reaches the Argonne.

15 Verdun captured. French retire from Maginot Line.

16 With the cause of France hopeless, Premier Reynaud resigns rather than give the word to "cease firing." The aged Marshal Pétain becomes premier.

17 Pétain announces in broadcast, "It is with a heavy heart that I tell you today that we must stop the fight." Chancellor Hitler and Premier Mussolini arrange to meet and decide terms of armistice.

21 French plenipotentiaries meet the Germans in Compiègne, where the

1918 armistice was signed. Germans dictate terms of armistice in 1940. In London General de Gaulle sets up a French Government-in-exile ("Free France").
22 Armistice signed. Fighting in France ends. Germans remain in occupation of a large part of France, including Paris.
25 Separate armistice with Italy signed.
27 Rumania submits to Russia's demand for Bessarabia and northern Bucovina.

July

9 France becomes a corporative state under Pétain, by vote of Parliament. Temporary capital at Vichy.
19 Hitler broadcasts plea for peace with England. Rejected.
21 Lithuania, Latvia, and Estonia absorbed into Soviet Union.

August

8 The Battle of England begins with waves of German bombers sweeping over southern ports.
14 British planes attack enemy bases in France and Netherlands.
15 Torpedoing of armed merchant cruiser *Transylvania* announced.

September

3 U.S. Government trades 50 overage destroyers to Britain for naval bases in Newfoundland and the West Indies.
6 King Carol of Rumania abdicates. His son Michael becomes king.
16 President Roosevelt signs Selective Service bill, drafting Americans between the ages of 21 and 35 for military service.
17 Italians force their way from Libya into Egypt.
23 British and French warships in battle at Dakar, West Africa.
24 Dakar expedition called off by the British and the "Free French" forces. French defenders refuse to surrender.
27 Japan joins the Rome-Berlin Axis, the three Powers agreeing to assist each other should any of the three be attacked by a fourth power.

October

7 Germans enter Rumania to guard petroleum fields.
16 Registration Day in the U.S. Over 16,000,000 men register for military training.
24 Adolf Hitler and the French Chief of State, Marshal Pétain, meet to promote a "new order" for Europe.
28 Italian Fascist troops in Albania invade Greece.

November

1 Athens and Salonika heavily bombed by Italians. British promise help to Greece.
10 Chamberlain, former British Premier who declared war, died at his home in Hampshire.
12 British planes of the fleet air arm attack Taranto Harbor, Italy.
15 Coventry, England, almost completely destroyed by mass bombing.
19 Greek forces rout Italians and advance into Albania.
20 Hungary allied with Germany and Italy.
23 Rumania joins Rome-Berlin Axis.

December

2 Capture of 5,000 Italians by Greek Army is announced.
12 British drive Italian invaders from Egypt: beginning of see-saw battles in North Africa.

1941

January

- 5 Bardia, Italy's stronghold in Libya, captured by Australian troops.
- 20 Hitler and Mussolini meet for conference.

February

- 7 Bengazi, Libya, taken by British.
- 10 Great Britain breaks relations with Rumania.
- 16 Bulgaria and Turkey sign non-aggression pact.
- 26 British forces, assisted by Africans, occupy Mogadiscio, Italian Somaliland.

March

- 1 Bulgaria signs the Axis Tripartite Pact.
- 8 U.S. Senate passes Lend-Lease bill empowering the President to give "all-out" aid to Britain or any other countries opposing the Axis.
- 11 France cedes territory in Indo-China to Thailand, under peace protocol arranged by the Japanese.
- 25 Yugoslav Government joins Axis, but military leaders overthrow government, make Peter king, and defy Germans.

April

- 3 German mechanized forces join Italians in North Africa. British retire from Bengazi.
- 6 Germany at war with Yugoslavia. Belgrade heavily bombed. Greece is also attacked, on the charge that the British intended to open a new war from there.
- 7 British and Imperial troops enter Addis Ababa, capital of Ethiopia. Practically all of Italian East Africa now under British control.
- 9 Salonika abandoned by the Greeks.
- 10 Greenland under U.S. protection.
- 13 Belgrade captured by Nazis. Russia and Japan sign five-year treaty of non-aggression and mutual friendship.
- 18 Yugoslav Army surrenders. British repel Nazi drive around Mt. Olympus, Greece.
- 23 King George of Greece flees to Crete, and later to Africa. Northern Greek Army surrenders.
- 25 British Empire forces begin withdrawal from Greece.
- 27 Athens occupied by Nazis.
- 29 Main part of British Expeditionary Forces embark from southern Greek ports. It is a second "Dunkirk."

May

- 7 Joseph Stalin becomes Premier of the Soviet Union.
- 9 Britain takes control of Iraq (Mesopotamia).
- 10-11 London suffers terrific bombing attacks.
- 12 Rudolf Hess, a Nazi leader, flies to Scotland and lands by parachute. He is placed in custody. It is later revealed that he had a private peace plan which attempted to take Great Britain out of the war.
- 18 Croatia, formerly part of Yugoslavia, is created a kingdom under an Italian duke.
- 20 Germans attack Crete with parachute and airborne troops.
- 24 British battle cruiser *Hood* sunk by German battleship *Bismarck* in North Atlantic.
- 27 With the aid of American-built planes, the *Bismarck*, attempting to return to port, is caught and sunk by planes and warships.

June

- 1 Britain announces surrender of Crete.

Chronology of the War

4 Ex-Kaiser William II, who fled from defeated Germany in 1919, dies in exile at Doorn, Holland.

8 British and "Free French" attack Syria. French defenders fight French attackers.

10 Sensation is caused by report that the U.S. ship *Robin Moor* was sunk by submarine off Cape Verde Islands, May 21. No lives lost.

16 U.S. State Department orders closing of all German consular and propaganda establishments in U.S.

19 Relations between Germany and Russia are strained by Hitler's drive into the Balkans.

21 Damascus taken by British and "Free French" in Syria campaign.

22 Germany declares war on Russia. Fighting starts on a 2,000-mile front ranging from the Black Sea to the Arctic. Italy at war with Russia. Rumania joins the Nazis to recover territory taken by the Russians. For the same reason Finland lines up with Germany.

28 Russian troops are forced back to the old Russian-Polish boundary.

July

7 American troops join British in occupation of Iceland.

13 Syria campaign ends, with defeat of defending French.

24 Japanese begin occupation of Indo-China with consent of the French.

25 President Roosevelt issues an order freezing Japanese assets in U.S. and halting all trade with Japan.

August

6 British and American Governments warn Japan not to attempt invasion of Thailand (Siam).

9-12 Prime Minister Churchill and President Roosevelt meet in secret conference on the high seas and issue an 8-point program of war aims, subsequently called the Atlantic Charter.

25 British and Russians invade Persia.

26 Russians, retreating, blow up great dam on the Dnieper River.

September

2 German spearhead approaches within 20 miles of Leningrad.

11 After several American vessels have been sunk or attacked by U-boats, President Roosevelt gives orders to "shoot at sight" any German or Italian vessel encountered by American ships or planes.

16 British and Russians attack Iran (Persia), force abdication of Riza Khan, and jointly occupy the kingdom.

19 Nazis capture Kiev, capital of the Ukraine.

21 The Crimea is isolated when Nazis break through to Sea of Azov.

25 German land troops, assisted by bombers, attack suburbs of Leningrad, but are driven back.

October

14 Nazis reach within 60 miles of Moscow.

16 Rumanian-Axis troops take Odessa, Black Sea Port. Temporary Soviet capital is set up at Kuibyshev, in the Volga region, while Moscow is besieged.

18 Lieutenant General Hideki Tojo, former war minister, is named Premier of Japan.

25 Kharkov, industrial center of the Ukraine, taken by Nazis.

29 German forces enter the Crimea.

31 U.S. destroyer *Reuben Jones,* while on convoy duty, is torpedoed and sunk, with a loss of 100 lives.

November

5 Japan sends special envoy to Washington to discuss Japanese-American relations.

10 Prime Minister Churchill announces that "should the United States become involved in war with Japan, a British declaration will follow within the hour."

16 Premier Tojo complains that the ABCD powers (America, Britain, China, Dutch East Indies) are encircling and blockading Japan economically, constituting measures little short of war.

26 Conversations between Japanese envoys and Secretary of State Hull in Washington reach crucial point. Japanese are plainly told they must get out of China and Indo-China.

December

7 At 7:50 A.M. in the Hawaiian Islands, Japanese planes begin surprise attack on Pearl Harbor, causing severe damage to American naval and military forces, with great loss of life. Japan declares war on the United States and Great Britain.

8 U.S. Congress adopts declaration of war against Japan. Churchill informs Parliament that Britain is at war with Japan.

10 Japanese air forces sink British battleship *Prince of Wales* and the cruiser *Repulse,* off the Malay peninsula. On the Russian front the Nazis have been driven back more than 50 miles from Rostov. Retreat continues in other sectors in bitter winter weather.

11 Germany and Italy, partners with Japan in the Tripartite Pact (Axis), declare war on the United States. Congress recognizes state of war with these countries.

22 Japanese make landings on Philippines. General Douglas MacArthur in command of defending forces.

25 Hongkong falls to Japs.

28 Manila is bombed, though it had been declared an open city.

1942

January

2 Japanese enter Manila. General MacArthur's army of the Philippines retires to Bataan peninsula, to begin heroic fight against fearful odds.

11 In tanks and planes and on bicycles, and even swinging from tree to tree, the Japs advance down the Malay peninsula, sweeping the British before them. Kuala Lumpur, largest town in Federated Malay States, is captured.

14 German U-boats attack tankers off American coast.

31 British Imperial troops withdraw from Malaya to Singapore and blow up causeway connecting island with mainland. In Burma, the British defenders are driven back from Moulmein.

February

6 Oil center in Borneo captured by Japanese.

10 Japanese troops pour into Singapore, across repaired causeway.

15 Singapore surrenders. Japanese general, Yamashita, receives surrender from General Percival.

24 In Burma campaign, British withdraw from Rangoon.

March

6 Batavia, capital of the Dutch East Indies, falls to the Japs.

10 Defending Dutch, British, and American troops in Java surrender unconditionally.

17 MacArthur, recalled from the Philippines, arrives in Australia by plane to take command of united forces there.

31 Native India Congress rejects plan of "Dominion status after the war," offered by Sir Stafford Cripps. Demand is for immediate independence.

April

8 German-Italian allies open offensive in Libya.

9 Bataan peninsula, Philippine Islands, long defended by General MacArthur and later by General Wainwright, falls to Japs, who inflict "March of Death" on American and Filipino prisoners. Wainwright, with small force, withdraws to Corregidor.

18 Tokyo is bombed by a squadron of American planes led by Brigadier General James H. Doolittle. The take-off was from carrier *Hornet*.

28 Corregidor island fortress is heavily bombed.

May

3 Mandalay falls to Japanese as invaders push into northern Burma. Lashio, terminus of the Burma Road into China, is reported captured.

4 British warships land troops in northern Madagascar. After three days' fighting, Diego Suarez, French naval base, is captured.

5 In Philippine campaign, Japs make landing on Corregidor island, launching attack from Bataan.

6 General Wainwright surrenders Corregidor and the other islands in Manila harbor.

8-9 Battle of the Coral Sea, won by Americans. Many Japanese warships destroyed in attempt to cut Allies' supply lines or invade Australia.

12 Germany resumes attack on Russians in the eastern Crimea.

18 Large American Expeditionary Force, with tanks and heavy artillery, reaches Northern Ireland.

19 Kerch peninsula, Crimea, falls to Germans, who report capture of over 100,000 Russians.

27 On Libyan front, two columns of German panzer divisions penetrate behind British defenses.

29 Following sinking of Mexican ships by U-boats, Mexico declares war on the Axis Powers, Germany, Italy, and Japan.

30 British bombers smash city of Cologne in mass night raid, using more than 1,000 planes.

June

2 Krupp works at Essen, Germany, are target for British bombers in second big raid.

4-6 Japanese attempts to capture Midway Island end in failure. In great sea and air fight, Japan loses four aircraft carriers and great numbers of planes.

17 In Libya campaign, General Erwin Rommel, commanding German-Italo forces, compels British to retreat from line protecting Tobruk.

21 Tobruk falls to the Axis after an overwhelming assault. Garrison of 25,000 men captured, with immense supplies.

25 Rommel carries the war more than 50 miles into Egypt.

30 Allied defensive line stiffens as Nazis reach within 100 miles of Alexandria.

July

1 Sevastopol, great stronghold on the Black Sea, falls to German and Rumanian troops after having been under siege for 25 days.

7 Hitler throws 1,000,000 men into a

vast wheeling operation aimed at the oil fields of the Caucasus.

27 Rostov-on-Don captured in terrific assault by Nazis, who push south and east in succeeding days.

August

6 India prepares for mass civil disobedience, recommended by Gandhi, unless Britain accepts India as a "free and independent partner" in the fight against aggression.

7 U.S. Marines land at Guadalcanal, Solomon Islands.

9 Gandhi and his chief supporters in the All-India Congress are imprisoned. Rioting ends after a few days.

10 Three American cruisers are lost in the battle of Savo Island, north of Guadalcanal.

19 British raid on Dieppe results in heavy losses to Canadian troops.

22 Brazil at war with Germany and Italy.

September

10 British begin occupation of Madagascar.

15 U.S. aircraft carrier *Wasp* torpedoed in Guadalcanal battle.

21 Violent street fighting in suburbs of Stalingrad. Germans are unable to advance.

23 Capital of Madagascar entered by British.

October

20 The Russians repulse a German mass attack at Stalingrad.

25 In the battle of Egypt, the British stand fast at El Alamein, despite heavy enemy attack.

November

4 British offensive, under General Montgomery, smashes Axis in Egypt.

6 Thousands of Italian and German troops surrender in Egyptian campaign. Rommel races back to Libya with remnants of army.

7 U.S. Army, Navy and Air Forces begin landing operations at numerous points on the shores of North Africa. They are supported by units of the Royal Navy and Royal Air Force. Operations are under command of General Dwight D. Eisenhower.

8 Pétain, French Chief of State, severs diplomatic relations with the U.S. Algiers quickly falls to Americans. Airports are seized at Oran and other points. Casablanca, on west coast of Morocco, is bombarded from the sea.

12 French admiral, Darlan, in Algiers, sides with Allies and orders all French forces in North Africa to cease resistance. Hitler sends his armies into Unoccupied France.

13 Tobruk is again taken by the British. Rommel retreats to Tripolitania, and finally to Tunisia.

15 Darlan appoints General Giraud as commander in chief of French armed forces in North Africa.

16 The Fighting French in London, led by General de Gaulle, declare that they will not accept arrangements to establish "a Vichy régime in Africa."

17 President Roosevelt announces that "French troops under the command of General Giraud have been in action against the enemy in Tunisia, fighting by the side of American and British soldiers."

27 French scuttle fleet at Toulon as Germans approach great naval base on the Mediterranean.

December

3 Russians break through German lines west of Rzhev. Germans have given up fight for Stalingrad.

17 Russian troops are now 80 miles west of Stalingrad.

24 Admiral Darlan assassinated in Algiers. General Giraud becomes High Commissioner of French Africa.

Chronology of the War

1943

January

5 Germans begin withdrawal from entire Stalingrad area.

14 President Roosevelt makes surprise flight to Casablanca, Morocco, to confer with Churchill and military leaders; called the "unconditional surrender" conference.

16 Russians open offensive on the upper Don.

18 Moscow announces that the seventeen-month siege of Leningrad has been raised.

27 After appalling losses, the Nazis establish new lines far to the west of Stalingrad.

30 British airmen bomb Berlin in daylight for the first time.

February

3 German radios announce three days of national mourning for those who died in Stalingrad battles.

9 Japanese finally abandon Guadalcanal area.

14-16 Rostov and Kharkov fall to Red Armies, climaxing a 375-mile drive from Stalingrad.

17 In Tunisia, U.S. forces are driven back by Nazis, who are using huge Mark VI tanks.

25 Americans recover lost ground in Tunisia.

March

2 The R.A.F. attacks Berlin in a devastating raid.

4 General MacArthur announces big victory over Japs in battle of Bismarck Sea, in New Guinea area.

10 Germans attempt new offensive in Kharkov area.

16 Russia admits evacuation of Kharkov, but claims victories in Smolensk area.

23 In Tunisia, British smash Axis defenses; break through Mareth Line.

April

7 Bolivia at war with the Axis Powers.

11 Americans retake Faïd Pass, Tunisia, where February retreat began.

12 British seize Sousse, last Axis-held supply port on Tunisian east coast.

26 Soviet Union breaks relations with Polish Government-in-exile, alleging contact between Germans and Poles.

May

7 In Tunisia, Americans take Bizerte and British enter Tunis.

11 Churchill in conference with Roosevelt at Washington.

12 Battle of North Africa ends with capture of General von Arnim and other German and Italian generals. Rommel flies back to Germany.

19 Churchill addresses U.S. Congress; declares, after Hitler's downfall we shall "lay the cities of Japan in ashes."

21 Stalin announces end of Comintern (Communist International).

30 Attu, Aleutian Islands, occupied by Japan in June, 1942, is recovered by Americans after hard battle.

June

3 In Algiers, Generals de Gaulle and Giraud head governing board for French Empire.

11 Italian island of Pantelleria, 80 miles from Sicily, surrenders to Allies after heavy sea and air bombardment.

12 Island of Lampedusa, in Mediterranean, is occupied by Allies.

30 U.S. forces land on Rendova Island in the central Solomons and destroy Jap defenders.

July

10 Sicily invaded by Canadian, American, and British troops, under supreme command of General Dwight D. Eisenhower. Two thousand ships involved in landing operations.

11 Allies establish beachheads and start north to cut off aid from continental Italy.

12 Syracuse falls to invaders.

19 Rome is bombed by U.S. Nineteenth Air Force. Objectives were railroad assembly yards and airdrome.

19 U.S. planes raid Japanese bases in Paramushiru Island in the Kuriles.

25 Mussolini resigns in favor of Marshal Badoglio.

August

1 U.S. Liberators bomb Ploesti oil fields and refineries in Rumania.

15 American and Canadian troops land on Kiska in the Aleutians, but find the Japanese have already fled.

17 President Roosevelt and Prime Minister Churchill confer at Quebec. The conquest of Sicily is completed.

23 The Russians retake Kharkov for the second time in the summer.

29 The Danes scuttle their fleet in revolt against the Germans who seize their king.

September

1 U.S. Task Force attacks Marcus Island in the Pacific, 1,100 miles from Tokyo.

3 Allies invade the toe of Italy across the Straits of Messina.

8 Italy surrenders unconditionally.

9 American Fifth Army lands at Salerno, Italy.

10 Germans shell and seize Rome, but the Italian fleet escapes them and is turned over to the Allies.

11 MacArthur's forces capture Salamaua in New Guinea.

17 Lae, important Japanese base in New Guinea, falls.

26 Russian troops retake Smolensk.

October

1 Fifth Army captures Naples in Italy.

13 Italy declares war on Germany.

19 United Nations' Foreign Secretaries open Moscow Conference. China is represented at some of the meetings.

November

6 The Russian Army recaptures Kiev.

20 U.S. troops land on Tarawa and Makin in the Gilbert Islands in the Pacific.

22 Roosevelt, Churchill, and Chiang Kai-shek begin the Cairo Conference in which a decision is reached to strip Japan of all her conquests. Makin and Tarawa are secured after bloody fighting in which 1,100 American lives were lost, 2,500 Americans were wounded.

December

4 Roosevelt, Churchill, and Stalin meet at Teheran.

16 U.S. Sixth Army lands on Arawe in New Britain.

24 Eisenhower named to direct the invasion of Europe as Supreme Commander.

26 Allied forces land on Cape Gloucester in New Britain.

Chronology of the War

1944

January

11 As Red Army enters Poland, a Moscow broadcast says the Soviet-Polish border established in 1939 must stand. Western Ukraine and western White Russia would thus come within the Soviet Union.

15 Russians open new offensive in Leningrad area.

20. Novgorod is evacuated by the Germans.

22 British, American, and Greek troops establish beachhead at Nettuno, on west coast of Italy, 32 miles south of Rome.

25 The Allies report capture of the port of Anzio, close to Nettuno.

30 Attempts to widen Anzio beachhead meet with failure. Germans, in heavy attack, report capture of several hundred American soldiers.

February

2 Estonia entered by Red Army. Offensive is launched against Latvia. U.S. Marines capture Roi Island, in the Marshalls, and land on Namur and Kwajalein: first occupation of pre-war Japanese territory in this war.

4 Admiral Chester W. Nimitz assumes control of the Kwajalein atoll as "military governor" of the Marshall Islands.

6 In Italian campaign, crack units of Heinrich Himmler's SS Élite Guard force British back 6 miles on Cassino front. Lieutenant General Mark Clark's beachhead battle at Anzio is stalled.

8 Russians capture important manganese center of Nikopol, after a four-day battle.

13 Soviet troops clear Nazis from entire east bank of Lake Peipus and are within 45 miles of Pskov, gateway to Latvia.

15 Heavy Allied bombing and shelling leaves historic Mount Cassino Abbey in ruins. British bombers drop 2,800 tons of explosives on Berlin.

17 It is revealed that a troopship, carrying mostly Americans, was sunk "by enemy action" in European waters on an undisclosed date; 1,000 men lost.

18 Admiral Nimitz announces strong attack on Truk Island.

21 In Japanese political shake-up, Hideki Tojo becomes chief of the army (military czar).

March

4 Red Army, under Marshal Zhukov, opens new offensive in western Ukraine, surging into Poland in a 31-mile advance.

6 Berlin bombed by hundreds of Flying Fortresses accompanied by fighter planes; 2,000 tons of explosives dropped.

8 Russians in advance on Tarnopol area reach within 60 miles of Rumania.

12 On failure of Eire to oust German and Japanese diplomatic agents, British Government stops all travel between Great Britain and Ireland.

15 In Italian campaign Cassino is completely destroyed, but German defenders remain in possession.

20 Red Army smashes into northern Rumania at Mogilev, crossing the Dniester River into Bessarabia. German troops invade Hungary because of the growing Russian threat to all the Balkans.

22 Japanese columns make their first penetration of India, pushing west

from Burma through the Manipur mountain country, in the direction of Imphal.

28 Allied drive at Cassino is admitted a "temporary failure."

April

4 Moscow radio calls on Rumanians to abandon the Germans and capitulate at once or their country will be destroyed. American forces in the Pacific capture 10 more atolls in the Marshall Islands.

5 Tarnopol, Nazi stronghold in Poland, falls to Russians. Charles de Gaulle becomes head of the Provisional Government of the French Republic.

10 Odessa, captured by the Germans in October, 1941, is again in Russian hands.

11 In Southwest Pacific, Japs retreat for last stand on New Britain. On Russian front, Red Army launches offensive on the Crimea.

12 Great air battles over German industrial cities; Americans use 2,000 planes.

14 Simferopol falls to Russians in Crimea campaign; 20,000 prisoners. British Government restricts privileges of diplomats; no more coded or uncensored communications. Diplomatic staff must not leave the country. Diplomatic pouches must not be dispatched unless submitted to censorship. Diplomatic staffs of the U.S., USSR, and British Dominions are exempt from decree. (Presumed purpose is to prevent leakage of invasion plans.)

18 Balaklava stormed by Russian Marines. American and British warplanes blast railroads, factories, and air fields in France and Germany in spectacular 30-hour air offensive. British and Indian troops drive back invading Japs in Manipur, India.

22 Under personal direction of General MacArthur, Americans make landings at Hollandia, Dutch New Guinea. Admiral Nimitz' Central Pacific naval forces coöperated in landing with naval and air bombardment.

25 Japanese offensive in Honan Province, China, menaces Chenghsien. Heavy attacks in Loyang and other sectors.

30 London reports U.S. and R.A.F. heavy bombers unloaded more than 80,000 tons of explosives on enemy territory in April.

May

3 Neutral Spain, at request of Britain and the U.S., agrees to curtail shipments of wolfram to Germany, and in return will receive shipments of petroleum from the Americas.

5 Gandhi, Indian Nationalist leader, is released from detention in the Aga Khan's summer palace at Poona, because of serious illness. He had been confined as a political prisoner since August, 1942.

10 Sevastopol is recaptured by Russians after a 24-day siege.

12 Japs are reported in temporary control of the Peiping-Hankow railroad. Action begins anew on Italian front, as Allies pursue retreating Germans at Pescara, near the Adriatic, and Cassino. Advance is under direction of General Sir Harold Alexander.

15 Led by French Moroccan troops, Allies break through German Gustav Line in Italy for gain of 7 miles.

17 All defenses on Gustav Line smashed. Allied Fifth Army reaches the Adolf Hitler Line in Italy. British Eighth Army establishes a bridgehead across the Rapido River. In China, the Japanese are engaged in street battle with the Chinese in Loyang.

18 Cassino is finally evacuated by the Germans. This monastery fortress

resisted attempts to capture it for more than two months.

22 Iceland, by referendum, votes for complete separation from Denmark. Republic to be proclaimed June 17. Allied Fifth Army, under Lieutenant General Mark W. Clark, begins strong offensive at long-dormant Anzio beachhead.

25 Germany yields whole coastline from Anzio to Terracina; Americans of the Anzio sector join with main armies to the south.

JUNE

4 Rome falls to Allies. Tanks and infantry troops of the Fifth Army battle German rearguards in suburbs and finally enter city. Berlin radio reports that Hitler had ordered evacuation to avoid bringing the Eternal City "under the peril of destruction." Rome is practically undamaged, except for railroad yards bombed by Allies.

6 D-Day. American, British, and Canadian troops, aided by thousands of ships and planes, land in northern France, beginning the long-awaited invasion of German-occupied Europe. The American general, Dwight D. Eisenhower, is in supreme command. Beachheads are secured on the sandy shores of Normandy, west of the mouth of the Seine River, and east of the Cotentin Peninsula, at the tip of which lies Cherbourg.

7 Landings in France are reported successful along a 100-mile front. Airborne troops and paratroops aid in struggle. In Italy, King Victor Emmanuel signs over his royal powers to Crown Prince Humbert as Lieutenant General of the Realm.

8 Bayeux, 5 miles inland from French coast, captured. Railroad to Cherbourg cut. In Italy, the Allied Fifth Army, under Lieutenant General Mark Clark, is 32 miles north of Rome.

9 Badoglio resigns as Premier of Italy; succeeded by Ivanoe Bonomi, a pre-Mussolini Premier.

11 Allies are halfway across the Cotentin Peninsula in drive to seal off Cherbourg. Russians begin new attack on southern Finland.

14 General de Gaulle, leader of French Committee of National Liberation visits France for the first time in 4 years; gets big welcome in liberated area. U.S. amphibious forces strike at Saipan, in Marianas; meet with strong resistance.

16 U.S. Superfortresses (B-29's) bomb southern Japan.

19 Germans bomb England with secret weapon (V-1), the pilotless plane, or flying bomb. Many subsequent attacks.

20 Viborg (Viipuri), Finland's second largest city, captured by Red Army. American invasion of the Marianas, 1,500 miles from Tokyo, draws out the Japanese fleet. In subsequent naval battle, 14 Jap ships are sunk or damaged, including a battleship, and Admiral Nimitz reports, "Darkness came to save the enemy, and he ran." Attack was directed by Admiral Raymond A. Spruance, with Vice Admiral Marc A. Mitscher leading carrier force.

25 American troops storm into Cherbourg in the face of desperate German resistance. On Russian front, First White Russian Army under General Rokossovsky goes into action in Bobruisk area; also Second Army under General Zakharov, and Third Army under General Cherniakhovsky in action to the south.

26 Stalin calls for salvos of Moscow's 224 guns to mark first great victory of summer offensive, as Vitebsk falls to Russians.

28 While Americans are completing occupation of Cherbourg, the British under General Sir Bernard L. Montgomery launch an attack on

Caen, on the east of the Normandy beachhead.

30 Hengyang, American air base in Hunan province, China, is abandoned by U.S. Fourteenth Air Force. Bobruisk, last German stronghold on "Fatherland Line," guarding road to Warsaw and Berlin, falls to Red Army. General Rokossovsky is made a Marshal of the Soviet Union.

JULY

3 Minsk is won by the Russians; this was heralded as "one of the decisive victories of the war."

6 General de Gaulle arrives in Washington for conference with President Roosevelt. Churchill discloses that in three weeks German robot bombs have killed 2,750 persons and seriously injured 8,000.

9 Caen, Normandy, falls to British and Canadians. U.S. Marines and infantry complete conquest of Saipan island, Marianas, after a bitter 25-day fight, with heavy casualties on both sides.

11 Russians cross border into Latvia. Red Army is reported 40 miles inside Lithuania.

12 East Prussia menaced by Soviet forces. German broadcasts cry: "The enemy is at the gates of the Reich." On the Western Front, American troops reach the fortress of St. Lô.

13 Wilno (Vilna) captured after five days of street fighting, opening the way to all the Baltic states.

14 Pinsk, German stronghold in the Pripet Marshes, is evacuated by the Nazis. Five Red armies are participating in offensives aimed squarely at Warsaw and Berlin.

17 Russians take Grodno. In South Pacific, Guam is bombarded by the U.S. Navy's biggest and newest battleships.

18 Japanese general, Hideki Tojo, admits "great disaster" of Saipan and is relieved of his post as chief of the General Staff. General Yoshijiro Umezu succeeds. In France, the British Second Army breaks through the German line at Caen in great tank battle. Units of American First Army smash into St. Lô.

19 In Jap political shake-up Tojo's entire cabinet resigns. Emperor Hirohito asks General Kuniaka Koiso to form a new cabinet. Hitler is reported "slightly burned and bruised" in bomb attempt on his life by one of a group of German officers who, according to Hitler, planned to take Germany out of the war.

21 U.S. Marines and infantry establish beachheads on Guam—a quick follow-up to the hard-won victory on Saipan. Russia's Third Baltic Army takes Pskov. Other forces are in Lublin and nearing Lwow. Moscow announces creation of a Polish Committee of National Liberation. (No reference to Polish Government-in-exile in London.)

25 Americans, under General Bradley, break through German lines in Normandy and begin great drive which routs enemy.

27 Russians enter Lwow. Hitler names Reichsmarshal Hermann Goering as Mobilization Director, "to adapt in every respect the entire public life to the necessities of total warfare." Goering names Propaganda Minister Goebbels "plenipotentiary for total war effort" to assist him. Heinrich Himmler is "dictator of the home front." Lieutenant General Leslie J. McNair killed by misdirected American aërial bomb in Normandy.

AUGUST

1 Americans enter the province of Brittany from Normandy.

2 Russian troops reach the Baltic Sea, 25 miles west of Riga, cutting off the Nazis in Estonia and Latvia from the main German Army. Fin-

Chronology of the War

land's president, Ryti, resigns; Marshal Mannerheim succeeds; talk of peace with Russia. Turkey breaks off diplomatic relations with Germany.

3 In western France, American tank columns race 30 miles toward Rennes and 25 miles toward St. Malo, threatening the port of Brest.

4 Americans take Rennes. Another American force sweeps west across the Breton peninsula, taking Dinan. A third force reaches Mortain, 150 miles from Paris.

7 Americans are fighting in outlying streets of Brest. Other American forces are at Lorient and St. Nazaire and driving toward Nantes. St. Malo is by-passed. The Battle of the Ports is won.

8 Having overrun the Brittany peninsula, the Yanks veer eastward in great drive toward Paris. In Italy, the British Eighth Army is at Florence, but does not cross the Arno.

9 Canadian and British forces smash German line southeast of Caen. U.S. troops close in on Le Mans, 110 miles from Paris. Nazi buzz-bomb offensive continues to take heavy toll in southern England. Thousands of mothers and children leave London, in evacuation program which enters its seventh week. General Eisenhower moves his headquarters from England to Normandy. Conquest of Guam completed after a 20-day battle.

11 On the Russian front, a giant tank battle is raging along the Riga-Warsaw sector.

12 Nazis evacuate Florence as Allies advance east and west of city. Historic buildings not damaged.

15 Invasion of southern France begins. American, British, and French troops storm ashore between Nice and Marseilles. Infantry lands under cover of a 70-minute naval bombardment. Invasion is directed by General Sir Henry Maitland Wilson, Supreme Commander in the Mediterranean theater.

17 In southern invasion of France, the U.S. Seventh Army, under Major General Alexander M. Patch, makes wide gains. French troops, which landed after the Yanks, are led by General de Tassigny. In northern France, General George S. Patton, commanding the American Third Army, is reported to have whipped his tanks within 40 miles of Paris.

18 General Patch gains French coast area from Cannes to Toulon, and advances 30 miles inland. German defense is weak.

21 Iron ring is closing on Germans in Paris area as American armored columns reach the Seine on both sides of the French capital. Aërial bombing adds to panic of retreating remnants of the German Seventh Army. French Underground patriots are aiding invaders.

22 Russia reopens offensive in Rumania and takes Iassy.

23 Belgian forces with Allies enter Deauville on the Channel coast. Exaggerated report declares Paris is liberated by French patriots, as Allied forces are poised halfway around the capital. Marseilles falls to French forces as Americans sweep inland 140 miles from the Mediterranean.

24 Rumania surrenders and joins the Allies. Bordeaux is captured by Allied forces and French patriots. Situation in Paris confused. Germans are still in capital. There is street fighting. Armistice is reported, to enable the Germans to get out. Late in the day, General Bradley, commanding the Twelfth Army Group, draws the 2nd French Armored Division out of the line and sends it, with some Yanks, to Paris.

25 German commandant surrenders to General Jacques LeClerc's men. Paris is officially "free." General de

Gaulle arrives; great Liberation Parade on the 26th.

27 General Eisenhower and high military officers of Allied forces enter Paris.

28 General Patton's Third Army crosses the Marne. Yanks are again in Chateau-Thierry, as their fathers were in 1918. Russians cross Carpathian Mountains and drive into Transylvania. Bulgaria is reported ready to join Allies.

29 U.S. troops capture Soissons, General Patch's Seventh Army wins great victories in the Rhone Valley, wiping out the bulk of the German Nineteenth Army. Russians win key seaport of Constantza, Rumania, on Black Sea.

30 Anglo-Canadian armies under Lieutenant General Miles Dempsey hold almost the entire line of the Seine west of Paris. Take Rouen and advance north to Gournay. American First Army under Lieutenant General Courtney H. Hodges advances from Soissons to Laon. Russians clear Germans out of rich Ploesti oil fields.

31 British Second Army drives into Amiens, virtually isolating a 100-mile stretch of the robot bomb coast of northern France. Nice, resort city on the Mediterranean, captured without opposition. Remnants of German Nineteenth Army retreating in the Lyon area. Bulgaria and Rumania get peace terms in Cairo and Moscow. Collapse of Germany's Balkan front. Revolt in Slovakia. Americans pass through Reims; reach Maginot Line.

September

1 Russian troops enter **Bucharest,** capital of Rumania.

4 British Second Army takes Brussels, also the port of Antwerp. Dutch border crossed. In the south, U.S. forces have driven 40 miles above Lyon.

5 Finnish-Soviet armistice halts 3-year war. Red Army pours through Rumania, reaches within 50 miles of Yugoslav border. Russia declares war on Bulgaria; a few hours later the Bulgarian Government asks Moscow for armistice.

6 U.S. First Army takes Namur; crosses Meuse.

7 Hungary at war with Rumania, in effort to retain Transylvania.

11 U.S. First Army units, under Lieutenant General Hodges, enter capital city of Luxembourg. German Siegfried Line bombarded from a dozen frontier posts. Roosevelt and Churchill in Quebec for eighth conference on war.

12 U.S. First Army crosses German border near Trier (Trèves), advancing 5 miles into Reich. British Second Army breaks across the frontier of Holland. U.S. Third Army seizes part of the old French Maginot Line intact. Troops of Seventh Army under General Patch coming up from the Mediterranean make contact with units of Patton's Third Army near Dijon. Soviet patrols cross border of East Prussia.

13 Le Havre, France's second largest port, is surrendered to the British. Rumania signs armistice with Allies.

14 Five thousand planes pound Germany from the Siegfried Line to Berlin. American troops reach Aachen. Russians are on the frontier of Czechoslovakia.

17 Airborne troops land deep inside Holland. Parachute troops and gliderborne infantrymen of the First Allied Airborne Army surprise German defenders and reach objectives without much opposition. In China the American Fourteenth Air Force abandons huge air base at Kweilin.

18 British 2nd Army foiled in attempt to form junction with airborne troops near Arnhem.

19 Finnish-Soviet armistice ratified by

Finnish Parliament. Finland cedes and leases much territory; agrees to drive Germans from country.

20 In the Pacific area the Americans win complete control of Anguar Island in the Palaus in the western Carolines.

21 British "Red Devil" paratroops in Arnhem sector fighting grimly, still unrelieved. Germans report sky troopers are being wiped out.

24 Russians advance from southern Poland 20 miles into Czechoslovakia and threaten Hungary. Estonian ports on Baltic taken by Soviet naval forces.

28 Battle of Arnhem ends in disaster for British airborne troops. Germans claim 6,400 prisoners; British say 1,700 to 1,800 escaped safely.

October

1 Japanese offensive sweeps through Kwangsi, forcing the Americans to abandon a fourth air base. On the Western European Front the Canadians complete capture of Calais, taking 5,000 prisoners. On the Eastern Front the Russians drive deeper into Yugoslavia and lower Hungary.

2 U.S. First Army begins new attack north of Aachen, smashing the Siegfried Line for a gain of 2 miles. Mud, mist, and rain hamper operations.

3 Warsaw patriots, who have been fighting the Germans since August, surrender. General Bor (Komorowski), leader of the patriot fighters, is a prisoner of the Germans. The official Polish Government-in-exile (in London) applauds General Bor's attempt as heroic. The rival Polish group organized in Russia denounces the "futile uprising which cost thousands of lives."

9 Dumbarton Oaks Conference ends. Plans made for a peace and security league to be organized by the United Nations—nations opposing any or all of the Axis powers: Italy, Germany, Japan.

10 Corinth occupied by British and Greek forces. Red Army reaches Baltic Sea north of Memel, isolating Nazi troops in Latvia.

14 Athens recovered by British and Greek troops. In the Pacific area, sea and air battles continue on the northern approaches to the Philippines off the island of Formosa.

19 Philippines invaded. Landing is made at Leyte, in central Philippines.

20 First communiqué headed "General MacArthur's Headquarters in the Philippines" thrills Americans. It reported: "In a major amphibious operation we have seized the eastern coast of Leyte Island.... Leyte in the Visayas is midway between Luzon and Mindanao and at one stroke splits into two the Japanese forces in the Philippines. The enemy expected the attack on Mindanao.... The landing was preceded by heavy air and naval bombardment which was devastating in its effect."

20 East Prussia invaded by Red Army. Belgrade, Yugoslav capital, taken by Russian and Partisan troops. Aachen finally falls to Americans after seven-day fight.

23 Tacloban, Leyte, becomes temporary capital of the Philippines. General MacArthur and President Osmeña re-establish government.

23-26 Crippling blow dealt Japanese Navy in battle for Leyte Gulf. Japanese losses: two battleships, four carriers, nine cruisers, and nine destroyers. American losses include the aircraft carrier *Princeton*.

28 General Stilwell, leader of the North Burma campaign, is recalled to U.S. and Major General Wedemeyer takes over.

November

5 B-29's bomb Singapore and Sumatra. Air-raid on Manila destroys 440 Japanese planes.
6 Stalin brands Japan as an aggressor nation.
7 Roosevelt re-elected for fourth term over Dewey.
13 U.S. Fourteenth Air Force abandons base in Liuchow in eastern China in face of advancing Japanese forces.
16 Allied winter offensive against Germans begins.
20 Allied troops under General Patton enter Metz.
24 Tokyo is bombed by Saipan-based B-29's.
25 U.S. Army breaks through Hurtgen Forest. Conquest of Peleliu virtually completed.
26 U.S. Fourteenth Air Force abandons its Nanning base in Kwangsi Province, China.
28 Third Army penetrates Saar Basin.
30 Canadian First Army invades Germany from the Nijmegen area in Holland.

December

3 Civil war breaks out in Greece as EAM and ELAS refuse to bow to British ultimatum to surrender arms.
5 Patton's forces battle through flaming Saarlautern.
11 France and Russia sign 20-year mutual assistance pact.
15 U.S. troops land in Mindoro Island in Philippines.
16 Germans begin a counteroffensive through Ardennes.
17 Germans break into Belgium and Luxembourg.
20 Germans smash toward Liége with 15 divisions, isolate American units at Bastogne.
22 Patton's army strikes at southern flank of Belgian Bulge of Germans.
24 Allied air might blasts Germans in the Bulge as ground forces dent the southern flank.
25 Eden and Churchill fly to Athens to settle Greek civil war. Russians reach Budapest. Leyte-Samar campaign against Japanese is considered concluded.
26 Germans reach Celles, 50 miles from Brussels, in their powerful drive. But Patton rams his rescue corridor to within five miles of besieged Bastogne.
27 Bastogne pocket is relieved. In the Pacific B-29's bomb Tokyo for the fifth time.
31 Lublin Poles, sponsored by Soviet Government, set up their own régime, break with London Polish Government-in-exile.

1945

January

3 On Western Front, Germans continue to jab at American lines, retaining initiative except in Belgium, where von Rundstedt withdraws some of his men and armor.
8 It is revealed that Field Marshal Montgomery has been placed in command of all American and British armies in the northern part of the Western Front—north of the German break-through. General Bradley is in command south of the Bulge.
9 Luzon, main island of the Philippines, invaded by U.S. Sixth Army troops under General MacArthur. Landing is made at Lingayen Gulf, 100 miles north of Manila.

Chronology of the War

12 Russians in big winter offensive drive into Poland, north and south of Warsaw.
15 Germans continue retreat from Belgium. MacArthur widens Luzon beachhead to 45 miles.
17 Warsaw is finally captured by the Russians in a brilliant encirclement maneuver. Capture is credited to Marshal Gregory H. Zhukov's First White Russian Army group and the Army of the Lublin Poles. In the south, Crakow is reported captured.
19 Russians take Lodz. German Armies are in complete and headlong retreat along the twisting 500-mile front.
22 Tannenberg taken by Russians in great smash into East Prussia. In Silesia the Red Army had reached within 10 miles of the Oder River. Armistice with Hungary signed.

February

5 MacArthur's troops enter Manila, but fighting continues for three weeks, with great damage of property, before Japs are driven out.
7 Roosevelt, Churchill, and Stalin meet in Yalta (Crimea) conference to plan for occupation of Germany after the war and to consider problems of liberated peoples. Report on conference issued February 12.
10 Tokyo is hit by 90 Superfortresses.
19 U.S. Marines make landing on Iwo Island, 750 miles from Tokyo. Japs make fanatical resistance in interior. Scottish and Canadian forces are given great credit for offensive against the German Siegfried Line.
21 Inter-American conference meets in Chapultepec Castle, Mexico City, to consider problems of war and peace. Argentina not represented.
23 U.S. Marines lose heavily in fight for islet of Iwo. On Western Front, U.S. Third Army, under Patton, crosses the Saar River. At north end of front, First Canadian Army advances on Wesel, gateway to Ruhr industrial district. Turkey votes to join Allies in war on Germany and Japan. Egypt also at war against Axis.
27 President Roosevelt returns from the Yalta conference. On his way back he was host, on his cruiser, to King Faruk of Egypt, Emperor Haile Selassie of Ethiopia, and King Ibn Saud of Arabia. He had hoped to meet General de Gaulle at Algiers, but De Gaulle refused the meeting.

March

7 Advanced infantry of Lieutenant General Hodges' First Army cross the Ludendorff Bridge over the Rhine at Remagen. First crossing of the Rhine in force.
8 Inter-American conference ends with general agreement as to united action in case of attack on any American republic (Chapultepec Pact).
14 U.S. First Army troops extend Remagen bridgehead on the Rhine and reach within 2 miles of the great *Autobahn* (motor highway) connecting Frankfort-on-Main with the industrial Ruhr.
17 U.S. Third Army seizes Coblenz as troops cross the Moselle. Central span of the Ludendorff Bridge collapses as engineers are strengthening span. Casualties few.
22 Various types of pontoon bridges are quickly thrown across the Rhine by British and American engineers, and the Allies continue pursuit of fleeing Germans. German Army leader von Rundstedt is reported replaced by Field Marshal Kesselring.
26 Entire Western Front has now moved east of the Rhine. Montgomery's Twenty-first Army Group, comprising British Second, Canadian First, and U.S. Ninth Armies, push on through Wesel in the north.

In the center, the U.S. First Army (General Hodges) extends bridgehead at Remagen to 33 miles. In south, the U.S. Third Army (Patton) crosses Rhine and moves on Frankfort. Further south, the U.S. Seventh Army (Patch) clears up final German pocket east of the Rhine (Karlsruhe sector).

27 Patton's Third Army takes Frankfort and races across Germany, 198 miles from Berlin. Chaos spreads in Reich. False victory rumors sweep the U.S. when a radio announcer misinterprets a dispatch from Washington. Russian troops are within 60 miles of Vienna. Argentina, pressed by the U.S., finally declares war on Axis powers.

APRIL

1 American troops invade Okinawa Island, 360 miles south of Japan.

2 Russians are within 50 miles of Berlin, but action is in south, pointing to Vienna.

4 Bratislava, capital of Slovakia, entered by Red Army. Suburbs of Vienna reached. Patton's Third Army spearheads to within 70 miles of Leipzig.

5 Premier Koiso and entire Japanese cabinet resign in face of mounting difficulties. Russia denounces neutrality pact with Japan, to expire in 1946. Admiral Suzuki becomes Japanese Premier.

6 Jap battleship *Yamato* sunk by American aircraft off the Ryuku Islands. Hard fighting on Okinawa, with heavy casualties.

9 Russian assault forces fight their way into Vienna. Soviet troops in Baltic area take Koenigsberg. Allied armies in west strike for the Elbe, last big stream before Berlin.

11 Vienna is finally won by Red Army. Yanks drive within 90 miles of Berlin. Units of Lieutenant General Wm. H. Simpson's Ninth U.S. Army reach the Elbe near Magdeburg. Canadians push into Holland. British advance on Bremen. American Seventh plunges into Bavaria. Over 300,000 prisoners in two weeks.

12 President Roosevelt dies at Warm Springs, Georgia. Harry S. Truman, Vice President, becomes President.

16 Russians begin push for Berlin on 45-mile front.

17 U.S. Seventh Army takes Nuremberg. British are within 2 miles of Bremen and 10 miles of Hamburg. Ernie Pyle, war correspondent, killed on Ie Jima, small island off Okinawa.

18 American troops take Leipzig and Magdeburg.

22 German High Command says the Red Army has entered Berlin and fierce street fighting rages in much-bombed capital. In the Dresden area Russians and Americans near junction, cutting Germany in two. In Italy, on the "forgotten front," British and American troops continue advance, taking Bologna and heading for Ferrara. Allied planes block Alpine passes. Field Marshal Sir Harold Alexander, Allied commander in the Mediterranean, declares the Germans in northern Italy have "no hope of escaping."

25 San Francisco conference of 46 nations, to prepare a charter for world peace and security, opens with speech broadcast by President Truman from Washington. Hitler's mountain chalet, Berchtesgaden, bombed by Royal Air Force.

28 Benito Mussolini, his mistress, and 16 of his Fascist henchmen are executed at the village of Dongo on Lake Como. Bodies were brought to Milan and thrown in the street, where they were kicked and spat upon by Italians who a few years before had cheered wildly for Il Duce. Burial was in potter's field; graves unmarked.

May

1 Adolf Hitler dies "fighting the Bolshevists in Berlin," according to Nazi radio from Hamburg. (Body which may be that of Hitler, smoke-blackened and charred, is found by Russians on June 6, in underground command post in the Reichschancellery where Hitler and his leading Nazis made their last-ditch stand. But it is not definitely proved.)

2 Berlin falls to Russians after 12 days of street fighting. German Army surrenders in Italy.

6 Grand Admiral Karl Doenitz, who is styled Fuehrer of the German Reich (succeeding the late Hitler) surrenders; orders U-boats to return to bases; orders armies to cease fighting.

7 Edward Kennedy, Associated Press correspondent, scoops the world with announcement that surrender of Reich is made in a school building at Reims, France, by Colonel General Gustav Jodl, chief of staff for German Army. Report correct, but was issued prematurely, for which Kennedy was ordered home.

8 Celebrated in United States as V-E Day (Victory in Europe). President Truman in radio broadcast announces surrender of Germany. King George speaks to Empire.

9 Moscow has big celebration of Victory Day. Ratification surrender signed in bomb-shattered Berlin, with Marshal Zhukoff, commander of the First White Russian Army, signing for the Soviets, and Field Marshal Wilhelm Keitel, commander-in-chief of the *Wehrmacht,* signing for the Germans. Russian troops parade through Prague, last European capital to be liberated.

10 U.S. Secretary of War Stimson reports that casualties for both the army and navy have neared the million mark.

15 Bodies of Nazi leader Goebbels and his wife and children are found in underground broadcasting station in Berlin. "Suicides," says Moscow. Allies disband the Doenitz régime; military-controlled government is planned. Advance in Philippines goes slowly, with hard fighting in Mindanao and Luzon.

17 It is revealed that 772 men were lost when the U.S. carrier *Franklin,* crowded with planes, was hit and partly destroyed by a Japanese dive bomber, 66 miles off the enemy's coast, March 19. Ship was kept afloat and brought back, 12,000 miles, to the Brooklyn Navy Yard. Japan has been sending bomb-carrying paper balloons against the western U.S. for several months. "No property damage," says Washington.

23 British Prime Minister Churchill resigns, in order to force a general election (first in 10 years). Will retain premiership until after election, July 5.

24 Heinrich Himmler, Nazi official, head of the dreaded Gestapo, called No. 1 war criminal, captured by British troops, commits suicide by swallowing poison hidden in vial in his mouth.

26 Tokyo is "laid waste" by American bombers. Fires were still burning on May 28.

June

5 A Four-Power declaration proclaiming the completion of Germany's defeat and the assumption of supreme authority in the Reich by the four victor Powers is signed in Berlin. General Eisenhower signs for the United States; Field Marshal Montgomery for Great Britain; Marshal Zhukov for the Soviet Union; General de Tassigny for France. Temporarily, Germany is returned to its pre-war boundaries and is divided into four zones: East zone (roughly half of Germany) to be controlled by Russia; northwest zone by Britain; west zone by

France; southwest zone by United States.

10 After a series of successful attacks on Japanese positions in eastern China, Chinese troops capture the port of Futing, 450 miles west of Okinawa. Australian troops invade Borneo and seize control of Brunei Bay on the northwest coast.

15 British soldiers capture Joachim von Ribbentrop, former German Foreign Minister, in a boarding house at Hamburg, completing the round-up of top Nazis known to be at large. Hess flew to Scotland and was detained as a prisoner of war. Goering is a prisoner. Hitler and Goebbels apparently died in the final battle of Berlin. Himmler committed suicide.

18 Lieutenant General Simon Bolivar Buckner, Jr., commander of all forces on Okinawa, dies in action; killed by a Japanese shell burst as he watched his U.S. Tenth Marines and doughboys drive toward final victory. General Eisenhower gets great reception in Washington on his return from Europe; addresses joint session of Congress. He commanded 3,000,000 men in Europe.

19 Eisenhower flies to La Guardia Field, New York, and is greeted by 4,000,000 on his 35-mile tour of the city.

21 Battle of Okinawa ends in victory for the Americans, who lost 6,900 men, killed or missing, and nearly 30,000 wounded, in the land operations of the army and Marines. Jap casualties were about 95,000. General Stilwell is placed in command of the Tenth Army, which conquered Okinawa.

26 World Security Charter signed at San Francisco by representatives of 50 United Nations.

27 373 are killed on the carrier *Bunker Hill* when a Japanese suicide plane and bomber score hits off Okinawa. The island of Luzon is announced reconquered, although some Japanese troops still hold out in mountains.

29 Chinese troops recapture Liuchow airbase; Americans occupy Kume Island.

30 Chinese troops invade Indo-China.

July

1 General MacArthur directs invasion of oil port of Balikpapan on the east coast of Borneo. Australian troops spearhead the attack.

3 Tokyo radio reports that nearly 5,000,000 casualties in killed, wounded, and homeless have been caused to date by American air raids.

4 MacArthur's headquarters announces the liberation of all the Philippine Islands.

5 General Spaatz is appointed commander of the Strategic Air Forces in the Pacific. The air war against Japan is stepped up in order to bring about a decision, if possible, before invasion of home islands is necessary.

9 Chinese retake another former U.S. air base in Tanchuk. The greatest air assault to date of the war hits the Japanese homeland.

15 Heavy air attacks by American fliers leave 10 Japanese cities in ruins, destroy or damage 128 enemy ships and 92 planes.

16 Admiral Nimitz describes powerful attack by U.S. Third Fleet, joined by British Forces, as pre-invasion stage of the war against Japan. 1,500 bombers roar over Japan.

17 Truman, Stalin, and Churchill meet at Potsdam for historic conference. British fleet joins in shelling of Japanese coast for the first time.

21 United States makes direct appeal by radio to Japan to quit war or face total destruction.

23 1,000 carrier-based planes drop fire

bombs on Nagoya and Osaka; over 600 B-29's blast Japanese naval base at Kure.

25 Tokyo radio broadcasts appeal for terms less severe than unconditional surrender.

26 U.S., Great Britain, and China reply with outline of terms laid down in the Cairo Declaration (November 22, 1943): Japan to be reduced to home islands, war criminals to be brought to justice, and Japan to be occupied. Results of British elections of July 5 are announced, giving the Labor Party, committed to a socialist program, an overwhelming majority in Parliament. Clement Attlee replaces Churchill as Prime Minister and returns to Potsdam to conclude conference with Truman and Stalin.

28 Chinese armies retake Kweilin, former American air base.

29 Japan formally rejects surrender ultimatum.

31 U.S. warns Japan that eight more of her cities face destruction.

August

1 Mounting air war over Japan sees 800 B-29's blast the enemy with 6,000 tons of blockbusters and fire bombs. U.S. Tenth Air Force shifts its operations from Burma to China.

2 Potsdam Declaration is released to the press. Among its terms, imposing a hard peace on defeated Germany, are complete demilitarization, continued occupation, drastic reduction of territory, and reparations to come out of present industrial equipment.

3. U.S. completes iron ring of blockade around Japanese home islands.

6 To an amazed world, President Truman announces that an atomic bomb has been dropped on Hiroshima, virtually wiping out the city. Truman also reveals that manufacture of this bomb, developed as the result of several years' scientific research, is at present controlled exclusively by the U.S.

8 Russia declares war on Japan. Soviet Far Eastern Armies attack Manchuria in a giant pincer movement from east and west.

9 The second atomic bomb is dropped on Nagasaki. Red troops penetrate deep into Manchuria. U.S. calls on the Japanese people to petition the Emperor to cease hostilities. 1,200 aircraft hammer northern Honshu after a naval bombardment of Kamaishi.

10 Once more Japan asks for peace, but inserts proviso that the Emperor retain his power. Russians invade Korea and southern Sakhalin Island.

11 Allies reply to Japanese peace offer: The Emperor must take orders from the victorious Powers. People throughout the United Nations await the Japanese reply expectantly.

12 A false radio flash over American networks sets off a premature celebration throughout the world.

14 After a delay of three days, the Japanese Government communicates acceptance of Allied peace terms. Emperor Hirohito broadcasts imperial rescript (directive) announcing Japanese defeat to his people.

19 Japanese surrender delegation arrives in Manila to receive instructions from General MacArthur. Russian airborne troops land at Harbin, Mukden, and Hsinking, headquarters of Kwantung Army in Manchuria.

20 Japanese emissaries leave Manila after conference on details of surrender. Russian forces in Far East cease firing on most fronts.

23 President Truman orders all Lend-Lease shipments halted to Allies because of the end of the war.

27 U.S. Third Fleet, under Admiral Halsey, moves into Sagami Bay.

28 Air-force technicians land at Atsugi airdrome, 18 miles from central

Tokyo, and prepare for arrival of transports bearing troops. Naval units enter Tokyo Bay.

29 Four major Allies name 24 top Nazis and Prussian militarists as defendants in first war crimes trial in German history, to be held in Nuremberg. Truman makes public the reports of official army and navy boards of inquiry on the Pearl Harbor disaster, which opened war with Japan. Secretary of State Hull, General Marshall, and Admiral Stark are censured. Truman brands criticism of Hull and Marshall unjustified.

30 General MacArthur lands at Atsugi airfield and is greeted by cheering paratroopers who preceded him. Additional troops pour in. Yokosuka base and neighboring fortress islands are occupied. MacArthur establishes headquarters in Yokohama.

31 American prisoners freed in occupation of Japan tell tales of harrowing experiences as Japanese captives.

SEPTEMBER

1 American control fans out smoothly through the entire area south of Tokyo.

2 The Japanese Premier and military leaders sign formal surrender documents on board the battleship U.S.S. *Missouri* in Tokyo Bay in presence of Allied representatives. Among latter is General Wainwright, who as commander of the forces in the Philippines was forced to surrender his battered troops on Bataan and Corregidor early in the war and had been a prisoner since that time.

WORLD CRISIS FOLLOWS WORLD WAR II

EVENTS developed with such rapidity following World War II that 1948-49-50 will be known as periods of world crisis. The problems of peace were as great as those of war. Tragic possibilities of a Third World War cast dark shadows over the nations. America, pledged to peace, took leadership in heroic efforts to save the world from another catastrophe.

Reconstruction of the devastated countries of Europe created many tense political, economic, and diplomatic controversies. The campaign for the election of a President of the United States for the term from 1948 to 1952 was fought peacefully at the polls while the world was engaged in what became known as a "cold War," a war of statesmanship and diplomacy with the nations upholding Democracy on one side and the totalitarian Soviet Union on the other side.

The United States, and other Democratic nations, had kept faith by demobilizing our military forces and reëstablishing themselves on a peace basis. Our former Soviet ally had maintained and strengthened their fighting forces and engaged in aggressions to place Europe under totalitarian control.

We, who had fought in World War II to save Democracy and individual freedom and human liberty from being demolished by Nazism and Fascism, were now facing the flickering embers of "world revolution" and Communism which would impose the will of the State over the people. The situation was grave. The future of civilization again was at stake.

Let us give you some of the high spots to supplement the chronology in the preceding pages. Two of these are of foremost importance: The establishment of the United Nations for the specific purpose of preserving world peace, and the War Crimes Trials which were to fix the responsibility and set a precedent for any future instigators of wars.

The United Nations is the direct result of World War II. Its birthplace was San Francisco, where its charter was drawn and signed (June 26, 1945) by fifty nations. Its total membership (1948) was fifty-seven nations. New York was selected as the seat or world capital for the United Nations and in parliamentary discussions it undertook the settlement of world problems.

The preamble to its charter specifically states its objectives: "We, the peoples of the United Nations, determined to save succeeding generations from the scourge of war, which twice in our lifetime has brought untold sorrow to mankind, and—To reaffirm faith in fundamental human rights, in the dignity and worth of the human person, in the equal right of men and women and of nations large and small, and—To establish conditions under which justice and respect for the obligations arising from treaties and other sources of international law can be maintained, and—To promote social progress and better standards of life in larger freedom and for these ends—To practice tolerance and live together in peace with one another as good neighbors, and—To unite our strength to maintain international peace and security, and—To insure, by the acceptance of principles and the institution of methods that armed force shall not be used, save in the common interest, and—To employ international machinery for the promotion of the economic and social advancement of all people, have resolved to combine our efforts to accomplish these aims."

Only by the betrayal of the principles so clearly set forth can any nation or group of nations instigate war. The defiance of these sacred principles, or the repudiation of the agreements reached by the United Nations, will bring shame, disgrace, and infamy upon its transgressors who will be damned forever in history as traitors to the human race. Such a mad adventure would mean the ultimate collapse of the nation that undertook it.

The second epochal result of World War II was the indictment of war instigators as criminals, branding them as murderers, and sentencing them to death or life imprisonment for their crimes. These "War Crimes Trials" in Germany, Japan, and other aggressor nations, set a new high standard for international morality.

The United Nations War Crimes Commission set up (Aug. 8, 1945) an International Military Tribunal signed by the United States, Great Britain, France, and Russia (and 19 other United Nations). The four-power court convened in Nuremberg, Germany (Nov. 20, 1945), and handed down its verdicts (Sept. 30-Oct. 1, 1946). The trial lasted 10 months and 10 days.

Twenty-two top-ranking Nazi leaders were convicted and sentenced: Martin Bormann, 46, Hitler's confidential secretary, tried in absentia, hanging; Hermann Goering, 53, commander of Hitler's Luftwaff, hanging; Wilhelm Keitel, 64, chief of Nazi High Command, hanging; Alfred Rosenberg, 53, Nazi racial persecutor, hanging; Fritz Sauckel, 52, director of slave labor conscription, hanging; Joachim Von Ribbentrop, 53, Foreign Minister, hanging; Alfred Jodl, 54, Colonel-General, hanging; Julius Streicher, 51, editor of anti-Jewish organ Der Stuermer, hanging; Dr. Arthur Seyss-Inquart, 54, Nazi Chancellor of Austria, and Administrator of Netherlands, hanging; Ernest Kaltenbrunner, 43, Chief of Gestapo, hanging; Hans Frank, 64, Governor of Occupied Poland, hanging; Wilhelm Frick, 69, Protector Bohemia and Moravia, hanging.

Rudolph Hess, 50, Deputy Fuehrer before he fled to Scotland (1941), life imprisonment; Erich Raeder, 70, Grand Admiral, life imprisonment; Walther Funk, 56, Economics Minister, life imprisonment; Baldur Von Schirach, 39, leader of Hitler Youth Movement, 20 years imprisonment; Albert Speer, 40, Minister of Armaments, 20 years imprisonment; Constantin Von Neurath, 73, former Foreign Minister, 15 years imprisonment; Karl Doenitz, 55, Grand Admiral and Hitler's successor as Fuehrer, 10 years imprisonment; Hjalmar Schacht, 69, Reichbank President and former Economics Minister, acquitted; Franz Von Papen, 67, wartime Ambassador to Turkey and ex-envoy to Austria, acquitted; Hans Fritzsche, 47, Deputy Propaganda Minister, acquitted.

Originally 24 war leaders were indicted, but Dr. Robert Ley, chief of Nazi Labor Front, hanged himself in his cell (Oct. 25, 1945). Gustav Krupp von Bohlen und Halback, munitions magnate, was adjudged unfit for trial because of mental and physical senility.

The hangings began at midnight (Oct. 16, 1946). Only Goering cheated the gallows by taking cyanide of potassium in his cell at the last minute. Hitler and Dr. Joseph Goebbels had committed suicide in their Chancellory hideaway in Berlin in the last days of the war. Similar trials were held in Japan where their atrocity leaders were executed.

Thus retribution caught up with the promulgators of World War II, and set a dire warning to instigators of any future wars.

INDEX

Aachen, 768-771, 796
Aaron Ward, destroyer, 528
Abbeville, 208-210, 214, 216, 418
Abele, destroyer, 923
Abemama, 492-493, 625
Abetz, Otto, 244
Acropolis, 288
Adak, 611
Adams, Lieutenant Sam, 514
Addis Ababa, 410-411
Administration of National Defense, 484; executive boards, 482-484
Admiral Hipper, 141
Admiral Luetzow, pocket battleship, 804
Admiral Scheer, pocket battleship, 804
Admiralty Islands, 643-645, 648, 655, 660
Adriatic Sea, 273, 287, 696, 721, 724, 806, 827
Aegean Islands, 290
Aegean Sea, 264, 287, 291, 700, 783
Africa, 249, 256-257, 259, 336, 371, 607; battle for, 550 (*see also* North Africa)
African Free Corps, Moroccan, 569
Afrika Korps, 411, 413, 543, 560, 569, 575-576, 579-580, 582, 585, 593, 603
Agattu, 516, 611
Agrigento, 672-673, 675
Aguinaldo, Emilio, 351, 454
Ailette River, 215
Ailifsen, Gunnar, 150
Ainsworth, Rear Admiral W. L., 638
Air control: Allied, 553, 567-568, 571, 573, 576-580, 584, 590, 737, 844; in Pacific, 470, 616
Air Transport Command, 620
Air warfare, 224
Aircraft carrier, task force built around, 488
Aisne River, 206, 214, 216, 217
Aitape, 645-647
Akagi, carrier, 512, 513
Akyab, 15, 501, 915
Alaska, 330, 442, 509, 612
Alaska Defense Command, 611
Alaskan Sea Frontier, 649
Albania, 5, 104, 278, 283-287, 289, 293, 783
Albert I, King of the Belgians, 161, 210
Albert W. Grant, destroyer, 877
Albert Canal, 156, 157
Aleutian Islands, 306, 509, 510, 515-516, 607, 611, 612
Alexander, King of Yugoslavia, 261, 277, 280
Alexander, A. V., First Lord of Admiralty, 685
Alexander, Captain George, Earl of Haig, 867
Alexander, General Harold R. L. G., 441, 500, 727; in Africa, 567, 585, 593, 604, 726, 729; Casablanca, 561; governor of Sicily, 673; supreme commander in Mediterranean, 784, 852
Alexandria, Egypt, 200, 240, 241, 411

Algeria, 539-540, 552-556, 566
Algiers, 536-537, 542-544, 549-550, 564, 727; frontier, 235; radio, 582, 671, 700
Alison, Colonel John R., 621
All-India Congress, 502
Allen, Major General Terry, 572, 673
Allied Control Commission, 694
Allied Control Council, 46-47
Allied First Airborne Army, 801-802
Allied Military Government (AMG), 675, 685, 693-694, 706, 713, 721
Alpine Chausseurs, 199
Alpine troops, German, 287; Italian, 284-285
Alsace, 234, 253, 256, 776, 795
Altmark, prison ship, 138
Amalienborg Castle, 130, 134
Amandola, Giovanni, 92
Amann, Max, 80, 82
Amaterasu-o-mi-Kami, Sun Goddess, 293, 294
Amboina, 447, 448
Amchitka, 611
American armies (*see* United States)
American Federation of Labor, 484
American Indians, 356, 628, 686, 697
American Red Cross, 461, 481-482; Blood Donors Service, 482; Information Service, 482; prisoners' packages, 482, 863, 868, 896; Volunteer Special Services Corps, 482
American Revolution, 192
Amiens, 208, 209, 215
Amsterdam, 168-171, 173, 175-176
Anapa, 390
Ancona, 717-718
Anderson, General Kenneth A. N., 541, 543, 582, 601, 605
Anderson, Sergeant Leroy C., 455
Andreanof Group, 611, 613
Andreev, Private Nicolai Ivanovitch, 846
Angaur Island, 656
Anglo-German Naval Agreement, 179
Anglo-German Payments Agreement, 179
Anglo-Japanese Alliance, 299-300
Ankara, 263
Antares, U.S.S., 324
Anti-Comintern Pact, 112, 133, 265, 271, 431
Anti-Fascists, 91, 713
Anti-Nazis, 47, 49, 67, 68, 101
Anti-Semitic laws, Vichy, 557
Anti-Semitism, 55, 56, 58, 59, 67, 96, 112, 267
Antiochus of Syria, 288
Antonescu, General Ion, 269-271
Antonescu, Victor, 267, 269-271
Antwerp, 154, 157, 158, 162, 173, 204, 766-767, 791
Anzio landing, 705-710
Aoos River, 285
Aosta, Duke of, 89, 90
Apassi, 348

970 Index

Appeasement, 110, 154, 179
Arafura Sea, 442, 615
Arawe Peninsula, 625, 627-628
Arbeitsfront, 70-73, 82
Arctic, route through, 365, 367
Ardennes Forest, 155, 204; German counter-offensive in, 774-777, 788-797, 806
Arezzo, 716-717
Argonaut, submarine, 609-610
Argonne Forest, 217, 751
Argyrokastron, 285
Arizona, battleship, 326, 328, 329, 333
Arnhem, 768-770, 801
Arnim, Colonel General Jurgen von, 558, 566, 568, 569, 581, 589, 604, 605
Arnold, Major General A. V., 928
Arnold, Lieutenant General Henry H., 16, 470, 480, 560, 621, 665, 737, 740, 901-902, 922
Arras, 208, 209, 219
Arundel Island, 615
Aryan doctrine, 55, 82, 83, 106, 116-117
Arzeu, 537
Ashbourne, Captain Lord, 884
Asia, 8, 434, 452, 510
Asia Minor, 607
Asiatic Fleet, United States, 446
Aslito Airfield, 650, 652
Assisi, 714
Astoria, heavy cruiser, 473, 475, 476, 504
Athenia, torpedoed, 190
Athens, 285-291, 783
Atlanta, antiaircraft cruiser, 517, 525, 528, 529
Atlantic, Battle of, 152
Atlantic Charter, 6-8, 320, 340, 366, 608
Atlantic Wall, 739
Atlas Mountains, 545
Attlee, Clement R., 558
Atoll warfare, 625-633
Atomic energy, 14
Atomic bomb, 17-21, 26, 38, 909, 936-937
Atsugi, 26, 29, 30, 40, 41
Attu, 510, 516, 607, 611-613, 650, 885, 926
Auchinleck, General Sir Claude, 411
August Wilhelm, Prince, 60
Augusta, cruiser, 17
Auriol, Vincent, 255
Australia, 17, 25, 29, 32, 190, 302, 411, 433, 442, 445, 449, 615, 617; declares war on Axis, 465; saved from invasion, 450, 465-470, 503, 507, 532; war effort, 465
Australia, cruiser, 505, 923
Australians: Air Forces, 570-571, 657, 664; Army, 231, 287, 288, 341, 410, 412, 413, 439, 518, 530, 614-617, 629, 640-642, 919; Navy, 664, 919
Austria, 55, 86, 261; annexation of, 5, 93-102, 105, 178, 293, 820, 838; first Nazi *Putsch*, 83; Hitler plebiscite, 105-107; liberation, 849, 850, 852; Russian advance into, 824-825, 828; Underground, 825
Austrian Republic, 93, 95, 98, 102
Austro-German Agreement, 98-99
Austro-Hungarian Dual Monarchy, 55, 93, 109, 272

Autobahnen, 774
Avanti, 86, 87
Avranches, 755, 756
Ayers, Colonel Russell G., 630
Azov, Sea of, 368, 370, 383, 389-391

B-29's, 16-18, 24, 33, 900-903, 908, 924, 925, 928
Bad Godesberg, 798, 802
Bad Orb, 865
Badger, Rear Admiral O. C., 904
Badoglio, Marshal Pietro, 677-678, 690, 692, 694, 698, 701, 702, 713
Baghdad, 261
Bagley, Vice Admiral David W., 338, 649
Bagramyan, General Ivan, 381, 807
Baguio, 348
Bailey, Marine Sergeant Thomas E., 330
Baka bombs, 923, 924, 927, 934
Baker, Lionel S., Pharmacist's Mate, 330
Baker, Sergeant Thomas, 653
Balaton, Lake, 807
Balbo, General Italo, 92
Bali, 449, 451
Balkan Entente, 261, 262, 268, 273
Balkan Wars (1912-1913), 261
Balkans, 83, 103-104, 119, 144, 200, 267, 271, 355, 698, 700, 820, 821, 827; blitz in, 261-266
Balloons, bomb-carrying, 922-923
Baltic Sea, 129, 181, 261, 806-807, 816-817, 829, 831, 838, 864
Baltic States, 123, 354, 366, 397
Banat, 267, 278, 279
Banda Island, 448
Banda Sea, 442, 615
Bangkok, 335, 902, 915
Banjermassin, 449
Barter, 268, 272
Barth, prison camp, 864
Barton, Major General R. O., 750-751
Barton, destroyer, 528
Baruch, Bernard M., 483
Bastogne, 768, 794-795
Bataan, 27, 45, 628, 661, 664; battle of, 452-461, 602, 890; "March of Death," 45, 459-461, 464, 893, 895
Bataan Peninsula, 346, 348, 351, 893, 894, 896
Batavia, 449, 450, 466
Batchka, 278, 279
Batt, William M., 483-485
Baudouin, Foreign Minister, 239-240, 253
Bavaria, 47, 57
Bayeux, 735-738
Bearn, aircraft carrier, 240
Beaverbrook, Lord, 224, 233, 374
Beck, General, 104
Beck, M., 180-181
Bedaux, Charles, 557
Beirut, 260
Belfort Gap, 767, 769, 771
Belgian Congo, 166
Belgium, 83, 86, 87, 167-169, 233, 791, 793, 796; alliance with France, 153; aid to Allies, 166, 206; appeal for aid, 168; German occu-

Index

pation, 153-166, 201-206, 208-209, 219; government in exile, 210; liberation of, 765-767; neutrality, 193; Underground, 165-166
Belgorod, 387-389
Belgrade, 273, 276-279
Belin, René, 247
Belleau Wood, carrier, 492, 493
Belleville-Sur-Mer, 420
Belloni, 92
Belousoff, Major, 836
Belsen, 845, 867, 868
Benes, Eduard, 109, 111, 117, 119, 166, 827
Bengal, Bay of, 441, 442, 500, 620
Benghazi, 411, 414
Benham, 529
Bennion, Captain Mervyn S., 328-329
Beran, Rudolf, 111
Berbey, Vice Admiral Daniel E., 627-628, 637, 644, 660, 665, 890
Berchtesgaden, 52, 53, 63, 99, 183, 265, 274, 846
Bergen, 139-142, 151
Bergeret, General, 557, 573
Beria, L. P., 366
Berkeley, destroyer, 427
Berkey, Admiral Russell S., 644, 890
Berlin, 44, 808, 821, 828; Allied control of, 47; battle of, 829-841; bombardment, 224, 226, 229, 366, 813, 837; broadcasts, 390, 721; surrender signed in, 3, 858-860
Berlin, University of, 75-76
Berlin to Bagdad, 261
Berlin Conference, 12, 46, 47
Berlin-Rome-Tokyo pact, 270
Berlin *Rundfunk*, 229
Berliner Tageblatt, 81
Bernadotte, Count Folke, 838, 847-849
Berne, 259
Berneval, 417, 419, 420
Bernhard zu Lippe-Biesterfeld, Prince, 171
Berr, Lieutenant Robert, 924
Bessarabia, 267-270, 365
Best, Dr. Werner, 133
Betio, 625
Biak Island, 648
Bianchi, Lieutenant Willibald C., 455
Bibolo Hill, 639
Bickell, Lieutenant Colonel George R., 327
Bidassoa River, international bridge, 236
Biddle, Francis, Attorney General, 479
Bilibid Prison, 895
Bill of Rights, 360
Billotte, General, 762
Bingham, Major Sidney V., 752
Bismarck, 109
Bismarck Archipelago, 446
Bismarck Sea, 442, 465, 616-617, 632, 645; Battle of, 616-617
Bismarck Sea, escort carrier, 906
Bissolati, 86
Bizerte, 218, 414, 554, 555, 558, 569, 683, 588-590, 593, 668, 732; drive for, 540-548, 588-597; fall of, 598-606
Black Dragon Society, 318, 319
"Black Hand" (Dutch underground), 176

Black Hand (Italian), 91
Black markets, 279
Black Sea, 263-264, 365, 369, 370, 387, 390, 392, 395; fleet, 384, 390, 391
Black Shirts, 90-91
Blamey, General Sir Thomas, 32-33
Blanchard, General Georges-Maurice-Jean, 215
Blandford, James B., Jr., 484
Blaskowitz, General von, 125
Blitzkrieg, 123, 127, 143-144, 154, 169, 170, 201, 226, 230, 361, 364-366, 675
Bloch, Rear Admiral Claude C., 331-333, 337-338
"Blood Brotherhood," 318
Blood Donors Service, 482
Bloody Nose Ridge, 654, 656
Bluecher, cruiser, 140
Blum, Léon, 244, 247, 250, 253, 845, 866
Boardman, Mabel T., 482
Bock, Field Marshal von, 104, 107, 365, 371
Bodelschwingh, Bishop, 67
Boer War, 416
Bohemia, 109, 115-117, 179
Bohr, Dr. Neils, 19
Boise, cruiser, 521, 689
Boisson, Pierre, 250-251
Bologna, 723, 725, 784, 785
Bolshevism, Fascist accusation of, 88-89, 104, 196, 360-362
Bone, 540, 541
Bonin Islands, 651, 652, 654, 900, 903, 904
Bonis, 494-495
Bonn, 778, 798, 800, 803
Bonnet, Georges, 115, 193
Bono, General de, 92
Bonomi, Ivanoe, 713
Booby traps, 693, 712
Bor, General, 126, 779-782, 866
Bordeaux, 215, 216, 219-223, 236, 238, 256, 765, 842-843
Boris III, King of Bulgaria, 262, 264-266
Borisov, 402
Borneo, 346, 431, 447-449
Borotra, Jean, 867
Borum, 641
Bose, Subhas Chandra, 622
Bosporus, 261
Botticelli, *Primavera*, 720
Bougainville, 489, 493-495, 519, 532, 615, 625, 642, 919
Bougie, 541
Boulogne, 160, 246, 765, 770
Bowles, Chester, 483
Boxer Rebellion, 299
Boys' festival (*tango no sekku*), 296
Bracknell, Pvt. Artie, 646
Bradley, Major General James L., 662, 928
Bradley, Major General Omar N., 593, 604, 730, 732, 736, 739, 741, 746, 748, 756, 767, 777, 789, 791, 867
Braeuer, Dr. Curt, 138, 139
Brandenburg, 813, 838
Bratislava, 114, 823-825
Brauchitsch, Field Marshal General Walther von, 104, 123, 374

Braun, Eva, 837
Brazil, 241, 564
Brazilian Expeditionary Force, 718, 725, 784, 787
Bredow, General von, 62
Breendonck, 164-165
Bremen, 804, 805, 846, 847
Brennus, 288
Breteton, General Lewis H., 412, 413, 437, 497
Breslau, 812, 814-816, 838
Brest-Litovsk, 123, 353
Bretagne, battleship, 239
Brett, Lieutenant General George H., 343, 451, 518, 524
Breznica, 282
Briand, Aristide, 59
Britain, Battle of, 126. (*See also* Great Britain)
British, 46; in Battle of France, 199-213; in Burma and China, 618-624; conquest of Germany, 842-861; Italian campaign, 686-725, 783-787; in North Africa, 533-606, 727; in Norway, 140-146; raid on *Altmark,* 138; in Sicily, 668-685; on Western Front, 726-778. (*See also* Great Britain)
British Broadcasting Corporation, 177, 418, 560, 586, 719
British Commonwealth of Nations, 178, 189-191, 465
British Medical Journal, 231
British Ministry of Information, 223
British Museum, 229
Brittany, 748, 755-756
Brooke, General Sir Alan, 560, 740
Brooke-Popham, Air Chief Marshal Sir Robert, 344
Brown, Major General Alfred F., 613
Brown, Lieutenant Harry, 327
Brown, Vice Admiral Wilson, 444, 487
Broz, Josip (*see* Tito)
Bruce, Major General Andrew D., 655, 923, 928
Bruening, Heinrich, 60-62
Brunel, Charles, 534
Brussels, 137, 154, 157, 158, 162, 163, 201, 204, 219, 765
Brussels, University of, 164
Bryansk, 383, 386, 389, 390
Buchanan, destroyer, 521
Buchenwald, 845, 867-870
Buckingham Palace, 229
Buckmaster, Captain Elliott, 507, 514, 515
Buckner, Lieutenant General Simon Bolivar, Jr., 611, 925-928, 930, 932-934, 936
Bucovina, 267, 269, 270
Buda, 821, 822
Budapest, 820-822, 865-866
Buddhism, 294-295
Budenny, Marshal Semyon, 365, 369, 370, 380, 381, 388
Buelow-Schwante, Vicco von, 154
Buerckel, Joseph, 107
Bug River, 270, 396
Buin, 494
Buka, 466, 494-495, 615, **629**
Bulatoff, Gregory. 826

Bulgaria, 166, 261-266, 269, 271, 274, 278, 286, 290-291, 807, 820, 827
Bulge, Battle of, 788-797
Bulkeley, Lieutenant Commander John D., 452-453, 467-468, 637
Bullitt, William C., 218
Buna, 471, 530-532, 614, 634-635
Bund Deutscher Maedel's (BDM) (Union of German Girls), 78
Bunker Hill, carrier, 936
Burma, invaded by Japanese, 301, 335, 339, 345, 438, 441, 445, 450, 500-501, 607-608, 649, 904; liberation, 15, 26, 29, 35, 619-623, 881, 911, 914-916, 920, 921
Burma-Ledo Road, 618-623
Burma Road, 344, 434, 438, 501, 620; loss of, 502; reopened, 623
Burns, Lieutenant John A., 647
Burrough, Admiral, 859
Busch, Field Marshal Ernst, 853
Bush, Dr. Vannevar, 19, 484
Bushi, 293, 294
Bushido, code, 293, 295-296, 456
But, 641
Butler, Major General William O., **612**
Buzz-bombs, 792
Byrnes, James F., 23, 25, 483

Cabanatuan prison camp, 895
Caen, 734, 735, 737, 738, 740; conquest by Canadians, 746-749
Cagliari, 582
Cairo, 289, 411, 700
Cairo Conference, 8, 703
Cairo Declaration, 24, 618
Calabria, 699, 701
Calais, 160, 209, 212-213, 233, 765, 770
California, Japanese shell coast, 450; submarines off coast, 342
California, battleship, 326, 333, 877, 923
Calippus, 288
Callaghan, Rear Admiral D. J., 527-528
Calugas, Sergeant José, 453-454
Cambon, Roger, 242
Cambrai, 208, 209, 211
Cameroons, 250, 254-255
Camino, Mount, 696
Camorra, 91
Camp John Hay, 348
Camp O'Donnell, 893, 895
Camp Ord, 348
Campbell, Sir Ronald I., 19
Canada, 19, 33, 190, 391, 484, 611
Canadians, 199, 231, 343-344, 419, 765-771; capture Caen, 746-749, 753; at Dieppe, 415-419, 577; in Italy, 724-725; in North Africa, 413, 727; in Sicily, 668-676; on the Western Front, 734-742, 745-749, 753-754, 756, 760, 763, 765, 770-771, 842, 846
Canberra, heavy cruiser, 473, 475, 476
Cannon, Lieutenant George H., 448
Canton-Hankow Railway, 15
Cap Bon, 413, 589-590, 593, 598, **600-606**
Cape Esperance, 518, 521-523, 531
Cape Gloucester, 627-628, 642

Index 973

Cap Negre Peninsula, 758
Cape Orlando, 682, 683
Cap Serrat, 569, 582
Capua, 694
Carentan, 739, 740
Carentan estuary, 734, 736, 738
Caribbean Sea, 240
Carinthia, 828
Carlson, Lieutenant Colonel Evans F., 531
Carlson's Raiders, 527, 531, 609-610, 644, 654
Carol, King of Rumania, 267-270
Caroline Islands, 302, 611, 631, 919
Carpathians, 806-808, 819-828
Carpender, Vice Admiral Arthur S., 636
Cartels, 57
Carter, Lieutenant David V., 933
Carter, Captain H. J., 637
Casablanca Conference, 8, 44, 237-238, 537, 539, 560-564, 805
Casablanca, Declaration of, 551, 560-562, 604
Caserta, 852
Cassin, destroyer, 326, 329
Cassino, battle at, 694, 697, 703-710, 722
Castellano, General, 701
Catania, 673, 675, 682
Catholic Church, persecution of, 66, 68, 69, 91, 164, 253-254
Catholic Youth, 108
Catroux, General Georges, 545-546, 573
Caucasus, 382-384, 390-392, 398, 406; oil, 370, 371, 377
Cavallero, General, 285
Cavell, Edith, 164
Cavite, 340, 348, 445, 454, 882
Cecil, Captain Charles P., 638
Celebes, 431, 448, 449
Celebes Sea, 442, 446, 615, 617, 654, 656
Cellette, Sergeant Albert H., 345
Central America, 240, 308
Central Pacific, 516, 609-611, 617
Central Pacific Force (*see* Fifth Fleet)
Centre Party, 190
Ceron, Staff Sergeant George R., 13
Ceylon, 441, 500
Chad, Lake, 250, 559
Chadwick, Sir James, 19
Chamberlain, Houston Stewart, 55
Chamberlain, Neville, 154, 169, 179-189, 192, 194-195, 200, 357, 361, 798
Chamberlain, Major William, 933
Chambers, Major Robert, Jr., 464
Changsha, 624
Channel (*see* English Channel)
Chapei, 5, 293, 319, 430
Charan Kanoa, 650
Charleroi, 157, 159, 208
Charles XII, King of Sweden, 353
Chase, Lieutenant William A., 512
Chase, Major General William C., 41
Chase, Brigadier General William M., 644
Chatel, Yves, 548, 557
Chautemps, Camille, 237
Chekiang Province, 608
Chemulpo, 300
Chen Cheng, General, 914, 918-919

Chennault, Lieutenant Colonel Claire L., 434, 437, 497, 608, 624, 918
Cherbourg, 216, 220, 735, 736, 742-745, 767
Cherbourg Peninsula, 737-742, 745
Chernykhovsky, General Ivan D., 807, 808, 810, 811, 813-815
Chester, heavy cruiser, 443, 444, 504, 523
Chetniks, 279-280
Chiang Kai-shek, Generalissimo, 15, 45, 317, 320, 322, 432, 434-435, 561, 564, 911, 914; at Cairo conference, 8, 703; Pacific War Council, 343; quoted on Japanese defeat, 435-436
Chiang Kai-shek, Madame, visit to United States, 608
Chiappe, Jean, 260
Chicago, heavy cruiser, 475, 476, 505
Child, Richard Washburn, 84
China, 9, 166, 253, 294-295, 298; Allied aid to, 315, 317, 563; Boxer Rebellion, 299; breach between Communists and Chungking, 432; Burma-Ledo Road, 618-624; declares war on Axis, 339, 429, 435; defense of homeland, 429-436; Japanese invasion and occupation, 5, 15, 293-307, 312-322, 335, 501, 607, 608, 654, 660; and Japanese surrender, 30-35, 41, 44; liberates Yunnan Province, 623; liberation of, 27, 29, 496, 881, 890, 897, 904, 921; at Moscow talks, 391; Potsdam Declaration, 12, 22, 25; publishes Tanaka memorial, 306; Republic, 8, 302, 608; "scorched earth" policy, 433; Twenty-one Demands on, 302-305
"China Affair," 318
"China Incident," 335, 339, 434, 442
Chinese Communists, 432, 911, 918
Chinese Republic, thirty-first anniversary, 608
Cho, Isamo, Lieutenant General, 934
Choiseul, 615, 642
Choltitz, General Dietrich von, 760, 762-764
Christ, 409
Christensen, Major James R., 632
Christian, King of Denmark, 127, 129-132, 134-136
Christian Socialist Party, 94, 95, 190
Christianity, Nazi attacks on, 76, 78-79
Chungking, 432-434, 658, 917
Churchill, Captain Randolph, 281
Churchill, Winston, 248, 263, 287, 502, 573, 584, 685, 693, 701, 720, 735, 740, 782, 891; appeals to the French, 221-223; to the Italians, 674; and Atlantic Charter, 6-8, 320, 366; and atomic bomb, 18; in Berlin, 12; broadcast to France, 256; at Cairo conference, 8, 703; at Casablanca, 560-564; crosses Rhine, 802; First Lord of Admiralty, 190; Pacific War Council, 516; pledges aid in Pacific, 636; Potsdam declaration, 45; proposes union with France, 219-220; Prime Minister, 155, 201, 209, 210; promises aid to Yugoslavia, 275; at Quebec, 9, 618; quoted on bombings, 228, 230; in Czechoslovakia, 110; on death of Sikorski, 126; on invasion of Britain, 233; on Italy, 606; on Narvik battle, 140; at Teheran, 9, 394, 703; warns on war progress, 391, 545; at Washington

974 Index

conferences, 342-343, 374, 385, 533; at Yalta, 814, 844
Churchill tanks, 566-567
Chust, 113
Chvalkovsky, Dr. Frantisek, 111, 112, 115-116
Ciano, Count, 269, 434, 678
City of Flint, merchantman, 137-138
Clark, Colonel George S., 454
Clark, Admiral J. J. ("Jocko"), 492, 651
Clark, General Mark W., 534-535, 561, 686, 689, 693, 702, 712, 718, 719, 722, 784, 787
Clark Field, 347, 658, 887, 893
Clarke, Brigadier General Bruce, 791
Class, Justizrat Heinrich, 56, 60
Clausen, Dr. Fritz, 135
Clay, Lieutenant General Lucius, 50
Clemenceau, Michel, 866
Cleves, 769
"Closed door" doctrine, 295
Coast Guard Reserve, 481
Coblentz, 778, 798-801
Coburg, Duke of, 60
Cochran, Colonel Philip G., 621
Collaborationists, 223, 249-250, 259, 536, 537
Collective farming, 359, 361, 408
Collective security, 8, 12, 262
Collins, Commander John A., 665
Collins, Major General Joseph T., 744
Cologne, 769, 772, 773, 777, 778, 788
Colombo, 500
Comacchio Lagoon, 784, 785
Combattant, destroyer, 740
Combined Chiefs of Staff (CCS), 449, 483
Combined Food Board, 484
Combined War Materials Board (CWM), 483
Comfort, hospital ship, 934
Comité National Français (see French National Committee)
Commandos, 152, 291, 472, 534, 546, 548, 555, 558, 609, 619, 668-669, 738, 757; Dieppe raid, 415-428
Committee of War Employment Practice, 484
Commonwealth of Nations (*see* British Commonwealth of Nations)
Communism, 123, 557; Russian, 353, 359-361, (*See also* Anti-Comintern Pact)
Communists, 61, 83, 89, 111, 194, 264, 266, 279, 432, 761, 911, 918
Compiègne, 221, 222
Compton, Dr. A. H., 19
Conant, President James B., 19
Concentration camps, 66, 67, 69, 81, 106-109, 116, 150-151, 176, 862-871; in conquered countries, 135-136, 164-165, 290, 352, 558, 782; evidence of barbarities, 845, 862-871
Confucianism, 294-295
Congress of Industrial Organizations, 484
Coningham, Air Vice Marshal Sir Arthur, 573, 792
Connally, Tom, Senator, 848
Connolly, Rear Admiral Richard L., 654, 890
Constantine, 711
Constantine, King of Greece, 282
Constitution, United States, 360
Cooley, Lieutenant Colonel, 520

Cooper, destroyer, 885
Coördination, of land, sea, air forces, 657, 671
Copenhagen, 127-130, 132, 134, 136
Coral Sea, battle, 471, 472, 503-509, 642, 649
Corbett, Corporal John C., 933
Corbin, Charles, 242
Corfu, 289, 783
Corinth, 783
Corlett, Major General Charles H., 630
Corregidor, 661-662, 664, 883; fall of, 27-28, 45, 348, 452-464, 657, 890
Corsica, 234, 690
Cossacks, 826, 829
Cost of War, 966
Coulondre, Robert, 114-115, 193
Courcel, Lieutenant de, 238
Courland Peninsula, 807
Coventry, 226, 229, 230, 375
Cowpens, carrier, 493
Cracow, 123, 810-812
Crerar, Lieutenant General H. D. G., 416, 746, 754, 767, 770, 801
Cressy, Battle of, 739
Crete, 278, 288, 289, 291, 619, 682, 683, 919
Crimea, 271, 368, 370, 371, 390-392, 394, 397, 406
Cripps, Sir Stafford, 502
Croatia, 274, 277-279
Croats, 93, 272
Cross, Lieutenant John L., Jr., 646
Crowley, Leo T., 483
Cruiser, support for aircraft carrier, 488
Crutchley, Admiral, 475
Culin, Colonel Frank L., Jr., 613
Cunningham, Admiral Sir Andrew, 410, 541, 553, 561, 700, 702
Cunningham, Brigadier General Julian W., 627
Cunninghame, Sir Thomas, 110
Curtiss, seaplane tender, 329
Curzon Line, 395
Cushing, destroyer, 528, 529
CV, CVL, CVE, 488
Cvetkovitch, Premier Dragisha, 272, 274, 275
Cyclops, 645, 646
Cyrenaica, 410
Czarne River, 808-809
Czechoslovakia, 48, 81, 83, 93, 97, 103, 105, 166, 261-262, 807, 821-828; German colonists, 117-118; Germany seizes, 109-119, 179; liberated, 838, 844, 850, 858; looting of, 112-113, 116-117; Partisans and Underground, 118-119, 827
Czechs, 93, 108-119; in armies abroad, 119, 231; resistance, 118-119, 827

D-Day, Allied landing in France, 712, 726-738
Dace, submarine, 873
Dachau, 67, 106, 165, 845, 867, 870
Dagua, 641
Dairen (Dalny), 300
Dakar, 241-242, 249, 251-252, 336, 533, 534, 540, 547, 564
Daladier, Edouard, 49, 159, 192, 194-195, 197, 198, 204, 215, 357, 845, 866
Dale, Lieutenant Jack C. K., 345

Index 975

Dalmatia, 278, 281, 827
Daluege, General Kurt, 134, 135
Dan, Baron Takuma, 318
Danes, aid to Allies, 136; resistance to Nazis, 131-136
d'Annunzio, Gabriele, 88
Danube Gateway, 808
Danube River, 264, 273, 277, 820-825, 846
Danubian Confederation, 261
Danzig, 121, 122, 179-184, 187, 195, 384, 811, 814, 815, 817-818
Dardanelles, 263, 264
Darlan, Admiral Jean-François, 193, 237, 259, 536-537, 539-540, 543, 546-548, 549-550
Darter, submarine, 873
Davao, 656-659, 898
Davet, General Achille, 672
Davies, Joseph E., 484
Davis, Elmer, 484, 599
Davis, Norman H., 482
Davis, William H., 483
Déat, Marcel, 245
Death March (*see* Bataan)
De Bono, General, 90
De Boyne Island, 504
Debuchi, Katsuji, 313, 429
Decoux, Admiral Jean, 251, 253
d'Entrecasteaux Islands, 615
De Gaulle, General Charles: appeals for French resistance, 237-238; BBC broadcasts, 221-223; on D-Day, 735; at Casablanca, 561-562, 564; condemned *in absentia*, 246-247; cooperation with Giraud, 550, 561, 573; heads Free French, 166, 237-238, 240-242, 244-260, 537, 540, 585, 596, 758, 760-761; National Defense, Undersecretary for, 214; President Provisional Government, 49; rallies Free French, 248-260; return to France, 740; enters Paris, 763-764; treatise on mechanized warfare, 202-203, 214-215, 548, 754
De Gaullists, 556-557, 607
De Larminat, 257
Delehanty, Staff Sergeant William J., 340-341
Delfosse, Antoine, 166
Democracy, 93, 95, 98, 102-104, 109, 135, 288, 336; Greek origin of word, 282; power as fighting force, 478
Demosthenes, 288
Dempsey, Lieutenant General Sir Miles C., 730-731, 736, 754, 765, 767, 796, 801, 849
Demyansk, 384
Den Helder, 173
Denis, Lieutenant General Henri, 156
Denmark, 175, 848, 849, 853; invasion of, 127-136; looting of, 131; resistance in, 131-136
Denny, Harold, 791, 869
Der Sturmer, 59
Derevyanko, Lieutenant General K. N., 32
Derrien, Admiral Edmond, 606
Deshazer, Corporal Jacob D., 500
Deutschkunde, 78
Devereux, Lieutenant Colonel James P. S., 27, 343
Devers, Lieutenant General Jacob L., 703, 854
DeWitt, Lieutenant General John L., 612

Dickens, Charles, 409
Dickinson, Lieutenant Clarence E., 328
Dickover, E. R., 314
Diego Saurez, 607
Dieppe, raid on, 415-428, 552, 577, 731, 735
Dietrich, Dr. Otto, 369
Dill, Field Marshal Sir John, 19, 784
Dillingen, 775
Dittmar, General, 847
Dixon, Commander Bob, 505
Djebel Garci, 590
Djedeida, 542-546
Djerba, Island of, 555
Djibouti, 235, 249
DNB, 83
Dnieper dam, 367, 391
Dnieper River, 368, 387-388, 390-396
Dniepropetrovsk, 403
Dniester River, 396-397
Dobruja, 269
Dodecanese Islands, 283, 700, 783
Doenitz, Grand Admiral Karl, 48, 835, 838, 843, 849, 850, 853-855
Dollfuss, Engelbert, 96-98
Dombaas, 143-144
Domei news agency, 22, 42
Don River, 368, 370, 375, 380-382, 398, 401
Donbas, 370, 371, 377, 387, 389, 392
Donets Basin, 368, 370, 372, 398, 407-408
Donets River, 387, 390
Donnelly, Captain Thomas J., 924
Doolittle, Lieutenant General James H., 16, 497-498, 541, 545, 731-732, 901, 904
Doorman, Rear Admiral, 487
Douai, 159, 241
Dover, 209, 226
Downes, destroyer, 326, 329
Drake, Brigadier General Charles C., 462
Drang nach Osten, 261
Drava River, 807
Dresden, 821, 831
Drexler, Anton, 58
Drexler, destroyer, 934
Dual Monarchy (*see* Austria-Hungary)
Duesseldorf, 777, 778, 800, 801, 846
Duisburg, 777, 778, 800-802
Dumbarton Oaks Conference, 9
Dun and Bradstreet, 485
Duncan, destroyer, 521, 522
Dunckel, Brigadier General William C., 886
Dunkerque, 239
Dunkirk, 161, 119, 209-215, 224, 233, 246, 434, 541, 552, 727, 729, 735, 765, 850
Durcansky, 114
Durgin, Admiral C. T., 890
Dutch, in Allied forces, 231, 341
Dutch East Indies, 174, 653
Dutch Harbor, 330, 442, 508, 510, 511, 926
Duzenbury, Staff Sergeant Wyatt E., 18
Dyess, Lieutenant Colonel William E., 459-461
Dykstra, Dr. Clarence A., 480

EAM, 783
Earle, Colonel Edwin P., 613
Earle, George H., 3rd, 265

Easley, Brigadier General Claudius M., 934
East Prussia, 807-808, 811-812, 815-817
Ebert, Frederick, 64
Eden, Anthony, 263, 391, 764
Edson's Raiders, 520
Efate, 469
Egypt, 8, 256, 533, 552, 600, 602, 606, 607, 727, 729; Battle of, 410-414
Ehrenburg, Ilya, 409
Eichelberger, Lieutenant General Robert L., 29, 40-43, 635, 893-894
Eighth Army, British, in Italy, 691-725, 784-785; in North Africa, 411-412, 544, 549, 552-605, 727, 729; in Sicily, 668, 671-672
Eighth Route Army, Communist, 609
Eindhoven, 768, 769
Eisenhower, General Dwight D., 50, 119, 126, 915; Allied Control Council, 46-47; broadcast on D-Day, 735; broadcast from Gibraltar, 536; Commander in Chief in Mediterranean, 533-703, in Italy, 685, 692, 700-702; in North Africa, 8, 414, 533-606, 610; in Sicily, 667, 673, 684-685, 703; farewell to armies of Italy and North Africa, 703; Commanding General, United States Forces in European Theatre (USFET), 46; and German surrender, 838, 854-855, 858-859; message from, 13; orders American halt before Berlin, 844; plot to kidnap, 775-776; ratifies French Provisional Government, 764; Supreme Commander Allied Expeditionary Force (SHAEF), Western Front, 46, 703, 712, 720, 726-805; testimony on concentration camps, 862, 867; triumphant return, 851; warning to Germans, 801, 802
Eisenlohr, German Minister, 105
Eisner, Kurt, 57
El Alamein, 291, 411, 414, 433, 573, 699, 708, 727, 784, 801
El Guettar, 572-573, 576-578, 580-581, 586
El Hamma, 577-579, 581
ELAS, 783
Elba, island of, 600, 714
Elbe River, 805, 844
Élite Guard (Schutzstaffel), 594
Elizabeth, Queen, 189
Ellice Islands, 611, 617
Ellyson, Lieutenant Eugene, 490
Elverum, 140, 141
Emden, cruiser, 141
Emirau Island, 644-645
Emmons, Lieutenant General D. C., 333, 337
Empress Augusta Bay, 494, 495
Enders, Robert, 455-456
Enfidaville, 588, 590-594
Engano, Cape, battle of, 873, 875, 879
England (*see* Great Britain)
English Channel, 158-160, 206, 208-219, 234, 416, 732, 734, 770
Eniwetok, 630-632, 650
Enna, 673-675
Enola Gay, B-29, 18
Entente Cordiale, 239
Enterprise, carrier, 443, 444, 487-488, 498, 509, 513, 514, 517, 518, 523, 525, 528, 529

Epirus, 283, 288
Epp, General Frank Ritter von, 60
Eritrea, 410
Erskine, Major General Graves B., 905
Espiritu Santo, 469
Essen, 800, 803, 805
Essener National Zeitung, 147
Essex, carrier, 488, 490, 491-493, 495-496, 651
Essex Scottish Regiment, 420, 422, 424
Estonia, 123, 124, 354, 361
Ethiopia, 5, 98, 103, 238, 293, 410, 678
Etna, Mount, 671, 672, 679, 682
Eupen, 768
European Advisory Commission, 391
Evans, 866
Evans, Lieutenant Colonel Robert, 792
Evzones, 286
Ewa, Marine base, 325, 326, 328
Extraterritorialty, end of, 608-609

Faïd Pass, 551-555, 569, 571, 572, 576, 587
Falaise pocket, 757, 759-760
Falkenhausen, Lieutenant General Baron Alexander von, 163
Falkenhorst, General Nikolaus von, 142, 144
Farenholt, destroyer, 521
Farinacci, Roberto, 92
Farrell, Brigadier General Thomas F., 19
Farrow, 1st Lieutenant William G., 500
Fascism, 238, 262, 557, 713, 786; campaigns, technique of, 104; in violent action, 103-108
Fascists, 88-92, 206, 273, 283-286, 289, 675-678, 685, 695, 715, 721
Fechteler, Admiral, 644, 894
Feder, Gottfried, 57, 58
Federal Bureau of Investigation (FBI), 308
Federal Communications Commission, 484
Federal Loan Agency (FLA), 484
Federal Works Agency, 484
Feinstein, Israel, 935
Fenner, 423
Fenno, Commander Frank W., 463
Ferdinand, Czar, 262
Ferebee, Major Thomas W., 18
Fermi, Dr. Enrico, 19
Ferryville, 589, 600
Fey, Major Emil, 95-98
FFI (*see* French Forces of Interior)
Fifth Army, United States, 686-697, 702-725, 784
Fifth Columnists, 93, 111, 170, 307, 336, 348, 500
Fifth Fleet, United States, 491, 650-652
Fighting French, 416, 469, 503, 537, 540, 552, 556-559, 570-585, 588, 607, 740, 758, 764
Fiji Islands 469, 473
Filippelli, 92
Filipinos, 347; liberation of, 661-664; guerrillas, 662, 892-895; troops, 346, 453-464
Fingerut, 407
Finland, 166; debt to U. S., 354; German alliance, 358, 373, 382, 397, 399; invaded by Russia, 197-198, 353-358, 361, 365, 395, 833

Index 977

Finns, history of, 353
Finschhafen, 466, 493, 616, 628, 641, 642
First Allied Airborne Army, 768-769
First Army, British, 540-542, 554, 555, 570, 577-578, 582, 588-589, 591-594, 596, 599-601
Fishburn, Francis, Medical Officer, 448
Fitch, Rear Admiral Aubrey W., 505
Fiume, 87-88, 281, 828
Five-Power Naval Treaty, 305, 431
Flanders, Battle of, 159-161, 209, 212, 215
Flandin, Pierre-Etienne, 260, 557
Fleischmann, Private Arnold, 707
Fleming, Major General Philip B., 484
Fleming, Captain Robert W., 891
Fletcher, Admiral, 472, 489, 504-507, 509, 649
Fletcher, destroyer, 528
Florence, 715-722; art treasures looted, 719-720
Flores Sea, 442
Florida Island, 473, 475, 504, 521
Florina, 264
Flushing, bombed, 173
Flying Fortresses, 325, 412, 413, 418, 438, 511, 512, 514, 522, 541, 544, 553, 558, 567-568, 582-583, 587-589, 610, 674, 702, 795, 900
"Flying Tigers," 344-345, 437, 608
Foch, Marshal, 207, 221
Foertsch, Lieutenant General, 854
Foggia, 691, 697
Foochow, 608, 917
Ford Field, 328
Ford Island, 329, 330
Foreign Economic Administration (FEA), 483
Foreign Legion, French, 538, 550
Forges-les-Eaux, 216
Formosa, 298, 301, 618, 659-660, 872, 888, 890, 892, 895, 900
Forrestal, James V., Secretary of Navy, 649, 653, 654, 659
Forster, Herr, 181, 184, 187
Fort Drum, 453, 462
Fort de l'Ecluse, 239
Fort de France, 240
Fort Frank, 453, 462
Fort Glenn, 510
Fort Hughes, 453, 462
Fort Mills, 350, 462
Four Freedoms, 6, 8
Four-Power Allied Control Council, 50
Four-Power Board, 41
Four-Power Treaty, 305
Four Winds Farm, 422-423
Fowler, R. B., 737
Fox, Lieutenant Anne G., 328
France, 33, 97, 104, 119, 123, 197, 298-299, 355, 357, 361; aids Little Entente, 262; alliance with Poland, 122, 124, 179-180, 187, 194; with Turkey, 195; Allied landing and Western Front, 726-738; Battle of, 214-223; in Battle of Flanders, 153-161; De Gaulle continues war, 248-260; Entente Cordiale, 239; enters war, 192-198; German plans to invade, 83, 93, 178; government in exile, 245; invaded by Germany, 121, 125, 199-213, 675, 754; liberation of, 712, 714, 719, 721, 754-764, 767, 842; looted, 243, 247, 253-254; Munich agreement, 110, 112-113; occupied by Nazis, 234-247; Potsdam declarations, 12; treason trials, 49; Underground, 759-760; Yellow Book, causes of war, 197; zone of occupation in Germany, 46, 47. (*See also* Dieppe; French; Fighting French; Free French; Vichy)
Francis Ferdinand, Archduke, 261
Franco, Francisco, 5, 293; "test case" in Spain, 103
Franco-Japanese Agreement, 434
Frank, Deputy Protector, 48, 118
Frankfort, 802, 813, 814, 817, 829, 831
Franklin, carrier, 910-911
Franzek, Sergeant, 231
Fraser, Admiral Sir Bruce A., 16, 32, 890, 891
Fredenhall, Major General Lloyd R., 541, 568, 571
Frederick the Great, 829
Free French (*see* De Gaulle)
Freemasons, 61, 79, 89, 91, 106
Freicorps, in Danzig, 181
French Air Force, 225
French armies, with Allies, 145-146, 170, 199-200, 203, 204, 208, 221, 668, 727, 805, 849; in Italy, 703-725; in North Africa, 533-606
French Equatorial Africa, 250
French First Army, 758, 759, 772, 774
French fleet, 196, 199, 200, 212, 220, 223, 235, 237-241, 257, 259; scuttled, 543
French Forces of the Interior (FFI), 736, 741, 758, 761-763, 765, 767, 842
French Indo-China, 27, 249-253, 260, 299, 301, 315, 335, 433, 892, 900, 916
French Morocco, 209, 237-238, 250, 668
French National Committee, 166, 223, 237, 239, 251, 573, 758, 760-762
French North Africa, 235, 243, 250
French Revolution, 192, 198
French Second Armored Division, 759
French Somaliland, 235, 249
French West Africa, 241, 249, 250
Freyberg, Lieutenant General Sir Bernard C., 289, 580, 605
Frick, Wilhelm, 48, 58
Friede, Major, 853
Friedeburg, Admiral Hans Georg von, 839, 849, 850, 853-859
Fritsch, General von, 105
Fritt Folk (Free People), 146, 147
Fuehrer Prinzip (leader principle), 77
Fuelling, Lieutenant Commander James L., 911
Fuglsang-Damgaard, Bishop, 135
Fullerton-Elphinstone, Captain Lord John Buller, 867
Funafuti atoll, 617
Funk, Walther, 48
Funston, Brigadier General Frederick, 454
Fuqua, Lieutenant Commander Samuel G., 328
Furlong, Rear Admiral William R., 329
Fusiliers Mont-Royal, 425-427
Futa Pass, 725, 784

978 Index

Gabès, 291, 544, 555, 558, 571-576, 579-581, 583, 586
Gabon, 257
Gabreski, Lieutenant Colonel Francis S., 864
Gafencu, Grigore, 268-269
Gafsa, 554-555, 569-572, 576, 584
Galicia, oil wells, 123
Galileo, 715
Gallup, Captain Brewster G., 461
Gallup, Captain George, 865
Gambier Bay, carrier, 878
Gamelin, General Maurice Gustave, 49, 155, 159, 193, 204, 206-208, 244, 247, 866
Gandhi, Mahatma, 437, 502
Garapan, 652
Gardelegen, concentration camp, 868
Garibaldi, 84
Garment Workers' Union, 484
Gary, Lieutenant (j.g.) Donald A., 911
Gauls, 288
Gauss, Ambassador Clarence E., 914
Gavutu, 474-475
Gay, Ensign George, 513
Gdynia, 123, 817-818
Geerds, Lieutenant Colonel Henry A., 530
Gehres, Captain Leslie E., 911
Geiger, Major General Roy S., 654, 926, 933
Gela, 668-672, 674
General Electric Company, 484
Geneva Convention, 864
George II, King of Greece, 282, 287-288, 291
George VI, King of England, 126, 146, 171, 189, 256, 604, 693, 718-719, 741-742
George, Brigadier General Harold H., 350, 466
Georgievsk, 405
Gerade Weg, 81
Gerbini, 679, 680
Gerlich, Dr. Fritz, 81
Gerling Insurance Company, 60
German-Austrians, 93
German Empire, centralization, 47
German Evangelical Youth, 76
German-Polish Agreement (1934), 180, 181
German Republic, 57, 60, 64, 73
German-Russian nonaggression pact, 121-122
German Workers' Party, 57-59
Germany, 40, 298-299, 311; Allied bombing of, 788, 804, 806; Army, Junkers, industrialists, 56-62, 64, 66, 70, 71; atrocities, 398-409, 862-871; Axis member, 4-10, 103, 316, 361-362; conquests, Austria, 93-108, 293, Czechoslovakia, 109-119, Poland, 120-126, Denmark, 127-136, Norway, 137-152, Belgium, 153-166, Netherlands, 167-177, France, conquests, 192-223, control of Vichy government, 248-260, Balkans, 261-266, Rumania, 267-271, Yugoslavia, 272-281, Greece, 282-291; D-Day, Allied invasion, occupied France, 726-764, Belgium and Netherlands, 765-771; destruction of cultural monuments, 400, 406-408; German soil invaded, 767-778, 798-805, Allies reach Rhine, 777-778, counterattack, Battle of Bulge, 774-775, 788-797; Germans driven from Hungary, Austria, Rumania, Bulgaria, 820-828; Great Britain, war with, 178-191, Battle of Britain, 224-233; Hitler and rise of Nazi party, 51-63; in Italian campaign, 686-725, 783-787, in Sicily, 667-685; leaves League of Nations, 431; Munich agreement, 110-113; Nazi education, 74-83; in North Africa, 410-414, 533-606; plot of world conquest, 4-5, 64-83; postwar, Allied plans for, 3, 9, 12-13; Russia invades, 806-819, fall of Berlin, 829-841; Russo-German pact, 361-362, invades Russia, 364-409, 411, 551, 598, Russia strikes back at, 380-409, 806-828, fall of Berlin, 829-841; surrender, 3-4, 842-861, text of, 857-858; Third Reich, 62; torture chambers, 862-871 (*See also* Concentration camps); United States declares war on, 308; United States, designs against, 336; war criminals, 13, 47-49; "war of nerves," 195; Warsaw, Battle of, 779-782; (*See also* Nazis)
Gerow, Lieutenant General L. T., 800, 803
Gesler, Count von, 408-409
Gestapo, 59, 66, 67, 70, 71, 73, 101, 105-108, 116, 118, 134, 135, 149, 150, 165, 177, 265, 271, 278, 279, 407, 780, 821
Gheorghieff, Khimon, 262
Ghormley, Vice Admiral R. L., 472, 517, 521, 523
Gibraltar, attack on, 241, 251, 533, 536, 606, 631
Giffen, Rear Admiral Robert C., 612
Gilbert Islands, 306, 340, 443, 492, 607, 610-611, 617, 625, 627, 629
Giolitti, Prime Minister, 88
Giraud, General Henri-Honoré, 204, 209; broadcasts, 537, 582; at Casablanca, 561-562, 564; conflict with De Gaulle, 556-559; cooperation with De Gaulle, 550, 573, 585; joins Allies, 535, 540, 544, 548, 596, 598, 601, 604-606, 667, 690; German reprisals against family, 605-606
Gironde, estuary of, 842-843
Glabrio, Manius Acilius, 288
Glassford, Rear Admiral William A., Jr., 449
Gliders, 733, 737
Gloucester, Cape, 627-628
Gluck, Mrs. Gemma, 866
Gneisenau, battleship, 141
Gobineau, 55
Godefroy, Rear Admiral René-Emile, 240-241
Goebbels, Dr. Joseph, 3, 59, 61, 66, 69, 96, 105, 107, 273, 748-749, 771, 832, 835, 837; *Angriff,* 82; Propaganda Minister, 79-80; suicide, 968
Goemboes, General, 97
Goering, Hermann, 58, 59, 61, 71, 100, 115, 147, 180, 184, 268, 270, 838, 847; inventor of concentration camps, 67; measures against Jews, 69; Minister of War, 66; 1934 purge, 62; on trial, 3, 48; orders for Russian slave labor, 403-404; suicide, 968
Golikoff, General Filip, 380
Golubovka, 400-401
Gona, 472, 530-532, 614, 634-635
Gonzales, Sgt. Manuel S., 687

Index 979

Good Hope, Cape of, 533
Gootee, Sergeant John M., 345
Gorizia, 587
Gothic Line, 714, 715, 720, 721, 784, 721-725
Govoroff, General Leonid N., 356, 380, 395
Grace, Commander, 935
Grace, Rear Admiral J. G., 505
Grand Alliance, 166
Grandi, Dino, 92
Graz, 108
Graziani, Marshal, 410, 411, 787
Grazzi, Emmanuele, 283
Great Britain, 97, 129, 153-154, 270, 279, 283, 299, 301, 314, 317, 355-357, 359, 361, 434; Allied Control Council; and atomic bomb project, 19-21; in Battle of Belgium, 153-166, Battle of Britain, 224-233, Battle of France, 192-223; blockades, 138, 243, 255; D-Day, and Western Front, 726-778, 788-805; De Gaulle backed by, 237-238, 245, 248-252; Dieppe raid, 415-428; Dumbarton Oaks, 9; Dunkirk, 161, 209-213; Entente Cordiale, 239; enters World War II, 178-192; Four-Power Board, 41; French alliance, 194; French ships interned by, 240-241; and German surrender, 842-861; and Greece, 284-289, 291, 410-411; in India, Burma, Malaya, and fall of Singapore, 437-441; informers in, 93; invasion of Italy, 677-725, of Sicily, 667-676; and Italian surrender, 701; and Japan, alliance, 299-300, declares war against, 339, and Japanese surrender, 22, 25, 31-33; Libyan campaign, 410-414; Munich agreement, 110, 112-113; in North Africa, 533-606; in Pacific War, 339-341; Poland, guarantees to, 122, 124, 179-180; and Russia, aid to, 378, 380, 381, 384-385, 391, mutual assistance pact with, 366; Turkish alliance, 195; White Paper, on concentration camps, 67, 869-870. (*See also* Britain; British)
"Greater East Asia Co-Prosperity Sphere," 249, 295, 609, 899
Greater Serbia, 272
Greco-Turkish War, 282
Greece, 261-264, 274; Battle of, 83, 282-291, 682, 919; British aid to, 284, 286-291, 410-411; British guarantee to, 180; heritage of, 282; liberation of, 283; republic, 282; troops with Allies, 725
Green, William, 484
Green (Nissen) Island, 629
Greenland agreement, 134
Greenwood, Arthur, 124, 187-188
Greim, Field Marshal Robert Ritter von, 847, 859
Greiner, Major General George W., 928
Grew, Joseph C., 293, 311-314, 323
Gromyko, Andrei A., 389
Groningen, 804
Groves, Major General Leslie R., 19
Gruber, Kurt, 76
Grummond, Douglass, 448
Grynzpan, Herschel, 67
Guadalcanal, 490, 494, 504, 609, 614-617,

634-636, 744; Battle of, 471-477, 517-532, 609, 614, 623, 628, 640, 656, 744
Guadeloupe, 253
Guam, 306; Japanese capture, 310, 313, 334-335, 340, 447; redeemed, 643, 650, 651, 654-656, 900, 903
Guderian, General Heinz, 104, 754, 756
Guerrillas, 272, 279, 290-291, 501, 662, 695
Gugel, Rudolf, 76
Guildhall, London, 227, 229
Guingard, Major General Sir Francis de, 855
Gurkhas, 586, 620, 708, 916
Gustav Line, 694-696, 706-707, 710
Guzzoni, General, 675
Gwin, destroyer, 529, 638
Gzhatsk, 384

Haakon VII, King of Norway, 137-139, 141-148, 735
Hacha, Dr. Emil, 111, 113-115
Hagelin, Albert Viljam, 147
Hague, The, 169-171, 173
Hague Convention, 163
Haimann, Chief Physician Baron von, 405-406
Hainan, island of, 433
Haiphong, 250, 252
Hale, Major General Willis H., 496, 617, 922
Halifax, Lord, 19, 122
Halligan, destroyer, 934-935
Hallmark, 1st Lieutenant Dean E., 500
Halmaharas, 656
Halsey, Vice Admiral William F., Jr., 15, 16, 29, 487-495, 523, 525, 629, 636, 649, 654, 656-660, 665, 873-880; character, 443-444; and Japanese surrender, 25, 30-32
Hamaguchi, Premier Yuko, 318
Hamar, 140
Hamburg, 845, 846, 849, 853
Hamel, Lieutenant Felix du, 867
Hamman, destroyer, 515
Hancock, John, 483
Hanfstaengl, Ernst "Putzie," 53, 58
Hanneken, Lieutenant Colonel H. H., 526
Hannibal, 715
Hannover, 226, 768, 804-805
Hansell, Brigadier General Haywood S., Jr., 901, 904
Hapsburg, Adelheid and Franz, 100
Hapsburg, Karl, 94
Hapsburg, House of, 93-95, 275
Hapsburg Empire, 54, 110
Hara, Premier Takashi, 304, 318
Hara-kiri, 296
Harbin, 21
Harding, Warren G., 304
Hardy, destroyer, 140
Harmon, Lieutenant General Millard F., 922
Harrill, Admiral W. K., 651
Harriman, Mrs. J. Borden, 138
Harriman, W. Averell, 368, 385, 561
Harris, Sir Arthur T., 732
Hart, Admiral Thomas C., 338, 343, 348, 445-446, 449, 487
Hart, Major General Verne B., 665
Haruna, battleship, 340, 341, 348, 876

Haskell, William N., 484
Hawaii, 309-311, 324, 332, 337, 442, 657
Hayashi, Senjuro, 318
Haynes, Brigadier General Caleb V., 608, 619
Hazelwood, Corporal Harold R., 448
Heiden, Konrad, 52
Heimwehr, 95-98, 100
Helena, cruiser, 326, 333, 521, 528, 638, 639
Helfrich, Vice Admiral C. E. L., 33, 449
Helldorf, Count von, 60
Helm, Major, 279
Helsinki, 355-357
Hemingway, Lieutenant Jack, 863
Henault, Dr. Charles, 165
Hendaye, 221
Henderson, Charles B., 484
Henderson, Leon, 484
Henderson, Major Lofton R., 477, 512
Henderson, Sir Nevile, 123, 182-186
Henderson Field, 477, 517-524, 526-529, 615, 635
Henry-Haye, Gaston, 252, 253, 256, 258
Heppenheim prison camp, 863
Hering, Captain Clyde E., Jr., 863
"Hermann Goering Werke," 107
Herriot, Édouard, 193
Hershey, Major General Lewis B., 480
Hess, Rudolf, 53, 58, 362
Hewitt, Rear Admiral Henry K., 541, 553, 686
Heydrich, Reinhardt (Butcher), 108, 118-119
Hickam Field, 323, 325-328, 330, 643
Hickox, destroyer, 911
Hideyoshi, Toyotomi, 297, 515
Higashi-Kuni, Prince, 40
Higgins, Lieutenant Walter, 616
Highlanders, 412, 419-420, 753, 777
Hill, Rear Admiral Harry W., 630, 655
Hill 192, 750
Hill 609, 596-597
Hillman, Sidney, 484
Hillsinger, Lieutenant Colonel L. B., 427
Himalayas, the "Hump," air route over, 438, 620, 623
Himmler, Henrich, 3, 59, 66, 67, 118, 134, 135, 163, 176, 265, 771, 803, 804, 812, 847-849, 870
Hindenburg, Reichspräsident Paul von, 61, 62, 64, 219, 812
Hiranuma, Premier Kiichiro, 318
Hirohito, Emperor, 17, 22-26, 39, 45, 322, 908, 937
Hiroshima, 17-21
Hiryu, carrier, 512-514
Hite, 1st Lieutenant Robert L., 500
Hitler, Adolf, 50, 136, 140, 144, 146-149, 151, 172, 195, 219-220, 226, 228-229, 233, 353, 362, 365, 431, 551, 590, 591, 636, 677, 739, 787, 800, 812, 813, 845; analysis of, 51-63, blunders, 333, 375, 380, 395, 788, character, 51, 63, paranoia, 788; attempts to assassinate, 196, 754; connivance with, 315; disappearance, 848-849, report of death, 3, 835, 837, 842, 847, 849; education, aims for, 75-75, 151 (*See also* Hitler Youth); German revolution, 312; Henderson, interviews with, 182-185; invasions, Austria, 93-108, Balkans, 261-266, Belgium, 153-166, Czechoslovakia, 109-119, France, 192-247, 301, 316, French surrender to, 221-222, entrance into Paris, 234, Netherlands, 167-177, 316, Poland, 120-126, 315, Rumania, 267-271, Russia, 70, 360-409 (*See also* Russia), blunder at Stalingrad, 375, 380, boast of riding through Red Square, 840, follows Napoleon's retreat, 390, in siege of Berlin, 753, 830, 832; Munich *Putsch,* 95, 848; and Mussolini, 286, 586, 677; plans for conquest of Europe, 178-179, of United States, 309, 311, 336, of the world, 63, 103, 153; reoccupies Rhineland, 5, 293; rise to power, 56-62, 96-97, 190, dictator, 62, 66, supreme command of German armies, 374; "secret weapon," 745; slave labor, orders for, 404; suicide, 968
Hitler, Alois, 52, 53
Hitler, William Patrick, 52-53
Hitler Youth, 72, 76-79, 108, 163; handbook, 78-79
Hobart, light cruiser, 505
Hobby, Colonel (Mrs.) Ovieta Culp, 481
Hodge, Lieutenant General John R., 42, 665, 926
Hodges, Lieutenant General Courtney H., 730, 753, 765, 768-772, 791-792, 795, 796, 798, 838, 843
Hoeffel, Captain Kenneth M., 463
Hoel, destroyer, 878
Hohenzollern family, 196
Holcomb, General Thomas, 480
Holland (*see* Netherlands)
Hollandia, 641, 645-647, 650
Homma, Lieutenant General Masaharu, 45, 351, 463
Homs, 414
Hongkong, 306, 310, 335, 339, 340, 343-344
Honjo, General, 430
Honolulu, 324, 325, 330
Honolulu, cruiser, 326, 333, 638
Honshu, 20, 42
Hoover, Herbert, 311-312, 355, 429
Hoover, Vice Admiral John H., 625
Hopkins, Harry L., 366, 483, 561
Horinouchi, Kensuke, 315-316, 319
Horne, Vice Admiral F. J., 488
Hornet, carrier, 497-499, 509, 513, 514, 519, 525, 651, 875, 880
Horserod, concentration camp, 135-136
Horstenau, Glaise von, 99, 100
Horthy, 775
Houston, 446; survivors, 28-29
Howard, Colonel Samuel L., 463
Howe, C. D., 19
Howie, Major Thomas D., 752-753
Hsiao I-Hsu, General, 623
Hsu Yung-chang, General, 32
Huber, Major Henry S., 865
Huertgen Forest, 773, 788
Huggenberg, Alfred, 60
Hughes, Charles Evans, 304
Hugo, Victor, 409; *Les Misérables,* **136**

Index 981

Hull, Cordell, 23, 134, 258, 266, 293, 311, 313-317, 320, 355, 479; denounces invasion of Yugoslavia, 276; favors end of extraterritoriality, 608; interview with Japanese diplomats, December 7, 1941, 322-323; Moscow conversations, 391
Hull, destroyer, 887
Humbert, Crown Prince, 713
Humboldt Bay, 645, 646
"Hump" (*see* Himalayas)
Hunan Province, 624
Hungary, Hungarians, 94, 97, 110, 112, 119, 125, 166, 261, 264, 269, 277, 279, 288, 365, 806-807; Axis member, 274; liberation, 820-824; at war with United States, 265-266, 271
Hunt, destroyer, 911
Hunter, Brigadier General Frank, 416
Hunter, destroyer, 140
Huntziger, General Charles, 204, 222, 223
Huon Gulf, 635, 637
Hurley, Major General Patrick J., 914
Hus, Jan, 109
Hutchins, Johnnie David, Seaman First Class, 642
Huy, concentration camp, 164
Hyde Park, New York, 11
Hyuga, battleship, 873

Iceland, 152
Ickes, Harold L., 479, 483, 484
Igorot infantry, 456
Il Popolo d'Italia, 87
Illustrious, carrier, 619, 923, 936
Ilmen, Lake, 384
Imamura, Lieutenant General Hitoshi, 450
Indefatigable, carrier, 936
Independence, carrier, 488, 491-493, 495
Independent Labor Party, England, 230
India, 371, 851, 911; Axis goal, 314, 410, 411, 437-441, 534, 607-608, 619, 622, Japanese raid on, 501; Cripps mission, 502; declares war on Hungary, Rumania, and Finland, 437; political divisions, 191, 437; troops, 410, 439, 605, 708, 721
Indian Ocean, 252, 336, 441, 465, 500, 533
Indians, Americans, 356, 686
Indo-China route, closed, 434
Inflation, 163; German, in France, 254
Informers, 93, 107
Ingino, Mt., 717
Inland Sea, 15-17, 909, 910
Inouye, Junnosuke, 318
Insumanai Island, 648
Inter-American Affairs, 484
Ionian Islands, 289
Iowa, battleship, 16, 880, 902
Iran, 9, 263, 289, 367, 375, 410, 437, 607
Iraq, 289, 410, 437
Irish volunteers, 413
Iron Guards, 268, 269
Irrawaddy River, 501
Irredentists, 86
Irving, Major General Frederick A., 665
Ise, battleship, 873
Isernia, 695, 696

Ishii, Colonel, 448
Isigny, 738-740
Isitt, Air Vice Marshal Leonard M., 33
Island hopping, 607-611
Ismay, General Sir Hastings, 561
Italian East Africa, 166
Italian Somaliland, 410
Italy, Italians, 93, 95, 97, 144, 166, 187, 240, 242, 253, 273-274, 276, 355; African Empire, 410-414, 551, 598, 698; Albania seized by, 5, 283; Allied invasion of, 126, 564, 599, 683-725, Salerno, 686-690, Naples, 691-697, Cassino and Anzio, 703-710, liberation of Rome, 711-714, Rome to Florence, battles, 715-725, invasion of Sicily, 667-685; Axis partner, 84-92, 103, 256, 277, 311; cobelligerent, 694, 697; declares war on France and Britain, 217, on Germany, 694, on Russia, 365; France attacked by, 199-210, 215-223, 234-235; German surrender in, 783-787, 850, 852; Greece attacked by, 263, 283-289, 678, occupies Ionian Islands, 289; industrialists, 89; invades Ethiopia, 5, 293; Libyan campaign, 410-414; Munich agreement, 110, 112; recognized by United Nations, 713; surrender, 3, 698-702; tradition of liberty, 84; troops, in Africa, 410-414, 533-534, 540, 543, 551, 565, 601-602, 606, 668, abandoned by Rommel, 559, in Sicily, 668-670; war on Tripoli, 86; in World War I, 87
Itter, Castle of, 866-867
Iwo, 16, 886, 887
Iwo Jima, 496, 900-909
Izanago and Izanami, 292

Janeff, Sotir, 265
Japan, 9, 12, 166, 411; Air Force, 487; Andaman Islands occupied by, 441; Anglo-Japanese Alliance, 299-300; Anti-Comintern Pact, 431; atomic bomb, 14-26; atrocities, 27, 459-461, 463-464; Australia, tide turned in, 465-470; Axis partnership, 64-73, 103, 292; Bataan, last stand, Corregidor, surrender and March of Death, 452-464; Bismarck Sea, 607-617; bombing of, 497-500, 900-909, 920; California coast shelled by, 450; China, undeclared war against, 5, 314-318, 429-438, 500-502, 618-624, Twenty-one Demands, 302-305, 430, Tanaka Memorial, 306-307, 312; Coral Sea, Battle, 503-509; Empire crumbles, 910-920; Five-Power Naval Treaty, 305; French Indo-China invaded by, 249-252: Guadalcanal, Solomons, 517-524; history and social system, 292-307, Shinto cult, 292-294, *Bushido* code, 292-296, warrior-priest combine, 295, 301-303; India, Axis goal, Burma, Malaya, Singapore, 191, 437-441; India, Burma, China, operations against, 500-502, 618-624; invincibility myth shattered, 433; Iwo Jima, 900-909; Korea annexed by, 302; leaves League of Nations, 5, 313, 431; London Agreement (1905), 301-302; Luzon invaded by, 663; MacArthur starts back—New Guinea, 471-477, on road

Japan (cont'd)
  back, 634-648, Navy and Air Force blast road for, 657-660, at Leyte, 661-666, Leyte Gulf, Battle for, 872-888, MacArthur at Luzon, enters Manila, 889-899, in Tokyo, 39-46; Manchuria, test cast in, 5, 103; Midway—Aleutians, 510-516; Mukden incident, 5, 293; Navy, 16, 909, 910, 925; "new order in East Asia," 315; Okinawa, 921-938; Pacific, bombing in, Guam redeemed, 654-656, Japanese holdings in (1943), 607, war in, 336-346, plans for, 262-263, rebirth of United States Navy and Air Force, 487-496; Pacific Islands, mandates on, 302-306, sweep through, 442-451; Pearl Harbor, events leading to, 292-307, attack, 308-335; Philippines, Battle of, and fall of Manila, 347-352; Portsmouth, Treaty of, 300-301; postwar attitude, 40; prison camps, 869; psychological warfare, 312; Russia, border troubles with, 431, joins war against Japan, 21; Russo-Japanese war, 300-301; Saipan and Philippine Sea, Battles, 649-653; Southwest Pacific, naval battles, 525-532; surrender, 3-4, 27-38, 937; Tarawa, conquest of atolls, 625-634; Tokyo, first raid on, 497-502; United States, occupied by, 39-46; plans for invasion of, 336, 509-510, 516; V-J Day, 3; war criminals, 42-45; war with, twenty-five highlights, 875; at Washington Conference, 304-305; Washington Naval Treaty terminated by, 431; a World Power, 303; in World War I, 302-304
Japanese-Americans, in Italian invasion, 686, 708, 784
Jarvis, 474
Jasar, Jules, 165
Java, 431, 440, 445, 448-451, 617
Java Sea, 442, 446; Battle of, 450, 487
Jean Bart, battleship, 537
Jefferson, Thomas, 11
Jehol Province, 430
Jeppson, Lieutenant M. U., 18
Jeschke, Colonel R. H., 526
Jesschonnek, General Hans, 381
Jews, persecution of, 48-49, 116-118, 134, 135, 151, 164, 176, 177; in Austria, 101, 106; in France, 246-247, 250, 253; German, 53, 55, 61, 66-69, 72, 112, 196, 206, 360, 402, 403, 869
Joassart, Gustave, 166
Jodl, Colonel General Gustav, 48, 288, 849, 850, 855-858
Joffre, Marshal, 49, 205, 207
John D. Ford, destroyer, 447
Johnson, Colonel J. M., 484
Johnson, Nelson T., 312
Johnston, William J., Pfc., 710
Johnston, destroyer, 878
Johnston Island, 342
Johore Strait, 439
Joint Assault Signal Company (JASCO), 903
Joint War Production Committee (JWP), 484
Jones, Brigadier General Albert M., 350
Jones, Colonel George M., 896

Jones, Jesse H., Secretary of Commerce, 479, 484
Jones, Brigadier General Lloyd E., 511
Jones, Marvin, 483
Jones, Vera N., 330
Jouhaux, Leon, 866
Jovanovich, Vice Premier Slovdan, 278
Juare, 530
Judaism, 79
Judo, 297
Jugendfuehrer (Youth Leader), 108
Juin, General Alphonse-Pierre, 536, 727, 857
Juliana, Princess, 171
Juneau, antiaircraft cruiser, 525, 528, 529
Jungklaus, General Richard, 163
Jungmaedel (Young Girls), 78
Jungvolk (Young Folk), 77
Junkers, 56-58, 61, 299
Jutland, 127-129, 135; battle, 140

Kaga, carrier, 512, 513
Kahr, Gustav von, 58, 62
Kairouan, 554, 558, 559, 578, 586-588
Kalamas River, 285
Kalamata, 290
Kalambaka, 290
Kalinin, 380, 400
Kamchatka Peninsula, 612
Kamenets-Podolsk, 403
Kami, 292-205
Kamikaze, suicide planes, 20, 923, 924, 927, 934-936
Kaneohe naval air base, 325, 326
Kaolikung Mountains, 623
Kaplan, Captain David, 707
Karachev, 386
Karageorgevitch dynasty, 275, 280
Karelian Isthmus, 353-354, 356, 358, 365, 380, 397, 400
Karlsruhe, cruiser, 140
Kasserine Pass, battle of, 555, 565-569, 571
Kastoria, 264
Kattegat strait, 140, 142
Katyn Forest, massacre, 385
Katyusha, rocket-firing gun, 833, 840
Kauffmann, Dr. Henrik de, 134
Kaupisch, General Leonhard, 130
Kavieng, 644
Kebili, 569, 580
Keitel, Field Marshal General Wilhelm, 48, 104, 222, 754, 839, 859-860
Kelibia, 602
Keller, Navy Lieutenant C. A., 345
Kellogg-Briand Treaty, 430
Kellogg Pact, 153
Kelly, Corporal Charles ("Commando"), 688
Kelly, Captain Colin P., Jr., 340-341, 348
Kelly, Corporal John, 743
Kemal Ataturk, 268
Kennard, Sir H., 181
Kenney, Lieutenant General George Churchill, 17, 494, 616, 632, 637, 641, 644, 656, 659, 877, 881-882; biography, 614; commands Allied air forces in Southwest Pacific, 657, 665

Index

Keppler, 115
Kerch, 370, 371, 374, 390-391, 397, 403
Keruma Islands, 924
Kesselring, Field Marshal General Albert, 589, 694, 713, 785
Kharitonoff, Major General Fedor M., 372
Kharkov, 365, 370, 383, 387, 389, 400, 402
Khartoum, 410
Kiaochow, 299
Kiev, 365, 368, 387, 388, 390, 392, 400, 403; recapture, 392, 394
Killin, William C., 345
Kimes, Lieutenant Colonel Ira L., 511
Kimmel, Admiral Husband E., 331, 333, 337
Kimpei-Tai, Japanese Gestapo, 42, 43
Kindertagestaedte (day nurseries), 77
King, Major General Edward P., Jr., 350, 458-459
King, Admiral Ernest J., 328, 493, 649, 659, 667, 737, 740, 922; at Casablanca, 560, 563; dual command, 470, 480; quoted, 476, 508-509, 654, 897
King George V, flagship, 16, 923
Kinkaid, Vice Admiral Thomas C., 505, 509, 523, 527, 644, 660, 665, 875-876, 878, 880, 890
Kinsel, General, 853, 854
Kirdorf, Emil, 60
Kirin, 429
Kirk, Rear Admiral Alan G., 685, 734; quoted, 515-516
Kiska, 510, 516, 607, 611-613, 926
Klatt, Sergeant Lowell V., 327
Klausner, Ministerial-Director, 62
Kleeberg, General, 124-125
Kleffens, E. N. van, 174
Klein, Lieutenant Albert, 604
Kleist, Colonel General Paul Ludwig von, 371, 372
Kluge, von, Field Marshal Gunther von, 387, 748, 751, 756, 765, 788
Knox, Frank, Secretary of the Navy, 330-331, 338, 449, 479, 649, 691-692
Knudsen, W. S., 483
Kobe, 15, 497, 908-910
Koch, Erich, 404
Kock, 125
Koelnische Zeitung, 81
Koenig, General Joseph-Pierre, 46, 764
Koenigsberg, 818-819
Koenigstein, prison, 557, 866
Koerner, Lieutenant Paul M., 707
Koga, Admiral Mineichi, 649
Koht, Foreign Minister Halvdan, 138
Koiso, General Kuniaka, "Tiger of Korea," 649, 654, 925
Kokoda, 472, 530
Kolombangara, 615
Komandorski, battle, 612
Koneff, Marshal Ivan S., 381, 392, 396-397; drive on Berlin, 807-812, 814-816, 820, 822, 826, 828-832, 838, 846
Kongo, Japanese battleship, 339, 345, 876
Königsberg, 384
Konoye, Prince Fumimaro, 44, 249, 315, 321

Koons, Corporal, 421
Korea, 21, 25-27, 35, 43, 294, 295, 297-302; annexed by Japan, 302; promise of freedom, 618, 619
Koritza, 284, 285
Korizis, Premier, 287
Korma, 399
Komorowski, Lieutenant General Tadeusz ("General Bor"), 779-782, 866
Korsun pocket, battle, 396
Kostikoff, Audrey, 381
Kramer, Josef, 868
Krasnaya Polyana, 402
Krause, Major General Fritz, 603-604
Kriebel, Lieutenant Colonel, 58
Krivoi Rog, 407-408
Krosigk, Count Ludwig Schwerin von, 849
Krueger, Lieutenant General Walter, 42, 614-615, 627-628, 636-637, 664-665, 885, 888, 890, 891, 893
Krug, James A., 483
Krupp, Gustave, 48
Krupp arms works, 800, 805
Kruse, Johan C. W., 134
Ksar Rhilane, 570, 571, 573, 574, 579
Kuban, 390, 406
Kuestrin, 813, 829, 831
Kula Gulf, 615, 638-639
Kung, H. H., Finance Minister, 914
Kurile Islands, 25, 654, 926
Kursk, 386, 387, 392, 402, 841
Kurusu, Saburo, 314, 318, 320-323, 434
Kusman, Rev. Stanley J., 697
Kwajalein, 624, 625, 629-630, 632, 885, 889
Kwantung Army, 21, 26
Kweichow Province, 917-918
Kyushu, 20

Labor, 117, 247, 484-485. (*See also* Unions)
Labor-management boards, 484
"Ladies from Hell," 753, 777
Ladoga, Lake, 357-358, 382
Lae, 466, 469, 504, 508, 518, 532, 616, 635, 641, 642
Laffey, destroyer, 521, 528, 934
LaGuardia, Fiorello H., 484, 866
La Haye, 746-749
Land, Rear Admiral Emory S., 483
Landrum, Major General Eugene M., 613
Lange, Pastor Ivar, 135
Langley, aircraft carrier, 348, 490
Laplanders, 354
Larsen, Major General Henry L., 903
Lascelles, Lieutenant Viscount George Henry, 867
Latvia, 123-125, 354, 361, 365, 400, 806
Laurel, Jose P., 45
Lausanne Loans, 96
Laval, Pierre, 49, 219, 238, 241, 251, 259-260, 536, 582, 607, 767; drafts charter, 239, 242
Lawrence, Professor Ernest, 19
Lawson, Brigadier J. K., 343-344
League of Nations, 5, 92, 94, 97, 112, 122, 127, 190, 261-262, 293, 303, 355, 430, 431; Covenant, 153; pitfalls, 10, 12

Leahy, Admiral William D., 483, 922
Leander, New Zealand cruiser, 638
Leapfrogging, 546, 681, 694, 771, 785
Lear, General Ben, 480
Leary, Vice Admiral Herbert F., 449
Leathers, Lord, 561
Lebanon, 252, 260
Lebensraum, 178
LeClerc, Brigadier General Jacques-Philippe, 254-255, 559, 579, 759, 761-764, 842
Leclerc, General Jacques Pierre, 33
Leclerq, Vice Admiral M. A. J., 606
Ledo Road, to China, 620, 623, 918
Lee, Vice Admiral W. A., Jr., 523, 529, 660
Leese, General Sir Oliver W. H., 703, 704, 722, 914
Legaspi, 897-898
Leghorn, 690, 715-718
Le Havre, 215, 216, 219, 232-233, 735, 760, 765, 789
Lehman, Herbert H., 484
Leigh-Mallory, Air Chief Marshal Sir Trafford, 416, 731, 732, 915
Leipzig, 831, 843
Leitzmann, General Karl, 60
LeMay, General, 904
Lend-Lease, 317, 319, 368, 373, 385, 391, 465, 478, 483, 502, 540, 548
Lenin, 86, 359, 840
Leningrad, 356, 365-367, 380, 395, 400, 406; siege, 368-379, 407
Lenks, Adolf, 76
Lentaigne, Major General W. D. A., 621
Leonberger, Harold, 448
Leonidas, King of Sparta, 288
Leopold, King of the Belgians, 153-156, 160-162, 845, 866; offer to mediate, 186, 196; surrender, 210, 211
Lessay, 749, 751, 755
Levin, Corporal Meyer, 340
Lewis, Captain Robert A., 18
Lexington, carrier, 444, 445, 487, 492-493, 504-507, 514, 627, 880
Ley, Dr. Robert, 48, 70-72, 82, 190
Leyte, 41, 65-69, 661-666, 881-886
Leyte Gulf, battle for, 872-888, 899
Lezaky, 119
Liaotung Peninsula of Manchuria (Kwantung), 298, 300
Liberators, 325, 553, 597, 616-617, 657, 668, 674, 795, 900
Libreville, 257
Libya, 126, 166, 263, 410-414, 533, 540, 552, 553, 559-560, 564
Licata, 668-671
Lichtenburg, 67
Lidice, 109, 119
Lie, Jonas, 150
Liège, 155-159, 162, 164, 766, 791, 792
Lille, 161, 209
Lillyman, Captain Frank, 733
Lincoln, Abraham, 11
Lingayen, 890-892, 897
Linlithgow, Marquess of, 438
Linz, 104, 105

Lipski, M., 186
Liscome Bay, carrier, 625-627
List, Sigmund, Field Marshal, 365
Lithuania, 123, 124, 126, 180, 354, 361, 365, 400
Little Entente, 261, 262
Litvinoff, Maxim, 361, 371, 389
Liutiaokou affair, 429, 432
Livadia, 290
Liversedge, Colonel Harry "The Horse" B., 907
Llewellin, Colonel J. J., 19
Locarno Pact, 5, 104, 153, 293
Lockard, Private Joseph L., 324-325
Lockwood, Vice Admiral Charles A., Jr., 16
Lofoten Islands, 150
Loire River, 221, 222, 745
Lombardy, 725
London, 172, 175, 177, 183, 245, 851; air raids, 189-190, 675, blitzkrieg, 226-231; East End, 227, 228, 230; Second Battle of, 767; treaties, 431
London Naval Conference, 318, 515
Longshaw, destroyer, 934
Longwy, 157
Lopatin, General, 372
Lorient, 232, 842, 850
Lorraine, 234, 253, 256, 258, 776, 795; Cross of, 241, 580, 761
Los Banos prison camp, 895
Los Negros Island, 643, 644
Lossow, General von, 58
Lothian, Lord, 317
Lotta di Classe, 86
Loudon, Alexander, 40
"Louie the Louse," 473, 527
Loustalot, Lieutenant E. D., 420
Louvain, 157, 158, 765; Library, 162
Lovat, Lieutenant Colonel, 420-421
Low Countries, 245, 675, 754, 765-771, 788 (*See also* Belgium; Netherlands)
Lublin, 125, 810
Luckenwalde, 845, 867
Ludendorf, General Erich, 58, 59
Ludendorff Bridge, 801
Ludlum, David, 709
Lueneburg Heath, 853
Luftwaffe, 123, 144, 225-226, 229, 233, 289, 376, 381, 411, 780, 833, 847
Lumsden, Lieutenant General William, 891
Lunga Point, 473, 531
Lunga Ridge, 519-520
Lupescu, Madame, 267, 270
Luxembourg, 130, 153, 154, 156, 158, 167-169, 201, 203, 214, 767, 768, 772, 793-795
Luzon, 41, 340, 342, 344-346, 348, 351, 496, 658-659, 662-664, 666, 872, 881-883, 886, 888, 892, 895, 897; Japanese attack, 311, 340; reconquest, 890-898
Lwow, 123, 403
Lytton Report, 313

Maas River, 169-171
McAfee, Captain Mildred H., 481
MacArthur, General Arthur, 349, 350, 614

Index 985

MacArthur, Captain Arthur, Jr., 349
MacArthur, General Douglas, 119, 126, 338; Australia, offensive based on, 465-470, 497, 500, stategy against Japan, 468, 872; biography, 349-350; cites stories of heroism, 455-456; commands army forces in Pacific theater, 922; message to American people, 34-35; Philippines, defense of, 338, 346-352, 452-456, 602, declares Manila open city, 344, 351-352, fall of Manila, 352, mission to Australia, 456, pledge to return, 467, 645; Philippines, return to, 471-477, 493-495, 503-510, 517, 532, 616-617, 627, 634-660, broadcast to Philippines, 661, at Leyte, 661-666, Leyte Gulf, battle, 872-888, at Luzon, 889-899, re-enters Manila, 894, Roosevelt message to, 664; promoted to full general, 342, to General of Army, 887; quoted, 458, 495, 617, 629, 640, 641, 648, 655-657, 664, 885; staff, 350-351; Supreme Commander for Allies, 24; Supreme Commander, Southwest Pacific, 466-467, 619; and surrender of Japanese, 25-34; in Tokyo, 39-46, arrests war criminals, 45, pledge to Japanese, 46, policy of occupation, 39-46
MacArthur, Mrs. Douglas, 466, 467
Macassar, 448, 449, 617
Macassar Strait, Battle of, 443, 446, 447, 487
McAuliffe, Brigadier General Anthony, 784
McCain, Vice Admiral John S., 33, 472-473, 490, 491, 882, 890
McCalla, destroyer, 521
McCawley, flagship, 473, 475
McClusky, Lieutenant Commander Clarence, 513
McCormick, Anne O'Hare, 720
McCoy, Commander Melvin H., 459, 464
Macedonia, 264, 278, 282, 287-290
McCreey, General, 785
MacFarland, destroyer, 523
McGee, Commander Homer F., 637
Mackenzie, Dean C. J., 19
McMorris, Rear Admiral C. H., 612
McNair, Lieutenant General Leslie J., 470, 480, 594, 684; death of, 754
McNaughton, Lieutenant General Andrew G. L., 668, 731, 736
McNutt, Paul V., 483
Madagascar, 252, 255, 607
Mafia, 91
Maffi, Cardinal, 91
Magdeburg, 805
Maginot, André, 190
Maginot Line, 154, 155, 158, 190, 193, 199, 203-205, 209, 214, 217-219, 225
Magwe, 501
Magyars, 110-111
Mahan, destroyer, 885
Mainz, 801
Makin, 492-493, 610, 613, 625-627
Maknassy, 574-578, 580-581
Malacca, Strait of, 442
Malaita Island, 521
Malaya, 27, 35, 301, 311, 335, 339-341, 346, 450, 487, 516; battle for, 438-441, 445, 447; rubber, 447
Malimbiu River, 526
Malinovsky, General Rodion Y., 381, 392, 397, 807, 820-826, 829
Malmédy, 768, 791-793
Malta, 462, 568, 577, 585, 667, 702
Manchukuo, 319, 430, 431
Manchuria, 5, 21, 25-27, 103, 298-302, 306, 319, 429-430, 618, 619, 901
Manchurian Incident, 307, 312-314
Manchus, fall of, 302
Mandalay, 15, 501, 914-916
Mandel, Georges, 205-206, 243-244, 247, 250, 255, 259
Mandl, Fritz, 97, 100
Manila, 25, 311, 335, 346, 464, 658; fall of, 347-352, proclaimed open city, 344, 351, reign of terror, 352; liberation, 41, 872, 882, 889-899
Manila Bay, 348, 452-454, 463, 658, 890-891, 894, 896
Mannerheim, Marshal, 358
Mannerheim Line, 354, 356, 357, 397
Maoris, 580
Mapia Islands, 884
Maquis, 759
Marathon, 288
Marco Polo Bridge, 432
Marcus Island, 35, 444, 488, 489, 491, 659, 919
Mareth Line, 291, 414, 552, 555, 558-560, 568-571, 573-586, 589, 679
Mariana Islands, 35, 302, 334, 643, 650-652, 654, 889, 901, 904, 919
Marines (see United States Marine Corps)
Maritime Alps, 219
Mark VI ("Tiger") tanks, 544, 551, 591, 687, 720
Markham, James E., 484
Marler, Sir Herbert, 314
Marne River, 217, 218
Marquat, Brigadier General William F., 350
Marquet, Adrien, 243, 244
Marseilles, 759, 763
Marshall, General George C., Chief of Staff, 19, 480, 560, 563, 619, 667, 723, 737, 740, 742, 771, 922
Marshall, Brigadier General Richard J., 456
Marshall, destroyer, 911
Marshall Islands, 302, 443, 469, 496, 610, 629-631, 919
Martin, Major General Frederick D., 333
Martin, Captain William I., 633, 650
Martinique, 240, 253, 258
Marx, Karl, 85; *Das Kapital*, 57
Marxists, 54, 79, 190
Maryland, battleship, 333, 651, 877, 930, 935-936
Masaryk, Jan, 109
Masaryk, Dr. Thomas Garrigue, 109
Masons, 246 (*See also* Freemasons)
Massigli, René, 764
"Master race" cult, 4, 120
Masurian Lakes, 807
Matanikau River, 520-523, 526. 627

Matchek, Dr., 274, 276, 278
Mateur, 542, 543, 545-547, 558, 569, 582-583, 595, 596, 599
Matheny, Colonel A., 610
Mathias, Sgt. James F., 753
Matteotti, Deputy Giacomo, 91, 92
Matthias, Colonel Franklin T., 19
Maui, 342
Mayotta, 608
Mazarakis, General Alexander, 287-288
Mead, Senator, James M., 124
Meauffe, 750
Mechanized warfare, 207; De Gaulle's views on, 202-203, 214
Meder, 1st Lieutenant Robert J., 500
Medici family, 715
Mediterranean Sea, 200, 234, 263, 410, 533, 553, 606, 672, 691, 700, 784; closed by Axis, 103; reopened to Allies, 606, 672
Medjerda Valley, 593
Medjez-el-Bab, 541, 547, 549, 550, 566, 568, 569, 589, 591-592, 600
Meehan, Colonel Arthur W., 610
Méharistes (camel corps), 544, 552, 559
Meidell, Birger Oivind, 147
Mein Kampf, 52, 59, 74, 78, 82, 117, 360
Meitner, Dr. Lise, 19
Melchukova, L. I., 403
Melitopol, 391
Mellnik, Lieutenant Colonel S. M., 459, 464
Memel, 180, 807, 813
Meredith, destroyer, 523
Merett, Lieutenant Samuel H., 345
Meretzkoff, General Kyrill A., 380, 395
Merkers, looted treasures in, 804
Merrill, Rear Admiral A. S., 636
Merrill, Brigadier General Frank D., 621-622
Merrill's Marauders, 621-622
Merritt, Lieutenant C. C. I., 423
Messerschmitts, 202, 225, 227, 273, 413
Messina, 672, 673, 680, 683, 684, 699; Strait of, 682, 698, 701
Metaxas, General, 282-285
Metz, 767, 768, 770, 771
Meuse, Belgian newspaper, 161
Meuse River, 155, 165, 770, 793; Battle of, 156-158, 204, 216
Middle East, 200, 289, 533, 534, 547, 553, 585
Midway Island, 310, 333-334, 447, 508, 516, 650; battle of, 477, 491, 509-516, 609-610
Mikado, 292-293, 296, 297
Mikhailovitch, General Draja, 279-281, 291
Miklas, President, 101, 105
Mikolajczyk, Premier Stanislaw, 780, 782
Mikuma, "cheat cruiser," 515
Milan, 90, 92, 678, 723, 725, 786
Miller, Dorris, 328
Milne Bay, 518, 519, 634, 655
Mindanao, 348, 456, 463, 468, 655-659, 897-898
Mindanao Sea, 873
Mindoro, 886-887
Mindoro Strait, 873
Mineralnye Vodi, 406-407
Minneapolis, flagship, 505, 517, 531

Minsk, 365, 397, 815
Miquelon, 249, 596
Missouri, flagship, 16, 25, 29, 30, 31, 33, 34, 36, 41, 44
Mitchell, Ruth, 276
Mitchell, General William L. ("Billy"), 276, 434
Mitscher, Vice Admiral Marc A., 489-491, 629, 632-633, 643, 645, 647, 650, 651, 654, 659-660, 665, 905; battle of Tokyo, 908; quoted, 880, 923
Mitsubishi arms plant, 20; bombers, 444-445
Mittel-Europa, 178, 261
Mittelhauser, General, 238, 242
Mius River, 387
Modi, Marshal Walther von, 788
Moerdyk Bridge, 171
Mogami, "cheat cruiser," 515
Mohammedans, 272
Molotov, Vyacheslaff M., 21, 355, 357, 362, 363; documentary letters on German atrocities, 398-403; Moscow conversations, 391
Moltke, von, 167
Molucca Sea, 615
Moluccas, 655-656
Momote airfield, 644
Monaghan, destroyer, 887
Mongolia, 302, 306
Monnet, Jean, 196
Monobe, 293, 295
Monroe Doctrine, 316
Monssen, destroyer, 528, 529
Mont St. Michel, 755
Monte Cassino, 125
Montgomery, Rear Admiral A. E., 489, 495, 625
Montgomery, Field Marshal Sir Bernard L.: on Allied Control Council, 46; biography, 727, 729; in French invasion, 727, 729-730, 736, 740-742, 748, 751, 753, 775, 784, 799-801, Battle of Bulge, 788, 791, 795-796; in Italy, 701-704; in North Africa, 126, 552, 590-597, 679, 708, 722; routs Rommel, 411-414, 569-589, 788; receives German surrender, 853-854; in Sicily, 668, 680; tribute to Eighth Army, 586
Montmédy, 209, 219; bridgehead, 156
Moore, Colonel B. E., 522
Moore, Major General George F., 350
Moore, Lieutenant Joseph H., 345
Moore-Cosgrave, Colonel Lawrence, 33
Morale, part played by radio and screen, 485-486
Moravia, 115-117, 179, 826
Moravian Gate, 808, 814, 826
Morgan, Lieutenant General Sir F. E., 855
Morgan, Major Robert, 902
Morgan, Lieutenant General W. D., 852
Morgenthau, Henry, Jr., Secretary of the Treasury, 479
Morocco, 537-540, 556, 595; Moroccans, 593, 596, *Goumiers*, 569, 586
Moscicki, President Ignace, 120
Moscow, 365-368, 387, 394, 397; battle for, 369-374; damage, 400, 408; victory celebration, 839-840

Moscow Conference, 1943, 8, 391
Moscow pictures, war effort, 486
Motobu Peninsula, 926-927
Motorized units, 122, 157, 170, 171 (*See also* Mechanized warfare)
Moulmein, 438
Mountbatten, Lord Louis, 415-416, 561, 563, 619, 622, 650, 731, 757, 911
Mubo, 635, 640
Mueller, Ludwig, 66-68
Mueller, Major General Paul J., 656
Mukden, 299, 306, 935
Mukden Incident, 5, 6, 293, 429-432
Mullinix, Rear Admiral Henry M., 625, 627
Munda airfield, 615, 639
Munich, 52, 53, 55, 56, 68, 220, 221, 845, 854, 870; bombed, 226; pact, 5, 109-110, 112, 179, 180, 193, 195, 197, 198, 244, 261, 361; *Putsch,* 58, 62, 74, 95, 196, 848
Munich University, 75
Munitions Assignment Board (MAB), 483
Munk, Dr. Kaj, 135
Munoz, Second Lieutenant Filbert, 706
Murmansk, 358, 365, 367, 382
Murphy, Robert D., 50, 534, 561
Murray, Philip, 484
Musashi, battleship, 876
Muselier, Vice Admiral Emile-Henri, 237, 596
Mushakoji, Kimitomo, 431
Mussert, Anton, 176-177
Mussolini, Alessandro, 85
Mussolini, Benito, 4, 5, 58, 136, 186, 215, 238, 367-368, 667, 676, 681, 694, 713, 716; abdication of, 677-678, 698; aim to restore Roman Empire, 103, 410-411, 551, 598; Albania seized by, 5, 283, 293, 431; and Austria, 96-100; claims Mediterranean, 200, 551; deal with Giolitti, 88; early life, 85; Ethopia invaded by, 103, 431; execution of, 4, 786; Fascist leader, 88-92; France "stabbed in back" by, 87; Greece invaded by, 282-287, asks German aid, 286; legend, 84-85; "march on Rome," 89-90; meetings with Hitler, 220-221, 586, 677; Prime Minister, 90-92; Matteotti murder, 91-92; "rescued" by Germans, 690, 715, 775; rise and fall of, 84-92; as Socialist, 85-88
Mutsuhito, Emperor, 297
Myer, Dillon S., 484
Myers, Sergeant Fred A., 923-924
Myitkyina, 622-623, 914, 915

Nagano, Admiral, 643
Nagasaki, 20, 21
Nagoya, 497, 908, 925
Naha, 930-932
Nairobi, 410
Namsos, 144
Namur, 155-159, 204, 630
Nanchang-Hankow Railroad, 608
Nancy, 767-769
Nanking, 302, 432
Nanumea, 492
Naples, 90, 553, 583, 585, 676, 697, 710; fall of, 690-694

Napoleon, 153, 167, 178, 234, 363, 374, 377, 764, 767, 788, 798, 829, 846; retreat from Moscow, 390
Narvik, 139, 142, 143, 145, 199, 200, 204
Narvik Fjord, 140
Nashville, cruiser, 923
Natal, 564
Natib, Mount, 453
National Committee (French, in London), (*see* French National Committee)
National Council of Resistance, 758-762
National Housing Agency, 484
National Socialist German Teachers' Union, 75
National Socialist German Workers' Party, 58
"National Socialist Government in Vienna," 101, 102
National Socialist Party (*see* Nazis)
National Socialist State, 62
Natunga, 531
Nauru Island, 340, 492-493, 617
Nautilus, submarine, 609-610
Nazis, 47-50, 58-60, 70, 83, 97, 772, 787, 870; barbarism in occupied territory, 398-409; barter system, 268, 272; conspiracies, 308; Constitution and civil rights suspended by, 80-81; educational system, 74-83; elimination of, 13; NSDAP, 75, 76; NSLB, 74-75; Nuremberg Congress, 360; philosophy, 55; plot to conquer world, 64-73, 79; press, control of, 79-83; "purge" of, 57, 66; race theory, 67, 861; spies, 93, 107. (*See also* names of countries attacked)
Nazism, 815; in action, 103-108; campaigns, technique of, 104
Near East, 268, 289
Neditch, General Milan, 278-280
Neenagh, Lieutenant William F., 345
Negro troops, American, 472, 479, 719, 722
Negroes, persecution of, 247
Nelson, Donald M., 483-485, 914
Nelson, Lieutenant Colonel Glen A., 613
Nelson, Lord, 681
Nelson, Pfc. Richard N., 18
Nelson, H.M.S., 692, 698-699
Neosho, tanker, 506, 507
Netherlands, 83, 158, 160; air forces, 342, 657; German invasion of, 102, 125, 153-155, 161, 167-177, 200-203, 219, 233, appeal for aid, 168, looting, 174-176, resistance, 174-177, water defense, 170; and Japanese surrender, 33; liberation of, 766-771, 789, 791, 804, 842, 846, 849; *Orange Book,* 168
Netherlands East Indies, 27, 301, 314, 315, 431, 440, 445-447, 450, 451, 469-470, 487, 503, 516, 615, 617, 631, 648, 650, 897-898
Netherlands New Guinea, 431
Nettuno, 705, 708
Neuhausen, Franz, 278-279
Neurath, Konstantin von, 48, 116, 118
Neutrality, 4, 155, 168, 193, 257, 803
Neva, River, 382
Nevada, battleship, 326, 329, 333, 905
New Britain, 35, 442, 443, 446, 448, 465, 469, 493, 503, 607, 615-616, 627, 635, 919

New Caledonia, 238, 469, 473, 503, 617
New Delhi, 501, 502
New Georgia, 532, 615, 636-640
New Guinea: attacked by Japanese, 35, 341, 442, 445, 446, 448, 465, 469; campaign in, Allied, 471, 493, 503-505, 517, 518, 525, 530, 614-617, 628-629, 634-636, 640-648, 655, 660, 889, 919; MacArthur in, 532, 640
New Hebrides, 249
New Ireland, 442, 503, 615, 919
New Mexico, battleship, 891
"New Order," 4, 83, 131, 149, 272
New Orleans, cruiser, 505, 517, 531
New South Wales, 503
New York, 336, 848
New York, battleship, 905
New York Times, 720, 791, 869
New Zealand, 25, 33, 190, 287, 302, 449, 471, 503, 615, 635, 640; troops, 231, 291, 410, 412-413, 580, 583, 605, 629, 657, 708-710, 719-721; war effort, 465
Newspapers (*see* Press)
Nicholas, Prince, 267
Nicholas, Colonel Kenneth D., 19
Nichols Field, 348, 658
Nicosia, 679
Nielson, 1st Lieutenant Chase J., 500
Niemoeller, Martin, 48-49, 866
Niimi, Vice Admiral Masaichi, 343
Nijmegen, 169, 769
Nikolaescu, Colonel, 401
Nikopol, 395-396
Nile Delta, 411, 412, 533
Nimitz, Admiral Chester W.: commands Pacific fleet, 126, 333, 338, 442-444, 490, 491, 493, 497, 611, 630, 656, 659, 886, 900, 903-905, 930, 933; on Four Power board, 41; and Japanese surrender, 30-32; Fleet Admiral, 887; joint operations, 649-650; quoted, 444, 624, 633, 904-905, 908, 917, on Okinawa, 928, losses, 927; stategy, 443, 507-508, 629-630, 645, at Midway, 515; supreme authority over naval resources, 922
Nine-Power Treaty, 305, 306, 312
Ninigi, Hikoho no, 292, 295
Nininger, Second Lieutenant Alexander R., Jr., 453
Nippon (*see* Japan)
Nishio, General Toshizo, 434
Nivelles, 162
Noble, Brigadier General Alfred H., 644
Noguès, General Charles, 238, 539, 556-557
Nomura, Admiral Kichisaburo, 319-323, 430, 434
Nordic theory, 75
Nordling, Raoul, 761, 763
Normandy, 220, 397, 733, 756; battles of, 739-745; *bocage,* 738
Norris, Major Benjamin W., 512
North Africa: Allied conquest of, 543-606; American landing in, 533-542; Casablanca, 8, 556-564; Libyan campaign, 410-414
North Carolina, battleship, 517
North Pacific, 516, 611-614
North Sea, 140, 142, 193, 218, 261, 770

Northampton, 525, 531
Norway, 49, 83, 125, 127, 128, 134, 199-200, 204, 850; aid to Allies, 152; German occupation of, 137-152; resistance, 138-152
Norwegian Air Force, 152
Norwegian Government in London, 152
Norwegian tanker fleet, 152
Novgorod, 367, 407
Novochaktinsk, 372
Novorossiisk, 384, 390
Noyes, Rear Admiral Leigh, 472
Nuremberg, 48, 183, 863
Nuremberg Laws, 68, 112
Nygaardsvold, Premier Johan, 142, 152

Oahu, 309, 324-325, 330, 333, 514
Oak Ridge, Tennessee, 19
O'Bannon, destroyer, 528
Oberammergau, 848
O'Brien, Lieutenant Colonel William J., 653
O'Brien, destroyer, 519
O'Callahan, Lieutenant Commander Joseph Timothy, 911
Ocean Island, 340
Oceania, 619
O'Connor, Basil, 482
O'Connor, Lieutenant General Sir Richard Nugent, 746-747
O'Daniel, Major General John W., 854
Odense, 133
Oder River, 813-817, 829, 831
Odessa, 365, 369, 397, 403, 406
O'Donnell, Brigadier General Emmett, 455, 901-902
O'Donnell, Camp, 460-461
Office of Alien Property Custodian, 484
Office of Censorship, 484
Office of Civilian Defense, 484
Office of Defense Transportation, 484
Office of Economic Stabilization (OES), 483
Office of Price Administration (OPA), 483
Office of Production Management (OPM), 483
Office of Scientific Research and Development, 19, 484
Office of War Information (OWI), 484
Office of War Mobilization and Reconversion (OWM), 483
Oglala, mine layer, 325, 326, 329
O'Hare, Lieutenant Commander Edward H. ("Butch"), 445, 627
Oil, 123, 152, 447, 449, 451, 821; Burma, 501, 619, 915, 916; Caucasus, 370, 371, 377; Iran, 263; pipe lines on Channel floor, 757; Rumanian, 267-271
Oise River, 206
Oka River, 374
O'Kane, Lieutenant Commander Richard H., 647
Okinawa, 15-17, 20, 30, 40, 41, 496; battle, 921-937
Oklahoma, battleship, 326, 329, 333
Okuma, Marquis Shigenobu, 302
Olden, Rudolf, 51-52
Oldendorf, Rear Admiral Jessse B., 876, 877, 880, 890

Olongapo, 452
Olympus, Mount, 287
"Open door" in China, 299, 303
Oppenheimer, Dr. J. Robert, 19
Oran, battle, 239, 241, 242, 537-539
Orel, 369, 383, 386-390, 392, 400, 841
Ormoc, 881-886
Oro Bay, 635
Osaka, 497, 908
Oslo, 139-144, 146-150
Oslo, University of, 151
Oslo Fjord, 138, 141-143
Oslo group, 128
Oslo Protocol, 137
Osmeña, President Sergio, 346, 347, 661, 897
Ostend, 158, 161-162, 206, 209, 210
Ostrava, 113
Oswiecim, concentration camp, 868
Outerbridge, Lieutenant Commander W. W., 324
OVRA, 91
Owen, Sergeant William J., 704
Owen Stanley Mountains, 530, 634
Oxenius, Major Wilhelm, 855

Pabst, Major Waldemar, 95
Pachino, 670
Pacific Fleet, 26, 337, 338, 442; Amphibious, 655; South Pacific Fleet, 449, 466, 472, 636
Pacific Ocean, 238, 301, 310, 465; Allied war aims in, 618, control returned to Allies, 487-496; atoll warfare in, 625-633; islands of, 8, 27, 302, 306, 315, 431, 654-656, Japanese conquests in, 442-451, 607, mandated to Japan, 302; Japan's holdings in (1943), 607; war in, 15-26, 292, 293, 296, 308-352, 442-477, 487-532, 607-617, 625-666, 872-937, Southwest Pacific, 25, 525-532, 614-617, 634-666. (*See also* North Pacific)
Pacific War Council, 343, 449, 516
Paderewski, Ignace Jan, 121
Palaus, 645, 654, 656, 919
Palawan, 897, 898
Palembang, 449
Palermo, 553, 676
Palestine, 238
Pan-German Union, 56
Pan-Germans, 56, 57, 60, 94, 163; plan of conquest, 4-5, 64-72, 102, 861
Panama Canal, 330, 442, 471, 509, 510
Panay, 658, 662, 897
Panay, gunboat, 314, 432, 442
Panfilov Division, 370
Pangalos, General, 282
Panteff, Colonel Athenas, 265
Pantelleria, 667
Panzer divisions, 158, 371
Papagos, Field Marshal Alexander, 284, 286
Papen, Franz von, 48, 61, 62, 98, 99
Papua, 341, 473
Parachute troops: Allied, 768-771, 802-804; American, 546, 641-642, 670, 733-736, 742, in Japan, 41, rescue parties, 27, 935; British, 916; German, 153-154, 169-171, 201, 209, 289, 546, 676, 709

Paris, 155-158, 172, 183, 192-194, 200, 202, 204, 209, 245-247, 737, 757, 851; capture by Germans, 215-218, Hitler enters, 234, Germans loot, 253; liberation of, 760-764
Paris, Pact of (*see* Kellogg-Briand Treaty)
Parker, Major General G. M., Jr., 27, 28, 350
Parodi, Alexandre, 760-762
Parr, Second Lieutenant George, 500
Parrot, destroyer, 447
Parry Island, 630-631
Parsons, Captain William S., 18
Partisans, 279-281, 291, 694, 716, 718, 720, 721, 723, 786-787, 822, 827
Pasco, Washington, 19
Passchendaele, 558
Patch, Major General Alexander McM., 503, 532, 757, 765, 767-769, 774-775, 777, 795, 801, 844, 846, 848
Patrol Torpedo (PT)-boats, 351, 452, 467, 637, 640, 733, 734, 876-877, 880, 883, 887
Patterson, Robert P., 747
Patterson, destroyer, 475, 476
Patton, General George S., Jr.: Battle of Bulge, 791-795; in France, 730, 736, 756-757, 765, 767-770, 774-778, sends troops to Paris, 762; in Germany, 798, 800-802, 843-844, 847-850, 863, liberates Dachau, 848, testimony on concentration camps, 867; in North Africa, 541, 571-572, 586, 592; in Sicily, 668, 670-671, 675, 679, 684; Third Army, 765-770, 773-778, 798-803, 844-850
Paul, Prince, of Yugoslavia, 274, 275
Paul Jones, destroyer, 447
Paulus, Colonel General Friedrich von, 379
Pavelitch, Ante, 277-279
Paviour, Lieutenant Robert F., 616
PBY scout planes, 511-512
Pearl Harbor, 7, 631; attack on, 3, 6, 8, 16, 20, 36, 44, 45, 271, 292, 293, 306-312, 320-325, 348, 374, 430, 435, 487, 516, 609, 633, 653, 664, 876, 885, inquiry into, 331-332, 449, recovery from, 333
Peary, destroyer, 466
Peiping, 432, 624
Peking, 299; Treaty of, 301
Peleliu, 656
Peloponnesus, 289, 290
Penang, 35
Penguin, mine-sweeper, 335, 340
Pennsylvania, flagship, 325, 326, 329, 333, 877
Pensacola, 531
Percival, Lieutenant General Sir Arthur E., 28, 31, 32, 439-440
Perekop Isthmus, 370
Pericles, 288
Periers, 749, 751, 755
Perkins, Frances, Secretary of Labor, 479
Permanent Joint Board of Defense (JBD), 484
Péronne, 215
Perry, Commodore Matthew C., 29, 30, 295, 297
Persians, 288, 289
Perth, survivors, 28-29
Perugia, 714, 715

Index

Pesaro, 722
Pescadores, 618, 659-660
Pest, 821, 822
Petacci, Clara, 786
Pétain, Marshal, 159, 205, 207; Chief of State, 243-245, 249-260; De Gaulle, reply to, 223, tribute to, 214; surrender, 219-221, 234; trial, 49; Vichy government, 236-239, 434, 535-536, 539-543, 582, 607, 845
Peter the Great, 353
Peter II, King of Yugoslavia, 275, 277-278, 281
Peterson, Lieutenant Commander J. V., 345
Petit Trianon, treaty, 267
Petroleum Administration for War, 484
Petsamo, 365, 366
Peyrouton, Marcel, 557-558
Pfriemer, Dr. Walter, 95, 96
Philippeville, 540, 541
Philippine Clipper, 334
Philippine Scouts, 348
Philippine Sea, Battle of, 650-652
Philippines, 321, 338, 516, 615, 872-873, 880-881, 904, 921; archipelago, 347; complete independence (1946), 347; Japanese conquest, 45, 301, 310, 335, 341-342, 435, 452-464; MacArthur defends, 342, 344-352, promise to return, 645; MacArthur's return to, 41, 634-666, 872-900, 919; Japanese surrender in, 28, 35
Phillips, Lieutenant Colonel J. P., 427
Phillips, Admiral Sir Tom Spencer Vaughan, 339
Philoff, Premier, 263, 265, 266
"Phony war," 196, 198, 205
Pichon, 586, 587
Pierlot, Prime Minister, 161, 166, 210
Pilsen, 113, 850
Pilsudski, Marshal Josef, 121, 182
Pimpf group, 77
Pinsk, 395
Pisa, 715, 717, 718, 722-723
Pius XII, Pope, 169, 186, 698, 705, 713, 714
Plattsburg, transport, 337
Ploesti, 271
"Plutocracies," 360
Po Valley, 723, 725, 785
Pocket battleships, 804
Poehner, Ernst, 58
Pola, 702, 723
Poland, Poles, 47, 93, 110, 112, 402, 478; army, 119, army in exile, 145-146, 206, 416, 418, 699, 710, 717, 721, 722, 768, 770-771, 785, 798, air force, navy, 231, 168, 686; British guarantee to, 179-184, Mutual Assistance Agreement, 122; Constitution of 1921, 121; deportations to, 69, 151, 258; "Facts and Figures," 121; France, alliance with, 194; German invasion of, 5, 83, 120-126, 158, 167, 169, 179, 183, 186-187, 192, 289, 293, 353, 361, 365, 551, 675; Government-in-exile, London, 125, 385, 395; Russians in, 392, 397, 814, 820, 828, fourth partition, 125, 194, nonaggression pact with Russia, 21-122; uprising (1944), 779-782

Poleck, Colonel Fritz, 854
Poletti, Lieutenant Colonel Charles, 694
Polish Corridor, 179, 180, 812, 816
Polish Naval Air Force, 120
Pomaret, Charles, 220, 221, 237
Pomerania, 121, 806, 813
Ponape, 631-632
Pont-du-Fahs, 544, 549
Pope, destroyer, 447
Poplawski, Lieutenant General, 810
Popoff, M. M., 381
Port Arthur, 299-301
Port Blair, 441
Port Darwin, 466
Port Gentil, 257
Port Lyautey, 537-539
Port Moresby, 445, 466, 470-472, 504, 505, 530, 532, 634
Portal, Air Chief Marshal Sir Charles, 560
Porter, 525
Portland, cruiser, 504, 517, 528, 529
Portsmouth, Treaty of, 300-301
Portugal, 257, 479
Posen, 812, 814, 816
Potsdam, 831-832
Potsdam Conference, 17, 20-23, 46
Potsdam Declaration, 12, 23-25, 31, 33, 34, 45
Pound, Admiral of Fleet Sir Dudley, 154-155, 560
Pourville, 419, 422, 423
Power, Admiral Sir Arthur J., 890
Pownall, Rear Admiral Charles Alan, 489, 491-492
Pownall, Lieutenant General Sir Henry, 344
Prague, 113-115, 179, 180, 821, 826, 838, 850
President's War Relief Control Board, 484
Press, free, 312, abolished by Mussolini, 90-91, part in war effort, 485; Japanese, 312; Nazi, weapon of aggression, 82-83, 114; Nazi-ruled, 79-83, 116, 175, 177, 246; underground, 118, 136, 152, 165-166, 177; unoccupied France, 249
Preston, destroyer, 348, 529
Price, Lieutenant Colonel Andrew, 705
Price, Byron, 484
Prince of Wales, flagship, 335, 339, 340, 344
Princeton, carrier, 492-495, 875, 879
Prioux, General René-Jacques-Adolphe, 161
Pripet Marshes, 395
Prisoners, of Germans, 862-871; of Japanese, 27-30, 34, 42, 44, 458-464
Propaganda: Communist, 360; French, 198; German, 79-83, 105, 130, 175, 177, 190-191, 195, 197-198, 265, 360-361, 365, 389, 390, 417, 713, 721, 829, Propaganda Ministry, 79-81; Japanese, 26, 42-43, 924; Mussolini's, 283
Protestants, Hitler and, 67, 68
Prussians, 55
Psychological warfare, 273, 775-776, 889
Pu Yi, Henry, 26, 430, 431
Puaux, Gabriel, 260
Pucheu, Pierre, 557-558
Puits, 419, 421-422
Punongbayen, Honorio, 461

Index

Putnam, Major Paul A., 343
Pye, Vice Admiral William S., 333

Quebec Conferences, 8, 9, 391, 618, 621, 698
Queen's Own Cameron Highlanders, 419-420, 423
Quezon, President Manuel, 346, 347, 349, 350, 661
Quincy, heavy cruiser, 473, 475, 476
Quisling, Vidkun, 49, 139, 146-152

Rabat, 538
Rabaul, 444, 466, 469, 487, 489-490, 517-518, 625, 635, 636, 642, 644, 919
Raczkiewicz, Wladyslaw, 125, 126
Raczynski, Count Edward, 122
Radar, 14
Radford, Rear Admiral Arthur W., 489, 490, 625, 627
Radio, in war effort, 14, 485-486
Raeder, Grand Admiral Erich, 48, 849
Ragsdale, Rear Admiral Van H., 625
Ragusa, 671
Raleigh, cruiser, 326, 333
Ralph Talbot, destroyer, 475, 476
Ramey, Brigadier General Howard, 610
Ramey, Brigadier General Roger M., 904
Ramsay, Admiral Sir Bertram Home, 727, 734
Ramsey, Captain Logan, 511
Randazzo, 682-683
Rangers, 415-416, 419-421, 536, 546, 738, 872, 895
Rangoon, 15, 345, 438, 440-441, 620, 900, 915, 916
Rankin, Jeannette, 310
Rapido River, 704-705, 709
Rath, von, 67
Rauschning, Dr. Hermann, 63
Ravensbrueck, concentration camp, 866
Ravenzwaai, C. van, 177
Rawlings, Vice Admiral Sir H. Bernard, 923
Raydon, Dr. H., 177
Reconstruction Finance Corporation (RFC), 484
Red Air Force, 376, 384, 386, 396-397, 840
Red Army, 21, 48, 119, 266, 353-358, 363-391, 398-399, 408, 693, 707, 779-782, 804, 806-841, 901; Partisans, 408
Red Cross, 41 (see also American Red Cross)
Red Navy, 370, 374
Refugees, 201-202, 206, 208, 219, 236-237
Reich Kultur Chamber, 80
Reich Press Association, 80
Reichenau, Walther von, Field Marshal, 104, 365
Reichs Press Chamber, 82
Reichstag fire, 61, 361; second, 835-837
Reichswehr, 57, 58, 61, 62, 104
Reid, Ensign Jewell, 511
Reid, destroyer, 885
Reims, 217, 850, 854, 855, 858
Remagen bridgehead, 798-801
Remizoff, General, 372
Rendova Island, 615, 636-637
Rennes, 220, 755

Renown, battle cruiser, 140-141
Renthe-Fink, Doctor von, 128
Republican Defense Corps, 95-98
Repulse, warship, 335, 339, 340, 344
Resistance, National Council of, 760-761
Reynaud, Paul, 49, 154, 158-160, 198-204, 208-210, 214-215, 218, 219, 244, 247, 253, 259, 845, 866
Reynaud, Paul, mayor of Cherbourg, 744
Rezhitsa, 389
Rheims (see Reims)
Rhine River, 157, 199, 769, 770, 772-778, 798-802
Rhineland, 47, 107, 117, 798; reoccupation of, 5, 104, 105, 153, 178, 293
Rhône Valley, 222, 239
Ribbentrop, Joachim von, 112, 115, 122, 152, 168, 180, 184-186, 195, 269, 276, 431, 434, 838, 849; trial, 48
Ribbentrop-Molotov pact, 121-122, 182, 184, 192, 194, 197, 353, 360-362
Richards, James, 329
Richards, Lieutenant William, 511
Richelieu, battleship, 241-242, 251
Richland Village, 19
Richmond, cruiser, 612
Ridgeway, Major General Matthew B., 792
Rieth, Doctor, 98
Riga, Treaty of, 395
Rimini, 724-725
Rio de Janeiro, troopship, 138
Riom, 247, 255, 259
Robb, Lieutenant James W., 328
Robert, Admiral Georges, 240, 258
Roberts, Colonel Harold C., 934
Roberts, Major General J. H., 416, 426
Roberts, Associate Justice Owen J., 331, 332
Roberts, destroyer escort, 878
Robertson, Second Lieutenant William D., 846-847
Robot bombs, 745, 748; sites, 767, 770
Rockefeller, Nelson A., 484
Rockey, Major General Keller E., 905
Rockwell, Rear Admiral Francis W., 446, 467, 612
Rodney, H.M.S., 140, 698-699
Roehm, Ernst, 57-59, 61, 62
Roer River, 774
Rogers, Lieutenant Robert, 327
Rokossovsky, Marshal Konstantin K., 379, 380, 392, 394, 397, 779; drive on Berlin, 807-808, 810-818, 828-829, 831, 837-838, 840
Rol, Colonel, 762
Roman Catholics, persecution of, 81
Rome, 273, 394, 676, 706; bombing of, 674-675, 732, 683, 729; "march on," 89; liberation of, 711-716
Rome-Berlin Axis, 98
Rommel, Marshal Erwin: African campaign, 410-414, 549, 551-555, 564-589, 729, 788; death, 751, 756; return to Europe, 595-596, 605, in France, 203, 737, in Italy, 694, 727
Roosevelt, Franklin D., 37, 134, 152, 198, 253, 276, 286-287, 321, 355, 436, 468, 489, 527, 656, 692, 701, 716, 782, 902; African land-

Roosevelt, Franklin D. (cont'd)
ing, broadcast on, 536, thanks to Allies, 604; arms embargo removed by, 355; Assistant Secretary of Navy, 337; Atlantic Charter, 6-8, 320, 340, 366; and atomic bomb, 18-19; Australia, MacArthur's organization in, 470; Bulgaria, Rumania, Hungary, recommends war against, 265; Cairo, 703; Casablanca, 560-564; crisis over Czechoslovakia, peace plea, 81; death, 10-12, 805, 825, 927, 936; democracies' war aims, statement of, 6-8; extraterritoriality, favors end of, 608; final (Jefferson Day) address, 10-11; freezes French assets, 240; freezes occupied countries' credits, 169; German attacks on, 77; Great Britain, convoys to, 362; Greek struggle recognized by, 285-286; Greeks, tribute to, 291, telegram, 286-287; Hirohito, message to, 322; Italians, appeal to, 674; Japan, proclaims state of war with, 309-311; Japanese shelling interrupts broadcasts, 450; Lend Lease, China, 502, North Africa, 540, Russia, 373; MacArthur's command, statement on, 467; Moscow, sends mission to, 368; and North African landing, 539-540; Pacific War Council, 449, 516; peace, efforts to preserve, 311; Pearl Harbor, appoints inquiry board into, 331; Philippine invasion, message on, 664; Philippines, pledges freedom of, 346; Poland, mediation offer, 186; Quebec, 8-9, 618; quoted, on Balkan war declarations, 271, on Doolittle flyers, 497, 499, on Lend-Lease, 317, on O'Hare's feat, 445, on rights of small nations, 128; Reynaud's plea to, 218; Sicilian invasion announced by, 667; Stalin, greetings to, 386; Stilwell backed by, 914; at Teheran Conference, 9, 394-395; third term, 362; Wainwright, messages to, 458, 462-463; war, warnings of, 487; War Cabinet, 479-480; Washington conferences, 343, 533; Yalta Conference, 10, 814-815, 844

Roosevelt, President Theodore, 300
Roosevelt, Brigadier General Theodore, 750-751
Roque, Colonel François de la, 866
Rosario, 893
Rosenberg, Alfred, 48, 55, 58, 61, 146, 409
Rosendahl, Captain Charles E., 531
Ross, Warrant Officer Donald K., 330
Ross, Malcolm, 484
Rostock, 837, 838
Rostov, 370-372, 381-383, 390, 401
Rota, 334, 654
Rotterdam, 167, 169-174, 375
Rouen, 217, 418
Rovno, 395
Royal Air Force (R.A.F.), 158, 173, 242, 345, 411, 418-419, 424, 427, 669, 685, 719; Battle of Britain, 225-233; Dunkirk, 211-212; exiles in, 119, 136, 152, 166, 231; Germany, 366, 800, 804, 813, 837, 846; North Africa, 544, 568, 577, 589, 593, 598; Western front, 729, 731-732, 742-743, 748, 763
Royal Australian Navy, 919
Royal Canadian Air Force, 418

Royal Canadian Engineers, 424, 425
Royal Engineers, 574-575
Royal Hamilton Light Infantry, 420, 424, 427
Royal Marine Commandos, 426-427
Royal Navy, 16, 140-143, 190, 199, 200, 211-213, 240, 251, 890
Royal Regiment of Canada, 419, 421-422
Royan, 843
Ruckman, Private George, 652-653
Ruegen, island of, 838
Ruge, General Otto, 145
Ruhr, 168, 815; pocket, 803-805, 844-845
Rumania, 123, 125, 166, 180, 261-271, 274, 827; Axis member, 270-271, 286; Nazi occupation, 179, 270, 820; oil, 267-271; Rumanians, 93, troops, 369, 379, 390, 397, 401, 807, 823; Russia, war against, 270, 365, 392
Rundstedt, von, Field Marshal Karl Rudolf Gerd, 365, 371, 747-748, 756, 773-775, 785, 788-791, 795-796, 800
Rupertus, Brigadier General William H., 473, 523, 526, 527
Russell Islands, 615-617
Russia, 280, 299, 389, 478, 534, 607; Allied aid to, 366-367, 373, 563; Allied Control Council, 41; and Baltic States, 354; and Bulgaria, 263-266; China, treaty with, 299; Finland, conflict with, 197, 353-358, 361; German invasion of, 270, 360-379, drives Germans from soil, 380-409, 564, "scorched earth" policy, 433, strategy, 388, tanks, 378, 381, 388; Germany, drive into, 803, 806-841, fall of Berlin, 829-841, German surrender, 842-861, zone occupied by Russia, 47-48; Germany, testimony on atrocities, in concentration camps, 862-871, in occupied territory, 398-409; industrial materials taken beyond Urals, 367; Japan, joint note to, 298-299, non-aggression pact denounced, 924-925, Russia enters Pacific war, 21, 25, and Japanese surrender, 22; Russia, liberated regions, restoration of, 408; life lines, 365, 367; magnitude of, 360-363; Moscow Conference, 8; Munich, 111; Poland invaded by, 120-126, 361, (1920), 207, 208, non-aggression pact with, 121-122; Portsmouth, Treaty of, 300-301; rivers, strategic importance of, 387-391; Rumania, demands on, 368-369; social and economic achievements, 359; Teheran, 9; United Nations, member of, 701; United States troops, meeting with, 846-847, 899; world power, 359-363; Yalta, 10, 814-815, 844. (See also Union of Soviet Socialist Republics)
Russo-German Non-Aggression Pact, 121-122, 182, 184, 192, 194, 197, 353, 360-362
Russo-Japanese Non-Aggression Treaty, 435
Russo-Japanese War, 300
Rust, Dr. Bernard, 75
Ruth, Babe, 318
Ruthenians, 93
Ruyijo, carrier, 517
Ruzycki, Stanley, 864
Ryder, Major General Charles, 541

Ryukaku, carrier, 505
Ryukyu Islands, 301, 659, 872, 890, 892, 920-922, 925
Rzhev, 374, 381, 384

SA, 57, 59, 62, 68, 70, 73, 82, 105, 181
Saar River, 157, 774-775, 777, 801; Basin, 773-775, 801; district, 107
Saar "plebiscite," 5, 153, 293
Saarbruecken, 194, 774, 777, 801
Sabang, 655
Sabotage, German, 155, 170, 772; Underground and Allied, 118, 132-133, 149, 165, 176, 177, 265, 290-291, 662, 700, 749
Sachsenburg, 67
Sachsenhausen, 67
Saidor, 628-629
St. Aubin airfield, 420, 423
St. Cloud, 537
St. Germain, Treaty of, 97, 267
St. Gilles prison, 164
St. Lo, 745-753, 755
St. Lo, carrier, 878
St. Louis, cruiser, 443, 638
St. Nazaire, 215, 216, 221, 223, 416, 842, 850
St. Paul's Cathedral, 227, 229
St. Phalle, Alexandre de, 762
St. Pierre, 249, 596
Saint-Vith, 791-794, 796
Saipan, 334, 643, 900, 901, 934; Battle, 650-655
Saito, Hirosi, 313
Sakai, Lieutenant General Takashi, 343
Sakhalin, 25
Salamaua, 466, 472, 504, 508, 518, 616, 635, 636, 641, 642
Salerno, landing, 702, 723; Battle of, 686-690
Salonika, 275, 284, 287, 288, 290-291
Salt Lake City, cruiser, 443, 521, 612
Salween River, 623
Saltzman, Lieutenant Stephen G., 327
Salzburg, 94, 867
Samar Island, 666; battle off, 875-880
Samothrace, 264
Samurai, 293-298
San Francisco, 336; conference, 6, 10-12, 804, 846, 848
San Francisco, cruiser, 521, 528
San Gimignano, 716-717
San Giovanni, 684
San Marino, 724-725
Sanananda Point, 532
Santa Cruz, battle of, 525, 875
Santa Fe, New Mexico, 19
Santa Fé, cruiser, 911
Santa Isabel, 615
Santee, carrier, 878
Santo Tomas, prison camp, 895
Sarajevo, 261, 277
Sarantyn, Clément, 194
Saratoga, carrier, 443, 490, 494, 495, 517, 630, 632, 910, 911
Sarawak, 346
Sardinia, 582, 587, 590, 690, 702
Sato, Ambassador, 21

Sauckel, Fritz, Gauleiter, 48, 404
Sautot, Henri, 249
Savo Island, 473, 475-476, 527-529, 872
Savoie (Savoy), 219; FFI rising, 758
Sayre, Francis B., 347, 468
Sbeitla, 553-555, 569
Sbiba, 565-566
Scanland, Captain Francis W., 329
Scavenius, Erik, 133
Schacht, Hjalmar Horace Greeley, 48, 60, 72, 273, 845, 866; barter scheme, 268
Schaefer, Herr, 81
Scharnhorst, 141
Scheldt River, 766, 768, 771
Schicklgruber, Alois, 52
Schiphol airdrome, 170
Schirach, Balder von, 66, 75, 76, 78, 108
Schittnig, Colonel, 400
Schleiben, Lieutenant General Carl Wilhelm von, 744
Schleicher, Kurt von, 60-62
Schleswig-Holstein, 127
Schleswig-Holstein, battleship, 122
Schlieffen plan, 155, 167
Schmidt, Dr. Guido, 99, 184
Schmidt, Major General Harry, 655, 905
Schoenauer, Second Lieutenant Lyle A., 616
Schofield Barracks, Wheeler Field, 327, 330
Schrier, Lieutenant Harold C., 907
Schroeder, Baron, 61
Schuschnigg, Kurt von, 98-102, 104, 105, 845, 866
Schutzstaffel (SS), 59, 66-68, 70, 72, 101, 106, 181, 792
Schwoedler, General, 371
Scorza, Carlo, 678
Scotland, 152, 478; Scots, 413, 590, 798
Scott, Rear Admiral Norman, 521, 527, 528
Scott, Colonel Robert L., 608
Sea guerrillas, 291
Sea power, American, rebirth of, 487-496
Seabees, 492, 626, 629, 630, 902-903, 931
Seals, Brigadier General Carl, 350
Seavy, Brigadier General William, 665
Sebree, Brigadier General E. D., 527
"Second Front" invasion, 726
Secret weapon, German, 708, 745
Sedan, 157, 158, 203-204, 535
Seeckt, General von, 97
Seine River, 217, 218
Seip, Doctor, 150
Seipel, Dr. Ignatz, 94, 95
Seisser, von, 58
Seitz, Captain George A., 936
Selective Training and Service Act, 440, 468, 480
Self-determination, 110
Sellmer, Lieutenant George, 616
Senegalese troops, 160
Sentani, 645, 646
Serbia, 261; Greater, 272
Serbs, 93
Sevastopol, 370, 374
Sevez, Major General François, 857, 858
Sèvres, Treaty of, 282

Seyffardt, Lieutenant General Hendrik A., 176-177
Seymour, Sir Horace James, 609
Seyss-Inquart, Dr. Arthur von, 48, 99-102, 105, 106, 175-176
Sfax, 544, 546-547, 551, 574, 584-589
SHAEF, 46, 776, 800, 854-855, 868-869
Shanghai, 5, 319, 335, 432, 433
"Shanghai Affair," 430
Shangri-La, 499, 901 (*See also* Hornet)
Shannon, Colonel Harold D., 516
Shantung Agreement, 305
Shantung Province, 299, 302, 304
Sharp, Brigadier General William, 350
Shaw, destroyer, 326, 329, 333
Shepherd, General Lemuel P., Jr., 654, 928
Sherman, Captain Frank C., 504, 507
Sherman, Rear Admiral Frederick Carl, 32, 489-490, 495
Sherman tanks, 412, 591, 753
Shigemitsu, Mamoru, Foreign Minister, 31, 32, 44
Shimada, Admiral Shigetaro, 651
Shimonoseki, Treaty of, 298
Shintoism, 292-297
Shoguns, 297, 298
Shoriki, Matsutaro, 318
Short, Lieutenant General Walter C., 331, 333, 337
Shuri, 930-932
Siberia, 298, 305, 360, 612
Sibert, Major General Franklin C., 665
Sicily, 410, 411, 570, 574, 576-578, 582, 585, 590; fall of, 126, 546, 599, 667-685, 699, 733
Sidi Barrani, 410
Sidi bou Zid, 550, 554-555, 569
Siegfried Line, 122, 190, 193, 768-771, 775, 777, 795
Siena, 715-716
Sikorski, General, 125-126, 782
Silesia, 806, 812, 813, 815-816, 829
Silesian Gate, 808
Simeon II, King of Bulgaria, 266
Simferopol, 371, 397
Simon, Sir John, 312-313
Simovitch, General Dusan, 275
Simpson, Lieutenant General William H., 730, 770, 792, 867
Sims, destroyer, 506, 507
Singapore, 25, 291, 335, 341, 631; fall of, 316, 344, 346, 438-440, 500, 900; reoccupied, 35
Sino-Japanese War, 298
Skagerrak, 140-142
Skoda arms plant, 117, 850
Skorzeny, Lieutenant Colonel Otto, 775-776
Slave labor, 71-73, 176, 247, 290, 401-405, 770, 810
Slavs, 266, 272-281, 407, 827
Slim, Lieutenant General Sir William J., 915
Slovakia, 824, 838
Slovaks, 93, 110-112; autonomists, 111, 113
Slovenes, 93, 272
Slovenia, 278
Smith, Rear Admiral A. E., 904

Smith, Lieutenant Colonel Baldwin B., 776
Smith, Technical Sergeant Ezra R., 461
Smith, Lieutenant General Holland McT., 625, 653, 905, 907
Smith, Major General Julian C., 625
Smith, Major General Ralph C., 625
Smith, Major General Walter B., 685, 701, 854-858
Smith, Rear Admiral William W., 505, 509
Smith, 525
Smolensk, 365, 366, 368, 371, 384-385, 390, 408
Smuts, Prime Minister Jan Christian, 740
Smyrna, 282
Social Democrats, 57, 61, 67; in Austria, 93-98, 100, 107
Socialist Party, Socialists, 55, 69, 85, 86, 91
Socrates, 288
Soddu, General Ubaldo, 285
Sofia, 265, 266, 274
Soissons, 216, 217
Solomon Islands, 17, 494, 503-504, 506, 607, 609-611, 614-617, 634, 636-642, 648, 919; seized by Japanese, 465, 466, 469, 493, 631, Eastern, Battle of, 471, 517-518, 525, 629
Solomons Sea, 442
Somervell, Lieutenant General Brehon B., 480, 560
Somerville, Admiral Sir James, 649
Somme River, 214-216
Soong, Dr. T. V., 608-609
Soryu, carrier, 512, 513
Sosnkowski, General Kazimierz, 126
Soule, Colonel Robert H., 895
Sousse, 586, 587, 589
South America, 308, 333, 336, 479
South Carolina, battleship, 880
South China Sea, 442
South Dakota, battleship, 30, 523, 525, 528, 529
South Manchurian Railway, 5, 293, 429
South Pacific Fleet, 449, 466, 472
South Saskatchewan Regiment, 419, 422-423
Southampton, 225, 229
Southan, Brigadier, 428
Southwest Pacific, 343, 614-617, 634-666; islands in, 25; naval battles in, 525-532
Soviet Guards, 833-834
Soviet Union, 8
Spa, 791-792, 795
Spaak, Foreign Minister, 161, 166
Spaatz, General Carl A., 16, 545, 553, 561, 589, 732, 839, 855, 859-860
Spaight, J. M., 230
Spain, 103, 105, 221, 236, 257, 293; Franco rebellion, 5; "neutrality," 676
Spanish, aid to FFI, 762
Spanish-American War, 333-334, 337, 338, 614
Spanish Morocco, 576
SPARS, 481
Spatz, Sergeant Harold A., 500
Speer, Albert, 849
Spellman, Archbishop, 718-719
Spence, destroyer, 887

Index

Spies, German, 93, 107
Spitfires, 225-227, 418, 424, 426-427, 567, 573, 579, 590
Spoleto, Duke of, 278
Sponeck, Major General Graf von, 605
Sportjugend (Sport Youth), 76
Sprague, Rear Admiral T. L., 877-878, 880
Spratly Islands, 433
Spruance, Admiral Raymond A., 15, 489, 491, 496, 509; at Midway, 511, 513-514, Tarawa, 625, Truk, 632-633, 643, Marianas, 650-651, Iwo, 905, Okinawa, 924-926
"Spruance Haircut," 629-630
Stachouwer, Governor-General A. W. I. Tjarda van Starkenborg, 450
Stahmer, Heinrich, 45
Stalin, Josef, 693, 782, 812, 833; announces fall of Berlin, 837; announces Korsun victory, 396; in Berlin, 12; brands Japan aggressor nation, 901; dictator, 360; enters Pacific war, 21, 26; invited to Casablanca, 561, Moscow meeting with Churchill, 562, 564; orders of the day, 810-811, 817, 839; quoted, on invasion of Germany, 806, on second front, 386; at Teheran, 9, 394-395; thanks for American aid, 391; victory address, 839, at victory celebration, 840; war leader, 362-367, 370, 373, 378, 388, orders stand at Stalingrad, 377; at Yalta, 10, 814, 844
Stalingrad, 271, 380, 388, 393-394, 433, 813, 822, 833, 841; battle for, 375-379, 381, 407
Stalino, 372, 389, 407
Standley, Admiral William H., 384-385
Starace, Achille, 786
Starhemberg, Prince Ernst Ruediger von, 95-98
Stark, Admiral R., 470
State Department, 314, 500, 803
Statendam, 173
Stauning, Premier Thorwald, 129, 132
Steiborik, Sergeant Joe A., 18
Steidle, Doctor, 95
Stern, General Gregory M., 356
Stettin, 817, 829, 831, 838
Stettinius, Edward R., Jr., 23
Stilwell, General Joseph W. ("Vinegar Joe"), 436, 497, 608, 620, 622-624, 911, 914, 936; Chinese troops reinforce British, 501-502
Stimson, Henry L., 19, 311-313, 429, 468, 479, 547, 599, 716, 787
Stockinger, 100
Stoessel, General Anatol Mikhailovitch, 300
Storm Troopers, 68, 96, 99, 101, 106, 147, 150, 834
Strakonice, munitions works, 118
Strasser, Gregor, 59, 61, 62, 80
Strasser, Otto, 69
Stratton, Lieutenant Commander Dorothy C., 481
Streicher, Julius, 48, 59, 76
Stresemann, Gustav, 59, 60
Strong, destroyer, 638
Struble, Rear Admiral A. D., 885
Stumpf, Colonel General Hans Juergen, 839, 859
Sturzo, Don, 89

Sub-Carpathian Russia, 111, 113
Subic Bay, 452, 453, 658, 888, 893-894
Submarines, Allied, 138, 470, 543; Axis, 138, 199, 336, 475, midget, 508
Suedetenland, Germans, 5, 83, 93, 110, 121, 283, 293, 844-845
Suez Canal, 256, 370, 410, 411, 533
Sugiyama, Field Marshal, 41, 643, 649
Sultan, Lieutenant General Daniel L., 911
Sulu Archipelago, 898
Sulu Sea, 442, 873
Sumatra, 431, 448, 449, 451, 500, 649, 655, 900
Sun Yat-sen, Dr., 302
"Super-race" mania, 4
Superfortresses, 16-18, 900-902, 908, 909, 922, 925
Supreme Headquarters Allied Expeditionary Force (*see* SHAEF)
Supreme War Council, 200, 207
Surabaya, 445, 448, 450, 617, 650
Suribachi, Mount, 906, 907
Surigao Strait, 885; Battle of, 873, 875-880
Susloparoff, Major General Ivan, 855, 857, 858
Sutherland, Lieutenant General Richard K., 29, 40, 43, 350, 456, 466
Suvorov, 833
Suwanee, carrier, 878
Suzuki, Baron Kantaro, 925, 932
Sweden, 128, 353, 355, 357, 479, 848; iron-ore fields, 142
Sweeney, Lieutenant Colonel Walter, Jr., 511, 512
Swift, Major General Palmer, 644
Switzerland, 85, 87, 190, 193, 196, 479, 786, 848
Sychevka, 384
Synchronization, Allies learn, 428, 727
Syria, 238, 242, 252, 256, 260, 371
Syrovy, General, 111

Taborek, Lieutenant, 345
Tacloban, 662, 664, 665
Taierhchwang, battle, 433
Talasea airfield, 645
Talbot, Commander, P. H., 447
Talienwan, 299
Tamera, 571, 573
Tanahmera, 645, 646
Tanaka, Baron, 431-432; Memorial, 306-307
Tanambogo, 474-475
Tang, submarine, 647
Tanks, Allied, 203, 425, 604; flail, 745, manless, 708; German, 158, 170, 202-204, 216-218, 543-544, 554, 566-567, 570, 604, 687; Russian, 811, 814, 823, 833; United States, 542, 591
Tannenberg, 183, 812
Tanner, Finnish Foreign Minister, 358
Tapotchau, Mount, 652
Tarawa, 445, 492-493, 611, 617, 644, 652, 934; conquest of, 625-626, 889
Tarhuna, 414
Tarlac, 348

Task force, rebirth of Pacific sea power through, 487-496, 517
Task Force 58, 488, 490-491, 632-633, 643, 645, 647, 649-652, 905
Tassafaronga, Battle of, 531
Tassigny, Major General Jean de Lattre de, 758, 839, 859-860
Taylor, Ensign Thomas H., 329
Tebessa, 566
Tebourba, 545-546, 599
Tedder, Air Chief Marshal Sir Arthur William, 291, 413, 552-553, 561, 727, 729, 731, 839, 858-860
Teheran, 9, 394, 703
Televaag, 150
Temryuk, 390-391
Ten-Year Non-Aggression Pact, Germany and Poland, 120
Tenaru, battle, 517
Tengyueh, 501
Tennessee, battleship, 326, 329, 333, 905
Terauchi, Field Marshal Count Juichi, 664, 883
Terboven, Josef, 147-149, 151
Terek River, 387
Teugels, 165
Texas, battleship, 905
Thailand, 15, 27-29, 252, 260, 335, 339, 902
Thala, 566-567
Thames River, 226-227
Thasos, 264
Theodosia, 371, 374
Thermopylæ, 288
Thessaly, 290
Third Reich, 261
Thirty Years' War, 175
Thoma, General Ritter von, 413
Thomas, James M., Private First Class, 630
Thomas, Major Rowan T., *Born in Battle*, 413-414
Thrace, 264, 282, 287, 289, 290
Three-Power Pact (*see* Tripartite Pact)
Thyssen, Fritz, 60
Tibbets, Colonel Paul W., Jr., 18
Tientsin, Treaty of, 298
Timor, 341
Timoshenko, Marshal Semyon, 365, 369-372, 380, 384, 388
Tinian, 643, 650, 654, 655, 900
Tinker, Major General Clarence L., 333, 515
Tiso, Joseph, 111, 113, 114
Tisza River, 277
Tito, Marshal (Broz, Josip), 279-281, 720, 807, 821, 826-827
Titulescu, 267
Tkachev, Volodya, 402
Tobruk, 291, 411, 414, 533, 919
Todt, Dr. Fritz, 190
Togo, Admiral, 300
Tojo, Premier Hideki, 4, 5, 44, 45, 321, 333, 338, 609, 653
Tokyo, battle of, 908-909; bombed, 15-17, 541, 901-905, 925, first raid on, 497-500; MacArthur enters, 39-43, 899; radio, 22, 42; surrender, 3, 22, 26, 28, 30, 36
Tokyo Bay, 26-27, 36, 44

Tokyo Express, 631, 638
"Tokyo Rose," 43
Tolbukhin, Marshal Fedor I., 381, 392, 397, 807, 820-825, 829
Tolman, Dr. Richard C., 19
Tolstoy, Alexei, quoted on atrocities, 406-407, 409
Tonghak rebellion, 298
Torgau, 846
Torgerson, Captain Harry L., 474
Toronto, Canada, 152
"Torpedo 8" squadron, 511-513
Torrés, Maître, 87
Toulon, 218, 258, 539, 543, 759, 763
Tournai, 162, 208
Tours, 217-219, 234
Towers, Rear Admiral John H., 489, 490
Toyama, Mitsuru, 319
Tozeur, 569
Trade unions, 48, 54, 69-72, 94, 100
Trans-Siberian Railroad, 299, 300
Transylvania, 267-269
Trasimeno, Lake, 715, 716
Trieste, 587, 787, 828
Trincomalee, 500-501
Tripartite Pact, 264, 265, 274, 286, 316-317, 434, 435
Triple Alliance, 86
Tripoli, 86, 255, 414, 544, 559, 581
Tripolitania, 549-550, 560, 585
Trnyi, 281
Troarn, 740-741, 756
Trobriand Islands, 615, 636, 637
Troina, 679-681
"Trojan Horse" traitors, 170
Trondheim, 139-144, 150, 199
Truk, 29, 302, 334, 504, 507, 630, 644, 647, 650, 919; attack on, 631-633, 643
Truman, President Harry S., 11-12, 17-24, 45, 840, 848, 851; victory broadcast, 36-38
Truscott, General, 850
Tschaikovsky, 373
Tsigantes, Christo, 291
Tsushima Strait, Battle of, 300
Tuka, Bela, 113
Tula, 372, 400
Tulagi, 473-476, 523
Tunis, 255; border, 235; drive for, 540-547, 554, 555, 580, 583, 586, 588-597; fall of, 598-606
Tunisia, 218, 668, 673, 679, 685, 727; battle for, 126, 291, 414, 539-606
Turati, Augusto, 92
Turin, massacre of, 92
Turkey, 195, 262-264, 269, 271, 275, 289
Turnage, Major General Allen H., 654
Turner, Vice Admiral Richmond K., 472, 527, 625, 655, 905, 926
Typhoon, on Leyte, 666
Typhoons, rocket-firing, 748, 887

Ubin Island, 439
Uji, warrior families, 293-295
Ukraine, 123, 360, 388-406; autonomists, 113; Germans invade, 365, 367, 368, 370, 371, 387

Index 997

Ullstein family, 81
Umezu, General Yoshijiro, 31, 32
Unalaska, 510
Unconditional surrender, 24-38, 551-563, 603, 605, 698, 701, 764, 815, 836, 838, 852-861, 937; Casablanca decision, 563
Underground: Belgium, 165-166, Denmark, 132-136, France, 737-738, 741, 743, 745, 749, 758-763, Holland, 176-177, Greece, 290-291, Norway, 149-152, Poland, 779-782, 810, Yugoslavia, 279-281; broadcasts to, D-Day, 735
Unimak Island, 510
Union of Soviet Socialist Republics (U. S. S. R.), 31-33; achievements, 359, 363; extent, 360-363; incorporates Lithuania, Latvia, and Estonia, 124. (*See also* Russia)
Unions, trade, 48, 54, 69-72, 94, 100
United Nations, 4, 14, 21, 30, 31, 38, 46, 50, 119, 125, 166, 278, 338, 339, 346, 374, 446, 449, 471-473, 500, 532, 534, 607, 648, 700, 701, 713, 779, 798, 806, 856; Charter, 10, 12, 13; Conference, San Francisco, 6, 10, 12, 804, 846; Declaration of, 8; diplomatic gains, 391; Dumbarton Oaks conference, created at, 9; responsibilty for peace, 841; victory of, 3-13
United States, 5, 192, 198, 222; arms shipments to Britain, 224; "Arsenal of Democracy," 478-486; Atlantic Charter, 6-8; brotherhood of races in, 478-479; Cairo, 8; Casablanca, 8, 556-564; China, credits to, 315, 317, concedes Japan's "special interests" in, 303, "open door" in, 299, 303; D-Day, Western front, 726-771, invasion of Germany, 772-778, 788-805, German surrender, 842-861, occupation of Germany, 46-50; declares war on Japan, 308, 310-311, on Germany and Italy, 308, 311, on Rumania, Bulgaria, Hungary, 265; Dumbarton Oaks, 9; Four Power Allied Control Council, 50, 694; Four Power Board, 41; economic depression, 312; Italian invasion, 92, 783-787; Japan, American administration of, 44-46, exports to, embargoed, 316; plans for invasion of United States, 336; war with (*see* Pacific Ocean); League of Nations, kept out of, 312-313; Moscow, 8; naval armaments, limitation of, 431; neutrality, 240; North Africa, 533-606; Pacific, war in, 336-346, in Philippines, 347-352, last stand at Bataan, Corregidor, surrender and March of Death, 452-464; MacArthur's Pacific campaign, 471-477, 503-532, 607-660, return to Philippines, 661-666, Leyte Gulf battle, 872-888, MacArthur enters Manila, 889-899, Iwo Jima, 900-909, Japanese empire crumbles, 910-920, Okinawa, 921-937, atomic bomb, 17-21, Japanese surrender, 22-38, occupation of Japan, 39-46; Pacific bases, 469; Pearl Harbor, attacked at, 324-335; Quebec, 8-9; Russia, aid to, 369-370, 373, 378, 380, 381, 384-385, 391; sea power, rebirth of, 487-496; self-government, 359-360; Sicilian invasion, 667-685; Teheran, 9; Tokyo, first raid on, 491-502; United Nations, 9, Charter, 10, San Francisco Conference, 11-13; Vichy, relations with, 249, 256-257; World War II, drawn into, 50, 152, 292, 308-323, 374; Yalta, 10
United States Army, in North Africa, 533-606, Sicily, 667-685, Italy, 683-725; Europe and Germany, 726-805, 830, 832, 842-860. (*See also* Pacific Ocean.)
United States Army Air Forces, 418, 437, 470, 608, 621, 813, 837; coöperate with Navy, 489-496, 657-660, 685, 753
United States Forces in European Theatre (USFET), 46
United States Marine Corps; in North Africa, 536; in Pacific, 333-334, 339, 340, 342, 470-476, 480, 494-495, 516-532, 616-617, 625-626, 628-632, 634-637, 644, 654-656, 900-909, 919, 921, 924, 926-934; at Pearl Harbor, 325-326; Women, 481
United States Navy, 470, 553, 671, 685-692, 705, 738; coördination with land and air forces, 525-532, 657; losses at Pearl Harbor, 326, 487; rebirth into world's greatest navy, 487-496; strength in 1945, 889-890
United States Relief and Rehabilitation Administration, 484
Upson, Lieutenant Commander Richard, 492
Urals, 360, 367
Urey, Professor Harold, 19
Ushijima, Mitsuri, Lieutenant General, 934
Utah, battleship, 326, 328, 333
Utrecht, 173
Utter, Navy Lieutenant H. T., 345

"V for Victory" campaign, 176
V-E Day, 3, 15, 851, 929
V-J Day, 3, 38
Valenciennes, 209, 241
Valiant, battleship, 689, 702
Valkenburgh, Captain van, 328, 329
Van Kirk, Captain Theodore, 18
Van Roey, Cardinal, 164
Vandegrift, Major General A. A., 471-477, 480, 494, 520, 522, 523, 526, 532
Vandervoort, Lieutenant Colonel Benjamin H., 747
Vangunu Island, 615, 636
Vares Majdan, 281
Vasilevsky, Marshal Alexander M., 21, 26, 381, 388, 397, 815-819, 829, 831
Vasterival, 420-421
Vateon, Major General Pedro A., 928
Vatican City, 674, 698
Vatutin, General Nikolai F., 380, 388, 392, 394-397, 815
Vecchi, General de, 92
Velikiye Luki, 381
Vella Lavella, 615
Venizelos, Venizelists, 261, 282
Verdun, 49, 157, 205, 215, 219, 237
Veronezh, 380
Versailles Peace Conference, 302, 303, 306
Versailles, Treaty of, 5, 77, 127, 153, 181, 234, 272, 293
Vestal, repair ship, 329-330

Vesuvius, 692
Viborg, 353, 357-358
Vichy, 234; Vichy France, 236-237, 241, 244-260; Government, 533-534, 539, 543, 740, 758, 767, adherents, 556-557, 573, 607, constitution, 239, 242; "war guilt" trials, 244, 246-247, 250, 255, 259
Victor Emanuel III, 86, 89-91, 262, 675-676, 698, 701-702, 713
Victorious, carrier, 936
Victory Road, 618-620
Vienna, 53-55, 93, 95-102, 104-108, 819-828
Vietinghoff-Scheel, Colonel General Heinrich von, 785, 787, 852
Vila River, 615
Villach, Carinthia, 108
Villamor, Captain Jesus, 455
Vilna, 124, 395, 397, 815
Vimy Ridge, 209
Vincennes, heavy cruiser, 473, 475, 476
Vinson, Fred M., 483
Viru Harbor, 637-639
Visayas, 658, 664
Vishinsky, Andrei Y., 859
Vistula River, 125, 181, 397, 781, 807, 809, 811, 815-816
Vitebsk, 397, 815
Vladivostok, 299, 300
Voelkischer Beobachter, 68, 82, 106, 273
Volcano Islands, 651, 654, 900, 903
Volga River, 375-377, 387
Volkhov, 380, 382, 395
von Epp plan, 155
Voronezh, 375, 380, 382, 387, 388, 392
Voronki, 402
Voronoff, Colonel General Nikolai N., 379, 381
Voroshiloff, Marshal Klementy E., 365, 369, 380-382, 388
Vosges mountains, 795, 796
Vraciu, Lieutenant Alex, 893
Vyazma, 384

Waechtler, Fritz, 75
Wagner, Lieutenant Boyd ("Buzz"), 342, 349, 456
Wagner, Rear Admiral, 853
Wainwright, General Jonathan, 338, 350, 351, 468, 895; at Bataan, 456-458, Corregidor, 461-463, surrender, 463-464, liberation, 27, 28, 935; honors to, 35; and Japanese surrender, 30-32
Wake Island, 27, 35, 306, 310, 334, 342, 343, 447, 488, 493, 610, 617, 919
Wakefield, U.S.S., 471
Waldron, Lieutenant Commander John C., 513
Walke, destroyer, 529
Walker, Frank C., 479
Walker, Colonel John T., 630
Wallace, Colonel Clarence R., 933
Wallace, Henry A., 19, 479
Wallace, Colonel William J., 520
Wandervoegel (Wanderbirds), 76
War Communications Board, 484
War Crimes Courts, 871
War criminals, 42-45, 47-49; trials of, 48-49, 968

War Food Administration (WFA), 483
"War guilt" trials, Vichy, 244, 246-247, 250, 255, 259
War Labor Board (WLB), 483
War Manpower Commission, 483
"War of nerves," 195-196, 273
War Production Board (WPB), 483
War Relocation Authority, 484
War Shipping Administration, 483
Ward, destroyer, 324, 885
Warren, Commander John T., 891
Warren, Whitney, 162
Warsaw: German conquest of, 120, 123-125, 167, 375, 675, Battle of, 779-782; Ghetto, 810; Russians liberate, 384, 807-808
Warspite, battleship, 142, 689, 702
Washington, D. C., 11, 35, 478, 851
Washington Disarmament Conference, 304-305, 307, 318-319, 343, 533
Washington, battleship, 521, 523, 525, 528, 529
Wasp, carrier, 490, 519, 880
Waterloo, 153
Waters, Colonel John K., 863
Watson, Brigadier General Thomas E., 630
Wau, 635
Wavell, Field Marshal Sir Archibald Percival, 286, 343, 410-411, 438, 440, 449
Weaver, Brigadier General James, 350
Wedemeyer, Major General Albert C., 619, 911, 914, 919
Wehrmacht, 276-277, 364, 371, 387-391, 806, 815, 836-837, 840
Wei Li-huang, General, 623
Wei Tao-ming, Dr., 608
Weimar Constitution, 57
Weimar Republic, 48, 56
Weizsäcker, Baron von, 182
Welles, Sumner, 253
"Werewolves," 803
Wermuth, Captain Arthur W. ("One-Man-Army"), 454
West Indies, 253, 479
West Point, 350-351
West Virginia, battleship, 326, 328, 333, 877
West Wall, 771, 772, 788
Western Desert Air Force, 578, 579, 586, 589
Westphalia, Treaty of, 175
Wewak, 493, 635, 640, 641, 919
Weygand, General Maxime, 49, 159, 206-208, 210, 214, 217, 237, 243, 867
Weyler, Rear Admiral, 876
Weymouth, 225
Wheeler Field, 325-327
Wheless, Captain Hewitt T., 345-346
Whitaker, John, 687
White Russia, 390, 392, 397-400, 402, 404
Whitehead, Major General Ennis C., 644
Whiteside, Arthur D., 485
Whitworth, Vice Admiral W. J., 142
Wickard, Claude B., 479, 484
Wigeland, Lieutenant Arthur, 865
Wilbur, Brigadier General William H., 563
Wilhelm II, Kaiser, 261, 299
Wilhelmina, Queen, 146, 168, 171, 174-175, 186, 196

Wilkins, Rear Admiral Theodore S., 665
Wilkinson, Vice Admiral, 660, 890
Will H. Berg, tanker, 450
William, Lieutenant Charles, Earl of Hopetoun, 867
William the Conqueror, 726
Williams, Corporal William W., 345
Willkie, Wendell, good-will tour, 608
Willoughby, Captain William H., 613
Wilson, Charles E., 484
Wilson, Field Marshal Sir Henry Maitland, 19, 700, 703, 784
Wilson, Woodrow, 87, 109, 110, 121, 198, 347
Wiltsie, Captain I. D., 627
Winant, Lieutenant John G., Jr., 863
Wingate, Brigadier General Orde C., 620
Wingate's Raiders, 620-621
Winkelman, General H. J., 171-174, 866
Wisconsin, battleship, 16
Wolff, Karl, 852
Wolff, Theodore, 81
Women, in war services, 480-482
Women Accepted for Volunteer Emergency Service (WAVES), 481
Women's Army Auxiliary Corps (WAACS), 548
Women's Army Corps (WACS), 480-481, 753
Woodlark Islands, 615, 636
Woodruff, Lieutenant William L., 522
World War I, 4, 10, 56, 58, 64, 73, 98, 109, 116, 120-121, 127, 128, 137, 153, 167, 192, 194, 197-198, 207, 210, 217, 261, 262, 272, 274, 282, 337, 338, 351, 353, 558, 737, 749, 751, 753, 812, 820; armistice, 848; costs of, 312, 325
World War II, 33, 50, 51, 62, 64, 73, 84, 92, 103, 109, 120, 121, 127, 137, 153, 167, 172, 191, 192, 198, 262, 267; causes and results of, 3, 6, 12, 13; cost of, 4; end of, 3-4, 10, 14
Wright, Admiral, 531
Wright, Captain Jerrauld, 535

Xerxes, 288

Yalta, 10, 21, 814, 844
Yamada, General Oto, 21, 26
Yamashita, General Tomayuki, 28, 351, 440, 459, 463, 881, 883-887
Yamato, superbattleship, 876, 925
Yangtze River, 432
Yap, 302, 304-306, 334, 645, 658
Yasnaya Polyana, 372
Yawn, Captain James Q., 632
Yeremenko, General A. I., 381, 397, 807, 814, 821, 826, 827, 829
Yi-sun, Admiral, 515
Yokohama, 41-43, 497
Yokosuka, 41, 43
Yorktown, carrier, 443, 491-493, 504-509, 513-515, 625, 629, 633, 647, 651
Young, Commander Cassin, 329, 330, 528
Young Plan, 60
Yugoslav-Bulgarian pact, 263-264
Yugoslav Volunteer and Guerrilla Army, 108, 272, 694, 720
Yugoslavia, 27, 87, 104, 261, 262, 274, 286, 479, 807, 821-822, 826-828; Battle of, 272-281
Yumasheff, Admiral Ivan, 21
Yunnan Province, 250, 501, 623, 917

Zaghouan, 603, 605
Zagreb, 276, 277, 279, 827
Zamboanga, 658
Zanana, 639
Zaporozhye, 391
Zay, Jean, 250
Zeebrugge, 209, 210
Zeilin, transport, 527
Zeitzler, General Kurt, 381
Zemke, Colonel Hubert, 864
Zernatto, Guido, 100
Zeros, 328, 340, 489, 504, 513, 514, 519, 524, 529, 641, 651
Zheleznovodsk, 406
Zhitomir, 394, 395
Zhukoff, Marshal Gregory K., 370; Allied Control Council, 46; Battle of Moscow, 371, 373, 381, 382, 388, 397; push toward Berlin, 807, 808, 810-812, 814-817, 819, 828, 829, 831-833, 838-840; German surrender to, 858-860
Zinchenko, 835-836